# TAX PLANNING (Chapter 4; PFP Sheets 20–22)

How is a taxable income determined? (Exhibit 4-1, page 100)

How is a federal income tax return prepared? (pages 107–112)

What type of tax assistance is available? (pages 113–116)

What if my tax return is audited? (pages 117–118)

## WEB SITES FOR TAX PLANNING

**Internal Revenue Service**
www.irs.ustreas.gov
**Tax forms & tips**
www.1040.com
www.taxweb.com

**File your taxes online**
www.taxsoft.com
**Ernst & Young**
www.ey.com/home.asp
**H&R Block**
www.hrblock.com

**TurboTax**
www.intuit.com/turbotax
**State income tax information**
www.taxadmin.org
www.intelligenttaxes.com

# BANKING SERVICES (Chapter 5; PFP Sheets 23–28)

How is electronic banking changing financial services? (pages 133–135)

How do changing interest rates affect financial service decisions? (page 136)

What are the main types of financial institutions? (pages 137–141)

How can I compare savings accounts and savings plans? (pages 146–149)

How do I reconcile my checking account? (page 161–162)

## WEB SITES FOR BANKING SERVICES

**Current rates for savings instruments**
www.bankrate.com
www.banx.com
www.usatoday.com/money/savebox.htm
**Federal Deposit Insurance Corporation**
www.fdic.gov
**U.S. Savings Bonds**
www.savingsbonds.gov

**Federal Reserve System**
www.federalreserve.gov
**Purchasing government notes & bonds**
www.frbsf.org
**Current value of U.S. savings bonds**
www.ny.frb.org
**American Bankers Association**
www.aba.com
**Credit union Information**
www.cuna.org

**Financial calculators for savings**
www.centura.com/personal/calculators/index.cfm
**Making payments on the Internet**
www.checkfree.com
**Online banking information**
www.orcc.com/banking.htm/
www.bankonline.com

# CONSUMER CREDIT (Chapters 6, 7; PFP Sheets 29–31)

What are the main types of consumer credit? (pages 169–176)

How much credit can I afford to use? (pages 176–177)

Should I cosign a loan for a friend or relative? (pages 177–178)

What information is in a person's credit file? (pages 177–178)

How is a credit application evaluated by a lender? (page 178–180)

What federal laws exist to protect the rights of borrowers?
(Exhibit 6-12, page 192)

What is the best way to compare different credit plans?
(pages 204–206)

How is the cost of credit determined? (pages 207–211)

What are some of the signs of credit overuse?
(Exhibit 7-4, page 216)

Where can I seek assistance in case of credit problems?
(pages 216–218)

## WEB SITES FOR USING CONSUMER CREDIT WISELY AND COMPARING CREDIT COSTS

**RAM Research Group**
www.ramresearch.com
**Comparison of costs & features**
www.cardtrak.com
**Current loan & credit card rates**
www.bankrate.com
www.banx.com
**National Center for Financial Education**
www.ncfe.org

**Credit reports information**
www.equifax.com
www.experian.com
www.tuc.com
**Consumer Credit law information**
www.ftc.gov
www.federalreserve.gov
www.pirg.org
**FinanCenter**
www.financenter.com

**National Foundation for Consumer Credit**
www.nfcc.org
**Debt Counselors of America**
www.dca.org
**Credit cost calculators**
www.centura.com/personal/calculators/index.cfm

# PERSONAL FINANCE

## Sixth Edition

### JACK R. KAPOOR
*College of DuPage*

### LES R. DLABAY
*Lake Forest College*

### ROBERT J. HUGHES
*Dallas County Community College*

Boston   Burr Ridge, IL   Dubuque, IA   Madison, WI   New York   San Francisco   St. Louis
Bangkok   Bogotá   Caracas   Lisbon   London   Madrid
Mexico City   Milan   New Delhi   Seoul   Singapore   Sydney   Taipei   Toronto

## McGraw-Hill Higher Education ⟨⟩

*A Division of The* **McGraw-Hill** *Companies*

PERSONAL FINANCE

Published by McGraw-Hill, an imprint of the McGraw-Hill Companies, Inc. 1221 Avenue of the Americas, New York, NY, 10020. Copyright © 2001, 1999, 1996, 1994, 1991, 1988, by The McGraw-Hill Companies, Inc. All rights reserved. No part of this publication may be reproduced or distributed in any form or by any means, or stored in a database or retrieval system, without the prior written consent of The McGraw-Hill Companies, Inc., including, but not limited to, in any network or other electronic storage or transmission, or broadcast for distance learning. Some ancillaries, including electronic and print components, may not be available to customers outside the United States.

This book is printed on acid-free paper.

6 7 8 9 0 DOW/DOW 0 9 8 7 6 5 4 3 2

ISBN 0-07-235084-9

Vice president/Editor-in chief:   *Michael W. Junior*
Publisher:   *John Biernat*
Developmental editor:   *Sarah Pearson*
Senior project manager:   *Jean Lou Hess*
Marketing manager:   *Rhonda Seelinger*
Production supervisor:   *Debra Bensen*
Coordinator freelance design:   *Kiera Cunningham*
Interior designer:   *Kay Fulton*
Cover designer:   *Joanne Schopler*
Cover images:   © Photodisc (four smaller images); ©2000 P Crowther/S Carter/Tony Stone Images (background image)
Supplement coordinator:   *Matthew Perry*
Media technology producer:   *Ann Rogula*
Compositor:   *Electronic Publishing Services, Inc. TN*
Typeface:   *10/12 Times Roman*
Printer:   *R. R. Donnelley & Sons Company*

**Library of Congress Cataloging-in-Publication Data**

Kapoor, Jack R.
    Personal finance / Jack R. Kapoor, Les R. Dlabay, Robert J. Hughes. — 6th ed.
      p.   cm.
    ISBN  0-07-235084-9 (The McGraw-Hill/Irwin series in finance, insurance, and real estate)
    Includes bibliographical references and index.
    1. Finance, Personal. I. Dlabay, Les R. II. Hughes, Robert James, 1946- III. Title.
IV. Series
    HG179.K37  2001
332.024dc—21                                               00042709

http://www.mhhe.com

The McGraw-Hill/Irwin Series in Finance, Insurance and Real Estate
Stephen A. Ross
Franco Modigliani Professor of Finance and Economics
*Sloan School of Management*
*Massachusetts Institute of Technology*
Consulting Editor

FINANCIAL MANAGEMENT

Benninga and Sarig
**Corporate Finance: A Valuation Approach**

Block and Hirt
**Foundations of Financial Management**
*Ninth Edition*

Brealey and Myers
**Principles of Corporate Finance**
*Sixth Edition*

Brealey, Myers and Marcus
**Fundamentals of Corporate Finance**
*Second Edition*

Brooks
**FinGame Online 3.0**

Bruner
**Case Studies in Finance: Managing for Corporate Value Creation**
*Third Edition*

Chew
**The New Corporate Finance: Where Theory Meets Practice**
*Second Edition*

Graduate Management Admissions Council, Robert F. Bruner, Kenneth Eades and Robert Harris
**Essentials of Finance: With an Accounting Review Fully Interactive CD-ROM derived from Finance Interactive 1997 Pre-MBA Edition**

Grinblatt and Titman
**Financial Markets and Corporate Strategy**

Helfert
**Techniques of Financial Analysis: A Modern Approach**
*Tenth Edition*

Higgins
**Analysis for Financial Management**
*Sixth Edition*

Hite
**A Programmed Learning Guide to Finance**

Kester, Fruhan, Piper and Ruback
**Case Problems in Finance**
*Eleventh Edition*

Nunnally and Plath
**Cases in Finance**
*Second Edition*

Ross, Westerfield and Jaffe
**Corporate Finance**
*Fifth Edition*

Ross, Westerfield and Jordan
**Essentials of Corporate Finance**
*Third Edition*

Ross, Westerfield and Jordan
**Fundamentals of Corporate Finance**
*Fifth Edition*

Smith
**The Modern Theory of Corporate Finance**
*Second Edition*

White
**Financial Analysis with an Electronic Calculator**
*Fourth Edition*

INVESTMENTS

Bodie, Kane and Marcus
**Essentials of Investments**
*Fourth Edition*

Bodie, Kane and Marcus
**Investments**
*Fourth Edition*

Cohen, Zinbarg and Zeikel
**Investment Analysis and Portfolio Management**
*Fifth Edition*

Corrado and Jordan
**Fundamentals of Investments: Valuation and Management**

Farrell
**Portfolio Management: Theory and Applications**
*Second Edition*

Hirt and Block
**Fundamentals of Investment Management**
*Sixth Edition*

Jarrow
**Modelling Fixed Income Securities and Interest Rate Options**

Morningstar, Inc. and Remaley
**U.S. Equities OnFloppy Educational Version**
*Annual Edition*

Shimko
**The Innovative Investor**
*Excel Version*

FINANCIAL INSTITUTIONS AND MARKETS

Cornett and Saunders
**Fundamentals of Financial Institutions Management**

Rose
**Commercial Bank Management**
*Fourth Edition*

Rose
**Money and Capital Markets: Financial Institutions and Instruments in a Global Marketplace**
*Seventh Edition*

Rose and Kolari
**Financial Institutions: Understanding and Managing Financial Services**
*Fifth Edition*

Santomero and Babbel
**Financial Markets, Instruments, and Institutions**
*Second Edition*

Saunders
**Financial Institutions Management: A Modern Perspective**
*Third Edition*

Saundus and Cornett
**Financial Markets & Institutions**

INTERNATIONAL FINANCE

Eun and Resnick
**International Financial Management**
*Second Edition*

Kester and Luehrman
**Case Problems in International Finance**
*Second Edition*

Levi
**International Finance**
*Third Edition*

To my parents, Ram and Sheila Kapoor; my wife, Theresa; and
my children, Karen, Kathryn, and Dave

To my mother, Mary Dlabay, and the memory of my father
Les; my wife, Linda; and my children, Carissa and Kyle

To my mother, Barbara Y. Hughes; and my wife, Peggy

# PREFACE

*"Double your money in five years"*
*"Eliminate your credit card debt"*
*"Obtain your dream job"*
*"Travel to a different country each year"*
*"Cut your automobile insurance rates by one-third"*

This book *cannot* promise you any of these. However, we CAN promise you the opportunity, along with your efforts, to achieve these and many other personal financial goals.

While technology, the global economy, and other social trends are changing the financial planning environment, many fundamentals remain constant. Your ability to make informed choices related to spending, saving, borrowing, and investing continues to be the foundation of long-term financial security.

## A FRAMEWORK FOR DECISION MAKING

Each day we are surrounded with new choices for shopping, television channels, and other activities. Money choices can be intense, however, *Personal Finance, Sixth Edition,* offers many tools to cope with these situations. The steps of the financial planning decision-making process are introduced in Chapter 1. This step-by-step approach will help you identify and evaluate choices as well as understand the consequences of your decisions in terms of opportunity costs.

## NEW CONTENT AND FEATURES TO THIS EDITION

Expanded emphasis on technology, real-world decision making, and practical advice from financial planning professionals are just a few of the new features in this edition of *Personal Finance*. In addition, many content and instructional features have been added or revised to better serve both students and instructors.

Chapter 1 includes expanded discussion and examples of the steps in the financial planning process along with increased information about online financial planning. Chapter 2 has increased coverage of planning and implementing a career search online.

Chapter 3 has expanded coverage of evaluating a person's financial situation using various ratios. Updated coverage of recent changes to tax laws and e-filing appears in Chapter 4.

Chapter 5 has updated and expanded coverage of online banking, identity theft, and financial privacy. The consumer credit material in Chapters 6 and 7 provides new information on shopping on the Internet with credit cards, updated coverage of cash advances, and expanded discussion on calculating finance charges.

The purchasing decision unit in Chapters 8 and 9 provides new coverage of online shopping, common consumer myths, and online home buying activities.

Chapters 10 through 12 have updated material on buying home and auto insurance. Expanded information on long-term care insurance along with new HMO and Medicare coverage are presented in Chapter 11. An updated discussion of term life insurance bargains and using the Internet for life insurance information are included in Chapter 12.

The investments unit, presented in Chapters 13 through 17, emphasizes the importance of your dedication and perseverance when building an investment program. Chapter 13 provides new information on employee sponsored retirement programs, global investment risk, and evaluating potential investments. More information on long-term returns offered by different investments is provided in Chapter 14. Updated information on buying and selling bonds is included in Chapter 15. Discussion of using the Internet to evaluate and select mutual funds has been added to Chapter 16. And, in Chapter 17, new information on buying collectibles online and investing in art is provided.

The retirement and estate planning is discussed in Chapters 18 and 19 and includes updated and expanded discussion of retirement housing alternatives, retirement plan options, and probate.

Several chapter and end-of-text appendices provide additional information and ideas for successful financial planning, such as "The Time Value of Money: Future Value and Present Value Computations," "Financial Planners and Other Financial Planning Information Sources," and "Consumer Agencies and Organizations."

## ACKNOWLEDGMENTS

We express our deepest appreciation for the efforts of the colleagues who provided extensive comments that contributed to the quality of the book you are using.

**Khurshid Ahmad**
Wright State University

**David Barr**
Blinn College

**Robert Bohn**
Golden Gate University

**Carlene Creviston**
Ball State University

**Gary Cutler**
Dyersburg State Community College

**Stephen Ferris**
University of Missouri, Columbia

**Marilyn Hood**
Texas A&M University

**James Johnson**
Black Hawk College

**Michael Johnson**
Madison Area Technical College

**Robert Lutz**
University of Utah

**Ken Mark**
Kansas City Kansas Community College

**Abbass Mamoozadeh**
Slippery Rock University

**Dianne Morrison**
University of Wisconsin, La Crosse

**Johnston Osagie**
Alcorn State University

**Barbara Poole**
Central Connecticut State University

**David Porras**
Quincy University

**Beth Scull**
University of South Carolina

**Judy Swisher**
Florida Atlantic University

Many talented professionals at McGraw-Hill Higher Education have contributed to the development of *Personal Finance,* Sixth Edition. We are especially grateful to Sarah Pearson, Jean Lou Hess, Kiera Cunningham, and Matthew Perry.

In addition, Jack Kapoor expresses special appreciation to Theresa and Dave Kapoor, Kathryn Thumme, and Karen Tucker for their typing, proofreading, and research assistance. Finally, we thank our wives and families for their patience, understanding, encouragement, and love throughout the years since we started this project.

## A NOTE OF APPRECIATION

Thousands of students at colleges and universities throughout the world have used the previous editions of *Personal Finance.* We are honored that professors and students have chosen our text to learn about personal financial decision making. A text should always be evaluated by the people who use it. We welcome your comments, suggestions, and questions. Finally, we truly hope that, as a result of studying personal finance, you will have a fulfilling life that brings economic prosperity along with satisfying personal relationships.

**Jack R. Kapoor**
*kapoorj@cdnet.cod.edu*

**Les R. Dlabay**
*dlabay@lfc.edu*

**Robert J. Hughes**
*rjh8410@dcccd.edu*

# GUIDED TOUR

Personal Finance continues to provide instructors and students with features and materials to create a learning environment that can be adapted to any educational setting.

## Chapter Opening Case

Each chapter starts with an opening case and related discussion questions to introduce the chapter content with a real-world situation.

### Personal Financial Planning: An Introduction

#### Financial Decisions for Two Sisters and a Child

How does a person cope with daily living expenses while also trying to plan for long-term financial security? For Tamara Lopez, this has not been easy. Since the death of her husband seven months ago, Tamara and her daughter Kelly, age 3, have lived with Tamara's sister. This arrangement has helped them handle the stress caused by their loss.

Tamara's husband died with less than $3,000 in savings and only $20,000 in life insurance. Tamara has not worked in recent years. Instead, she has stayed home to take care of Kelly. Tamara now needs to return to work and obtain child care services. She also wants to help her sister Boni, who has provided emotional and financial support for her and Kelly.

Boni has a different financial situation. Three years ago, Boni had a skiing accident that left her partially paralyzed. She faces several financial concerns, such as maintenance costs for her electric wheelchair. Boni's disability insurance benefits have provided only 60 percent of her previous salary, and she now needs to obtain employment.

After eight months of physical therapy, Boni worked to expand her computer skills. The Americans with Disabilities Act (ADA) requires that employers make accommodations for applicants who have disabilities but are otherwise qualified for employment. ADA allows Boni more opportunities than were available before this law was enacted. Of the 15.2 million adults ages 21 to 64 with moderate disabilities, 77 percent—about 11.7 million—are employed.

She has been offered a job in the accounting department of an investment company located near the mall," Boni told

"That's great!" responded Tamara. "What about their health, life, and disability insurance plans?"

"They are just about what I need," said Boni. "The company also offers options for long-term-care insurance, which could be important for me as I get older. Now how about you? Have you been able to find a sitter for Kelly?"

"Well, not yet," replied Tamara, "but I'm sure we'll work out something. Together we have gotten through all our difficulties so far."

#### Questions

1. What financial goals and activities should be a priority for Tamara as a single parent?
2. What actions should Boni consider to manage her financial situation?
3. How might Tamara and Boni work together to manage their current and future financial needs?
4. Conduct a web search to obtain information that could be useful to Tamara and Boni. Recommend a website that they might consult when making financial planning decisions.

SOURCES: Patricia Braus, "When the Helpers Need a Hand," *American Demographics,* September 1998, pp. 66–72; Susan Decker, "Caring for Another's Finances," *USA Today,* June 4, 1999, p. 3B; Stuart Drown, "Special Cases: Families Learn to Cope Financially When Members Have Chronic Medical Conditions," *Chicago Tribune,* June 25, 1999, sec. 6, pp. 1, 7; Mary Beth Franklin, "Insuring Against Life's Frailties," *Kiplinger's Personal Finance Magazine,* July 1999, pp. 78–82; Jennifer Lach, "Disability Not Liability," *American Demographics,* June 1999, pp. 21–22.

---

Chapter 1  Personal Financial Planning    3

### Learning Objectives

**Obj. 1**  Analyze the process for making personal financial decisions.

**Obj. 2**  Develop personal financial goals.

**Obj. 3**  Assess personal and economic factors that influence personal financial planning.

**Obj. 4**  Determine personal and financial opportunity costs associated with personal financial decisions.

**Obj. 5**  Identify strategies for achieving personal financial goals for different life situations.

## Learning Objectives

Learning Objectives are presented at the start of each chapter. These objectives are highlighted at the start of each major section in the chapter, and appear again in the end-of-chapter summary. The learning objectives are also used to organize the end-of-chapter questions, problems, and exercises, as well as materials in the Instructor's Manual, Student Resource Manual, and the Test Bank.

---

### THE FINANCIAL PLANNING PROCESS

**Obj. 1**
Analyze the process for making personal financial decisions.

*personal financial planning*  The process of managing your money to achieve personal economic satisfaction.

Everywhere you turn, someone is talking about money. When it comes to handling your finances, are you an *explorer,* someone who is always searching through uncharted areas? Are you a *passenger,* just along for the ride on the money decision-making trip of life? Or are you a *researcher,* seeking answers to the inevitable money questions of life?

Most people want to handle their finances so that they get full satisfaction from each available dollar. Typical financial goals include such things as a new car, a larger home, advanced career training, extended travel, and self-sufficiency during working and retirement years. To achieve these and other goals, people need to identify and set priorities. Financial and personal satisfaction are the result of an organized process that is commonly referred to as *personal money management* or *personal financial planning.*

**Personal financial planning** is the process of managing your money to achieve personal economic satisfaction. This planning process allows you to control your financial situation. Every person, family, or household has a unique financial position, and any financial activity therefore must also be carefully planned to meet specific needs and goals.

A comprehensive financial plan can enhance the quality of your life and increase your satisfaction by reducing uncertainty about your future needs and resources. The specific advantages of personal financial planning include

- Increased effectiveness in obtaining, using, and protecting your financial resources throughout your lifetime.
- Increased control of your financial

## Key Terms

Key terms appear in bold type with margin definitions.

# In this edition, boxed features are used in each chapter to build student interest and highlight important topics. Three different types of boxed features are used:

## Financial Planning for Life's Situations

This box offers information that can assist students when faced with special situations and unique financial planning decisions. Many emphasize the use of Internet sources.

### Financial Planning for Life's Situations

#### USING THE INTERNET FOR FINANCIAL PLANNING

Web . . . e-mail . . . URL . . . cybercash!

Just a few years ago, these terms made no sense to most people. Even now, many people are still not quite sure about all this stuff. However, most know that good financial planning requires information, and the Internet is the most efficient source of information.

Throughout this book, the financial planning content presented can be expanded and updated using the Internet. The websites we suggest, along with others you locate yourself, will allow you to quickly obtain information for making financial decisions appropriate to your life situation. In addition, at the end of each chapter, a feature called "Creating an E-Plan: Financial Decisions Using the Web" will give you an opportunity to plan, research, and implement various components necessary for a comprehensive financial plan.

As you study the personal financial topics discussed in this book, you will find the following Internet topic areas especially useful:

- *Cyber-info for personal financial planning:* With thousands of personal finance websites available, where does a person begin? Some of the most useful ones include www.personalwealth.com, www.financenter.com, www.quicken.com, www.moneycentral.msn.com, and www.fool.com.
- *Online banking:* No more lines. No more rude bank tellers. No more inhaling exhaust fumes while waiting in the drive-through lane. In addition to existing banks that are online, web-only banks include www.sfnb.com and www.telebank.com.

- *Online tax information and advice:* Tax planning should not occur only around April 15. For assistance, go to www.irs.gov, www.1040.com, and www.taxweb.com.
- *Applying for a mortgage online:* Instead of waiting days or even weeks, prospective home buyers can not obtain financing online at www.eloan.com and www.lendingtree.com.
- *Buying a car online:* Information that used to be difficult to get is now available to everyone. Over 70 percent of car buyers research their planned purchases online to obtain information about vehicle features and costs at websites such as www.autoweb.com and www.carpoint.msn.com.
- *Selecting investments online:* As everyone knows, "information is power." This axiom is especially true when investing. You can obtain company information and investment assistance at www.quote.yahoo.com, www.quicken.com, and www.fool.com.
- *Being your own investment broker:* You already know which investments you want to buy? Then it's time to get into the market by going to www.etrade.com or www.ameritrade.com.
- *Planning for retirement:* Whether you are 40 years or 40 minutes away from retiring, you can get lots of help at www.lifenet.com.

Note: Additional websites appear on the end sheets of this book and in the end-of-chapter exercises. Refer to the appendix for this chapter for information on conducting Internet searches. Also, be aware that websites may change or no longer be in use.

---

### Financial Planning Calculations

#### ANNUAL CONTRIBUTIONS TO ACHIEVE A FINANCIAL GOAL

Achieving specific financial goals often requires regular deposits to a savings or investment account. By using time value of money calculations, you can determine the amount you should save or invest to achieve a specific goal for the future.

##### EXAMPLE 1

Jonie Emerson has two children who will start college in 10 years. She plans to set aside $1,500 a year for her children's college educations during that period and estimates she will earn an annual interest rate of 5 percent on her savings. What amount can Jonie expect to have available for her children's college educations when they start college?

##### CALCULATION:

$1,500 × Future value of a series of deposits, 5%, 10 years

$1,500 × 12.578 (Exhibit 1–8B) = $18,867

##### EXAMPLE 2

Don Calder wants to accumulate $50,000 over the next 10 years as a reserve fund for his parents' retirement living expenses and health care. If he earns an average of 8 percent on his investments, what amount must he invest each year to achieve this goal?

##### CALCULATION:

$50,000 ÷ Future value of a series of deposits, 8%, 10 years

$50,000 ÷ 14.487 (Exhibit 1–8B) = $3,452.80

Don needs to invest approximately $3,450 a year for 10 years at 8 percent to achieve the desired financial goal.

## Financial Planning Calculations

This feature presents more than 90 mathematical applications relevant to personal financial situations.

---

**Advice from a Pro**

#### ELLEN ROGIN ON PERSONAL FINANCIAL PLANNING

"Spend less than you earn" is the foundation of long-term financial security according to Ellen Rogin, president of Strategic Financial Designs in Northfield, Illinois, a fee-based investment advisory company.

Although it sounds simple, most people do not follow this basic requirement for financial planning success. Ms. Rogin has been advising people about their money for over 12 years. While the typical client of her company ranges in age from 30 to 50, some are younger or older. Most of her clients are professionals and executives who have a common concern: a secure retirement. But Ms. Rogin is quick to point out that she works with people with a variety of needs, life situations, and investment philosophies. She has even advised a lottery winner, although she doesn't recommend that expectation as a steady path to long-term financial security!

The availability of information, Ms. Rogin believes, is the most significant change in the financial planning marketplace in recent years. With the Internet, television programs, and an extensive number of magazines and books,

people can be better informed regarding personal finance topics and investments. However, Ms. Rogin warns that people must assess the validity of the information. She suggests "avoiding specific investment advice from magazines and other sources that may not be appropriate for your individual situation."

When planning your own financial direction, Ms. Rogin recommends three actions:

1. Set specific financial goals.
2. Reduce your debts.
3. Save for retirement.

Even if someone else is managing your finances, Ms. Rogin encourages you to "be involved." Be aware of your personal economic situation and the financial marketplace. Communicate your money views, risk acceptance, and financial priorities. Never let a financial planner, your spouse, or another family member have complete control.

Additional information about Strategic Financial Designs is available on the company's website at www.sfd-inc.com.

## Advice from a Pro

This feature provides unique perspectives from industry professionals.

## Did You Know

Each chapter contains several "Did You Know?" features with facts, information, and financial planning assistance.

## Personal Financial Planner

The integrated use of the *Personal Financial Planner* is highlighted with a PFP graphic in the margin. This visual, near the text material needed to complete each Personal Financial Planner worksheet, helps students better integrate this instructional supplement into the teaching-learning process.

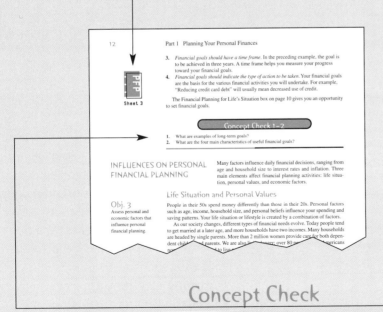

## Concept Check

The *Concept Check* at the end of each major section provides questions to help students assess their knowledge of the main ideas covered in that section.

# A variety of end of chapter features are offered to support the concepts presented throughout the chapter.

## Financial Planning Activities

The *Financial Planning Activities* provide ways to research and apply financial planning topics. These activities now include references to the *S&P Personal Finance* website, which are designated by an S&P icon.

## Life Situation Case

The enhanced *Life Situation Case* enables students to understand how personal finance works in the real world.

## Internet Case

Based on the wealth of information available on the Internet, the *Internet Case* provides a common scenario showing how this important resource can make financial planning easier. *Creating an E-Plan: Financial Decisions Using the Web* provides specific website addresses and learning activities to research specific personal financial decisions.

---

### (Reproduced page 26)

26    Part 1  Planning Your Personal Finances

#### Financial Planning Activities

1. *Researching Personal Finance on the Internet.* Using websites such as www.personalwealth.com, www.quicken.com, or www.kiplinger.com and search engines, obtain information about commonly suggested actions related to various personal financial planning decisions. What are some of the best sources of information on the Internet to assist you with financial planning?   (Obj. 1)
2. *Comparing Financial Planning Actions.* Survey friends, relatives, and others to determine the process they use when making financial decisions. How do these people measure risk when making financial decisions?   (Obj. 1)
3. *Using Financial Planning Experts.* Prepare a list of financial planning specialists (investment advisers, credit counselors, insurance agents, real estate brokers, tax preparers) in your community who can assist people with personal financial planning. Prepare a list of questions that might be asked of these financial planning professionals by (a) a young person just starting out on his or her own, (b) a young couple planning for their children's education and for their own retirement, and (c) a person nearing retirement.   (Obj. 1, 3)
4. *Setting Financial Goals.* Using Sheet 3 in the *Personal Financial Planner,* create one short-term and one long-term goal for people in these life situations: (a) a young single person, (b) a single parent with a child age 8, (c) a married person with no children, and (d) a retired person.   (Obj. 2)
5. *Analyzing Changing Life Situations.* Ask friends, relatives, and others how their spending, saving, and borrowing

activities changed when they decided to continue their education, change careers, or have children.   (Obj. 3)
6. *Researching Economic Conditions.* Use library resources, such as *The Wall Street Journal,* the "Economy" section of www.personalwealth.com, or other websites to determine recent trends in interest rates, inflation, and other economic indicators. Information about the consumer price index (measuring changes in the cost of living) may be obtained at www.bls.gov. Report how this economic information might affect your financial planning decisions.   (Obj. 3)
7. *Comparing Alternative Financial Actions.* What actions would be necessary to compare a financial planner who advertises "One Low Fee Is Charged to Develop Your Personal Financial Plan" and one that advertises "You Are Not Charged a Fee, My Services Are Covered by the Investment Company for Which I Work"?   (Obj. 4, 5)
8. *Determining Opportunity Costs.* What is the relationship between current interest rates and financial opportunity costs? Using time value of money calculations, state one or more goals in terms of an annual savings amount and the future value of this savings fund.   (Obj. 2, 4)
9. *Researching Financial Planning Software.* Visit software retailers to obtain information about the features and costs of various personal financial planning activities. Information about programs such as Microsoft Money and Quicken may be obtained on the Internet.   (Obj. 5)

#### LIFE SITUATION CASE

**TRIPLE TROUBLE FOR THE "SANDWICH GENERATION"**

Until recently, Fran and Ed Blake's personal finances ran smoothly. Both have maintained well-paying jobs while raising two children. The Blakes have a daughter who is completing her freshman year of college and a son three years younger. Currently they have $22,000 in various savings and investment funds set aside for the children's education. With education costs increasing faster than inflation, they are uncertain whether this amount is adequate.

In recent months, Fran's mother has required extensive medical attention and personal care. Unable to live alone, she is now a resident of a long-term care facility.

increases of about 7 percent. While a major portion of the cost is covered by her Social Security and pension, Fran's mother is unable to cover the entire cost. Their desire to help adds to the Blakes' financial burden.

The Blakes are like millions of other Americans who have financial responsibilities for both dependent children and aging parents. Commonly referred to as the "sandwich generation," this group is squeezed on one side by the cost of raising and educating children and on the other side by the financial demands of caring for aging parents.

Finally, the Blakes, ages 47 and 43, are also concerned about saving for their own retirement. While they have consistently made annual deposits to a retirement fund, various

---

### (Reproduced page 126)

126    Part 1  Planning Your Personal Finances

#### INTERNET CASE    Online Tax Assistance

For decades, people have complained about preparing their federal income tax return. Either they bemoaned the time and effort needed to prepare their own return or they complained about the cost of having someone else prepare their return.

With the availability of information on the Internet, the tax preparation process has become faster, easier, and less expensive. However, taxpayers must still make a commitment to finding, learning, and using tax information.

Jan and Karl Mueller want to use the Web to save money on their taxes while preparing their federal tax return and filing online. The Muellers own their home and pay for child care. Each has an employee-sponsored retirement program.

**Questions**

1. What types of tax information would you recommend the Muellers seek through a web search?
2. Locate specific websites that would meet the Muellers' tax information needs.
3. The Muellers have heard about people getting audited by the IRS. What information is available online to reduce the chance of being audited?
4. Based on web research, what things do the Muellers need to know about filing their federal tax return online? What websites can provide assistant with this process?

#### Creating an E-Plan: Financial Decisions Using the Web

**TAX PLANNING ACTIVITIES**

Taxes are a fact of financial planning. However, various actions can be taken to reduce the time and money that goes toward taxes.

**Websites for Tax Planning**

- Access to federal tax forms, IRS regulations, and other tax information at **www.irs.gov.**
- Tax planning suggestions from Ernst & Young at **www.ey.com/us/tax** and H&R Block at **www.hrblock.com.**
- Federal forms and tax tips at **www.1040.com, www.taxweb.com,** and **www.intelligenttaxes.com.**
- Preparing your tax form and filing online at **www.taxsoft.com.**
- Software information for TurboTax at **www.intuit.com/turbotax.**
- State income tax information and forms at **www.taxadmin.org,** and **www.intelligentaxes.com.**

(Note: Addresses and content of websites change, and new sites are created daily. Use search engines discussed to

**PFP sheets: 20–22**

**Short-Term Financial Planning Activities**

1. Develop a system for filing and storing various tax records related to income, deductible expenses, and current tax forms (see Exhibit 4-2).
2. Using the IRS and other websites, identify recent changes in tax laws that may affect your financial planning decisions.
3. Using current IRS tax forms and tax tables, estimate your tax liability for the current year (see PFP Sheet 20).
4. Compare the cost of tax preparation services (see PFP Sheet 21).

**Long-Term Financial Planning Activities**

1. Identify saving and investing decisions that would minimize future income taxes.
2. Develop a plan for actions to take related to your current and future tax situation (see PFP Sheet 22).

# Video Case

In connection with the *Dollars & Sense* videos, a *Video Case* builds upon a particular topic and provides questions to support how it relates to the chapter concepts.

# Continuous Case

The six-part continuous case, which appears at the end of each text part (after Chapters 4, 7, 9, 12, 17, and 19), allows students to apply course concepts in an evolving life situation. This feature encourages students to evaluate the changes that affect a family and then respond to the resulting shift in needs, resources, and priorities.

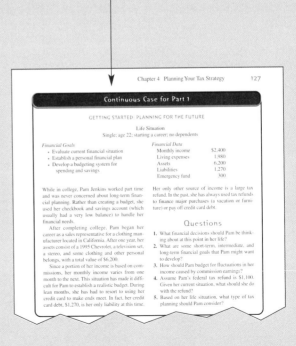

# SUPPLEMENTS

Few textbooks provide the innovative and practical instructional resources for both students and teachers. The comprehensive teaching-learning package for Personal Finance includes the following:

## For Students

- The *Personal Financial Planner* comes free with each copy of the text. This valuable learning tool consists of over 60 worksheets for creating and implementing a personal financial plan. Icons appear in each chapter indicating which worksheet relates to a particular topic.
(ISBN 0072395567)

- The *Student Resource Manual with Readings and Cases* allows students to review and apply text concepts. Each chapter contains a chapter overview, a pretest, self-guided study questions, a post-test, problems, applications, cases, and recent articles from *BusinessWeek*. Together, these exercises reinforce important text concepts and offer students additional opportunities to use their critical thinking and writing skills.
(ISBN 0072410027)

- *Student CD-ROM* – Available with each new text, this rich resource includes:
  - *Personal Financial Planning Software* consisting of a Windows-based, computerized version of the Personal Financial Planner and other financial tools for handling personal finance calculations;
  - The *PowerPoint Presentation System*, prepared by Professor Virginia Junk of the University of Idaho, offers more than 300 visual presentations that enhance lectures, handouts and class exercises;
  - The *S&P Personal Wealth Site Guide* provides a highly detailed guide to the #1 personal finance site on the Internet. It includes such features as a site overview and introduction, how to create your own personal financial plan, how to manage and track your own portfolio, and much more.
  - *Practice Quizzes* are provided to thoroughly test the concepts in the text for better test preparation;
  - *Weblinks* from the book are listed in order of chapter for easy access to the Internet.

## For Instructors

- The *Instructor's Manual* includes a "Course Planning Guide" with instructional strategies, course projects, and supplementary resource lists. The "Chapter Teaching Materials" section of the Instructor's Manual provides a chapter overview, the chapter objectives with summaries, introductory

activities, and detailed lecture outlines with teaching suggestions. This section also includes concluding activities, ready-to-duplicate quizzes, supplementary lecture materials and activities, and answers to concept checks, end-of-chapter questions, problems, and cases.
(ISBN 0072350857)

- The *PowerPoint Presentation System*, found on the Student and Instructor CD-ROMs and the Online Learning Center, offers more than 300 visual presentations that may be edited and manipulated to fit a particular course format.

- The *Transparency Acetates* package consists of 60 ready-to-use transparency acetates that highlight the major concepts of each chapter.
(ISBN 0072380780)

- The *Transparency Masters* supplement, part of the Instructor's Manual, contains over 60 ready-to-duplicate transparency masters that may be used to create transparencies or handouts.

- The *Test Bank* consists of over 1,500 true-false, multiple choice, and essay questions. These test items are organized by the learning objectives for each chapter. This manual also includes answers, text page references, and an indication of difficulty level.
(ISBN 0072350865)

- Our *Brownstone Diploma Testing System* offers the test items for *Personal Finance* on computer disk. This program makes it possible to create tests based on chapter, type of questions, and difficulty level. It allows instructors to combine their own questions with test items created by the authors of *Personal Finance*. This system can be used to edit existing questions and create numerous different versions of each test. The program accepts graphics, allows password protection of saved tests, and may be used on a computer network.
(ISBN 0072395559)

- The *Instructor's CD-ROM* provides the instructor with one resource for all supplementary material, including the Instructor's Manual, Test Bank, PowerPoint, the S&P Personal Wealth Site Guide, and related weblinks.
(ISBN 0072380772)

# Technology to Enhance Financial Decision Making

Online financial planning, use of the Web, and other technology are emphasized throughout the book with text content, examples, applications, problem-solving exercises, and financial decision situations. In addition to the Student and Instructor CD-ROMs, the Online Learning Center to accompany *Personal Finance* includes up-to-date information and instructional resources. This rich and useful tool provides online supplements, direct links to related websites, such as S&P Personal Wealth; e-Learning Sessions, a walk-through study session for each chapter; and much more. The *Personal Finance* website is located at www.mhhe.com/kdh6e.

# PageOut: The Course Website Development Center and PageOut Lite

*www.pageout.net*

This web page generation software, free to adopters, is designed to help professors just beginning to explore website options. In just a few minutes, even the most novice computer user can have a course website.

Simply type your material into the template provided and PageOut Lite instantly converts it to HTML—a universal Web language. Next, choose your favorite of three easy-to-navigate designs and your Web homepage is created, complete with online syllabus, lecture notes, and bookmarks. You can even include a separate instructor page and an assignment page.

PageOut offers enhanced point-and-click features including a Syllabus Page that applies real-world links to original text material, an automated grade book, and a discussion board where instructors and your students can exchange questions and post announcements.

# Brief Contents

# CONTENTS

# PART 2 MANAGING YOUR PERSONAL FINANCES

PART

3

# MAKING YOUR PURCHASING DECISIONS

PART  INSURING YOUR RESOURCES

PART 5

# INVESTING YOUR FINANCIAL RESOURCES

PART **6** CONTROLLING YOUR FINANCIAL FUTURE

1

# PLANNING YOUR PERSONAL FINANCES

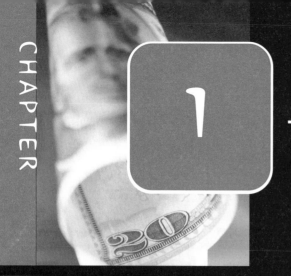

# 1

# Personal Financial Planning: An Introduction

## Financial Decisions for Two Sisters and a Child

How does a person cope with daily living expenses while also trying to plan for long-term financial security? For Tamara Lopez, this has not been easy. Since the death of her husband seven months ago, Tamara and her daughter Kelly, age 3, have lived with Tamara's sister. This arrangement has helped them handle the stress caused by their loss.

Tamara's husband died with less than $3,000 in savings and only $20,000 in life insurance. Tamara has not worked in recent years. Instead, she has stayed home to take care of Kelly. Tamara now needs to return to work and obtain child care services. She also wants to help her sister Boni, who has provided emotional and financial support for her and Kelly.

Boni has a different financial situation. Three years ago, Boni had a skiing accident that left her partially paralyzed. She faces several financial concerns, such as maintenance costs for her electric wheelchair. Boni's disability insurance benefits have provided only 60 percent of her previous salary, and she now needs to obtain employment.

After eight months of physical therapy, Boni worked to expand her computer skills. The Americans with Disabilities Act (ADA) requires that employers make accommodations for applicants who have disabilities but are otherwise qualified for employment. ADA allows Boni more opportunities than were available before this law was enacted. Of the 15.2 million adults ages 21 to 64 with moderate disabilities, 77 percent—about 11.7 million—are employed.

"I've been offered a job in the accounting department of that investment company located near the mall," Boni told Tamara.

"That's great!" responded Tamara. "What about their health, life, and disability insurance plans?"

"They are just about what I need," said Boni. "The company also offers options for long-term-care insurance, which could be important for me as I get older. Now how about you? Have you been able to find a sitter for Kelly?"

"Well, not yet," replied Tamara, "but I'm sure we'll work out something. Together we have gotten through all our difficulties so far."

## Questions

1. What financial goals and activities should be a priority for Tamara as a single parent?
2. What actions should Boni consider to manage her financial situation?
3. How might Tamara and Boni work together to manage their current and future financial needs?
4. Conduct a web search to obtain information that could be useful to Tamara and Boni. Recommend a website that they might consult when making financial planning decisions.

SOURCES: Patricia Braus, "When the Helpers Need a Hand," *American Demographics,* September 1998, pp. 66–72; Susan Decker, "Caring for Another's Finances," *USA Today,* June 4, 1999, p. 3B; Stuart Drown, "Special Cases: Families Learn to Cope Financially When Members Have Chronic Medical Conditions," *Chicago Tribune,* June 25, 1999, sec. 6, pp. 1, 7; Mary Beth Franklin, "Insuring Against Life's Frailties," *Kiplinger's Personal Finance Magazine,* July 1999, pp. 78–82; Jennifer Lach, "Disability Not Liability," *American Demographics,* June 1999, pp. 21–22.

## Learning Objectives

**Obj. 1**   Analyze the process for making personal financial decisions.

**Obj. 2**   Develop personal financial goals.

**Obj. 3**   Assess personal and economic factors that influence personal financial planning.

**Obj. 4**   Determine personal and financial opportunity costs associated with personal financial decisions.

**Obj. 5**   Identify strategies for achieving personal financial goals for different life situations.

## THE FINANCIAL PLANNING PROCESS

**Obj. 1**
Analyze the process for making personal financial decisions.

Everywhere you turn, someone is talking about money. When it comes to handling your finances, are you an *explorer,* someone who is always searching through uncharted areas? Are you a *passenger,* just along for the ride on the money decision-making trip of life? Or are you a *researcher,* seeking answers to the inevitable money questions of life?

Most people want to handle their finances so that they get full satisfaction from each available dollar. Typical financial goals include such things as a new car, a larger home, advanced career training, extended travel, and self-sufficiency during working and retirement years. To achieve these and other goals, people need to identify and set priorities. Financial and personal satisfaction are the result of an organized process that is commonly referred to as *personal money management* or *personal financial planning.*

**Personal financial planning** is the process of managing your money to achieve personal economic satisfaction. This planning process allows you to control your financial situation. Every person, family, or household has a unique financial position, and any financial activity therefore must also be carefully planned to meet specific needs and goals.

*personal financial planning*   The process of managing your money to achieve personal economic satisfaction.

A comprehensive financial plan can enhance the quality of your life and increase your satisfaction by reducing uncertainty about your future needs and resources. The specific advantages of personal financial planning include

- Increased effectiveness in obtaining, using, and protecting your financial resources throughout your lifetime.
- Increased control of your financial affairs by avoiding excessive debt, bankruptcy, and dependence on others for economic security.
- Improved personal relationships resulting from well-planned and effectively communicated financial decisions.
- A sense of freedom from financial worries obtained by looking to the future, anticipating expenses, and achieving your personal economic goals.

We all make hundreds of decisions each day. Most of these decisions are quite simple and have few consequences. Some are complex and have long-term effects on our personal and financial situations. While everyone makes decisions, few people consider how to make better decisions. As Exhibit 1–1 shows, the financial planning process is a logical, six-step procedure: (1) determining your current financial situation,

**Sheet 1**

## EXHIBIT 1–1   The Financial Planning Process

Determine current financial situation

(2) developing financial goals, (3) identifying alternative courses of action, (4) evaluating alternatives, (5) creating and implementing a financial action plan, and (6) reevaluating and revising the plan.

## Step 1: Determine Your Current Financial Situation

In this first step of the financial planning process, you will determine your current financial situation with regard to income, savings, living expenses, and debts. Preparing a list of current asset and debt balances and amounts spent for various items gives you a foundation for financial planning activities. The personal financial statements discussed in Chapter 3 will provide the information you need to match your goals with your current income and potential earning power.

Step 1 Example:    Within the next two months, Kent Mullins will complete his undergraduate studies with a major in international studies. He has worked part time in various sales jobs. He has a small savings fund ($1,700) and over $8,500 in student loans. What additional information should Kent have available when planning his personal finances?

## Step 2: Develop Financial Goals

You should periodically analyze your financial values and goals. This involves identifying how you feel about money and why you feel that way. Are your feelings about money based on factual knowledge or on the influence of others? Are your financial priorities based on social pressures, household needs, or desires for luxury items? How will economic conditions affect your goals and priorities? The purpose of this analysis is to differentiate your needs from your wants.

Specific financial goals are vital to financial planning. Others can suggest financial goals for you; however, *you* must decide which goals to pursue. Your financial goals can range from spending all of your current income to developing an extensive savings and investment program for your future financial security.

Step 2 Example:    Kent Mullins has several goals, including paying off his student loans, obtaining an advanced degree in global business management, and working in Latin America for a multinational company. What other goals might be appropriate for Kent?

## Step 3: Identify Alternative Courses of Action

Developing alternatives is crucial for making good decisions. Although many factors will influence the available alternatives, possible courses of action usually fall into these categories:

- *Continue the same course of action.* For example, you may determine that the amount you have saved each month is still appropriate.
- *Expand the current situation.* You may choose to save a larger amount each month.
- *Change the current situation.* You may decide to use a money market account instead of a regular savings account.
- *Take a new course of action.* You may decide to use your monthly saving budget to pay off credit card debts.

Not all of these categories will apply to every decision situation; however, they do represent possible courses of action. For example, if you want to stop working full time to go to school, you must generate several alternatives under the category "Take a new course of action."

Creativity in decision making is vital to effective choices. Considering all of the possible alternatives will help you make more effective and satisfying decisions. For instance, most people believe they must own a car to get to work or school. However, they should consider other alternatives such as public transportation, carpooling, renting a car, shared ownership of a car, or a company car.

Remember, when you decide not to take action, you elect to "do nothing," which can be a dangerous alternative.

Step 3 Example:    Kent Mullins has several options available for the near future. He could work full time and save for graduate school; he could go to graduate school full time by taking out an additional loan; or he could go to school part time and work part time. What additional alternatives might he consider?

## Step 4: Evaluate Alternatives

You need to evaluate possible courses of action, taking into consideration your life situation, personal values, and current economic conditions. How will the ages of dependents affect your saving goals? How do you like to spend leisure time? How will changes in interest rates affect your financial situation?

*Opportunity cost*
What a person gives
up by making a choice.

### Consequences of Choices

Every decision closes off alternatives. For example, a decision to invest in stock may mean you cannot take a vacation. A decision to go to school full time may mean you cannot work full time. **Opportunity cost** is what you give up by making a choice. This cost, commonly referred to as the *trade-off* of a decision, cannot always be measured in dollars. It may refer to the money you forgo by attending school rather than working, but it may also refer to the time you spend shopping around to compare brands for a major purchase. In either case, the resources you give up (money or time) have a value that is lost.

Decision making will be an ongoing part of your personal and financial situation. Thus, you will need to consider the lost opportunities that will result from your decisions. Since decisions vary based on each person's situation and values, opportunity costs will differ for each person.

### Evaluating Risk

Uncertainty is a part of every decision. Selecting a college major and choosing a career field involve risk. What if you don't like working in this field or cannot obtain employment in it? Other decisions involve a very low degree of risk, such as putting money in a savings account or purchasing items that cost only a few dollars. Your chances of losing something of great value are low in these situations.

In many financial decisions, identifying and evaluating risk is difficult (see Exhibit 1–2). The best way to consider risk is to gather information based on your experience and the experiences of others and to use financial planning information sources.

### Financial Planning Information Sources

When you travel, you often need a road map. Traveling the path of financial planning requires a different kind of map. Relevant information is required at each stage of the decision-making process. This book provides the foundation you need to make personal financial planning

## EXHIBIT 1-2

### Types of Risk

- Rising prices cause lost buying power.
- Decide whether to buy something now or later. If you buy later, you may have to pay more.

- Changing interest rates affect your costs (when you borrow) and your benefits (when you save or invest).
- Borrowing at a low interest rate when interest rates are rising can be to your advantage. But if you save when interest rates are dropping, you will earn a lower return with a six-month savings certificate than with a certificate having a longer maturity.

- The loss of a job could be the result of such things as changes in consumer spending.
- Individuals who face the risk of unemployment need to save while employed or acquire skills they can use to obtain a different type of work.

- Tangible and intangible factors can create a less than desirable situation. Purchasing a certain brand or from a certain store may entail the risk of having to obtain repairs at an inconvenient location.
- Personal risk may also take the form of the health risks, safety risks, or additional costs associated with various purchases or financial decisions.

- Some savings and investments have potential for higher earnings. However, they may be more difficult to convert to cash or to sell without significant loss in value.

Step 5 Example:   Kent Mullins has decided to work full time for a few years while he (1) pays off his student loans, (2) saves money for graduate school, and (3) takes a couple of courses in the evening and on weekends. What are the benefits and drawbacks of this choice?

## Step 6: Reevaluate and Revise Your Plan

Financial planning is a dynamic process that does not end when you take a particular action. You need to regularly assess your financial decisions. You should do a complete review of your finances at least once a year. Changing personal, social, and economic factors may require more frequent assessments.

When life events affect your financial needs, this financial planning process will provide a vehicle for adapting to those changes. Regularly reviewing this decision-making process will help you make priority adjustments that will bring your financial goals and activities in line with your current life situation.

Step 6 Example:   Over the next 6 to 12 months, Kent Mullins should reassess his financial, career, and personal situations. What employment opportunities or family circumstances might affect his need or desire to take a different course of action?

### Concept Check 1–1

1. What are the main elements of every decision we make?
2. What are some risks associated with financial decisions?
3. What are some common sources of financial planning information?
4. Why should you reevaluate your actions after making a personal financial decision?
5. What website feature of www.personalwealth.com or www.financenter.com would provide assistance with your financial decisions?

## PING PERSONAL FINANCIAL GOALS

Since the United States is one of the richest countries in the world, it is difficult to understand why so many Americans have money problems. The answer seems to be the result of two main factors. The first is poor planning and weak money management habits in areas such as spending and the use of credit. The other is extensive advertising, selling efforts, and product availability. Achieving personal financial satisfaction starts with clear financial goals.

### Types of Financial Goals

Two factors commonly influence your financial aspirations for the future. The first is the time frame in which you would like to achieve your goals. The second is the type of financial need that drives your goals.

#### Timing of Goals

What would you like to do tomorrow? Believe it or not, that question involves goal setting. *Short-term goals* are goals to be achieved within the next year or so, such as saving for a vacation or paying off small debts. *Intermediate goals* have a time frame of two to five years. *Long-term goals* involve financial plans that are more than five years off, such as retirement savings, money for children's college educations, or the purchase of a vacation home.

## EXHIBIT 1-3

Financial Planning
Information
Sources

- newsletters
- periodicals
- books

Computer
World Wide
Online Informa

Financial Specialists

- financial planners
- bankers
- accountants
- insurance agents
- lawyers
- tax preparers

**PFP**

**Sheet 2**

decisions. Changing personal, social, and econom
continually supplement and update your knowledge
the informational resources available when making
Financial Planning for Life's Situation box and the
additional information.

Step 4 Example:    As Kent Mullins evaluates hi
must consider his income needs for both the short t
also assess career opportunities with his current skill
training. What risks and trade-offs should Kent consi

## Step 5: Create and Impleme Financial Action Plan

In this step of the financial planning proce
This requires choosing ways to achieve yc
increase your savings by reducing your s
income through extra time on the job. If yo
tax payments, you may increase the amoun
file quarterly tax payments, or shelter cu
retirement program. As you achieve your im
goals next in priority will come into focus.

To implement your financial action plan,
others. For example, you may use the service
chase property insurance or the services of an
stocks, bonds, or mutual funds. Your own et
achieving your financial goals.

**Did You Know**

? Research
indicates that
people with a
financial plan
(developed
themselves or by a
professional) had
significantly higher
amounts in savings
than those who
didn't. (Andrea Rock,
"You've Gotta Have a
Plan," *Money,* March
1999, pp. 117–20,
123, 125–27.)

DEV

Obj
Devel
finan

# Financial Planning for Life's Situations

## USING THE INTERNET FOR FINANCIAL PLANNING

Web . . . e-mail . . . URL . . . cybercash!

Just a few years ago, these terms made no sense to most people. Even now, many people are still not quite sure about all this stuff. However, most know that good financial planning requires information, and the Internet is the most efficient source of information.

Throughout this book, the financial planning content presented can be expanded and updated using the Internet. The websites we suggest, along with others you locate yourself, will allow you to quickly obtain information for making financial decisions appropriate to your life situation. In addition, at the end of each chapter, a feature called "Creating an E-Plan: Financial Decisions Using the Web" will give you an opportunity to plan, research, and implement various components necessary for a comprehensive financial plan.

As you study the personal financial topics discussed in this book, you will find the following Internet topic areas especially useful:

- *Cyber-info for personal financial planning:* With thousands of personal finance websites available, where does a person begin? Some of the most useful ones include www.personalwealth.com, www.financenter.com, www.quicken.com, www.moneycentral.msn.com., and www.fool.com
- *Online banking:* No more lines. No more rude bank tellers. No more inhaling exhaust fumes while waiting in the drive-through lane. In addition to existing banks that are online, web-only banks include www.sfnb.com and www.telebank.com.

- *Online tax information and advice:* Tax planning should not occur only around April 15. For assistance, go to www.irs.gov, www.1040.com, and www.taxweb.com.
- *Applying for a mortgage online:* Instead of waiting days or even weeks, prospective home buyers can now obtain financing online at www.eloan.com and www.lendingtree.com.
- *Buying a car online:* Information that used to be difficult to get is now available to everyone. Over 70 percent of car buyers research their planned purchases online to obtain information about vehicle features and costs at websites such as www.autoweb.com and www.carpoint.msn.com.
- *Selecting investments online:* As everyone knows, "information is power." This axiom is especially true when investing. You can obtain company information and investment assistance at www.quote.yahoo.com, www.quicken.com, and www.fool.com.
- *Being your own investment broker:* You already know which investments you want to buy? Then it's time to get into the market by going to www.etrade.com or www.ameritrade.com.
- *Planning for retirement:* Whether you are 40 years or 40 minutes away from retiring, you can get lots of help at www.lifenet.com.

Note: Additional websites appear on the end sheets of this book and in the end-of-chapter exercises. Refer to the appendix for this chapter for information on conducting Internet searches. Also, be aware that websites may change or no longer be in use.

Long-term goals should be planned in coordination with short-term and intermediate ones. Setting and achieving short-term goals is commonly the basis for moving toward success of long-term goals. For example, saving for a down payment to buy a house is a short-term goal that can be a foundation for a long-term goal: owning your own home.

Goal frequency is another ingredient in the financial planning process. Some goals, such as vacations or money for gifts, may be set annually. Other goals, such as a college education, a car, or a house, occur less frequently.

## Goals for Different Financial Needs

A goal of obtaining increased career training is different than a goal of saving money to pay a semiannual auto insurance premium. *Consumable-product goals* usually occur on a periodic basis and involve items that are used up relatively quickly, such as food, clothing, and entertainment. Such purchases, if made unwisely, can have a negative effect on your financial situation.

*Durable-product goals* usually involve infrequently purchased, expensive items such as appliances, cars, and sporting equipment; these consist of tangible items. In contrast, many people overlook *intangible-purchase goals*. These goals may relate to personal relationships, health, education, and leisure. Goal setting for these life circumstances is also necessary for your overall well-being.

## Goal-Setting Guidelines

An old saying goes, "If you don't know where you're going, you might end up somewhere else and not even know it." Goal setting is central to financial decision making. Your financial goals are the basis for planning, implementing, and measuring the progress of your spending, saving, and investing activities. Exhibit 1–4 offers typical goals and financial activities for various life situations.

# Financial Planning for Life's Situations

## CREATING FINANCIAL GOALS

Based on your current situation or expectations for the future, create two financial goals, one short-term and one long-term, using the following guidelines:

**Step 1.** Create realistic goals based on your life situation.

### A. SHORT-TERM GOAL

_____
_____
_____
_____
_____

### B. LONG-TERM GOAL

_____
_____
_____
_____

**Step 2.** State your goals in specific, measurable terms.

a. _____
_____

b. _____
_____

**Step 3.** Describe the time frame for accomplishing your goals.

a. _____
_____

b. _____
_____

**Step 4.** Indicate an action to be taken to achieve your goals.

a. _____
_____

b. _____
_____

**EXHIBIT 1-4**   Financial Goals and Activities for Various Life Situations

Common Financial Goals and Activities

- Obtain appropriate career training.
- Create an effective financial recordkeeping system.
- Develop a regular savings and investment program.

- Accumulate an appropriate emergency fund.
- Purchase appropriate types and amounts of insurance coverage.
- Create and implement a flexible budget.

- Evaluate and select appropriate investments.
- Establish and implement a plan for retirement goals.
- Make a will and develop an estate plan.

| Life Situation | Specialized Financial Activities |
|---|---|
| Young, single (18–35) | • Establish financial independence.<br>• Obtain disability insurance to replace income during prolonged illness.<br>• Consider home purchase for tax benefit. |
| Young couple with children under 18 | • Carefully manage the increased need for the use of credit.<br>• Obtain an appropriate amount of life insurance for the care of dependents.<br>• Use a will to name guardian for children. |
| Single parent with children under 18 | • Obtain adequate amounts of health, life, and disability insurance.<br>• Contribute to savings and investment fund for college.<br>• Name a guardian for children and make other estate plans. |
| Young dual-income couple, no children | • Coordinate insurance coverage and other benefits.<br>• Develop savings and investment program for changes in life situation (larger house, children).<br>• Consider tax-deferred contributions to retirement fund. |
| Older couple (+50), no dependent children at home | • Consolidate financial assets and review estate plans.<br>• Obtain health insurance for postretirement period.<br>• Plan retirement housing, living expenses, recreational activities, and part-time work. |
| Mixed-generation household (elderly individuals and children under 18) | • Obtain long-term health care insurance and life/disability income for care of younger dependents.<br>• Use dependent care service if needed.<br>• Provide arrangements for handling finances of elderly if they become ill.<br>• Consider splitting of investment cost, with elderly getting income while alive and principal going to surviving relatives. |
| Older (+50), single | • Make arrangement for long-term health care coverage.<br>• Review will and estate plan.<br>• Plan retirement living facilities, living expenses, and activities. |

Your financial goals should be stated to take the following factors into account:

1. *Financial goals should be realistic.* Financial goals should be based on your income and life situation. For example, it is probably not realistic to expect to buy a new car each year if you are a full-time student.

2. *Financial goals should be stated in specific, measurable terms.* Knowing exactly what your goals are will help you create a plan designed to achieve them. For example, the goal of "accumulating $5,000 in an investment fund within three years" is a clearer guide to planning than the goal of "putting money into an investment fund."

**Sheet 3**

3. *Financial goals should have a time frame*. In the preceding example, the goal is to be achieved in three years. A time frame helps you measure your progress toward your financial goals.

4. *Financial goals should indicate the type of action to be taken*. Your financial goals are the basis for the various financial activities you will undertake. For example, "Reducing credit card debt" will usually mean decreased use of credit.

The Financial Planning for Life's Situation box on page 10 gives you an opportunity to set financial goals.

## Concept Check 1–2

1. What are examples of long-term goals?
2. What are the four main characteristics of useful financial goals?

# INFLUENCES ON PERSONAL FINANCIAL PLANNING

Many factors influence daily financial decisions, ranging from age and household size to interest rates and inflation. Three main elements affect financial planning activities: life situation, personal values, and economic factors.

## Life Situation and Personal Values

**Obj. 3**
Assess personal and economic factors that influence personal financial planning.

People in their 50s spend money differently than those in their 20s. Personal factors such as age, income, household size, and personal beliefs influence your spending and saving patterns. Your life situation or lifestyle is created by a combination of factors.

As our society changes, different types of financial needs evolve. Today people tend to get married at a later age, and more households have two incomes. Many households are headed by single parents. More than 2 million women provide care for both dependent children and parents. We are also living longer; over 80 percent of all Americans now living are expected to live past age 65.

*adult life cycle*
The stages in the family situation and financial needs of an adult.

As Exhibit 1–5 shows, the **adult life cycle**—the stages in the family and financial needs of an adult—is an important influence on your financial activities and decisions. Your life situation is also affected by marital status, household size, and employment, as well as events such as

- Graduation (at various levels of education).
- Engagement and marriage.
- The birth or adoption of a child.
- A career change or a move to a new area.
- Dependent children leaving home.
- Changes in health.
- Divorce.
- Retirement.
- The death of a spouse, family member, or other dependent.

*values*  Ideas and principles that a person considers correct, desirable, and important.

In addition to being defined by your family situation, you are defined by your **values**—the ideas and principles that you consider correct, desirable, and important. Values have a direct influence on such decisions as spending now versus saving for the future or continuing school versus getting a job.

Life Situation
Influences on
Your Financial
Decisions

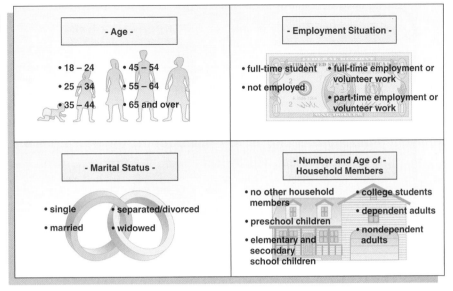

## Economic Factors

*economics*   The study of
how wealth is created and
distributed.

Daily economic activities are another important influence on financial planning. In our society, the forces of supply and demand play an important role in setting prices. **Economics** is the study of how wealth is created and distributed. The economic environment includes various institutions, principally business, labor, and government, that must work together to satisfy our needs and wants.

### Market Forces
Prices of goods and services are generally determined by supply and demand. Just as a high demand for a consumer product forces its price up, a high demand for money pushes up interest rates. This price of money reflects the limited supply of money and the demand for it.

At times, the price of an item may seem to be unaffected by the forces of supply and demand, but in fact at such times other economic factors may also be influencing its price. Although factors such as production costs and competition influence prices, the market forces of supply and demand remain in operation.

### Financial Institutions
Banks, savings and loan associations, credit unions, insurance companies, and investment companies are the financial institutions with which most people do business. Financial institutions provide services that facilitate financial activities in our economy. They accept savings, handle checking accounts, sell insurance, and make investments on behalf of others.

While various government agencies regulate financial activities, the Federal Reserve System, our nation's central bank, has significant responsibility in our economy. *The Fed,* as it is called, is concerned with maintaining an adequate money supply. It achieves this by influencing borrowing, interest rates, and the buying or selling of government securities. The Fed attempts to make adequate funds available for consumer spending and business expansion while keeping interest rates and consumer prices at an appropriate level.

## ELLEN ROGIN ON PERSONAL FINANCIAL PLANNING

"Spend less than you earn" is the foundation of long-term financial security according to Ellen Rogin, president of Strategic Financial Designs in Northfield, Illinois, a fee-based investment advisory company.

Although it sounds simple, most people do not follow this basic requirement for financial planning success. Ms. Rogin has been advising people about their money for over 12 years. While the typical client of her company ranges in age from 30 to 50, some are younger or older. Most of her clients are professionals and executives who have a common concern: a secure retirement. But Ms. Rogin is quick to point out that she works with people with a variety of needs, life situations, and investment philosophies. She has even advised a lottery winner, although she doesn't recommend that expectation as a steady path to long-term financial security!

The availability of information, Ms. Rogin believes, is the most significant change in the financial planning marketplace in recent years. With the Internet, television programs, and an extensive number of magazines and books,

people can be better informed regarding personal finance topics and investments. However, Ms. Rogin warns that people must assess the validity of the information. She suggests "avoiding specific investment advice from magazines and other sources that may not be appropriate for your individual situation."

When planning your own financial direction, Ms. Rogin recommends three actions:

1. Set specific financial goals.
2. Reduce your debts.
3. Save for retirement.

Even if someone else is managing your finances, Ms. Rogin encourages you to "be involved." Be aware of your personal economic situation and the financial marketplace. Communicate your money views, risk acceptance, and financial priorities. Never let a financial planner, your spouse, or another family member have complete control.

Additional information about Strategic Financial Designs is available on the company's website at www.sfd-inc.com.

### Global Influences
The global marketplace also influences financial activities. Our economy is affected by both the financial activities of foreign investors and competition from foreign companies. American businesses compete against foreign companies for the spending dollars of American consumers.

When the level of exports of U.S.-made goods is lower than the level of imported goods, more U.S. dollars leave the country than the dollar value of foreign currency coming into the United States. This reduces the funds available for domestic spending and investment. Also, if foreign companies decide not to invest their dollars in the United States, the domestic money supply is reduced. This reduced money supply may cause higher interest rates.

### Economic Conditions
Newspapers and business periodicals regularly publish current economic statistics. Exhibit 1–6 provides an overview of some economic indicators that influence financial decisions. Your personal financial decisions are most heavily influenced by consumer prices, consumer spending, and interest rates.

*inflation* A rise in the general level of prices.

### 1. Consumer Prices
**Inflation** is a rise in the general level of prices. In times of inflation, the buying power of the dollar decreases. For example, if prices increased 5 percent during the last year, items that cost $100 then would now cost $105. This means it now takes more money to buy the same amount of goods and services.

| EXHIBIT 1–6 | Changing Economic Conditions and Financial Decisions | |
| --- | --- | --- |
| **Economic Factor** | **What It Measures** | **How It Influences Financial Planning** |
| Consumer prices | The value of the dollar; changes in inflation | If consumer prices increase faster than your income, you are unable to purchase the same amount of goods and services; higher consumer prices will also cause higher interest rates. |
| Consumer spending | The demand for goods and services by individuals and households | Increased consumer spending is likely to create more jobs and higher wages; high levels of consumer spending and borrowing can also push up consumer prices and interest rates. |
| Interest rates | The cost of money; the cost of credit when you borrow; the return on your money when you save or invest | Higher interest rates make buying on credit more expensive; higher interest rates make saving and investing more attractive and discourage borrowing. |
| Money supply | The dollars available for spending in our economy | Interest rates tend to decline as more people save and invest; but higher saving (and lower spending) may also reduce job opportunities. |
| Unemployment | The number of people without employment who are willing and able to work | People who are unemployed should reduce their debt level and have an emergency savings fund for living costs while out of work; high unemployment reduces consumer spending and job opportunities. |
| Housing starts | The number of new homes being built | Increased home building results in more job opportunities, higher wages, more consumer spending, and overall economic expansion. |
| Gross domestic product (GDP) | The total value of goods and services produced within a country's borders, including items produced with foreign resources | The GDP provides an indication of a nation's economic viability resulting in employment and opportunities for personal financial wealth. |
| Trade balance | The difference between a country's exports and its imports | If a country exports more than it imports, interest rates may rise and foreign goods and foreign travel will cost more. |
| Dow Jones Average, S&P 500, other stock market indexes | The relative value of stocks represented by the index | These indexes provide an indication of the general movement of stock prices. |

The main cause of inflation is an increase in demand without a comparable increase in supply. For example, if people have more money to spend because of pay increases or borrowing but the same amounts of goods and services are available, the increased demand can bid up prices for those goods and services.

Inflation is most harmful to people living on fixed incomes. Due to inflation, retired people and others whose incomes do not change are able to afford smaller amounts of goods and services.

Inflation can also adversely affect lenders of money. Unless an adequate interest rate is charged, amounts repaid by borrowers in times of inflation have less buying power than the money they borrowed. If you pay 10 percent interest on a loan and the inflation rate is 12 percent, the dollars you pay the lender have lost buying power. For this reason, interest rates rise in periods of high inflation.

The rate of inflation varies. During the late 1950s and early 1960s, the annual inflation rate was in the 1 to 3 percent range. During the late 1970s and early 1980s, the cost of living increased 10 to 12 percent annually. At a 12 percent annual inflation rate, prices double (and the value of the dollar is cut in half) in about six years. To find out how fast prices (or your savings) will double, use the *rule of 72:* Just divide 72 by the annual inflation (or interest) rate. An annual inflation rate of 8 percent, for example, means prices will double in nine years ($72 \div 8 = 9$).

More recently, the annual price increase for most goods and services as measured by the consumer price index has been in the 3 to 5 percent range. The *consumer price index (CPI),* published by the Bureau of Labor Statistics, is a measure of the average change in the prices urban consumers pay for a fixed "basket" of goods and services. For current CPI information, go to www.bls.gov.

**2. Consumer Spending**   Total demand for goods and services in the economy influences employment opportunities and the potential for income. As consumer purchasing increases, the financial resources of current and prospective employees expand. This situation improves the financial condition of many households.

In contrast, reduced spending causes unemployment, since staff reduction commonly results from a company's reduced financial resources. The financial hardships of unemployment are a major concern of business, labor, and government. Retraining programs, income assistance, and job services can help people adjust.

**3. Interest Rates**   In simple terms, interest rates represent the cost of money. Like everything else, money has a price. The forces of supply and demand influence interest rates. When consumer saving and investing increase the supply of money, interest rates tend to decrease. However, as consumer, business, government, and foreign borrowing increase the demand for money, interest rates tend to rise.

Interest rates affect your financial planning. The earnings you receive as a saver or an investor reflect current interest rates as well as a *risk premium* based on such factors as the length of time your funds will be used by others, expected inflation, and the extent of uncertainty about getting your money back. Risk is also a factor in the interest rate you pay as a borrower. People with poor credit ratings pay a higher interest rate than people with good credit ratings. Interest rates influence many financial decisions. Current interest rate data may be obtained at www.federalreserve.gov.

**PFP**

**Sheet 4**

## Concept Check 1-3

1.  How do age, marital status, household size, employment situation, and other personal factors affect financial planning?
2.  How might the uncertainty of inflation make personal financial planning difficult?
3.  What factors influence the level of interest rates?

# OPPORTUNITY COSTS AND THE TIME VALUE OF MONEY

**Obj. 4**
Determine personal and financial opportunity costs associated with personal financial decisions.

Have you noticed that you always give up something when you make choices? In every financial decision, you sacrifice something to obtain something else that you consider more desirable. For example, you might forgo current consumption to invest funds for future purchases or long-term financial security. Or you might gain the use of an expensive item now by making credit payments from future earnings. These *opportunity costs* may be viewed in terms of both personal and financial resources (see Exhibit 1–7).

## Personal Opportunity Costs

An important personal opportunity cost involves time that when used for one activity cannot be used for other activities. Time used for studying, working, or shopping will not be available for other uses. The allocation of time should be viewed like any decision: Select your use of time to meet your needs, achieve your goals, and satisfy personal values.

Other personal opportunity costs relate to health. Poor eating habits, lack of sleep, or avoiding exercise can result in illness, time away from school or work, increased health care costs, and reduced financial security. Like financial resources, your personal resources (time, energy, health, abilities, knowledge) require management.

## Financial Opportunity Costs

*time value of money*
Increases in an amount of money as a result of interest earned.

You are constantly making choices among various financial decisions. In making those choices, you must consider the **time value of money**, the increases in an amount of money as a result of interest earned. Saving or investing a dollar instead of spending it today results in a future amount greater than a dollar. Every time you spend, save, invest, or borrow money, you should consider the time value of that money as an opportunity cost. Spending money from your savings account means lost interest earnings; however, what you buy with that money may have a higher priority than those earnings. Borrowing to make a purchase involves the opportunity cost of paying interest on the loan, but your current needs may make this trade-off worthwhile.

**EXHIBIT 1-7**

Opportunity Costs and Financial Results Should Be Evaluated When Making Financial Decisions

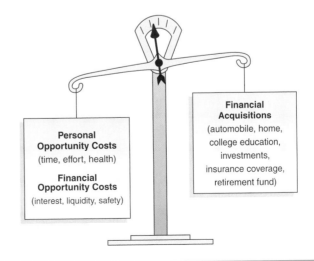

**Personal Opportunity Costs** (time, effort, health)

**Financial Opportunity Costs** (interest, liquidity, safety)

**Financial Acquisitions** (automobile, home, college education, investments, insurance coverage, retirement fund)

The opportunity cost of the time value of money is also present in these financial decisions:

- Setting aside funds in a savings plan with little or no risk has the opportunity cost of potentially higher returns from an investment with greater risk.
- Having extra money withheld from your paycheck in order to receive a tax refund has the opportunity cost of the lost interest the money could earn in a savings account.
- Making annual deposits in a retirement account can help you avoid the opportunity cost of having inadequate funds later in life.
- Purchasing a new automobile or home appliance has the potential benefit of saving you money on future maintenance and energy costs.

## Interest Calculations

Three amounts are used to calculate the time value of money for savings in the form of interest earned:

- The amount of the savings (commonly called the *principal*).
- The annual interest rate.
- The length of time the money is on deposit.

These three items are multiplied to obtain the amount of interest. Simple interest is calculated as follows:

$$\boxed{\text{Amount in savings}} \times \boxed{\text{Annual interest rate}} \times \boxed{\text{Time period}} = \boxed{\text{Interest}}$$

For example, $500 on deposit at 6 percent for six months would earn $15 ($500 × 0.06 × $^6\!/_{12}$, or ½ year).

You can calculate the increased value of your money from interest earned in two ways: You can calculate the total amount that will be available later (future value), or you can determine the current value of an amount desired in the future (present value).

## Future Value of a Single Amount

Deposited money earns interest that will increase over time. **Future value** is the amount to which current savings will increase based on a certain interest rate and a certain time period. For example, $100 deposited in a 6 percent account for one year will grow to $106. This amount is computed as follows:

$$\text{Future value} = \$100 + (\$100 \times 0.06 \times 1 \text{ year}) = \$106$$

Original amount in savings        Amount of interest earned

*future value* The amount to which current savings will increase based on a certain interest rate and a certain time period; also referred to as compounding.

The same process could be continued for a second, third, and fourth year, but the computations would be time consuming. Future value tables simplify the process (see Exhibit 1–8). To use a future value table, multiply the amount deposited by the factor for the desired interest rate and time period. For example, $650 at 8 percent for 10 years would have a future value of $1,403.35 ($650 × 2.159). The future value of an amount will always be greater than the original amount. As Exhibit 1–8A shows, all the future value factors are larger than 1.

Future value computations may be referred to as *compounding*, since interest is earned on previously earned interest. Compounding allows the future value of a deposit to grow faster than it would if interest were paid only on the original deposit.

The sooner you make deposits, the greater the future value will be. Depositing $1,000 in a 5 percent account at age 40 will give you $3,387 at age 65. However, making the $1,000 deposit at age 25 would result in an account balance of $7,040 at age 65.

**EXHIBIT 1-8**

Time Value of
Money Tables
(condensed)

**A. Future Value of $1 (single amount)**

Percent

| Year | 5% | 6% | 7% | 8% | 9% |
|---|---|---|---|---|---|
| 5 | 1.276 | 1.338 | 1.403 | 1.469 | 1.539 |
| 6 | 1.340 | 1.419 | 1.501 | 1.587 | 1.677 |
| 7 | 1.407 | 1.504 | 1.606 | 1.714 | 1.828 |
| 8 | 1.477 | 1.594 | 1.718 | 1.851 | 1.993 |
| 9 | 1.551 | 1.689 | 1.838 | 1.999 | 2.172 |
| 10 | 1.629 | 1.791 | 1.967 | 2.159 | 2.367 |

**B. Future Value of a Series of Annual Deposits (annuity)**

Percent

| Year | 5% | 6% | 7% | 8% | 9% |
|---|---|---|---|---|---|
| 5 | 5.526 | 5.637 | 5.751 | 5.867 | 5.985 |
| 6 | 6.802 | 6.975 | 7.153 | 7.336 | 7.523 |
| 7 | 8.142 | 8.394 | 8.654 | 8.923 | 9.200 |
| 8 | 9.549 | 9.897 | 10.260 | 10.637 | 11.028 |
| 9 | 11.027 | 11.491 | 11.978 | 12.488 | 13.021 |
| 10 | 12.578 | 13.181 | 13.816 | 14.487 | 15.193 |

**C. Present Value of $1 (single amount)**

Percent

| Year | 5% | 6% | 7% | 8% | 9% |
|---|---|---|---|---|---|
| 5 | 0.784 | 0.747 | 0.713 | 0.681 | 0.650 |
| 6 | 0.746 | 0.705 | 0.666 | 0.630 | 0.596 |
| 7 | 0.711 | 0.665 | 0.623 | 0.583 | 0.547 |
| 8 | 0.677 | 0.627 | 0.582 | 0.540 | 0.502 |
| 9 | 0.645 | 0.592 | 0.544 | 0.500 | 0.460 |
| 10 | 0.614 | 0.558 | 0.508 | 0.463 | 0.422 |

**D. Present Value of a Series of Annual Deposits (annuity)**

Percent

| Year | 5% | 6% | 7% | 8% | 9% |
|---|---|---|---|---|---|
| 5 | 4.329 | 4.212 | 4.100 | 3.993 | 3.890 |
| 6 | 5.076 | 4.917 | 4.767 | 4.623 | 4.486 |
| 7 | 5.786 | 5.582 | 5.389 | 5.206 | 5.033 |
| 8 | 6.463 | 6.210 | 5.971 | 5.747 | 5.535 |
| 9 | 7.108 | 6.802 | 6.515 | 6.247 | 5.995 |
| 10 | 7.722 | 7.360 | 7.024 | 6.710 | 6.418 |

See Appendix A at the end of the book for more complete future value and present value tables.

**Future Value of a Series of Deposits**   Quite often, savers and investors make regular deposits. An *annuity* is a series of equal deposits or payments. To determine the future value of equal yearly savings deposits, use Exhibit 1–8B. For this table to be used, the deposits must earn a constant interest rate. If you deposit $50 a year at 7 percent for six years, starting at the end of the first year, you will have $357.65 at the end of that time ($50 × 7.153). The Financial Planning Calculations box on page 20, presents examples of using future value to achieve financial goals.

*present value*   The current value for a future amount based on a certain interest rate and a certain time period; also referred to as *discounting*.

## Present Value of a Single Amount

Another aspect of the time value of money involves determining the current value of a desired amount for the future. **Present value** is the current value for a future amount based on a certain interest rate and a certain time period. Present value computations, also called *discounting,* allow you to determine how much to deposit now to obtain a desired total in the future. Present value tables (Exhibit 1–8C) can be used to make the computations. If you want $1,000 five years from now and you earn 5 percent on your savings, you need to deposit $784 ($1,000 × 0.784).

The present value of the amount you want in the future will always be less than the future value, since all of the factors in Exhibit 1–8C are less than 1 and interest earned will increase the present value amount to the desired future amount.

## Present Value of a Series of Deposits

You can also use present value computations to determine how much you need to deposit so that you can take a certain amount out of the account for a desired number of years. For example, if you want to take $400 out of an investment account each year for nine years and your money is earning an annual rate of 8 percent, you can see from Exhibit 1–8D that you would need to make a current deposit of $2,498.80 ($400 × 6.247).

## Financial Planning Calculations

### ANNUAL CONTRIBUTIONS TO ACHIEVE A FINANCIAL GOAL

Achieving specific financial goals often requires regular deposits to a savings or investment account. By using time value of money calculations, you can determine the amount you should save or invest to achieve a specific goal for the future.

#### EXAMPLE 1

Jonie Emerson has two children who will start college in 10 years. She plans to set aside $1,500 a year for her children's college educations during that period and estimates she will earn an annual interest rate of 5 percent on her savings. What amount can Jonie expect to have available for her children's college educations when they start college?

**CALCULATION:**

$1,500 × Future value of a series of deposits, 5%, 10 years

$1,500 × 12.578 (Exhibit 1–8B) = $18,867

#### EXAMPLE 2

Don Calder wants to accumulate $50,000 over the next 10 years as a reserve fund for his parents' retirement living expenses and health care. If he earns an average of 8 percent on his investments, what amount must he invest each year to achieve this goal?

**CALCULATION:**

$50,000 ÷ Future value of a series of deposits, 8%, 10 years

$50,000 ÷ 14.487 (Exhibit 1–8B) = $3,452.80

Don needs to invest approximately $3,450 a year for 10 years at 8 percent to achieve the desired financial goal.

**Sheet 5**

The formulas for calculating future and present values, as well as tables covering a wider range of interest rates and time periods, are presented in Appendix A. Computer programs for calculating time value of money are also available.

## Concept Check 1-4

1. How can you use future value and present value computations to measure the opportunity cost of a financial decision?
2. Use the time value of money tables in Exhibit 1–8 to calculate the following:
    a. The future value of $100 at 7 percent in 10 years.
    b. The future value of $100 a year for six years earning 6 percent.
    c. The present value of $500 received in eight years with an interest rate of 8 percent.

# ACHIEVING FINANCIAL GOALS

**Obj. 5**
Identify strategies for achieving personal financial goals for different life situations.

Throughout life, our needs usually can be satisfied with the intelligent use of financial resources. Financial planning involves deciding how to obtain, protect, and use those resources. By using the eight major areas of personal financial planning to organize your financial activities, you can avoid many common money mistakes.

## Components of Personal Financial Planning

This book is designed to provide a framework for the study and planning of personal financial decisions. Exhibit 1–9 presents an overview of the eight major personal financial planning areas. To achieve a successful financial situation, you must coordinate these components through an organized plan and wise decision making.

### Obtaining (Chapter 2)
You obtain financial resources from employment, investments, or ownership of a business. Obtaining financial resources is the foundation of financial planning, since these resources are used for all financial activities.

Key Websites for Obtaining:   www.hotjobs.com   www.monster.com

### Planning (Chapters 3, 4)
Planned spending through budgeting is the key to achieving goals and future financial security. Efforts to anticipate expenses and financial decisions can also help reduce taxes. The ability to pay your fair share of taxes—no more, no less—is vital to increasing your financial resources.

Key Websites for Planning:   www.personalwealth.com   www.quicken.com

### Saving (Chapter 5)
Long-term financial security starts with a regular savings plan for emergencies, unexpected bills, replacement of major items, and the purchase of special goods and services, such as a college education, a boat, or a vacation home. Once you have established a basic savings plan, you may use additional money for investments that offer greater financial growth.

*liquidity*  The ability to readily convert financial resources into cash without a loss in value.

An amount of savings must be available to meet current household needs. **Liquidity** refers to the ability to readily convert financial resources into cash without a loss in value. The need for liquidity will vary based on a person's age, health, and family situation. Savings plans such as interest-earning checking accounts, money market accounts, and money market funds earn money on your savings while providing liquidity.

**Components of Personal Financial Planning**

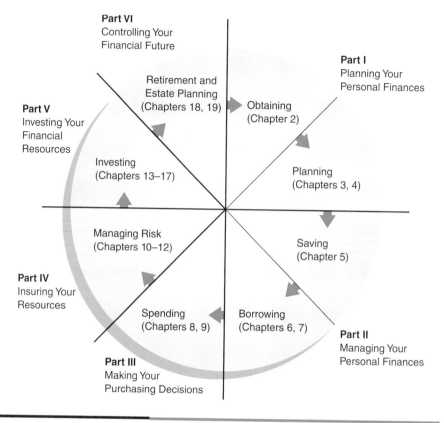

**Part VI**
Controlling Your
Financial Future

**Part I**
Planning Your
Personal Finances

Retirement and
Estate Planning
(Chapters 18, 19)

Obtaining
(Chapter 2)

**Part V**
Investing Your
Financial
Resources

Investing
(Chapters 13–17)

Planning
(Chapters 3, 4)

Managing Risk
(Chapters 10–12)

Saving
(Chapter 5)

**Part IV**
Insuring Your
Resources

Spending
(Chapters 8, 9)

Borrowing
(Chapters 6, 7)

**Part II**
Managing Your
Personal Finances

**Part III**
Making Your
Purchasing Decisions

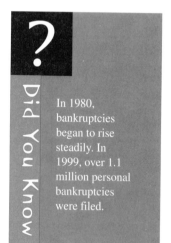

**Did You Know?**

In 1980, bankruptcies began to rise steadily. In 1999, over 1.1 million personal bankruptcies were filed.

*bankruptcy*  A set of federal laws that allow you to either restructure your debts or remove certain debts.

**Key Websites for Saving:**   www.bankrate.com   www.banx.com

**Borrowing (Chapters 6, 7)**   Maintaining control over your credit-buying habits will contribute to your financial goals. The overuse and misuse of credit may cause a situation in which a person's debts far exceed the resources available to pay those debts. **Bankruptcy** is a set of federal laws that allow you to either restructure your debts or remove certain debts. The people who declare bankruptcy each year may have avoided this trauma with wise spending and borrowing decisions. Chapter 7 discusses bankruptcy in detail.

**Key Websites for Borrowing:**   www.financenter.com   www.cardtrak.com

**Spending (Chapters 8, 9)**   Financial planning is designed not to prevent your enjoyment of life but to help you obtain the things you want. Too often, however, people make purchases without considering the financial consequences. Some people shop compulsively, creating financial difficulties. You should detail your living expenses and your other financial obligations in a spending plan. Spending less than you earn is the only way to achieve long-term financial security.

**Key Websites for Spending:**   www.consumerworld.org   www.consumer.gov

**Managing Risk (Chapters 10–12)**   Adequate insurance coverage is another component of personal financial planning. Certain types of insurance are commonly overlooked in financial plans. For example, the number of people who suffer disabling injuries or diseases at age 50 is greater than the number who die at that age, so people may need disability insurance more than they need life insurance. Yet surveys reveal that most people have adequate life insurance but few have disability insurance. The insurance industry is more aggressive in selling life insurance than in selling disability insurance, thus putting the burden of obtaining adequate disability insurance on you.

Many households have excessive or overlapping insurance coverage. Insuring property for more than it is worth may be a waste of money, as may both a husband and a wife having similar health insurance coverage.

**Key Websites for Managing Risk:**   www.insure.com   www.insuremarket.com

**Investing (Chapters 13–17)**   While many types of investment vehicles are available, people invest for two primary reasons. Those interested in *current income* select investments that pay regular dividends or interest. In contrast, investors who desire *long-term growth* choose stocks, mutual funds, real estate, and other investments with potential for increased value in the future.

You can achieve investment diversification by including a variety of assets in your *portfolio*—for example, stocks, bond mutual funds, real estate, and collectibles such as rare coins. Obtaining general investment advice is easy; however, it is more difficult to obtain specific investment advice to meet your individual needs and goals.

**Key Websites for Investing:**   www.personalwealth.com   www.investorama.com

**Retirement and Estate Planning (Chapters 18, 19)**   Most people desire financial security upon completion of full-time employment. But retirement planning also involves thinking about your housing situation, your recreational activities, and possible part-time or volunteer work.

**Key Websites for Retirement and Estate Planning:**   www.lifenet.com www.aarp.org

Transfers of money or property to others should be timed, if possible, to minimize the tax burden and maximize the benefits for those receiving the financial resources. A knowledge of property transfer methods can help you select the best course of action for funding current and future living costs, educational expenses, and retirement needs of dependents.

## Developing a Flexible Financial Plan

*financial plan*
A formalized report that summarizes your current financial situation, analyzes your financial needs, and recommends future financial activities.

A **financial plan** is a formalized report that summarizes your current financial situation, analyzes your financial needs, and recommends future financial activities. You can create this document on your own, seek assistance from a financial planner, or use a money management software package (see the chapter appendix). Exhibit 1–10 offers a framework for developing and implementing a financial plan, along with examples for several life situations.

## Implementing Your Financial Plan

You must have a plan before you can implement it. However, once you have clearly assessed your current situation and identified your financial goals, what do you do next?

The most important strategy for success is the development of financial habits that contribute to both short-term satisfaction and long-term financial security, including the following:

1.  Using a well-conceived spending plan will help you stay within your income while you save and invest for the future. The main source of financial difficulties is overspending.

**EXHIBIT 1-10**    Financial Planning in Action

2.  Having appropriate insurance protection will help you prevent financial disasters.
3.  Becoming informed about tax and investment alternatives will help you expand your financial resources.

Achieving your financial objectives requires two things: (1) a willingness to learn and (2) appropriate information sources. *You* must provide the first element; the chapters that follow will provide the second. For successful financial planning, know where you are now, know where you want to be, and be persistent in your efforts to get there.

## Concept Check 1-5

1.  What are the main components of personal financial planning?
2.  What is the purpose of a financial plan?
3.  Identify some common actions taken to achieve financial goals.

# Summary of Objectives

**Obj. 1**   **Analyze the process for making personal financial decisions.**

Personal financial planning involves the following process: (1) determine your current financial situation; (2) develop financial goals; (3) identify alternative courses of action; (4) evaluate alternatives; (5) create and implement a financial action plan; and (6) reevaluate and revise the financial plan.

**Obj. 2**   **Develop personal financial goals.**

Financial goals should (1) be realistic; (2) be stated in specific, measurable terms; (3) have a time frame; and (4) indicate the type of action to be taken.

**Obj. 3**   **Assess personal and economic factors that influence personal financial planning.**

Financial decisions are affected by a person's life situation (income, age, household size, health), personal values, and economic factors (prices, interest rates, and employment opportunities).

**Obj. 4**   **Determine personal and financial opportunity costs associated with personal financial decisions.**

Every decision involves a trade-off with things given up. Personal opportunity costs include time, effort, and health. Financial opportunity costs are based on the time value of money. Future value and present value calculations enable you to measure the increased value (or lost interest) that results from a saving, investing, borrowing, or purchasing decision.

**Obj. 5**   **Identify strategies for achieving personal financial goals for different life situations.**

Successful financial planning requires specific goals combined with spending, saving, investing, and borrowing strategies based on your personal situation and various social and economic factors.

# Financial Planning Problems

(Note: Some of these problems require the use of the time value of money tables in Appendix A.)

1. *Calculating Future Value of Property.* Ben Collins plans to buy a house for $65,000. If that real estate is expected to increase in value by 5 percent each year, what will its approximate value be seven years from now?   (Obj. 3)

2. *Using the Rule of 72.* Using the rule of 72, approximate the following amounts.   (Obj. 3)
   a. If land in an area is increasing 6 percent a year, how long will it take for property values to double?
   b. If you earn 10 percent on your investments, how long will it take for your money to double?
   c. At an annual interest rate of 5 percent, how long will it take for your savings to double?

3. *Determining the Inflation Rate.* In the late 1980s, selected automobiles had an average cost of $12,000. The average cost of those same automobiles is now $15,000. What was the rate of increase for these automobiles between the two time periods?   (Obj. 3)

4. *Computing Future Living Expenses.* A family spends $28,000 a year for living expenses. If prices increase by 4 percent a year for the next three years, what amount will the family need for their living expenses after three years?   (Obj. 3)

5. *Calculating Earnings on Savings.* What would be the yearly earnings for a person with $6,000 in savings at an annual interest rate of 5.5 percent?   (Obj. 4)

6. *Computing Time Value of Money.* Using time value of money tables, calculate the following.   (Obj. 4)
   a. The future value of $450 six years from now at 7 percent.
   b. The future value of $800 saved each year for 10 years at 8 percent.
   c. The amount a person would have to deposit today (present value) at a 6 percent interest rate to have $1,000 five years from now.
   d. The amount a person would have to deposit today to be able to take out $500 a year for 10 years from an account earning 8 percent.

7. *Calculating Future Value of a Series of Amounts.* Elaine Romberg prepares her own income tax return each year. A tax preparer would charge her $60 for this service. Over a period of 10 years, how much does Elaine gain from preparing her own tax return? Assume she can earn 6 percent with a savings certificate.   (Obj. 4)

# Financial Planning Activities

1. *Researching Personal Finance on the Internet.* Using websites such as www.personalwealth.com, www. quicken.com, or www. kiplinger.com and search engines, obtain information about commonly suggested actions related to various personal financial planning decisions. What are some of the best sources of information on the Internet to assist you with financial planning?   (Obj. 1)

2. *Comparing Financial Planning Actions.* Survey friends, relatives, and others to determine the process they use when making financial decisions. How do these people measure risk when making financial decisions?   (Obj. 1)

3. *Using Financial Planning Experts.* Prepare a list of financial planning specialists (investment advisers, credit counselors, insurance agents, real estate brokers, tax preparers) in your community who can assist people with personal financial planning. Prepare a list of questions that might be asked of these financial planning professionals by *(a)* a young person just starting out on his or her own, *(b)* a young couple planning for their children's education and for their own retirement, and *(c)* a person nearing retirement.   (Obj. 1, 3)

4. *Setting Financial Goals.* Using Sheet 3 in the *Personal Financial Planner,* create one short-term and one long-term goal for people in these life situations: *(a)* a young single person, *(b)* a single parent with a child age 8, *(c)* a married person with no children, and *(d)* a retired person.   (Obj. 2)

5. *Analyzing Changing Life Situations.* Ask friends, relatives, and others how their spending, saving, and borrowing activities changed when they decided to continue their education, change careers, or have children.   (Obj. 3)

6. *Researching Economic Conditions.* Use library resources, such as *The Wall Street Journal,* the "Economy" section of www.personalwealth.com, or other websites to determine recent trends in interest rates, inflation, and other economic indicators. Information about the consumer price index (measuring changes in the cost of living) may be obtained at www.bls.gov. Report how this economic information might affect your financial planning decisions.   (Obj. 3)

7. *Comparing Alternative Financial Actions.* What actions would be necessary to compare a financial planner who advertises "One Low Fee Is Charged to Develop Your Personal Financial Plan" and one that advertises "You Are Not Charged a Fee, My Services Are Covered by the Investment Company for Which I Work"?   (Obj. 4, 5)

8. *Determining Opportunity Costs.* What is the relationship between current interest rates and financial opportunity costs? Using time value of money calculations, state one or more goals in terms of an annual savings amount and the future value of this savings fund.   (Obj. 2, 4)

9. *Researching Financial Planning Software.* Visit software retailers to obtain information about the features and costs of various personal financial planning activities. Information about programs such as Microsoft Money and Quicken may be obtained on the Internet.   (Obj. 5)

# LIFE SITUATION CASE

## TRIPLE TROUBLE FOR THE "SANDWICH GENERATION"

Until recently, Fran and Ed Blake's personal finances ran smoothly. Both have maintained well-paying jobs while raising two children. The Blakes have a daughter who is completing her freshman year of college and a son three years younger. Currently they have $22,000 in various savings and investment funds set aside for the children's education. With education costs increasing faster than inflation, they are uncertain whether this amount is adequate.

In recent months, Fran's mother has required extensive medical attention and personal care assistance. Unable to live alone, she is now a resident of a long-term care facility. The cost of this service is $2,050 a month, with annual increases of about 7 percent. While a major portion of the cost is covered by her Social Security and pension, Fran's mother is unable to cover the entire cost. Their desire to help adds to the Blakes' financial burden.

The Blakes are like millions of other Americans who have financial responsibilities for both dependent children and aging parents. Commonly referred to as the "sandwich generation," this group is squeezed on one side by the cost of raising and educating children and on the other side by the financial demands of caring for aging parents.

Finally, the Blakes, ages 47 and 43, are also concerned about saving for their own retirement. While they have consistently made annual deposits to a retirement fund, various current financial demands may force them to tap into this money.

## Questions

1. What actions have the Blakes taken that would be considered wise financial planning choices?
2. What areas of financial concern do the Blakes face? What actions might be appropriate to address these concerns?
3. Using time value of money calculations (tables in Appendix A), compute the following:
   *a.* At 12 percent, what would be the value of the $22,000 education funds in three years?
   *b.* If the cost of long-term care is increasing at 7 percent a year, what will be the approximate monthly cost for Fran's mother eight years from now?
   *c.* Fran and Ed plan to deposit $1,500 a year to their retirement fund for 35 years. If they earn an average annual return of 9 percent, what will be the value of their retirement fund after 35 years?

## VIDEO CASE   The Personal Financial Plan

People have different attitudes toward money and financial planning. Some view spending as the ultimate purpose of making money, with nothing or very little for saving. Others, due to their family situation or age, understand the need to plan, save, and invest.

Following a logical process for developing a personal financial plan is the foundation of effective money management. By setting goals, people are able to provide a direction for the short term and long term. Specific goals can also prevent various financial planning pitfalls.

As you may already realize, different financial activities are usually appropriate for different ages. People in their 30s have many expenses; they also need to have a plan for long-term financial security. In contrast, people in their 50s need to reassess their retirement investments and start thinking about living arrangements and housing during their later years.

### Questions

1. What are some common personal financial planning mistakes people make?
2. How does goal setting help a person to achieve long-term financial security?
3. What factors affect the need to take different financial actions for different ages in life, such as in your 30s, 40s, and 50s?

# Creating an E-Plan: Financial Decisions Using the Web

## STARTING YOUR FINANCIAL PLAN

Planning is the foundation for success in every aspect of life. Assessing your current financial situation along with setting goals is the key to successful financial planning.

Websites for Financial Planning

- Goal-setting information and investment planning at **www.personalwealth.com.**
- The FinanCenter provides answers to questions and calculations related to budgeting, automobiles, savings, investments, credit, and housing at **www.financenter.com/.**
- "The Motley Fool" offers a wide range of personal finance information at **www.fool.com/,** as does **www.quicken.com (www.qfn.com),** the Cable News Network financial news service at **cnnfn.com/ index.html**, and Money Central at **www. moneycentral.msn.com.**
- Selected articles from *Money* magazine at **www.money. com**, from *Kiplinger's Personal Finance Magazine* at **www.kiplinger.com,** and *Business Week* at **www.businessweek.com.**
- Information on Federal Reserve activities, publications, and access to the websites of the 12 Federal Reserve Banks at **www.federalreserve.gov.** Each Federal Reserve Bank has a website with publications, links to other websites, and current economic data; these include the Boston Federal Reserve Bank at **www.bos.frb.org** and the New York Federal Reserve Bank at **www.ny.frb.org.**
- Current consumer price index and inflation information at **www.bls.gov,** **www.stls.frb.org/fred/data/cupdate.html,** and **www.westegg.com/inflation.**
- Current economic data at **www.stats. bls.gov/eag.table.htm.**
- Financial planning calculators for computing the time value of money at **www.centura.com/formulas/calc.html,** and **www.moneyadvisor.com/calc.**

(Note: Addresses and content of websites change, and new sites are created daily. Use the search engines discussed in the chapter appendix to update and locate websites for your current financial planning needs.)

*PFP sheets: 1–5*

Short-Term Financial Planning Activities

1. Prepare a list of personal and financial information for yourself and family members. Also create a list of financial service organizations that you use (see PFP Sheets 1, 2).
2. Set financial goals related to various current and future needs (see PFP Sheet 3).
3. Monitor current economic conditions (inflation, interest rates) to determine possible actions to take related to your personal finances (see PFP Sheet 4).

Long-Term Financial Planning Activities

1. Based on various financial goals, calculate the savings deposits necessary to achieve those goals.
2. Identify various financial planning actions for you and other household members for the next two to five years.

CHAPTER
1

# Financial Planners and Other Financial Planning Information Sources

"ATM fees rise"

"Global currency fluctuations may affect consumer prices."

"Mortgage interest rates remain constant."

These are just a few of the possible influences on personal financial decisions that occur each day. While this book offers the foundation for successful personal financial planning, changing social trends, economic conditions, and technology influence the decision-making environment. Your ability to continually supplement and update your knowledge is a skill that will serve you for a lifetime.

Various resources are available to assist you with personal financial decisions. These resources include printed materials, financial institutions, courses and seminars, the Internet, computer software, and financial planning specialists.

## CURRENT PERIODICALS

As Exhibit 1–A shows, a variety of personal finance periodicals are available to expand and update your knowledge. These periodicals, along with books on various personal finance topics, can be found in libraries.

## FINANCIAL INSTITUTIONS

Some financial advisers, such as insurance agents and investment brokers, are affiliated with companies that sell financial services. Through national marketing efforts or local promotions, banks, savings and loan associations, credit unions, insurance companies, investment brokers, and real estate offices offer suggestions on budgeting, saving, investing, and other aspects of financial planning. These organizations frequently offer booklets, financial planning worksheets, websites, and other materials and information.

PERSONAL FINANCIAL PLANNING PERIODICALS

The area of personal finance is constantly changing. You can keep up with changes by reading the following periodicals. You can subscribe to them, read them at your school or community library, or access them on the Internet.

**Bottom Line/Personal**
Box 1027
Milburn, NJ 07041
Website: www.boardroom.com

**Business Week**
1221 Avenue of the Americas
New York, NY 10020
Website: www.businessweek.com

**Consumers Digest**
5705 North Lincoln Ave.
Chicago, IL 60659
Website: www.consumersdigest.com

**Consumer Reports**
Consumers Union
101 Truman Avenue
Yonkers, NY 10703-1057
Website: www.consumerreports.org

**Forbes**
60 Fifth Avenue
New York, NY 10011
Website: www.forbes.com

**Fortune**
Time & Life Building
Rockefeller Center
New York, NY 10020-1393
Website: www.fortune.com

**Kiplinger's Personal Finance Magazine**
1729 H Street, NW
Washington, DC 20006
Website: www.kiplinger.com

**Money**
Time & Life Building
Rockefeller Center
New York, NY 10020-1393
Website: www.money.com

**Smart Money**
224 West 57th Street
New York, NY 10019
Website: www.smartmoney.com

**U.S. News & World Report**
2400 N Street, NW
Washington, DC 20037-1196
Website: www.usnews.com

**The Wall Street Journal**
200 Burnett Road
Chicopee, MA 01020
Website: www.wsj.com

**Worth**
575 Lexington Avenue
New York, NY 10022
Website: www.worth.com

## COURSES AND SEMINARS

Colleges and universities offer courses in investments, real estate, insurance, taxation, and estate planning to enhance your knowledge of personal financial planning. The Cooperative Extension Service, funded through the U.S. Department of Agriculture, has offices located at universities in every state and in many counties (see your local telephone directory). Programs of these offices include community seminars and continuing education courses in the areas of family financial management, housing, consumer purchasing, health care, and food and nutrition. In addition, Cooperative Extension Service offices offer a variety of publications, videos, and software to assist consumers.

Civic clubs and community business organizations often schedule free or inexpensive programs featuring speakers and workshops on career planning, small-business management, budgeting, life insurance, tax return preparation, and investments. Financial institutions and financial service trade associations present seminars for current and prospective customers and members.

## PERSONAL FINANCE SOFTWARE

Personal computer software is available to help you perform a variety of personal financial planning activities, from selecting a career to writing a will. These programs help you analyze your current financial situation and project your future financial position. Specialized computer programs are also available for conducting investment analyses, preparing tax returns, and determining the costs of financing and owning a home. Remember, a personal computer cannot change your saving, spending, and borrowing habits; only *you* can do that. However, your computer can provide fast and current analyses of your financial situation and progress. For information about the latest software, visit a computer store or read the articles and advertisements in magazines such as *PC Computing, PC Magazine, Computer Life, Windows, Family PC,* and *Home PC.*

## Spreadsheets

A spreadsheet program such as Excel or Lotus 1-2-3 can assist with various financial planning tasks. Spreadsheet software can store, manipulate, create projections, and report data for activities such as

- Creating budget categories and recording spending patterns.
- Maintaining tax records for different types of expenses such as mileage, travel expenses, materials and supplies, and business-related costs.
- Calculating the growth potential of savings accounts and investments.
- Monitoring changes in the market value of investments.
- Keeping records of the value of items for a home inventory.
- Projecting needed amounts of life insurance and retirement income.

## Money Management and Financial Planning Programs

Integrated financial planning programs can help you maintain home financial records, create a budget, observe spending patterns, write checks, keep tax records, select and monitor investments, and project retirement needs. The most popular of these software packages are

| *MS Money* | *Quicken* |
|---|---|
| Microsoft | Intuit |
| 1–800–426–9400 | 1-800-446-8848 |
| (www.microsoft.com) | (www.quicken.com) |

## Tax Software

Each year the software available to prepare federal and state tax returns becomes more helpful. Besides preparation and printing of the various forms and schedules, programs include tax-planning tips (with audio and video clips), audit warnings, and the ability to file your tax return electronically. The most readily available tax software includes

| *TurboTax* | *Kiplinger's TaxCut* |
|---|---|
| Quicken | Kiplinger |
| 1–800–446–8848 | 1–800–235–4060 |
| (www.turbotax.com) | (www.taxcut.com) |

## Investment Analysis Programs

Software designed for researching, trading, and monitoring an investment portfolio is also available. Most of these programs may be connected to online services to obtain current stock quotes and to buy and sell investments.

# THE WORLD WIDE WEB AND PERSONAL FINANCIAL PLANNING

The World Wide Web makes it possible to access more information from your home or office than libraries offer. You may use the Web for a variety of personal financial planning activities, including (1) researching current financial information; (2) obtaining programs to do financial planning calculations; (3) monitoring current stock and investment values; and (4) asking questions of experts and others through help lines, bulletin board services, and discussion forums. Some of the most useful websites providing current information on various personal finance topics include

- Standard and Poor's Personal Wealth at www.personalwealth.com
- FinanCenter at www.financenter.com
- "The Motley Fool" at www.fool.com
- The Quicken Web site at www.quicken.com
- Money Central at www.moneycentral.msn.com
- *Money* magazine at www.money.com; *Kiplinger's Personal Finance Magazine* at www.kiplinger.com; and *Business Week* at www.businessweek.com
- The Federal Reserve System at www.federalreserve.gov

Additional websites are offered at the end of each chapter in the "Using the Internet to Create a Personal Financial Plan" feature and on the inside front and back covers of this book.

## USING SEARCH ENGINES

A search engine is a website that allows you to locate information related to specific topics. Some of the most commonly used search engines include

| | |
|---|---|
| www.altavista.com | www.excite.com |
| www.hotbot.com | www.infoseek.com |
| www.lycos.com | www.northernlight.com |
| www.search.com | www.webcrawler.com |
| www.yahoo.com | www.mamma.com |
| www.go.com | www.snap.com |

Various search engines operate in different ways and provide various features. Some search engines look for topic areas; others seek specific words. When conducting web searches, be precise with your descriptive words. For example, use "mortgage rates" instead of "interest rates" to obtain information on the cost of borrowing to buy a home. Use "resumes" instead of "career planning" for assistance on developing a personal data sheet.

## FINANCIAL PLANNING SPECIALISTS

Various specialists provide specific financial assistance and advice:

- *Accountants* specialize in tax matters and financial documents.
- *Bankers* assist with financial services and trusts.
- *Credit counselors* suggest ways to reduce spending and eliminate credit problems.
- *Certified financial planners* coordinate financial decisions into a single plan.
- *Insurance agents* sell insurance coverage to protect your wealth and property.
- *Investment brokers* provide information and handle transactions for stocks, bonds, and other investments.
- *Lawyers* help in preparing wills, estate planning, tax problems, and other legal matters.
- *Real estate agents* assist with buying and selling a home or other real estate.
- *Tax preparers* specialize in the completion of income tax returns and other tax matters.

Many of these specialists offer services that include various aspects of financial planning. A financial planner's background or the company he or she represents is a good gauge of the financial planner's principal area of expertise. An accountant is likely to be most knowledgeable about tax laws, while an insurance company representative will probably emphasize how to use insurance for achieving financial goals.

## Who Are the Financial Planners?

Many financial planners represent major insurance companies or investment businesses. Financial planners may also be individuals whose primary profession is tax accounting, real estate, or law. Approximately 250,000 people call themselves financial planners. Financial planners are commonly categorized based on four methods of compensation:

1. **Fee-only planners** charge an hourly rate that may range from $75 to $200, or may charge a fixed fee of between less than $500 and several thousand dollars. Other fee-only planners may charge an annual fee ranging from .04 percent to 1 percent of the value of your assets.
2. **Fee-offset planners** start with an hourly fee or an annual fee. This charge is reduced by any commission earned from the sale of investments or insurance.
3. **Fee-and-commission planners** earn commissions from the investment and insurance products purchased and charge a fixed fee (ranging from $250 to $2,000) for a financial plan.
4. **Commission-only planners** receive their revenue from the commissions on sales of insurance, mutual funds, and other investments.

Consumers must be cautious about the fees charged and how these fees are communicated. A study by the Consumer Federation of America revealed that more than half of financial planners who told "mystery shoppers" that they offer "fee-only" services actually earned commissions or other financial rewards for implementing the recommendations made to their clients.

## Do You Need a Financial Planner?

The two main factors that determine whether you need financial planning assistance are (1) your income and (2) your willingness to make independent decisions. If you earn less than $40,000 a year, you probably do not need a financial planner. Income of less than this amount does not allow for many major financial decisions once you have allocated for the spending, savings, insurance, and tax elements of your personal financial planning.

Taking an active role in your financial affairs can reduce the need for a financial planner. Your willingness to keep up to date on developments related to investments, insurance, and taxes can reduce the amount you spend on financial advisers. This will require an ongoing investment of time and effort; however, it will enable you to control your own financial direction.

When deciding whether to use a financial planner, also consider the services he or she provides. First, the financial planner should assist you in assessing your current financial position with regard to spending, saving, insurance, taxes, and potential investments. Second, the financial planner should offer a clearly written plan with different courses of action. Third, the planner should take time to discuss the components of the plan and help you monitor your financial progress. Finally, the financial planner should guide you to other experts and sources of financial services as needed.

## How Should You Select a Financial Planner?

You can locate financial planners by using a telephone directory, contacting financial institutions, or obtaining references from friends, business associates, or professionals with whom you currently deal, such as insurance agents or real estate brokers.

When evaluating a financial planner, ask the following:

- Is financial planning your primary activity, or are other activities primary?
- Are you licensed as an investment broker or as a seller of life insurance?
- What is your educational background and formal training?
- What are your areas of expertise?
- Do you use experts in other areas, such as taxes, law, or insurance, to assist you with financial planning recommendations?
- What professional titles and certifications do you possess?
- Am I allowed a free initial consultation?
- How is the fee determined? (Is this an amount I can afford?)
- Do you have an independent practice, or are you affiliated with a major financial services company?
- What are sample insurance, tax, and investment recommendations you make for clients?
- My major concern is _____. What would you suggest?
- May I see a sample of a written financial plan?
- May I see the contract you use with clients?
- Who are some of your clients whom I might contact?

Also, make sure you are comfortable with the planner and that the planner can clearly communicate. This type of investigation takes time and effort; however, remember that you are considering placing your entire financial future in the hands of one person.

## How Are Financial Planners Certified?

While state and federal regulation of financial planners is expanding, the requirements for becoming a financial planner vary from state to state. For example, Kansas requires that new financial advisers pass an exam that measures knowledge of stocks, bonds, and other investment products. Some states license individual investment advisers; other states license firms but not individual advisers. A few states regulate neither individual advisers nor firms. Recent federal regulation requires that the Securities and Exchange Commission (SEC) monitor the largest financial advisers.

Many financial planners use abbreviations for the titles they have earned. Some of these abbreviations are quite familiar, for example, CPA (certified public accountant), JD (doctor of law), and MBA (master of business administration); others include CFP (Certified Financial Planner), ChFC (Chartered Financial Consultant, in the life insurance industry), PFS (Personal Financial Specialist), AFC (Accredited Financial Counselor), CFA (Chartered Financial Analyst, handling stock and bond portfolios), AEP (Accredited Estate Planner), CRP (Certified Retirement Planner), RIA (Registered Investment Adviser, registered with SEC), EA (Enrolled Agent, tax specialist), and RFC (Registered Financial Consultant).

While these credentials provide some assurance of expertise, not all planners are licensed. The Better Business Bureau estimates that fraudulent planners take consumers for tens of millions of dollars in bad investments and advice each year. Financial planning activities such as insurance and investment security sales do come under regulatory control. Be wary of and investigate any financial planning action you are considering.

You may contact the following organizations and agencies for further information about certification and regulation of financial planners:

- National Association of Personal Financial Advisors at 1–888–333–6659 (www.napfa.org).
- Certified Financial Planners Board of Standards at 1–888–273–6275 (www.cfpboard.org).
- Financial Planning Association at 1–800–945–4237 (www.fpanet.org).
- North American Securities Administrators Association at 1–888–846–2722 (www.nasaa.org).
- National Association of Insurance Commissioners at 816–842–3600 (www.naic.org).
- Securities and Exchange Commission at 1–800–732–0330 (www.sec.gov).
- American Institute of Certified Public Accountants at 1–800–862–4272 (www.aicpa.org).

# 2

# Financial Aspects of Career Planning

## If you stay ready, you don't have to get ready

He knew it was going to happen, he just didn't know when. But, Kevin Larkin was ready.

When Kevin's company, Sun Electronics, announced it would lay off 600 workers, most people in the organization panicked. In contrast, Kevin volunteered to leave!

Kevin didn't have another job, nor was he offered a generous severance package. However, he did have a knowledge of his career skills and an ability to find another employment position. In other words, Kevin was prepared for the uncertainty that occurs in a volatile economy with increased foreign competition and technology. Through ongoing training, he continually upgraded his technical skills while also improving his ability to work on project teams.

Since Kevin knew things were changing in the electronics industry, he was not surprised when the downsizing announcement came. However, unlike most other Sun employees, Kevin was prepared for that moment. In addition to getting ongoing training, he maintained a strong dedication to Sun. His on-the-job performance, creativity, and initiative were admired by both supervisors and coworkers. When investigating other employment opportunities, Kevin used vacation days and made sure that others made up or covered his work.

Kevin used several of the thousands of websites related to career planning. He researched companies online that had employment opportunities available and also compared the employee benefits these organizations offered.

In case he was not able to get another position immediately, Kevin also investigated working as a consultant in the electronics industry. With over 20 million people serving as independent contractors, part-time workers, on-call employees, and temporaries, this career path offers many opportunities.

Finally, Kevin also prepared himself financially. He worked to increase his savings to cover periods of lower income. He informed his family of a possible need for reduced spending and budget cuts.

Overall, Kevin is an ideal example of a person who manages his or her career. He did not let changes in the economy and the employment marketplace surprise him. He continuously readied himself for those inevitable events.

## Questions

1. What actions did Kevin take to ensure his future employment potential?
2. What factors commonly affect future employment opportunities?
3. Explain how Kevin's actions could be adapted to most career situations.
4. In what ways could information from various websites be useful for a person seeking employment?

SOURCES: David R. Francis, "Part-Time Workers Face Full-Time Problems," *The Christian Science Monitor,* July 1, 1999, p. 11; Charles A. Jaffee, "Separation Anxiety: Soften the Blow of a Job Loss by Making Financial Preparations while Employed," *Chicago Tribune,* April 30, 1999, sec. 6, pp. 1, 7; Shelley Donald Coolidge, "Why More Job Hunters Are Stalking the Web," *The Christian Science Monitor,* August 16, 1999, pp. 11, 14–15.

## Learning Objectives

**Obj. 1**   Describe the activities associated with career planning and advancement.

**Obj. 2**   Evaluate the factors that influence employment opportunities.

**Obj. 3**   Implement employment search strategies.

**Obj. 4**   Assess the financial and legal concerns related to obtaining employment.

**Obj. 5**   Analyze the techniques available for career growth and advancement.

# FINANCIAL AND PERSONAL ASPECTS OF CAREER CHOICE

**Obj. 1**

Describe the activities associated with career planning and advancement.

*job*   An employment position obtained mainly to earn money, without regard for interests or opportunities for advancement.

*career*   A commitment to a profession that requires continued training and offers a clear path for occupational growth.

"Boring!" "Oh no!" "Excellent!" These are some common responses to "It's time to get up for work."

Have you ever wondered why some people find great satisfaction in their work while others want only to put in their time? As with other personal financial decisions, career selection and professional growth require planning. The average person changes jobs about seven times during a lifetime. Most likely, therefore, you will reevaluate your choice of a job on a regular basis.

The lifework you select is a key to your financial well-being and personal satisfaction. You may select a **job,** an employment position obtained mainly to earn money. Many people work in one or more jobs during their lives without considering their interests or opportunities for advancement. Or you may select a **career,** a commitment to a profession that requires continued training and offers a clear path for occupational growth.

## Trade-Offs of Career Decisions

While many factors affect daily living habits and financial choices, your employment situation probably affects them the most. Your income level, business associates, and available leisure time are a direct result of the work you do.

Like other decisions, career choice and professional development alternatives have risks and opportunity costs. In recent years, many people in our society have placed family values and personal fulfillment above monetary reward and professional recognition. Career choices require periodic evaluation of trade-offs related to personal, social, and economic factors. For example:

- Some people select employment that is challenging and offers strong personal satisfaction rather than employment in which they can make the most money.
- Some people refuse a transfer or a promotion that would require moving their families to a new area or reducing leisure time.
- Many parents opt for part-time employment or flexible hours to allow more time for their children.
- Many people give up secure job situations because they prefer to operate their own businesses.

**EXHIBIT 2-1**

**Education and Income**

SOURCE: U.S. Bureau of the Census.

As of the late-1990s, estimated lifetime earnings for workers, based on the completed level of education, was:

**Non–high school graduate**

$608,810

**High school graduate**

$820,870

**Some college**

$992,890

**College graduate (bachelor's degree)**

$1,420,850

**Professional degree**

$3,012,530

## Career Training and Skill Development

Your level of formal training affects your financial success. Exhibit 2–1 shows the influence of education on income. The statistics in this exhibit do not mean you will automatically earn a certain amount because you have a college degree. They imply that more education increases your *potential* earning power. Other factors, such as field of study, also influence future income.

In addition to formal career training, successful managers, employers, and career counselors stress the importance of traits adaptable to most work situations. While some of these traits can be acquired in school, others require experiences in other situations. The traits that successful people usually possess include

- An ability to work well with others in a variety of settings.
- A desire to do tasks better than they have to be done.
- An interest in reading a wide variety of materials.
- A willingness to cope with conflict and adapt to change.
- An awareness of accounting, finance, and marketing fundamentals.
- A knowledge of technology and computer software such as word processing, spreadsheet, database, web search, and graphics programs.
- An ability to solve problems creatively in team settings.
- A knowledge of research techniques and library resources.
- Well-developed written and oral communication skills.
- An understanding of both their own motivations and the motivations of others.

## FINANCIAL PLANNING FOR LIFE'S SITUATIONS

### *DEVELOPING A CAREER ACTION PLAN*

For each of the following elements of career planning,

a. Describe your current situation in this area.

b. State a specific goal you have in this area.

c. Describe the time frame for accomplishing this goal.

d. Indicate actions to take to achieve the goal.

1. *Personal and Career Interests:* What do you enjoy doing? How would you like to improve or expand your interests?

a. _____

b. _____

c. _____

d. _____

2. *Career Skills:* What type of work situation do you enjoy? How would you like to improve or expand your career skills? What new career skills do you desire?

a. _____

b. _____

c. _____

d. _____

3. *Education:* What education and career training do you desire?

a. _____

b. _____

c. _____

d. _____

4. *Employment Position:* Have you selected career fields of interest to you? What type of employment situation do you desire?

a. _____

b. _____

c. _____

d. _____

These competencies give people flexibility, making it easy to move from one organization to another and to successfully change career fields. How are *you* working to develop these traits?

## Personal Factors

You might be able to identify a satisfying career using guidance tests that measure your abilities, interests, and personal qualities. Aptitude tests, interest inventories, and other types of career assessment tests are available at school career counseling offices. You can use a book that allows you to take these tests at home. For a fee, testing services will mail you the results of your completed test, or tests may be taken online.

*Aptitudes* are natural abilities that people possess. The ability to work well with numbers, problem-solving skills, and physical dexterity are examples of aptitudes.

*Interest inventories* determine the activities that give you satisfaction. These instruments measure qualities related to various types of work. People with strong social tendencies may be best suited for careers that involve dealing with people, while people with investigative interests may be best suited for careers in research areas.

**EXHIBIT 2-2**   Stages of Career Planning, Advancement, and Career Changes

Test results will not tell you which career to pursue. They will only give you an indication of your aptitudes and interests. Another important dimension of career selection is your personality. Do you perform best in structured or high-pressure situations, or do you prefer unstructured or creative work environments? The financial aspects of the career are also likely to be a concern.

Many people are able to obtain employment based on various interests and experiences. A person with volunteer experience might be hired as executive director of a community organization. Or a person who enjoys planning parties and other events may work as a meeting planner. The Financial Planning for Life's Situations box on page 39 can help you plan actions for obtaining a job or changing careers.

## Career Decision Making

Changing personal and social factors will require you to continually assess your work situation. Exhibit 2–2 provides an approach to career planning, advancement, and career change. As you can see, the different entry points depend on your personal situation. Your career goals will also affect how you use this process. If you desire more responsibility on the job, for example, you may obtain advanced training or change career fields. This process is a suggested framework for planning, changing, or advancing in a career.

## Concept Check 2-1

1. How does a *job* differ from a *career?*
2. What opportunity costs are associated with career decisions?
3. What skills would be of value in most employment situations?

# CAREER OPPORTUNITIES: NOW AND IN THE FUTURE

Your job search should start with an assessment of the career choice factors shown in Exhibit 2–3.

**Obj. 2**

Evaluate the factors that influence employment opportunities.

## Social Influences

Various demographic and geographic trends influence employment opportunities. Demographic trends affecting the job market include the following:

- An increase in the number of working parents expands the demand for food service and child care.
- An increase in leisure time among some segments of the population results in an increased interest in personal health, physical fitness, and recreational products and services.
- An increase in the number of older people raises the demand for travel services, health care, and retirement facilities.
- An increased demand for additional employment training increases career opportunities for teachers and trainers within business organizations.

What other employment opportunities might be influenced by demographic trends?

## EXHIBIT 2-3

Factors Influencing Your Career Opportunities

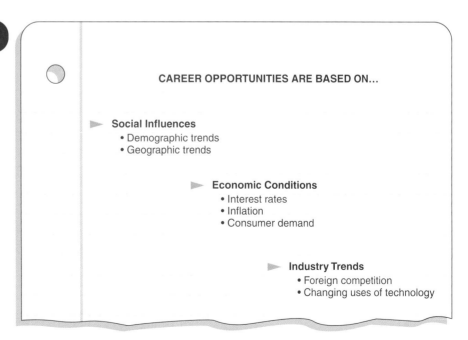

**CAREER OPPORTUNITIES ARE BASED ON...**

▶ **Social Influences**
- Demographic trends
- Geographic trends

▶ **Economic Conditions**
- Interest rates
- Inflation
- Consumer demand

▶ **Industry Trends**
- Foreign competition
- Changing uses of technology

Changes in the locations of jobs influence employment opportunities. In recent years, some of the fastest-growing job markets include major cities in Florida, North Carolina, and Arizona; Atlanta, Georgia; Boulder, Colorado; Boise, Idaho; San Jose, California; Austin, Texas; Salt Lake City, Utah; and Albuquerque, New Mexico.

In considering geographic areas, be sure to assess salary levels. Average incomes are high in such metropolitan areas as Boston, New York, and Chicago; however, the prices of food, housing, and other living expenses are also high.

What appears to be a big salary may actually mean a lower standard of living than in a geographic area with lower salaries and lower living costs.

For example, in recent years, the cost of living for a single employee earning $30,000 annually was 60 percent higher in the District of Columbia than the national city average. In contrast, the cost of living in Fayetteville, Arkansas, was only 90 percent of the national city average.

To compare living costs and salaries in different cities, you may use the following "Geographic Buying Power" formula:

$$\frac{\text{City 1}}{\text{City 2}} \quad \frac{\text{Index number} \times \text{Salary}}{\text{Index number}} = \$ \text{ buying power}$$

For example,

$$\frac{\text{Chicago}}{\text{Omaha}} \quad \frac{123 \times \$30{,}000}{93.3} = \$39{,}550$$

A person earning $30,000 in Omaha, Nebraska, would need to earn $39,550 in Chicago to have comparable buying power.

Additional information on geographic cost-of-living differences may be obtained at www.erieri.com.

## Economic Conditions

High interest rates, price increases, or decreased demand for goods and services can reduce career opportunities. While you cannot eliminate the effects of economic factors on employment trends, these factors affect some businesses more than others. For example, high interest rates reduce employment in housing-related industries, since people are less likely to buy homes when interest rates are high.

## Trends in Industry and Technology

Two factors have caused a decline in manufacturing employment in our economy. First, increased competition from companies in Asia, Europe, and other regions has reduced demand for American-made products. Second, automated production methods have decreased the need for manual workers and other entry-level employees in factories.

Employment stability has a strong influence on a person's financial situation for both the short and long term. For example, workers in various technology fields, where scientific advances can quickly make products (and jobs) obsolete, must be ready to cope with personal financial uncertainty. (See the Financial Planning for Life's Situations box.)

While career opportunities have dwindled in some sectors of our economy, opportunities in other sectors have grown. Service industries that are expected to have the greatest employment potential for the 21st century include

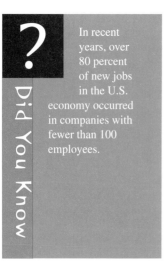

**Did You Know**

**?** In recent years, over 80 percent of new jobs in the U.S. economy occurred in companies with fewer than 100 employees.

# Financial Planning for Life's Situations

## COMMUTING TO THE NEXT ROOM

To meet the needs of family situations and reduce business costs, many organizations allow some employees to do all or some work at home. *Telecommuting* involves using a computer and other technology (fax machine, videoconferencing, computer networking, e-mail) to work at home instead of at a company office or factory. Workers can care for children or dependent parents while saving time and energy by not traveling to a different location. Companies save money by requiring less office space.

Telecommuting is best suited to jobs that do not require regular in-person contact with others. The work must be of a type that can be done through computer networks and other telecommunications equipment. This employment arrangement is most common among staff writers, researchers, economists, accounting clerks, word processing clerks, database supervisors, and computer programmers. Companies find that telecommuting helps them to keep talented employees who do not want to work in a structured environment.

Another flexible employment arrangement is operating a business out of your home. Over 5 million people in the United States operate home businesses. The most common home-based businesses are sales, information processing, construction and contracting, personal care services, arts and crafts, consulting, and clerical support.

Would running your own business be an appropriate career for you? That depends on your personality and abilities. Are you a highly motivated, confident individual? Do you have the ability to manage different phases of a business? Are you someone who enjoys challenges and is willing to take risks?

If you are planning to start your own business, consider three main issues. First, become knowledgeable about your product or service. Next, identify your potential customers, select an appropriate location, and study competitors. Finally, consider your financial sources. Most entrepreneurs use a combination of personal funds and loans.

You can obtain assistance with starting a home-based business from a lawyer, a local banker, an accountant, or an insurance agent. For additional information about running your own business, contact the Small Business Administration, Attn.: Public Information Office, 1441 L St. NW, Washington, DC 20416; website: www.sba.gov. Also useful is the website of the National Association for the Self-Employed at selfemployed.nase.org/NASE.

- *Computer technology*—systems analysts, computer operators, website developers, network operations managers, and repair personnel and service technicians for data processing equipment.
- *Health care*—medical assistants, physical therapists, home health workers, biotech analysts, laboratory technicians, registered nurses, and health care administrators.
- *Business services*—web consultants, foreign language translators, employee benefit managers, operations consultants, and research data analysts.
- *Social services*—child care workers, elder care coordinators, family counselors, and social service agency administrators.
- *Sales and retailing*—web promotion producers, marketing representatives, and sales managers with technical knowledge in the areas of electronics, medical products, and financial services.
- *Hospitality and food services*—travel agents, resort and hotel administrators, food service managers, online customer service representatives, and meeting planners.
- *Management and human resources*—clerical supervisors, recruiters, interviewers, employee benefit administrators, and employment service workers.

- *Education*—corporate trainers, special education teachers, adult education instructors, educational administrators, and teachers for elementary, secondary, and postsecondary schools.
- *Financial services*—risk assessment managers, actuaries, e-commerce accountants, investment brokers, and others with a knowledge of accounting and taxes.

Business demands in the 21st century will include expanded reading and communication skills. More and more employees are being called on to read scientific and technical journals and financial reports and to write speeches and journal articles. Your career success is likely to be dependent on communication skills, computer skills, and the ability to communicate in a second language.

**Sheet 6**

### Concept Check 2–2

1. What are some demographic and economic factors that affect career opportunities?
2. How does technology affect available employment positions?

## EMPLOYMENT SEARCH STRATEGIES

We have all heard about job applicants who send out hundreds of résumés with very little success, while others get several offers. What are the differences between these two groups? The answer usually involves an ability to expand one's experiences and use job search techniques effectively.

**Obj. 3**
Implement employment search strategies.

### Obtaining Employment Experience

A common concern among people seeking employment is a lack of work experience. Many opportunities are available to obtain work-related training.

#### Part-Time Employment
Summer and part-time work can provide experience along with the chance to see if you enjoy a particular career field. The increased use of temporary employees has opened up opportunities to obtain experience in many career areas. Part-time work may also be of value for people who are changing careers and need experience in a different career field.

More and more workers are taking advantage of temporary job assignments as a channel to a full-time position. The number of temporary employment services and "interim" workers continues to increase. Working as a "temp" can give you valuable experience as well as contacts in various fields of employment. Further information may be obtained at the website of the National Association of Temporary and Staffing Services (NATSS) at www.natss.org.

#### Volunteer Work
Involvement in community organizations and government agencies can provide excellent opportunities to acquire skills, establish good work habits, and make contacts. Volunteering to work at the gift shop of a museum, for example, gives you experience in retailing. You may participate in a recycling project, assist at a senior citizens' center, or help supervise youth activities at a park district. These activities will help you develop skills applicable to other types of work situations.

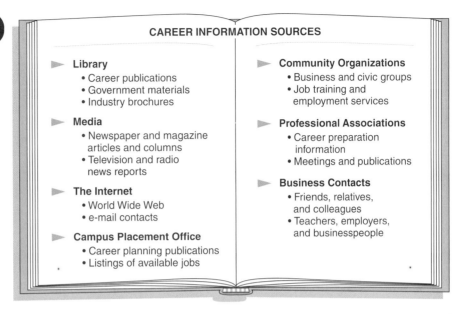

**EXHIBIT 2-4**

Career Information Sources

**CAREER INFORMATION SOURCES**

► **Library**
  • Career publications
  • Government materials
  • Industry brochures

► **Media**
  • Newspaper and magazine articles and columns
  • Television and radio news reports

► **The Internet**
  • World Wide Web
  • e-mail contacts

► **Campus Placement Office**
  • Career planning publications
  • Listings of available jobs

► **Community Organizations**
  • Business and civic groups
  • Job training and employment services

► **Professional Associations**
  • Career preparation information
  • Meetings and publications

► **Business Contacts**
  • Friends, relatives, and colleagues
  • Teachers, employers, and businesspeople

**Internships**    In very competitive fields, an internship will give you the experience you need to obtain employment. During an internship, you can make contacts about available jobs. Applying for an internship is similar to applying for a job. Most colleges and universities offer cooperative education and internships as part of their academic programs.

**Campus Projects**    Class assignments and campus activities are frequently overlooked as work-related experience. You can obtain valuable career skills on campus from experience in

• Managing, organizing, and coordinating people and activities as an officer or a committee chairperson of a campus organization.
• Public speaking in class, campus, and community presentations.
• Goal setting, planning, supervising, and delegating responsibility in community service and class projects.
• Financial planning and budgeting gained from organizing fund-raising projects, managing personal finances, and handling funds for campus organizations.
• Conducting research for class projects, community organizations, and campus activities.

## Using Career Information Sources

Career planning and advancement, like other financial decisions, are enhanced by the use of current and relevant information. Exhibit 2–4 provides an overview of the main sources of career information.

**Library Materials**    Most school and community libraries have extensive career information sources. The *Occupational Outlook Handbook* covers all aspects of career planning and job search and provides detailed information on jobs in various career clusters. Other helpful government resources related to careers are the *Dictionary of Occupational Titles* and the *Occupational Outlook Quarterly.*

## JONATHAN HOENIG ON PERSONAL CAREER STRATEGIES

In the 1950s, large corporations regularly recruited staff with the understanding that "work" was a commitment in the truest sense. You were "in" for life, a gold watch waiting patiently in the storage closet.

Times have changed: The "company man" is dead. Then again, so is the company. In its stead lies an unfortunate assemblage of temp jobs, freelance gigs, and internships. All without benefits. All without perks. All featuring wages not seen since the abolishment of indentured servitude.

Enter the entrepreneur! Entrepreneurship is not merely working for yourself but *thinking* for yourself.

Regardless of who signs your paychecks, don't be misled: *You work for yourself.* An entrepreneurial attitude is a realistic response to corporate America's increasingly frigid indifference. Don't concern yourself with the "company"; your interest should always be *you.*

But you've got nothing to worry about. Never before has there been a better time to ditch the suit and work for yourself. Technology is cheaper, faster, and more accessible than at any time in history. With a modem and fax machine, you can sell to Indonesia just as easily as to Indiana. No excuses: Get a laptop and get crankin'!

Armed with sufficient technology and a tangy dollop of moxie, you can compete with any Fortune 500, no questions asked. One of the inherent advantages of being an entrepreneur is the ability to work faster, cheaper, and more effectively than the big shots. No permission, approval, or signatures needed. You can easily fill the lucrative "cracks" big corporations leave behind. Chances are they will hire you to do so. The nimble entrepreneur will find an abundance of opportunity.

A disclaimer: The mythology is a bit misleading. Poser entrepreneurs boast of being able to "miss work for a ballgame," but the real ones find they don't have an abundance of time. You'll work hard—arguably harder than you did while working for big business—*but you'll enjoy the pain!* Enjoyment is key: You could be miserable in corporate America, so at least enjoy what you're doing.

**Mass Media Career Information**   Most newspapers offer articles and columns about job searches and career trends. Newspapers, television reports, and radio reports also provide useful information about economic and social influences on careers. Changes in interest rates, consumer demand, and foreign trade are good indicators of job availability in various career areas.

**World Wide Web**   The Internet offers a variety of information sources related to job opportunities, preparing a résumé, interviewing, and other career planning topics. See the "Financial Planning for Life's Situations" box on page 47 for additional information on using the Web for career planning.

**Campus Placement Office**   Your school probably has a career planning and placement service. This office is likely to have materials on various career planning topics and can assist you in creating a résumé and preparing for an interview.

**Community Organizations**   Every community has business and civic groups you can use in your career search. Public meetings featuring industry leaders and business owners provide opportunities to become acquainted with local businesspeople.

## Financial Planning for Life's Situations

### ONLINE CAREER PLANNING

Each day, more and more people are using the Internet for their career planning activities. Obtaining information, making contacts, and upgrading employment skills are just a few of the web-based career tasks growing in popularity.

*Career Planning Assistance:*
For tips on preparing a résumé and dressing for an interview, go to www.hotjobs.com, www.careers.wsj. com, and www.careerpath.com.

*Identifying Employment Opportunities:*
To research career trends and employment opportunities, go to websites such as www.ajb.dni.us, campus. monster.com, and www.careerbuilder.com.

*Posting Your Résumé on the Web:*
When creating a résumé for online distribution, keep the format simple and avoid e-mail attachments that some computer systems may be unable to open. Many websites exist for posting résumés; some of the most popular ones include www.careerpath.com,

www.careermosaic.com, www.hotjobs.com, and www. monster.com.

*Cyber-Interviews:*
A preliminary interview may take place via e-mail. You may be asked to respond online about your background and experience. Additional information about online interviews is available at www.headhunter.net and www.jobtrak.com.

*Online Career Advancement:*
Online courses to expand your career skills, along with information from professional organizations, may be accessed at www.ama.org (the American Marketing Association) and with a web search for "online courses."

*Career Resource Centers:*
Several websites and search engines offer a variety of career information, such as www.aol.com, www. excite.com, www.yahoo.com, www.lycos.com, www. webcrawler.com, and www.hotbot.com/jobs.

**Professional Associations**   Various professions have organizations to promote their career areas. These organizations include the American Marketing Association, the Independent Insurance Agents of America, the American Society of Women Accountants, and the National Association of Real Estate Brokers. The *Encyclopedia of Associations* can help you identify organizations representing careers that interest you.

**Business Contacts**   Professional contacts can advise you about career preparation and job opportunities. Friends, relatives, people you meet through community and professional organizations, and people you meet through school, work, church, or other activities are all potential business contacts. **Networking** is the process of making and using contacts to obtain and update career information. Campus programs such as organizations, sports, and lectures can provide valuable contacts. Every person you talk to is a potential career contact who may provide career information or assistance.

Although the contacts you make may not be able to hire you, if jobs are available they can refer you to the right person. They can also help you get an **informational interview,** a meeting at which you gather information about a career or an organization. When planning and using informational interviews, consider the following:

*networking*  The process of making and using contacts for obtaining and updating career information.

*informational interview*  A company visit or meeting at which one gathers information about a career or an organization.

- Prepare a list of industries and organizations for which you would like to work. Talk to family, friends, coworkers, and others for names of people you might contact.

- Prepare a list of open-ended questions that will help you obtain information about current trends in the industry and potential employment opportunities.
- Make an appointment for a 20-minute meeting; emphasize to the person that the meeting is for information only.
- Try to interact with the person at his or her place of work to gain better awareness of the work environment.
- Follow up with a thank-you note, and, if possible, send some information (such as an article) that might be of interest to your contact.

## Identifying Job Opportunities

**Sheet 7**

Before you apply for employment, you need to identify job openings that match your interests and abilities.

### Job Advertisements

Advertisements in newspapers and professional periodicals can be valuable sources of available positions. Newspapers such as *The Wall Street Journal,* the *New York Times,* the *Chicago Tribune,* and the *Los Angeles Times* have job listings covering a wide geographic area. You should also check local and regional newspapers. For opportunities in a specific career field, refer to specialized publications such as *Advertising Age, Marketing News,* the *Journal of Accountancy,* and *American Banker.* Since 80 to 90 percent of available jobs are not advertised to the general public, other job search techniques are critical.

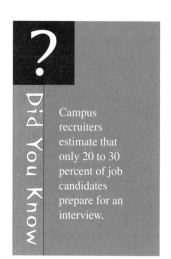

Campus recruiters estimate that only 20 to 30 percent of job candidates prepare for an interview.

### Career Fairs

Career fairs, commonly held on campuses and at convention centers, offer an opportunity to make contact with several firms in a short time span. Be prepared to quickly communicate your potential contributions to an organization. By making yourself memorable to the recruiter, you are likely to be called for a follow-up interview.

### Employment Agencies

Another possible source of job leads is employment agencies. These for-profit organizations match job hunters with prospective employers. Often the hiring company pays the fee charged by the employment agency; however, be careful when you are asked to pay a fee and have no guarantee of a job. Be sure you understand any contracts before signing them.

Government-supported employment services are also available. Contact your state employment service or your state department of labor for further information.

*job creation*   The development of an employment position that matches your skills with the needs of an organization.

### Job Creation

After researching a particular company or industry, present how your abilities would contribute to that organization. **Job creation** involves developing an employment position that matches your skills with the needs of an organization.

As you develop skills in areas you enjoy, you may be able to create a demand for your services. For example, a person who enjoyed researching business and economic trends was hired by a major corporation to make presentations for its managers at various company offices. Other people with an ability to design promotions and advertising might be hired by a nonprofit organization that needs to expand its public visibility.

### Other Job Search Methods

Your ability to locate existing and potential employment positions is limited only by your imagination and initiative. Commonly overlooked sources of jobs include the following:

- Visit companies where you would like to work, and make face-to-face contacts. Create an impression that you are someone who can contribute. Calling or visiting before 8 a.m. or after 4 p.m. increases your chance of talking to someone who is not busy.
- Successful organizations continually look for quality employees. Telephone and business directories can provide names of organizations that employ people with your qualifications.
- Search the World Wide Web for information about potential jobs and organizations that may be in search of someone with your abilities and skills.
- Talk with alumni who work in your field. Graduates who are familiar with your school and major can help you focus your career search.

To improve your job search efforts, work as many hours a week *getting* a job as you expect to work each week *on* the job. Maintaining an ongoing relationship with contacts can be a valuable source of information about future career opportunities.

## Applying for Employment

Many qualified people never get the job they deserve without a presentation of skills and experiences. This process usually involves three elements.

*résumé*   A summary of a person's education, training, experience, and other job qualifications.

1. The **résumé,** a summary of education, training, experience, and qualifications, provides prospective employers with an overview of your potential contributions to an organization.

*cover letter*   A letter that accompanies a résumé and is designed to express interest in a job and obtain an interview.

2. A **cover letter** is the correspondence you send with a résumé to communicate your interest in a job and to obtain an interview.
3. The *interview* is the formal meeting used to discuss your qualifications in detail.

The appendix to this chapter presents additional information on résumés, cover letters, and interviews.

### Concept Check 2-3

1. How can a person obtain employment-related experiences without working in a job situation?
2. What types of career information sources can be helpful in identifying job opportunities?
3. How does the information in a cover letter differ from the information in a résumé?

## FINANCIAL AND LEGAL ASPECTS OF EMPLOYMENT

### Obj. 4
Assess the financial and legal concerns related to obtaining employment.

"We would like you to work for us." When offered an employment position, you should examine a range of factors. Carefully assess the organization, the specific job, and the salary and other benefits.

### Accepting an Employment Position

Before accepting a position, do additional research about the job and the company. Request information about your specific duties and job expectations. If someone currently has a similar position, ask to talk to that person. If you are replacing a person who is no longer with the company, obtain information about the circumstances of that person's departure.

### The Work Environment

Investigate the work environment. The term *corporate culture* refers to management styles, work intensity, dress codes, and social interactions within an organization. For example, some companies have rigid lines of communication, while others have an open-door atmosphere. Are the values, goals, and lifestyles of current employees similar to yours? If not, you may find yourself in an uncomfortable situation that doesn't allow you to perform according to your capabilities.

Consider company policies and procedures for salary increases, evaluations of employees, and promotions. Talk with current workers to obtain this information.

### Factors Affecting Salary

Your initial salary will be influenced by your education and training, company size, and salaries for comparable positions. To ensure a fair starting salary, talk to people in similar positions and check business journals for information about salary levels. In addition, make sure you clearly understand company procedures and policies for raises. In recent years, increased emphasis has been placed on team results for salary increases and on rewards for expanded learning.

Performance quality and work responsibilities are the main influences on salary advances. Meet regularly with your supervisor to obtain performance evaluations and suggestions for professional growth. Communicate your desire for increased work responsibilities and greater financial rewards. Meeting and exceeding organizational expectations should enhance your monetary position. If not, you may wish to consider other employment opportunities.

## Evaluating Employee Benefits

Escalating health care costs, changing family situations, and concerns about retirement have increased the attention given to supplementary compensation benefits.

### Meeting Employee Needs

In recent years, nonsalary employee benefits have expanded to meet the needs of different life situations. The increasing number of two-income and single-parent households has resulted in a greater need for child care benefits and leaves of absence to care for newborn children, newly adopted children, and other dependents. The need for elder care benefits for employees with dependent parents or grandparents also increases. Child care benefits are offered in a variety of forms, ranging from direct payments for child care to facilities on company premises.

Other employee benefits designed to meet employees' needs include flexible work schedules; work-at-home arrangements; legal assistance; counseling for health, emotional, and financial needs; and exercise and fitness programs. Such benefits not only enhance the quality of employees' lives but are profitable for organizations because happier, healthier employees miss fewer workdays and have a higher level of productivity. (See the accompanying Financial Planning for Life's Situations box.)

**Cafeteria-style employee benefits** are programs that allow workers to base their job benefits on a credit system and personal needs. Flexible selection of employee benefits has become common. A married employee with children may opt for increased life and health insurance, while a single parent may use benefit credits for child care services. The Financial Planning for Life's Situations box on page 52 suggests benefits for different life situations. Like any financial decision, employee benefits involve a trade-off, or opportunity cost, that you must assess.

**Did You Know?**

About 70 percent of all professionals find positions through personal contacts and networking. Responding to job ads accounts for about 15 percent of jobs. (Source: *Chicago Sun-Times,* August 1, 1999, p. 1C.)

*cafeteria-style employee benefits*  Programs that allow workers to base their job benefits on a credit system and personal needs.

## Financial Planning for Life's Situations

### EMPLOYEE BENEFITS TO MEET VARIED NEEDS

At Wilton Conner Packaging Company (Charlotte, NC), employees get their laundry done on premises for $1 a load. Long-term employees at John Nuveen Company (Chicago, IL) qualify for college tuition payments for their children. At some locations of MBNA America Bank (Wilmington, DE), workers may use services such as an espresso bar, a barber shop, shoe repair, film processing, and a travel agency.

These are some attempts companies make to meet the varied needs of employees. Organizations are realizing that a strong effort to maintain a loyal, committed work force benefits their long-term financial success. One survey reports that about 30 percent of companies offer on-site gift stores, while 22 percent have on-site medical care.

To allow parents more time with their families, some companies are using a compressed workweek known as the *9/80*. Employees on this schedule put in 80 hours of work over 9 days instead of the usual 10. This gives employees a three-day weekend every other week.

Other methods used to meet the needs of workers with children or dependent parents include flextime, job sharing, on-site child care, and telecommuting.

Electronic technology is also contributing to meeting employee needs. Many companies use interactive computer technology to allow workers to access benefits information, make changes in their benefits package, and conduct related business using personal computers. Once connected to this type of system, employees can obtain real-time information on the market value of pension plan investments. In addition, they can choose a health plan, research HMOs, and select a doctor.

SOURCES: Stephanie Armour, "Perking Up Employees: Fringe Benefits on the Rise," *USA Today,* October 8, 1997, pp. 1B, 2B; Lynn Asinof, "Click & Shift: Workers Control Their Benefits On-Line," *The Wall Street Journal,* November 21, 1997, pp. C1, C17; Kathy M. Kristof, "Up to Date: No Time Like the Present to Bone Up on Your Defined Benefit Plan," *Chicago Tribune,* September 7, 1999, sec. 6, pp. 1, 7; Kelly Smith, "America's Best Company Benefits," *Money,* October, 1999, pp. 117–26.

Many organizations offer *flexible spending plans,* also called *expense reimbursement accounts.* This arrangement allows you to set aside part of your salary for paying medical or dependent care expenses. These funds are not subject to income or Social Security taxes. However, money not used for the specified purpose is forfeited. Therefore, you must carefully plan the amount to be designated for a flexible spending plan.

In a similar manner, a *medical-spending account (MSA)* allows people who are self-employed or work for a company with 50 or fewer employees the opportunity to pay health care costs with pretax dollars. The MSA has two components: (1) health insurance coverage with a high deductible and (2) a tax-deferred savings account for paying medical expenses. Money in this account may be taken out for other uses; however, the funds are then taxed, along with an additional 15 percent tax penalty. While MSAs have tax-saving implications, the high deductible may not be affordable for many households.

When matching dependent health care needs and medical insurance plans, consider the following:

- Types of services available and location of health care providers.
- Direct costs (insurance premiums) to you.
- Anticipated out-of-pocket costs (deductibles and coinsurance amounts).

Chapter 11 discusses medical and disability insurance in detail.

As people live longer, profit-sharing plans and retirement programs are increasing in importance. In addition to Social Security benefits, some employers contribute to a pension plan. *Vesting* is the point at which retirement payments made by the organization on

## Financial Planning for Life's Situations

### SELECTING EMPLOYEE BENEFITS

Commonly recommended employee benefits for various life situations are listed below. Based on your current life situation or expectations for the future, list the employee benefits that would be most important to you.

#### SINGLE, NO CHILDREN

- Disability income insurance to maintain earning power
- Health insurance
- Contributions to a retirement program
- Educational assistance, such as tuition reimbursement

#### YOUNG FAMILY

- Comprehensive health insurance
- Life insurance
- Child care services

#### SINGLE PARENT

- Health insurance
- Life insurance
- Disability income insurance
- Dependent care benefits

#### MARRIED, NO CHILDREN

- Health and disability insurance
- Retirement program contributions
- Maternity coverage and parental leave (young couple)
- Long-term health care needs (older couple)

#### MIXED-GENERATION HOUSEHOLD

- Health and disability insurance
- Child care services
- Elder care benefits

Life situation _____

_____

Desired employee benefits _____

_____

_____

_____

_____

_____

your behalf belong to you even if you no longer work for the organization. Vesting schedules vary, but all qualified plans (those for which an employer may deduct contributions to the plan for tax purposes) must (1) be 100 percent vested on completion of five years of service or (2) have 20 percent vesting after three years and full vesting, in stages, after seven years. Vesting refers only to the employer's pension contributions; employee contributions belong to the employees regardless of the length of their service with the organization.

Workers are commonly allowed to make personal contributions to company-sponsored retirement programs. These plans usually involve a variety of investments, making it easy for employees to create a diversified portfolio for their retirement funds. Retirement plans are discussed in Chapters 4 and 18.

**Comparing Benefits**    Two methods used to assess the monetary value of employee benefits are market value calculations and future value calculations.

*Market value* calculations determine the specific monetary value of employee benefits—the cost of the benefits if you had to pay for them. For example, you may view the value of one week's vacation as $\frac{1}{52}$ of your annual salary, or you may view the value of a life insurance benefit as what it would cost you to obtain the same coverage. You can use this method to determine the difference between two job offers with different salaries and employee benefits.

## FINANCIAL PLANNING CALCULATIONS

### TAX-EQUIVALENT EMPLOYEE BENEFITS

Employee benefits that are nontaxable have a higher financial value than you may realize. A $100 employee benefit on which you are taxed is not worth as much as a nontaxable $100 benefit. This formula is used to calculate the *tax-equivalent value* of a nontaxable benefit:

$$\frac{\text{Value of the benefit}}{(1 - \text{Tax rate})}$$

For example, receiving a life insurance policy with a nontaxable annual premium of $350 is comparable to receiving a taxable employee benefit worth $486 if you are in the 28 percent tax bracket. This tax-equivalent amount is calculated as follows:

$$\frac{\$350}{(1 - 0.28)} = \frac{\$350}{0.72} = \$486$$

A variation of this formula, which would give the *after-tax* value of an employee benefit, is

Taxable value of the benefit $(1 - \text{Tax rate})$

For the above example, the calculation would be

$$\$486(1 - 0.28) = \$486(0.72) = \$350$$

In other words, a taxable benefit with a value of $486 would have an after-tax value of $350 since you would have to pay $136 ($486 × 0.28) in tax on the benefit.

These calculations can help you assess and compare different employee benefits within a company or in considering different jobs. Remember to also consider the value of employee benefits in terms of your personal and family needs and goals.

---

**Sheet 12**

*Future value* calculations, as discussed in Chapter 1, enable you to assess the long-term worth of employee benefits such as pension programs and retirement plans. For example, you can compare the future value of payments contributed to a company retirement fund to that of other saving and investment options.

You should also take tax considerations into account when you assess employment benefits. A *tax-exempt* benefit is one on which you won't have to pay income tax, but a *tax-deferred* benefit requires the payment of income tax at some future time, such as at retirement. In recent years, the federal government has required that taxes be paid on certain types of nonfinancial benefits. For example, the value of a company car used for personal travel is considered taxable income.

To be exempt from federal income tax, a benefit plan must be "nondiscriminatory"; that is, lower-paid workers must receive benefits comparable to those given to highly paid executives. If executives are given life insurance coverage in which the premium constitutes a higher proportion of their salaries, the excess value of the insurance premium is taxable. When assessing employment compensation and benefits, consider their taxability, since an untaxed benefit of lower value may be worth more than a benefit of higher value that is subject to taxation (see the accompanying Financial Planning Calculations box).

## Your Employment Rights

Employees have legal rights both during the hiring process and on the job. For example, an employer cannot refuse to hire a woman or terminate her employment because of pregnancy, nor can it force her to go on leave at an arbitrary point during her pregnancy. In addition, a woman who stops working due to pregnancy must get full credit for previous service, accrued retirement benefits, and accumulated seniority. Other employment rights include the following:

**Did You Know?**

More and more employers are using credit reports as hiring tools. Federal law requires that job applicants be told if credit histories are being used in the hiring process.

- A person may not be discriminated against in the employment selection process on the basis of age, race, color, religion, sex, marital status, national origin, or mental or physical disabilities.
- Minimum-wage and overtime pay legislation apply to individuals in certain work settings.
- Workers' compensation (for work-related injury or illness), Social Security, and unemployment insurance are required benefits.

## Concept Check 2-4

1. How does a person's life situation determine the importance of certain employee benefits?
2. What methods can be used to measure the monetary value of employee benefits?

# LONG-TERM CAREER DEVELOPMENT

## Obj. 5
Analyze the techniques for career growth and advancement.

A job is for today, but a career can be for a life-time. Will you always enjoy the work you do today? Will you be successful in the career you select? These questions cannot be answered right away; however, certain skills and attitudes can lead to a fulfilling work life.

Everyday you can perform duties that contribute to your career success. Communicating and working well with others will enhance your chances for financial advancement and promotion. Flexibility and openness to new ideas will expand your abilities, knowledge, and career potential.

Develop efficient work habits. Use lists, goal setting, note cards, and other time management techniques. Combine increased productivity with quality. All of your work activities should reflect your best performance. This extra effort will be recognized and rewarded.

Finally, learn to anticipate problems and areas for action. Creativity and a willingness to assist others can help the entire organization and contribute to your work enjoyment and career growth.

## Training Opportunities

Many technology-work situations did not exist a few years ago. Many of the job skills you will need in the future have yet to be created. Your desire for increased education is a primary determinant of your career success and financial advancement. Continue to learn about new technology and the global economy.

Various methods for updating and expanding your knowledge are available. Formal methods include company programs, seminars offered by professional organizations, and graduate and advanced college courses. Many companies encourage and pay for continuing education.

Informal methods for updating and expanding your knowledge include reading and discussion with colleagues. Newspapers, news magazines, business periodicals, and professional journals offer a wealth of information on business, economic, and social trends. Informal meetings with coworkers and associates from other companies are a valuable source of current career information.

## Career Paths and Advancement

As with other financial decisions, career choices must be reevaluated in light of changing values, goals, economic conditions, and social trends. As Exhibit 2–5 shows, you will evolve through a series of career stages, each with specific tasks and challenges. A

**EXHIBIT 2-5**

Stages of Career Development: Characteristics and Concerns

| Stage | Characteristics | Concerns |
|---|---|---|
| Preentry and career exploration stage | • Assess personal interests and set career goals<br>• Obtain necessary training<br>• Gain initial employment | • Matching interests and abilities to employment<br>• Dealing with shock of unfulfilled expectations |
| Establishment and professional growth stage | • Gain in experience, effectiveness, and respect of colleagues<br>• Concentrate on an area of specialization | • Developing career contacts<br>• Avoiding overinvolvement and career burnout |
| Advancement and mid-career adjustment stage | • Continue to obtain experience and knowledge to win promotions<br>• Seek new challenges and expanded responsibility | • Finding continued satisfaction<br>• Maintaining sensitivity toward colleagues and subordinates |
| Late-career and preretirement stage | • Make financial and personal plans for retirement<br>• Assist in training successor | • Determining the extent of professional involvement after retirement<br>• Planning involvement in community activities |

*mentor*   An experienced employee who serves as a teacher and counselor for a less experienced person in a career field.

**Sheet 13**

successful technique for coping with the anxieties associated with career development is to gain the support of an established person in your field. A **mentor** is an experienced employee who serves as a teacher and counselor for a less experienced person in a career field. A relationship with a mentor can provide such benefits as personalized training, access to influential people, and emotional support during difficult times.

Your efforts to attract a mentor start with excellent performance. Show initiative, be creative, and be alert to meeting the needs of others. Maintain visibility and display a desire to learn and grow by asking questions and volunteering for new assignments.

A prospective mentor should be receptive to assisting others and to helping them grow in both the technical and social areas of a career. Many organizations have formal mentor programs with an experienced employee assigned to oversee the career development of a new employee. Some mentor relationships involve retired individuals who desire to share their knowledge and experience.

## Changing Careers

At some time in their lives, most workers change jobs. About 10 million career moves occur each year. People change jobs to obtain a better or different position within the same career field or to move into a new career field. Changing jobs may be more difficult than selecting the first job. Unless their present situation is causing mental stress or physical illness, most people are unwilling to exchange the security of an existing position for the uncertainty of an unfamiliar one.

The following may be indications that it is time to move on:

- Low motivation toward your current work.
- Physical or emotional distress caused by your job.
- Consistently poor performance evaluations.
- A lack of social interactions with coworkers.
- Limited opportunity for salary or position advancement.
- A poor relationship with your superior.

A decision to change careers may require minor alterations in your life (such as going from retail sales to industrial sales), or it may mean extensive retraining and starting at an entry level in a new field. As with every other financial decision, no exact formula exists for deciding whether you should make a career change. However, follow these guidelines. First, carefully assess the financial and personal costs and benefits of changing careers in relation to your needs and goals and those of your household. Giving up benefits such as health insurance may be costly to a family, but the expanded career opportunities in a new field may be worth the trade-off. Then determine whether a career change will serve your needs and goals and those of other household members.

In many industries, job security is a thing of the past. Company mergers, downsizing, and economic conditions may result in forced career changes. Layoffs cause emotional and financial stress for individuals and families. To cope with job termination while seeking new employment, counselors recommend that you

- Maintain appropriate eating, sleep, and exercise habits.
- Get involved in family and community activities; new career contacts are possible anywhere.
- Improve your career skills through personal study, formal classes, or volunteer work.
- Target your job search to high-growth industries or small businesses.
- Consider opportunities with nonprofit organizations, government agencies, temporary employment, or consultant work.
- Target your skills and experience to the needs of an organization.

## Concept Check 2-5

1. What types of activities would you recommend for people who desire career advancement and professional growth?
2. What factors should a person consider before changing jobs or career fields?

## KEY FORMULAS

| Page | Topic | Formula |
|------|-------|---------|
| 42 | Geographic buying power | $\text{Geographic Buying Power} = \dfrac{\text{City 1}}{\text{City 2}} \dfrac{\text{Index number} \times \text{Salary}}{\text{Index number}}$ |

*Example:*

$$= \frac{123 \times 50{,}000}{98.8}$$

$$= \$62{,}247$$

| 53 | Tax-equivalent employee benefits | Tax-equivalent of a nontaxable benefit $= \dfrac{\text{Value of the benefit}}{(1 - \text{Tax rate})}$ |

*Example:*

$$= \frac{\$1{,}250}{(1 - 0.28)}$$

$$= \$1{,}736$$

## Summary of Objectives

**Obj. 1   Describe the activities associated with career planning and advancement.**

Career planning and advancement involve the following stages and activities: (1) assess and research personal goals, abilities, and career fields; (2) evaluate the employment market and identify specific employment opportunities; (3) develop a résumé and cover letter for use in applying for available positions; (4) interview for available positions; (5) evaluate financial and other elements of the positions you are offered; and (6) plan and implement a program for career development.

**Obj. 2   Evaluate the factors that influence employment opportunities.**

Consider the selection of a career in relation to personal abilities, interests, experience, training, and goals; social influences affecting employment, such as demographic trends; changing economic conditions; and industrial and technological trends.

**Obj. 3   Implement employment search strategies.**

For successful career planning and development, consider doing the following. Obtain employment or related experiences by working part-time or by participating in campus and community activities. Use career information sources to learn about employment fields and identify job opportunities. Prepare a résumé and cover letter that effectively present your qualifications for a specific employment position. Practice interview skills that project enthusiasm and competence.

**Obj. 4   Assess the financial and legal concerns related to obtaining employment.**

Evaluate the work environment and compensation package of prospective employers. Assess employee benefits on the basis of their market value, future value, and taxability and your personal needs and goals. Prospective and current employees have legal rights with regard to fair hiring practices and equal opportunity on the job.

**Obj. 5   Analyze the techniques available for career growth and advancement.**

Informal and formal education and training opportunities are available to foster professional development and facilitate career changes.

## Financial Planning Problems

1. *Determining the Future Value of Education.* Jenny Franklin estimates that as a result of completing her master's degree, she will earn $6,000 a year more for the next 40 years.   (Obj. 1)

   a. What would be the total amount of these additional earnings?

   b. What would be the *present value* of these additional earnings based on an annual interest rate of 6 percent? (Use Table A–4 in Appendix A.)

2. *Comparing Living Costs.* Brad Edwards is earning $42,000 a year in a city located in the Midwest. He is interviewing for a position in a city with a cost of living

12 percent higher than where he currently lives. What would be the minimum salary he would need at his new job to maintain the same standard of living?   (Obj. 2)

3. *Calculating Future Value of Salary.* During a job interview, Pam Thompson is offered a salary of $23,000. The company gives annual raises of 6 percent. What would be Pam's salary during her fifth year on the job?   (Obj. 3)

4. *Computing Future Value.* Calculate the future value of a retirement account in which you deposit $2,000 a year for 30 years with an annual interest rate of 8 percent. (Use the tables in Appendix A.)   (Obj. 4)

5. *Comparing Taxes for Employee Benefits.* Which of the following employee benefits has the greater value? Use the formula given in the Financial Planning Calculations box on page 53 to compare these benefits. (Assume a 28 percent tax rate.)   (Obj. 4)

   a. A nontaxable pension contribution of $4,300 or the use of a company car with a taxable value of $6,325.

   b. A life insurance policy with a taxable value of $450 or a nontaxable increase in health insurance coverage valued at $340.

6. *Comparing Employment Offers.* Bill Mason is considering two job offers. Job 1 pays a salary of $36,500 with $4,500 of nontaxable employee benefits. Job 2 pays a salary of $34,700 and $6,120 of nontaxable benefits. Which position would have the higher monetary value? Use a 28 percent tax rate.   (Obj. 4)

## Financial Planning Activities

1. *Researching Career Views.* Interview several people about influences on their current employment situation. How did various personal, economic, and social factors affect their career choices and professional development?   (Obj. 1)

2. *Researching Career Planning Activities.* Interview a person who recently made a major career change. What personal and economic factors influenced this decision? What specific career planning activities did the person use?   (Obj. 1)

3. *Comparing Career Alternatives.* Using Sheet 6 in the *Personal Financial Planner,* research two careers you might consider. Compare employment requirements, duties on the job, and future potential.   (Obj. 2)

4. *Projecting Future Career Opportunities.* Based on a web search or library resources, obtain articles, employment data projections, and other information about the careers with the most future potential. Prepare a report or visual presentation (slides, poster, or video) communicating the types of careers likely to be most in demand in the future.   (Obj. 2)

5. *Searching Employment Opportunities on the Internet.* Using websites such at www.ajb.dni.us or www.careermosiac.com (or web search engines), obtain information about positions available in your areas of interest.   (Obj. 3)

6. *Participating in an Informational Interview.* Arrange an informational interview at a local company or with a business contact you have made. Prepare questions to ask related to needed skills in this employment field, current trends for the industry, and future prospects for this career area.   (Obj. 3)

7. *Searching the Web for Benefit Information.* Using a web search or the library, obtain information about various employee benefits such as health insurance, retirement plans, child care, life insurance, and tuition reimbursement.   (Obj. 4)

8. *Analyzing Employee Benefits.* Using Sheet 12 in the *Personal Financial Planner,* obtain information about various employee benefits from current or prospective employers.   (Obj. 4)

9. *Obtaining Career Advancement Information.* Talk with several people employed in various types of careers (large company, international business, individual entrepreneur, nonprofit, or government). Prepare an outline or other visual presentation describing the training and professional development activities they have found most valuable.   (Obj. 5)

10. *Creating a Personal Data Sheet.* Using Sheet 8 in the *Personal Financial Planner,* plan the content and format for a résumé that you might use in the near future.   (Ch. App.)

11. *Preparing for an Interview.* Based on library research, a web search, and experiences of others, obtain information about effective interviewing techniques. Prepare a video that presents appropriate and inappropriate actions one might take when preparing for and participating in an interview.   (Ch. App.)

## LIFE SITUATION CASE

### BEING YOUR OWN BOSS

"I can't stand it anymore. It was another one of those days!" Stan Vernon proclaimed as he walked in the door.

"Well, stop complaining and change jobs," his wife Calley retorted.

"But it's been the same everywhere," complained Stan. "I think it's time to take a different approach."

Later that week, while looking through the classified section of the newspaper, Stan spotted an opportunity to buy a company that provided computerized accounting, payroll, and financial analysis services to small businesses. This investment would allow Stan to use his career skills while giving him experience in running his own company.

"This seems to be an opportunity for you to do what you enjoy and not have to answer to others," advised Calley. "Let's go over and talk to the current owner."

"That's a good idea," commented Stan. "But how much should we pay for the company?"

Calley responded, "Start by asking how much they want for it!"

### Questions

1. What might affect a person's decision to own a business rather than work for someone else?
2. What factors should Stan analyze when placing a value on the business he is considering for purchase?
3. If Stan can invest his funds at 6 percent and expects to have an annual profit from the business of $60,000 for 10 years, what would be the present value of that series of cash inflows? (See Appendix A.)
4. In addition to running his own business, what other employment alternatives could give Stan more flexibility in his career?

## INTERNET CASE   Starting Your Own Business

After seven years as a staff programmer for a software company, Ellen Kendall is looking for a new challenge. She has enjoyed her work; however, she wants to use her creative skills to develop software for use by small-business owners and families. Some of the programs she plans to develop would

- Help companies monitor customer needs and concerns.
- Provide an easy method for creating and updating websites.
- Assist young entrepreneurs with starting their own business.

Ellen has about $30,000 in savings that she plans to use to start her business. A friend with sales and marketing experience has indicated an interest in becoming a partner in the proposed business.

The major drawback of Ellen's career change is giving up her secure job with many benefits, including health insurance, life insurance, paid holidays and vacation, and a retirement plan.

### Questions

1. What personal and financial factors might Ellen consider when assessing this career change?
2. Locate websites that might be useful to Ellen when planning and operating her business.
3. What skills are commonly needed for success when starting and running a business?
4. Describe how Ellen might use the Internet in the operation of her business.

# Creating an E-Plan: Financial Decisions Using the Web

## PLANNING YOUR CAREER

Your selection of a career and professional development activities will influence many aspects of your life, including financial resource availability, leisure time, living location, and acquaintances.

Websites for Career Planning

- Career planning tips at **www.jobtrak.com/jobguide, www.careers.wsj.com,** and **www.mapping-your-future.org.**
- Listings of available jobs at **www.careermosiac.com, www.careerpath.com, www.hotjobs.com,** and **www.monster.com.**
- Résumé preparation information and other career planning assistance at **www.occ.com** and **www.jobweb.com.**
- Career information from U.S. Department of Labor and state agencies at **www.ajb.dni.us.**
- Current career planning articles from *Money* magazine at **www.money.com,** from *Kiplinger's Personal Finance Magazine* at **www.kiplinger.com,** and *Business Week* at **www.businessweek.com.**

- Employee benefit information at **www.ebri.org, www.ifebp.org,** and **www.benefitslink.com.**
- Information on starting your own business at **www.sba.gov** and **www.inc.com.**

(NOTE: Addresses and content of websites change, and new sites are created daily. Use search engines to update and locate websites for your current financial planning needs.)

*PFP sheets: 6–13*

Short-Term Financial Planning Activities

1. Explore various career areas in relation to your interests, abilities, and goals  (see PFP Sheet 6).
2. Develop a résumé and sample cover letter for use in a job search  (see PFP Sheets 8, 9).
3. Research prospective employers and develop a strategy for effective interviewing  (see PFP Sheets 10, 11).

Long-Term Financial Planning Activities

1. Analyze employee benefits based on your current and possible future financial needs  (see PFP Sheet 12).
2. Develop a plan of action for professional development and career advancement  (see PFP Sheet 13).

CHAPTER
2

# Résumés, Cover Letters, and Interviews

## DEVELOPING A RÉSUMÉ

Every business must present its product or service to potential customers in an effective manner. In the same way, you must market yourself to prospective employers by developing a résumé, creating a letter to obtain an interview, and interviewing for available positions.

### Résumé Elements

A *résumé* is a summary of your education, training, experience, and other job qualifications. This personal-information sheet is vital in your employment search. The main components of a résumé are as follows.

**1. The Personal Data Section**   Start with your name, address, and telephone number. Both a school and home address and telephone number may be appropriate. Do not include your birth date, sex, height, and weight in a résumé unless they apply to specific job qualifications.

**2. The Career Objective Section**   You may omit this section from your résumé. A vague career objective will be meaningless to a prospective employer, and one that is too specific might prevent you from being considered for another position within the organization. Your career objective is probably best communicated in your cover letter. As an alternative, consider a "Summary" section with a synopsis of your capabilities.

**3. The Education Section**   This section should include dates, schools attended, fields of study, and degrees earned. Courses directly related to your career field may be highlighted. If your grade point average is exceptionally high, include it to demonstrate your ability to excel.

**EXHIBIT 2–A**

Sample Action Verbs to Communicate Career-Related Experiences

- Achieved...
- Administered...
- Coordinated...
- Created...
- Designed...
- Developed...
- Directed...
- Edited...
- Initiated...
- Implemented...

- Managed...
- Monitored...
- Organized...
- Planned...
- Produced...
- Researched...
- Summarized...
- Supervised...
- Trained...
- Updated...

**4. The Experience Section**    In this section, list organizations, dates of involvement, and responsibilities for all previous employment, work-related school activities, and community service. Highlight computer skills, technical abilities, and other specific competencies that are in demand by organizations. Use action verbs to communicate how your experience and talents will benefit the organization (see Exhibit 2–A). Focus this information on results and accomplishments, not characteristics.

**5. The Related Information Section**    List honors or awards to communicate your ability to produce quality work. List other interests and activities if they relate to your career. However, avoid a long list of hobbies and other interests, which can give the impression that work is not your top priority.

**6. The References Section**    In this section, list people who can verify your skills and competencies. These individuals may be teachers, previous employers, supervisors, or business colleagues. Be sure to obtain permission from the people you plan to use as references. References are usually not included in a résumé; however, you will need to have this information available if a prospective employer requests it.

## Types of Résumés

Three commonly used types of résumés are the chronological résumé, the functional résumé, and the targeted résumé. The *chronological résumé* (see Exhibit 2–B) presents your education, work experience, and other information in a reverse-time sequence (the most recent item first). This type of résumé is most appropriate for people with a continuous school and work record. Many people find it to be the best vehicle for presenting their career qualifications.

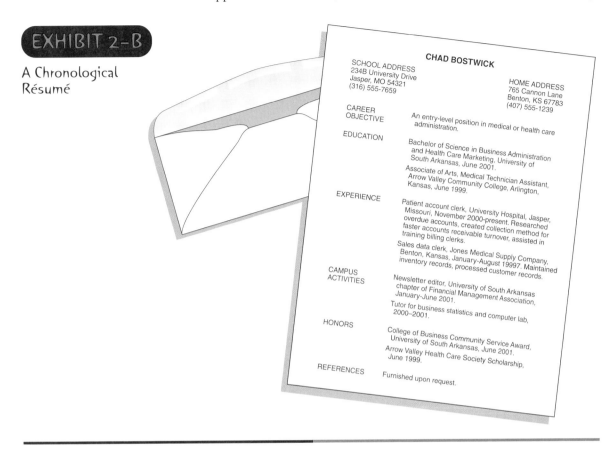

**EXHIBIT 2-B**

A Chronological Résumé

**CHAD BOSTWICK**

SCHOOL ADDRESS
234B University Drive
Jasper, MO 54321
(316) 555-7659

HOME ADDRESS
765 Cannon Lane
Benton, KS 67783
(407) 555-1239

CAREER OBJECTIVE — An entry-level position in medical or health care administration.

EDUCATION — Bachelor of Science in Business Administration and Health Care Marketing, University of South Arkansas, June 2001.
Associate of Arts, Medical Technician Assistant, Arrow Valley Community College, Arlington, Kansas, June 1999.

EXPERIENCE — Patient account clerk, University Hospital, Jasper, Missouri, November 2000–present. Researched overdue accounts, created collection method for faster accounts receivable turnover, assisted in training billing clerks.
Sales data clerk, Jones Medical Supply Company, Benton, Kansas, January–August 19997. Maintained inventory records, processed customer records.

CAMPUS ACTIVITIES — Newsletter editor, University of South Arkansas chapter of Financial Management Association, January–June 2001.
Tutor for business statistics and computer lab, 2000–2001.

HONORS — College of Business Community Service Award, University of South Arkansas, June 2001.
Arrow Valley Health Care Society Scholarship, June 1999.

REFERENCES — Furnished upon request.

---

The *functional résumé* (see Exhibit 2–C) is suggested for people with diverse skills and time gaps in their experience. This résumé emphasizes your abilities and skills in categories such as communication, supervision, project planning, human relations, and research. Each section provides information about experiences and qualifications rather than dates, places, and job titles. This type of résumé is especially appropriate if you are changing careers or your most recent experiences are not directly related to the available position.

You may want to develop a *targeted résumé,* that is, a résumé for a specific job. Such a résumé highlights the capabilities and experiences most appropriate to the available position. The format may be similar to the chronological or functional résumé except it includes a very specific career objective. The targeted résumé takes extra time and research to prepare; however, this effort increases your opportunity for obtaining an interview.

*E-résumés,* used when applying for a job online, should consider the following factors:

- Keep the format simple; avoid bold type, underline, italics, and tabs.
- Do not use attached files that may be difficult to open or decipher.
- Résumés posted on an Internet database may be viewed by your current employer, whom you may not want to know about your job search.
- An Internet résumé is less personal than a printed one or a phone call; over 90 percent of jobs are found offline through ads, job fairs, and networking.

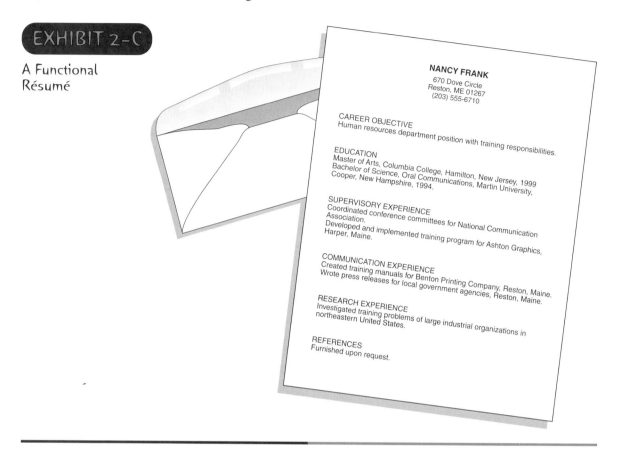

**EXHIBIT 2-C**

A Functional Résumé

**NANCY FRANK**
670 Dove Circle
Reston, ME 01267
(203) 555-6710

CAREER OBJECTIVE
Human resources department position with training responsibilities.

EDUCATION
Master of Arts, Columbia College, Hamilton, New Jersey, 1999
Bachelor of Science, Oral Communications, Martin University,
Cooper, New Hampshire, 1994.

SUPERVISORY EXPERIENCE
Coordinated conference committees for National Communication
Association.
Developed and implemented training program for Ashton Graphics,
Harper, Maine.

COMMUNICATION EXPERIENCE
Created training manuals for Benton Printing Company, Reston, Maine.
Wrote press releases for local government agencies, Reston, Maine.

RESEARCH EXPERIENCE
Investigated training problems of large industrial organizations in
northeastern United States.

REFERENCES
Furnished upon request.

## Résumé Preparation

No formula exists for the preparation of an effective résumé; however, a résumé must be presented in a professional manner. Many candidates are disqualified due to poor résumés. Personal computers and laser printers make the résumé design process easier. Many quick-print businesses specialize in the preparation and reproduction of résumés.

Limit your résumé to one page. Send a two-page résumé only if you have enough material to fill three pages; then use the most valid information to prepare an impressive two-page presentation.

Use a format that highlights how your experiences will contribute to the company's needs. Underline or italicize items if appropriate. Remember, résumés are usually skimmed very quickly; some companies use scanners to check for key words related to education and technical expertise.

Words and phrases that commonly impress prospective employers include "foreign language skills," "computer experience," "achievement," "research experience," "flexible," "team projects," and "overseas study or experience."

For best results, seek guidance in preparing and evaluating your résumé. Counselors, the campus placement office, and friends may find errors and suggest improvements.

PFP

Sheet 8

## Résumé Delivery Methods

Traditionally, résumés have been mailed or hand delivered. When presenting a résumé in person, you have an opportunity to observe the company environment and make a positive impression about your career potential. Electronic résumé delivery may be done by fax, by e-mail, or posting on websites such as www.monster.com and www.careermosaic.com.

## Résumé Alternatives

Thousands of résumés are sent each day. To stand out, applicants have tried various creative approaches. Employers report receiving résumés in the form of comic strips, "wanted" posters, advertisements, and menus; résumés attached to balloons, pizzas, and plants; and résumés on video and computer disks. Some of these efforts were effective; however, most employers view them as frivolous. A creative approach is probably most appropriate in fields such as advertising, journalism, photography, and public relations.

Instead of a résumé, some career counselors recommend a *targeted application letter* describing your background, experience, and accomplishments. After researching a position and company, you can communicate how your specific skills will benefit the organization.

Finally, you might create a *performance portfolio* containing tangible evidence of your experience. This printed or website presentation could include product designs, advertisements, marketing plans, published articles, photos, tables of sales results, financial charts, or video clips.

## CREATING A COVER LETTER

Your résumé must be targeted to a specific organization and job. A cover letter is designed to express your interest in a job and help you obtain an interview. This letter accompanies your résumé and usually consists of an introductory paragraph, one or two development paragraphs, and a concluding paragraph.

### Introduction

The introductory paragraph should get the reader's attention. Indicate your reason for writing by referring to the job or type of employment in which you are interested. Communicate what you have to offer the company based on your experience and qualifications.

### Development

The development section should highlight the aspects of your background that specifically qualify you for the job. Refer the employer to your résumé for more details. At this point, elaborate on experiences and training that will contribute to the organization's needs in the future.

### Conclusion

The concluding paragraph should request action from the employer. Ask for the opportunity to discuss your qualifications and potential with the employer in more detail; in other words, get an interview! Include information to make contacting you convenient, such as telephone numbers and the times when you are available. Close your letter by summarizing how you can benefit the organization.

You should create a separate cover letter (see Exhibit 2–D) for each position for which you apply. A poorly prepared cover letter usually guarantees rejection. Be sure to address your correspondence to the appropriate person in the organization.

Sheet 9

**EXHIBIT 2-D**

Sample Cover
Letter

May 23, 2001

Ms. Hanna Cabral
Human Resources Director
Global Translation Services
3400 Superior Boulevard
Jamestown, NY 13456

Dear Ms. Cabral:

Based on my background and studies in international relations, this is to express my interest in the position available with your organization. Brenda Kelly in your accounting department recommended that I contact you. My studies have included courses in global business practices along with an internship with the exporting department of an electronics company.

My ability to work in a cross-cultural environment provides your organization with a person who can adapt to varied business settings. As a result of my work with companies in other countries, I am able to meet the diverse needs of your clients. My language skills have allowed me to handle customer relations activities with international customers.

I look forward to the opportunity to discuss my qualifications with you in further detail. You may contact me at 501–963–4556 or at jhopkins1@internet.com. I believe my training and background will allow me to contribute to the continued success of your organization.

Sincerely,

*Jerry Hopkins*

Jerry Hopkins
5678 Collins Road
West Barrington, NY 14332

A résumé and cover letter are your ticket to the interview. You may possess outstanding qualifications and career potential, but you need an interview to communicate this information. The time, effort, and care you take to present yourself on paper will help you achieve your career goal.

## THE JOB INTERVIEW

"Why should we hire you?" This may be an unexpected question; however, you may need to answer it. The interview phase of job hunting is limited to candidates who possess the specific qualifications the employer wants. Being invited for an interview puts you closer to receiving a job offer.

### Preparing for the Interview

Prepare for your interview by obtaining additional information about your prospective employer. The best sources of company information include

PFP

Sheet 10

- Library resources such as annual reports or recent articles.
- Internet searches of company and industry information.
- Observations during company visits.
- Observations of company products in stores or other places.
- Informal interviews with current and past employees.
- Discussions with people knowledgeable about the company or industry.

During your research, try to obtain information about the company's past and current activities. Facts about its operations, competitors, recent successes, planned expansion, and personnel policies will be helpful when you discuss your potential contributions to the company.

Another preinterview activity is preparation of questions such as

- What training opportunities are available to employees who desire advancement?
- What qualities do your most successful employees possess?
- What do your employees like best about working here?
- What actions of competitors are likely to affect the company in the near future?

Also, prepare questions about your specific interests and about the particular organization with which you are interviewing. Request information about company policies and employee benefits.

**Sheet 11**

Successful interviewing requires practice. By using a video recorder or working with friends, you can develop the confidence needed for effective interviewing. Work to organize ideas, speak clearly and calmly, and communicate enthusiasm. Prepare specific answers regarding your strengths. Many campus organizations and career placement offices offer opportunities for practice by conducting mock interviews. Prepare concise answers for specific questions (see Exhibit 2–E) explaining how your experience will contribute to the future of the company. If appropriate, plan to bring photos or other evidence of your past efforts.

As you get ready for the interview, keep in mind that proper dress and grooming are important. Current employees are the best source of information about how to dress. In general, dress more conservatively than employees do. A business suit is usually appropriate for both men and women. Avoid trendy and casual styles, and don't wear too much jewelry. Confirm the time and location of the interview. Take copies of your résumé, your reference list, and a small notebook for writing down ideas during the interview. Plan to arrive about 10 minutes earlier than your appointed time.

## The Interview Process

A *screening interview* is an initial, usually brief meeting with applicants that reduces the pool of job candidates. In the screening interview, interviewees are processed on the basis of overall impression and a few general questions. Screening interviews may be conducted on college campuses by corporate recruiters. Success qualifies you for closer consideration by the employer.

Organizations are expanding the use of online screening interviews in which applicants provide basic personal and background information. In addition, these "e-interviews" may ask you to respond to questions such as "Would you rather have structure or flexibility in your work?" and "What approach do you use to solve difficult problems?" Computerized interviewing may also be used to test an applicant's ability in job-related situations such as those that a bank teller or retail clerk might encounter.

Once you are judged to be a strong candidate for a job, your next interview can last from one hour to several days. The *selection interview,* which is reserved for the finalists in the job search, may involve a series of activities, including responses to questions, meetings with several people on the staff, and a seminar presentation.

The first part of the selection interview usually occurs in an informal setting. This arrangement is designed to help you relax and to establish rapport. Next, a brief discussion of the available position may take place. The main part of the interview

**Common Interview Questions**

### Education and Training Questions

What education and training qualify you for this job?

Why are you interested in working for this company?

In addition to going to school, what activities have helped you to expand your interests and knowledge?

What did you like best about school?

What did you like least?

### Work and Other Experience Questions

In what types of situations have you done your best work?

Describe the supervisors who motivated you most.

Which of your past accomplishments are you most proud of?

Have you ever had to coordinate the activities of several people?

Describe some people whom you have found difficult to work with.

Describe a situation in which your determination helped you achieve a specific goal.

What situations frustrate you?

Other than past jobs, what experiences have helped prepare you for this job?

What methods do you consider best for motivating employees?

### Personal Qualities Questions

What are your major strengths?

What are your major weaknesses? What have you done to overcome your weaknesses?

What do you plan to be doing 5 or 10 years from now?

Which individuals have had the greatest influence on you?

What traits make a person successful?

How well do you communicate your ideas orally and in writing?

How would your teachers and your past employers describe you?

What do you do in your leisure time?

How persuasive are you in presenting ideas to others?

involves questions to assess your abilities, potential, and personality. Interviews may include situations or questions to determine how you react under pressure. Remain calm. Answer clearly in a controlled manner. In the last portion of the interview, you are usually given an opportunity to ask questions.

An interviewer *cannot* ask:

- where you were born.
- your age.
- if you have any disabilities.
- about marital status, religion, or responsibility for children.

However, an interviewer *can* ask:

- if you are a U.S. citizen.
- you to prove you are over 18.
- if you have the physical ability to perform the job for which you have applied.
- if there are any days or times when you can't work.

The use of *behavioral interviewing* is expanding to better evaluate an applicant's on-the-job potential. In these situations, prospective employees are asked about how they might handle various work situations. Behavioral interview questions typically begin with "describe" or "tell me about . . . " to encourage interviewees to better explain their work style.

Most interviewers conclude the selection interview by telling you when you can expect to hear from the company. While waiting, consider doing two things. First, send a follow-up letter within a day or two expressing your appreciation for the opportunity to interview. If you don't get the job, this thank-you letter can make a positive impression that improves your chances for future consideration. Second, do a self-evaluation of your interview performance. Write down the areas that you could improve. Try to remember the questions you were asked that were different than what you expected.

Finally, the more interviews you have, the better you will present yourself. And the more interviews you have, the better the chance of being offered a job.

# 3

# Money Management Strategy: Financial Statements and Budgeting

## "We Spent How Much on What?"

"Here we go again," complained Ben. "Everytime we try to use a budget, we end up arguing and still don't have enough money."

Yolanda replied, "Maybe if we kept track of everything we spend, we would have some idea of where our money goes."

"No, not that!" Ben exclaimed. "I have a friend who keeps a notebook and lists everything he spends. That would drive me crazy."

"Well, we can't keep going like we have," responded Yolanda. "A year ago, we owed $4,500 on the credit cards. Now it's up to $7,000. And we don't have anything in savings. How will we ever be able to have a down payment for a house?"

Ben and Yolanda decided to sort all their check stubs, receipts, and credit card statements to see where their money was going. Last year, they spent over $2,000 in restaurants and charged over $800 on their vacation.

"I didn't realize we spent that much on those things," commented Ben. "We also had auto maintenance costs of $1,650 and donated $1,800 to the homeless shelter and church. Those are things we had to do and wanted to do."

Yolanda replied, "But now that we know how we spend our money, what do we do next?"

"Maybe we should get a computerized money management program," Ben suggested.

Yolanda countered, "Maybe we should just start with spending a few dollars on a notebook and file folders to record and sort our receipts."

## Questions

1. What would Ben and Yolanda learn by sorting their expenses into various categories? What categories should they use?
2. How can knowing where their money goes help Ben and Yolanda plan their spending?
3. What financial goals might Ben and Yolanda consider to address some of their money management concerns?
4. Locate a website that would help Ben and Yolanda improve their money management skills.

## Learning Objectives

**Obj. 1** Recognize relationships among financial documents and money management activities.

**Obj. 2** Create a system for maintaining personal financial records.

**Obj. 3** Develop a personal balance sheet and cash flow statement.

**Obj. 4** Create and implement a budget.

**Obj. 5** Calculate savings needed to achieve financial goals.

# PLANNING FOR SUCCESSFUL MONEY MANAGEMENT

## Obj. 1

Recognize relationships among financial documents and money management activities.

*money management*
Day-to-day financial activities necessary to manage current personal economic resources while working toward long-term financial security.

"Each month I have too much month and not enough money. If the month were only 20 days long, budgeting would be easy." Most of us have heard a comment like this when it comes to budgeting and money management.

Your daily spending and saving decisions are at the center of financial planning. You must coordinate these decisions with your needs, goals, and personal situation. When people watch a baseball or football game, they usually know the score. In financial planning, knowing the score is also important. Maintaining financial records and planning your spending are essential to successful personal financial management. The time and effort you devote to these recordkeeping activities will yield benefits. **Money management** refers to the day-to-day financial activities necessary to manage current personal economic resources while working toward long-term financial security.

## Opportunity Cost and Money Management

Consumers can choose from more than 25,000 items in a supermarket, from more than 11,000 periodicals, and from as many as 500 cable television stations. Daily decision making is a fact of life, and trade-offs are associated with each choice made. Selecting an alternative means you give up something else. In terms of money management decisions, examples of trade-off situations, or *opportunity costs,* include the following:

- Spending money on current living expenses reduces the amount you can use for saving and investing for long-term financial security.
- Saving and investing for the future reduce the amount you can spend now.
- Buying on credit results in payments later and a reduction in the amount of future income available for spending.
- Using savings for purchases results in lost interest earnings and an inability to use savings for other purposes.
- Comparison shopping can save you money and improve the quality of your purchases but uses up something of value you cannot replace: your time.

As you develop and implement various money management activities, you need to assess financial and personal costs and benefits associated with financial decisions.

## EXHIBIT 3-1   MONEY MANAGEMENT ACTIVITIES

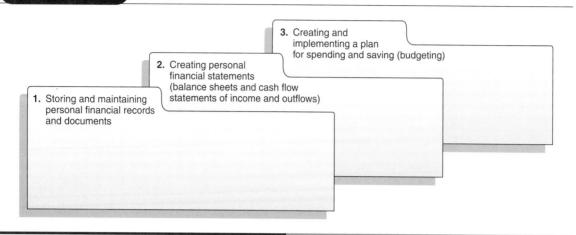

3. Creating and implementing a plan for spending and saving (budgeting)

2. Creating personal financial statements (balance sheets and cash flow statements of income and outflows)

1. Storing and maintaining personal financial records and documents

## Components of Money Management

As Exhibit 3–1 shows, three major money management activities are interrelated. Personal financial records and documents are the foundation of systematic resource use. They provide written evidence of business transactions, ownership of property, and legal matters. Personal financial statements enable you to measure and assess your financial position and progress. Your spending plan, or budget, is the basis for effective money management.

### Concept Check 3-1

1.  What opportunity costs are associated with money management activities?
2.  What are the three major money management activities?

## A SYSTEM FOR PERSONAL FINANCIAL RECORDS

**Obj. 2**
Create a system for maintaining personal financial records.

Experts once predicted that computers would result in fewer paper documents. How wrong they were! Today computers are generating more paperwork than ever. Much of that paperwork relates to financial matters. Invoices, credit card statements, insurance policies, and tax records are the basis of financial recordkeeping and personal economic choices.

An organized system of financial records provides a basis for

*   Handling daily business affairs, including payment of bills on time.
*   Planning and measuring financial progress.
*   Completing required tax reports.
*   Making effective investment decisions.
*   Determining available resources for current and future buying.

As Exhibit 3–2 shows, most financial records are kept in one of three places: a home file, a safe deposit box, or a home computer. A home file should be used to keep records for current needs and documents with limited value. Your home file may be a series of folders, a cabinet with several drawers, or even a cardboard box. Whatever method you use, it is most important that your home file be organized to allow quick access to required documents and information.

## EXHIBIT 3–2    WHERE TO KEEP YOUR FINANCIAL RECORDS

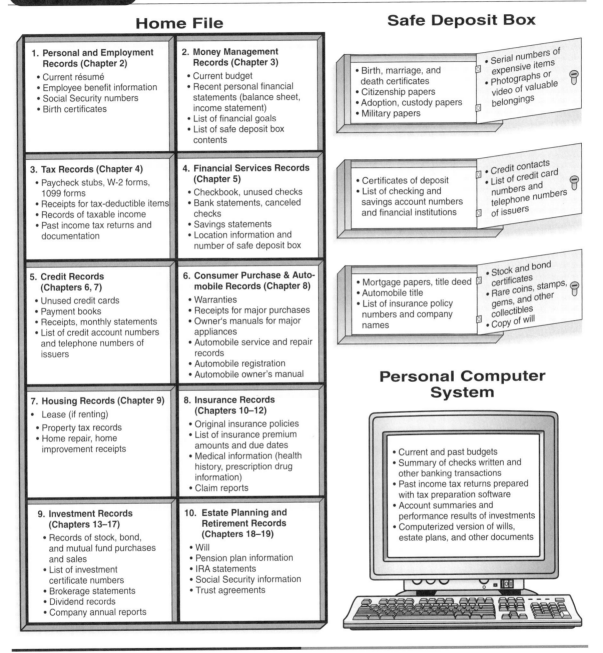

### Home File

**1. Personal and Employment Records (Chapter 2)**
- Current résumé
- Employee benefit information
- Social Security numbers
- Birth certificates

**2. Money Management Records (Chapter 3)**
- Current budget
- Recent personal financial statements (balance sheet, income statement)
- List of financial goals
- List of safe deposit box contents

**3. Tax Records (Chapter 4)**
- Paycheck stubs, W-2 forms, 1099 forms
- Receipts for tax-deductible items
- Records of taxable income
- Past income tax returns and documentation

**4. Financial Services Records (Chapter 5)**
- Checkbook, unused checks
- Bank statements, canceled checks
- Savings statements
- Location information and number of safe deposit box

**5. Credit Records (Chapters 6, 7)**
- Unused credit cards
- Payment books
- Receipts, monthly statements
- List of credit account numbers and telephone numbers of issuers

**6. Consumer Purchase & Automobile Records (Chapter 8)**
- Warranties
- Receipts for major purchases
- Owner's manuals for major appliances
- Automobile service and repair records
- Automobile registration
- Automobile owner's manual

**7. Housing Records (Chapter 9)**
- Lease (if renting)
- Property tax records
- Home repair, home improvement receipts

**8. Insurance Records (Chapters 10–12)**
- Original insurance policies
- List of insurance premium amounts and due dates
- Medical information (health history, prescription drug information)
- Claim reports

**9. Investment Records (Chapters 13–17)**
- Records of stock, bond, and mutual fund purchases and sales
- List of investment certificate numbers
- Brokerage statements
- Dividend records
- Company annual reports

**10. Estate Planning and Retirement Records (Chapters 18–19)**
- Will
- Pension plan information
- IRA statements
- Social Security information
- Trust agreements

### Safe Deposit Box

- Birth, marriage, and death certificates
- Citizenship papers
- Adoption, custody papers
- Military papers
- Serial numbers of expensive items
- Photographs or video of valuable belongings

- Certificates of deposit
- List of checking and savings account numbers and financial institutions
- Credit contacts
- List of credit card numbers and telephone numbers of issuers

- Mortgage papers, title deed
- Automobile title
- List of insurance policy numbers and company names
- Stock and bond certificates
- Rare coins, stamps, gems, and other collectibles
- Copy of will

### Personal Computer System

- Current and past budgets
- Summary of checks written and other banking transactions
- Past income tax returns prepared with tax preparation software
- Account summaries and performance results of investments
- Computerized version of wills, estate plans, and other documents

*safe deposit box*
A private storage area at a financial institution with maximum security for valuables.

Important financial records and valuable articles should be kept in a location that provides better security than a home file. A **safe deposit box** is a private storage area at a financial institution with maximum security for valuables and difficult-to-replace documents. Access to the contents of a safe deposit box requires two keys. One key is issued to you; the other is kept by the financial institution where the safe deposit box is located. Items commonly kept in a safe deposit box include stock certificates, contracts, a list of insurance policies, and valuables such as rare coins and stamps.

The number of financial records and documents may seem overwhelming; however, they can easily be organized into 10 categories (see Exhibit 3–2). These groups correspond to the major topics covered in this book. You may not need to use all of these records and documents at present. As your financial situation changes, you will add others.

How long should you keep personal finance records? The answer to this question differs for various documents. Records such as birth certificates, wills, and Social Security data should be kept permanently. Records on property and investments should be kept as long as you own these items. Federal tax laws dictate the length of time you should keep tax-related information. Copies of tax returns and supporting data should be saved for six years. Normally, an audit will go back only three years; however, under certain circumstances, the Internal Revenue Service may request information from six years back. Financial experts recommend keeping documents related to the purchase and sale of real estate indefinitely.

**PFP**

**Sheet 14**

## Concept Check 3-2

1. What are the benefits of an organized system of financial records and documents?
2. What suggestions would you give for creating a system for organizing and storing financial records and documents?
3. What influences the length of time you should keep financial records and documents?

# PERSONAL FINANCIAL STATEMENTS FOR MEASURING FINANCIAL PROGRESS

**Obj. 3**
Develop a personal balance sheet and cash flow statement.

Every journey starts somewhere. You need to know where you are before you can go somewhere else. Personal financial statements tell you the starting point of your financial journey.

Most of the financial documents we have discussed come from financial institutions, other business organizations, or the government. Two documents that you create yourself, the personal balance sheet and the cash flow statement, are called *personal financial statements*. These reports provide information about your current financial position and present a summary of your income and spending. The main purposes of personal financial statements are to

• Report your current financial position in relation to the value of the items you own and the amounts you owe.
• Measure your progress toward your financial goals.
• Maintain information about your financial activities.
• Provide data you can use when preparing tax forms or applying for credit.

## The Personal Balance Sheet: Where Are You Now?

*balance sheet*
A financial statement that reports what an individual or a family owns and owes; also called a *net worth statement.*

The current financial position of an individual or a family is a common starting point for financial planning. A **balance sheet,** also called a *net worth statement* or *statement of financial position,* reports what you own and what you owe. You prepare a personal balance sheet to determine your current financial position using the following process:

$$\boxed{\text{Item of value}\atop\text{(what you own)}} - \boxed{\text{Amounts owed}\atop\text{(what you owe)}} = \boxed{\text{Net worth}\atop\text{(your wealth)}}$$

For example, if your possessions are worth $4,500 and you owe $800 to others, your net worth is $3,700.

### Step 1: Listing Items of Value

Available cash and money in bank accounts combined with other items of value are the foundation of your current financial position. **Assets** are cash and other tangible property with a monetary value. The balance sheet for Rose and Edgar Gomez (Exhibit 3–3) lists their assets under four categories:

*assets*  Cash and other property with a monetary value.

*liquid assets*  Cash and items of value that can easily be converted to cash.

1. **Liquid assets** are cash and items of value that can easily be converted to cash. Money in checking and savings accounts is liquid and is available to the Gomez family for current spending. The cash value of their life insurance may be borrowed if needed. While assets other than liquid assets can also be converted into cash, the process is not quite as easy.

2. *Real estate* includes a home, a condominium, vacation property, or other land that a person or family owns.

3. *Personal possessions* are a major portion of assets for most people. Included in this category are automobiles and other personal belongings. While these items have value, they may be difficult to convert to cash. You may decide to list your possessions on the balance sheet at their original cost. However, these values probably need to be revised over time, since a five-year-old television set, for example, is worth less now than when it was new. Thus, you may wish to list your possessions at their current value (also referred to as *market value*). This method takes into account the fact that such things as a home or rare jewelry may increase in value over time. You can estimate current value by looking at ads for the selling price of comparable automobiles, homes, or other possessions. Or you may use the services of an appraiser.

4. *Investment assets* are funds set aside for long-term financial needs. The Gomez family will use their investments for such things as financing their children's education, purchasing a vacation home, and planning for retirement. Since investment assets usually fluctuate in value, the amounts listed should reflect their value at the time the balance sheet is prepared.

### Step 2: Determining Amounts Owed

Looking at the total assets of the Gomez family, you might conclude that they have a strong financial position. However, their debts must also be considered. **Liabilities** are amounts owed to others but do not include items not yet due, such as next month's rent. A liability is a debt you owe now, not something you may owe in the future. Liabilities fall into two categories:

*liabilities*  Amounts owed to others.

*current liabilities*  Debts that must be paid within a short time, usually less than a year.

*long-term liabilities*  Debts that are not required to be paid in full until more than a year from now.

1. **Current liabilities** are debts you must pay within a short time, usually less than a year. These liabilities include such things as medical bills, tax payments, insurance premiums, cash loans, and charge accounts.

2. **Long-term liabilities** are debts you do not have to pay in full until more than a year from now. Common long-term liabilities include auto loans, educational loans, and mortgages. A *mortgage* is an amount borrowed to buy a house or other real estate that will be repaid over a period of 15, 20, or 30 years. Similarly, a home improvement loan may be repaid to the lender over the next 5 to 10 years.

# EXHIBIT 3-3   CREATING A PERSONAL BALANCE SHEET

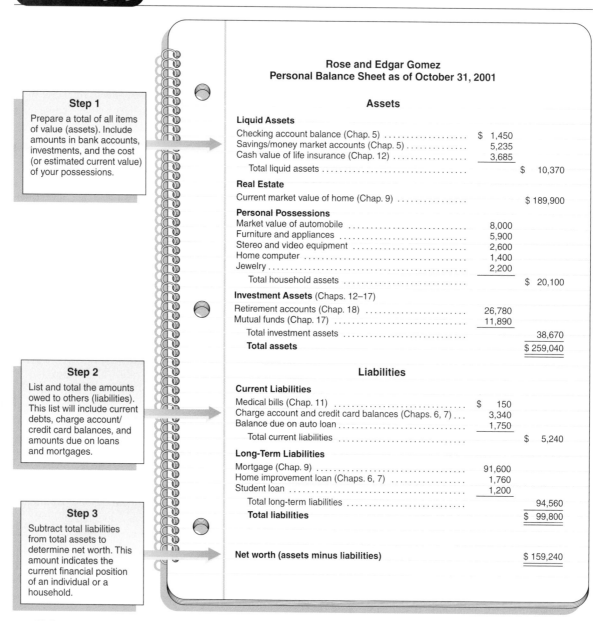

**Step 1**

Prepare a total of all items of value (assets). Include amounts in bank accounts, investments, and the cost (or estimated current value) of your possessions.

**Step 2**

List and total the amounts owed to others (liabilities). This list will include current debts, charge account/credit card balances, and amounts due on loans and mortgages.

**Step 3**

Subtract total liabilities from total assets to determine net worth. This amount indicates the current financial position of an individual or a household.

**Rose and Edgar Gomez**
**Personal Balance Sheet as of October 31, 2001**

## Assets

**Liquid Assets**

| | | |
|---|---:|---:|
| Checking account balance (Chap. 5) | $ 1,450 | |
| Savings/money market accounts (Chap. 5) | 5,235 | |
| Cash value of life insurance (Chap. 12) | 3,685 | |
| Total liquid assets | | $    10,370 |

**Real Estate**

| | |
|---|---:|
| Current market value of home (Chap. 9) | $ 189,900 |

**Personal Possessions**

| | | |
|---|---:|---:|
| Market value of automobile | 8,000 | |
| Furniture and appliances | 5,900 | |
| Stereo and video equipment | 2,600 | |
| Home computer | 1,400 | |
| Jewelry | 2,200 | |
| Total household assets | | $    20,100 |

**Investment Assets** (Chaps. 12–17)

| | | |
|---|---:|---:|
| Retirement accounts (Chap. 18) | 26,780 | |
| Mutual funds (Chap. 17) | 11,890 | |
| Total investment assets | | 38,670 |
| **Total assets** | | **$ 259,040** |

## Liabilities

**Current Liabilities**

| | | |
|---|---:|---:|
| Medical bills (Chap. 11) | $      150 | |
| Charge account and credit card balances (Chaps. 6, 7) | 3,340 | |
| Balance due on auto loan | 1,750 | |
| Total current liabilities | | $      5,240 |

**Long-Term Liabilities**

| | | |
|---|---:|---:|
| Mortgage (Chap. 9) | 91,600 | |
| Home improvement loan (Chaps. 6, 7) | 1,760 | |
| Student loan | 1,200 | |
| Total long-term liabilities | | 94,560 |
| **Total liabilities** | | **$   99,800** |

| | |
|---|---:|
| **Net worth (assets minus liabilities)** | $ 159,240 |

NOTE: Various asset and liability items are discussed in the chapters listed next to them.

The debts listed in the liability section of a balance sheet represent the amount owed at the moment; they do not include future interest payments. However, each debt payment is likely to include a portion of interest. Chapters 6 and 7 discuss the cost of borrowing further.

## Step 3. Computing Net Worth

*net worth* The difference between total assets and total liabilities.

Your **net worth** is the difference between your total assets and your total liabilities. This relationship can be stated as

$$\text{Assets} - \text{Liabilities} = \text{Net worth}$$

Net worth is the amount you would have if all assets were sold for the listed values and all debts were paid in full. Also, total assets equal total liabilities plus net worth. The balance sheet of a business is commonly expressed as

$$\text{Assets} = \text{Liabilities} + \text{Net worth}$$

As Exhibit 3–3 shows, Rose and Edgar Gomez have a net worth of $159,240. Since very few people, if any, liquidate all assets, the amount of net worth has a more practical purpose: It provides a measurement of your current financial position.

*insolvency* The inability to pay debts when they are due because liabilities far exceed the value of assets.

A person may have a high net worth but still have financial difficulties. Having many assets with low liquidity means not having the cash available to pay current expenses. **Insolvency** is the inability to pay debts when they are due; it occurs when a person's liabilities far exceed available assets. Bankruptcy, discussed in Chapter 7, may be an alternative for a person in this position.

You can increase your net worth in various ways, including

**Sheet 15**

- Increasing your savings.
- Reducing spending.
- Increasing the value of investments and other possessions.
- Reducing the amounts you owe.

Remember, your net worth is *not* money available for use but an indication of your financial position on a given date.

## Evaluating Your Financial Position

A personal balance sheet helps you measure progress toward financial goals. Your financial situation improves if your net worth increases each time you prepare a balance sheet. It will improve more rapidly if you are able to set aside money each month for savings and investments.

As with net worth, the relationship among various balance sheet items can give an indication of your financial position. The Financial Planning Calculations box on the next page explains several commonly used financial ratios.

## The Cash Flow Statement: Where Did Your Money Go?

*cash flow* The actual inflow and outflow of cash during a given time period.

*cash flow statement* A financial statement that summarizes cash receipts and payments for a given period.

Each day, financial events can affect your net worth. When you receive a paycheck or pay living expenses, your total assets and liabilities change. **Cash flow** is the actual inflow and outflow of cash during a given time period. Income from employment will probably represent your most important *cash inflow;* however, other income, such as interest earned on a savings account, should also be considered. In contrast, payments for items such as rent, food, and loans are *cash outflows.*

A **cash flow statement,** also called a *personal income and expenditure statement,* (Exhibit 3–4 on page 79) is a summary of cash receipts and payments for a given period, such as a month or a year. This report provides data on your income and spending

# Financial Planning Calculations

## RATIOS FOR EVALUATING FINANCIAL PROGRESS

Financial ratios provide guidelines for measuring changes in your financial situation. These relationships can indicate progress toward an improved financial position.

| Ratio | Calculation | Example | Interpretation |
|---|---|---|---|
| Debt ratio | Liabilities divided by net worth | $25,000/$50,000 = 0.5 | Shows relationship between debt and net worth; a low debt ratio is best. |
| Current ratio | Liquid assets divided by current liabilities | $4,000/$2,000 = 2 | Indicates $2 in liquid assets for every $1 of current liabilities; a high current ratio is desirable to have cash available to pay bills. |
| Liquidity ratio | Liquid assets divided by monthly expenses | $10,000/$4,000 = 2.5 | Indicates the number of months in which living expenses can be paid if an emergency arises; a high liquidity ratio is desirable. |
| Debt-payments ratio | Monthly credit payments divided by take-home pay | $540/$3,600 = 0.15 | Indicates how much of a person's earnings goes for debt payments (excluding a home mortgage); most financial advisers recommend a debt-payments ratio of less than 20 percent. |
| Savings ratio | Amount saved each month divided by gross income | $648/$5,400 = 0.12 | Financial experts recommend monthly savings of at least 10 percent. |

These financial ratios, and other financial analysis methods, can assist you in assessing your spending and saving patterns to help you reach your financial goals.

patterns, which will be helpful when preparing a budget. A checking account can provide information for your cash flow statement. Deposits to the account are your *inflows;* checks written are your *outflows.* Of course, in using this system, when you do not deposit the entire amounts received, you must also note the spending of undeposited amounts in your cash flow statement.

The process for preparing a cash flow statement is

| Total cash received during the time period | − | Cash outflows during the time period | = | Cash surplus or deficit |
|---|---|---|---|---|

### Step 1: Record Income
Creating a cash flow statement starts with identifying the cash received during the time period involved. **Income** is the inflows of cash for an individual or a household. For most people, the main source of income is money received from a job. Other common income sources include

*income*   Inflows of cash to an individual or a household.

- Wages, salaries, and commissions.
- Self-employment business income.
- Saving and investment income (interest, dividends, rent).

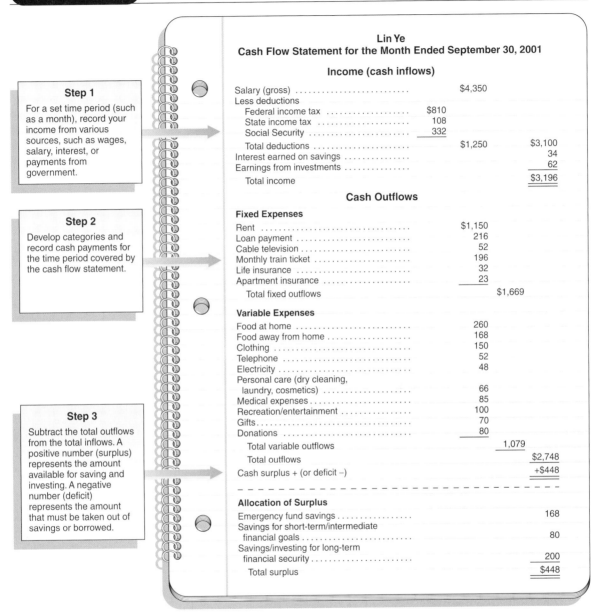

## EXHIBIT 3-4   CREATING A CASH FLOW STATEMENT OF INCOME AND OUTFLOWS

**Step 1**

For a set time period (such as a month), record your income from various sources, such as wages, salary, interest, or payments from government.

**Step 2**

Develop categories and record cash payments for the time period covered by the cash flow statement.

**Step 3**

Subtract the total outflows from the total inflows. A positive number (surplus) represents the amount available for saving and investing. A negative number (deficit) represents the amount that must be taken out of savings or borrowed.

**Lin Ye**
**Cash Flow Statement for the Month Ended September 30, 2001**

### Income (cash inflows)

| | | | |
|---|---|---|---|
| Salary (gross) | | $4,350 | |
| Less deductions | | | |
| Federal income tax | $810 | | |
| State income tax | 108 | | |
| Social Security | 332 | | |
| Total deductions | $1,250 | $3,100 | |
| Interest earned on savings | | 34 | |
| Earnings from investments | | 62 | |
| Total income | | $3,196 | |

### Cash Outflows

**Fixed Expenses**

| | | |
|---|---|---|
| Rent | $1,150 | |
| Loan payment | 216 | |
| Cable television | 52 | |
| Monthly train ticket | 196 | |
| Life insurance | 32 | |
| Apartment insurance | 23 | |
| Total fixed outflows | | $1,669 |

**Variable Expenses**

| | | |
|---|---|---|
| Food at home | 260 | |
| Food away from home | 168 | |
| Clothing | 150 | |
| Telephone | 52 | |
| Electricity | 48 | |
| Personal care (dry cleaning, laundry, cosmetics) | 66 | |
| Medical expenses | 85 | |
| Recreation/entertainment | 100 | |
| Gifts | 70 | |
| Donations | 80 | |
| Total variable outflows | 1,079 | |
| Total outflows | | $2,748 |
| Cash surplus + (or deficit –) | | +$448 |

**Allocation of Surplus**

| | |
|---|---|
| Emergency fund savings | 168 |
| Savings for short-term/intermediate financial goals | 80 |
| Savings/investing for long-term financial security | 200 |
| Total surplus | $448 |

- Gifts, grants, scholarships, and educational loans.
- Government payments, such as Social Security, public assistance, and unemployment benefits.
- Amounts received from pension and retirement programs.
- Alimony and child support payments.

*take-home pay*
Earnings after deductions for taxes and other items; also called *disposable income.*

In Exhibit 3–4, notice that Lin Ye's monthly salary (or *gross income*) of $4,350 is her main source of income. However, she does not have use of the entire amount. **Take-home pay,** also called *net pay,* is a person's earnings after deductions for taxes and other items. Lin's deductions for federal, state, and Social Security taxes are $1,250. Her take-home pay is $3,196. This amount, plus earnings from savings and investments, is the income she has available for use during the current month.

*discretionary income*
Money left over after paying for housing, food, and other necessities.

Take-home pay is also called *disposable income,* the amount a person or household has available to spend. **Discretionary income** is money left over after paying for housing, food, and other necessities. Studies report that discretionary income ranges from less than 5 percent for people under age 25 to more than 40 percent for older people.

## Step 2: Record Cash Outflows

Cash payments for living expenses and other items make up the second component of a cash flow statement. Lin Ye divides her cash outflows into two major categories: fixed expenses and variable expenses. While every individual and household has different cash outflows, these main categories, along with the subgroupings Lin uses, can be adapted to most situations.

1. *Fixed expenses* are payments that do not vary from month to month. Rent or mortgage payments, installment loan payments, cable television service fees, and a monthly train ticket for commuting to work are examples of constant or fixed cash outflows.

For Lin, another type of fixed expense is the amount she sets aside each month for payments due once or twice a year. For example, Lin pays $384 every March for life insurance. Each month, she records a fixed outflow of $32 for deposit in a special savings account so that the money will be available when her insurance payment is due.

2. *Variable expenses* are flexible payments that change from month to month. Common examples of variable cash outflows are food, clothing, utilities (such as electricity and telephone), recreation, medical expenses, gifts, and donations. The use of a checkbook or some other recordkeeping system is necessary for an accurate total of cash outflows.

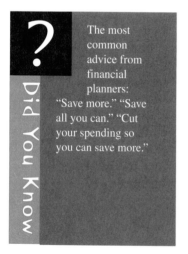

The most common advice from financial planners: "Save more." "Save all you can." "Cut your spending so you can save more."

## Step 3: Determine Net Cash Flow

The difference between income and outflows can be either a positive (*surplus*) or a negative (*deficit*) cash flow. A deficit exists if more cash goes out than comes in during a given month. This amount must be made up by withdrawals from savings or by borrowing. The effect of a net cash flow on net worth is shown in the Financial Planning for Life's Situations feature on page 81.

When you have a cash surplus, as Lin did (Exhibit 3–4), this amount is available for saving, investing, or paying off debts. Each month, Lin sets aside money for her *emergency fund* in a savings account that she would use for unexpected expenses or to pay living costs if she did not receive her salary. She deposits the rest of the surplus in savings and investment plans that have two purposes. The first is the achievement of short-term and intermediate financial goals, such as a new car, a vacation, or reenrollment in school; the second is long-term financial security—her retirement.

A cash flow statement provides the foundation for preparing and implementing a spending, saving, and investment plan, discussed in the next section.

Sheet 16

## Concept Check 3-3

1. What are the main purposes of personal financial statements?
2. What does a personal balance sheet tell about your financial situation?
3. How can you use a balance sheet for personal financial planning?
4. What information does a cash flow statement present?

# Financial Planning for Life's Situations

## MEASURING YOUR FINANCIAL PROGRESS

People commonly prepare a balance sheet on a periodic basis, such as every three or six months. Between those points in time, use your budget and cash flow statement to plan and measure spending and saving activities. For example, during a certain calendar year, you might prepare a balance sheet on January 1, June 30, and December 31. Your budget would serve to plan your spending and saving between these points in time, and your cash flow statement of income and outflows would document your actual spending and saving. This relationship may be illustrated as shown below.

Changes in your net worth are the result of the relationship between cash inflows and outflows. In periods when your outflows exceed your inflows, you must draw on savings or borrow (buy on credit). When this happens, lower assets (savings) or higher liabilities (due

to the use of credit) result in a lower net worth. When inflows exceed outflows, putting money into savings or paying off debts will result in a higher net worth. In general, the relationship between the cash flow statement and the balance sheet may be expressed as follows:

| Cash Flow Statement | Balance Sheet |
|---|---|
| If cash inflows (income) are greater than cash outflows . . . . | Net worth increases |
| If cash outflows (payments) are greater than cash inflows (income) . . . . . . . . . . | Net worth decreases |

Using a budget, creating a cash flow statement, and developing a balance sheet on a periodic basis can help you improve your financial situation.

(January 1 to June 30)          (July 1 to December 31)

# BUDGETING FOR SKILLED MONEY MANAGEMENT

## Obj. 4
Create and implement a budget.

*budget*   A specific plan for spending income.

A **budget,** or *spending plan,* is necessary for successful financial planning. The common financial problems of overusing credit, lacking a regular savings program, and failing to ensure future financial security can be minimized through budgeting. The main purposes of a budget are to help you

- Live within your income.
- Spend your money wisely.
- Reach your financial goals.
- Prepare for financial emergencies.
- Develop wise financial management habits.

Budgeting may be viewed in four major phases as shown in Exhibit 3–5.

## Starting the Budgeting Process

The financial statements and documents discussed in the first sections of this chapter provide a starting point for your daily money management activities. A personal balance sheet is an effective scorecard for measuring financial progress. Increases in net

**EXHIBIT 3-5**   CREATING AND IMPLEMENTING A BUDGET

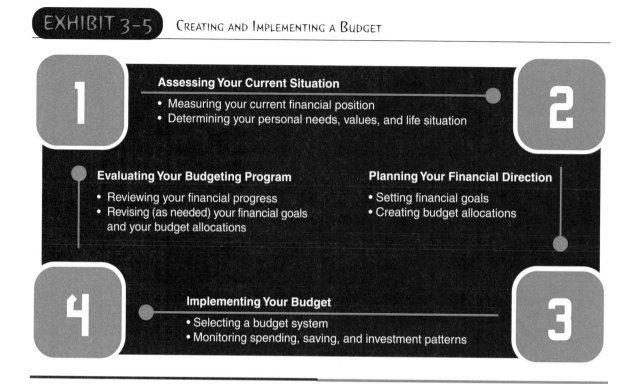

worth as a result of increased assets or decreased debt are evidence of an improved financial position. A regular assessment of your financial standing using a personal balance sheet can provide a point of reference for money management decisions.

Each day, you make many decisions that communicate your *lifestyle* by indicating how you spend your time and money. The clothes you wear, the food you eat, and the interests you pursue contribute to your lifestyle. Some people spend time and money on automobiles or stereo equipment; other people travel, plant gardens, or engage in church or community activities. These actions reflect a lifestyle influenced by three factors:

- *Career.* Your job situation will influence the amount of income, the way you spend your leisure time, and even the people with whom you associate.
- *Family.* The size of your household and the ages of its members will also affect your lifestyle. The spending priorities of a couple without children will differ from those of a couple with several youngsters.
- *Values.* Ideas and beliefs you regard as important will strongly influence your interests, activities, and purchasing habits.

These factors combine to create planned spending patterns that your financial goals reflect.

### Step 1: Setting Financial Goals
Future plans are an important dimension of your financial direction. Financial goals are plans for future activities that require you to plan your spending, saving, and investing. Exhibit 3–6 gives examples of common financial goals based on life situation and time.

## EXHIBIT 3-6   COMMON FINANCIAL GOALS

| Personal Situation | Short-Term Goals (less than 2 years) | Intermediate Goals (2–5 years) | Long-Term Goals (over 5 years) |
|---|---|---|---|
| Single person | • Complete college<br>• Pay off auto loan | • Take a vacation to Europe<br>• Pay off education loan<br>• Return to school for graduate degree | • Buy a vacation home in the mountains<br>• Provide for retirement income |
| Married couple (no children) | • Take an annual vacation<br>• Buy a new car | • Remodel home<br>• Build a stock portfolio | • Buy a retirement home<br>• Provide for retirement income |
| Parent (young children) | • Increase life insurance<br>• Increase savings | • Increase investments<br>• Buy a new car | • Accumulate a college fund for children<br>• Move to a larger home |

NOTE: As discussed in Chapter 1, your goals should be realistic, specific, and measurable for a definite time frame.

As discussed in Chapter 1, financial goals should be realistic; be stated in specific, measurable terms; have a definite time frame; and imply the type of action to be taken. Your personal financial statements and budgeting allow you to achieve your financial goals with

1. Your cash flow statement: telling you what you received and spent over the past month.
2. Your balance sheet: reporting your current financial position—where you are now.
3. Your budget: planning spending and saving to achieve financial goals.

### Step 2: Estimating Income

As Exhibit 3–7 shows, you should first estimate available money for a given time period. A common budgeting period is a month, since many payments, such as rent or mortgage, utilities, and credit cards, are due each month. In determining available income, include only money that you are sure you'll receive. Bonuses, gifts, or unexpected income should not be considered until the money is actually received.

If you get paid once a month, planning is easy since you will work with a single amount. But if you get paid weekly or twice a month, you will need to plan how much of each paycheck will go for various expenses. If you get paid every two weeks, plan your spending based on the two paychecks you will receive each month. Then, during the two months each year that have three paydays, you can put additional amounts into savings, pay off some debts, or make a special purchase.

Budgeting income may be difficult if your earnings vary by season or your income is irregular, as with sales commissions. In these situations, attempt to estimate your income based on the past year and on your expectations for the current year. Estimating your income on the low side will help you avoid overspending and other financial difficulties.

### Step 3: Budgeting Emergency Fund and Savings

To set aside money for unexpected expenses as well as future financial security, the Braziers (see Exhibit 3–7) have budgeted several amounts for savings and investments. Financial advisers suggest that an emergency fund representing three to six months of living expenses be established for use in periods of unexpected financial difficulty. This

EXHIBIT 3-7   THE FRAZIERS DEVELOP AND IMPLEMENT A MONTHLY BUDGET

**Step 1**
Set financial goals

**Step 2**
Estimate expected income from all sources; this amount is to be allocated among various outflow categories

**Step 3**
Budget amount for an emergency fund, periodic expenses, and financial goals

**Step 4**
Budget set amounts that you are obligated to pay

**Step 5**
Budget estimated amounts that are to be spent for various household and living expenses

**Step 6**
Record actual amounts for inflows and outflows. Compare actual amounts with budgeted amounts to determine variances

**Step 7**
Evaluate whether revisions are needed in your spending and savings plan

## Monthly Budget

| Financial goals | Budgeted Amounts (dollars) | (percent) | Actual Amounts | Variance |
|---|---|---|---|---|
| **Projected Inflows (income)** | | | | |
| Salary | 2874 | 100 | 2874 | — |
| **Projected Outflows (disbursements)** | | | | |
| **Emergency Fund and Savings:** | | | | |
| Emergency fund savings | 115 | 4 | 115 | — |
| Savings for auto insurance | 29 | 1 | 29 | — |
| Savings for vacation | 57 | 2 | 57 | — |
| Savings for investments | 57 | 2 | 57 | — |
| Total savings | 258 | 9 | 258 | — |
| **Fixed Expenses** | | | | |
| Mortgage payment | 518 | 18 | 518 | — |
| Property taxes | 115 | 4 | 115 | — |
| Auto loan payment | 144 | 5 | 144 | — |
| Life insurance | 29 | 1 | 29 | — |
| Total fixed expenses | 806 | 28 | 806 | — |
| **Variable expenses** | | | | |
| Food | 402 | 14 | 417 | −15 |
| Utilities (telephone, heat, electric, water) | 172 | 6 | 164 | +8 |
| Clothing | 116 | 4 | 93 | +23 |
| Transportation (automobile operation, repairs, public transportation) | 460 | 16 | 471 | −11 |
| Personal and health care | 172 | 6 | 163 | +9 |
| Entertainment | 172 | 6 | 201 | −29 |
| Reading, education | 86 | 3 | 78 | +8 |
| Gifts, donations | 144 | 5 | 150 | −6 |
| Personal allowances, miscellaneous expenses | 86 | 3 | 90 | −4 |
| Total variable expenses | 1810 | 63 | 1827 | −17 |
| Total outflow | 2874 | 100 | 2891 | −17 |

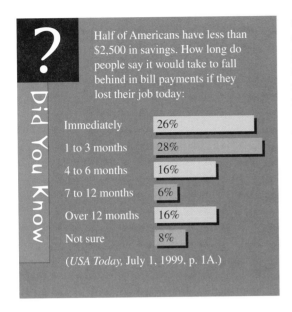

amount will vary based on a person's life situation and employment stability. A three-month emergency fund is probably adequate for a person with a stable income or secure employment, while a person with erratic or seasonal income may need to set aside an emergency fund sufficient for six months or more of living expenses.

The Fraziers also set aside an amount each month for their automobile insurance payment, which is due every six months. Both this amount and the emergency fund are put into a savings account that will earn interest. The *time value of money*, discussed in Chapter 1, refers to increases in an amount of money as a result of interest earned. Savings methods for achieving financial goals are discussed later in this chapter.

A very common budgeting mistake is to spend the amount you have left at the end of the month. When you do that, you often have *nothing* left for savings. Since savings are vital to long-term financial security, advisers suggest that an amount be budgeted as a fixed expense.

### Step 4: Budgeting Fixed Expenses

Definite obligations are the basis for this portion of a budget. As Exhibit 3–7 shows, the Fraziers have fixed expenses for housing, taxes, and loan payments. They make a monthly payment of $29 for life insurance. The budgeted total for the Fraziers' fixed expenses is $806, or 28 percent of estimated available income.

Assigning amounts to spending categories requires careful consideration. The amount you budget for various items will depend on your current needs and plans for the future. The following sources can help you plan your spending:

• Your cash flow statement.
• Consumer expenditure data for the Bureau of Labor Statistics (http://stats.bls.gov).
• Articles in magazines such as *Kiplinger's Personal Finance Magazine* and *Money*.
• Estimates of future income and expenses and anticipated changes in inflation rates.

Exhibit 3–8 provides suggested budget allocations for different life situations. Although this information can be of value when creating budget categories, maintaining a detailed record of your spending for several months is a better source for your personal situation. However, don't become discouraged. Use a simple system, such as a notebook or your checkbook. This "spending diary" will help you know where your money is going. Remember, a budget is an *estimate* for spending and saving intended to help you make better use of your money, not to reduce your enjoyment of life.

### Step 5: Budgeting Variable Expenses

Planning for variable expenses is not as easy as budgeting for savings or fixed expenses. Variable expenses will fluctuate by household situation, time of year, health, economic conditions, and a variety of other factors. A major portion of the Fraziers' planned spending—over 60 percent of their budgeted income—is for variable living costs.

The Fraziers base their estimates on their needs and desires for the items listed and on expected changes in the cost of living. The *consumer price index (CPI)* is a measure of the general price level of consumer goods and services in the United States. This

| EXHIBIT 3-8 | TYPICAL AFTER-TAX BUDGET ALLOCATIONS FOR DIFFERENT LIFE SITUATIONS |

| Budget Category | Student | Working Single (no dependents) | Couple (children under 18) | Single Parent (young children) | Parents (children over 18 in college) | Couple (over 55, no dependent children) |
|---|---|---|---|---|---|---|
| Housing (rent or mortgage payment; utilities; furnishings and appliances) | 0–25% | 30–35% | 25–35% | 20–30% | 25–30% | 25–35% |
| Transportation | 5–10 | 15–20 | 15–20 | 10–18 | 12–18 | 10–18 |
| Food (at home and away from home) | 15–20 | 15–25 | 15–25 | 13–20 | 15–20 | 18–25 |
| Clothing | 5–12 | 5–15 | 5–10 | 5–10 | 4–8 | 4–8 |
| Personal and health care (including child care) | 3–5 | 3–5 | 4–10 | 8–12 | 4–6 | 6–12 |
| Entertainment and recreation | 5–10 | 5–10 | 4–8 | 4–8 | 6–10 | 5–8 |
| Reading and education | 10–30 | 2–4 | 3–5 | 3–5 | 6–12 | 2–4 |
| Personal insurance and pension payments | 0–5 | 4–8 | 5–9 | 5–9 | 4–7 | 6–8 |
| Gifts, donations, and contributions | 4–6 | 5–8 | 3–5 | 3–5 | 4–8 | 3–5 |
| Savings | 0–10 | 4–15 | 5–10 | 5–8 | 2–4 | 3–5 |

SOURCES: Bureau of Labor Statistics (http://stats.bls.gov); *American Demographics; Money; The Wall Street Journal.*

government statistic indicates changes in the buying power of a dollar. As consumer prices increase due to inflation, people must spend more to buy the same amount. Changes in the cost of living will vary depending on where you live and what you buy.

As mentioned in Chapter 1, the *rule of 72* can help you budget for price rises. At a 6 percent inflation rate, prices will double in 12 years (72/6); at an 8 percent inflation rate, prices will double in only 9 years (72/8).

### Step 6: Recording Spending Amounts
After you have established your spending plan, you will need to keep records of your actual income and expenses similar to those you keep in preparing an income statement. In Exhibit 3–7, notice that the Fraziers estimated specific amounts for income and expenses. These are presented under "Budgeted Amounts." The family's actual spending was not always the same as planned. A **budget variance** is the difference between the amount budgeted and the actual amount received or spent. The total variance for the Fraziers was a $17 **deficit,** since their actual spending exceeded their planned spending by this amount. The Fraziers would have had a **surplus** if their actual spending had been less than they had planned.

Variances for income should be viewed as the opposite of variances for expenses. Less income than expected would be a deficit, while more income than expected would be a surplus.

*budget variance* The difference between the amount budgeted and the actual amount received or spent.

*deficit* The amount by which actual spending exceeds planned spending.

*surplus* The amount by which actual spending is less than planned spending.

**Sheet 17**

Spending more than planned for an item may be justified by reducing spending for another item or putting less into savings. However, it may be necessary to revise your budget and financial goals.

## Step 7: Reviewing Spending and Saving Patterns   Like most decision-making activities, budgeting is a circular, ongoing process. You will need to review and perhaps revise your spending plan on a regular basis.

### Reviewing Your Financial Progress   The results of your budget may be obvious: having extra cash in checking, falling behind in your bill payments, and so on. However, such obvious results may not always be present. Occasionally, you will have to sit down (with other household members, if appropriate) and review areas where spending has been more or less than expected.

**Sheet 18**

As Exhibit 3–9 shows, you can prepare an annual summary to compare actual spending with budgeted amounts. This type of summary may also be prepared every three or six months. A spreadsheet computer program can be useful for this purpose. The summary will help you see areas where changes in your budget may be necessary. This review process is vital to both successful short-term money management and long-term financial security.

### Revising Your Goals and Budget Allocations   What should you cut first when a budget shortage occurs? This question doesn't have easy answers, and the answers will vary for different household situations. The most common overspending areas are entertainment and food, especially away-from-home meals. Purchasing less expensive brand items, buying quality used products, avoiding credit card purchases, and renting rather than buying are common budget adjustment techniques.

At this point in the budgeting process, you may also revise your financial goals. Are you making progress toward achieving your objectives? Have changes in personal or economic conditions affected the desirability of certain goals? Have new goals surfaced that should be given a higher priority than those that have been your major concern? Addressing these issues while creating an effective saving method will help ensure accomplishment of your financial goals.

## Characteristics of Successful Budgeting

Having a spending plan will not eliminate financial worries. A budget will work only if you follow it. Changes in income, expenses, and goals will require changes in your spending plan. Money management experts advise that a successful budget should be

- *Well planned.* A good budget takes time and effort to prepare. Planning a budget should involve everyone affected by it. Children can learn important money management lessons by helping to develop and use the family budget.
- *Realistic.* If you have a moderate income, don't immediately expect to save enough money for an expensive car or a lavish vacation. A budget is designed not to prevent you from enjoying life but to help you achieve what you want most.
- *Flexible.* Unexpected expenses and changes in your cost of living will require a budget that you can easily revise. Also, special situations, such as two-income families or the arrival of a baby, may require an increase in certain types of expenses.
- *Clearly communicated.* Unless you and others involved are aware of the spending plan, it will not work. The budget should be written and available to all household

## EXHIBIT 3-9  An Annual Budget Summary

| Item | Monthly Budget | Jan. | Feb. | Mar. | Apr. | May | June | July | Aug. | Sept. | Oct. | Nov. | Dec. | Annual Totals Actual | Annual Totals Budgeted* |
|---|---|---|---|---|---|---|---|---|---|---|---|---|---|---|---|
| | | | | | | Actual Spending (cash outflows) | | | | | | | | | |
| Income | 2,730 | 2,730 | 2,730 | 2,730 | 2,940 | 2,730 | 2,730 | 2,730 | 2,730 | 2,850 | 2,850 | 2,850 | 2,850 | 33,450 | 32,760 |
| Savings | 150 | 150 | 150 | 200 | 150 | 90 | 50 | 30 | 100 | 250 | 250 | 150 | 40 | 1,610 | 1,800 |
| Mortgage/rent | 826 | 826 | 826 | 826 | 826 | 826 | 826 | 826 | 826 | 826 | 826 | 826 | 826 | 9,912 | 9,912 |
| Housing costs (insurance, utilities) | 190 | 244 | 238 | 187 | 176 | 185 | 188 | 146 | 178 | 198 | 199 | 201 | 195 | 2,283 | 2,280 |
| Telephone | 50 | 43 | 45 | 67 | 56 | 54 | 52 | 65 | 45 | 43 | 52 | 49 | 41 | 618 | 600 |
| Food (at home) | 280 | 281 | 291 | 245 | 234 | 298 | 261 | 298 | 320 | 301 | 298 | 298 | 324 | 3,409 | 3,360 |
| Food (away from home) | 80 | 67 | 98 | 84 | 89 | 123 | 109 | 89 | 83 | 67 | 76 | 83 | 143 | 1,089 | 960 |
| Clothing | 100 | 98 | 98 | 123 | 156 | 86 | 76 | 111 | 124 | 89 | 95 | 123 | 111 | 1,268 | 1,200 |
| Transportation (auto operation, public transportation) | 340 | 302 | 312 | 333 | 345 | 291 | 281 | 390 | 313 | 299 | 301 | 261 | 301 | 3,809 | 4,080 |
| Credit payments | 249 | 249 | 249 | 249 | 249 | 249 | 249 | 249 | 249 | 249 | 249 | 249 | 249 | 2,988 | 2,988 |
| Insurance (life, health, other) | 45 | — | — | 135 | — | — | 135 | — | — | 135 | — | — | 135 | 540 | 540 |
| Health care | 140 | 176 | 145 | 187 | 122 | 111 | 156 | 186 | 166 | 134 | 189 | 193 | 147 | 1,912 | 1,680 |
| Recreation | 80 | 67 | 98 | 123 | 98 | 67 | 45 | 89 | 98 | 65 | 89 | 89 | 111 | 1,033 | 960 |
| Reading, education | 40 | 32 | 54 | 44 | 34 | 39 | 54 | 12 | 38 | 54 | 34 | 76 | 45 | 516 | 480 |
| Gifts, donations | 100 | 102 | 110 | 94 | 89 | 123 | 89 | 95 | 94 | 113 | 89 | 99 | 134 | 1,229 | 1,200 |
| Personal miscellaneous expense | 60 | 89 | 45 | 61 | 54 | 98 | 59 | 54 | 49 | 71 | 65 | 90 | 56 | 799 | 720 |
| Total | 2,730 | 2,702 | 2,705 | 2,964 | 2,614 | 2,626 | 2,642 | 2,638 | 2,743 | 2,892 | 2,786 | 2,771 | 2,864 | 33,009 | 32,760 |
| Surplus (deficit) | | 28 | 25 | (234) | 266 | 104 | 88 | 92 | (13) | (42) | 64 | 79 | (14) | 443 | — |

*Monthly amount times 12.

## Financial Planning for Life's Situations

### SELECTING A BUDGETING SYSTEM

Although your checkbook will give you a fairly complete record of your expenses, it does not serve the purpose of planning for spending. A budget requires that you outline how you will spend available income. Various types of budgeting systems exist, from informal procedures to computerized spending plans.

A *mental budget* exists only in a person's mind. This simple system may be appropriate if you have limited resources and minimal financial responsibilities. The major drawback of a mental budget is the danger of forgetting what amounts you plan to spend on various items.

A *physical budget* involves the use of envelopes, folders, or containers to hold the money or slips of paper that represent amounts allocated for spending categories. This system allows you to actually see where your money goes. Envelopes would contain the amount of cash or a note listing the amount to be used for "Food," "Rent," "Clothing," "Auto Payment," "Entertainment," and other expenses.

Experienced financial advisers recommend a *written budget*. The exact system and the amount of detail will depend on the time, effort, and information that you put into the budgeting process. A written budget can be kept on notebook paper or in a specialized budgeting book available in office supply stores. A common budget format is a spreadsheet that has several monthly columns for comparing budgeted and actual amounts for various expense items.

The use of *computerized budgeting systems* is increasing. In addition to creating a spreadsheet budget, a home computer is capable of doing other financial recordkeeping tasks such as writing checks and projecting the future value of savings accounts. Software packages such as Microsoft Money (www.msn.com/money) and Quicken (www.quicken.com) can assist you. While it takes time and effort to learn the software and enter data, a computerized budgeting and recordkeeping procedure can yield fast and accurate financial planning data.

members. Many variations of written budgets are possible, including a notebook or a computerized system (see the accompanying Financial Planning for Life's Situations box).

### Concept Check 3-4

1. What are the main purposes of a budget?
2. How does a person's life situation affect goal setting and amounts allocated for various budget categories?
3. What are the main steps in creating a budget?
4. What are commonly recommended qualities of a successful budget?
5. What actions might you take when evaluating your budgeting program?

## SAVING TO ACHIEVE FINANCIAL GOALS

**Obj. 5**
Calculate savings needed for achieving financial goals.

Saving of current income (as well as investing, which is discussed in Part 5) is the basis for an improved financial position and long-term financial security. Common reasons for saving include the following:

- To set aside money for irregular and unexpected expenses.
- To pay for the replacement of expensive items, such as appliances or an automobile, or to have money for a down payment on a house.
- To buy special items such as home video or recreational equipment or to pay for a vacation.

- To provide for long-term expenses such as the education of children or retirement.
- To earn income from the interest on savings for use in paying living expenses.

## Selecting a Saving Technique

Traditionally, the United States ranks fairly low among industrial nations in savings rate. A low savings rate tends to slow economic growth with fewer funds available for business borrowing and for creation of new jobs. Low savings also affect the personal financial situations of people. Studies reveal that the majority of Americans do not have an adequate amount set aside for emergencies.

Since most people find saving difficult, financial advisers suggest several methods to make it easier. One method is to write a check each payday and deposit it in a special savings account at a distant financial institution. This savings deposit can be a percentage of income, such as 5 or 10 percent, or a specific dollar amount. Always "pay yourself first." To guarantee setting something aside for savings, view savings as a fixed expense in your spending plan.

Another method is *payroll deduction,* which is available at many places of employment. Under a *direct deposit* system, an amount is automatically deducted from your salary and deposited in a savings or investment account.

Finally, saving coins or spending less on certain items can help you save. Each day, put your change in a container. In a short time, you will have enough money to make a substantial deposit in a savings account. You can also increase your savings by taking a sandwich to work instead of buying lunch or refraining from buying snacks or magazines.

How you save, however, is less important than making regular periodic savings deposits that will help you achieve financial goals. Small amounts of savings can grow faster than most people realize. For example, at 5 percent interest, compounded daily, just $1 a day for 10 years will give you $4,700.

## Calculating Savings Amounts

**Sheet 19**

To achieve your financial objectives, you should convert your savings goals into specific amounts. While certain saving methods involve keeping money at home, those funds should be deposited in an interest-earning savings plan on a regular basis. To earn interest, you must learn to "hide" money, not in your home but in an account at a financial institution or with an investment company.

Your use of a savings or investment plan is vital to the growth of your money. As Exhibit 3–10 shows, using the time value of money calculations, introduced in Chapter 1, can help you achieve your financial goals.

## Concept Check 3-5

1. What are some suggested methods to make saving easy?
2. What methods are available to calculate amounts needed to reach savings goals?

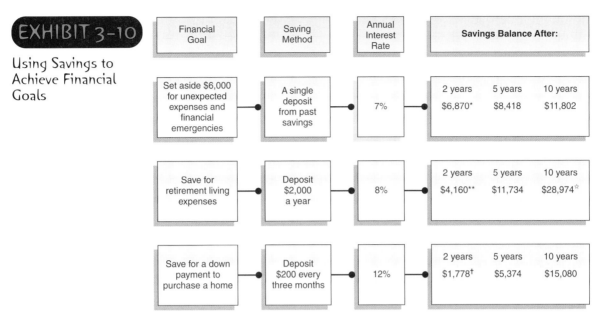

**EXHIBIT 3-10**

Using Savings to Achieve Financial Goals

* Based on the future value of $1 tables in Chapter 1 and Appendix A.
** Based on the future value of a series of deposits tables in Chapter 1 and Appendix A.
☆ With annual $2,000 deposits, this same retirement account would grow to over $500,000 in 40 years.
† Based on quarterly compounding, explained in Chapter 5.

## KEY FORMULAS

| Page | Topic | Formula |
|------|-------|---------|
| 77 | Net Worth | Net worth = Total assets − Total liabilities<br>*Example:* = $125,000 − $53,000<br>= $72,000 |
| 78 | Debt ratio | Debt ratio = Liabilities/Net worth<br>*Example:* = $7,000/$21,000<br>= 0.33 |
| 78 | Current ratio | Current ratio = Liquid assets/Current liabilities<br>*Example:* = $8,500/$4,500<br>= 1.88 |
| 78 | Liquidity ratio | Liquidity ratio = Liquid assets/Monthly expenses<br>*Example:* = $8,500/$3,500<br>= 2.4 |
| 78 | Debt-payments ratio | Debt-payments ratio = Monthly credit payments/Take-home pay<br>*Example:* = $760/$3,800<br>= 0.20 |

| 78 | Savings ratio | Savings ratio = Amount saved per month/Gross monthly income |
| | | *Example:*    = $460/$3,800 |
| | | = 0.12 |
| 78 | Cash surplus (or deficit) | Cash surplus (or deficit) = Total inflows − Total outflows |
| | | *Example:*        = $5,600 − $4,970 |
| | | = $630 (surplus) |

## Summary of Objectives

**Obj. 1**   **Recognize relationships among financial documents and money management activities.**

Successful money management requires effective coordination of personal financial records, personal financial statements, and budgeting activities.

**Obj. 2**   **Create a system for maintaining personal financial records.**

An organized system of financial records and documents is the foundation of effective money management. This system should provide ease of access as well as security for financial documents that may be impossible to replace.

**Obj. 3**   **Develop a personal balance sheet and cash flow statement.**

A personal balance sheet, also known as a *net worth statement,* is prepared by listing all items of value (assets) and all amounts owed to others (liabilities). The difference between your total assets and your total liabilities is your net worth. A cash flow statement, also called a *personal income and expenditure statement,* is a summary of cash receipts and payments for a given period, such as a month or a year. This report provides data on your income and spending patterns.

**Obj. 4**   **Create and implement a budget.**

The budgeting process involves four phases: (1) assessing your current personal and financial situation, (2) planning your financial direction by setting financial goals and creating budget allowances, (3) implementing your budget, and (4) evaluating your budgeting program.

**Obj. 5**   **Calculate savings needed for achieving financial goals.**

Future value and present value calculations may be used to compute the increased value of savings for achieving financial goals.

## Financial Planning Problems

1. *Creating Personal Financial Statements.* Based on the procedures presented in the chapter, prepare your current personal balance sheet and a cash flow statement for the next month.   (Obj. 3)

2. *Calculating Balance Sheet Amounts.* Based on the following data, compute the total assets, total liabilities, and net worth.   (Obj. 3)

   Liquid assets, $3,670
   Investment assets, $8,340
   Current liabilities, $2,670
   Household assets, $89,890
   Long-term liabilities, $76,230

3. *Preparing a Personal Balance Sheet.* Use the following items to prepare a balance sheet and a cash flow statement.

   Determine the total assets, total liabilities, net worth, total cash inflows, and total cash outflows.   (Obj. 3)

   Rent for the month, $650
   Monthly take-home salary, $1,950
   Cash in checking account, $450
   Savings account balance, $1,890
   Spending for food, $345
   Balance of educational loan, $2,160
   Current value of automobile, $7,800
   Telephone bill paid for month, $65
   Credit card balance, $235
   Loan payment, $80
   Auto insurance, $230
   Household possessions, $3,400
   Stereo equipment, $2,350

Payment for electricity, $90
Lunches/parking at work, $180
Donations, $70
Home computer, $1,500
Value of stock investment, $860
Clothing purchase, $110
Restaurant spending, $130

4. *Computing Balance Sheet Amounts.* For each of the following situations, compute the missing amount.   (Obj. 3)
   a.  Assets $45,000; liabilities $16,000; net worth $_____
   b.  Assets $76,500; liabilities $_____; net worth $18,700.
   c.  Assets $34,280; liabilities $12,965; net worth $_____
   d.  Assets $_____; liabilities $38,345; net worth $52,654

5. *Determining Budget Variances.* Fran Bowen created the
following budget:
Food, $350
Transportation, $320
Housing, $950
Clothing, $100
Personal expenses and recreation, $275
She actually spent $298 for food, $337 for transportation,
$982 for housing, $134 for clothing, and $231 for personal

expenses and recreation. Calculate the variance for each
of these categories, and indicate whether it was a *deficit*
or a *surplus.*   (Obj. 4)

6. *Calculating the Effect of Inflation.* Bill and Sally Kaplan
have an annual spending plan that amounts to $36,000. If
inflation is 5 percent a year for the next three years, what
amount will the Kaplans need for their living expenses
three years from now?   (Obj. 4)

7. *Computing Time Value of Money for Savings.* Use future
value and present value calculations (see tables in Appendix A) to determine the following.   (Obj. 5)
   a.  The future value of a $500 savings deposit after eight
       years at an annual interest rate of 7 percent.
   b.  The future value of saving $1,500 a year for five years
       at an annual interest rate of 8 percent.
   c.  The present value of a $2,000 savings account that will
       earn 6 percent interest for four years.

8. *Calculating Present Value of a Savings Fund.* Hal
Thomas wants to establish a savings fund from which a
community organization could draw $800 a year for 20
years. If the account earns 6 percent, what amount would
he have to deposit now to achieve this goal?   (Obj. 5)

## Financial Planning Activities

1. *Researching Money Management Information.* Using the
   "Basics" section of www.personalwealth.com, other websites, library sources, friends, relatives, and others,
   obtain information on common suggestions for successful money management.   (Obj. 1)
2. *Developing a Financial Document System.* Working with
   two or three others in your class, use Sheet 14 in the *Personal Financial Planner* to develop a system for filing
   and maintaining personal financial records.   (Obj. 2)
3. *Comparing Financial Record Systems.* Conduct a survey
   of people of various ages to determine the system they
   use to keep track of various financial documents and
   records.   (Obj. 2)
4. *Creating Personal Financial Statements.* Using Sheets 15
   and 16 in the *Personal Financial Planner,* or some other
   format, prepare a personal balance sheet and cash flow
   statement.   (Obj. 3)
5. *Researching Household Asset Information on the Internet.* Using the World Wide Web or library research, find
   information about the assets commonly held by households in the United States. How have the values of assets,
   liabilities, and net worth of U.S. consumers changed in
   recent years?   (Obj. 3)

6. *Researching Money Management Software.* Use the
   World Wide Web, store visits, or advertisements to determine the software a person might use to prepare personal
   financial statements, create a budget, and monitor spending, saving, and investing.   (Obj. 3, 4)
7. *Analyzing Budgeting Situations.* Discuss with several
   people how the budget in Exhibit 3–7 (p. 84) might be
   changed based on various budget variances. If the household faced a decline in income, what spending areas
   might be reduced first?   (Obj. 4)
8. *Comparing Budgeting Systems.* Ask two or three friends
   or relatives about their budgeting systems. Obtain information on how they maintain their spending records. Create a visual presentation (video or slide presentation) that
   communicates wise budgeting techniques.   (Obj. 4)
9. *Analyzing Saving Habits.* Interview a young single person, a young couple, and a middle-aged person about
   their financial goals and savings habits. What actions do
   they take to determine and achieve various financial
   goals?   (Obj. 5)

## LIFE SITUATION CASE

### OUT OF WORK BUT NOT OUT OF BILLS

Due to lower sales, the company for which Ed Weston works was cutting back on its work force. Even though Ed had been with the company for seven years, most of his duties were being performed by new, automated equipment.

After getting the word about losing his job, Ed talked with his wife, Alice, and their two children (ages 12 and 9) about ways they could reduce spending. The Westons started by making up a list of three things: (1) bills they had to pay each month, (2) areas where they could reduce spending, and (3) sources of funds to help them pay current expenses. Each family member had several ideas to help them cope with the difficult financial burden that was likely to occur over the next few weeks and months.

Before Ed was unemployed, the Westons had a monthly take-home income of $3,165. Each month, the money went for the following items: $880 for rent, $180 for utilities, $560 for food, $480 for automobile expenses, $300 for clothing, $280 for insurance, $250 for savings, and $235 for personal and other items. After the loss of Ed's job, the household's monthly income is $1,550, from his wife's wages and his unemployment benefits. The Westons also have savings accounts, investments, and retirement funds of $28,000.

### Questions

1. What budget items might the Westons consider reducing to cope with their financial difficulties?
2. How should the Westons use their savings and retirement funds during this financial crisis? What additional sources of funds might be available to them during this period of unemployment?
3. What other current and future financial actions would you recommend to the Westons?

## VIDEO CASE   The Road to There

Harry and Michelle are concerned that they have not started saving for their daughter's college education. Although Melissa is only five years old, putting away money for this goal should start as soon as possible. Building a college savings fund has become a major priority for Harry and Michelle.

In the process of getting their finances organized, Harry and Michelle discover a need to create a system for various documents and records. They also realize the value of a balance sheet and cash flow statement when planning and implementing personal financial decisions. While the budgeting process seems easy at first, Harry and Michelle soon learn that they are unable to account for several hundred dollars each month.

### Questions

1. In addition to saving for their daughter's education, what other short-term and long-term financial goals might be appropriate for Harry and Michelle? What savings methods and other financial activities could help them achieve these goals?
2. What guidelines would you recommend for Harry and Michelle for organizing their financial documents and records?
3. According to the video, Harry and Michelle have a balance sheet appropriate for people in their 20s. What actions should they take to maintain and improve their financial position as they get older?
4. What would you suggest for Harry and Michelle to create and implement an effective budget?

## Creating an E-Plan: Financial Decisions Using the Web

### DEVELOPING PERSONAL FINANCIAL STATEMENTS AND A SPENDING PLAN

Money management activities are the basis for most financial planning activities. Creation of a financial document filing system, a personal balance sheet, a cash flow statement, and a budget provide you with tools for setting, implementing, and achieving financial goals.

Websites for Money Management

- Goal-setting and money management information at **www.personalwealth.com** and **www.quicken.com.**
- The FinanCenter and Money Central provide answers to questions and calculations related to budgeting, automobiles, savings, investments, credit, and housing at **www.financenter. com/** and **www.moneycentral.msn.com.**
- Current data from the Consumer Expenditure Survey of the Bureau of Labor Statistics, U.S. Dept. of Labor, available at **www.stats.bls.gov.**
- Budgeting information at **www.lifeadvice.com** and **www.americanexpress.com/student.**
- Money management information from the National Center for Financial Education at **www.ncfe.org.**
- Savings information at **www.savingsnet.com.**

(Note: Addresses and content of websites change, and new sites are created daily. Use search engines to update and locate websites for your current financial planning needs.)

*PFP sheets: 14–19*

Short-Term Financial Planning Activities

1. Develop a filing system to organize your financial records and documents. (see PFP Sheet 14).
2. Create a personal balance sheet (see PFP Sheet 15) and a personal cash flow statement (see PFP Sheet 16).
3. Based on your current financial situation, set short-term financial goals and develop a budget (see PFP Sheet 17). Monitor your spending for various categories (see PFP Sheet 18).
4. Accumulate an appropriate amount for an emergency fund.

Long-Term Financial Planning Activities

1. Set long-term financial goals related to education, housing, or retirement (see PFP Sheet 3).
2. Develop a savings plan, such as automatic withdrawals, to achieve long-term financial goals.

# 4

# Planning Your Tax Strategy

## We Owe How Much in Taxes?

Now that his daughter, Mandy, is 2, Melvin Eckert has decided to restart his full-time business. Since Mandy's birth, Melvin has stayed home to care for her while his wife, Nina, continued her career as a human resources supervisor for a health care products company. Her salary and employee benefits provide the family with adequate financial resources. However, Melvin misses his career activities.

Before Mandy's birth, Melvin worked as an independent distributor and technical consultant for companies that made computer software used by small businesses. He represented several software companies and earned a commission based on sales. He also earned fees for helping companies set up computer networks.

When Melvin resumes his full-time career activities, he will need a car, business clothes, equipment, and supplies. The family will have child care expenses for Mandy. In addition, with two working parents, the Eckerts will likely eat meals away from home more often.

While certain business-related expenses are deductible from Melvin's income, the net earnings from his business will be subject to two types of federal taxes. First, the profit will be added to the family's tax return as ordinary income at a tax rate of 28 percent. Second, Melvin will have to pay a self-employment tax on his net earnings of about 15 percent as contributions for future Social Security benefits. In all, after deducting his business expenses, Melvin will pay about 43 cents of federal income tax for every dollar earned. And he still has to pay the state income tax.

"By the time we pay our extra household expenses, business expenses, and taxes, we'll have less than 20 cents per dollar I earn," Melvin commented to Nina. "Is it worth it?"

"That depends," replied Nina. "If you enjoy your work, that has to count for something."

"Well," responded Melvin, "I'm sure the government will enjoy my work, since they'll get a big chunk of the money."

## Questions

1. What financial and personal factors can affect a person's decision to work?
2. What are the tax benefits and drawbacks associated with owning your own business?
3. How might the Eckerts evaluate the financial and personal benefits of Melvin's working?

## Learning Objectives

**Obj. 1**   Describe the importance of taxes for personal financial planning.

**Obj. 2**   Calculate taxable income and the amount owed for federal income tax.

**Obj. 3**   Prepare a federal income tax return.

**Obj. 4**   Identify tax assistance sources.

**Obj. 5**   Select appropriate tax strategies for different financial and personal situations.

## TAXES AND FINANCIAL PLANNING

**Obj. 1**
Describe the importance of taxes for personal financial planning.

Taxes are an everyday financial fact of life. You pay some taxes every time you get a paycheck or make a purchase. However, most people concern themselves with taxes only in April. With about one-third of each dollar you earn going for taxes, an effective tax strategy is vital for successful financial planning. Understanding tax rules and regulations can help you reduce your tax liability.

The U.S. Bureau of the Census reports that about two out of three American households have no money left after paying for taxes and normal living expenses. For most of us, taxes are a significant factor in financial planning. Each year, the Tax Foundation determines how long the average person works to pay taxes. In recent years, "Tax Freedom Day" came in early May. This means that the time people worked from January 1 until early May represents the portion of the year worked to pay their taxes.

This financial obligation includes the many types of taxes discussed later in this section. To help you cope with these taxes, common goals related to tax planning include

- Knowing the current tax laws and regulations that affect you.
- Maintaining complete and appropriate tax records.
- Making purchase and investment decisions that can reduce your tax liability.

You should gear tax planning efforts toward paying your fair share of taxes while taking advantage of tax benefits appropriate to your personal and financial situation.

The principal purpose of taxes is to finance government activities. As citizens, we expect government to provide services such as police and fire protection, schools, road maintenance, parks and libraries, and safety inspection of food, drugs, and other products. Most people pay taxes in four major categories: taxes on purchases, taxes on property, taxes on wealth, and taxes on earnings.

**? Did You Know**

A recent survey reveals significant differences among state and local tax bills around the country. In Wyoming, the average annual income, property, and sales tax bill is $2,748. In contrast, in Buffalo, New York, a household with a comparable income, home value, and spending habits pays $12,664 in taxes. Other states with the lowest average tax bills are Nevada, Tennessee, Louisiana, and South Dakota. (Marc L. Schulhof, "Taxing Geography," *Kiplinger's Personal Finance Magazine*, October 1998, pp. 99–102.)

## Taxes on Purchases

You probably pay sales tax on many of your purchases. This state and local tax is added to the purchase prices of products. Many states exempt food and drugs from sales tax to reduce the economic burden of this tax on the poor. In recent years, all but five states (Alaska, Delaware, Montana, New Hampshire, and Oregon) have had a general sales tax. An **excise tax** is imposed by the federal and state governments on specific goods and services, such as gasoline, cigarettes, alcoholic beverages, tires, air travel, and telephone service.

*excise tax*   A tax imposed on specific goods and services, such as gasoline, cigarettes, alcoholic beverages, tires, and air travel.

## Taxes on Property

Real estate property tax is a major source of revenue for local governments. This tax is based on the value of land and buildings. The increasing amount of real estate property taxes is a major concern of homeowners. Retired people with limited pension incomes may encounter financial difficulties if local property taxes increase rapidly.

Some areas also impose personal property taxes. State and local governments may assess taxes on the value of automobiles, boats, furniture, and farm equipment.

## Taxes on Wealth

*estate tax*   A tax imposed on the value of a person's property at the time of his or her death.

An **estate tax** is imposed on the value of a person's property at the time of his or her death. This federal tax is based on the fair market value of the deceased individual's investments, property, and bank accounts less allowable deductions and other taxes. Estate taxes are discussed in greater detail in Chapter 19.

*inheritance tax*   A tax levied on the value of property bequeathed by a deceased person.

Money and property passed on to heirs may also be subject to a state tax. An **inheritance tax** is levied on the value of property bequeathed by a deceased person. This tax is paid for the right to acquire the inherited property.

Individuals are allowed to give money or items valued at $10,000 or less in a year to a person without being subject to taxes. Gift amounts greater than $10,000 are subject to federal tax. Amounts given for the payment of tuition or medical expenses are not subject to federal gift taxes. Some states impose a gift tax on amounts that a person, before his or her death, transfers to another person since the action may have been intended to avoid estate and inheritance taxes.

In the late 1990s, total taxes as a percentage of income for a two-earner family were estimated at over 38 percent. For a single-earner family, total taxes as a percentage of income were estimated at over 36 percent.

## Taxes on Earnings

The two main taxes on wages and salaries are Social Security and income taxes. Social Security taxes are used to finance the retirement, disability, and life insurance benefits of the federal government's Social Security program. Chapters 11 and 18 discuss various aspects of Social Security. Income tax is a major financial planning factor for most people. Some workers are subject to federal, state, and local income taxes. Currently only seven states do not have a state income tax.

Throughout the year, your employer will withhold income tax payments from your paycheck, or you may be required to make estimated tax payments if you own your own business. Both types of payments are only estimates of your income taxes. You may need to pay an additional amount, or you may get a tax refund. The following sections will assist you in preparing your federal income tax return and planning your future tax strategies.

## Concept Check 4-1

1. How should you consider taxes in your financial planning?
2. What types of taxes do people frequently overlook when making financial decisions?

## INCOME TAX FUNDAMENTALS

### Obj. 2

Calculate taxable income and the amount owed for federal income tax.

*taxable income*   The net amount of income, after allowable deductions, on which income tax is computed.

*earned income*   Money received for personal effort, such as wages, salary, commission, fees, tips, or bonuses.

*investment income*   Money received in the form of dividends, interest, or rent from investments. Also called *portfolio income.*

*passive income*   Income resulting from business activities in which you do not actively participate.

*exclusion*   An amount not included in gross income.

*tax-exempt income*   Income that is not subject to tax.

*tax-deferred income*   Income that will be taxed at a later date.

*adjusted gross income (AGI)*   Gross income reduced by certain adjustments, such as contributions to an individual retirement account (IRA) and alimony payments.

Each year, millions of Americans are required to pay their share of income taxes to the federal government. The process involves computing taxable income, determining the amount of income tax owed, and comparing this amount with the income tax payments withheld or made during the year.

### Step 1: Determining Adjusted Gross Income

**Taxable income** is the net amount of income, after allowable deductions, on which income tax is computed. Exhibit 4–1 presents the components of taxable income and the process used to compute it.

Types of Income   Most, but not all, income is subject to taxation. Your gross, or total, income can consist of three main components:

1. **Earned income** is money received for personal effort. Earned income is usually in the form of wages, salary, commission, fees, tips, or bonuses.
2. **Investment income** (sometimes referred to as *portfolio income*) is money received in the form of dividends, interest, or rent from investments.
3. **Passive income** results from business activities in which you do not actively participate, such as a limited partnership.

Other types of income subject to federal income tax include alimony, awards, lottery winnings, and prizes. Cameron Clark won $30,533 in prizes on the television game show "Wheel of Fortune." In addition to paying California sales tax of $1,154, Cameron had to sell the car stereo, ping-pong table, camping gear, water ski equipment, bass guitar, and art drawing table and chair he won to pay the federal income tax. He did get to keep the Toyota Tercel, Honda Scooter, Gucci watches, and Australian vacation.

Total income is also affected by exclusions. An **exclusion** is an amount not included in gross income. For example, the foreign income exclusion allows U.S. citizens working and living in another country to exclude a certain portion ($74,000) of their incomes from federal income taxes.

Exclusions are also referred to as **tax-exempt income,** or income that is not subject to tax. For example, interest earned on most state and city bonds is exempt from federal income tax. **Tax-deferred income** is income that will be taxed at a later date. The earnings on an individual retirement account (IRA) are an example of tax-deferred income. While these earnings are credited to the account now, you do not pay taxes on them until you withdraw them from the account.

Adjustments to Income   **Adjusted gross income (AGI)** is gross income after certain reductions have been made. These reductions, called *adjustments to income,* include contributions to an individual retirement account (IRA) or a Keogh retirement plan, penalties for early withdrawal of savings, and alimony payments. Adjusted gross income is used as the basis for computing various income tax deductions, such as medical expenses.

**EXHIBIT 4-1**    Computing Taxable Income and Your Tax Liability

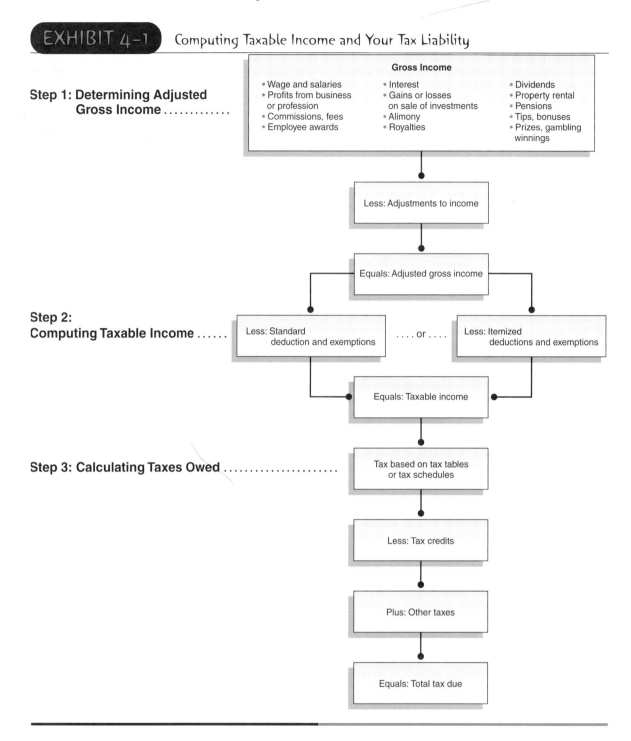

**Step 1: Determining Adjusted Gross Income** . . . . . . . . . . . . .

**Gross Income**
- Wage and salaries
- Profits from business or profession
- Commissions, fees
- Employee awards
- Interest
- Gains or losses on sale of investments
- Alimony
- Royalties
- Dividends
- Property rental
- Pensions
- Tips, bonuses
- Prizes, gambling winnings

Less: Adjustments to income

Equals: Adjusted gross income

**Step 2: Computing Taxable Income** . . . . . .

Less: Standard deduction and exemptions    . . . . or . . . .    Less: Itemized deductions and exemptions

Equals: Taxable income

**Step 3: Calculating Taxes Owed** . . . . . . . . . . . . . . . . . . . . . .

Tax based on tax tables or tax schedules

Less: Tax credits

Plus: Other taxes

Equals: Total tax due

*tax shelter* An investment that provides immediate tax benefits and a reasonable expectation of a future financial return.

Certain adjustments to income, such as tax-deferred retirement plans, are a type of tax shelter. **Tax shelters** are investments that provide immediate tax benefits and a reasonable expectation of a future financial return. In recent years, tax court rulings and changes in the tax code have disallowed various types of tax shelters that were considered excessive.

## Step 2: Computing Taxable Income

**Deductions**   A **tax deduction** is an amount subtracted from adjusted gross income to arrive at taxable income. Every taxpayer receives at least the **standard deduction,** a set amount on which no taxes are paid. As of 1999, single people receive a standard deduction of $4,300 (married couples filing jointly receive $7,200). Blind people and individuals 65 and older receive higher standard deductions.

Many people qualify for more than the standard deduction. **Itemized deductions** are expenses a taxpayer is allowed to deduct from adjusted gross income. Common itemized deductions include the following:

- *Medical and dental expenses,* including doctors' fees, prescription medications, hospital expenses, medical insurance premiums, hearing aids, eyeglasses, and medical travel that has not been reimbursed or paid by others. The amount of this deduction is the medical and dental expenses that exceed 7.5 percent (as of 2000) of adjusted gross income. If your AGI is $20,000, for example, you must have more than $1,500 in unreimbursed medical and dental expenses before you can claim this deduction. If your medical and dental bills amount to $1,600, you qualify for a $100 deduction.
- *Taxes*—state and local income tax, real estate property tax, and state or local personal property tax.
- *Interest*—mortgage interest, home equity loan interest, and investment interest expense up to an amount equal to investment income.
- *Contributions* of cash or property to qualified charitable organizations. Contribution totals greater than 20 percent of adjusted gross income are subject to limitations.
- *Casualty and theft losses*—financial losses resulting from natural disasters, accidents, or unlawful acts. Deductions are for the amount exceeding 10 percent of AGI, less $100, for losses *not* reimbursed by an insurance company or other source. California residents commonly report casualty losses due to earthquake damage.
- *Moving expenses* when a change in residence is associated with a new job that is at least 50 miles farther from your former home than your old main job location. Deductible moving expenses include only the cost of transporting taxpayer and household members and the cost of moving household goods and personal property.
- *Job-related and other miscellaneous expenses* such as unreimbursed job travel, union dues, required continuing education, work clothes or uniforms, investment expenses, tax preparation fees, and safe deposit box rental (for storing investment documents). The total of these expenses must exceed 2 percent of adjusted gross income to qualify as a deduction. Such miscellaneous expenses as gambling losses to the extent of gambling winnings and physical or mental disability expenses that limit employability are not subject to the 2 percent limit.

The standard deduction *or* total itemized deductions, along with the value of your exemptions (see the next section), is subtracted from adjusted gross income to obtain your taxable income. The accompanying Financial Planning for Life's Situations box can help you determine which items to include in your taxable income when you calculate your federal income tax.

You are required to maintain records to document tax deductions. Financial advisers recommend a home filing system (see Exhibit 4–2) for storing receipts and other tax documents. Canceled checks can serve as proof of payment for such deductions as

*tax deduction*   An amount subtracted from adjusted gross income to arrive at taxable income.

*standard deduction*   A set amount on which no taxes are paid.

*itemized deductions*   Expenses that can be deducted from adjusted gross income, such as medical expenses, real estate property taxes, home mortgage interest, charitable contributions, casualty losses, and certain work-related expenses.

# Financial Planning for Life's Situations

## IS IT TAXABLE INCOME? IS IT DEDUCTIBLE?

Certain financial benefits individuals receive are not subject to federal income tax. Indicate whether each of the following items would or would not be included in taxable income when you compute your federal income tax.

Indicate whether each of the following items would or would not be deductible when you compute your federal income tax.

| Is it taxable income . . . ? | Yes | No |
|---|---|---|
| **1.** Lottery winnings | ___ | ___ |
| **2.** Child support received | ___ | ___ |
| **3.** Worker's compensation benefits | ___ | ___ |
| **4.** Life insurance death benefits | ___ | ___ |
| **5.** Municipal bond interest earnings | ___ | ___ |
| **6.** Bartering income | ___ | ___ |

| Is it deductible . . . ? | Yes | No |
|---|---|---|
| **7.** Life insurance premiums | ___ | ___ |
| **8.** Cosmetic surgery for improved looks | ___ | ___ |
| **9.** Fees for traffic violations | ___ | ___ |
| **10.** Mileage for driving to volunteer work | ___ | ___ |
| **11.** An attorney's fee for preparing a will | ___ | ___ |
| **12.** Income tax preparation fee | ___ | ___ |

Note: These taxable income items and deductions are based on the 1999 tax year and may change due to changes in the tax code.

Answers: 1, 6, 10, 12—yes; 2, 3, 4, 5, 7, 8, 9, 11—no.

---

charitable contributions, medical expenses, and business-related expenses. Travel expenses can be documented in a daily log with records of mileage, tolls, parking fees, and away-from-home costs.

Generally, you should keep tax records for three years from the date you file your return. However, you may be held responsible for providing back documentation up to six years. Records such as past tax returns and housing documents should be kept indefinitely.

*exemption* A deduction from adjusted gross income for yourself, your spouse, and qualified dependents.

## Exemptions

An **exemption** is a deduction from adjusted gross income for yourself, your spouse, and qualified dependents. A dependent must not earn more than a set amount unless he or she is under age 19 or is a full-time student under age 24; you must provide more than half of the dependent's support; and the dependent must reside in your home or be a specified relative and must meet certain citizenship requirements. The Social Security number of each dependent must be reported on the tax return, regardless of age.

For 1999, taxable income was reduced by $2,750 for each exemption claimed. This amount is revised annually based on inflation. Increased exemptions and standard deductions eliminate or reduce the taxes many low-income Americans pay. For 1999, a family of four did not have to pay federal income tax on the first $18,200 of gross income ($7,200 for the standard deduction and $11,000 for four exemptions). After deducting the amounts for exemptions, you obtain your taxable income, which is the amount used to determine taxes owed.

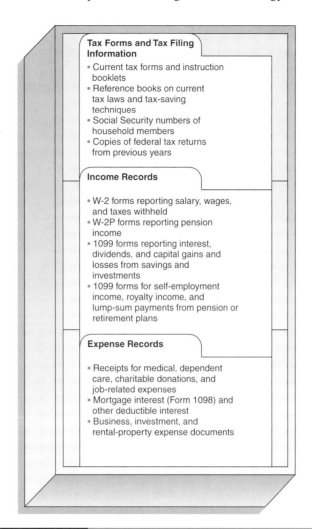

**EXHIBIT 4-2**

A Tax
Recordkeeping
System

**Tax Forms and Tax Filing Information**
- Current tax forms and instruction booklets
- Reference books on current tax laws and tax-saving techniques
- Social Security numbers of household members
- Copies of federal tax returns from previous years

**Income Records**
- W-2 forms reporting salary, wages, and taxes withheld
- W-2P forms reporting pension income
- 1099 forms reporting interest, dividends, and capital gains and losses from savings and investments
- 1099 forms for self-employment income, royalty income, and lump-sum payments from pension or retirement plans

**Expense Records**
- Receipts for medical, dependent care, charitable donations, and job-related expenses
- Mortgage interest (Form 1098) and other deductible interest
- Business, investment, and rental-property expense documents

## Step 3: Calculating Taxes Owed

Your taxable income is the basis for computing the amount of your income tax. The use of tax rates and the benefits of tax credits are the final phase of the tax computation process.

Tax Rates   Use your taxable income in conjunction with the appropriate tax table or tax schedule. Before 1987, there were 14 tax rates, ranging from 11 to 50 percent. For 1999, the five-rate system for federal income tax was as follows:

| Rate on Taxable Income | Single Taxpayers | Married Taxpayers | Heads of Household |
|---|---|---|---|
| 15% | Up to $25,750 | Up to $43,050 | Up to $34,550 |
| 28 | $25,750–$62,450 | $43,050–$104,050 | $34,550–$89,150 |
| 31 | $62,450–$130,250 | $104,050–$158,550 | $89,150–$144,400 |
| 36 | $130,250–$283,150 | $158,550–$283,150 | $144,400–$283,150 |
| 39.6 | Over $283,150 | Over $283,150 | Over $283,150 |

## Financial Planning Calculations

### TAX CREDITS VERSUS TAX DEDUCTIONS

Many people confuse *tax credits* with *tax deductions.* Is one better than the other? A tax *credit,* such as eligible child care or dependent care expenses, results in a dollar-for-dollar reduction in the amount of taxes owed. A *tax deduction,* such as an itemized deduction in the form of medical expenses, mortgage interest, or charitable contributions, reduces the taxable income on which your taxes are based.

Here is how a $100 tax credit compares with a $100 tax deduction:

As you might expect, tax credits are less readily available than tax deductions. To qualify for a $100 child care tax credit, you may have to spend $500 in child care expenses. In some situations, spending on deductible items may be more beneficial than qualifying for a tax credit. A knowledge of tax law and careful financial planning will help you use both tax credits and tax deductions to maximum advantage.

$100 Tax Deduction

↓

Reduces your taxable income by $100. The amount of your tax reduction depends on your tax bracket. Your taxes will be reduced by $15 if you are in the 15 percent tax bracket and by $28 if you are in the 28 percent tax bracket.

$100 Tax Credit

↓

Reduces your taxes by $100.

A separate tax rate schedule exists for married persons who file separate income tax returns.

*marginal tax rate* The rate used to calculate tax on the last (and next) dollar of taxable income.

The 15, 28, 31, 36, and 39.6 percent rates are referred to as **marginal tax rates.** These rates are used to calculate tax on the last (and next) dollar of taxable income. After deductions and exemptions, a person in the 28 percent tax bracket pays 28 cents in taxes for every dollar of taxable income in that bracket.

*average tax rate* Total tax due divided by taxable income.

In contrast, the **average tax rate** is based on the total tax due divided by taxable income. Except for taxpayers in the 15 percent bracket, this rate is less than a person's marginal tax rate. For example, a person with taxable income of $40,000 and a total tax bill of $4,200 would have an *average tax rate* of 10.5 percent ($4,200 ÷ $40,000). Self-employed people are likely to have a higher average tax rate due to self-employment taxes, which include payments toward future Social Security benefits.

Taxpayers who benefit from the special treatment given to certain income and receive special deductions may be subject to an additional tax. The *alternative minimum tax (AMT)* is designed to ensure that those who receive tax breaks also pay their fair share of taxes. Further discussion of the AMT is beyond the scope of this book; you may obtain information from the Internal Revenue Service (IRS).

*tax credit* An amount subtracted directly from the amount of taxes owed.

Tax Credits   The tax owed may be reduced by a **tax credit,** an amount subtracted directly from the amount of taxes owed. One example of a tax credit is the credit given for child care and dependent care expenses. This amount lowers the tax owed by an individual or a couple. A tax credit differs from a deduction in that a tax credit has a full dollar effect in lowering taxes, whereas a deduction reduces the taxable income on which the tax liability is computed. (See the accompanying Financial Planning Calculations box.)

EXHIBIT 4-3

W-2 Form

| a Control number | | OMB No. 1545-0008 | | |
|---|---|---|---|---|
| b Employer's identification number  37 – 19876541 | | | 1 Wages, tips, other compensation  23,972.09 | 2 Federal income tax withheld  2,678.93 |
| c Employer's name, address, and ZIP code | | | 3 Social security wages  23,972.09 | 4 Social security tax withheld  1,725.99 |
| Information Data, Inc.  9834 Collins Blvd.  Benton, NJ 08734 | | | 5 Medicare wages and tips | 6 Medicare tax withheld |
| | | | 7 Social security tips | 8 Allocated tips |
| d Employee's social security number  123-45-6789 | | | 9 Advance EIC payment | 10 Dependent care benefits |
| e Employee's name, address, and ZIP code | | | 11 Nonqualified plans | 12 Benefits included in box 1 |
| Barbara Victor  124 Harper Lane  Parmont, NJ 07819 | | | 13 See Instrs. for box 13 | 14 Other |

| 15 Statutory employee | Deceased | Pension plan | Legal rep. | Hshld. emp. | Subtotal | Deferred compensation |
|---|---|---|---|---|---|---|
| ☐ | ☐ | ☐ | ☐ | ☐ | ☐ | ☐ |

| 16 State   Employer's state I.D. No.  37 – 19876541 | 17 State wages, tips, etc. | 18 State income tax | 19 Locality name | 20 local wages, tips, etc. | 21 Local income tax |
|---|---|---|---|---|---|

(1)                                                        Department of the Treasury—Internal Revenue Service

Form **W-2** **Wage and Tax Statement**
Copy B To Be Filed With Employee's FEDERAL Tax Return

This information is being furnished to the Internal Revenue Service.

Low-income workers can benefit from the *earned-income credit (EIC)*. This federal tax regulation, for working parents with taxable income under a certain amount ($30,580 with more than one child in 1999), can result in a tax credit of more than $2,500. Families that do not earn enough to owe federal income taxes are also eligible for the EIC. When these families file a tax return and attach Schedule EIC, they receive a check from the IRS for the amount of their credit.

## Making Tax Payments

You will make your payment of income taxes to the federal government in one of two ways: through payroll withholding or through estimated tax payments.

Withholding     The pay-as-you-go system requires an employer to deduct federal income tax from your pay and send it to the government. The withheld amount is based on the number of exemptions and the expected deductions claimed on the W-4 form. For example, a married person with children would have less withheld than a single person with the same salary, since the married person will owe less tax at year-end.

After the end of the year, you will receive a W-2 form (see Exhibit 4–3), which reports your annual earnings and the amounts that have been deducted for federal income tax, Social Security, and, if applicable, state income tax. A copy of the W-2 form is filed with your tax return to document your earnings and the amount you have paid in taxes. The difference between the amount withheld and the tax owed is either the additional amount you must pay or the refund you will receive.

Many taxpayers view an annual tax refund as a "windfall," extra money they can count on each year. However, these taxpayers are forgetting the opportunity cost of withholding excessive amounts. Others view their extra tax withholding as "forced savings." However, a payroll deduction plan for savings could serve the same purpose and would enable them to earn the interest instead of giving the government an interest-free loan.

Students and low-income individuals may file for exemption from withholding if they paid no federal income tax last year and do not expect to pay any in the current year. Dependents may not be exempt from withholding if they have any unearned income and if their total gross income will exceed $500. Being exempt from withholding results in not having to file for a refund and allows you to make more use of your money during the year. However, even if federal income tax is not withheld, Social Security taxes will still be deducted.

**Estimated Payments**    People with income from savings, investments, independent contracting, royalties, and lump-sum payments from pensions or retirement plans have their earnings reported on Form 1099. People in these situations and others who do not have taxes withheld may be required to make tax payments during the year (April 15, June 15, September 15, and January 15 as the last payment for the previous tax year). These payments are based on the person's estimate of taxes due at year-end. Underpayment or failure to make these estimated payments can result in penalties and interest charges. These penalties are usually avoided if withholding and estimated payments total more than your tax liability for the previous year or at least 90 percent of the current year's tax.

## Deadlines and Penalties

Most people are required to file their federal income tax return each April 15. If you are not able to file on time, you can use Form 4868 to obtain an automatic four-month extension. This extension is for the 1040 form and other documents, but it does not delay your payment liability. You must submit the estimated amount owed along with Form 4868 by April 15. Failure to file on time can result in a penalty of 5 percent for just one day.

People who make quarterly deposits for estimated taxes must submit their payments by April 15, June 15, and September 15 of the current tax year, with the final payment due by January 15 of the following year.

The IRS can impose penalties and interest for violations of the tax code. Failure to file a tax return can result in a 25 percent penalty in addition to the taxes owed.

Underpayment of quarterly estimated taxes requires paying interest on the amount you should have paid. Underpayment due to negligence or fraud can result in penalties of 50 to 75 percent. The good news is that if you claim a refund several months or years late, the IRS will pay you interest. Refunds must be claimed within three years of filing the return or within two years of paying the tax.

**Sheet 20**

## Concept Check 4-2

1.  How does tax-exempt income differ from tax-deferred income?
2.  What information is needed to compute taxable income?
3.  When would you use the standard deduction instead of itemized deductions?
4.  What is the difference between your marginal tax rate and your average tax rate?
5.  How does a tax credit affect the amount owed for federal income tax?

# FILING YOUR FEDERAL INCOME TAX RETURN

## Obj. 3
Prepare a federal income tax return.

As you stare at those piles of papers, you know it's time to do your taxes! Submitting your federal income tax return requires several decisions and activities. First, you must determine whether you are required to file a return. Next, you need to decide which basic form best serves your needs and whether you are required to submit additional schedules or supplementary forms. Finally, you must prepare your return.

## Who Must File?

Every citizen or resident of the United States and every U.S. citizen who is a resident of Puerto Rico is required to file a federal income tax return if his or her income is above a certain amount. The amount is based on the person's *filing status* and other factors such as age. For example, single persons under 65 had to file a return on April 15, 2000 (for tax year 1999), if their gross income exceeded $7,050; single persons over 65 had to file if their gross income exceeded $8,100. The amount at which you are required to file will change each year based on changes in the standard deduction and in the allowed personal exemptions. If your gross income is less than this amount but taxes were withheld from your earnings, you will need to file a return to obtain a refund.

Your filing status is affected by such factors as marital status and dependents. The five filing status categories are as follows:

- *Single*—never-married, divorced, or legally separated individuals with no dependents.
- *Married, filing joint return*—combines the income of a husband and a wife.
- *Married, filing separate returns*—each spouse is responsible for his or her own tax. Under certain conditions, a married couple can benefit from this filing status.
- *Head of household*—an unmarried individual or a surviving spouse who maintains a household (paying for more than half of the costs) for a child or a dependent relative.
- *Qualifying widow or widower*—an individual whose spouse died within the past two years and who has a dependent; this status is limited to two years after the death of the spouse.

In some situations, you may have a choice of filing status. In such cases, compute your taxes under the available alternatives to determine the most advantageous filing status.

## Which Tax Form Should You Use?

Although about 400 federal tax forms and schedules exist (see Exhibit 4–4), you have a choice of three basic forms when filing your income tax. Recently about 20 percent of taxpayers used Form 1040EZ or Form 1040A; about 60 percent used the regular Form 1040. Your decision in this matter will depend on your type of income, the amount of your income, the number of your deductions, and the complexity of your tax situation.

### Form 1040EZ    You may use Form 1040EZ if

- You are single or married filing a joint return, under age 65, and claim no dependents.
- Your income consisted only of wages, salaries, and tips and not more than $400 of taxable interest.
- Your taxable income is less than $50,000.
- You do not itemize deductions or claim any adjustments to income or any tax credits.

**EXHIBIT 4-4**   THE MOST COMMONLY USED FEDERAL INCOME TAX FORMS

| Form | Title | Purpose |
|---|---|---|
| 1040EZ | Income Tax Return | For single taxpayers or married taxpayers filing jointly with no dependents, taxable income of less than $50,000, no deductions |
| 1040A | Income Tax Return | For taxpayers with taxable income of less than $50,000 and no itemized deductions who may take an IRA deduction and have certain tax credits |
| 1040 | Income Tax Return | For taxpayers with more complex tax situations who do not qualify for use of 1040EZ or 1040A |
| 1040PC | Income Tax Return for Computerized Returns | For filing a tax return prepared on a personal computer |
| 1040X | Amended Income Tax Return | To correct income or deductions reported in a previous year |
| Schedule A | Itemized Deductions | To claim deductions for medical expenses, certain state and local taxes, interest, donations, casualty losses, moving expenses, and other deductible expenses |
| Schedule B | Interest and Dividend Income | To report interest and/or dividend income of over $400 |
| Schedule C | Profit or Loss from Business or Profession | To report income and expenses from self-employment |
| Schedule C-EZ | Net Profit from Business | To report net profit of a sole proprietorship with gross receipts of less than $25,000 and expenses of less than $2,000 |
| Schedule D | Capital Gains and Losses | To report gains and losses on the sale of investments |
| Schedule E | Supplemental Income Schedule | To report income and expenses from rental property, royalties, partnerships, estates, and trusts |
| Schedule EIC | Earned-Income Credit | To calculate tax credit for low-income working families |
| Schedule R | Credit for the Elderly or Disabled | To claim a tax credit for elderly or disabled persons in low-income categories |
| Schedule SE | Social Security Self-Employment Tax | To calculate self-employment Social Security tax based on profit from a business or profession |
| 2106 | Employee Business Expenses | To report employee-related travel expenses and reimbursements for these expenses |
| 2119 | Sale of Your Home | To report the sale and/or exchange of your primary place of residence |
| 2441 | Credit for Child and Dependent Care Expenses | To calculate the tax credit for child care or dependent care costs for individuals in certain income groups |
| 3903 | Moving Expenses | To calculate the deductible expenses related to a change of residence based on job-distance restrictions |
| 4562 | Depreciation and Amortization | To calculate business depreciation expenses for various types of assets |
| 4684 | Casualties and Thefts | To report nonbusiness casualty and theft losses less any reimbursement from insurance or other sources |
| 4868 | Application for Automatic Extension | To request a four-month delay in filing your federal tax return; does not delay time for payment of taxes |
| 5329 | Return for IRA and Qualified Retirement Plans Taxes | To report excess contributions, premature distributions, or excess distributions related to a retirement plan |
| 8283 | Noncash Charitable Contributions | To report a charitable deduction of property or services |
| 8606 | Nondeductible IRA Contributions | To report contributions to an individual retirement arrangement that are not deductible for tax purposes |
| 8615 | Computation of Tax for Children under Age 14 Who Have Investment Income of More than $1,300 | To report income and capital gains from investments |
| 8829 | Expenses for Business Use of Your Home | To report expenses related to the use of your home for business purposes |
| 8839 | Qualified Adoption Expenses | To report expenses associated with adoption of a child |

Form 1040EZ allows people with less complicated situations to file with minimal effort. For example, Margie Collins, a college freshman, had a part-time job at a health center. Since she was single, earned less than the amount needed to file, and had $43 in interest income, Margie was able to use Form 1040EZ to obtain a refund of income tax withheld during the past year.

**Form 1040A**   This form would be used by people who have less than $50,000 in taxable income from wages, salaries, tips, unemployment compensation, interest, or dividends and use the standard deduction. With Form 1040A, you can also take deductions for individual retirement account (IRA) contributions and a tax credit for child care and dependent care expenses.

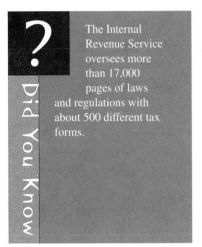

The Internal Revenue Service oversees more than 17,000 pages of laws and regulations with about 500 different tax forms.

If you qualify for either Form 1040EZ or Form 1040A, you may wish to use one of them to simplify filing your tax return. You may not want to use either the Form 1040EZ or Form 1040A if Form 1040 allows you to pay less tax.

**Form 1040**   Form 1040 is an expanded version of Form 1040A that includes sections for all types of income. You are required to use this form if your income is over $50,000 or if you can be claimed as a dependent on your parents' return *and* you had interest or dividends over a set limit.

Form 1040 allows you to itemize your deductions. You can list various allowable expenses (medical costs, home mortgage interest, real estate property taxes) that will reduce taxable income and the amount you owe the government. You should learn about all the possible adjustments to income, deductions, and tax credits for which you may qualify.

**Form 1040X**   This form is used to amend a previously filed tax return. If you discovered income that was not reported, or if you found additional deductions, you should file Form 1040X to pay the additional tax or obtain a refund.

## Completing the Federal Income Tax Return

The major sections of Form 1040 (see Exhibit 4–5) correspond to tax topics discussed in the previous sections of this chapter:

1. *Filing status and exemptions.* Your tax rate is determined by your filing status and allowances for yourself, your spouse, and each person you claim as a dependent.
2. *Income.* Earnings from your employment (as reported by your W-2 form) and other income, such as savings and investment income, are reported in this section of Form 1040.
3. *Adjustments to income.* As discussed later in the chapter, if you qualify, you may deduct contributions (up to a certain amount) to an individual retirement account (IRA) or other qualified retirement program.
4. *Tax computation.* In this section, your adjusted gross income is reduced by your itemized deductions (see Exhibit 4–6) or by the standard deduction for your tax situation. In addition, an amount is deducted for each exemption to arrive at your taxable income. That income is the basis for determining the amount of your tax (see Exhibit 4–7).
5. *Tax credits.* Any tax credits for which you qualify are subtracted at this point.

**EXHIBIT 4-5**    Federal Income Tax Return—Form 1040

**1.**
Your marriage and household situation will affect your taxable income and tax rate

**2.**
Your earnings and other sources of income will be reported in this section

**3.**
Adjusted gross income results from certain deductions and will be used as a basis for computing other deductions

---

**6.** *Other taxes.* Any special taxes, such as self-employment tax, are included at this point.

**7.** *Payments.* Your total withholding and other payments are indicated in this section.

**8.** *Refund or amount you owe.* If your payments exceed the amount of income tax you owe, you are entitled to a refund. If the opposite is true, you must make an additional payment. Taxpayers who want their refunds sent directly to a bank will no longer need to complete a separate form. Instead, the necessary account information will be recorded directly on Form 1040, 1040A, or 1040EZ.

**9.** *Your signature.* Forgetting to sign a tax return is one of the most common filing errors.

## EXHIBIT 4-5 (continued)

**4.**
In this section, you subtract your itemized deductions or the standard deduction and exemptions to obtain taxable income; your tax is based on the tax tables or schedule

**5.**
Tax credits are deducted at this point

**6.**
Any additional taxes owed are added at this point

**7.**
The federal income tax you have had withheld or payments you have made are recorded here

**8.**
Your total tax is compared to your total payments to determine your refund or amount due

**9.**
Don't forget to sign the form and your check !!!

Form 1040    Page 2

**Tax and Credits**

| | | | |
|---|---|---|---|
| 34 | Amount from line 33 (adjusted gross income) | 34 | 51,502 |
| 35a | Check if: ☐ You were 65 or older, ☐ Blind; ☐ Spouse was 65 or older, ☐ Blind. Add the number of boxes checked above and enter total here ▶ 35a | | |
| b | If you are married filing separately and your spouse itemizes deductions or you are a dual-status alien, see page 30 and check here ▶ 35b ☐ | | |

Standard Deduction for Most People

Single: $4,300
Head of household: $6,350
Married filing jointly or Qualifying widow(er): $7,200
Married filing separately: $3,600

| | | | |
|---|---|---|---|
| 36 | Enter your **itemized deductions** from Schedule A, line 28, **OR standard deduction** shown on the left. **But** see page 30 to find your standard deduction if you checked any box on line 35a or 35b **or** if someone can claim you as a dependent | 36 | 14,372 |
| 37 | Subtract line 36 from line 34 | 37 | 37,130 |
| 38 | If line 34 is $94,975 or less, multiply $2,750 by the total number of exemptions claimed on line 6d. If line 34 is over $94,975, see the worksheet on page 31 for the amount to enter | 38 | 11,000 |
| 39 | **Taxable income.** Subtract line 38 from line 37. If line 38 is more than line 37, enter -0- | 39 | 26,130 |
| 40 | **Tax** (see page 31). Check if any tax is from a ☐ Form(s) 8814 b ☐ Form 4972 ▶ | 40 | 3,919 |
| 41 | Credit for child and dependent care expenses. Attach Form 2441 | 41 | |
| 42 | Credit for the elderly or the disabled. Attach Schedule R | 42 | |
| 43 | Child tax credit (see page 33) | 43 | |
| 44 | Education credits. Attach Form 8863 | 44 | |
| 45 | Adoption credit. Attach Form 8839 | 45 | |
| 46 | Foreign tax credit. Attach Form 1116 required | 46 | |
| 47 | Other. Check if from a ☐ Form 3800 b ☐ Form 8396 c ☐ Form 8801 d ☐ Form (specify) | 47 | |
| 48 | Add lines 41 through 47. These are your **total credits** | 48 | |
| 49 | Subtract line 48 from line 40. If line 48 is more than line 40, enter -0- ▶ | 49 | 3,919 |

**Other Taxes**

| | | | |
|---|---|---|---|
| 50 | Self-employment tax. Attach Schedule SE | 50 | |
| 51 | Alternative minimum tax. Attach Form 6251 | 51 | |
| 52 | Social security and Medicare tax on tip income not reported to employer. Attach Form 4137 | 52 | |
| 53 | Tax on IRAs, other retirement plans, and MSAs. IAttach Form 5329 if required | 53 | |
| 54 | Advance earned income credit payments from Form(s) W-2 | 54 | |
| 55 | Household employment taxes. Attach Schedule H | 55 | |
| 56 | Add lines 49 through 55. This is your **total tax** ▶ | 56 | |

**Payments**

| | | | |
|---|---|---|---|
| 57 | Federal income tax withheld from Forms W-2 and 1099 | 57 | 4,142 |
| 58 | 1999 estimated tax payments and amount applied from 1998 return | 58 | |
| 59a | **Earned income credit.** Attach Sch. EIC if you have a qualifying child | | |
| b | Nontaxable earned income: amount ▶ and type ▶ | 59a | |
| 60 | Additional child tax credit. Attach Form 8812 | 60 | |
| 61 | Amount paid with request for extension to file (see page 48) | 61 | |
| 62 | Excess social security and RRTA tax withheld (see page 48) | 62 | |
| 63 | Other payments. Check if from a ☐ Form 2439 b ☐ Form 4136 | 63 | |
| 64 | Add lines 57, 58, 59a, 60 through 63. These are your **total payments** ▶ | 64 | 4,142 |

**Refund**
Have it directly deposited! See page 48 and fill in 66b, 66c, and 66d.

| | | | |
|---|---|---|---|
| 65 | If line 64 is more than line 56, subtract line 56 from line 64. This is the amount you **OVERPAID** | 65 | 223 |
| 66a | Amount of line 615 you want **REFUNDED TO YOU** ▶ | 66a | 223 |
| ▶ b | Routing number ▶ c Type: ☐ Checking ☐ Savings | | |
| ▶ d | Account number | | |
| 67 | Amount of line 65 you want **APPLIED TO YOUR 2000 ESTIMATED TAX** ▶ 67 | | |

**Amount You Owe**

| | | | |
|---|---|---|---|
| 68 | If line 56 is more than line 64, subtract line 64 from line 56. This is the **AMOUNT YOU OWE.** For details on how to pay, see page 49 ▶ | 68 | |
| 69 | Estimated tax penalty. Also include on line 68. | 69 | |

**Sign Here**
Joint return? See page 18.
Keep a copy of this return for your records.

Under penalties of perjury, I declare that I have examined this return and accompanying schedules and statements, and to the best of my knowledge and belief, they are true, correct, and complete. Declaration of preparer (other than taxpayer) is based on all information of which preparer has any knowledge.

| Your signature | Date | Your occupation | Daytime telephone number (optional) |
|---|---|---|---|
| *Edward L. Rameriz* | 4-10-01 | PRODUCTION SUPERVISOR | |
| Spouse's signature. If a joint return, BOTH must sign. | Date | Spouse's occupation | |
| *Marge S. Rameriz* | 4-10-01 | SALES REPRESENTATIVE | |

**Paid Preparer's Use Only**

| Preparer's signature | Date | Check if self-employed ☐ | Preparer's social security no. |
|---|---|---|---|
| Firm's name (or yours if self-employed) and address | | E.I. No. | |
| | | ZIP code | |

*U.S.GPO:0000-419-539

⊛ Printed on recycled paper

NOTE: These forms are used in a recent year; the current forms may not be exactly the same. Obtain current income tax forms and current tax information from your local IRS office, post office, public library, or at www.irs.gov.

## Filing State Income Tax Returns

All but seven states (Alaska, Florida, Nevada, South Dakota, Texas, Washington, and Wyoming) have a state income tax. In most states, the tax rate ranges from 1 to 10 percent and is based on some aspect of your federal income tax return, such as adjusted gross income or taxable income. For further information about the income tax in your state, contact the state department of revenue. States usually require income tax returns to be filed when the federal income tax return is due. For help in planning your tax activities, see Exhibit 4–8.

**EXHIBIT 4-6**    Schedule A for Itemized Deductions—Form 1040

Health care expenses (not covered by insurance) are listed here, but must exceed 7.5% of adjusted gross income to be deductible

Deductible interest payments are listed here

A variety of other expenses may qualify under these deduction categories

Certain other taxes may be deducted

Donations and charitable contributions are reported here

The total of your itemized deductions is transferred to Form 1040 in the "Tax Computation" section

---

**SCHEDULES A&B** (Form 1040)

Department of the Treasury
Internal Revenue Service

**Schedule A—Itemized Deductions**
(Schedule B is on back)

▶ Attach to Form 1040. ▶ See Instructions for Schedules A and B (Form 1040).

OMB No. 1545-0074

Attachment Sequence No. **07**

Name(s) shown on Form 1040: EDWARD L. & MARGE S. RAMERIZ

Your social security number: 124 45 6789

| | | | | | |
|---|---|---|---|---|---|
| **Medical and Dental Expenses** | Caution: Do not include expenses reimbursed or paid by others. | | | | |
| | 1 | Medical and dental expenses (see page A-1). | 1 | 2,462 — | |
| | 2 | Enter amount from Form 1040, line 34. | 2 | 51,502 — | |
| | 3 | Multiply line 2 above by 7.5% (.075) | 3 | 3,863 — | |
| | 4 | Subtract line 3 from line 1. If line 3 is more than line 1, enter -0- | | 4 | — 0 — |
| **Taxes You Paid** (See page A-2.) | 5 | State and local income taxes | 5 | 812 — | |
| | 6 | Real estate taxes (see page A-2) | 6 | 2,840 — | |
| | 7 | Personal property taxes | 7 | | |
| | 8 | Other taxes. List type and amount ▶ | 8 | | |
| | 9 | Add lines 5 through 8 | | 9 | 3,652 — |
| **Interest You Paid** (See page A-3.) | 10 | Home mortgage interest and points reported to you on Form 1098 | 10 | 6,490 — | |
| | 11 | Home mortgage interest not reported to you on Form 1098. If paid to the person from whom you bought the home, see page A-3 and show that person's name, identifying no., and address ▶ | | | |
| Note: Personal interest is not deductible. | 11 | | 11 | | |
| | 12 | Points not reported to you on Form 1098. See page A-3 for special rules | 12 | | |
| | 13 | Investment interest. Attach Form 4952 if required. (See page A-3.) | 13 | | |
| | 14 | Add lines 10 through 13 | | 14 | 6,490 — |
| **Gifts to Charity** If you made a gift and got a benefit for it, see page A-4. | 15 | Gifts by cash or check. If made any gift of $250 or more, see page A-4. | 15 | 4,230 — | |
| | 16 | Other than by cash or check. If any gift of $250 or more, see page A-4. You **MUST** attach Form 8283 if over $500 | 16 | | |
| | 17 | Carryover from prior year | 17 | | |
| | 18 | Add lines 15 through 17 | | 18 | 4,230 — |
| **Casualty and Theft Losses** | 19 | Casualty or theft loss(es). Attach Form 4684. (See page A-5.) | | 19 | — 0 — |
| **Job Expenses and Most Other Miscellaneous Deductions** (See page A-5 for expenses to deduct here.) | 20 | Unreimbursed employee expenses—job travel, union dues, job education, etc. You **MUST** attach Form 2106 or 2106-EZ if required. (See page A-5.) ▶ UNION DUES | 20 | 625 — | |
| | 21 | Tax preparation fees | 21 | | |
| | 22 | Other expenses—investment, safe deposit box, etc. List type and amount ▶ | 22 | | |
| | 23 | Add lines 20 through 22 | 23 | 625 — | |
| | 24 | Enter amount from Form 1040, line 34. | 24 | 51,502 — | |
| | 25 | Multiply line 24 above by 2% (.02) | 25 | 1,030 — | |
| | 26 | Subtract line 25 from line 23. If line 25 is more than line 23, enter -0- | | 26 | — 0 — |
| **Other Miscellaneous Deductions** | 27 | Other—from list on page A-6. List type and amount ▶ | 27 | | |
| | 28 | | 28 | | |
| **Total Itemized Deductions** | 29 | Is Form 1040, line 34, over $126,600 (over $63,300 if married filing separately)? **NO.** Your deduction is not limited. Add the amounts in the far right column for lines 4 through 27. Also, enter this amount on Form 1040, line 36. **YES.** Your deduction may be limited. See page A-5 for the amount to enter. | ▶ | 29 | 14,372 — |

For paperwork Reduction Act Notice, see Form 1040 instructions.     Cat. No. 11330X     Schedule A (Form 1040)

---

## Concept Check 4-3

1. In what ways does your filing status affect preparation of your federal income tax return?
2. What factors affect your choice of a 1040 form?

---

# TAX ASSISTANCE AND THE AUDIT PROCESS

In the process of completing your federal income tax return, you may seek additional information or assistance. After filing your return, you may be identified for a tax audit. If this happens, several policies and procedures protect your rights.

**EXHIBIT 4-7**   Tax Tables and Tax Rate Schedules

## Tax Table

| If (taxable income) is– | | And you are– | | | |
|---|---|---|---|---|---|
| At least | But less than | Single | Married filing jointly* | Married filing separately | Head of a household |
| | | | Your tax is– | | |

**26,000**

| At least | But less than | Single | Married filing jointly* | Married filing separately | Head of a household |
|---|---|---|---|---|---|
| 26,000 | 26,050 | 3,940 | 3,904 | 4,489 | 3,904 |
| 26,050 | 26,100 | 3,954 | 3,911 | 4,503 | 3,911 |
| 26,100 | 26,150 | 3,968 | 3,919 | 4,517 | 3,919 |
| 26,150 | 26,200 | 3,982 | 3,926 | 4,531 | 3,926 |
| 26,200 | 26,250 | 3,996 | 3,934 | 4,545 | 3,934 |
| 26,250 | 26,300 | 4,010 | 3,941 | 4,559 | 3,941 |
| 26,300 | 26,350 | 4,024 | 3,949 | 4,573 | 3,949 |
| 26,350 | 26,400 | 4,038 | 3,956 | 4,587 | 3,956 |
| 26,400 | 26,450 | 4,052 | 3,964 | 4,601 | 3,934 |
| 26,450 | 26,500 | 4,066 | 3,971 | 4,615 | 3,971 |
| 26,500 | 26,550 | 4,080 | 3,979 | 4,629 | 3,979 |
| 26,550 | 26,600 | 4,094 | 3,986 | 4,643 | 3,986 |
| 26,600 | 26,650 | 4,108 | 3,994 | 4,657 | 3,994 |
| 26,650 | 26,700 | 4,122 | 4,001 | 4,671 | 4,001 |
| 26,700 | 26,750 | 4,136 | 4,009 | 4,685 | 4,009 |
| 26,750 | 26,800 | 4,150 | 4,016 | 4,699 | 4,016 |
| 26,800 | 26,850 | 4,164 | 4,024 | 4,713 | 4,024 |
| 26,850 | 26,900 | 4,178 | 4,031 | 4,727 | 4,031 |
| 26,900 | 26,950 | 4,192 | 4,039 | 4,741 | 4,039 |
| 26,950 | 27,000 | 4,206 | 4,046 | 4,755 | 4,046 |

* This column must also be used by a qualifying widow(er).

## Tax Rate Schedules

**Schedule Y-1**—Use if your filing status is **Married filing jointly or Qualifying widow(er)**

| If the amount on Form 1040, line 38, is: Over– | But not over– | Enter on Form 1040, line 39 | of the amount over– |
|---|---|---|---|
| $0 | $43,050 | ------------ 15% | $0 |
| 43,050 | 104,050 | $6,457.50 + 28% | 43,050 |
| 104,050 | 158,550 | 23,537.50 + 31% | 104,050 |
| 158,550 | 283,150 | 40,432.50 + 36% | 158,550 |
| 283,150 | ---------- | 85,288.50 + 39.6% | 283,150 |

**Caution:** *Use only if your taxable income (Form 1040, line 39) is $100,000 or more. If less, use the* **Tax Table***. Even though you cannot use the tax rate schedules above if your taxable income is less than $100,000, all levels of taxable income are shown so taxpayers can see the tax rate that applies to each level.*

NOTE: These were the federal income tax rates for a recent year. Current rates may vary due to changes in the tax code and adjustments for inflation. Obtain current income tax booklets from your local IRS office, post office, bank, public library, or at www.irs.gov.

**Obj. 4**
Identify tax assistance sources.

## Tax Information Sources

As with other aspects of personal financial planning, many resources are available to assist you with your taxes. The IRS offers a wide variety of services to taxpayers. Libraries and bookstores offer books and other publications that are updated annually.

**IRS Services**   If you wish to do your own tax return or just to expand your knowledge of tax regulations, the IRS has four main methods of assistance:

1. *Publications.* The IRS offers hundreds of free booklets and pamphlets. You can obtain these publications at a local IRS office, by mail request, or by a telephone call to the office listed in your tax packet or your local telephone directory. Especially helpful is *Your Federal Income Tax* (IRS Publication 17). You may obtain IRS publications and tax forms by calling 1–800–TAX–FORM or online at www.irs.gov.

2. *Recorded messages.* The IRS Tele-Tax system allows you access to about 150 telephone tax tips covering everything from filing requirements to reporting gambling income. Your push-button phone gives you 24-hour-a-day access to

**EXHIBIT 4-8**

Tax-Planner
Calendar

| January | February | March |
|---|---|---|
| • Establish a recordkeeping system for your tax information<br>• If you expect a refund, file your tax return for the previous year<br>• Make your final estimated quarterly payment for the previous year for income not covered by withholding | • Check to make sure you received W-2 and 1099 forms from all organizations from which you had income during the previous year; these should have been received by January 31; if not, contact the organization | • Organize your records and tax information in preparation for filing your tax return; if you expect a refund, file as soon as possible |

| April | May | June |
|---|---|---|
| • April 15 is the deadline for filing your federal tax return; if it falls on a weekend, you have until the next business day (usually Monday)<br>• If necessary, file for an automatic extension for filing your tax forms | • Review your tax return to determine whether any changes in withholding, exemptions, or marital status have not been reported to your employer | • The second installment for estimated tax is due June 15 for income not covered by withholding |

| July | August | September |
|---|---|---|
| • With the year half over, consider or implement plans for a personal retirement program such as an IRA or a Keogh | • Tax returns are due August 15 for those who received the automatic four-month extension | • The third installment for estimated tax is due September 15 for income not covered by withholding |

| October | November | December |
|---|---|---|
| • Determine the tax benefits of selling certain investments by year-end<br>• Prepare a preliminary tax form to determine the most advantageous filing status | • Make any last-minute changes in withholding by your employer to avoid penalties for too little withholding<br>• Determine if you qualify for an IRA; if so, consider opening one | • Determine if it would be to your advantage to make payments for next year before December 31 of the current year<br>• Decide if you can defer income for the current year until the following year |

NOTE: Children born before the end of the year give you a full-year exemption, so plan accordingly!

this recorded information. Telephone numbers can be found in your tax packet or your telephone directory, or call 1–800–829–4477.

3. *Phone hot line.* You can obtain information about specific problems through an IRS-staffed phone line. The appropriate telephone number is listed in your local telephone directory, or call 1–800–829–1040. You are not asked to give your name when you use this service, so your questions are anonymous.

4. *Walk-in service.* You can visit your local or district IRS office to obtain assistance with your taxes. More than 500 of these facilities are available to taxpayers. Be

## Financial Planning for Life's Situations

### ONLINE TAX PLANNING

Various tax activities are made easier and faster with the Web. These include:

- *Tax planning.* Information on current tax laws and suggestions for reducing taxes may be obtained at www.personalwealth.com, www.intelligenttaxes.com, and www.quicken.com.
- *Obtaining tax forms.* Federal tax forms and tax tips are available at www.irs.gov., www.1040.com. and www.taxweb.com.
- *Preparing your tax return.* Information about software that you can use to prepare your federal

and state income tax returns may be accessed at www.turbotax.com and www.taxcut.com.

- *Filing your tax return.* E-filing may be done by contacting www.taxsoft.com.
- *Current tax developments.* Developments regarding tax news, important filing dates, and other tax suggestions are available at www.tax.org, www.taxprophet.com, and www.taxlogic.com.
- *Obtaining state tax information.* State income tax information and forms are available at www.intelligenttaxes.com, www.taxworld.org and www.tax-admin.org.

aware, however, that information IRS employees provide is not always reliable. Various studies in recent years have reported incorrect answers over 30 percent of the time. You can be held liable for taxes owed even if you based your calculations on information provided by IRS employees.

5. *CD-ROM.* The Internal Revenue Service also sells a CD-ROM with over 2,000 tax forms and publications.

In addition, the IRS has videos, free speakers for community groups, and teaching materials for schools to assist taxpayers.

### Tax Publications

Each year, several tax guides are published and offered for sale. These publications include *J. K. Lasser's Your Income Tax* and *Consumer Reports Books Guide to Income Tax Preparation.* You can purchase them at bookstores, drugstores, or supermarkets or use them at your library.

### The Internet

As with other personal finance topics, extensive information may be found on the Internet, especially the World Wide Web. The Internal Revenue Service (www.irs.gov) is a good starting point. Personal finance magazines, such as *Kiplinger's Personal Finance Magazine* and *Money,* as well as other financial planning information services, offer a variety of tax information. In addition, the websites of companies that sell tax software and tax-related organizations can be useful (see the Financial Planning for Life's Situations box).

### Tax Preparation Software and Electronic Filing

More and more taxpayers are using personal computers for tax recordkeeping and tax form preparation. A spreadsheet program can be very helpful in maintaining and updating tax data on various income and expense categories. Software packages such as *Tax-Cut* and *TurboTax* allow you to complete needed tax forms and schedules and either print for mailing or file online. See www.turbotax.com or www.taxcut.com for additional information.

## JONATHAN HOENIG SPEAKS ON TAX PLANNING

Any attempt to calculate your investment return must include the least exciting, most annoying financial subject: taxes. Even the word makes me cringe!

The government *will* get their share of your money—no exceptions. Smart tax planning helps you pay less tax legally. The federal government isn't fooling around: Those who avoid paying taxes get socked with high-priced penalties or jail time. Pay your taxes on time.

Toward the first of the year, you will begin to receive a series of statements from the jobs at which you have worked or financial institutions where you hold accounts. This includes brokerage firms, banks, mutual funds, and other intermediaries. Scrounge up the receipts from any charitable donations you've made (canceled checks are OK) and proof of any work-related expenses you plan on writing off. Keep these materials together: Lost forms waste time and money!

Form 1040 has several sections to be aware of. "Filing Status" determines the filing category in which you belong. Married? Single? Each category has a particular schedule of taxes. Generally, your income should be added up, including any losses. Figure your taxable income, factor in additional credits or taxes, and write a check. *You've just paid your taxes!*

For those with a home business, complicated returns, or sketchy paperwork, some professional tax guidance is highly recommended—*and worth it!* Spending some money on a tax preparer or CPA might seem daunting, but will ensure that your return is filed accurately and rapidly.

The average cost (including postage, copies, books, software, and phone) for filing a federal tax return is over $80. In addition, Americans spend over 5 billion hours each year preparing federal tax forms. Between 1984 and 1999, the number of federal tax forms increased by more than 100.

The IRS has been expanding its acceptance of computer-readable tax forms. Electronic filing of federal taxes now exceeds 30 million returns annually. With electronic filing, taxpayers have received their refunds within three weeks. The additional cost tax preparers charge for this service is usually between $15 and $70. The IRS also allows filing of tax returns through various websites.

Telefile is a file-by-phone system that has been tested in various geographic areas. It allows taxpayers to call a toll-free number, using a touch-tone phone, to file their tax returns. A follow-up written or voice "signature" confirmation is required.

## Tax Preparation Services

Over 40 million U.S. taxpayers pay someone to do their income taxes. The fee for this service can range from $40 at a tax preparation service for a simple return to more than $2,000 to a certified public accountant for a complicated return.

Many people do their own taxes. This experience can help you improve your understanding of your financial situation. The average person takes about 3½ hours to complete Form 1040, compared with about an hour for Form 1040A and under 30 minutes for the one-page 1040EZ. Doing your own taxes, however, can be complicated, particularly if you have sources of income other than salary. The sources available for professional tax assistance include the following:

- Tax services range from local, one-person operations to national firms with thousands of offices, such as H&R Block.
- Enrolled agents—government-approved tax experts—prepare returns and provide tax advice. You may contact the National Association of Enrolled Agents at 1–800–424–4339 for information about enrolled agents in your area.
- Many accountants offer tax assistance along with other business services. A certified public accountant (CPA) with special training in taxes can help with tax planning and the preparation of your annual tax return.
- Attorneys usually do not complete tax returns; however, you can use an attorney's services when you are involved in a tax-related transaction or when you have a difference of opinion with the IRS.

Even if you hire a professional tax preparer, you are responsible for supplying accurate and complete information. Hiring a tax preparer will not guarantee that you pay the *correct* amount. A study conducted by *Money* magazine of 41 tax preparers reported fees ranging from $375 to $3,600, with taxes due ranging from $31,846 to $74,450 for the same fictional family. If you owe more tax because your return contains errors or you have made entries that are not allowed, it is your responsibility to pay that additional tax, plus any interest and penalties.

Beware of tax preparers and other businesses that offer your refund in advance. These "refund anticipation loans" frequently charge very high interest rates for this type of consumer credit. Studies reveal interest rates sometimes exceeding 300 percent (on an annualized basis).

**Sheet 21**

## What If Your Return Is Audited?

*tax audit*   A detailed examination of your tax return by the Internal Revenue Service.

The Internal Revenue Service reviews all returns for completeness and accuracy. If you make an error, your tax is automatically refigured and you receive either a bill or a refund. If you make an entry that is not allowed, you will be notified by mail. A **tax audit** is a detailed examination of your tax return by the IRS. In most audits, the IRS requests more information to support the entries on your tax return. Be sure to keep accurate records to support your return. Keep receipts, canceled checks, and other evidence to prove amounts that you claim. Avoiding common filing mistakes (see Exhibit 4–9) helps to minimize your chances of an audit.

### Who Gets Audited?
Just under 1.3 percent of all tax filers—about 1.5 million people—are audited each year. While the IRS does not reveal its basis for auditing returns, several indicators are evident. People who claim large or unusual deductions increase their chances of an audit.

Tax advisers suggest including a brief explanation or a copy of receipts for deductions that may be questioned. Individuals with high incomes who report large losses due to tax shelters or partnerships, or who have had their tax returns questioned in the past, may also be targeted for an audit.

### Types of Audits
The simplest and most common type of audit is the *correspondence audit*. This mail inquiry requires you to clarify or document minor questions about your tax return. You usually have 30 days to provide the requested information.

The *office audit* requires you to visit an IRS office to clarify some aspect of your tax return. This type of audit usually takes an hour or two.

- Organize all tax-related information for easy access.
- Follow instructions carefully. Many people deduct total medical and dental expenses rather than the amount of these expenses that exceeds 7.5 percent of adjusted gross income.
- Use the proper tax rate schedule or tax table column.
- Be sure to claim the correct number of exemptions and the correct amounts of standard deductions.
- Consider the alternative minimum tax that may apply to your situation. Be sure to pay self-employment tax and tax on early IRA withdrawals.
- Check your arithmetic several times.
- Sign your return (both spouses must sign a joint return), or the IRS won't process it.
- Be sure to include the correct Social Security number(s) and to record amounts on the correct lines.
- Attach necessary documentation such as your W-2 forms and required supporting schedules.
- Put your Social Security number, the tax year, and a daytime telephone number on your check—and be sure to sign the check!
- Make the check payable to "U.S. Treasury," and include your Social Security number on your check.
- Keep a photocopy of your return.
- Put the proper postage on your mailing envelope.
- Finally, check everything again—and file on time! Care taken when you file your income tax can result in "many happy returns."

The *field audit* is more complex. An IRS agent visits you at your home, your business, or the office of your accountant so you have access to records. A field audit may be done to verify whether an individual has an office in the home as claimed.

**Your Audit Rights**   When you receive an audit notice, you have the right to request time to prepare. Also, you can ask the IRS for clarification of items being questioned. When you are audited, use the following suggestions:

- Decide whether you will bring your tax preparer, accountant, or lawyer.
- Be on time for your appointment; bring only relevant documents.
- Present tax records and receipts in a logical, calm, and confident manner; maintain a positive attitude.
- Make sure the information you present is consistent with the tax law.
- Keep your answers aimed at the auditor's questions. Answer questions clearly and completely. Be as brief as possible; you can never tell an auditor too little.

People under stress tend to talk too much. IRS auditors are trained to create silence and listen in case the taxpayer blurts out damaging information. The five best responses to questions during the audit are "Yes," "No," "I don't recall," "I'll have to check on that," and "What specific items do you want to see?"

If you disagree with the results of an audit, you may request a conference at the Regional Appeals Office. Although most differences of opinion are settled at this stage, some taxpayers take their cases further. A person may go to the U.S. tax court, the U.S. claims court, or the U.S. district court. Some tax disputes have gone to the U.S. Supreme Court.

## Concept Check 4-4

1. What are the main sources available to help people prepare their taxes?
2. What actions can reduce the chances of an IRS audit?
3. What appeal process do taxpayers have if they disagree with an audit decision of the IRS?

## TAX PLANNING STRATEGIES

### Obj. 5

Select appropriate tax strategies for different financial and personal situations.

*tax avoidance*   The use of legitimate methods to reduce one's taxes.

*tax evasion*   The use of illegal actions to reduce one's taxes.

Most people want to pay their fair share of taxes—no more, no less. They do this by practicing **tax avoidance,** the use of legitimate methods to reduce one's taxes. In contrast, **tax evasion** is the use of illegal actions to reduce one's taxes. To minimize taxes owed, follow these guidelines:

- If you expect to have the *same* or a *lower* tax rate next year, *accelerate deductions* into the current year. Pay real estate property taxes or make your January mortgage payment in December. Make charitable donations by December 31.
- If you expect to have a *lower* or the *same* tax rate next year, *delay the receipt of income* until next year. This means income will be taxed at a lower rate or at a later date.
- If you expect to have a *higher* tax rate next year, consider *delaying deductions,* since they will have a greater benefit. A $1,000 deduction at 28 percent lowers your taxes $280; at 31 percent, your taxes are lowered $310.
- If you expect to have a *higher* tax rate next year, *accelerate the receipt of income* to have it taxed at the current lower rate.

As Exhibit 4–10 shows, people in different life situations can take advantage of various tax rules. When considering financial decisions in relation to your taxes, remember that purchasing, investing, and retirement planning are the areas most heavily affected by tax laws.

### Consumer Purchasing

The buying decisions most directly affected by taxes are the purchase of a residence, the use of credit, and job-related expenses.

**Place of Residence**   Owning a home is one of the best tax shelters. Both real estate property taxes and interest on the mortgage are deductible (as itemized deductions) and thus reduce your taxable income. While renting may seem less expensive than owning, the after-tax cost of owning a home often makes owning financially advantageous. Chapter 9 presents specific calculations for comparing renting and buying.

**Consumer Debt**   Current tax laws allow homeowners to borrow for consumer purchases. You can deduct interest on loans (of up to $100,000) secured by your primary or secondary home up to the actual dollar amount you have invested in it—the difference between the market value of the home and the amount you owe on it. These *home equity loans,* which are *second mortgages,* are discussed in greater detail in Chapters 6 and 9. Current tax laws allow you to use that line of credit to buy a car, consolidate credit card or other debts, or finance other personal expenses. Some states place restrictions on home equity loans.

## Did You Know

**?** Each year, over 90,000 taxpayers do not receive their refunds. The undeliverable checks total over $60 million, an average of more than $600 per check. These refund checks were returned by the post office because it was unable to deliver them. Taxpayers due a refund may contact the IRS at 1–800–829–1040.

## EXHIBIT 4-10   Special Tax Situations

| | |
|---|---|
| Business in your home | • You may deduct any ordinary and necessary expenses related to starting and maintaining your business, including a portion of your rent or mortgage if that portion of your home is used exclusively for business. It must be your principal place of business. (Individuals who are employed elsewhere and claim an office at home are likely to be challenged by the IRS on this deduction.) |
| Divorced persons | • Child support payments have no tax consequences. They are neither deductible by the payer nor included in the recipient's income. Alimony is tax deductible by the payer and must be included as income by the recipient. Exemptions for children are generally claimed by the parent who has custody for a longer period during the tax year. |
| Single parents | • A single parent may claim "head of household" filing status, which has greater advantages than "single" status. Working parents may qualify for a child care tax credit. Low-income families may qualify for the earned-income credit (EIC). |
| Retired persons | • Individuals over age 59½ may withdraw tax-deferred funds from a retirement plan without penalty. Of course, these funds must be reported as ordinary income. As of 1999, retirees with total incomes, including Social Security, exceeding $44,000 (couples) and $34,000 (others) pay income tax on up to 85 percent of their Social Security benefits. Those with incomes between $25,000 and $34,000 (singles) or $32,000 and $44,000 (couples) continue to be taxed on up to 50 percent of their benefits. |

NOTE: Individual circumstances and changes in the tax laws can affect these examples.

A person may also claim a deduction for interest expense on qualified education loans. This deduction is allowed only for interest paid during the first 60 months in which interest payments are required.

### Job-Related Expenses

As previously mentioned, certain work expenses, such as union dues, some travel and education costs, and business tools, may be included as itemized deductions. Job search expenses are also deductible if you incur them when seeking employment in your current occupational category. Such expenses may include transportation to interviews, résumé preparation and duplication, and employment agency or career counseling fees. Remember, only the portion of these expenses that exceeds 2 percent of adjusted gross income is deductible. Expenses related to finding your first job or obtaining work in a different field are not deductible.

### Investment Decisions

A major area of tax planning involves the wide variety of decisions related to investing.

### Tax-Exempt Investments

Interest income from municipal bonds, which are issued by state and local governments, and other tax-exempt investments is not subject to federal income taxes. While municipal bonds have lower interest rates than other investments, the *after-tax* income may be higher. For example, if you are in the 28 percent tax bracket, earning $100 of tax-exempt income would be worth more to you than earning $125 in taxable investment income. The $125 would have an after-tax value of $90: $125 less $35 (28 percent of $125) for taxes.

## Financial Planning Calculations

### SHORT-TERM AND LONG-TERM CAPITAL GAINS

You will pay a lower tax rate on the profits from stocks and other investments if you hold the asset for more than 18 months. As of 1999, a taxpayer in the 28 percent tax bracket would pay $280 in taxes on a $1,000 short-term capital gain (assets held for less than 18 months). However, that same taxpayer would pay only $200 on the $1,000 (a 20 percent capital gains tax) if the investment were held for more than 18 months.

| | Short-Term Capital Gain (assets held less than 18 months) | Long-Term Capital Gain (assets held 18 months or more) |
|---|---|---|
| Capital gain | $1,000 | $1,000 |
| Capital gains tax rate | 28% | 20% |
| Capital gains tax | $280 | $200 |
| Tax savings | | $80 |

Tax-Deferred Investments    Although, from a tax standpoint, tax-deferred investments, whose income will be taxed at a later date, are less beneficial than tax-exempt investments, they also have financial advantages. According to basic opportunity cost, paying a dollar in the future instead of today gives you the opportunity to invest (or spend) it now. Examples of tax-deferred investments include

- *Tax-deferred annuities,* usually issued by insurance companies. These investments are discussed in Chapter 19.
- *Series EE U.S. Treasury bonds.* Interest on these bonds is exempt from federal income tax if it is used to pay tuition at a college, university, or qualified technical school. Chapter 5 gives further details.
- *Retirement plans* such as IRA, Keogh, or 401(k) plans. The next section discusses the tax implications of these plans.

*capital gains* Profits from the sale of a capital asset such as stocks, bonds, or real estate.

**Capital gains,** profits from the sale of a capital asset such as stocks, bonds, or real estate, are also tax deferred; you do not have to pay the tax on these profits until the asset is sold. In recent years, *long-term* capital gains (on investments held more than 18 months) have been taxed at 20 percent. Certain assets, however, such as art, antiques, stamps, and other collectibles, are still taxed at the pre-1997 capital gains rate—28 percent. Starting in 2001, the capital gains tax rate on assets held for more than five years will be 18 percent.

*Short-term* capital gains (on investments held for less than 18 months) are taxed as ordinary income (see the Financial Planning Calculations box). Taxpayers in the 15 percent tax bracket have lower capital gains tax rates for both short-term and long-term investments.

The sale of an investment for less than its purchase price is, of course, a *capital loss.* Capital losses can be used to offset capital gains and up to $3,000 of ordinary income. Unused capital losses may be carried forward into future years to offset capital gains or ordinary income up to $3,000 per year.

Capital gains of $500,000 on the sale of a home may be excluded by a couple filing a joint return ($250,000 for singles). This exclusion is allowed each time a taxpayer sells or exchanges a principal residence—however, only once every two years.

### Self-Employment

Owning your own business has certain tax advantages. Self-employed persons may deduct expenses such as health and life insurance as business costs. However, business owners have to pay self-employment tax (Social Security) in addition to the regular tax rate.

### Children's Investments

In past years, parents made investments on their children's behalf and listed the children as owners. This process, known as *income shifting*, attempted to reduce the taxable income of parents by shifting the ownership of investments to children in lower tax brackets. A child under 14 with investment income of more than $1,300 is taxed at the parent's top rate. For investment income under $1,300, the child receives a deduction of $650 and the next $650 is taxed at his or her own rate, which is probably lower than the parent's rate. This income-shifting restriction does not apply to children 14 and older, so it is possible to take advantage of income shifting with them.

## Retirement Plans

A major tax strategy of benefit to working people is the use of tax-deferred retirement plans such as individual retirement arrangements (IRAs), Keogh plans, and 401(k) plans.

### Traditional IRA

When IRAs were first established, every working person was allowed to deduct up to $2,000 per year for IRA contributions. The contributions to and earnings from these accounts are not taxed until they are withdrawn. Today a regular IRA deduction is available only to people who do not participate in employer-sponsored retirement plans and have an adjusted gross income under a certain amount. In 1999, this amount was $41,000 for single taxpayers and $61,000 for jointly filing taxpayers. These amounts are scheduled to increase over the next 10 years.

In general, amounts withdrawn from deductible IRAs are included in gross income. An additional 10 percent penalty is usually imposed on withdrawals made before age 59½ unless the withdrawn funds are on account of death or disability, for medical expenses, or for qualified higher education expenses.

### Roth IRA

The Roth IRA (also called the IRA Plus) allows a $2,000 annual contribution which is not tax deductible; however, the earnings on the account are tax free after five years. The funds from the Roth IRA may be withdrawn before age 59½ if the account owner is disabled, for educational expenses, or for the purchase of a first home. Like the regular IRA, the Roth IRA is limited to people with an adjusted gross income under a certain amount.

Deductible IRAs provide tax relief up front as contributions reduce current taxes. However, taxes must be paid when the withdrawals are made from the deductible IRA. In contrast, the Roth IRA does not have immediate benefits, but the investment grows in value on a tax-free basis. Withdrawals from the Roth IRA are exempt from federal and state taxes.

### Education IRA

The Education IRA is designed to assist parents in saving for the college education of their children. Once again, the annual contribution (limited to $500) is not tax deductible and is limited to taxpayers with an adjusted gross income under a certain amount. However, as with the Roth IRA, the earnings accumulate tax free.

Keogh Plan    If you are self-employed and own your own business, you can establish a Keogh plan. This retirement plan, also called an HR10 plan, may combine a profit-sharing plan and a pension plan of other investments purchased by the employee. In general, with a Keogh, people may contribute 25 percent of their annual income, up to a maximum of $30,000, to this tax-deferred retirement plan.

401(k) Plan    The part of the tax code called 401(k) authorizes a tax-deferred retirement plan sponsored by an employer. This plan allows you to contribute a greater tax-deferred amount (a maximum of $10,000 for 1999) than you can contribute to an IRA. However, most companies set a limit on your contribution, such as 15 percent of your salary. Many employers provide a matching contribution in their 401(k) plans. For example, a company may contribute 50 cents for each $1 contributed by an employee. This results in an immediate 50 percent return on your investment.

Tax planners advise people to contribute as much as possible to a Keogh or 401(k) plan since (1) the increased value of the investment accumulates on a tax-free basis until the funds are withdrawn and (2) contributions reduce your adjusted gross income for computing your current tax liability. Chapter 18 discusses these retirement plans in greater detail.

## Changing Tax Strategies

Sheet 22

Someone once said that "death and taxes are the only certainties of life." Changing tax laws seem to be another certainty. Each year, the IRS modifies the tax form and filing procedures. In addition, Congress frequently passes legislation that changes the tax code. These changes require that you regularly determine how to take best advantage of the tax laws for personal financial planning. Finally, carefully consider changes in your personal situation and your income level. You should carefully monitor your personal tax strategies to best serve both your daily living needs and your long-term financial goals.

### Concept Check 4–5

1.  How does tax avoidance differ from tax evasion?
2.  What common tax-saving methods are available to most individuals and households?

## Summary of Objectives

Obj. 1    **Describe the importance of taxes for personal financial planning.**

Tax planning can influence spending, saving, borrowing, and investing decisions. A knowledge of tax laws and maintenance of accurate tax records allow you to take advantage of appropriate tax benefits. An awareness of income taxes, sales taxes, excise taxes, property taxes, estate taxes, inheritance taxes, gift taxes, and Social Security taxes is vital for successful financial planning.

Obj. 2    **Calculate taxable income and the amount owed for federal income tax.**

Taxable income is determined by subtracting adjustments to income, deductions, and allowances for exemptions from gross income. Your total tax liability is based on the published tax tables or tax schedules, less any tax credits.

Obj. 3    **Prepare a federal income tax return.**

The major sections of Form 1040 require you to calculate (1) your filing status, (2) exemptions, (3) income from all sources, (4) adjustments to your income, (5) standard deduction or itemized deductions, (6) tax credits for which you qualify, (7) other taxes you owe, (8) amounts you have withheld or paid in advance, and (9) your refund or the additional amount you owe.

## Obj. 4   Identify tax assistance sources.

The main sources of tax assistance are IRS services and publications, other publications, the Internet, computer software, and professional tax preparers such as commercial tax services, enrolled agents, accountants, and attorneys.

## Obj. 5   Select appropriate tax strategies for different financial and personal situations.

You may reduce your tax burden through careful planning and making financial decisions related to consumer purchasing, the use of debt, investments, and retirement planning.

## Financial Planning Problems

1. *Computing Taxable Income.* Thomas Franklin arrived at the following tax information:

   Gross salary, $41,780
   Interest earnings, $225
   Dividend income, $80
   One personal exemption, $2,650
   Itemized deductions, $3,890
   Adjustments to income, $1,150

   What amount would Thomas report as taxable income? (Obj. 1)

2. *Determining Tax Deductions.* If Lola Harper had the following itemized deductions, should she use Schedule A or the standard deduction? The standard deduction for her tax situation is $6,050. (Obj. 2)

   Donations to church and other charities, $1,980
   Medical and dental expenses exceeding 7.5 percent of adjusted gross income, $430
   State income tax, $690
   Job-related expenses exceeding 2 percent of adjusted gross income, $1,610

3. *Calculating Average Tax Rate.* What would be the average tax rate for a person who paid taxes of $4,864.14 on a taxable income of $39,870? (Obj. 2)

4. *Determining a Refund or Taxes Owed.* Based on the following data, would Ann and Carl Wilton receive a refund or owe additional taxes? (Obj. 2)

   Adjusted gross income, $43,190
   Itemized deductions, $11,420

   Child care tax credit, $80
   Federal income tax withheld, $6,784
   Amount for personal exemptions, $7,950
   Tax rate on taxable income, 15 percent

5. *Selecting Federal Tax Forms.* Which 1040 form should each of the following individuals use? (Obj. 3)
   a. A high school student with an after-school job and interest earnings of $480 from savings accounts.
   b. A college student who, due to ownership of property, is able to itemize deductions rather than take the standard deduction.
   c. A young, entry-level worker with no dependents and income only from salary.

6. *Using Federal Tax Tables.* Using the tax table in Exhibit 4–7 (p. 113), determine the amount of taxes for the following situations:
   a. A head of household with taxable income of $26,210.
   b. A single person with taxable income of $26,888.
   c. A married person filing a separate return with taxable income of $26,272. (Obj. 3)

7. *Comparing Taxes on Investments.* Would you prefer a fully taxable investment earning 10.7 percent or a tax-exempt investment earning 8.1 percent? Why? (Obj. 5)

8. *Future Value of a Tax Savings.* On December 30, you decide to make a $1,000 charitable donation. If you are in the 28 percent tax bracket, how much will you save in taxes for the current year? If you deposit that tax savings in a savings account for the next five years at 8 percent, what will be the future value of that account? (Obj. 5)

## Financial Planning Activities

1. *Searching the Internet for Tax Information.* Using websites such as S&P *Personal Wealth* at www.personalwealth.com, *Kiplinger's Personal Finance Magazine* at www.kiplinger.com, or *Money* magazine at www. money. com, or library resources, obtain information about the tax implications of various financial planning decisions. (Obj. 1)

2. *Researching Tax-Exempt Income.* Using library resources or the World Wide Web, determine the types of income that are exempt from federal income tax. (Obj. 2)

3. *Planning Your Tax Payment.* Survey several people about whether they get a federal tax refund or owe taxes each year. Obtain information about the following: *(a)* Do they usually get a refund or owe taxes when they file their

federal tax return? *(b)* Is their situation (refund or payment) planned? *(c)* What are the reasons they want to get a refund each year? *(d)* Are there situations where getting a refund may not be a wise financial decision?   (Obj. 2)

4. *Researching Current Tax Forms.* Obtain samples of current tax forms you would use to file your federal income tax return. These may be ordered by mail, obtained at a local IRS office or post office, or obtained on the Internet at www.irs.gov.   (Obj. 4)

5. *Researching Tax Questions.* Use IRS publications and other reference materials to answer a specific tax question. Contact an IRS office to obtain an answer for the same question. What differences, if any, exist between the information sources?   (Obj. 4)

6. *Analyzing Tax Preparation Software.* Visit a retailer that sells tax preparation software, such as www.turbotax.

com, or visit the websites of software companies to determine the costs and features of programs you may use to prepare and file your federal income tax return.   (Obj. 4)

7. *Reducing Tax Errors.* Create a visual presentation (video or slide presentation) that demonstrates actions a person might take to reduce errors when filing a federal tax return.   (Obj. 4)

8. *Comparing Tax Services.* Using Sheet 21 in the *Personal Financial Planner,* obtain information from two different tax preparation companies about the services they offer and the costs of their services.   (Obj. 4)

9. *Determining Tax Planning Activities.* Survey friends and relatives about their tax planning strategies. You may use Sheet 22 from the *Personal Financial Planner* to obtain questions for your survey.   (Obj. 5)

# LIFE SITUATION CASE

## A SINGLE FATHER'S TAX SITUATION

Ever since his wife's death, Eric Stanford has faced difficult personal and financial circumstances. His job provides him with a fairly good income but keeps him away from his daughters, ages 8 and 10, nearly 20 days a month. This requires him to use in-home child care services that consume a large portion of his income. Since the Stanfords live in a small apartment, this arrangement has been very inconvenient.

Due to the costs of caring for his children, Eric has only a minimal amount withheld from his salary for federal income taxes. This makes more money available during the year, but for the last few years he has had to make large payments in April—another financial burden.

Although Eric has created an investment fund for his daughters' college education and for his retirement, he has not sought to select investments that offer tax benefits. Overall, he needs to look at several aspects of his tax planning activities to find strategies that will best serve his current and future financial needs.

Eric has assembled the following information for the current tax year:

Earnings from wages, $42,590
Interest earned on savings, $125
IRA deduction, $2,000

Checking account interest, $65
Three exemptions at $2,750 each
Current standard deduction for filing status, $6,350
Amount withheld for federal income tax, $3,178
Tax credit for child care, $400
Filing status: head of household

## Questions

1. What are Eric's major financial concerns in his current situation?
2. In what ways might Eric improve his tax planning efforts?
3. Is Eric typical of many people in our society with regard to tax planning? Why or why not?
4. What additional actions might Eric investigate with regard to taxes and personal financial planning?
5. Calculate the following
   *a.* What is Eric's taxable income? (Refer to Exhibit 4–1, page 100.)
   *b.* What is his total tax liability? (Use Exhibit 4–7, page 113.) What is his average tax rate?
   *c.* Based on his withholding, will Eric receive a refund or owe additional tax? What is the amount?

## INTERNET CASE   Online Tax Assistance

For decades, people have complained about preparing their federal income tax return. Either they bemoaned the time and effort needed to prepare their own return or they complained about the cost of having someone else prepare their return.

With the availability of information on the Internet, the tax preparation process has become faster, easier, and less expensive. However, taxpayers must still make a commitment to finding, learning, and using tax information.

Jan and Karl Mueller want to use the Web to save money on their taxes while preparing their federal tax return and filing online. The Muellers own their home and pay for child care. Each has an employee-sponsored retirement program.

### Questions

1. What types of tax information would you recommend the Muellers seek through a web search?
2. Locate specific websites that would meet the Muellers' tax information needs.
3. The Muellers have heard about people getting audited by the IRS. What information is available online to reduce the chance of being audited?
4. Based on web research, what things do the Muellers need to know about filing their federal tax return online? What websites can provide assistance with this process?

## Creating an E-Plan: Financial Decisions Using the Web

### TAX PLANNING ACTIVITIES

Taxes are a fact of financial planning. However, various actions can be taken to reduce the time and money that goes toward taxes.

Websites for Tax Planning

- Access to federal tax forms, IRS regulations, and other tax information at **www.irs.gov.**
- Tax planning suggestions from Ernst & Young at **www.ey.com/us/tax** and H&R Block at **www.hrblock.com.**
- Federal forms and tax tips at **www.1040.com, www.taxweb.com,** and **www.intelligenttaxes.com.**
- Preparing your tax form and filing online at **www.taxsoft.com.**
- Software information for TurboTax at **www.intuit.com/ turbotax.**
- State income tax information and forms at **www.taxadmin.org,** and **www.intelligentaxes.com.**

(Note: Addresses and content of websites change, and new sites are created daily. Use search engines discussed to update and locate websites for your current financial planning needs.)

*PFP sheets: 20–22*

Short-Term Financial Planning Activities

1. Develop a system for filing and storing various tax records related to income, deductible expenses, and current tax forms (see Exhibit 4–2).
2. Using the IRS and other websites, identify recent changes in tax laws that may affect your financial planning decisions.
3. Using current IRS tax forms and tax tables, estimate your tax liability for the current year (see PFP Sheet 20).
4. Compare the cost of tax preparation services (see PFP Sheet 21).

Long-Term Financial Planning Activities

1. Identify saving and investing decisions that would minimize future income taxes.
2. Develop a plan for actions to take related to your current and future tax situation (see PFP Sheet 22).

## Continuous Case for Part 1

### GETTING STARTED: PLANNING FOR THE FUTURE

Life Situation
Single; age 22; starting a career; no dependents

*Financial Goals*
- Evaluate current financial situation
- Establish a personal financial plan
- Develop a budgeting system for spending and savings

*Financial Data*

| | |
|---|---|
| Monthly income | $2,400 |
| Living expenses | 1,980 |
| Assets | 6,200 |
| Liabilities | 1,270 |
| Emergency fund | 300 |

While in college, Pam Jenkins worked part time and was never concerned about long-term financial planning. Rather than creating a budget, she used her checkbook and savings account (which usually had a very low balance) to handle her financial needs.

After completing college, Pam began her career as a sales representative for a clothing manufacturer located in California. After one year, her assets consist of a 1995 Chevrolet, a television set, a stereo, and some clothing and other personal belongs, with a total value of $6,200.

Since a portion of her income is based on commissions, her monthly income varies from one month to the next. This situation has made it difficult for Pam to establish a realistic budget. During lean months, she has had to resort to using her credit card to make ends meet. In fact, her credit card debt, $1,270, is her only liability at this time.

Her only other source of income is a large tax refund. In the past, she has always used tax refunds to finance major purchases (a vacation or furniture) or pay off credit card debt.

### Questions

1. What financial decisions should Pam be thinking about at this point in her life?
2. What are some short-term, intermediate, and long-term financial goals that Pam might want to develop?
3. How should Pam budget for fluctuations in her income caused by commission earnings?
4. Assume Pam's federal tax refund is $1,100. Given her current situation, what should she do with the refund?
5. Based on her life situation, what type of tax planning should Pam consider?

# MANAGING YOUR PERSONAL FINANCES

CHAPTER

# 5

# Banking Services: Savings Plans and Payment Accounts

Press One to Withdraw Cash...
Press Two to Deposit Cash...
Press Three for High Banking Fees!

Carter Yuma was visiting the cash machine near his place of work for the third time this week. "Wow! Another cash withdrawal," commented his friend Edwin. "You must have tons of money in that checking account."

"Well, not really," Carter confessed. "I can use this ATM card to access either my checking or savings account."

"You mean after you've used up everything in your checking account, you start taking money out of your savings?" asked Edwin. "Doesn't this machine make it too easy for you to overspend?"

"It's just that I've been very busy at work the last few weeks. I've been eating at restaurants a lot, and my cash is used up quickly," replied Carter.

A couple of weeks later, Carter received his bank statement, which included a couple of surprises. "Oh no!" he exclaimed. "Withdrawing cash from my checking account made me fall below the minimum balance for the account, so they charged me $8.50. My 11 cash withdrawals resulted in more fees. And what's this? Another charge for an overdraft! All those cash withdrawals and fees really hit me hard! And my savings account is down to $78!"

## Questions

1. What benefits and costs are associated with automatic teller machines?
2. How does the use of financial services like ATMs affect a person's overall financial plan?
3. What could Carter do to reduce his banking fees and manage his money more wisely?
4. Locate a website that provides information suggesting methods for reducing banking fees.

SOURCES: *ATMs: Always Taking Money,* April 1999, U.S. Public Interest Research Group, 218 D St., SE, Washington, DC 20003; Allison Kaplan, "Who Wants to Pay $300 for Convenience?" *Daily Herald* (Arlington Heights, IL), February 19, 1999, sec. 1, pp. 1, 11; Noelle Knox, "Her Money Gets Caught in the Net," *Chicago Sun-Times,* June 20, 1999, p. 53A; Robert Hershey, Jr., "At Banks, the Fees Just Keep on Coming," *The New York Times,* November 1, 1998, Business Section, p. 11; John Schmeltzer, "95% of Banks in Illinois Impose ATM Surcharges," *Chicago Tribune,* April 2, 1999, sec. 3, pp. 1, 4.

## Learning Objectives

Obj. 1 Analyze factors that affect selection and use of financial services.

Obj. 2 Compare the types of financial institutions.

Obj. 3 Compare the costs and benefits of various savings plans.

Obj. 4 Identify the factors used to evaluate different savings plans.

Obj. 5 Compare the costs and benefits of different types of checking accounts.

## A STRATEGY FOR MANAGING CASH

**Obj. 1**
Analyze factors that affect selection and use of financial services.

With over 11,000 banks, 2,000 savings and loan associations, and 12,000 credit unions, an extensive financial services market exists. These organizations provide a variety of services for your daily payment and savings needs. Today a trip to "the bank" may mean a visit to a credit union, an automatic teller machine in a shopping mall, or checking an account balance on the Web. In recent years, financial services have expanded. A bank is not the only source of checking accounts. Mortgages are available from several types of financial institutions.

While some financial decisions relate directly to goals, your daily activities require the use of financial services for various business transactions. Exhibit 5–1 provides an overview of financial services for managing cash flows and moving toward financial goals. In simplest terms, you can increase current savings only by spending less than you take in.

### Meeting Daily Money Needs

Buying groceries, paying the rent, and other routine spending activities require a cash management plan.

**Managing Cash**  Cash, check, credit card, or automatic teller machine (ATM) card are the common payment choices. While most people desire ease of payment, they must also consider fees and the potential for impulse buying and overspending. For example, in recent years ATM fees have risen from nothing to $1 or $2 per cash withdrawal and even higher charges for balance inquiries. If you are charged two $1 transaction fees a week and could invest your money at 5 percent, this convenience will cost you more than $570 over a five-year period.

Common mistakes made when managing current cash needs include

- Overspending as a result of impulse buying and using credit cards.
- Having insufficient liquid assets (cash, checking account) to pay current bills.
- Using savings or borrowing to pay for current expenses.
- Failing to put unneeded funds in an interest-earning savings account or investment plan to achieve long-term goals.

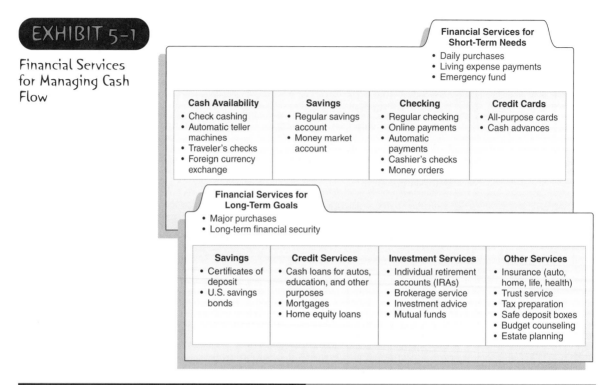

**EXHIBIT 5-1**

Financial Services for Managing Cash Flow

**Financial Services for Short-Term Needs**
- Daily purchases
- Living expense payments
- Emergency fund

**Cash Availability**
- Check cashing
- Automatic teller machines
- Traveler's checks
- Foreign currency exchange

**Savings**
- Regular savings account
- Money market account

**Checking**
- Regular checking
- Online payments
- Automatic payments
- Cashier's checks
- Money orders

**Credit Cards**
- All-purpose cards
- Cash advances

**Financial Services for Long-Term Goals**
- Major purchases
- Long-term financial security

**Savings**
- Certificates of deposit
- U.S. savings bonds

**Credit Services**
- Cash loans for autos, education, and other purposes
- Mortgages
- Home equity loans

**Investment Services**
- Individual retirement accounts (IRAs)
- Brokerage service
- Investment advice
- Mutual funds

**Other Services**
- Insurance (auto, home, life, health)
- Trust service
- Tax preparation
- Safe deposit boxes
- Budget counseling
- Estate planning

**Sources of Quick Cash**   No matter how carefully you manage your money, there may be times when you will need more cash than you currently have available. To cope with that situation, you have two basic choices: liquidate savings or borrow. A savings account, certificate of deposit, mutual fund, or other investment may be raided when you need funds. Alternatively, a credit card cash advance or a personal loan may be appropriate. Remember, however, that both using savings and increasing borrowing reduce your net worth and your potential to achieve long-term financial security.

## Types of Financial Services

Banks and other financial institutions offer services to meet a variety of needs. These services fall into four main categories.

**1. Savings**   Safe storage of funds for future use is a basic need for everyone. These services, commonly referred to as *time deposits,* include money in savings accounts and certificates of deposit. Selection of a savings plan is commonly based on the interest rate earned, liquidity, safety, and convenience. These factors are discussed later in the chapter.

**2. Payment Services**   The ability to transfer money to other parties is a necessary part of daily business activities. Checking accounts and other payment methods, commonly called *demand deposits,* are also covered later in the chapter.

**3. Borrowing**   Most people use credit at some time during their lives. Credit alternatives range from short-term accounts, such as credit cards and cash loans, to long-term borrowing, such as a home mortgage. Chapters 6 and 7 discuss the types and costs of credit.

## 4. Other Financial Services

Insurance protection, investment for the future, real estate purchases, tax assistance, and financial planning are additional services you may need for successful financial management. With some financial plans, someone else manages your funds. A **trust** is a legal agreement that provides for the management and control of assets by one party for the benefit of another. This type of arrangement is most commonly created through a commercial bank or a lawyer. Parents who want to set aside certain funds for their children's education may use a trust. The investments and money in the trust are managed by a bank, and the necessary amounts go to the children for their educational expenses. Trusts are covered in more detail in Chapter 19.

To simplify the maze of financial services and to attract customers, many financial institutions offer all-in-one accounts. An **asset management account,** also called a *cash management account,* provides a complete financial services program for a single fee. Investment brokers and other financial institutions offer this all-purpose account, which usually includes

- A minimum balance of $5,000, $10,000, or as much as $25,000.
- A checking account and an ATM card.
- An all-purpose credit card.
- A line of credit to obtain quick cash loans.
- Access to various types of investments such as stocks, bonds, mutual funds, commodities, and government securities; one account allows customers access to over 1,600 mutual funds.
- Online services for banking transactions and for investing.
- A *sweep,* a feature in which cash that is not needed in the checking account or invested earns a money market interest rate.
- A single monthly statement that summarizes all transactions and types of accounts.

Asset management accounts are offered by companies such as American Express (www.americanexpress.com) and Charles Schwab (www.schwab.com).

## Electronic Banking Services

Years ago, people had to conduct banking activities only during set business hours, usually nine in the morning to three in the afternoon. Today things are different. Several million Americans bank or pay bills online. Computerized financial services (see Exhibit 5–2) provide fast, convenient, and efficient systems for recording inflows and outflows of funds.

### Direct Deposit

Each year, more and more workers are receiving only a pay stub on payday. Their earnings are automatically deposited into checking or savings accounts. This process saves time, effort, and money. Government agencies are also increasing use of direct deposits to reduce costs. State and federal government checks going to contractors and to Social Security and welfare recipients are deposited electronically into the payees' bank accounts.

### Automatic Payments

Many utility companies, lenders, and other businesses allow customers to use an automatic payment system with bills paid through direct withdrawal from a bank account. Experts recommend that you stagger your payments based on when paychecks are received. This allows you to

---

*trust*   A legal agreement that provides for the management and control of assets by one party for the benefit of another.

*asset management account*   An all-in-one account that includes savings, checking, borrowing, investing, and other financial services for a single fee; also called a *cash management account.*

**Sheet 23**

**? Did You Know**

A study by the Federal Reserve Bank of St. Louis revealed that just over half of those surveyed have paychecks or benefits sent directly to their bank account through electronic direct deposit service. Only a third paid some of their bills through electronic payments. The study also revealed that 97 percent of the users of direct deposit are "extremely" or "very" satisfied with that service.

EXHIBIT 5-2

Electronic Banking
Transactions

pay bills in an orderly fashion while stabilizing your cash flow. Be sure to check bank statements regularly to ensure that the correct amounts have been deducted from your account. A minor error can result in an overdrawn account and expensive fees.

## Automatic Teller Machines

*automatic teller machine (ATM)* A computer terminal used to conduct banking transactions.

An **automatic teller machine (ATM)**, or simply *cash machine,* is a computer terminal that allows customers to conduct banking transactions. In addition, some ATMs sell bus passes, postage stamps, gift certificates, and mutual funds.

With more than 120,000 cash machines, most people are aware of ATM convenience. In addition to cash machines at banks, malls, and movie theaters, temporary ATMs are placed at sporting events, fairs, and community events.

*debit card* A plastic access card used in computerized banking transactions; also called a *cash card* or *ATM card.*

A **debit card** or *cash card,* activates ATM transactions and is linked to a bank account. A debit card is in contrast to a *credit card,* since you are spending existing funds rather than borrowing additional money. Using a debit card, along with your personal identification number (PIN), is similar to writing a check with the amount of the transaction (cash withdrawal or purchase) deducted from your bank account.

## ATM Fees

ATM convenience can be expensive. As the opening case points out, a person who uses an ATM several times a week can incur service charges of several hundred dollars a year. Surveys reveal that in casinos, ATM surcharges often add up to $3 to $5 per transaction. An ATM transaction on a cruise ship can cost $9 or more.

To reduce ATM fees, experts suggest that you

- Compare ATM fees at different financial institutions before opening an account. Get the fee schedule in writing.
- Use your own bank's ATM whenever possible to avoid surcharges imposed when using the ATM of another financial institution.

- Withdraw larger cash amounts, as needed, to avoid fees on several small transactions.
- Consider using personal checks, traveler's checks, credit cards, and prepaid cash cards when away from home.

### Lost Debit Cards

A lost or stolen debit card can be expensive. If you notify the financial institution within two days of losing the card, your liability for unauthorized use is $50. If you wait any longer, you can be liable for up to $500 of unauthorized use for up to 60 days; beyond that time, your liability is unlimited. However, some card issuers use the same rules for lost or stolen debit cards as used for credit cards: a $50 maximum.

You are not liable for unauthorized use if, for example, a con artist uses your account number to make a purchase. Reporting the fraud within 60 days of receiving your bank statement protects your right not to be charged for this transaction.

### Plastic Payments

While cash and checks are still very common methods of paying, various access cards are gaining in acceptance and use.

### 1. Point-of-Sale Transactions

ATM cards are accepted by many retail stores and restaurants. Your financial institution may issue two types of debit cards for these transactions. An *online card* operates like an ATM card, with an instant transfer of funds from your account. Online transactions require that you enter your secret personal identification number (PIN) to authorize the transaction.

*Offline card* transactions are processed like credit card charges; your PIN is not required. However, these transactions do not increase the amount owed. Instead, the funds are deducted from your bank account after a day or two.

**Did You Know?**

A national study of 336 banks found that more than 9 out of 10 banks charge consumers an ATM surcharge above the fee already charged by almost all banks for using another bank's ATM. This policy effectively doubles the cost of an ATM transaction. Consumers pay an average of $2.57 per ATM transaction at machines not owned by their own financial institution. (*Always Taking Money: A Fourth National Survey of ATM Surcharging Rates*, U.S. Public Interest Research Group, 218 D St., SE, Washington, DC 20003; website: www.pirg.org/consumer.)

### 2. Stored-Value Cards

Prepaid cards for buying telephone service, transit fares, highway tolls, laundry service, library fees, and school lunches are becoming very common. While some of these access cards, such as phone cards, are disposable (or become collector's items), others are reloadable "stored-value" cards.

At the 1996 Summer Olympics in Atlanta, cards in denominations of $10, $20, $50, and $100 were issued by Visa USA. The price of a purchase is subtracted by an electronic card reader in the store. The remaining value is stored in a microchip implanted in the card.

### 3. Smart Cards

"Smart cards," sometimes called "electronic wallets," look like ATM cards; however, they also include a microchip. This minicomputer stores prepaid amounts for buying goods and services. In addition, the card stores data about a person's account balances, transaction records, insurance information, and medical history. Smart cards are expected to see expanded use in the future as the services they offer increase.

### 4. Electronic Cash

CyberCash Inc. (www.cybercash.com) is one of the main contenders in the market that is developing electronic money. The company plans to create electronic replicas of all existing payment systems—cash, checks, credit cards, and coins.

EXHIBIT 5-3

Changing Interest
Rates and
Decisions
Related to
Financial
Services

**When interest rates are rising...**

- Use long-term loans to take advantage of current low rates
- Select short-term savings instruments to take advantage of higher rates when they mature

- Use short-term loans to take advantage of lower rates when you refinance the loans
- Select long-term savings instruments to "lock in" earnings at current high rates

**When interest rates are falling...**

## Opportunity Costs of Financial Services

When making decisions about spending and saving, consider the trade-off between current satisfaction and long-term financial security. In a similar manner, you consider opportunity cost—what you give up—when you evaluate, select, and use financial services. The money you save by shopping around for a low-cost checking account must be balanced against the value of the time you spend gathering information. Other common trade-offs related to financial services include the following:

- Higher returns of long-term savings and investment plans may be achieved at the cost of *low liquidity,* the inability to obtain your money quickly.
- The convenience of a 24-hour automatic teller machine or a bank branch office near your home or place of work must be weighed against service fees.
- The "no fee" checking account that requires a non-interest-bearing $500 minimum balance means lost interest of nearly $400 at 6 percent compounded over 10 years.

You should evaluate costs and benefits in both monetary and personal terms to choose the financial services that best serve your needs.

## Financial Services and Economic Conditions

Changing interest rates, rising consumer prices, and other economic factors also influence financial services. For successful financial planning, be aware of the current trends and future prospects for interest rates (see Exhibit 5–3 and the Financial Planning for Life's Situations box on page 137). You can learn about these trends and prospects by reading *The Wall Street Journal* (www.wsj.com), the business section of daily newspapers, and business periodicals such as *Business Week* (www.businessweek.com), *Forbes* (www.forbes.com), and *Fortune* (www.fortune.com).

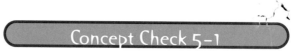

### Concept Check 5-1

1. What is the relationship between financial services and overall financial planning?
2. What are the major categories of financial services?
3. What financial services are available through electronic banking systems?
4. Why shouldn't you select financial services only on the basis of monetary factors?
5. How do changing economic conditions affect the use of financial services?

# Financial Planning for Life's Situations

## UNDERSTANDING INTEREST RATES

When people discuss higher or lower interest rates, they could be talking about one of many types of interest rates. Some interest rates refer to the cost of borrowing by a business; others refer to the cost of buying a home. Your awareness of various types of interest rates can help you plan your spending, saving, borrowing, and investing. The accompanying table describes the most commonly reported interest rates and gives their *annual average* for selected years.

Using the business section of a newspaper, *The Wall Street Journal*, the website of the Federal Reserve System (www.federalreserve.gov) or other business information sources, obtain current numbers for some or all of these interest rates. How might the current trend in interest rates affect your financial decisions?

|  | 1970 | 1975 | 1980 | 1985 | 1990 | 1995 | 1999 | Current |
|---|---|---|---|---|---|---|---|---|
| *Prime rate*—an indication of the rate banks charge large corporations | 7.91% | 7.85% | 15.26% | 9.93% | 10.01% | 8.83% | 8.00% | _____% |
| *Discount rate*—the rate financial institutions are charged to borrow funds from Federal Reserve banks | 5.95 | 6.25 | 11.77 | 7.69 | 6.98 | 5.21 | 4.62 | _____ |
| *T-bill rate*—the yield on short-term (13-week) U.S. government debt obligations | 6.39 | 5.78 | 11.43 | 7.48 | 7.51 | 5.51 | 4.66 | _____ |
| *Treasury bond rate*—the yield on long-term (30-year) U.S. government debt obligations | 6.86 | 8.19 | 11.39 | 10.97 | 8.61 | 6.88 | 5.87 | _____ |
| *Mortgage rate*—the amount individuals are paying to borrow for the purchase of a new home | 8.45 | 9.00 | 12.66 | 11.55 | 10.13 | 7.95 | 7.43 | _____ |
| *Corporate bond rate*—the cost of borrowing for large U.S. corporations | 8.04 | 8.83 | 11.94 | 11.37 | 9.32 | 7.59 | 7.05 | _____ |
| *Certificate of deposit rate*—the rate for six-month time deposits at savings institutions | 7.65 | 6.89 | 12.99 | 8.25 | 8.17 | 5.93 | 5.46 | _____ |

SOURCE: Federal Reserve Statistical Release: *Selected Interest Rates* (H-15), www.federalreserve.gov.

# TYPES OF FINANCIAL INSTITUTIONS

**Obj. 2**

Compare the types of financial institutions.

Many types of businesses, such as insurance companies, investment brokers, and credit card companies, have become involved in financial services previously limited to banks. Companies such as General Motors, Sears, and AT&T now issue or sponsor credit cards. Banks have also expanded their competitive efforts by opening offices that specialize in financial services such as investments, insurance, or real estate. Increased competition has brought about the opening of many limited-service offices, sometimes called *nonbanks*. These limited-service offices specialize in a particular banking activity, such as savings or personal loans.

EXHIBIT 5-4

Types of Financial
Institutions

| Deposit-Type Institutions | Nondeposit Institutions |
| --- | --- |
| • Commercial banks<br>• Savings and loan associations<br>• Mutual savings banks<br>• Credit unions | • Life insurance companies<br>• Investment companies<br>• Finance companies<br>• Mortgage companies<br>• Pawnshops<br>• Check-cashing outlets |

In contrast, *financial supermarkets* or *superbanks* offer a range of financial services. One advantage of financial supermarkets is the convenience of one-stop shopping. The trade-off for this convenience may be higher costs and less personalized service. Also, many of these financial institutions are not covered by federal deposit insurance.

Despite changes in the banking environment, many familiar financial institutions still serve your needs. Most of these institutions have expanded their services. As Exhibit 5–4 shows, financial institutions fall into two major categories: deposit-type institutions and nondeposit institutions.

## Deposit-Type Institutions

The financial institutions that most people use serve as intermediaries between suppliers (savers) and users (borrowers) of funds. These deposit-type institutions include commercial banks, savings and loan associations, mutual savings banks, and credit unions.

### Commercial Banks

A **commercial bank** offers a full range of financial services, including checking, savings, and lending, along with many other services. Commercial banks are organized as corporations, with individual investors (stockholders) contributing the capital the banks need to operate. National banks are chartered by the federal government and state banks by state governments. State-chartered banks are usually subject to fewer restrictions than federally chartered banks.

In recent years, some banks have opened full-service branch offices in grocery stores. These are truly "financial supermarkets," offering everything from automatic teller machines and loans to safe deposit boxes.

### Savings and Loan Associations

While the commercial bank traditionally served businesses and individuals with large amounts of money, the **savings and loan association (S&L)** specialized in savings accounts and loans for mortgages. In recent years, savings and loan associations have expanded their services to include checking accounts, specialized savings plans, loans to businesses, and other investment and financial planning services. Like banks, savings and loan associations have either federal or state charters.

### Mutual Savings Banks

Another financial institution that serves individuals is the **mutual savings bank,** which is owned by depositors and, like the traditional savings and loan association, specializes in savings accounts and mortgage loans. Mutual savings banks are located mainly in the northeastern United States. Unlike the profits

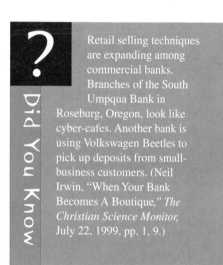

*commercial bank*
A financial institution that offers a full range of financial services to individuals, businesses, and government agencies.

*savings and loan association (S&L)*
A financial institution that traditionally specialized in savings accounts and mortgage loans.

*mutual savings banks*
A financial institution that is owned by depositors and specializes in savings accounts and mortgage loans.

of other types of financial institutions, the profits of a mutual savings bank go to the depositors, paying higher rates on savings.

## Credit Unions

*credit union*
A user-owned, nonprofit cooperative financial institution that is organized for the benefit of its members.

A **credit union** is a user-owned, nonprofit, cooperative financial institution. Traditionally, credit union members had to have a common bond such as work, church, or community affiliation. As the common bond restriction was loosened, the membership of credit unions increased. Today more than 10 million people belong to over 12,000 credit unions in the United States.

Each year, surveys conducted by consumer organizations and others report lower fees for checking accounts, lower loan rates, and higher levels of user satisfaction for credit unions compared to other financial institutions. Most credit unions offer credit cards, mortgages, home equity loans, direct deposit, cash machines, safe deposit boxes, and investment services.

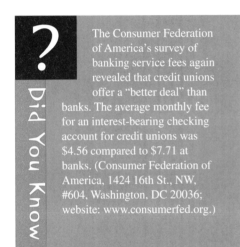

**Did You Know?** The Consumer Federation of America's survey of banking service fees again revealed that credit unions offer a "better deal" than banks. The average monthly fee for an interest-bearing checking account for credit unions was $4.56 compared to $7.71 at banks. (Consumer Federation of America, 1424 16th St., NW, #604, Washington, DC 20036; website: www.consumerfed.org.)

## Nondeposit Institutions

Financial services are also available from institutions such as life insurance companies, investment companies, finance companies, mortgage companies, pawnshops, and check-cashing outlets.

### Life Insurance Companies

While the main purpose of life insurance is to provide financial security for dependents, many life insurance policies contain savings and investment features. Chapter 12 discusses these policies. In recent years, life insurance companies have expanded their financial services to include investment and retirement planning.

### Investment Companies

Investment companies, also referred to as *mutual funds,* offer banking-type services. A common service of these organizations is the **money market fund,** a combination savings-investment plan in which the investment company uses your money to purchase a variety of short-term financial instruments. Your earnings are based on the interest the investment company receives. Unlike accounts at most banks, savings and loan associations, and credit unions, investment company accounts are not covered by federal deposit insurance.

*money market fund*
A savings-investment plan offered by investment companies, with earnings based on investments in various short-term financial instruments.

Investors in money market funds are usually allowed to write a limited number of checks on their accounts. This service gives the convenience of liquidity.

### Finance Companies

Making loans to consumers and small businesses is the main function of finance companies. These loans have short and intermediate terms with higher rates than most other lenders charge. Some finance companies have expanded their activities to offer other financial planning services.

### Mortgage Companies

Mortgage companies are organized primarily to provide loans to purchase homes. Chapter 9 discusses the activities of mortgage companies.

### Pawnshops

Pawnshops make loans based on the value of tangible possessions such as jewelry or other valuable items. Many low- and moderate-income families use these organizations to obtain cash loans quickly. Pawnshops charge higher fees than other financial institutions.

# Financial Planning for Life's Situations

## *BEWARE OF HIGH-COST FINANCIAL SERVICES*

Would you pay $8 to cash a $100 check? Or pay $20 to borrow $100 for two weeks? Many people without ready access to financial services (especially low-income consumers) commonly use the services of check-cashing outlets, pawnshops, payday loan stores, and rent-to-own centers. Offers of "quick cash" and "low payments" attract consumers without a bank account or credit cards.

*Pawnshops.*
Since 1988, the number of pawnshops has doubled to between 13,000 and 15,000. Despite a thriving economy in recent years, thousands of consumers are increasingly in need of small loans—usually $50 to $75, to be repaid in 30 to 45 days. Pawnshops have become the "neighborhood bankers" and the "local shopping malls," since they provide both lending and retail shopping services, selling items that owners do not redeem.

*Payday Loans.*
Debt Counselors of America and other organizations warn of increased use of *payday loans,* also referred to as *cash advances, check advance loans, postdated check loans,* and *delayed deposit loans.* Desperate borrowers pay annual interest rates of as much as 780 percent and more to obtain needed cash from payday loan companies. These enterprises have increased to more than 8,000 in the United States from 300 seven years ago. The most common users of payday loans are workers who have become trapped by debts run up by free spending or have been driven into debt by misfortune.

In a typical payday loan, a consumer writes a personal check for $115 to borrow $100 for 14 days. The payday lender agrees to hold the check until the next payday. This $15 finance charge for the 14 days translates into an annual percentage rate of 391 percent. Some consumers "roll over" their loans, paying another $15 for the $100 loan for the next 14 days. After a few

rollovers, the finance charge can exceed the amount borrowed. The Chicago Department of Consumer Services has reported annual rates ranging from 659 to 1,300 percent for some payday loans.

*Rent-to-Own Centers.*
Years ago, people who rented furniture and appliances found few deluxe items available. Today rental businesses offer big-screen televisions, seven-piece cherry-wood bedroom sets, and personal computers. Since 1992, annual revenues in the rental-purchase industry—defined as stores that lease products to consumers who can own the item if they complete a certain number of monthly or weekly payments—have increased 26 percent to $4.4 billion. An estimated 8,300 rental-purchase stores are in operation. About 30 percent of rental-purchase customers have household incomes below $24,000, and about 40 percent earn between $24,000 and $36,000.

In Wisconsin, more than 10,000 customers of the Rent-A-Center chain became part of a class action lawsuit seeking refunds of finance charges for rented merchandise. The suit accused the rental chain of illegally charging interest rates as high as 100 percent to rent televisions and other appliances, often to customers in low-income areas. The rental agreements were disguised as leases to get around a Wisconsin law that requires disclosure of any credit sale interest rate above 5 percent.

SOURCES: Genevieve Buck, "More Credence Lent as Pawn-shops Grow," *Chicago Tribune,* July 18, 1998, sec. 2, pp. 1–2; Consumer Federation of America, 1424 16th St., NW, #604, Washington, DC 20036; 202–387–6121; Debt Counselors of America, 1–800–680–3328 (www.dca.org); Dave Daley, "Rent-A-Center Suit Ruled Class-Action," *Milwaukee Journal Sentinel,* July 10, 1998, sec. B., p. 1; Peter T. Kilborn, "Payday Loans Drawing Many into a World of Onerous Fees," *The New York Times,* June 18, 1999, pp. A1, A20; Jennifer Lach, "This Space for Rent," *American Demographics,* August 1999, pp. 41–43.

## Check-Cashing Outlets

Most financial institutions will not cash a check unless the person has an account. The more than 6,000 check-cashing outlets (CCOs) charge anywhere from 1 to 20 percent of the face value of a check; the average cost is between 2 and 3 percent. However, for a low-income family, that can be a significant portion of the total household budget (see the accompanying "Financial Planning for Life's Situations" box).

CCOs offer a wide variety of services, including electronic tax filing, money orders, private postal boxes, utility bill payment, and the sale of bus and subway tokens. You can usually obtain most of these services for less at other locations.

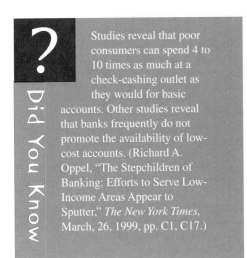

## Cyberbanking

Banking through the telephone, the personal computer, and online services continues to expand. Hundreds of banks now have "cyber" branches where customers can check balances, pay bills, transfer funds, compare savings plans, and apply for loans on the Internet. Wells Fargo (www.wellsfargo.com) and Bank of America (www.bankamerica.com) were two of the first banks to do business on the Web.

The Security First Network Bank (www.sfnb.com) was one of the first financial institutions to operate exclusively on the Internet. Access to all accounts and transactions is available 24 hours a day, seven days a week. (See the Financial Planning for Life's Situations box on page 142.)

## Comparing Financial Institutions

The basic concerns of a financial services customer are simple:

- Where can I get the best return on my savings?
- How can I minimize the cost of checking and payments services?
- Will I be able to borrow money when I need it?

As you use financial services, decide what you want from the organization that will serve your needs. With the financial marketplace constantly changing, you must assess the various services and other factors before selecting an organization (see Exhibit 5–5).

The services the financial institution offers are likely to be a major factor. Personal service is important to many customers. Convenience may be provided by business hours, branch offices, automatic teller machines, and online service. Convenience and service have a cost, so be sure to compare fees and other charges at several financial institutions.

Finally, you should consider safety factors and interest rates. Obtain information about earnings you will receive on savings and checking accounts and the rate you will pay for borrowed funds. Most financial institutions have deposit insurance to protect customers against losses; however, not all of them are insured by federal government programs. Investigate the type of protection you will have.

**How Should You Choose a Financial Institution?**

- Services offered
- Rates
- Fees and charges
- Financial advice

- Safety (deposit insurance)
- Convenience
- Location
- Online services
- Special programs

# Financial Planning for Life's Situations

## BANKING ONLINE

"We never close." "Highest savings rates anywhere." "Lowest checking account fees ever."

These impressive banking services are now possible with the use of the World Wide Web. Banks, like other businesses and financial service companies, are now online with cyber-versions of their traditional activities.

*Comparing Banking Services.*
As you start or expand your use of online banking services, several websites provide a wide range of banking information. These include www.bankrate.com, www.financenter.com, and www.quicken.com.

*Online Bank Branches.*
Traditional banks are expanding to offer services online. Some examples include www.wellsfargo.com, www.citibank.com, www.bankamerica.com, and www.americanexpress.com/banking.

*Paying Bills Online.*
Internet delivery of household bills will soon occur when you hear "You have bills" as you log on to a website or access your e-mail. Paperless bill delivery is currently limited in use to a few banks. However, several financial, utility, and technology companies are planning

systems that will enable consumers to view, pay, scan details, and summarize monthly charges with the click of a mouse. For information on paying bills online, go to www.msn.com, www.quicken.com, www.yahoo.com, www.aol.com, www.checkfree.com, or www.paytrust.com.

*Web-Only Banks.*
Many of today's best checking and saving deals come from branchless banks doing business solely on the Internet. Web banks usually require little or no minimum balance on checking accounts. Many Internet banks also pay higher interest on checking accounts than traditional banks. While ATMs are not readily available from web banks, these online financial companies usually offer banking and customer service over the telephone. Some Internet banks include www.sfnb.com, www.telebank.com, and www.net.b@nk.com (www.netbank.com).

Be cautious! You may access the website of the Federal Deposit Insurance Corporation (www.fdic.gov) to obtain information on fraudulent cyberbanks. The FDIC can tell you if a web bank has a legitimate charter to operate as a financial institution. You may also want to check out the information at www.badbanks.com.

Your selection of a financial institution should be based on valid information. Never assume that one will provide a better interest rate or service than another. You need to compare banks, savings and loan associations, and credit unions with other providers of financial services.

## Concept Check 5-2

1.  What are examples of deposit-type financial institutions?
2.  What factors do consumers usually consider when selecting a financial institution to meet their saving and checking needs?

# TYPES OF SAVINGS PLANS

**Obj. 3**
Compare the costs and benefits of various savings plans.

As Chapter 3 emphasized, you need a savings program to attain financial goals. Evaluation of various savings plans is the starting point of this process.

Changes in financial services have created a wide choice of savings alternatives (see Exhibit 5–6). While the number of savings plans may seem overwhelming, they can be grouped into these main categories: regular savings accounts, club accounts, certificates

## EXHIBIT 5-6   SAVINGS ALTERNATIVES

| Type of Account | Benefits | Drawbacks |
|---|---|---|
| Regular savings accounts/passbook accounts/share accounts | Low minimum balance<br>Ease of withdrawal<br>Insured | Low rate of return |
| Certificates of deposit (CDs) | Guaranteed rate of return for time of CD<br>Insured | Possible penalty for early withdrawal<br>Minimum deposit |
| Interest-earning checking accounts | Checking privileges<br>Interest earned<br>Insured | Service charge for going below minimum balance<br>Cost for printing checks; other fees may apply |
| Money market accounts | Favorable rate of return (based on current interest rates)<br>Allows some check writing<br>Insured | Higher minimum balance than regular savings accounts<br>No interest or service charge if below a certain balance |
| Money market funds | Favorable rate of return (based on current interest rates)<br>Some check writing | Minimum balance<br>Not insured |
| U.S. savings bonds | Fairly good rate of return (varies with current interest rates)<br>Low minimum deposit<br>Government guaranteed<br>Exempt from state and local income taxes | Lower rate when redeemed before five years |

of deposit, interest-earning checking accounts, money market accounts and funds, and savings bonds. Investment vehicles, such as U.S. Treasury bills, are discussed in later chapters.

## Regular Savings Accounts

*Regular savings accounts,* traditionally called *passbook accounts,* usually involve a low or no minimum balance. Today, instead of a passbook showing deposits and withdrawals, savers receive a monthly or quarterly statement with a summary of transactions.

A regular savings account usually allows you to withdraw money as needed. However, these *time deposits* may require a waiting period of up to 30 days to obtain your funds.

Banks, savings and loan associations, and other financial institutions offer regular savings accounts. At a credit union, these savings plans are called **share accounts**.

*share account*
A regular savings account at a credit union.

## Club Accounts

*Club accounts,* offered mainly at smaller financial institutions, are designed to meet a specific goal. Examples are vacation and Christmas club accounts in which you make a weekly deposit. Usually you cannot withdraw money until a certain time (such as November 1 for Christmas clubs) without incurring a penalty. A club account is a forced-savings method that usually pays very low interest.

## Certificates of Deposit

*certificate of deposit (CD)*  A savings plan requiring that a certain amount be left on deposit for a stated time period to earn a specified interest rate.

Higher earnings are commonly available to savers when they leave money on deposit for a set time period. A **certificate of deposit (CD)** is a savings plan requiring that a certain amount be left on deposit for a stated time period (ranging from 30 days to five or more years) to earn a specific rate of return. These time deposits can be an attractive and safe savings alternative. However, most financial institutions impose a penalty for early withdrawal of CD funds.

### Types of CDs
Financial institutions offer certificates of deposit with a variety of features:

1. *Rising-rate* or *bump-up CDs* may have higher rates at various intervals, such as every six months. However, beware of ads that highlight a higher rate in the future. This rate may be in effect only for the last couple of months for an 18- or 24-month CD. Also, some bump-ups may require a rather large minimum investment.

2. *Stock-indexed CDs* have earnings based on the stock market. In times of strong stock performance, your CD earnings can be higher than those on other CDs. At other times, however, you may earn no interest and may even lose part of your savings.

3. *Callable CDs* start with higher rates and usually have long-term maturities, as high as 10 to 15 years. These savings plans also have the benefit of federal deposit insurance. However, the bank may "call" the account after a stipulated period, such as one or two years, if interest rates drop. When the call option is exercised, the saver receives the original investment principal and any interest that has been earned. Remember, don't be drawn in by the high initial rate on a callable CD; it could change in a few years. Also, if it is not called, you may not have the flexibility to withdraw funds without a substantial penalty.

4. *Global CDs* combine higher interest with a hedge on future changes in the dollar compared to other currencies. As exchange rates change, your earnings can fluctuate. A weaker U.S. dollar (compared to a given foreign currency) can result in a higher return on your savings. In contrast, a stronger dollar will result in a lower rate of return. Some global CDs offered by U.S. banks have federal deposit insurance; others do not.

5. *Promotional CDs* attempt to attract savers with gifts or special rates. A Boulder, Colorado, bank offered Rolex watches, archery equipment, and Zodiac inflatable boats in lieu of interest. Be sure to balance the value of the item against the lost interest.

### Managing CDs
When saving with a CD or *rolling over* a CD (buying a new one at maturity), carefully assess all earnings and costs. Do not allow your financial institution to automatically roll over your money into another CD for the same term. If interest rates have dropped, you might consider a shorter maturity. Or if you believe rates are at a peak and you won't need the money for some time, obtain a CD with a longer term.

Consider creating a CD *portfolio* with CDs maturing at different times, for example, $2,000 in a three-month CD, $2,000 in a six-month CD, $2,000 in a one-year CD, and $2,000 in a two-year CD. This will give you some degree of liquidity and flexibility when you reinvest your funds.

Don't hesitate to buy CDs by mail from a financial institution in another state. You might earn as much as a full percentage point higher than your local bank offers. Also, when interest rates stay low, consider other savings alternatives such as savings bonds, mutual funds, and government securities. Current information about CD rates at various financial institutions may be obtained at www.bankrate/com.

## Interest-Earning Checking Accounts

Checking accounts can also be savings vehicles. These interest-earning accounts, which usually pay a low interest rate, are discussed in the next section of this chapter.

## Money Market Accounts and Funds

*money market account*
A savings account offered by banks, savings and loan associations, and credit unions that requires a minimum balance and has earnings based on market interest rates.

To meet consumer demand for higher savings rates, a savings plan with a floating interest rate was created. A **money market account** is a savings account that requires a minimum balance and has earnings based on market interest rates. Money market accounts allow you to write a limited number of checks to make large payments or to transfer money to other accounts. Since money market accounts may impose a fee when you go below the required minimum balance, usually $1,000, consider a regular savings account or a payroll deduction savings plan.

Both money market accounts and money market funds offer earnings based on current interest rates, and both have minimum-balance restrictions and allow check writing. The major difference is in safety. Money market *accounts* at banks and savings and loan associations are covered by federal deposit insurance. This is not true of money market *funds,* which are a product of investment and insurance companies. Since money market funds invest mainly in short-term (less than a year) government and corporate securities, however, they are usually quite safe.

## U.S. Savings Bonds

Years ago, the low return on savings bonds made their purchase a patriotic act rather than a wise saving choice. In recent years, however, the Treasury Department has used a floating interest rate on savings bonds. Earnings rise and fall based on changes in the level of interest rates in the economy.

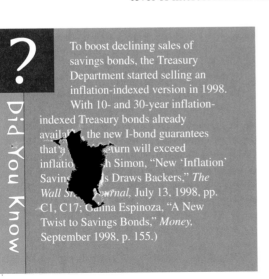

To boost declining sales of savings bonds, the Treasury Department started selling an inflation-indexed version in 1998. With 10- and 30-year inflation-indexed Treasury bonds already availa[...] the new I-bond guarantees that [...]turn will exceed inflatio[...]h Simon, "New 'Inflation' Savin[...]s Draws Backers," *The Wall S[...]urnal,* July 13, 1998, pp. C1, C17; Gilna Espinoza, "A New Twist to Savings Bonds," *Money,* September 1998, p. 155.)

Series EE bonds may be purchased for amounts ranging from $25 to $15,000 (face values of $50 to $30,000, respectively). You must hold bonds at least five years to earn the stated rate. If redeemed within five years of purchase, you earn a lower rate. Between the time the bond is six months and five years old, your money earns a slightly higher rate every six months. Series EE bonds continue to earn interest for 30 years, well beyond the time at which the face value is reached.

The main tax advantages of Series EE bonds are that (1) the interest earned is exempt from state and local taxes and (2) you do not have to pay federal income tax on earnings until the bonds are redeemed.

EE bonds that have reached face value may be exchanged for Series HH bonds to defer the taxes. The taxes owed for interest earned on the EE bonds will not be due until the HH bonds are cashed in or reach maturity.

Series HH bonds pay interest in cash twice a year. This interest is taxed as current income. The semiannual interest payments of HH bonds make them a popular source of retirement income.

Investors may purchase up to $15,000 ($30,000 maturity face) of U.S. savings bonds a year. This amount applies to any person, so parents may buy an additional $15,000 in each child's name.

Redeemed Series EE bonds may be exempt from federal income tax if the funds are used to pay tuition and fees at a college, university, or qualified technical school for yourself or a dependent. The bonds must be purchased by an individual who is at least 24 years old, and they must be issued in the names of one or both parents. These provisions have been designed to assist low- and middle-income households; people whose incomes exceed a certain amount do not qualify for the exemption.

Banks and other financial institutions that sell U.S. savings bonds no longer issue the actual bond. Instead, you receive a receipt or, if desired, a "gift certificate." The bonds are then sent from the Federal Reserve bank within 15 business days. For an update on U.S. savings bond rates and other information, call 1–800–US BONDS. Websites for savings bond information are www.savingsbonds.gov and www.ny.frb.org..

Lost, stolen, or destroyed savings bonds will be replaced by the government free of charge. A table of savings bond redemption values (Form PD 3600) is available from the Savings Bond Marketing Office, 800 K St., NW, Washington, DC 20226.

**Sheet 24**

## Concept Check 5-3

1.  What are the main types of savings plans offered by financial institutions?
2.  How does a money market *account* differ from a money market *fund*?
3.  What are the benefits of U.S. savings bonds?

# EVALUATING SAVINGS PLANS

## Obj. 4
Identify the factors used to evaluate different savings plans.

*rate of return*  The percentage of increase in the value of savings as a result of interest earned; also called *yield.*

*compounding*  A process that calculates interest based on previously earned interest.

Your selection of a savings plan will be influenced by the rate of return, inflation, tax considerations, liquidity, safety, restrictions, and fees.

## Rate of Return

Earnings on savings can be measured by the **rate of return,** or *yield,* the percentage of increase in the value of your savings from earned interest. For example, a $100 savings account that earned $5 after a year would have a rate of return, or yield, of 5 percent. This rate of return was determined by dividing the interest earned ($5) by the amount in the savings account ($100).

### Compounding
The yield on your savings usually will be greater than the stated interest rate. **Compounding** refers to interest that is earned on previously earned interest. Each time interest is added to your savings, the next interest amount is computed on the new balance in the account. Future value and present value calculations, introduced in Chapter 1, take compounding into account.

The more frequent the compounding, the higher your rate of return will be. For example, $100 in a savings account that earns 6 percent compounded annually will increase $6 after a year. But the same $100 in a 6 percent account compounded daily will earn $6.19 for the year. Although this difference may seem slight, large amounts held in savings for long periods of time will result in far higher differences (see Exhibit 5–7).

**EXHIBIT 5-7**

Compounding
Frequency
Increases the
Savings Yield

Shorter compounding periods result in higher yields. This chart shows the growth of $10,000, five-year CDs paying the same rate of 8 percent, but with different compounding methods.

| End of Year | Compounding Method | | | |
| --- | --- | --- | --- | --- |
| | Daily | Monthly | Quarterly | Annually |
| 1 | $10,832.78 | $10,830.00 | $10,824.32 | $10,800.00 |
| 2 | 11,743.91 | 11,728.88 | 11,716.59 | 11,664.00 |
| 3 | 12,712.17 | 12,702.37 | 12,682.41 | 12,597.12 |
| 4 | 13,770.82 | 13,756.66 | 13,727.85 | 13,604.89 |
| 5 | 14,917.62 | 14,898.46 | 14,859.46 | 14,693.28 |
| Annual yield | 8.33% | 8.30% | 8.24% | 8.00% |

Truth in Savings    The *Truth in Savings* law (Federal Reserve Regulation DD) requires financial institutions to disclose the following information on savings account plans:

- Fees on deposit accounts.
- The interest rate.
- The annual percentage yield (APY).
- Other terms and conditions of the savings plan.

*annual percentage yield (APY)*   The percentage rate expressing the total amount of interest that would be received on a $100 deposit based on the annual rate and frequency of compounding for a 365-day period.

Truth in Savings (TIS) defines **annual percentage yield (APY)** as the percentage rate expressing the total amount of interest that would be received on a $100 deposit based on the annual rate and frequency of compounding for a 365-day period. This law defines a year as 365 days rather than 360, 366, or some other number. TIS eliminates the confusion caused by the more than 8 million variations of interest calculation methods previously used by financial institutions. APY reflects the amount of interest a saver should expect to earn. (See the Financial Planning Calculations box on page 148 for additional information on APY.)

In addition to setting the formula for computing the annual percentage yield, Truth in Savings (1) requires disclosure of fees and APY earned on any statements provided to customers, (2) establishes rules for advertising deposit accounts, and (3) restricts the method of calculating the balance on which interest is paid. Financial institutions are also required to calculate interest on the full principal balance in the account each day.

## Inflation

The rate of return you earn on your savings should be compared with the inflation rate. When the inflation rate was over 10 percent, people with money in savings accounts earning 5 or 6 percent were experiencing a loss in the buying power of that money. In general, as the inflation rate increases, the interest rates offered to savers also increase. This gives you an opportunity to select a savings option that will minimize the erosion of your dollars on deposit.

## Tax Considerations

Like inflation, taxes reduce interest earned on savings. For example, a 10 percent return for a saver in a 28 percent tax bracket means a real return of 7.2 percent (the Financial Planning Calculations feature on page 149 shows how to compute the after-tax savings rate of return). As discussed in Chapter 4 and discussed further in Part 5, several tax-exempt and tax-deferred savings plans and investments can increase your real rate of return.

## Financial Planning Calculations

### ANNUAL PERCENTAGE YIELD

The Truth in Savings law, which took effect in 1993, requires that financial institutions report in advertisements, if a rate is quoted, and to savings plan customers the annual percentage yield (APY). The formula for APY is

$$APY = 100\,[(1 + Interest/Principal)^{365/days\ in\ term} - 1]$$

The *principal* is the amount of funds on deposit. *Interest* is the total dollar amount earned during the term on the principal. *Days in term* is the actual number of days over which interest is earned.

When the number of days in the term is 365 (that is, where the stated maturity is 365 days) or where the account does not have a stated maturity, the APY formula is simply

$$APY = 100\ (Interest/Principal)$$

APY provides a consistent comparison for savings plans with different interest rates, different compounding frequencies, and different time periods. APY may be easily viewed in terms of a $100 deposit for a 365-day year. For example, an APY of 6.5 percent would mean $6.50 interest for a year.

Also, remember that taxes usually are not withheld from savings and investment income. Consequently, you may owe additional taxes at year-end due to earnings on savings.

## Liquidity

Liquidity allows you to withdraw your money on short notice without a loss of principal or fees. Some savings plans impose penalties for early withdrawal or have other restrictions. With certain types of savings certificates and accounts, early withdrawal may be penalized by a loss of interest or a lower earnings rate.

You should consider the degree of liquidity you desire in relation to your savings goals. To achieve long-term financial goals, many people trade off liquidity for a higher return.

## Safety

Most savings plans at banks, savings and loan associations, and credit unions are insured by agencies affiliated with the federal government. This protection prevents a loss of money due to the failure of the insured institution.

While a few financial institutions have failed in recent years, savers with deposits covered by federal insurance have not lost any money. Depositors of failed organizations have either been paid the amounts in their accounts or have had the accounts taken over by a financially stable institution.

The Federal Deposit Insurance Corporation (FDIC) administers separate insurance funds: the Bank Insurance Fund and the Savings Association Insurance Fund. Credit unions may obtain deposit insurance through the National Credit Union Association (NCUA). Some state-chartered credit unions have opted for a private insurance program.

The FDIC insures deposits of up to $100,000 per person per financial institution; a joint account is considered to belong proportionally to each name on the account. For example, if you have a $70,000 individual account and an $80,000 joint account with a relative in the same financial institution, $10,000 of your savings will not be covered by federal deposit insurance ($70,000 plus one-half of $80,000 exceeds the $100,000 limit). However, by using combinations of individual, joint, and trust accounts in different

# Financial Planning Calculations

## AFTER-TAX SAVINGS RATE OF RETURN

The taxability of interest on your savings reduces your real rate of return. In other words, you lose some portion of your interest to taxes. This calculation consists of the following steps:

1. Determine your top tax bracket for federal income taxes.
2. Subtract this rate, expressed as a decimal, from 1.0.
3. Multiply the result by the yield on your savings account.
4. This number, expressed as a percentage, is your after-tax rate of return.

For example,

1. You are in the 28 percent tax bracket.
2. $1.0 - 0.28 = 0.72$.
3. If the yield on your savings account is 6.25 percent, $0.0625 \times 0.72 = 0.045$.
4. Your after-tax rate of return is 4.5 percent.

You may use the same procedure to determine the *real rate of return* on your savings based on inflation. For example, if you are earning 6 percent on savings and inflation is 5 percent, your real rate of return (after inflation) is 5.7 percent: $0.06 \times (1 - 0.05) = 0.057$.

financial institutions, it may be possible to have federal deposit insurance cover amounts that exceed $100,000. Remember, the maximum coverage of federal deposit insurance is based on each depositor, not on each account. The best advice is to never keep more than $100,000 in one financial institution. Be careful, however, since different branch offices count as the same institution. Also, mergers in the financial service industry may bring accounts from different banks together. Further information on deposit insurance is available at www.fdic.gov.

Since not all financial institutions have federal deposit insurance, investigate this matter when you are selecting a savings plan. Additional information on the regulation and consumer protection aspects of financial institutions is included in Appendix B.

## Restrictions and Fees

Other limitations can affect your choice of a savings program. For example, there may be a delay between the time interest is earned and the time it is added to your account. This means it will not be available for your immediate use. Also, some institutions charge a transaction fee for each deposit or withdrawal.

In the past, some financial institutions had promotions offering a "free" gift when a certain savings amount was deposited. To receive this gift, you had to leave your money on deposit for a certain time period, or you may have received less interest, since some of the earnings were used to cover the cost of the "free" items. Economists tell us that "there is no such thing as a free lunch"; the same holds true for toasters and television sets.

**Sheet 25**

## Concept Check 5-4

1. When would you prefer a savings plan with high liquidity over one with a high rate of return?
2. What is the relationship between compounding and the future value of an amount?
3. How do inflation and taxes affect earnings on savings?

# SELECTING PAYMENT METHODS

**Obj. 5**
Compare the costs
and benefits of
different types of
checking accounts.

With about 90 percent of business transactions conducted by check, a checking account is a necessity for most people.

## Types of Checking Accounts

Checking accounts fall into three major categories: regular checking accounts, activity accounts, and interest-earning checking accounts.

One study determined that consumers pay $218.27 a year on average for a checking account at a big bank, compared to $190.33 at smaller financial institutions. (Galina Espinoza, "How to Deal with Your Bank," *Money,* November 1998, pp. 157–58, 160.)

### Regular Checking Accounts
*Regular checking accounts* usually have a monthly service charge that you may avoid by keeping a minimum balance in the account. Some financial institutions will waive the monthly fee if you keep a certain amount in savings. Avoiding the monthly service charge can be beneficial. For example, a monthly fee of $7.50 results in $90 a year. However, you lose interest on the minimum-balance amount in a non-interest-earning account.

### Activity Accounts
*Activity accounts* charge a fee for each check written and sometimes a fee for each deposit in addition to a monthly service charge. However, you do not have to maintain a minimum balance. An activity account is most appropriate for people who write only a few checks each month and are unable to maintain the required minimum balance.

### Interest-Earning Checking Accounts
*Interest-earning checking accounts,* sometimes called *NOW accounts* (NOW stands for *negotiable order of withdrawal*), usually require a minimum balance. If the account balance goes below this amount, you may not earn interest and will likely incur a service charge.

*share draft account* An interest-bearing checking account at a credit union.

The **share draft account** is an interest-earning checking account at a credit union. Credit union members write checks, called *share drafts,* against their account balances.

## Evaluating Checking Accounts

Would you rather have a checking account that pays interest and requires a $1,000 minimum balance or an account that doesn't pay interest and requires a $300 minimum balance? This decision requires evaluating factors such as restrictions, fees and charges, interest, and special services (see Exhibit 5–8).

Banks are making billion-dollar profits off of bounced-check fees. Each year, the banking industry collects over $5 billion from consumers in bounced-check charges. Banks charge 11 to 32 times what it actually costs them to process bounced checks. (Consumer Federation of America, 1424 16th St., NW, #604, Washington, DC 20036; 202–387–6121; www.consumerfed.org.)

### Restrictions
The most common limitation on checking accounts is the amount you must keep on deposit to earn interest or avoid a service charge. Until recently, financial institutions also placed various restrictions on the holding period for deposited checks; that is, they required a period of time for checks to clear before you were allowed to use the funds. The Expedited Funds Availability Act requires that funds from local checks be available within two business days and funds from out-of-town checks be withheld for no more than five business days.

### Fees and Charges
Nearly all financial institutions require a minimum balance or impose service charges for checking accounts. When using an interest-bearing checking

**EXHIBIT 5-8**

Checking Account
Selection Factors

**CHECKING ACCOUNT SELECTION FACTORS**

| Restrictions | Fees and Charges |
|---|---|
| • Minimum balance | • Monthly fee |
| • Federal deposit insurance | • Fees for each check or deposit |
| • Hours and location of branch offices | • Printing of checks |
| • Holding period for deposited checks | • Fee to obtain canceled check copy |
| | • Overdraft, stop-payment order, certified check fee |
| | • Fees for preauthorized bill payment, fund transfer, or home banking activity |

| Special Services | Interest |
|---|---|
| • Direct deposit of payroll and government checks | • Interest rate |
| • 24-hour teller machines | • Minimum deposit to earn interest |
| • Overdraft protection | • Method of compounding |
| • Banking-at-home | • Portion of balance used to compute interest |
| • Discounts or free checking for certain groups (students, senior citizens, employees of certain companies) | • Fee charged for falling below necessary balance to earn interest |
| • Free or discounted services, such as traveler's checks | |

**Sheet 26**

account, compare your earnings with any service charge or fee. Also, consider the cost of lost or reduced interest due to the need to maintain the minimum balance.

Checking account fees have increased in recent years. Items such as check printing, overdraft fees, and stop-payment orders have doubled or tripled in price at some financial institutions. Some institutions will "bait" you with fancy checks at a low price and then charge a much higher price when you reorder. You may be able to purchase checks at a lower cost from a mail-order company that advertises in magazines or the Sunday newspaper.

**Interest**   As discussed earlier, the interest rate, the frequency of compounding, and the interest computation method will affect the earnings on your checking account.

**Special Services**   Financial institutions commonly offer checking account customers services such as 24-hour teller machines and home banking services. Financial institutions are also attempting to reduce the paper and postage costs associated with checking accounts. One solution is to not return canceled checks to customers. The financial institution then uses microfilm to store checks and provides customers with detailed statements summarizing the checks written. If a customer requests a copy of a canceled check, the institution reproduces the copy from its microfilm file for a fee.

**Overdraft protection** is an automatic loan made to checking account customers for checks written in excess of the available balance. This service is convenient but costly. Most overdraft plans make loans based on $50 or $100 increments. An overdraft of just

*overdraft protection*
An automatic loan made to checking account customers to cover the amount of checks written in excess of the available balance in the checking account.

## STEVE DOLE ON IDENTITY THEFT AND FINANCIAL PRIVACY

"People who put their Social Security and drivers license numbers of their checks are making identity theft fairly easy," according to Steve Dole, senior banking analyst at Hawthorn Bank in Illinois. "With one check, a con artist could know your Social Security, driver's license, and bank account numbers as well as your address, phone number, and perhaps even a sample of your signature."

Identity fraud can range from passing bad checks and using stolen credit cards to theft of another person's total financial existence. While situations as portrayed in the movie *The Net* are rare, people need to be aware that they can easily become a victim.

Dole also suggests that you not mail your bills from your home mailbox, especially if the box is out by the street. This gives a potential scam artist easy access to a variety of financial and personal information.

The ease of obtaining Social Security numbers and more than 3 billion credit solicitations a year make identity theft a fairly simple scam. Each day, more than 1,000 people have their identities stolen by a con artist applying for credit in the victim's name. After obtaining a loan or racking up credit card charges, the thief disappears, leaving a ruined credit rating that may take years to correct.

Banks and other financial institutions work to protect the identities and privacy of their depositors. Mr. Dole reminds bank customers that the slight inconvenience of being asked for identification or having an account balance checked protects you and others from financial losses.

Other recommendations to protect yourself from identity fraud include the following:

- Shred or burn financial information containing account or Social Security numbers.
- Use passwords other than maiden names.
- Don't put your Social Security number on any document unless it is legally required.
- Check your credit report once or twice a year to make sure it is correct.
- Have your name removed from mailing lists operated by credit agencies and companies offering credit promotions.
- If you become a victim, notify the credit card company and other businesses with specific details. Also, file a police report to provide documentation of the scam.

Websites with additional information on financial privacy and identity theft include www.identitytheft.org, www.idfraud.org, www.privacyrights.org, and www.pirg.org/calpirg/consumer/privacy.

**Sheet 27**

$1 might trigger a $50 loan and corresponding finance charges of perhaps 18 percent. But overdraft protection can be less costly than the fee charged for a check you write when you do not have enough money on deposit to cover it. That fee may be $20 or more. Many financial institutions will allow you to cover checking account overdrafts with an automatic transfer from a savings account for a nominal fee.

Beware of checking accounts that offer several services (safe deposit box, traveler's checks, low-rate loans, and travel insurance) for a single monthly fee. This may sound like a good value; however, financial experts observe that such accounts benefit only a small group of people who make constant use of the services offered.

# Financial Planning Calculations

## COMPARING CHECKING ACCOUNT COSTS

Comparisons of interest earned and service charges and fees for checking accounts can be confusing. To assist you with this analysis, use the following calculation. Remember: Not all items listed here will apply to every type of checking account.

### INFLOWS

*Step 1.*

Multiply average monthly balance $ _____
by average rate of return _____ percent to
determine annual earnings

Total estimated annual inflow         $ _____

### OUTFLOWS

*Step 2.*

Monthly service
    charge $ _____ × 12 =            $ _____
Average number of checks written
    per month _____ × charge
    per check × 12                     $ _____
Average number of deposits per
    month _____ × charge per
    deposit × 12                       $ _____
Fee for dropping below minimum
    balance $ _____ × number
    of times below minimum             $ _____
Lost interest: Opportunity cost
    _____ percent × required
    minimum balance $ _____         $ _____

Total estimated annual outflow         $ _____

*Step 3.*

Estimated annual inflows less annual outflows =
    + Net earnings for account (Step 1)
    − Net cost for account (Step 2)

+/− $ _____

NOTE: This calculation does not take into account charges and fees for services such as overdrafts, stop-payments, ATM use, and check printing. Be sure to also consider these costs when selecting a checking account.

The accompanying Financial Planning Calculations box offers a method for comparing the costs of various types of checking accounts.

## Other Payment Methods

While personal checks are the most common payment form, other methods are available. A *certified check* is a personal check with guaranteed payment. The amount of the check is deducted from your balance when the financial institution certifies the check. A *cashier's check* is a check of a financial institution. You may purchase one by paying the amount of the check plus a fee. You may purchase a *money order* in a similar manner from financial institutions, post offices, and stores. Certified checks, cashier's checks, and money orders allow you to make a payment that the recipient knows is valid.

*Traveler's checks* allow you to make payments when you are away from home. This payment form requires you to sign each check twice. First, you sign the traveler's checks when you purchase them. Then, to identify you as the authorized person, you sign them again as you cash them.

Electronic traveler's checks, in the form of a prepaid travel card, are becoming more common. The card allows travelers visiting other nations to get local currency from an ATM.

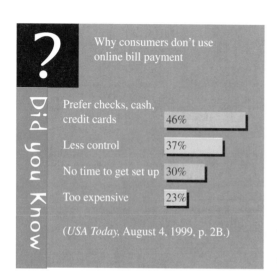

**Did you Know**

? Why consumers don't use online bill payment

Prefer checks, cash, credit cards    46%

Less control    37%

No time to get set up    30%

Too expensive    23%

(*USA Today,* August 4, 1999, p. 2B.)

## Concept Check 5-5

1. What factors are commonly considered when selecting a checking account?
2. Are checking accounts that earn interest preferable to regular checking accounts? Why or why not?

# KEY FORMULAS

| Page | Topic | Formula |
|------|-------|---------|
| 148 | Annual percentage yield (APY) | $APY = 100\,[(1 + Interest/Principal)^{365/\text{days in term}} - 1]$ |
| | | Principal = The amount of funds on deposit |
| | | Interest = The total dollar amount earned on the principal |
| | | Days in term = The actual number of days in the term of the account |
| | When the number of days in the term is 365 or where the account does not have a stated maturity, the APY formula is simply | $APY = 100\,(Interest/Principal)$ |
| | | *Example:* |
| | | $100\left[\left(1 + \dfrac{\$56.20}{\$1,000}\right)^{\frac{365}{365}} - 1\right] = 0.0562 = 5.62\%$ |
| 149 | After-tax rate of return | Interest rate $\times$ (1 − Tax rate) |
| | | *Example:* |
| | | $0.05 \times (1 - 0.28) = 0.036 = 3.6\%$ |

# Summary of Objectives

**Obj. 1** **Analyze factors that affect selection and use of financial services.**

Financial products such as savings plans, checking accounts, loans, and trust services are used for managing daily financial activities. Technology, opportunity costs, and economic conditions affect the selection and use of financial services.

**Obj. 2** **Compare the types of financial institutions.**

Commercial banks, savings and loan associations, mutual savings banks, credit unions, life insurance companies, investment companies, finance companies, mortgage companies, pawnshops, and check-cashing outlets may be compared on the basis of services offered, rates and fees, safety, convenience, and special programs available to customers.

**Obj. 3** **Compare the costs and benefits of various savings plans.**

Commonly used savings plans include regular savings accounts, club accounts, certificates of deposit, interest-earning checking accounts, money market accounts, money market funds, and U.S. savings bonds.

**Obj. 4** **Identify the factors used to evaluate different savings plans.**

Savings plans may be evaluated on the basis of rate of return, inflation, tax considerations, liquidity, safety, restrictions, and fees.

**Obj. 5** **Compare the costs and benefits of different types of checking accounts.**

Regular checking accounts, activity accounts, and interest-earning checking accounts can be compared with regard to restrictions (such as a minimum balance), fees and charges, interest, and special services.

# Financial Planning Problems

1. *Determining Savings Goals.* What would be common savings goals for a person who buys a five-year CD paying 8.75 percent instead of an 18-month savings certificate paying 7.5 percent?  (Obj. 4)
2. *Computing Future Value.* What would be the value of a savings account started with $500, earning 6 percent (compounded annually) after 10 years?  (Obj. 5)
3. *Calculating Present Value.* Brenda Young desires to have $10,000 eight years from now for her daughter's college fund. If she will earn 7 percent (compounded annually) on her money, what amount should she deposit now? Use the present value of a single amount calculation.  (Obj. 5)
4. *Computing Future Value of Annual Deposits.* What amount would you have if you deposited $1,500 a year for 30 years at 8 percent (compounded annually)? (Use Appendix A.)  (Obj. 5)
5. *Comparing Taxable and Tax-Free Yields.* With a 28 percent marginal tax rate, would a tax-free yield of 7 percent or a taxable yield of 9.5 percent give you a better return on your savings? Why?  (Obj. 5)
6. *Computing APY.* What would be the annual percentage yield for a savings account that earned $56 in interest on $800 over the past 365 days?  (Obj. 5)
7. *Calculating Opportunity Cost.* What is the annual opportunity cost of a checking account that requires a $350 minimum balance to avoid service charges? Assume an interest rate of 6.5 percent.  (Obj. 5)
8. *Comparing Costs of Checking Accounts.* What would be the net *annual* cost of the following checking accounts?  (Obj. 5)
   a. Monthly fee, $3.75; processing fee, 25 cents per check; checks written, an average of 22 a month.
   b. Interest earnings of 6 percent with a $500 minimum balance; average monthly balance, $600; monthly service charge of $15 for falling below the minimum balance, which occurs three times a year (no interest earned in these months).
9. *Computing Checking Account Costs.* Based on the following information, determine the true balance in your checking account.  (Ch. App.)
   Balance in your checkbook, $356
   Balance on bank statement, $472
   Service charge and other fees, $15
   Interest earned on the account, $4
   Total of outstanding checks, $187
   Deposits in transit, $60

# Financial Planning Activities

1. *Researching Financial Services.* Using the World Wide Web or library resources, obtain information about new developments in financial services. How have technology, changing economic conditions, and new legislation affected the types and availability of various saving and checking financial services? (Obj. 1)

2. *Monitoring Economic Conditions.* Research current economic conditions (interest rates, inflation) using *The Wall Street Journal,* other library resources, the "Economy" section of www.personalwealth.com, or other  websites. Based on current economic conditions, what actions would you recommend to people who are saving and borrowing money? (Obj. 1)

3. *Comparing Financial Institutions.* Collect advertisements and promotional information from several financial institutions, or locate the websites of financial institutions such as Wells Fargo Bank (www.wellsfargo.com) and Bank of America (www.bankamerica.com). Create a list of factors that a person might consider when comparing costs and benefits of various savings plans and checking accounts. (Obj. 2)

4. *Obtaining Opinions about Financial Services.* Survey several people to determine awareness and use of various financial services such as online banking, "smart cards," and check-writing software. (Obj. 2)

5. *Researching Credit Unions.* Using the website for the Credit Union National Association (www.cuna.org) or other sources, obtain information about joining a credit union and the services this type of financial institution offers. (Obj. 2)

6. *Comparing Savings Plans.* Collect advertisements from several financial institutions with information about the savings plans they offer. (You may do this using the websites of various financial institutions.) Using Sheet 25 in the *Personal Financial Planner,* compare the features and potential earnings of two or three savings plans. (Obj. 3, 4)

7. *Researching Current Savings Rates.* Using library sources (such as *The Wall Street Journal* and other current business periodicals) or websites (such as www. bankrate.com and www.personalwealth.com), pre-  pare a summary of current rates of return for various savings accounts, money market accounts, certificates of deposit, and U.S. savings bonds. (Obj. 3, 4)

8. *Comparing Checking Accounts.* Using Sheets 26 and 27 in the *Personal Financial Planner,* compare the features and costs of checking accounts at two different financial institutions. Online searches of bank websites may be useful. (Obj. 5)

9. *Analyzing Check-Writing Software.* Visit software retailers to obtain information about the features in various personal computer programs used for maintaining a checking account. Information about programs such as Managing Your Money, Microsoft Money, and Quicken may be obtained on the Internet. (Obj. 5)

10. *Researching Checking Accounts.* Several states require that banks offer basic checking accounts. For example, in Illinois, New York, New Jersey, and Minnesota, check services with minimal fees must be made available for consumers making a limited number of transactions. Obtain information about the availability of these types of *life-line* accounts in your area. (Obj. 5)

# LIFE SITUATION CASE

## CHECKING OUT FINANCIAL SERVICES

Carla and Ed Johnson have separate checking accounts. Each pays part of the household and living expenses. Carla pays the mortgage and telephone bill, while Ed pays for food and utilities and makes the insurance and car payments. This arrangement allows them the freedom to spend whatever extra money they have each month without needing to explain their actions to each other. Carla and Ed believe their separate accounts have minimized disagreements about money. Since both spend most of their money each month,

they have low balances in their checking accounts, resulting in a monthly charge totaling $15.

In the same financial institution where Carla has her checking account, the Johnsons have $600 in a passbook savings account that earns 2.2 percent interest. If the savings account balance exceeded $1,000, they would earn 3.15 percent. If the balance stayed above $1,000, they would not have to pay the monthly service charge on Carla's checking account. The financial institution has a program that moves money from checking to savings. This program would allow the Johnsons to increase their savings and work toward a secure financial future.

Ed has his checking account at a bank that offers an electronic banking system allowing a customer to obtain cash at many locations 24 hours a day. Ed believes this feature is valuable when cash is needed to cover business expenses and personal spending. For an additional monthly fee, the bank would also provide Ed with a credit card, a safe deposit box, and a single monthly statement summarizing all transactions.

While most people plan their spending for living expenses, few plan their use of financial services. Therefore, many people are charged high fees for checking accounts and earn low interest on their savings. Despite a wide choice of financial institutions and services, you can learn to compare their costs and benefits. Your awareness of financial services and your ability to evaluate them are vital skills for a healthy personal economic future.

## Questions

1. Which financial services are most important to Carla and Ed Johnson?
2. What efforts are the Johnsons currently making to assess their use of financial services in relation to their other financial activities?
3. How should the Johnsons assess their needs for financial services? On what bases should they compare financial services?
4. What should the Johnsons do to improve their use of financial services?

## INTERNET CASE   Selecting Online Financial Services

Each month, Margo Bostrom becomes more frustrated with the fees she pays for financial services. Recently her checking account and ATM fees were over $15 a month. In addition, Margo is frustrated by the lower quality of customer service. Whenever she uses the drive-through window, she has to wait more than 10 minutes.

Margo is considering a "web-only" bank that offers continuous access to account information along with electronic bill-paying service. She would earn 6 percent interest on funds in her checking account, which is about three times higher than what she currently earns. But since the web-only bank doesn't have its own ATMs, she could incur significant fees when obtaining cash. On the positive side, she would have access to low-cost, online investment trading.

The web-only bank will require direct deposit of paychecks. Cash deposits would have to be handled through an ATM or through an electronic transfer at a traditional bank.

Margo's current bank is expanding its services to include 24-hour access to account balances and electronic bill paying through its website. This added service might entice her to continue doing business with the bank. She is also concerned about deposit insurance with the web-only bank.

## Questions

1. What factors should Margo consider when comparing a "web-only" bank and online banking with her current financial institution?
2. Locate websites that Margo might use while considering online banking.
3. What actions would you recommend for Margo?

# Creating an E-Plan: Financial Decisions Using the Web

## SELECTING SAVINGS AND CHECKING SERVICES

The use of payment services and savings programs influences other aspects of financial planning. Attempts to minimize banking fees while maximizing earnings on funds are common objectives.

Websites for Selecting Banking Services

- Current rates for various savings instruments at **usatoday.com/money/savebox.htm, www.bankrate.com,** and **www.banx.com.**
- The Federal Deposit Insurance Corporation provides access to consumer information, press releases, and banking statistics at **www.fdic.gov.**
- Current information on U.S. savings bonds at **www.savingsbonds.gov** and **www.ny.frb.org.**
- Information on Federal Reserve activities, publications, and access to the websites of other Federal Reserve Banks is available at **www.federalreserve.gov.**
- Information about banking services from the American Bankers Association at **www.aba.com.**
- Financial calculators for savings at **www.centura.com/formulas/calc.html.**
- Information on making payments on the Internet at **www.checkfree.com.**
- Online banking information at **www.orcc.com/banking.htm/.**

(Note: Addresses and content of websites change, and new sites are created daily. Use search engines to update and locate websites for your current financial planning needs.)

*PFP sheets: 23–28*

Short-Term Financial Planning Activities

1. Identify various financial services needed for savings, payment, and money management activities. Identify financial institutions that you might use to obtain these financial services (see PFP sheet 23).
2. Compare the rates of return, fees, and other factors for different savings plans that you might use to meet your financial goals (see PFP Sheets 24, 25).
3. Compare the features and costs of checking services at various financial institutions (see PFP Sheet 26, 27).

Long-Term Financial Planning Activities

1. Identify saving decisions that would best help you achieve long-term financial goals.
2. List the economic conditions (inflation, current interest rates) and personal factors related to the costs and benefits of financial services that you should monitor as your personal life situation changes over time.

# Using a Checking Account

## OPENING A CHECKING ACCOUNT

Deciding who the owner of the account will be is your starting point for opening a checking account. Only one person is allowed to write checks on an *individual account*. A *joint account* has two or more owners, with any authorized person allowed to write checks if it is specified as an "or" account. In contrast, an "and" account with two owners requires the signatures of both owners on checks. This arrangement is commonly used by businesses and other organizations.

Both an individual account and a joint account require a signature card. This document is a record of the official signatures of the person or persons authorized to write checks on the account.

## MAKING DEPOSITS

A *deposit ticket* is the form you use for adding money to your checking account (see Exhibit 5–A on page 160). On this document, you list the amounts of the cash and checks being deposited. Each check you deposit requires an *endorsement*—your signature on the back of the check—to authorize the transfer of the funds into your account. The following are three common endorsement forms:

- A *blank endorsement* is your signature. Use this endorsement form only when you are actually depositing or cashing a check, since a check could be cashed by anyone once its back has been signed.
- A *restrictive endorsement* consists of the words *for deposit only,* followed by your signature. This endorsement form is especially useful when you are depositing checks by mail.
- A *special endorsement* allows you to transfer a check to an organization or another person. On this endorsement form, the words *pay to the order of* are followed by the name of the organization or person and then by your signature.

**EXHIBIT 5-A**

Deposit Ticket

DEPOSIT TICKET

Barbara Carter
7640 Moontree Lane
Elton, NE 67844

DATE _____ *April 10* _____ 19 *2001*

_____

First National Bank
of Elton

⑆000000000⑆ ⑈5 5 303 79⑈" 3323

CHECKS AND OTHER ITEMS ARE RECEIVED FOR DEPOSIT SUBJECT TO THE PROVISIONS OF THE UNIFORM COMMERCIAL CODE OR ANY APPLICABLE COLLECTION AGREEMENT.

| CASH | CURRENCY | 17 | – |
| | COIN | 2 | 50 |
| LIST CHECKS SINGLY | | 16 | 25 |
| | | 11 | 37 |
| TOTAL FROM OTHER SIDE | | | |
| **TOTAL** | | 47 | 12 |
| LESS CASH RECEIVED | | 10 | – |
| **NET DEPOSIT** | | 37 | 12 |

00-0000/0000

USE OTHER SIDE FOR
ADDITIONAL LISTING

BE SURE EACH ITEM IS
PROPERLY ENDORSED

Federal regulations require that endorsements be on the reverse of the left side of the check, using no more than 1½ inches of space from the top. They may be hand-written, typed, rubber-stamped, or printed.

## WRITING CHECKS

Before writing a check, record the information in your check register and deduct the amount of the check from your balance; otherwise, you will think you have more money available than you really do. Many checking account customers use duplicate checks to maintain a record of their current balance.

The procedure for proper check writing, displayed in Exhibit 5–B, consists of the following steps:

1. Record the current date.
2. Write the name of the person or organization receiving the payment.
3. Record the amount of the check in figures.
4. Write the amount of the check in words; checks for less than a dollar should be written as "only 79 cents," for example, with the word *dollars* on the check crossed out.
5. Sign the check in the same way you signed the signature card when you opened your account.
6. Make a note of the reason for payment to assist with budget and tax preparation.

Check-writing software is available as a separate program or as part of a financial planning package such as Microsoft Money (www.msn.com/money) or Quicken (www.quicken.com). These programs can easily prepare checks while maintaining your financial records such as the check register, personal financial statements, and a budget.

A *stop-payment order* may be necessary if a check is lost or stolen or if a business transaction was not completed in a satisfactory manner. A verbal stop-payment order is valid for 14 days; a written order stays in effect for six months. After that time, it may be necessary to renew the order and fill out a new stop-payment form. Most banks, however, do not honor checks with "stale" dates, usually six months old or older. The fee for a stop-payment commonly ranges from $10 to $20. If several checks are missing or you lose your checkbook, the bank may suggest closing that account and opening a new one. This action is likely to be less costly than paying several stop-payment fees.

**EXHIBIT 5-B**

A Personal Check

Kenneth Buckley
7828 Carl Drive
Westover, OR 98123

3693

① *February 6* 20 *01*

PAY TO THE
ORDER OF ② *Midland College*          ③ $ *862.75*

④ *Eight-hundred sixty-two and 75/100* ————— DOLLARS

Oregon State Employees
Credit Union

MEMO ⑥ *spring tuition*          ⑤ *Kenneth Buckley*

⑈000000000⑈  1505  303079⑈  3693

## MAINTAINING A CHECKING ACCOUNT

Each month you will receive a *bank statement*, a summary of the transactions for a checking account. This document reports deposits made, checks paid, interest earned, and fees for items such as service charges and printing of checks. The balance reported on the bank statement probably will differ from the balance in your checkbook. Reasons for a difference are checks that you have written but have not yet cleared, deposits you have made since the bank statement was prepared, interest added to your account, and deductions for fees and charges.

To determine your true balance, you should prepare a *bank reconciliation.* This report accounts for differences between the bank statement and your checkbook balance. The steps you take in this process, shown in the Financial Planning Calculations box on page 162, are as follows:

1.  Compare the checks you have written over the past month with those reported as paid on your bank statement. Use the canceled checks from the financial institution, or compare your check register with the check numbers reported on the bank statement (many financial institutions no longer return canceled checks to customers). *Subtract* from the *bank statement balance* the total of the checks written but not yet cleared.
2.  Determine whether any recent deposits are not on the bank statement. If so, *add* the amount of the outstanding deposits to the *bank statement balance.*
3.  *Subtract* any fees or charges on the bank statement and ATM withdrawals from your *checkbook balance.*
4.  *Add* any interest earned to your *checkbook balance.*

At this point, the revised balances for both your checkbook and the bank statement should be the same. If the two do not match, check your math, making sure every check and deposit was recorded correctly in your checkbook and on the bank statement.

Many people do not take the time to reconcile their accounts; however, failure to do this could cost you money. If the bank subtracts more for a check than the amount for which you wrote it and you don't complain within a year, the bank may not be liable for correcting the error. Regulations covering this situation vary from state to state.

# Financial Planning Calculations

## RECONCILING YOUR CHECKING ACCOUNT

The process of comparing your checkbook balance to the bank statement is vital for determining any errors that may have occurred. Use the following steps to reconcile your account.

| THE BANK STATEMENT | | | YOUR CHECKBOOK | | |
|---|---|---|---|---|---|
| Balance on current bank statement | $ | 643.96 | Current balance in your checkbook | $ | 295.91 |

| | Date | Amount | | | |
|---|---|---|---|---|---|
| **Step 1.** Add up outstanding checks (checks that you have written but have not yet cleared the banking system) and withdrawals still outstanding. | 10-4 | 70.00 | **Step 3.** Subtract total of fees or other charges listed on bank statement. | $ | −15.75 |
| | 10-6 | 130.00 | | | |
| | 10-7 | 111.62 | Subtract ATM withdrawals. | $ | −100.00 |
| Subtract the total. | $ | −311.62 | **Step 4.** Add interest earned. | $ | +2.18 |
| **Step 2.** Add up deposits in transit (deposits that have been made but are not reported on the current statement). | 10-2 | 60.00 | Add direct deposits. | $ | +300.00 |
| | 10-5 | 90.00 | | | |
| Add the total. | $ | +150.00 | Adjusted checkbook balance | $ | 482.34 |
| Adjusted bank balance | $ | 482.34 | | | |

# 6

# Introduction to Consumer Credit

## A Rising House of Cards?   Poorer Borrowers Use More Plastic

What, me worry? With the strong economy, hefty income growth, and bulging stock portfolios, consumers have been spending—and borrowing—with abandon. Indeed, credit card debt jumped by $22.5 billion in the six months ending in January 1999, more than double the rise of the prior 12 months.

An interesting question is how consumers with credit card debt will fare. A recent analysis by Federal Reserve Bank of New York economists suggests that a new class of borrowers may be especially at risk. It notes that the credit card charge-off rate, a measure of bad loans written off by banks, jumped sharply when the economy slowed moderately in 1995 and continued to rise to a 25-year high in 1997, even after growth rebounded.

Fed survey data help explain why. From 1989 to 1995, as the percentage of households with plastic rose from 56 to 67 percent, the share of cardholders with incomes less than $25,000 increased from 22 to 28 percent. Meanwhile, the average credit card balance rose from $1,000 to $1,700, and the typical cardholder's liquid assets fell more than 25 percent.

Consider this: Total household debt is now perilously close, at 98 percent, to total disposable annual income. At the end of the famously debt-happy 1980s, consumer IOUs stood at only 80 percent of total household earnings.

In sum, poorer, riskier borrowers joined the credit card ranks in the 1990s and apparently took on a lot of debt in the process. And it's this group, many of whose members have low-level blue-collar jobs, that seems highly vulnerable to even a modest cyclical slowdown.

### Credit-Card Debt Leaps Higher

6-month growth in consumer revolving credit

6 months ending in: July '97  Jan '98  July '98  Jan '99

▲ Billions of Dollars    Data: Federal Reserve

## Questions

1. Why are today's consumers spending and borrowing heavily?
2. Why do some experts suggest that a new class of borrowers may be especially at risk if economic growth slows?
3. Visit the Federal Reserve Bank of New York's website at www.ny.frb.org or other Federal Reserve websites and obtain the latest information on consumer credit card debt. Is this debt stable or rising?

SOURCES: Gene Koretz, "A Rising House of Cards," *Business Week,* April 5, 1999, p. 28; Michael J. Mandel, "Is the U.S. Building a Debt Bomb?" *Business Week,* November 1, 1999, pp. 40–42. Reprinted from the November 1, 1999 issue of *Business Week* by special permission. © 1999 McGraw-Hill Companies, Inc.

## Learning Objectives

**Obj. 1**   Define consumer credit and analyze its advantages and disadvantages.

**Obj. 2**   Differentiate among various types of credit.

**Obj. 3**   Assess your credit capacity and build your credit rating.

**Obj. 4**   Describe the information creditors look for when you apply for credit.

**Obj. 5**   Identify the steps you can take to avoid and correct credit mistakes.

**Obj. 6**   Describe the laws that protect you if you have a complaint about consumer credit.

## WHAT IS CONSUMER CREDIT?

**Obj. 1**
Define consumer credit and analyze its advantages and disadvantages.

*credit*   An arrangement to receive cash, goods, or services now and pay for them in the future.

*consumer credit*   The use of credit for personal needs (except a home mortgage).

"Charge it!" "Cash or credit?" "Put it on my account." As these phrases indicate, the use of credit is a fact of life in personal and family financial planning. When you use credit, you satisfy needs today and pay for this satisfaction in the future. While the use of credit is often necessary and even advantageous, responsibilities and disadvantages are associated with its use.

**Credit** is an arrangement to receive cash, goods, or services now and pay for them in the future. **Consumer credit** refers to the use of credit for personal needs (except a home mortgage) by individuals and families in contrast to credit used for business purposes.

Although Polonius cautioned, "Neither a borrower nor a lender be," using and providing credit have become a way of life for many people and businesses in today's economy. In January, you pay a bill for electricity that you used in December. A statement arrives in the mail for medical services that you received last month. You write a check for $40, a minimum payment on a $300 department store bill. With a bank loan, you purchase a new car. These are all examples of using credit: paying later for goods and services obtained now.

Most consumers have three alternatives in financing current purchases: They can draw on their savings, use their present earnings, or borrow against their expected future income. Each of these alternatives has trade-offs. If you continually deplete your savings, little will be left for emergencies or retirement income. If you spend your current income on luxuries instead of necessities, your well-being will eventually suffer. And if you pledge your future income to make current credit purchases, you will have little or no spendable income in the future.

Consumer credit is based on trust in people's ability and willingness to pay bills when due. It works because people by and large are honest and responsible. But how does consumer credit affect our economy, and how is it affected by our economy?

### The Importance of Consumer Credit in Our Economy

Consumer credit dates back to colonial times. While credit was originally a privilege of the affluent, farmers came to use it extensively. No direct finance charges were imposed; instead, the cost of credit was added to the prices of goods. With the advent of the automobile in the early 1900s, installment credit, in which the debt is repaid in equal installments over a specified period of time, exploded on the American scene.

All economists now recognize consumer credit as a major force in the American economy. Any forecast or evaluation of the economy includes consumer spending trends and consumer credit as a sustaining force. To paraphrase an old political expression, as the consumer goes, so goes the U.S. economy.

The aging of the baby boom generation has added to the growth of consumer credit. This generation currently represents about 30 percent of the population but holds nearly 60 percent of the outstanding debt. The people in this age group have always been disproportionate users of credit, since consumption is highest as families are formed and homes are purchased and furnished. Thus, while the extensive use of debt by this generation is nothing new, the fact that it has grown rapidly has added to overall debt use.

## Uses and Misuses of Credit

Using credit to purchase goods and services may allow consumers to be more efficient or more productive or to lead more satisfying lives. There are many valid reasons for using credit. A medical emergency may leave a person strapped for funds. A homemaker returning to the work force may need a car. It may be possible to buy an item now for less money than it will cost later. Borrowing for a college education is another valid reason. But it probably is not reasonable to borrow for everyday living expenses or finance a Corvette on credit when a Ford Escort is all your budget allows.

"Shopaholics" and young adults are most vulnerable to misusing credit. College students are a prime target for credit card issuers, and issuers make it very easy for students to get credit cards. Wendy Leright, a 25-year-old teacher in Detroit, knows this all too well. As a college freshman, she applied for and got seven credit cards, all bearing at least an 18.9 percent interest rate and a $20 annual fee. Although unemployed, she used the cards freely, buying expensive clothes for herself, extravagant Christmas presents for friends and family, and even a one-week vacation in the Bahamas. "It got to a point where I didn't even look at the price tag," she said. By her senior year, Wendy had amassed $9,000 in credit card debt and couldn't make the monthly payments of nearly $200. She eventually turned to her parents to bail her out. "Until my mother sat me down and showed me how much interest I had to pay, I hadn't even given it a thought. I was shocked," Wendy said. "I would have had to pay it off for years."[1]

Using credit increases the amount of money a person can spend to purchase goods and services now. But the trade-off is that it decreases the amount of money that will be available to spend in the future. However, many people expect their incomes to increase and therefore expect to be able to make payments on past credit purchases and still make new purchases.

Here are some questions you should consider before you decide how and when to make a major purchase, for example, a car:

- Do I have the cash I need for the down payment?
- Do I want to use my savings for this purchase?
- Does the purchase fit my budget?
- Could I use the credit I need for this purchase in some better way?
- Could I postpone the purchase?
- What are the opportunity costs of postponing the purchase? (Alternative transportation costs, a possible increase in the price of the car)

- What are the dollar costs and the psychological costs of using credit? (Interest, other finance charges, being in debt and responsible for making a monthly payment)

If you decide to use credit, make sure the benefits of making the purchase now (increased efficiency or productivity, a more satisfying life, etc.) outweigh the costs (financial and psychological) of using credit. Thus, credit, when effectively used, can help you have more and enjoy more. When misused, credit can result in default, bankruptcy, and loss of creditworthiness.

## Advantages of Credit

Consumer credit enables people to enjoy goods and services now—a car, a home, an education, help in emergencies—and pay for them through payment plans based on future income.

Credit cards permit the purchase of goods even when funds are low. Customers with previously approved credit may receive other extras, such as advance notice of sales and the right to order by phone or to buy on approval. In addition, many shoppers believe it is easier to return merchandise they have purchased on account. Credit cards also provide shopping convenience and the efficiency of paying for several purchases with one monthly payment.

Credit is more than a substitute for cash. Many of the services it provides are taken for granted. Every time you turn on the water tap, flick the light switch, or telephone a friend, you are using credit.

It is safer to use credit, since charge accounts and credit cards let you shop and travel without carrying a large amount of cash. You need a credit card to make a hotel reservation, rent a car, and shop by phone. You may also use credit cards for identification when cashing checks, and the use of credit provides you with a record of expenses.

The use of credit cards can provide up to a 50-day "float," the time lag between when you make the purchase and when the lender deducts the balance from your checking account when the payment is due. This float, offered by many credit card issuers, includes a grace period of 20 to 25 days. During the grace period, no finance charges are assessed on current purchases if the balance is paid in full each month within 25 days after billing.

Some large corporations, such as General Electric Company and General Motors Corporation, issue their own Visa and MasterCard and offer rebates on purchases. For example, every time you make a purchase with the GM MasterCard, 5 percent of the purchase price is set aside for you in a special GM Card Rebate account. When you are ready to buy or lease a GM car or truck, you just cash in your rebate at the GM dealership. Similarly, with a Discover card, you can earn a cash bonus of up to 1 percent based on your total purchases during the year. In the late 1990s, however, some corporations began to eliminate these cards.

Platinum credit cards offered by American Express provide emergency medical evacuation for travelers. In 1994, Stephen Bradley of New York was vacationing in tiny, isolated Coruripe, Brazil. He ate something that made him gravely ill. With no doctor nearby, a friend frantically called American Express about its guarantee to arrange emergency medical evacuation and treatment for Platinum Card users. AmEx moved fast: It lined up a car to rush Bradley to the nearest large town, managed to book a room in a sold-out hotel, and sent a doctor there to make a house call. The physician even accompanied Bradley's travel partner, Richard Laermer, to a local pharmacy for medicine. "When we went home to see our doctor, he told us she had saved Steve's life," recalls Laermer. "For the last five years we have been indebted to Platinum." Merrill Lynch and Company has introduced a new card with many of the same benefits, but with a lower annual fee.[2]

Finally, credit indicates stability. The fact that lenders consider you a good risk usually means you are a responsible individual. However, if you do not repay your debts in a timely manner, you will find that credit has many disadvantages.

## Disadvantages of Credit

Perhaps the greatest disadvantage of using credit is the temptation to overspend, especially during periods of inflation. It seems easy to buy today and pay tomorrow using cheaper dollars. But continual overspending can lead to serious trouble.

Whether or not credit involves security (something of value to back the loan), failure to repay a loan may result in loss of income, valuable property, and your good reputation. It can even lead to court action and bankruptcy. Misuse of credit can create serious long-term financial problems, damage to family relationships, and a slowing of progress toward financial goals. Therefore, you should approach credit with caution and avoid using it more extensively than your budget permits.

Although credit allows more immediate satisfaction of needs and desires, it does not increase total purchasing power. Credit purchases must be paid for out of future income; therefore, credit ties up the use of future income. Furthermore, if your income does not increase to cover rising costs, your ability to repay credit commitments will diminish. Before buying goods and services on credit, consider whether they will have lasting value, whether they will increase your personal satisfaction during present and future income periods, and whether your current income will continue or increase.

Finally, credit costs money. It is a service for which you must pay. Paying for purchases over a period of time is more costly than paying for them with cash. Purchasing with credit rather than cash involves one very obvious trade-off: the fact that it will cost more due to monthly finance charges and the compounding effect of interest on interest.

## Summary: Advantages and Disadvantages of Credit

The use of credit provides immediate access to goods and services, flexibility in money management, safety and convenience, a cushion in emergencies, a means of increasing resources, and a good credit rating if you pay your debts back in a timely manner. But remember, the use of credit is a two-sided coin. An intelligent decision as to its use demands careful evaluation of your current debt, your future income, the added cost, and the consequences of overspending.

### Concept Check 6-1

1. How might consumers with credit card debt fare if a cyclical slowdown occurs?
2. What is consumer credit?
3. Why is consumer credit important to our economy?
4. What are the uses and misuses of credit?
5. What are the advantages and disadvantages of credit?

| EXHIBIT 6-1 | **Closed-End Credit** | **Open-End Credit** |
|---|---|---|
| Examples of Closed-End and Open-End Credit | • Mortgage loans<br>• Automobile loans<br>• Installment loans (Installment sales contract, installment cash credit, single lump-sum credit) | • Cards issued by department stores, bank cards (Visa, MasterCard, American Express)<br>• Travel & entertainment (T&E)<br>• Overdraft protection |

## TYPES OF CREDIT

**Obj. 2**

Differentiate among various types of credit.

*closed-end credit* One-time loans that the borrower pays back in a specified period of time and in payments of equal amounts.

*open-end credit* A line of credit in which loans are made on a continuous basis and the borrower is billed periodically for at least partial payment.

Two basic types of consumer credit exist: closed-end credit and open-end credit. With **closed-end credit,** you pay back one-time loans in a specified period of time and in payments of equal amounts. With **open-end credit,** loans are made on a continuous basis and you are billed periodically for at least partial payment. Exhibit 6–1 shows examples of closed-end and open-end credit.

### Closed-End Credit

Closed-end credit is used for a specific purpose and involves a specified amount. Mortgage loans, automobile loans, and installment loans for purchasing furniture or appliances are examples of closed-end credit. An agreement, or contract, lists the repayment terms: the number of payments, the payment amount, and how much the credit will cost. Closed-end payment plans usually involve a written agreement for each credit purchase. A down payment or trade-in may be required, with the balance to be repaid in equal weekly or monthly payments over a period of time. Generally, the seller holds title to the merchandise until the payments have been completed.

The three most common types of closed-end credit are installment sales credit, installment cash credit, and single lump-sum credit. *Installment sales credit* is a loan that allows you to receive merchandise, usually high-priced items such as large appliances or furniture. You make a down payment and usually sign a contract to repay the balance, plus interest and service charges, in equal installments over a specified period.

*Installment cash credit* is a direct loan of money for personal purposes, home improvements, or vacation expenses. You make no down payment and make payments in specified amounts over a set period.

*Single lump-sum credit* is a loan that must be repaid in total on a specified day, usually within 30 to 90 days. Lump-sum credit is generally, but not always, used to purchase a single item. As Exhibit 6–2 shows, consumer installment credit reached over $1.2 trillion in 1997.

### Open-End Credit

*line of credit* The dollar amount, which may or may not be borrowed, that a lender makes available to a borrower.

*interest* A periodic charge for the use of credit.

Using a credit card issued by a department store, using a bank credit card (Visa, MasterCard) to make purchases at different stores, charging a meal at a restaurant, and using overdraft protection are examples of open-end credit. As you will soon see, you do not apply for open-end credit to make a single purchase, as you do with closed-end credit. Rather, you can use open-end credit to make any purchases you wish if you do not exceed your **line of credit,** the maximum dollar amount of credit the lender has made available to you. You may have to pay **interest,** a periodic charge for the use of credit, or other finance charges. Some creditors allow you a grace period of 20 to 25 days to pay a bill in full before you incur any interest charges.

You may have had an appointment with a doctor or a dentist that you did not pay for until later. Professionals and small businesses often do not demand immediate payment

## Volume of Consumer Credit

All economists now recognize consumer credit as a major force in the American economy.

SOURCE: Statistical Abstract of the United States 1998, Table 820, p. 523.

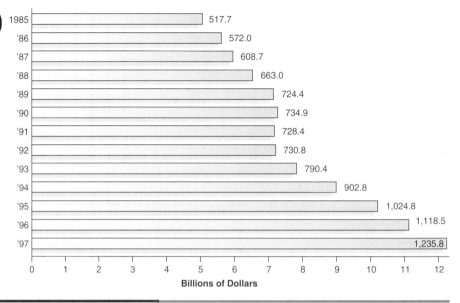

| Year | Billions of Dollars |
|------|---------------------|
| 1985 | 517.7 |
| '86 | 572.0 |
| '87 | 608.7 |
| '88 | 663.0 |
| '89 | 724.4 |
| '90 | 734.9 |
| '91 | 728.4 |
| '92 | 730.8 |
| '93 | 790.4 |
| '94 | 902.8 |
| '95 | 1,024.8 |
| '96 | 1,118.5 |
| '97 | 1,235.8 |

*revolving check credit*
A prearranged loan from a bank for a specified amount; also called a *bank line of credit.*

but will charge interest if you do not pay the bill in full within 30 days. *Incidental credit* is a credit arrangement that has no extra costs and no specific repayment plan.

Many retailers use open-end credit. Customers can purchase goods or services up to a fixed dollar limit at any time. Usually you have the option to pay the bill in full within 30 days without interest charges or to make set monthly installments based on the account balance plus interest.

Many banks extend **revolving check credit.** Also called a *bank line of credit,* this is a prearranged loan for a specified amount that you can use by writing a special check. Repayment is made in installments over a set period. The finance charges are based on the amount of credit used during the month and on the outstanding balance.

### Credit Cards

Credit cards are extremely popular. According to a recent *American Banker* survey, 8 out of 10 U.S. households carry one or more credit cards. Two out of three households have at least one retail credit card, 56 percent have one or more Visa cards, and 47 percent have at least one MasterCard.[3]

One-third of all credit card users generally pay off their balances in full each month. These cardholders are often known as *convenience users.* Others are borrowers; they carry balances beyond the grace period and pay finance charges. As Exhibit 6–3 illustrates, consumers use more than 1.4 billion credit cards to buy clothing, meals, vacations, gasoline, groceries, doctor visits, and other goods and services on credit.

While cash advances on credit cards can look attractive, remember that interest usually accrues from the moment you accept the cash, and you must also pay a transaction fee. One cash advance could cost you the money you were saving for a birthday gift for that special someone.

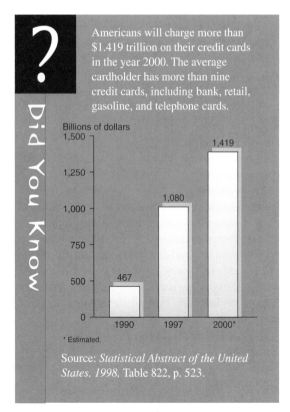

### Did You Know?

Americans will charge more than $1.419 trillion on their credit cards in the year 2000. The average cardholder has more than nine credit cards, including bank, retail, gasoline, and telephone cards.

Billions of dollars

| Year | Amount |
|------|--------|
| 1990 | 467 |
| 1997 | 1,080 |
| 2000* | 1,419 |

* Estimated.

Source: *Statistical Abstract of the United States, 1998,* Table 822, p. 523.

## EXHIBIT 6-3

### Credit Card Holders and Credit Cards Held

About 157 million people use more than 1.4 billion credit cards to buy goods and services.

SOURCE: *Statistical Abstract of the United States 1998*, Table 822, p. 523.

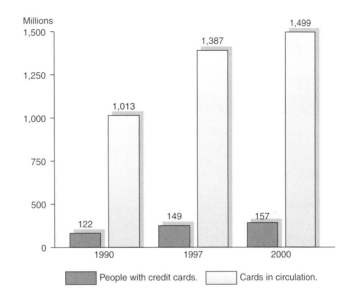

Millions

| | 1990 | 1997 | 2000 |
|---|---|---|---|
| People with credit cards. | 122 | 149 | 157 |
| Cards in circulation. | 1,013 | 1,387 | 1,499 |

About 25,000 financial institutions participate in the credit card business, and the vast majority of them are affiliated with Visa International or the Interbank Card Association, which issues MasterCard. The Financial Planning for Life's Situations box on page 172 provides a few helpful hints for choosing a credit card.

*Cobranding* is the linking of a credit card with a business trade name offering "points" or premiums toward the purchase of a product or service. Cobranding has become increasingly popular since the success of General Motors Corporation's credit card, launched in 1992. Cobranded credit cards offer rebates on products and services such as health clubs, tax preparation services from H&R Block, and gasoline purchases. Banks are realizing that cobranded credit cards help build customer loyalty. *Smart cards,* the ultimate plastic, embedded with a computer chip that can store 500 times the data of a credit card, are on their way.

Smart cards combine credit cards, a driver's license, a health care ID with your medical history and insurance information, frequent-flier miles, and telephone cards. A single smart card, for example, can be used to buy an airline ticket, store it digitally, and track frequent-flier miles. In the near future, smart cards will provide a crucial link between the World Wide Web and the physical world. "The Internet combined with the development of electronic cash will finally start the smart-card revolution in the U.S.," according to Keith S. Kendrick, senior vice president at AT&T Universal Card. Citibank, Chase Manhattan Corporation, and Wells Fargo & Company have begun testing the smart credit/debit cards.[4]

At Florida State University, smart cards have become practically indispensable. Students use smart cards to pay tuition, buy meals in the cafeteria, borrow library books, rent videos, and gain access to dormitories and online study groups.[5]

Don't confuse credit cards with debit cards. Debit cards are often called *bank cards, ATM cards, cash cards,* and *check cards.* Although they may look alike, the **debit card**, as the name implies, electronically subtracts from your account at the moment you buy goods or services, while the credit card extends credit and delays your payment. Debit cards are most commonly used at automatic teller machines, but they are increasingly being used to purchase goods at point-of-sale terminals in stores and service stations. It is estimated that in 2000, over 9.4 billion transactions worth $368 billion took place with 353 million debit cards.[6]

*debit card*   Electronically subtracts the amount of a purchase from the buyer's account at the moment the purchase is made.

# Financial Planning for Life's Situations

## CHOOSING A CREDIT CARD?

When choosing a credit card, it pays to shop around. Follow these suggestions to select the card that best meets your needs.

1. Department stores and gasoline companies are good places to obtain your first credit card. Pay your bills in full and on time, and you will begin to establish a good credit history.

2. Bank cards are offered through banks and savings and loan associations. Fees and finance charges vary considerably (from 8 to 21.6 percent), so shop around.

3. If you usually pay your bill in full, try to deal with a financial institution with an interest-free grace period, which is the time after a purchase has been made and before a finance charge is imposed, typically 25 to 30 days.

4. If you're used to paying monthly installments, look for a card with a low monthly finance charge. Be sure you understand how that finance charge is calculated.

5. Consider obtaining a card from an out-of-state financial institution if it offers better terms than those offered locally.

6. Be aware of some credit cards that offer "no fee" or low interest but start charging interest from the day you purchase an item.

7. Watch out for credit cards that do not charge annual fees but instead charge a "transaction fee" each time you use the card.

8. If you're paying only the minimum amounts on your monthly statement, you need to plan your budget more carefully. The longer it takes for you to pay off a bill, the more interest you pay. The finance charges you pay on an item could end up being more than the item is worth.

9. With a grace period of 25 days, you actually get a free loan when you pay bills in full each month.

10. To avoid delays that may result in finance charges, follow the card issuer's instructions as to where, how, and when to make bill payments.

11. If you have a bad credit history and problems getting a credit card, look for a savings institution that will give you a secured credit card if you open a savings account. Your line of credit will be determined by the amount you have on deposit.

12. Beware of offers of easy credit. No one can guarantee to get you credit.

13. Think twice before making a 900 number telephone call for a credit card. You will pay from $2 to $50 for the 900 call and may never receive a credit card.

14. Be aware of credit cards offered by "credit repair" companies or "credit clinics." These firms may also offer to clean up your credit history for a fee. But remember, only time and good credit habits will repair your credit report if you have a poor credit history.

15. If you don't have a list of your credit issuers' telephone numbers, you may be able to obtain them by calling the 800 number directory assistance at 1–800–555–1212.

16. Travel and entertainment (T&E) cards often charge higher annual fees than most credit cards. Usually you must make payment in full within 30 days of receiving your bill or typically no further purchases will be approved on the account.

17. Often additional credit cards on your account for a spouse or child (over 18) are available with a minimum additional fee or no fee at all.

18. Be aware that debit cards are not credit cards but simply a substitute for a check or cash. The amount of the sale is subtracted from your checking account.

SOURCES: American Institute of Certified Public Accountants; U.S. Office of Consumer Affairs; Federal Trade Commission.

You are never responsible for charges on a debit card you haven't accepted. If you report a lost or stolen debit card within two days, federal regulations limit your liability to $50. After two days, your liability is limited to $50 plus any amount resulting from your failure to notify the issuer. If your debit card is lost or stolen, you must work directly with the issuer.

**Protecting Yourself against Debit/Credit Card Fraud**   In a country where consumers owe more than $1 trillion on their credit cards, estimates of $2 billion to $3 billion in credit fraud losses—just two to three one-thousandths of 1 percent—may not

### JONATHAN HOENIG ON CREDIT CHAOS

According to Jonathan Hoenig, a radio show host and a columnist, "the bubonic plague of personal finance comes in the form of a 17 percent or higher interest rate on your credit card. You'll have to do a lot of bargain shopping and coupon clipping to compensate for your constantly compounding finance charges. Bummer? *Yes.* Your fault? *Yes.* Just because you have access to credit doesn't mean you should necessarily partake of the plastic." He cautions that credit cards can be a useful part of personal finance or a painful experience. Rule of thumb: *Don't buy things you can't afford.*

Thankfully, most young people seem to be following the rules these days. According to *Scholars and Cents,* an independent study sponsored by Visa USA, more than half of young people surveyed pay their credit card balance in full each month. Compared to the majority of cardholders, 60 percent of whom carry a balance, young people are demonstrating their financial savvy in record numbers.

Paying cash? You'll still deal with debt. Certain types, like school loans, car payments, and mortgages, are designed to be paid over longer periods of time. This is reflected in a lower interest rate. A credit card bill, and other types of "unsecured" debt, however, should be paid as soon as possible, advises Hoenig.

The Visa survey suggests young people are headed in the right direction. Ninety-four percent of college students recognize the importance of establishing and maintaining a good credit history.

seem all that terrible. But it *is* terrible for victims of fraud. Though they may be protected financially, they are forced to endure major inconvenience. Many fraud victims are devastated emotionally. The negative effects can linger for years. Moreover, all of us pay the costs of credit card fraud through higher prices, higher interest rates, and increased inconvenience.

How can you protect yourself against credit card fraud? You can take several measures:

- Sign your new cards as soon as they arrive.
- Treat your cards like money. Store them in a secure place.
- Shred anything with your account number before throwing it away.
- Don't give your card number over the phone or online unless you initiate the call.
- Don't write your card number on a postcard or the outside of an envelope.
- Remember to get your card and receipt after a transaction, and double-check to be sure it's yours.
- If your billing statement is incorrect or your credit cards are lost or stolen, notify your card issuers immediately.
- If you don't receive your billing statement, notify the company immediately.
- If you are a victim of credit card fraud, call Experian at 1–888–EXPERIAN.
- Request a copy of your credit report every few years. Reviewing your report will tell you if anyone has applied for credit in your name and whether any accounts are being used without your knowledge, with the billing statement being sent to a different address.[7]

The Internet has joined the telephone and television as an important part of our lives. Every day, more consumers use the Internet for financial activities like investing, banking, and shopping.

When you make purchases online, make sure your transactions are secure, your personal information is protected, and your fraud sensors are sharpened. Although you

## Financial Planning for Life's Situations

### A NEW BLUE CARD FOR THE TECHIES

American Express wants tech-savvy customers for its new Blue credit card, designed for online buyers. AmEx is pitching its Blue card as an ultrasafe way to shop online. Equipped with a built-in computer chip, the card can be plugged into a special reader attached to the user's computer to verify the shopper's identity and unlock the digital wallet. The digital wallet service, offered in late 1999, will store all of a customer's key shopping information, such as credit card numbers, on a secure AmEx site. For "e-tailers" that accept the wallet, including Amazon.com, CDnow, and Gap Online, AmEx will zap that information to the merchant.

Not to be outdone by AmEx, other Internet credit card issuers are aiming at online buyers. NextCard, the Internet credit card issuer based in San Francisco, has high hopes for its Dilbert card, which features characters from the popular comic strip. The card features instant approvals, no late fees, and double frequent-flier miles, and if you don't need paper statements, the card pays you a "reverse" fee. Applicants who apply through the Dilbert.com website can adorn their cards with a picture of a Dilbert character and a title under their own name.

SOURCES: Mike McNamee, "Don't Leave Home Without a Freebie," *Business Week,* November 8, 1999, pp. 150–51; Pamela Black, "Just Put It on My Dilbert," *Business Week,* October 18, 1999, p. 8.

can't control fraud or deception on the Internet, you can take steps to recognize it, avoid it, and report if it does occur. Here's how:

- *Use a secure browser,* software that encrypts or scrambles the purchase information you send over the Internet, to guard the security of your online transactions. Most computers come with a secure browser already installed. You can also download some browsers for free over the Internet.
- *Keep records of your online transactions.* Read your e-mail. Merchants may send you important information about your purchases.
- *Review your monthly bank and credit card statements* for any billing errors or unauthorized purchases. Notify your credit card issuer or bank immediately if your credit card or checkbook is lost or stolen.
- *Read the policies of websites you visit,* especially the disclosures about a site's security, its refund policies, and its privacy policy on collecting and using your personal information. Some websites' disclosures are easier to find than others; look at the bottom of the home page, on order forms, or in the "About" or "FAQS" section of a site. If you can't find a privacy policy, consider shopping elsewhere.
- *Keep you personal information private.* Don't disclose personal information—your address, telephone number, Social Security number, or e-mail address—unless you know who's collecting the information, why they're collecting it, and how they'll use it.
- *Give payment information only to businesses you know and trust,* and only in appropriate places such as electronic order forms.
- *Never give your password to anyone online,* even your Internet service provider.
- *Do not download files sent to you by strangers or click on hyperlinks from people you don't know.* Opening a file could expose your computer system to a virus.[8]

The accompanying Financial Planning for Life's Situations box describes what American Express and other card issuers have planned for online buyers.

# Financial Planning Calculations

## HOW MUCH CAN YOU BORROW WITH A HOME EQUITY LOAN?

Depending on your income and the equity in your home, you can apply for a line of credit for anywhere from $10,000 to $250,000 or more.

Some lenders let you borrow only up to 75 percent of the value of your home, less the amount of your first mortgage. At some banks you may qualify to borrow up to 85 percent! This higher lending limit may make the difference in your ability to get the money you need for home improvements, education, or other expenses.

Use the following chart to calculate your home loan value, which is the approximate amount of your home equity line of credit.

|  | Example | Your Home |
| --- | --- | --- |
| Approximate market value of your home | $100,000 | $ _____ |
| Multiply by .85 | ×.85 | ×.85 |
| Approximate loan value | 85,000 | _____ |
| Subtract balance due on mortgage(s) | 50,000 | _____ |
| Approximate credit limit available | $35,000 | $ _____ |

In the above example, your home loan value (the amount for which you could establish your account) is $35,000.

Once your account is established, you can write a check for any amount you need up to $35,000.

In choosing a home equity loan,

1. Find out if your lending institution protects you against rising interest rates.
2. Compare the size of your lender's fee with those of other institutions.
3. Find out if your lender charges an inactivity fee.
4. Make sure high annual fees and other costs do not outweigh the tax advantage of a home equity loan, especially if you are borrowing only a small amount.
5. Be careful of interest-only payments on home equity loans.
6. Find out whether your lender has the right to change the terms and conditions of your plan or to terminate your plan.
7. Make sure that all of the interest you hope to finally deduct on your home equity loan is in fact deductible.
8. Carefully evaluate your reasons for using the equity in your home for loans.
9. Know the full costs and risks of home equity loans before you make a commitment to a lending institution.

SOURCES: *Home Equity Loan Guide,* Household Bank, F.S.B., August 1991, p. 3; *Home Equity Loans: A Consumer's Guide,* American Institute of CPAs, n.d.

**Travel and Entertainment (T&E) Cards**   T&E cards are really not credit cards, because the monthly balance is due in full. However, most people think of Diners Club or American Express cards as credit cards because they don't pay the moment they purchase goods or services.

*home equity loan*
A loan based on the current market value of a home less the amount still owed on the mortgage.

**Home Equity Loans**   A **home equity loan** is based on the difference between the current market value of your home and the amount you still owe on your mortgage. With such a loan, you can borrow up to $100,000 or more on your home. Depending on the value of the home, you can borrow up to 85 percent of its appraised value, less the amount you still owe on your mortgage. The interest you pay on a home equity loan is tax deductible, unlike interest on other types of loans.

A home equity loan is usually set up as a revolving line of credit, typically with a variable interest rate. A *revolving line of credit* is an arrangement whereby borrowings are permitted up to a specified limit and for a stated period, usually 5 to 10 years. Once the line of credit has been established, you draw from it only the amount you need at any one time (see the accompanying Financial Planning Calculations box). Today many lenders offer home equity lines of credit. But your home is your largest asset. You should use the home equity loan only for major items such as education, home improvements, or medical bills and not for daily expenses. Remember, if you miss payments on a home equity loan, you can lose your home. Furthermore, when you sell your home, you probably will be required to pay off your equity line in full. If you plan to sell your house in the near future, consider whether annual fees to maintain the account and other costs of setting up an equity credit line make sense.

## Concept Check 6-2

1. What are the two main types of consumer credit?
2. What is a debit card?
3. What is a home equity loan?

## MEASURING YOUR CREDIT CAPACITY

### Obj. 3
Assess your credit capacity and build your credit rating.

The only way to determine how much credit you can assume is to first learn how to make an accurate and sensible personal or family budget. Budgets, as you learned in Chapter 3, are simple, carefully considered spending plans. With budgets, you first provide for basic necessities such as rent or mortgage, food, and clothing. Then you provide for items such as home furnishings and other heavy, more durable goods.

### Can You Afford a Loan?

Before you take out a loan, ask yourself whether you can meet all of your essential expenses and still afford the monthly loan payments. You can make this calculation in two ways. One is to add up all of your basic monthly expenses and then subtract this total from your take-home pay. If the difference will not cover the monthly payment and still leave funds for other expenses, you cannot afford the loan.

A second and more reliable method is to ask yourself what you plan to give up to make the monthly loan payment. If you currently save a portion of your income that is greater than the monthly payment, you can use these savings to pay off the loan. But if you do not, you will have to forgo spending on entertainment, new appliances, or perhaps even necessities. Are you prepared to make this trade-off? Although it is difficult to precisely measure your credit capacity, you can follow certain rules of thumb.

### General Rules of Credit Capacity

#### Debt Payments-to-Income Ratio
The debt payments–to–income ratio is calculated by dividing your monthly debt payments (not including house payment, which is a long-term liability) by your net monthly income. Experts suggest that you spend no more than 20 percent of your net (after-tax) income on consumer credit payments. Thus, as Exhibit 6–4 shows, a person making $1,068 per month after taxes should spend no more than $213 on credit payments per month.

The 20 percent estimate is the maximum; however, 15 percent is much better. The 20 percent estimate is based on the average family, with average expenses; it does not take major

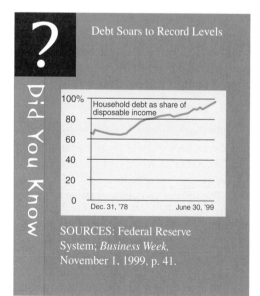

Did You Know?

**Debt Soars to Record Levels**

Household debt as share of disposable income

Dec. 31, '78          June 30, '99

SOURCES: Federal Reserve System; *Business Week*, November 1, 1999, p. 41.

### EXHIBIT 6-4

**How to Calculate Debt Payments-to-Income Ratio**

Spend no more than 20 percent of your net (after-tax) income on credit payments.

| | |
|---|---:|
| Monthly gross income | $1,500 |
| Less: | |
|     All taxes | 270 |
|     Social Security | 112 |
|     Monthly IRA contribution | 50 |
| Monthly net income | $ 1,068 |
| Monthly installment credit payments: | |
|     Visa | 25 |
|     MasterCard | 20 |
|     Discover card | 15 |
|     Education loan | — |
|     Personal bank loan | — |
|     Auto loan | 153 |
| Total monthly payments | $  213 |
| Debt payments-to-income ratio ($213/$1,068) | 19.94% |

**Sheet 29**

emergencies into account. If you are just beginning to use credit, you should not consider yourself safe if you are spending 20 percent of your net income on credit payments.

**Debt-to-Equity Ratio**     The debt-to-equity ratio is calculated by dividing your total liabilities by your net worth. In calculating this ratio, do not include the value of your home and the amount of its mortgage. If your debt-to-equity ratio is about 1—that is, if your consumer installment debt roughly equals your net worth (not including your home or the mortgage)—you have probably reached the upper limit of debt obligations.

The debt-to-equity ratio for business firms in general ranges between 0.33 and 0.50. The larger this ratio, the riskier the situation for lenders and borrowers. Of course, you can lower the debt-to-equity ratio by paying off debts.

None of the above methods is perfect for everyone; the limits given are only guidelines. Only you, based on the money you earn, your current obligations, and your financial plans for the future, can determine the exact amount of credit you need and can afford. You must be your own credit manager.

Keep in mind that you adversely affect your credit capacity if you cosign a loan for a friend or a relative.

## Cosigning a Loan

What would you do if a friend or a relative asked you to cosign a loan? Before you give your answer, make sure you understand what cosigning involves. Under a recent Federal Trade Commission rule, creditors are required to give you a notice to help explain your obligations. The cosigner's notice says,

> You are being asked to guarantee this debt. Think carefully before you do. If the borrower doesn't pay the debt, you will have to. Be sure you can afford to pay if you have to, and that you want to accept this responsibility.
>
> You may have to pay up to the full amount of the debt if the borrower does not pay. You may also have to pay late fees or collection costs, which increase this amount.
>
> The creditor can collect this debt from you without first trying to collect from the borrower. The creditor can use the same collection methods against you that can be used against the borrower, such as suing you, garnishing your wages, etc. If this debt is ever in default, that fact may become a part of *your* credit record.[9]

**Cosigners Often Pay**     Some studies of certain types of lenders show that as many as three of four cosigners are asked to wholly or partially repay the loan. That statistic should not surprise you. When you are asked to cosign, you are being asked to take a risk that a professional lender will not take. The lender would not require a cosigner if the borrower met the lender's criteria for making a loan.

In most states, if you do cosign and your friend or relative misses a payment, the lender can collect the entire debt from you immediately without pursuing the borrower first. Also, the amount you owe may increase if the lender decides to sue to collect. If the lender wins the case, it may be able to take your wages and property.

### If You Do Cosign

Despite the risks, at times you may decide to cosign. Perhaps your child needs a first loan or a close friend needs help. Here are a few things to consider before you cosign:

1. Be sure you can afford to pay the loan. If you are asked to pay and cannot, you could be sued or your credit rating could be damaged.
2. Consider that even if you are not asked to repay the debt, your liability for this loan may keep you from getting other credit you want.
3. Before you pledge property such as your automobile or furniture to secure the loan, make sure you understand the consequences. If the borrower defaults, you could lose the property you pledge.
4. Check your state law. Some states have laws giving you additional rights as a cosigner.
5. Request that a copy of overdue-payment notices be sent to you so that you can take action to protect your credit history.

## Building and Maintaining Your Credit Rating

If you apply for a charge account, credit card, car loan, personal loan, or mortgage, your credit experience, or lack of it, will be a major consideration for the creditor. Your credit experience may even affect your ability to get a job or buy life insurance. A good credit rating is a valuable asset that should be nurtured and protected. If you want a good rating, you must use credit with discretion: Limit your borrowing to your capacity to repay, and live up to the terms of your contracts. The quality of your credit rating is entirely up to you.

In reviewing your creditworthiness, a creditor seeks information from a credit bureau. Most creditors rely heavily on credit reports in considering loan applications.

*credit bureau*
A reporting agency that assembles credit and other information about consumers.

### Credit Bureaus

**Credit bureaus** collect credit and other information about consumers. There are three major credit bureaus: Experian Information Solutions (formerly TRW, Inc.), Trans Union Credit Information Company, and Equifax Services, Inc. Each bureau maintains over 200 million credit files on individuals based on 2½ billion items of information received each month from lenders.[10] In addition, several thousand regional credit bureaus collect credit information about consumers. These firms sell the data to creditors that evaluate credit applications.

The Federal Trade Commission receives more consumer complaints about credit bureaus than about any other industry, on average 11,000 a year. A common complaint involves mixups between people with identical surnames. However, the accuracy of credit reports has improved recently, due primarily to public outcry and the threat of stricter federal laws.

### Who Provides Data to Credit Bureaus?

Credit bureaus obtain their data from banks, finance companies, merchants, credit card companies, and other creditors. These sources regularly send reports to credit bureaus containing information about the kinds of credit they extend to customers, the amounts and terms of that credit, and customers' paying habits. Credit bureaus also collect some information from other sources, such as court records.

## EXHIBIT 6-5

### Sample Credit Report

All credit reports contain your name, address, Social Security number, and birth date.

SOURCE: Courtesy of Equifax Services, Inc.

## What Is in Your Credit Files?

As the sample credit report in Exhibit 6–5 shows, the credit bureau file contains your name, address, Social Security number, and birth date. It may also include the following information:

Your employer, position, and income.
Your former address.
Your former employer.
Your spouse's name, Social Security number, employer, and income.
Whether you own your home, rent, or board.
Checks returned for insufficient funds.

Your credit file may also contain detailed credit information. Each time you buy from a reporting store on credit or take out a loan at a bank, a finance company, or some other reporting creditor, a credit bureau is informed of your account number and the date, amount, terms, and type of credit. As you make payments, your file is updated

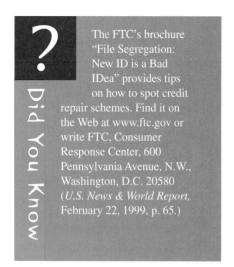

The FTC's brochure "File Segregation: New ID is a Bad IDea" provides tips on how to spot credit repair schemes. Find it on the Web at www.ftc.gov or write FTC, Consumer Response Center, 600 Pennsylvania Avenue, N.W., Washington, D.C. 20580 (*U.S. News & World Report*, February 22, 1999, p. 65.)

*Fair Credit Reporting Act*   Regulates the use of credit reports, requires the deletion of obsolete information, and gives consumers access to their files and the right to have erroneous data corrected.

to show the outstanding balance, the number and amounts of payments past due, and the frequency of 30-, 60-, or 90-day delinquencies. Any suits, judgments, or tax liens against you may appear as well. However, a federal law protects your rights if the information in your credit file is erroneous.

### Fair Credit Reporting

You can see that fair and accurate credit reporting is vital to both creditors and consumers. In 1971, Congress enacted the **Fair Credit Reporting Act**, which regulates the use of credit reports, requires the deletion of obsolete information, and gives consumers access to their files and the right to have erroneous data corrected. Furthermore, the act allows only authorized persons to obtain credit reports.

In the early 1990s, TRW, Inc. (now Experian Information Solutions, Inc.), settled lawsuits alleging that the credit-reporting giant used sloppy procedures that created errors in consumer credit files, inadequately investigated consumer complaints about inaccuracies, allowed errors to recur in credit files, and illegally sold consumer data to firms for their mailing lists.

Credit bureaus provide lists of creditworthy consumers for companies to offer credit. These are called prescreened lists. You can remove your name from all Experian-generated mail and telephone lists by sending your full name and addresses for the past five years to Experian, Consumer Opt Out, P.O. Box 919, Allen, TX 75013, or call 1–800–353–0809. Your name will be shared with Equifax and Trans Union, the other two national credit reporting systems.

### Who May Obtain a Credit Report?

Your credit report may be issued only to properly identified persons for approved purposes. It may be furnished to prospective employers in response to a court order or in accordance with your own written request. A credit report may also be provided to someone who will use it in connection with a credit transaction, underwriting of insurance, or some other legitimate business need or in determining eligibility for a license or other benefit granted by a government agency. Your friends and neighbors may not obtain credit information about you. If they request such information, they may be subject to fine and imprisonment.

The credit bureaus contend that current laws protect consumers' privacy, but many consumer organizations believe that anyone with a personal computer and a modem can easily access credit bureau files.

### Time Limits on Adverse Data

Most of the information in your credit file may be reported for only seven years. If you have declared personal bankruptcy, however, that fact may be reported for 10 years. After 7 or 10 years, a credit reporting agency can't disclose the information in your credit file unless you are being investigated for a credit application of $75,000 or more or for an application to purchase life insurance of $150,000 or more.

### Incorrect Information in Your Credit File

Credit bureaus are required to follow reasonable procedures to ensure that subscribing creditors report information accurately. However, mistakes may occur. Your file may contain erroneous data or records of someone with a name similar to yours. When you notify the credit bureau that you dispute the accuracy of its information, it must reinvestigate and modify or remove inaccurate data. You should give the credit bureau any pertinent data you have

## EXHIBIT 6-6

### Sample Dispute Letter

The law requires credit card companies to correct inaccurate or incomplete information in your credit report.

SOURCE: Federal Trade Commission. June 1999.

Date

Your Name
Your Address
Your City, State, Zip Code

Complaint Department
Name of Credit Reporting Agency
Address
City, State, Zip Code

Dear Sir or Madam:

I am writing to dispute the following information in my file. The items I dispute are also encircled on the attached copy of the report I received. (Identify item(s) disputed by name of source, such as creditor or tax court, and identify type of item, such as credit account, judgment, etc.)

This item is (inaccurate or incomplete) because (describe what is inaccurate or incomplete and why). I am requesting that the item be deleted (or request another specific change) to correct the information.

Enclosed are copies of (use this sentence if applicable and describe any enclosed documentation, such as payment records, court documents) supporting my position. Please reinvestigate this (these) matter(s) and (delete or correct) the disputed item(s) as soon as possible.

Sincerely,
Your name

Enclosures: (List what you are enclosing)

concerning an error. If you contest an item on your credit report, the reporting agency must remove the item unless the creditor verifies that the information is accurate (see Exhibit 6–6).

If you are denied credit, insurance, employment, or rental housing based on the information in the report, you can get a copy of your credit report free within 60 days of your request. You should review your credit files every few years even if you are not planning to apply for a big loan. Married women and young adults should make sure that all accounts for which they are individually and jointly liable are listed in their credit files.

What Are the Legal Remedies?  Any consumer reporting agency or user of reported information that willfully or through negligence fails to comply with the provisions of the Fair Credit Reporting Act may be sued by the affected consumer. If the agency or the user is found guilty, the consumer may be awarded actual damages, court costs, and attorneys' fees and, in the case of willful noncompliance, punitive damages as allowed by the court. The action must be brought within two years of the occurrence or within two years after the discovery of material and willful misrepresentation of information. An unauthorized person who obtains a credit report under false pretenses may be fined up to $5,000, imprisoned for one year, or both. The same penalties apply to anyone who willfully provides credit information to someone not authorized to receive it.

Exhibit 6–7 outlines the steps you can take if you are denied credit.

**EXHIBIT 6-7**    What If You Are Denied Credit?

Steps you can take if you are denied credit.

*If a creditor receives no more than 150 applications during a calendar year, the disclosures may be oral.

SOURCE: Reprinted courtesy of Office of Public Information, Federal Reserve Bank Minneapolis, Minneapolis, MN 55480.

## Concept Check 6-3

1.  What are the general rules for measuring credit capacity?
2.  What can happen if you cosign a loan?
3.  What can you do to build and maintain your credit rating?
4.  What is the Fair Credit Reporting Act?
5.  How do you correct erroneous information in your credit file?
6.  What are your legal remedies if a credit reporting agency engages in unfair reporting practices?

# APPLYING FOR CREDIT     A Scenario from the Past

**Obj. 4**
Describe the information creditors look for when you apply for credit.

Mary and John Jones have a joint income that is more than enough for them to make payments on their dream house. Yet they are turned down for a mortgage loan. The lender says Mary might become pregnant and leave her job.

In fact, however, it is illegal for a creditor to ask or assume anything about a woman's childbearing plans. It is even illegal to discourage the Joneses from applying for a loan because Mary is of childbearing age. Also, the lender must fully acknowledge Mary's income.

*Equal Credit Opportunity Act (ECOA)* Bans discrimination in the extension of credit on the basis of race, color, age, sex, marital status, and other factors.

When you are ready to apply for credit, you should know what creditors think is important in deciding whether you are creditworthy. You should also know what they cannot legally consider in their decisions. The **Equal Credit Opportunity Act (ECOA)** starts all credit applicants off on the same footing. It states that race, color, age, sex, marital status, and certain other factors may not be used to discriminate against you in any part of a credit dealing. Credit rights of women are protected under the ECOA. Women should build and protect their own credit histories, using the checklist shown in the Financial Planning for Life's Situations box on page 184.

## What Creditors Look For: The Five Cs of Credit Management[11]

When a lender extends credit to its customers, it recognizes that some customers will be unable or unwilling to pay for their purchases. Therefore, lenders must establish policies for determining who will receive credit. Most lenders build their credit policies around the *five Cs of credit:* **character, capacity, capital, collateral,** and **conditions** (see the Financial Planning for Life's Situations box on page 186).

*character* The borrower's attitude toward his or her credit obligations.

**Character** is the borrower's attitude toward credit obligations. Most credit managers consider character the most important factor in predicting whether you will make timely payments and ultimately repay your loan.

*capacity* The borrower's financial ability to meet credit obligations.

**Capacity** is your financial ability to meet credit obligations, that is, to make regular loan payments as scheduled in the credit agreement. Therefore, the lender checks your salary statements and other sources of income, such as dividends and interest. Your other financial obligations and monthly expenses are also considered before credit is approved.

*capital* The borrower's assets or net worth.

*collateral* A valuable asset that is pledged to ensure loan payments.

**Capital** refers to your assets or net worth. Generally, the greater your capital, the greater your ability to repay a loan. The lender determines your net worth by requiring you to complete a credit application (see Exhibit 6–8). You must authorize your employer and financial institutions to release information to confirm the claims made in the credit application.

*conditions* The general economic conditions that can affect a borrower's ability to repay a loan.

---

**EXHIBIT 6-8**

Sample Credit Application Questions

- Amount of loan requested
- Proposed use of the loan
- Your name and birth date
- Social Security and driver's license numbers
- Present and previous street addresses
- Present and previous employers and their addresses
- Present salary
- Number and ages of dependents
- Other income and sources of other income
- Have you ever received credit from us?

- If so, when and at which office?
- Checking account number, institution, and branch
- Savings account number, institution, and branch
- Name of nearest relative not living with you
- Relative's address and telephone number
- Your marital status
- Information regarding joint applicant: same questions as above

# Financial Planning for Life's Situations

## WOMEN'S CHECKLIST FOR BUILDING AND PROTECTING THEIR CREDIT HISTORIES

It is simple and sensible to build and protect your own credit history. Here are some steps to get you started.

*If you are single:*
- Open a checking or savings account, or both.
- Apply for a local department store card.
- Take out a small loan from your bank. Make timely payments.

*If you are already married:*
- Establish credit in your maiden name or your first name.
- Open your own accounts.
- Try to have separate credit card accounts in your own name.
- Review your joint accounts.
- Make sure that creditors report your credit history to credit bureaus in both names.

*If you are getting married:*
- Write to your creditors and ask them to continue maintaining your credit file separately.
- You can choose to use your first name and your maiden name (Sue Smith), your first name and your husband's last name (Sue Jones), or your first name and a combined last name (Sue Smith-Jones).
- Once you have picked a name, use it consistently.

*If you have recently been separated or divorced:*
- Close all of your joint accounts. Your credit record could suffer if your ex-partner is delinquent.
- Meet your creditors and clear your credit record if your ex-partner has hurt your credit rating.

*If you are widowed:*
- Notify all creditors and tell them whether you or the executor of the estate will handle payment.

- Transfer all existing joint loans to your name alone. You may also want to renegotiate repayment terms.
- Transfer joint credit card accounts to your name alone or reapply for new accounts.
- Seek professional advice, if needed.

And remember that a creditor *cannot:*
1. Refuse you individual credit in your own name if you are creditworthy.
2. Require a spouse to cosign a loan. Any creditworthy person can be your cosigner if one is required.
3. Ask about your birth control practices or family plans or assume that your income will be interrupted to have children.
4. Consider whether you have a telephone listing in your own name.

A creditor *must:*
5. Evaluate you on the same basis as applicants who are male or who have a different marital status.
6. Consider income from part-time employment.
7. Consider reliable alimony, child support, or separate-maintenance payments.
8. Consider the payment history of all joint accounts that accurately reflects your credit history.
9. Report the payment history on an account if you use the account jointly with your spouse.
10. Disregard information on accounts if you can prove that it does not reflect your ability or willingness to repay.

SOURCE: Reprinted courtesy of Office of Public Information, Federal Reserve Bank of Minneapolis, Minneapolis, MN 55480.

**Collateral** is an asset that you pledge to a financial institution to obtain a loan. If you fail to honor the terms of the credit agreement, the lender can repossess the collateral and then sell it to satisfy the debt.

**Conditions** refer to general economic conditions that can affect your ability to repay a loan. The basic question focuses on security—of both your job and the firm that employs you.

Creditors use different combinations of the five Cs to reach their decisions. Some creditors set unusually high standards, and others simply do not make certain kinds of loans. Creditors also use different kinds of rating systems. Some rely strictly on their own instinct and experience. Others use a credit-scoring or statistical system to predict

## EXHIBIT 6-9

**How a Consumer's Application Is Scored**

Creditors use different kinds of rating systems to grant credit.

| Occupation | Points Awarded |
|---|---|
| Supervisor for 5 yrs | 25 |
| Clerk for one year | 5 |
| Temporary construction worker | 0 |
| Unemployed | –20 |

+

| Monthly Income | Points Awarded |
|---|---|
| Less than $400 | 0 |
| $400–$650 | 3 |
| $651–$800 | 7 |
| $801–$1,200 | 12 |
| More than $1,200 | 15 |

| Age | Points Awarded |
|---|---|
| 21–28 | 11 |
| 28–35 | 5 |
| 36–48 | 2 |
| 48–61 | 12 |
| 61 | 15 |

| Home | Points Awarded |
|---|---|
| Homeowner | 25 |
| Renter (same place for five years) | 15 |
| New renter | 0 |
| Boarder | –10 |

+

| Telephone in Home | Points Awarded |
|---|---|
| Yes | 12 |
| No | 0 |

whether an applicant is a good credit risk. They assign a certain number of points to each characteristic that has proven to be a reliable sign that a borrower will repay. Then they rate the applicant on this scale.

Typical questions in a credit application appear in Exhibit 6–8. Exhibit 6–9 shows how your credit application might be scored. In addition, during the loan application process, the lender may evaluate many of the following criteria to determine whether you are a good credit risk.

### Age

Eugene and Ethel Esposito, a retired couple, and many older people have complained that they were denied credit because they were over a certain age or that when they retired, their credit was suddenly cut off or reduced.

The ECOA is very specific about how a person's age may be used in credit decisions. A creditor may ask about your age, but if you're old enough to sign a binding contract (usually 18 or 21 years old, depending on state law), a creditor may not

Turn you down or decrease your credit because of your age.
Ignore your retirement income in rating your application.
Close your credit account or require you to reapply for it because you have reached a
    certain age or retired.
Deny you credit or close your account because credit life insurance or other credit-
    related insurance is not available to people of your age.

### Public Assistance

You may not be denied credit because you receive Social Security or public assistance. But, as with age, certain information related to this source of income could have a bearing on your creditworthiness.

### Housing Loans

The ECOA covers your application for a mortgage or a home improvement loan. It bans discrimination due to characteristics such as your race, color, or sex or to the race or national origin of the people in the neighborhood where you live or want to buy your home. Creditors may not use any appraisal of the value of your property that considers the race of the people in your neighborhood.

# Financial Planning for Life's Situations

## THE FIVE CS OF CREDIT

Here is what lenders look for in determining your creditworthiness.

### CREDIT HISTORY

**1. Character: Will you repay the loan?**      Yes      No

Do you have a good attitude toward credit obligations?      ____  ____

Have you used credit before?      ____  ____

Do you pay your bills on time?      ____  ____

Have you ever filed for bankruptcy?      ____  ____

Do you live within your means?      ____  ____

### STABILITY

How long have you lived at your present address?      ____ yrs.

Do you own your home?      ____  ____

How long have you been employed by your present employer?      ____ yrs.

### INCOME

**2. Capacity: Can you repay the loan?**

Your salary and occupation?      $____ ; ____

Place of occupation?      _____

How reliable is your income?      Reliable ___ ; Not reliable ___

Any other sources of income?      $_____

### EXPENSES

Number of dependents?      _____

Do you pay any alimony or child support?      Yes ___ ; No ___

Current debts?      $_____

### NET WORTH

**3. Capital: What are your assets and net worth?**

What are your assets?      $_____

What are your liabilities?      $_____

What is your net worth?      $_____

### LOAN SECURITY

**4. Collateral: What if you don't repay the loan?**

What assets do you have to secure the loan? (Car, home, furniture?)      _____

What sources do you have besides income? (Savings, stocks, bonds, insurance?)      _____

### JOB SECURITY

**5. Conditions: What general economic conditions can affect your repayment of the loan?**

How secure is your job?      Secure ___ ; Not secure ___

How secure is the firm you work for?      Secure ___ ; Not secure ___

SOURCE: Adapted from William M. Pride, Robert J. Hughes, and Jack R. Kapoor, *Business,* 6th ed. (Boston: Houghton Mifflin, 1999), pp. 498–500.

## What If Your Application Is Denied?

**Ask Questions If Your Application Is Denied**      If you receive a notice that your application has been denied, the ECOA gives you the right to know the specific reasons for denial. If the denial is based on a credit report, you are entitled to know the specific information in the credit report that led to it. After you receive this information from the creditor, you should contact the local credit bureau to find out what information it reported. The bureau cannot charge you a disclosure fee if you ask for a copy of your credit report within 60 days of being notified of a denial based on a credit report. You may ask the bureau to investigate any inaccurate or incomplete information and correct its records.

1. What is the Equal Credit Opportunity Act?
2. What are the five Cs of credit?
3. What can you do if your credit application is denied?

# AVOIDING AND CORRECTING CREDIT MISTAKES

**Obj. 5**
Identify the steps you can take to avoid and correct credit mistakes.

*Fair Credit Billing Act (FCBA)* Sets procedures for promptly correcting billing mistakes, refusing to make credit card payments on defective goods, and promptly crediting payments.

Has a department store's computer ever billed you for merchandise that you returned to the store or never received? Has a credit company ever charged you for the same item twice or failed to properly credit a payment on your account?

The best way to maintain your credit standing is to repay your debts on time. But complications may still occur. To protect your credit and save your time, money, and future credit rating, you should learn how to correct any mistakes and misunderstandings that crop up in your credit accounts. If a snag occurs, first try to deal directly with the creditor. The credit laws can help you settle your complaints.

The **Fair Credit Billing Act (FCBA),** passed in 1975, sets procedures for promptly correcting billing mistakes, refusing to make credit card or revolving credit payments on defective goods, and promptly crediting your payments.

The act defines a billing error as any charge for something you did not buy or for something bought by a person not authorized to use your account. Also included among billing errors is any charge that is not properly identified on your bill (that is, for an amount different from the actual purchase price) or that was entered on a date other than the purchase date. A billing error may also be a charge for something you did not accept on delivery or was not delivered according to agreement.

Billing errors also include errors in arithmetic; failure to reflect a payment or other credit to your account; failure to mail the statement to your current address, provided you notified the creditor of an address change at least 20 days before the end of the billing period; and questionable items, or items about which you need additional information.

## In Case of a Billing Error

If you think your bill is wrong or you want more information about it, follow these steps. First, notify the creditor *in writing* within 60 days after the bill was mailed. A telephone call will not protect your rights. Be sure to write to the address the creditor lists for billing inquiries. Give the creditor your name and account number, say that you believe the bill contains an error, and explain what you believe the error to be. State the suspected amount of the error or the item you want explained. Then pay all the parts of the bill that are not in dispute. While waiting for an answer, you do not have to pay the disputed amount or any minimum payments or finance charges that apply to it.

The creditor must acknowledge your letter within 30 days, unless it can correct your bill sooner. Within two billing periods, but in no case longer than 90 days, either your account must be corrected or you must be told why the creditor believes the bill is correct. If the creditor made a mistake, you need not pay any finance charges on the disputed amount. Your account must be corrected, and you must be sent an explanation of any amount you still owe.

If no error is found, the creditor must promptly send you an explanation of the reasons for that determination and a statement of what you owe, which may include any finance charges that have accumulated and any minimum payments you missed while you were questioning the bill. Exhibit 6–10 summarizes the steps in resolving a billing dispute.

**EXHIBIT 6-10**   Steps in the Process of Resolving a Billing Dispute

A creditor may not threaten your credit rating while you are resolving a billing dispute.

SOURCE: Courtesy of Charge-It-System®, Billing Errors Section, *Cardholder Tips*, March 1992, n.p.

## Your Credit Rating during the Dispute

A creditor may not threaten your credit rating while you are resolving a billing dispute. Once you have written about a possible error, a creditor is prohibited from giving out information that would damage your credit reputation to other creditors or credit bureaus. And until your complaint has been answered, the creditor may not take any action to collect the disputed amount.

After explaining the bill, the creditor may report you as delinquent on the amount in dispute and take action to collect if you do not pay in the time allowed. Even so, you can still disagree in writing. Then the creditor and the credit bureau must report that you have challenged your bill and give you the name and address of each recipient of information about your account. When the matter has been settled, the creditor must report the outcome to each recipient of the information. Remember, you may also place your version of the dispute in your credit record.

## Defective Goods or Services

Your new sofa arrives with only three legs. You try to return it, but no luck. You ask the merchant to repair or replace it; still no luck. The Fair Credit Billing Act provides that you may withhold payment on any damaged or shoddy goods or poor services that you have purchased with a credit card as long as you have made a sincere attempt to resolve the problem with the merchant.

## Identity Crisis: What to Do If Your Identity Is Stolen

"I don't remember charging those items. I've never even been in that store."

Maybe you never charged those goods and services, but someone else did—someone who used your name and personal information to commit fraud. When impostors take your name, Social Security number, credit card number, or some other piece of your personal information for their use, they are committing a crime.

The biggest problem is that you may not know your identity has been stolen until you notice that something is amiss: You may get bills for a credit card account you never opened, your credit report may include debts you never knew you had, a billing cycle may pass without you receiving a statement, or you may see charges on your bills that you didn't sign for, didn't authorize, and know nothing about.

If someone has stolen your identity, the Federal Trade Commission recommends that you take three actions immediately:

1. *Contact the fraud departments of each of the three major credit bureaus* (see the table that follows). Tell them to flag your file with a fraud alert, including a statement that creditors should call you for permission before they open any new accounts in your name.

|  | **To Report Fraud** | **To Order Credit Report** | **Website** |
| --- | --- | --- | --- |
| Equifax | 1–800–525–6285 | 1–800–685–1111 | www.equifax.com |
| Experian | 1–888–EXPERIAN | 1–888–EXPERIAN | www.experian.com |
| Trans Union | 1–800–680–7289 | 1–800–916–8800 | www.transunion.com |

2. *Contact the creditors for any accounts that have been tampered with or opened fraudulently.* Ask to speak with someone in the security or fraud department, and follow up in writing.
3. *File a police report.* Keep a copy in case your creditors need proof of the crime.

To prevent an identity thief from picking up your trash to capture your personal information, tear or shred your charge receipts, copies of credit applications, insurance forms, bank checks and statements, expired charge cards, and credit offers you get in the mail.

If you believe an identity thief has accessed your bank accounts, checking account, or ATM card, close the accounts immediately. When you open new accounts, insist on password-only access. If your checks have been stolen or misused, stop payment. If your ATM card has been lost, stolen, or otherwise compromised, cancel the card and get another with a new personal identification number (PIN).

If, after taking all these steps, you are still having identity problems, stay alert to new instances of identity theft. Notify the company or creditor immediately, and follow up in writing. Also, contact the Privacy Rights Clearinghouse, which provides information on how to network with other identity theft victims. Call 619–298–3396 or visit www.privacyrights.org.

The U.S. Secret Service has jurisdiction over financial fraud cases. Although the service generally investigates cases where the dollar loss is substantial, your information may provide evidence of a larger pattern of fraud that requires its involvement. Contact your local field office.

The Social Security Administration may issue you a new Social Security number if you still have difficulties after trying to resolve problems resulting from identity theft. Unfortunately, however, there is no guarantee that a new Social Security number will resolve your problems.

Finally, you can file a complaint with the Federal Trade Commission (FTC) through a toll-free consumer help line at 1–877–FTC–HELP; by mail at Consumer Response Center, Federal Trade Commission, 600 Pennsylvania Ave., NW, Washington, DC 20580; or at its website, www.ftc.gov using the online complaint form. Although the FTC cannot resolve individual problems for consumers, it can act against a company if it sees a pattern of possible law violations.

### Concept Check 6-5

1. What is the Fair Credit Billing Act?
2. What must you do to protect your rights if a billing error occurs?
3. What happens to your credit rating during the billing dispute?
4. What can you do if your identity is stolen?

## COMPLAINING ABOUT CONSUMER CREDIT

**Obj. 6**
Describe the laws that protect you if you have a complaint about consumer credit.

If you have a complaint about credit, first try to solve your problem directly with the creditor. Only if that fails should you use more formal complaint procedures. This section describes how to file a complaint with the federal agencies responsible for administering consumer credit protection laws.

### Complaints about Banks

If you have a complaint about a bank in connection with any of the federal credit laws, or if you think any part of your business with a bank has been handled in an unfair or deceptive way, you may get advice and help from the Federal Reserve System. You don't need to have an account at the bank to file a complaint. (See Exhibit 6–11.)

### Protection under Consumer Credit Laws

You may also take legal action against a creditor. If you decide to file a lawsuit, there are important consumer credit laws you should know about.

### Truth in Lending and Consumer Leasing Acts

If a creditor fails to disclose information required under the Truth in Lending Act or the Consumer Leasing Act, gives inaccurate information, or does not comply with the rules regarding credit cards or the right to cancel them, you may sue for actual damages, that is, any money loss you suffer. Class action suits are also permitted. A class action suit is a suit filed on behalf of a group of people with similar claims.

## EXHIBIT 6-11

Complaint Form to Report Violations of Federal Credit Laws

SOURCE: Board of Governors of the Federal Reserve System.

**COMPLAINT FORM**                                    **Federal Reserve System**

Name _____   Name of Bank _____

Address _____   Address _____
               Street                                        City              State        Zip

City          State          Zip

Daytime telephone _____   Account number (if applicable) _____
               (include area code)

The complaint involves the following service:   Checking Account ☐     Savings Account ☐     Loan ☐

Other: Please specify _____

I have attempted to resolve this complaint directly with the bank:     No ☐     Yes ☐

If "No", an attempt should be made to contact the bank and resolve the complaint.

If "Yes", name of person or department contacted is _____
                                                                                          Date

MY COMPLAINT IS AS FOLLOWS (Briefly describe the events in the order in which they happened, including specific dates and the bank's actions to which you object. Enclose copies of any pertinent information or correspondence that may be helpful. Do not send us your only copy of any document):

_____

_____

_____

_____

_____

_____

_____

_____

This information is solicited under the Federal Trade Commission Improvement Act. Providing the information is voluntary, complete information is necessary to expedite investigation of your complaint. Routine use of the information may include disclosing it to bank(s) or others involved or to other governmental agencies as deemed appropriate.

Date _____                          Signatures _____

                                                            _____

### Equal Credit Opportunity Act

If you think you can prove that a creditor has discriminated against you for any reason prohibited by the ECOA, you may sue for actual damages plus punitive damages (that is, damages for the fact that the law has been violated) of up to $10,000.

### Fair Credit Billing Act

A creditor that fails to comply with the rules applying to the correction of billing errors automatically forfeits the amount owed on the item in question and any finance charges on it, up to a combined total of $50, even if the bill was correct. You may also sue for actual damages plus twice the amount of any finance charges.

### Fair Credit Reporting Act

You may sue any credit-reporting agency or creditor for violating the rules regarding access to your credit records and correction of errors in your credit file. You are entitled to actual damages plus any punitive damages the court allows if the violation is proven to have been intentional.

### Consumer Credit Reporting Reform Act

An unfavorable credit report can force you to pay a higher interest rate on a loan or cost you a loan, an insurance policy, an apartment rental, or even a job offer. The **Consumer Credit Reporting Reform Act** of 1997 places the burden of proof for accurate credit information on the credit reporting agency rather than on you. Under this law, the creditor must certify that disputed data are accurate. If a creditor or the credit bureau verifies incorrect data, you can sue for damages. The federal government and state attorneys general can also sue creditors for civil damages.

*Consumer Credit Reporting Reform Act* Places the burden of proof for accurate credit information on the credit reporting agency.

Exhibit 6–12 on page 192 summarizes the major federal consumer credit laws. The Federal Reserve System has set up a separate office, the Division of Consumer and Community Affairs, in Washington to handle consumer complaints. Contact the director

**EXHIBIT 6-12**   SUMMARY OF FEDERAL CONSUMER CREDIT LAWS

| Act (date effective) | Major Provisions |
|---|---|
| *Truth in Lending Act* (July 1, 1969) | Provides specific cost disclosure requirements for the annual percentage rate and the finance charges as a dollar amount<br>Requires disclosure of other loan terms and conditions<br>Regulates the advertising of credit terms<br>Provides the right to cancel a contract when certain real estate is used as security |
| (January 25, 1971) | Prohibits credit card issuers from sending unrequested cards; limits a cardholder's liability for unauthorized use of a card to $50 |
| (October 1, 1982) | Requires that disclosures for closed-end credit (installment credit) be written in plain English and appear apart from all other information<br>Allows a credit customer to request an itemization of the amount financed if the creditor does not automatically provide it |
| *Fair Credit Reporting Act* (April 24, 1971) | Requires disclosure to consumers of the name and address of any consumer reporting agency that supplied reports used to deny credit, insurance, or employment<br>Gives consumers the right to know what is in their files, have incorrect information reinvestigated and removed, and include their versions of a disputed item in the file<br>Requires credit-reporting agencies to send the consumer's version of a disputed item to certain businesses or creditors<br>Sets forth identification requirements for consumers wishing to inspect their files<br>Requires that consumers be notified when an investigative report is being made<br>Limits the amount of time certain information can be kept in a credit file |
| *Fair Credit Billing Act* (October 28, 1975) | Establishes procedures for consumers and creditors to follow when billing errors occur on periodic statements for revolving credit accounts<br>Requires creditors to send a statement setting forth these procedures to consumers periodically<br>Allows consumers to withhold payment for faulty or defective goods or services (within certain limitations) when purchased with a credit card<br>Requires creditors to promptly credit customers' accounts and to return overpayments if requested |
| *Equal Credit Opportunity Act* (October 28, 1975) | Prohibits credit discrimination based on sex and marital status<br>Prohibits creditors from requiring women to reapply for credit upon a change in marital status<br>Requires creditors to inform applicants of acceptance or rejection of their credit application within 30 days of receiving a completed application<br>Requires creditors to provide a written statement of the reasons for adverse action |
| (March 23, 1977) (June 1, 1977) | Prohibits credit discrimination based on race, national origin, religion, age, or the receipt of public assistance<br>Requires creditors to report information on an account to credit bureaus in the names of both husband and wife if both use the account and both are liable for it |
| *Fair Debt Collection Practices Act* (March 20, 1978) | Prohibits abusive, deceptive, and unfair practices by debt collectors<br>Establishes procedures for debt collectors contacting a credit user<br>Restricts debt collector contacts with a third party<br>Specifies that payment for several debts be applied as the consumer wishes and that no money be applied to a debt in dispute |
| *Consumer Credit Reporting Reform Act* (September 30, 1997) | Places the burden of proof for accurate credit information on credit issuers rather than on consumers<br>Requires creditors to certify that disputed credit information is accurate<br>Requires "credit repair" companies to give consumers a written contract that can be canceled within three business days<br>Requires the big three credit bureaus (Experian, Equifax, and Trans Union) to establish a joint toll-free system that allows consumers to call and remove their names permanently from all prescreened lists<br>Places the maximum cost of a credit report at $8; however, indigent persons, welfare recipients, unemployed persons, and jobhunters can get one free report annually |

SOURCES: *Managing Your Credit*, rev. ed. (Prospect Heights, IL: Money Management Institute, Household Financial Services, 1988), p. 36; © Household Financial Services, Prospect Heights, Illinois; *Banking Legislation & Policy,* Federal Reserve Bank of Philadelphia, April–June 1997, pp. 3–4.

**EXHIBIT 6-13**   FEDERAL GOVERNMENT AGENCIES THAT ENFORCE CONSUMER CREDIT LAWS

| If you think you've been discriminated against by: | You may file a complaint with the following agency: |
|---|---|
| A retailer, nonbank credit card issuer, consumer finance company, state-chartered credit union or bank, noninsured savings and loan institution | Federal Trade Commission (FTC) Equal Credit Opportunity Washington, DC 20580 |
| A national bank | Comptroller of the Currency Consumer Affairs Division Washington, DC 20219 |
| A Federal Reserve member bank | Board of Governors of the Federal Reserve System Director, Division of Consumer Affairs Washington, DC 20551 |
| Other insured banks | Federal Deposit Insurance Corporation Office of Bank Customer Affairs Washington, DC 20429 |
| Insured savings and loan institutions | Federal Home Loan Bank Board Equal Credit Opportunity Washington, DC 20552 |
| The FHA mortgage program | Housing and Urban Development (HUD) Department of Health, Education and Welfare Washington, DC 20410 |
| A federal credit union | National Credit Union Administration 2025 M Street, N.W. Washington, DC 20455 |

of this division in Washington, DC 20551. This division also writes regulations to carry out the consumer credit laws, enforces these laws for state-chartered banks that are members of the Federal Reserve System, and helps banks comply with these laws.

## Your Rights under Consumer Credit Laws

If you believe you have been refused credit due to discrimination, you can do one or more of the following:

1. Complain to the creditor. Let the creditor know you are aware of the law.
2. File a complaint with the government. You can report any violations to the appropriate government enforcement agency (see Exhibit 6–13). Although the agencies use complaints to decide which companies to investigate, they cannot handle private cases. When you are denied credit, the creditor must give you the name and address of the appropriate agency to contact.
3. If all else fails, sue the creditor. You have the right to bring a case in a federal district court. If you win, you can recover your actual damages and punitive damages of up to $10,000. You can also recover reasonable attorneys' fees and court costs. A private attorney can advise you on how to proceed.

**Concept Check 6-6**

1. What federal laws protect you if you have a complaint regarding consumer credit?
2. What are your rights under the consumer credit laws?

# Summary of Objectives

**Obj. 1**   Define *consumer credit* and analyze its advantages and disadvantages.

Consumer credit is the use of credit by individuals and families for personal needs. Among the advantages of using credit are the ability to purchase goods when needed and pay for them gradually, the ability to meet financial emergencies, convenience in shopping, and establishment of a credit rating. Disadvantages are that credit costs money, encourages overspending, and ties up future income.

**Obj. 2**   Differentiate among various types of credit.

Closed-end and open-end credit are two types of consumer credit. With closed-end credit, the borrower pays back a one-time loan in a stated period of time and with a specified number of payments. With open-end credit, the borrower is permitted to take loans on a continuous basis and is billed for partial payments periodically.

**Obj. 3**   Assess your credit capacity and build your credit rating.

Two general rules for measuring credit capacity are the debt payments–to–income ratio and the debt-to-equity ratio. In reviewing your creditworthiness, a creditor seeks information from one of the three national credit bureaus or a regional credit bureau.

**Obj. 4**   Describe the information creditors look for when you apply for credit.

Creditors determine creditworthiness on the basis of the five Cs: character, capacity, capital, collateral, and conditions.

**Obj. 5**   Identify the steps you can take to avoid and correct credit mistakes.

If a billing error occurs on your account, notify the creditor in writing within 60 days. If the dispute is not settled in your favor, you can place your version of it in your credit file. You may also withhold payment on any defective goods or services you have purchased with a credit card as long as you have attempted to resolve the problem with the merchant.

**Obj. 6**   Describe the laws that protect you if you have a complaint about consumer credit.

If you have a complaint about credit, first try to deal directly with the creditor. If that fails, you can turn to the appropriate consumer credit law. These laws include the Truth in Lending Act, the Consumer Leasing Act, the Equal Credit Opportunity Act, the Fair Credit Billing Act, the Fair Credit Reporting Act, and the Consumer Credit Reporting Reform Act.

# Financial Planning Problems

1. *Calculating the Amount for a Home Equity Loan.* A few years ago, Michael Tucker purchased a home for $100,000. Today the home is worth $150,000. His remaining mortgage balance is $50,000. Assuming Michael can borrow up to 80 percent of the market value of his home, what is the maximum amount he can borrow? (Obj. 2)

2. *Determining the Debt Payments–to–Income Ratio.* Louise McIntyre's monthly gross income is $2,000. Her employer withholds $400 in federal, state, and local income taxes and $160 in Social Security taxes per month. Louise contributes $80 per month for her IRA. Her monthly credit payments for Visa, MasterCard, and Discover cards are $35, $30, and $20, respectively. Her monthly payment on an automobile loan is $285. What is Louise's debt payments–to–income ratio? Is Louise living within her means? Explain. (Obj. 3)

3. *Calculating the Debt-to-Equity Ratio.* Robert Thumme owns a $140,000 townhouse and still has an unpaid mortgage of $110,000. In addition to his mortgage, he has the following liabilities:

| | |
|---|---|
| Visa | $565 |
| MasterCard | 480 |
| Discover card | 395 |
| Education loan | 920 |
| Personal bank loan | 800 |
| Auto loan | 4,250 |
| Total | $7,410 |

Robert's net worth (not including his home) is about $21,000. This equity is in mutual funds, an automobile, a coin collection, furniture, and other personal property. What is Robert's debt-to-equity ratio? Has he reached the upper limit of debt obligations? Explain. (Obj. 3)

4. *Calculating the Net Worth and Determining a Safe Credit Limit.*
   a. Calculate your net worth based on your present assets and liabilities.
   b. Refer to your net worth statement and determine your safe credit limit. Use the debt payments–to–income and debt-to-equity formulas. (Obj. 3)

**5.** *Using Credit Cards as an Identification.* Dinesh D'Souza flew to New York to attend his brother's wedding. Knowing that his family would be busy, he did not ask anyone to meet him at the airport. Instead, he planned to rent a car to use while in New York. He has no nationally known credit cards but is prepared to pay cash for the rental car. The car rental agency refuses to rent him a car, even though it has several cars available. Why do you think Dinesh is unable to rent a car?   (Obj. 4)

**6.** *Determining What Creditors Look for in Approving Loans.* Jim Moniz, a recent college graduate, has accepted a teaching position at Hubbleville High School. Jim moved to Hubbleville and applied for a car loan at First National Bank. He had never used credit or obtained

a loan. The bank notified him that it will not approve the loan unless he has a cosigner. On what basis has the bank denied Jim credit?   (Obj. 4)

**7.** *Analyzing Feasibility of a Loan.* Fred Reinero has had a student loan, two auto loans, and three credit cards. He has always made timely payments on all obligations. He has a savings account of $2,400 and an annual income of $25,000. His current payments for rent, insurance, and utilities are about $1,100 per month. Fred has accumulated $12,800 in an individual retirement account. Fred's loan application asks for $10,000 to start up a small restaurant with some friends. Fred will not be an active manager; his partner will run the restaurant. Will he get the loan? Explain your answer.   (Obj. 4)

## Financial Planning Activities

**1.** *Determining Whether or Not to Use Credit.* Survey friends and relatives to determine the process they used in deciding whether or not to use credit to purchase an automobile or a major appliance. What risks and opportunity costs did they consider?   (Obj. 1)

**2.** *Analyzing Opportunity Costs Using Credit.* Think about the last three major purchases you made.   (Obj. 1)
  *a.* Did you pay cash? If so, why?
  *b.* If you paid cash, what opportunity costs were associated with the purchase?
  *c.* Did you use credit? If so, why?
  *d.* What were the financial and psychological opportunity costs of using credit?

**3.** *Comparing Reasons for Using Credit.* Prepare a list of similarities and differences in the reasons the following individuals might have for using credit.   (Obj. 2)
  *a.* A teenager.
  *b.* A young adult.
  *c.* A growing family of four.
  *d.* A retired couple.

**4.** *Using the Internet to Obtain Information about Credit Cards.* Choose one of the following organizations and visit its website. Then prepare a report that summarizes the information the organization provides. How could this information help you in choosing your credit card?
  *a.* Credit Card Network—provides information on credit card rates. (www.creditnet.com)
  *b.* Federal Trade Commission—provides information on how to regain financial health, uses and misuses of credit cards, and many other related topics. (www. ftc.gov)   (Obj. 2)

**5.** *Using your Home Equity to Obtain a Loan.* Visit your local financial institutions, such as commercial banks, federal savings banks, and credit unions, to obtain information about getting a home equity loan. Compare their requirements for the loan.   (Obj. 2)

**6.** *Determining Whether to Cosign a Loan.* Talk to a person who has cosigned a loan. What experiences did this person have as a cosigner?   (Obj. 3)

**7.** *Determining Net Worth and Credit Capacity.* What changes might take place in your personal net worth during different stages of your life? How might these changes affect your credit capacity?   (Obj. 4)

**8.** *Assessing How Lenders Determine Creditworthiness.* Survey credit representatives such as bankers, managers of credit departments in retail stores, managers of finance companies, credit union officers, managers of credit bureaus, and savings and loan officers. Ask what procedures they follow in granting or refusing a loan. Write a report of your survey.   (Obj. 4)

**9.** *Analyzing Credit-Related Problems.* Bring to class examples of credit-related problems of individuals or families. Suggest ways in which these problems might be solved.   (Obj. 5)

**10.** *Evaluating Creditors and Seeking Help with Credit-Related Problems.* Compile a list of places a person can call to report dishonest credit practices, get advice and help with credit problems, and check out a creditor's reputation before signing a contract.   (Obj. 6)

## LIFE SITUATION CASE

### A HARD LESSON ON CREDIT CARDS

Parents of college students, beware: The empty-nest syndrome you're experiencing may end up as empty-wallet syndrome. The moment your kids step on campus, they become highly-sought-after credit card customers. To establish relationships, they hope will extend well beyond the college years, card marketers are offering students everything from free T-shirts to chances to win airline tickets as enticements to sign up. As a result, college students now have heavy card debts. Some 14 percent have balances of $3,000 to $7,000, and 10 percent owe amounts exceeding $7,000, according to Nellie Mae, a nonprofit student loan provider in Braintree, Massachusetts.

"Students who have no history with credit are being handed it on a silver platter," say Gerri Detweiler, education adviser for Debt Counselors of America, a consumer advocacy group in Rockville, Maryland. As long as they are over 18, students can get a card without asking mom or dad to cosign. But when they get into trouble, they often go running to their folks for help. Jason Britton did—and then some. Now 21 and a senior at Georgetown University in Washington, Britton racked up $21,000 in debt on 16 cards over four years. "When I first started, my attitude was: 'I'll get a job after college to pay off all my debt,'" he says. He realized he dug himself into a hole when he couldn't meet the minimum monthly payments. Now he works three part-time jobs, and his parents are helping him pay his tuition and loans.

### Questions

1. Why should parents of college students beware?
2. How do credit card marketers entice college students?
3. Where do students turn for help when they get into debt trouble?

SOURCE: Adapted from Marcia Vickers, "A Hard Lesson on Credit Cards," *Business Week,* March 15, 1999, p. 107. Reprinted from the March 15, 1999 issue of *Business Week* by special permission. © 1999 McGraw-Hill Companies, Inc.

## VIDEO CASE   Consumer Credit

How does the use of credit affect your financial plan? What types of credit are available to you? How do you obtain credit? What factors do lenders consider before extending credit? How do you improve your chances of obtaining the credit you need?

A young woman faces the above questions. She is tempted to buy clothing that she really likes but knows she can't afford. However, when she makes the decision to use her credit card, she suddenly goes on a shopping spree. She joins most consumers who have a limited understanding of consumer credit and the pros and cons of using it.

Credit is *not* free money. In addition to repaying the amount she charged, she must pay an additional expense in interest until the full balance is repaid.

When used responsibly, credit is a valuable financial tool. When used excessively, credit can destroy financial plans.

### Questions

1. What are the pros and cons of using credit cards?
2. What suggestions might you offer the young woman regarding the use of her credit card?
3. Assuming the young woman does not pay the full balance, which type of credit card would you recommend for her?

# Creating an E-Plan: Financial Decisions Using the Web

## ESTABLISHING AND MAINTAINING CREDIT RECORD

The wise use of credit requires a knowledge of the process for establishing credit. In addition, you should develop an awareness of credit reports and the legal rights associated with using consumer credit.

Websites for Wise Use of Credit

- Credit card information from RAM Research Group at **www.ramresearch.com** and comparison of credit card costs and features at **www.cardtrak.com.**
- Current rates for mortgages, home equity loans, credit cards, and consumer loans are at **www.bankrate.com/ bankrate/publ/tips.htm** and **www.banx.com.**
- Wise use of credit information from the National Center for Financial Education at **www.ncfe.org.**
- Information on credit reports at **www.equifax.com**, **www.experian.com**, and **www.transunion.com.**
- Credit law information at **www.ftc.gov, www.bog.frb.fed. us,** and **www.pirg.org.**

(Note: Addresses and content of websites change, and new sites are created daily. Use search engines to update and locate websites for your current financial planning needs.)

*PFP sheet: 29*

Short-Term Financial Planning Activities

1. Prepare an inventory of current credit balances and monthly payments (see PFP Sheet 29).
2. Review your credit file for current accuracy of information.
3. Become familiar with consumer credit laws that may relate to various aspects of your use of credit.

Long-Term Financial Planning Activities

1. Describe actions you may take to reduce your credit balances (if applicable).
2. Create a plan for spending that provides for using credit at an appropriate level.

# 7

# Choosing a Source of Credit: The Costs of Credit Alternatives

Remember Jason Britton from the previous chapter, who racked up $21,000 in credit card debt? Having educated himself on the pitfalls of credit, Britton now speaks to student groups on the issue. Since card issuers' pitches may be confusing, he and other experts offer this advice: Beware of teaser rates. Credit card marketers may advertise a low annual percentage rate (APR), but it often jumps substantially after three to nine months. First USA's Student Visa has a 9.9 percent introductory rate that soars to 17.99 percent after five months. Teaser rates aren't unique to student cards, but a 1998 study by the Washington-based U.S. Public Interest Research Group found that 26 percent of college students found them misleading.

Because students move often and may not get their mail forwarded quickly, bills can get lost. Then the students fall prey to late-payment fees. Some cards, such as Wells Fargo & Company's Student MasterCard, have late fees as high as $30. If one or two payments are overdue, many cards bump interest rates up as well.

Students are often unaware that rates on cash advances are much higher than those on card balances. Citibank's student card has an APR on advances of 19.9 percent versus 17.5 percent for regular balances. Some cards also impose a fee of as much as 4 percent of the advance.

The moral? *Don't ask for extra credit.* Instead, find a card that has a restrictive credit line. The limit on the American Express Credit Card for College Students ranges from $500 to $4,000, depending on age and credit history. Another option: Get a secured credit card. Its credit limit depends on your savings at the issuing bank. Debt advisers say students should hold only a credit card on which they can carry a small balance and a charge card they must pay off monthly. They should pay more than the minimum on credit cards. And they should not charge purchases they can pay for in cash, such as pizza and gas.

If you are a parent, talk to your kids about responsible credit card use. College Parents of America, a Washington advocacy group, has tips on its website, www.collegeparents.org. Among them: Make sure your kids know a card isn't a way of getting items they can't afford.

## Questions

1. What is Jason Britton's advice to student groups?
2. Are teaser rates unique to student credit cards?
3. Should you get a secured credit card? Why or why not?
4. Visit Debt Counselors of America at www.dca.org, or the National Fraud Information Center at www.fraud.org to find the latest consumer credit costs. What are your findings?

## Learning Objectives

**Obj. 1**  Analyze the major sources of consumer credit.

**Obj. 2**  Determine the cost of credit by calculating interest using various interest formulas.

**Obj. 3**  Develop a plan to manage your debts.

**Obj. 4**  Evaluate various private and governmental sources that assist consumers with debt problems.

**Obj. 5**  Assess the choices in declaring personal bankruptcy.

## SOURCES OF CONSUMER CREDIT

**Obj. 1**
Analyze the major sources of consumer credit.

Credit costs got you down? Well, you are not alone. Credit costs money; therefore, always weigh the benefits of buying an item on credit now versus waiting until you have saved enough money to pay cash. We can all get into credit difficulties if we do not understand how and when to use credit.

Financial and other institutions, the sources of credit, come in all shapes and sizes. They play an important role in our economy, and they offer a broad range of financial services. By evaluating your credit options, you can reduce your finance charges. You can reconsider your decision to borrow money, discover a less expensive type of loan, or find a lender that charges a lower interest rate.

Before deciding whether to borrow money, ask yourself these three questions: Do I need a loan? Can I afford a loan? Can I qualify for a loan? We discussed the affordability of loans and the qualifications required to obtain loans in the last chapter. Here we wrestle with the first question.

You should avoid credit in two situations. The first situation is one in which you do not need or really want a product that will require financing. Easy access to installment loans or possession of credit cards sometimes encourages consumers to make expensive purchases they later regret. The solution to this problem is simple: After you have selected a product, resist any sales pressure to buy immediately and take a day to think it over.

The second situation is one in which you can afford to pay cash. Consider the trade-offs and opportunity costs involved. Paying cash is almost always cheaper than using credit. In fact, some stores even offer a discount for payment in cash.

### What Kind of Loan Should You Seek?

As discussed in the last chapter, two types of credit exist: closed-end and open-end credit. Because installment loans may carry a lower interest rate, they are the less expensive credit option for loans that are repaid over a period of many months or years. However, because credit cards usually provide a float period—a certain number of days during which no interest is charged—they represent the cheaper way to make credit purchases that are paid off in a month or two. Also, once you have a credit card, using it is always easier than taking out an installment loan. An alternative to a credit card is a travel and entertainment (T&E) card, such as an American Express or Diners Club card. A T&E card requires full payment of the balance due each month but does not impose a finance charge. Annual fees, however, can be high.

In seeking an installment loan, you may think first of borrowing from a bank or a credit union. However, less expensive credit sources are available.

### Inexpensive Loans

Parents or family members are often the source of the least expensive loans. They may charge you only the interest they would have earned had they not made the loan—as little as the 3 percent they would have earned on a passbook account. Such loans, however, can complicate family relationships. All loans to or from family members should be in writing and state the interest rate, if any, repayment schedule, and the final payment date.

Also relatively inexpensive is money borrowed on financial assets held by a lending institution, for example, a bank certificate of deposit or the cash value of a whole life insurance policy. The interest rate on such loans typically ranges from 7 to 10 percent. But the trade-off is that your assets are tied up until you have repaid the loan.

### Medium-Priced Loans

Often you can obtain medium-priced loans from commercial banks, federal savings banks (Savings and Loan Associations), and credit unions. New-car loans, for example, may cost 8 to 12 percent; used-car loans and home improvement loans may cost slightly more.

Borrowing from credit unions has several advantages. These institutions provide free credit life insurance, are generally sympathetic to borrowers with legitimate payment problems, and provide personalized service. Credit unions can now offer the same range of consumer loans that banks and other financial institutions do. Over 72 million Americans belong to credit unions, and the number of credit union members has been growing steadily. About 11,500 credit unions exist in the United States today.

### Expensive Loans

Though convenient to obtain, the most expensive loans available are from finance companies, retailers, and banks through credit cards. Finance companies often lend to people who cannot obtain credit from banks or credit unions. Typically, the interest ranges from 12 to 25 percent. If you are denied credit by a bank or a credit union, you should question your ability to afford the higher rate a loan company charges.

Borrowing from car dealers, appliance stores, department stores, and other retailers is also relatively expensive. The interest rates retailers charge are usually similar to those charged by finance companies, frequently 20 percent or more.

Banks lend funds not only through installment loans but also through cash advances on MasterCard or Visa cards. (See the Financial Planning Calculations box on page 201.) According to Stephen Brobeck, executive director of the Consumer Federation of America in Washington, DC, the average household has more than 10 credit cards and owes $7,000 on them. More than 3 billion credit card solicitations are mailed to consumers each year.[1] Credit card cobranding has become increasingly popular with banks and industries. Cobranded credit cards, such as Yahoo! Visa card will make shopping over the Internet easier and faster. Yahoo! will designate Visa as its "preferred card" and will promote Visa throughout its websites and to online merchants worldwide.

One type of loan from finance companies is currently less expensive than most other credit. Loans of this kind, which often can be obtained at a rate of under 8 percent, are available from the finance companies of major automakers—General Motors

## Financial Planning Calculations

### CASH ADVANCES

A cash advance is a loan billed to your credit card. You can obtain a cash advance with your credit card at a bank or an automated teller machine (ATM) or by using checks linked to your credit card account.

Most cards charge a special fee when a cash advance is taken out. The fee is based on a percentage of the amount borrowed, usually about 2 or 3 percent.

Some credit cards charge a minimum cash advance fee, as high as $5. You could get $20 in cash and be charged $5, a fee equal to 25 percent of the amount you borrowed.

Most cards do not have a grace period on cash advances. This means you pay interest every day until you repay the cash advance, even if you do not have an outstanding balance from the previous statement.

On some cards, the interest rate on cash advances is higher than the rate on purchases. Be sure you check the details on the contract sent to you by the card issuer.

Here is an example of charges that could be imposed for a $200 cash advance that you pay off when the bill arrives:

Cash advance fee = $4 (2% of $200)
Interest for one month = $3 (18% APR on $200)
**Total cost for one month** = $7 ($4 + $3)

In comparison, a $200 purchase on a card with a grace period could cost $0 if paid off promptly in full.

**The bottom line:** It is usually much more expensive to take out a cash advance than to charge a purchase to your credit card. Use cash advances only for real emergencies.

SOURCE: A pamphlet provided by the office of Public Responsibility, American Express Company and Consumer Action, San Francisco, CA 94105. (n.p; n.d.)

Acceptance Corporation, Ford Motor Credit Corporation, and others. But a car dealer that offers you such a rate may be less willing to discount the price of the car or throw in free options.

Exhibit 7–1 on pages 202 and 203 summarizes the major sources of consumer credit: commercial banks, consumer finance companies, credit unions, life insurance companies, and savings and loan associations. This exhibit attempts to generalize the information and give an average picture of each source regarding the type of credit available, lending policies, and customer services. Due to the dramatic fluctuations in interest rates during the 1990s, it is no longer possible to provide a common range of annual percentage rates for each source of credit. Check with your local lender for current interest rates. Study and compare the differences to determine which source can best meet your needs and requirements.

Today borrowing and credit are more complex than ever. As more and more types of financial institutions offer financial services, your choices of what and where to borrow will widen. Online computer services such as America Online, CompuServe, and Prodigy may be used to compare interest rates for different loan sources and credit cards. Smart cards, or chip cards, will allow you to access accounts from your banks, transfer funds, and obtain account balances. These cards will facilitate electronic banking and bill payment. You will be able to access these smart card services from point-of-sale terminals, ATMs, the Internet, touch-tone phones, interactive TVs, screen phones, personal digital assistants, and cellular phones. For further information, see Appendix B. Shopping for credit is just as important as shopping for an automobile, furniture, or major appliances.

**EXHIBIT 7-1**    SOURCES OF CONSUMER CREDIT AND THEIR MAJOR FEATURES

| Credit Source | Commercial Banks | Consumer Finance Companies |
|---|---|---|
| Type of loan | Single-payment loans<br>Personal installment loans<br>Passbook loans<br>Check-credit plans<br>Credit card loans<br>Second mortgages | Personal installment loans<br>Second mortgages |
| Lending policies | Seek customers with established credit history<br>Often require collateral or security<br>Prefer to deal in large loans, such as auto, home improvement, and home modernization, with the exception of credit card and check-credit plans<br>Determine repayment schedules according to the purpose of the loan<br>Vary credit rates according to the type of credit, time period, customer's credit history, and the security offered<br>May require several days to process a new credit application | Often lend to consumers without established credit history<br>Often make unsecured loans<br>Often vary rates according to the size of the loan balance<br>Offer a variety of repayment schedules<br>Make a higher percentage of small loans than other lenders<br>Maximum loan size limited by law<br>Process applications quickly, frequently on the same day the application is made |
| Cost | Lower than some lenders because they:<br>  Take fewer credit risks<br>  Lend depositors' money, which is a relatively inexpensive source of funds<br>  Deal primarily in large loans, which yield a larger dollar income without an increase in administrative costs | Higher than some lenders because they:<br>  Take greater credit risks<br>  Must borrow and pay interest on money to lend<br>  Deal frequently in small loans, which are costly to make and yield a small amount of income |
| Services | Offer several types of consumer credit plans<br>May offer financial counseling<br>Handle credit transactions confidentially | Provide credit promptly<br>Make loans to pay off accumulated debts willingly<br>Design repayment schedules to fit the borrower's income<br>Usually offer financial counseling<br>Handle credit transactions confidentially |

| Credit Unions | Life Insurance Companies | Federal Savings Banks (Savings and Loan Associations) |
|---|---|---|
| Personal installment loans<br>Share draft–credit plans<br>Credit card loans<br>Second mortgages | Single-payment or partial-payment loans | Personal installment loans (generally permitted by state-chartered savings associations)<br>Home improvement loans<br>Education loans<br>Savings account loans<br>Second mortgages |
| Lend to members only<br>Make unsecured loans<br>May require collateral or cosigner for loans over a specified amount<br>May require payroll deductions to pay off loan<br>May submit large loan applications to a committee of members for approval<br>Offer a variety of repayment schedules | Lend on cash value of life insurance policy<br>No date or penalty on repayment<br>Deduct amount owed from the value of policy benefit if death or other maturity occurs before repayment | Will lend to all creditworthy individuals<br>Often require collateral<br>Loan rates vary depending on size of loan, length of payment, and security involved |
| Lower than some lenders because they:<br>Take fewer credit risks<br>Lend money deposited by members, which is less expensive than borrowed money<br>Often receive free office space and supplies from the sponsoring organization<br>Are managed by members whose services are usually donated<br>Enjoy federal income tax exemptions | Lower than some lenders because they:<br>Take no risk<br>Pay no collection costs<br>Secure loans by cash value of policy | Lower than some lenders because they:<br>Lend depositors' money, which is a relatively inexpensive source of funds<br>Secure most loans by savings accounts or real estate |
| Design repayment schedules to fit the borrower's income<br>Generally provide credit life insurance without extra charge<br>May offer financial counseling<br>Handle credit transactions confidentially | Permit repayment at any time<br>Handle credit transactions confidentially | Often offer financial counseling<br>Specialize in mortgages and other housing-related loans<br>Handle credit transactions confidentially |

SOURCE: *Managing Your Credit* (Household International, 1988), pp. 18–19. © Household Financial Services, Prospect Heights, Illinois.

Concept Check 7-1

1. Why do students fall prey to late-payment fees?
2. What are the major sources of consumer credit?
3. What are some advantages and disadvantages of securing a loan from a credit union? From a finance company?

## THE COST OF CREDIT

### Obj. 2

Determine the cost of credit by calculating interest using various interest formulas.

*Truth in Lending law* A federal law that requires creditors to disclose the annual percentage rate (APR) and the finance charge as a dollar amount.

*finance charge* The total dollar amount paid to use credit.

*annual percentage rate (APR)* The percentage cost (or relative cost) of credit on a yearly basis. The APR yields a true rate of interest for comparisons with other sources of credit.

The **Truth in Lending law** of 1969 was a landmark piece of legislation. For the first time, creditors were required to state the cost of borrowing as a dollar amount so that consumers would know exactly what the credit charges were and thus could compare credit costs and shop for credit.

If you are thinking of borrowing money or opening a credit account, your first step should be to figure out how much it will cost you and whether you can afford it. Then you should shop for the best terms. Two key concepts that you should remember are the finance charge and the annual percentage rate.

### Finance Charge and Annual Percentage Rate (APR)

Credit costs vary. If you know the finance charge and the annual percentage rate (APR), you can compare credit prices from different sources. Under the Truth in Lending law, the creditor must inform you, in writing and before you sign any agreement, of the finance charge and the APR.

The **finance charge** is the total dollar amount you pay to use credit. It includes interest costs and sometimes other costs such as service charges, credit-related insurance premiums, or appraisal fees.

For example, borrowing $100 for a year might cost you $10 in interest. If there is also a service charge of $1, the finance charge will be $11. The **annual percentage rate (APR)** is the percentage cost (or relative cost) of credit on a yearly basis. The APR is your key to comparing costs, regardless of the amount of credit or how much time you have to repay it.

Suppose you borrow $100 for one year and pay a finance charge of $10. If you can keep the entire $100 for the whole year and then pay it all back at once, you are paying an APR of 10 percent:

| Amount Borrowed | Month Number | Payment Made | Loan Balance |
|---|---|---|---|
| $100 | 1 | 0 | $100 |
| | 2 | 0 | 100 |
| | 3 | 0 | 100 |
| | . | . | . |
| | . | . | . |
| | . | . | . |
| | . | . | . |
| | 12 | 100 | 0 |
| | | (plus $10 interest) | |

On average, you had full use of $100 throughout the year. To calculate the average use, add the loan balance during the first and last month, then divide by 2:

$$\text{Average balance} = \frac{\$100 + \$100}{2} = \$100$$

## Financial Planning Calculations

### THE ARITHMETIC OF THE ANNUAL PERCENTAGE RATE (APR)

There are two ways to calculate the APR: using an APR formula and using the APR tables. The APR tables are more precise than the formula. The formula, given below, only approximates the APR:

$$r = \frac{2 \times n \times I}{P(N + 1)}$$

where

r = Approximate APR
n = Number of payment periods in one year (12, if payments are monthly; 52, if weekly)
I = Total dollar cost of credit
P = Principal, or net amount of loan
N = Total number of payments scheduled to pay off the loan

Let us compare the APR when the $100 loan is paid off in one lump sum at the end of the year and when the same loan is paid off in 12 equal monthly payments. The stated annual interest rate is 10 percent for both loans.

Using the formula, the APR for the lump-sum loan is

$$r = \frac{2 \times 1 \times \$10}{\$100(1 + 1)} = \frac{\$20}{\$100(2)} = \frac{\$20}{\$200} = 0.10$$

or 10 percent

Using the formula, the APR for the monthly payment loan is

$$r = \frac{2 \times 12 \times \$10}{\$100(12 + 1)} = \frac{\$240}{\$100(13)} = \frac{\$240}{\$1,300}$$

$$= 0.1846, \text{ or } 18.46 \text{ percent (rounded to } 18.5 \text{ percent)}$$

But if you repay the $100 and the finance charge (a total of $110) in 12 equal monthly payments, you don't get use of the $100 for the whole year. In fact, as shown next, you get use of less and less of that $100 each month. In this case, the $10 charge for credit amounts to an APR of 18.5 percent.

| Amount Borrowed | Month Number | Payment Made | Loan Balance |
|---|---|---|---|
| $100 | 1 | 0 | $100.00 |
| | 2 | 8.33 | 91.67 |
| | 3 | 8.33 | 83.34 |
| | 4 | 8.33 | 75.01 |
| | 5 | 8.33 | 66.68 |
| | 6 | 8.33 | 58.35 |
| | 7 | 8.33 | 50.02 |
| | 8 | 8.33 | 41.69 |
| | 9 | 8.33 | 33.36 |
| | 10 | 8.33 | 25.03 |
| | 11 | 8.33 | 16.70 |
| | 12 | 8.33 | 8.37 |

Note that you are paying 10 percent interest even though you had use of only $91.67 during the second month, not $100. During the last month, you owed only $8.37 (and had use of $8.37), but the $10 interest is for the entire $100. As calculated in the previous example, the average use of the money during the year is $100 + $8.37 ÷ 2, or $54.18.

The accompanying Financial Planning Calculations feature shows how to calculate the APR.

### UNDERSTANDING CREDIT AND FINANCIAL MANAGEMENT

Maxine Sweet, vice president of consumer education at Experian, states that her goal is to prevent credit problems by helping consumers understand credit and financial management and to serve as a resource to those who help educate consumers.

According to Sweet, whenever you apply for a new credit card, a loan, or an extension of credit, the potential lender almost certainly will review your credit report before making a decision. She suggests that you take the time to ensure your credit report is accurate and complete.

Experian publishes the *Reports on Credit* series. Each of the 10 reports covers a different topic, ranging from how to get your credit report to protecting yourself from credit card fraud. The "Divorce & Credit" report, for example, is distributed to divorce attorneys, marriage counselors, and others who have the opportunity to reach consumers.

On the Internet, you can find much of Experian's educational material at www. experian.com. Be sure to check out the "Ask Max" advice column.

All creditors—banks, stores, car dealers, credit card companies, and finance companies—must state the cost of their credit in terms of the finance charge and the APR. The law does not set interest rates or other credit charges, but it does require their disclosure so that you can compare credit costs and tackle the trade-offs.

## Tackling the Trade-Offs

When you choose your financing, there are trade-offs between the features you prefer (term, size of payments, fixed or variable interest, or payment plan) and the cost of your loan. Here are some of the major trade-offs you should consider.

### Term versus Interest Costs
Many people choose longer-term financing because they want smaller monthly payments. But the longer the term for a loan at a given interest rate, the greater the amount you must pay in interest charges. Consider the following analysis of the relationship between the term and interest costs.

### A Comparison
Even when you understand the terms a creditor is offering, it's easy to underestimate the difference in dollars that different terms can make. Suppose you're buying a $7,500 used car. You put $1,500 down, and you need to borrow $6,000. Compare the following three credit arrangements:

|  | APR | Length of Loan | Monthly Payment | Total Finance Charge | Total Cost |
|---|---|---|---|---|---|
| Creditor A | 14% | 3 years | $205.07 | $1,382.52 | $7,382.52 |
| Creditor B | 14 | 4 years | 163.96 | 1,870.08 | 7,870.08 |
| Creditor C | 15 | 4 years | 166.98 | 2,015.04 | 8,015.04 |

How do these choices compare? The answer depends partly on what you need. The lowest-cost loan is available from creditor A. If you are looking for lower monthly payments, you could repay the loan over a longer period of time. However, you would have to pay more in total costs. A loan from creditor B—also at a 14 percent APR, but for four years—would add about $488 to your finance charge.

If that four-year loan were available only from creditor C, the APR of 15 percent would add another $145 to your finance charges. Other terms, such as the size of the down payment, will also make a difference. Be sure to look at all the terms before you make your choice.

**Lender Risk versus Interest Rate**   You may prefer financing that requires low fixed payments with a large final payment or only a minimum of up-front cash. But both of these requirements can increase your cost of borrowing because they create more risk for your lender.

If you want to minimize your borrowing costs, you may need to accept conditions that reduce your lender's risk. Here are a few possibilities.

**Variable Interest Rate**   A variable interest rate is based on fluctuating rates in the banking system, such as the prime rate. With this type of loan, you share the interest rate risks with the lender. Therefore, the lender may offer you a lower initial interest rate than it would with a fixed-rate loan.

**A Secured Loan**   If you pledge property or other assets as collateral, you'll probably receive a lower interest rate on your loan.

**Up-Front Cash**   Many lenders believe you have a higher stake in repaying a loan if you pay cash for a large portion of what you are financing. Doing so may give you a better chance of getting the other terms you want. Of course, by making a large down payment, you forgo interest that you might earn in a savings account.

**A Shorter Term**   As you have learned, the shorter the period of time for which you borrow, the smaller the chance that something will prevent you from repaying and the lower the risk to the lender. Therefore, you may be able to borrow at a lower interest rate if you accept a shorter-term loan, but your payments will be higher.

In the next section, you will see how the above-mentioned trade-offs can affect the cost of closed-end and open-end credit.

## Calculating the Cost of Credit

The two most common methods of calculating interest are compound and simple interest formulas. Perhaps the most basic method is the simple interest calculation. Simple interest on the declining balance, add-on interest, bank discount, and compound interest are variations of simple interest.

*simple interest* Interest computed on the principal only and without compounding.

**Simple Interest**   **Simple interest** is the interest computed on principal only and without compounding; it is the dollar cost of borrowing money. This cost is based on three elements: the amount borrowed, which is called the *principal;* the rate of interest; and the amount of time for which the principal is borrowed.

You can use the following formula to find simple interest:

$$\text{Interest} = \text{Principal} \times \text{Rate of interest} \times \text{Time}$$

or

$$I = P \times r \times T$$

**Example 1**   Suppose you have persuaded a relative to lend you $1,000 to purchase a laptop computer. Your relative agreed to charge only 5 percent interest, and you agreed to repay the loan at the end of one year. Using the simple interest formula, the interest will be 5 percent of $1,000 for one year, or $50, since you have the use of $1,000 for the entire year:

$$I = \$1,000 \times 0.05 \times 1$$
$$= \$50$$

Using the APR formula discussed earlier,

$$APR = \frac{2 \times n \times I}{P(N + 1)} = \frac{2 \times 1 \times \$50}{\$1,000(1 + 1)} = \frac{\$100}{\$2,000} = 0.05, \text{ or } 5 \text{ percent}$$

Note that the stated rate, 5 percent, is also the annual percentage rate.

## Simple Interest on the Declining Balance

*declining balance method*   A method of computing interest when more than one payment is made on a simple interest loan.

When more than one payment is made on a simple interest loan, the method of computing interest is known as the **declining balance method.** Since you pay interest only on the amount of the original principal that you have not yet repaid, the more frequent the payments, the lower the interest you will pay. Most credit unions use this method for their loans.

Example 2    Using simple interest on the declining balance to compute interest charges, the interest on a 5 percent, $1,000 loan repaid in two payments, one at the end of the first half-year and another at the end of the second half-year, would be $37.50, as follows:

First payment:

$$I = P \times r \times T$$
$$= \$1,000 \times 0.05 \times \frac{1}{2}$$
$$= \$25 \text{ interest plus } \$500, \text{ or } \$525$$

Second payment:

$$I = P \times r \times T$$
$$= \$500 \times 0.05 \times \frac{1}{2}$$
$$= \$12.50 \text{ interest plus the remaining balance of } \$500, \text{ or } \$512.50$$

Total payment on the loan:

$$\$525 + \$512.50 = \$1,037.50$$

Using the APR formula,

$$APR = \frac{2 \times n \times I}{P(N + 1)} = \frac{2 \times 2 \times \$37.50}{\$1,000(2 + 1)} = \frac{\$150}{\$3,000} = 0.05, \text{ or } 5 \text{ percent}$$

Note that using simple interest under the declining balance method, the stated rate, 5 percent, is also the annual percentage rate. The add-on interest, bank discount, and compound interest calculation methods differ from the simple interest method as to when, how, and on what balance interest is paid. For these methods, the real annual rate, or the annual percentage rate, differs from the stated rate.

## Add-On Interest

*add-on interest method*   A method of computing interest in which interest is calculated on the full amount of the original principal.

With the **add-on interest method,** interest is calculated on the full amount of the original principal. The interest amount is immediately added to the original principal, and payments are determined by dividing principal plus interest by the number of payments to be made. When only one payment is required, this method produces the same APR as the simple interest method. However, when two or more payments are to be made, the add-on method results in an effective rate of interest that is higher than the stated rate.

Example 3    Consider again the two-payment loan in Example 2. Using the add-on method, interest of $50 (5 percent of $1,000 for one year) is added to the $1,000 borrowed, giving $1,050 to be repaid—half (or $525) at the end of the first half-year and the other half at the end of the second half-year.

Even though your relative's stated interest rate is 5 percent, the real interest rate is

$$\text{APR} = \frac{2 \times n \times I}{P(N + 1)} = \frac{2 \times 1 \times \$50}{\$1,000(2 + 1)} = \frac{\$100}{\$3,000} = 0.066, \text{ or } 6.6 \text{ percent}$$

Note that using the add-on interest method means that no matter how many payments you are to make, the interest will always be $50. As the number of payments increases, you have use of less and less credit over the year. For example, if you make four quarterly payments of $262.50, you have use of $1,000 during the first quarter, about $750 during the second quarter, about $500 during the third quarter, and about $250 during the fourth and final quarter. Therefore, as the number of payments increases, the true interest rate, or APR, also increases.

The appendix to this chapter presents various other methods of determining the cost of credit, such as the bank discount method, the compound interest formula, amortization, and the use of tables.

## Cost of Open-End Credit
As discussed earlier, open-end credit includes credit cards, department store charge cards, and check overdraft accounts that allow you to write checks for more than your actual balance. You can use open-end credit again and again until you reach a prearranged borrowing limit. The Truth in Lending law requires that open-end creditors let you know how the finance charge and the APR will affect your costs.

First, creditors must tell you how they calculate the finance charge. Creditors use various systems to calculate the balance on which they assess finance charges. Some creditors add finance charges after subtracting payments made during the billing period; this is called the **adjusted balance method.** Other creditors give you no credit for payments made during the billing period; this is called the **previous balance method.** Under the third—and the fairest—method, the **average daily balance method,** creditors add your balances for each day in the billing period and then divide by the number of days in the period. The average daily balance may include or exclude new purchases during the billing period.

Here is how some different methods of calculating finance charges affect the cost of credit:

*adjusted balance method*
The assessment of finance charges after payments made during the billing period have been subtracted.

*previous balance method*
A method of computing finance charges that gives no credit for payments made during the billing period.

*average daily balance method*   A method of computing finance charges that uses a weighted average of the account balance throughout the current billing period.

|  | Average Daily Balance (*including* new purchases) | Average Daily Balance (*excluding* new purchases) |
|---|---|---|
| Monthly rate | 1½% | 1½% |
| APR | 18% | 18% |
| Previous balance | $400 | $400 |
| New purchases | $50 on 18th day | $50 on 18th day |
| Payments | $300 on 15th day (new balance = $100) | $300 on 15th day (new balance = $100) |
| Average daily balance | $270* | $250** |
| Finance charge | $4.05 (1½% × $270) | $3.75 (1½% × $250) |

*To figure average daily balance (*including* new purchases):
($400 × 15 days) + ($100 × 3 days) + ($150 × 12 days) ÷ 30 days
($6,000 + $300 + $1,800) ÷ 30 or, $8,100 ÷ 30 days = $270

**To figure average daily balance (*excluding* new purchases):

$$(\$400 \times 15 \text{ days}) + (\$100 \times 15 \text{ days}) \div 30 \text{ days}$$
$$(\$6,000 + \$1,500) \div 30 \text{ or}, \$7,500 \div 30 \text{ days} = \$250$$

|                        | Adjusted Balance           | Previous Balance           |
|------------------------|----------------------------|----------------------------|
| Monthly rate           | 1½%                        | 1½%                        |
| APR                    | 18%                        | 18%                        |
| Previous balance       | $400                       | $400                       |
| Payments               | $300                       | $300                       |
| Average daily balance  | N/A                        | N/A                        |
| Finance charge         | $1.50 (1½% × $100)         | $6.00 (1½% × $400)         |

As the example shows, the finance charge varies for the same pattern of purchases and payments.

Second, creditors must tell you when finance charges on your credit account begin so that you know how much time you have to pay your bills before a finance charge is added. Some creditors, for example, give you a 20- to 25-day grace period to pay your balance in full before imposing a finance charge. But in most cases, the grace period applies only if you have no outstanding balance on your card. Therefore, if you want to take advantage of the interest-free period on your card, you must pay your bill in full every month.

The Truth in Lending law does not set rates or tell the creditor how to make interest calculations. It requires only that the creditor tell you the method that will be used. You should ask for an explanation of any terms you don't understand.

**Sheet 30**

## Cost of Credit and Expected Inflation

As you have seen, interest rates dictate when you must pay future dollars to receive current dollars. Borrowers and lenders, however, are less concerned about dollars, present or future, than about the goods and services those dollars can buy—that is, their purchasing power.

Inflation erodes the purchasing power of money. Each percentage point increase in inflation means a decrease of approximately 1 percent in the quantity of goods and services you can purchase with a given quantity of dollars. As a result, lenders, seeking to protect their purchasing power, add the expected rate of inflation to the interest rate they charge. You are willing to pay this higher rate because you expect inflation to enable you to repay the loan with cheaper dollars.

For example, if a lender expects a 4 percent inflation rate for the coming year and desires an 8 percent return on its loan, it will probably charge you a 12 percent nominal or stated rate (a 4 percent inflation premium plus an 8 percent "real" rate).

Return to Example 1, in which you borrowed $1,000 from your relative at the bargain rate of 5 percent for one year. If the inflation rate was 4 percent during that year, your relative's real rate of return was only 1 percent (5 percent stated interest minus 4 percent inflation rate) and your "real" cost was not $50 but only $10 ($50 minus $40 inflation premium).

## Cost of Credit and Tax Considerations

Before the Tax Reform Act of 1986, the interest you paid on consumer credit reduced your taxable income. The new law did not affect the deductibility of home mortgage interest, but now you can no longer deduct interest paid on consumer loans.

## Avoid the Minimum Monthly Payment Trap

The "minimum monthly payment" is the smallest amount you can pay and still be a cardholder in good standing. Banks often encourage you to make the minimum payment, such as 2 percent of your outstanding balance or $20, whichever is greater. Some statements refer to the minimum as the "cardholder amount due." But that is not the total amount you owe.

Consider the following examples. In each example, the minimum payment is based on $\frac{1}{36}$ of the outstanding balance or $20, whichever is greater.

Example 1   You are buying new books for college. If you spend $500 on textbooks using a credit card charging 19.8 percent interest and make only the minimum payment, it will take you more than 2½ years to pay off the loan, adding $150 in interest charges to the cost of your purchase. The same purchase on a credit card charging 12 percent interest will cost only $78 extra.

Example 2   You purchase a $2,000 stereo system using a credit card with 19 percent interest and a 2 percent minimum payment. If you pay just the minimum every month, it will take you 265 months—over 22 years—to pay off the debt and will cost you nearly $4,800 in interest payments. Doubling the amount paid each month to 4 percent of the balance owed would allow you to shorten the payment time to 88 months from 265 months—or 7 years as opposed to 22 years—and save you about $3,680.

Example 3   You charge $2,000 in tuition and fees on a credit card charging 18.5 percent interest. If you pay off the balance by making the minimum payment each month, it will take you more than 11 years to repay the debt. By the time you have paid off the loan, you will have spent an extra $1,934 in interest alone—almost the actual cost of your tuition and fees. Again, to be prudent, pay off the balance as quickly as possible.

See the Financial Planning for Life's Situations feature on page 212 for guidance in choosing the card that is right for you.

## When the Repayment Is Early: The Rule of 78s

*rule of 78s*
A mathematical formula to determine how much interest has been paid at any point in a loan term.

Creditors sometimes use tables based on a mathematical formula called the **rule of 78s,** also called *the sum of the digits,* to determine how much interest you have paid at any point in a loan. This formula dictates that you pay more interest at the beginning of a loan, when you have the use of more of the money, and pay less and less interest as the debt is reduced. Because all of the payments are the same in size, the part going to pay back the amount borrowed increases as the part representing interest decreases.

The laws of several states authorize the use of the rule of 78s as a means of calculating finance charge rebates when you pay off a loan early. The Truth in Lending law requires that your creditor disclose whether or not you are entitled to a rebate of the finance charge if you pay off the loan early. Loans for a year or less, however, usually do not allow for a finance charge rebate.

## Credit Insurance

*credit insurance*
Any type of insurance that ensures repayment of a loan in the event the borrower is unable to repay it.

**Credit insurance** ensures the repayment of your loan in the event of death, disability, or loss of property. The lender is named the beneficiary and directly receives any payments made on submitted claims.

There are three types of credit insurance: credit life, credit accident and health, and credit property. The most commonly purchased type of credit insurance is credit life insurance, which provides for the repayment of the loan if the borrower dies. According to the Consumer Federation of America and the National Insurance Consumer Organization, most borrowers don't need credit life insurance. Those who don't have life insurance can buy term life insurance for less. Term life insurance is discussed in Chapter 12.

Credit accident and health insurance, also called *credit disability insurance,* repays your loan in the event of a loss of income due to illness or injury. Credit property

# Financial Planning for Life's Situations

## To Choose It, First Decide How You Plan to Use It

Many bank cards offer added value through enhancements such as discounts on merchandise, rebates on purchases, travel and accident insurance, frequent-flier mileage, emergency card replacement, donations to nonprofit groups, and 24-hour customer service. The trick to finding the bank card that's right for you is to balance the benefits with the right price. You should consider interest rates and fees based on how you plan to use the card.

- *Annual fee.* If you plan to pay your balance in full each month, shop for a card that has a grace period and carries no annual fee, or a low annual fee, even if the trade-off is a higher interest rate. You plan to pay little or no interest anyway. Gold or platinum cards often charge $100 or more in annual fees.
- *Low rates.* If you prefer to stretch out repayment, aim for a card with a lower interest rate. In general, lower-interest-rate cards tend to have tougher credit approval requirements, may not offer a grace period, and often have slightly higher annual fees. But if you qualify, the money you save on interest is likely to offset a higher fee.
- *Variable rates.* Some credit cards promote variable interest rates tied to an index like *The Wall Street Journal* "prime rate." You may benefit from lower interest rates when the index is low, but remember that when the index rises, you'll pay the higher rate even on purchases you've already made.
- *Grace period.* Not all credit cards offer a grace period. When you use such a card, the bank begins charging you interest on the day you make the purchase or the day the purchase is recorded on your account. Try to

pay off your balance in full each month to maintain the grace period and avoid paying interest.

- *Other fees.* Most automated teller machine (ATM) cards charge a special fee when you take a cash advance. Usually the fee is about 2 or 3 percent of the amount borrowed.

Many banks impose late fees even when payment arrives a day after the due date. Some banks charge a set fee, such as $25 or $30, while others charge a percentage, such as 5 percent, of the minimum payment due.

Most cards assess an over-credit-limit fee. For instance, if you charge $400 over your limit and the penalty is 5 percent, you will pay a $20 fee in addition to interest charges. A few companies charge lost-card replacement fees, usually $5 or $10.

Some credit card issuers allow you to skip a payment without a penalty. While this sounds like the bank is giving you a break, you will be charged interest during this period and will owe more in interest than you did before.

Once you decide on the right combination of features and price, you can begin shopping. Federal law requires that every mail solicitation, "take one" application, and application brochure carry a special box listing the interest rate, annual fee, length of grace period, and other fees. This will allow you to easily compare the costs of different card plans.

SOURCES: American Bankers Association; *Understanding Credit Card Costs* (San Francisco: Consumer Action, March 1994); *Choosing and Using Credit Cards* (Washington, DC: Federal Trade Commission, January 1999). © American Bankers Association. Reprinted with permission.

**Sheet 31**

insurance provides coverage for personal property purchased with a loan. It may also insure collateral property, such as a car or furniture. However, premiums for such coverages are quite high.

## Concept Check 7-2

1. Distinguish between the finance charge and the annual percentage rate.
2. What are the three variations of the simple interest formula?
3. Distinguish among the adjusted balance, previous balance, and average daily balance methods of calculating the cost of open-end credit.
4. What is the rule of 78s?

## MANAGING YOUR DEBTS

### Obj. 3
Develop a plan to manage your debts.

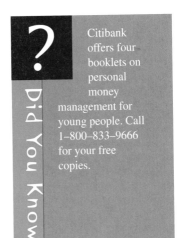

Citibank offers four booklets on personal money management for young people. Call 1–800–833–9666 for your free copies.

A sudden illness or the loss of your job may make it impossible for you to pay your bills on time. If you find you cannot make your payments, contact your creditors at once and try to work out a modified payment plan with them. If you have paid your bills promptly in the past, they may be willing to work with you. Do not wait until your account is turned over to a debt collector. At that point, the creditor has given up on you.

Automobile loans present special problems. Most automobile financing agreements permit your creditor to repossess your car anytime you are in default on your payments. No advance notice is required. If your car is repossessed and sold, you will still owe the difference between the selling price and the unpaid debt, plus any legal, towing, and storage charges. Try to solve the problem with your creditor when you realize you will not be able to meet your payments. It may be better to sell the car yourself and pay off your debt than to incur the added costs of repossession.

If you are having trouble paying your bills, you may be tempted to turn to a company that claims to offer assistance in solving debt problems. Such companies may offer debt consolidation loans, debt counseling, or debt reorganization plans that are "guaranteed" to stop creditors' collection efforts. Before signing with such a company, investigate it. Be sure you understand what services the company provides and what they will cost you. Do not rely on verbal promises that do not appear in your contract. Also, check with the Better Business Bureau and your state or local consumer protection office. It may be able to tell you whether other consumers have registered complaints about the company.

A constant worry for a debtor who is behind in payments is the fear of debt collection agencies. However, as you will see in the next section, a federal agency protects certain legal rights that you possess in your dealings with such agencies.

### Debt Collection Practices

*Fair Debt Collection Practices Act (FDCPA)*
A federal law, enacted in 1978, that regulates debt collection activities.

The Federal Trade Commission enforces the **Fair Debt Collection Practices Act (FDCPA),** which prohibits certain practices by agencies that collect debts for creditors. The act does not apply to creditors that collect debts themselves. While the act does not erase the legitimate debts consumers owe, it does regulate the ways debt collection agencies do business. Exhibit 7–2 summarizes the steps you may take if a debt collector calls.

### Warning Signs of Debt Problems

Bill Kenney, in his early 30s, has a steady job with an annual income of $40,000. Bill, his wife, and their two children enjoy a comfortable life. A new car is parked in the driveway of their home, which is furnished with such modern conveniences as a new microwave oven, a new freezer, an electric washer and dryer, a videocassette recorder, and a large-screen color television set.

However, Bill Kenney is in debt. He is drowning in a sea of bills, with most of his income tied up in repaying debts. Foreclosure proceedings on his home have been instituted, and several stores have court orders to repossess practically every major appliance in it. His current car payment is overdue, and three charge accounts at local stores are several months delinquent.

This case is neither exaggerated nor isolated. Unfortunately, a large number of people are in the same floundering state. These people's problem is immaturity. Mature consumers have certain information; they demonstrate self-discipline, control their impulses, and use sound judgment; they accept responsibility for

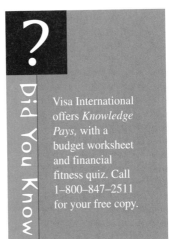

Visa International offers *Knowledge Pays,* with a budget worksheet and financial fitness quiz. Call 1–800–847–2511 for your free copy.

## EXHIBIT 7-2    What to Do If a Debt Collector Calls

The Federal Trade Commission enforces the Fair Debt Collection Practices Act. The law dictates how and when a debt collector may contact you.

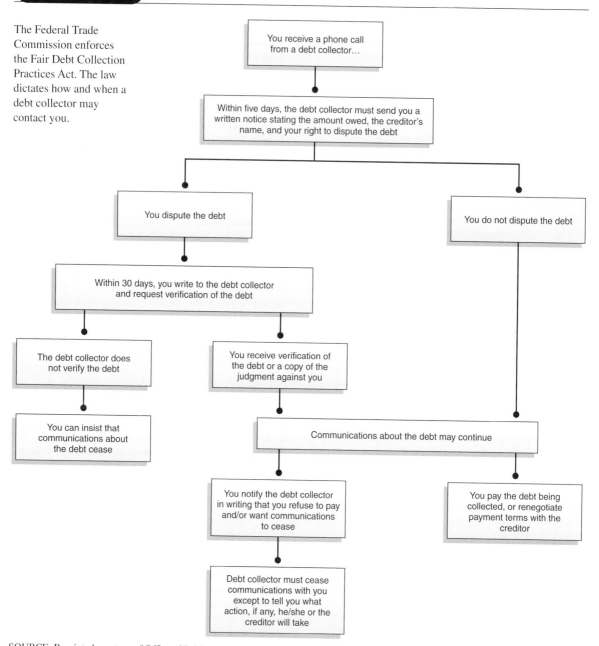

SOURCE: Reprinted courtesy of Office of Public Information, Federal Reserve Bank of Minneapolis, Minneapolis, MN 55480.

money management; and they are able to postpone and govern expenditures when overextension of credit appears likely. As Exhibit 7–3 on page 215 shows, overextension of credit is the second most common reason consumers are unable to pay their bills on time.

| | Primary or Contributing Cause |
|---|---|
| **Reason for Default** | **of Default (percent of cases)** |
| Loss of income | 48 |
|    Unemployment | 24 |
|    Illness | 16 |
|    Other | 8 |
| Overextension | 25 |
| Defective goods or services or other perceived consumer fraud | 20 |
| Fraudulent use of credit | 4 |
| Other | 3 |

**EXHIBIT 7-3**

**Why Consumers Don't Pay**

Loss of income due to unemployment or illness and over-indebtedness are the major reasons consumers don't pay.

SOURCE: Reprinted courtesy of Office of Public Information, Federal Reserve Bank of Minneapolis, Minneapolis, MN 55480.

Referring to overindebtedness as the nation's number two family financial problem, a nationally noted columnist on consumer affairs lists the following as frequent reasons for indebtedness:[2]

1. *Emotional problems,* such as the need for instant gratification, as in the case of a man who can't resist buying a costly suit or a woman who impulsively purchases an expensive dress in a trendy department store.
2. *The use of money to punish,* such as a husband who buys a new car without consulting his wife, who in turn buys a diamond watch to get even.
3. *The expectation of instant comfort* among young couples who assume that by use of the installment plan, they can have immediately the possessions their parents acquired after years of work.
4. *Keeping up with the Joneses,* which is more apparent than ever, not only among prosperous families but among limited-income families too.
5. *Overindulgence of children,* often because of the parents' own emotional needs, competition with each other, or inadequate communication regarding expenditures for the children.
6. *Misunderstanding or lack of communication among family members.* For example, a salesperson visited a Memphis family to sell them an expensive freezer. Although the freezer was beyond the means of this already overindebted family and too large for their needs anyway, the husband thought his wife wanted it. Not until later, in an interview with a debt counselor, did the wife relate her concern when she signed the contract; she had wanted her husband to say no.
7. *The amount of the finance charges,* which can push a family over the edge of their ability to pay, especially when they borrow from one company to pay another and these charges pyramid.

Exhibit 7–4 on page 216 lists the danger signals of potential debt problems.

## The Serious Consequences of Debt

Just as the causes of indebtedness vary, so too does a mixture of other personal and family problems that frequently result from overextension of credit.

Loss of a job because of garnishment proceedings may occur in a family that has a disproportionate amount of income tied up in debts. Another possibility is that such a family is forced to neglect vital areas. In the frantic effort to rob Peter to pay Paul,

**EXHIBIT 7-4**

**Danger Signals of Potential Debt Problems**

Seek help from your local Consumer Credit Counseling Service if you experience these danger signals.

SOURCES: *Advice for Consumers Who Use Credit* (Silver Springs, MD: Consumer Credit Counseling Service of Maryland, Inc.); *How to Be Credit Smart* (Washington, DC: Consumer Credit Education Foundation).

1. Paying only the minimum balance on credit card bills each month
2. Increasing the total balance due on credit accounts each month
3. Missing payments, paying late, or paying some bills this month and others next month
4. Intentionally using the overdraft or automatic loan features on checking accounts or taking frequent cash advances on credit cards
5. Using savings to pay routine bills such as groceries or utilities
6. Receiving second or third payment notices from creditors
7. Not talking to your spouse about money or talking *only* about money
8. Depending on overtime, moonlighting, or bonuses to meet everyday expenses
9. Using up your savings
10. Borrowing money to pay old debts
11. Not knowing how much you owe until the bills arrive
12. Going over your credit limit on credit cards
13. Having little or nothing in savings to handle unexpected expenses
14. Being denied credit because of a negative credit bureau report
15. Getting a credit card revoked by the issuer
16. Putting off medical or dental visits because you can't afford them right now

If your household is experiencing more than two of these warning signals, it's time to examine your budget for ways to reduce expenses.

skimping may seriously affect the family's health and neglect the educational needs of children. Excessive indebtedness may also result in heavy drinking, neglect of children, marital difficulties, and drug abuse. But help is available to those debtors who seek it.

See the accompanying Financial Planning for Life's Situations feature to obtain free credit information on the Internet.

**Concept Check 7-3**

1. What is the Fair Debt Collection Practices Act?
2. What are the most frequent reasons for indebtedness?
3. What are common danger signals of potential debt problems?

## CONSUMER CREDIT COUNSELING SERVICES

**Obj. 4**
Evaluate various private and governmental sources that assist consumers with debt problems.

*Consumer Credit Counseling Service (CCCS)* A local, nonprofit organization that provides debt counseling services for families and individuals with serious financial problems.

If you are having problems paying your bills and need help, you have several options. You can contact your creditors and try to work out an adjusted repayment plan yourself, or you can check your telephone directory for a nonprofit financial counseling program to get help.

The **Consumer Credit Counseling Service (CCCS)** is a local, nonprofit organization affiliated with the National Foundation for Consumer Credit (NFCC). Branches of the CCCS provide debt counseling services for families and individuals with serious financial problems. It is not a charity, a lending institution, or a governmental or legal agency. The Consumer Credit Counseling Service is supported by contributions from banks, consumer finance companies, credit unions, merchants, and other community-minded organizations and individuals.

According to the NFCC, every year millions of consumers contact CCCS offices for help with their personal financial problems. More than 225 CCCS offices opened in 1996, bringing the total number of locations to about 1,300. Now more than 90 percent of the U.S. population has convenient access to CCCS services.

# Financial Planning for Life's Situations

## *Money Management in Cyberspace*

Whether you're developing a plan for reaching your financial goals or searching for a low-interest credit card, you can look to the Internet for a world of free information. Many websites provide interactive worksheets that allow you to plug in personal information and obtain customized reports. Here are some suggestions.

**www.financenter.com** (FinanCenter) This site provides nifty payment calculators that help you figure out the actual dollars paid in interest over the period of a credit card debt or the maximum amount you should borrow at your current income. If your payments have been piling up, take a deep breath before traveling here.

**www.bankrate.com** (Bank Rate Monitor) Looking for the best credit card rates available or up-to-the-minute news on the credit industry? Then log on here. This site posts a survey of card rates and even lets you apply online for some cards. You can also scroll through a list of suggestions for cutting your credit card debt.

**www.ramresearch.com** (RAM Research) Created by this independent bank research organization, the site contains everything you ever wanted to know about credit cards. It includes a database of 10,000 financial institutions, and news and statistics on the credit industry. If you've had credit problems and want to reestablish your credit rating, see the section on secured cards.

**www.aaii.org** (American Association of Individual Investors) The AAII website covers the fundamentals of investing, with an array of subjects that will interest both the novice and the advanced investor. You can dive into portfolio management or brush up on investment terminology. There's also a special section on using computers to manage your finances.

**www.napfa.org** (National Association of Personal Financial Advisors) NAPFA offers consumer information on what to expect from a financial planner, as well as how and why to choose one. A handy search tool lets you pinpoint an adviser close to home.

**www.iafp.org** (International Association for Financial Planning) Check here to learn how to assess your financial situation and ways to set budget goals. The site also features a section on determining whether or not you need a financial planner.

**www.sec.gov** (Securities and Exchange Commission) Here you'll find a wealth of information about this U.S. government regulatory agency, including a straightforward discussion on the essentials of investing. You can tap into the EDGAR database to view the information that the SEC requires companies to file.

**www.personalwealth.com** (Standard & Poor's Personal Wealth) This home page also covers many financial topics and can be customized for your preferences.

**www.money.com** (*Money* magazine) This site covers virtually all topics related to money, including credit information, current money indexes, and a financial calculator.

**www.consumercredit.com** (American Consumer Credit Counseling, Inc.) This site is a good place to go if you have a credit problem or are heading that way.

**www.nfcc.org** (National Foundation for Consumer Credit) This is the home page for a network of local nonprofit organizations that provide consumer credit education and services.

SOURCES: *Teacher$ Talk*, TIAA-CREF (New York: Spring 1997), p. 5; *Dollars & Sense: Personal Finance for the 21st Century*, Telecourse Study Guide (Burr Ridge, IL: Irwin McGraw-Hill, 1999), p. 82.

To find an office near you, check the white pages of your local telephone directory under Consumer Credit Counseling Service, or call 1–800–388–CCCS. All information is kept strictly confidential. Exhibit 7–5 on page 218 reveals the characteristics of the typical CCCS client.

## What the CCCS Does

Credit counselors are aware that most people who are in debt over their heads are basically honest people who want to clear up their indebtedness. Too often, the problems of such people arise from a lack of planning or a miscalculation of what they earn.

**Profile of a CCCS Client**

Following are the characteristics of the typical client of the Consumer Credit Counseling Service:

| | |
|---|---|
| Age: | 35 |
| Sex: | Male 51%, female 49% |
| Marital status: | Single 25%, married 52% |
| | Separated, divorced, or widowed 23% |
| Number in family: | 3.3 |
| Buying or own home: | 38% |
| Average monthly gross income: | $2,056 |
| Average total debt: | $18,312 |
| Average number of creditors: | 11 |

SOURCES: National Foundation for Consumer Credit, Inc. (Silver Springs, MD); Consumer Credit Insurance Association (Chicago); Consumer Credit Counseling Service (Chicago); TransUnion Corporation; *Chicago Tribune*, August 9, 1992, sec. 6, p. 10.

Therefore, the CCCS is as concerned with preventing the problems as with solving them. As a result, its activities are divided into two parts:

1. Aiding families with serious debt problems by helping them manage their money better and setting up a realistic budget and plan for expenditures.
2. Helping people prevent debt problems by teaching them the necessity of family budget planning, providing education to people of all ages regarding the pitfalls of unwise credit buying, suggesting techniques for family budgeting, and encouraging credit institutions to provide full information about the costs and terms of credit and to withhold credit from those who cannot afford to repay it.

Anyone who is overburdened by credit obligations can phone, write, or visit a CCCS office. The CCCS requires that an applicant complete an application for credit counseling and then arranges an appointment for a personal interview with the applicant.

CCCS counseling is usually free. However, when the CCCS administers a debt repayment plan, it sometimes charges a nominal fee to help defray administrative costs.

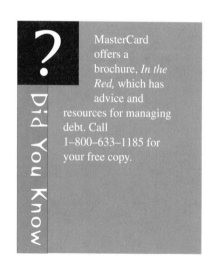

**Did You Know**

MasterCard offers a brochure, *In the Red,* which has advice and resources for managing debt. Call 1–800–633–1185 for your free copy.

## Alternative Counseling Services

In addition to the CCCS, universities, military bases, credit unions, local county extension agents, and state and federal housing authorities sometimes provide nonprofit counseling services. These organizations usually charge little or nothing for such assistance. You can also check with your local bank or consumer protection office to see whether it has a listing of reputable, low-cost financial counseling services.

But what if a debtor suffers from an extreme case of financial woes? Is there any relief? The answer is yes: bankruptcy proceedings.

## Concept Check 7-4

1. What is the Consumer Credit Counseling Service?
2. What are the two major activities of the Consumer Credit Counseling Service?
3. What options other than the CCCS do consumers have for financial counseling?

# DECLARING PERSONAL BANKRUPTCY

**Obj. 5**

Assess the choices in declaring personal bankruptcy.

Jan Watson typifies the new face of bankruptcy. A 43-year-old freelance commercial photographer from Point Reyes, California, she was never in serious financial trouble until she began incurring big medical costs last year and reached for her credit cards to pay the bills. Since Jan didn't have health insurance, her debt quickly mounted and soon reached $17,000. It was too much for her to pay off with her $25,000-a-year free-lance income. Her solution: Declare personal bankruptcy and the immediate freedom it would bring from creditors' demands.

Ms. Watson's move put her in familiar company, demographically speaking. An increasing number of bankruptcy filers are well-educated, middle-class baby boomers with an overwhelming level of credit card debt. These baby boomers make up 44 percent of the adult population, but they account for 59 percent of personal bankruptcies. In that group, the people most likely to be in bankruptcy are between 40 and 44 years old, an age group that is usually assumed to be economically established. Increasingly, too, the bankruptcy debtor is likely to be female. Women now account for 28.6 percent of bankruptcy filers, up from 17 percent only a decade ago.

In 1994, the U.S. Senate unanimously passed a bill that will reduce the time and cost of bankruptcy proceedings. The bill strengthens creditor rights and enables more individuals to weather bankruptcy proceedings without selling their assets.

Unfortunately for some debtors, bankruptcy has become an acceptable tool of credit management. During the last nine years, the personal bankruptcy rate has increased 20 percent annually. According to the American Bankruptcy Institute, a record 1.48 million people declared bankruptcy in 1998, the highest rate since the U.S. bankruptcy code took effect in 1979 (see Exhibit 7–6). Bankruptcy courts have turned to regular Saturday sessions to handle the overflow.

## The U.S. Bankruptcy Act of 1978: The Last Resort

Nationwide, the overwhelming majority of bankruptcies like Jan Watson's are filed under Chapter 7 of the U.S. bankruptcy code. You have two choices in declaring personal bankruptcy: Chapter 7 (a straight bankruptcy) and Chapter 13 (a wage earner plan) bankruptcy. Both choices are undesirable, and neither should be considered an easy way out.

**EXHIBIT 7-6**

**U.S. Bankruptcies, 1961–98**

SOURCES: Administrative Office of the United States Courts; *Economic Policy Review,* Federal Reserve Bank of New York, July 1997, p. 84; *Credit Union Executive,* March–April 1999, p. 24.

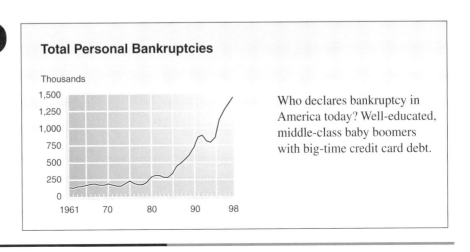

**Total Personal Bankruptcies**

Thousands

Who declares bankruptcy in America today? Well-educated, middle-class baby boomers with big-time credit card debt.

*Chapter 7 bankruptcy*
One type of personal (or straight) bankruptcy in which many debts are forgiven.

## Chapter 7 Bankruptcy

In a **Chapter 7 bankruptcy,** a debtor is required to draw up a petition listing his or her assets and liabilities. The debtor submits the petition to a U.S. district court and pays a filing fee. A person filing for relief under the bankruptcy code is called a *debtor;* the term *bankrupt* is not used.

Chapter 7 is a straight bankruptcy in which many, but not all, debts are forgiven. Most of the debtor's assets are sold to pay off creditors. However, certain assets of the debtor are protected to some extent. For example, Social Security payments, unemployment compensation, and limited values of your equity in a home, car, or truck, household goods and appliances, trade tools, books, and so forth are protected.

However, some creditors still try to collect. In 1997, for example, the Federal Trade Commission negotiated a settlement agreement with Sears, Roebuck and Company ensuring that Sears makes full refunds totaling more than $100 million to consumers. More than 200,000 consumers whose debts were discharged in bankruptcy proceedings had been forced by Sears to continue payments or face illegal collection efforts.

The discharge of debts in Chapter 7 does not affect alimony, child support, certain taxes, fines, certain debts arising from educational loans, or debts that you fail to properly disclose to the bankruptcy court. At the request of a creditor, the bankruptcy judge may also exclude from the discharge debts resulting from loans you received by giving the lender a false financial statement. Furthermore, debts arising from fraud, embezzlement, driving while intoxicated, larceny, or certain other willful or malicious acts may also be excluded.

According to recent research by Purdue's Credit Research Center, Chapter 7 bankrupts average $19,800 in annual after-tax income and credit card debts of $17,544. Increasingly, credit card issuers have been targeting less affluent consumers. From 1993 to 1996, the proportion of households with incomes under $20,000 that received credit card offers rose from 40 to 58 percent. In addition, issuers are increasingly marketing to recent bankrupts and teenagers.[3]

*Chapter 13 bankruptcy*
A voluntary plan that a debtor with regular income develops and proposes to a bankruptcy court.

## Chapter 13 Bankruptcy

In a **Chapter 13 bankruptcy,** a debtor with a regular income proposes to a bankruptcy court a plan for extinguishing his or her debts from future earnings or other property over a period of time. In such a bankruptcy, the debtor normally keeps all or most of the property.

During the period the plan is in effect, which can be as long as five years, the debtor makes regular payments to a Chapter 13 trustee. The trustee, in turn, distributes the money to the creditors. Under certain circumstances, the bankruptcy court may approve a plan permitting the debtor to keep all property even though the debtor repays less than the full amount of the debts. Certain debts not dischargeable in Chapter 7, such as those based on fraud, may be discharged in Chapter 13 if the debtor successfully completes the plan. To file a Chapter 13 bankruptcy, a person must have regular income and not more than $250,000 in unsecured debts or $750,000 in secured debts.[4]

## Effect of Bankruptcy on Your Job and Your Future Credit

Different people have different experiences in obtaining credit after they file bankruptcy. Some find obtaining credit more difficult. Others find obtaining credit easier because they have relieved themselves of their prior debts or because creditors know they cannot file another bankruptcy case for a period of time. Obtaining credit may be easier for people who file a Chapter 13 bankruptcy and repay some of their debts than for people who file a Chapter 7 bankruptcy and make no effort to repay. The bankruptcy law prohibits your employer from discharging you simply because you have filed a bankruptcy case.

One caution: Don't confuse a personal bankruptcy with a business (or Chapter 11) bankruptcy. The Chapter 11 bankruptcy is a reorganization requested by a business and ordered by the court because a business is unable to pay its debts.

## Should a Lawyer Represent You in a Bankruptcy Case?

When 29-year-old Lynn Jensen of San Gabriel, California, lost her $35,000-a-year job, she ended up filing for bankruptcy using a "how to file for bankruptcy" book because she could not afford a lawyer. Like Lynn, you have the right to file your own bankruptcy case and to represent yourself at all court hearings. In any bankruptcy case, however, you must complete and file with a bankruptcy court several detailed forms concerning your property, debts, and financial condition. Many people find it easier to complete these forms with the assistance of experienced bankruptcy counsel. In addition, you may discover that your case will develop complications, especially if you own a substantial amount of property or your creditors object to the discharge of your debts. Then you will require the advice and assistance of a lawyer.

Choosing a bankruptcy lawyer may be difficult. Some of the least reputable lawyers make easy money by handling hundreds of bankruptcy cases without adequately considering individual needs. Recommendations from those you know and trust and from employee assistance programs are most useful.

### What Are the Costs?   The monetary costs to the debtor under Chapter 13 bankruptcy include the following:

1. *Court costs.* The debtor must pay a filing fee to the clerk of the court at the time of filing his or her petition. The filing fee may be paid in up to four installments if the court grants authorization.
2. *Attorneys' fees.* These fees are usually the largest single item of cost. Often the attorney does not require them to be paid in advance at the time of filing but agrees to be paid in installments after receipt of a down payment.
3. *Trustees' fees and costs.* The trustees' fees are established by the bankruptcy judge in most districts and by a U.S. trustee in certain other districts.

Although it is possible to reduce these costs by purchasing the legal forms in a local stationery store and completing them yourself, an attorney is strongly recommended.

There are also intangible costs to bankruptcy. For example, obtaining credit in the future may be difficult, since bankruptcy reports are retained in credit bureaus for 10 years. Therefore, you should take the extreme step of declaring personal bankruptcy only when no other options for solving your financial problems exist.

Since you now know everything you ever wanted to know about consumer credit, read the Financial Planning for Life's Situations feature on page 222 to test your credit IQ.

## Concept Check 7-5

1. What is the purpose of Chapter 7 bankruptcy?
2. What is the difference between Chapter 7 and Chapter 13 bankruptcy?
3. How does bankruptcy affect your job and future credit?
4. What are the costs of declaring bankruptcy?

# Financial Planning for Life's Situations

## WHAT'S YOUR CREDIT IQ?

### CREDIT-ABILITY SCORECARD

Test your credit IQ. For each question, circle the letter that best describes your credit habits.

**1. I pay my bills when they are due.**
(A) Always    (B) Almost Always    (C) Sometimes

**2. After paying my regular bills each month, I have money left from my income.**
(A) Yes    (B) Sometimes    (C) Never

**3. I know how much I owe on my credit cards each month before I receive my bills.**
(A) Yes    (B) Sometimes    (C) No

**4. When I get behind in my payments, I ignore the past-due notices.**
(A) Never or Not Applicable    (B) Sometimes
(C) Always

**5. When I need more money for my regular living expenses, I take out a loan or use my line of credit on my credit card or checking account.**
(A) Never    (B) Sometimes    (C) Often

**6. If I want to see a copy of my credit report, I would contact . . .**
(A) A credit reporting agency    (B) My lenders
(C) My lawyer

**7. My credit record shows that I am current on all my loans and charge accounts.**
(A) Yes    (B) Don't know    (C) No

**8. I pay more than the minimum balance due on my credit card accounts.**
(A) Always    (B) Sometimes    (C) Never

**9. To pay off my current credit and charge card accounts, it would take me . . .**
(A) 4 months or less    (B) 5 to 8 months
(C) Over 8 months

**10. My consumer loans (including auto loans, but not mortgage payment) and credit card bills each month average more than 20% of my take-home pay.**
(A) No    (B) Sometimes    (C) Always

**11. If I had serious credit problems, I would contact my creditors to explain the problem.**
(A) Yes    (B) Probably    (C) No

**12. If I default (don't repay) on a loan, that fact can stay on my credit report for . . .**
(A) 7 years    (B) 3 years    (C) 1 year

Assign a score of 3 for each "A" answer, 2 for each "B" answer, and 1 for each "C" response. Total the score.

*If you scored:*

31–36   You have an excellent knowledge of credit and its responsible use.

24–30   You should take steps toward a better understanding of your personal finances and of the credit process.

18–23   You probably need to take a serious look at your personal finances; consider controlling your spending and keeping on a tight budget.

12–17   You may be heading for serious trouble; consider seeking help, such as nonprofit consumer credit counseling services.

SOURCE: *How to Be Credit Smart.* AFSA Education Foundation, 1997.

# KEY FORMULAS

| Page | Topic | Formula |
|------|-------|---------|
| 205 | Calculating annual percentage rate (APR) | $APR = \dfrac{2 \times \text{Number of payment periods in one year} \times \text{Dollar cost of credit}}{\text{Loan amount (Total number of payments to pay off the loan} + 1)}$ $= \dfrac{2 \times n \times I}{P(N + 1)}$ |

*Example:*

P = Principal borrowed, \$100; n = number of payments in one year, 1;
I = Dollar cost of credit, \$8

$$APR = \frac{2 \times 1 \times \$8}{\$100(1 + 1)} = \frac{\$16}{\$200} = 0.08, \text{ or 8 percent}$$

For 12 equal monthly payments,

$$APR = \frac{2 \times 12 \times \$8}{\$100(12 + 1)} = \frac{\$192}{\$1,300} = 0.1476, \text{ or 14.76 percent}$$

| 207 | Calculating simple interest | $\text{Interest (in dollars)} = \text{Principal borrowed} \times \text{Interest rate} \times \text{Length of loan in years}$ |

$$I = P \times r \times T$$

*Example:*

From above:  P = \$100; r = 0.08; T = 1

$$I = \$100 \times 0.08 \times 1 = \$8$$

| 229 | Calculating compound interest | $\text{Total future value of a loan} = \text{Principal}(1 + \text{Rate of interest})^{\text{Time in years}}$ |

$$F = P(1 + r)^T$$

*Example:*

From above:  P = \$100; r = 0.08; T = 1

$$F = \$100(1 + 0.08)^1 = \$100(1.08) = \$108$$

| 230 | Calculating total monthly payment (principal + interest) on a conventional loan | $\frac{\text{Monthly payment}}{} = \frac{\text{Loan} \times \text{Monthly interest rate} \times (1 + \text{Monthly interest rate})^{\text{Time in months}}}{(1 + \text{Monthly interest rate})^{\text{Time in months}} - 1}$ |

$$MP = P \times \frac{i \times (1 + i)^T}{(1 + i)^T - 1}$$

*Example:*

From above:  P = \$100; i = 0.08

In a 12-month loan,

$$MP = \frac{\$100 \times 0.08(1 + 0.08)^{12}}{(1 + 0.08)^{12} - 1} = \frac{\$100 \times 0.08/12 \times (1 + 0.0066)^{12}}{(1 + 0.0066)^{12} - 1} = \$8.70$$

## Summary of Objectives

**Obj. 1   Analyze the major sources of consumer credit.**

The major sources of consumer credit are commercial banks, savings and loan associations, credit unions, finance companies, life insurance companies, and family and friends. Each of these sources has unique advantages and disadvantages.

Parents or family members are often the source of the least expensive loans. They may charge you only the interest they would have earned had they not made the loan. Such loans, however, can complicate family relationships.

**Obj. 2   Determine the cost of credit by calculating interest using various interest formulas.**

Compare the finance charge and the annual percentage rate (APR) as you shop for credit. Under the Truth in Lending law, creditors are required to state the cost of borrowing so that you can compare credit costs and shop for credit.

For a borrower, the most favorable method of calculating the cost of open-end credit is the adjusted balance method. In this period, creditors add finance charges after subtracting payments made during the billing period. The Rule of 78s favors lenders. This formula dictates that you pay more interest at the beginning of a loan, when you have the use of more money, and pay less and less interest as the debt is reduced. Because all the payments are the same size, the part going to pay back the amount borrowed increases as the part representing interest decreases.

## Obj. 3   Develop a plan to manage your debts.

The Fair Debt Collection Practices Act prohibits certain practices by debt collection agencies. Debt has serious consequences if a proper plan for managing it is not implemented.

Most people agree that emotional problems, the use of money to punish, the expectation of instant comfort, keeping up with the Joneses, overindulgence of children, misunderstanding or lack of communication among family members, and the amount of finance charge are common reasons for indebtedness.

## Obj. 4   Evaluate various private and governmental sources that assist consumers with debt problems.

If you cannot meet your obligations, contact your creditors immediately. Before signing up with a debt consolidation company, investigate it thoroughly. Better yet, contact your local Consumer Credit Counseling Service or other debt counseling organizations.

Such organizations help people manage their money better by setting up a realistic budget and plan for expenditures. These organizations also help people prevent debt problems by teaching them the necessity of family budget planning and providing education to people of all ages.

## Obj. 5   Assess the choices in declaring personal bankruptcy.

A debtor's last resort is to declare bankruptcy, permitted by the U.S. Bankruptcy Act of 1978. Consider the financial and other costs of bankruptcy before taking this extreme step. A debtor can declare Chapter 7 (straight) bankruptcy or Chapter 13 (wage earner plan) bankruptcy.

Some people find obtaining credit more difficult after filing bankruptcy. Others find obtaining credit easier because they have relieved themselves of their prior debts or because creditors know they cannot file another bankruptcy case for a period of time. Obtaining credit may be easier for people who file a Chapter 13 bankruptcy and repay some of their debts than for people who file a Chapter 7 bankruptcy and make no effort to repay their debts.

## Financial Planning Problems

1. *Calculating the Finance Charge on a Loan.* Dave borrowed $500 for one year and paid $50 in interest. The bank charged him a $5 service charge. What is the finance charge on this loan?   (Obj. 2)
2. *Calculating the Annual Percentage Rate.* In problem 1, Dave borrowed $500 on January 1, 2001, and paid it all back at once on December 31, 2001. What was the APR? (Obj. 2)
3. *Calculating the Annual Percentage Rate.* If Dave paid the $500 in 12 equal monthly payments, what was the APR? (Obj. 2)
4. *Comparing the Costs of Credit Cards.* Bobby is trying to decide between two credit cards. One has no annual fee and an 18 percent interest rate, and the other has a $40 annual fee and an 8.9 percent interest rate. Should he take the card that's free or the one that costs $40?   (Obj. 2)
5. *Calculating Cash Advance Fee and the Dollar Amount of Interest.* Sidney took a $200 cash advance by using checks linked to her credit card account. The bank charges a 2 percent cash advance fee on the amount borrowed and offers no grace period on cash advances. Sidney paid the balance in full when the bill arrived. What

was the cash advance fee? What was the interest for one month at an 18 percent APR? What was the total amount she paid? What if she had made the purchase with her credit card (assuming no overcredit limit) and paid off the bill in full promptly?   (Obj. 2)
6. *Comparing the Cost of Credit during Inflationary Periods.* Dorothy lacks cash to pay for a $600 dishwasher. She could buy it from the store on credit by making 12 monthly payments of $52.74. The total cost would then be $632.88. Instead, Dorothy decides to deposit $50 a month in the bank until she has saved enough money to pay cash for the dishwasher. One year later, she has saved $642—$600 in deposits plus interest. When she goes back to the store, she finds the dishwasher now costs $660. Its price has gone up 10 percent, the current rate of inflation. Was postponing her purchase a good trade-off for Dorothy?   (Obj. 2)
7. *Comparing Costs of Credit Using Three Calculation Methods.* You have been pricing a compact disk player in several stores. Three stores have the identical price of $300. Each store charges 18 percent APR, has a 30-day grace period, and sends out bills on the first of the month.

On further investigation, you find that store A calculates the finance charge by using the average daily balance method, store B uses the adjusted balance method, and store C uses the previous balance method. Assume you purchased the disk player on May 5 and made a $100 payment on June 15. What will the finance charge be if you made your purchase from store A? From store B? From store C?   (Obj. 2)

**8.** *Determining Interest Cost Using the Simple Interest Formula.* What are the interest cost and the total amount due on a six-month loan of $1,500 at 13.2 percent simple annual interest?   (Obj. 2)

**9.** *Calculating the Total Cost of a Purchase, the Monthly Payment, and an APR.* After visiting several automobile dealerships, Richard selects the used car he wants. He likes its $10,000 price, but financing through the dealer is no bargain. He has $2,000 cash for a down payment, so he needs an $8,000 loan. In shopping at several banks for an installment loan, he learns that interest on most automobile loans is quoted at add-on rates. That is, during the life of the loan, interest is paid on the full amount borrowed even though a portion of the principal has been paid back. Richard borrows $8,000 for a period of four years at an add-on interest rate of 11 percent. What is the total interest on Richard's loan? What is the total cost of the car? What is the monthly payment? What is the annual percentage rate (APR)?   (Obj. 2)

## Financial Planning Activities

**1.** *Determining Criteria If a Loan Is Needed.* Survey friends and relatives to find out what criteria they used to determine the need for credit.   (Obj. 1)

**2.** *Comparing Costs of Loans from Various Lenders.* Prepare a list of sources of inexpensive loans, medium-priced loans, and expensive loans in your area. What are the trade-offs in obtaining a loan from an "easy" lender?   (Obj. 1)

**3.** *Using Current Information on Obtaining the Best Credit Terms.* Choose a current issue of *Worth, Money, Kiplinger's Personal Finance Magazine,* or *Business Week* and summarize an article that provides suggestions on how you can choose the best, yet least expensive source of credit.   (Obj. 2)

**4.** *Using the Internet to Obtain Information about the Costs of Credit.* As pointed out at the beginning of this chapter, credit costs money; therefore, you must conduct a cost/benefit analysis before making any major purchase. While most people consider credit costs, others simply ignore them and eventually find themselves in financial difficulties. To help consumers avoid this problem, each of the following organizations has a home page on the Internet:

*Finance Center, Inc.,* helps consumers save money when purchasing, financing, or refinancing a new home or a car, or making a credit card transaction. (www.financenter.com)

*Debtors Anonymous* offers financial counseling to debt-ridden consumers. (www.debtorsanonymous.org)

*Bank Rate Monitor*™ is America's consumer rate source for mortgages, credit cards, auto loans, home equity loans, and personal loans. (www.bankrate.com)

Choose one of the above organizations and visit its website. Then prepare a report that summarizes the information the organization provides. Finally, decide how this information could help you better manage your credit and its costs.   (Obj. 2)

**5.** *Choosing between the Features and Costs of a Loan.* When you choose financing, what are the trade-offs between the features you prefer (term, size of payments, fixed or variable interest, or payment plan) and the cost of your loan?   (Obj. 2)

**6.** *Calculating the Cost of Credit Using Three APR Formulas.* How are the simple interest, simple interest on the declining balance, and add-on interest formulas used in determining the cost of credit?   (Obj. 2)

**7.** *Handling Harassment from Debt Collection Agencies.* Your friend is drowning in a sea of overdue bills and is being harassed by a debt collection agency. Prepare a list of the steps your friend should take if the harassment continues.   (Obj. 3)

**8.** *Seeking Assistance from the Consumer Credit Counseling Services.* Visit a local office of the Consumer Credit Counseling Service. What assistance can debtors obtain from this office? What is the cost of this assistance, if any?   (Obj. 4)

**9.** *Assessing the Choices in Declaring Personal Bankruptcy.* What factors would you consider in assessing the choices in declaring personal bankruptcy? Why should personal bankruptcy be the choice of last resort?   (Obj. 4)

## LIFE SITUATION CASE

### FINANCING SUE'S HYUNDAI EXEL

After shopping around, Sue Wallace decided on the car of her choice, a used Hyundai Exel. The dealer quoted her a total price of $8,000. Sue decided to use $2,000 of her savings as a down payment and borrow $6,000. The salesperson wrote this information on a sales contract that Sue took with her when she set out to find financing.

When Sue applied for a loan, she discussed loan terms with the bank lending officer. The officer told her that the bank's policy was to lend only 80 percent of the total price of a used car. Sue showed the officer her copy of the sales contract, indicating that she had agreed to make a $2,000, or 25 percent, down payment on the $8,000 car, so this requirement caused her no problem. Although the bank was willing to make 48-month loans at an annual percentage rate of 15 percent on used cars, Sue chose a 36-month repayment schedule. She believed she could afford the higher payments, and she knew she would not have to pay as much interest if she paid off the loan at a faster rate. The bank lending officer provided Sue with a copy of the Truth-in-Lending Disclosure Statement shown here.

**Truth-in-Lending Disclosure Statement (Loans)**

| Annual Percentage Rate | Finance Charge | Amount Financed | Total of Payments   36 |
|---|---|---|---|
| The cost of your credit as a yearly rate. | The dollar amount the credit will cost you. | The amount of credit provided to you or on your behalf. | The amount you will have paid after you have made all payments as scheduled. |
| 15% | $1,487.64 | $6,000.00 | $7,487.64 |

You have the right to receive at this time an itemization of the Amount Financed.

☒ I want an itemization.          ❏ I do not want an itemization.

Your payment schedule will be:

| Number of Payments | Amount of Payments | When Payments Are Due |
|---|---|---|
| 36 | $207.99 | 1st of each month |

Sue decided to compare the APR she had been offered with the APR offered by another bank, but the 20 percent APR of the second bank (bank B) was more expensive than the 15 percent APR of the first bank (bank A). Here is her comparison of the two loans:

|  | Bank A 15% APR | Bank B 20% APR |
|---|---|---|
| Amount financed | $6,000.00 | $6,000.00 |
| Finance charge | 1,487.64 | 2,027.28 |
| Total of payments | 7,487.64 | 8,027.28 |
| Monthly payments | 207.99 | 222.98 |

The 5 percent difference in the APRs of the two banks meant Sue would have to pay $15 extra every month if she got her loan from the second bank. Of course, she got the loan from the first bank.

### Questions

1. What is perhaps the most important item shown on the disclosure statement? Why?
2. What is included in the finance charge?
3. What amount will Sue receive from the bank?
4. Should Sue borrow from bank A or bank B? Why?

# VIDEO CASE   Credit Problems

This video case features a couple who are dining at a fine restaurant and realize they have exceeded their credit limit on both of their credit cards. The couple seems unaware of some important warning signs of potential credit problems.

Credit counselor Joanne Budde explains the three goals of the Consumer Credit Counseling Service: to educate consumers, provide confidential counseling, and develop personalized debt management plans.

Gerri Detweiler of Debt Counselors of America states that one reason many people have credit problems is that credit is so easily available. A financial adviser explains that credit counseling may be a better alternative to bankruptcy.

Maxine Sweet of Experian states that missed payments can stay on a credit report for up to 7 years and bankruptcies for up to 10 years. She also advises consumers to beware of some credit repair scams. Finally, financial adviser Dianne Wilkman explains how some credit counselors can negotiate with lenders to work out a repayment plan.

## Questions

1. What are some important warning signs of potential credit problems? Do you believe the couple in the video are experiencing these signs?
2. What are the major functions of Consumer Credit Counseling Service? Would you suggest the couple seek CCCS assistance? Why or why not?
3. Do you believe credit is too easily available? If so, explain and give examples.
4. Why would credit counseling be a better alternative to bankruptcy?

# Creating an E-Plan: Financial Decisions Using the Web

## COMPARING CREDIT SOURCES AND COSTS

Credit is available from many sources. Becoming aware of the differences among financial institutions related to borrowing costs and other factors while wisely managing your debt will help you avoid financial difficulties.

Websites for Comparing Credit Costs

- RAM Research provides an opportunity to compare credit card costs and features at **www.cardtrak.com** and a library of credit information at **www.ramresearch.com.**
- Current rates for mortgages, home equity loans, credit cards, and consumer loans at **www.bankrate.com/ bankrate/publ/tips.htm** and **www.banx.com.**
- Credit card information from the FinanCenter at **www.financenter.com**.
- The National Foundation for Consumer Credit provides information on financial problems and credit reports at **www.nfcc.org.**
- National Credit Counseling Services assistance may be obtained at **www.nccs.org** and the Debt Counselors of America at **www.dca.org.**

- Information for the Bankcard Holders of America at **www.epn.com/bha.**
- Financial calculators for cost of credit at **www.centura.com/formulas/calc.html.**

(Note: Addresses and content of websites change, and new sites are created daily. Use search engines to update and locate websites for your current financial planning needs.)

*PFP Sheets: 30–31*

Short-Term Financial Planning Activities

1. Evaluate your current use of credit cards. Compare various credit card offers related to APR, annual fee, grace period, and other fees (see PFP Sheet 30).
2. Compare various credit sources for loans related to various financial needs (see PFP Sheet 31).

Long-Term Financial Planning Activities

1. Investigate various actions commonly taken to avoid debt problems.
2. Prepare a spending plan to minimize the use of credit.

## CHAPTER 7

# Other Methods of Determining the Cost of Credit

## BANK DISCOUNT METHOD

When the *bank discount rate* method is used, interest is calculated on the amount to be paid back and you receive the difference between the amount to be paid back and the interest amount. For instance, if your relative lends you $1,000 less $50 (interest at 5 percent), you receive $950.

Example 1    Using the APR formula, you find the true interest rate, or the annual percentage rate, is 5.263 percent, not the stated 5 percent:

$$\text{APR} = \frac{2 \times n \times I}{P(N + 1)} = \frac{2 \times 1 \times \$50}{\$950(1 + 1)} = \frac{\$100}{\$1,900} = 0.05263, \text{ or } 5.263 \text{ percent}$$

## COMPOUND INTEREST

Unlike simple interest, *compound interest* is the interest paid on the original principal *plus* the accumulated interest. With interest compounding, the greater the number of periods for which interest is calculated, the more rapidly the amount of interest on interest and interest on principal builds.

Annual compounding means there is only *one* period annually for the calculation of interest. With such compounding, interest charges on a *one-year* loan are identical whether they are figured on a simple interest basis or on an annual compound basis. However, a new interest formula, based on the simple interest formula, must be used if there is annual compounding for two or more years or compounding with more than one compound period per year.

## COMPOUND FORMULA

A compact formula that describes compound interest calculations is

$$F = P(1 + r)^T$$

where

F = Total future repayment value of a loan (principal *plus* total accumulated or compound interest)

P = Principal

r = Rate of interest per year, or annual interest rate

T = Time in years

Before the compound interest formula can be used for *multiple*-period compounding, two important adjustments must be made.

First, adjust the *annual* interest rate (r) to reflect the number of compounding periods per year. For example, a 5 percent annual rate of interest, compounded half-yearly, works out to 2.5 percent (5 percent divided by 2) per half-year.

Second, adjust the time factor (T), which is measured in years, to reflect the *total* number of compounding periods. For example, your loan for one year compounded half-yearly works out to two compound periods (1 year multiplied by 2 compounding periods per year) over the length of the loan.

Example 2    Suppose your relative compounds interest semiannually and you make two payments, six months apart. Using the compound interest formula, here is the annual percentage rate:

$$F = P(1 + r)^T$$

$$F = \$1{,}000(1 + 0.05)^{1 \times 2}$$

$$= \$1{,}000(1 + 0.025)^2$$

$$= \$1{,}000(1.050625)$$

$$= \$1{,}050.625$$

That is, you are paying $50.63 in interest for a one-year, $1,000 loan. Now, using the APR formula, you find the APR is 6.75 percent:

$$APR = \frac{2 \times n \times I}{P(N + 1)}$$

$$= \frac{2 \times 2 \times \$50.63}{\$1{,}000(2 + 1)}$$

$$= \frac{\$202.52}{\$3{,}000}$$

$$= 0.0675, \text{ or } 6.75 \text{ percent}$$

If your relative chose to compound interest daily (365 compounding periods per year), the solution to this problem would be quite complicated. A calculator or a compound interest table can make interest calculations more manageable.

The following table summarizes the effects on the APR when the interest on a one-year, $1,000 loan is calculated using the simple interest, declining balance, add-on interest, bank discount, and compound interest methods:

| Method | Amount Borrowed | Stated Interest | Total Interest | Number of Payments | APR |
|--------|----------------|-----------------|----------------|--------------------|-----|
| Simple interest* | $1,000 | 5% | $50.00 | 1 | 5.00% |
| Declining balance* | 1,000 | 5 | 37.50 | 2 | 5.00 |
| Add-on* | 1,000 | 5 | 50.00 | 2 | 6.60 |
| Bank discount | 1,000(–50) | 5 | 50.00 | 1 | 5.26 |
| Compound interest | 1,000 | 5 | 50.63 | 2 | 6.75 |

*Discussed in the chapter.

The methods of calculating interest described here are just some of the more common methods in use. As you have seen, the method of interest calculation can substantially affect the amount of interest paid, and you should be aware not only of the stated or nominal interest rates but also of how the stated rates are used in calculating total interest charges. Furthermore, the simple interest and bank discount methods assume you have the full use of the principal over the length of the loan. Rather than making periodic payments, you are obligated to repay the loan in one or two lump sums. Most borrowers, however, are unable to repay loans, especially home loans (mortgages) and auto loans, in one or two lump-sum payments. They must make equal periodic payments to pay off a loan and interest over the length of the loan. This concept is known as *amortization*.

## AMORTIZATION

*Amortization* is the process of gradually reducing a debt through scheduled periodic payments. For example, if a five-year auto loan is repaid in 60 equal monthly payments, each of these payments is applied to reduce the principal and pay interest on the total amount borrowed. Over the initial years of the loan, most of the monthly payment is used to pay interest; the rest reduces the principal. As the loan approaches maturity, more of the monthly payment is used to pay off the principal than to pay interest.

The following formula can be used to calculate the monthly payment (principal and interest) on an installment loan or a conventional mortgage loan:

$$\text{Monthly payment} = \text{Loan} \times \frac{\text{Monthly interest rate} \times (1 + \text{Monthly interest rate})^{T \times 12}}{(1 + \text{Monthly interest rate})^{T \times 12} - 1}$$

Because a monthly mortgage payment is required, both the annual interest rate and the total length of the loan must be adjusted by 12 (months).

*Example 3*    On a 30-year mortgage loan for $60,000 at a 12 percent annual interest rate, what is the monthly payment (MP)? Substitute the numbers into the formula:

$$MP = \$60,000 \times \frac{\frac{0.12}{12} \times \left(1 + \frac{0.12}{12}\right)^{30 \times 12}}{\left(1 + \frac{0.12}{12}\right)^{30 \times 12} - 1}$$

$$= \$60,000 \times \frac{0.01 \times (1 + 0.01)^{360}}{(1 + 0.01)^{360} - 1}$$

$$= \$60,000 \times \frac{0.01 \times 35.9496}{35.9496 - 1}$$

$$= \$60,000 \times \frac{0.359496}{34.9496}$$

$$= \$60,000 \times 0.010286$$

$$= \$617.17$$

## USE OF TABLES

Finding the monthly payment on a mortgage or consumer installment loan may become rather complicated when the problem must be solved manually. Fortunately, the use of tables can simplify the task. Notice how easily the problem in Example 3 is solved by using the table at the end of this appendix.

Just find the P&I constant for 12 percent and a 30-year term, which is 10.29 for a $1,000 loan. Since the loan in Example 3 is for $60,000, multiply 10.29 by 60. The result, $617.40, is fairly close to the $617.17 found by using the formula.

Example 4    What is the total finance charge on a 30-year, $60,000 loan at a 10.5 percent annual interest rate?

Using the table on the next page, you find the constant for a 10.5 percent, $1,000 loan with a 30-year term is 9.15. Since the loan is for $60,000, multiply the constant by 60. The result is a $549 monthly payment, which includes principal and interest.

For a 30-year loan, you must make 360 monthly payments of $549, totaling $197,640. Since you borrowed $60,000 but repaid $197,640, the difference must be the finance charge, which amounts to $137,640! Surprised?

You will come to a similar conclusion if you use the monthly payment formula presented in Example 3.

## P&I Constants per $1,000 of Loan Amount

| Interest Rate | 15 Years | 20 Years | 25 Years | 30 Years | Interest Rate | 15 Years | 20 Years | 25 Years | 30 Years |
|---|---|---|---|---|---|---|---|---|---|
| 6.00% | 8.44 | 7.16 | 6.44 | 6.00 | 10.62% | 11.13 | 10.07 | 9.53 | 9.24 |
| 6.12 | 8.51 | 7.24 | 6.52 | 6.08 | 10.75 | 11.21 | 10.15 | 9.62 | 9.33 |
| 6.25 | 8.57 | 7.31 | 6.60 | 6.16 | 10.87 | 11.29 | 10.24 | 9.71 | 9.43 |
| 6.37 | 8.64 | 7.38 | 6.67 | 6.24 | 11.00 | 11.37 | 10.32 | 9.80 | 9.52 |
| 6.50 | 8.71 | 7.46 | 6.75 | 6.32 | 11.12 | 11.44 | 10.41 | 9.89 | 9.62 |
| 6.62 | 8.78 | 7.53 | 6.83 | 6.40 | 11.25 | 11.52 | 10.49 | 9.98 | 9.71 |
| 6.75 | 8.85 | 7.60 | 6.91 | 6.49 | 11.37 | 11.60 | 10.58 | 10.07 | 9.81 |
| 6.87 | 8.92 | 7.68 | 6.99 | 6.57 | 11.50 | 11.68 | 10.66 | 10.16 | 9.90 |
| 7.00 | 8.99 | 7.75 | 7.07 | 6.65 | 11.62 | 11.76 | 10.75 | 10.26 | 10.00 |
| 7.12 | 9.06 | 7.83 | 7.15 | 6.74 | 11.75 | 11.84 | 10.84 | 10.35 | 10.09 |
| 7.25 | 9.13 | 7.90 | 7.23 | 6.82 | 11.87 | 11.92 | 10.92 | 10.44 | 10.19 |
| 7.37 | 9.20 | 7.98 | 7.31 | 6.91 | 12.00 | 12.00 | 11.01 | 10.53 | 10.29 |
| 7.50 | 9.27 | 8.06 | 7.39 | 6.99 | 12.12 | 12.08 | 11.10 | 10.62 | 10.38 |
| 7.62 | 9.34 | 8.13 | 7.47 | 7.08 | 12.25 | 12.16 | 11.19 | 10.72 | 10.48 |
| 7.75 | 9.41 | 8.21 | 7.55 | 7.16 | 12.37 | 12.24 | 11.27 | 10.81 | 10.58 |
| 7.87 | 9.48 | 8.29 | 7.64 | 7.25 | 12.50 | 12.33 | 11.36 | 10.90 | 10.67 |
| 8.00 | 9.56 | 8.36 | 7.72 | 7.34 | 12.62 | 12.41 | 11.45 | 11.00 | 10.77 |
| 8.12 | 9.63 | 8.44 | 7.80 | 7.42 | 12.75 | 12.49 | 11.54 | 11.09 | 10.87 |
| 8.25 | 9.70 | 8.52 | 7.88 | 7.51 | 12.87 | 12.57 | 11.63 | 11.18 | 10.96 |
| 8.37 | 9.77 | 8.60 | 7.97 | 7.60 | 13.00 | 12.65 | 11.72 | 11.28 | 11.06 |
| 8.50 | 9.85 | 8.68 | 8.05 | 7.69 | 13.12 | 12.73 | 11.80 | 11.37 | 11.16 |
| 8.62 | 9.92 | 8.76 | 8.14 | 7.78 | 13.25 | 12.82 | 11.89 | 11.47 | 11.26 |
| 8.75 | 9.99 | 8.84 | 8.22 | 7.87 | 13.37 | 12.90 | 11.98 | 11.56 | 11.36 |
| 8.87 | 10.07 | 8.92 | 8.31 | 7.96 | 13.50 | 12.98 | 12.07 | 11.66 | 11.45 |
| 9.00 | 10.14 | 9.00 | 8.39 | 8.05 | 13.62 | 13.07 | 12.16 | 11.75 | 11.55 |
| 9.12 | 10.22 | 9.08 | 8.48 | 8.14 | 13.75 | 13.15 | 12.25 | 11.85 | 11.65 |
| 9.25 | 10.29 | 9.16 | 8.56 | 8.23 | 13.87 | 13.23 | 12.34 | 11.94 | 11.75 |
| 9.37 | 10.37 | 9.24 | 8.65 | 8.32 | 14.00 | 13.32 | 12.44 | 12.04 | 11.85 |
| 9.50 | 10.44 | 9.32 | 8.74 | 8.41 | 14.12 | 13.40 | 12.53 | 12.13 | 11.95 |
| 9.62 | 10.52 | 9.40 | 8.82 | 8.50 | 14.25 | 13.49 | 12.62 | 12.23 | 12.05 |
| 9.75 | 10.59 | 9.49 | 8.91 | 8.59 | 14.37 | 13.57 | 12.71 | 12.33 | 12.15 |
| 9.87 | 10.67 | 9.57 | 9.00 | 8.68 | 14.50 | 13.66 | 12.80 | 12.42 | 12.25 |
| 10.00 | 10.75 | 9.65 | 9.09 | 8.78 | 14.62 | 13.74 | 12.89 | 12.52 | 12.35 |
| 10.12 | 10.82 | 9.73 | 9.18 | 8.87 | 14.75 | 13.83 | 12.98 | 12.61 | 12.44 |
| 10.25 | 10.90 | 9.82 | 9.26 | 8.96 | 14.87 | 13.91 | 13.08 | 12.71 | 12.54 |
| 10.37 | 10.98 | 9.90 | 9.35 | 9.05 | 15.00 | 14.00 | 13.17 | 12.81 | 12.64 |
| 10.50 | 11.05 | 9.98 | 9.44 | 9.15 | | | | | |

# Continuous Case for Part 2

## USING FINANCIAL SERVICES: SAVINGS, CHECKING, AND CREDIT

### Life Situation
Recently married couple: Pam, 26; Josh, 28; renting an apartment

*Financial Goals*
- Develop a savings fund for emergencies and long-term financial security
- Reduce monthly debt payments

*Financial Data*

| | |
|---|---|
| Monthly income | $ 5,840 |
| Living expenses | 3,900 |
| Assets | 13,500 |
| Liabilities | 7,800 |
| Emergency Fund | 1,000 |

Pam Jenkins recently married Josh Brock. Pam continues to work as a sales representative for a clothing manufacturer, and her monthly income has averaged $2,840 a month over the past year. Josh is employed as a computer programmer and earns $3,000 a month.

The Brocks' combined monthly income, $5,840, allows them to enjoy a comfortable lifestyle. Yet they have been unable to save any money for emergencies. According to Josh, "It's hard to believe, but we don't even have a savings account because we spend everything we make each month." Every month, they deposit each of their paychecks in separate checking accounts. Josh pays the rent and makes the car payment. Pam buys the groceries and pays the monthly utilities. They use the money left over to purchase new clothes and the other "necessities" of life that they both want. To make matters worse, they often resort to using their seven credit cards for everyday purchases when they both run out of money at the end of the month. As a result, they have credit card debts totaling $2,800.

## Questions

1. What is the minimum amount that the Brocks should have in an emergency fund?
2. What should the Brocks do to increase the amount of money they set aside for emergencies?
3. Pam and Josh have separate checking accounts. Do you think they should give up their separate checking accounts and open a joint checking account?
4. If you were Pam or Josh, how would you go about paying off your credit card debts and other liabilities?
5. What would you recommend to the Brocks regarding their future use of credit?

3

# MAKING YOUR PURCHASING DECISIONS

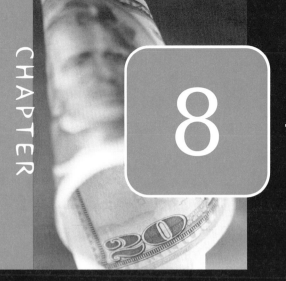

# 8

# Consumer Purchasing Strategies and Legal Protection

## Buying Online without Going Out of Your Mind

As Mallory Zonic was finishing her long workday, she realized that she needed to get her mother a birthday gift. The stores were closed; however, Mallory had recently seen some ads for *www.something-or-other.com* while doing research online at work.

While first feeling overwhelmed by the many online shopping websites, she was able to locate three that would be useful. On one website (*www.gifts-for-mom.com*), Mallory saw a sweater her mother would probably like. "This looks very nice," she thought. "And it's quite reasonably priced."

Mallory placed an order online using her credit card. Within a week, she received it. But, when she opened the package, she noticed the style of the sweater was different than it looked online. "Oh no, this isn't what I wanted," she thought.

Mallory called the clothing company to find out how to return the item. The company told her to send the sweater back for a refund. However, Mallory had to pay the return postage and was not refunded the original shipping and handling charges.

Later that day, Mallory saw a table lamp in a catalog. "This is a nice gift for Mother," she thought. She sent in a check for the lamp and within a week received a notice that the item would not be available for four to six weeks.

Frustrated by her online and catalog shopping experiences, Mallory was not sure what to do next. She thought maybe it was time to forget about buying online and with catalogs and consider the Home Shopping Network!

## Questions

1. What benefits and drawbacks are associated with online shopping?
2. What actions might a consumer take before making an online purchase?
3. What options are available to consumers who are dissatisfied with an online purchase or other buying situation?
4. Locate a website that could be of use to consumers before making an online purchase or when a problem arises from an online purchase.

## Learning Objectives

**Obj. 1**   Assess the financial implications of consumer purchasing decisions.

**Obj. 2**   Evaluate the alternatives in consumer purchasing decisions.

**Obj. 3**   Implement strategies for effective purchasing.

**Obj. 4**   Identify steps to take to resolve consumer problems.

**Obj. 5**   Evaluate the legal alternatives available to consumers.

## FINANCIAL IMPLICATIONS OF CONSUMER DECISIONS

**Obj. 1**

Assess the financial implications of consumer purchasing decisions.

Every person making personal financial decisions is a consumer. Regardless of age, income, or household situation, we all use goods and services. Daily buying decisions involve a trade-off between current spending and saving for the future. While some people shop for recreation and others only when necessary, both groups use techniques to get the most for their money. Wise buying decisions contribute to both your current personal satisfaction and your long-term financial security.

Various economic, social, and personal factors affect daily buying habits (see Exhibit 8–1). These factors are the basis for spending, saving, investing, and achieving personal financial goals. In very simple terms, the only way you can have long-term financial security is to not spend all of your current income. In addition, as Exhibit 8–1 shows, overspending leads to misuse of credit and financial difficulties.

Throughout your life, your buying decisions reflect many influences. You should consider opportunity costs to maximize the satisfaction you obtain from available financial resources. Commonly overlooked trade-offs when buying include

- Paying a higher price over time by using credit to buy items that you need now.
- Buying unknown, possibly poor-quality brands that are less expensive.
- Selecting brands that may be difficult to service or repair.
- Ordering by mail or online, which saves time and money but may make it harder to return, replace, or repair purchases.
- Taking time and effort to comparison-shop to save money and obtain better after-sale service.

Your buying decisions reflect many aspects of your personality, life situation, values, and goals. Combine this fact with the complexity of the marketplace, and you can see that most purchase decisions require analysis.

**? Did You Know**

In 1998, America's 30.9 million teens purchased $141 billion worth of goods and services. Each month, young consumers ages 8 to 17 take an average of a dozen trips to the mall, where they spend $25 per visit. (Mary Lord, "It's Never Too Soon for Econ 101," *U.S. News and World Report*, June 14, 1999, pp. 58–59.)

**EXHIBIT 8-1**

Consumer Buying Influences and Financial Implications

**Economic Factors**
• Consumer prices (inflation)
• Interest rates
• Product quality
• National income
• Tax rates
• Government regulations
• Supply and demand
• Convenience
• Product safety
• Brand name
• Maintenance costs
• Warranty

**Social Factors**
• Lifestyle
• Interests
• Hobbies
• Attitudes
• Peer group
• Social class
• Culture
• Advertisements
• Media (magazines, radio, television, newspapers)
• Opinion leaders

**Personal Factors**
• Sex
• Age
• Occupation
• Income
• Education
• Marital status
• Family size
• Geographic region
• Type of housing
• Ethnic background
• Religious affiliation

Budgeting – Planned spending and saving

Spending Path

Saving Path

Actual spending/ cash management

Saving and investments

Overspending

Appropriate spending patterns

$      $
**Achievement of financial goals**
$      $

Potential misuse of credit

! **Financial difficulties** !

## Concept Check 8-1

1. What factors commonly influence a person's daily buying choices?
2. How are daily buying decisions related to overall financial planning?

# CONSUMER PURCHASING: A RESEARCH-BASED APPROACH

## Obj. 2
Evaluate the alternatives in consumer purchasing decisions.

Shopping decisions are based on a specific decision-making process. Exhibit 8–2 presents steps for effective purchasing. This process will be most valuable with large purchases such as appliances, sports equipment, electronic products, home improvements, and vacations. When buying such items, most people want to get the most for their money.

You probably make many routine purchases of low-cost items, such as food and clothing, without thinking about them, and often this is exactly what you should do. Following all of the steps in the consumer buying process for low-cost items may not be the best use of your time.

## Phase 1: Preshopping Activities

First, define your needs and obtain relevant product information. These activities are the foundation for buying decisions to help you achieve your goals.

### Problem Identification
Objective decision making should start with an open mind. Some people always buy the same brand when another brand at a lower price would also serve their needs, or when another brand at the same price may provide better quality. A narrow view of the problem is a weakness in problem identification. You may think the problem is "I need to have a car" when the real problem is "I need transportation."

**EXHIBIT 8-2**   A RESEARCH-BASED APPROACH TO CONSUMER PURCHASES

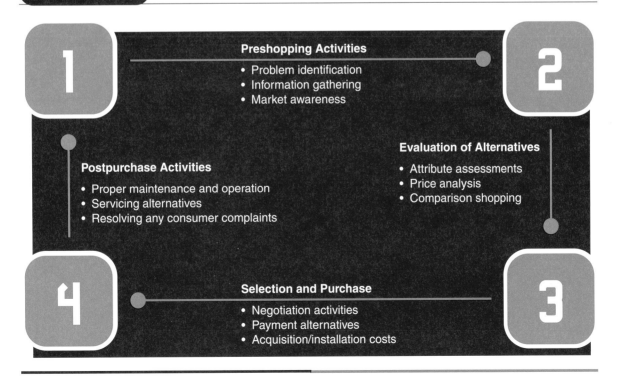

**1 — Preshopping Activities**
- Problem identification
- Information gathering
- Market awareness

**2 — Evaluation of Alternatives**
- Attribute assessments
- Price analysis
- Comparison shopping

**3 — Selection and Purchase**
- Negotiation activities
- Payment alternatives
- Acquisition/installation costs

**4 — Postpurchase Activities**
- Proper maintenance and operation
- Servicing alternatives
- Resolving any consumer complaints

## Information Gathering

Information is power. The better informed you are, the better buying decisions you will make. Knowing the least expensive place to buy an appliance can enhance your financial well-being. Information for buying decisions commonly falls into three areas:

1. *Costs*—what is the price at various locations?
2. *Options*—who offers which items, brands, and services?
3. *Consequences*—how might a purchase affect my time, health, and financial situation?

Some people spend very little time gathering and evaluating buying information. At the other extreme are people who spend much time obtaining consumer information. While information is necessary for wise purchasing, too much information can create confusion and frustration. The best course of action lies somewhere between these extremes. Many simple, routine purchases may require no information other than experience, while expensive items merit some information gathering. The main sources of consumer information should be evaluated for reliability, completeness, relevance, and objectivity.

### Personal Contacts

Besides gaining knowledge from past purchases, you can learn from the experiences of others. Information about product performance, brand quality, and prices can be valuable.

### Business Organizations

Advertising is the most common source of consumer information. Each day you are exposed to several hundred ads on billboards, in publications, at stores, and on television, on radio, and online. Advertising that provides information about product price, quality, and availability can be helpful. Many ads, however, appeal to emotions and provide little assistance when making purchase decisions.

Other business information sources are the product label and the package. Like advertising, a product label contains helpful information such as ingredients, weight, and price, as well as attempts to stimulate sales. Despite state and federal laws prohibiting false advertising, deceptive or misleading ads may be present.

### Media Information

Television, radio, newspapers, magazines, and websites are the most valuable, easily available, and least expensive consumer information sources. Besides advertisements, these media sources provide purchasing advice and consumer information.

### Independent Testing Organizations

Since 1936, Consumers Union has been providing information about the quality of products and services. Each month *Consumer Reports* (www.consumerreports.org) presents test results on items ranging from automobiles, vacuum cleaners, and computers to hand soap, orange juice, and hot dogs. Consumers Union has increased its coverage of subjects such as apartment renting, health care, insurance, investments, legal services, tax preparers, and banking services. *Consumer Reports* and other consumer publications may be accessed on the Web.

Underwriters Laboratories (UL) is a business-sponsored organization that tests products for electrical and fire safety. Items that pass the tests display the UL symbol. This emblem assures consumers that the product has met safety standards.

### Government Agencies

Local, state, and federal governments provide publications and other information services for consumers (for example, see Exhibit 8–3 on page 241). Government agencies inform consumers through toll-free telephone numbers,

**EXHIBIT 8-3**

Telemarketing
Sales Rule

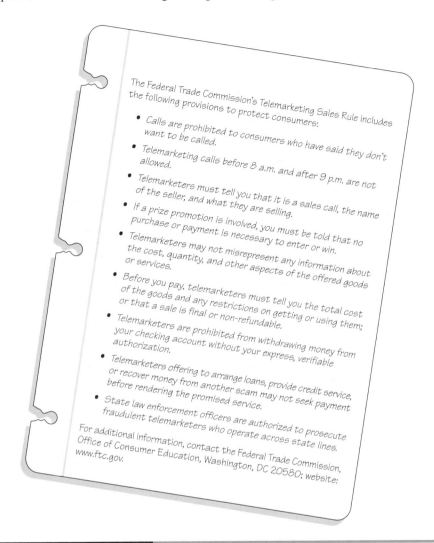

The Federal Trade Commission's Telemarketing Sales Rule includes the following provisions to protect consumers:

- Calls are prohibited to consumers who have said they don't want to be called.
- Telemarketing calls before 8 a.m. and after 9 p.m. are not allowed.
- Telemarketers must tell you that it is a sales call, the name of the seller, and what they are selling.
- If a prize promotion is involved, you must be told that no purchase or payment is necessary to enter or win.
- Telemarketers may not misrepresent any information about the cost, quantity, and other aspects of the offered goods or services.
- Before you pay, telemarketers must tell you the total cost of the goods and any restrictions on getting or using them; or that a sale is final or non-refundable.
- Telemarketers are prohibited from withdrawing money from your checking account without your express, verifiable authorization.
- Telemarketers offering to arrange loans, provide credit service, or recover money from another scam may not seek payment before rendering the promised service.
- State law enforcement officers are authorized to prosecute fraudulent telemarketers who operate across state lines.

For additional information, contact the Federal Trade Commission, Office of Consumer Education, Washington, DC 20580; website: www.ftc.gov.

websites, and community programs at shopping centers, county fairs, and libraries. Appendix B details government sources of information on various consumer topics.

**Online Sources**   The Internet now provides one of the most extensive sources of consumer information. Most companies, magazines, newspapers, consumer organizations, and government agencies have websites with product information and shopping suggestions. For additional information on using the Internet and World Wide Web for consumer information, see the accompanying Financial Planning for Life's Situations box on page 242.

**Marketplace Awareness**   Preshopping research results in expanded awareness of the buying environment. This includes an awareness of

- Store, mail-order, and online sources of an item.
- Available brands and features.
- Pricing techniques for the item.
- The most reliable sources of information.

# Financial Planning for Life's Situations

## ONLINE BUYING

You would think that a merchant that doesn't pay retail store rent would be able to pass on the savings. Yet, with few exceptions, consumers pay no less online than they do through conventional retail channels. As of the late 1990s, about 10 percent of U.S. households have made at least one online purchase. The total value of goods and services bought online in 1999 was over $6 billion, and this amount has doubled every 12 months.

If you dislike fighting shopping mall traffic or dealing with surly store clerks, online shopping may be an attractive alternative. The most frequently visited online retailing websites include amazon.com, cdnow.com, buy.com, ebay.com, columbiahouse.com, bmgmusicservice.com, beyond.com, qvc.com, onsale.com, aol.com, and yahoo.com.

### ONLINE BUYING CONCERNS

Most online shoppers insist on brand-name familiarity before making a cyberspace purchase using a credit card. The major concerns related to e-commerce are security of payment, reliability of the business, privacy, returning items, and resolving differences with merchants.

### ONLINE PHARMACIES

Organizations such as Drug-store.com, Soma.com, and PlanetRx (www.planetrx.com) are attempting to persuade consumers to purchase medications, personal care products, and disposable diapers by computer. These online pharmacies boast of an inventory three times greater than those of traditional drugstores, which tend to carry only the fastest-moving items. Internet pharmacies also offer privacy and lower prices. But beware: Some unlicensed drug dispensers have set up business online.

### ONLINE AUCTIONS

"Cyber-bidding" occurs during an online auction for collectibles or other items. Unlike in a traditional "live" auction, the highest bidder does not deal with the auction house. Instead, the buyer makes payment and delivery arrangements with the seller of the item. Buyers must beware, since some online sellers require payment in advance and never deliver the merchandise.

In most basic terms, eBay is an online flea market, where everything is sold by auction. With more than 1 million registered users, eBay processes some 700,000 auctions a day and ranks as the number two website in time spent on the service per month. Many eBay sellers use the site as an online garage sale. Others are professionals, making eBay an online extension of their antique stores and music shops.

### CONSUMER PROTECTION WEBSITES

Some of the best websites for consumer information and assistance are www.consumerworld.org, www.consumerreports.org, www.consumer.gov, www.pueblo.gsa.gov, www.consumerlaw.org, and www.consumerlawpage.com.

SOURCES: *Consumer Alert: Online Auctions: Going, Going, Gone*, April 1998, Federal Trade Commission, Bureau of Consumer Protection, Washington, DC 20580 (www.ftc.gov); Jane Bennett Clark, "Online Pharmacies vs. Corner Drugstore," *Kiplinger's Personal Finance Magazine*, July 1999, p. 52; Preston Gralla, "Leave the Mall Behind," *Family PC*, February 1999, pp. 54–56, 58, 60, 62, 64; "Most Popular Web Retailers," *Advertising Age*, July 5, 1999, p. 27; "Shopping Goes Online," *Consumer Reports*, November 1998, pp. 18–23.

## Phase 2: Evaluation of Alternatives

Every purchasing situation usually has several acceptable alternatives. Ask yourself: Is it possible to delay the purchase or to do without the item? Should I pay for the item with cash or buy it on credit? Which brands should I consider? How do the price, quality, and service compare at different stores? Is it possible to rent the item instead of buying it? Considering such alternatives will result in more effective purchasing decisions.

### Attribute Assessments
Each alternative should be evaluated based on personal values and goals; available time and money; costs and benefits; and specific needs with regard to product size, quality, quantity, and features. Exhibit 8–4 presents

**EXHIBIT 8-4**   Consumer Buying Matrix

Item _NOTEBOOK COMPUTER_

Information Sources/Comments _CONSUMER MAGAZINE/BRAND C SLOW COMPARED TO_
_OTHERS TESTED; FRIEND/BRAND B PERFORMS WELL_

| | | Alternatives | | | | | |
|---|---|---|---|---|---|---|---|
| | | **Brand** _A_ | | _B_ | | _C_ | |
| **Attribute** | **Weight** | **Price** _$2,150_ | | _$2,029_ | | _$1,899_ | |
| | | Rating (1-10) | Weighted Score | Rating (1-10) | Weighted Score | Rating (1-10) | Weighted Score |
| FEATURES | .3 | 6 | 1.8 | 8 | 2.4 | 10 | 3 |
| PERFORMANCE | .4 | 9 | 3.6 | 7 | 2.8 | 5 | 2 |
| DESIGN | .1 | 8 | .8 | 8 | .8 | 7 | .7 |
| WARRANTY | .2 | 9 | 1.8 | 6 | 1.2 | 4 | .8 |
| ■ Totals | 1.0 | | 8.0 | | 7.2 | | 6.5 |

Step 2 → (Brand/Price row)

Step 1 → (Attribute rows: FEATURES, PERFORMANCE, DESIGN, WARRANTY)

Step 4 → (Totals row)

Step 3 → (Weighted Score columns)

a buying matrix that may be used to evaluate alternatives. In this exhibit, a consumer is considering the purchase of one of three brands of notebook computers using the following steps:

Step 1.  Identify attributes such as features, performance, design, and warranty, and assign a weight based on the importance of each attribute.

Step 2.  Select the brands to be evaluated.

Step 3.  Rate (from 1 to 10) each brand based on the attributes identified in step 1. Multiply the rating number by the weight. For example, in Exhibit 8–4, brand A received a rating of 6 for "features," giving a weighted score of 1.8 ($6 \times .3$).

Step 4.  Total and assess the results. Besides this numeric evaluation, consider other factors such as price, store reputation, and your personal situation.

As you research a consumer purchase, identify the attributes that are important to you. Helpful sources for this task are friends who own the product, salespeople, periodicals such as *Consumer Reports,* and the Web. The specific attributes will vary depending on the product or service. When buying a cordless telephone, for example, you might consider sound quality, ring loudness, number memory, and the range of use; you might assess a microwave oven on the basis of size, ease of operation, power settings, and exterior finish; and you are likely to select a provider of services based on training, experience, and reputation.

## Price Analysis

Research shows that prices can vary for all types of products. For a camera, prices may range from under $200 to well over $500. The price of aspirin may range from less than $1 to over $3 for 100 five-grain tablets. While differences in quality and attributes may exist among the cameras, the aspirin are the same in quantity and quality.

Differences in quality (based on information from others and on your personal evaluation of product attributes) need to be assessed in relation to price. When the quality and quantity are the same (as with aspirin), the lowest price is likely to be the wisest choice, except, perhaps, if the place of purchase is not convenient.

When prices and quality differ (as in the buying matrix in Exhibit 8–4), you have two alternatives. If all the choices are within your available resources, you may purchase the item with the highest number of weighted "quality points," or you may divide the price of each item by its quality points to determine which item gives you the best value per dollar spent.

Always be cautious of the common belief that "you get what you pay for." Many studies have revealed low relationships between price and quality, especially for expensive, highly technical products. To obtain the best value for your dollar, you should use other comparison shopping activities.

**Sheet 32**

## Comparison Shopping

Many people view comparison shopping as a waste of time. While this may be true in certain situations, comparison shopping can be beneficial when

- Buying expensive or complex items.
- Buying items that you purchase often.
- Comparison shopping can be done easily (with advertisements, catalogs, or online).
- Different sellers offer different prices and services.
- Product quality or prices vary greatly.

## Phase 3: Selection and Purchase

Once you've done your research and evaluations, some other activities and decisions may be appropriate. Certain products, such as real estate or automobiles, may be purchased using price negotiation. Negotiation may also be used in other buying situations to obtain a lower price or additional features. Two vital factors in negotiation are (1) having all the necessary information about the product and buying situation and (2) dealing with a person who has the authority to give you a lower price or additional features, such as the owner or store manager.

Whether to pay cash or use credit should be considered in terms of the costs and benefits. Paying cash gives you the benefit of not paying finance charges, but you have the opportunity costs of not earning interest on the amount paid and not having the amount in savings for emergencies. Before using credit, evaluate the various financial and opportunity costs based on

- Different places to borrow.
- Different types of credit accounts.
- Different down payment amounts.
- Different payment periods.

## Financial Planning for Life's Situations

### COMMON CONSUMER MYTHS

The National Association of Consumer Agency Administrators recently identified a list of misconceptions among consumers. These common myths include the following:

- "I can return my car within three days of purchase." While many people believe this (including many lawyers), there is no cooling-off period for motor vehicles.
- "My credit report information is confidential." Although wrongfully obtaining another person's credit report is a crime, there are many ways the information can be legally distributed. Recently enacted federal laws allow corporate affiliates to share most information.
- "My creditors can't call me at work." In most states, creditors (but not third-party debt collectors) can call and write—days, nights, weekends, and holidays—until the debts are repaid.
- "You can't repossess my car; it's on private property." While state laws differ, the general rule is that repossession cannot occur if it involves force, a breach of the peace, or entry into a dwelling. Vehicles in driveways and unlocked garages are usually fair game.

- "An auto lease is like a rental; if I have problems with the car or problems paying, I can just bring it back." Most leases require payments for the duration of the contract. Early termination often results in various additional charges.
- "If I lose my credit cards, I'm liable for purchases." Credit card companies perpetuate this myth in an attempt to sell "credit card protection" coverage. Federal laws limit charges on lost or stolen cards to $50. Most national credit card companies will not charge the $50 if the consumer makes a good-faith effort to notify the lender quickly of lost or stolen cards.
- "It says right here that I've won; it must be true." Fake prize notifications continue to become more convincing. Some consumers actually go to the company office to try to pick up their prizes.

SOURCE: "Ten Top Consumer Law 'Urban Myths'" National Association of Consumer Agency Administrators, 1010 Vermont Ave., NW, #514, Washington, DC 20005; 202–347–7395; website: www.nacaanet.org.

Finally, get all acquisition and installation costs and conditions in writing. Many bargains have disappeared due to "add-on" costs such as hookup charges, delivery fees, and the like. Know exactly what the purchase price includes.

## Phase 4: Postpurchase Activities

Federal law allows three business days to cancel a contract for $25 or more if the agreement was signed away from the seller's regular place of business. This "cooling-off" law does not apply to purchases made at a retail business in a fixed location or for transactions made by mail or phone. This law was originally designed to protect consumers from questionable door-to-door salespeople. The cancellation right also applies to home equity loans, health club memberships, and discount buying clubs, no matter where the contract is signed. Most states allow a cooling-off period when buying time-share vacation property; others also cover campground memberships.

Maintenance and ownership costs may be associated with some purchases. Correct use can result in improved performance and fewer repairs. When you need repairs not covered by a warranty, follow a pattern similar to that used when making the original purchase. Investigate, evaluate, and negotiate a variety of servicing options.

If you are not satisfied with a purchase, know how to cope with complaint situations. The final two sections of this chapter discuss how to handle consumer complaints and the legal alternatives available to consumers.

One final point: The purchasing process can be an ongoing activity that requires continual reevaluation. You have to consider what you have learned from gathering information and from buying experiences as well as changes in your values, goals, resources, and life situation. (See "Financial Planning for Life's Situations" feature.) These changes make every purchasing decision a new experience with different alternatives and different opportunity costs.

## Concept Check 8-2

1. What are the major sources of consumer information?
2. What are the benefits and drawbacks of using advertising to gather information for a consumer purchase?
3. What relationship exists between a person's life situation and the attributes the person desires in a consumer purchase?

## PRACTICAL PURCHASING STRATEGIES

**Obj. 3**
Implement strategies for effective purchasing.

People have different buying styles. Some shoppers look for ways to save on the brands they regularly buy, while others buy the lowest-priced brands or look for the best bargains. To achieve your buying goals, use the techniques listed in Exhibit 8–5.

### Timing Purchases

In the past, certain items would go on sale the same time each year. People could obtain bargains by buying winter clothing in mid- or late winter, or summer clothing in mid- or late summer. Many people save by buying holiday items and other products at reduced prices in late December and early January. In recent years, as retail competition has intensified, sales and discounts occur throughout the year. Also, "back-to-school" sales have broadened to include anything a college student might need.

Weather reports and other news can also help you plan your purchasing strategies. A crop failure can quickly result in higher prices for certain food products. Changing

## EXHIBIT 8-5

Practical Purchasing Strategies

economic conditions and political difficulties in foreign countries may result in higher prices and reduced supplies of certain products. Awareness of such situations can help you buy when prices are relatively low.

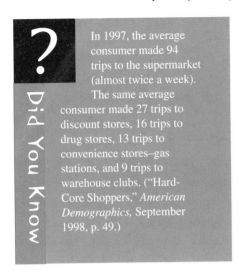

In 1997, the average consumer made 94 trips to the supermarket (almost twice a week). The same average consumer made 27 trips to discount stores, 16 trips to drug stores, 13 trips to convenience stores–gas stations, and 9 trips to warehouse clubs. ("Hard-Core Shoppers," *American Demographics*, September 1998, p. 49.)

*cooperative*   A nonprofit organization whose member-owners may save money on certain products or services.

*impulse buying* Unplanned purchasing.

## Store Selection

Your decision to shop at a particular store is probably influenced by the quality and variety of merchandise. Also important are the store's policies on matters such as check cashing, exchanges, and frequency of sales. Most stores offer customers various services, including free parking and delivery, telephone and mail orders, and product advice. Finally, your selection of a store is affected by store hours, location, reputation, and the accessibility of shopping alternatives. Exhibit 8–6 provides an overview of the major types of retailers.

Social, economic, and technological influences have resulted in alternatives to store shopping. One alternative is the **cooperative,** a nonprofit organization whose member-owners may save money on certain products or services. As discussed in Chapter 5, a credit union is an example of a financial services cooperative. Food cooperatives, usually based in a community group or church, buy grocery items in large quantities. The savings on these bulk purchases are passed on to the co-op's members in the form of lower food prices. Although most food co-ops have a limited scope, some have thousands of members and have expanded their services to provide low-cost groceries to nonmembers. Cooperatives have also been organized to provide less expensive child care, recreational equipment, health care, cable television, and burial services.

## Brand Comparison

Comparison shopping is the process of considering alternative stores, brands, and prices. In contrast, **impulse buying** is unplanned purchasing. Some impulse buying may be acceptable; too much can cause financial problems.

Since food and other products come in different brands, customers have a choice. *National-brand* products are highly advertised items available in many stores. You are probably familiar with brands such as Green Giant, Nabisco, Del Monte, Kellogg's, Kraft, Levi-Strauss, Sony, Kodak, and Tylenol. Brand-name products are usually more expensive than nonbrand products, but they offer a consistency of quality for which people are willing to pay.

*Store-brand* products, sold by one chain of stores, are low-cost alternatives to famous-name products. These products have labels that identify them with a specific retail chain, such as Safeway, Kroger, A&P, Osco, Walgreen's, and Kmart. Since store-brand products are commonly manufactured by the same companies that produce brand-name counterparts, they allow consumers to save money. Private and store-brand items can result in extensive savings over time.

## Label Information

Certain label information is helpful; however, other information is nothing more than advertising. Federal law requires that food labels contain information about the common name of the product, the name and address of the manufacturer or distributor, the net weight of the product, and a list of the ingredients in decreasing order of weight. Food labels (1) must have nutrition information on all processed foods; (2) must define

**EXHIBIT 8-6**   TYPES OF RETAILERS

|  | Benefits | Limitations |
|---|---|---|
| **Traditional Stores** | | |
| Department stores | Wide variety of products grouped by department | Possible inexperience or limited knowledge of sales staff |
| Specialty stores | Wide selection of a specific product line; knowledgeable sales staff | Prices generally higher; location and shopping hours may not be convenient |
| Discount stores | Convenient parking; low prices | Self-service format; minimal assistance from sales staff |
| **Contemporary Retailers** | | |
| Convenience stores | Convenient location; long hours; fast service | Prices generally higher than those of other types |
| Catalog showroom | Brand-name items; discount prices | Limited services from sales staff; no delivery or installation |
| Factory outlet | Brand-name items; low prices | May offer only "seconds" or "irregulars"; few services; returns may not be allowed |
| Hypermarket | Full supermarket combined with general merchandise discount store | Clerks not likely to offer specialized service or product information |
| Warehouse, superstore | Large quantities of items at discount prices | May require membership fee; limited services; inventory items may vary |
| **Nonstore Shopping** | | |
| Cooperative | Nonprofit, member owned and operated, resulting in lower prices | Limited product line; few customer services; may sell only to members |
| Direct selling (mail order, telephone sales, home demonstrations, television home shopping, online shopping) | Convenience; saves time and perhaps money | Possible delays in delivery; companies may not give what they promise; sometimes difficult to return purchases and get refunds |

terms such as *low fat, light, low sodium,* and *high fiber;* and (3) allow scientifically established health claims that have been shown to help reduce the risk of disease. Product labeling for appliances includes information about operating costs that can assist you in selecting the most energy-efficient models of refrigerators, washing machines, and air conditioners.

**Open dating,** information that describes the freshness or shelf life of a perishable product, also appears on labels. Open dating was originally used for bakery and dairy products; now it is also used for most other foods. Phrases such as "Use before May 2001" or "Not to be sold after October 8" appear on most grocery items.

## Price Comparison

*open dating*   Information about freshness or shelf life found on the package of a perishable product.

*unit pricing*   The use of a standard unit of measurement to compare the prices of packages of different sizes.

**Unit pricing** uses a standard unit of measurement to compare the prices of packages of different sizes. The process for calculating and using the unit price is as follows:

1.  Determine the common unit of measurement, such as ounces, pounds, gallons, or number of sheets (for items such as paper towels and facial tissues).
2.  Divide the price by the number of common units; for example, an 8-ounce package of breakfast cereal selling for $1.52 has a unit price of 19 cents per ounce, while an 11-ounce package costing $1.98 has a unit price of 18 cents per ounce.

# Financial Planning Calculations

## NET PRESENT VALUE OF A CONSUMER PURCHASE

The time value of money (see Chapter 1 and Appendix A) may be used to evaluate the financial benefits of buying home appliances and other items. For example, when you purchase a washing machine and a clothes dryer, the money you save by not driving to and using a laundromat could be considered a cash *inflow* (since money not going out is like money coming in). The cost of the appliances would be the current cash *outflow*. If the appliances have an expected life of 10 years, the *net present value* calculations might be as shown below.

You can use this calculation format to assess the financial benefits of a consumer purchase by comparing the cost savings achieved by the purchase over time with the current price of the item purchased.

| | |
|---|---:|
| **Step 1.** Estimated amount saved on weekly washing and drying at laundromat: | |
| $4.75 times 52 weeks | $ 247.00 |
| Savings from not driving to laundromat: 6 miles a week at 15 cents a mile times 52 weeks | 46.80 |
| Less: Estimated cost of hot water and electricity to operate appliances at home | −13.80 |
| Total annual savings | $ 280.00 |
| **Step 2.** Multiply annual savings by the present value of a series | |
| (Exhibit 1–8D in Chapter 1 or Exhibit A–4 in Appendix A) for 6 percent over 10 years | 7.360 |
| (6 percent is the average expected return from a savings account). | 2,060.80 |
| **Step 3.** Subtract the cost of the washing machine and the clothes dryer. | −875.00 |
| The result is the net present value of the savings obtained by buying the appliances.* | $1,185.80 |

*A negative net present value would indicate that the financial aspects of the purchase are not desirable.

3. Compare the unit prices for various sizes, brands, and stores to determine the best buy for your situation.

Remember, the package with the lowest unit price may not be the best buy for you since it may contain more food than you would use before spoilage occurs.

Two common techniques that offer customers reduced prices are coupons and rebates. Each year, billions of coupons are distributed on packages and through newspapers, magazines, and the mail. Coupons are especially valuable if you already plan to buy the products. A family saving about $8 a week on their groceries by using coupons will save $416 over a year and $2,080 over five years (not counting interest earned had that amount been put in a savings account). Coupons are available online at www.coolsavings.com, www.centsoff.com, and www.couponsurfer.com.

A **rebate** is a partial refund of the price of a product. This technique was originally used to promote sales of automobiles, but it is now used for selling almost every type of product.

The following guidelines are helpful in comparing prices:

- More convenience (location, hours, sales staff) usually means higher prices.
- Ready-to-use products (convenience foods, preassembled toys, furniture) usually have higher prices.
- Large packages are usually the best buy; however, be sure to use unit pricing to compare different sizes, brands, and stores.
- "Sale" may not always mean saving money; the sale price at one store may be higher than the regular price at another store.

**Sheet 34**

*rebate* A partial refund of the price of a product.

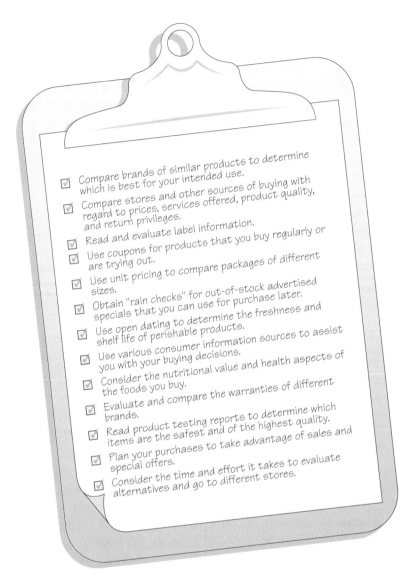

**EXHIBIT 8-7**

Wise Buying
Techniques: A
Summary

☑ Compare brands of similar products to determine which is best for your intended use.

☑ Compare stores and other sources of buying with regard to prices, services offered, product quality, and return privileges.

☑ Read and evaluate label information.

☑ Use coupons for products that you buy regularly or are trying out.

☑ Use unit pricing to compare packages of different sizes.

☑ Obtain "rain checks" for out-of-stock advertised specials that you can use for purchase later.

☑ Use open dating to determine the freshness and shelf life of perishable products.

☑ Use various consumer information sources to assist you with your buying decisions.

☑ Consider the nutritional value and health aspects of the foods you buy.

☑ Evaluate and compare the warranties of different brands.

☑ Read product testing reports to determine which items are the safest and of the highest quality.

☑ Plan your purchases to take advantage of sales and special offers.

☑ Consider the time and effort it takes to evaluate alternatives and go to different stores.

## Warranty Evaluation

*warranty* A written guarantee from the manufacturer or distributor of a product that specifies the conditions under which the product can be returned, replaced, or repaired.

Most products come with some guarantee of quality. A **warranty** is a written guarantee from the manufacturer or distributor that specifies the conditions under which the product can be returned, replaced, or repaired. Federal law requires that sellers of products that cost more than $15 and have a warranty make this document available to customers before purchase. Frequently this disclosure is printed in the catalog or on the package.

An *express warranty,* usually in written form, is created by the seller or manufacturer and has two forms: the full warranty and the limited warranty. A *full warranty* states that a defective product can be fixed or replaced during a reasonable amount of time. A *limited warranty* covers only certain aspects of the product, such as parts, or requires the buyer to incur part of the costs for shipping or repairs.

An *implied warranty* covers a product's intended use or other basic understandings that are not in writing. For example, an implied *warranty of title* indicates that the seller has the right to sell the product. An implied *warranty of merchantability* guarantees that the product is fit for the ordinary uses for which it is intended: A toaster must toast bread, and a stereo must play CDs or tapes. Implied warranties vary from state to state.

*service contract*
An agreement between a business and a consumer to cover the repair costs of a product.

A **service contract** is an agreement between a business and a consumer to cover the repair costs of a product. Even though service contracts are frequently called *extended warranties,* they are not warranties. For a fee, they insure the buyer of a product against losses due to the cost of certain repairs. Owners of automobiles, home appliances, and other equipment buy these contracts to protect themselves against large repair expenses. Service contracts are very profitable for businesses, since many more people buy them than need repair service. Buying a service contract may not be the best use of your money. Most companies that sell service contracts pay out less than 10 cents in costs for every dollar received from consumers. A wiser action may be to set aside money for needed repairs.

Exhibit 8–7 summarizes techniques that can assist you in your buying decisions.

## Concept Check 8–3

1. What types of brands are commonly available to consumers?
2. What information on food labels can be helpful to consumers?
3. In what situations can comparing prices help in purchasing decisions?
4. How does a service contract differ from a warranty? What rights do purchasers of products have even if no written warranty exists?

## RESOLVING CONSUMER COMPLAINTS

**Obj. 4**
Identify steps to take to resolve consumer problems.

Most customer complaints result from defective products, low quality, short product lives, unexpected costs, deceptive pricing, and poor repairs. These problems are most commonly associated with products and services listed in Exhibit 8–8. Federal consumer agencies estimate annual consumer losses from fraudulent business activities at $10 billion to $40 billion for telemarketing and mail order, $3 billion for credit card fraud and credit "repair" scams, and $10 billion for investment swindles. (See "Financial Planning for Life's Situations" feature.)

Most people do not anticipate or have problems with their purchases. Since problems do arise, however, it's best to be prepared for them. The process for resolving differences between buyers and sellers includes the steps presented in Exhibit 8–9 on page 253. To help ensure success when you make a complaint, keep a file of receipts, names of people you talked to, dates of attempted repairs, copies of letters you wrote, and costs incurred.

## EXHIBIT 8–8

**Sources of Common Consumer Complaints**

SOURCES: Council of Better Business Bureaus, National Association of Attorneys General, National Fraud Information Center.

Motor vehicle purchases, repairs
Mail-order purchases
Magazine subscriptions
Work-at-home, business opportunities
Landlord–tenant relations
Investment scams
Telemarketing
Computers, home electronics
Health clubs, diet programs
Online buying, product sales

Home remodeling, home repairs
Credit card promotions, practices
Contests and sweepstakes
Dry cleaning, laundry companies
Travel services, travel packages
Rent-to-own companies
Cramming (telephoning customers for optional services never ordered)
Slamming (switching phone service to another carrier without permission)
Spamming (unsolicited e-mail messages)

# Financial Planning for Life's Situations

## BEWARE OF THESE COMMON (AND NOT SO COMMON) FRAUDS

**FOREIGN SCAMS.** About 800 people received a letter from a Nigerian bank promising all or part of $30 million. The letter requested the recipient's bank account number so the money could be transferred. There was another catch: To receive the fortune, the recipient would have to pay between $100,000 to $1 million in taxes—in advance! Fourteen people, none of them U.S. residents, sent checks totaling about $20 million.

**TELEMARKETING SCAMS.** Telemarketing fraud and common telephone scams include prize offers, travel packages, investments, charities, work-at-home schemes, magazine sales, and business opportunities.

**ADVANCE-FEE LOANS.** Fraudulent loan brokers misrepresenting the availability of credit use the "advance-fee" loan scam. They guarantee to get you a loan or other type of credit—but you must pay *before* you apply. After getting the money in advance, the con artists disappear.

**CREDIT REPAIR.** Companies offer to clean up the credit reports of consumers with poor credit histories. After paying hundreds of dollars, consumers find out these companies can do nothing to improve their credit reports.

**AUTOMATIC DEBIT SCAMS.** Automatic debiting of your checking account can be a legitimate payment method for monthly bills. However, many fraudulent telemarketers use this technique to take money from a person's checking account. *Do not* give out checking account information over the phone unless you are familiar with the company.

**FRAUDULENT DIET PRODUCTS AND HEALTH CLAIMS.** Americans spend an estimated $6 billion a year on fraudulent diet products such as "The Amazing Skin Patch Melts Away Body Fat," "Lose Weight While You Sleep," and "Lose All the Weight You Can for Just $99." Spotting false health claims may be as easy as being cautious of phrases such as "scientific breakthrough," "miraculous cure," "exclusive product," "secret ingredient," or "ancient remedy." Common health fraud schemes occur in the areas of cancer, AIDS-HIV, and arthritis.

**MAGAZINE SUBSCRIPTION SCAMS.** Beware of telephone sales pitches for "free," "prepaid," or "special" magazine offers. One consumer received a call stating that as a "preferred customer" the company had prepaid seven magazine subscriptions for 60 months. All that would be required would be a "small" weekly service fee of $3.43. The magazines would cost nearly $900 over five years.

**TOLL-FREE SCAMS.** Calls to 800, 888, and 877 numbers are almost always free. However, there are some exceptions. Companies that provide audio entertainment or information services may charge for calls to toll-free numbers, but only if they follow the Federal Trade Commission's 900-number rule.

**BOGUS "CAMPUS CARD."** Consumer protection offices in 20 states warned about "campus cards" available for a $25 fee. These prepaid debit cards were being promoted as "required" for many services and privileges at whichever college or university the student decided to attend. While the company appeared to be affiliated with the school, it was actually a for-profit business.

**INTERNET PYRAMID SCHEME.** The Council of Better Business Bureaus issued an alert about an "international program of wealth distribution" called "Pentagono" or "Future Strategies International." The plan, based in Italy and promoted on the Internet, advertised that consumers could receive up to $116,000 for an initial investment of about $120. Participants were asked to purchase three certificates and sell those to three other people. Tied to the promotion was a discount shopping card that allegedly offered deep discounts from merchants worldwide. For everyone to profit in the scheme, there had to be a never-ending supply of potential and willing participants.

**BADGE FRAUD.** Less than one week after the death of an Anchorage, Alaska, police officer, fundraisers began calling local residents. One organization, operating under several names, collected $5,445. Not one cent of those funds were ever seen by the police officer's family.

**FRAUDULENT HOTLINE.** The attorney general in Missouri obtained a court order to shut down a fraudulent consumer telemarketing "hotline" that was being used to divert inquiries and complaints about a vacation company from legitimate consumer protection agencies. The enterprise would solicit customers to buy vacation packages or timeshares. When customers asked how to check the legitimacy of the company, they were referred to the hotline run by the company under a different name.

Further information about various frauds and deceptive business practices is available at www.fraud.org and www.ftc.gov.

Written documents can help to resolve a problem in your favor. An automobile owner kept detailed records and receipts for all gasoline purchases, oil changes, and repairs. When a warranty dispute occurred, the owner was able to prove proper maintenance and received a refund for the defective vehicle.

**EXHIBIT 8-9**

Suggested Steps for Resolving Consumer Complaints

**Step 1**   Local communication...          Return to the place of purchase

**Step 2**   Higher-level communication...   Contact the company's main office

**Step 3**   Third-party involvement...      Obtain assistance from a consumer agency

**Step 4**   Litigation...                   Take legal action

## Step 1: Return to Place of Purchase

Most consumer complaints are resolved at the original sales location. Since most business firms are concerned about their reputations, they usually honor legitimate complaints. As you talk with the salesperson, customer service person, or store manager, avoid yelling, threatening a lawsuit, or demanding unreasonable action. In general, a calm, rational, yet persistent approach is recommended.

**Did You Know**

Just over half of consumers (52 percent) said they would go back to the source when they have a complaint about a product or service. A third (34 percent) would report the company to the Better Business Bureau, while fewer than one in five (17 percent) said they would contact the manufacturer or company headquarters. (*Consumer Behavior, Experiences, and Attitudes: a Comparison by Age Group,* AARP, 601 E St., NW, Washington, DC 20049.)

## Step 2: Contact Company Headquarters

Express your dissatisfaction to the corporate level if a problem is not resolved at the local store. A letter like the one in Exhibit 8–10 may be appropriate. You can obtain addresses of companies you may wish to contact from the *Consumer's Resource Handbook,* published by the federal government; Standard & Poor's *Register of Corporations, Directors, and Executives;* Dun & Bradstreet's *Million Dollar Directory;* or other reference books available at your library. The websites of major companies also offer a method to communicate with these organizations; see www.hoovers.com.

You can obtain a company's consumer hotline number by using a directory of toll-free numbers or calling 1–800–555–1212, the toll-free information number. Some companies print the toll-free hotline number on product packages. Studies reveal that over 70 percent of consumer complaints made to company toll-free numbers are resolved on the first contact.

## Step 3: Obtain Consumer Agency Assistance

If you do not receive satisfaction from the company, several consumer, business, and government organizations are available. These include national organizations specializing in issues such as automobile safety, health care, and nutrition, and local organizations that handle complaints, conduct surveys, and provide legal assistance.

**EXHIBIT 8-10**    SAMPLE COMPLAINT LETTER

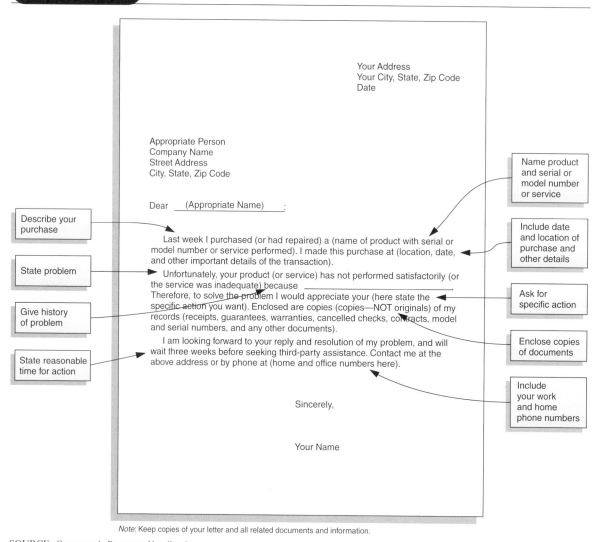

Describe your purchase

State problem

Give history of problem

State reasonable time for action

Your Address
Your City, State, Zip Code
Date

Appropriate Person
Company Name
Street Address
City, State, Zip Code

Dear _____ (Appropriate Name) _____ :

    Last week I purchased (or had repaired) a (name of product with serial or model number or service performed). I made this purchase at (location, date, and other important details of the transaction).
    Unfortunately, your product (or service) has not performed satisfactorily (or the service was inadequate) because _____
    Therefore, to solve the problem I would appreciate your (here state the specific action you want). Enclosed are copies (copies—NOT originals) of my records (receipts, guarantees, warranties, cancelled checks, contracts, model and serial numbers, and any other documents).
    I am looking forward to your reply and resolution of my problem, and will wait three weeks before seeking third-party assistance. Contact me at the above address or by phone at (home and office numbers here).

Sincerely,

Your Name

Name product and serial or model number or service

Include date and location of purchase and other details

Ask for specific action

Enclose copies of documents

Include your work and home phone numbers

*Note*: Keep copies of your letter and all related documents and information.

SOURCE: *Consumer's Resource Handbook.*

*mediation*   The attempt by an impartial third party to resolve a difference between two parties through discussion and negotation.

*arbitration*   The settlement of a difference by a third party whose decision is legally binding.

    The Better Business Bureaus are a network of offices that resolve complaints against local merchants. Better Business Bureaus are sponsored by local business organizations, and companies are not obligated to respond to the complaints. The Better Business Bureau in your area can be of value before you make a purchase. Its files will tell you about the experiences of others who dealt with a firm with which you are planning to do business.

    **Mediation** involves the use of a third party to settle grievances. In mediation, an impartial person—the *mediator*—tries to resolve a conflict between a customer and a business through discussion and negotiation. Mediation is a nonbinding process. It can save time and money compared to other dispute settlement methods.

    **Arbitration** is the settlement of a difference by a third party—the *arbitrator*—whose decision is legally binding. After both sides agree to the arbitration process, each side presents its case to the arbitrator. Arbitrators are selected from volunteers trained for this purpose. Most major automobile manufacturers and many industry organizations have arbitration programs to resolve consumer complaints.

A vast network of government agencies is also available. Problems with local restaurants or food stores may be handled by a city or county health department. Every state has agencies to handle problems involving deceptive advertising, fraudulent business practices, banking, insurance companies, and utility rates.

Federal agencies available to help resolve consumer difficulties and provide information are listed in Appendix B. When you are uncertain about which agency to use, contact your U.S. representative in Washington, DC. This office can help channel your concern to the appropriate consumer protection agency.

## Step 4: Take Legal Action

The next section discusses the various alternatives available to resolve consumer problems.

> **?**
> **Did You Know**
>
> Without realizing it, many consumers sign contracts with provisions that stipulate arbitration as the method to resolve disputes. As a result, consumers face various risks, including rules vastly different from a jury trial, higher costs for the arbitrator's time, and selection of an arbitrator by the defendant. ("The Arbitration Trap: How Consumers Pay for 'Low Cost' Justice," *Consumer Reports*, August 1999, pp. 64–65.)

### Concept Check 8-4

1. What are common causes of consumer problems and complaints?
2. How can most consumer complaints be resolved?
3. How does arbitration differ from mediation?

## LEGAL OPTIONS FOR CONSUMERS

**Obj. 5**
Evaluate the legal alternatives available to consumers.

*small claims court*
A court that settles legal differences involving amounts below a set limit and employs a process in which the litigants usually do not use a lawyer.

What should you do if all of the previously mentioned avenues of action fail to bring about a resolution of a consumer complaint? One of the following legal actions may be appropriate.

### Small Claims Court

Every state has a court system to settle minor disagreements. In **small claims court,** a person may file a claim involving amounts below a set dollar limit. The maximum varies from state to state, ranging from $500 to $10,000; most states have a limit of between $1,500 and $3,000. The process usually takes place without a lawyer, although in many states attorneys are allowed in small claims court.

To make best use of small claims court, experts suggest the following tips:

- Become familiar with the court's location, procedures, and filing fees (usually from $5 to $50).
- Observe other cases to learn more about the process.
- Present your case in a polite, calm, and concise manner.
- Submit evidence such as photographs, contracts, receipts, and other documents.
- Use witnesses who can testify on your behalf.

While obtaining a favorable judgment in small claims court may be easy, the collection process is frequently difficult. Since the defendant may not appear, you may have to pay a sheriff to serve a court order or use a collection agency to get your money.

## Class-Action Suits

Occasionally a number of people have the same complaint—for example, people who were injured by a defective product, customers who were overcharged by a utility company, or travelers who were cheated by a tour business. Such people may qualify for a class-action suit. A **class-action suit** is a legal action taken by a few individuals on behalf of all the people who have suffered the same alleged injustice. These people, called a *class,* are represented by one lawyer or by a group of lawyers working together.

*class-action suit*
A legal action taken by a few individuals on behalf of all the people who have suffered the same alleged injustice.

Once a situation qualifies as a class-action suit, all of the affected parties must be notified of the suit. At this point, a person may decide not to participate in the class-action suit and instead file an individual lawsuit. If the court ruling is favorable to the class, the funds awarded may be divided among all the people involved, used to reduce rates in the future, or assigned to public funds for government use. Recent class-action suits included auto owners who were sold unneeded replacement parts for their vehicles and a group of investors who sued a brokerage company for unauthorized buy-and-sell transactions that resulted in high commission charges.

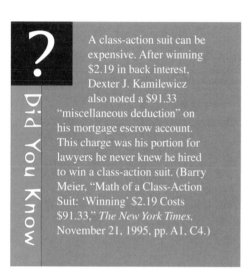

Did You Know

A class-action suit can be expensive. After winning $2.19 in back interest, Dexter J. Kamilewicz also noted a $91.33 "miscellaneous deduction" on his mortgage escrow account. This charge was his portion for lawyers he never knew he hired to win a class-action suit. (Barry Meier, "Math of a Class-Action Suit: 'Winning' $2.19 Costs $91.33," *The New York Times,* November 21, 1995, pp. A1, C4.)

## Using a Lawyer

When small claims court or a class-action suit is not appropriate, you may seek the services of an attorney. The most common sources of available lawyers are referrals from people you know, the local branch of the American Bar Association, and telephone directory listings. Lawyers advertise in newspapers, on television, and in other media. Be aware that impressive advertising does not mean competent legal counsel.

Deciding when to use a lawyer is difficult. In general, straightforward legal situations such as appearing in small claims court, renting an apartment, or defending yourself on a minor traffic violation usually do not require legal counsel. But for more complicated matters such as writing a will, settling a real estate purchase, or suing for injury damages caused by a product, it is probably wise to obtain the services of an attorney.

PFP

**Sheet 35**

When selecting a lawyer, you should consider several questions. Is the lawyer experienced in your type of case? Will you be charged on a flat fee basis, at an hourly rate, or on a contingency basis? Is there a fee for the initial consultation? How and when will you be required to make payment for services?

## Other Legal Alternatives

The cost of legal services can be a problem, especially for low-income consumers. A **legal aid society** is one of a network of publicly supported community law offices that provide legal assistance to people who cannot afford their own attorney. These community agencies provide this assistance at a minimal cost or without charge.

*legal aid society*   One of a network of publicly supported community law offices that provide legal assistance to consumers who cannot afford their own attorney.

*Prepaid legal services* provide unlimited or reduced-fee legal assistance for a set fee. Some of these programs provide certain basic services, such as telephone consultation and preparation of a simple will, for an annual fee ranging from $50 to $150 or more. More complicated legal assistance requires an additional fee, usually at a reduced rate. Other programs do not charge an advance fee but allow members to obtain legal services at discount rates. In general, prepaid legal programs are designed to prevent minor troubles from becoming complicated legal problems. Legal questions may be researched online at www.nolo.com.

# Financial Planning for Life's Situations

## IS IT LEGAL?

The following situations are common problems for consumers. How would you respond to the question at the end of each situation?

|  | Yes | No |
|---|---|---|

**1.** A store advertised a bottle of shampoo as "the $1.79 size, on sale for 99¢." If the store never sold the item for $1.79 but the manufacturer's recommended price was $1.79, was this a legitimate price comparison?    ____ ____

**2.** You purchase a stereo system for $650. Two days later, the same store offers the same item for $425. Is this legal?    ____ ____

**3.** You receive an unordered sample of flower seeds in the mail. You decide to plant them to see how well they will grow in your yard. A couple of days later, you receive a bill for the seeds. Do you have to pay for the seeds?    ____ ____

**4.** A store has a "going out of business sale—everything must go" sign in its window. After six months, the sign is still there. Is this a deceptive business practice?    ____ ____

**5.** A 16-year-old injured while playing ball at a local park is taken to a hospital for medical care. The parents refuse to pay the hospital since they didn't request the service. Can the parents be held legally responsible for the charges?    ____ ____

**6.** You purchase a shirt for a friend. The shirt doesn't fit, but when you return it to the store, you are offered an exchange since the store policy is no cash refunds. Is this legal?    ____ ____

**7.** A manufacturer refuses to repair a motorcycle that is still under warranty. The manufacturer can prove that the motorcycle was used improperly. If this is true, must the manufacturer honor the warranty?    ____ ____

**8.** An employee of a store incorrectly marks the price of an item at a lower amount. Is the store obligated to sell the item at the lower price?    ____ ____

Circumstances, interpretations of the law, and store policies, as well as state and local laws, can affect the above situations. The generally accepted answers are *no* for 1, 3, 7, and 8; *yes* for 2, 4, 5, and 6.

## Personal Consumer Protection

While many laws, agencies, and legal tools are available to protect your rights, none will be of value unless you use them. (See "Financial Planning for Life's Situations" feature.) Consumer protection experts suggest that to prevent being taken in by deceptive business practices, you should

1. Do business only with reputable companies with a record of satisfying customers.
2. Avoid signing contracts and other documents you do not understand.
3. Be cautious about offerings that seem too good to be true—they probably are!
4. Compare the cost of buying on credit with the cost of paying cash; also, compare the interest rates the seller offers with those offered by a bank or a credit union.
5. Avoid rushing to get a good deal; successful con artists depend on impulse buying.

### Concept Check 8-5

1. In what types of situations would small claims court and class-action suits be helpful?
2. Describe some situations in which you might use the services of a lawyer.

# Summary of Objectives

**Obj. 1** Assess the financial implications of consumer purchasing decisions.

A variety of economic, social, and personal factors influence daily buying decisions. Overspending and poor money management are frequent causes of overuse of credit and other financial difficulties.

**Obj. 2** Evaluate the alternatives in consumer purchasing decisions.

A research-based approach to consumer buying involves problem identification, information gathering, and increased marketplace awareness. In this approach, purchase alternatives are assessed on the basis of quality, price, performance, style, company reputation, and service.

**Obj. 3** Implement strategies for effective purchasing.

Timing purchases, comparing stores and brands, using label information, computing unit prices, and evaluating warranties are common strategies for effective purchasing.

**Obj. 4** Identify steps to take to resolve consumer problems.

Most consumer problems can be resolved by following these steps: (1) Return to the place of purchase; (2) contact the company's main office; (3) obtain assistance from a consumer agency; and (4) take legal action.

**Obj. 5** Evaluate the legal alternatives available to consumers.

Small claims court, class-action suits, the services of a lawyer, legal aid societies, and prepaid legal services are legal means for handling consumer problems that cannot be resolved through communication with the business involved or through the help of a consumer protection agency.

# Financial Planning Problems

1. *Analyzing Influences on Consumer Buying.* Use advertisements, recent news articles, and personal observations to point out the economic, social, and personal factors that influence the purchases of people in the following life situations. (Obj. 1)

   a. A retired person.

   b. A single parent with children ages 5 and 9.

   c. A dual-income couple with no children.

   d. A person with a dependent child and a dependent parent.

2. *Comparing Buying Alternatives.* Tammy Monahan is considering the purchase of a home entertainment center. The product attributes she plans to consider and the weights she gives to them are as follows:

   | | |
   |---|---|
   | Portability | .1 |
   | Sound projection | .6 |
   | Warranty | .3 |

   Tammy related the brands as follows:

   | | Portability | Sound Projection | Warranty |
   |---|---|---|---|
   | Brand A | 6 | 8 | 7 |
   | Brand B | 9 | 6 | 8 |
   | Brand C | 5 | 9 | 6 |

   Using the consumer buying matrix (Exhibit 8–4), conduct a quantitative product evaluation rating for each brand.

   What other factors is Tammy likely to consider when making her purchase? (Obj. 2)

3. *Researching Consumer Purchases.* Using the consumer buying matrix (Exhibit 8–4), analyze a consumer purchase you plan to make sometime in the future. What factors affected the selection of the attributes and weights you chose for this purchase analysis? (Obj. 2)

4. *Calculating the Cost of Credit.* John Walters is comparing the cost of credit to the cash price of an item. If John makes a $60 down payment and pays $32 a month for 24 months, how much more will that amount be than the cash price of $685? (Obj. 2)

5. *Computing Unit Prices.* Calculate the unit price of each of the following items: (Obj. 3)

   | Item | Price | Size | Unit Price |
   |---|---|---|---|
   | Motor oil | $1.95 | 2.5 quarts | ___ cents/quart |
   | Cereal | 2.17 | 15 ounces | ___ cents/ounces |
   | Canned fruit | 0.89 | 13 ounces | ___ cents/ounces |
   | Facial tissue | 2.25 | 300 tissues | ___ cents/100 tissues |
   | Shampoo | 3.96 | 17 ounces | ___ cents/ounces |

6. *Calculating the Present Value of a Consumer Purchase.* What would be the net present value of a microwave oven that costs $159 and will save you $68 a year in time and food away from home? Assume an average return on your savings of 7 percent. (Obj. 3)

**7.** *Computing Net Present Value.* Use the feature "Financial Planning Calculations: Net Present Value of a Consumer Purchase" (p. 249) to analyze a past or a future purchase. (Obj. 3)

**8.** *Calculating Future Value.* You can purchase a service contract for all of your major appliances for $160 a year. If the appliances are expected to last for 10 years and you earn 5 percent on your savings, what would be the future value of the amount you will pay for the service contract? (Obj. 3)

**9.** *Comparing Automobile Purchases.* Based on financial and opportunity costs, which of the following do you believe would be the wiser purchase?   (Chapter Appendix)

*Vehicle 1:* A three-year-old car with 45,000 miles, costing $6,700 and requiring $385 of immediate repairs.

*Vehicle 2:* A five-year-old car with 62,000 miles, costing $4,500 and requiring $760 of immediate repairs.

**10.** *Calculating Motor Vehicle Operating Costs.* Calculate the approximate yearly operating cost of the following vehicle.   (Chapter Appendix)

Annual depreciation, $2,500
Annual mileage, 13,200
Current year's loan interest, $650
Miles per gallon, 24
Insurance, $680
License and registration fees, $65
Average gasoline price, $1.18 per gallon
Oil changes/repairs, $370
Parking/tolls, $420

## Financial Planning Activities

**1.** *Obtaining Consumer Information.* Using the World Wide Web, library resources, or a survey of acquaintances, determine the major factors people consider when *(a)* buying food, *(b)* selecting a store at which to shop, and *(c)* using information from advertisements.   (Obj. 1)

**2.** *Comparing Consumer Information Sources.* Obtain a recent issue of *Consumer Reports* (or go to www.Consumer Reports.org) to evaluate and compare different brands of a product. Also obtain information on this product from people who sell this item and those who have recently purchased it. Compare the information received from these sources.   (Obj. 2)

**3.** *Evaluating Consumer Information Sources.* Develop guidelines that consumers could use to evaluate different sources of consumer information (advertising, salespeople, friends, government publications, Internet sites). Consider the *(a)* objectivity, *(b)* accuracy, *(c)* clarity, and *(d)* usefulness of these sources. Prepare a video or other visual presentation to communicate your guidelines. (Obj. 2)

**4.** *Researching Consumer Information on the Internet.* Locate websites that would provide you with useful information when buying various consumer products. (Obj. 3)

**5.** *Determining Brand Loyalty.* Conduct a survey of several people regarding brand loyalty. For what products do these people usually buy a certain brand? What factors (price, location, information) may influence their selection of another brand?   (Obj. 3)

**6.** *Solving Consumer Problems.* Interview one or two people who have had a complaint about a product or company.

What difficulties did they encounter? What actions did they take? Was the complaint resolved in a satisfactory manner?   (Obj. 4)

**7.** *Identifying and Solving Consumer Problems.* Collect magazine or newspaper advertisements that appear to be "too good to be true." Why are these ads deceptive? Should government agencies take action against any of the companies presenting these ads? (Additional information about common frauds may be obtained at www. fraud.org.)   (Obj. 4)

**8.** *Comparing Legal Services.* Prepare a survey of legal services available to students and others in your community. Use Sheet 35 in the *Personal Financial Planner* to compare the fees and services provided by lawyers and other sources of legal assistance.   (Obj. 5)

**9.** *Comparing Used Cars.* Use Sheet 37 in the *Personal Financial Planner* to compare different sources of used motor vehicles.   (Chapter Appendix)

**10.** *Searching the Internet for Transportation Information.* Using various search engines, identify websites that could assist consumers with evaluating and comparing automobile prices.   (Chapter Appendix)

**11.** *Evaluating Motor Vehicle Leases.* Use Sheet 38 in the *Personal Financial Planner* to compare the costs of buying and leasing a motor vehicle.   (Chapter Appendix)

**12.** *Comparing Auto Service.* Compare the prices different types of automotive service businesses (specialty shops, dealers, service stations) charge for the purchase and installation of a battery, muffler, and tires.   (Chapter Appendix)

## LIFE SITUATION CASE

### MAKING MARKETPLACE DECISIONS

Anthony Carlton just completed his college degree and has taken a job in a nearby city. As he prepares to move into his new apartment, Anthony realizes he must make a purchasing decision regarding furniture. He starts the buying process by talking to his parents and friends.

His dad suggests that Anthony lease some furniture until he is sure how long he will live in this area. "No sense buying things that you might have to sell or move a long distance," he advises.

"I can get you a great deal on some furniture," offered Anthony's friend Steve. Anthony responded, "I don't have that much cash available." Steve replied, "No problem, we have an easy payment plan at our store."

While continuing to think about the situation, Anthony comes across an advertisement by a "rent-to-buy" store. He calls the company and finds out that the very low payments

make it possible to get the furniture available almost immediately. In addition, the salesperson on the phone commented that "within just a few years, these items can be yours to keep."

Anthony continues to read articles about buying furniture and talks to others about the purchase. As he obtains more buying information, Anthony becomes increasingly uncertain about what action to take. Finally, he exclaims, "Maybe I can just sit on the floor!"

### Questions

1. What information sources are likely to be most helpful to Anthony?
2. How should Anthony evaluate the costs and benefits of the alternatives available for resolving his buying problem?
3. What other alternatives may be available to Anthony?

## INTERNET CASE   Complaining Online

"I'm never going to return this to the store."

That's a common response when dissatisfied with a purchase. But what happens when the store is *www.just-try-to-return-it.com*?

With almost 60 percent of all Internet users buying something online, there will be problems. One study revealed that one in five survey respondents had a problem with online shopping. The two most common concerns were that they paid for something and didn't get it, or paid for something and got something different than what was expected. While consumers have a strong concern about being charged for something they never agreed to, only three percent said they had this problem.

When shopping online, consumer experts warn to consider all costs associated with the purchase and delivery. Many online shopping websites charge a "restocking" fee for an item that is returned. Most will also make the consumer pay for the shipping when returning a product. Studies also

reveal that most shopping websites either do not include their return policies or hide them in the fine print.

### Questions

1. What items on a website can help consumers make well informed, safe, trouble-free purchases?
2. What information could be useful to online shoppers at www.safeshopping.org?
3. Locate an online shopping website to determine the return policies and procedures of this company.

SOURCES: "Proceed with Caution: Shopping Online Is Convenient but It Does Have Its Drawbacks," by Jeffrey Steele, *Chicago Tribune,* December 14, 1999, Section 6, pp. 1, 7. "Online Returns Aren't Easy," *The News-Sun* (Waukegan, IL), December 16, 1999, Section C, pp. C1, C3.

## Creating an E-Plan: Financial Decisions Using the Web

### COMPARISON SHOPPING AND BUYING MOTOR VEHICLES

Daily buying actions such as comparing prices, evaluating brands, and avoiding fraud allow you to wisely use resources for both current living expenses and long-term financial security.

Websites for Comparison Shopping

- Current *Consumer Reports* articles at **www.ConsumerReports.org;** extensive information on various consumer topics are at links to other sites at **www.consumerworld.org.**
- A comparison of brands, prices, and features for various products may be accessed at **www.compare.net** and **www.pricescan.com.**
- Consumer information related to food, health, money, product safety, and transportation at **www.consumer.gov**; access to publications from the Consumer Information Center at **www.pueblo.gsa.gov**; Federal Trade Commission consumer information at **www.ftc.gov.**
- The National Fraud Information Center website offers fraud warnings and links to federal, state, and local consumer agencies at **www.fraud.org**; the Better Business Bureau offers a directory of BBB offices, information on marketplace scams, and links to other BBB websites at **www.bbb.org.**
- Legal information related to various consumer and personal finance topics at **www.nolo.com** and **www.consumerlawpage.com.**
- CARveat Emptor has links to various aspects of researching, selecting, negotiating, and leasing motor vehicles at **www.well.com/user/kr2**; new- and used-car prices at **www.edmunds.com** and **www.kbb.com;** auto leasing information at **www.leasesource.com.**
- Driving safety information at **www.hwysafety.org** and crash data and insurance injury, collision, and theft loss information at **www.carsafety.org.**

(Note: Addresses and content of websites change, and new sites are created daily. Use search engines to update and locate additional websites.)

*PFP sheets: 32–39*

Short-Term Financial Planning Activities

1. Compare the use of cash and credit, and various brands, for the purchase of a major consumer item you may need in the near future (see PFP Sheets 32, 33).
2. Conduct a unit pricing comparison at several stores (see PFP Sheet 34).
3. Determine current transportation needs related to new and used motor vehicles and compare buying and leasing options (see PFP Sheets 36–38).

Long-Term Financial Planning Activities

1. Determine buying guidelines for major purchases (appliances, furniture, home entertainment equipment). Identify brands, store locations, and savings plans to avoid buying on credit.
2. Identify and compare various legal services available for use (see PFP Sheet 35).
3. Identify motor vehicles that would provide the lowest operating and insurance costs (see PFP Sheet 39).

# CHAPTER 8

# Buying and Operating a Motor Vehicle

## BUYING A USED VEHICLE

The average used car costs about $10,000 less than the average new car. The cost of a new car exceeds $20,000. New cars cost an average of about 50 cents a mile to own and operate; used cars cost an average of about 35 cents a mile. While many people prefer a previously owned vehicle, higher new-car prices have created increased demand and higher costs for used cars. Americans spend over $100 billion a year to purchase more than 20 million used cars.

### Sources of Used Vehicles

**New-Car Dealers**    New-car dealers usually also sell used vehicles. These automobiles are late-model vehicles received as trade-ins for new-car purchases. New-car dealers generally give you a better warranty on a used car than other sellers and have a service department to recondition the cars. These services mean higher used-car prices at new-car dealers than at other sources.

**Used-Car Dealers**    Used-car dealers specialize in previously owned vehicles. They usually offer vehicles that are older than those offered by new-car dealers. If they give warranties, the coverage is likely to be limited. In exchange for these drawbacks, you will probably be able to obtain a lower price from a used-car dealer. Be aware that some used-car dealers obtain vehicles that have been poorly maintained.

**Private Parties**    Individuals selling their own cars are another common source. A private-party sale can be a bargain if the vehicle was well maintained; it can also be a nightmare. Few consumer protection regulations apply to private-party sales. Caution is suggested when using this used-car source. Ask past owners if they have a record of regular maintenance and repairs.

Other Sources   Some of the other sources available for purchasing a used motor vehicle include:

- Auctions and dealers that sell automobiles previously owned by businesses, auto rental companies, and government agencies. While these vehicles have probably been serviced regularly, most have also had many drivers or have undergone extreme use—such as police cars.
- Used-car superstores such as CarMax offer a large inventory of previously-owned vehicles at competitive prices.
- Online used-car businesses, such as www.dealernet.com and www.americasautomall.com.

## Consumer Protection for Used-Car Buyers

The Federal Trade Commission (FTC) requires businesses that sell used cars to place a buyer's guide sticker in the windows of cars for sale. This disclosure must state whether the car comes with a warranty and, if so, what protection the dealer will provide. If no warranty is offered, the car is sold "as is" and the dealer assumes no responsibility for any repairs, regardless of any oral claims. About one-half of all the used cars sold by dealers come without a warranty, and if you buy such a car, you must pay for any repairs needed to correct problems. Be sure to get in writing any promises made by the salesperson.

While a used car may not have an *express warranty,* most states have *implied warranties* that protect basic rights of the used-car buyer. An implied warranty of merchantability means the product is guaranteed to do what it is supposed to do. The used car is guaranteed to run—at least for awhile!

The buyer's guide required by the FTC encourages you to have the used car inspected by a mechanic and to get all promises in writing. You also receive a list of the 14 major systems of an automobile and some of the major problems that may occur in these systems. This list can be helpful in comparing the vehicles and warranties offered by different dealers. FTC used-car regulations do not apply to vehicles purchased from private owners.

Follow two general rules when you buy a used vehicle. First, buy your vehicle from a source that gives some assurance of the vehicle's reliability. Second, make a detailed investigation of the vehicle's condition and performance potential.

## The Inspection Process

The appearance of a used car can be deceptive. A well-maintained engine may be inside a body with rust; a clean, shiny exterior may conceal major operational problems. Therefore, conduct a used-car inspection as outlined in Exhibit 8–A.

Have a trained and trusted mechanic of *your* choice check the car to estimate the costs of potential repairs. This service will help you avoid surprises.

Although federal law makes odometer tampering illegal, the problem still exists. Mileage may be turned back to give a vehicle a newer appearance. Signs of possible odometer fraud are the failure of digits to line up straight or the presence of broken plastic in the speedometer case. If the brake pedal or upholstery looks very old or very new for the number of miles on the odometer, odometer tampering may have occurred.

Before making your final decision, find out whether there have been safety recalls on the car. If so, have the necessary adjustments been made? Information about recalls may be

## EXHIBIT 8-A    CHECKING OUT A USED CAR

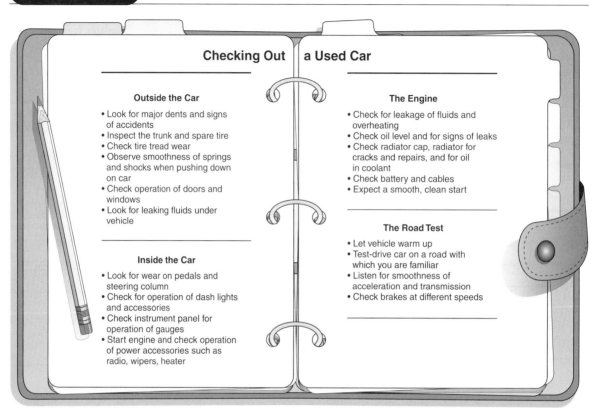

### Checking Out a Used Car

**Outside the Car**

- Look for major dents and signs of accidents
- Inspect the trunk and spare tire
- Check tire tread wear
- Observe smoothness of springs and shocks when pushing down on car
- Check operation of doors and windows
- Look for leaking fluids under vehicle

**Inside the Car**

- Look for wear on pedals and steering column
- Check for operation of dash lights and accessories
- Check instrument panel for operation of gauges
- Start engine and check operation of power accessories such as radio, wipers, heater

**The Engine**

- Check for leakage of fluids and overheating
- Check oil level and for signs of leaks
- Check radiator cap, radiator for cracks and repairs, and for oil in coolant
- Check battery and cables
- Expect a smooth, clean start

**The Road Test**

- Let vehicle warm up
- Test-drive car on a road with which you are familiar
- Listen for smoothness of acceleration and transmission
- Check brakes at different speeds

obtained from the National Highway Traffic Safety Administration, a division of the U.S. Department of Transportation. This agency has an auto safety hotline (1–800–424–9393) for consumers to check on auto recalls; the website is www.nhtsa.gov.

## Used-Car Price Negotiation

Begin to determine a fair price by checking newspaper ads for the prices of comparable vehicles. Other sources of current used-car prices are *Edmund's Used Car Prices* and the National Automobile Dealers Association's *Official Used Car Guide,* commonly called the *blue book.* These publications are available at banks, credit unions, libraries, and bookstores. Websites are also available.

A number of factors influence the basic price of a used car. The number of miles the car has been driven, along with features and options, affect price. A low-mileage car will have a higher price than a comparable car with high mileage. The condition of the vehicle and the demand for the model also affect price.

Used-car prices follow the trend in new-car sales. If more people buy new cars and trade in or sell their present cars, the increased supply of used cars keeps their prices down. However, when the demand for new cars is low and people keep their cars longer, the prices of used cars increase. Information about the market value and safety of used motor vehicles may be obtained online; see the Financial Planning for Life's Situations box on page 265.

**Sheet 37**

## Financial Planning for Life's Situations

### ONLINE CAR BUYING

You can't use your mouse to kick the tires. However, you can do just about everything else related to planning a car purchase online.

- Planning a motor vehicle purchase: Basic information about car buying may be obtained at www.edmunds.com, www.well.com/user/kr2, www.caranddriver.com, www.autoweb.com, www.autoconnect.com, and http://carpoint.msn.com.
- Comparing vehicle prices: Current car price information is available at www.edmunds.com and www.kbb.com.
- Auto financing information: You can research and apply for an auto loan at www.bankrate.com, www.carfinance.com, and www.quicken.com.
- Auto manufacturers: Most carmakers have a website to obtain information on current models, such as

www.gm.com, www.chrysler.com, www.toyota.com, www.honda.com, and www.ford.com.

- Car-buying services: You can order your motor vehicle online through car-buying services such as www.acscorp.com, www.autobytel.com, and www.autoadvisor.com.
- Leasing information: Information on leasing a motor vehicle may be obtained at www.leasesource.com and http://carinfo.com.
- Buying a used car: Information on buying a previously owned vehicle is available at www.cars.com and www.nada.com.
- Auto safety: For information on vehicle safety and recalls, visit www.hwysafety.org, www.carsafety.org, and www.nhtsa.dot.gov.

## PURCHASING A NEW VEHICLE

You may be interested in a vehicle with "AC, pwr mrrs, ABS, and P/S." When you decode these abbreviations, you will know the vehicle has air conditioning, power mirrors, antilock brakes, and power steering. Gathering information, selecting options, and determining price are the primary actions when buying a new car.

### Gathering Information

An important source of new-car price information is the *sticker price*. This is a printed form on the vehicle with the suggested retail price of the new car. This information label presents the base price of the car as well as the costs of accessories and other items. The dealer's cost, or *invoice price,* is an amount less than the sticker price.

The difference between the sticker price and the dealer's cost is the range available for negotiation. This range is larger for full-size, luxury cars; subcompacts usually do not have a wide negotiation range. Dealer's cost for a vehicle (in relation to the sticker price) varies based on the size of the car. For example, on subcompact and compact cars, the dealer's cost is usually between 87 and 94 percent of the sticker price. On full-size cars and vans, the cost is between 80 and 84 percent of the list price.

Information about dealer's cost is available from several sources. *Edmund's New Car Prices,* available in libraries and bookstores, is helpful. More sophisticated car cost data can be obtained from computerized services such as Consumers Union, publisher of *Consumer Reports* (www.consumerreports.org).

Obtaining a favorable deal may depend on the time of day, the month, and the year. Usually you will get the most attention during the morning or early afternoon. Salespeople may give you a better price near the end of the month to make their quota. Finally, some experts recommend that you buy your new car in winter or early spring, when auto sales tend to be slow.

## Selecting Options

Optional equipment falls into three categories:

1.  Mechanical devices that improve performance and operation, such as a larger engine, the transmission, power steering, power brakes, and cruise control.
2.  Comfort and convenience options, including power seats, air conditioning, stereo systems, power locks, rear window defoggers, and tinted glass.
3.  Aesthetic features that add to the vehicle's visual appeal, such as metallic paint, special trim, and upholstery.

Color is an option that can make your car safer. Tests that involved viewing vehicles on backgrounds of concrete, meadows, and snow determined that the most visible colors were luminous orange, white (although white was difficult to see in snow and bright sunshine), and light shades of orange, gray, and blue. The colors most difficult to see were browns, greens, dark gray, dark blue, and black.

You may save money on optional equipment by selecting the deluxe edition of a model. Items that cost extra with the basic, low-price edition may be included as standard equipment with the higher-priced limited edition. Be sure you want all of the options, and compare the prices of the two editions to make sure the additional accessories justify the cost difference.

A *service contract* can cover the cost of repairs not included in the manufacturer's warranty. Service contracts range from $400 to over $1,000; however, they do not always include everything you might expect. Most of these contracts contain a list of parts not covered, along with other provisions. All service contracts cover failure of the engine cooling system; however, some contracts exclude coverage of such failures if caused by overheating.

Because of costs and exclusions, service contracts may not be a wise financial decision. You can minimize your concern about expensive repairs by setting aside a fund of money to pay for them. Then, if you need repairs, the money to pay for them will be available.

## Determining a Purchase Price

Traditionally, car buyers negotiated prices. However, many auto dealers are using various forms of one-price selling.

### Price Bargaining
Start price bargaining by comparing the prices of similar automobiles at several dealers. This information provides background on selling prices in relation to the sticker price. Be prepared to be flexible about the car you choose. Determination to buy a specific make, model, and style weakens your negotiating position.

Use dealer cost information to get a price that is only a couple of hundred dollars over the cost. The closer your price is to the dealer's cost, the better the deal you are getting. Don't be fooled by a price far below the sticker price; the dealer's cost is the number that should be of concern.

Will you receive a better deal by purchasing a car off the lot or by ordering one from the factory? The answer is not clear. Selling a car in stock helps a dealer clear inventory; however, you may not get a good price deal on the car if it is in high demand. Moreover, the car on the lot may have options you don't want. Ordering a car means waiting several weeks or months, but it eliminates the dealer's inventory carrying cost.

To prevent confusion in determining the true price of the new car, do not mention a trade-in vehicle until the cost of the car has been settled. Then ask how much the dealer is willing to pay for your old car. If the offer price is not acceptable, sell the old car on your own.

# Financial Planning for Life's Situations

## MOTOR VEHICLE SALES TECHNIQUES

*Be cautious.* To avoid buying a vehicle you do not want or cannot afford, be on guard for sales pitches like these:

- "My manager won't approve this deal. But if you are willing to pay for shipping, we have a deal." *Lowballing* occurs when a new-car buyer is quoted a very low price that increases when add-on costs are included at the last moment.
- "We can easily give you $8,000 on your trade-in. That's more than $1,200 above its market value." *Highballing* occurs when a new-car buyer is offered a very high amount for a trade-in vehicle, with the extra amount made up by increasing the new-car price.
- "How much can you afford per month?" Be sure to also ask how many months. Also, compare the total finance charge and annual percentage rate (APR) among different lenders.
- "What will it take to put you in this car today?" "I have this car ready for you today." "Take it overnight and see how you like it." Each of these types of subtle pressure is designed to lower your guard and give the seller an edge in negotiating a deal.
- "A small deposit will hold this vehicle for you." Never leave a deposit unless you are ready to buy a vehicle or are willing to lose that amount. Very few dealers will refund a deposit.
- "Your price is only $100 above our cost." However, many hidden costs may have been added in to get the dealer's cost.
- "You can have this $8,000 car for $7,000 with our 12 percent financing over five years." The total cost of the vehicle will be over $9,300. Once again, compare financing terms among different lenders.

Beware of sales agreements with preprinted amounts. Cross out numbers you believe are not appropriate for your purchase.

A typical negotiating conversation might go like this:

*Customer:* "I'm willing to give you $15,600 for the car. That's my top offer."
*Auto salesperson:* "Let me check with my manager." After returning, "My manager says $16,200 is the best we can do."
*Customer* (who should be willing to walk out at this point): "I can go to $15,650."
*Auto salesperson:* "We have the car you want, ready to go. How about $15,700?"

If the customer agrees, the dealer has gotten $100 more than the customer's "top offer!" Also see "Financial Planning for Life's Situation" box.

**Set-Price Dealers**   An increasing number of auto dealers and manufacturers now use no-haggling car selling. The prices are presented for customers to accept or reject as stated. Instead of spending time negotiating price, emphasis shifts to the features and benefits of the vehicle.

**Car-Buying Services**   You may also consider a *car-buying service,* a business that helps you obtain a specific new car at a reasonable price with minimal effort. Also referred to as an *auto broker,* these businesses offer desired models with options for prices ranging between $50 and $200 over the dealer's cost. First, the auto broker charges a small fee for price information on desired models. Then, if you decide to buy a car, the auto broker arranges the purchase with a dealer near your home.

**Online Car Buying**   At first, the World Wide Web was a dynamic source of auto buying information. As this marketplace of ideas has expanded to a marketplace of products, consumers can now buy a car online. Some traditional dealers have set up websites to attract customers from outside their usual geographic areas (see the Financial Planning for Life's Situations box on page 265).

### The Sales Agreement
Before the sale is completed, you must sign a *sales agreement,* a legal document that contains the specific details of an automobile purchase. As with any contract, make sure you understand the sales agreement before signing. Also, be sure everything you expect from the deal is presented in the sales agreement. If an item isn't in writing, you have no assurance it will be included.

The sales agreement or another receipt will serve as proof of any deposit you pay. Obtain in writing the conditions that would allow you to get back your deposit. Make your deposit as small as possible to cut your losses in case you cancel the deal and are unable to get a refund.

## Consumer Protection for New-Car Buyers

New-car warranties provide buyers with some assurance of quality. These warranties vary in the time and mileage of the protection they offer and in the parts they cover. The main conditions of a warranty are (1) coverage of basic parts against manufacturer's defects; (2) power train coverage for the engine, transmission, and drive train; and (3) the corrosion warranty, which usually applies only to holes due to rust, not to surface rust. Other important conditions of a warranty are a statement regarding whether the warranty is transferable to other owners of the car and details about the charges, if any, that will be made for major repairs in the form of a *deductible.*

In the past, when major problems occurred with a new car and the warranty didn't solve the difficulty, many consumers lacked a course of action. As a result, all 50 states and the District of Columbia enacted *lemon laws* that require a refund for the vehicle after the owner has made repeated attempts to obtain servicing. In general, these laws apply to situations in which a person has made four attempts to get the same problem corrected and situations in which the vehicle has been out of service for more than 30 days within 12 months of purchase or the first 12,000 miles. The terms of the state laws vary; contact your state consumer protection office for details (see Appendix B). The lemon laws resulted in various arbitration programs of automobile manufacturers.

## Financing an Automobile Purchase

You may pay cash for your car. However, as motor vehicles increase in cost, most people buy them on credit.

### Financing Sources
As discussed in Chapter 7, car loans are available from banks, credit unions, consumer finance companies, and other financial institutions. Many lenders will *preapprove* you for a certain loan amount. This lets you know how much you can afford to spend. Preapproval also separates financing from negotiating the price of the car. Until the new-car price is set, you should not indicate that you intend to use the dealer's credit plan. Studies have revealed that low-cost loans are frequently offset by increased vehicle prices.

Dealer financing is another option. In an effort to make automobile buying more attractive, General Motors Acceptance Corporation, Ford Motor Credit Company, and Chrysler Financial Corporation have created credit plans such as balloon payment loans, variable-rate loans, and special loans for recent college graduates. With a *balloon payment loan,* which is illegal in some states, you make payments smaller than the payments on a regular loan for 48 months. After 48 months, you have the option to (1) continue to make payments until the balance has been paid; (2) return the car to the dealer for a fee; or (3) sell the car, pay off the loan, and keep any leftover funds.

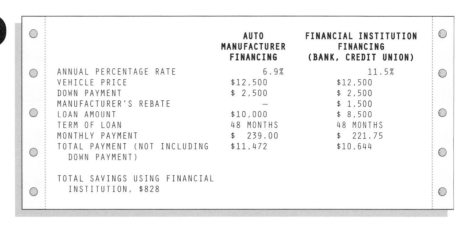

**EXHIBIT 8-B**

Comparing
Rebates
and Special
Financing:
An Example

| | AUTO MANUFACTURER FINANCING | FINANCIAL INSTITUTION FINANCING (BANK, CREDIT UNION) |
|---|---|---|
| ANNUAL PERCENTAGE RATE | 6.9% | 11.5% |
| VEHICLE PRICE | $12,500 | $12,500 |
| DOWN PAYMENT | $ 2,500 | $ 2,500 |
| MANUFACTURER'S REBATE | — | $ 1,500 |
| LOAN AMOUNT | $10,000 | $ 8,500 |
| TERM OF LOAN | 48 MONTHS | 48 MONTHS |
| MONTHLY PAYMENT | $ 239.00 | $ 221.75 |
| TOTAL PAYMENT (NOT INCLUDING DOWN PAYMENT) | $11,472 | $10,644 |
| TOTAL SAVINGS USING FINANCIAL INSTITUTION, $828 | | |

Obtaining the Best Financing    The lowest interest rate or the lowest payment does not necessarily mean the best credit plan. Select the length of your auto loan carefully. Otherwise, after two or three years, the value of your car may be less than the amount you still owe; this situation is referred to as *upside-down* or *negative equity*. If you default on your loan or sell the car at this time, you will have to pay the difference.

The annual percentage rate (APR) is the best indicator of the true cost of credit. The federal truth in lending law requires that the APR be clearly stated in advertising and other communications. Low payments may seem to be a good deal, but they mean you will be paying longer and your total finance charges will be higher. Consider both the APR and the finance charge when comparing credit terms of different lenders.

Automobile manufacturers frequently offer opportunities for low-interest financing. They may offer rebates at the same time, giving buyers a choice between a rebate and a low-interest loan. Carefully compare low-interest financing and the rebate (see Exhibit 8–B). Special rebates are sometimes offered to students, teachers, credit union members, real estate agents, and other groups.

## LEASING A MOTOR VEHICLE

More than one-fourth of all new motor vehicles are leased. When federal tax laws eliminated deductions for consumer loan interest and sales tax, buying an automobile had fewer financial benefits and leasing became more attractive. *Leasing* is a contractual agreement with monthly payments for the use of an automobile over a set time period, typically three, four, or five years. At the end of the lease term, the vehicle is usually returned to the leasing company.

### Advantages of Leasing

The main advantages of leasing a vehicle include the following:

- Leasing requires only a small cash outflow for the security deposit, usually amounting to two monthly payments, whereas buying can require a large cash outflow for the purchase price or a down payment.
- The monthly lease payments are usually lower than monthly financing payments for a purchased automobile.
- The lease agreement provides detailed records for people who use their automobiles for business purposes.

## Disadvantages of Leasing

Common drawbacks of automobile leasing include the following:

- You have no ownership interest in the vehicle.
- You must meet requirements similar to those for qualifying for credit.
- You may have additional costs for extra mileage, certain repairs, turning the car in early, or even a move to another state.

## Types of Leases

With a *closed-end,* or "walk-away," lease, the most common type, you return the vehicle at the end of the lease after paying any additional costs for damage or extra mileage. This type of lease commits you for the full term; getting out early will probably require a large fee. Since you have no risk with regard to the residual value of the car, your payments are higher with a closed-end lease than with an open-end lease.

An *open-end,* or "finance," lease, which is easier to terminate than a closed-end lease, may require you to pay the difference between the expected value of the leased automobile and the amount for which the leasing company sells it. The current market value will probably be determined by an independent appraiser. If the appraised value is equal to or greater than the estimated ending value specified in the lease, you will not owe an additional amount. However, if the appraised value is less than that value, you will be required to make an *end-of-lease* payment.

The *single-payment* lease allows you to obtain a discount on the motor vehicle rental agreement. The manufacturer or finance company reduces its default risk and administrative costs. You must decide whether the discount available with this prepaid lease is worth the lost earnings (opportunity costs) from savings.

## Financial Aspects of Leasing

When leasing, you arrange for the dealer to sell the vehicle through a financing company. As a result, be sure you know the true cost, including

1. The *capitalized cost,* which is the price of the vehicle. The average car buyer pays about 92 percent of the list price for a vehicle; the average leasing arrangement has a capitalized cost of 96 percent of the list price.
2. The *money factor,* which is the interest rate being paid on the capitalized cost.
3. The monthly payment and number of payments.
4. The *residual value,* or the expected value of the vehicle at the end of the lease. After the final payment, you may need to decide whether to return, keep, or sell the vehicle. If the current market value is greater than the residual value, you may be able to sell it for a profit. If the residual value is less than the market value (which is the typical case), returning the vehicle to the leasing company is usually the best decision. However, you may want to buy the vehicle for continued use.

A recommended guideline for evaluating leases is the "2 percent rule." A two-year, no-money-down lease may be a good deal if the monthly payment is 2 percent or less of the car's suggested retail price. After this guideline is met, you should investigate other terms of the lease.

Individuals who lease automobiles are protected by the Consumer Leasing Act, administered by the Federal Trade Commission, which requires disclosure of various terms and conditions of the leasing agreement (see Exhibit 8–C).

**EXHIBIT 8–C**

Terms and Conditions of an Automobile Lease

### Terms and Conditions of an Automobile Lease

▶ **Initial Costs**
- Security deposit
- Advance payments
- Insurance requirements
- Sales tax and license fees
- "Capitalized cost reduction" (really a down payment) to reduce amount of monthly payments

▶ **Continuing and End-of-Lease Costs**
- Monthly payment
- Length of agreement (number of payments)
- Mileage charges (for exceeding the mileage specified in the lease agreement)
- Charges for excessive wear and tear
- End-of-lease and disposition charges

## Avoiding Lease Traps

When considering a lease agreement for a motor vehicle, beware of the following common pitfalls:

**Sheet 38**

- Not knowing the total cost of the agreement, including the cost of the vehicle, not just the monthly payment.
- Making a larger up-front payment than is required or paying unnecessary add-on costs.
- Negotiating the monthly payment rather than the capitalized cost of the vehicle.
- Not having the value of any trade-in vehicle reflected in the lease.
- Signing a contract you don't understand.

Compare monthly payments and other terms among several leasing companies. People have been known to pay over $24,000 to lease a vehicle worth only $20,000 at the start of the lease agreement. Comparison of leasing terms is available at websites such as www.leasesource.com. For further information see Appendix B. The Financial Planning Calculations feature on page 272 provides a guideline for comparing buying and leasing.

## FINANCIAL ASPECTS OF AUTOMOBILE OWNERSHIP

Most people spend more of their income on transportation than on any other item except housing and food. For many households, when insurance, license plates, and road taxes are included, the amount spent on an automobile also exceeds the amount spent on food. Over a period of 50 years, you can expect to spend over $200,000 on automobile costs, more than seven times the amount an average person spends on education.

## Automobile Operating Costs

Your driving costs will vary based on two main factors: the size of your automobile and the number of miles you drive. The American Automobile Association recently estimated that, given an annual mileage of 10,000, a subcompact would cost over 40 cents

# Financial Planning Calculations

## BUYING VERSUS LEASING AN AUTOMOBILE

To compare the costs of purchasing and leasing a vehicle, use the following framework.

| Purchase Costs | Example | Your Figures |
|---|---|---|
| Total vehicle cost, including sales tax ($15,000) | | |
| Down payment (or full amount if paying cash) | $2,000 | $_____ |
| Monthly loan payment: $336 × 48-month length of financing (this item is zero if vehicle is not financed) | 16,128 | _____ |
| Opportunity cost of down payment (or total cost of the vehicle if it is bought for cash): $2,000 × 4 years of financing/ownership × 6 percent | 480 | _____ |
| Less: Estimated value of vehicle at end of loan term/ownership period | 23,000 − | _____ |
| Total cost to buy | $15,608 | |

| Leasing Costs | Example | Your Figures |
|---|---|---|
| Security deposit ($300) Monthly lease payments: $300 × 48-month length of lease | $14,400 | $_____ |
| Opportunity cost of security deposit: $300 security deposit × 4 years × 6 percent | 72 | _____ |
| End-of-lease charges (if applicable)* | 1,500 | _____ |
| Total cost to lease | $15,972 | |

*With a closed-end lease, charges for extra mileage or excessive wear and tear; with an open-end lease, end-of-lease payment if appraised value is less than estimated ending value.

a mile, a midsize car nearly 50 cents, and a full-size car over 60 cents. These cost estimates are obtained by considering two categories of expenses:

| Fixed Ownership Costs | Variable Operating Costs |
|---|---|
| Depreciation | Gasoline and oil |
| Interest on auto loan | Tires |
| Insurance | Maintenance and repairs |
| License, registration, taxes, and fees | Parking and tolls |

Fixed Ownership Costs    The largest fixed expense associated with a new automobile is *depreciation,* the loss in the vehicle's value due to time and use. For example, federal tax guidelines assume a motor vehicle depreciates 52 percent during the first two years of its expected five-year life. For a $15,000 car, that means someone who can deduct the cost of the vehicle for tax purposes would have $7,800 in business expenses over the first two years.

Since money is not paid out for depreciation, many people do not consider it an expense. However, this decreased value of an automobile is a cost that owners incur.

While depreciation is considered a fixed cost of automobile ownership, the actual amount of the decreased value depends on two factors: (1) the extent to which the automobile is used and (2) the care taken to maintain it. Low-mileage, well-maintained automobiles retain a larger portion of their original value than do other automobiles. Also, certain high-quality, expensive models, such as BMWs and Lexus, depreciate at a slower rate than other models. Not all automobiles depreciate. Very old vehicles in excellent condition may even *appreciate*, or increase in value.

Another fixed ownership cost is the interest charged when financing an automobile purchase. This charge is based on the loan amount, the interest rate, and the length of the loan. Other fixed costs associated with automobile ownership are insurance, license and registration fees, and taxes. Fixed costs are easier to anticipate than variable costs.

**Sheet 39**

### Variable Operating Costs
Costs such as gasoline, oil, and tires increase with the number of miles an automobile is driven. Planning for these expenses is easier if the number of miles you drive during a given period of time is fairly constant. Unexpected trips will increase such costs.

As a car gets older, maintenance and repair costs usually increase. Expect to replace relatively low-priced components such as fan belts, hoses, the battery, or the muffler. Budgeting an amount for more costly repairs, such as repair of brakes, can minimize the financial burden.

### Automobile Expense Records
Awareness of the total cost of owning and operating an automobile can help your overall financial planning. An automobile expense record should include the dates of odometer readings. Recording your mileage each time you buy gas will allow you to compute fuel efficiency. For tax-deductible travel, the Internal Revenue Service requires specific information about the mileage, locations, dates, and purposes of trips. Use a notebook to keep records of regular operating expenses such as gas, oil, parking, and tolls. Also, consider keeping files on maintenance, repair, and replacement part costs. Finally, keep a record of infrequent expenditures such as insurance payments and license and registration fees (see Exhibit 8–D).

## Proper Maintenance

People who sell, repair, or drive automobiles for a living stress the importance of regular vehicle care. While owner's manuals and articles suggest mileage or time intervals for certain servicing, more frequent oil changes or tune-ups can minimize major repairs and maximize the life of your car.

Automotive systems that should be monitored and maintained on a regular basis are the engine, cooling system, transmission, brakes, steering mechanism, exhaust components, and suspension. Exhibit 8–E presents additional details on automobile maintenance. This list is not intended to be a complete guide; however, it should serve as a reminder of areas that could result in expensive problems.

## Automobile Servicing Sources

A variety of businesses offer automobile maintenance and repair service.

### Car Dealers
The service department of a car dealer offers a wide range of car care services. Since car dealers are required to perform routine maintenance, major repairs, and body work, they have a complete inventory of parts for most vehicles. Service charges at a car dealer may be higher than those of other repair businesses.

### Service Stations
Gas stations may provide convenience and reasonable prices for routine maintenance and repairs. However, the number of full-service stations has declined due to lower profits and competition from other automobile servicing businesses. Today most people buy gas at a combination gas station and convenience store. For automobile servicing, drivers must consider other alternatives.

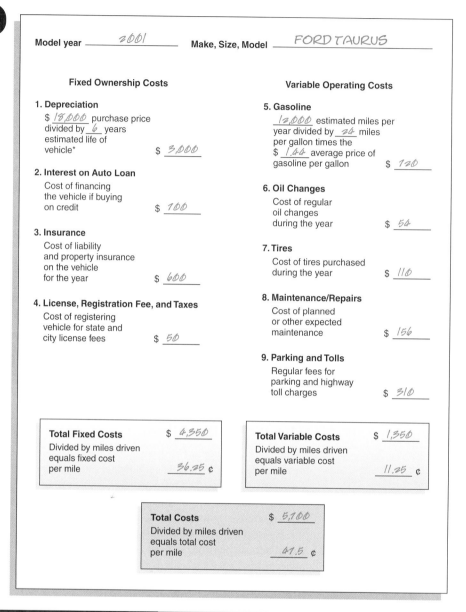

## EXHIBIT 8-D

### Estimating Annual Automobile Ownership and Operating Costs

*This estimate of vehicle depreciation is based on a *straight-line* approach—equal depreciation each year. A more realistic approach would be larger amounts in the early years of ownership, such as 25 to 30 percent the first year and 30 to 35 percent the second year. Most cars lose 90 percent of their value by the time they are seven years old.

Model year ____2001____          Make, Size, Model ____FORD TAURUS____

**Fixed Ownership Costs**

**1. Depreciation**
$ _18,000_ purchase price
divided by _6_ years
estimated life of
vehicle*                                $ _3,000_

**2. Interest on Auto Loan**
Cost of financing
the vehicle if buying
on credit                               $ _100_

**3. Insurance**
Cost of liability
and property insurance
on the vehicle
for the year                            $ _600_

**4. License, Registration Fee, and Taxes**
Cost of registering
vehicle for state and
city license fees                       $ _50_

**Variable Operating Costs**

**5. Gasoline**
_12,000_ estimated miles per
year divided by _24_ miles
per gallon times the
$ _1.44_ average price of
gasoline per gallon          $ _120_

**6. Oil Changes**
Cost of regular
oil changes
during the year              $ _54_

**7. Tires**
Cost of tires purchased
during the year              $ _110_

**8. Maintenance/Repairs**
Cost of planned
or other expected
maintenance                  $ _156_

**9. Parking and Tolls**
Regular fees for
parking and highway
toll charges                 $ _310_

**Total Fixed Costs**          $ _4,350_
Divided by miles driven
equals fixed cost
per mile                       _36.25_ ¢

**Total Variable Costs**       $ _1,350_
Divided by miles driven
equals variable cost
per mile                       _11.25_ ¢

**Total Costs**                $ _5,700_
Divided by miles driven
equals total cost
per mile                       _47.5_ ¢

## Automobile Repair Shops

Independent repair shops serve a wide variety of automobile servicing needs at fairly competitive prices. As with any service, the quality of these repair shops varies. Talk with previous customers before selecting a repair shop.

## Department and Discount Stores

Mass merchandise retailers such as Sears and Wal-Mart offer convenient automobile service. These retailers usually emphasize the sale of tires, batteries, mufflers, and other replacement parts. They also replace brakes and do oil changes and tune-ups.

**EXHIBIT 8–E**

**EXTENDED VEHICLE LIFE THROUGH PROPER MAINTENANCE**

- Get regular oil changes
- Check fluids (brake, power steering, transmission)
- Inspect hoses and belts for wear
- Get a tune-up (new spark plugs, fuel filter, air filter) 12,000–15,000 miles
- Check and clean battery cables and terminals
- Check spark plug wires after 50,000 miles
- Flush radiator and service transmission every 25,000 miles
- Keep lights, turn signals, and horn in good working condition
- Check muffler and exhaust pipes
- Check tires for wear; rotate tires every 7,500 miles
- Check condition of brakes

**Specialty Shops**   These businesses offer a single product or service at a reasonable price with fast service. Mufflers, tires, automatic transmissions, and oil changes are among the items these limited-service businesses provide.

Since automobile maintenance and repairs can be expensive, be sure to seek out competent service for your money. To avoid unnecessary expenses, be aware of the common repair frauds presented in Exhibit 8–F. Remember to deal with reputable auto service businesses. Be sure to get a written, detailed estimate in advance as well as a detailed, paid receipt for the service completed. Studies of consumer problems consistently rank auto repairs as one of the top consumer ripoffs.

Many people avoid problems and minimize costs by working on their own vehicles. This can save money for routine maintenance and minor repairs such as oil changes, tune-ups, and replacement of belts, hoses, and batteries. Many books on automobile servicing are available. Some high schools and community colleges offer basic automobile maintenance courses.

## Selling Your Automobile

At some time, you may be on the selling side of an automobile transaction. The selling process starts with awareness of documents you must file with your state vehicle registration department. Contact this agency to obtain the necessary forms as well as information about the regulations that affect the sale of an automobile.

**EXHIBIT 8–F**

**Common Automobile Repair Frauds**

The majority of automobile servicing sources are fair and honest. Sometimes, however, consumers waste dollars when they fall prey to the following tricks:

- When checking the oil, the attendant puts the dipstick only partway down and then shows you that you need oil.
- An attendant cuts a fan belt or punctures a hose. Watch carefully when someone checks under your hood.
- A garage employee puts some liquid on your battery and then tries to convince you that it is leaking and you need a new battery.
- Removing air from a tire instead of adding air to it can make an unwary driver open to buying a new tire or paying for an unneeded patch on a tire that is in perfect condition.
- The attendant puts grease near a shock absorber or on the ground and then tells you your present shocks are dangerous and you need new ones.
- You are charged for two gallons of antifreeze with a radiator flush when only one gallon was put in.

Dealing with reputable businesses and a basic knowledge of your automobile are the best methods of avoiding deceptive repair practices.

Use current advertisements in local newspapers, along with the used-car price guides, to assist you in setting a sales price. Maintenance and minor repairs will help improve the vehicle's appearance and increase its customer appeal.

Next, make others aware of the car. Put a "for sale" sign, with a telephone number on it, in a location that will allow many people to see it. Information about the car can be distributed through store, church, or community bulletin boards, and in advertisements in local newspapers.

Ask people who express interest in buying your car to provide you with their addresses and telephone numbers, and have them make appointments to see and test-drive the car. As a precaution, be sure to accompany prospective buyers on the road test. If you have kept a file of maintenance and repair receipts, use this information to document the condition of the car.

When completing the transaction, be sure to meet the necessary legal requirements, such as payment of title, vehicle registration, and other fees. To avoid getting a bad check or handling large amounts of cash, insist that the car be paid for with a cashier's check or a money order. Provide the buyer with a receipt containing the details of the transaction.

# The Housing Decision: Factors and Finances

## Two Can Buy More Cheaply Than One

During a time when mortgage rates were fairly high, Nina Cortez and her sister, Cathy, were unable to buy the house they wanted. Their parents had given them $4,000 for a down payment, but that was not enough for the type of house they wanted.

After finishing college, Nina rented an apartment for seven years. During that time, she was able to save $8,000 for a down payment on a home. Also, she now earns enough money to afford the monthly costs of a home.

During the past eight months, mortgage rates in their area of the country have declined 1.5 percentage points. Nina and Cathy have decided to combine their resources to purchase a home. The *co-ownership* arrangement allows them to buy a home valued at $15,000 more than they could have afforded a year ago.

However, Nina and Cathy should ask themselves a few questions before buying the house. What happens to the house if one of them marries or accepts a job transfer to another city? What if one of them can no longer meet the financial requirements of the home? How will they share maintenance responsibilities and costs?

Nina and Cathy need to answer these and other questions before entering a co-ownership housing arrangement.

### Questions

1. What factors affect a person's ability to buy a house?
2. What are common sources for a down payment? Why should home buyers not use all of their savings to make the down payment on a home?
3. What problems could arise in a co-ownership housing arrangement?
4. Locate websites that provide housing information that would be of value to Nina and Cathy during their home-buying activities.

SOURCES: Deborah Donovan, "New Loan Options for Home Buyers," *Daily Herald* (Arlington Heights, IL), August 4, 1999, sec. 7, pp. 1–2; Galina Espinoza, "Are Two Homes Better Than One?" *Money,* August 1999, pp. 98–102; Doug Levy, "Net Takes Legwork Out of House Hunt," *USA Today,* July 20, 1999, p. 3B; Sara Nathan, "Twenty-Somethings Buying Homes," *USA Today,* April 8, 1999, p. 3B.

## Learning Objectives

**Obj. 1**   Evaluate available housing alternatives.

**Obj. 2**   Analyze the costs and benefits associated with renting.

**Obj. 3**   Implement the home-buying process.

**Obj. 4**   Calculate the costs associated with purchasing a home.

**Obj. 5**   Develop a strategy for selling a home.

## EVALUATING HOUSING ALTERNATIVES

**Obj. 1**
Evaluate available housing alternatives.

**Sheet 40**

As you walk around various neighborhoods, you are likely to see a variety of housing types. When you assess housing alternatives, you need to identify the factors that will influence your choice.

### Your Lifestyle and Your Choice of Housing

While the concept of lifestyle—how you spend your time and money—may seem intangible, it materializes in consumer purchases. Every buying decision is a statement about your lifestyle. Your lifestyle, needs, desires, and attitudes are reflected in your choice of a place to live. For example, some people want a kitchen large enough for family gatherings. Career-oriented people may want a lavish bathroom or a home spa where they can escape the pressures of work. As you select housing, you might consider the alternatives in Exhibit 9–1 on page 280.

While personal preferences are the foundation of a housing decision, financial factors may modify the final choice. Traditional financial guidelines suggest that "you should spend no more than 25 or 30 percent of your take-home pay on housing" or "your home should cost about 2½ times your annual income." While changes in our economy and our society no longer make these guidelines completely valid, you need some sort of financial guideline to determine the amount to spend on housing. A budget and other financial records discussed in Chapter 3 can help you evaluate your income, living costs, and other financial obligations to determine an appropriate amount for your housing expenses.

### Opportunity Costs of Housing Choices

Although the selection of housing is usually based on life situation and financial factors, you should also consider what you might have to give up. While the opportunity costs of your housing decision will vary, some common trade-offs include

- The interest earnings lost on the money used for a down payment on a home or the security deposit for an apartment.

- The time and cost of commuting to work when you live in an area that offers less expensive housing or more living space.

**EXHIBIT 9-1**

Possible Housing for Different Life Situations

| Life Situation | Possible Housing Types |
|---|---|
| Young single | Rental housing requires limited maintenance activities and offers mobility in the event of a job transfer |
| | Purchase a home or a condominium for financial and tax benefits |
| Single parent | Rental housing provides a suitable environment for children and some degree of home security |
| | Purchase low-maintenance housing that meets the financial and social needs of family members |
| Young couple, no children | Rental housing offers convenience and flexibility of lifestyle |
| | Purchase housing for financial benefits and to build long-term financial security |
| Couple, young children | Rental housing can provide appropriate facilities for children in a family-oriented area |
| | Purchase a home to meet financial and other family needs |
| Couple, children no longer at home | Rental housing offers convenience and flexibility for changing needs and financial situations |
| | Purchase housing that requires minimal maintenance and meets lifestyle needs |
| Retired person | Rental housing can meet financial, social, and physical needs |
| | Purchase housing that requires minimal maintenance, offers convenience, and provides needed services |

- The loss of tax advantages and equity growth when you rent a city apartment to be close to your work.
- The time and money you spend when you repair and improve a lower-priced home.
- The time and effort involved when you have a home built to your personal specifications.

Like every other financial choice, a housing decision requires consideration of what you give up in time, effort, and money.

## Renting versus Buying Housing

The choice between renting and buying your residence should be analyzed based on lifestyle and financial factors. Exhibit 9–2 can help you assess renting and buying alternatives. Mobility is a primary motivator of renters, while buyers usually want permanence.

As you can see in the Financial Planning Calculations feature on page 282, the choice between renting and buying usually is not clear-cut. In general, renting is less costly in the short run, but homeownership usually has long-term financial advantages.

## Housing Information Sources

As with other consumer purchases, housing information is available. Start your data search with basic resources such as this book and books available in libraries. Consult the real estate section of your newspaper for articles about renting, buying, financing, remodeling, and other housing topics. Other helpful information sources are friends, real estate agents, and government agencies (see Appendix B).

Sheet 41

**EXHIBIT 9-2**

Evaluating
Housing
Alternatives

**EVALUATING
HOUSING ALTERNATIVES**

**Renting**
Apartment

| Advantages | Disadvantages |
|---|---|
| • Easy to move<br>• Fewer responsibilities for maintenance<br>• Minimal financial commitment | • No tax benefits<br>• Limitations regarding remodeling<br>• May have restrictions regarding pets, other activities |

**Renting**
House

| Advantages | Disadvantages |
|---|---|
| • Easy to move; less maintenance<br>• More room than apartment<br>• Minimal financial commitment | • Higher utility expenses than apartment<br>• Limitations regarding remodeling |

**Owning**
New house

| Advantages | Disadvantages |
|---|---|
| • No previous owner<br>• Pride of ownership<br>• Tax benefits | • Financial commitment<br>• Higher living expenses than renting<br>• Limited mobility |

**Owning**
Previously owned house

| Advantages | Disadvantages |
|---|---|
| • Pride of ownership<br>• Established neighborhood<br>• Tax benefits | • Financial commitment<br>• Possibility of repairs or replacements<br>• Limited mobility |

**Owning**
Condominium

| Advantages | Disadvantages |
|---|---|
| • Tax benefits<br>• Fewer maintenance responsibilities than house<br>• Usually good accessibility to recreation and business districts | • Less privacy than house<br>• Financial commitment<br>• Uncertain demand affecting property value<br>• Potential disagreements with condominium association regarding rules<br>• Assessment fees |

**Owning**
Cooperative

| Advantages | Disadvantages |
|---|---|
| • Ownership in form of nonprofit organization<br>• Stable property values | • Frequently difficult to sell<br>• Potential disagreements among members<br>• Other members may have to cover costs of unrented units |

**Owning**
Manufactured home (mobile home)

| Advantages | Disadvantages |
|---|---|
| • Less expensive than other ownership options<br>• Flexibility in selection of home features and appliances | • May be difficult to sell in future<br>• Financing may be difficult to obtain<br>• Construction quality may be poor |

# Financial Planning Calculations

## RENTING VERSUS BUYING YOUR PLACE OF RESIDENCE

Comparing the costs of renting and buying involves consideration of a variety of factors. The following framework and example provide a basis for assessing these two housing alternatives. The apartment in the example has a monthly rent of $700, and the home costs $85,000. A 28 percent tax rate is assumed.

Although the numbers in this example favor buying, remember that in any financial decision, calculations provide only part of the answer. You should also consider your needs and values and assess the opportunity costs associated with renting and buying.

|  | Example | Your Figures |
|---|---|---|
| **Rental Costs** | | |
| Annual rent payments | $ 8,400 | $ _____ |
| Renter's insurance | 170 | _____ |
| Interest lost on security deposit (amount of security deposit | | |
|   times after-tax savings account interest rate) | 80 | _____ |
|   Total annual cost of renting . . . . . . . . . . . . . . . . . . . . . . . . . . | $ 8,650 | |
| **Buying Costs** | | |
| Annual mortgage payments | $10,500 | _____ |
| Property taxes (annual costs) | 2,000 | _____ |
| Homeowner's insurance (annual premium) | 400 | _____ |
| Estimated maintenance and repairs (1%) | 850 | _____ |
| After-tax interest lost on down payment and closing costs | 1,030 | _____ |
| *Less* (financial benefits of home ownership): | | |
|   Growth in equity | 264 | – _____ |
|   Tax savings for mortgage interest (annual mortgage interest times tax rate) | 2,866 | – _____ |
|   Tax savings for property taxes (annual property taxes times tax rate) | 560 | – _____ |
|   Estimated annual appreciation (3%)* | 2,550 | – _____ |
|   Total annual cost of buying . . . . . . . . . . . . . . . . . . . . . . . . . . | $ 8,540 | _____ |

*This is a nationwide average; actual appreciation of property will vary by geographic area and economic conditions.

The World Wide Web has become an important source of housing information. In addition to providing home-buying tips and mortgage rates, online sites can be used to access available housing in an area (see the Financial Planning for Life's Situations feature on page 283).

## Concept Check 9–1

1. How does a person's employment and household situation influence the selection of housing?
2. What are some common opportunity costs associated with the selection of housing?

## Financial Planning for Life's Situations

### USING THE INTERNET FOR HOME BUYING

Instead of getting in the car on Sunday afternoon to go house hunting, home buyers are going online. The Web offers many home-buying services including the following:

- *Planning your home purchase online:* Information on the basics of home buying may be obtained at www.homefair.com, www.homes.wsj.com, www.homebuyer.com, www.realestate.com, www.homeadvisor.msn.com, and www.mortgage.quicken.com.

- *Cyber-info for finding a home:* Homes available for sale in your area and in other areas of the country may be accessed at www.realtor.com, www.century 21.com, www.remax.com, and www.ads4homes. com, as well as at websites for major newspapers such as www.chicagotribune.com.

- *Comparing mortgage rates:* To compare current rates from various mortgage sources, go to www. bankrate.com, www.amo-mortgage.com, www.hsh. com, or www.homeshark.com.

- *Applying for a mortgage online:* Instead of waiting days and even weeks, prospective home buyers can now obtain financing online at www.eloan.com and www.lendingtree.com.

- *Selling your own home:* Information about selling your home without a real estate agent may be obtained at www.owners.com.

- *Housing complaints:* If you don't have a "home, sweet home," you can contact the Department of Housing at www.hud.gov.

## RENTING YOUR RESIDENCE

### Obj. 2
Analyze the costs and benefits associated with renting.

Are you interested in a "2-bd. garden apt, a/c, crptg, mod bath, lndry, sec $850"? Not sure? Translated, this means a two-bedroom garden apartment (at or below ground level) with air conditioning, carpeting, a modern bath, and laundry facilities. An $850 security deposit is required.

At some point in your life, you are likely to rent your place of residence. You may rent when you are first on your own or later in life when you want to avoid the activities required to maintain your own home. About 35 percent of U.S. households live in rental units.

As a tenant, you pay for the right to live in a residence owned by someone else. Exhibit 9–3 on page 284 presents the activities involved in finding and living in a rental unit.

### Selecting a Rental Unit

An apartment is the most common type of rental housing. Apartments range from modern, luxury units with extensive recreational facilities to simple one- and two-bedroom units in quiet neighborhoods.

If you need more room, you should consider renting a house. The increased space will cost more, and you will probably have some responsibility for maintaining the property. If you need less space, you may rent a room in a private house.

The main sources of information on available rental units are newspaper ads, real estate and rental offices, and people you know. When comparing rental units, consider the factors presented in Exhibit 9–4 on page 285.

### Advantages of Renting

The three main advantages of renting are mobility, fewer responsibilities, and lower initial costs.

Housing Rental Activities

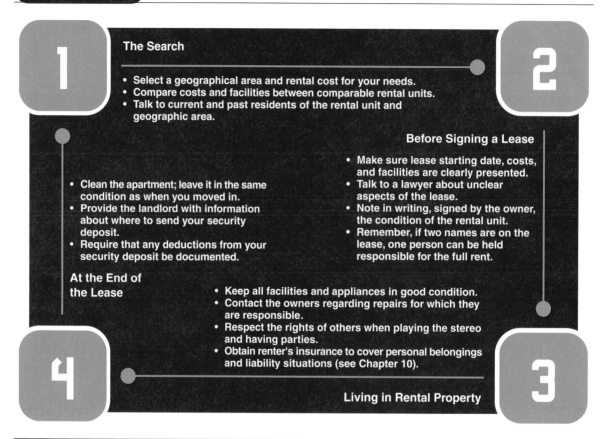

**1**

**The Search**

- Select a geographical area and rental cost for your needs.
- Compare costs and facilities between comparable rental units.
- Talk to current and past residents of the rental unit and geographic area.

**2**

**Before Signing a Lease**

- Make sure lease starting date, costs, and facilities are clearly presented.
- Talk to a lawyer about unclear aspects of the lease.
- Note in writing, signed by the owner, the condition of the rental unit.
- Remember, if two names are on the lease, one person can be held responsible for the full rent.

- Clean the apartment; leave it in the same condition as when you moved in.
- Provide the landlord with information about where to send your security deposit.
- Require that any deductions from your security deposit be documented.

**At the End of the Lease**

- Keep all facilities and appliances in good condition.
- Contact the owners regarding repairs for which they are responsible.
- Respect the rights of others when playing the stereo and having parties.
- Obtain renter's insurance to cover personal belongings and liability situations (see Chapter 10).

**Living in Rental Property**

**4**

**3**

Mobility    Renting offers mobility when a location change is necessary or desirable. A new job, a rent increase, the need for a larger apartment, or the desire to live in a different community can make relocation necessary. It is easier to move when you are renting than when you own a home. After you have completed school and started your career, renting makes it easier for job transfers.

Fewer Responsibilities    Renters have fewer responsibilities than homeowners since they usually do not have to be concerned with maintenance and repairs. However, they are expected to do regular household cleaning. Renters also have fewer financial concerns. Their main housing costs are rent and utilities, while homeowners incur expenses related to property taxes, property insurance, and upkeep.

Lower Initial Costs    It is less expensive to take possession of a rental unit than to buy a home. While new tenants usually pay a security deposit, a new home buyer is likely to have a down payment and closing costs of several thousand dollars.

## Disadvantages of Renting

Renting has few financial benefits, may impose a restricted lifestyle, and involve legal details.

EXHIBIT 9-4

Selecting an
Apartment

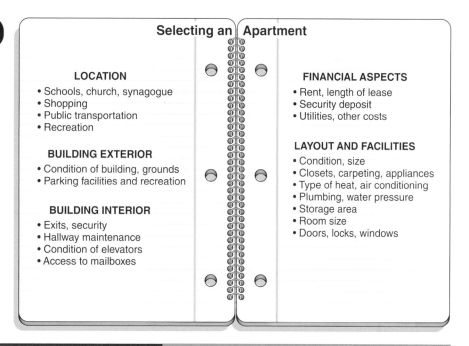

**Selecting an Apartment**

**LOCATION**
• Schools, church, synagogue
• Shopping
• Public transportation
• Recreation

**BUILDING EXTERIOR**
• Condition of building, grounds
• Parking facilities and recreation

**BUILDING INTERIOR**
• Exits, security
• Hallway maintenance
• Condition of elevators
• Access to mailboxes

**FINANCIAL ASPECTS**
• Rent, length of lease
• Security deposit
• Utilities, other costs

**LAYOUT AND FACILITIES**
• Condition, size
• Closets, carpeting, appliances
• Type of heat, air conditioning
• Plumbing, water pressure
• Storage area
• Room size
• Doors, locks, windows

**Few Financial Benefits**     Renters do not enjoy the financial advantages home-owners do. Tenants cannot take tax deductions for mortgage interest and property taxes or benefit from the increased value of real estate. They are subject to rent increases over which they have little control.

**Restricted Lifestyle**     Renters are generally limited in the types of activities they can pursue in their place of residence. Noise from a stereo system or parties may be monitored closely. Tenants are often subject to restrictions regarding pets and decorating the property.

*lease  A legal document that defines the conditions of a rental agreement.*

**Legal Details**     Most tenants sign a **lease,** a legal document that defines the conditions of a rental agreement. This document provides the following information:

* A description of the property, including the address.
* The name and address of the owner/landlord (the *lessor*).
* The name of the tenant (the *lessee*).
* The effective date of the lease.
* The length of the lease.
* The amount of the security deposit.
* The amount and due date of the monthly rent.
* The location at which the rent must be paid.
* The date and amount due of charges for late rent payments.
* A list of the utilities, appliances, furniture, or other facilities that are included in the rental amount.
* The restrictions regarding certain activities (pets, remodeling).
* The tenant's right to sublet the rental unit.
* The charges for damages or for moving out of the rental unit later (or earlier) than the lease expiration date.
* The conditions under which the landlord may enter the apartment.

Standard lease forms include conditions you may not want to accept. The fact that a lease is printed does not mean you must accept it as is. Negotiate with the landlord about lease terms you consider unacceptable.

Some leases give you the right to *sublet* the rental unit. Subletting may be necessary if you must vacate the premises before the lease expires. Subletting allows you to have another person take over rent payments and live in the rental unit.

Most leases are written, but oral leases are also valid. With an oral lease, one party must give a 30-day written notice to the other party before terminating the lease or imposing a rent increase.

A lease provides protection to both landlord and tenant. The tenant is protected from rent increases during the lease term unless the lease contains a provision allowing an increase. In most states, the tenant cannot be locked out or evicted without a court hearing. The lease gives the landlord the right to take legal action against a tenant for nonpayment of rent or destruction of property.

## Costs of Renting

A *security deposit* is usually required when you sign a lease. This money is held by the landlord to cover the cost of any damages done to the rental unit during the lease period. The security deposit is usually one month's rent.

Several state and local governments require that the landlord pay interest on a security deposit. After you vacate the rental unit, your security deposit should be refunded within a reasonable time. Many states require that it be returned within 30 days of the end of the lease. If money is deducted from your security deposit, you have the right to an itemized list of the cost of repairs.

As a renter, you will incur other living expenses besides monthly rent. For many apartments, water is covered by the rent; however, other utilities may not be covered. If you rent a house, you will probably pay for heat, electricity, water, and telephone. When you rent, you should obtain insurance coverage for your personal property. Renter's insurance is discussed in Chapter 10.

**? Did You Know** Renter's insurance is one of the most overlooked expenses of apartment dwellers. Damage or theft of personal property (clothing, furniture, stereo equipment, jewelry) usually is not covered by the landlord's insurance policy.

**PFP Sheet 42**

### Concept Check 9-2

1.   What are the main benefits and drawbacks of renting a place of residence?
2.   Which components of a lease are likely to be most negotiable?

# THE HOME-BUYING PROCESS

**Obj. 3**
Implement the home-buying process.

Many people dream of having a place of residence they can call their own. Homeownership is a common financial goal. Exhibit 9–5 presents the process for achieving this goal.

## Step 1: Determine Homeownership Needs

In the first phase of the home-buying process, you should consider the benefits and drawbacks of this major financial commitment. Also, evaluate different types of housing units and determine the amount you can afford.

### Evaluate Owning Your Place of Residence

What Are the Benefits of Homeownership?   Whether you purchase a house, a condominium, or a manufactured home, you can enjoy the pride of ownership, financial benefits, and lifestyle flexibility of homeownership.

**EXHIBIT 9-5**        The Home-Buying Process

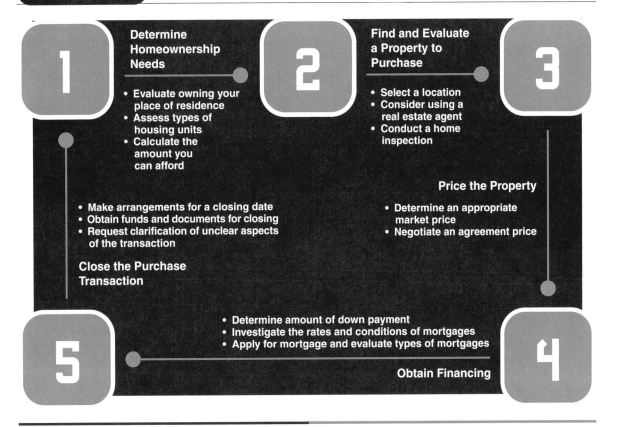

**1**  Determine Homeownership Needs

- Evaluate owning your place of residence
- Assess types of housing units
- Calculate the amount you can afford

**2**

**3**  Find and Evaluate a Property to Purchase

- Select a location
- Consider using a real estate agent
- Conduct a home inspection

**Price the Property**

- Determine an appropriate market price
- Negotiate an agreement price

**Close the Purchase Transaction**

- Make arrangements for a closing date
- Obtain funds and documents for closing
- Request clarification of unclear aspects of the transaction

**5**

**Obtain Financing**

- Determine amount of down payment
- Investigate the rates and conditions of mortgages
- Apply for mortgage and evaluate types of mortgages

**4**

1. *Pride of ownership.* Having a place to call their own is a primary motive of many home buyers. Stability of residence and a personalized living location can be important.

2. *Financial benefits.* One financial benefit is the deductibility of mortgage interest and real estate tax payments for federal income taxes. A potential benefit is increases in the value of the property. Finally, homeowners in most states may be able to borrow against the equity in their homes. *Equity* is the home value less the amount owed on the mortgage.

3. *Lifestyle flexibility.* While renting gives you mobility, homeownership gives you more opportunity to express individuality. Homeowners have greater freedom than renters in decorating their dwellings and entertaining guests.

**What Are the Drawbacks of Homeownership?**   The American dream of buying one's own home does not guarantee a glamorous existence. This investment can result in financial uncertainty, limited mobility, and higher living costs.

1. *Financial uncertainty.* Among the financial uncertainties associated with buying a home is obtaining money for a down payment. Obtaining mortgage financing may be a problem due to your personal situation or current economic conditions. Finally, changing property values in an area can affect your financial investment.

2. *Limited mobility.* Homeownership does not provide ease of changing living location as does renting. If changes in your situation make it necessary to sell your home, doing so may be difficult. High interest rates and other factors can result in a weak demand for housing.

**3.** *Higher living costs.* Owning your place of residence can be expensive. The homeowner is responsible for maintenance and costs of repainting, repairs, and home improvements.

Real estate taxes are a major expense of homeowners. Higher property values and higher tax rates mean higher real estate taxes. Higher taxes affect homeowners more directly than renters, who pay them in the form of higher rent. It is harder for homeowners to counter the effects of high taxes by moving to less expensive housing.

## Assess Types of Housing Available

Seven common options are available to home buyers:

**1.** *Single-family dwellings* are the most popular form of housing. These residences include previously owned houses, new houses, and custom-built houses. Older houses may be preferred by people who want a certain style and quality of housing.

**2.** *Multiunit dwellings,* dwellings with more than one living unit, include duplexes and townhouses. A *duplex* is a building that contains two separate homes. A *townhouse* contains two, four, or six single-family living units.

*condominium* An individually owned housing unit in a building with several such units.

**3. Condominiums** are individually owned housing units in a building with several units. Individual ownership does not include the common areas, such as hallways, outside grounds, and recreational facilities. These areas are owned by the condominium association, which is run by the people who own the housing units. The condominium association oversees the management and operation of the housing complex. Condominium owners are charged a monthly fee to cover the maintenance, repairs, improvements, and insurance for the building and common areas. A condominium is not a type of building structure; it is a legal form of homeownership.

*cooperative housing* A form of housing in which a building containing a number of housing units is owned by a nonprofit organization whose members rent the units.

**4. Cooperative housing** is a form of housing in which a building containing a number of units is owned by a nonprofit organization whose members rent the units. The living units of a co-op, unlike condominiums, are owned not by the residents but by the co-op. Rents in a co-op can increase quickly if living units become vacant, since the remaining residents must cover the maintenance costs of the building.

*manufactured home* A housing unit that is fully or partially assembled in a factory before being moved to the living site.

**5. Manufactured homes** are housing units that are fully or partially assembled in a factory and then moved to the living site. There are two basic types of manufactured homes. One type is the *prefabricated home,* with components built in a factory and then assembled at the housing site. With this type of housing, mass production can keep building costs lower.

**6.** *Mobile homes* are a second type of manufactured home. Since very few mobile homes are moved from their original sites, the term is not completely accurate. These housing units are typically less than 1,000 square feet in size; however, they usually offer the same features as a conventional house—fully equipped kitchens, fireplaces, cathedral ceilings, and whirlpool baths. The site for a mobile home may be either purchased or leased in a development specifically designed for such housing units.

The safety of mobile homes is continually debated. Fires occur no more frequently in these housing units than in other types of homes. But due to the construction of mobile homes, a fire spreads faster than in conventional houses. Manufacturers' standards for the fire safety of mobile homes are higher than in the past. Still, when a fire occurs in a mobile home, the unit is often completely destroyed. This type of housing is also vulnerable to wind.

Another common concern about mobile homes is their tendency to depreciate in value. When this occurs, an important benefit of homeownership is eliminated. Depreciation may make it difficult to obtain financing to purchase a mobile home.

**7.** *Building a home* is another option. Some people want a home built to their specifications. Before you begin such a project, be sure you possess the necessary knowledge, money, and perseverance. When choosing a contractor to coordinate the project, consider the following:

- Does the contractor have the experience needed to handle the type of building project you require?
- Does the contractor have a good working relationship with the architect, materials suppliers, electricians, plumbers, carpenters, and other personnel needed to complete the project?
- What assurance do you have about the quality of materials?
- What arrangements must be made for payments during construction?
- What delays in the construction process will be considered legitimate?
- Is the contractor licensed and insured?
- Is the contractor willing to provide names, addresses, and phone numbers of satisfied customers?
- Have local consumer agencies received any complaints about this contractor?

Your written contract should include a time schedule, cost estimates, a description of the work, and a payment schedule.

You can save as much as 25 percent of the cost of a new house by supervising its construction. Home-building suppliers and owners of homes under construction can suggest quality tradespeople. Inexpensive blueprints are available from the U.S. Department of Housing and Urban Development; these building plans can save you thousands of dollars in architect fees.

## Determine How Much You Can Afford

As you determine how much of your budget you will spend on a home, consider the price of the house along with its size and quality.

## Price and Down Payment

The amount you can spend is affected by funds available for a down payment, your income, and your current living expenses. Other factors you should consider are current mortgage rates, the potential future value of the property, and your ability to make monthly mortgage, tax, and insurance payments. To determine how much you can afford to spend on a home, have a loan officer at a mortgage company or other financial institution prequalify you. This service is provided without charge.

## Size and Quality

You may not get all the features you want in your first home, but financial advisers suggest you get into the housing market by purchasing what you can afford. As you move up in the housing market, your second or third home can include more of the features you want.

Ideally, the home you buy will be in good condition. In certain circumstances, you may be willing to buy a *handyman's special*, a home that needs work and that you are able to get at a lower price because of its condition. You will then need to put more money into the house for repairs and improvements or to invest *sweat equity* by doing some of the work yourself. Home improvement information and assistance are available from hardware stores and other home product retailers.

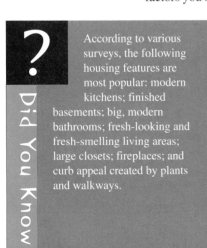

**Did You Know**

According to various surveys, the following housing features are most popular: modern kitchens; finished basements; big, modern bathrooms; fresh-looking and fresh-smelling living areas; large closets; fireplaces; and curb appeal created by plants and walkways.

## Step 2: Find and Evaluate a Property to Purchase

Next, you should select a location, consider using the services of a real estate agent, and conduct a home inspection.

### Selecting a Location

An old adage among real estate people is that the three most important factors to consider when buying a home are *location, location,* and *location!* Perhaps you prefer an urban, a suburban, or a rural setting. Or perhaps you want to live in a small town or in a resort area. In selecting a neighborhood, compare your values and lifestyle with those of current residents.

*zoning laws*   Restrictions on how the property in an area can be used.

Be aware of **zoning laws**, restrictions on how the property in an area can be used. The location of businesses and the anticipated construction of industrial buildings or a highway may influence your buying decision.

If you have or plan to have a family, you should assess the school system. Educators recommend that schools be evaluated on program variety, achievement level of students, percentage of students who go on to college, dedication of faculty members, facilities, school funding, and involvement of parents. Homeowners without children also benefit from strong schools, since the educational advantages of a community help maintain property values.

### Using a Real Estate Agent

A real estate agent can help you assess your housing needs and determine the amount you can afford to spend. Real estate agents have information about areas of interest to you and housing available to buy.

The main services a real estate agent provides include (1) presenting your offer to the seller, (2) negotiating a settlement price, (3) assisting you in obtaining financing, and (4) representing you at the closing. A real estate agent will also recommend lawyers, insurance agents, home inspectors, and mortgage companies to serve your needs.

Since the seller of the home usually pays the real estate agent's commission, the buyer may not incur a direct cost. However, this expense may be reflected in the price paid for the home. In some states, the agent could be working for the seller. In others, the agent may be working for the buyer and may be a *dual agent,* working for both the buyer and the seller. When dual agency exists, some states require that buyers sign a disclosure acknowledging that they are aware the agent is working for both buyer and seller.

Many states now have *buyer agents* who represent the buyer's interests. In these situations, the buyer agent may be paid by either the seller or the buyer.

### Conducting a Home Inspection

Before reaching your decision about a specific home, conduct a complete evaluation of the property. An evaluation by a trained home inspector can minimize future problems. Do not assume everything is in proper working condition because someone lives there now. Being cautious and determined will save you headaches and unplanned expenses.

Some states, cities, and lenders require inspection documents. The mortgage company will usually conduct an *appraisal* to determine the fair market value of the property; although the appraisal is not a detailed inspection, it does help to assess the condition of the home. Exhibit 9–6 presents a detailed format for inspecting a home. A home purchase agreement may include the right to have a contractor or several professionals (roofer, plumber, electrician) inspect the property.

## Step 3: Price the Property

After you have selected a home, determine an offer price and negotiate a final buying price.

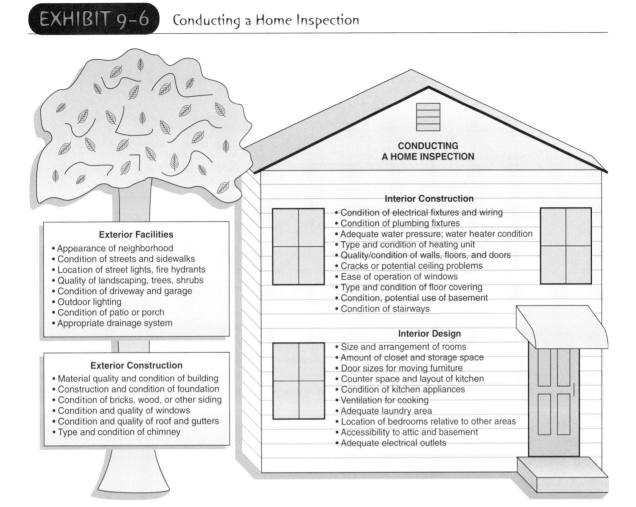

**EXHIBIT 9-6**   Conducting a Home Inspection

CONDUCTING
A HOME INSPECTION

**Interior Construction**
- Condition of electrical fixtures and wiring
- Condition of plumbing fixtures
- Adequate water pressure; water heater condition
- Type and condition of heating unit
- Quality/condition of walls, floors, and doors
- Cracks or potential ceiling problems
- Ease of operation of windows
- Type and condition of floor covering
- Condition, potential use of basement
- Condition of stairways

**Interior Design**
- Size and arrangement of rooms
- Amount of closet and storage space
- Door sizes for moving furniture
- Counter space and layout of kitchen
- Condition of kitchen appliances
- Ventilation for cooking
- Adequate laundry area
- Location of bedrooms relative to other areas
- Accessibility to attic and basement
- Adequate electrical outlets

**Exterior Facilities**
- Appearance of neighborhood
- Condition of streets and sidewalks
- Location of street lights, fire hydrants
- Quality of landscaping, trees, shrubs
- Condition of driveway and garage
- Outdoor lighting
- Condition of patio or porch
- Appropriate drainage system

**Exterior Construction**
- Material quality and condition of building
- Construction and condition of foundation
- Condition of bricks, wood, or other siding
- Condition and quality of windows
- Condition and quality of roof and gutters
- Type and condition of chimney

**Determining the Home Price**    What price should you offer for the home? The main factors to consider are recent selling prices in the area, current demand for housing, the length of time the home has been on the market, the owner's need to sell, financing options, and features and condition of the home. Each of these factors can affect your offer price. For example, you will have to offer a higher price in times of low interest rates and high demand for homes. On the other hand, a home that has been on the market for over a year could mean an opportunity to offer a lower price. The services of a real estate agent or an appraiser can assist you in assessing the current value of the home.

Your offer will be in the form of a *purchase agreement*, or contract (see Exhibit 9–7). This document constitutes your legal offer to purchase the home. Your first offer price usually will not be accepted.

**Negotiating the Purchase Price**    If your initial offer is accepted, you have a valid contract. If your offer is rejected, you have several options, depending on the seller. A *counteroffer* from the owner indicates a willingness to negotiate a price settlement. If the counteroffer is only slightly lower than the asking price, you are expected

## EXHIBIT 9-7

### The Components of a Home Purchase Agreement

SOURCE: *Homeownership: Guidelines for Buying and Owning a Home* (Richmond, VA: Federal Reserve Bank of Richmond).

**Components of a Home Purchase Agreement**

In a real estate transaction, the contract between buyer and seller contains the following information:

- ❏ The names and addresses of the buyer and seller
- ❏ A description of the property
- ❏ The price of the property
- ❏ The amount of the mortgage that will be needed
- ❏ The amount of the earnest money deposit
- ❏ The date and time of the closing
- ❏ Where the closing will take place
- ❏ A provision for extension of the closing date

- ❏ A provision for disposition of the deposit money if something goes wrong
- ❏ Adjustments to be made at the closing
- ❏ Details of what is included in the sale—home appliances, drapes, carpeting, and other items
- ❏ Special conditions of the sale
- ❏ Inspections the buyer can make before the closing
- ❏ Property easements, such as the use of an area of the property for utility lines or poles

to move closer to that price with your next offer. If the counteroffer is quite a bit off the asking price, you are closer to the point where you might split the difference to arrive at the purchase price. If no counteroffer is forthcoming, you may wish to make another offer to see whether the seller is willing to do any negotiating. Be cautious in your negotiations if the seller is using a buyer agent. Remember, in that situation, the agent represents the interests of the seller.

In times of high demand for housing, negotiating may be minimized; this situation is referred to as a *seller's market,* since the current homeowner is likely to have several offers for the property. In contrast, when home sales are slow, a *buyer's market* exists and a lower price is likely.

When you buy a previously owned home, your negotiating power is based on current market demand and the current owner's need to sell. When you buy a new home, a slow market may mean lower prices or an opportunity to obtain various amenities (fireplace, higher-quality carpeting) from the builder at a lower cost.

Once a price has been agreed on, the purchase contract becomes the basis for the real estate transaction. As part of the offer, the buyer must present **earnest money**, a portion of the purchase price deposited as evidence of good faith to show that the purchase offer is serious. At the closing of the home purchase, the earnest money is applied toward the down payment. This money is usually returned if the sale cannot be completed due to circumstances beyond the buyer's control.

Home purchase agreements often contain a *contingency clause*. This contract condition states that the agreement is binding only if a certain event occurs. For example, a real estate contract may stipulate that the contract will not be valid unless the buyer obtains financing for the purchase within a certain period of time, or it may make the purchase of a home contingent on the sale of the buyer's current home.

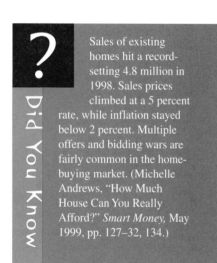

**Did You Know?**

Sales of existing homes hit a record-setting 4.8 million in 1998. Sales prices climbed at a 5 percent rate, while inflation stayed below 2 percent. Multiple offers and bidding wars are fairly common in the home-buying market. (Michelle Andrews, "How Much House Can You Really Afford?" *Smart Money,* May 1999, pp. 127–32, 134.)

*earnest money*
A portion of the price of a home that the buyer deposits as evidence of good faith to indicate a serious purchase offer.

## Concept Check 9-3

1.   What are the advantages and disadvantages of owning a home?
2.   What guidelines can be used to determine the amount to spend for a home purchase?
3.   How can the quality of a school system benefit even homeowners in a community who do not have school-age children?
4.   What services are available to home buyers from real estate agents?
5.   How does a *seller's* market differ from a *buyer's* market?

## THE FINANCES OF HOME BUYING

**Obj. 4**
Calculate the costs associated with purchasing a home.

After you have decided to purchase a specific home and have agreed on a price, you will probably obtain a loan. Financing a home purchase requires obtaining a mortgage, an awareness of types of mortgages, and settling the real estate transaction.

### Step 4: Obtain Financing

#### Determine Amount of Down Payment

The amount of cash available for a down payment will affect the size of the mortgage loan you require. A large down payment, such as 20 percent or more, will make it easier for you to obtain a mortgage.

Personal savings, pension plan funds, sales of investments or other assets, and assistance from relatives are the most common sources of a down payment. Parents can help their children purchase a home by giving them a cash gift or a loan, depositing money with the lender to reduce the interest rate on the loan, cosigning the loan, or acting as comortgagors.

Private mortgage insurance (PMI) is usually required if the down payment is less than 20 percent. This coverage protects the lender from financial loss due to default. PMI charges, which the borrower pays, vary depending on the amount of the down payment. These costs may be paid in full at closing or are sometimes financed over the life of the mortgage, depending on the type of financing.

After building up 20 or 25 percent equity in a home, a home buyer should contact the lender to cancel PMI. The Homeowners Protection Act of 1998 requires that a PMI policy be terminated automatically when a homeowner's equity reaches 22 percent of the property value at the time the mortgage was executed. Homeowners can request termination earlier if they can provide proof that the equity in the home has grown to 20 percent of the current market value. Additional information is available at www.privatemi.com.

**Did You Know?**

A home buyer bought a $100,000 house with a $105,000 loan and then borrowed an additional $25,000 for renovations. Between 1996 and 1997, the no-equity lending business grew from $3.5 billion to $10 billion. Most over-equity mortgages carry an adjustable rate of between 12 and 14 percent and are made to borrowers with excellent credit. Since most over-equity loans are used for consolidating credit card debt or home improvements, financial advisers suggest applying for a low-interest credit card instead. (Eric C. Evarts, "'Over-Equity' Mortgage Can Put House at Risk," *Chicago Sun-Times*, July 5, 1998, pp. 35C–36C.)

#### Qualifying for a Mortgage

Do you have funds for a down payment? Do you earn enough to make mortgage payments while covering other living expenses? Do you have a good credit rating? Unless you pay cash for a home, a favorable response to these questions is necessary. A **mortgage** is a long-term loan on a specific piece of property such as a home or other real estate. Payments on a mortgage are usually made over 15,

*mortgage*   A long-term loan on a specific piece of property such as a home or other real estate.

## EXHIBIT 9-8   Housing Affordability and Mortgage Qualification Amounts

| | Example A | Example B |
|---|---|---|
| Step 1: Determine your monthly gross income (annual income divided by 12). | $36,000 ÷ 12 | |
| Step 2: With a down payment of at least 10 percent, lenders use 28 percent of monthly gross income as a guideline for PITI (principal, interest, taxes, and insurance) and 36 percent of monthly gross income as a guideline for PITI plus other debt payments. | $ 3,000 <br> × .36 <br> $ 1,080 | $ 3,000 <br> × .28 <br> $  840 |
| Step 3: Subtract other debt payments (e.g., payments on an auto loan) and an estimate of the monthly costs of property taxes and homeowner's insurance. | − 280 <br> − 200 | — <br> − 200 |
| *(a) Affordable monthly mortgage payment* | $  600 | $  640 |
| Step 4: Divide this amount by the monthly mortgage payment per $1,000 based on current mortgage rates—a 10 percent, 30-year loan, for example (see Exhibit 9–9)—and multiply by $1,000. | ÷ $  8.78 <br> × $ 1,000 | ÷ $  8.78 <br> × $ 1,000 |
| *(b) Affordable mortgage amount* | $68,337 | $72,893 |
| Step 5: Divide your affordable mortgage amount by 1 minus the fractional portion of your down payment (e.g., 12.1 with a 10 percent down payment). | ÷ .9 | ÷ .9 |
| *(c) Affordable home purchase price* | $75,930 | $80,992 |

Note: The two ratios lending institutions use (step 2) and other loan requirements may vary based on a variety of factors, including the type of mortgage, the amount of the down payment, your income level, and current interest rates.

20, or 30 years. Banks, savings and loan associations, credit unions, and mortgage companies are the most common home financing sources. *Mortgage brokers* can help home buyers obtain financing, since they are in contact with several financial institutions. A mortgage broker may charge higher fees than a lending institution with which you deal directly.

To qualify for a mortgage, you must meet criteria similar to those for other loans. The home you buy serves as security, or *collateral*, for the mortgage. The major factors that affect the affordability of your mortgage are your income, other debts, the amount available for a down payment, the length of the loan, and current mortgage rates. The results calculated in Exhibit 9–8 are (*a*) the monthly mortgage payment you can afford, (*b*) the mortgage amount you can afford, and (*c*) the home purchase price you can afford.

The procedures in Exhibit 9–8 include the following:

1. Indicate your monthly gross income.
2. Multiply your monthly gross income by 0.28 (or 0.36 if you have other debts, such as an auto loan). Lenders commonly use 28 and 36 percent as guidelines to determine the amount most people can comfortably afford for housing.
3. After subtracting the monthly debt payments and an estimate of the monthly cost for property taxes and homeowner's insurance, you arrive at your *affordable monthly mortgage payment* (*a*).
4. Divide (*a*) by the factor from Exhibit 9–9, based on your mortgage term (in years) and rate. Then multiply your answer by $1,000 to convert your figure to thousands of dollars. This gives you your *affordable mortgage amount* (*b*). Exhibit 9–9 provides the amount you need to pay back $1,000 over 15, 20, 25, or 30 years based on various interest rates.
5. To obtain your *affordable home purchase price* (*c*), divide (*b*) by the amount you will be financing, such as 0.9 when you make a 10 percent down payment.

Sheet 43

**EXHIBIT 9-9**

Mortgage Payment Factors (principal and interest factors per $1,000 of loan amount)

| Term Rate | 30 Years | 25 Years | 20 Years | 15 Years |
|---|---|---|---|---|
| 6.0% | $ 6.00 | $ 6.44 | $ 7.16 | $ 8.43 |
| 6.5 | 6.32 | 6.67 | 7.45 | 8.71 |
| 7.0 | 6.65 | 7.06 | 7.75 | 8.98 |
| 7.5 | 6.99 | 7.39 | 8.06 | 9.27 |
| 8.0 | 7.34 | 7.72 | 8.36 | 9.56 |
| 8.5 | 7.69 | 8.05 | 8.68 | 9.85 |
| 9.0 | 8.05 | 8.39 | 9.00 | 10.14 |
| 9.5 | 8.41 | 8.74 | 9.32 | 10.44 |
| 10.0 | 8.78 | 9.09 | 9.65 | 10.75 |
| 10.5 | 9.15 | 9.44 | 9.98 | 11.05 |
| 11.0 | 9.52 | 9.80 | 10.32 | 11.37 |
| 11.5 | 9.90 | 10.16 | 10.66 | 11.68 |
| 12.0 | 10.29 | 10.53 | 11.01 | 12.00 |
| 12.5 | 10.67 | 10.90 | 11.36 | 12.33 |
| 13.0 | 11.06 | 11.28 | 11.72 | 12.65 |
| 13.5 | 11.45 | 11.66 | 12.07 | 12.98 |
| 14.0 | 11.85 | 12.04 | 12.44 | 13.32 |
| 14.5 | 12.25 | 12.42 | 12.80 | 13.66 |
| 15.0 | 12.64 | 12.81 | 13.17 | 14.00 |

These sample calculations are typical of those most financial institutions use; the actual qualifications for a mortgage may vary by lender and by the type of mortgage. In addition, current mortgage interest rates will affect the amount of the mortgage loan for which you qualify.

The mortgage loan for which you can qualify is larger when interest rates are low than when they are high. For example, a person who can afford a monthly mortgage payment of $700 will qualify for a 30-year loan of

$105,263 at 7 percent
$ 95,368 at 8 percent
$ 86,956 at 9 percent
$ 79,726 at 10 percent
$ 73,529 at 11 percent
$ 68,027 at 12 percent

As interest rates rise, fewer people are able to afford the cost of an average-priced home.

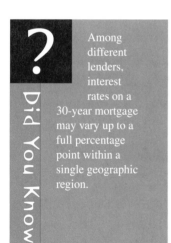

Among different lenders, interest rates on a 30-year mortgage may vary up to a full percentage point within a single geographic region.

**Did You Know**

*points*   Prepaid interest charged by a lending institution for the mortgage; each discount point is equal to 1 percent of the loan amount.

Evaluating Points    When you compare costs at several mortgage companies, the interest rate you are quoted is not the only factor to consider. The required down payment and the points charged will affect the interest rate.

**Points** are prepaid interest charged by the lender. Each *discount point* is equal to 1 percent of the loan amount and should be viewed as a premium you pay for obtaining a lower mortgage rate. In deciding whether to take a lower rate with more points or a higher rate with fewer points, do the following:

1. Determine the difference between the monthly payments you will make for two different situations.
2. Determine the difference between the points charged for the two different rates or at two different lenders.
3. Divide the result in step 2 by the result in step 1. This will tell you how many months it will take for the lower monthly payment to offset the higher cost of the points.

If you plan to live in your home longer than the time calculated in step 3, paying the points and taking the lower mortgage rate is probably the best action. This decision will, however, be affected by the amount of funds available to pay the points at the time of closing. If you plan to sell your home sooner than the time calculated in step 3, the higher mortgage rate with fewer discount points may be better. Online research may be used to compare current mortgage rates and to apply for a mortgage.

## The Application Process

Applying for a mortgage involves three main phases:

1. After completing the mortgage application, a meeting between lender and borrower is scheduled. The borrower presents evidence of employment, income, ownership of assets, and amounts of existing debts. At this point, most lenders charge an application fee of between $100 and $300.
2. The lender obtains a credit report and verifies other aspects of the borrower's application and financial status.
3. The mortgage is either approved or denied. The decision is based on the potential borrower's credit and financial history and an evaluation of the home, including its location, condition, and value. This process will indicate the maximum mortgage for which you qualify. This amount may not be loaned on every house you are considering.

The loan commitment is the financial institution's decision to provide the funds needed to purchase a specific property. At this point, the purchase contract for the home becomes legally binding. The approved mortgage application usually *locks in* an interest rate for 30 to 60 days.

## Fixed-Rate, Fixed-Payment Mortgages

As Exhibit 9–10 shows, fixed-rate, fixed-payment mortgages are one of the two major types of mortgages.

*conventional mortgage*
A fixed-rate, fixed-payment home loan with equal payments over 15, 20, or 30 years.

*amortization* The reduction of a loan balance through payments made over a period of time.

### Conventional Mortgages

The **conventional mortgage** usually has equal payments over 15, 20, or 30 years based on a fixed interest rate. This mortgage offers home buyers certainty about future loan payments. The mortgage payments are set at a level that allows **amortization** of the loan; that is, the balance owed is reduced with each payment. Since the amount borrowed is large, the payments made during the early years of the mortgage are applied mainly to interest, with only small reductions in the principal of the loan. As the amount owed declines, the monthly payments have an increasing impact on the loan balance. Near the end of the mortgage term, nearly all of each payment is applied to the balance.

For example, a $75,000, 30-year, 10 percent mortgage would have monthly payments of $658.18. The payments would be divided as follows:

|  | Interest | | Principal | Remaining Balance | |
|---|---|---|---|---|---|
| For the first month | $625.00 | ($75,000 × 0.10 × ¹⁄₁₂) | $ 33.18 | $74,966.82 | ($75,000 − $33.18) |
| For the second month | 624.72 | ($74,966.82 × 0.10 × ¹⁄₁₂) | 33.46 | 74,933.36 | ($74,966.82 − $33.46) |
| For the 360th month | 5.41 | | 649.54 | − 0 − | |

In the past, many conventional mortgages were *assumable*. This feature allowed a home buyer to continue with the seller's original agreement. Assumable mortgages were especially attractive if the mortgage rate was lower than market interest rates at the time of the sale. Today, due to volatile interest rates, few assumable mortgages are offered.

## EXHIBIT 9-10   Types of Mortgage Loans

| Loan Type | Benefits | Drawbacks |
|---|---|---|
| **Fixed-Rate, Fixed-Payment** | | |
| 1. Conventional 30-year mortgage | • Fixed monthly payments for 30 years provide certainty of principal and interest payments. | • Higher initial rates than adjustables. |
| 2. Conventional 15- or 20-year mortgage | • Lower rate than 30-year fixed; faster equity buildup and quicker payoff of loan. | • Higher monthly payments. |
| 3. FHA/VA fixed-rate mortgage (30-year and 15-year) | • Low down payment requirements and fully assumable with no prepayment penalties. | • May require substantial points; may have application red tape and delays. |
| 4. "Balloon" loan (3–10-year terms) | • May carry discount rates and other favorable terms, particularly when the home seller provides the loan. | • At the end of the 3–10-year term, the entire remaining balance is due in a lump-sum or "balloon" payment, forcing the borrower to find new financing. |
| **Adjustable-Rate, Variable-Payment** | | |
| 5. Adjustable-rate mortgage (ARM)—payment changes on 1-year, 3-year, and 5-year schedules | • Lower initial rates than fixed-rate loans, particularly on the one-year adjustable. Generally assumable by new buyers. Offers possibility of future rate and payment decreases. Loans with rate "caps" may protect borrowers against increases in rates. Some may be convertible to fixed-rate plans. | • Shifts far greater interest rate risk onto borrowers than fixed-rate loans. May push up monthly payments in future years. |
| 6. Graduated-payment mortgage (GPM)—payment increases by prearranged increments during first 5 to 7 years, then levels off | • Allows buyers with marginal incomes to qualify. Higher incomes over next 5–7 years expected to cover gradual payment increases. May be combined with adjustable-rate mortgage to further lower initial rate and payment. | • May have higher annual percentage rate (APR) than standard fixed-rate or adjustable-rate loans. May involve negative amortization—increasing debt owed by lender. Income may not increase as expected. |
| 7. Growing-equity mortgage (GEM)—contributes rising portions of monthly payments to payoff of principal debt. Typically pays off in 15–18 years rather than 30 | • Lower up-front payments, quicker loan payoff than conventional fixed-rate or adjustable-rate loans. | • May have higher effective rates and higher down payments than other loans in the marketplace. |

SOURCE: Reprinted from *Home Guide*, published by the National Association of Realtors® © 1989. All rights reserved.

**Government-Guaranteed Financing Programs**   *Government-guaranteed financing programs* include loans insured by the Federal Housing Authority (FHA) and loans guaranteed by the Veterans Administration (VA). These government agencies do not provide the mortgage money; rather, they help home buyers obtain low-interest, low-down-payment loans.

To qualify for an FHA-insured loan, a person must meet certain conditions related to the down payment and fees. Most low- and middle-income people can qualify for

**EXHIBIT 9-11**

Mortgage Rates through the Years

SOURCE: Board of Governors of the Federal Reserve System.

the FHA loan program. The minimum down payment ranges from 3 to 5 percent, depending on the loan size. This lower down payment makes it easier for a person to purchase a home. FHA-insured loans have interest rates slightly lower than market interest rates, since the FHA's involvement reduces the risk for the lending institution. The borrower is required to pay a fee for insurance that protects the lender from financial loss due to default. Despite the protection given the lender, the lower-than-market interest rate can result in extra prepaid interest, *points*, as a condition of the loan.

The VA-guaranteed loan program assists eligible armed services veterans with home purchases. As with the FHA program, the funds for VA loans come from a financial institution or a mortgage company, with the risk reduced by government participation. A VA loan can be obtained without a down payment. The points charged by the lending institution must be paid by the home seller; however, the veteran is usually responsible for other charges, such as origination and funding fees.

Both FHA-insured loans and VA-guaranteed loans can be attractive financing alternatives and are assumable by future owners when the house is sold to qualifying individuals. Both impose limits on the amount one can borrow, and a backlog of processing applications and approving loans may occur during periods of high demand.

**?**

**Did You Know**

By taking out a 15-year instead of a 30-year mortgage, a home buyer borrowing $200,000 can save over $150,000 in interest over the life of the loan. The faster equity growth with the shorter mortgage is also a benefit. A 15-year mortgage may not make sense for everyone, since the additional monthly payment may be needed to pay off credit cards or for other living expenses. (Carlos Tajada, "Sweet Fifteen," *The Wall Street Journal*, September 17, 1998, p. C1.)

**Balloon Mortgages**   The high mortgage rates of the early 1980s (Exhibit 9–11) led to innovative lending plans for home buyers. One such plan is the **balloon mortgage,** which has fixed monthly payments and a very large final payment, usually after three, five, or seven years. This financing plan is designed for people who wish to buy a home during periods of high interest rates but expect to be able to refinance the loan or sell the home before or when the balloon payment is due. Most balloon mortgages allow conversion to a conventional mortgage (for a fee) after a year if certain conditions are met. Some financial counselors advise against the use of a balloon mortgage, since you have to pay mortgage processing and closing costs when you refinance. Beware that an inability to refinance in time can result in a major financial loss.

*balloon mortgage*
A home loan with fixed monthly payments and a large final payment, usually after three, five or seven years.

Adjustable-Rate, Variable-Payment Mortgages     As noted in Exhibit 9–10, adjustable-rate, variable-payment mortgages are a major category of financing available to home buyers.

Adjustable-Rate Mortgages     The **adjustable-rate mortgage (ARM),** also referred to as a *flexible-rate mortgage* or a *variable-rate mortgage,* has an interest rate that increases or decreases during the life of the loan. When mortgage rates were at record highs, many people took out variable-rate home loans, expecting rates would eventually go down. ARMs usually have a lower initial interest rate than fixed-rate mortgages; however, the borrower, not the lender, bears the risk of future interest rate increases.

*adjustable-rate mortgage (ARM)* A home loan with an interest rate that can change during the mortgage term due to changes in market interest rates; also called a *flexible-rate mortgage* or a *variable-rate mortgage.*

A **rate cap** restricts the amount by which the interest rate can increase or decrease during the ARM term. This limit prevents the borrower from having to pay an interest rate significantly higher than the one in the original agreement. Most rate caps limit increases (or decreases) in the mortgage rate to one or two percentage points in a year and to no more than five points over the life of the loan.

*rate cap* A limit on the increases and decreases in the interest rate charged on an adjustable-rate mortgage.

A **payment cap** keeps the payments on an adjustable-rate mortgage at a given level or limits the amount to which those payments can rise. When mortgage payments do not rise but interest rates do, the amount owed can increase in months in which the mortgage payment does not cover the interest owed. This increased loan balance, called *negative amortization,* means the amount of the home equity is decreasing instead of increasing. As a result of these increases in the amount owed, the borrower usually has to make payments for a period longer than planned. Beware: Some adjustable-rate mortgages may stretch out as long as 40 years.

*payment cap* A limit on the payment increases for an adjustable-rate mortgage.

Consider several factors when you evaluate adjustable-rate mortgages: (1) determine the frequency of and restrictions on allowed changes in interest rates; (2) consider the frequency of and restrictions on changes in the monthly payment; (3) investigate the possibility that the loan will be extended due to negative amortization, and find out whether the mortgage agreement limits the amount of negative amortization; (4) find out what index the lending institution will use to set the mortgage interest rate over the term of the loan.

A lending institution will revise the rate for an adjustable-rate mortgage based on changes in the rates on U.S. Treasury securities, the Federal Home Loan Bank Board's mortgage rate index, or its own cost-of-funds index. Studies reveal that an ARM can be less costly over the life of a mortgage as long as interest rates remain fairly stable.

*Convertible ARMs* allow the home buyer to change an adjustable-rate mortgage to a fixed-rate mortgage during a certain period, such as the time between the second and fifth year of the loan. A conversion fee, typically between $250 and $500, must be paid to obtain a fixed rate, usually 0.25 to 0.50 percent higher than the current rates for conventional 30-year mortgages.

**Sheet 44**

Graduated-Payment Mortgages     A **graduated-payment mortgage** is a financing agreement in which payments rise to different levels every 5 or 10 years during the term of the loan. In the early years, the loan payments could lead to a negative amortization with an increase in the amount owed. This type of mortgage is especially beneficial for people who anticipate increases in income in the future.

*graduated-payment mortgage* A home financing agreement in which payments rise to different levels every 5 or 10 years during the loan term.

Growing-Equity Mortgages     A **growing-equity mortgage** provides for increases in payments that allow the amount owed to be paid off more quickly. With such a mortgage, a person would be able to pay off a 30-year home loan in 15 to 18 years. A growing-equity mortgage may be desired by individuals who want to build equity in their homes quickly.

*growing-equity mortgage* A home loan agreement that provides for payment increases to allow the amount owed to be paid off more quickly.

## Other Financing Methods

To assist first-time home buyers, builders and financial institutions offer financing plans to make the purchase easier.

*buy-down* An interest rate subsidy from a home builder or a real estate developer that reduces a home buyer's mortgage payments during the first few years of the loan.

### Buy-Downs

A **buy-down** is an interest rate subsidy from a home builder or a real estate developer that reduces the mortgage payments during the first few years of the loan. This assistance is intended to stimulate sales among home buyers who cannot afford conventional financing. After the buy-down period, the mortgage payments increase to the level that would have existed without the financial assistance.

*shared appreciation mortgage (SAM)* A home loan agreement in which the borrower agrees to share the increased value of the home with the lender when the home is sold.

### Shared Appreciation Mortgages

The **shared appreciation mortgage (SAM)** is an arrangement in which the borrower agrees to share the increased value of the home with the lender when the home is sold. This agreement provides the home buyer with a below-market interest rate and lower payments than a conventional loan. To obtain these conditions, the borrower typically must agree to give the lending institution 30 to 50 percent of the home's appreciation when the home is sold or after a set number of years. Shared appreciation agreements are also common when parents provide financial assistance to their children for the purchase of a home.

*second mortgage* A cash advance based on the paid-up value of a home; also called a *home equity loan.*

### Second Mortgages

A **second mortgage,** more commonly called a *home equity loan,* allows a homeowner to borrow on the paid-up value of the property. Traditional second mortgages allow a homeowner to borrow a lump sum against the equity and repay it in monthly installments. Recently lending institutions have offered a variety of home equity loans, including a line of credit program that allows the borrower to obtain additional funds. You need to be careful when using a home equity line of credit. This revolving credit plan can keep you continually in debt as you request new cash advances.

A home equity loan makes it possible to deduct the interest on consumer purchases on your federal income tax return. However, it creates the risk of losing the home if required payments on both the first and second mortgages are not made. To help prevent this financial disaster, some states restrict the use of home equity loans. Be cautious of home equity loans for amounts that exceed 100 percent of your equity in the home.

*reverse mortgage* A loan based on the equity in a home, that provides elderly homeowners with tax-free income and is paid back with interest when the home is sold or the homeowner dies.

### Reverse Mortgages

Programs are available to assist people who have a high equity in their homes and need cash. **Reverse mortgages** provide elderly homeowners with tax-free income in the form of a loan that is paid back (with interest) when the home is sold or the homeowner dies. You must be 62 to qualify. These financing plans, also called *home equity conversion mortgages,* have two main formats. A *reverse mortgage annuity* guarantees the homeowner a monthly income for life. In contrast, a reverse mortgage may have a *set term,* at the end of which the loan would be due. This format is likely to offer a higher monthly income; however, an elderly person faces the prospect of having to sell the home before he or she desires to do so. Reverse mortgages are increasing in availability through both government programs and private lending institutions.

*refinancing* The process of obtaining a new mortgage on a home to get a lower interest rate.

### Refinancing

During the term of your mortgage, you may want to **refinance** your home, that is, obtain a new mortgage on your current home at a lower interest rate. Before taking this action, be sure the costs of refinancing do not offset the savings of a lower interest rate. Refinancing is most advantageous when you can get a rate 2 or 3 percent lower than your current rate and when you plan to own your present home for at least two more years. Divide the costs of refinancing by the amount saved each month to determine the time you need to

**? Did You Know**

If you still owe $60,000 on a $100,000, 0.5 percent mortgage with 20 years left to pay, refinancing the $60,000 for 30 years at 7.5 percent will reduce your monthly payments from $834 to $417. This will result in savings of over $106,000 in interest. Refinancing with a 20-year mortgage would result in even larger savings.

# Financial Planning for Life's Situations

## SHOULD YOU PAY OFF YOUR MORTGAGE EARLY?

If you have a mortgage, you might consider paying it off early. Make sure the mortgage does not include a *prepayment penalty*, a fee you pay for the privilege of retiring a loan early. Most mortgages do not include this penalty. Before paying off your mortgage early, however, consider the tax deductions you may lose and your lost earnings on the money you use to retire this debt.

Instead of paying off your entire mortgage early, consider paying an additional amount each month—for example, $25. Since this amount will be applied to the loan principal, you will save interest and pay off the mortgage in a shorter time than the contracted period.

Paying an additional $25 a month on a $75,000, 30-year, 10 percent mortgage will save you over $34,000 in interest and enable you to pay off the loan in less than 25 years.

Beware of organizations that promise to help you make additional payments on your mortgage. This is something you could do on your own, and they are likely to charge you a fee for doing it. In addition, these organizations frequently collect money from you every two weeks but make a payment only once a month, which gives them the use of thousands of *your* dollars to invest for *their* gain.

**Sheet 45**

cover your costs. Also, be sure to consider the tax deductibility of refinancing costs. Another financing decision involves making extra payments on your mortgage (see the Financial Planning for Life's Situations feature).

## Step 5: Close the Purchase Transaction

Before finalizing the transaction, do a *walk-through* to inspect the conditions and facilities of the home you plan to buy. You can use a Polaroid or video camera to collect evidence for any last-minute items you may need to negotiate.

The *closing* involves a meeting among the buyer, seller, and lender of funds, or representatives of each party, to complete the transaction. Documents are signed, last-minute details are settled, and appropriate amounts are paid. A number of expenses are incurred at the closing. The **closing costs,** also referred to as *settlement costs,* are the fees and charges paid when a real estate transaction is completed (see Exhibit 9–12 on page 302).

**Title insurance** is one closing cost. This coverage has two phases. First, the title company defines the boundaries of the property being purchased and conducts a search to determine whether the property is free of claims such as unpaid real estate taxes. Second, during the mortgage term, the title company protects the owner and the lender against financial loss resulting from future defects in the title and from other unforeseen property claims not excluded by the policy.

Also due at closing time is the deed recording fee. The **deed** is the document that transfers ownership of property from one party to another. With a *warranty deed*, the seller guarantees the title is good. This document certifies that the seller is the true owner of the property, there are no claims against the title, and the seller has the right to sell the property.

Mortgage insurance is another possible closing cost. If required, mortgage insurance protects the lender from loss resulting from a mortgage default.

The Real Estate Settlement Procedures Act (RESPA) helps home buyers understand the closing process and closing costs. This legislation requires that loan applicants be

*closing costs* Fees and charges paid when a real estate transaction is completed; also called *settlement costs.*

*title insurance* Insurance that, during the mortgage term, protects the owner or the lender against financial loss resulting from future defects in the title and from other unforeseen property claims not excluded by the policy.

*deed* A document that transfers ownership of property from one party to another.

## EXHIBIT 9–12   Common Closing Costs

At the transaction settlement of a real estate purchase and sale, the buyer and seller will encounter a variety of expenses that are commonly referred to as *closing costs*.

| | Cost Range Encountered | |
| --- | --- | --- |
| | By the Buyer | By the Seller |
| Title search fee | $50–$150 | — |
| Title insurance | $100–$600 | $100–$600 |
| Attorney's fee | $50–$700 | $50–$700 |
| Property survey | — | $100–$400 |
| Appraisal fee | $100–$300 | — |
| Recording fees; transfer taxes | $15–$30 | $15–$30 |
| Credit report | $25–$75 | — |
| Termite inspection | $50–$150 | — |
| Lender's origination fee | 1–3% of loan amount | — |
| Reserves for home insurance and property taxes | Varies | — |
| Interest paid in advance (from the closing date to the end of the month) and "points" | Varies | — |
| Real estate broker's commission | — | 5–7% of purchase price |

Note: The amounts paid by the buyer are in addition to the down payment.

given certain information, including an estimate of the closing costs, before the actual closing. Obtaining this information as early as possible will allow you to plan for the closing costs. Information on RESPA is available online at www.hud.gov/fha/res/respa_hm.html.

At the closing and when you make your monthly payments, you will probably deposit money to be used for home expenses. For example, the lender will require that you have property insurance. An **escrow account** is money, usually deposited with the lending institution, for the payment of property taxes and homeowner's insurance. This account protects the lender from financial loss due to unpaid real estate taxes or damage from fire or other hazards.

*escrow account*
Money, usually deposited with the lending financial institution, for the payment of property taxes and homeowner's insurance.

As a new home buyer, you might also consider purchasing an agreement that gives you protection against defects in the home. *Implied warranties* created by state laws may cover some problem areas; other repair costs can occur. Home builders and real estate sales companies offer warranties to buyers. Coverage offered commonly provides protection against structural, wiring, plumbing, heating, and other mechanical defects. Most home warranty programs have many limitations.

In addition, a new homeowner may purchase a service contract from a real estate company such as Century 21 or Remax. This agreement warrants appliances, plumbing, air conditioning and heating systems, and other items for one year. As with any service contract, you must decide whether the coverage provided and the chances of repair expenses justify the cost.

## Home Buying: A Final Word

For most people, buying a home is the most expensive decision they will undertake. As a reminder, Exhibit 9–13 provides an overview of the major elements to consider when making this critical financial decision.

**EXHIBIT 9-13**

The Main Elements of Buying a Home

- **Location.** Consider the community and geographic region. A $150,000 home in one area may be an average-priced house, while in another part of the country it may be fairly expensive real estate. The demand for homes is largely affected by the economy and the availability of jobs.
- **Down payment.** While making a large down payment reduces your mortgage payments, you will also need the funds for closing costs, moving expenses, repairs, or furniture.
- **Mortgage application.** When applying for a home loan, you will usually be required to provide copies of recent tax returns, a residence and employment history, information about bank and investment accounts, a listing of debts, and evidence of auto and any real estate ownership.
- **Points.** You may need to select between a higher rate with no discount points and a lower rate requiring points paid at closing.
- **Closing costs.** Settlement costs can range from 2 to 6 percent of the loan amount. This means you could need as much as $6,000 to finalize a $100,000 mortgage; this amount is in addition to your down payment.
- **PITI.** Your monthly payment for principal, interest, taxes, and insurance is an important budget item. Beware of buying "too much house" and not having enough for other living expenses.
- **Maintenance costs.** As any homeowner will tell you, owning a home can be expensive. Set aside funds for repair and remodeling expenses.

## Concept Check 9-4

1.  What are the main sources of money for a down payment?
2.  What factors affect a person's ability to qualify for a mortgage?
3.  How do changing interest rates affect the amount of mortgage a person can afford?
4.  How do discount points affect the cost of a mortgage?
5.  Under what conditions might an adjustable-rate mortgage be appropriate?
6.  When might refinancing a mortgage be advisable?
7.  How do closing costs affect a person's ability to afford a home purchase?

## SELLING YOUR HOME

Obj. 5
Develop a strategy for selling a home.

Most people who buy a home will eventually be on the other side of a real estate transaction. Selling your home requires preparing it for selling, setting a price, and deciding whether to sell it yourself or use a real estate agent.

### Preparing Your Home for Selling

The effective presentation of your home can result in a fast and financially favorable sale. Real estate salespeople recommend that you make needed repairs and paint worn exterior and interior areas. Clear the garage and exterior areas of toys, debris, and old vehicles, and keep the lawn cut and the leaves raked. Keep the kitchen and bathroom clean. Avoid offensive odors by removing garbage and keeping pets and their areas clean. Remove excess furniture and dispose of unneeded items to make the house, closets, and storage areas look larger. When showing your home, open drapes and turn on lights to give it a pleasant atmosphere. This effort will give your property a positive image and make it attractive to potential buyers.

## Determining the Selling Price

Putting a price on your home can be difficult. You risk not selling it immediately if the price is too high, and you may not get a fair amount if the price is too low. An **appraisal,** an estimate of the current value of the property, can provide a good indication of the price you should set. An asking price is influenced by recent selling prices of comparable homes in your area, demand in the housing market, and available financing based on current mortgage rates.

The home improvements you have made may or may not increase the selling price. A hot tub or an exercise room may have no value for potential buyers. Among the most desirable improvements are energy-efficient features, a remodeled kitchen, an additional or remodeled bathroom, added rooms and storage space, a converted basement, a fireplace, and an outdoor deck or patio.

The time to think about selling your home is when you buy it and every day you live there. Daily maintenance, timely repairs, and home improvements will increase the future sales price.

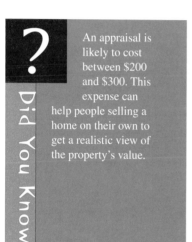

An appraisal is likely to cost between $200 and $300. This expense can help people selling a home on their own to get a realistic view of the property's value.

## Sale by Owner

Each year, about 10 percent of home sales are made by the home's owners. If you decide to sell your home without using a real estate professional, price the home and advertise it through local newspapers and with an information sheet describing it in detail. Obtain a listing sheet from a real estate office as an example of the information to include on your flier. Distribute the sheet at stores and in other public areas.

When selling your home on your own, obtain information about the availability of financing and financing requirements. This information will help you and potential buyers to determine whether a sale is possible. Use the services of a lawyer or title company to assist you with the contract, the closing, and other legal matters.

Require potential buyers to provide their names, addresses, telephone numbers, and background information, and show your home only by appointment. As a security measure, show it only when two or more adults are at home. Selling your own home can save you several thousand dollars in commission, but it requires an investment of time and effort.

## Listing with a Real Estate Agent

You may decide to sell your home with the assistance of a real estate agent. These businesses range from firms owned by one person to nationally franchised companies. Primary selection factors should be the real estate agent's knowledge of the community and the agent's willingness to actively market your home.

Your real estate agent will provide you with various services. These services include suggesting a selling price, making potential buyers and other agents aware of your home, providing advice on features to highlight, conducting showings of your home, and handling the financial aspects of the sale. A real estate agent can also help screen potential buyers to determine whether they will qualify for a mortgage.

Discount real estate brokers are available to assist sellers who are willing to take on certain duties and want to reduce selling costs. Companies such as Save More Real Estate and Help-U-Sell Real Estate charge a flat fee or 1 to 2 percent of the selling price instead of the customary 6 percent.

## Concept Check 9-5

1. What actions are recommended when planning to sell your home?
2. What factors affect the selling price of a home?
3. What should you consider when deciding whether to sell your home on your own or use the services of a real estate agent?

## Summary of Objectives

**Obj. 1   Evaluate available housing alternatives.**

Your needs, life situation, and financial resources are the major factors that influence your selection of housing. Assess renting and buying alternatives in terms of their financial and opportunity costs.

**Obj. 2   Analyze the costs and benefits associated with renting.**

The main advantages of renting are mobility, fewer responsibilities, and lower initial costs. The main disadvantages of renting are few financial benefits, a restricted lifestyle, and legal concerns.

**Obj. 3   Implement the home-buying process.**

Home buying involves five major stages: (1) determining homeownership needs, (2) finding and evaluating a property

to purchase, (3) pricing the property, (4) financing the purchase, and (5) closing the real estate transaction.

**Obj. 4   Calculate the costs associated with purchasing a home.**

The costs associated with purchasing a home include the down payment; mortgage origination costs; closing costs such as a deed fee, prepaid interest, attorney's fees, payment for title insurance, and a property survey; and an escrow account for homeowner's insurance and property taxes.

**Obj. 5   Develop a strategy for selling a home.**

When selling a home, you must decide whether to make certain repairs and improvements, determine a selling price, and choose between selling the home yourself and using the services of a real estate agent.

## Financial Planning Problems

1. *Determining Appropriate Housing.* What type of housing would you suggest for people in the following life situations?   (Obj. 1)
   a. A single parent with two school-age children.
   b. A two-income couple without children.
   c. A person with both dependent children and a dependent parent.
   d. A couple near retirement with grown children.
2. *Comparing Renting and Buying.* Based on the following data, would you recommend buying or renting?

| Rental Costs | Buying Costs |
|---|---|
| Annual rent, $7,380 | Annual mortgage payments, $9,800 ($9,575 is interest) |
| Insurance, $145 | Property taxes, $1,780 |
| Security deposit, $650 | Insurance/maintenance, $1,050 |
| | Down payment/closing costs, $4,500 |
| | Growth in equity, $225 |
| | Estimated annual appreciation, $1,700 |

Assume an after-tax savings interest rate of 6 percent and a tax rate of 28 percent.   (Obj. 2)

3. *Analyzing the Buy-versus-Rent Decision.* Use the buy-versus-rent analysis on page 282 to compare two residences you might consider.   (Obj. 2)
4. *Estimating a Monthly Mortgage Payment.* Estimate the affordable monthly mortgage payment, the affordable mortgage amount, and the affordable home purchase price for the following situation (see Exhibit 9-8).   (Obj. 4)

   Monthly gross income, $2,950
   Down payment to be made—15 percent of purchase price
   Other debt (monthly payment), $160
   Monthly estimate for property taxes and insurance, $210
   30-year loan at 10.5 percent.
5. *Calculating Monthly Mortgage Payments.* Based on Exhibit 9-9, what would be the monthly mortgage payments for each of the following situations?
   a. A $40,000, 15-year loan at 11.5 percent.
   b. A $76,000, 30-year loan at 9 percent.
   c. A $65,000, 20-year loan at 10 percent.
   What relationship exists between the length of the loan and the monthly payment? How does the mortgage rate affect the monthly payment?   (Obj. 4)

6. *Comparing Total Mortgage Payments.* Which mortgage would result in higher total payments?   (Obj. 4)
   Mortgage A: $985 a month for 30 years
   Mortgage B: $780 a month for 5 years and $1,056 for 25 years
7. *Evaluating a Refinance Decision.* Kelly and Tim Jones plan to refinance their mortgage to obtain a lower interest rate. They will reduce their mortgage payments by $56 a month. Their closing costs for refinancing will be $1,670. How long will it take them to cover the cost of refinancing? (Obj. 4)
8. *Future Value of an Amount Saved.* You estimate that you can save $3,800 by selling your home yourself rather than using a real estate agent. What would be the future value of that amount if invested for five years at 7 percent? (Obj. 5)

## Financial Planning Activities

1. *Comparing Housing Alternatives.* Interview several people about the factors that influenced their current residence.   (Obj. 1)
2. *Comparing Rental Situations.* Using Sheet 42 in the *Personal Financial Planner,* compare the costs, facilities, and features of apartments and other rental housing in your area. You may obtain this information through newspaper advertisements, rental offices, or online searches.   (Obj. 2)
3. *Researching Rental Agreements.* Interview a tenant and a landlord to obtain their views about potential problems associated with renting. How do their views on tenant–landlord relations differ?   (Obj. 2)
4. *Comparing Home-Buying Alternatives.* Visit the sales office for a condominium, a new home, and a mobile home. Based on the information obtained, prepare a written or an oral presentation comparing the benefits and potential concerns of these housing alternatives.   (Obj. 3)
5. *Using a Real Estate Agent.* Interview a real estate agent about the process involved in selecting and buying a home. Ask about housing prices in your area and the services the agent provides. Also, find out the agent's opinion as to what will happen to housing prices and interest rates over the next six months.   (Obj. 3)
6. *Comparing Types of Mortgages.* Talk with people who have different types of mortgages. What suggestions do they offer about obtaining home financing? What were their experiences with closing costs when they purchased their homes?   (Obj. 4)
7. *Comparing Mortgage Companies.* Using Sheet 44 in the *Personal Financial Planner,* contact several mortgage companies and other financial institutions to obtain information about current mortgage rates, application fees, and the process for obtaining a mortgage.   (Obj. 4)
8. *Searching the Web for Mortgage Rates.* Using websites such as www.financenter.com, www.interest.com, or www.bestrate.com, obtain information on current mortgage rates available in different parts of the country.   (Obj. 4)
9. *Analyzing Homes for Sales.* Visit a couple of homes for sale. What features do you believe would appeal to potential buyers? What efforts were made to attract potential buyers to the open houses?   (Obj. 5)

## LIFE SITUATION CASE

### HOUSING DECISIONS

When Mark and Valerie Bowman first saw the house, they didn't like it. However, it was a dark, rainy day. They viewed the house more favorably on their second visit, which they had expected to be a waste of time. Despite cracked ceilings, the need for a paint job, and a kitchen built in the 1950s, the Bowmans saw a potential to create a place they could call their own.

Beth Franklin purchased her condominium four years ago. She obtained a mortgage rate of 9.75 percent, a very good rate then. Recently, when interest rates dropped, Beth was considering refinancing her mortgage at a lower rate.

Matt and Peggy Zoran had been married for five years and were still living in an apartment. Several of the Zorans' friends had purchased homes recently. However, Matt and Peggy were not sure they wanted to follow this example. Although they liked their friends' homes and had viewed photographs of homes currently on the market, they also liked the freedom from maintenance responsibility they enjoyed as renters.

### Questions

1. How could the Bowmans have benefited from buying a home that needed improvements?
2. How might Beth Franklin have found out when mortgage rates were at a level that would make refinancing her condominium more affordable?
3. Although the Zorans had good reasons for continuing to rent, what factors might make it desirable for an individual or a family to buy a home?

# VIDEO CASE   The Home-Buying Process

After renting for awhile, Janet and Jeff are now planning to buy their first home. They believe the time has come to take a big step forward in their housing choice.

City or suburbs? Condominium or townhouse? Existing home or new construction? Conventional mortgage or FHA? Fixed-rate mortgage or ARM?

"Wow, this gets a bit confusing," exclaimed Jeff.

"I'm sure we'll be able to get through this," responded Janet.

While they are a bit overwhelmed by this decision, Janet and Jeff also know that many information sources and housing professionals are available to assist them.

## Questions

1. What factors commonly influence renters to buy a home?
2. How can Janet and Jeff determine how much they can afford when buying a home?
3. What professionals will be most useful to Janet and Jeff when buying a home?
4. Are Janet and Jeff financially qualified to purchase a home? What factors will influence the decision to grant them a mortgage?

## Creating an E-Plan: Financial Decisions Using the Web

### SELECTING AND FINANCING HOUSING

Housing represents a major budget expenditure. This area of financial planning requires careful analysis of needs along with a comparison of the costs and benefits of housing alternatives.

Websites for Housing

- Comparing renting and buying at **www.financenter.com.**
- A step-by-step guide to buying a home at **www.maxsol.com/homes/steps.htm.**
- Assistance with various aspects of home buying (housing prices, mortgage rates) at **www.homes. wsj.com, www. homefair.com/home, www. homeshark.com,** and **www. ired.com.**
- Mortgage rate information at **www.bankrate.com, www.loan-page.com, www.hsh.com,** and **www. microsurf.com.**
- Adjustable-rate mortgage information at **www. maxsol. com/homes/comparm.htm.**
- Fannie Mae's website at **www.homepath.com** includes information on home buying, mortgages, refinancing, and other homeownership topics.
- Housing and mortgage information from the Department of Housing and Urban Development at **www.hud.gov.**
- Information on prepaying a mortgage at **alfredo. wustl. edu/mort/.**

- Information about reverse mortgages at **www.hud. gov/rvrsmort.html.**
- Financial calculators for mortgage costs at **www.centura.com/formulas/ca/c.html.**

(Note: Addresses and content of websites change, and new sites are created daily. Use search engines to update and locate websites for your current financial planning needs.)

*PFP sheets: 40–45*

Short-Term Financial Planning Activities

1. Compare your current housing situation with your housing needs and financial situation (see PFP Sheet 40).
2. Conduct an analysis to compare renting and buying of housing (see PFP Sheet 41).
3. Compare various rental alternatives as needed (see PFP Sheet 42).
4. Determine your housing and mortgage affordability, and compare various sources of mortgages (see PFP Sheets 43).

Long-Term Financial Planning Activities

1. Monitor changing interest rates and assess refinancing alternatives (see PFP Sheet 45).
2. Develop a plan for assessing housing needs and costs in the future.

# Continuous Case for Part 3

SPENDING PATTERNS FOR FINANCIAL SECURITY

**Life Situation**
Young married couple: Pam, 30; Josh, 32; two children, ages 1 and 3

*Financial Goals*
- Improve daily spending habits
- Purchase a new home
- Acquire a second motor vehicle

*Financial Data*

| | |
|---|---|
| Monthly income | $ 3,600 |
| Living expenses | 3,125 |
| Assets | 33,850 |
| Liabilities | 1,520 |

The Brocks now have two preschool-age children. Their household income has declined because Pam has "retired" for awhile to care for the children. To compensate for their lower monthly income, Pam and Josh have cut back to the basics and purchase only the "necessities" each month. Still, their expenses total $3,125 a month. However, the Brocks have managed to pay down their liabilities over the past four years; now their liabilities total $1,520.

Housing needs are also changing for the Brocks as their family increases in size. At present, they pay $750 in rent for a two-bedroom apartment. To purchase a home for a comparable monthly payment, the Brocks would have to relocate farther from Josh's place of employment.

In addition to buying a home, the Brocks need to purchase a second automobile. Currently Pam must drive Josh to the train station (creating many inconveniences for her and the children) if she wants to use the car for various business and education activities. If they move to the suburbs, the situation will only get worse.

## Questions

1. What major factors are affecting the Brocks' spending habits?
2. Based on a monthly income of $3,600, an estimated $240 per month for property taxes and homeowner's insurance, current mortgage interest rates of 9 percent, and a down payment of at least 10 percent, what would it cost the Brocks to purchase a home?
3. What tax advantages will the Brocks realize by purchasing a home rather than renting?
4. What transportation alternatives should the Brocks consider? If they decide that they need a second motor vehicle, how should they finance it?

# INSURING YOUR RESOURCES

# 10

# Home and Automobile Insurance

José and Marty are excited about their spring break trip to Florida. They decided to rent a car because Marty drives an old car and José doesn't want to put miles on the Honda his parents gave him as a graduation gift. When they go to pick up the car, the sales agent asks them if they want a loss-damage and collision-damage waiver, which would cost them $10 per day. They don't want to spend an extra $70 on this trip, but neither one knows if his personal insurance covers rental cars. What should they do?

Motorists usually decline trip insurance. They get the same or better protection from their personal auto insurance. However, sometimes there are gaps in personal coverage. If you don't know the rules and decline the rental agency's offer, you may be driving uninsured. For example, Marty may not have comprehensive and collision coverage on his old car because he knows it isn't worth the additional coverage. This means he also won't be covered on the rental car.

If Marty's or José's auto policy doesn't cover collision or theft when driving a rental car, they have another option. Certain credit cards will protect them against damage or theft if the card is used when paying for the rental. But again, there may be limitations.

If José and Marty don't know their rental car insurance rules, they should check with their auto insurer or credit card company before signing the rental agreement. Otherwise, the safest thing might be to pay the additional $10 per day.

## Questions

1. Why do most motorists decline additional coverage when they rent a car? What are the limitations of this strategy?
2. What other option do Marty and José have if their personal auto insurance does not cover rental cars?
3. What web research could they do before they rent a car again?

## Learning Objectives

**Obj. 1**  Develop a risk management plan using insurance.

**Obj. 2**  Discuss the importance of property and liability insurance.

**Obj. 3**  Explain the insurance coverages and policy types available to homeowners and renters.

**Obj. 4**  Analyze factors that influence the amount of coverage and cost of home insurance.

**Obj. 5**  Identify the important types of automobile insurance coverages.

**Obj. 6**  Evaluate factors that affect the cost of automobile insurance.

## INSURANCE AND RISK MANAGEMENT: AN INTRODUCTION

### Obj. 1
Develop a risk management plan using insurance.

*insurance*  Protection against possible financial loss.

*insurance company*  A risk-sharing firm that assumes financial responsibility for losses that may result from an insured risk.

*insurer*  An insurance company.

*policy*  A written contract for insurance.

*premium*  The amount of money a policyholder is charged for an insurance policy.

*insured*  A person covered by an insurance policy.

*policyholder*  A person who owns an insurance policy.

Insurance involves property and people. By providing protection against the risks of financial uncertainty and unexpected losses, insurance makes it possible to plan for the future.

### What Is Insurance?

**Insurance** is protection against possible financial loss. Although many types of insurance exist, they all have one thing in common: They give you the peace of mind that comes from knowing that money will be available to meet the needs of your survivors, pay medical expenses, protect your home and belongings, and cover personal or property damage caused by you when driving.

Life insurance replaces income that would be lost if the policyholder died. Health insurance helps meet medical expenses when the policyholder becomes ill. Automobile insurance helps cover property and personal damage caused by the policyholder's car. Home insurance covers the policyholder's place of residence and its associated financial risks, such as damage to personal property and injuries to others.

An **insurance company,** or **insurer,** is a risk-sharing firm that agrees to assume financial responsibility for losses that may result from an insured risk. A person joins the risk-sharing group (the insurance company) by purchasing a **policy** (a contract). Under the policy, the insurance company agrees to assume the risk for a fee (the **premium**) that the person (the **insured,** or the **policyholder**) pays periodically.

Insurance provides protection against many risks of financial uncertainty and unexpected losses. The financial consequences of failing to obtain the right amount and type of insurance can be disastrous.

### Types of Risks

You face risks every day. You can't cross the street without some danger that you'll be hit by a car. You can't own property without taking the chance that it will be lost, stolen, damaged, or destroyed. Insurance companies offer financial protection against such dangers and losses by promising to compensate the insured for a relatively large loss in return for the payment of a much smaller but certain expense called the *premium.*

*Risk, peril,* and *hazard* are important terms in insurance. While in popular use these terms tend to be interchangeable, each has a distinct, technical meaning in insurance terminology.

Basically, **risk** is uncertainty or lack of predictability. In this instance, it refers to the uncertainty as to loss that a person or a property covered by insurance faces. Insurance companies frequently refer to the insured person or property as the *risk.*

**Peril** is the cause of a possible loss. It is the contingency that causes someone to take out insurance. People buy policies for financial protection against perils such as fire, windstorms, explosions, robbery, accidents, and premature death.

**Hazard** increases the likelihood of loss through some peril. For example, defective house wiring is a hazard that increases the likelihood of the peril of fire.

The most common risks are classified as personal risks, property risks, and liability risks. *Personal risks* are the uncertainties surrounding loss of income or life due to premature death, illness, disability, old age, or unemployment. *Property risks* are the uncertainties of direct or indirect losses to personal or real property due to fire, windstorms, accidents, theft, and other hazards. *Liability risks* are possible losses due to negligence resulting in bodily harm or property damage to others. Such harm or damage could be caused by an automobile, professional misconduct, injury suffered on one's property, and so on.

Personal risks, property risks, and liability risks are types of **pure risk,** or *insurable risk,* since there would be a chance of loss only if the specified events occurred. Pure risks are accidental and unintentional risks for which the nature and financial cost of the loss can be predicted.

A **speculative risk** is a risk that carries a chance of either loss or gain. Starting a small business that may or may not succeed is an example of speculative risk. So is gambling. Speculative risks are legally defined as uninsurable.

*risk* Chance or uncertainty of loss; also used to mean "the insured."

*peril* The cause of a possible loss.

*hazard* A factor that increases the likelihood of loss through some peril.

*pure risk* A risk in which there is only a chance of loss; also called *insurable risk.*

*speculative risk* A risk in which there is a chance of either loss or gain.

## Risk Management Methods

*Risk management* is an organized strategy for protecting assets and people. It helps reduce financial losses caused by destructive events. Risk management is a long-range planning process. People's risk management needs change at various points in their lives. If you understand risks and how to manage them, you can provide better protection for yourself and your family. In this way, you can reduce your financial losses and thereby improve your chances for economic, social, physical, and emotional well-being. Since you will probably be unable to afford to cover all risks, you need to understand how to obtain the best protection you can afford.

Most people think of risk management as buying insurance. However, insurance is not the only method of dealing with risk; in certain situations, other methods may be less costly. Four general risk management techniques are commonly used.

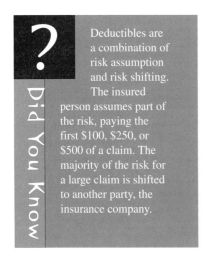

**1. Risk Avoidance**   You can avoid the risk of an automobile accident by not driving to work. General Motors can avoid the risk of product failure by not introducing new cars. Risk avoidance would be practiced in both instances, but at a very high cost. You might have to give up your job, and General Motors might lose out to competitors that introduce new models.

In some situations, however, risk avoidance is practical. At the personal level, people avoid risks by not smoking or by not walking through high-crime neighborhoods. At the business level, jewelry stores avoid losses through robbery by locking their merchandise in vaults. Obviously, no person or business can avoid all risks.

**2. Risk Reduction**   While avoiding risks completely may not be possible, reducing risks may be a cause of action. You can reduce the risk of injury in an auto accident by wearing a seat belt. You can install smoke alarms and fire extinguishers to protect life and reduce potential fire damage. You can reduce the risk of illness by eating a balanced diet and exercising.

**3. Risk Assumption**   Risk assumption means taking on responsibility for the loss or injury that may result from a risk. Generally, it makes sense to assume a risk when the potential loss is small, when risk management has reduced the risk, when insurance coverage is expensive, and when there is no other way to obtain protection. For instance, you might decide not to purchase collision insurance on an older car. Then, if an accident occurs, you will bear the costs of fixing the car.

*self-insurance*   The process of establishing a monetary fund to cover the cost of a loss.

**Self-insurance** is the process of establishing a monetary fund to cover the cost of a loss. Self-insurance does not eliminate risks; it only provides means for covering losses. Many people self-insure by default, not by choice.

**4. Risk Shifting**   The most common method of dealing with risk is to shift, or transfer, it to an insurance company or some other organization. Insurance is the protection against loss afforded by the purchase of an insurance policy from an insurance company.

Exhibit 10–1 summarizes various risks and appropriate strategies for managing them.

## Planning an Insurance Program

Because all people have their own needs and goals, many of which change over the years, a personal insurance program should be tailored to those changes. In the early years of marriage, when the family is growing, most families need certain kinds of insurance protection. This protection may include property insurance on an apartment or a house, life and disability insurance for wage earners and caretakers of dependents, and adequate health insurance for the whole family.

Later, when the family has a higher income and a different financial situation, protection needs will change. There might be a long-range provision for the children's education, more life insurance to match higher income and living standards, and revised health insurance protection. Still later, when the children have grown and are on their own, retirement benefits will be a consideration, further changing the family's personal insurance program.

### EXHIBIT 10-1   EXAMPLES OF RISKS AND RISK MANAGEMENT STRATEGIES

| Risks | | Strategies for Reducing Financial Impact | | |
| --- | --- | --- | --- | --- |
| Personal Events | Financial Impact | Personal Resources | Private Sector | Public Sector |
| Disability | Loss of one income<br>Loss of services<br>Increased expenses | Savings, investments<br>Family observing<br>safety precautions | Disability insurance | Disability insurance |
| Illness | Loss of one income<br>Catastrophic hospital<br>expenses | Health-enhancing<br>behavior | Health insurance<br>Health maintenance<br>organizations | Military health care<br>Medicare, Medicaid |
| Death | Loss of one income<br>Loss of services<br>Final expenses | Estate planning<br>Risk reduction | Life insurance | Veteran's life<br>insurance<br>Social Security<br>survivor's benefits |
| Retirement | Decreased income<br>Unplanned living<br>expenses | Savings<br>Investments<br>Hobbies, skills | Retirement and/or<br>pensions | Social Security<br>Pension plan for<br>government<br>employees |
| Property loss | Catastrophic storm<br>damage to property<br>Repair or replacement<br>cost of theft | Property repair and<br>upkeep<br>Security plans | Automobile insurance<br>Homeowner's<br>insurance<br>Flood insurance (joint<br>program with<br>government) | Flood insurance<br>(joint program<br>with business) |
| Liability | Claims and settlement<br>costs<br>Lawsuits and legal<br>expenses<br>Loss of personal<br>assets and income | Observing safety<br>precautions<br>Maintaining property | Homeowner's<br>insurance<br>Automobile insurance<br>Malpractice insurance | |

The Financial Planning for Life's Situations feature on page 316 suggests several guidelines to follow in planning your insurance program. Exhibit 10–2 outlines the steps in developing a personal insurance program.

### Step 1: Set Insurance Goals

In managing risks, your goals are to minimize personal, property, and liability risks. Your insurance goals should define what to do to cover the basic risks present in your life situation. Covering the basic risks means providing a financial resource to cover costs resulting from a loss.

Suppose your goal is to buy a new car. You must plan to make the purchase and to protect yourself against financial losses from accidents. Auto insurance on the car lets you enjoy the car without worrying that an auto accident might leave you worse off, financially and physically, than before.

Each individual has unique goals. Income, age, family size, lifestyle, experience, and responsibilities influence the goals you set, and the insurance you buy must reflect those goals. In general, financial advisers say that a basic risk management plan must set goals to reduce

## EXHIBIT 10-2   CREATING A PERSONAL INSURANCE PROGRAM

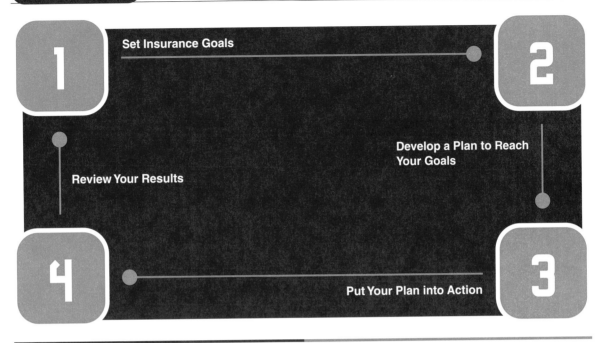

- Potential loss of income due to the premature death, illness, accident, or unemployment of a wage earner.
- Potential loss of income and extra expense resulting from the illness, disability, or death of a spouse.
- Additional expenses due to the injury, illness, or death of other family members.
- Potential loss of real or personal property due to fire, theft, or other hazards.
- Potential loss of income, savings, and property due to personal liability.

### Step 2: Develop a Plan to Reach Your Goals

Planning is a sign of maturity, a way of taking control of life instead of letting life happen to you. What risks do you face? Which risks can you afford to take without having to back away from your goals? What resources—public programs, personal assets, or private risk-sharing plans—are available to you?

To understand and use the resources at your command, you need good information. In terms of insurance, this means a clear picture of the available insurance, the reliability of different insurers, and the comparative costs of the coverage needed.

### Step 3: Put Your Plan into Action

As you carry out your plan, obtain financial and personal resources, budget them, and use them to reach risk management goals. If, for example, you find the insurance protection you have is not enough to cover your basic risks, you may purchase additional coverage, change the kind of insurance coverage, restructure your budget to cover additional insurance costs, and strengthen your savings or investment programs to reduce long-term risk.

The best risk management plans have flexibility. Savings accounts or other cash, for example, should be available as emergency funds for unexpected financial problems. The best plans are also flexible enough to allow you to respond to changing life situations.

## Financial Planning for Life's Situations

### HOW CAN YOU PLAN AN INSURANCE PROGRAM?

**DID YOU:**                                                                        YES   NO

- Seek advice from a competent and reliable insurance adviser?                        ☐     ☐
- Determine what insurance you need to provide your family with sufficient protection if you die?   ☐     ☐
- Consider what portion of the family protection is met by Social Security and by group insurance?   ☐     ☐
- Decide what other needs insurance must meet (funeral expenses, savings, retirement annuities, etc.)?   ☐     ☐
- Decide what types of insurance best meet your needs?                                ☐     ☐
- Plan an insurance program and implement it except for periodic reviews of changing needs and changing conditions?   ☐     ☐
- Avoid buying more insurance than you need or can afford?                            ☐     ☐
- Would you drop one policy for another that provides the same coverage for less money?   ☐     ☐

Note: *Yes* answers reflect wise actions for insurance planning.

Your goal should be an insurance program that expands (or contracts) with changing protection needs.

To put your risk management plan to work, you must answer four basic questions: (1) What should be insured, (2) for how much, (3) what kind of insurance should I buy, and (4) from whom?

### 4. Review Your Results

Evaluate your insurance plan periodically, at least every two or three years or whenever your family circumstances change. Among the questions you should ask yourself are: Does it work? Does it adequately protect my plans and goals? An effective risk manager consistently checks the outcomes of decisions and is alert to changes that may reduce the effectiveness of the current risk management plan.

A young working couple may be entirely happy with their life and health insurance coverage. When they add an infant to the family, a review of protection is appropriate. Suddenly the risk of financial catastrophe to the family (should one or both parents die or become disabled) is much greater.

The needs of a single person differ from those of a family, a single parent, a couple, or a group of unrelated adults living in the same household. While these people face similar risks, their financial responsibility to others differs greatly. In each case, the vital question is: Have I provided the financial resources and risk management strategy needed to take care of my basic responsibilities for my own well-being and the well-being of others?

**Sheet 46**

### Concept Check 10-1

1. What is the purpose of insurance?
2. How are the most common risks classified?
3. What is the difference between pure risk and speculative risk?
4. What are the methods of managing risk?
5. What are the steps in planning your personal insurance coverage?

### JONATHAN HOENIG SPEAKS ON INSURANCE

Ever been to Vegas? Ever made a bet?

Buying insurance is essentially making a bet that you *don't* want to win. While you can't *plan* on experiencing many of life's calamities, you *should* plan for them. Without the appropriate insurance, a single event, such as a major accident, can completely trash your hard-earned assets.

Never smoked? Healthy as a horse? It doesn't matter! Insurance is specifically designed for those situations you hope will never occur. When those situations do occur, however, you'll find that savvy spending on appropriate insurance was money well spent.

Life insurance takes care of your dependents if you die. If you have a spouse, children, or other loved ones who are directly dependent on your income, life insurance is a *must.* Young people generally find they don't need life insurance.

Health insurance "foots" the medical bills if you get sick. If you've ever paid full price for a medical prescription, you are probably aware that health care costs have skyrocketed. Even a seemingly simple procedure can often cost thousands of dollars. So everyone needs health insurance, and thankfully many employers offer group plans at reasonable rates. Be sure to inquire about health insurance when applying for a job; the level of insurance offered might affect your interest in working for a particular company. Working solo? Individuals who purchase private policies will pay more for equivalent coverage.

Keep in mind that there are insurance products available for any number of scenarios, so do your homework and evaluate your needs. As always, read everything and ask questions.

Statistics show that each year 1 out of 106 people die, 1 out of 70 have an automobile accident, and 1 out of 88 households catch on fire. That "1" could be you.

## PROPERTY AND LIABILITY INSURANCE

**Obj. 2**
Discuss the importance of property and liability insurance.

Major disasters have caused catastrophic amounts of property loss in the United States. Hurricane Hugo cost $4.2 billion in damages in 1989. Fires in Oakland, California in 1991 caused insured losses of $1.7 billion. Hurricane Andrew resulted in $15 billion of insurance claims in 1992. The Midwest floods of 1993 resulted in over $2 billion of damage.

Since most people invest large amounts of money in their homes and motor vehicles, protecting these assets from loss is a great concern. Each year, homeowners and renters lose billions of dollars from more than 3 million burglaries, 500,000 fires, and 200,000 instances of damage from other hazards. The cost of injuries and property damage caused by automobiles is also very great. Most people use insurance to reduce their chances of economic loss from these risks.

The price you pay for home and automobile insurance may be viewed as an investment in financial protection against these losses. Although the costs of home and automobile insurance may seem high, the financial losses from which insurance protects you are much higher. Property and liability insurance offer protection from financial losses that may arise from a wide variety of situations.

The main types of risks related to a home and an automobile are (1) property damage or loss and (2) your responsibility for injuries to others or damage to the property of others.

### Potential Property Losses

Houses, automobiles, furniture, clothing, and other personal belongings are a substantial financial commitment. Property owners face two basic types of risks. The first is

**liability**  Legal responsibility for the financial cost of another person's losses or injuries.

**negligence**  Failure to take ordinary or reasonable care in a situation.

**strict liability**  A situation in which a person is held responsible for intentional or unintentional actions.

**vicarious liability**  A situation in which a person is held legally responsible for the actions of another person.

*physical damage* caused by hazards such as fire, wind, water, and smoke. These hazards can cause destruction of your property or temporary loss of its use. For example, if a windstorm causes a large tree branch to break your automobile windshield, you lose the use of the vehicle while it is being repaired. The second type of risk property owners face is *loss of use* due to robbery, burglary, vandalism, or arson.

## Liability Protection

In a wide variety of circumstances, a person may be judged legally responsible for injuries or damages. For example, if a child walks across your property, falls, and sustains severe injuries, the child's family may be able to recover substantial damages from you as a result of the injuries. If you accidentally damage a rare painting while assisting a friend with home repairs, the friend may take legal action against you to recover the cost of the painting.

**Liability** is legal responsibility for the financial cost of another person's losses or injuries. Your legal responsibility is commonly caused by **negligence,** failure to take ordinary or reasonable care. Doing something in a careless manner, such as improperly supervising children at a swimming pool or failing to remove items from a frequently used staircase, may be ruled as negligence in a liability lawsuit.

Despite taking great care, a person may still be held liable in a situation. **Strict liability** is present when a person is held responsible for intentional or unintentional actions. **Vicarious liability** occurs when a person is held responsible for the actions of another person. If the behavior of a child causes financial or physical harm to others, the parent may be held responsible; if the activities of an employee cause damage, the employer may be held responsible.

### Concept Check 10-2

1. What property and liability risks might some people overlook?
2. How could a person's life situation influence the need for certain types of property and liability insurance?

## PRINCIPLES OF HOME AND PROPERTY INSURANCE

### Obj. 3
Explain the insurance coverages and policy types available to homeowners and renters.

**homeowner's insurance**  Coverage for a place of residence and its associated financial risks.

Your home and personal belongings are probably a major portion of your assets. Whether you rent your dwelling or own a home, property insurance is vital. **Homeowner's insurance** is coverage for your place of residence and its associated financial risks, such as damage to personal property and injuries to others (see Exhibit 10–3).

### Homeowner's Insurance Coverages

A homeowner's policy provides coverages for the building and other structures, additional living expenses, personal property, personal liability and related coverages, and specialized coverages.

### Building and Other Structures
The main component of homeowner's insurance is protection against financial loss due to damage or destruction to a house or other structures. Your dwelling and attached structures are covered for fire and other

**EXHIBIT 10-3**   Home Insurance Coverage

**Building and
other structures**

**Personal
property**

**Loss of use/additional
living expenses while home
is uninhabitable**

**Personal liability and
related coverages**

damages. Detached structures on the property, such as a garage, toolshed, or gazebo, are also protected. The coverage also includes trees, shrubs, and plants.

### Additional Living Expenses

If damage from a fire or other event prevents the use of your home, *additional living expense coverage* pays for the cost of living in a temporary location while your home is being repaired. Some policies limit additional living expense coverage to 10 to 20 percent of the home's coverage and limit payments to a maximum of six to nine months; other policies pay the full cost incurred for up to a year.

### Personal Property

Your household belongings, such as furniture, appliances, and clothing, are covered for damage or loss up to a portion of the insured value of the home, usually 55, 70, or 75 percent. For example, a home insured for $80,000 might have $56,000 (70 percent) of coverage for household belongings.

Personal property coverage commonly has limits for the theft of certain items, such as $1,000 for jewelry, $2,000 for firearms, and $2,500 for silverware. Items with a value exceeding these limits can be protected with a **personal property floater,** which covers the damage or loss of a specific item of high value. A floater requires a detailed description of the item and periodic appraisals to verify the current value. This coverage protects the item regardless of location; thus, the item is insured while you are traveling or transporting it.

Floaters to protect home computers and related equipment are recommended. This additional coverage can prevent financial loss due to damage or loss of your computer. Contact your insurance agent to determine whether the equipment is covered against damage from mischievous pets, spilled drinks, dropping, or power surges.

Personal property coverage usually provides protection against the loss or damage of articles taken with you when away from home. For example, possessions taken on vacation or used while at school are usually covered up to a policy limit. Property that you rent, such as some power tools or a rug shampoo machine, is insured while in your possession.

In the event of damage or loss of property, you must be able to prove both ownership and value. A **household inventory** is a list or other documentation of personal belongings, with purchase dates and cost information. You can get a form for such an inventory from an insurance agent. Exhibit 10–4 provides a reminder of the items you should include in the inventory. For items of special value, you should have receipts, serial numbers, brand names, model names, and written appraisals of value.

*personal property floater* Additional property insurance to cover the damage or loss of a specific item of high value.

*household inventory* A list or other documentation of personal belongings, with purchase dates and cost information.

**EXHIBIT 10-4**    HOUSEHOLD INVENTORY CONTENTS

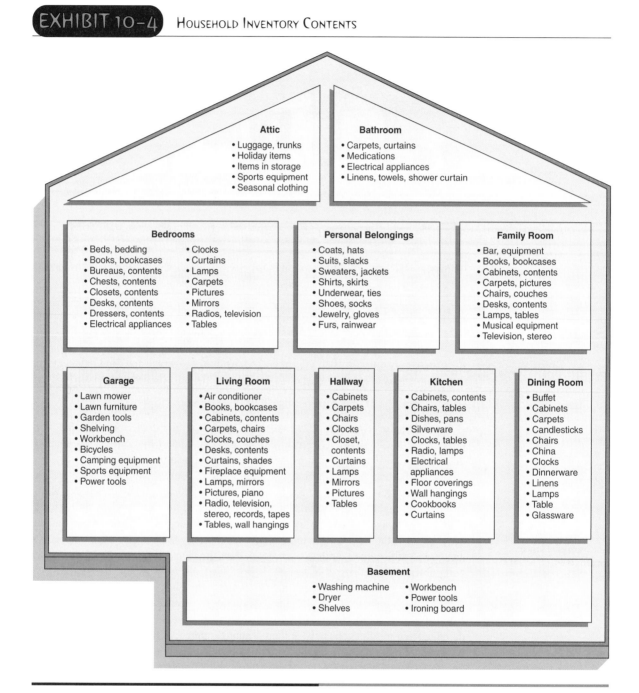

**Attic**
- Luggage, trunks
- Holiday items
- Items in storage
- Sports equipment
- Seasonal clothing

**Bathroom**
- Carpets, curtains
- Medications
- Electrical appliances
- Linens, towels, shower curtain

**Bedrooms**
- Beds, bedding
- Books, bookcases
- Bureaus, contents
- Chests, contents
- Closets, contents
- Desks, contents
- Dressers, contents
- Electrical appliances
- Clocks
- Curtains
- Lamps
- Carpets
- Pictures
- Mirrors
- Radios, television
- Tables

**Personal Belongings**
- Coats, hats
- Suits, slacks
- Sweaters, jackets
- Shirts, skirts
- Underwear, ties
- Shoes, socks
- Jewelry, gloves
- Furs, rainwear

**Family Room**
- Bar, equipment
- Books, bookcases
- Cabinets, contents
- Carpets, pictures
- Chairs, couches
- Desks, contents
- Lamps, tables
- Musical equipment
- Television, stereo

**Garage**
- Lawn mower
- Lawn furniture
- Garden tools
- Shelving
- Workbench
- Bicycles
- Camping equipment
- Sports equipment
- Power tools

**Living Room**
- Air conditioner
- Books, bookcases
- Cabinets, contents
- Carpets, chairs
- Clocks, couches
- Desks, contents
- Curtains, shades
- Fireplace equipment
- Lamps, mirrors
- Pictures, piano
- Radio, television, stereo, records, tapes
- Tables, wall hangings

**Hallway**
- Cabinets
- Carpets
- Chairs
- Clocks
- Closet, contents
- Curtains
- Lamps
- Mirrors
- Pictures
- Tables

**Kitchen**
- Cabinets, contents
- Chairs, tables
- Dishes, pans
- Silverware
- Clocks, tables
- Radio, lamps
- Electrical appliances
- Floor coverings
- Wall hangings
- Cookbooks
- Curtains

**Dining Room**
- Buffet
- Cabinets
- Carpets
- Candlesticks
- Chairs
- China
- Clocks
- Dinnerware
- Linens
- Lamps
- Table
- Glassware

**Basement**
- Washing machine
- Dryer
- Shelves
- Workbench
- Power tools
- Ironing board

**Sheet 47**

Your household inventory can include photographs or a video recording of your home and contents. Make sure the closet and storage area doors are photographed open. On the backs of the photographs, indicate the date and the value of the objects. Regularly update your inventory, photos, and appraisal documents. Keep a copy of each document in a secure location such as a safe deposit box.

## Personal Liability and Related Coverages

Each day, you face the risk of financial loss due to injuries to others or damage to property for which you are responsible. The following are examples of this risk:

- A neighbor or guest falls on your property, resulting in permanent disability.
- A spark from burning leaves on your property starts a fire that damages a neighbor's roof.
- A member of your family accidentally breaks an expensive glass statue while at another person's house.

In each of these situations, you could be held responsible for the costs incurred. The personal liability component of a homeowner's policy protects you from financial losses resulting from legal action or claims against you or family members due to damages to the property of others. This coverage includes the cost of legal defense.

Not all individuals who come to your property are covered by your liability insurance. While a baby-sitter or others who assist you occasionally are probably covered, regular employees, such as a housekeeper or a gardener, may require worker's compensation coverage.

*umbrella policy*
Supplementary personal liability coverage; also called a *personal catastrophe policy.*

Most homeowner's policies provide a basic personal liability coverage of $100,000, but additional amounts are frequently recommended. An **umbrella policy,** also called a *personal catastrophe policy,* supplements your basic personal liability coverage. This added protection covers you for personal injury claims such as libel, slander, defamation of character, and invasion of property. Extended liability policies are sold in amounts of $1 million or more and are useful for individuals with substantial net worth. If you are a business owner, you may need other types of liability coverage.

*medical payments coverage*   Home insurance that pays the cost of minor accidental injuries on one's property.

**Medical payments coverage** pays the costs of minor accidental injuries on your property and minor injuries caused by you, family members, or pets away from home. Settlements under medical payments coverage are made without determining fault. This protection allows fast processing of small claims, generally up to $5,000. Suits for more severe personal injuries are covered by the personal liability portion of the homeowner's policy. Medical payments coverage does not cover the people who live in the home being insured.

Should you or a family member accidentally damage another person's property, the *supplementary coverage* of homeowner's insurance will pay for these minor mishaps. This protection is usually limited to $500 or $1,000. Again, payments are made regardless of fault. Any property damage claims for greater amounts would require action under the personal liability coverage.

## Specialized Coverages

Homeowner's insurance usually does not cover losses from floods and earthquakes. People living in areas with these two risks need special coverage. In various communities, the National Flood Insurance Program makes flood insurance available. This protection is separate from the homeowner's policy. An insurance agent or the Federal Emergency Management Agency of the Federal Insurance Administration (see Appendix B) can give you additional information about this coverage. Fewer than half of the people who live in flood-prone areas have this coverage.

*endorsement*
An addition of coverage to a standard insurance policy.

Earthquake insurance can be obtained as an **endorsement,** or addition of coverage, to the homeowner's policy. Since the most severe earthquakes occur in the Pacific Coast region, most insurance against this risk is bought in that region. Remember, however, that every state is vulnerable to earthquakes and this insurance coverage is available in all areas. Lenders frequently require insurance against both floods and earthquakes for a mortgage to buy a home in areas with these risks.

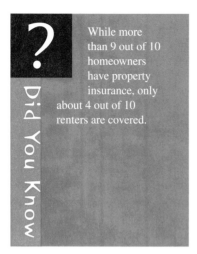

## Renter's Insurance

For people who rent, home insurance coverages include personal property protection, additional living expenses coverage, and personal liability and related coverages. Protection against financial loss due to damage or loss of personal property is the main component of renter's insurance. Often renters believe they are covered under the insurance policy of the building owner. In fact, the building owner's property insurance does not cover tenants' personal property unless the building owner can be proven liable. If faulty wiring causes a fire and damages a tenant's property, the renter may be able to collect for damages from the building owner. Renter's insurance is relatively inexpensive and provides protection from financial loss due to many of the same risks covered in homeowner's policies.

## Home Insurance Policy Forms

Until the mid-1950s, a homeowner had to buy separate coverage for fire, theft, and other risks. Then the insurance industry developed a series of package policies. The *basic form (HO–1)* and the *broad form (HO–2)* were the first such policies; they provided the primary coverages shown in Exhibit 10–5.

The *special form (HO–3)* of a homeowner's policy covers the building for all causes of loss or damage except those specifically excluded by the policy. Common exclusions are flood, earthquake, war, and nuclear accidents (see also Exhibit 10–6 on page 324). Personal property is covered for the risks listed in the policy.

The *tenants form (HO–4)* protects the personal property of renters against the specific risks listed in the policy. As mentioned, renter's insurance does not include coverage on the building or other structures.

*Condominium owner's insurance (HO–6)* protects personal property of condominium owners and any additions or improvements made to the living unit, such as bookshelves, electrical fixtures, and wall or floor coverings. Insurance on the building and other structures is purchased by the condominium association.

The *modified coverage form (HO–8)*, or older-home policy, provides the same coverages as the basic form at a more reasonable cost because the homes are older and more difficult to replace.

Manufactured housing units and mobile homes usually qualify for insurance coverage with conventional policies. However, certain mobile homes may require a special arrangement and higher rates since their construction makes them more prone to fire and wind damage. The cost of mobile home insurance coverage is most heavily affected by location and by the method used to attach the housing unit to the ground. This type of property insurance is quite expensive; a $20,000 mobile home can cost as much to insure as a $60,000 house.

In addition to the property and liability risks previously discussed, home insurance policies include coverage for

- Credit card fraud, check forgery, and counterfeit money.
- The cost of removing damaged property.
- Emergency removal of property to protect it from damage.
- Temporary repairs after a loss to prevent further damage.
- Fire department charges in areas with such fees.

**EXHIBIT 10-5**

Types of Home
Insurance Policies

The policies below cover perils provided for in the basic and broad forms, including

| Basic Form (HO–1) | • Fire, lightning<br>• Windstorm, hail<br>• Explosion<br>• Riot or civil commotion<br>• Aircraft<br>• Vehicles | • Smoke<br>• Vandalism or malicious mischief<br>• Theft<br>• Glass breakage<br>• Volcanic eruption |
|---|---|---|
| **Broad Form (HO–2)** | Covers all basic-form risks, plus<br>• Falling objects<br>• Weight of ice, snow, or sleet<br>• Discharge of water or steam | • Tearing apart of heating system or appliance<br>• Freezing<br>• Accidental damage from electrical current |
| **Special Form (All risk) (HO–3)** | Covers all basic and broad-form risks, plus any other risks except those specifically excluded from the policy, such as<br>• Flood      • War<br>• Earthquake      • Nuclear accidents | |
| **Tenants Form (HO–4)** | Covers personal belongings against the risks covered by the basic and broad forms of the homeowner's policies | |
| **Comprehensive Form (HO–5)** | Expands coverage of HO–3 to include endorsements for items such as replacement cost coverage on contents and guaranteed replacement cost coverage on buildings | |
| **Condominium Form (HO–6)** | Covers personal belongings and additions to the living unit | |
| **Country Home Form (HO–7)** | For nonfarm business rural residents with coverage on agricultural buildings and equipment | |
| **Modified Coverage Form (HO–8)** | This older-home policy covers residences with high replacement cost relative to current market value. For example, decorative woodwork in a Victorian home would be very costly to duplicate; coverage pays for the restoration of property, but not necessarily with the same materials as used in the original. | |

The other major coverages of each policy are
• Personal liability
• Medical payments for guests on the property
• Additional living expenses

Note: HO–1 and HO–2 policies are no longer sold in many areas.

## Concept Check 10-3

1.   What main coverages are included in home insurance policies?
2.   What is the purpose of personal liability coverage?
3.   How does renter's insurance differ from other home insurance policies?

## HOME INSURANCE COST FACTORS

**Obj. 4**

Analyze factors that influence the amount of coverage and cost of home insurance.

Studies reveal that as many as two-thirds of homes in the United States are not insured or are underinsured. Financial losses caused by fire, theft, wind, and other risks amount to billions of dollars each year. Since most homeowners have a mortgage on their property, their lending institutions usually require insurance. When purchasing insurance, you can get the best value by selecting the appropriate coverage amount and being aware of factors that affect insurance costs.

**Not Everything Is Covered**

Certain personal property is specifically excluded from the coverage provided by homeowner's insurance:

- Articles separately described and specifically insured, such as jewelry, furs, boats, or expensive electronic equipment.
- Animals, birds, or fish.
- Motorized land vehicles, except those used to service an insured's residence, that are not licensed for road use.
- Any device or instrument for the transmission and recording of sound, including any accessories or antennas, while in or on motor vehicles. This includes stereo tape players, stereo tapes, and citizens' band radios.
- Aircraft and parts.
- Property of roomers, boarders, and other tenants who are not related to any insured.
- Property contained in an apartment regularly rented or held for rental to others by any insured.
- Property rented or held for rental to others away from the residence premises.
- Business property in storage, or held as a sample, or for sale, or for delivery after sale.
- Business property pertaining to business actually conducted on the residence premises.
- Business property away from the residence premises.

**EXHIBIT 10–7**

**Determining the Amount of Home Insurance You Need**

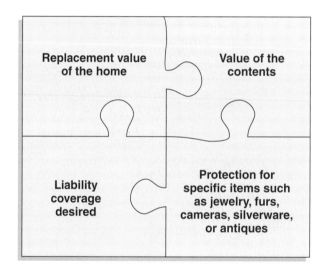

## How Much Coverage Do You Need?

Several factors affect the insurance coverage needed for your home and property (see Exhibit 10–7). Your insurance protection should be based on the amount needed to rebuild or repair your house, not the amount you paid for it. As construction costs rise, you should increase the amount of coverage. In recent years, most insurance policies have had a built-in inflation clause that increases coverage as property values increase.

In the past, most homeowner's policies contained a provision requiring that the building be insured for at least 80 percent of the replacement value. Under this **coinsurance clause,** the homeowner would have to pay for part of the losses if the property was not insured for the specified percentage of the replacement value. While a few companies still use a coinsurance clause, most companies today suggest full coverage.

*coinsurance clause*
A policy provision that requires a homeowner to pay for part of the losses if the property is not insured for the specified percentage of the replacement value.

If you are financing a home, the lending institution will require you to have property insurance in an amount that covers its financial investment. Remember, too, that the amount of insurance on your home will determine the coverage on the contents. Personal belongings are generally covered up to an amount ranging from 55 to 75 percent of the insurance amount on the dwelling.

Insurance companies base claim settlements on one of two methods. Under the **actual cash value (ACV)** method, the payment you receive is based on the current replacement cost of a damaged or lost item less depreciation. This means you would get $180 for a five-year-old television set that cost you $400 and had an estimated life of eight years if the same set now costs $480. Your settlement amount is determined by taking the current cost of $480 and subtracting five years of depreciation from it— $300 for five years at $60 a year.

*actual cash value (ACV)*
A claim settlement method in which the insured receives payment based on the current replacement cost of a damaged or lost item, less depreciation.

*replacement value*
A claim settlement method in which the insured receives the full cost of repairing or replacing a damaged or lost item.

Under the **replacement value** method for settling claims, you receive the full cost of repairing or replacing a damaged or lost item; depreciation is not considered. However, many companies limit the replacement cost to 400 percent of the item's actual cash value. Replacement value coverage costs about 10 to 20 percent more than ACV coverage.

## Factors That Affect Home Insurance Costs

**Sheet 48**

The main influences on the premium paid for home and property insurance are the location of the home, the type of structure, the coverage amount and policy type, discounts, and differences among insurance companies.

### Location of Home
The location of the residence affects insurance rates. So do the efficiency of the fire department, distance from the fire station, the available water supply, and the frequency of thefts in the area. If more claims have been filed in an area, home insurance rates for people living there will be higher. Weather events such as a hailstorm or a hurricane also affects insurance costs.

**Did You Know?**
One in 10 insured American homeowners reports an insured loss annually. However, in Milwaukee only 1 in 11 insured homeowners has a claim each year, and the average $2,036 claim is half that of Los Angeles. Los Angeles had the highest average payment per claim—$4,052. These findings are based on data from the Insurance Research Council. (Michele Derus, "Low-Loss Leader," *Chicago Tribune*, October 11, 1997, sec. 4, p. 21.)

### Type of Structure
The type of home and the construction materials influence the costs of insurance coverage. A brick house, for example, would cost less to insure than a similar house made of wood. However, earthquake coverage is more expensive for a brick home than for a wood dwelling. Also, the age and style of the house can create potential risks and increase insurance costs.

### Coverage Amount and Policy Type
The policy you select and the financial limits of coverage affect the premium you pay. It costs more to insure a $150,000 home than a $100,000 home. The comprehensive form of homeowner's policy costs more than a tenant's policy.

The *deductible* amount in your policy also affects the cost of your insurance. If you increase the amount of your deductible, your premium will be lower since the company will pay out less in claims. The most common deductible amount is $250. Increasing the deductible from $250 to $500 or $1,000 can reduce the premium 15 percent or more.

**Sheet 49**

## Reducing Home Insurance Costs

**Home Insurance Discounts**    Most companies offer incentives that reduce home insurance costs. Your premium may be lower if you have smoke detectors or a fire extinguisher. Deterrents to burglars, such as dead bolt locks or an alarm system, can also save you money. Some companies offer home insurance discounts to policyholders who are nonsmokers or may give a discount for being "claim free" for a certain number of years.

**Company Differences**    Studies show that you can save up to 25 percent on homeowner's insurance by comparing companies. Contact both insurance agents who work for one company and independent agents who represent several. The information you obtain will enable you to compare rates. Home insurance rates may be compared using information from websites such as www.insuremarket.com.

Don't select a company on the basis of price alone. Also consider service and coverage. Not all companies settle claims in the same way. For example, a number of homeowners had two sides of their houses dented by hail. Since the type of siding used in these houses was no longer available, all of the siding had to be replaced. Some insurance companies paid for complete replacement of the siding, while others paid only for replacement of the damaged areas. State insurance commissions, other government agencies, and consumer organizations can provide information about the reputations of insurance companies. *Consumer Reports* (www.consumerreports.org) regularly publishes a satisfaction index of property insurance companies.

### Concept Check 10-4

1.  What major factors influence the cost of home insurance?
2.  What actions can a person take to reduce the cost of home insurance?

## AUTOMOBILE INSURANCE COVERAGES

**Obj. 5**
Identify the important types of automobile insurance coverages.

*financial responsibility law*   State legislation that requires drivers to prove their ability to cover the cost of damage or injury caused by an automobile accident.

Each year, motor vehicle crashes cost over $150 billion in lost wages and medical costs. The National Traffic Safety Administration estimates that alcohol use is a factor in over 60 percent of automobile accidents. Such accidents result in thousands of highway deaths and injuries and over $30 billion in costs. These automobile accidents create a risk that affects many people financially and emotionally. Automobile insurance cannot eliminate the costs of automobile accidents; however, it does reduce the financial impact.

A **financial responsibility law** is state legislation that requires drivers to prove their ability to cover the cost of damage or injury caused by an automobile accident. All states have such laws to protect the public from physical harm and property damage losses caused by drivers. When injuries or significant property damage occur in an accident, the drivers involved are required to file a report with the state and to show financial responsibility. As of 2000, over 45 states had compulsory automobile insurance laws. In other states, most people meet the financial responsibility requirement by buying insurance, since very few have the financial resources to meet this legal requirement on their own. Exhibit 10–8 presents each state's minimum limits for financial responsibility. These amounts represent the minimum state requirement; higher coverage is recommended to protect the financial assets of individuals.

**EXHIBIT 10-8**

Automobile
Financial
Responsibility/
Compulsory
Insurance
Minimum Limits
(as of 2000)

SOURCE: Insurance
Information Institute
(www.iii.org).

| State | Liability Limits | State | Liability Limits |
|-------|------------------|-------|------------------|
| Alabama* | 20/40/10 | Montana* | 25/50/10 |
| Alaska* | 50/100/25 | Nebraska* | 25/50/25 |
| Arizona* | 15/30/10 | Nevada* | 15/30/10 |
| Arkansas* | 25/50/15 | New Hampshire | 25/50/25 |
| California* | 15/30/5 | New Jersey* | 15/30/5 |
| Colorado* | 25/50/15 | New Mexico* | 25/50/10 |
| Connecticut* | 20/40/10 | New York*† | 25/50/10 |
| Delaware* | 15/30/5 | North Carolina* | 25/50/15 |
| District of Columbia* | 25/50/10 | North Dakota* | 25/50/25 |
| Florida* | 10/20/10 | Ohio* | 12.5/25/7.5 |
| Georgia* | 15/30/10 | Oklahoma* | 10/20/10 |
| Hawaii* | 20/40/10 | Oregon* | 25/50/10 |
| Idaho* | 25/50/15 | Pennsylvania* | 15/30/5 |
| Illinois* | 20/40/15 | Rhode Island* | 25/50/25 |
| Indiana* | 25/50/10 | South Carolina* | 15/30/10 |
| Iowa* | 20/40/15 | South Dakota* | 25/50/25 |
| Kansas* | 25/50/10 | Tennessee | 25/50/10 |
| Kentucky* | 25/50/10 | Texas* | 20/40/15 |
| Louisiana* | 10/20/10 | Utah* | 25/50/15 |
| Maine* | 50/100/25 | Vermont* | 20/50/10 |
| Maryland* | 20/40/10 | Virginia | 25/50/20 |
| Massachusetts* | 20/40/5 | Washington* | 25/50/10 |
| Michigan* | 20/40/10 | West Virginia* | 20/40/10 |
| Minnesota* | 30/60/10 | Wisconsin | 25/50/10 |
| Mississippi | 10/20/5 | Wyoming* | 25/50/20 |
| Missouri* | 25/50/10 | | |

*State with compulsory automobile liability insurance.
†50/100 in cases where injury results in death.

The main coverages provided by automobile insurance fall into two categories: bodily injury coverages and property damage coverages (see Exhibit 10–9). Other coverages include wage loss insurance, towing service, accidental death, and car rental when a vehicle is undergoing repairs due to an accident.

## Motor Vehicle Bodily Injury Coverages

Most of the money automobile insurance companies pay in claims goes for legal expenses of injury lawsuits, medical expenses, and related costs. The main bodily injury coverages are bodily injury liability, medical payments coverage, and uninsured motorist's protection. No-fault systems in a number of states have influenced the process of settling bodily injury claims.

**bodily injury liability**
Coverage for the risk of financial loss due to legal expenses, medical costs, lost wages, and other expenses associated with injuries caused by an automobile accident for which the insured was responsible.

### Bodily Injury Liability   **Bodily injury liability** covers the risk of financial loss due to legal expenses, medical expenses, lost wages, and other expenses associated with injuries caused by an automobile accident for which you were responsible. This insurance protects you from extensive financial losses.

Bodily injury liability is usually expressed as a split limit, such as 50/100 or 100/300. These amounts represent thousands of dollars of coverage. The first number (see Exhibit 10–10) is the limit for claims that can be paid to one person; the second number is the limit for each accident; the third number is discussed in the section on

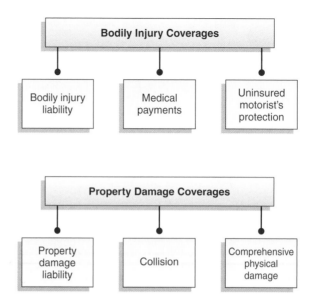

**EXHIBIT 10-9**

Two Major Categories of Automobile Insurance

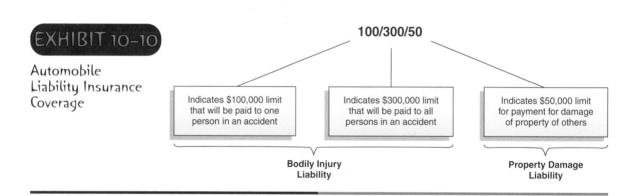

**EXHIBIT 10-10**

Automobile Liability Insurance Coverage

property damage coverages. With 100/300 bodily injury coverage, for example, a driver would have a limit of $100,000 that could be paid to one person in an accident for claims. In addition, there would be a $300,000 limit for all bodily injury claims from a single accident.

### Medical Payments Coverage

While bodily injury liability pays for the costs of injuries to persons who were not in your automobile, **medical payments coverage** covers the costs of health care for people who were injured in your automobile, including yourself. This protection covers friends, carpool members, and others who ride in your vehicle. Medical payments insurance also provides medical benefits if you or a member of your family is struck by an automobile or injured while riding in another person's automobile.

### Uninsured Motorist's Protection

If you are in an accident caused by a person without insurance, **uninsured motorist's protection** covers the cost of injuries to you and your family; in most states, however, it does not cover property damage. This insurance also provides protection against financial losses due to injuries caused by a hit-and-run driver or by a driver who has insufficient coverage to cover the cost of

*medical payments coverage* Automobile insurance that covers medical expenses for people injured in one's car.

*uninsured motorist's protection* Automobile insurance coverage for the cost of injuries to a person and members of his or her family caused by a driver with inadequate insurance or by a hit-and-run driver.

*no-fault system*   An automobile insurance program in which drivers involved in accidents collect medical expenses, lost wages, and related injury costs from their own insurance companies.

your injuries. *Underinsured motorist's coverage* provides financial protection when another driver has insurance but less coverage than needed to cover the financial damages brought on you.

### No-Fault Insurance

Difficulties and high costs of settling claims for medical expenses and personal injuries resulted in the creation of the **no-fault system,** in which drivers involved in accidents collect medical expenses, lost wages, and related injury costs from their own insurance companies. The system is intended to provide fast, smooth methods of paying for damages without taking the legal action frequently necessary to determine fault.

In 1971, Massachusetts was the first state to implement no-fault insurance. As of 2000, nearly 30 states had some variation of the system. While no-fault automobile insurance was intended to reduce the time and cost associated with the settlement of automobile injury cases, this has not always been the result. One reason for continued difficulties is that no-fault systems vary from state to state. Some no-fault states set limits on medical expenses, lost wages, and other claim settlements, while other states allow lawsuits under certain conditions, such as permanent paralysis or death. Some states include property damage in no-fault insurance. Drivers should investigate the coverages and implications of no-fault insurance in their states.

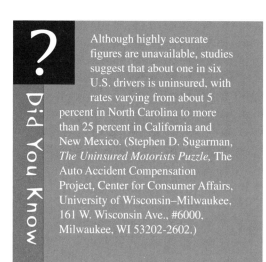

**Did You Know?**

Although highly accurate figures are unavailable, studies suggest that about one in six U.S. drivers is uninsured, with rates varying from about 5 percent in North Carolina to more than 25 percent in California and New Mexico. (Stephen D. Sugarman, *The Uninsured Motorists Puzzle,* The Auto Accident Compensation Project, Center for Consumer Affairs, University of Wisconsin–Milwaukee, 161 W. Wisconsin Ave., #6000, Milwaukee, WI 53202-2602.)

## Motor Vehicle Property Damage Coverages

Three coverages protect you from financial loss due to damage of property of others and damage to your vehicle: (1) property damage liability, (2) collision, and (3) comprehensive physical damage. (See the accompanying Financial Planning for Life's Situations feature on page 330.)

*property damage liability*   Automobile insurance coverage that protects a person against financial loss when that person damages the property of others.

### Property Damage Liability

When you damage the property of others, **property damage liability** protects you against financial loss. This coverage applies mainly to other vehicles; however, it also includes damage to street signs, lampposts, buildings, and other property. Property damage liability protects you and others covered by your policy when driving another person's automobile with permission. The policy limit for property damage liability is commonly stated with your bodily injury coverages. The last number in 50/100/25 and 100/300/50, for example, is for property damage liability ($25,000 and $50,000, respectively).

*collision*   Automobile insurance that pays for damage to the insured's car when it is involved in an accident.

### Collision

When your automobile is involved in an accident, **collision** insurance pays for the damage to the automobile regardless of fault. However, if another driver caused the accident, your insurance company may try to recover the repair costs for your vehicle through the other driver's property damage liability. The insurance company's right to recover the amount it pays for the loss from the person responsible for the loss is called *subrogation*.

The amount you can collect with collision insurance is limited to the retail value of the automobile at the time of the accident. This amount is usually based on the figures provided by some appraisal service such as the *Official Used Car Guide* of the National

## Financial Planning for Life's Situations

### ARE YOU COVERED?

Often people believe their insurance will cover various financial losses. For each of the following situations, name the type of home or automobile insurance that would protect you.

1. While you are on vacation, clothing and other personal belongings are stolen. _____

2. Your home is damaged by fire, and you have to live in a hotel for several weeks. _____

3. You and members of your family suffer injuries in an automobile accident caused by a hit-and-run driver. _____

4. A deliveryperson is injured on your property and takes legal action against you. _____

5. Your automobile is accidentally damaged by some people playing baseball. _____

6. A person takes legal action against you for injuries you caused in an automobile accident. _____

7. Water from a local lake rises and damages your furniture and carpeting. _____

8. Your automobile needs repairs because you hit a tree. _____

9. You damaged a valuable tree when your automobile hit it, and you want to pay for the damage. _____

10. While riding with you in your automobile, your nephew is injured in an accident and incurs various medical expenses. _____

ANSWERS: (1) Personal property coverage of home insurance; (2) additional living expenses of home insurance; (3) uninsured motorist's protection; (4) personal liability coverage of home insurance; (5) comprehensive physical damage; (6) bodily injury liability; (7) flood insurance—requires coverage separate from home insurance; (8) collision; (9) property damage liability of automobile insurance; (10) medical payments.

Association of Automobile Dealers. If you have an automobile with many add-on features or one that is several years old and has been restored, you should obtain a documented statement of its condition and value before an accident occurs.

*comprehensive physical damage* Automobile insurance that covers financial loss from damage to a vehicle caused by a risk other than a collision, such as fire, theft, glass breakage, hail, or vandalism.

### Comprehensive Physical Damage

Another protection for your automobile involves financial losses from damage caused by a risk other than a collision. **Comprehensive physical damage** covers you for risks such as fire, theft, glass breakage, falling objects, vandalism, wind, hail, flood, tornado, lightning, earthquake, avalanche, or damage caused by hitting an animal. Certain articles in your vehicle, such as some radios and stereo equipment, may be excluded from this insurance. These articles may be protected by the personal property coverage of your home insurance. Like collision insurance, comprehensive coverage applies only to your car, and claims are paid without considering fault. (See the Financial Planning Calculations feature.)

## Other Automobile Insurance Coverages

In addition to basic bodily injury and property damage coverages, other protection is available. Wage loss insurance will reimburse you for any salary or income lost due to injury in an automobile accident. Wage loss insurance is usually required in states with a no-fault insurance system; in other states, it is available on an optional basis.

## Financial Planning Calculations

### CLAIM SETTLEMENTS AND DEDUCTIBLES

Both collision and comprehensive coverage are commonly sold with a *deductible* to help reduce insurance costs. If a broken windshield costs $250 to replace and you have a $100 deductible on your comprehensive coverage, the insurance company will pay $150 of the damages.

Deductibles keep insurance premiums lower by reducing the number of small claims companies pay. Going from full-coverage comprehensive insurance to a $100 deductible may reduce the cost of that coverage by as much as 40 percent.

Towing and emergency road service coverage pays for the cost of breakdowns and mechanical assistance. This coverage can be especially beneficial on long trips or during inclement weather. Towing and road service coverage pays for the cost of getting the vehicle to a service station or starting it when it breaks down on the highway, not for the cost of repairs. If you belong to an automobile club, your membership may include towing coverage. Purchasing duplicate coverage as part of your automobile insurance could be a waste of money. Rental reimbursement coverage pays for a rental car if your vehicle is stolen or is in the shop for repairs after an accident.

### Concept Check 10-5

1. What is the purpose of financial responsibility laws?
2. What are the main coverages included in most automobile insurance policies?
3. What is no-fault insurance?
4. How does collision coverage differ from comprehensive physical damage coverage?

## AUTOMOBILE INSURANCE COSTS

**Obj. 6**
Evaluate factors that affect the cost of automobile insurance.

The average household spends over $1,000 for auto insurance each year. Automobile insurance premiums reflect the amounts insurance companies pay for injury and property damage claims. Your automobile insurance is directly related to coverage amounts and factors such as the vehicle, your place of residence, and your driving record.

### Amount of Coverage

"How much coverage do I need?" This question affects the amount you pay for insurance. Our legal environment and increasing property values influence coverage amounts.

**Legal Concerns**   As discussed earlier, every state has laws that require or encourage automobile liability insurance coverage. Since very few people can afford to pay an expensive court settlement with personal assets, most drivers buy automobile liability insurance.

In the past, bodily injury liability coverage of 10/20 was considered adequate. In fact, some states still use these amounts as their minimum limits for financial responsibility. However, in recent injury cases, some people have been awarded millions of dollars; thus, legal and insurance advisers now recommend 100/300. As discussed earlier in this chapter, an umbrella policy can provide additional liability coverage of $1 million or more.

Property Values    Just as medical expenses and legal settlements have increased, so has the cost of automobiles. Therefore, a policy limit of more than $10,000 for property damage liability is appropriate; $50,000 or $100,000 is usually suggested.

## Automobile Insurance Premium Factors

Several factors influence the premium you pay for automobile insurance. The main factors are vehicle type, rating territory, and driver classification.

### Automobile Type    The year, make, and model of your motor vehicle strongly influence automobile insurance costs. Expensive replacement parts and complicated repairs due to body style contribute to higher rates. Also, certain makes and models are stolen more often than others.

*rating territory*   The place of residence used to determine a person's automobile insurance premium.

### Rating Territory    In most states, your **rating territory** is the place of residence used to determine your automobile insurance premium. Various geographic locations have different costs due to differences in the number of claims made. For example, fewer accidents and less vandalism occur in rural areas than in large cities. New York City, Los Angeles, and Chicago have the highest incidence of automobile theft.

*driver classification*  A category based on the driver's age, sex, marital status, driving record, and driving habits; used to determine automobile insurance rates.

### Driver Classification    You are compared with other drivers to set your automobile insurance premium. **Driver classification** is a category based on the driver's age, sex, marital status, driving record, and driving habits; drivers' categories are used to determine automobile insurance rates. In general, young drivers (under 25) and those over 70 have more frequent and severe accidents. As a result, they pay higher premiums.

Accidents and traffic violations influence your driver classification. A poor driving record increases your insurance costs. Finally, you pay less for insurance if you do not drive to work than if you use your automobile for business. Belonging to a carpool instead of driving to work alone can reduce insurance costs.

Your credit history may also be considered when applying for auto insurance. While several states limit the use of credit scoring in auto insurance, the practice is common in other areas.

The number of claims you file with your insurance company also affects your premiums. Expensive liability settlements or extensive property damage will increase your rates. If you have many expensive claims or a poor driving record, your company may cancel your policy, making it difficult for you to obtain coverage from another company. To deal with this problem, every state has an **assigned risk pool** consisting of people who are unable to obtain automobile insurance. Some of these people are assigned to each insurance company operating in the state. They pay several times the normal rates, but they do get coverage. Once they establish a good driving record, they can reapply for insurance at regular rates.

*assigned risk pool*  Consists of people who are unable to obtain automobile insurance due to poor driving or accident records and must obtain coverage at high rates through a state program that requires insurance companies to accept some of them.

## Reducing Automobile Insurance Premiums

Methods for lowering automobile insurance costs include comparing companies and taking advantage of commonly offered discounts.

# Financial Planning for Life's Situations

## WHAT TO DO IF YOU HAVE AN AUTO ACCIDENT

No one plans to have an auto accident; nevertheless, more than 18 million auto accidents occur each year. If you are involved in an auto accident, you should take the following actions:

- Stop your vehicle, turn off your ignition, and remain at the scene of the accident.
- Seek medical assistance for anyone who is injured. Do not move an injured person; that should be done by medical personnel.
- Obtain the names and addresses of other drivers, passengers, and witnesses; make notes regarding the circumstances of the accident.

- Assist in the preparation of a police report, if required, by providing your name, address, license number, and vehicle and insurance information. Do not admit fault.
- Obtain a copy of the police accident report, if any; file the necessary accident documents with your insurance company and state or local government agencies.
- Additional information is available at www.accidentprep.com.

## Comparing Companies

Rates and service vary among automobile insurance companies. Among companies in the same area, premiums can vary as much as 100 percent. If you relocate, don't assume your present company will offer the best rates in your new living area. Rates may be compared online at www.insuremarket.com.

Also consider the service the local insurance agent provides. Will this company representative be available to answer questions, change coverages, and handle claims as needed? You can check a company's reputation for handling automobile insurance claims and other matters with sources such as *Consumer Reports* or your state insurance department. Most states publish information with sample auto insurance rates for different companies to help consumers save money. See Appendix B for the address of your state insurance regulator.

## Premium Discounts

The best way to keep your rates down is to establish and maintain a safe driving record. Taking steps to avoid accidents and traffic violations will mean lower automobile insurance premiums. In addition, most insurance companies offer various discounts. Drivers under 25 can qualify for reduced rates by completing a driver training program or maintaining good grades in school. When young drivers are away at school without a car, families are likely to get reduced premiums since the student will not be using the vehicle on a regular basis.

Installing security devices such as a fuel shutoff switch, a second ignition switch, or an alarm system will decrease your chances of theft and lower your insurance costs. Being a nonsmoker can qualify you for lower automobile insurance premiums. Discounts are also offered for participating in a carpool and insuring two or more vehicles with the same company. Ask your insurance agent about other methods for lowering your automobile insurance rates.

**? Did You Know**

The Insurance Research Council reports that automobile crashes are resulting in fewer severe injuries. Also, a lower proportion of injury claims involve lawyer representation. Reduced injuries are the result of several factors, including seat belt use laws, better air bag design, campaigns against drinking and driving, intensified auto insurance fraud investigations, and increased use of technology to improve claims review. (*Injuries in Auto Accidents: An Analysis of Auto Insurance Claims*, Insurance Research Council, 718 Providence Road, Box 3025, Malvern, PA 19355-0725; www.ircweb.org.)

Increasing the amount of deductibles will result in a lower premium. Also, some people believe an old car is not worth the amount paid for collision and comprehensive coverages and therefore dispense with them. However, before doing this, be sure to compare the value of your car for getting you to school or work with the cost of these coverages.

If you change your driving habits, get married, or alter your driving status in other ways, be sure to notify the insurance company. Premium savings can result. Also, some employers make group automobile insurance available to workers. Before you buy a motor vehicle, find out which makes and models have the lowest insurance costs. This information can result in a purchasing decision with many financial benefits.

## Concept Check 10-6

1.   What factors influence how much a person pays for automobile insurance?
2.   What actions can a person take to reduce the cost of automobile insurance?

## Summary of Objectives

**Obj. 1**   **Develop a risk management plan using insurance.**

The four general risk management techniques are risk avoidance, risk reduction, risk assumption, and risk shifting. In planning a personal insurance program, set your goals, make a plan to reach your goals, put your plan into action, and review your results.

**Obj. 2**   **Discuss the importance of property and liability insurance.**

Owners of homes and automobiles face the risks of (1) property damage or loss and (2) legal actions by others for the costs of injuries or property damage. Property and liability insurance offer protection from financial losses that may arise from a wide variety of situations faced by owners of homes and users of automobiles.

**Obj. 3**   **Explain the insurance coverages and policy types available to homeowners and renters.**

Homeowner's insurance includes protection for the building and other structures, additional living expenses, personal property, and personal liability. Renter's insurance includes the same coverages excluding protection for the building and other structures, which is the concern of the building owner. The main types of home insurance policies are the basic, broad, special, tenants, comprehensive, condominium, country home, and modified coverage forms. These policies differ in the risks and property they cover.

**Obj. 4**   **Analyze factors that influence the amount of coverage and cost of home insurance.**

The amount of home insurance coverage is determined by the replacement cost of your dwelling and personal belongings. The cost of home insurance is influenced by the location of the home, the type of structure, the coverage amount, the policy type, discounts, and insurance company differences.

**Obj. 5**   **Identify the important types of automobile insurance coverages.**

Automobile insurance is used to meet states' financial responsibility laws and to protect drivers against financial losses associated with bodily injury and property damage. The major types of automobile insurance coverages are bodily injury liability, medical payments, uninsured motorist's, property damage liability, collision, and comprehensive physical damage.

**Obj. 6**   **Evaluate factors that affect the cost of automobile insurance.**

The cost of automobile insurance is affected by the amount of coverage, automobile type, rating territory, driver classification, differences among insurance companies, and premium discounts.

## Financial Planning Problems

1. *Calculating Property Loss Claim Coverage.* Most home insurance policies cover jewelry for $1,000 and silverware for $2,500 unless items are covered with additional insurance. If $3,500 worth of jewelry and $3,800 worth of silverware were stolen from a family, what amount of the claim would not be covered by insurance?   (Obj. 2)

2. *Computing Actual Cash Value Coverage.* What amount would a person with actual cash value (ACV) coverage receive for two-year-old furniture destroyed by a fire? The furniture would cost $1,000 to replace today and had an estimated life of five years.   (Obj. 3)

3. *Determining Replacement Cost.* What would it cost an insurance company to replace a family's personal property that originally cost $18,000? The replacement costs for the items have increased 15 percent.   (Obj. 3)

4. *Calculating a Coinsurance Claim.* If Carissa Dalton has a $130,000 home insured for $100,000, based on the 80 percent coinsurance provision, how much would the insurance company pay on a $5,000 claim?   (Obj. 3)

5. *Determining the Claim Amount (with Deductibles).* For each of the following situations, what amount would the insurance company pay?   (Obj. 3)

   *a.* Wind damage of $785; the insured has a $500 deductible.

   *b.* Theft of a stereo system worth $1,300; the insured has a $250 deductible.

   *c.* Vandalism that does $375 of damage to a home; the insured has a $500 deductible.

6. *Calculating Auto Liability Claim Coverage.* Becky Fenton has 25/50/10 automobile insurance coverage. If two other people are awarded $35,000 each for injuries in an auto accident in which Becky was judged at fault, how much of this judgment would the insurance cover?   (Obj. 4)

7. *Determining a Property Damage Liability Claim.* Kurt Simmons has 50/100/15 auto insurance coverage. One evening he lost control of his vehicle, hitting a parked car and damaging a storefront along the street. Damage to the parked car was $5,400, and damage to the store was $12,650. What amount will the insurance company pay for the damages? What amount will Kurt have to pay?   (Obj. 4)

8. *Calculating Future Value of Insurance Savings.* Beverly and Kyle Nelson currently insure their cars with separate companies, paying $450 and $375 a year. If they insured both cars with the same company, they would save 10 percent on the annual premiums. What would be the future value of the annual savings over 10 years based on an annual interest rate of 6 percent?   (Obj. 5)

## Financial Planning Activities

1. *Determining Insurance Coverages.* Survey friends and relatives to determine the types of insurance coverages they have. Also, obtain information about the process used to select these coverages.   (Obj. 1)

2. *Researching Insurance on the Internet.* Locate websites that provide useful information for selecting and comparing various insurance coverages.   (Obj. 1)

3. *Developing a Personal Insurance Plan.* Outline a personal insurance plan with the following phases: (*a*) identify personal, financial, and property risks; (*b*) set goals you might achieve when obtaining needed insurance coverages; and (*c*) describe actions you might take to achieve these insurance goals.   (Obj. 1)

4. *Analyzing Insurance Coverages.* Talk to a financial planner or an insurance agent about the financial difficulties faced by people who lack adequate home and auto insurance. What common coverages do many people overlook?   (Obj. 2)

5. *Maintaining a Household Inventory.* Survey several people about their household inventory records. In the event of damage or loss, would they be able to prove the value of their personal property and other belongings?   (Obj. 3)

6. *Comparing Home Insurance Costs.* Contact two or three insurance agents to obtain information about home or renter's insurance. Use Sheet 49 in the *Personal Financial Planner* to compare the coverages and costs.   (Obj. 3)

7. *Analyzing Home Insurance Policies.* Examine a homeowner's or renter's insurance policy. What coverages does the policy include? Does the policy contain unclear conditions or wording?   (Obj. 3)

8. *Reducing Home Insurance Costs.* Talk to several homeowners about the actions they take to reduce the cost of their home insurance. Locate websites that offer information about reducing home insurance costs. Prepare a video or other visual presentation to communicate your findings.   (Obj. 4)

9. *Determining Auto Insurance Coverages.* Survey several people to determine the types and amounts of automobile insurance coverage they have. Do most of them have adequate coverage? (Obj. 5)

10. *Comparing Auto Insurance Costs.* Contact two or three insurance agents to obtain information about automobile insurance. Use Sheet 50 in the *Personal Financial Planner* to compare costs and coverages for various insurance companies. (Obj. 6)

11. *Reducing Auto Insurance Costs.* Search the World Wide Web or talk to an insurance agent to obtain suggestions for reducing automobile insurance costs. (Obj. 6)

## LIFE SITUATION CASE

### WE RENT, SO WHY DO WE NEED INSURANCE?

"Have you been down in the basement?" Nathan asked his wife, Erin, as he entered their apartment.

"No, what's up?" responded Erin.

"It's flooded because of all that rain we got last weekend!" he exclaimed.

"Oh no! We have the extra furniture my mom gave us stored down there. Is everything ruined?" Erin asked.

"The couch and coffee table are in a foot of water; the loveseat was the only thing that looked OK. Boy, I didn't realize the basement of this building wasn't waterproof. I'm going to call our landlady to complain."

As Erin thought about the situation, she remembered that when they moved in last fall, Kathy, their landlady, had informed them that her insurance policy covered the building but not the property belonging to each tenant. Because of this, they had purchased renter's insurance. "Nathan, I think our renter's insurance will cover the damage. Let me give our agent a call."

When Erin and Nathan purchased their insurance, they had to decide whether they wanted to be insured for cash value or for replacement costs. Replacement was more expensive, but it meant they would collect enough to go out and buy new household items at today's prices. If they had opted for cash value, the couch Erin's mother had paid $1,000 for five years ago would be worth less than $500 today.

Erin made the call and found out their insurance did cover the furniture in the basement, and at replacement value after they paid the deductible. The $300 they had invested in renter's insurance last year was well worth it!

Not every renter has as much foresight as Erin and Nathan. Fewer than 4 in 10 renters have renter's insurance. Some aren't even aware they need it. They may assume they are covered by the landlord's insurance, but they aren't. This mistake can be costly.

Think about how much you have invested in your possessions and how much it would cost to replace them. Start with your stereo equipment or the color television and VCR that you bought last year. Experts suggest that people who rent start thinking about these things as soon as they move into their first apartment. Your policy should cover your personal belongings and provide funds for living expenses if you are dispossessed by a fire or other disaster.

### Questions

1. Why is it important for people who rent to have insurance?

2. Does the building owner's property insurance ever cover the tenant's personal property?

3. What is the difference between cash value and replacement value?

4. When shopping for renter's insurance, what coverage features should you look for?

## INTERNET CASE   Buying Insurance on the Web

Hector and Lisa Marek recently purchased a new sports utility vehicle for use in their family business as well as for recreation. They have always bought their auto insurance from the same agent. Now they are considering a different approach.

Many insurance companies make it possible to shop, compare, and purchase auto insurance on the Web. This convenience is not without a cost of your time and effort. Consumers must be knowledgeable about various types of coverage available, as well as about financial needs and insurance costs.

Buying auto insurance on the Internet can be fast, easy, and inexpensive. However, Lisa and Hector must take some time and effort to ensure they have the right coverage at an appropriate price.

### Questions

1. As Hector and Lisa start to compare different insurance companies and coverages, what factors should they consider?
2. Locate websites that could help Lisa and Hector to compare and select auto insurance.
3. What auto insurance recommendations would you make to Hector and Lisa?

## Creating an E-Plan: Financial Decisions Using the Web

### OBTAINING HOME AND AUTO INSURANCE

Creation of an insurance plan including appropriate coverage for your home, personal property, and motor vehicles helps to avoid financial difficulties.

Websites for Home and Auto Insurance

- The website of the Insurance Research Council offers current information on various insurance research studies, policy issues, and IRC publications, along with links to related websites, at **www.ircweb.org.**
- Answers to questions about basic information and current developments about auto and home insurance may be obtained at **www.insure.com.**
- Home and auto insurance information at **www.iiaa. iix.com** and **www.iii.org.**
- Insurance rate information at **www.insuremarket.com.**
- Information about trends and current issues in the home, auto, and property insurance industry at **www.ircweb.org.**

(Note: Addresses and content of websites change, and new sites are created daily. Use search engines to update and locate websites for your current financial planning needs.)

*PFP sheets: 46–50*

Short-Term Financial Planning Activities

1. List current and needed insurance coverages (see PFP Sheet 46).
2. (a) Prepare an inventory of personal belongings (see PFP Sheet 47). (b) Compare the cost of homeowner's or renter's insurance from two or more companies (see PFP Sheet 49).
3. Compare the cost of auto insurance from two or more companies (see PFP Sheet 50).

Long-Term Financial Planning Activities

1. Identify buying decisions that could reduce your future home and auto insurance costs.
2. Develop a plan to monitor changes in your life situation that would affect the need to change home or auto insurance coverages.

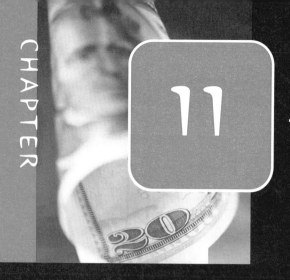

# Health and Disability Insurance

## A CHECKUP FOR YOUR HEALTH PLAN

Eddie Toohey knew it was time to make a change in his company's indemnity health plan. The 18 employees at his Brown Hearing Aid Centers, based in Orange, Texas, had complained repeatedly about the high co-payments and limited coverage. While Toohey wanted to switch over to a managed care plan and was even willing to pay a little more for a good one, he didn't know how to choose. What he needed was a set of benchmarks to help judge a plan's quality. Toohey obtained several pamphlets that helped him ask the right questions when comparing health plans. Now, Toohey says, "I am requesting turnover rates. If members are dropping out, that's not a good sign."

Almost 60 percent of large companies with more than 10,000 employees routinely use quality indicators to choose their health plans, according to a 1998 survey by the Washington Business Group on Health and Watson Wyatt Worldwide, a benefits consulting firm in Bethesda, Maryland. But small employers haven't had easy access to such data or even known of its existence. Quality is gauged by a number of factors, such as access to care, which includes the ability to see specialists or use an emergency room while out of town. It's also measured by the coverage of specific clinical treatments and by consumer satisfaction.

How can you judge a particular plan? One of the best sources is the National Committee for Quality Assurance (NCQA), a nonprofit Washington think tank that publishes the industry bible, *Quality Compass*. You can get a free synopsis of this information, "The State of Managed Care Quality," at the NCQA website (www.ncqa.org); this report reviews 300 managed care plans. NCQA's accreditation is like the Good Housekeeping seal of approval.

## Questions

1. Visit the NCQA website and see how your health care provider is rated by the National Committee for Quality Assurance. What are your findings?
2. Why were the 18 employees at Brown Hearing Aid Centers complaining to Eddie Toohey?
3. How is the quality of a health care provider judged?
4. Why is NCQA's accreditation like the Good Housekeeping seal of approval?

SOURCE: Adapted from, "A Checkup for Your Health Plan," *Business Week*, March 1, 1999, p. 16. Reprinted from the March 1, 1999 issue of *Business Week* by special permission. © 1999 McGraw-Hill Companies, Inc.

## Learning Objectives

**Obj. 1**   Explain why the costs of health insurance and health care have been increasing.

**Obj. 2**   Define *health insurance* and *disability income insurance* and explain their importance in financial planning.

**Obj. 3**   Recognize the need for disability income insurance.

**Obj. 4**   Analyze the benefits and limitations of the various types of health care coverage.

**Obj. 5**   Evaluate private sources of health insurance and health care.

**Obj. 6**   Appraise the sources of government health care programs.

## HEALTH CARE COSTS

**Obj. 1**
Explain why the costs of health insurance and health care have been increasing.

Health insurance is one way people protect themselves against economic losses due to illness, accident, or disability. Health coverage is available through private insurance companies, service plans, health maintenance organizations, and government programs.

Employers often offer health insurance as part of an employee benefit package, called *group health insurance,* and health care providers sell it to individuals.

Affordable health care has become one of the most important social issues of our time. News broadcasts abound with special reports on "America's health care crisis" or politicians demanding "universal health insurance."

### High Medical Costs

The United States has the highest per capita medical expenditures of any industrialized country in the world. In 1999, average per capita spending on health care totaled $4,340 a year, up from $1,000 in 1980. The United States spends twice as much on health care as the average for the 24 industrialized countries in Europe and North America (see Exhibit 11–1).

U.S. health care costs were estimated at $1.2 trillion in 1999, a 5.6 percent increase over 1998 (see Exhibit 11–2). In the next five years, health care costs are expected to increase 6.5 percent annually. Since 1993, health care spending as a percentage of gross domestic product (GDP) has remained relatively constant at 13.6 percent, except in 1997, when it fell to 13.4 percent. During the next five years, health care spending as a percentage of GDP will range from 13.4 to 13.5 percent.

**Rapid Increase in Medical Expenditures**   Since federally sponsored health care began in 1965, U.S. health care expenditures rose from $41.6 billion, or about 6 percent of GDP, to over $1.2 trillion in 1999, or 13.4 percent of GDP (see Exhibit 11–3).[1]

**High Administrative Costs**   In the United States, administrative costs consume nearly 26 percent of health care dollars compared to 1 percent under Canada's socialized system. These costs include activities such as enrolling beneficiaries in a

**EXHIBIT 11-1**

Health Care
Expenditures as
a Percentage of
GDP for Selected
Countries, 1995

SOURCES: Health Industry
Manufacturers Association;
U.S. Department of
Commerce, International
Trade Administration;
*U.S. Industry and Trade
Outlook, 1999* (Washington,
DC: U.S. Department of
Commerce, 1998), p. 44-1.

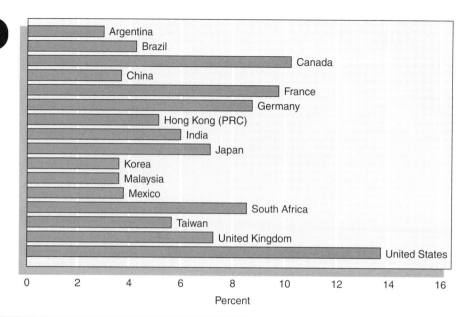

**EXHIBIT 11-2**   U.S. NATIONAL HEALTH EXPENDITURES, 1960–1999

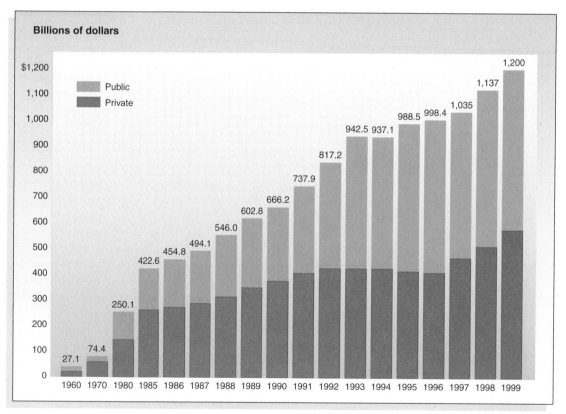

SOURCES: U.S. Department of Health and Human Services; Health Care Financing Administration; *U.S. Industry and Trade Outlook,*
*1999* (Washington, DC: U.S. Department of Commerce, 1999), p. 44-3; HCFA press release, January 27, 1997; *Chicago Tribune,*
January 13, 1998, p. 5.

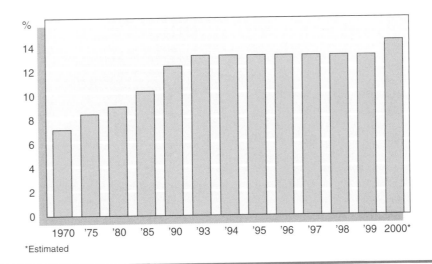

**EXHIBIT 11-3**

U.S. Health Care Expenditures as a Percentage of GDP, 1970-2000

SOURCES: U.S. Department of Health and Human Services; Healthcare Financing Administration; *U.S. Industry and Trade Outlook, 1999* (Washington, DC: U.S. Department of Commerce, 1999), p. 44-2.

health plan, paying health insurance premiums, checking eligibility, obtaining authorizations for specialist referrals, and filing reimbursement claims. More than 1,100 different insurance forms are now in use in the United States.

## Why Does Health Care Cost So Much?

The high and rising costs of health care are attributable to many factors, including

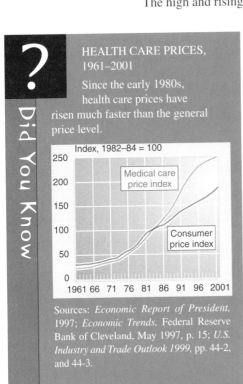

**Did You Know?**

HEALTH CARE PRICES, 1961–2001

Since the early 1980s, health care prices have risen much faster than the general price level.

Index, 1982–84 = 100

Medical care price index

Consumer price index

Sources: *Economic Report of President, 1997; Economic Trends,* Federal Reserve Bank of Cleveland, May 1997, p. 15; *U.S. Industry and Trade Outlook 1999,* pp. 44-2, and 44-3.

- The use of sophisticated, expensive technologies.
- Duplication of tests and sometimes duplication of technologies that yield similar results.
- Increases in the variety and frequency of treatments, including allegedly unnecessary tests.
- The increasing number and longevity of elderly people.
- Regulations that result in cost shifting rather than cost reduction.
- The increasing number of accidents and crimes that require emergency medical services.
- Limited competition and restrictive work rules in the health care delivery system.
- Labor intensiveness and rapid average earnings growth for health care professionals and executives.
- Using more expensive medical care than necessary, such as going to an emergency room with a bad cold.
- Built-in inflation in the health care delivery system.
- Other major factors that cost billions of dollars each year, including fraud, administrative waste, malpractice insurance, excessive surgical procedures, a wide range of prices for similar services, and double health coverage.

According to the General Accounting Office, fraud and abuse account for nearly 10 percent of all dollars spent on health care. In 1999, that was a loss of about $20 billion to Medicare. "Rather than look for people who are nickel-and-diming the program, we've ratcheted up," says Donna Shalala, secretary of health and human services. "We have to demonstrate that we have the guts to go after the big players in health care."[2]

## Financial Planning for Life's Situations

### WHEN AN OUNCE OF PREVENTION COSTS TOO MUCH

Want to know why health premiums are heading up? In 1997, Kaiser Permanente HMO spent about $500,000 on antipsychotic medications for its members. In 1998, with the arrival of Eli Lilly & Company's more effective Zyprexa, the tab soared to $8 million. Xalatan, a hot new glaucoma medication, generated bills of $7 million for Kaiser in 1998—up from $400,000 for the drugs it replaced. "This is not sustainable," say David Campen, head of Kaiser's California drug formulary board.

Drugmakers are churning out a flood of expensive products and advertising them heavily. Patients want the new treatments, and their doctors are obliging. Pharmaceutical claims soared by up to 18 percent in 1998, says Merrill Lynch & Company analyst Roberta Walter; in many plans, drugs account for 15 percent of total medical costs. Are the new drugs worth the price?

Now HMO plans are guiding consumers to lower-price drugs by setting tiered copayments. For approved branded drugs, patients pay $10 or $15 per prescription. If they choose the generic equivalent, the cost is $5. An unapproved product costs $25 or more. It's not a perfect arrangement. For patients with chronic conditions, $25 per prescription adds up quickly. But the alternative is unchecked demand and wasted resources. "Bringing in some accountability does bring the best of both worlds in terms of value and choice," says Nicholas A. Hanchak, Aetna's head of pharmacy management. Consumers should enjoy the bounty of drugmakers' research labs—but they should help pay their way, too. Don't fault HMOs for trying to bring some sanity to the system.

SOURCE: Adapted from Keith H. Hammonds, "When An Ounce of Prevention Costs Too Much," *Business Week,* January 25, 1999, p. 46. Reprinted from the January 25, 1999 issue of *Business Week* by special permission. © 1999 McGraw-Hill Companies, Inc.

Because third parties—private health insurers and government—pay such a large part of the nation's health care bill, hospitals, doctors, and patients often lack the incentive to make the most economical use of health care services. See the accompanying Financial Planning for Life's Situations box above.

## What Is Being Done about the High Costs of Health Care?

In the private sector, concerned groups such as employers, labor unions, health insurers, health care professionals, and consumers have undertaken a wide range of innovative activities to contain the costs of health care. These activities include

- Programs to carefully review health care fees and charges and the use of health care services.
- The establishment of incentives to encourage preventive care and provide more services out of hospitals where this is medically acceptable.
- Involvement in community health planning to help achieve a better balance between health needs and health care resources.
- The encouragement of prepaid group practices and other alternatives to fee-for-service arrangements.
- Community health education programs that motivate people to take better care of themselves.

**?**

**Did You Know**

BIG PREMIUM HIKES:
The Predictions Come True

SOURCES: Watson Wyatt Worldwide; *Business Week,* September 27, 1999, p. 52.

## What Can You Do to Reduce Personal Health Care Costs?

The best way to avoid the high cost of illness is to stay well. The prescription is the same as it has always been:

1. Eat a balanced diet, and keep your weight under control.
2. Avoid smoking, and don't drink to excess.
3. Get sufficient rest, relaxation, and exercise.
4. Drive carefully, and watch out for accident and fire hazards in the home.

### Concept Check 11-1

1. What are the reasons for rising health care expenditures?
2. What are various groups doing to curb the high costs of health care?
3. What can you do to reduce health care costs?

## HEALTH INSURANCE AND FINANCIAL PLANNING

### Obj. 2

Define *health insurance* and *disability income insurance* and explain their importance in financial planning.

Although the United States spent about $1.2 trillion on health care in 1999 (see Exhibit 11–2 on page 340), the number of Americans without basic health insurance has been growing. In this wealthy country of over 285 million people, 42 million citizens have no health insurance. Two-thirds of uninsured persons are either full-time workers or family members of full-time employees.

According to recent government reports, two-thirds of uninsured pregnant women fail to receive adequate prenatal care. Among children, 40 percent fail to receive basic childhood vaccinations, 25 percent don't see a doctor even once a year, and 31 percent in low-income families lack health coverage.[3]

A growing number of college students have been uninsured due to the growth of an older student population not covered by family policies. Today 40 percent of college students are older than 25.

### What Is Health Insurance?

Health insurance is a form of protection to alleviate the financial burdens individuals suffer from illness or injury. According to the Health Care Financing Administration, health insurance includes both medical expense insurance and disability income insurance.[4]

**Health Insurance**   Health insurance, like other forms of insurance, reduces the financial burden of risk by dividing losses among many individuals. It works in the same way as life insurance, homeowner's insurance, and automobile insurance. You pay the insurance company a specified premium, and the company guarantees you some degree of financial protection. Like the premiums and benefits of other types of insurance, the premiums and benefits of health insurance are figured on the basis of average experience. To establish rates and benefits, insurance company actuaries rely on general statistics that tell them how many people in a certain population group will become ill and how much their illnesses will cost.

Medical expense insurance and disability income insurance, discussed in the next section, are an important part of your financial planning. To safeguard your family's economic security, both protections should be a part of your overall insurance program.

There are many ways individuals or groups of individuals can obtain health insurance protection. Planning a health insurance program takes careful study because the protection should be shaped to the needs of the individual or family. For many families, the task is simplified because the group health insurance they obtain at work already provides a foundation for their coverage.

## Group Health Insurance

Group plans comprise more than 85 percent of all the health insurance issued by health and life insurance companies. Most of these plans are employer sponsored, and the employer often pays part or most of their cost. Group insurance will cover you and your immediate family. Group insurance seldom requires evidence that you are insurable if you enroll when you first become eligible for coverage.

The *Health Insurance Portability and Accountability Act of 1996 (HIPA)* legislates new federal standards for health insurance portability, nondiscrimination in health insurance, and guaranteed renewability. The law provides tax breaks for long-term care insurance, authorizes various government agencies to investigate Medicare/Medicaid fraud and abuses, and permits establishing experimental *medical savings accounts (MSAs)*. The MSA allowed small businesses and self-employed people to open medical savings accounts for the first time in 1997. The law permitted 750,000 people to open tax-free MSAs for routine health care costs and to buy high-deductible health insurance for major medical expenses.

This landmark legislation gives millions of workers the comfort of knowing that if they change jobs, they need not lose their health insurance. For example, a parent with a sick child can move from one group plan to another without lapses in health insurance and without paying more than other employees for coverage. In addition to providing health care portability, this law created a stable source of funding for fraud control activities.

The protection group insurance provides varies from plan to plan. The plan may not cover all of your health insurance needs; therefore, you will have to consider supplementing it with individual health insurance.

## Individual Health Insurance

Individual health insurance covers either one person or a family. If the kind of health insurance you need is not available through a group or if you need coverage in addition to the coverage a group provides, you should obtain an individual policy—a policy tailored to your particular needs—from the company of your choice. This requires careful shopping, because coverage and cost vary from company to company. For example, the premiums for similar coverage can vary up to 50 percent for the same person, according to Mark Gurda, president of Castle Group Health in Northbrook, Illinois. Moreover, the rules and regulations vary from state to state.

Find out what your group insurance will pay for and what it won't. Make sure you have enough insurance, but don't waste money by overinsuring.

## Supplementing Your Group Insurance

A sign that your group coverage needs supplementing would be its failure to provide benefits for the major portion of your medical care bills, mainly hospital, doctor, and surgical charges. If, for example, your group policy will pay only $500 per day toward a hospital room and the cost in your area is $1,000, you should look for an individual policy that covers most of the remaining amount. Similarly, if your group policy will pay only about half the going rate for surgical procedures in your area, you need individual coverage for the other half.

In supplementing your group health insurance, consider the health insurance benefits your employer-sponsored plan provides for family members. Most group policy contracts have a **coordination of benefits (COB)** provision. The COB is a method of integrating the benefits payable under more than one health insurance plan so that the benefits received from all sources are limited to 100 percent of allowable medical expenses.

*coordination of benefits (COB)* A method of integrating the benefits payable under more than one health insurance plan.

If you have any questions about your group plan, you should be able to get answers from your employer, union, or association. If you have questions about an individual policy, talk with your insurance company representative.

## Medical Coverage and Divorce

Medical coverage of nonworking spouses is a concern when couples divorce. Under federal law, coverage under a former spouse's medical plan can be continued for 36 months if the former spouse works for a company with 20 or more employees.

Premiums will be totally paid by the individual and can run as high as $4,000 annually. If there are children and the custodial parent doesn't work, the working parent usually can still cover the children under an employer's group plan.

The federal *Consolidated Omnibus Budget Reconciliation Act of 1986 (COBRA)* requires many employers to offer employees and dependents who would otherwise lose group health insurance the option to continue their group coverage for a set period of time. Employees of private companies and state and local governments are covered by this law; employees of the federal government and religious institutions are not.

> ## Concept Check 11-2
>
> 1. What is health insurance, and what is its purpose?
> 2. What are group health and individual health insurance?
> 3. What is a coordination of benefits provision?

## DISABILITY INCOME INSURANCE

### Obj. 3
Recognize the need for disability income insurance.

*disability income insurance* Provides payments to replace income when an insured person is unable to work.

Because you feel young and healthy now, you may overlook the very real need for disability income insurance. Disability income insurance protects your most valuable asset: your ability to earn income. Most people are more likely to lose their incomes due to disability than to death. The fact is that for all age groups, disability is more likely than death.

**Disability income insurance** provides regular cash income lost by employees as the result of an accident, illness, or pregnancy. Disability income insurance is probably the most neglected form of available insurance protection. Many people who insure their houses, cars, and other property fail to insure their most valuable resource: their earning power. Disability can cause even greater financial problems than death. In fact, disability is often called "the living death." Disabled persons lose their earning power while continuing to incur normal family expenses. In addition, they often face huge expenses for the medical treatment and special care their disabilities require.

If you are between ages 35 and 65, your chances of being unable to work for 90 days or more due to a disabling illness or injury are about equal to your chances of dying. To be more specific, at age 40 you face a 12 percent chance of dying before reaching age 65 and a 19 percent chance of having at least one disability lasting 90 days or longer.[5] If you have no disability income protection, you are betting that you will not become disabled, and that could be a very costly bet.

The probability of a male becoming temporarily or permanently disabled between ages 20 and 30 is 1.3 percent, but between ages 20 and 60 it increases to 19.1 percent. Females are less prone to disability during their lifetimes and have only a 15.3 percent chance of becoming disabled between 20 and 60 years of age.[6]

## Definition of Disability

*Disability* has several definitions. Some policies define it simply as the inability to do your regular work. Others have stricter definitions. For example, a dentist who is unable to do his or her regular work because of a hand injury but can earn income through related duties such as teaching dentistry would not be considered permanently disabled under certain policies.

Good disability plans pay when you are unable to work at your regular job; poor disability plans pay only when you are unable to work at any job. A good disability plan will also make partial disability payments when you return to work on a part-time basis.

## Disability Insurance Trade-offs

Following are some important trade-offs you should consider in purchasing disability income insurance.

### Waiting or Elimination Period
Benefits don't begin on the first day you become disabled. Usually there is a waiting or elimination period of between 30 and 90 days. Some waiting periods may be as long as 180 days. Generally, disability income policies with longer waiting periods have lower premiums. If you have substantial savings to cover three to six months of expenses, the reduced premiums of a policy with a long waiting period may be attractive. But if you need every paycheck to cover your bills, you are probably better off paying the higher premium for a short waiting period. Short waiting periods, however, are very expensive.

### Duration of Benefits
The maximum time a disability income policy will pay benefits may be a few years, to age 65, or for life. You should seek a policy that pays benefits for life. If you became permanently disabled, it would be financially disastrous if your benefits ended at age 55 or 65.

### Amount of Benefits
You should aim for a benefit amount that, when added to your other income, will equal 60 to 70 percent of your gross pay. Of course, the greater the benefits, the greater the cost.

### Accident and Sickness Coverage
Consider both accident and sickness coverage. Some disability income policies will pay only for accidents, but you want to be insured for illness, too.

### Guaranteed Renewability
Ask for noncancelable and guaranteed renewable coverage. Either coverage will protect you against your insurance company dropping you if your health becomes poor. The premium for these coverages is higher, but the coverages are well worth the extra cost. Furthermore, look for a disability income policy that waives premium payments while you are disabled.

**Approximate Monthly Social Security Benefits If You Became Disabled in 1999 and Had Steady Earnings**

| Your Age | Your Family | Your Earnings in 1998 | | | | |
|---|---|---|---|---|---|---|
| | | $20,000 | $30,000 | $40,000 | $50,000 | $68,400 or More* |
| 25 | You | $ 826 | $1,092 | $1,310 | $1,435 | $1,644 |
| | You, your spouse, and your child† | 1,239 | 1,639 | 1,965 | 2,152 | 2,466 |
| 35 | You | 826 | 1,092 | 1,310 | 1,435 | 1,649 |
| | You, your spouse, and your child† | 1,239 | 1,639 | 1,965 | 2,152 | 2,474 |
| 45 | You | 826 | 1,092 | 1,310 | 1,409 | 1,624 |
| | You, your spouse, and your child† | 1,239 | 1,639 | 1,965 | 2,113 | 2,436 |
| 55 | You | 826 | 1,092 | 1,307 | 1,435 | 1,539 |
| | You, your spouse, and your child† | 1,239 | 1,639 | 1,961 | 2,152 | 2,309 |
| 64 | You | 773 | 1,023 | 1,208 | 1,285 | 1,384 |
| | You, your spouse, and your child† | 1,159 | 1,535 | 1,813 | 1,928 | 2,076 |

SOURCE: *Social Security: Understanding the Benefits* (Washington, DC: Social Security Administration, January 1999), p. 36.
*Earnings equal to or greater than the OASDI wage base from age 22 through 1998.
†Equals the maximum family benefit.
NOTE: The accuracy of these estimates depends on your actual earnings, which may vary significantly from those shown here.

See whether you qualify for a lower premium if you agree to forgo part of your monthly benefit when Social Security, company retirement benefits, or worker's compensation benefits begin. Most disability income policies coordinate their benefits with these programs.

## Sources of Disability Income

Before you buy disability income insurance, remember that you may already have some form of such insurance. This coverage may come to you through your employer, Social Security, or worker's compensation.

**Employer**   Many, but not all, employers provide disability income protection for their employees through group insurance plans. Your employer may have some form of wage continuation policy that lasts a few months or an employee group disability plan that provides long-term protection. In most cases, your employer will pay part or all of the cost of this plan.

**Social Security**   Most salaried workers in the United States participate in the Social Security program. In this program, your benefits are determined by your salary and by the number of years you have been covered under Social Security. Your dependents also qualify for certain benefits, as Exhibits 11–4 and 11–5 show. However, Social Security has very strict rules. You must be totally disabled for 12 months or more, and you must be unable to do any work.

**Worker's Compensation**   If your accident or illness occurred at your place of work or resulted from your type of employment, you could be entitled to worker's compensation benefits in your state. Like Social Security benefits, these benefits are determined by your earnings and work history.

**EXHIBIT 11–5** APPROXIMATE MONTHLY SOCIAL SECURITY SURVIVORS' BENEFITS FOR YOUR FAMILY IF YOU DIED IN 1999 AND HAD STEADY EARNINGS

| Your Age Age | Your Family | Your Earnings in 1998 | | | | |
|---|---|---|---|---|---|---|
| | | $20,000 | $30,000 | $40,000 | $50,000 | $68,400 or More* |
| 35 | Your spouse and one child[†] | $1,239 | $1,639 | $1,965 | $2,132 | $2,484 |
| | Your spouse and two children[††] | 1,459 | 1,962 | 2,292 | 2,511 | 2,898 |
| | One child only | 619 | 819 | 982 | 1,076 | 1,242 |
| | Your spouse at age 60[§] | 590 | 781 | 936 | 1,026 | 1,184 |
| 45 | Your spouse and one child[†] | 1,239 | 1,639 | 1,965 | 2,152 | 2,445 |
| | Your spouse and two children[††] | 1,459 | 1,962 | 2,292 | 2,511 | 2,853 |
| | One child only | 619 | 819 | 982 | 1,076 | 1,222 |
| | Your spouse at age 60[§] | 590 | 781 | 936 | 1,026 | 1,165 |
| 55 | Your spouse and one child[†] | 1,239 | 1,639 | 1,961 | 2,113 | 2,309 |
| | Your spouse and two children[††] | 1,459 | 1,962 | 2,288 | 2,466 | 2,694 |
| | One child only | 619 | 819 | 980 | 1,056 | 1,154 |
| | Your spouse at age 60[§] | 590 | 781 | 934 | 1,007 | 1,100 |

SOURCE: *Social Security: Understanding the Benefits* (Washington, DC: Social Security Administration, January 1999), p. 37.
* Earnings equal to or greater than the OASDI wage base from age 22 through 1998.
[†] Amounts shown also equal the benefits paid to two children if no parent survives or surviving parent has substantial earnings.
[††] Equals the maximum family benefit.
[§] Amounts payable in 1999. Spouses turning 60 in the future would receive higher benefits.
NOTE: The accuracy of these estimates depends on your actual earnings, which may vary significantly from those shown here.

Other possible sources of disability income include Veterans Administration pension disability benefits, civil service disability benefits for government workers, state vocational rehabilitation benefits, state welfare benefits for low-income people, Aid to Families with Dependent Children, group union disability benefits, automobile insurance that provides benefits for disability from an auto accident, and private insurance programs such as credit disability insurance, which covers loan payments when you are disabled. Use Exhibit 11–6 to determine how much income you will have available if you become disabled.

The availability and extent of these and other disability income sources vary widely in different parts of the country. Be sure to look into such sources carefully before calculating your need for additional disability income insurance.

## Determining Your Disability Income Insurance Requirements

Once you have found out what your benefits from the numerous public and private disability income sources would be, you should determine whether those benefits are sufficient to meet your disability income needs. If the sum of your disability benefits approaches your after-tax income, you can safely assume that should disability strike, you'll be in good shape to pay your day-to-day bills while recuperating.

You should know how long you would have to wait before the benefits begin (the waiting or elimination period) and how long they would be paid (the benefit period).

**Disability Income Worksheet**

How much income will you have available if you become disabled?

| | Monthly Amount | After Waiting: | For a Period of: |
|---|---|---|---|
| Sick leave or short-term disability | _____ | _____ | _____ |
| Group long-term disability | _____ | _____ | _____ |
| Social Security | _____ | _____ | _____ |
| Other government programs | _____ | _____ | _____ |
| Individual disability insurance | _____ | _____ | _____ |
| Credit disability insurance | _____ | _____ | _____ |
| Other income: | _____ | _____ | _____ |
|     Savings | _____ | _____ | _____ |
|     Spouse's income | _____ | _____ | _____ |
| Total monthly income while disabled: | $_____ | | |

**Sheet 51**

What if, as is often the case, Social Security and other disability benefits are not sufficient to support your family? In that case, you may want to consider buying disability income insurance to make up the difference.

Don't expect to insure yourself for your full salary. Most insurers limit benefits from all sources to no more than 70 to 80 percent of your take-home pay. For example, if you earn $400 a week, you could be eligible for disability insurance of about $280 to $320 a week. You will not need $400, because while you are disabled, your work-related expenses will be eliminated and your taxes will be far lower or may be even zero.

The Financial Planning for Life's Situations box on page 350 shows you how to compare different features among disability income policies.

## Concept Check 11–3

1. What is disability income insurance?
2. What are the three main sources of disability income?
3. How can you determine the amount of disability income insurance you need?

## TYPES OF HEALTH INSURANCE COVERAGES

**Obj. 4**
Analyze the benefits and limitations of the various types of health care coverage.

With today's high cost of health care, it makes sense to be as fully insured as you can afford. Combining the group plan available where you work with the individual policies insurance companies offer will enable you to put together enough coverage to give you peace of mind. A good health insurance plan should

- Offer basic coverage for hospital and doctor bills.
- Provide at least 120 days' hospital room and board in full.
- Provide at least a $1 million lifetime maximum for each family member.
- Pay at least 80 percent for out-of-hospital expenses after a yearly deductible of $500 per person or $1,000 per family.
- Impose no unreasonable exclusions.
- Limit your out-of-pocket expenses to no more than $3,000 to $5,000 a year, excluding dental, optical, and prescription costs.

Several types of health insurance coverage are available under group and individual policies.

## Financial Planning for Life's Situations

### DISABILITY INCOME POLICY CHECKLIST

Every disability income policy may have different features. The following checklist will help you compare policies you may be considering.

| | Policy A | Policy B |
|---|---|---|
| **1.** How is disability defined? | | |
| Inability to perform your own job? | | |
| Inability to perform any job? | ____ | ____ |
| **2.** Does the policy cover | | |
| Accident? | ____ | ____ |
| Illness? | ____ | ____ |
| **3.** Are benefits available | | |
| For total disability? | ____ | ____ |
| For partial disability? | ____ | ____ |
| Only after total disability? | ____ | ____ |
| Without a prior period of total disability? | ____ | ____ |
| **4.** Are full benefits paid, whether or not you are able to work, for loss of | | |
| Sight? | ____ | ____ |
| Speech? | ____ | ____ |
| Hearing? | ____ | ____ |
| Use of limbs? | ____ | ____ |

| | Policy A | Policy B |
|---|---|---|
| **5.** What percentage of your income will the maximum benefit replace? | ____ | ____ |
| **6.** Is the policy noncancelable, guaranteed renewable, or conditionally renewable? | ____ | ____ |
| **7.** How long must you be disabled before premiums are waived? | ____ | ____ |
| **8.** Is there an option to buy additional coverage, without evidence of insurability, at a later date? | ____ | ____ |
| **9.** Does the policy offer an inflation adjustment feature? | ____ | ____ |
| If so, what is the rate of increase? | ____ | ____ |
| How often is it applied? | ____ | ____ |
| For how long? | ____ | ____ |

| | Policy A | | Policy B | |
|---|---|---|---|---|
| **10.** What does the policy cost? | **With Inflation Feature** | **Without Inflation Feature** | **With Inflation Feature** | **Without Inflation Feature** |
| For a waiting period of | | | | |
| _____ days and (30–180) | _____ | _____ | _____ | _____ |
| For a benefit period of | | | | |
| _____ ? 1 yr.–lifetime | _____ | _____ | _____ | _____ |
| **Total** | _____ | _____ | _____ | _____ |

SOURCE: Health Insurance Association of America, Washington DC.

## Hospital Expense Insurance

*hospital expense insurance* Pays part or all of hospital bills for room, board, and other charges.

**Hospital expense insurance** pays part or the full amount of hospital bills for room, board, and other charges. Frequently a maximum amount is allowed for each day in the hospital, up to a maximum number of days. More people have hospital insurance than any other kind of health insurance.

## Surgical Expense Insurance

**Surgical expense insurance** pays part or the full amount of the surgeon's fees for an operation. A policy of this kind usually lists a number of specific operations and the maximum fee allowed for each. The higher the maximum fee allowed in the policy, the higher the premium charged. People often buy surgical expense insurance in combination with hospital expense insurance.

## Physician Expense Insurance

**Physician expense insurance** helps pay for physician's care that does not involve surgery. Like surgical expense insurance, it lists maximum benefits for specific services. Its coverage may include visits to the doctor's office, X rays, and lab tests. This type of insurance is usually bought in combination with hospital and surgical insurance. The three types of insurance combined are called **basic health insurance coverage.**

## Major Medical Expense Insurance

**Major medical expense insurance** protects against the large expenses of a serious injury or a long illness. It adds to the protection offered by basic health insurance coverage. The costs of a serious illness can easily exceed the benefits under hospital, surgical, and physician expense policies. Major medical pays the bulk of the additional costs. The maximum benefits payable under major medical insurance are high—up to $1 million. Because major medical insurance offers such a wide range of benefits and provides high maximums, it contains two features to help keep the premium within the policyholder's means.

One of these features is a **deductible** provision that requires the policyholder to pay a basic amount before the policy benefits begin—for example, the first $500 per year under an individual plan and a lesser amount under a group plan. (Sometimes part or all of the deductible amount is covered by the benefits of a basic hospital and surgical plan.) The other feature is a **coinsurance** provision that requires the policyholder to share expenses beyond the deductible amount. Many policies pay 75 or 80 percent of expenses above the deductible amount; the policyholder pays the rest.

Some major medical policies contain a **stop-loss** provision. This requires the policyholder to pay up to a certain amount, after which the insurance company pays 100 percent of all remaining covered expenses. Typically, the out-of-pocket payment is between $3,000 and $5,000.

## Comprehensive Major Medical Insurance

**Comprehensive major medical insurance** is a type of major medical insurance that has a very low deductible amount, often $200 or $300, and is offered without a separate basic plan. This all-inclusive health insurance helps pay hospital, surgical, medical, and other bills. Many major medical policies have specific maximum benefits for certain expenses, such as hospital room and board and the cost of surgery.

## Hospital Indemnity Policies

A **hospital indemnity policy** pays benefits only when you are hospitalized, but these benefits, stipulated in the policy, are paid to you in cash and you can use the money for medical, nonmedical, or supplementary expenses. While such policies have limited coverage, their benefits can have wide use. The hospital indemnity policy is not a substitute for basic or major medical protection but a supplement to it. Many people buy hospital indemnity policies in the hope that they will make money if they get sick, but the average benefit return does not justify the premium cost.

## Dental Expense Insurance

*Dental expense insurance* provides reimbursement for the expenses of dental services and supplies and encourages preventive dental care. The coverage normally provides for oral examinations (including X rays and cleanings), fillings, extractions, inlays, bridgework, and dentures, as well as oral surgery, root canal therapy, and orthodontics.

## Vision Care Insurance

A recent development in health insurance coverage is *vision care insurance*. An increasing number of insurance companies and prepayment plans are offering this insurance, usually to groups.

Vision and eye health problems are the second most prevalent chronic health care concerns, affecting 120 million Americans. Good vision care insurance should cover diagnosing and treating eye diseases such as glaucoma, periodic eye examinations, eyeglasses, contact lenses, and eye surgery.

In considering vision and dental coverages, you should analyze their costs and benefits. Sometimes these coverages cost more than they are worth.

*long-term care insurance (LTC)*
Provides day-in, day-out care for long-term illness or disability.

## Other Insurance Policies

Dread disease, trip accident, death insurance, and cancer policies, which are usually sold through the mail, in newspapers and magazines, or by door-to-door salespeople working on commission, are notoriously poor values. Their appeal is based on unrealistic fears, and a number of states have prohibited their sale. Such policies provide coverage only for very specific conditions and are no substitute for comprehensive insurance.

## Long-Term Care Insurance

**Long-term care insurance (LTC),** virtually unknown 20 years ago, is growing faster than any other form of insurance in the country. *Long-term care* is day-in, day-out assistance that you might need if you ever have an illness or a disability that lasts a long time and leaves you unable to care for yourself. You may or may not need lengthy care in a nursing home, but you may need help at home with daily activities such as dressing, bathing, and doing household chores.

In the late-1990s, about 8 million men and women over age 65 were estimated to need long-term care. The number is expected to increase to 12 million by the year 2020. Most of these older Americans will be cared for at home; family members and friends are the sole caregivers for 70 percent of the elderly population.

**Did You Know?**

? Why do people buy long-term care insurance?

- 23% To avoid losing savings and assets
- 25% To avoid dependence
- 25% For other reasons
- 15% To protect standard of living
- 12% To guarantee affordable services

SOURCES: Based on unpublished data from the Health Insurance Association, *1995 Long-Term Care Buyer/Non-Buyer Survey,* and LifePlans, Inc., 1995; Teachers Insurance and Annuity Association, 1996.

## Financial Planning for Life's Situations

### IS LONG-TERM CARE INSURANCE RIGHT FOR YOU?

Is long-term care (LTC) insurance worth buying? It's a tough call. Nursing home costs average $40,000 a year, and can be twice that in markets such as New York. But LTC insurance itself can be pricey, especially if you're already retired when you buy it. The policies make sense mostly for middle-class people who can't afford to bear the risk themselves but don't qualify for Medicaid. Policies are offered by most of the big insurers, such as Travelers, CNA, and John Hancock, as well as more specialized companies, such as UNUM. The policies contain variables such as daily benefits, length of coverage, and deductibles.

Not everyone needs LTC insurance. A 65-year-old man has only a 14 percent chance of spending more than a year in a nursing home, according to a 1991 *New England Journal of Medicine* estimate. For women, the odds are higher, but less than 30 percent. Still, many middle-income families may want to consider an LTC policy. Medicaid covers nursing home care, but only after you have depleted your assets (excluding home and car). So retirement-age couples with less than $150,000 in savings may be better off paying out of their pocket than buying a costly LTC policy. That also applies if your annual income is $30,000 or less. By the same token, if you have a seven-figure nest egg, you should be able to pay nursing home costs out of your savings. "If people have liquid assets of $1 million or

more, they can probably self-insure," says St. Louis financial planner Eileen Dorsey.

Don't just think about dollars, though. LTC insurance makes more sense if your relatives have a history of ailments that require extended care. "If you have diabetes or Alzheimer's in your family, you should react very differently than if your relatives drop dead of heart attacks at age 92," says Anne Werner, president of United Seniors Health Cooperative, a Washington, DC, nonprofit organization. Also, consider your age: The younger you are, the cheaper the premiums. At 45, a decent policy runs $500 a year. Your premium will be locked in at a 45-year-old's rate, but you'll make the payment for 30 years. Wait until 70, and premiums can be six times higher, "I recommend it as early as age 50," says James M. Knaus, a Troy, Michigan, financial planner.

You'll need to decide how much daily coverage you want and how long the benefits should run. Also, consider the deductible, or "elimination period." That is the number of days of care you will have to pay for before the policy kicks in. If you can handle, say, 100 days, you'll save a lot. Get an inflation rider, especially if you're young. And, as always, read the fine print. Long-term care is a major obligation, and it pays to make sure you're getting the coverage you expect.

SOURCE: "Is This Insurance Right for You?" *Business Week,* March 29, 1999, p. 182. Reprinted from the March 29, 1999 issue of *Business Week* by special permission. © 1999 McGraw-Hill Companies, Inc.

Long-term care can be very expensive. As a national average, a year in a nursing home can cost $40,000. In some regions, it can cost as much as $60,000. The average cost for one year of nursing home care is projected to be $48,200 by 2001. Bringing an aide into your home just three times a week to help with dressing, bathing, preparing meals, and similar household chores can easily cost $1,000 a month.

The annual premium for LTC policies can range from under $900 up to $15,000, depending on your age and the choices you make. The older you are when you enroll, the higher your annual premium. Typically, individual insurance plans are sold to the 50-to-80 age group, pay benefits for a maximum of two to six years, and carry a dollar limit on the total benefits they will pay. (See the Financial Planning for Life's Situations box above.)

The number of policies in effect has more than doubled since 1990, to about 4 million. About 120 insurance companies cover 12 percent of people age 65 and over. But long-term care insurance is not for everyone; it is rarely recommended for people under 60. If you are over 60, you may consider it if you wish to protect your assets, but if you have substantial wealth ($1 million or more), or very little (less than $150,000),

## LONG-TERM CARE INSURANCE

Wendy Miller, head of benefits research at Merck & Company, laments that when offered LTC policies, Merck employees have been slow to purchase them. The company has offered LTC coverage since 1991, but fewer than 10 percent of its 18,500 eligible employees have signed on. "People think of it as old-age insurance," says Miller. "They tend to be overinsured in life insurance, yet don't have key elements of income protection, such as long-term care."

The best LTC policies cover both home care and nursing home stays. Policies offer a range of benefits from $50 per day for a year or $200 per day for a lifetime. You may need an inflation protection option, especially if you buy when young.

the premium can be a waste of money.[7] However, if your employer pays the premium, the Health Insurance Portability and Accountability Act of 1996 treats a long-term care premium as a tax-deductible expense for the employer.[8]

Explore services available in your community to help meet long-term care needs. Care given by family members can be supplemented by visiting nurses, home health aides, friendly visitor programs, home-delivered meals, chore services, adult day care centers, and respite services for caregivers who need a break from daily responsibilities.

These services are becoming more widely available. Some or all of them may be found in your community. Your local Area Agency on Aging or Office on Aging can help you locate the services you need. Call the Eldercare Locator at 1–800–677–1116 to locate your local office.

The Financial Planning for Life's Situations box on page 355 can help you compare the features of long-term care policies.

An insurance company usually allows you a minimum of 10 days to review your health insurance policy, so be sure to check the major provisions that affect your coverage. Deductible, coinsurance, and stop-loss provisions were discussed under major medical expense insurance. Other major provisions are described in the following sections.

## Major Provisions in a Health Insurance Policy

All health insurance policies have certain provisions in common. Be sure you understand what your policy covers. Even the most comprehensive policy may be of little value if a provision in small print limits or denies benefits.

**Eligibility**    The eligibility provision defines who is entitled to benefits under the policy. Age, marital status, and dependency requirements are usually specified in this provision. For example, foster children usually are not automatically covered under the family contract, but stepchildren may be. Check with your insurance company to be sure.

LONG-TERM CARE: Growing Demand

SOURCES: Health Insurance Association; *Business Week,* March 29, 1999, p. 181.

# Financial Planning for Life's Situations

## LONG-TERM CARE POLICY CHECKLIST

The following checklist will help you compare LTC policies you may be considering:

|  | Policy A | Policy B |
| --- | --- | --- |
| **1.** What services are covered? |  |  |
| Skilled care | ____ | ____ |
| Intermediate care | ____ | ____ |
| Custodial care | ____ | ____ |
| Home health care | ____ | ____ |
| Adult day care | ____ | ____ |
| Other | ____ | ____ |
| **2.** How much does the policy pay per day? |  |  |
| For skilled care | ____ | ____ |
| For intermediate care | ____ | ____ |
| For custodial care | ____ | ____ |
| For home health care | ____ | ____ |
| For adult day care | ____ | ____ |
| **3.** How long will benefits last? |  |  |
| In a nursing home for: |  |  |
| Skilled nursing care | ____ | ____ |
| Intermediate nursing care | ____ | ____ |
| Custodial care | ____ | ____ |
| At home: | ____ | ____ |
| **4.** Does the policy have a maximum lifetime benefit? If so, what is it? |  |  |
| For nursing home care | ____ | ____ |
| For home health care | ____ | ____ |
| **5.** Does the policy have a maximum length of coverage for each period of confinement? If so, what is it? |  |  |
| For nursing home care | ____ | ____ |
| For home health care | ____ | ____ |
| **6.** How long must I wait before pre-existing conditions are covered? | ____ | ____ |
| **7.** How many days must I wait before benefits begin? |  |  |
| For nursing home care | ____ | ____ |
| For home health care | ____ | ____ |
| **8.** Are Alzheimer's disease and other organic mental and nervous disorders covered? |  |  |

|  | Policy A | Policy B |
| --- | --- | --- |
| **9.** Does this policy require: |  |  |
| Physician certification of need? | ____ | ____ |
| An assessment of activities of daily living? | ____ | ____ |
| A prior hospital stay for: |  |  |
| Nursing home care? | ____ | ____ |
| Home health care? | ____ | ____ |
| A prior nursing home stay for home health care coverage? | ____ | ____ |
| Other? | ____ | ____ |
| **10.** Is the policy guaranteed renewable? | ____ | ____ |
| **11.** What is the age range for enrollment? | ____ | ____ |
| **12.** Is there a waiver-of-premium provision: |  |  |
| For nursing home care? | ____ | ____ |
| For home health care? | ____ | ____ |
| **13.** How long must I be confined before premiums are waived? | ____ | ____ |
| **14.** Does the policy offer an inflation adjustment feature? If so: |  |  |
| What is the rate of increase? | ____ | ____ |
| How often is it applied? | ____ | ____ |
| For how long? | ____ | ____ |
| Is there an additional cost? | ____ | ____ |
| **15.** What does the policy cost: |  |  |
| Per year? |  |  |
| With inflation feature | ____ | ____ |
| Without inflation feature | ____ | ____ |
| Per month? |  |  |
| With inflation feature | ____ | ____ |
| Without inflation feature | ____ | ____ |
| **16.** Is there a 30-day free look? | ____ | ____ |

SOURCE: *Guide to Long-Term Care Insurance* (Washington, DC: Health Insurance Association of America, 1994), pp. 11–12.

### Assigned Benefits

When you assign benefits, you sign a paper allowing your insurance company to make payments to your hospital or doctor. Otherwise, the payments will be made to you when you turn in your bills and claim forms to the company.

### Internal Limits

A policy with internal limits will pay only a fixed amount for your hospital room no matter what the actual rate is, or it will cover your surgical expenses only to a fixed limit no matter what the actual charges are. For example, if your policy has an internal limit of $200 per hospital day and you are in a $300-a-day hospital room, you will have to pay the difference.

### Copayment

*copayment* A provision under which the insured pays a flat dollar amount each time a covered medical service is received after the deductible has been met.

**Copayment** is a type of cost sharing. Most major medical plans define copayment as the amount the patient must pay for medical services after the deductible has been met. You pay a flat dollar amount each time you receive a covered medical service. Copayments of $3 to $10 for prescriptions and $5 to $15 for doctors' office visits are common. The amount of copayment does not vary with the cost of service.

### Service Benefits

In a service benefits provision, insurance benefits are expressed in terms of entitlement to receive specified hospital or medical care rather than entitlement to receive a fixed dollar amount for each procedure. Service benefits are always preferable to a coverage stated in dollar amounts.

### Benefit Limits

The benefit limits provision defines the maximum benefits possible, in terms of either a dollar amount or a number of days in the hospital. Many policies today have benefit limits ranging from $250,000 to unlimited payments.

### Exclusions and Limitations

The exclusions and limitations provision specifies the conditions or circumstances for which the policy does not provide benefits. For example, the policy may exclude coverage for pre-existing conditions, cosmetic surgery, or routine checkups.

### Coordination of Benefits

As discussed earlier, the coordination of benefits provision prevents you from collecting benefits from two or more group policies that would in total exceed the actual charges. Under this provision, the benefits from your own and your spouse's policies are coordinated to allow you up to 100 percent payment of your covered charges.

### Guaranteed Renewable

With this policy provision, the insurance company cannot cancel a policy unless you fail to pay premiums when due. Also, it cannot raise premiums unless a rate increase occurs for all policyholders in that group.

### Cancellation and Termination

This provision explains the circumstances under which the insurance company can terminate your health insurance policy. It also explains your right to convert a group contract into an individual contract.

## Which Coverage Should You Choose?

Now that you are familiar with the types of health insurance available and some of their major provisions, how do you choose one? The most important thing to understand is that the more money you can pay for health insurance, the more coverage you can get.

For medical insurance, you have three choices. You can buy (1) basic, (2) major medical, or (3) both basic and major medical. If your budget is very limited, it is a toss-up between choosing a basic plan or a major medical plan. In many cases, either plan will handle a major share of your hospital and doctor bills. In the event of an illness involving catastrophic costs, however, you will need the protection a major medical policy offers. Ideally, you should get a basic plan and a major medical supplementary plan or a comprehensive major medical policy that combines the values of both these plans in a single policy.

## Health Insurance Trade-offs

The benefits of health insurance policies differ, and the differences can have a significant impact on your premiums. Consider the following trade-offs.

### Reimbursement versus Indemnity

A reimbursement policy provides benefits based on the actual expenses you incur. An indemnity policy provides specified benefits, regardless of whether the actual expenses are greater or less than the benefits.

### Internal Limits versus Aggregate Limits

A policy with internal limits stipulates maximum benefits for specific expenses, such as the maximum reimbursement for daily hospital room and board. Other policies may limit only the total amount of coverage, such as $1 million major expense benefits, or may have no limits.

### Deductibles and Coinsurance

The cost of a health insurance policy can be greatly affected by the size of the deductible (the amount you must pay toward medical expenses before the insurance company pays), the degree of coinsurance, and the share of medical expenses you must pay (for example, 20 percent).

### Out-of-Pocket Limit

A policy that limits the total of the coinsurance and deductibles you must pay (for example, $2,000) will limit or eliminate your financial risk, but it will also increase the premium.

### Benefits Based on Reasonable and Customary Charges

A policy that covers "reasonable and customary" medical expenses limits reimbursement to the usual charges of medical providers in an area and helps prevent overcharging.

## Health Information Online

**Sheet 52**

Recent studies indicate that consumers are seeking information on health and health care online to supplement traditional medical counsel. By far, the most consumer-friendly part of the Internet is the World Wide Web. While the rest of the Internet displays text only, the Web has the ability to display graphics and multimedia. Many legitimate providers of reliable health and medical information, including the federal Food and Drug Administration, are taking advantage of the Web's popularity by offering brochures and in-depth information on specific topics at their websites. The Financial Planning for Life's Situations feature on page 358 lists some good health care websites.

### Concept Check 11-4

1. What are several types of health insurance coverage available under group and individual policies?
2. What are the major provisions of a health insurance policy?
3. How do you decide which coverage to choose?
4. How can you analyze the costs and benefits of your health insurance policy?

## Financial Planning for Life's Situations

### HEALTH CARE WEBSITES ON THE INTERNET

**http://www.HouseCall.com** is an online encyclopedia of more than 30,000 pages of health information that incorporates data from news sources, including television, radio, newspapers, magazines, and medical journals.

**http://www.centerwatch.com** provides information on ongoing international clinical research trials, new drug therapies, and a confidential patient notification service.

**http://healthnet.ivi.com** explains medical headlines, current issues, and newly approved drugs and answers other questions with advice from physicians.

**http://pharminfo.com** has health news from the publishers of *The New England Journal of Medicine* and is a pharmaceutical information network.

**http://www.icic.nci.nin.gov** is a National Cancer Institute database that includes information about cancer and its treatment. All information is reviewed by oncology experts.

**http://www.cdc.gov** provides information from the Centers for Disease Control and Prevention on chronic diseases, injuries and disabilities, health risks, and prevention guidelines.

**http://medicus.marhall.edu/medicus.htm** is an online interactive patient service that simulates an actual patient encounter.

**http://www.cpmc.columbia.edu/list.html** is a site provided by Columbia University and Presbyterian Hospital in New York. It has information on cholesterol in clinical vocabulary terms.

**http://www.nih.gov** provides online health care information from the National Institutes of Health, a federal agency, and a biomedical research center, with materials on AIDS research, women's health, and bone marrow transplantation.

**http://www.nlm.nih.gov** is the National Library of Medicine's web page offering resources and information from more than 5 million medical books, journals, pamphlets, rare manuscripts, and films.

**http://nhic-nt.health.org** is the National Health Information Center's web page, an online directory of more than 1,100 health-related organizations that provide health information.

**http://chmis.org** lists materials available from Community Health Management Information Systems. Communities across the country collaborate to address the need for comprehensive health information systems.

**http://www.fda.gov** is the Food and Drug Administration's site. It has documents from the Center for Drug Evaluation and Research, the National Center for Toxicological Research, and the Center for Food Safety and Applied Nutrition. The site includes the latest information from the FDA, including press statements, testimony, federal register notices, and enforcement reports.

SOURCE: *NCL Bulletin,* November–December 1996, p. 2.

## PRIVATE SOURCES OF HEALTH INSURANCE AND HEALTH CARE

**Obj. 5**
Evaluate private sources of health insurance and health care.

Health insurance is available from more than 800 private insurance companies. Moreover, service plans such as Blue Cross/Blue Shield, health maintenance organizations, preferred provider organizations, government programs such as Medicare, fraternal organizations, and trade unions provide health insurance.

### Private Insurance Companies

Insurance companies sell health insurance through either group or individual policies. Of these two types, group health insurance represents about 90 percent of all medical expense insurance and 80 percent of all disability income insurance.

The policies insurance companies issue provide for payment either directly to the insured for reimbursement of expenses incurred or, if assigned by the insured, to the provider of services.

Most private insurance companies sell health insurance policies to employers, who in turn offer them as fringe benefits to employees and employees' dependents. The premiums may be partially paid by employers. The Health Insurance Portability and Accountability Act, as discussed earlier, requires employers to keep detailed records of all employees and dependents covered by the company's health plan. Employers must be able to provide certificates of coverage for any employee covered since July 1, 1996.

## Hospital and Medical Service Plans

Blue Cross and Blue Shield are statewide organizations similar to commercial health insurance companies. Each state has its own Blue Cross and Blue Shield. The Blues plans play an important role in providing private health insurance to millions of Americans.

**Blue Cross** plans provide *hospital care benefits* on essentially a "service type" basis. Through a separate contract with each member hospital, Blue Cross reimburses the hospital for covered services provided to the insured.

**Blue Shield** plans provide benefits for *surgical and medical services* performed by physicians. The typical Blue Shield plan provides benefits similar to those provided under the benefit provisions of hospital-surgical policies issued by insurance companies.

During the 1970s and 1980s, increasing health care costs spurred the growth of managed care. **Managed care** refers to prepaid health plans that provide comprehensive health care to members. Managed care is offered by health maintenance organizations, preferred provider organizations, exclusive provider organizations, point-of-service plans, and traditional indemnity insurance companies.

A recent industry survey estimated that 85 percent of employed Americans are enrolled in some form of managed care. Managed care companies now provide information that helps you better manage your health care needs. Health plans have launched Internet programs that allow you to access medical research, support groups, and professional advice, and to exchange e-mail with health care providers. The best-known managed care plans are health maintenance organizations (HMOs) and preferred provider organizations (PPOs), which offer a wide range of preventive services.

## Health Maintenance Organizations (HMOs)

Prepaid managed care is designed to make the provision of health care services cost effective by controlling their use. Health maintenance organizations are an alternative to basic and major medical insurance plans. A **health maintenance organization (HMO)** is a health insurance plan that directly employs or contracts with selected physicians, surgeons, dentists, and optometrists to provide health care services in exchange for a fixed, prepaid monthly premium. HMOs operate on the premise that maintaining health through preventive care will minimize future medical problems.

The preventive care HMOs provide includes periodic checkups, screening programs, diagnostic testing, and immunizations. HMOs also provide a comprehensive range of other health care services. These services are divided into two categories: basic and supplemental. *Basic health services* include inpatient, outpatient, maternity, mental health, substance abuse, and emergency care. *Supplemental services* include vision, hearing, and pharmaceutical care, which are usually available for an additional fee.

Your membership in a typical HMO should cover office visits, routine checkups, hospital and surgical care, eye exams, laboratory and X-ray services, hemodialysis for kidney failure, and mental health services. See the Financial Planning for Life's Situations feature on page 361 for tips on how to choose and use an HMO.

*Blue Cross*
An independent, nonprofit membership corporation that provides protection against the cost of hospital care.

*Blue Shield*
An independent, nonprofit membership corporation that provides protection against the cost of surgical and medical care.

*managed care*   Prepaid health plans that provide comprehensive health care to members.

*health maintenance organization (HMO)*
A health insurance plan that provides a wide range of health care services for a fixed, prepaid monthly premium.

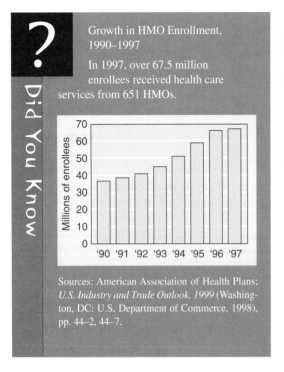

**Did You Know**

Growth in HMO Enrollment, 1990–1997

In 1997, over 67.5 million enrollees received health care services from 651 HMOs.

Sources: American Association of Health Plans; *U.S. Industry and Trade Outlook, 1999* (Washington, DC: U.S. Department of Commerce, 1998), pp. 44–2, 44–7.

In the late 1990s, HMOs were coming under fire from patients, doctors, unions, and federal and state governments. In 1997, President Clinton appointed a 34-member advisory committee to draft a patients' bill of rights and study what kind of legislation may be needed to enforce it. "Many Americans worry that lower costs mean lower quality and less attention to their rights," said the president. Senator Edward Kennedy charged that "too many managed-care firms and other insurance companies have decided that the shortest route to highest profits and a competitive edge is by denying patients the care they need and deserve." Furthermore, Health Access, a coalition of 215 consumer organizations, is drafting a very comprehensive state bill of rights for HMO members. It would set legal standards for everything from when HMOs can deny care to how long they can keep patients waiting on the telephone. In 1996, 35 states passed 56 laws to "regulate or weaken HMOs," according to Thomas Bodenheimer of the University of San Francisco School of Medicine.[9]

In 1999, Aetna's U.S. Healthcare HMO was fighting an $800 million lawsuit against the HMO and two of its medical directors. Allegedly, the medical directors had denied and delayed drug rehabilitation benefits for a man who ultimately died of a drug overdose. Earlier the same HMO was hit with one of the largest managed care verdicts ever when a California jury ordered Aetna to pay $120.5 million in damages to a stomach cancer patient.[10]

Responding to new state laws that could cost HMOs millions of dollars in lawsuits, some managed care companies are paying for medical services and procedures they previously rejected. In addition, 22 states have enacted laws permitting patients to appeal managed care companies' coverage decisions to outside, independent review panels.[11]

## Preferred Provider Organizations (PPOs)

*preferred provider organization (PPO)*
A group of doctors and hospitals that agree to provide health care at rates approved by the insurer.

A **preferred provider organization (PPO)** is a group of doctors and hospitals that agree to provide health care at rates approved by the insurer. In return, PPOs expect prompt payment and the opportunity to serve an increased volume of patients. The premiums for PPOs are slightly higher than those for HMOs. An insurance company or your employer contracts with a PPO to provide specified services at predetermined fees to PPO members.

Preferred provider organizations combine the best elements of the fee-for-service and HMO systems. PPOs offer the services of doctors and hospitals at discount rates or give breaks in copayments and deductibles.

PPOs provide their members with essentially the same benefits HMOs offer. However, while HMOs require members to seek care from HMO providers only (except for emergency treatment), PPOs allow members to use a preferred provider—or another provider for a higher copayment—each time a medical need arises. This combination of allowing free choice of physicians and low-cost care makes PPOs popular.

*exclusive provider organization (EPO)*
Renders medical care from affiliated health care providers.

The **exclusive provider organization (EPO)** is the extreme form of the PPO. Services rendered by nonaffiliated providers are not reimbursed. Therefore, if you belong to an EPO, you must receive your care from affiliated providers or pay the entire cost yourself. Providers typically are reimbursed on a fee-for-service basis according to a negotiated discount or fee schedule.

# Financial Planning for Life's Situations

## TIPS ON USING AND CHOOSING AN HMO

### HOW TO USE AN HMO

When you first enroll in an HMO, you must choose a plan physician (family practitioner, internist, pediatrician, or obstetrician-gynecologist) who provides or arranges for all of your health care services. It is extremely important that you receive your care through the plan physician. If you don't, you are responsible for the cost of the service rendered.

The only exceptions to the requirement that care be received through the plan physician are medical emergencies. A medical emergency is a sudden onset of illness or a sudden injury that would jeopardize your life or health if not treated immediately. In such instances, you may use the facilities of the nearest hospital emergency room. All other care must be provided by hospitals and doctors under contract with the HMO.

### HOW TO CHOOSE AN HMO

If you decide to enroll in an HMO, you should consider these additional factors:

1. *Accessibility.* Since you must use plan providers, it is extremely important that they be easily accessible from your home or office.
2. *Convenient office hours.* Your plan physician should have convenient office hours.
3. *Alternative physicians.* Should you become dissatisfied with your first choice of a physician, the HMO should allow you the option to change physicians.
4. *Second opinions.* You should be able to obtain second opinions.

5. *Type of coverage.* You should compare the health care services offered by various HMOs, paying particular attention to whether you will incur out-of-pocket expenses or copayments.
6. *Appeal procedures.* The HMO should have a convenient and prompt system for resolving problems and disputes.
7. *Price.* You should compare the prices various HMOs charge to ensure that you are getting the most services for your health care dollar.

### WHAT TO DO WHEN AN HMO DENIES TREATMENT OR COVERAGE

- *Get it in writing.* To better defend your case, ask for a letter detailing the clinical reasons your claim was denied and the name and medical expertise of the HMO staff member responsible.
- *Know your rights.* The plan document or your HMO's member services department will tell you how experimental treatments are defined and covered and how the appeals process works.
- *Keep records.* Make copies of any correspondence, including payments and any reimbursements. Also, keep a written log of all conversations relevant to your claim.
- *Find advocates.* Enlist the help of your doctor, employer, and state insurance department to lobby your case before the HMO.

SOURCE: Reprinted from the May 19, 1997 issue of *Business Week* by special permission. © 1999 McGraw-Hill Companies, Inc.

---

*point-of-service plan (POS)* A network of selected contracted, participating providers; also called an *HMO-PPO hybrid* or *open-ended HMO.*

A **point-of-service plan (POS),** sometimes called an *HMO-PPO hybrid* or *open-ended HMO,* combines characteristics of both HMOs and PPOs. POSs use a network of selected contracted, participating providers. Employees select a primary care physician who controls referrals for medical specialists. If you receive care from a plan provider, you pay little or nothing, as in an HMO, and do not file claims. Medical care provided by out-of-plan providers will be reimbursed, but you must pay significantly higher copayments and deductibles. Hybrid plans are useful if you want to try managed care but don't want to be locked into a network of doctors. A drawback is that they cost more than HMOs.

The distinction among HMOs, PPOs, EPOs, and POSs is becoming blurred. As cost reduction pressures mount and these alternative delivery systems try to increase their market share, each tries to make its system more attractive. The evolution of health care plans will likely continue so that it will become increasingly difficult to characterize a particular managed care delivery system as adhering to any particular model.

Cost of Inpatient Care Compared to Home Care for Selected
Medical Conditions (current dollars)

| Condition | Per-Patient Per-Month Hospital Costs | Per-Patient Per-Month Home Care Costs | Per-Patient Per-Month Dollar Savings |
|---|---|---|---|
| Low birth weight | 26,190 | 330 | 25,860 |
| Ventilator-dependent adults | 21,570 | 7,050 | 14,520 |
| Oxygen-dependent children | 12,090 | 5,250 | 6,840 |
| Chemotherapy for children with cancer | 69,870 | 55,950 | 13,920 |
| Congestive heart failure among the elderly | 1,758 | 1,605 | 153 |
| Intravenous antibiotic theraphy for cellulitis, osteomyelitis, others | 12,510 | 4,650 | 7,860 |

SOURCES: National Association for Home Care; *U.S. Industry and Trade Outlook, 1999* (Washington, DC: U.S. Department of Commerce, 1998), p. 44-11.

## Home Health Care Agencies

Home health care providers furnish and are responsible for the supervision and management of preventive medical care in a home setting in accordance with a medical order. Rising hospital care costs, new medical technology, and the increasing number of elderly and infirm people have helped make home care one of the fastest-growing areas of the health care industry.

Spending on home health care has been growing at an annual rate of about 20 percent over the past few years. This rapid growth reflects (1) the increasing proportion of older people in the U.S. population, (2) the lower costs of home health care compared to the costs of institutional health care, (3) insurers' active support of home health care, and (4) Medicare's promotion of home health care as an alternative to institutionalization.

Home health care consists of home health agencies, home care aide organizations, and hospices. Recently the National Association for Home Care identified over 20,200 home care institutions in the United States. These agencies provide services to over 7 million people with an acute illness, a long-term medical condition, a permanent disability, or a terminal illness.[12] Exhibit 11–7 provides some examples of cost savings for certain medical conditions.

## Employer Self-Funded Health Plans

Certain types of health insurance coverage are made available by plans that employers, labor unions, fraternal societies, or communities administer. Usually these groups provide the amount of protection a specific group of people desires and can afford.

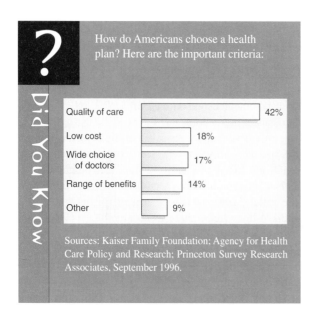

How do Americans choose a health plan? Here are the important criteria:

| | |
|---|---|
| Quality of care | 42% |
| Low cost | 18% |
| Wide choice of doctors | 17% |
| Range of benefits | 14% |
| Other | 9% |

Sources: Kaiser Family Foundation; Agency for Health Care Policy and Research; Princeton Survey Research Associates, September 1996.

Self-funded groups must assume the financial burden if medical bills are greater than the amount covered by premium income. While private insurance companies have the assets needed in such situations, self-funded plans often do not. The results can be disastrous.

In addition to the private sources of health insurance and health care discussed in this section, government health care programs cover over 45 million people. The next section discusses these programs.

## Concept Check 11-5

1. What are the major sources of health insurance and health care?
2. What are Blue Cross and Blue Shield plans? What benefits does each plan provide?
3. What are the differences among HMOs, PPOs, EPOs, and POSs?
4. What are home health care agencies?
5. What are employer self-funded health plans?

## GOVERNMENT HEALTH CARE PROGRAMS

**Obj. 6**

Appraise the sources of government health care programs.

Public opinion polls consistently show that Americans are unhappy with the nation's health care system. Increasingly, businesses and citizens have been calling for some kind of national health program.

Federal and state governments offer health coverage in accordance with laws that define the premiums and benefits they can offer. Specific requirements as to age, occupation, length of service, and family income may be used to determine eligibility for coverage. Two sources of government health insurance are Medicare and Medicaid.

### Medicare

*Medicare,* established in 1965, is a federal health insurance program for people 65 or older, people of any age with permanent kidney failure, and people with certain disabilities. The program is administered by the Health Care Financing Administration. Local Social Security Administration offices take applications for Medicare, assist beneficiaries in filing claims, and provide information about the program.

Medicare has two parts: hospital insurance (Part A) and medical insurance (Part B). Medicare *hospital insurance* helps pay for inpatient hospital care, inpatient care in a skilled nursing facility, home health care, and hospice care. Hospital insurance is financed from a portion of the Social Security tax. Part A pays for all covered services for inpatient hospital care after you pay a single annual deductible ($768 in 1999).

Medicare *medical insurance* helps pay for doctors' services and a variety of other medical services and supplies not covered by hospital insurance. Each year, as soon as you meet the annual medical insurance deductible, medical insurance will pay 80

**Did You Know?**

Assuming that Congress makes no changes in current law, Medicare spending will increase from $187 billion in 1997, to $246 billion in 2002, to $393 billion by 2008.

Source: *U.S. Industry and Trade Outlook, 1999* (Washington, DC: U.S. Department of Commerce, 1999), p. 44-8.

percent of the approved charges for the covered services that you receive during the rest of the year. In 1999, the annual deductible was $100. Voluntary medical insurance is financed from the monthly premiums paid by people who have enrolled in it and from general federal revenues.

And now the bad news. The recent budget agreement would slash Medicare growth by $115 billion over the next five years, extending the program's solvency until 2008.[13]

### Mending Medicare

Without changes, the nation's $207 billion-a-year system for providing health care to seniors is projected to go broke in 2008. That's decades before Social Security could exhaust its trust fund, but before 77 million baby boomers start collecting Medicare benefits. Medicare is a much smaller program, but due to a combination of rising health care costs and a growing elderly population, Medicare spending will soar at a faster rate than Social Security, from 12 percent of the budget in 1999 to more than 27 percent by 2030. "With all due respect for all the hoopla over Social Security, Medicare is a far more important and more difficult issue," says Brandeis University health policy expert Stuart H. Altman. "Anything we do still leaves a huge gap between the available money and the program's cost."[14]

The Balanced Budget Act of 1997 created the new Medicare + Choice program. The act expands managed care options by encouraging wider availability of HMOs and allows other types of health plans to participate in Medicare. It gives you the option to remain in the original Medicare (Parts A and B) or to enroll in a Medicare + Choice plan.

The act also created the Medical Savings Account (MSA), a test program limited to 390,000 Medicare beneficiaries. MSAs are tax-free savings accounts that can be used to pay medical bills. MSA funds withdrawn for nonmedical purposes are taxable and subject to a penalty. The act also contains provisions to slow the growth in Medicare spending.

In 1999, President Clinton asked Congress to support his Medicare reforms. His plan attempts to modernize and strengthen the Medicare program and prepare it for the health, demographic, and financing challenges it faces in the 21st century. The plan would

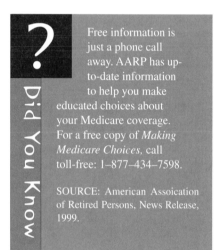

Did You Know?

Free information is just a phone call away. AARP has up-to-date information to help you make educated choices about your Medicare coverage. For a free copy of *Making Medicare Choices*, call toll-free: 1–877–434–7598.

SOURCE: American Assoication of Retired Persons, News Release, 1999.

- *Preserve the current system.* The government would allow for some competition from private insurers but maintain the basic federally operated program.
- *Add a drug benefit.* Seniors would get generous new coverage for prescription drugs, although they may have to pay slightly higher premiums.
- *Restore Medicare solvency.* The government would shift nearly $800 billion in income tax revenues over 15 years to shore up the health care trust fund.[15]

Exhibit 11–8 compares Medicare HMO plans, and Exhibit 11–9 compares features of different Medicare options.

### What Is Not Covered by Medicare?

Although Medicare is very helpful for meeting medical costs, it does not cover everything. In addition to the deductibles and coinsurance mentioned earlier, Medicare does not cover some medical expenses at all, including

- Care in a skilled nursing facility (SNF) beyond 100 days per benefit period.
- Skilled nursing care in facilities not approved by Medicare.
- Intermediate and custodial nursing care (the kind many nursing home residents need).
- Out-of-hospital prescription drugs.

| | Plan 1 | Plan 2 | Plan 3 |
|---|---|---|---|
| **Hospital Services:** | | | |
| Hospitalization | | | |
| Outpatient services | | | |
| Hospital emergency room | | | |
| Psychiatric inpatient care | | | |
| Other | | | |
| **Professional Services:** | | | |
| Physician office visits | | | |
| Laboratory and X ray | | | |
| Chiropractic care | | | |
| Outpatient mental illness treatment | | | |
| Other | | | |
| **Other Services:** | | | |
| Skilled nursing facility care | | | |
| Home health care | | | |
| Durable medical equipment | | | |
| Ambulance services | | | |
| Out-of-area urgent/emergency care | | | |
| Prescription drugs | | | |
| Other | | | |
| **Routine Care:** | | | |
| Routine physical exam | | | |
| Routine eye exam | | | |
| Prescription eyeglasses/lenses | | | |
| Prescription eyeglasses/frames | | | |
| Routine hearing exam | | | |
| Hearing aid | | | |
| Mammograms/pap smears | | | |
| Other | | | |
| **Statistics:** | | | |
| Plan membership | | | |
| Number of primary care doctors available | | | |
| Counties serviced | | | |
| Out-of-pocket maximum | | | |
| Other | | | |
| **Miscellaneous:** | | | |
| Contract type | | | |
| Monthly premium | | | |

**EXHIBIT 11-8**

**Medicare HMO Comparison Chart**

SOURCE: *1999 Medicare Supplement Premium Comparison Guide,* Illinois Department of Insurance.

- Private-duty nursing.
- Routine checkups, dental care, most immunizations, cosmetic surgery, routine foot care, eyeglasses, and hearing aids.
- Care received outside the United States except in Canada and Mexico, and then only in limited circumstances.
- Services Medicare does not consider medically necessary.
- Physician charges above Medicare's approved amount. The government has a fee schedule for physician charges and places limits on charges in excess of the Medicare-approved amount when the physician does not accept Medicare's approved amount as payment in full.

**EXHIBIT 11-9**   A Comparison of Various Medicare Plans

| | Current Options | New Options (Medicare and Choice) | Plan Description |
|---|---|---|---|
| Original Medicare | ✓ | ✓ | • You choose your health care providers.<br>• Medicare pays your providers for covered services.<br>• Most beneficiaries choose Medicare supplemental insurance to cover deductible and copayments. |
| Medicare<br>Health maintenance organization (HMO) | ✓ | ✓ | • You must live in the plan's service area.<br>• You agree to use the plan network of doctors, hospitals, and other health providers, except in an emergency.<br>• Medicare pays the HMO to provide all medical services. |
| Preferred provider organization (PPO) | | ✓ | • Works like an HMO, except you have the choice to see a health provider out of the network.<br>• If you do see an out-of-network provider, you will pay a higher cost. |
| Provider-sponsored organization (PSO) | | ✓ | • Works like a Medicare HMO, except the networks are managed by health care providers (doctors and hospitals) rather than an insurance company. |
| Private fee for service | | ✓ | • Medicare pays a lump sum to a private insurance health plan.<br>• Providers can bill more than what the plan pays; you are responsible for paying the balance.<br>• The plan may offer more benefits than original Medicare. |
| Medical savings account (MSA) | | ✓ | • A test program is limited to 390,000 Medicare beneficiaries.<br>• Medicare MSAs are a special type of savings account that can be used to pay medical bills.<br>• HCFA will make an annual lump-sum deposit into an enrollee's account (only Medicare can deposit funds into this account).<br>• MSAs work with a special private insurance company and carry a very high deductible.<br>• Funds withdrawn for nonmedical purposes are taxable and subject to a penalty. |

SOURCE: Medicare & You (Washington, DC, Health Care Financing Administration, 1999).

For a more complete description of Medicare coverage and costs, ask your local Social Security Administration office for a copy of *The Medicare Handbook*. For more information, call the Medicare Hotline at 1–800–772–1213.

**Medigap**   Medicare was never intended to pay all medical costs. To fill the gap between Medicare payments and medical costs not covered by Medicare, many companies sell medigap insurance policies. **Medigap** or **MedSup insurance** is not sold or serviced by the federal government or state governments. Contrary to the claims made by advertising and insurance agents, Medicare supplement insurance is not a government-sponsored program.

*medigap (MedSup) insurance* Supplements Medicare by filling the gap between Medicare payments and medical costs not covered by Medicare.

Most states now have 10 standardized Medicare supplement policies designated by the letters A through J. These newly standardized policies make it much easier to compare the costs of policies issued by different insurers. All Medicare policies must cover certain gaps in Medicare coverage, such as the daily coinsurance amount for hospitalization.

In addition to the basic benefits that must now be included in all newly issued Medicare supplement policies in most states, you should consider other policy features.

## Medicaid

Title XIX of the Social Security Act provides for a program of medical assistance to certain low-income individuals and families. In 1965 the program, known as *Medicaid,* became federal law.

Medicaid is administered by each state within certain broad federal requirements and guidelines. Financed by both state and federal funds, it is designed to provide medical assistance to groups or categories of persons who are eligible to receive payments under one of the cash assistance programs such as Aid to Families with Dependent Children and Supplemental Security Income. The states may also provide Medicaid to medically needy individuals, that is, to persons who fit into one of the categories eligible for public assistance.

Many members of the Medicaid population are also covered by Medicare. Where such dual coverage exists, most state Medicaid programs pay for the Medicare premiums, deductibles, and copayments and for services not covered by Medicare. Medicaid differs from Medicare because eligibility for Medicaid depends on having very low income and assets. Once a person is eligible, Medicaid provides more benefits than does Medicare. Because Medicaid coverage is so comprehensive, people using it do not need to purchase supplemental insurance.

To qualify for federal matching funds, state programs must include inpatient hospital services; outpatient hospital services; laboratory and X-ray services; skilled nursing and home health services for individuals age 21 and older; family planning services; early and periodic screening, diagnosis, and treatment for individuals under 21; and physicians' services in the home, office, hospital, nursing home, or elsewhere.

**?**

**Did You Know**

You can call
1–800–HHS–TIPS to
report fraud and abuse
in Medicare and
Medicaid programs.

## Fight against Medicare/Medicaid Fraud and Abuse

Nearly 70 percent of consumers believe the Medicare program would not go broke if fraud and abuse were eliminated. Moreover, nearly 80 percent are not aware of any efforts to reduce health care fraud and abuse. In 1997, President Clinton introduced the Medicare/Medicaid Anti-Waste, Fraud and Abuse Act, which established tough new requirements for health care providers that wish to participate in the Medicare/Medicaid program.

The Financial Planning for Life's Situations feature on page 368 provides some consumer tips on health and disability insurance.

## Government Consumer Health Information Websites

With more than 60 central World Wide Web sites on eight separate web domains, the Department of Health and Human Services (HHS) maintains one of the richest and most reliable sources of information on the Internet (www.hhs.gov). HHS documents on the Web include information on health issues, research-related data, and access to HHS services, including interactive sites. Major HHS health information websites include the following.

**Healthfinder**   Healthfinder includes links to more than 1,250 websites, including over 250 federal sites and 1,000 state, local, not-for-profit, university, and other consumer health resources. Topics are organized in a subject index. With more than 7 million hits in its first two months of operation, Healthfinder is currently rated fifth among consumers' favorite websites on the "Web 100" list (www.hhs.gov).

## Financial Planning for Life's Situations

### CONSUMER TIPS ON HEALTH AND DISABILITY INSURANCE

1. If you pay your own premiums directly, try to arrange to pay them on an annual or quarterly basis rather than a monthly basis. It is cheaper.

2. Policies should be delivered to you within 30 days. If not, contact your insurer and find out, in writing, why. If a policy is not delivered in 60 days, contact the state department of insurance.

3. When you receive a policy, take advantage of the free-look provision. You have 10 days to look it over and obtain a refund if you decide it is not for you.

4. Unless you have a policy with no internal limits, read over your contract every year to see whether its benefits are still in line with medical costs.

5. Don't replace a policy because you think it is out of date. Switching may subject you to new waiting periods and new exclusions. Rather, add to what you have if necessary.

6. On the other hand, don't keep a policy because you've had it a long time. You don't get any special credit from the company for being an old customer.

7. Don't try to make a profit on your insurance by carrying overlapping coverages. Duplicate coverage is expensive. Besides, most group policies now contain a coordination of benefits clause limiting benefits to 100 percent.

8. Use your health emergency fund to cover small expenses.

9. If you're considering the purchase of a dread disease policy such as cancer insurance, understand that it is supplementary and will pay for only one disease. You should have full coverage before you consider it. Otherwise, it's a gamble.

10. Don't lie on your insurance application. If you fail to mention a pre-existing condition, you may not get paid. You can usually get paid even for that condition after one or two years have elapsed if you have had no treatment for the condition during that period.

11. Keep your insurance up to date. Some policies adjust to inflation better than others. Some insurers check that benefits have not been outdistanced by inflation. Review your policies annually.

12. Never sign a health insurance application (such applications are lengthy and detailed for individually written policies) until you have recorded full and complete answers to every question.

SOURCE: Health Insurance Association of America.

**MEDLINEplus**    MEDLINEplus, the world's most extensive collection of published medical information, is coordinated by the National Library of Medicine. Originally designed for health professionals and researchers, MEDLINEplus is also valuable for students and for those seeking more specific information about health care (www.nlm.nih.gov/medlineplus).

**NIH Health Information Page**    This website provides a single access point to the consumer health information resources of the National Institutes of Health, including the NIH Health Information Index, NIH publications and clearinghouses, and the Combined Health Information Database (www.nih.gov).

### Concept Check 11-6

1.   What are the two sources of government health insurance?
2.   What benefits do Part A and Part B of Medicare provide?
3.   What is medigap, or MedSup, insurance?

# Summary of Objectives

Obj. 1  **Explain why the costs of health insurance and health care have been increasing.**

Health care costs, except during 1994–96, have gone up faster than the rate of inflation. Among the reasons for high and rising health care costs are the use of expensive technologies, duplication of tests and sometimes technologies, increases in the variety and frequency of treatments, unnecessary tests, the increasing number and longevity of elderly people, regulations that shift rather than reduce costs, the increasing number of accidents and crimes requiring emergency services, limited competition and restrictive work rules in the health care delivery system, rapid earnings growth among health care professionals, built-in inflation in the health care delivery system, and other factors.

Obj. 2  **Define** *health insurance* **and** *disability income insurance* **and explain their importance in financial planning.**

Health insurance is protection that provides payment of benefits for a covered sickness or injury. Disability income insurance protects a person's most valuable asset: the ability to earn income.

Health insurance and disability income insurance are two protections against economic losses due to illness, accident, or disability. Both protections should be a part of your overall insurance program to safeguard your family's economic security.

Disability can cause even greater financial problems than death. In fact, disability is often called "the living death." Disabled persons lose their earning power while continuing to incur normal family expenses. In addition, they often face huge expenses for the medical treatment and special care their disabilities require.

Obj. 3  **Recognize the need for disability income insurance.**

Disability income insurance provides regular cash income lost by employees as the result of an accident, illness, or pregnancy. Sources of disability income insurance include the employer, Social Security, worker's compensation, the Veterans Administration, the federal and state governments, unions, and private insurance.

Obj. 4  **Analyze the benefits and limitations of the various types of health care coverage.**

Five basic types of health insurance are available under group and individual policies: hospital expense insurance, surgical expense insurance, physician's expense insurance, major medical expense insurance, and comprehensive major medical insurance. The benefits and limitations of each policy differ. Ideally, you should get a basic plan and a major medical supplementary plan, or a comprehensive major medical policy that combines the values of both of these plans in a single policy.

Major provisions of a health insurance policy include eligibility requirements, assigned benefits, inside limits, copayment, service benefits, benefit limits, exclusions and limitation, coordination of benefits, guaranteed renewability, and cancellation and termination.

Obj. 5  **Evaluate private sources of health insurance and health care.**

Health insurance and health care are available from private insurance companies, hospital and medical service plans such as Blue Cross/Blue Shield, health maintenance organizations (HMOs), preferred provider organizations (PPOs), exclusive provider organizations (EPOs), point-of-service plans (POSs), home health care agencies, and employer self-funded health plans.

Obj. 6  **Appraise the sources of government health care programs.**

The federal and state governments offer health coverage in accordance with laws that define the premiums and benefits. Two well-known government health programs are Medicare and Medicaid.

# Financial Planning Problems

1. *Calculating the Effect of Inflation on Health Care Costs.* As of 1995, per capita spending on health care in the United States was about $3,600. If this amount increased by 5 percent a year, what would be the amount of per capita spending for health care in 10 years?  (Obj. 1)
2. *Calculating the Amount of Disability Benefits.* Georgia Braxton, a widow, has take-home pay of $600 a week. Her disability insurance coverage replaces 70 percent of her earnings after a four-week waiting period. What amount would she receive in disability benefits if an illness kept Georgia off work for 16 weeks?  (Obj. 3)
3. *Calculating the Amount of Reimbursement from an Insurance Company.* The Kelleher family has health insurance coverage that pays 80 percent of out-of-hospital expenses after a $500 deductible per person. If one family member has doctor and prescription medication expenses of $1,100, what amount would the insurance company pay? (Obj. 4)

4. *Comparing the Costs of a Regular Health Insurance Policy and an HMO.* A health insurance policy pays 65 percent of physical therapy costs after a $200 deductible. In contrast, an HMO charges $15 per visit for physical therapy. How much would a person save with the HMO if he or she had 10 physical therapy sessions costing $50 each? (Obj. 5)

## Financial Planning Activities

1. *Identifying Financial Resources Needed to Pay for Health Care Services.* List health care services that you and other members of your family have used during the past year. Assign an approximate dollar cost to each of these services, and identify the financial resources (savings, health insurance, government sources, etc.) you used to pay for them. (Obj. 1)
2. *Using Current Information to Obtain Costs of Health Care.* Choose a current issue of *Consumer Reports, Money, Business Week,* or *Kiplinger's Personal Finance Magazine* and summarize an article that updates the costs of health care. How might you use this information to reduce your health care costs? (Obj. 1)
3. *Reviewing an Employer's Health Benefit Package.* List the benefits included in your employee benefit package, such as health insurance, disability income insurance, and life insurance. Discuss the importance of such a benefit package to the consumer. (Obj. 2)
4. *Determining Social Security Disability Benefits.* Visit the Social Security Administration's web page to determine approximate monthly Social Security disability benefits if you became disabled in the current year. Or call your Social Security office to request the latest edition of *Social Security: Understanding the Benefits.* (Obj. 3)
5. *Comparing Major Provisions in a Health Care Insurance Policy.* Obtain sample health insurance policies from insurance agents or brokers, and analyze the policies for definitions, coverages, exclusions, limitations on coverage, and amounts of coverage. In what ways are the policies similar? In what ways are do they differ? (Obj. 4)
6. *Using the Internet to Obtain Information about Various Types of Health Insurance Coverages.* Visit the following Department of Health and Human Services websites to gather information about various types of health insurance coverages. Prepare a summary report on how this information may be useful to you. (Obj. 4)
   a. Healthfinder (http://www.healthfinder.gov)
   b. MEDLINE (http://www.medline.gov)
7. *Choosing a Source of Health Insurance and Health Care.* Visit the National Health Information Center's web page (http://nhic-nt.health.org). The NHIC is an online directory of more than 1,100 health-related organizations that can provide health care information. Describe in a two-page report the types of health insurance and health care available to consumers. (Obj. 5)
8. *Using Current Information for People with Medicare.* Write to the U.S. Department of Health and Human Services (Health Care Financing Administration, Baltimore, MD 21207), and ask for the latest edition of *Guide to Health Insurance for People with Medicare.* On the basis of the information contained in this source, describe the changes that have been made in the hospital insurance and medical insurance provided by Medicare. (Obj. 6)

## LIFE SITUATION CASE

### HEALTH INSURANCE: YOU CAN TAKE IT WITH YOU

Hadiya had been experiencing chronic back pain for the past year-and-a-half at her job as an assembly line worker in a microchip plant. She was receiving treatment that was covered by her health insurance and had decided to look for a new career. A friend told her about a new employer in her area that offered retraining for office positions; this seemed ideal because the work would be less physical.

Unfortunately, Hadiya heard that if she changed jobs, her new insurance would not cover her pre-existing medical condition. A pre-existing condition is an illness or injury you had before you switched jobs, that you are receiving treatment for at the time you switch, or that you have been treated for in the past but that might recur. This meant she would not be able to continue her current treatment or get the back surgery her doctor recommended. She felt helpless and forced to stay with a job that was actually exacerbating her back problem.

Hadiya is not alone, but thanks to a law that took effect July 1, 1997, her health insurance is now "portable." In other words, when she moves from one company to another, Hadiya will continue to receive coverage or will eventually be able to get coverage for her back problem even though it is a pre-existing medical condition.

The Health Insurance Portability and Accountability Act (HIPAA) works like this: If you or your family were covered under a former employer's health plan for at least 12 months, without an interruption of 63 or more days, a new plan will have to provide coverage with no limitation on pre-existing conditions. Hadiya just needs to request a certificate of insurance coverage from her former employer to prove her eligibility under a new plan.

Under HIPAA, Hadiya's new plan can refuse to cover her condition if it was diagnosed within six months before the date she enrolled. However, since her back problems began 18 months before she decided to change jobs, she cannot be refused coverage. Even people who fall within the six-month date will be able to get coverage for a pre-existing condition if they stay with the new plan for 12 months.

## Questions

1. What is portability?
2. How does the HIPAA work?
3. What does Hadiya need to do to prove she had insurance coverage?

SOURCES: Grace W. Weinstein, "Health Insurance: You Can Take It with You," *Investor's Business Daily,* June 17, 1997, p. A1; "Answering Your Questions on Health Insurance Reform," *Gannett News Service,* June 11, 1997.

# INTERNET CASE   Making Sense of Medicare

Eugenio Costa, 65, received a 56-page booklet from Uncle Sam called *Medicare and You 2000.* It doesn't have much of a plot, but it might be the most important reading he does this year.

For seniors or their adult children, the booklet outlines the choices Medicare recipients face in the fast-changing world of health care. But Medicare is mind-numbingly complicated, and it is too easy to get lost in a maze of options.

Eugenio is fully aware, however, that Medicare, Medicare HMO (Medicare + Choice), or Medigap do not cover long-term nursing home or at-home care. For that, he will have to buy private insurance, which can cost thousands of dollars a year if he signs up now.

All of these choices allow seniors to tailor a plan to their needs. But it also makes picking insurance much more complicated. Eugenio knows that a mistake can be costly in terms of both health and money.

## Questions

1. What factors should Eugenio Costa consider in making the choice among various types of Medicare, Medigap, or HMO health care insurance policies?
2. Visit the following websites for Medicare resources to obtain general information, guides on buying Medigap or HMO coverage, and price quotations with insurance company ratings on Medigap insurance carriers.

### General Information
Medicare
1–800–633–4227
www.medicare.gov

ElderCare Locator
1–800–677–1116

### Guides on Buying Medigap or HMO Coverage
Medicare Rights Center
www.medicarerights.org

United Seniors Health Cooperative
www.ushc-online.org

### Quotes and Ratings on Medigap Carriers
Weiss Rating
1–800–289–9222
www.weissratings.com

Quotesmith.com
1–800–566–9393
www.quotesmith.com

SOURCE: Adapted from Howard Gleckman, "Making Sense of Medicare," *Business Week,* November 1, 1999, pp. 210–12.

# Creating an E-Plan: Financial Decisions Using the Web

## COMPARING HEALTH INSURANCE PLANS

Changing programs and regulations influence your ability to be properly covered for health care and disability insurance coverage. Awareness of policy types, coverages, and limitations will help you plan this phase of your financial plan.

Websites for Health Insurance

- Links to various health websites may be accessed at **www.healthseek.com.**
- Information from the Life and Health Information Foundation for Education at **www.life-line.org.**
- Information about health insurance options at **www.north coast.com/unlimited/services_listing/ greg_connors/gci.html.**
- Answers to common questions about long-term care at **www.service.com/answers/health_insurance. html.**
- Medicare from Social Security Administration at **www. ssa.gov.**
- Supplemental Medicare information from the National Association of Insurance Commissioners at **www.naic. org.**
- Current health insurance articles from *Money* magazine at **www.money.com,** *Kiplinger's Personal*

*Finance Magazine* at **www.kiplinger.com,** *Business Week* at **www.businessweek.com,** *Worth* magazine at **www. worth.com,** and *Smart Money* at **www.dowjones.com/ smartmoney.**

(Note: Addresses and content of websites change, and new sites are created daily. Use search engines to update and locate websites for your current financial planning needs.)

*PFP sheets: 50–51*

Short-Term Financial Planning Activities

1. Assess your current habits that could improve your health and reduce medical costs.
2. Evaluate your need for expanded disability income insurance (see PFP Sheet 50).
3. Analyze current health insurance coverage in relation to family and household needs (see PFP Sheet 51).
4. Compare the cost of health insurance programs available from various sources.

Long-Term Financial Planning Activities

1. Identify possible future needs for supplemental Medicare and long-term-care insurance coverages.
2. Develop a plan for reducing health care and medical insurance costs.

# Life Insurance

## STAYING AFLOAT WHEN YOUR HEALTH SINKS

Harry Mills had just bought a second dental practice when he was stricken with plasma cell cancer. For two years, he battled to make payments on his new office. By 1997, debilitated by both illness and intensive treatments, the Oshkosh (Nebraska) dentist had fallen far behind.

But Mills still had one big asset: a $250,000 life insurance policy. So last year, he tapped it for $100,000. By the time he died in July, all his debts were paid off. "He didn't have to think he was a failure," says his widow, Shirley. "He was able to die with dignity."

As the Mills learned, it is not easy to raise cash once you're diagnosed with a terminal illness. But there are ways to stay financially afloat in your final months. "Look at where the dollars are," says Herbert Daroff, a Boston financial planner. "The value of your house, your life insurance, and your retirement assets." If you get a terminal diagnosis, give yourself time to absorb the doctor's words. Then get in touch with a financial expert—a planner, broker, or lawyer you trust. The choices you make will depend on your family, resources, and life expectancy. If you have young children, holding on to assets may be a key goal. But if you have three years to live and can no longer work, you may need steady income to pay medical costs and living expenses.

An often overlooked source of income is life insurance. You can tap policies that have cash value, such as whole or universal life, in several ways. The simplest: Take a loan. Most are at near-market rates. And ask about accelerated death benefit riders. If you have less than six months to live, such policies will pay up to half their value before you die. These options are not available if you have more common term insurance. But you can sell any policy to investors at a discount to its face value, an arrangement called a *viatical settlement*.

Check out the company; make sure it is regulated by a state insurance commission. You can also contact the Viatical Association of America for a list of member companies (1–800–842–9811; www.viatical.org). Shop around. "Contact several different companies to get the best offer," says Gary Chodes, president of Viaticus, a unit of insurer CNA Financial. Instead of selling a term policy, you can borrow using the policy as a collateral.

Harry Mills got a loan from Salt Lake City's LifeWise Family Financial Security (1–800–219–7385; www.lifewise financial.com). The company will lend up to 85 percent of a policy's value, depending on your life expectancy, and pays your premiums. You repay nothing while you live, but your interest obligations will be compounding all the while. After you die, the company deducts interest and fees, and returns to your heirs any of the policy's remaining value. Shirley Mills says her loan cost about $16,000. "We don't claim this is cheap money," says LifeWise chief executive Mark Livingston. None of these alternatives is easy. And scrambling for money in the face of terminal illness may be the toughest financial decision you'll ever have to make.

### Questions

1. How can the Internet help you create a life insurance program? (Visit the Insurance.com and Insure.com websites.)
2. What was Harry Mills's biggest asset? Were all his debts paid off when he died?
3. What is an overlooked source of income for terminally ill people?

SOURCE: Reprinted from the June 28, 1999 issue of *Business Week* by special permission. © 1999 McGraw-Hill Companies, Inc.

## Learning Objectives

**Obj. 1** Define *life insurance* and describe its purpose and principle.

**Obj. 2** Determine your life insurance needs.

**Obj. 3** Distinguish between the two types of life insurance companies and analyze various types of life insurance policies these companies issue.

**Obj. 4** Select important provisions in life insurance contracts.

**Obj. 5** Create a plan to buy life insurance.

**Obj. 6** Recognize how annuities provide financial security.

## LIFE INSURANCE: AN INTRODUCTION

Even though it is impossible to put a price on your life, you probably own some life insurance—through a group plan where you work, as a veteran, or through a policy you bought. Perhaps you are considering the purchase of additional life insurance to keep pace with inflation or cover your growing family. If so, you should prepare for that purchase by learning as much as possible about life insurance and how it can help you meet your needs.

Most American families face substantial loss when one spouse dies unexpectedly. Unfortunately, 45 percent of widows and 37 percent of widowers say their spouse had been inadequately insured. Life for the surviving spouse becomes a financial struggle.

Life insurance is one of the most important and expensive purchases you may ever make. Deciding whether you need it and choosing the right policy from dozens of options takes time, research, and careful thought. This chapter will help you make decisions about life insurance. It describes what life insurance is and how it works, the major types of life insurance coverages, and how you can use life insurance to protect your family.

Consumer awareness of life insurance has changed little over the years. Life insurance is still more often sold than bought. In other words, while most people actively seek to buy insurance for their property and health, they avoid a life insurance purchase until an agent approaches them. Still, at the beginning of 1999, life insurance in force reached a new high of $19.84 trillion. About 185 million Americans (78 percent of all households) now have life insurance.[1]

### What Is Life Insurance?

**Obj. 1**
Define *life insurance* and describe its purpose and principle.

Life insurance is neither mysterious nor difficult to understand. It works in the following manner. A person joins a risk-sharing group (an insurance company) by purchasing a contract (a policy). Under the policy, the insurance company promises to pay a sum of money at the time of the policyholder's death to the person or persons selected by him or her (the beneficiaries). In the case of an endowment policy, the money is paid to the policyholder (the insured) if he or she is alive on the future date (the maturity date) named in the policy. The insurance company makes this promise in return for the insured's agreement to pay it a sum of money (the premium) periodically.

## The Purpose of Life Insurance

Most people buy life insurance to protect someone who depends on them from financial losses caused by their death. That someone could be the nonworking spouse and children of a single-income family. It could be the wife or husband of a two-income family. It could be an aging parent. It could be a business partner or a corporation.

Life insurance proceeds may be used to

- Pay off a home mortgage or other debts at the time of death.
- Provide lump-sum payments through an endowment to children when they reach a specified age.
- Provide an education or income for children.
- Make charitable bequests after death.
- Provide a retirement income.
- Accumulate savings.
- Establish a regular income for survivors.
- Set up an estate plan.
- Make estate and death tax payments.

Life insurance is one of the few ways to provide liquidity at the time of death.

## The Principle of Life Insurance

The principle of home insurance, discussed in Chapter 10, can be applied to the lives of persons. From records covering many years and including millions of lives, mortality tables have been prepared to show the number of deaths among various age groups during any year. In the 1950s, the life insurance industry developed and the National Association of Insurance Commissioners (NAIC) approved a mortality table known as the Commissioners 1958 Standard Ordinary (CSO) Mortality Table. In 1980, the NAIC approved a new Standard Ordinary Mortality Table based on experience during 1970–75. Unlike the 1958 CSO table, which combined the mortality experience of males and females, the 1980 CSO table separates the experience by sex.

## How Long Will You Live?

No one really knows how long a particular individual will live. But life expectancy in the United States has been steadily increasing since 1900. For example, in 1900, the life expectancy of a man was 46.3 years and of a woman 48.3 years. By 1996, life expectancy had increased to 73.0 years for males and 79.0 for females. Exhibit 12–1 shows the most recent life expectancy table, issued in 1997 by the National Center for Health Statistics. The life expectancy shown does not indicate the age at which a person has the highest probability of dying. For example, the exhibit shows that the life expectancy of a male at age 30 is 44.9 years. This does not mean 30-year-old males will probably die at age 74.9 years. It means 44.9 is the average number of additional years all males alive at age 30 may expect to live.

### Concept Check 12–1

1. How can the Internet help you create a life insurance plan?
2. What is the meaning of life insurance?
3. What is the purpose of life insurance?
4. What is the principle of life insurance?
5. What do life expectancy tables indicate?

**EXHIBIT 12–1**

Life Expectancy
Tables
(All races, 1996)

SOURCE: National Center for Health Statistics, U.S. Department of Health and Human Services, 1997.

Life expectancy does not indicate the age at which a person has the highest probability of dying.

| Age | Remaining Years of Life | | |
| | Both Sexes | Male | Female |
| --- | --- | --- | --- |
| 0 | 76.1 | 73.0 | 79.0 |
| 1 | 75.6 | 72.6 | 78.6 |
| 5 | 71.7 | 68.7 | 74.7 |
| 10 | 66.8 | 63.8 | 69.7 |
| 15 | 61.9 | 58.9 | 64.8 |
| 20 | 57.1 | 54.2 | 59.9 |
| 25 | 52.4 | 49.6 | 55.1 |
| 30 | 47.7 | 44.9 | 50.2 |
| 35 | 43.0 | 40.4 | 45.4 |
| 40 | 38.4 | 35.9 | 40.7 |
| 45 | 33.9 | 31.5 | 36.0 |
| 50 | 29.4 | 27.1 | 31.5 |
| 55 | 25.2 | 23.0 | 27.1 |
| 60 | 21.2 | 19.2 | 22.9 |
| 65 | 17.5 | 15.7 | 18.9 |
| 70 | 14.1 | 12.5 | 15.3 |
| 75 | 11.1 | 9.8 | 11.9 |
| 80 | 8.3 | 7.3 | 8.9 |
| 85 | 6.1 | 5.4 | 6.4 |

# DETERMINING YOUR LIFE INSURANCE NEEDS

**Obj. 2**
Determine your life insurance needs.

You should consider a number of factors before you buy life insurance. These factors include your present and future sources of income, other savings and income protection, group life insurance, group annuities (or other pension benefits), net worth, and Social Security. First, however, you should determine whether you *need* life insurance.

## Do You Need Life Insurance?

If your death would cause financial stress for your spouse, children, parents, or anyone else you want to protect, you should consider purchasing life insurance. Your stage in the life cycle and the type of household you live in will influence this decision. Single persons living alone or with their parents usually have little or no need for life insurance. Consider Brian Brickman, 28, a bachelor who does not smoke, is in excellent health, and has no dependents. Brian owns a $100,000 condominium with a $90,000 mortgage. Since his employer provides a $100,000 group term life policy, he needs no additional life insurance. Larry Lucas, 32, and his wife, Liz, 30, are professionals, each earning $45,000 a year. The Lucases have no dependents. This two-earner couple may have a moderate need for life insurance, especially if they have a mortgage or other large debts. Households with small children usually have the greatest need for life insurance.

## Determining Your Life Insurance Objectives

Before you consider types of life insurance policies, you must decide what you want your life insurance to do for you and your dependents.

First, how much money do you want to leave to your dependents should you die today? Will you require more or less insurance protection to meet their needs as time goes on?

Second, when would you like to be able to retire? What amount of income do you believe you and your spouse would need then?

Third, how much will you be able to pay for your insurance program? Are the demands on your family budget for other living expenses likely to be greater or lower as time goes on?

When you have considered these questions and developed some approximate answers, you are ready to select the types and amounts of life insurance policies that will help you accomplish your objectives.

Once you have decided what you want your life insurance to accomplish, the next important decision is how much to buy.

## Estimating Your Life Insurance Requirements

How much life insurance should you carry? This question is important for every person who owns or intends to buy life insurance. Because of the various factors involved, the question cannot be answered by mathematics alone. Nevertheless, an insurance policy puts a price on the life of the insured person, and therefore methods are needed to estimate what that price should be.

There are four general methods for determining the amount of insurance you may need: the easy method, the DINK method, the "nonworking" spouse method, and the "family need" method.

### The Easy Method    Simple as this method is, it is remarkably useful. It is based on the insurance agent's rule of thumb that a "typical family" will need approximately 70 percent of your salary for seven years before they adjust to the financial consequences of your death. In other words, for a simple estimate of your life insurance needs, just multiply your current gross income by 7 (7 years) and 0.70 (70 percent).

Example:

$30,000 current income × 7 = $210,000; $210,000 × 0.705 = $147,000

Your figures:

$_____ current income × 7 = $_____ × 0.70 = $_____

This method assumes your family is "typical." You may need more insurance if you have four or more children, if you have above-average family debt, if any member of your family suffers from poor health, or if your spouse has poor employment potential. On the other hand, you may need less insurance if your family is smaller.

### The DINK (Dual Income, No Kids) Method    If you have no dependents and your spouse earns as much as or more than you do, you have very simple insurance needs. Basically, all you need to do is ensure that your spouse will not be unduly burdened by debts should you die. Here is an example of the DINK method:

|  | Example | Your Figures |
|---|---|---|
| Funeral expenses | $ 5,000 | $ _____ |
| One-half of mortgage | 60,000 | _____ |
| One-half of auto loan | 7,000 | _____ |
| One-half of credit card balance | 1,500 | _____ |
| One-half of personal debt | 1,500 | _____ |
| Other debts | 1,000 | _____ |
| Total insurance needs | $76,000 | $ _____ |

**EXHIBIT 12-2**

A Worksheet to Calculate Your Life Insurance Needs

SOURCES: *About Life Insurance,* Metropolitan Life Insurance Company, February 1997, p. 3; *The TIAA Guide to Life Insurance Planning for People in Education* (New York: Teachers Insurance and Annuity Association, January 1997), p. 3.

1. Five times your personal yearly income _____ (1)

2. Total approximate expenses above and beyond your daily living costs for you and your dependents (e.g., tuition, care for a disabled child or parent) amount to = _____ (2)

3. Your emergency fund (3 to 6 months of living expenses) amounts to = _____ (3)

4. Estimated amount for your funeral expenses (U.S. average is $5,000 to $10,000) + _____ (4)

5. Total estimate of your family's financial needs (add lines 1 through 4) = _____ (5)

6. Your total liquid assets (e.g., savings accounts, CDs, money market funds, existing life insurance both individual and group, pension plan death benefits, and Social Security benefits) − _____ (6)

7. Subtract line 6 from line 5 and enter the difference here. = _____ (7)

The net result (line 7) is an estimate of the shortfall your family would face upon your death. Remember, these are just rules of thumb. For a complete analysis of your needs, consult a professional.

---

This method assumes your spouse will continue to work after your death. If your spouse suffers poor health or is employed in an occupation with an uncertain future, you should consider adding an insurance cushion to see him or her through hard times.

The "Nonworking" Spouse Method   Insurance experts have estimated that extra costs of up to $10,000 a year may be required to replace the services of a homemaker in a family with small children. These extra costs may include the cost of a housekeeper, child care, more meals out, additional carfare, laundry services, and so on. They do not include the lost potential earnings of the surviving spouse, who often must take time away from the job to care for the family.

To estimate how much life insurance a homemaker should carry, multiply the number of years before the youngest child reaches age 18 by $10,000:

Example:

$$10 \text{ years} \times \$10,000 = \$100,000$$

Your figures:

_____ years × $10,000 = $ _____

If there are teenage children, the $10,000 figure can be reduced. If there are more than two children under age 13, or anyone in the family suffers poor health or has special needs, the $10,000 figure should be adjusted upward.

The "Family Need" Method   The first three methods assume you and your family are "typical" and ignore important factors such as Social Security and your liquid assets. Exhibit 12–2 provides a detailed worksheet for making a thorough estimation of your life insurance needs.

Although this method is quite thorough, you may believe it does not address all of your special needs. If so, you should obtain further advice from an insurance expert or a financial planner.

As you determine your life insurance needs, don't forget to consider the life insurance you may already have. You may have ample coverage through your employer and through any mortgage and credit life insurance you have purchased.

**PFP**

**Sheet 53**

**Concept Check 12-2**

1. How do you determine the need for life insurance?
2. What determines your life insurance objectives?
3. What are the four methods of estimating your life insurance requirements?

## TYPES OF LIFE INSURANCE COMPANIES AND POLICIES

### Obj. 3
Distinguish between the two types of life insurance companies and analyze various types of life insurance policies these companies issue.

*nonparticipating policy*
Life insurance that does not provide policy dividends; also called a *nonpar policy.*

*participating policy*
Life insurance that provides policy dividends; also called a *par policy.*

### Types of Life Insurance Companies

You can purchase the new or extra life insurance you need from two types of life insurance companies: stock life insurance companies, owned by shareholders, and mutual life insurance companies, owned by their policyholders. About 95 percent of U.S. life insurance companies are stock companies, and about 5 percent are mutuals.

Stock companies generally sell **nonparticipating** (or *nonpar*) policies, while mutual companies specialize in the sale of **participating** (or *par*) policies. A participating policy has a somewhat higher premium than a nonparticipating policy, but a part of the premium is refunded to the policyholder annually. This refund is called the *policy dividend.*

There has been long and inconclusive debate about whether stock companies or mutual companies offer less expensive life insurance. You should check with both stock and mutual companies to determine which type offers the best policy for your particular needs at the lowest price.

If you wish to pay exactly the same premium each year, you should choose a nonparticipating policy with its guaranteed premiums. However, you may prefer life insurance whose annual price reflects the company's experience with its investments, the health of its policyholders, and its general operating costs, that is, a participating policy.

Nevertheless, as with other forms of insurance, price should not be your only consideration in choosing a life insurance policy. You should consider the financial stability, reliability, and service the insurance company provides. Currently about 1,700 life insurance companies in the United States sell life insurance.

### Types of Life Insurance Policies

Both mutual insurance companies and stock insurance companies sell two basic types of life insurance: temporary and permanent insurance. Temporary insurance can be term, renewable term, convertible term, or decreasing term insurance. Permanent insurance is known by different names, including *whole life, straight life, ordinary life,* and *cash value life insurance.* As you will learn in the next section, permanent insurance can be limited payment, variable, adjustable, or universal life insurance. Other types of insurance policies—group life and credit life insurance—are generally temporary forms of insurance. Exhibit 12–3 shows the types of policies issued recently, and Exhibit 12–4 shows major types and subtypes of life insurance.

### Term Life Insurance

*term insurance* Life insurance protection for a specified period of time; sometimes called *temporary life insurance.*

**Term insurance** is protection for a specified period of time, usually 1, 5, 10, or 20 years or up to age 70. A term insurance policy pays a benefit only if you die during the period it covers. If you stop paying the premiums, the insurance stops. Term insurance is therefore sometimes called *temporary life insurance.*

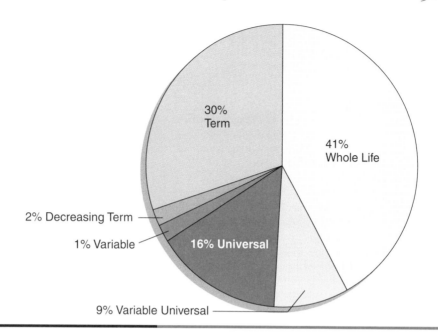

**EXHIBIT 12-3**

Types of Life
Insurance Policies
Issued

SOURCE: *1999 Life
Insurance Fact Book*
(Washington, DC:
American Council
of Life Insurance), p. 6.

30%
Term

41%
Whole Life

2% Decreasing Term

1% Variable

16% Universal

9% Variable Universal

**EXHIBIT 12-4**

Major Types and
Subtypes of Life
Insurance

| Term (temporary) | Whole, Straight, or Ordinary Life | Other Types |
|---|---|---|
| • Term<br>• Renewable term<br>• Multiyear level term<br>• Convertible term<br>• Decreasing term | • Limited payment<br>• Single premium<br>• Modified life<br>• Variable life<br>• Adjustable life<br>• Universal life<br>• Variable universal life | • Group life<br>• Credit life |

Term insurance is a basic, "no frills" form of life insurance and is the best value for most consumers. The premiums for people in their 20s and 30s are less expensive than those for whole life insurance, discussed in the next section.

You need insurance coverage most while you are raising young children. Although term life insurance premiums increase as you get older, you can reduce your coverage as your children grow up and your assets (the value of your savings, investments, home, autos, etc.) increase.

Here are various options in choosing your term insurance. Also, see the Financial Planning for Life's Situations box on page 382.

Renewability Option   The coverage of term insurance ends at the conclusion of the term, but you can continue it for another term if you have a renewability option. For example, the term insurance of The Teachers Insurance and Annuity Association is renewable at your option for successive five-year periods to age 70 without medical reexamination. Level premiums are paid during each five-year period. The premiums increase every five years.

# Financial Planning for Life's Situations

## TERM LIFE BARGAIN DAYS

What costs less than half what it did two years ago? Term life insurance. Term insurance buyers have been enjoying some of the lowest rates in history, thanks to increased competition and the ability to buy policies on the Internet or over the phone without going through an agent.

Let's say you're a 45-year-old man in good health who wants a 20-year, $1 million term policy with level premiums. Back in 1997, that would have cost more than $1,800 a year, says Moody's Investors Service. Today the annual premium can be as little as $964.

But this bargain hunter's paradise may not last. The National Association of Insurance Commissioners has approved regulations that would require insurers to raise the reserves they set aside to cover claims. To finance the reserve additions, insurers will likely increase premiums and limit interest rate guarantees. So it's smart to buy now if you're considering life insurance.

Term life policies provide insurance for a set period—5, 10, or even 50 years—*without* the savings and investment features you'll find in whole or universal life coverage. Unlike with other types of life insurance, you can drop coverage without penalty. Today, thanks to toll-free calling and the Net, you have plenty of choices. If you want to review options with a live person, you can visit an agent or a broker though you'll pay a commission to buy. If you feel confident about shopping alone, direct sales over the phone or on the Net are the cheapest routes. You might also check out deals through your college or credit card issuer.

You can find quotes online at these websites:

www.accuquote.com          www.consumerquote.com
www.instantquote.com       www.insuremarket.com
www.masterquote.com        www.quotesmith.com
www.quickquote.com         www.selectquote.com

PREMIUMS PLUNGE
Sample annual premium for a $1 million, 20-year term policy for a "preferred risk" male, 45

Reprinted from the July 5, 1999 issue of *Business Week* by special permission. © 1999 McGraw-Hill Companies, Inc.

Adapted from Kerry Hannon. "Term Life Bargain Days," *Business Week,* July 5, 1999, pp. 92–93

## Multiyear Level Term (or Straight Term)

*Multiyear term life* is a relatively new policy. It guarantees that you will pay the same premium for the life of your policy. In 1998, 40 percent of new term policies guaranteed a set rate for 20 years or longer, compared to none in 1995.[2]

## Conversion Option

If you have convertible term insurance, you can exchange it for a whole life policy without a medical examination and at a higher premium. The premium for the whole life policy stays the same for the rest of your life. Consider this option if you want cash-value life insurance and can't afford it now but expect to do so in the future.

## Decreasing Term Insurance

Term insurance is also available in a form that pays less to the beneficiary as time passes. The insurance period you select might depend on your age or on how long you decide you will need the coverage. For example, a decreasing term contract for 25 years might be appropriate as coverage of a mortgage loan balance on a house because the coverage will decrease as the balance on the mortgage decreases. You could get the same result by purchasing annual renewable term policies of diminishing amounts during the period of the mortgage loan. An annual renewable policy would offer more flexibility to change coverage if you were to sell or remortgage the house. Mortgage insurance therefore is a form of decreasing term insurance, decreasing to keep pace with the principal balance on your mortgage loan. Recently a 35-year-old person buying a $100,000, 20-year decreasing term policy from the Teachers Insurance and Annuity Association would pay a first-year premium of $141.

## Whole Life Insurance

*whole life policy*
An insurance plan in which the policyholder pays a specified premium each year for as long as he or she lives; also called a *straight life policy,* a *cash-value life policy,* or an *ordinary life policy.*

*cash value*  The amount received after giving up a life insurance policy.

The most common type of permanent life insurance is the **whole life policy** (also called a *straight life policy,* a *cash-value life policy,* or an *ordinary life policy*), for which you pay a specified premium each year for as long as you live. In return, the insurance company promises to pay a stipulated sum to the beneficiary when you die. The amount of your premium depends primarily on the age at which you purchase the insurance.

One important feature of the whole life policy is its cash value. **Cash value** (or *cash surrender value*) is an amount that increases over the years that you receive if you give up the insurance. Hence, cash-value policies provide a death benefit *and* a savings account. Insurance salespeople often emphasize the "forced savings" aspect of cash value insurance. A table in the whole life policy enables you to tell exactly how much cash value the policy has at any given time (see Exhibit 12–5 on page 384).

Cash-value policies may make sense for people who intend to keep the policies for the long term or for people who must be forced to save. But you should not have too low a death benefit just because you would like the savings component of a cash-value life policy. The Consumer Federation of America Insurance Group (formerly known as NICO) suggests that you explore other savings and investment strategies before investing your money in a permanent life insurance policy.

The insurance company accumulates a substantial reserve during the early years of the whole life policy to pay the benefits in the later years, when your chances of dying are greater. At first, the annual premium for whole life insurance is higher than that for term insurance. However, the premium for a whole life policy remains constant throughout your lifetime, whereas the premium for a term policy increases with each renewal.

Several types of whole life insurance have been developed to meet different objectives. A few of the more popular types are discussed next.

### Limited Payment Policy

One type of whole life policy is called the *limited payment policy.* With this plan, you pay premiums for a stipulated period, usually 20 or 30 years, or until you reach a specified age, such as 60 or 65 (unless your death occurs earlier). Your policy then becomes "paid up," and you remain insured for life. The company will pay the face amount of the policy at your death. Because the premium payment period for a limited payment policy is shorter than that for a whole life policy, the annual premium is higher. For example, recently a 35-year-old person buying a $25,000, 20-payment life policy at a preferred risk rate from the Teachers Insurance and Annuity Association (TIAA) would pay a $236.25 premium during the first year. In contrast, the premium for an ordinary life policy would be $183.50 for the same coverage. How do you qualify for preferred risk rates? See the accompanying Financial Planning for Life's Situations feature on page 385.

A special form of the limited payment plan is the single-premium policy. In this type of contract, you make only one very large premium payment.

**An Example of Guaranteed Cash Values**

SOURCE: *Sample Life Insurance Policy* (Washington, DC: American Council of Life Insurance, n.d.), p. 2.

| Plan and Additional Benefits | Amount | Premium | Years Payable |
|---|---|---|---|
| Whole life (premiums payable to age 90) | $10,000 | $229.50 | 55 |
| Waiver of premium (to age 65) | | 4.30 | 30 |
| Accidental death (to age 70) | 10,000 | 7.80 | 35 |

A premium is payable on the policy date and every 12 policy months thereafter. The first premium is $241.60.

*Explanation:* To cancel the policy in the 10th year, the insured would get $1,719 in savings (cash value). He or she could use the $1,719 to purchase a $3,690 paid-up life policy or purchase an extended term policy that would be in effect for 19 years and 78 days.

**Table of Guaranteed Values**

| End of Policy Year | Cash or Loan Value | Paid-up Insurance | Extended Term Insurance | |
|---|---|---|---|---|
| | | | Years | Days |
| 1 | $ 14 | $ 30 | 0 | 152 |
| 2 | 174 | 450 | 4 | 182 |
| 3 | 338 | 860 | 8 | 65 |
| 4 | 506 | 1,250 | 10 | 344 |
| 5 | 676 | 1,640 | 12 | 360 |
| 6 | 879 | 2,070 | 14 | 335 |
| 7 | 1,084 | 2,500 | 16 | 147 |
| 8 | 1,293 | 2,910 | 17 | 207 |
| 9 | 1,504 | 3,300 | 18 | 177 |
| 10 | 1,719 | 3,690 | 19 | 78 |
| 11 | 1,908 | 4,000 | 19 | 209 |
| 12 | 2,099 | 4,300 | 19 | 306 |
| 13 | 2,294 | 4,590 | 20 | 8 |
| 14 | 2,490 | 4,870 | 20 | 47 |
| 15 | 2,690 | 5,140 | 20 | 65 |
| 16 | 2,891 | 5,410 | 20 | 66 |
| 17 | 3,095 | 5,660 | 20 | 52 |
| 18 | 3,301 | 5,910 | 20 | 27 |
| 19 | 3,508 | 6,150 | 19 | 358 |
| 20 | 3,718 | 6,390 | 19 | 317 |
| Age 60 | 4,620 | 7,200 | 18 | 111 |
| Age 65 | 5,504 | 7,860 | 16 | 147 |

Paid-up additions and dividend accumulations increase the cash values; indebtedness decreases them.

**Direct Beneficiary:** Helen M. Benson, wife of the insured
**Owner:** Thomas A. Benson, the insured
**Insured:** Thomas A. Benson    **Age and Sex:** 37 Male
**Policy Date:** November 1, 2001    **Policy Number:** 000/00
**Date of Issue:** November 1, 2001

**Variable Life Insurance Policy**     The cash values of a *variable life* insurance policy fluctuate according to the yields earned by a separate fund, which can be a stock fund, a money market fund, or a long-term bond fund. A minimum death benefit is guaranteed, but the death benefit can rise above that minimum depending on the

# Financial Planning for Life's Situations

## GUIDELINES FOR PREFERRED RATES

Do you qualify for preferred rates? These guidelines are used to determine preferred rates; standard rates are higher.

- **Blood profile:** All favorable values for cholesterol, triglycerides, and lipids.
- **Blood pressure:** May not exceed 140/90.
- **Urinalysis:** No abnormal findings. Presence of nicotine will disqualify the applicant for no-tobacco rates.
- **Personal history:** No history of or current treatment for high blood pressure, cancer, diabetes, mental or nervous disorders, or disorders of the heart, lungs, liver, or kidneys.

- **Build:** Weight may not exceed 115 percent of average for height.
- **Driving:** No convictions for reckless driving or driving under the influence of alcohol or drugs in the past five years; no more than three moving violations in the past three years; no more than one moving violation in the past six months.
- **Family history:** No family history (natural parents and siblings) of death from heart disease, cardiovascular impairments, cancer, or diabetes prior to age 60.

SOURCE: Ameritas Life Insurance Corporation.

---

earnings of the dollars invested in the separate fund. The premium payments for a variable life policy are fixed.

When you purchase a variable life policy, you assume the risk of poor investment performance. Therefore, the cash value of a variable life policy is not guaranteed. Life insurance agents selling variable life policies must be registered representatives of a broker-dealer licensed by the National Association of Securities Dealers and registered with the Securities and Exchange Commission. If you are interested in a variable life policy, be sure your agent gives you a prospectus that includes an extensive disclosure about the policy.

## Adjustable Life Insurance Policy

The *adjustable life* insurance policy is another relatively recent type of whole life insurance. You can change such a policy as your needs change. For example, if you want to increase or decrease your coverage, you can change either the premium payments or the period of coverage.

## Universal Life

*universal life* A whole life policy that combines term insurance and investment elements.

Subject to certain minimums, **universal life** insurance, first introduced in 1979, is designed to let you pay premiums at any time in virtually any amount. The amount of insurance can be changed more easily in a universal life policy than in a traditional policy. The increase in the cash value of a universal life policy reflects the interest earned on short-term investments. Thus, the universal life policy clearly combines term insurance and investment elements. Recently about $2.6 trillion of universal life insurance was in force.

Like the details of other types of policies, the details of universal life policies vary from company to company. The key distinguishing features of universal life policies are explicit, separate accounting reports to policyholders of (1) the charges for the insurance element, (2) the charges for company expenses (commissions, policy fees, etc.), and (3) the rate of return on the investment (cash value) of the policy. The rate of return is flexible; it is guaranteed to be not less than a certain amount (usually 4 percent), but it may be more, depending on the insurance company's decision.

## EXHIBIT 12-6   COMPARISON OF TERM, WHOLE LIFE, UNIVERSAL LIFE, AND VARIABLE LIFE INSURANCE

| | Type of Policy | Period Covered | Cash Value | Insurance Protection | Premium | Coverage | Comments |
|---|---|---|---|---|---|---|---|
| **Temporary** | Term | | | | | | |
| | Level | For a stated number of years, such as 1, 5, 20 | None | High | Stays the same until renewal | Stays the same | Pure insurance coverage |
| | Decreasing | For a stated number of years, such as 1, 5, 20 | None | High | Stays the same | Decreases | Least expensive type of insurance |
| **Permanent** | Whole life | | | | | | Part insurance, part savings |
| | Straight | Whole life | Low | Moderate | Stays the same | Stays the same | |
| | Limited payment | Whole life | Low | Moderate | Stays the same | Stays the same | Paid up after a certain number of years |
| | Universal life | Varies | Low to high | Low to high | Varies | Varies | Combines renewable term insurance with a savings account paying market interest rates |
| | Variable life | Varies | Low to high | Low to high | Varies | Varies | Part insurance, part investments in stock, bond, or money market funds |

What are the differences between universal life and whole life insurance? While both policy types have cash value, universal life gives you more direct control. With universal life, you control your outlay and can change your premium without changing your coverage. Whole life, in contrast, requires you to pay a specific premium every year, or the policy will lapse. Universal life allows you access to your cash value by a policy loan or withdrawal. Whole life allows only for policy loans.

Since your primary reason for buying a life insurance policy is the insurance component, the cost of that component should be your main consideration. Thus, universal life policies, which offer a high rate of return on the cash value but charge a high price for the insurance element, generally should be avoided. (See the accompanying Financial Planning for Life's Situations box on page 387.)

Exhibit 12–6 compares some important features of term, whole life, and universal life policies.

Over the years, variations on term and whole life insurance have been developed. The details of these policies may differ among companies. Therefore, check with individual companies to determine the best policy for your needs.

## Other Types of Life Insurance Policies

**Group Life Insurance**   In recent decades, *group life insurance* has become quite popular. A group insurance plan insures a large number of persons under the terms of a single policy without requiring medical examinations. In general, the principles that apply to other forms of insurance also apply to group insurance.

# Financial Planning for Life's Situations

## SO YOU THINK YOU'RE COVERED

If you bought life insurance in the 1980s or early 1990s, your mail may bring you unpleasant news: Your policy may be about to burst. Low interest rates have undermined millions of cash-value life insurance policies sold when rates were at historic double-digit highs. Insurers designed these policies around the premise that healthy investment earnings could reduce, or eventually eliminate, the premiums policyholders had to pay.

But as rates fell, insurers' investment returns couldn't keep up with the low-premium promise. The result was more holders getting notices that their policies' cash values are spiraling downward, forcing hefty boosts in costs. "I've seen premiums double, triple, even quadruple—it all depends on how far off the mark the sale presentation was," says Stanley Hargrave, a certified financial planner and insurance consultant with IMS/CPAs in Riverside, California. The alternative to paying more is to let the policy lapse—an option that may mean going without insurance for clients whose age or poor health makes them uninsurable.

Given those choices, it's little wonder lawyers are filing lawsuits. Class-action suits charging Prudential Insurance and dozens of other insurers with misleading sales practices have already reaped billions of dollars in damages to policyholders and millions in legal fees. The biggest suits involved so-called "vanishing premium" policies, where agents promised that high investment returns would make the policies self-funding in just a few years. Most of those cases have been settled, and policyholders are getting notice of their awards, usually in the form of discounts on new policies.

The policies most likely to implode are those called universal, or adjustable-premium, life. Most universal life buyers took high interest rates as an opportunity to buy more insurance for less cost, paying the minimum premium necessary, based on rates when they bought the policy.

But those low premiums aren't guaranteed: If the insurance company suffers rising mortality costs (the funds needed to pay death benefits) or falling interest rates, you may be forced to pay more premium or reduce the death benefit. Mortality costs have actually trended down, but interest rates have fallen faster.

If you have a universal life policy, you will receive an annual statement showing how your policy is performing. Locate your latest statement and, if you can find it, the sales illustration—the forecast your agent prepared when you bought your policy showing how its costs and cash value were projected to build over time. The illustration was probably based on a rosy view of interest rates at the time of purchase; the annual statement uses actual current rates. Compare what the illustration shows your cash value should be by now with the actual cash value from the statement. If your cash value isn't keeping up with the projection, your policy is headed for trouble. If you see trouble, call the agent who sold you the policy and ask for a set of "in-force illustrations" that recalculate the policy's future.

You want to know two things: how long the policy will last if you keep paying the current premium and how much more you'd have to pay to maintain the current death benefit until your target age.

Some experts suggest you hire a fee-only insurance consultant to analyze your situation and represent you. Low Load Insurance Services (877–254–4429; e-mail: lowload@gte.net) or the National Association of Personal Financial Advisors (www.napfa.org) can give referrals.

### Anatomy of a Life Insurance Implosion

**Universal life policy:** Bought by a 41-year-old man in 1984

**Death benefit:** $1 million

**Interest rates at time of purchase:** 12%

**Annual premium:** $4,720

Now the holder is told his policy will lapse when he's 68—not at age 95, as originally projected—because it is earning only 6% interest.

The policyholder's options:
  Boost annual premiums to $14,184.
  Cut the death benefit to $401,000.
  Let the policy lapse at age 68.

Reprinted from the August 30, 1999 issue of *Business Week* by special permission. © 1999 McGraw-Hill Companies, Inc.

## BE AN INFORMED INSURANCE BUYER

Glen S. Daily, a fee-only insurance consultant, states that Americans make thousands of costly decisions about life insurance. He advises that when you are in doubt about which life insurance to purchase, buy term. It is the least expensive, easy to understand, and a good start. If you want a whole life policy, buy a low-

load cash-value policy. These policies are sold directly to the public or through fee-for-service advisers. Ask your agent to explain plausible risk in writing. Review annual statements and ask your agent for an in-force illustration every few years to determine if the current premium is still adequate.

Fundamentally, group insurance is term insurance, which was described earlier. Usually the cost of group insurance is split between the employer and the employees so that the cost of insurance per $1,000 is the same for each employee, regardless of age. For older employees, the employer pays a larger portion of the costs of the group policy.

However, group life insurance is not always a good deal. Insurance advisers offer countless stories about employer-sponsored plans, or group plans offered through professional associations, offering coverage that costs 20, 50, or even 100 percent more than policies their clients could buy on the open market.

If you want to compare rates and avoid a high-pressure pitch for permanent insurance, contact a low-load, no-commission insurer. One life insurance adviser recommends either USAA Life & Health Insurance Company (1–800–531–8000) or Ameritas Life Insurance Corporation (1–800–552–3553); both give quotes over the phone.

### Endowment Life Insurance

*Endowment life insurance* provides coverage from the beginning of the contract to maturity and guarantees payment of a specified sum to the insured, even if he or she is still living at the end of the endowment period. The face value of the policy is paid to beneficiaries upon the death of the insured. The endowment period typically has a duration of 10 to 20 years or the attainment of a specified age.

### Credit Life Insurance

*Credit life insurance* is used to repay a personal debt should the borrower die before doing so. It is based on the belief that "no person's debts should live after him or her." It was introduced in the United States in 1917, when installment financing and purchasing became popular.

Credit life insurance policies for auto loans and home mortgages are not the best buy for the protection they offer. Instead, buy less expensive decreasing term insurance, discussed earlier. In fact, some experts claim that credit life insurance policies are the nation's biggest ripoff.

Exhibit 12–7 shows the growth of individual, group, and credit life insurance in the United States.

### Industrial Life Insurance

With industrial life insurance policies, also known as home service or debit insurance, agents collect weekly, bimonthly, or monthly premiums at the insured's home. Industrial life insurance is the least popular form, and its appeal continues to drop rapidly.

## EXHIBIT 12-7

### Growth of Individual, Group, and Credit Life Insurance in Force in the United States

Most group life insurance contracts are issued to employers, though many are issued to unions, professional associations, and other groups.

SOURCE: *1999 Life Insurance Fact Book* (Washington, DC: American Council of Life Insurance), p. 3.

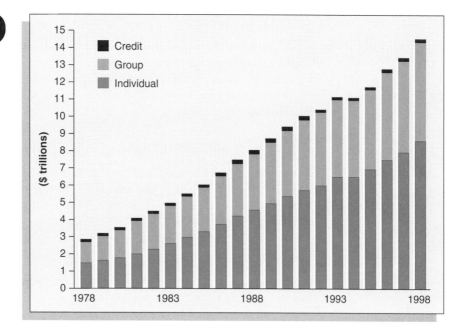

Modern life insurance policies contain numerous provisions whose terminology can be confusing. Therefore, an understanding of these provisions is very important for the insurance buyer.

In our dynamic economy, inflation and interest rates change often. Therefore, experts recommend that you reevaluate your insurance coverage every two years. Be sure to update your insurance whenever your situation changes substantially. For example, the birth of another child or an increase in your home mortgage can boost your insurance needs.

## Concept Check 12-3

1. What are the two types of life insurance companies?
2. What are the major types and subtypes of life insurance?

## IMPORTANT PROVISIONS IN A LIFE INSURANCE CONTRACT

### Obj. 4
Select important provisions in life insurance contracts.

*beneficiary*   A person designated to receive something such as life insurance proceeds, from the insured.

Your life insurance policy is valuable only if it meets your objectives. When your objectives change, however, it may not be necessary to give up the policy. Instead, study the policy carefully and discuss its provisions with your agent. Following are some of the most common provisions.

### Naming Your Beneficiary

An important provision in every life insurance policy is the right to name your beneficiary. A **beneficiary** is a person who is designated to receive something, such as life insurance proceeds, from the insured. In your policy, you can name one or more persons as contingent beneficiaries who will receive your policy proceeds if the primary beneficiary dies before you do.

## The Grace Period

When you buy a life insurance policy, the insurance company agrees to pay a certain sum of money under specified circumstances and you agree to pay a certain premium regularly. The *grace period* allows 28 to 31 days to elapse, during which time you may pay the premium without penalty. After that time, the policy lapses if you have not paid the premium.

## Policy Reinstatement

A lapsed policy can be put back in force, or reinstated, if it has not been turned in for cash. To reinstate the policy, you must again qualify as an acceptable risk, and you must pay overdue premiums with interest. There is a time limit on reinstatement, usually one or two years.

## Nonforfeiture Clause

*nonforfeiture clause*
A provision that allows the insured not to forfeit all accrued benefits.

One important feature of the whole life policy is the **nonforfeiture clause.** This provision prevents the forfeiture of accrued benefits if you choose to drop the policy. For example, if you decide not to continue paying premiums, you can exercise specified options with your cash value.

To illustrate workings of the whole life policy and its cash value, let us suppose a 30-year-old woman buys $30,000 worth of coverage. She might pay an annual premium of $435 for a whole life policy with no policy dividends. Here's how the cash would grow:

| | |
|---|---|
| Age 35 | $1,830 |
| Age 40 | 4,260 |
| Age 45 | 6,990 |
| Age 50 | 9,960 |

## Incontestability Clause

*incontestability clause*
A provision stating that the insurer cannot dispute the validity of a policy after a specified period.

The **incontestability clause** stipulates that after the policy has been in force for a specified period (usually two years), the insurance company cannot dispute its validity during the lifetime of the insured for any reason, including fraud. One reason for this provision is that the beneficiaries, who cannot defend the company's contesting of the claim, should not be forced to suffer because of the acts of the insured.

## Suicide Clause

*suicide clause*
A provision stating that if the insured dies by suicide during the first two years the policy is in force, the death benefit will equal the amount of the premium paid.

The **suicide clause** provides that if the insured dies by suicide during the first two years the policy is in force, the death benefit will equal the amount of the premium paid. Generally, after two years, the suicide becomes a risk covered by the policy and the beneficiaries of a suicide receive the same benefit that is payable for death from any other cause.

## Automatic Premium Loans

With an automatic premium loan option, if you do not pay the premium within the grace period, the insurance company automatically pays it out of the policy's cash value if that cash value is sufficient in your whole life policy. This prevents you from inadvertently allowing the policy to lapse.

## Misstatement of Age Provision

The misstatement of age provision says that if the company finds out that your age was incorrectly stated, it will pay the benefits your premiums would have bought if your age had been correctly stated. The provision sets forth a simple procedure to resolve what could otherwise be a complicated legal matter.

## Policy Loan Provision

A loan from the insurance company is available on a whole life policy after the policy has been in force for one, two, or three years, as stated in the policy. This feature, known as the *policy loan provision,* permits you to borrow any amount up to the cash value of the policy. However, a policy loan reduces the death benefit by the amount of the loan plus interest if the loan is not repaid.

## Riders to Life Insurance Policies

*rider*   A document attached to a policy that modifies its coverage.

An insurance company can change the provisions of a policy by attaching a rider to it. A **rider** is any document attached to the policy that modifies its coverage by adding or excluding specified conditions or altering its benefits. A whole life insurance policy may include a waiver of premium disability benefit, an accidental death benefit, or both.

### Waiver of Premium Disability Benefit

Under this provision, the company waives any premiums that are due after the onset of total and permanent disability. In effect, the company pays the premiums. The disability must occur before you reach a certain age, usually 60.

The waiver of premium rider is sometimes desirable. Don't buy it, however, if the added cost will prevent you from carrying needed basic life insurance. Some insurance companies include this rider automatically in all policies issued through age 55.

### Accidental Death Benefit

*double indemnity*
A benefit under which the company pays twice the face value of the policy if the insured's death results from an accident.

Under this provision, the insurance company pays twice the face amount of the policy if the insured's death results from an accident. The accidental death benefit is often called **double indemnity.** Accidental death must occur within a certain time period after the injury, usually 90 days, and before the insured reaches a certain age, usually 60 or 65.

The accidental death benefit is expensive. Moreover, your chances of dying in the exact manner stated in the policy are very small, as are the chances that your beneficiary will collect the double payment.

### Guaranteed Insurability Option

This option allows you to buy specified additional amounts of life insurance at stated intervals without proof of insurability. Thus, even if you do not remain in good health, you can increase the amount of your insurance as your income rises. This option is desirable if you anticipate the need for additional life insurance in the future.

### Cost of Living Protection

This special rider is designed to help prevent inflation from eroding the purchasing power of the protection your policy provides. A *loss, reduction,* or *erosion of purchasing power* refers to the impact inflation has on a fixed amount of money. As inflation increases the costs of goods and services, that fixed amount will not buy as much in the future as it does today. Exhibit 12–8 shows the effects of inflation on a $100,000 life insurance policy. However, your insurance needs are likely to be smaller in later years.

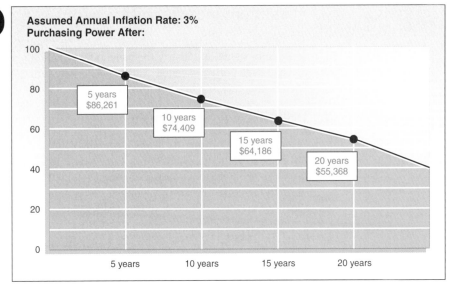

**EXHIBIT 12-8**

Effects of Inflation on a $100,000 Life Insurance Policy

SOURCE: *The TIAA Guide to Life Insurance Planning for People in Education* (New York: Teachers Insurance and Annuity Association, January 1997), p. 8.

Assumed Annual Inflation Rate: 3%
Purchasing Power After:

5 years
$86,261

10 years
$74,409

15 years
$64,186

20 years
$55,368

## Accelerated Benefits

*Accelerated benefits*, also known as *living benefits*, are life insurance policy proceeds paid to the policyholder who is terminally ill *before* he or she dies. The benefits may be provided for directly in the policies, but more often they are added by riders or attachments to new or existing policies. A representative list of insurers that offer accelerated benefits is available from the National Insurance Consumer Helpline (NICH) at 1–800–942–4242. Although more than 150 companies offer some form of accelerated benefits, not all plans are approved in all states. NICH cannot tell you whether a particular plan is approved in any given state. For more information, check with your insurance agent or your state department of insurance.

## Second-to-Die Option

A *second-to-die life insurance* policy, also called *survivorship life,* insures two lives, usually husband and wife. The death benefit is paid when the second spouse dies. Usually a second-to-die policy is intended to pay estate taxes when both spouses die. However, some attorneys claim that with the right legal advice, you can minimize or avoid estate taxes completely.

Now that you know the various types of life insurance policies and the major provisions of and riders to such policies, you are ready to make your buying decisions.

### Concept Check 12-4

1. What are the most common provisions in life insurance contracts?
2. What is a beneficiary?
3. What is a rider?
4. What is the concept of double indemnity?

## BUYING LIFE INSURANCE

**Obj. 5**

Create a plan to buy life insurance.

You should consider a number of factors before buying life insurance. As discussed earlier in this chapter, these factors include your present and future sources of income, other savings and income protection, group life insurance, group annuities (or other pension benefits), Social Security, and, of course, the financial strength of the company.

**EXHIBIT 12-9**

Rating Systems
of Major Rating
Agencies

| | A. M. Best | Standard & Poor's<br>Duff & Phelps | Moody's | Weiss Research |
|---|---|---|---|---|
| Superior | A++<br>A+ | AAA | Aaa | A+ |
| Excellent | A<br>A− | AA+<br>AA<br>AA− | Aa1<br>Aa2<br>Aa3 | A<br>A−<br>B+ |
| Good | B++<br>B+ | A+<br>A<br>A− | A1<br>A2<br>A3 | B<br>B−<br>C+ |
| Adequate | B<br>B− | BBB+<br>BBB<br>BBB− | Baa1<br>Baa2<br>Baa3 | C<br>C−<br>D+ |
| Below average | C++<br>C+ | BB+<br>BB<br>BB− | Ba1<br>Ba2<br>Ba3 | D<br>D−<br>E+ |
| Weak | C<br>C−<br>D | B+<br>B<br>B− | B1<br>B2<br>B3 | E<br>E− |
| Nonviable | E<br>F | CCC<br>CC<br>C, D | Caa<br>Ca<br>C | F |

## From Whom to Buy?

Look for insurance coverage from financially strong companies with professionally qualified representatives. It is not unusual for a relationship with an insurance company to extend over a period of 20, 30, or even 50 years. For that reason alone, you should choose carefully when deciding on an insurance company or an insurance agent. Fortunately, you have a choice of sources.

Sources    Protection is available from a wide range of private and public sources, including insurance companies and their representatives; private groups such as employers, labor unions, and professional or fraternal organizations; government programs such as Medicare and Social Security; and financial institutions and manufacturers offering credit insurance.

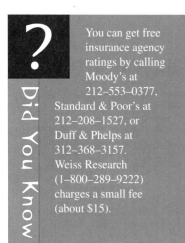

You can get free insurance agency ratings by calling Moody's at 212–553–0377, Standard & Poor's at 212–208–1527, or Duff & Phelps at 312–368–3157. Weiss Research (1–800–289–9222) charges a small fee (about $15).

Rating Insurance Companies    Some of the strongest, most reputable insurance companies in the nation provide excellent insurance coverage at reasonable costs. In fact, the financial strength of an insurance company may be a major factor in holding down premium costs for consumers.

Locate an insurance company by checking the reputations of local agencies. Ask members of your family, friends, or colleagues about the insurers they prefer.

For a more official review, consult *Best's Agents Guide* or *Best's Insurance Reports* at your public library. Exhibit 12–9 describes the rating systems used by A. M. Best and the other big four rating agencies. As a rule, you should deal with companies rated A11, A1, or A. In addition, *Consumer Reports, Kiplinger's Personal Finance Magazine,* and *Money* periodically provide satisfaction ratings on various types of insurance and insurance companies. For the latest ratings, visit www.stanardandpoor.com and http://inforseek.go.com/.

## Financial Planning for Life's Situations

### CHECKLIST FOR CHOOSING AN INSURANCE AGENT

|  | Yes | No |
|---|---|---|
| **1.** Is your agent available when needed? Clients sometimes have problems that need immediate answers. | ☐ | ☐ |
| **2.** Does your agent advise you to have a financial plan? Each part of the plan should be necessary to your overall financial protection. | ☐ | ☐ |
| **3.** Does your agent pressure you? You should be free to make your own decisions about insurance coverage. | ☐ | ☐ |
| **4.** Does your agent keep up with changes in the insurance field? Agents often attend special classes or study on their own so that they can serve their clients better. | ☐ | ☐ |
| **5.** Is your agent happy to answer questions? Does he or she want you to know exactly what you are paying for with an insurance policy? | ☐ | ☐ |

**Choosing Your Insurance Agent**    An insurance agent handles the technical side of insurance. However, that's only the beginning. The really important part of the agent's job is to apply his or her knowledge of insurance to help you select the proper kind of protection within your financial boundaries.

Choosing a good agent is among the most important steps in building your insurance program. How do you find an agent? One of the best ways to begin is by asking your parents, friends, neighbors, and others for their recommendations. However, note that you will seldom have the same agent all your life. The accompanying Financial Planning for Life's Situations feature offers guidelines for choosing an insurance agent.

*chartered life underwriter (CLU)*
A life insurance agent who has passed a series of college-level examinations on insurance and related subjects.

You may also want to investigate an agent's membership in professional groups. Agents who belong to a local Life Underwriters Association are often among the more experienced agents in their communities. A **chartered life underwriter (CLU)** is a life insurance agent who has passed a series of college-level examinations on insurance and related subjects. Such agents are entitled to use the designation CLU after their names. Agents who have passed a series of examinations on property and casualty insurance are designated as *chartered property and casualty underwriters (CPCUs)*.

Once you have found an agent, you must decide which policy is right for you. The best way to do this is to talk to your agent, which does not obligate you to buy insurance.

## Comparing Policy Costs

Each life insurance company designs the policies it sells to make them attractive and useful to many policyholders. One policy may have features another policy doesn't; one company may be more selective than another company; one company may get a better return on its investments than another company. These and other factors affect the prices of life insurance policies.

In brief, five factors affect the price a company charges for a life insurance policy: the company's cost of doing business, the return on its investments, the mortality rate it expects among its policyholders, the features the policy contains, and competition among companies with comparable policies.

The prices of life insurance policies therefore vary considerably among life insurance companies. Moreover, a particular company will not be equally competitive for all policies. Thus, one company might have a competitively priced policy for 24-year-olds but not for 35-year-olds.

*interest-adjusted index*
A method of evaluating the cost of life insurance by taking into account the time value of money.

Ask your agent to give you interest-adjusted indexes. An **interest-adjusted index** is a method of evaluating the cost of life insurance by taking into account the time value of money. Highly complex mathematical calculations and formulas combine premium payments, dividends, cash-value buildup, and present value analysis into an index number that makes possible a fairly accurate cost comparison among insurance companies. The lower the index number, the lower the cost of the policy. The Consumer Federation of America Insurance Group offers a computerized service for comparing policy costs. Contact them at 1424 16th St. NW, Suite 604, Washington, DC, 20036, or at 202–387–6121. Insurance Information, Inc., in South Dennis, Massachusetts, provides price quotes for term insurance. For $50 it will run your age, health status, and occupation through computer data banks covering about 650 different policies and send you the names of the five policies suitable for you and sold in your state. Contact this company at 1–800–472–5800.

Price quote services offer convenient and free, no-obligation premium comparisons. TermQuote in Dayton, Ohio, represents about 100 insurance companies, and Select Quote in San Francisco represents about 20 insurance companies.

Here are the web addresses and telephone numbers of some price quote services:

AccuQuote (www.accuquote.com) 1–800–442–9899
InsuranceQuote Services (www.iquote.com) 1–800–972–1104
InstantQuote (www.instantquote.com) 1–888–223–2220
MasterQuote (www.masterquote.com) 1–800–627–LIFE
QuickQuote (www.quickquote.com) 1–800–867–2404
TermQuote (www.rcinet.com/~termquote) 1–800–444–8376

These services are not always unbiased, since most sell life insurance themselves; they may recommend more coverage than you need. Ask them to quote you the rate each insurer charges most of its policyholders, not the best rate, for which few persons qualify. Compare quotes from several additional sources listed in the accompanying Financial Planning for Life's Situations feature on page 396.

The accompanying Financial Planning Calculations feature on page 397 shows how to use an interest-adjusted index to compare the costs of insurance.

## Obtaining a Policy

A life insurance policy is issued after you submit an application for insurance and the insurance company accepts the application. The application usually has two parts. In the first part, you state your name, age, and sex, what type of policy you desire, how much insurance you want, your occupation, and so forth. In the second part, you give your medical history. While a medical examination is frequently required for ordinary policies, usually no examination is required for group insurance.

The company determines your insurability by means of the information in your application, the results of the medical examination, and the inspection report. Of all applicants, 98 percent are found to be insurable, though some may have to pay higher premiums because of an existing medical condition.

# Financial Planning for Life's Situations

## ARE YOU COVERED?

Online insurance is beginning to emerge as regulatory hurdles are cleared. But there are still a lot of different kinds of insurance sites—with different strengths and weaknesses for consumers.

| Name | What It Does | How It Stacks Up |
|------|--------------|------------------|
| ebix.com (www.ebix.com) | Reverse auction in which insurers and agents bid for customers. | Boasts a reasonable mix of 170 agents in 46 states. Offers both consumer and business insurance. But the process confuses some customers. |
| eCoverage (www.ecoverage.com) | Developing auto, homeowner, and marine insurance with an underwriting partner for sale only on the Web. Says it can cut costs and pass savings on to customers. | No agent fees, and it's backed by big Web investor Softbank. But because it sells only policies developed with its partner, it doesn't have comparison quotes. |
| InsWeb (www.insweb.com) | Comparison site that generates leads for insurers and agents. | Policies from 46 carriers, fewer than Quotesmith. It can be tough to complete transactions on the site because many underwriting partners insist on closing deals offline. |
| Quicken Insurance (www.insuremarket.com) | "Mall" with quotes from 21 carriers of auto, health, home, disability, small business, life, and other insurance. | Promises instant, binding quotes. But critics say customer service is weak on offerings and general information about buying insurance. |
| Quotesmith.com (www.quotesmith.com) | Instant quotes on auto, life, medical, dental, and other insurance. | Database includes more than 300 insurers in 50 states, the most of any site. But critics say quotes can change as insurers ask more questions before policies close. |

SOURCE: Diane Brady, "Insurers Step Gingerly into Cyberspace," *Business Week*, November 22, 1999, pp. 160–62.

## Examining a Policy

**Before the Purchase**   When you buy a life insurance policy, read every word of the contract and, if necessary, ask your agent for a point-by-point explanation of the language. Many insurance companies have rewritten their contracts to make them more understandable. These are legal documents, and you should be familiar with what they promise, even though they use technical terms.

**After the Purchase**   After you buy new life insurance, you have a 10-day "free-look" period during which you can change your mind. If you do so, the company will return your premium without penalty.

It's a good idea to give your beneficiaries and your lawyer a photocopy of your policy. Your beneficiaries should know where the policy is kept, because to obtain the insurance proceeds, they will have to send it to the company upon your death, along with a copy of the death certificate.

# Financial Planning Calculations

## DETERMINING THE COST OF INSURANCE

In determining the cost of insurance, don't overlook the time value of money. You must include as part of that cost the interest (opportunity cost) you would earn on money if you did not use it to pay insurance premiums. For many years, insurers did not assign a time value to money in making their sales presentations. Only recently has the insurance industry widely adopted interest-adjusted cost estimates.

If you fail to consider the time value of money, you may get the false impression that the insurance company is giving you something for nothing. Here is an example. Suppose you are 35 and have a $10,000 face amount, 20-year, limited-payment, participating policy. Your annual premium is $210, or $4,200 over the 20-year period. Your dividends over the 20-year payment period total $1,700, so your total net premium is $2,500 ($4,200 − $1,700). Yet the cash value of your policy at the end of 20 years is $4,600. If you disregard the interest your premiums could otherwise have earned, you might get the impression that the insurance company is giving you $2,100 more than you paid ($4,600 − $2,500). But if

you consider the time value of money (or its opportunity cost), the insurance company is not giving you $2,100. What if you had invested the annual premiums in a conservative stock mutual fund? At an 8 percent annual yield, your account would have accumulated to $6,180 in 20 years. Therefore, instead of having received $2,100 from the insurance company, you have paid the company $1,580 for 20 years of insurance protection:

| | |
|---|---|
| Premiums you paid over 20 years | $4,200 |
| Time value of money | 1,980 ($6,180 − $4,200) |
| Total cost | 6,180 |
| Cash value | 4,600 |
| Net cost of insurance | 1,580 ($6,180 − $4,600) |

Be sure to request interest-adjusted indexes from your agent; if he or she doesn't give them to you, look for another agent. As you have seen in the example, you can compare the costs among insurance companies by combining premium payments, dividends, cash value buildup, and present value analysis into an index number.

## Choosing Settlement Options

A well-planned life insurance program should cover the immediate expenses resulting from the death of the insured. However, that is only one of its purposes. In most instances, the primary purpose of life insurance is to protect dependents against a loss of income resulting from the premature death of the primary wage earner. Thus, selecting the appropriate settlement option is an important part of designing a life insurance program. The most common settlement options are lump-sum payment, limited installment payment, life income option, and proceeds left with the company.

### Lump-Sum Payment
The insurance company pays the face amount of the policy in one installment to the beneficiary or to the estate of the insured. This form of settlement is the most widely used option.

### Limited Installment Payment
This option provides for payment of the life insurance proceeds in equal periodic installments for a specified number of years after your death.

### Life Income Option
Under the life income option, payments are made to the beneficiary for as long as she or he lives. The amount of each payment is based primarily on the sex and attained age of the beneficiary at the time of the insured's death.

## Financial Planning for Life's Situations

### TEN GOLDEN RULES OF BUYING LIFE INSURANCE

Remember that your need for life insurance coverage will change over time. Your income may go up or down, or your family size might change. Therefore, it is wise to review your coverage periodically to ensure that it keeps up with your changing needs.

**Follow these rules when buying life insurance:**                                                **Done**

1. Understand and know what your life insurance needs are before you make any purchase, and make sure the company you choose can meet those needs.  ☐
2. Buy your life insurance from a company that is licensed in your state.  ☐
3. Select an agent who is competent, knowledgeable, and trustworthy.  ☐
4. Shop around and compare costs.  ☐
5. Buy only the amount of life insurance you need and can afford.  ☐
6. Ask about lower premium rates for nonsmokers.  ☐
7. Read your policy and make sure you understand it.  ☐
8. Inform your beneficiaries about the kinds and amount of life insurance you own.  ☐
9. Keep your policy in a safe place at home, and keep your insurance company's name and your policy number in a safe-deposit box.  ☐
10. Check your coverage periodically, or whenever your situation changes, to ensure that it meets your current needs.  ☐

SOURCE: American Council of Life Insurance, 1001 Pennsylvania Avenue, NW, Washington, DC 20004-2599.

**Proceeds Left with the Company**   The life insurance proceeds are left with the insurance company at a specified rate of interest. The company acts as trustee and pays the interest to the beneficiary. The guaranteed minimum interest rate paid on the proceeds varies among companies.

## Switching Policies

**Sheet 54**

Think twice if your agent suggests that you replace the whole life or universal life insurance you already own. According to a recent study by the Consumer Federation of America, consumers lose billions of dollars each year because they don't hold onto their cash life insurance policies long enough or because they purchase the wrong policies. The author of the study, James Hunt, Vermont's former insurance commissioner, notes that half of those who buy whole or universal life policies drop them within 10 years.

Before you give up this protection, make sure you are still insurable (check medical and any other qualification requirements). Remember that you are now older than you were when you purchased your policy, and a new policy will therefore cost more. Moreover, the older policy may have provisions that are not duplicated in some of the new policies. This does not mean you should reject the idea of replacing your present policy; rather, you should proceed with caution. We recommend that you ask your agent or company for an opinion about the new proposal to get both sides of the argument.

The insurance industry is regulated by state insurance commissioners. Recently many states passed new laws to protect consumers from overzealous sales agents. The National Association of Insurance Commissioners, state regulators, and insurance companies plan to develop new standards to protect consumers.

The Financial Planning for Life's Situations feature on page 398 presents important guidelines for purchasing life insurance.

## Concept Check 12-5

1. How do insurance companies price their products?
2. How do insurance companies determine your insurability?
3. What should you do in examining a policy before and after the purchase?
4. What are the four most common settlement options?
5. Should you switch life insurance policies?

## FINANCIAL PLANNING WITH ANNUITIES

**Obj. 6**

Recognize how annuities provide financial security.

*annuity*   A contract that provides a regular income for as long as the person lives.

As you have seen so far, life insurance provides a set sum of money at your death. However, if you want to enjoy benefits while you are still alive, you might consider annuities. An annuity protects you against the risk of outliving your assets.

An **annuity** is a financial contract written by an insurance company that provides you with a regular income. Generally, you receive the income monthly, often with payments arranged to continue for as long as you live. The payments may begin at once (*immediate annuity*) or at some future date (*deferred annuity*). According to a recent Gallup Organization survey, the average owner of an annuity is a 66-year-old, retired person with an annual household income of less than $75,000. About 95 percent of annuities issued were deferred annuities. The remainder were immediate annuities used to provide retirement income. The annuity is often described as the opposite of life insurance: It pays while you live, while life insurance pays when you die.

As with the life insurance principle, discussed earlier, the predictable mortality experience of a large group of individuals is fundamental to the annuity principle. By determining the average number of years a large number of persons in a given age group will live, the insurance company can calculate the annual amount to pay to each person in the group over his or her entire life.

For example, for annuity purposes, the life expectancy of males age 76 is about 10 years (see Exhibit 12–10). Thus, if 1,000 males age 76 each pay a $10,000 premium (a total of $10 million), each is guaranteed a payment of $1,000 per year for life. Those who live beyond the 10-year average have their "excess" payments funded by those who die before 10 years have elapsed.

Because the annual payouts per premium amount are determined by average mortality experience, annuity contracts are more attractive for people whose present health, living habits, and family mortality experience suggest that they are likely to live longer than average. As a general rule, annuities are not advisable for people in poor health, although exceptions to this rule exist, read the accompanying Financial Planning for Life's Situations feature on page 401.

### Why Buy Annuities?

A primary reason for buying an annuity is to give you retirement income for the rest of your life. You should fully fund your IRAs, Keoghs, and 401(K)s before considering annuities. We discuss retirement income in Chapter 18, "Retirement Planning."

Although people have been buying annuities for many years, the appeal of variable annuities has increased recently due to a rising stock market. A *fixed annuity* states that the annuitant (the person who is to receive the annuity) will receive a fixed amount of

**EXHIBIT 12-10**

Individual Annuity
Mortality Table

SOURCE: *1997 Life
Insurance Fact Book*
(Washington,
DC: American
Council of Life
Insurance), pp. 107–08.

| Age of Male | U.S. Population Deaths per 1,000 | U.S. Population Life Expectancy (years) | Age of Male | U.S. Population Deaths per 1,000 | U.S. Population Life Expectancy (years) |
|---|---|---|---|---|---|
| 50 | 5.89 | 27.94 | 71 | 33.15 | 12.72 |
| 51 | 6.42 | 27.10 | 72 | 35.93 | 12.14 |
| 52 | 6.99 | 26.28 | 73 | 38.82 | 11.58 |
| 53 | 7.61 | 25.46 | 74 | 41.84 | 11.02 |
| 54 | 8.30 | 24.65 | 75 | 45.07 | 10.48 |
| 55 | 9.02 | 23.85 | 76 | 48.67 | 9.95 |
| 56 | 9.78 | 23.06 | 77 | 52.74 | 9.44 |
| 57 | 10.59 | 22.29 | 78 | 57.42 | 8.93 |
| 58 | 11.51 | 21.52 | 79 | 62.77 | 8.45 |
| 59 | 12.54 | 20.76 | 80 | 68.82 | 7.98 |
| 60 | 13.68 | 20.02 | 81 | 75.52 | 7.53 |
| 61 | 14.93 | 19.29 | 82 | 82.78 | 7.11 |
| 62 | 16.28 | 18.58 | 83 | 90.41 | 6.70 |
| 63 | 17.67 | 17.88 | 84 | 98.42 | 6.32 |
| 64 | 19.11 | 17.19 | 85 | 107.25 | 5.96 |
| 65 | 20.59 | 16.51 | 86 | 117.12 | 5.61 |
| 66 | 22.16 | 15.85 | 87 | 127.17 | 5.29 |
| 67 | 23.89 | 15.20 | 88 | 137.08 | 4.99 |
| 68 | 25.85 | 14.56 | 89 | 147.28 | 4.70 |
| 69 | 28.06 | 13.93 | 90 | 158.68 | 4.43 |
| 70 | 30.52 | 13.32 | | | |

income over a certain period or for life. With a *variable annuity,* the monthly payments vary because they are based on the income received from stocks or other investments.

Some of the growth in the use of annuities can be attributed to the passage of the Employee Retirement Income Security Act (ERISA) of 1974. Annuities are often purchased for individual retirement accounts (IRAs), which ERISA made possible. They may also be used in Keogh-type plans for self-employed people. As you will see in Chapter 18, contributions to both IRA and Keogh plans are tax deductible up to specified limits.

## Tax Considerations

When you buy an annuity, the interest on the principal, as well as the interest compounded on that interest, builds up free of current income tax. The Tax Reform Act of 1986 preserves the tax advantages of annuities (and insurance) but curtails deductions for IRAs. With an annuity, there is no maximum annual contribution. Also, if you die during the accumulation period, your beneficiary is guaranteed no less than the amount invested.

Exhibit 12–11 shows the difference between an investment in an annuity and an investment in a certificate of deposit (CD). Remember, federal income tax on an annuity is deferred, whereas the tax on interest earned on a CD must be paid currently.

As with any other financial product, the advantages of annuities are tempered by drawbacks. In the case of variable annuities, these drawbacks include reduced flexibility and fees that lower investment return.

# Financial Planning for Life's Situations

## IS YOUR ANNUITY A DUD?

Annuities—tax deferred investment plans that come with such discouraging terms as "surrender charge" and "mortality expense"—are the financial world's deadliest topic. Are you satisfied with your annuity? Mary Sandrowski wasn't. A retired medical transcriber in California Sandrowski was appalled at how little her Hartford fixed annuity paid: just 4 percent. "I thought, 'I can do this on a bank CD any day of the week,'" she recalls. So she enlisted her son, Phillip Cook, a Torrance, California financial planner (CFP), to find a better deal. He put together a similar contract paying one-half a percentage point more a year, but with a first-year 4 percent bonus that more than offset a 1 percent surrender fee on the old contract.

Dumping an annuity isn't something to do lightly because taxes and fees can be considerable. But if the reasons you bought it no longer apply, why not try to do better? "The annuity marketplace is so competitive now, there are lots of deals," say Fort Worth CFP E. Kim Dignum. Dignum formed this four-step plan to help you see if it's worth switching.

First, determine the current value of your contract and the "surrender charge," or percentage fee, you would have to pay to end it. It likely ranges from 0 to 10 percent. Then call one of the firms offering no-load annuities without surrender charges, such as Scudder (1–800–225–2470), T. Rowe Price (1–800–469–5304), or Vanguard (1–800–522–5555), and learn the return on a comparable contract. Fidelity (1–800–544–2442) also offers low-cost annuities, but with surrender charges.

Next, do the following worksheet to get a quick idea of whether you pay a surrender charge to exit your current annuity for a better one. Melbourne (Florida) CFP Mary Ellen Baldwin suggests that if your surrender charge is 2 percent or less, a swap may put you ahead.

|  | Current Annuity | Proposed Annuity |
|---|---|---|
| **1.** Current annuity value | $100,000 | $0 |
| **2.** Surrender charge | 2% | |
| **3.** Cash available to reinvest | | $98,000 |
| **4.** Annual return on annuity | 4% | 5% |
| **5.** Value after 1 year (annuity balance times 1 plus annual rate of return) | $104,000 | $102,900 |
| **6.** Value after 2 years (value in line 5 times 1 plus annual rate of return) | $108,160 | $108,045 |
| **7.** Value after 3 years (value in line 6 times 1 plus annual rate of return) | 112,486 | $113,447 |

Third, if you switch, do it via a 1035 exchange, which allows you to move your money without paying the tax due on withdrawn earnings at ordinary income rates. It's akin to rolling over an individual retirement account. Call the company where you want the money to go and say the magic words, "1035 exchange." The company will send you the paperwork, contact your current annuity issuer, and walk you through the swap. Keep a record of your investments, or "basis," in the old annuity. You'll need it to pay the lowest tax when you take your money out.

Finally, if you decide the surrender charge is still too high for a switch, be patient since these fees typically decline each year. Meanwhile, you probably can withdraw some of your capital, often 10 percent, without paying a fee. Instead of taking income from a lower-cost or higher-return account, tap the annuity for cash—unless you're under age 59 1/2, when you would be hit with a 10 percent tax penalty. Rethinking your annuity takes some work, but it's a task with one clear beneficiary—you.

Reprinted from the July 5, 1999 issue of *Business Week* by special permission. © 1999 McGraw-Hill Companies, Inc.

## Concept Check 12-6

1. What is an annuity?
2. Why do people buy annuities?
3. How are annuities taxed?

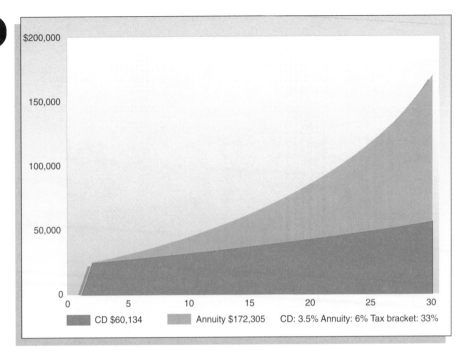

**EXHIBIT 12-11**

Tax-Deferred Annuity versus Taxable CD (a 30-year projection of performance; single deposit of $30,000)

CD $60,134    Annuity $172,305    CD: 3.5% Annuity: 6% Tax bracket: 33%

# Summary of Objectives

**Obj. 1  Define *life insurance* and describe its purpose and principle.**

Life insurance is a contract between an insurance company and a policyholder under which the company agrees to pay a specified sum to a beneficiary upon the insured's death. Most people buy life insurance to protect someone who depends on them from financial losses caused by their death. Fundamental to the life insurance principle is the predictable mortality experience of a large group of individuals.

**Obj. 2  Determine your life insurance needs.**

In determining your life insurance needs, you must first determine your insurance objectives and then use the easy method, the DINK method, the "nonworking" spouse method, or the "family need" method. The "family need" method is recommended. You should consider a number of factors before you buy insurance, including your present and future sources of income, other savings and income protection, group life insurance, group annuities (or other pension benefits), and Social Security.

**Obj. 3  Distinguish between the two types of life insurance companies and analyze various types of life insurance policies these companies issue.**

The two types of life insurance companies are stock companies, owned by stockholders, and mutual companies, owned

by policyholders. In general, stock companies sell nonparticipating policies and mutual companies sell participating policies. The three basic types of life insurance are term, whole life, and endowment policies. Many variations and combinations of these types are available. You should check with both stock and mutual companies to determine which type offers the best policy for your particular needs at the lowest price.

Nevertheless, as with other forms of insurance, price should not be your only consideration in choosing a life insurance policy. You should also consider the financial stability, reliability, and service the insurance company provides.

**Obj. 4  Select important provisions in life insurance contracts.**

The naming of the beneficiary, the grace period, policy reinstatement, the incontestability clause, the suicide clause, automatic premium loans, the misstatement of age provision, and the policy loan provision are important provisions in most life insurance policies. Common riders in life insurance policies are the waiver of premium disability benefit, the accidental death benefit, the guaranteed insurability option, cost of living protection, and accelerated benefits.

**Obj. 5  Create a plan to buy life insurance.**

Before buying life insurance, consider your present and future sources of income, group life insurance, group annuities (or other pension benefits), and Social Security. Then compare the costs of several life insurance policies. Examine your policy before and after the purchase, and choose appropriate settlement options. The most common settlement options are lump-sum payment, limited installment payment, life income option, and proceeds left with the company. Online computer services provide a wealth of information about all topics related to life insurance.

## Obj. 6   Recognize how annuities provide financial security.

An annuity is the opposite of life insurance: It pays while you live, whereas life insurance pays when you die. An annuity provides you with a regular income during your retirement years. The Tax Reform Act of 1986 gives annuities favorable income tax treatment.

The appeal of fixed annuities has increased recently. With a fixed annuity, the annuitant receives a fixed amount of income over a certain period or for life. With a *variable annuity,* the monthly payments vary because they are based on the income received from stocks or other investments.

## Financial Planning Problems

1. *Calculating the Amount of Life Insurance Needed Using the Easy Method.* You are the wage earner in a "typical family," with $30,000 gross annual income. Use the easy method to determine how much life insurance you should carry.   (Obj. 2)

2. *Estimating Life Insurance Needs Using the DINK Method.* You and your spouse are in good health and have reasonably secure careers. Each of you makes about $28,000 annually. You own a home with an $80,000 mortgage, and you owe $10,000 on car loans, $5,000 in personal debts, and $3,000 on credit card loans. You have no other debts. You have no plans to increase the size of your family in the near future. Estimate your total insurance needs using the DINK method.   (Obj. 2)

3. *Using the "Nonworking" Spouse Method to Determine Life Insurance Needs.* Tim and Allison are married and have two children, ages 4 and 7. Allison is a "nonworking" spouse who devotes all of her time to household activities. Estimate how much life insurance Tim and Allison should carry.   (Obj. 2)

4. *Comparing the Costs of Life Insurance and Various Provisions in a Life Insurance Policy.* Obtain premium rates for $25,000 whole life, universal life, and term life policies from local insurance agents. Compare the costs and provisions of these policies.   (Obj. 3)

5. *Calculating Your Life Insurance Needs.* Use Exhibit 12–2 to calculate your life insurance needs.   (Obj. 3)

6. *Choosing the Settlement Options.* Review the settlement options on your family's life insurance policies, and discuss with your family which option would be the best choice for them at this time.   (Obj. 5)

7. *Calculating Accumulated Account Values.* Assume you have $10,000 to invest for 10 years. You can invest in a certificate of deposit at 8.5 percent or a 10-year, tax-deferred annuity at 8.5 percent. Assume a 33 percent federal tax bracket. Use Exhibit 12–11 to find your accumulated account values. Which investment is better, and by how much?   (Obj. 6)

## Financial Planning Activities

1. *Planning for Life Insurance.* Choose a current issue of *Money, Kiplinger's Personal Finance Magazine, Consumer Reports,* or *Worth* and summarize an article that provides information on human life expectancy and how life insurance may provide financial security.   (Obj. 1)

2. *Assessing the Need for Life Insurance.* Interview relatives and friends to determine why they purchased life insurance. Prepare an essay summarizing your findings.   (Obj. 1)

3. *Comparing the Methods of Determining Life Insurance Requirements.* Analyze the four methods of determining life insurance requirements. Which method is best, and why?   (Obj. 2)

4. *Comparing Premiums for Life Insurance Policies.* Choose one stock and one mutual life insurance company. Obtain and compare premiums for
   a. Term life insurance for $50,000.
   b. Whole life insurance for $50,000.
   c. Universal life insurance for $50,000.
   Prepare a summary table indicating which policy you would consider and why.   (Obj. 3)

5. *Using the Internet to Obtain Information about Various Types of Life Insurance.* All major life insurance companies now maintain a web page. Visit a few websites of companies such as Metropolitan Life, New York Life, Transamerica Life, Lincoln Benefit Life, or others of

your choice. Then prepare a report that summarizes the various types of insurance coverages available from these companies.   (Obj. 4)

6. *Comparing the Provisions of Life Insurance Policies.* Examine your life insurance policies and the policies of other members of your family. Note the contractual provisions of each policy. What does the company promise to do in return for premiums?   (Obj. 4)

7. *Using the Services Provided by State Insurance Departments.* Contact your state insurance department to get information about whether your state requires interest-adjusted cost disclosure. Prepare a summary report of your finding.   (Obj. 5)

8. *Assessing the Use and Need for Annuities.* Interview friends, relatives, and others who have bought annuities. Which type of annuity did they purchase, and why?   (Obj. 6)

## LIFE SITUATION CASE

### HOW MUCH IS ENOUGH?

Joanne and Glenn Kitsos recently had their second child and decided to make a change to their life insurance. "We've got two kids now, and we have to start thinking about the future." Joanne said.

The Kitsos and other new parents are among the people experts say ought to have life insurance. Anyone who has someone financially dependent on them or anyone whose death would cause someone to lose money should be insured.

"Term life insurance is extraordinarily cheap when people are in their 20s and 30s, so people with children should purchase a sufficient amount," says Elliot S. Lipson, an Atlanta financial planner. "All too often, people buy expensive policies that offer savings or investment components but lack a basic benefit that is large enough to provide for their needs."

The amount you need isn't easy to determine because the total can be as little as 5 times and as much as 10 times your annual salary.

Jim Hunt, consultant to the Consumer Federation of America's insurance group, says the total need for an average couple with two young children is close to six to eight times their salary. For example, the Kitsos's combined income is $100,000, so they probably need a minimum of $600,000 in insurance and maybe a little more if they have no group life insurance at work.

Here are a few questions to ask when figuring how much life insurance you need:

• How much income will your dependents need every year if you die?

• How much income will your dependents have from other sources, such as investments, pensions, or savings, if you die?

• How much income will your dependents have access to from sources such as your spouse's salary or Social Security?

Once you've come up with a total, you have to decide whether you want term, whole life, or some hybrid variation.

Your goal, Hunt says, is to buy as much insurance as you need. But because of the costs of whole life insurance, that often means term. While whole life costs more in the early years, it guarantees that you will pay the same premium 10, 15, or even 20 years down the road.

The Kitsos started out with whole life insurance, but they have decided to switch to term insurance that will last until their kids graduate from college. They want to have enough insurance to cover their funeral costs and the cost of their children's college educations. But rather than using their insurance as an investment, they plan to invest more in mutual funds.

### Questions

1. What is the advantage of buying life insurance when you are younger and what is a good reason for having it?

2. What would be the total coverage needed for an average couple with two children and a combined income of $45,000?

3. What is one advantage of whole life insurance?

4. Is term insurance the right choice for the Kitsos? Why or why not?

SOURCES: Earl C. Gottschalk, Jr. "Avoiding the Big Mistakes Along Life's Path," *The Wall Street Journal,* May 27, 1997, p. C1; Candy McCampbell, "How Much Insurance to Carry Is a Question Not Easily Answered," *Gannett News Service,* July 9, 1997, p. S12.

# INTERNET CASE   Insurers Step into Cyberspace

Sonalee Patel, a newly married dentist and a potential life insurance buyer, knows that the sleepy old insurance industry is getting an Internet wake-up call. Net upstarts such as InsWeb, eCoverage, Quotesmith.com, and ebix.com are fighting to grab a fat slice of the $250 billion Americans spend each year on all kinds of insurance. The net upstarts know the Web has the potential to cut the costs of insurance and make the experience of buying life insurance more pleasant.

Forester Research, Inc., projects that online insurance sales to consumers will jump to $2.1 billion by 2001, from $250 million in 1999. Allstate Corporation thinks the opportunity is big enough that it cut 10 percent of its work force and began selling insurance over the Net.

Insurance agents are the most threatened by the Internet. The 1.8 million agents in the United States take an average of 11.3 percent of what consumers pay for insurance, according to the Insurance Information Institute, and that figure can top 20 percent for some insurers. Selling insurance over the Net could eliminate or drastically reduce the fees, saving Sonalee and other insurance buyers billions of dollars each year.

After checking out insurance sites on the Net, Sonalee discovered that comparing the prices of insurance policies is much easier than in the past. For example, Quotesmith offers prices from more than 300 underwriters in one place.

## Questions

1. What factors should Sonalee consider in purchasing her life insurance through the Internet?
2. What additional Internet resources should she visit on the Web?
3. Do you think buying insurance online will become popular in the 21st century? State your reasons.

SOURCE: Adapted from Diane Brady, "Insurance Steps Gingerly into Cyberspace," *Business Week,* November 22, 1999, pp. 160–62.

---

## Creating an E-Plan: Financial Decision Using the Web

### DETERMINING LIFE INSURANCE NEEDS

Providing for the financial needs of dependents is the primary goal of a life insurance program. Comparing policy types, coverage amounts, and other provisions will help you meet this financial purpose.

Websites for Life Insurance

- Life insurance needs may be assessed at **www.rightquote. com.**
- Compare types of life insurance policies and costs for various insurers at **www.quickquote.com/, www.quotesmith.com, www.quickquote.com,** and **www. accuquote.com.**
- Answers to questions about basic information and current developments about auto, home, and life insurance at **www.insure.com.**
- Life insurance rates and insurance planning assistance at **insuremarket.com** and **www.lifenet.com.**
- Information on state insurance regulatory agencies from the National Association of Insurance Commissioners at **www.naic.org.**

(Note: Addresses and content of websites change, and new sites are created daily. Use search engines to update and locate websites for your current financial planning needs.)

*PFP sheets: 53–54*

Short-Term Financial Planning Activities

1. Determine life insurance needs for your current life situation (see PFP Sheet 53).
2. Compare rates and coverages for different life insurance policies and companies (see PFP Sheet 54).
3. Evaluate the use of annuities in your financial plan.

Long-Term Financial Planning Activities

1. Identify information sources to monitor changes in life insurance coverages and costs offered by life insurance companies.
2. Develop a plan for reassessing life insurance needs as family and household situations change.

# Continuous Case for Part 4

## MANAGING RISKS FOR EFFECTIVE FINANCIAL PLANNING

### Life Situation
Pam, 36; Josh, 38; three children, ages 9, 7, and 4

*Financial Goals*
- Evaluate property and liability insurance needs
- Assess the need for disability insurance
- Determine additional life insurance needs

*Financial Data*

| | |
|---|---|
| Monthly income | $4,300 |
| Living expenses | 4,075 |
| Assets | 150,850 |
| Liabilities | 99,520 |

Both Pam and Josh Brock are comfortable. They now have three children, are happy with their home, and are more financially secure than they were six years ago. In fact, everything seems to be right on track. Yet the Brocks still have financial needs they must address. Several changes have affected their financial planning:

- The value of their home has increased due to inflation and home improvements.
- They have purchased a used car to meet additional transportation needs.
- Josh's current employer offers him only 30 days of sick leave.
- Pam's life insurance policy is only for $2,000. Josh has life insurance coverage equal to approximately eight times his annual salary.

## Questions

1. How should the Brocks determine whether they have enough insurance coverage for their home?
2. What factors should the Brocks consider in deciding whether to purchase collision insurance coverage for their used car?
3. When considering disability income insurance, what length of waiting period and duration of benefits should the Brocks consider?
4. Do you think Pam and Josh Brock have enough life insurance? If not, what changes would you recommend? Explain your answer.

# INVESTING YOUR FINANCIAL RESOURCES

# Investing Fundamentals

## Standard & Poor's Personal Wealth Website: Help You Can Use

Need some help establishing an investment program? Why not go to the Internet? That's what Kelly and Brian Hernandez did. Six months ago, they purchased a computer for their two kids to use for schoolwork. Little did they realize how the computer would affect their investment planning and other financial decisions.

One afternoon, Kelly was helping one of the kids with a homework assignment to determine the five richest people in the United States. They began by typing the words "personal wealth," but they forgot the space between the two words. To Kelly's surprise, the computer responded with a reference for the Standard & Poor's Personal Wealth website when they clicked on the computer's search button. While it didn't give the information needed to complete the homework assignment, Kelly decided to investigate this website. Although there were no "get rich quick" schemes, the website did contain practical information on how to establish an investment program. Two hours later, the homework assignment was still incomplete, but Kelly had explored the website and vowed to show Brian the type of information that could help them manage the family's finances.

Today, more and more Americans are using the Internet to help plan their financial future, evaluate investment alternatives, and monitor the value of their investments. Although just one of many, the Standard & Poor's Personal Wealth website (www.personalwealth.com) is an excellent choice for beginning investors like Kelly and Brian Hernandez, as well as more experienced investors. Kelly and Brian began by examining the material in a section called Basics of Smart Investing. Topics in this section include (1) Risks & Rewards, (2) Battling Inflation, (3) Compounding, (4) Rate of Return,

(5) Asset Types, (6) Diversification, and (7) material on stocks, bonds, and mutual funds. There is even a section called Getting Started.

After reading the material in the Getting Started section, both Kelly and Brian decided it was time to take charge of their family's finances. They began by paying off some high-interest credit card bills and saving some money they could use for emergencies. Then they started saving the money needed to finance an investment program. During this time, they also continued to learn. They studied additional material in the S&P website, visited other financial planning websites, and began to read *Money* and *Worth* magazines. They even began tracking some potential stock and mutual fund investments in anticipation of when they could actually purchase their first investments. According to Brian, their financial planning was not only rewarding but also fun. For the first time since they got married, they were getting their financial affairs in order.

### Questions

1. How important is an investment program for financial planning?
2. Kelly and Brian Hernandez began their search for investment information by examining S&P's Personal Wealth website. If you were seeking help to establish an investment program, where would you obtain the needed information?

SOURCE: Standard & Poor's Personal Wealth website (www.personalwealth.com), August 10, 1999, Standard & Poor's Corporation, 25 Broadway, New York, NY 10004.

## Learning Objectives

**Obj. 1** Explain why you should establish an investment program.

**Obj. 2** Describe how safety, risk, income, growth, and liquidity affect your investment decisions.

**Obj. 3** Identify the major types of investment alternatives.

**Obj. 4** Recognize the role of the professional financial planner and your role in a personal investment program.

**Obj. 5** Use various sources of financial information that can reduce risks and increase investment returns.

## PREPARING FOR AN INVESTMENT PROGRAM

**Obj. 1**
Explain why you should establish an investment program.

The old saying goes "I've been rich and I've been poor, but believe me, rich is better." While being rich doesn't guarantee happiness, the accumulation of money does provide financial security and is a worthy goal. Kelly and Brian Hernandez, the couple in the opening case, began their financial planning and investment program by examining the material in Standard & Poor's Personal Wealth website. As a student who purchased a new text and enrolled in this course, you enjoy free access to this website for one full term. Why not take a look and see the type of financial and investment information that it offers? To view the material that the Hernandezes used to create their financial plan, follow these steps:

1. Type in the following web address: www.personalwealth.com.
2. Click on the section titled Basics.
3. Click on the section titled Tutorials.
4. Under the Tutorials section, click on the section titled Basics of Smart Investing.

By studying the material contained in this website and following the basic investment principles presented in this chapter, along with the information on stocks, bonds, mutual funds, real estate, and other investments in the remaining chapters in Part 5, you can create a financial plan that is custom-made for you.

The decision to establish an investment plan is an important first step to accomplishing your long-term financial goals. Like other decisions, the decision to start an investment plan is one you must make for yourself. No one is going to make you save the money you need to fund an investment plan. These things won't be done unless you want to do them. In fact, the *specific* goals you want to accomplish must be the driving force behind your investment plan.

### Establishing Investment Goals

Some people say they want to be rich. Others say they want to be financially secure. But it takes more than just wishing. While it would be nice if you could magically accumulate wealth, it takes careful planning and discipline to achieve the financial freedom you desire. For most people, the first step is to establish investment goals. Without investment goals, you cannot know what you want to accomplish.

Sheet 55

To be useful, investment goals must be specific and measurable. They must be tailored to your particular financial needs. Some financial planners suggest that investment goals be stated in terms of money: By December 31, 2008, I will have total assets of $120,000. Other financial planners believe investors are more motivated to work toward goals that are stated in terms of the particular things they desire: By January 1, 2008, I will have accumulated enough money to purchase a second home in the mountains. The following questions will help you establish valid investment goals:

1.  What will you use the money for?
2.  How much money do you need to satisfy your investment goals?
3.  How will you obtain the money?
4.  How long will it take you to obtain the money?
5.  How much risk are you willing to assume in an investment program?
6.  What possible economic or personal conditions could alter your investment goals?
7.  Considering your economic circumstances, are your investment goals reasonable?
8.  Are you willing to make the sacrifices necessary to ensure that you meet your investment goals?
9.  What will the consequences be if you don't reach your investment goals?

Your investment goals are always oriented toward the future. In Chapter 1, we classified goals as short term (less than two years), intermediate (two to five years), or long term (over five years). These same classifications are also useful in planning your investment program. For example, you may establish a short-term goal of accumulating $3,000 in a savings account over the next 18 months. You may then use the $3,000 to purchase stocks or mutual funds to help you obtain your intermediate or long-term investment goals.

## Performing a Financial Checkup

Before beginning an investment program, your personal financial affairs should be in good shape. In this section, we examine several factors you should consider before making your first investment.

### Work to Balance Your Budget

Often people must learn to live within their means before they begin investing. Many individuals regularly spend more than they make. They purchase items on credit and then must make monthly installment payments and pay finance charges ranging between 12 and 18 percent or higher. With this situation, it makes no sense to start an investment program until credit card and installment purchases, along with the accompanying finance charges, are reduced or eliminated. Therefore, you should limit credit purchases to only the necessities or to purchases required to meet emergencies. A good rule of thumb is to limit installment payments to 10 percent of your monthly pay after taxes. Eventually, the amount of cash remaining after the bills are paid will increase and can be used to start a savings program or finance investments. A word of caution: Corrective measures take time, and it is impossible to improve a bad situation overnight.

### Obtain Adequate Insurance Protection

We discussed insurance in detail in Part 4, and will not cover that topic again here. However, it is essential that you consider insurance needs before beginning an investment program. The types of insurance and the amount of coverage will vary from one person to the next. Before you start investing, examine the amount of your insurance coverage for life insurance, hospitalization, your home and other real estate holdings, automobiles, and any other assets that may need coverage.

### Start an Emergency Fund

*emergency fund* An amount of money you can obtain quickly in case of immediate need.

Most financial planners suggest that an investment program should begin with the accumulation of an emergency fund. An **emergency fund** is an amount of money you can obtain quickly in case of immediate need. This money should be deposited in a savings account paying the highest available interest rate or in a money market mutual fund that provides immediate access to cash if needed.

The amount of money to be put away in the emergency fund varies from person to person. However, most financial planners agree that an amount equal to three to nine months' living expenses is reasonable. For example, Debbie Martin earns $30,000 a year. Her monthly expenses total $1,600. Before Debbie can begin investing, she must save at least $4,800 ($1,600 × 3 months = $4,800) in a savings account or other near-cash investments to meet emergencies.

### Have Access to Other Sources of Cash for Emergency Needs

*line of credit* A short-term loan that is approved before the money is actually needed.

You may also want to establish a line of credit at a commercial bank, savings and loan association, credit union, or credit card company. A **line of credit** is a short-term loan that is approved before you actually need the money. Because the paperwork has already been completed and the loan has been preapproved, you can later obtain the money as soon as you need it. The cash advance provision offered by major credit card companies can also be used in an emergency.

However, both lines of credit and credit cards have a ceiling, or maximum dollar amount, that limits the amount of available credit. If you have already exhausted both of these sources of credit on everyday expenses, they will not be available in an emergency.

## Getting the Money Needed to Start an Investment Program

Once you have established your investment goals and completed your personal financial checkup, it's time to start investing—assuming you have enough money to finance your investments. Unfortunately, the money doesn't automatically appear. In today's world, you must work to accumulate the money you need to start any type of investment program.

### Priority of Investment Goals

How badly do you want to achieve your investment goals? Are you willing to sacrifice some purchases to provide financing for your investments? The answers to both questions are extremely important. Take Rita Johnson, a 32-year-old nurse in a large St. Louis hospital. As part of a divorce settlement in 1996, she received a cash payment of almost $55,000. At first, she was tempted to spend this money on a trip to Europe, a new BMW, and new furniture. But after some careful planning, she decided to save $35,000 in a certificate of deposit and invest the remainder in a conservative mutual fund. On May 31, 2000, these investments were valued at $79,000.

As pointed out earlier in this chapter, no one can make you save money to finance your investment program. You have to *want* to do it.

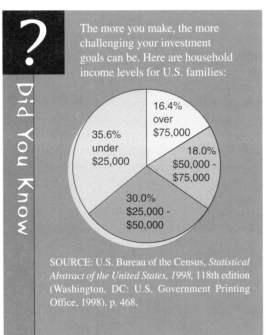

**Did You Know?**

The more you make, the more challenging your investment goals can be. Here are household income levels for U.S. families:

- 16.4% over $75,000
- 35.6% under $25,000
- 18.0% $50,000 - $75,000
- 30.0% $25,000 - $50,000

SOURCE: U.S. Bureau of the Census, *Statistical Abstract of the United States, 1998*, 118th edition (Washington, DC: U.S. Government Printing Office, 1998), p. 468.

And *you* may be the most important part of a successful investment program. What is important to you? What do you value? Each of these questions affects your investment goals. At one extreme are people who save or invest as much of each paycheck as they can. Their savings and investment program and the satisfaction they get from attaining their intermediate and long-term financial goals is more important than the more immediate satisfaction of spending a large part of their paychecks on new clothes, a meal at an expensive restaurant, or a weekend getaway. At the other extreme are people who spend everything they make and run out of money before their next paycheck. Most people find either extreme unacceptable and take a more middle-of-the-road approach. These people often spend money on the items that make their life more enjoyable and still save enough to fund an investment program. As you will see later in this section, even a small amount of money saved or invested on a regular basis can amount to a large sum over a period of time.

Here are some suggestions to help you obtain the money you need.

1. *Pay yourself first.* Too often, people save or invest what is left over after they have paid everything else. As you might guess, nothing is left over in many cases, and the investment program is put on hold for another month. A second and much better approach is to (1) pay your monthly bills, (2) save a reasonable amount of money, and (3) use whatever money is left over for personal expenses such as new clothes or entertainment.

2. *Take advantage of employer-sponsored retirement programs.* Many employers will match part or all of the contributions you make to a retirement program. Here's how a matching program works. For every dollar the employee contributes, the employer matches it with a specified amount such as 25 cents, 50 cents, or even $1. To make this option even more attractive, many matching programs are often part of an employer-sponsored retirement program that receives favorable tax treatment. (The tax benefits of different types of retirement programs are discussed later in Chapter 18.)

3. *Participate in an elective savings program.* You can elect to have money withheld from your paycheck each payday and automatically deposited in a savings account. When you choose this option, it is much easier to put money into the account than it is to get money out of it. You can also make investing easier by arranging with a mutual fund or brokerage firm to take a fixed sum from your bank account automatically every month and invest it. An elective savings program is an excellent way to fund a traditional IRA or Roth IRA (both topics are discussed in Chapters 4 and 18).

4. *Make a special savings effort one or two months each year.* Some financial planners recommend that you cut back to the basics for one or two months each year to obtain additional money for investment purposes.

5. *Take advantage of gifts, inheritances, and windfalls.* During your lifetime, you will likely receive gifts, inheritances, salary increases, year-end bonuses, or federal income tax refunds. Often people opt to spend this extra money on something they could not afford under normal circumstances. A better approach is to use the money to fund your investment program.

## The Value of Long-Term Investment Programs

Many people never start an investment program because they have only small sums of money. But even small sums grow over a long period of time. The Millers, the couple described in the Financial Planning for Life's Situations feature on page 413, began their investment program by investing $2,000 *each year* when they were in their 20s; yet they expect their investment portfolio to be worth more than $1.5 million by the time Peter reaches age 65. How did they do it? Simple: They took advantage of the

## Financial Planning for Life's Situations

### REALITY 101: THE TIME VALUE OF MONEY

Should college students worry about planning for retirement? You bet! There is no better time to begin an investment program than when you are young. The reason is quite simple: If you start an investment program when young, let the time value of money work for you, and make sound investments, you won't have to worry about finances when you reach retirement age. With these facts in mind, it's even possible for a person with an average salary to retire early.

Take Mary and Peter Miller. Mary, 32, is a high school history teacher. Peter, 35, runs his own computer consulting business. Together they earn about $80,000 a year and enjoy their careers. Both want to make sure they have enough money to retire on when Peter reaches age 65.

When the Millers married just over 10 years ago, they established a long-term goal to accumulate a retirement nest egg of $1.5 million. They consulted with Gina Reynolds, a financial planner whom a friend recommended. Reynolds explained that if they chose quality investments that earned a 12 percent average annual return and invested just $2,000 each year, their investment portfolio would be worth $1,534,180 at the end of

40 years, when Peter reached age 65. She explained that most of this amount was the result of the time value of money, an investment concept that allows all interest, dividends, and the dollar appreciation that occurs when investments increase in value to accumulate over a long period of time.

According to Reynolds, there is no better time to begin an investment program than right now. To drive this point home, she calculated that if the Millers waited 10 years before starting their investment program and made the same investments for a 30-year period, their investment portfolio would be worth only $482,660. They would lose over $1 million! Needless to say, the Millers realized they had to start their investment program now.

Today, after 10 years of investing in long-term stocks and mutual funds, the Millers estimate that their investments are worth approximately $45,000. And while the current value of their investment portfolio is a long way from $1.5 million, Gina Reynolds promises that if they keep investing in the same types of investments, the time value of money will enable their portfolio to grow to more than $1.5 million by the time Peter reaches age 65.

time value of money. You can achieve the same type of result. For instance, if you invest $2,000 each year for 40 years at a 6 percent annual rate of return, your investment will grow to $309,520. The rate of return and the length of time your money is invested *do* make a difference. Exhibit 13–1 shows how much your investment portfolio will be worth at the end of selected time periods and with different rates of return.

Notice that the value of your investments increases each year because of two factors. First, it is assumed you will invest another $2,000 each year. For example, at the end of 40 years, you will have invested a total of $80,000 ($2,000 × 40 years). Second, all investment earnings are allowed to accumulate and are added to your yearly deposits. Thus, the totals illustrated in Exhibit 13–1 are a result of continuous yearly deposits *plus* earnings on your investments.

Also, notice that if investments earn a higher rate of return, total portfolio values increase dramatically. For example, a $2,000 annual investment that earns 6 percent a year is worth $309,520 at the end of 40 years. But if the same $2,000 annual investment earns 12 percent each year, your investment portfolio value increases to $1,534,180 at the end of the same 40-year period. The search for higher returns is one reason many investors choose stocks and mutual funds that offer higher potential returns compared to certificates of deposit or savings accounts. You should know that to earn higher returns, you must take more chances. In fact, the material in the next section will help you determine if you should invest in these higher risk investments.

**EXHIBIT 13–1**

Growth Rate for $2,000 Invested at the End of Each Year at Various Rates of Return for Different Time Periods

| Rate of Return | Balance at End of Year | | | | | |
|---|---|---|---|---|---|---|
| | 1 | 5 | 10 | 20 | 30 | 40 |
| 6% | $2,000 | $11,274 | $26,362 | $73,572 | $158,116 | $309,520 |
| 7 | 2,000 | 11,502 | 27,632 | 81,990 | 188,922 | 399,280 |
| 8 | 2,000 | 11,734 | 28,974 | 91,524 | 226,560 | 518,120 |
| 9 | 2,000 | 11,970 | 30,386 | 102,320 | 272,620 | 675,780 |
| 10 | 2,000 | 12,210 | 31,874 | 114,550 | 328,980 | 885,180 |
| 11 | 2,000 | 12,456 | 33,444 | 128,406 | 398,040 | 1,163,660 |
| 12 | 2,000 | 12,706 | 35,098 | 144,104 | 482,660 | 1,534,180 |

The investment earnings illustrated in Exhibit 13–1 are taxable as ordinary income under current Internal Revenue Service guidelines. To avoid or postpone taxation, you may want to invest your money in a traditional individual retirement account (IRA), a Roth IRA, a 401(k) or 403(b) retirement account offered through your employer, or one of the tax-free investments described later in Part 5. The details about different types of retirement accounts are presented in Chapter 18. Although taxes are always a consideration, this complication does not reduce the importance of the time value of money. In fact, the time value of money is so important for a successful investment program that you may want to review this concept (see Chapter 1) before you begin to invest.

### Concept Check 13–1

1. How can the Internet help you create a financial plan or establish an investment program?
2. Why should an investor develop specific investment goals?
2. What factors should you consider when performing a financial checkup?
4. How can an investor accumulate the money needed to fund an investment program?
5. Explain the time value of money concept and how it could affect your investment program.

## FACTORS AFFECTING THE CHOICE OF INVESTMENTS

**Obj. 2**
Describe how safety, risk, income, growth, and liquidity affect your investment decisions.

**Sheet 56**

Millions of Americans buy stocks, bonds, or mutual funds, purchase gold and silver, or make similar investments. And they all have reasons for investing their money. Some people want to supplement their retirement income when they reach age 65, while others want to become millionaires before age 40. Although each investor may have specific, individual goals for investing, all investors must consider a number of factors before choosing an investment alternative.

### Safety and Risk

The safety and risk factors are two sides of the same coin. You cannot evaluate any investment without assessing how safety relates to risk. Safety in an investment means minimal risk of loss. On the other hand, risk in an investment means a measure of uncertainty about the outcome. Investments range from very safe to very risky. At one end of the investment spectrum are very safe investments that attract conservative investors. Investments in this category include government bonds, savings accounts, certificates of deposit, and certain stocks and bonds. Mutual funds and real estate may also be very safe investments. Investors pick such investments because they know there is very little chance that investments of this kind will become worthless. Although anyone can choose investments like those just listed, there is usually a reason someone chooses conservative investments. Many investors choose conservative investments because of the individual life situations in which they find themselves. As people approach retirement, for example, they usually choose more conservative investments with less chance of losing a large part of the nest egg they have built up over the years. Today one interesting change in investment philosophy is that most financial planners recommend that retirees still invest a small portion of their money in investments that will increase in value. The reason is simple: People are living longer, and they need more money for their retirement years. Some people choose to invest one-time windfalls or inheritances in a conservative investment because they know it may be impossible to replace the money if it is lost. Finally, some investors simply dislike taking chances.

*speculative investment*
A high-risk investment made in the hope of earning a relatively large profit in a short time.

At the other end of the investment spectrum are speculative investments. A **speculative investment** is a high-risk investment made in the hope of earning a relatively large profit in a short time. Such investments offer the possibility of a larger dollar return, but if they are unsuccessful, you may lose most or all of your initial investment. Speculative stocks, certain bonds, mutual funds, real estate, derivatives, commodities, options, precious metals, precious stones, and collectibles are risk-oriented investments. Although many of these investments are discussed in detail in later chapters, they are often considered too risky for beginning investors.

By now, you probably realize the safety and risk factors are more complex than the simple definitions just presented. From an investor's standpoint, one basic rule sums up the relationship between the factors of safety and risk: *The potential return on any investment should be directly related to the risk the investor assumes.* For example, Ana Luna was injured in a work-related accident three years ago. After a lengthy lawsuit, she received a legal settlement totaling $420,000. As a result of the injury, she was no longer qualified to perform her old job as an assembler for an electronics manufacturer. When she thought about the future, she knew she needed to get a job, but realized she would be forced to acquire new employment skills. She also realized she had received a great deal of money that could be invested to provide a steady source of income not only for the next two years while she obtained job training but also for the remainder of her life. Having never invested before, she quickly realized her tolerance for risk was minimal. She had to conserve her $420,000 settlement. Eventually, after much discussion with professionals and her own research, she chose to save about half of her money in certificates of deposit. For the remaining half, she chose three stocks that offered a 4 percent average dividend, a potential for growth, and a high degree of safety because of the financial stability of the corporations that issued the stocks.

A more risk-oriented investor might have criticized Ana's decisions as too conservative. In fact, this second type of investor might have chosen to invest in more speculative stocks that offer a greater potential for growth and increase in market value even though the corporations issuing the stocks are not paying dividends at the present time. Often beginning investors are afraid of the risk associated with many investments. But it helps to remember that without the risk, it is impossible to obtain the larger returns that really make an investment program grow. The key is to determine how much risk you are willing to assume, and then choose quality investments that offer higher returns without an unacceptably high risk. The bottom line is: What is right for one investor may not be right for another.

The problem of assessing safety and risk is further complicated by the large number of potential investments from which to choose. You must determine how much risk you are willing to assume. Once you have determined the amount of risk you are comfortable

# Financial Planning for Life's Situations

## A QUICK TEST TO MEASURE INVESTMENT RISK

The following quiz, adapted from one prepared by the T. Rowe Price group of mutual funds, can help you discover how comfortable you are with varying degrees of risk. Other things being equal, your risk tolerance score is a useful guide in deciding how heavily you should weight your portfolio toward safe investments versus more risk-oriented, speculative investments.

1. You're the winner on a TV game show. Which prize would you choose?
   - ☐ $2,000 in cash (1 point).
   - ☐ A 50 percent chance to win $4,000 (3 points).
   - ☐ A 20 percent chance to win $10,000 (5 points).
   - ☐ A 2 percent chance to win $100,000 (9 points).

2. You're down $500 in a poker game. How much more would you be willing to put up to win the $500 back?
   - ☐ More than $500 (8 points).
   - ☐ $500 (6 points).
   - ☐ $250 (4 points).
   - ☐ $100 (2 points).
   - ☐ Nothing—you'll cut your losses now (1 point).

3. A month after you invest in a stock, it suddenly goes up 15 percent. With no further information, what would you do?
   - ☐ Hold it, hoping for further gains (3 points).
   - ☐ Sell it and take your gains (1 point).
   - ☐ Buy more—it will probably go higher (4 points).

4. Your investment suddenly goes down 15 percent one month after you invest. Its fundamentals still look good. What would you do?
   - ☐ Buy more. If it looked good at the original price, it looks even better now (4 points).

   - ☐ Hold on and wait for it to come back (3 points).
   - ☐ Sell it to avoid losing even more (1 point).

5. You're a key employee in a start-up company. You can choose one of two ways to take your year-end bonus. Which would you pick?
   - ☐ $1,500 in cash (1 point).
   - ☐ Company stock options that could bring you $15,000 next year if the company succeeds, but will be worthless if it fails (5 points).

**Your total score:** _____

### SCORING

**5–18 points** You are a more conservative investor. You prefer to minimize financial risks. The lower your score, the more cautious you are. When you choose investments, look for high credit ratings, well-established records, and an orientation toward stability. In stocks, bonds, and real estate, look for a focus on income.

**19–30 points** You are a less conservative investor. You are willing to take more chances in pursuit of greater rewards. The higher your score, the bolder you are. When you invest, look for high overall returns. You may want to consider bonds with higher yields and lower credit ratings, the stocks of newer companies, and real estate investments that use mortgage debt.

A primer on the ABCs of investing is available from T. Rowe Price, 100 E. Pratt St., Baltimore, MD 21202 (1–800–638–5660).

---

with, you can choose different investments that hopefully will provide the expected return. To help you determine how much risk you are willing to assume, take the test for risk tolerance presented in the Financial Planning for Life's Situations feature at the top of this page.

## Components of the Risk Factor

The risk factor associated with a specific investment does change from time to time. For example, the stock of Computer-Tabulating-Recording Company was once considered a high-risk investment. Then this company changed its name to IBM and eventually became a leader in the computer industry. By the early 1980s, many conservative investors were purchasing IBM stock because of its safety and earnings potential. But in the early 1990s, many of these same investors sold their IBM stock because changes in the computer industry had brought financial problems for IBM. IBM was once again considered too risky for many investors. Now, as a result of solving many of its financial problems, IBM is once again considered an excellent choice for most investors.

When choosing an investment, you must carefully evaluate changes in the risk factor. In fact, the overall risk factor can be broken down into five components.

Inflation Risk   Your investments can provide a way to keep up with or stay ahead of inflation. While inflation rates have fallen sharply from the high levels of the early 1980s, the dollar is still shrinking in value. One dollar placed in a safe-deposit box in 1980 had less than 50 cents of buying power in early 1999.[1] As defined in Chapter 1, inflation is a rise in the general level of prices.

During periods of high inflation, there is a risk that the financial return on an investment will not keep pace with the inflation rate. To see how inflation reduces your buying power, let's assume you have deposited $10,000 in the bank at 4 percent interest. At the end of one year, your money will have earned $400 in interest ($10,000 $\times$ 4% = $400). Assuming an inflation rate of 6 percent, it will cost you an additional $600 ($10,000 $\times$ 6% = $600), or a total of $10,600, to purchase the same amount of goods you could have purchased for $10,000 a year earlier. Thus, even though you earned $400, you lost $200 in purchasing power. And after paying taxes on the $400 interest, your loss of purchasing power is even greater.

The rate of return when adjusted for inflation will vary from one investment to another. For example, common stocks had an inflation adjusted compounded return of 7.4 percent over the period 1926 to 1996. By comparison, corporate bonds had an inflation-adjusted compounded return of 2.4 percent and U.S. Treasury bills returned only 0.6 percent during the same period.[2] Before you rush out and invest in common stocks, however, realize that you should consider other factors when choosing an investment. On the other hand, rate of return is a major concern during periods of high inflation.

Interest Rate Risk   The interest rate risk associated with a fixed-return investment in preferred stocks or government or corporate bonds is the result of changes in the interest rates in the economy. The value of preferred stocks, government bonds, or corporate bonds decreases when overall interest rates increase. In contrast, the value of these same investments rises when overall interest rates decrease. For example, suppose you purchase a $1,000 corporate bond issued by AMR, the parent company of American Airlines, that matures in 2012 and pays 9 percent interest until maturity. This means AMR will pay $90 ($1,000 $\times$ 9% = $90) each year until the maturity date in 2012. If bond interest rates for comparable bonds increase to 11 percent, the market value of your 9 percent bond will decrease. No one will be willing to purchase your bond at the price you paid for it, since a comparable bond that pays 11 percent can be purchased for $1,000. As a result, you will have to sell your bond for less than $1,000 or hold it until maturity. If you decide to sell your AMR bond, the approximate dollar price you could sell it for would be $818 ($90 $\div$ 11% = $818). This price would provide the purchaser with an 11 percent return, and you would lose $182 ($1,000 − $818 = $182) because you owned a bond with a fixed interest rate of 9 percent during a period when overall interest rates in the economy increased.

Of course, if overall interest rates declined, your bond would increase in value. Let's assume that interest rates on comparable corporate bonds declined to 7 percent. As a result, the value of your AMR bond that pays 9 percent would increase in value. The approximate price you could sell it for would be $1,286 ($90 ÷ 7% = $1,286). This price would provide the purchaser with a 7 percent return, and you would earn a profit of $286 ($1,286 − 1,000 = $286) because you owned a bond with a fixed interest rate of 9 percent during a period when overall interest rates in the economy declined.

### Business Failure Risk

The risk of business failure is associated with investments in common stock, preferred stock, and corporate bonds. With each of these investments, you face the possibility that bad management, unsuccessful products, competition, or a host of other factors will cause the business to be less profitable than originally anticipated. Lower profits usually mean lower dividends or no dividends at all. If the business continues to operate at a loss, even interest payments and repayment of bonds may be questionable. The business may even fail and be forced to file for bankruptcy, in which case your investment may become totally worthless. Of course, the best way to protect yourself against such losses is to carefully evaluate the companies that issue the stocks and bonds you purchase. It also helps to purchase stock in more than one company and thus diversify your investments.

### Market Risk

The prices of stocks, bonds, mutual funds, and other investments may fluctuate because of the behavior of investors in the marketplace. As a result, economic growth is not as systematic and predictable as most investors might believe. Generally, a period of rapid expansion is followed by a period of recession. During periods of recession, it may be quite difficult to sell investments such as real estate. Fluctuations in the market price for stocks and bonds may have nothing to do with the fundamental changes in the financial health of corporations. Such fluctuations may be caused by political or social conditions. For example, the price of petroleum stocks may increase or decrease as a result of political activity in the Middle East. In late 1997, the stock markets in Asia experienced substantial losses. As a result, investors who had purchased stocks listed on these exchanges lost money.

### Global Investment Risk

Today more investors are investing in stocks and bonds issued by foreign firms and in global mutual funds. While we discuss these investments in more detail in the remainder of Part 5, you should know that investing in global securities creates additional risk. An investor can purchase stocks or bonds issued by individual foreign firms or, as most financial analysts recommend, purchase shares in a global mutual fund. For the small investor who has less than $200,000 to invest and is unaccustomed to the risks in foreign investments, global mutual funds offer more safety. Here are two factors to consider before taking the plunge.

First, *global investments must be evaluated just like domestic investments.* But evaluating foreign firms and global mutual funds may be difficult because reliable accounting information on foreign firms is often scarce. Of course, you can get an annual report, but you won't know whether the foreign firm uses the generally accepted accounting principles used by U.S. firms or follows its own national accounting rules.

Second, *changes in the currency exchange rate may affect the return on your investment.* The foreign currency exchange rate is applied whenever securities are bought and sold and whenever dividends are paid. For instance, if you want to purchase stock issued by a French firm, your U.S. currency must be converted into French francs. And the French francs you receive when you sell your shares in the foreign firm must  be converted back to U.S. dollars. Your potential return is determined not only by how well your investment performed but also by whether the currency exchange rate became more or less favorable during the time you held the investment.

| EXHIBIT 13–2 | Corporation | Dividends Since | Type of Business |
|---|---|---|---|
| | AT&T Corporation | 1881 | Telephone utility |
| | DuPont (E. I.) de Nemours & Co. | 1904 | Chemicals |
| | Exxon Corporation | 1882 | Chemical and petroleum products |
| | General Electric Company | 1899 | Electrical equipment |
| | Procter & Gamble Company | 1891 | Soap products |
| | Texaco | 1903 | Chemical and petroleum products |
| | Union Pacific Corporation | 1900 | Railroad |

**Corporations with Consecutive Dividend Payments for at Least 95 Years**

## Investment Income

Investors sometimes purchase certain investments because they want a predictable source of income. The safest investments—passbook savings accounts, certificates of deposit, U.S. savings bonds, and U.S. Treasury bills—are also the most predictable sources of income. With these investments, you know exactly what the interest rate is and how much income will be paid on a specific date.

If investment income is a primary objective, you can also choose government bonds, corporate bonds, preferred stocks, utility stocks, or selected common stock issues. When purchasing stocks or corporate bonds for potential income, most investors are concerned about the issuing corporation's overall profits, future earnings picture, and dividend policies. For example, some corporations are very proud of their long record of consecutive dividend payments and will maintain that policy if at all possible (see Exhibit 13–2).

Other investments that may provide income potential are mutual funds and real estate rental property. Although the income from mutual funds is not guaranteed, you can choose funds whose primary objective is income. Income from rental property is not guaranteed because the possibility of either vacancies or unexpected repair bills always exists. The more speculative investments, such as commodities, options, precious metals, gemstones, and collectibles, offer little, if any, potential for regular income.

## Investment Growth

To investors, *growth* means their investments will increase in value. Often the greatest opportunity for growth is an investment in common stock. During the 1990s, investors found that stocks issued by corporations in the electronics, technology, energy, and health care industries provided the greatest growth potential. In fact, goods and services provided by companies in these industries promise to be in even greater demand in the 21st century.

When purchasing growth stocks, investors often sacrifice immediate cash dividends in return for greater dollar value in the future. Companies like Microsoft, Dell, America Online, and other technology firms are considered to be growth companies and pay little or no dividends. For most growth companies, profits that would normally be paid to stockholders in the form of dividends are reinvested in the companies in the form of *retained earnings*. The money the companies keep can provide at least part of the financing they need for future growth and expansion and control the cost of borrowing money. As a result, they grow at an even faster pace. Growth financed by retained earnings normally increases the dollar value of a share of stock for the investor.

Government bonds, corporate bonds, mutual funds, and real estate may also offer growth possibilities. Precious metals, gemstones, and collectibles are more speculative investments that offer less predictable growth potential. Investments in commodities and options are more speculative investments that usually stress immediate returns as opposed to continued long-term growth.

## Investment Liquidity

*liquidity*   The ability to buy or sell an investment quickly without substantially affecting the investment's value.

**Liquidity** is the ability to buy or sell an investment quickly without substantially affecting the investment's value. Investments range from near-cash investments to frozen investments from which it is impossible to get your money. Checking and savings accounts are very liquid because they can be quickly converted to cash. Certificates of deposit impose penalties for withdrawing money before the maturity date.

With other investments, you may be able to sell quickly, but market conditions, economic conditions, or many other factors may prevent you from regaining the amount you originally invested. For example, the owner of real estate may have to lower the asking price to find a buyer. And it may be difficult to find a buyer for investments in collectibles such as antiques and paintings.

### Concept Check 13-2

1. Why are safety and risk two sides of the same coin?
2. What are the five components of the risk factor?
3. How do income, growth, and liquidity affect the choice of an investment?

## AN OVERVIEW OF INVESTMENT ALTERNATIVES

### Obj. 3
Identify the major types of investment alternatives.

Once you have considered the risks involved, established your emergency fund and have some money accumulated for investment purposes, it's time to consider the investment alternatives most people choose. You should begin by gathering as much information as possible about investment alternatives. Then you will be able to decide whether purchasing stocks, bonds, mutual funds, real estate, or other investment alternatives is a better use of your money than putting it in the bank. The remainder of this section provides a brief overview of different investment alternatives. The remaining chapters of Part 5 provide more detailed information on stocks, bonds, mutual funds, real estate, and other investment alternatives.

## Stock or Equity Financing

*equity capital*   Money that a business obtains from its owners.

**Equity capital** is money that a business obtains from its owners. If a business is a sole proprietorship or a partnership, it acquires equity capital when the owners invest their own money in the business. For a corporation, equity capital is provided by stockholders, who buy shares of its stock. Since all stockholders are owners, they share in the success of the corporation. This can make buying stock an attractive investment opportunity.

However, you should consider at least two factors before investing in stock. First, a corporation is not required to repay the money obtained from the sale of stock or to repurchase the stock at a later date. Assume you purchased 100 shares of Southwest Airlines stock. Later you decide to sell your Southwest stock. Your stock is sold to another investor, not back to the company. In many cases, a stockholder sells a stock because he or she thinks its price is going to decrease in value. The purchaser, on the other hand, buys that stock because he or she thinks its price is going to increase. This creates a situation in which either the seller or the buyer earns a profit while the other party to the transaction experiences a loss.

Second, a corporation is under no legal obligation to pay dividends to stockholders. A **dividend** is a distribution of money, stock, or other property that a corporation pays to stockholders. Dividends are paid out of earnings, but if a corporation that usually pays dividends has a bad year, its board of directors can vote to omit dividend payments to help pay necessary business expenses. Corporations may also retain earnings to make additional financing available for expansion, research and product development, or other business activities.

*dividend*   A distribution of money, stock, or other property that a corporation pays to stockholders.

There are two basic types of stock: *common stock* and *preferred stock.* Both types have advantages and disadvantages that you should consider before deciding which to use for an investment program. A share of common stock represents the most basic form of corporate ownership. People often purchase common stock because this type of investment can provide (1) a source of income if the company pays dividends, (2) growth potential if the dollar value of the stock increases, and (3) growth potential if the company splits its common stock. And because it is a popular type of investment, most large corporations sell common stock to satisfy a large part of their financing needs.

The most important priority an investor in preferred stock enjoys is receiving cash dividends before common stockholders are paid any cash dividends. This factor is especially important when a corporation is experiencing financial problems and cannot pay cash dividends to both preferred and common stockholders. Other factors you should consider before purchasing both common or preferred stock are discussed in Chapter 14.

## Corporate and Government Bonds

*corporate bond*
A corporation's written pledge to repay a specified amount of money, along with interest.

*government bond*
The written pledge of a government or a municipality to repay a specified sum of money, along with interest.

There are two types of bonds an investor should consider. A **corporate bond** is a corporation's written pledge to repay a specified amount of money, along with interest. A **government bond** is the written pledge of a government or a municipality to repay a specified sum of money, along with interest. Thus, when you buy a bond, you are loaning a corporation or government entity money for a period of time. Regardless of who issues the bond, you need to consider two major questions before investing in bonds. First, will the bond be repaid at maturity? The maturity dates for most bonds range between 1 and 30 years. An investor who purchases a bond has two options: keep the bond until maturity and then redeem it, or sell the bond to another investor. In either case, the value of the bond is closely tied to the ability of the corporation or government agency to repay the bond at maturity. Second, will the corporation or government agency be able to maintain interest payments to bondholders? Bondholders normally receive interest payments every six months. Again, if a corporation or government agency cannot pay the interest on its bonds, the value of those bonds will decrease.

Receiving periodic interest payments until maturity is one method of making money on a bond investment. Investors also use two other methods that can provide more liberal returns on bond investments. Chapter 15 discusses each of these methods.

## Mutual Funds

*mutual fund*
An investment alternative chosen by people who pool their money to buy stocks, bonds, and other securities selected by professional managers employed by an investment company.

A **mutual fund** is an investment alternative chosen by people who pool their money to buy stocks, bonds, and other securities selected by professional managers employed by an investment company. Professional management is an especially important factor for investors with little or no previous experience in financial matters. Another reason investors choose mutual funds is *diversification.* Since mutual funds invest in a number of different securities, an occasional loss in one security is often offset by gains in other securities. As a result, the diversification provided by a mutual fund reduces risk.

The goals of one investor often differ from those of another. The managers of mutual funds realize this and tailor their funds to meet individual needs and objectives. Some invest in U.S. companies, while others invest in stocks and bonds issued by companies in foreign countries. As a result of all the different investment alternatives, mutual funds range from very conservative to extremely speculative investments.

*Although investing money in a mutual fund provides professional management, even the best managers can make errors in judgment. The responsibility for choosing the right mutual fund is still based on the investor's evaluation of a mutual fund investment.* Chapter 16 presents more information on the different types of mutual funds, the costs involved, and techniques for evaluating these investments.

## Real Estate

As a rule, real estate increases in value and eventually sells at a profit, but there are no guarantees. Although many beginning investors believe real estate values increase by 10 or 15 percent a year, in reality the nationwide average annual increase is about 3 percent. This growth rate makes real estate a long-term investment and not a get-rich-quick scheme.

Success in real estate investments depends on how well you evaluate alternatives. Experts often tell would-be investors that the three most important factors when evaluating a potential real estate investment are *location, location,* and *location.* While location may be the most important factor, other factors may determine whether or not a piece of real estate is a good investment. For example, you should answer the following questions before making a decision to purchase any property:

1. Is the property priced competitively with similar properties?
2. What type of financing is available, if any?
3. How much are the taxes?
4. What is the condition of the buildings and houses in the immediate area?
5. Why are the present owners selling the property?
6. Is there a chance that the property will decrease in value?

Any investment has disadvantages, and real estate is no exception. Many people were "taken" by unscrupulous promoters who sold inaccessible land in the Florida Everglades. Poor location can cause a piece of property to decrease in value. Also, to sell your property, you must find an interested buyer who is able to obtain enough money or financing to complete the transaction. Finding a buyer can be difficult if loan money is scarce, the real estate market is in a decline, or you overpaid for the property. If you are forced to hold your investment longer than you originally planned, you must also consider taxes and loan payments. Chapter 17 presents additional information on how to evaluate a real estate investment.

## Other Investment Alternatives

As defined earlier in this chapter, a speculative investment is a high-risk investment made in the hope of earning a relatively large profit in a short time. By its very nature, any investment may be speculative; that is, it may be quite risky. However, a *true* speculative investment is speculative because of the methods investors use to earn a quick profit. Typical speculative investments include

**EXHIBIT 13-3**

Factors Used to
Evaluate Typical
Investment
Alternatives

N/A = Not applicable.

| | Type of Investment | Factors to Be Evaluated | | | | |
| --- | --- | --- | --- | --- | --- | --- |
| | | Safety | Risk | Income | Growth | Liquidity |
| Traditional investments | Common stock | Average | Average | Average | High | Average |
| | Preferred stock | Average | Average | High | Average | Average |
| | Corporate bonds | Average | Average | High | Low | Average |
| | Government bonds | High | Low | Low | Low | High |
| | Mutual funds | Average | Average | Average | Average | Average |
| | Real estate | Average | Average | Average | Average | Low |
| Speculative investments | Options | Low | High | N/A | Low | Average |
| | Derivatives | Low | High | N/A | Low | Average |
| | Commodities | Low | High | N/A | Low | Average |
| | Precious metals, gemstones, and collectibles | Low | High | N/A | Low | Low |

- Call options
- Put options
- Derivatives
- Commodities
- Precious metals
- Gemstones
- Coins
- Stamps
- Antiques and collectibles

Without exception, investments of this kind are normally referred to as speculative for one reason or another. For example, the gold market has many unscrupulous dealers who sell worthless gold-plated lead coins to unsuspecting, uninformed investors. With any speculative investment, it is extremely important to deal with reputable dealers and recognized investment firms. It pays to be careful. While investments in this category can lead to large dollar gains, they should not be used by anyone who does not fully understand the risks involved. Chapter 14 presents information on options. Chapter 17 discusses precious metals, gemstones, and collectibles.

## Summary of Factors That Affect Investment Choices

Earlier in this chapter, we examined how safety, risk, income, growth, and liquidity affect your investment choices. In the preceding section, we looked at available investment alternatives. Now let's compare the factors that affect the choice of investments with each alternative. Exhibit 13–3 ranks the alternatives in terms of safety, risk, income, growth, and liquidity.

It is now appropriate to introduce the topic of diversification. **Diversification** is the process of spreading your assets among several types of investments to lessen risk. *In fact, diversification can reduce the risk associated with putting all your eggs in one basket—a common mistake made by investors. To avoid this mistake,* many financial planners suggest that you think of your investment program as a pyramid consisting of four levels, as illustrated in Exhibit 13–4. This approach to investing can provide financial growth and protection regardless of your age, marital status, income, or level of financial sophistication.

*diversification* The process of spreading your assets among several types of investments to lessen risk.

**EXHIBIT 13-4**

Possible
Investments for
Financial Security,
Safety and Income,
Growth, and
Speculation

**EXHIBIT 13-5**

Steps for Effective
Investment
Planning

1. Establish your investment goals.
2. Determine the amount of money you need to obtain your goals.
3. Specify the amount of money you currently have available to fund your investments.
4. List different investments that you want to evaluate.
5. Evaluate (a) the risk factor and (b) the potential return for all investments.
6. Reduce possible investments to a reasonable number.
7. Choose at least two different investments.
8. Continue to evaluate your investment program.

In Exhibit 13–4, the investments in level 1 provide the foundation for an investment program. After the foundation is established in level 1, most investors choose from the investment alternatives in level 2 and level 3. Be warned: Many investors may decide the investments in level 4 are too speculative for their investment programs. While investments at this level may provide spectacular dollar gains, they pose the risk that they will lose value or even become totally worthless.

Once you understand the risk factors associated with different investment alternatives and the principle of diversification, the next step is to develop a personal investment plan.

## A Personal Investment Plan

To be a successful investor, you must develop a plan and then implement it. Most people use a series of steps like those listed in Exhibit 13–5 to develop their own personal plan for investing.

You begin investment planning by establishing realistic goals. The second step is to determine the amount of money you will obtain by a specific date. The total amount of money specified in step 2 should be based on your goals. The amount of money you now have available for investment purposes is specified in step 3. For most investors, the money currently available for investment purposes has accumulated over a period of time. For example, Shannon and Fred Rogers began saving $200 a month to finance a future investment program over three years ago. They deposited the money in an interest-bearing savings account. Now, after three years, they have accumulated over $8,000 that they can use to purchase different investments. In step 4, you list specific investment alternatives that you want to evaluate.

Because of the relationship between risks and returns for each investment, step 5 is divided into two components. In step 5a, you examine the risk factor for each investment alternative. In step 5b, you examine the potential return associated with each

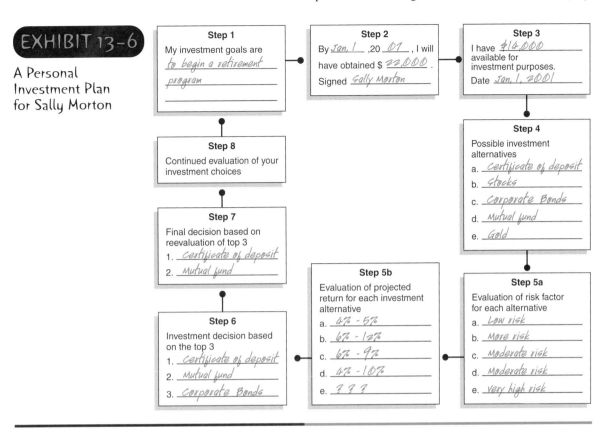

**EXHIBIT 13-6**

A Personal Investment Plan for Sally Morton

**Step 1**
My investment goals are *to begin a retirement program*

**Step 2**
By *Jan. 1* ,20 *01* , I will have obtained $ *22,000* .
Signed *Sally Morton*

**Step 3**
I have *$14,000* available for investment purposes.
Date *Jan. 1, 2001*

**Step 8**
Continued evaluation of your investment choices

**Step 4**
Possible investment alternatives
a. *Certificate of deposit*
b. *Stocks*
c. *Corporate Bonds*
d. *Mutual fund*
e. *Gold*

**Step 7**
Final decision based on reevaluation of top 3
1. *Certificate of deposit*
2. *Mutual fund*

**Step 5b**
Evaluation of projected return for each investment alternative
a. *4% - 5%*
b. *6% - 12%*
c. *6% - 9%*
d. *4% -10%*
e. *???*

**Step 5a**
Evaluation of risk factor for each alternative
a. *Low risk*
b. *More risk*
c. *Moderate risk*
d. *Moderate risk*
e. *Very high risk*

**Step 6**
Investment decision based on the top 3
1. *Certificate of deposit*
2. *Mutual fund*
3. *Corporate Bonds*

alternative. The information needed to complete steps 5a and 5b should be based on your research of potential investments. At the very least, this requires some expert advice, careful study, and a commitment of your time. In step 6, you reduce potential investments to a reasonable number. In step 7, you make a final decision to choose at least two different investments. By choosing at least two alternatives, you build a certain amount of diversification into your investment program. As the total dollar value of your investments grows, you will probably want to continue to consider additional investments. After all, spreading potential risks among different investments is a key factor in diversifing your investment program.

Step 8 provides for continued evaluation of your investments. Investors' circumstances often change as they go through life. As a result, investors are often forced to adapt their planning to new situations. For example, if you accept a new job at a substantially higher salary, changes in investment goals may make your present personal plan of action obsolete. Also, different investments may become more or less attractive because of changes in economic and financial conditions. During the early 1980s, for example, many investors sold their common stocks and placed their money in certificates of deposit that paid high guaranteed interest. During the 1990s, many of the same investors cashed in their certificates of deposit, which were now paying lower interest rates, and purchased common stocks and mutual funds that offered more potential.

To illustrate the above planning process, let's use the case of Sally Morton, who accepted a position in advertising after college. After four years, Sally is earning $30,000 a year. Her take-home pay after deductions is $2,000 a month. Her living expenses are about $1,600 a month, which leaves a surplus of $400. After graduating from college, she immediately began saving a portion of each month's surplus. First, she established an emergency fund. Now she has $14,000 available for investment purposes. After much thought, Sally developed the personal plan of action illustrated in Exhibit 13–6.

## DOC'S PRESCRIPTION FOR A HEALTHY INVESTMENT PROGRAM

According to Doc Gallagher, life is not a dress rehearsal. This is all we've got!! The host of a popular radio program on financial planning in the Dallas/Fort Worth metroplex and founder of the Gallagher Financial Group, says that retire means getting up in the morning and doing what YOU want to do. He often asks potential clients a basic question: What worthy goal would you pursue if money were no object? It is towards THIS goal that you start investing.

In addition to helping clients determine goals that are important, Doc Gallagher also encourages clients to adopt the 15/15/70 rule. He recommends that you first give away 15 percent. You must learn that money is a servant, not a master. You must learn that it really is "more blessed to give than to receive." Then give yourself 15 percent. Most people say I'll pay all the bills, then I'll invest whatever is left. It won't happen. Pay yourself off the top. Finally, live on the remaining 70 percent. Learn to discipline youself in order to pay those bills.

Once a client has accumulated enough money to finance an investment program, Doc Gallagher encourages his clients and radio listeners to choose long-term investments. For many beginning investors, he often suggests good mutual funds with a 4-star or 5-star rating, excellent long-term performance, and good management. Above all, Doc believes that you should pick investments that are suitable for your risk comfort level.

Your own plan may be quite different from Sally's, but the principle is the same. Each person has different ideas and goals. Establish your investment goals first, and then follow through. Often the follow-through is the most important component when it comes to developing a successful investment plan. Simply put: How important are your investment goals, and are you willing to work to attain them?

### Concept Check 13-3

1. Of all the investment alternatives presented in this chapter, which one do you think would help you obtain your investment goals? Why?
2. Why do investors purchase stocks?
3. What are two chief advantages of investing in mutual funds?
4. What factors should you consider before purchasing real estate for investment purposes?
5. How can the investment pyramid presented in Exhibit 13–4 help you build an investment program to reach your financial goals?
6. What are the steps required for a personal investment plan?

## FACTORS THAT REDUCE INVESTMENT RISK

In this section, we examine the factors that can spell the difference between success and failure for an investor. We begin by reviewing the role of a financial planner. Then we consider your role in the investment process.

**Obj. 4**
Recognize the role of the professional financial planner and your role in a personal investment program.

### The Role of a Financial Planner

To achieve their financial goals, many people seek professional help. In many cases, they turn to stockbrokers, lawyers, accountants, bankers, or insurance agents. However, these professionals are specialists in one specific field and may not be qualified to provide the type of advice required to develop a thorough financial plan.

A qualified financial planner has had at least two years of training in securities, insurance, taxes, real estate, and estate planning and has passed a rigorous examination. As evidence of training and successful completion of a 10-hour qualifying examination, the Institute of Certified Financial Planners in Denver allows individuals to use the designation Certified Financial Planner (CFP). Similarly, the American College in Bryn Mawr, Pennsylvania, allows individuals to use the designation Chartered Financial Consultant (ChFC) if they complete the necessary requirements, have a minimum of three years' experience, and pass 10 two-hour exams. For more information on how to choose a financial planner, review the material in Appendix 1 presented after Chapter 1.

## Your Role in the Investment Process

Successful investors continually evaluate their investments. They never sit back and let their investments manage themselves. Obviously, different types of investments will require different methods of evaluation. Some factors to consider when choosing different investments are described next.

### Evaluate Potential Investments

Let's assume you have $25,000 to invest. Also assume your investment will earn a 10 percent return the first year. At the end of one year, you will have earned $2,500 and your investment will be worth $27,500. Not a bad return on your original investment! Now ask yourself: How long would it take to earn $2,500 if I had to work for this amount of money at a job? For some people, it might take a month; for others, it might take longer. The point is that if you want this type of return, you should be willing to work for it, but the work takes a different form than a job. When choosing an investment, the work you invest is the time it takes to research different investments so that you can make an informed decision.

Some people invest large sums of money and never research the investments they purchase. Obviously, this is a flawed approach that can lead to large dollar losses. On the other hand, an informed investor has a much better chance of choosing the types of investments that will increase in value. In fact, much of the information in the remainder of Part 5 will help you learn how to evaluate different investment opportunities. But you have to be willing to work and learn if you want to be a successful investor. As you will see in the next section, evaluation doesn't stop once you make a decision to purchase an investment. It continues as long as you own the investment.

### Monitor the Value of Your Investments

Would you believe that some people invest large sums of money and don't know what their investments are worth? They don't know if their investments have increased or decreased in value. They don't know if they should sell their investments or continue to hold them. A much better approach is to monitor the value of your investments. If you choose to invest in stocks, bonds, mutual funds, commodities, or options, you can determine the value of your holdings by looking at the price quotations reported on the Internet, on cable financial news programs, and in newspapers. Your real estate holdings may be compared with similar properties currently for sale in the surrounding area. Finally, you can determine the value of your precious metals, gemstones, and collectibles by checking with reputable dealers and investment firms. Regardless of which type of investment you choose, close surveillance will keep you informed of whether your investment increases or decreases in value. The Financial Planning Calculations box on page 428 presents further information on monitoring the value of your investments.

### Keep Accurate and Current Records

Accurate recordkeeping can help you spot opportunities to maximize profits or reduce dollar losses when you sell your

## Financial Planning Calculations

### CHARTING THE VALUE OF YOUR INVESTMENT

To monitor the value of their investments, many investors use a simple chart like the one illustrated here. To construct a chart like this one, place the original purchase price of your investment in the middle on the side of the chart.

Then use price increments of a logical amount to show increases and decreases in dollar value.

Place individual dates along the bottom of the chart. For stocks, bonds, mutual funds, and similar investments, you may want to graph every two weeks and chart current values on, say, a Friday. For longer-term investments like real estate, you can chart current values every six months.

### A WORD OF CAUTION

If an investment is beginning to have a large increase or decrease in value, you should watch that investment more closely. You can still continue to chart at regular intervals, but you may want to check dollar values more frequently—in some cases, daily.

investments. Accurate recordkeeping can also help you decide whether you want to invest additional funds in a particular investment. At the very least, you should keep purchase records for each of your investments that include the actual dollar cost of the investment, plus any commissions or fees you paid. It is also useful to keep a list of the sources of information (Internet addresses, business periodicals, research publications, etc.), along with copies of the material you used to evaluate each investment. Then, when it is time to reevaluate an existing investment, you will know where to begin your search for current information. As you will see in the next section, accurate record-keeping is also necessary for tax purposes.

## Tax Considerations

Generally, investment income falls into three categories: tax-exempt income, tax-deferred income, and taxable income. *Tax-exempt income* is income that is *not* subject to tax. For example, the interest paid on most state and municipal bonds (see Chapter 15) is exempt from federal income tax. Also, the income earned on a Roth individual retirement account is tax free. *Tax-deferred income* is income that will be taxed at a later date. The most common type of tax-deferred income is the income earned on a traditional individual retirement account (IRA). Both contributions and earnings on traditional IRAs accumulate tax free until you withdraw them at a later date; then you must pay federal income tax. The 401(k) and 403(b) retirement accounts provided by many employers also provide tax-deferred income. Chapter 18 discusses individual retirement accounts and employer-sponsored retirement plans in greater detail. The income from all other investments is *taxable income.*

With all three types of investment income, it is your responsibility to determine how taxes affect your investments. Areas of concern include dividend, interest, and rental income, and capital gains and capital losses.

### Dividends, Interest Income, and Rental Income

As defined earlier in this chapter, a dividend is a distribution of money, stock, or other property that a corporation pays to stockholders. Like wages or salaries, cash dividends are reported on your federal tax return as ordinary income. If you own shares of a corporation and receive additional shares of the same company as a stock dividend, the dividend is *generally* not taxable unless you decide to sell the additional shares. A corporation will send you a Form 1099-DIV that states how much dividend income has been reported to the Internal Revenue Service in your name.

Interest from banks, credit unions, and savings and loan associations is subject to federal taxation. Usually the payer will send you a Form 1099-INT that states how much interest income has been reported to the Internal Revenue Service in your name. Interest that you receive from promissory notes, loans, bonds, and U.S. securities must also be reported as income. With the exception of tax-free bonds, there is no exclusion for interest income. You must report the total of such income as ordinary income on your tax return.

Net income from rental property is also subject to federal taxation and is treated as ordinary income like wages or salaries. Generally, you must report all income and expenses on rental property on IRS Schedule E.

### Capital Gains and Capital Losses

Under current tax laws, profit resulting from the sale of stocks, mutual funds, bonds, land, and some personal property held for 12 months or less is a short-term capital gain and taxed as ordinary income. For example, assume Joe Coit sold 100 shares of General Electric stock for a profit of $1,000. If this investment was held for less than 12 months and Joe is in the 28 percent tax bracket, Joe's tax on the $1,000 profit is $280 ($1,000 × 28% = $280). Investments held for longer than 12 months are treated as long-term capital gains and are taxed at reduced tax rates. Under the current tax law, the tax rate on long-term capital gains is 20 percent for most taxpayers and 10 percent for people in the 15 percent tax bracket. If Joe Coit had held his General Electric stock for longer than 12 months, his profit would be treated as a long-term capital gain. His tax on the $1,000 long-term capital gain would be $200 ($1,000 × 20% = $200). Long-term capital gains on assets purchased after December 31, 2000, and held for more than five years will be taxed at even lower rates. For these assets, the 20 percent rate will drop to 18 percent and the 10 percent rate will drop to 8 percent.

Under current tax laws, capital losses are first used to offset capital gains. Up to $3,000 in capital losses may then be used each year to offset ordinary income. Any capital losses in excess of $3,000 may be used in future tax years.

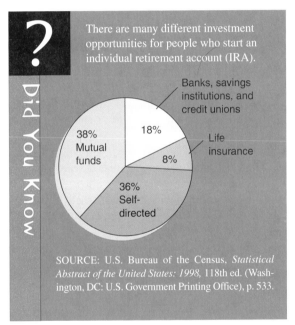

**Did You Know?**

There are many different investment opportunities for people who start an individual retirement account (IRA).

Banks, savings institutions, and credit unions — 18%
Life insurance — 8%
Self-directed — 36%
Mutual funds — 38%

SOURCE: U.S. Bureau of the Census, *Statistical Abstract of the United States: 1998*, 118th ed. (Washington, DC: U.S. Government Printing Office), p. 533.

## Concept Check 13-4

1. What type of training does a qualified financial planner have?
2. What is your role in the investment process?
3. How do dividends, interest, and rental income differ from short-term and long-term capital gains and losses?

# SOURCES OF INVESTMENT INFORMATION

## Obj. 5
Use various sources of financial information that can reduce risks and increase investment returns.

With most investments, more information is available than you can read and comprehend. Therefore, you must be selective in the type of information you use for evaluation purposes. With some investments, however, only a limited amount of information is available. For example, a wealth of information is available on individual stocks and mutual funds, whereas the amount of information on a metal such as cobalt or manganese may be limited to one source. Regardless of the number or availability of sources, always determine how reliable and accurate the information is. Following are sources of information you can use to evaluate present and future investments.

## The Internet and Online Computer Services

While no one knows the exact number, experts estimate that there are more than 100 million Internet users worldwide.[3] In the United States alone, over 9.5 million Americans use the Internet.[4] Today more people have access to information provided by computers located in their homes or at libraries, universities, or businesses than ever before. And this number is growing. More important, a wealth of information is available on most personal finance topics and different investment alternatives. For example, you can obtain interest rates for certificates of deposit; current price information for stocks, bonds, and mutual funds; and brokers' recommendations to buy, hold, or sell a corporation's stock. You can even trade securities online just by pushing the right button on your computer keyboard. You can also use computers and financial planning software to develop a personal financial plan.

To use your computer to generate information you really need, you must be selective. One of the best ways to access needed information is to use a search engine. Search engines like Yahoo, Alta Vista, Infoseek, and WebCrawler allow you to do a word search for either the personal finance topic or investment alternative that you want to explore. Federal, state, and local governments and most corporations also have a home page where you can obtain valuable information.

Today thousands of Internet service providers allow users to connect to the Internet and use search engines, newsgroups, mailing lists, and e-mail. If you're a beginner, you may find it easier to use one of the commercial online companies like America Online, CompuServe, Prodigy, and Microsoft Network. These companies usually provide subscribers with access to a broad range of information on a variety of topics as well as a connection to the Internet. While it is impossible to list all the Internet sites related to personal finance, those listed in Exhibit 13–7 will get you started. We will examine other specific Internet sites in the remaining chapters in Part 5. Also, read the Appendix at the end of Chapter 1 for information on how to use the Internet for personal financial planning.

## Newspapers and News Programs

One of the most readily available sources of information for the average investor is the financial page of a metropolitan newspaper or *The Wall Street Journal*. There you will find a summary of the day's trading on the two most widely quoted stock exchanges in the United States, the New York Stock Exchange and the American Stock Exchange. In addition to stock coverage, most newspapers provide information on stocks traded in the over-the-counter markets, mutual funds, corporate and government bonds, commodities and options, and general economic news. Detailed information on how to read price quotations for stocks, bonds, mutual funds, and other investments is presented in the remaining chapters of Part 5.

**Useful Internet Sites for Personal Financial Planning**

The following five Internet sites provide information that you can use to establish a financial plan and begin an investment program.

| Sponsor and Description | Web Address |
|---|---|
| **Standard & Poor's Personal Wealth** website provides current financial news and material that can help both beginning and experienced investors sharpen their investment skills. | www.personalwealth.com |
| **The Quicken** website provides information about investments, home mortgages, insurance, taxes, banking and credit, and different types of retirement programs. | www.quicken.com |
| **Financial Center, Inc.** helps consumers calculate the cost of purchasing autos, homes, and investments. The site also helps individuals establish savings programs and retirement programs. | www.financcenter.com |
| **The Motley Fool** website provides lighthearted but excellent investment advice. It also provides educational materials if you want to learn more about financial planning and investments. | www.fool.com |
| **The Invest-O-Rama** website contains a very useful web directory of more than 11,500 links to investment information. It also provides feature articles and tools that can help you invest. | www.investorama.com |

It is also possible to obtain economic and investment information on radio or television. Many stations broadcast investment market summaries and economic information as part of their regular news programs. Cable providers like CNN Financial and CNBC provide ongoing market coverage, investment information, and economic news. See Exhibit 13–8 for publications and news programs used by successful investors.

## Business Periodicals and Government Publications

Most business periodicals are published weekly, twice a month, or monthly. *Barron's, Business Week, Fortune, Forbes, Harvard Business Review,* and similar business periodicals provide not only general news about the overall economy but detailed financial information about individual corporations. Some business periodicals—for example, *Advertising Age* and *Business Insurance*—focus on information about the firms in a specific industry. In addition to business periodicals, more general magazines such as *U.S. News & World Report, Time,* and *Newsweek* provide investment information as a regular feature. Finally, *Money, Consumer Reports, Smart Money, Kiplinger's Personal Finance Magazine, Worth,* and similar periodicals provide information and advice designed to improve your investment skills.

The U.S. government is the world's largest provider of information. Much of this information is of value to investors and is either free or available at minimal cost. U.S. government publications that investors may find useful include the *Federal Reserve Bulletin,* published by the Federal Reserve System, and the *Survey of Current Business,* published by the Department of Commerce.

## Corporate Reports

The federal government requires corporations selling new issues of securities to disclose information about corporate earnings, assets and liabilities, products or services, and the qualifications of top management in a *prospectus* that they must give to investors. In addition to the prospectus, all publicly owned corporations send their stockholders an annual report and quarterly reports that contain detailed financial data.

A Personal
Reading List for
Successful
Investing

While individual investors have their favorite sources for investment information, it is quite likely that most successful investors use some of the following newspapers, periodicals, and news programs on a regular basis.

**Newspapers**
- Metropolitan newspapers—published daily
- *The Wall Street Journal*—published Monday through Friday each week
- *USA Today*—published daily
- *The New York Times*—published daily

**Cable Television**
- CNN Financial—ongoing
- CNBC—ongoing

**Business Periodicals**
- *Barron's*—published weekly
- *Business Week*—published weekly
- *Fortune*—published twice a month
- *Forbes*—published twice a month
- *Newsweek*—published weekly
- *U.S News & World Report*—published weekly

**Personal Financial Publications**
- *Consumer Reports*—published monthly
- *Kiplinger's Personal Finance Magazine*—published monthly
- *Money*—published monthly
- *Smart Money*—published monthly
- *Worth*—published monthly

Included in annual and quarterly corporate reports is a statement of financial position, which describes changes in assets, liabilities, and owners' equity. Also included in these reports is an income statement, which provides dollar amounts for sales, expenses, and profits or losses.

## Statistical Averages

Investors often gauge the value of their investments by following one or more widely recognized statistical averages. Such an average is a statistical measure that indicates whether a broad investment category (stocks, bonds, mutual funds, etc.) is increasing or decreasing in value.

How much importance should you attach to statistical averages? These averages show trends and direction, but they do not pinpoint the actual value of a specific investment. Some of the more widely used statistical averages are listed in Exhibit 13–9. The remaining chapters of Part 5 describe many of these averages.

## Investor Services and Newsletters

Many stockbrokers and financial planners mail a free monthly or quarterly newsletter to their clients. In addition, investors can subscribe to services that provide investment information. The fees for investor services generally range from $30 to $750 a year.

Five widely used services are available for investors who specialize in stocks, bonds, and mutual funds:

**EXHIBIT 13-9**

Statistical Averages Used to Evaluate Investments

| Statistical Average | Type of Investment |
| --- | --- |
| Dow Jones Industrial Average | Stocks |
| Standard & Poor's 500 Stock Index | Stocks |
| Value Line Stock Index | Stocks |
| New York Stock Exchange Index | Stocks on New York Stock Exchange |
| American Stock Exchange Index | Stocks on American Stock Exchange |
| NASDAQ Composite Stock Index | Over-the-counter stocks |
| Lipper Mutual Funds Index | Mutual funds |
| Dow Jones Bond Average | Corporate bonds |
| *Barron's* Money Rates | Interest rates |
| New One-Family House Price Index | Real estate |
| Dow Jones Spot Market Index | Commodities |
| Sotheby's Fine Art Index | Art/paintings |
| Linn's Trends of Stamp Values | Stamps |

1. *Standard & Poor's Stock Reports.* These up-to-date reports on corporations cover such topics as recommendations, sales and earnings, prospects, recent developments, income statements, and statements of financial position.
2. *Value Line.* These reports supply detailed information about major corporations—earnings, dividends, sales, liabilities, and other financial data.
3. *Moody's Investors Service.* Moody's reports help investors evaluate potential investments in corporate securities and provide information similar to that contained in Standard & Poor's and Value Line reports.
4. *Morningstar Investment Reports.* Morningstar tracks thousands of mutual funds and issues monthly reports on safety, financial performance, and other important information that investors can use to evaluate a mutual fund.
5. *Wiesenberger Investment Reports.* The mutual fund information provided by Wiesenberger is similar to Morningstar's detailed reports.

Other investment publications that may help you evaluate potential investments include Dun & Bradstreet's *Key Business Ratios; Hoover's Handbook of American Business,* published by the Referance Press; the *Commodity Yearbook;* and publications by the International Monetary Fund.

In addition to the preceding publications, each of the following securities exchanges provides information through printed materials and the Internet:

**Sheet 57**

- American Stock Exchange (www.amex.com).
- Chicago Mercantile Exchange (www.cme.com).
- New York Stock Exchange (www.nyse.com).
- Stock exchange markets—foreign exchanges (www.qualisteam.com).
- Nasdaq market (www.nasdaq.com).

Each of these websites provides basic information about the exchange, offers educational material and a glossary of important terms, and describes how investors can profit from transactions through the exchange.

The preceding discussion of investor services and newsletters is not exhaustive, but it gives you some idea of the amount and scope of the information available to serious investors. Although most small investors find many of the services and newsletters described here too expensive for personal subscriptions, this information may be available from stockbrokers or financial planners. This type of information is also available at many public libraries.

## Concept Check 13-5

1. What do you think is the most readily available source of information for the average investor? Explain your answer.
2. What type of information can you obtain using the Internet?
3. Briefly describe the additional sources of information you can use to evaluate a potential investment and lessen risk.

## KEY FORMULAS

| Page | Topic | Formula |
|------|-------|---------|
| 417 | Interest calculation for a corporate bond | Dollar amount of annual interest $=$ Issue price $\times$ Interest rate |
| | *Example:* | Dollar amount of interest $=$ $\$1,000 \times 7\%$ |
| | | $= \$1,000 \times 0.07$ |
| | | $= \$70$ |
| 417 | Approximate market price | Approximate market price $= \dfrac{\text{Annual interest amount}}{\text{Comparable interest rate}}$ |
| | *Example:* | Approximate market price $= \dfrac{\$80}{9\%}$ |
| | | $= \dfrac{\$80}{0.09}$ |
| | | $= \$888.89$ |

## Summary of Objectives

**Obj. 1**   **Explain why you should establish an investment program.**

Investment goals must be specific and measurable and should be classified as short term, intermediate, and long term. Before beginning an investment program, you must make sure your personal financial affairs are in order. This process begins with learning to live within your means and obtaining adequate insurance protection. The next step is the accumulation of an emergency fund equal to three to nine months' living expenses. Then, and only then, is it time to save the money needed to establish an investment program.

**Obj. 2**   **Describe how safety, risk, income, growth, and liquidity affect your investment decisions.**

Although each investor may have specific, individual reasons for investing, all investors must consider the factors of safety, risk, income, growth, and liquidity. Especially important is the relationship between safety and risk. Basically, this concept can be summarized as follows: The potential return for any investment should be directly related to the risk the investor assumes. The risk factor can be broken down into five components: inflation risk, interest rate risk, business failure risk, market risk, and global investment risk.

Obj. 3   **Identify the major types of investment alternatives.**

Investment alternatives include stocks, bonds, mutual funds, and real estate. More speculative investment alternatives include options, derivatives, commodities, precious metals, gemstones, and collectibles. Before choosing a specific investment, you should evaluate all potential investments on the basis of safety, risk, income, growth, and liquidity. You should also diversify your investments to lessen risk. With all of these factors in mind, the next step is to develop a specific, personal investment plan to help you accomplish your goals.

Obj. 4   **Recognize the role of the professional financial planner and your role in a personal investment program.**

A qualified financial planner has had at least two years of training in securities, insurance, taxes, real estate, and estate planning, and has passed a rigorous examination. Financial planners can help people achieve their investment goals, but choosing a qualified planner is your responsibility. It is also your responsibility to evaluate and to monitor the value of your investments and to keep accurate and current records.

Obj. 5   **Use various sources of financial information that can reduce risks and increase investment returns.**

Because more information on investments is available than most investors can read and comprehend, you must be selective in the type of information you use for evaluation purposes. Sources of information include the Internet, newspapers and news programs, business periodicals, government publications, corporate reports, statistical averages, and investor services.

## Financial Planning Problems

1. *Calculating the Amount for an Emergency Fund.* Beth and Bob Martin have total take-home pay of $3,200 a month. Their monthly expenses total $2,800. Calculate the minimum amount this couple needs to establish an emergency fund. How did you calculate this amount? (Obj. 1)

2. *Using the Standard & Poor's Personal Wealth Website.* Visit the Standard & Poor's Personal Wealth Website and complete the five steps required to develop a financial plan. To complete this activity, follow these steps:   (Obj. 1)
   a. Go to www.personalwealth.com.
   b. Click on Plan and Recommendations. (Note: If you are not registered for the free services offered by this website, you will need to complete the registration process to obtain a user name and a password.)
   c. Read the introductory material and then click on the Create a Plan button at the bottom of this screen.
   d. Complete all five steps required to create your personalized financial plan. Answer all questions to the best of your ability.
   e. Take a moment and review, and, if necessary, revise your answers to all questions.
   f. Print out your financial plan.
   Based on the information contained in your financial plan, how can the savings and asset allocation recommendations help you obtain your investment goals? Explain your answers.

3. *Determining Interest and Approximate Bond Value.* Assume that three years ago, you purchased a corporate bond that pays 9.5 percent. The purchase price was $1,000. Also assume that three years after your bond investment, comparable bonds are paying 8 percent.   (Obj. 2)

   a. What is the annual dollar amount of interest that you receive from your bond investment?
   b. Assuming that comparable bonds are paying 8 percent, what is the approximate dollar price for which you could sell your bond?
   c. In your own words, explain why your bond increased or decreased in value.

4. *Analyzing Income and Growth Investments.*
   a. List three personal factors that might lead some investors to emphasize income rather than growth in their investment planning.
   b. List three personal factors that might lead some investors to emphasize growth rather than income.   (Obj. 2)

5. *Comparing Investment Alternatives.* Choose three of the investment alternatives presented in this chapter, then rank them from high to low on safety, risk, and liquidity. Assume that 3 is the highest score and 1 is the lowest score for each factor. Based on your ranking, which of the three alternatives would you choose for your own investment program? Why?   (Obj. 3)

6. *Developing a Financial Plan.* Assume you are single and have graduated from college. Your monthly take-home pay is $2,100, and your monthly expenses total $1,800, leaving you with a monthly surplus of $300. Develop a personal plan of action for investing like the one illustrated in Exhibit 13–6.   (Obj. 3)

7. *Monitoring an Investment's Financial Performance.* Based on the following information, construct a graph that illustrates price movement for a share of the New York Venture Mutual Fund. Note: You may want to review the material presented in the Financial Planning Calculations feature on page 428.   (Obj. 4)

| | | | |
|---|---|---|---|
| January | $18.70 | July | $16.10 |
| February | 18.00 | August | 15.50 |
| March | 20.30 | September | 16.40 |
| April | 21.35 | October | 16.90 |
| May | 19.50 | November | 18.40 |
| June | 17.80 | December | 17.20 |

8. *Using Financial Information.* Suppose you just inherited 500 shares of General Motors stock. List five sources of information you could use to evaluate your inheritance. Beside each source, briefly state how the information it contains could help in your evaluation.   (Obj. 5)

## Financial Planning Activities

1. *Using Investment Information.* Choose a current issue of *Kiplinger's Personal Finance Magazine, Money,* or *Consumer Reports* and summarize an article that provides suggestions on how you could use your money more effectively.   (Obj. 1)

2. *Planning for an Investment Program.* Assume you are 28 years old, your take-home pay totals $2,200 a month, you have monthly living expenses that total $1,200, your monthly car payment is $300, and your credit card debts total $4,900. Using the information presented in this chapter, develop a three-part plan to (*a*) reduce your monthly expense, (*b*) establish an emergency fund, and (*c*) save $4,000 to establish an investment program.   (Obj. 1)

3. *Using the Internet to Obtain Information about Money Management.* As pointed out at the beginning of this chapter, it doesn't make sense to establish an investment program until credit card and installment purchases are reduced or eliminated. While most people are responsible and make payments when they're supposed to, some people get in trouble. To help avoid this problem, each of the following organizations has a home page on the Internet:
   *Debt Counselors of America* provides information about how to manage consumer debt (www.dca.org).
   *Equifax* provides information about how you can obtain your credit report (www.equifax.com).
   *Finance Center, Inc.* helps you save money when purchasing, financing, or refinancing a new home, car, or credit card transactions (www.financenter.com).
   Choose one of the above organizations and visit its home page. Then prepare a report that summarizes the information provided by the organization. Finally, indicate if this information could help you manage your consumer debt.   (Obj. 1)

4. *Choosing Investment Alternatives.* From the investment alternatives described in this chapter, choose two specific investments you believe would help an individual who is 35 years old, is divorced, and earns $20,000 a year begin an investment program. Assume this person has $30,000 to invest at this time. As part of your recommendation, compare each of your investment suggestions on safety, risk, income, growth, and liquidity.   (Obj. 2)

5. *Choosing Investment Alternatives.* Choose one of the investment alternatives presented in this chapter (stocks, bonds, mutual funds, real estate, or speculative investments) and prepare a two-page report describing why this

investment would be appropriate for a woman who is 68 years old and has just lost her husband. Assume she is debt free and has inherited $175,000.   (Obj. 3)

6. *Explaining the Principle of Diversification.* Prepare a two-minute presentation describing why the principle of diversification is important when establishing an investment program.   (Obj. 3)

7. *Choosing a Financial Planner.* More than 200,000 people call themselves financial planners. Describe the process you would use to choose one financial planner to help you develop an investment program.   (Obj. 4)

8. *Reporting Investment Income for Tax Purposes.* Choose four of the following sources of investment income. Then describe how each type is taxed by the federal government.   (Obj. 4)
   *a.* Dividend income.
   *b.* Interest income.
   *c.* Rental income.
   *d.* Short-term and long-term capital gains.
   *e.* Capital losses.

9. *Using Investment Information.* Assume you have established an emergency fund and have saved an additional $12,000 to fund an investment in common stock issued by AT&T Corporation. Using the sources of information discussed in this chapter, go to the library and obtain information about this company. Summarize your findings in a three-page report describing AT&T's current operations and the firm's past and present financial performance. Finally, indicate if you would purchase AT&T common stock based on the information in your report.   (Obj. 5)

10. *Using Investment Information.* Each year the publishers of *Fortune* provide a special edition called the *Fortune Investor's Guide* devoted to helping people learn about different investment alternatives. At the time of publication of this text, the latest guide was published on December 20, 1999. Obtain a copy of either this guide or one published on a later date, and summarize one of the articles highlighting an investment that could help you reach your investment goals.   (Obj. 5)

11. *Using the Internet to Obtain Investment Information.* One of the most useful Internet search engines available is Yahoo. Visit the Yahoo Finance site (http://finance.yahoo.com). Then describe in a two-page report the type of information available and how it could help you become a better investor.   (Obj. 5)

# LIFE SITUATION CASE

## FIRST BUDGET, THEN INVEST FOR SUCCESS!

Joe and Mary Garner, married 12 years, have an eight-year-old child. Six years ago, they purchased a home on which they owe about $110,000. They also owe $6,000 on their two-year-old automobile. All of their furniture is paid for, but they owe a total of $3,170 on two credit cards. Joe is employed as an engineer and makes $48,000 a year. Mary works as a part-time computer analyst and earns about $18,000 a year. Their combined monthly income after deductions is $3,950.

About six months ago, the Garners had what they now describe as a "financial meltdown." It all started one Monday afternoon when their air conditioner stopped cooling. Since their home was only six years old, they thought the repair ought to be a simple one—until the repair technician diagnosed their problem as a defective compressor. Unfortunately, the warranty on the compressor had run out about three months before the compressor broke down. According to the technician, it would cost over $1,200 to replace the compressor. At the time, they had about $2,000 in their savings account, which they had been saving for their summer vacation, and now they had to use their vacation money to fix the air conditioner.

For the Garners, the fact that they didn't have enough money to take a vacation was like a wake-up call. They realized they were now in their mid-30s and had serious cash problems. According to Joe, "We don't waste money, but there just never seems to be enough money to do the things we want to do." But according to Mary, "The big problem is that we never have enough money to start an investment program that could pay for our daughter's college education or fund our retirement."

They decided to take a "big" first step in an attempt to solve their financial problems. They began by examining their monthly expenses for the past month. Here's what they found:

### Income (cash inflow)

| | | |
|---|---|---|
| Joe's take-home salary | $2,800 | |
| Mary's take-home salary | 1,150 | |
| Total income | | $3,950 |

### Cash outflows

Monthly fixed expenses:

| | | |
|---|---|---|
| Home mortgage payment, including taxes and insurance | $1,190 | |
| Automobile loan | 315 | |
| Automobile insurance | 130 | |
| Life insurance premium | 50 | |
| Total fixed expenses | | $1,685 |

Monthly variable expenses:

| | | |
|---|---|---|
| Food and household necessities | $ 480 | |
| Electricity | 115 | |
| Natural gas | 50 | |
| Water | 35 | |
| Telephone | 55 | |
| Family clothing allowance | 130 | |
| Gasoline and automobile repairs | 120 | |
| Personal and health care | 100 | |
| Recreation and entertainment | 600 | |
| Gifts and donations | 300 | |
| Minimum payment on credit cards | 80 | |
| Total variable expenses | | $2,065 |
| **Total monthly expenses** | | **$3,750** |
| **Surplus for savings or investments** | | **$ 200** |

Once the Garners realized they had a $200 surplus each month, they began to replace the $1,200 they had taken from their savings account to pay for repairing the air conditioner. Now it was time to take the next step.

## Questions

1. How would you rate the financial status of the Garners before the air conditioner broke down?
2. The Garners have a $200 surplus at the end of each month. Based on their current financial condition, what do you think they should do with this money?
3. The Garners' take-home pay is almost $4,000 a month. Yet, after all expenses are paid, there is only a $200 surplus each month. Based on the information presented in this case, what expenses, if any, seem out of line and could be reduced to increase the surplus at the end of each month?
4. Given that both Joe and Mary Garner are in their mid-30s and want to retire when they reach age 65, what type of investment goals would be most appropriate for them?
5. How does the time value of money concept affect the types of long-term goals and the investments that a couple like the Garners might use to build their financial nest egg?
6. Based on the different investments described in this chapter, what specific types of investments (stocks, mutual funds, real estate, etc.) would you recommend for the Garners? Why?

## VIDEO CASE    Fundamental of Investing

Why do we spend so much time on financial planning in this course?

Good question. Now for some answers. The fact is that a personal financial course is all about planning and investing. As illustrated in the video, personal financial planning is important because it allows you to manage your money to achieve personal economic satisfaction and provides funding for your investment program. The first step is always to perform a financial checkup. Specifically, you should

1. Develop a budget and determine if you can live within it.
2. Make sure you are adequately insured.
3. Establish an emergency fund.

Once you have completed the financial checkup and made any necessary changes in your spending patterns, you can establish investment goals. Factors that influence your investment goals include your age, how long before you need the money, and your tolerance for risk.

Based on your goals, and assuming you have accumulated the money needed to fund your investment program, it's time to make some investment decisions. Most beginning investors think all they have to do is find *one* good investment. Unfortunately, that's not true. A much better approach is to use asset allocation to minimize your risk. A simple definition of asset allocation is putting your investment dollars into different baskets. Separate "baskets" might include cash, stocks, bonds, mutual funds, and other investment alternatives. Specific investments within each category are chosen based on the individual investor's attitude toward safety and risk. As pointed out in the video and the text, safety in an investment means minimal risk of loss, while risk in an investment means a measure of uncertainty about the outcome. Today most investors break the risk factor into different components.

In addition to analyzing the risk/reward offered by different investment alternatives, many investors research different investment alternatives by visiting a college or public library or using the Internet. Other investors choose to use a financial planner, an investment manager, or other professionals. Once a decision to purchase a specific investment is made, good investors continue to evaluate their investments by monitoring the investments' value, keeping accurate records, performing financial calculations, and revising their goals if necessary. In some cases, it is necessary to sell one investment and purchase another.

## Questions

1. Assume you were just notified that you have inherited $5,000. What would you do with the money? Justify your answer.
2. Many individuals choose their own investments. Others use a financial planner, an investment manager, or other professional. Which approach seems right for you? How would you go about choosing a professional to help you make investment decisions?
3. As pointed out in the video case, an informed investor is a wise investor. Choose a specific investment alternative, and describe the types of information you could use to evaluate it. Where would you get this information?

## Creating an E-Plan: Financial Decisions Using the Web

### DEVELOPING AN INVESTMENT PLAN

An investment program should consider safety, current income, growth potential, liquidity, and taxes. Your ability to set financial goals and select investment vehicles is crucial to long-term financial prosperity.

Websites for Investment Planning

- Investment planning information at **www.personalwealth.com, www.quicken.com,** the FinanCenter at **www.financenter.com/,** "The Motley Fool" at **www.fool. com/,** the Cable News Network at **www.cnnfn.com,** Bloomberg Personal at **www.bloomberg.com,** Money Line at **www.moneyline.com,** the Daily Rocket at **www.dailyrocket.com,** and **www.investorama.com.**
- Current investment articles from *Money* magazine at **www.money.com,** *Kiplinger's Personal Finance Magazine* at **www.kiplinger.com,** *Business Week* at **www.businessweek.com,** *Worth* magazine at **www.worth.com,** and *Smart Money* at **www.smartmoney. com.**
- Basic information about investing at **www.investfaq.com.**
- Investment newsletters, glossary, market data, and financial calculators from the National Association of Securities dealers at **www.investor.nasd.com.**

- Information from the American Association of Individual Investors at **www.aaii.org.**
- Investment club information at **www.better-investing.org.**
- Information about online financial swindles from the Securities and Exchange Commission at **www.sec/gov.**

(Note: Addresses and content of websites change, and new sites are created daily. Use search engines to update and locate websites for your current financial planning needs.)

*PFP sheets: 55, 56, 57*

Short-Term Financial Planning Activities

1. Set investment goals for various financial needs (see PFP Sheet 55).
2. Assess various types of investments for market risk, inflation, interest rate risk, and liquidity (see PFP Sheet 56).
3. Identify and evaluate investment information sources. (See PFP Sheet 57.)

Long-Term Financial Planning Activities

1. Identify saving and investing decisions that would serve your changing life situations.
2. Develop a plan for revising investments as family and household situations change.

# Investing in Stocks

Can the Yahoo Internet search engine help you pick stocks that will increase in value? The answer is a definite yes. Today, a wealth of information is available on the Internet, and the Yahoo Finance website is an excellent place to start your search for a quality investment. That's what Jason Godwin did three years ago.

It all started when Jason, 26, moved to a small town in East Texas. While he enjoyed the more relaxed lifestyle, he missed a lot of the conveniences he took for granted when he lived in the metropolitan Dallas area. The convenience he missed the most was his trips to the public library. Ironically, he had never considered himself a bookworm, but he did enjoy researching different investments. Unfortunately, the local library in the nearest small town just didn't have the "stuff" that Jason used to make his investment decisions. In fact, it didn't even have a copy of *Moody's Handbook of Common Stocks* or *Value Line*, two sources he had become accustomed to using.

Jason quickly realized he would have to find other sources of information if he were to continue investing. A friend suggested that he consider going online, but Jason was reluctant. Just the thought of making important financial decisions based on information from cyberspace was frightening. But if he wanted current and valid information, he had to do something. So he purchased a computer and began surfing the Net for useful investment information. He found that by accessing the Internet, he could obtain more than enough information to evaluate stocks and other investments that caught his interest.

After five months of surfing the Net and examining different websites, Jason now uses the Yahoo Finance website as a starting point when evaluating potential stock investments. By simply entering Yahoo's address (http://finance.yahoo.com), typing in the name of a corporation or its stock symbol, and clicking his mouse, he can obtain information about management, new products and marketing activities, and financial data. Of particular interest to Jason are the recommendations made by brokers that follow a corporation's stock, the firm's earnings per share and earnings history, and access to research abstracts. And he can get current price information for a stock, along with graphs that show historical market values, current news about the firm, information submitted by the corporation to the Securities and Exchange Commission, a profile of the company, and messages posted by investors. Now Jason admits he has become a better investor than before he started using a computer. More important, his computer-based investment decisions are increasing in value.

## Questions

1. How important are evaluation of a stock issue and the financial condition of a company when making a decision to buy or sell the company's stock? Explain your answer.
2. If you needed to obtain financial data to make a decision to buy or sell a company's stock, would you go to the library or the Internet? Why?

SOURCE: Yahoo Finance website (http://finance.yahoo.com), August 15, 1999, Yahoo, Inc., 3420 Central Expressway, Santa Clara, CA 95051.

Reproduced with permission of Yahoo! Inc. 1999 by Yahoo! Inc. Yahoo! and Yahoo! Logo are trademarks of Yahoo! Inc.

## Learning Objectives

**Obj. 1**   Identify the most important features of common stock.

**Obj. 2**   Discuss the most important features of preferred stock.

**Obj. 3**   Explain how you can evaluate stock investments.

**Obj. 4**   Describe how stocks are bought and sold.

**Obj. 5**   Explain the trading techniques used by long-term investors and short-term speculators.

## COMMON STOCK

**Obj. 1**

Identify the most important features of common stock.

Many beginning investors face two concerns when they begin an investment program. First, they don't know where to get the information they need to evaluate potential investments. In reality, more information is available than most investors can read. And, as pointed out in the opening case, quality investment information is available not only in libraries but also on the Internet. Jason Godwin found more information than he needed to make informed investment decisions by accessing the Yahoo Finance website.

Second, beginning investors sometimes worry that they won't know what the information means when they do find it. Yet common sense goes a long way when evaluating potential investments. For example, consider the following questions:

1. Is an increase in sales a healthy sign for a corporation? (Answer: yes)
2. Should a firm's profits increase or decrease over time? (Answer: increase)
3. Should a corporation's earnings per share increase or decrease over time? (Answer: increase)

Although the answers to these questions are obvious, you will find more detailed answers to these and other questions in this chapter. In fact, that's what this chapter is all about. We want you to learn how to evaluate a stock and to make money from your investment decisions. That's the way it's supposed to work.

Investors provide the money; the corporation uses the money to generate sales and earn profits; and the stockholders earn a return on their investment. Today a lot of people buy and sell stocks. Why? The most obvious answer is simple: They want larger returns than those more conservative investments offer. As pointed out in the last chapter, significant differences exist between the rates of return offered by stock investments compared to those of corporate bonds and U.S. Treasury bills. Between 1926 and 1996, the common stocks included in the Standard & Poor's 500 Stock Index provided an average 10.7 percent annual return before adjusting for inflation and a 7.4 percent return after adjustment. During the same period, corporate bonds returned only 5.6 before adjusting for inflation and 2.4 percent after adjustment for inflation, and U.S. Treasury bills returned only 3.7 percent before adjustment and 0.6 percent after adjustment.[1] Clearly, stocks outperformed the more conservative investment alternatives.

**EXHIBIT 14-1**

A Common Stock
Certificate

Want more proof? Stocks, as measured by the same index, had a 19.18 percent average annual return before adjusting for inflation between 1982 and 1996. And during the last three years (mid-1996 to mid-1999), the stocks in the same index averaged an annual return of 29.70 percent.[2] Not bad when compared to returns offered by certificates of deposit and more conservative investments! However, before you decide to invest in stocks, you should realize that this type of investment involves more risk and greater potential for loss.

*securities* Investments, including stocks and bonds, mutual funds, options, and commodities, traded on securities exchanges or the over-the-counter markets.

The term **securities** encompasses a broad range of investments, including stocks and bonds, mutual funds, options, and commodities traded on security exchanges or the over-the-counter markets. In this chapter, we examine stocks. There are two types of stocks: common and preferred stock. We discuss common stock in this section and preferred stock in the next. Exhibit 14–1 shows a common stock certificate. Since common stockholders are the actual owners of the corporation, they share in its success. But before investing your money, it helps to understand why corporations issue common stock and why investors purchase that stock.

## Why Corporations Issue Common Stock

Corporations issue common stock to finance their business start-up costs and help pay for their ongoing business activities. Today corporations are classified as either private corporations or public corporations. A *private corporation* is a corporation whose stock is owned by relatively few people and is not traded openly in stock markets. A *public corporation* is a corporation whose stock is traded openly in stock markets and may be purchased by individuals. Public corporations may have thousands or even millions of stockholders. American Telephone & Telegraph, for example, has over 2 million stockholders, while General Motors has almost 1 million. Corporate managers prefer selling common stock as a method of financing for several reasons.

### A Form of Equity    Corporations don't have to repay the money a stockholder pays for stock. Generally, a stockholder in a public corporation may sell his or her stock to another individual. The selling price is determined by how much a buyer is

willing to pay for the stock. Simply put, if the demand for a particular stock increases, the market value of the stock will increase. If the demand for a particular stock decreases, the market value of the stock will decrease. Demand for a stock changes when information about the firm or its future prospects is released to the general public. For example, information about expected sales revenues, earnings, expansions or mergers, or other important developments within the firm can increase or decrease the demand for, and ultimately the market value of, the firm's stock.

### Dividends Not Mandatory

Dividends are paid out of profits, and dividend payments must be approved by the corporation's board of directors. Dividend policies vary among corporations, but most firms distribute between 30 and 70 percent of their earnings to stockholders. However, some corporations follow a policy of smaller or no dividend distributions to stockholders. In general, these are rapidly growing firms, like Amazon (online sales), Michaels (crafts), and Staples (office supplies), that retain a large share of their earnings for research and development, expansion, or major projects. On the other hand, utility companies and other financially secure enterprises may distribute 80 to 90 percent of their earnings. Always remember that if a corporation has had a bad year, dividend payments may be reduced or omitted. Although board members may vote to continue paying dividends when a corporation is operating at a loss, they often vote to completely omit dividend payments to stockholders.

### Voting Rights and Control of the Company

In return for the financing provided by selling common stock, management must make concessions to stockholders that may restrict corporate policies. For example, corporations are required by law to have an annual meeting at which stockholders have a right to vote, usually casting one vote per share of stock. Stockholders may vote in person or by proxy. A **proxy** is a legal form that lists the issues to be decided at a stockholders' meeting and requests that stockholders transfer their voting rights to some individual or individuals. The common stockholders elect the board of directors and must approve major changes in corporate policies. Typical changes in corporate policy include (1) an amendment of the corporate charter, (2) the sale of certain assets, (3) possible mergers, (4) the issuance of preferred stock or corporate bonds, and (5) changes in the amount of common stock.

Many state laws provide that a corporation may include a provision for preemptive rights in its corporate charter. A **preemptive right** is the right of current stockholders to purchase any new stock the corporation issues before it is offered to the general public. By exercising their preemptive rights, stockholders are able to maintain their current proportion of corporate ownership. This may be important when the corporation is small and management control is a matter of concern to stockholders.

Finally, corporations are required by law to distribute annual and quarterly reports to stockholders. These reports contain details about sales, earnings, and other vital information.

## Why Investors Purchase Common Stock

How do you make money by buying common stock? Basically, common stock investments can increase in three ways: income from dividends, dollar appreciation of stock value, and the possibility of increased value from stock splits.

### Income from Dividends

While the corporation's board members are under no legal obligation to pay dividends, most board members like to keep stockholders happy (and prosperous). Few things will unite stockholders into a powerful opposition

*proxy*   A legal form that lists the issues to be decided at a stockholders' meeting and requests that stockholders transfer their voting rights to some individual or individuals.

*preemptive right*   The right of current stockholders to purchase any new stock the corporation issues before it is offered to the general public.

TYPICAL INFORMATION ON CORPORATION DIVIDENDS AS PRESENTED IN THE WALL STREET JOURNAL

Republished with permission of Dow Jones, Inc. from *The Wall Street Journal,* January 31, 2000; permission conveyed through Copyright Clearance Center, Inc.

## CORPORATE DIVIDEND NEWS

### Dividends Reported January 28

| Company | Period | Amt. | Payable date | Record date |
|---|---|---|---|---|
| **REGULAR** | | | | |
| AMB Finl Corp | Q | .08 | 2 – 25 – 00 | 2 – 11 |
| Alexander&Baldwin | Q | .22½ | 3 – 2 – 00 | 2 – 14 |
| Allen Organ clB | Q | .14 | 3 – 3 – 00 | 2 – 18 |
| Analogic Corp | Q | .07 | 2 – 25 – 00 | 2 – 11 |
| Avery Dennison | Q | .27 | 3 – 15 – 00 | 3 – 1 |
| CENIT Bancorp | Q | .15 | 2 – 19 – 00 | 2 – 7 |
| Cabot Oil & Gas | Q | .04 | 2 – 25 – 00 | 2 – 11 |
| Cash America Intl | Q | .01¼ | 2 – 23 – 00 | 2 – 9 |
| Cleco Corp | Q | .41½ | 2 – 15 – 00 | 2 – 4 |
| Community Finl | Q | .08 | 2 – 23 – 00 | 2 – 9 |
| Correctional Props | Q | .36½ | 2 – 17 – 00 | 2 – 3 |
| D&E Communications | Q | .10 | 3 – 15 – 00 | 2 – 25 |

force more rapidly than omitted or lowered dividends. Therefore, board members usually declare dividends if the corporation's after-tax profits are sufficient for them to do so. Since dividends are a distribution of profits, investors must be concerned about future after-tax profits. In short, how secure is the dividend?

Corporate dividends for common stock may take the form of cash, additional stock, or company products. However, the last type of dividend is extremely unusual. If the board of directors declares a cash dividend, each common stockholder receives an equal amount per share. Although dividend policies vary, most corporations pay dividends on a quarterly basis. Some corporations, particularly those experiencing large swings in earnings, declare special year-end or extra dividends in addition to their regular quarterly dividends.

Notice in Exhibit 14–2 that AMB Financial Corporation has declared a quarterly dividend of $0.08 per share to stockholders who own the stock on the record date of February 11. The **record date** is the date on which a stockholder must be registered on the corporation's books in order to receive dividend payments. When a stock is traded around the record date, the company must determine whether the buyer or the seller is entitled to the dividend. To solve this problem, this rule is followed: *Dividends remain with the stock until two business days before the record date.* On the second day before the record date, the stock begins selling ex-dividend. Investors who purchase an ex-dividend stock are not entitled to receive dividends for that quarter, and the dividend is paid to the previous owner of the stock.

For example, AMB Financial declared a quarterly dividend of $0.08 per share to stockholders who owned its stock on Friday, February 11. The stock went ex-dividend on Wednesday, February 9, 2000, two *business* days before the February 11 date. A stockholder who purchased the stock on February 9 or after was not entitled to this quarterly dividend payment. AMB Financial made the actual dividend payment on February 25 to stockholders who owned the stock on the record date. Investors are generally very conscious of the date on which a stock goes ex-dividend, and the dollar value of the stock may go down by the value of the quarterly dividend.

*record date*  The date on which a stockholder must be registered on the corporation's books in order to receive dividend payments.

Dollar Appreciation of Stock Value    In most cases, you purchase stock and then hold onto that stock for a period of time. If the market value of the stock increases, you must decide whether to sell the stock at the higher price or continue to

**Sample Stock Transaction for Eastman Kodak**

**Assumptions**

100 shares of common stock purchased July 23, 1997, sold July 23, 1999; dividends of $3.52 per share for the two-year period.

| Costs when purchased | | Return when sold | |
|---|---|---|---|
| 100 shares @ $67 = | $6,700 | 100 shares @ $76 = | $7,600 |
| Plus commission | + 55 | Minus commission | − 80 |
| Total investment | $6,755 | Total return | $7,520 |

| Transaction summary | |
|---|---|
| Total return | $7,520 |
| Minus total investment | −6,755 |
| Profit from stock sale | $ 765 |
| Plus dividends | + 352 |
| Total return for the transaction | $1,117 |

hold it. If you decide to sell the stock, the dollar amount of difference between the purchase price and the selling price represents your profit.

Let's assume that on July 23, 1997, you purchased 100 shares of Eastman Kodak stock at a cost of $67 a share. Your cost for the stock was $6,700 plus $55 in commission charges, for a total investment of $6,755. (Note: Commissions, a topic covered later in this chapter, are charged when you purchase stock *and* when you sell stock.) Let's also assume you held your 100 shares until July 23, 1999, and then sold them for $76 a share. During the two-year period you owned Eastman Kodak, the company paid dividends totaling $3.52 a share. Exhibit 14–3 shows your return on the investment. In this case, you made money because of quarterly dividend distributions and through an increase in stock value from $67 to $76 per share. As Exhibit 14–3 shows, your total return is $1,117. Of course, if the stock's value should decrease, or if the firm's board of directors reduces or votes to omit dividends, your return may be less than the original investment. For help in deciding if it's time to sell stock, read the Financial Planning for Life's Situations box on page 446.

## Possibility of Increased Value from Stock Splits

*stock split* A procedure in which the shares of common stock owned by existing stockholders are divided into a larger number of shares.

Investors can also increase potential profits through a stock split. A **stock split** is a procedure in which the shares of stock owned by existing stockholders are divided into a larger number of shares. In 1999, for example, Tommy Hilfiger's board of directors approved a 2-for-1 stock split. After the stock split, a stockholder who had previously owned 100 shares now owned 200 shares. The most common stock splits are 2-for-1, 3-for-1, and 4-for-1.

Why do corporations split their stock? In many cases, a firm's management has a theoretical ideal price range for the firm's stock. If the market value of the stock rises above the ideal range, a stock split brings the market value back in line. In the case of Tommy Hilfiger, the 2-for-1 stock split reduced the market value to about one-half of the stock's previous market value. The lower market value for each share of stock was the result of dividing the dollar value of the company by a larger number of shares of common stock. Also, a decision to split a company's stock and the resulting lower market value makes the stock more attractive to the investing public. This attraction is based on the belief that most corporations split their stock only when their financial future is improving and on the upswing. As a result, investors have an expectation of future financial growth. This expectation of future growth can mean increases in the firm's sales and profits *and* increase in the market value of the firm's stock. *Be warned: There are no guarantees that a stock's market value will go up after a split.*

# Financial Planning for Life's Situations

## WHEN SHOULD YOU SELL A STOCK?

In January 1997, Martha Parker purchased 100 shares of stock of Johnson & Johnson, one of the world's largest pharmaceutical companies, for $49 a share. According to Martha, all the financial information about Johnson & Johnson looked good. Two years later, when the value of Johnson & Johnson had increased to $96 a share, Martha decided to sell the stock for a profit. During that two-year period, she had thought about selling her stock at least four times. But she just couldn't make the decision to sell.

According to financial experts, the value of a share of stock may go up or down, but investors like Martha Parker always have trouble deciding when to sell. Generally, most investors have a reason for buying a stock, but when it is time to sell that same stock, they are often blinded by a sense of loyalty to "their" investments, whether deserved or not. Although no sure cures for this problem exist, the following suggestions may help:

1. *Follow your stock's value.* Too often, investors purchase a stock and then forget about it. They assume everything is OK and the stock will magically increase in value. A much better approach is to graph the dollar value of your stock on a weekly basis.

2. *Watch the company's financials.* Smart investors evaluate a stock investment before they make it. The smartest investors use all the available information to continuously evaluate their stocks. If the amounts reported or projected for sales, profits, or other important financial measures are declining or are well below industry averages, it may be time to sell the stock. If you would not buy the same investment today, it's time to sell it no matter how much you have gained or lost.

3. *Track the firm's product line.* Simply put, if the firm's products become obsolete and the company fails to introduce state-of-the-art new products, its sales—and ultimately profits—may take a nosedive. The failure to introduce new products may destroy the firm's ability to compete.

4. *Monitor economic developments.* An economic recession or an economic recovery may cause the value of a stock investment to increase or decrease. For example, most consumers who are unemployed don't buy new cars. Therefore, manufacturing firms like General Motors or Ford may experience lower sales, lower profits, and lower stock values until the employment outlook brightens. Also, watch the inflation rate, interest rates, productivity rates, and similar economic indicators that may be a red flag.

5. *Be patient.* The secret of success for making money with stocks is time. As pointed out earlier in this chapter, stocks have returned over 10 percent before adjusting for inflation each year for over a 40-year period and, assuming you purchased good stocks, your investments will eventually increase in value.

A less common type of stock split occurs when the number of outstanding shares of common stock is reduced. This usually occurs when the market value of a corporation's stock has dropped to a point where the directors consider it too low. In a *reverse split,* stockholders exchange their shares for a proportionately smaller number of shares. As a result, the market value is adjusted upward by a proportionate amount.

## Concept Check 14–1

1. If you needed information about a stock investment, would you go to the library or the Internet. Why?
2. Why do corporations issue common stock?
3. What are the typical issues on which stockholders vote?
4. Describe three reasons stockholders purchase common stock.
5. Why do corporations split their stock? Is a stock split good or bad for investors?

# PREFERRED STOCK

## Obj. 2

Discuss the most important features of preferred stock.

*par value*  An assigned (and often arbitrary) dollar value that is printed on a stock certificate.

*callable preferred stock*  Stock that a corporation may exchange, at its option, for a specified amount of money.

In addition to or instead of purchasing common stock, you may purchase preferred stock. The most important priority an investor in preferred stock enjoys is receiving cash dividends before common stockholders are paid any cash dividends. This factor is especially important when a corporation is experiencing financial problems and cannot pay cash dividends to both preferred and common stockholders. Unlike the amount of the dividend on common stock, the dollar amount of the dividend on preferred stock is known before the stock is purchased. The dividend amount is either a stated amount of money for each share of preferred stock or a certain percentage of the par value of the stock. The **par value** is an assigned (and often arbitrary) dollar value that is printed on a stock certificate. For example, if the par value for a preferred stock issue is $50 and the dividend rate is 6 percent, the dollar amount of the dividend is $3 ($50 × 6% = $3).

Preferred stocks are often referred to as "middle" investments because they represent an investment midway between common stock (an ownership position) and corporate bonds (a creditor position). When compared to corporate bonds, the yield on preferred stocks is often smaller than the yield on bonds. When compared to common stocks, preferred stocks are safer investments that offer more secure dividends. They are often purchased by individuals who need a predictable source of income. They are also purchased by other corporations, because corporations receive a tax break on the dividend income from preferred stock. For all other investors, preferred stocks lack the growth potential that common stocks offer and the safety of many corporate bond issues. As a result, preferred stocks are generally considered a poor investment for most individuals.

While preferred stock does not represent a legal debt that must be repaid, if the firm is dissolved or declares bankruptcy, preferred stockholders do have first claim to the corporation's assets after creditors (including bondholders).

Generally, preferred stock is callable. **Callable preferred stock** is stock that a corporation may exchange, at its option, for a specified amount of money. To understand why a corporation would call in a preferred stock issue, you must first realize that dividend rates paid by similar investments increase and decrease. If dividends are decreasing and similar investments provide a smaller return than the corporation's preferred stock issue, management may decide to call in their existing preferred issue and substitute a new preferred stock that pays a lower dividend. Management may also decide to call in the preferred stock and issue common stock with no specified dividend. The dividend amount paid on a preferred issue can also affect the market value of the stock. For example, the preferred stock issue in the last example paid a 6 percent dividend. When the corporation issued that preferred stock, the 6 percent dividend was competitive with the dividends paid by corporations issuing preferred stocks at that time. If dividend rates on similar investments decrease, the market value of the 6 percent preferred stock issue will go up due to its higher dividend. On the other hand, if dividends paid on similar investments increase, the market value of the 6 percent preferred stock issue will fall due to its lower dividend rate.

When compared to corporations selling common stock, preferred stock is used less often by only a few corporations, Yet it is an alternative method of financing that may attract investors who do not wish to buy common stock. Preferred stock, like common stock, is equity financing that does not have to be repaid. And dividends on preferred stock, as on common stock, may be omitted by action of the board of directors.

Many small investors consider preferred stock to be as safe as corporate bonds. Generally, however, it is less safe, because corporate bonds represent borrowed money that must be repaid. Bondholders are more likely to receive interest payments until maturity and eventual repayment of their initial investment than preferred stockholders are to continue receiving dividends or recover their initial investment in the stock. To make preferred stock issues more attractive, some corporations may offer three additional features.

## The Cumulative Feature of Preferred Stock

*cumulative preferred stock*   Stock whose unpaid dividends accumulate and must be paid before any cash dividend is paid to common stockholders.

If the corporation's board of directors believes that omitting dividends is justified, it can vote to omit both the dividends paid to common stockholders and the dividends paid to preferred stockholders. One way preferred stockholders can protect themselves against omitted dividends is to purchase cumulative preferred stock. **Cumulative preferred stock** is stock whose unpaid dividends accumulate and must be paid before any cash dividend is paid to the common stockholders. If a corporation does not pay dividends to the cumulative preferred stockholders during one dividend period, the amount of the missed dividends is added to the following period's preferred dividends. If you own noncumulative preferred stock, an omitted dividend will not be made up later.

## The Participation Feature of Preferred Stock

To make a preferred stock issue more attractive, corporations sometimes add a *participation feature*. This feature allows preferred stockholders to share with the common stockholders in the corporation's earnings. Participating preferred stock is rare; this feature is used only when special measures are necessary to attract investors.[3]

The participation feature of preferred stock works like this: (1) The required dividend is paid to preferred stockholders; (2) a stated dividend, usually equal to the dividend amount paid to preferred stockholders, is paid to common stockholders; and (3) the remainder of the earnings available for distribution is shared by both preferred and common stockholders.

## The Conversion Feature of Preferred Stock

*Convertible preferred stock* can be exchanged, at the stockholder's option, for a specified number of shares of common stock. The conversion feature provides the investor with the added safety of preferred stock and the possibility of greater speculative gain through conversion to common stock.

All the information relating to the number of shares of common stock that may be obtained through conversion of preferred stock is stated in the corporate records and is usually printed on the preferred stock certificate. For example, assume Martin & Martin Manufacturing Corporation has issued a convertible preferred stock. Each share of preferred stock in this issue is convertible into two shares of common stock. Assume the market price of Martin & Martin's convertible preferred stock is $24 and the stock pays an annual dividend of $1.60 a share. Also assume the market price of the company's common stock is $9 and the common stock currently pays an annual dividend of $0.54 a share. Under these circumstances, you would keep the preferred stock. If the market price of the common stock increased to above $12 a share, however, you would have an incentive to exercise the conversion option.

The decision to convert preferred stock to common stock is complicated by three factors. First, the dividends paid on preferred stock are more secure than the dividends paid on common stock. Second, the amount of the dividend for preferred stock is generally higher than the amount of the dividend for common stock. Third, because of the conversion option, the market value of convertible preferred stock usually increases as the market value of common stock increases.

The next section discusses additional factors you should evaluate before purchasing either preferred stock or common stock.

## Concept Check 14-2

1. What is the most important priority a preferred stockholder has compared to common stockholders?
2. Why would a corporation call in preferred stock?
3. Why do corporations issue preferred stock?
4. Describe three features corporations can offer to make preferred stock more attractive.

## EVALUATION OF A STOCK ISSUE

**Obj. 3**
Explain how you can evaluate stock investments.

Many investors expect to earn a 10 percent or higher return on their investments, yet they are unwilling to spend the time required to become a good investor. In fact, many people purchase investments without doing *any* research. They wouldn't buy a car without a test drive or purchase a residence without comparing different houses, but for some unknown reason they invest without doing their homework. The truth is that there is no substitute for a few hours of detective work when choosing an investment. This section explains how to evaluate a potential stock investment.

A wealth of information is available to stock investors. Sources of this information include newspapers, the Internet, business periodicals, corporate reports, and investor services. Most local newspapers carry several pages of business news. *The Wall Street Journal* (published weekdays) and *Barron's* (published once a week) are devoted almost entirely to financial and economic news. And with the recent economic upturn, more people are using the Internet to evaluate or monitor the value of their investments. Obviously, different types of investments require different methods of evaluation, but a logical place to start the evaluation process for stock is with the classification of different types of stock investments.

### Classification of Stock Investments

When evaluating a stock investment, stockbrokers, financial planners, and investors often classify stocks into different categories. We describe eight commonly used classifications.

*blue-chip stock*   A safe investment that generally attracts conservative investors.

A **blue-chip stock** is a safe investment that generally attracts conservative investors. Stocks of this kind are issued by the strongest and most respected companies, such as AT&T, General Electric, and Kellogg. Characteristics to watch for when evaluating this type of stock include leadership in an industrial group, a history of stable earnings, and consistency in paying dividends.

*income stock*   A stock that pays higher-than-average dividends.

An **income stock** pays higher-than-average dividends. To be able to pay above-average dividends, a corporation must have a steady, predictable source of income. Stocks issued by Bristol-Myers Squibb, Dow Chemical, and Royal Dutch/Shell are often purchased for their higher-than-average dividends. Also, stocks issued by electric, gas, telephone, and other utility companies are generally classified as income stocks. Many investors seeking income may also include quality preferred stock issues in their portfolios.

*growth stock*   A stock issued by a corporation that has the potential of earning profits above the average profits of all firms in the economy.

A **growth stock** is issued by a corporation that has the potential to earn profits above the average profits of all firms in the economy. Key factors to evaluate when choosing a growth stock include an expanding product line of quality merchandise and an effective research and development department. Retail expansion, state-of-the-art manufacturing facilities, and expansion into international markets are also characteristic of growth stocks. In fact, most growth companies retain a large part of their earnings to pay for their research and development efforts. As a result, such companies generally pay out less than 30 percent of their earnings in dividends to their stockholders. In the late-1990s, typical growth stocks included Adobe Systems; Southwest Airlines; Just For Feet, Inc.; and Home Depot.

*cyclical stock*   A stock that follows the business cycle of advances and declines in the economy.

A **cyclical stock** follows the business cycle of advances and declines in the economy. When the economy expands, the market value of a cyclical stock increases; when the economy declines, the market value decreases. Most cyclical stocks are in basic industries such as automobiles, steel, paper, and heavy manufacturing. Investors try to buy cyclical stocks just before the economy expands and sell them just before it declines. Assuming the economy continues to expand, most financial experts are predicting that Ford (automotive), Phelps Dodge (metals), and Centex (construction) will increase in value because of increased demand for their products during the first part of the 21st century.

*defensive stock*   A stock that remains stable during declines in the economy.

A **defensive stock** remains stable during declines in the economy. Generally, companies that issue such stocks have a history of stable earnings and are able to maintain dividend payments to stockholders during periods of economic decline. Many stocks that are classified as income stocks or blue-chip stocks are also classified as defensive stocks because of their stable earnings and consistent dividend policies. Stocks in this classification include Procter & Gamble, Kellogg, and stocks issued by utility companies.

*large-cap stock*
A stock issued by a large corporation that has a large amount of stock outstanding and a large amount of capitalization.

*capitalization*   The total amount of securities—stocks and bonds—issued by a corporation.

*small-cap stock*   A stock issued by a company that has a capitalization of $150 million or less.

Stocks may also be classified as large caps or small caps. A **large-cap stock** is issued by a large corporation that has a large amount of stock outstanding and a large amount of capitalization. In financial circles, **capitalization** is usually defined as the total amount of securities—stocks and bonds—issued by a corporation. Typically, the companies listed in the Dow Jones averages are considered large caps. Because many large-cap stocks are often considered much more secure than small-cap stocks, they may appeal to more conservative investors. A **small-cap stock** is generally defined as a stock issued by a company that has a capitalization of $150 million or less. Since these stocks are issued by smaller companies, they tend to be more speculative and are often purchased by speculators hoping to make a quick profit.

*penny stock*   A stock that typically sells for less than $1 per share.

A **penny stock** typically sells for less than $1 a share.[4] These are stocks issued by new companies or companies with erratic sales and earnings. Therefore, penny stocks are more volatile than more conservative stocks. These stocks are classified as high-risk investments and are more difficult to research because information about them is hard to find. They are also more difficult to track, and dramatic increases and decreases in market value are common. Unfortunately, when the bubble bursts, these stocks can become worthless. As a result, penny stocks should by purchased only by investors who understand *all* the risks.

## How to Read the Financial Section of the Newspaper

Most metropolitan newspapers contain information about stocks listed on the New York Stock Exchange, the American Stock Exchange, and other major stock exchanges, and stocks of local interest. Although not all newspapers print exactly the same information, they usually provide the basic information. Stocks are listed alphabetically, so your first task is to move down the table to find the stock you're interested in. Then, to read the stock quotation, you simply read across the table. The first row in Exhibit 14–4 gives detailed information about Eastman Kodak. (Each numbered entry in the list below the enlarged stock table refers to a numbered column of the stock table.)

## EXHIBIT 14-4

Financial Information about Common Stock Given in The Wall Street Journal

Republished with permission of Dow Jones, Inc. from *The Wall Street Journal*, November 5, 1999; permission conveyed through Copyright Clearance Center, Inc.

| | 52 Weeks | | | | Yld | | Vol | | | | | Net |
|---|---|---|---|---|---|---|---|---|---|---|---|---|
| | Hi | Lo | Stock | Sym | Div | % | PE | 100s | Hi | Lo | Close | Chg |
| | 79¹³⁄₁₆ | 56⅝ | EKodak | EK | 1.76 | 2.9 | 14 | 13452 | 62¹³⁄₁₆ | 61¹⁄₁₆ | 61¾ | + ¹⁄₁₆ |
| | 103½ | 62 | Eaton | ETN | 1.76 | 2.5 | 8 | 3850 | 72¾₁₆ | 70 | 70¹⁄₁₆ | − 1⅜ |
| | 45 | 18¹⁄₁₆ | EatonVance | EV | .38 | .9 | ... | 403 | 41⅞ | 41⁹⁄₁₆ | 41½ | + ³⁄₁₆ |
| | 15⅝ | 10¾ | EtnVnc MIT | EVN | .83 | 7.0 | ... | 564 | 12 | 11¾ | 11¹³⁄₁₆ | − ⅛ |
| | 10 | 9⅛ | EatnVancInco | EVF | .89 | 9.2 | ... | 862 | 9¹¹⁄₁₆ | 9⁹⁄₁₆ | 9⅝ | ... |
| | 33⅜ | 18½ | EchelonInt | EIN | ... | 40 | 181 | 32½ | 32¹⁄₁₆ | 32½ | − ¹⁄₁₆ |
| | 44⁷⁄₁₆ | 31¹¹⁄₁₆ ♣ | Ecolab | ECL | .48f | 1.4 | 27 | 3621 | 35¹³⁄₁₆ | 33¾ | 34½ | − 1⁹⁄₁₆ |
| | 29⅝ | 21⅝ | EdisonInt | EIX | 1.08 | 3.8 | 14 | 8675 | 29 | 28¼ | 28¼ | − ¾ |
| | 38⁵⁄₁₆ | 24¼ ♣ | EdwardsAG | AGE | .60 | 1.8 | 9 | 3950 | 32¾ | 32⁹⁄₁₆ | 32⁷⁄₁₆ | − ⅝ |
| | 21⅜ | 16 | 1838BondFd | BDF | 1.45 | 8.7 | ... | 58 | 16¾ | 16¹¹⁄₁₆ | 16¾ | + ¹⁄₁₆ |
| n | 22 | 14¾ | Eircom ADS | EIR | .06p | ... | ... | 242 | 16⅝ | 15⅞ | 16⅜ | + ⅛ |
| n | 24¹³⁄₁₆ | 20¹⁵⁄₁₆ | EIX QUIPS A | | 1.97 | 9.0 | ... | 300 | 22 | 21¹¹⁄₁₆ | 22 | + ¼ |
| n | 25¼ | 23½ | EIX QUIPS B | | .19p | ... | ... | 121 | 24¾₁₆ | 24 | 24¾₁₆ | + ¹⁄₁₆ |
| | 28⅛ | 24⅜ | Eksprtfinans pf | | 2.18 | 8.7 | ... | 7 | 25¼ | 25 | 25 | ... |
| | 43⁷⁄₁₆ | 30⅝ | ElPasoEngy | EPG | .82f | 2.6 | 20 | 23792 | 32½ | 31¼ | 31¼ | − ⁵⁄₁₆ |
| | 25⅜ | 16¾ | ElPasoPtnr | EPN | 2.10 | 10.4 | 33 | 240 | 20⅜ | 19⅞ | 20⅛ | − ⅜ |

1. Highest price paid for one share of Eastman Kodak during the past 52 weeks: $79.81
2. Lowest price paid for one share of Eastman Kodak in the past 52 weeks:  $56⅝, or $56.63
3. Name of the company:  Eastman Kodak
4. Ticker symbol or letters that identify a stock for trading:  EK
5. Projected annual dividend for next year based on the amount of the firm's last dividend: $1.76
6. Yield percentage, or the percentage of return based on the dividend and current price of the stock:  $1.76 ÷ $61.75 = 0.029 = 2.9%
7. Price-earnings (PE) ratio—the price of a share of stock divided by the corporation's earnings per share of stock outstanding over the last 12 months:  14
8. Number of shares of Eastman Kodak traded during the day, expressed in hundreds of shares:  1,345,200
9. Highest price paid for one share of Eastman Kodak during the day:  $62¹³⁄₁₆, or $62.81
10. Lowest price paid for one share of Eastman Kodak during the day:  $61¹⁄₁₆, or $61.06
11. Price paid in the close transaction of the day:  $61¾, or $61.75
12. Difference between the price paid for the last share today and the price paid for the last share on the previous day:  + ¹⁄₁₆, or plus $0.06 (in Wall Street terms, Eastman Kodak "closed up ¹⁄₁₆" on this day)

If a corporation has more than one stock issue, the common stock is always listed first. Then the preferred stock issues are listed and are indicated by the letters *pf* behind the firm's name.

## The Internet

As pointed out in the last chapter, it is impossible to describe all of the websites that deal with personal finance and investments. We will examine some websites that are logical starting points when evaluating a stock investment, but there are many more than those described in this section. Let's begin with information about the corporation that is available on the Internet.

Today most corporations have a home page, and the information these pages provide is especially useful. First, it is easily accessible. All you have to do is use a search engine to locate the corporation's home page. Second, the information on the home page may be more up to date than printed material obtained from the corporation or outside sources. Finally, this information may be more complete than that in the corporation's annual report, quarterly report, or other publications. Look at the financial information for Microsoft displayed in Exhibit 14–5. By clicking on a button, you can access Microsoft's latest annual report, information on the firm's earnings, and other factors that could affect the value of the company's stock.

**FIGURE 14–5**

Financial
Information
Available on
Microsoft's
Investor Relations
Web Page

SOURCE: The Microsoft
Website (www.microsoft.
com) May 5, 2000,
Microsoft Corporation,
One Microsoft Way,
Redmond, Washington,
98052.

You can also use websites like Yahoo and other search engines to obtain information about stock investments. Take a look at a portion of the opening page of the Yahoo Finance website in Exhibit 14–6. This website provides a wealth of information. For example, under the research category on the left-hand side, there is a stock screener that will help you pick stock investments, information on upgrades and downgrades for specific stock issues, data on earnings, information the company has submitted to the Securities and Exchange Commission, financial information about the corporation, and historical market quotes. You can also get current market values by entering a corporation's stock symbol and clicking on the Get Quotes button. If you don't know the symbol, just click on the Symbol Lookup button and follow the directions. In addition to the current market value, the Yahoo Finance website provides even more specific information about a particular company. By clicking on the Profile, Research, News, SEC, Messages, or Insider information buttons, that are part of the screen for each corporation, it is possible to obtain even more information. How about picking a company like Texas Instruments (symbol TXN) or Home Depot (symbol HD) and going exploring on the Internet? To begin, enter the web address for Yahoo Finance (http://finance.yahoo.com). Then enter the symbol for one of the above corporations in the Get Quotes section. You'll be surprised at the amount of information you can obtain with a click of your mouse.

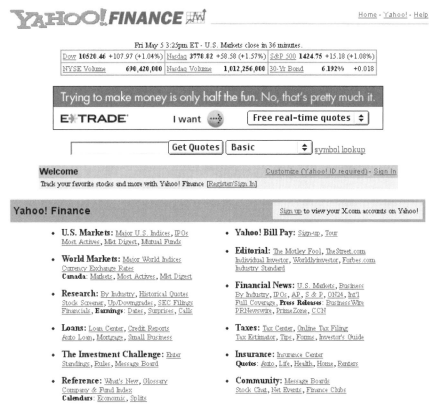

In addition, you can use professional advisory services like Standard & Poor's Financial Information Services (www.standardpoor.com), Moody's Investors Service (www.moodys.com), and Value Line (www.valueline.com). While some of the information provided by these services is free, there is a charge for the more detailed information you may need to evaluate a stock investment. For more information about professional advisory services and the type of information they provide, read the next section.

## Stock Advisory Services

In addition to newspapers and the Internet, sources of information you can use to evaluate potential stock investments are the printed materials provided by stock advisory services. In choosing among the hundreds of stock advisory services that charge fees for their information, you must consider both the quality and the quantity of the information they provide. The information ranges from simple alphabetical listings to detailed financial reports.

Standard & Poor's reports, Value Line, and Moody's Investors Service were briefly described in the last chapter. Here we will examine a detailed report for Reebok International, Ltd., a worldwide manufacturer and distributor of athletic footwear and apparel, that is published in *Moody's Handbook of Common Stock* (see Exhibit 14–7).

The basic report illustrated in Exhibit 14–7 consists of six main sections. The top section provides information about stock prices and capitalization, earnings, and dividends for Reebok. The "Background" section describes the company's major operations

## REEBOK INTERNATIONAL, LTD.

| EXCH. | SYM. | REC. PRICE | P/E RATIO | YLD. | MKT. CAP. | RANGE (52-WK.) | '98 Y/E PR. |
|---|---|---|---|---|---|---|---|
| NYSE | RBK | 18⅝ (6/30/99) | 23.3 | … | $1.05 bill. | 29¼ - 12⁹⁄₁₆ | 14⅞ |

MEDIUM GRADE. NEAR-TERM EARNINGS MAY BE DAMPENED BY A 10.4% DECREASE IN WORLDWIDE BACK-LOG OF OPEN CUSTOMER ORDERS.

**INTERIM EARNINGS (Per Share):**

| Qtr. | Mar. | June | Sept. | Dec. |
|---|---|---|---|---|
| 1995① | 0.80 | 0.26 | 0.96 | 0.02 |
| 1996 | 0.64 | 0.27 | 0.75 | 0.35 |
| 1997① | 0.69 | 0.35 | 1.26 | 0.01 |
| 1998① | d0.06 | 0.11 | 0.50 | d0.13 |
| 1999 | 0.32 | … | … | … |

**INTERIM DIVIDENDS (Per Share):**

| Amt. | Decl. | Ex. | Rec. | Pay. |
|---|---|---|---|---|
| Last div., 0.08Q, 9/11/96 | | | | |

**CAPITALIZATION (12/31/98):**

| | ($000) | (%) |
|---|---|---|
| Long-Term Debt .............. | 554,432 | 49.9 |
| Minority Interest .............. | 31,972 | 2.9 |
| Common & Surplus ......... | 524,377 | 47.2 |
| Total ............................. | 1,110,781 | 100.0 |

*7 YEAR PRICE SCORE 35.0      *12 MONTH PRICE SCORE 101.0
*NYSE COMPOSITE INDEX=100

### BUSINESS:

Reebok International, Ltd. is a worldwide designer, developer, marketer and distributors of sports, fitness and casual footwear, apparel and equipment under the REEBOK, ROCKPORT, and GREG NORMAN brands and footwear under the POLO RALPH LAUREN brand. Categories in the Reebok footwear division include: aerobic, tennis, fitness, running, basketball, cycling, volleyball, walking and children's ath-

letic footwear. The apparel division designs men's, women's and children's sportswear for aerobics, fitness and running in addition to offering casual clothes. The Rockport Co. is a market leader in casual and dress comfort shoes for men and women. Ellesse designs and markets high-end sports apparel, sportswear and athletic shoes. Avia Group International was sold in June 1996.

### RECENT DEVELOPMENTS:

For the quarter ended 3/31/99, net income totaled $17.9 million compared with a net loss of $3.4 million in the corresponding previous-year quarter. Results for 1998 included a special pre-tax charge of $35.0 million related to restructuring activities. Total revenues were $787.0 million, down 10.6% from $879.9 million a year ago. Worldwide

Reebok sales dropped 13.2% to $651.5 million compared with $750.5 million in the prior-year quarter. U.S. Reebok footwear sales declined 9.3% to $266.3 from $293.7 million in the first quarter of 1998. Sales of the Reebok brand outside the U.S. dropped 11.9% to $317.0 million versus $360.0 million a year earlier.

### PROSPECTS:

The overall industry outlook is not improving, and the economic conditions in certain regions may continue to negatively affect the Company's results. In addition, near-term earnings may be dampened by a 10.4% decrease in worldwide backlog of open customer orders. However, the Company plans to launch two new products durning 1999

for its Polo Ralph Lauren business. These new product introductions combined with a strong demand in the footwear division should benefit earnings going forward. Meanwhile, the Company will continue to focus on improving its operating cash while strengthening its balance sheet.

### ANNUAL FINANCIAL DATA:

| FISCAL YEAR | TOT. REVS. ($mill.) | NET INC. ($mill.) | TOT. ASSETS ($mill.) | OPER. PROFIT % | NET PROFIT % | RET. ON EQUITY % | RET. ON ASSETS % | CURR. RATIO | EARN. PER SH. $ | CASH FL. PER SH. $ | TANG. BK. VAL. $ | DIV. PER SH. $ | PRICE RANGE | AVG. P/E RATIO | AVG. YIELD % |
|---|---|---|---|---|---|---|---|---|---|---|---|---|---|---|---|
| 12/31/98 | 3,205.4 | ① 23.9 | 1,739.6 | 3.8 | 0.7 | 4.6 | 1.4 | 2.2 | ① 0.42 | 1.26 | 8.05 | … | 33³⁄₁₆ - 12⁹⁄₁₆ | 54.5 | … |
| 12/31/97 | 3,637.4 | ① 135.1 | 1,756.1 | 7.4 | 3.7 | 26.6 | 7.7 | 2.5 | ① 2.32 | 3.13 | 8.27 | … | 52⅞ - 27⅝ | 17.3 | … |
| 12/31/96 | 3,482.9 | 139.0 | 1,786.2 | 7.7 | 4.0 | 36.4 | 7.8 | 2.8 | 2.00 | 2.65 | 5.58 | 0.30 | 45¼ - 25⅜ | 17.7 | 0.8 |
| 12/31/95 | 3,484.6 | ① 164.8 | 1,656.2 | 10.5 | 4.7 | 18.4 | 10.0 | 3.1 | ① 2.07 | 2.57 | 11.11 | 0.30 | 39⅝ - 24⅛ | 15.4 | 0.9 |
| 12/31/94 | 3,287.6 | 254.5 | 1,649.5 | 13.0 | 7.7 | 25.7 | 15.4 | 2.6 | 3.02 | 3.46 | 11.05 | 0.30 | 40¼ - 28⅜ | 11.4 | 0.9 |
| 12/31/93 | 2,893.9 | ① 223.4 | 1,391.7 | 13.6 | 7.7 | 26.4 | 16.1 | 2.8 | ① 2.53 | 2.93 | 8.99 | 0.30 | 38⅝ - 23 | 12.2 | 1.0 |
| 12/31/92 | 3,060.6 | ① 114.8 | 1,345.3 | 14.0 | 3.8 | 13.7 | 8.5 | 2.7 | ① 1.24 | 1.72 | 8.23 | 0.30 | 35⅝ - 21⅜ | 23.0 | 1.1 |
| 12/31/91 | 2,736.1 | 234.7 | 1,430.8 | 14.9 | 8.6 | 28.5 | 16.4 | 2.4 | 2.37 | 2.76 | 6.36 | 0.30 | 35⅛ - 10¾ | 9.7 | 1.3 |
| 12/31/90 | 2,158.4 | 176.6 | 1,403.2 | 13.8 | 8.2 | 17.7 | 12.6 | 3.5 | 1.54 | 1.86 | 6.48 | 0.30 | 20 - 8⅛ | 9.1 | 2.1 |
| 12/31/89 | 1,833.5 | 175.0 | 1,166.4 | 16.0 | 9.5 | 20.7 | 15.0 | 3.9 | 1.53 | 1.78 | 5.12 | 0.30 | 19⅝ - 11⅛ | 10.0 | 2.0 |

**Statistics are as originally reported.** ① Incl. non-recurr. chrg. 1998, $35.0 mill.; 1997, $58.2 mill.; 1995, $72.1 mill.; 1993, $8.4 mill.; 1992, $155.0 mill.

**OFFICERS:**
P. B. Fireman, Chmn., Pres., C.E.O.
K. I. Watchmaker, Exec. V.P., C.F.O.
L. S. Vannoni, Treas.
B. Nagler, Sr. V.P., Gen. Couns.

**PRINCIPAL OFFICE:** 100 Technology Center Drive, Stoughton, MA 02072

**TELEPHONE NUMBER:** (781) 401-5000
**WEB:** www.reebok.com

**NO. OF EMPLOYEES:** 6,600 (approx.)

**SHAREHOLDERS:** 6,895

**ANNUAL MEETING:** In May

**INCORPORATED:** MA, Jul., 1979

**INSTITUTIONAL HOLDINGS:**
No. of Institutions: 135
Shares Held: 39,216,987
% Held: 70.1

**INDUSTRY:** Rubber and plastics footwear (SIC: 3021)

**TRANSFER AGENT(S):** BankBoston, N.A., Boston, MA.

in detail. It lists specific products, including footwear; apparel for men, women, and children; and other business lines that complement the firm's existing product line. The next section, "Recent Developments," provides current information about the company's net income and sales revenue. Reebok reported net income of $17.9 million during the quarter ended March 31, 1999. During the same period, sales decreased 10.6

## Financial Planning for Life's Situations

### GETTING TO THE BASICS OF ANNUAL REPORTS

One of the best resources you can use to determine the soundness of a stock investment is a corporation's annual report. These reports are an excellent tool for learning about a company, its management, its past performance, and its goals. But while thumbing through these glossy publications, you must always keep in mind that corporations use this medium to "toot their own horn." The letter from the chair of the board, the upbeat, smiling faces of the employees, and the artistic layout and beautiful photographs are nice to look at, but it's the accounting statements and footnotes that give the true picture of the financial health of a corporation. Understanding the items presented on these pages tucked away in the back of the report is the real key to determining if a company is making a profit. Once you know the basics of reading annual reports, you will be in a better position to evaluate different investment opportunities.

Experts recommend that before investing, you review and compare the annual reports a corporation has published over the last three years. Read the shareholders' letters to see if they met their goals each year. Are any areas of concern mentioned? Are the facts presented in a straightforward manner, or do you have to struggle to interpret their meaning? Learn to read between the lines to separate the hype from the truth. And watch for words like *except for, challenges,* and *contingencies.*

Next, turn to the statement of financial position (sometimes called the balance sheet). This is where you can compare the corporation's financial position by noting changes in its current assets, current liabilities, inventories, total liabilities, and owners' equity. Information on the income statement will enable you to determine if the corporation earned a profit. Be sure to look at the amounts reported for sales, expenses, and profit or loss figures.

Finally, don't overlook the footnotes: They contain (and sometimes hide) important information.

percent to $787 million. The "Prospects" section describes the company's outlook. It states, "The overall industry outlook is not improving, and the economic conditions in certain regions may continue to negatively affect the company's results." The "Statistics" section provides important data on the company for the past 10 years. Among the topics included in this section are total revenues, operating profit margin, return on equity, and net profit. The final section of the report states, among other things, when and where the company was incorporated, where its principal office is located, who its transfer agent is, and who its main corporate officers are.

Exhibit 14–8 on page 456 presents a detailed research report for Reebok published by Value Line. While other stock advisory services provide basically the same types of information as that in Exhibits 14–7 and 14–8, it is the investor's job to interpret such information and decide whether the company's stock is a good investment.

## Corporate News

As mentioned in Chapter 13, the federal government requires corporations selling new issues of securities to disclose information about corporate earnings, assets and liabilities, products or services, and the qualifications of top management in a prospectus that they must give to investors. In addition to a prospectus, all publicly owned corporations send their stockholders an annual report and quarterly reports that contain detailed financial data. Even if you're not a stockholder, you can obtain an annual report from the corporation. For most corporations, all it takes is a call to an 800 number. A written request to the corporation's headquarters can also help you obtain an annual report. To see how the information contained in an annual report can help you choose stock investments, read the accompanying Financial Planning for Life's Situations feature.

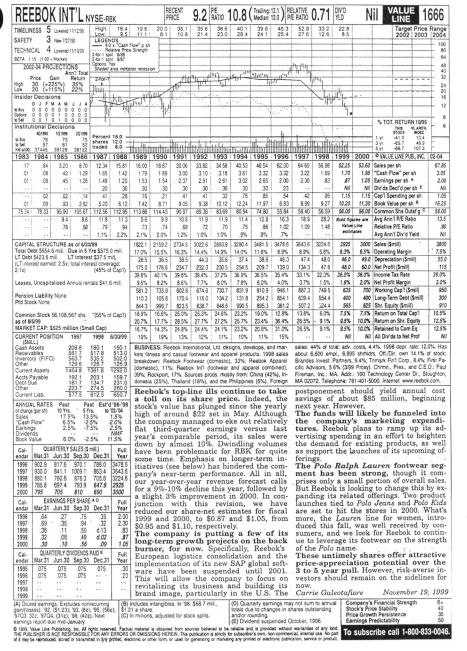

In addition to corporate publications, many periodicals can help you evaluate a corporation and its stock issues. *Business Week, Fortune,* and *Forbes* provide not only general economic news but detailed financial information about individual corporations. Magazines like *Money, Kiplinger's Personal Finance Magazine, Smart Money, Worth,* and *Consumer Reports* provide information to help you make informed investment decisions. Trade or industry publications like *Advertising Age* provide information about firms within a specific industry. Finally, news magazines like *U.S. News and World Report, Time,* and *Newsweek* feature financial news on a regular basis.

# Factors That Influence the Price of a Stock

*bull market*   Occurs when investors are optimistic about a nation's economy and buy stocks.

*bear market*   Occurs when investors are pessimistic about a nation's economy and sell stocks.

A **bull market** occurs when investors are optimistic about the nation's economy and buy stocks. In a bull market, the fact that more investors are buying stock causes the value of both individual stocks and the stock market as a whole to increase. A **bear market** occurs when investors are pessimistic about the nation's economy and sell stocks. Because more investors are selling stock, the value of both individual stocks and the stock market as a whole declines.

How do you determine whether it is the right time to buy or sell a particular stock? Many factors affect the market value of a stock. Therefore, you must also consider potential sales revenues, profits or losses, cash flow, and other important fundamentals when determining whether a stock will increase or decrease in value. In the remainder of this section, we examine numerical measures for a corporation and the fundamental, technical, and efficient market theories that investors use to determine whether a stock is priced right.

### Numerical Measures for a Corporation

*book value*   Determined by deducting all liabilities from the corporation's assets and dividing the remainder by the number of outstanding shares of common stock.

Although little correlation may exist between the market value of a stock and its book value, book value is widely reported in financial publications. Therefore, it deserves mention. The **book value** for a share of stock is determined by deducting all liabilities from the corporation's assets and dividing the remainder by the number of outstanding shares of common stock. For example, assume XYZ Corporation has assets of $6 million and liabilities of $3 million and has issued 100,000 shares of common stock. In this situation, the book value for a share of XYZ stock is $30 per share, as follows:

$$\frac{\overset{\textit{Assets}}{\$6,000,000} - \overset{\textit{Liabilities}}{\$3,000,000}}{100,000 \text{ shares of stock}} = \$30 \text{ per share}$$

Some investors believe they have found a bargain when a stock's market value is about the same as or lower than its book value. *Be warned:* Book value calculations may be misleading, because the dollar amount of assets used in the above formula may be understated or overstated on the firm's financial statements. For example, buildings are depreciated like the firm's other assets, yet buildings may increase, not decrease, in value. This dollar increase for buildings is not reported on a firm's financial statements. As a result, the book value may be incorrect. From a practical standpoint, most financial experts suggest that book value is just one piece of the puzzle and you must consider other factors along with book value when evaluating a possible stock investment.

*current yield*   The yearly dollar amount of income generated by an investment divided by the investment's current market value.

One of the most common calculations investors use to monitor the value of their investments is the current yield. The **current yield** is the yearly dollar amount of income generated by an investment divided by the investment's current market value. For example, assume you purchase stock in Ford Motor Company. Also assume Ford pays an annual dividend of $1.84 and is currently selling for $49 a share. The current dividend yield is 3.8 percent, calculated as follows:

$$\text{Current yield} = \frac{\text{Annual income amount}}{\text{Market value}}$$

$$= \frac{\$1.84}{\$49}$$

$$= 0.038, \text{ or } 3.8 \text{ percent.}$$

*total return*
A calculation that includes the yearly dollar amount of income as well as any increase or decrease in the original purchase price of the investment.

As a general rule, an increase in current yield is a healthy sign for any investment. A current yield of 6 percent is better than a 3.8 percent current yield.

Although the current yield calculation is useful, you should also consider whether the investment is increasing or decreasing in dollar value. **Total return** is a calculation that includes not only the yearly dollar amount of income but also any increase or decrease in the original purchase price of the investment. The following formula is used to calculate total return:

$$\text{Total return} = \text{Current return} + \text{Capital gain}$$

While this concept may be used for any investment, let's illustrate it by using the assumptions for Ford stock presented in the preceding example. Assume, in addition, that you own 100 shares of the stock that you purchased for $49.00 a share and hold your stock for two years before deciding to sell it at the current market price of $61.50 a share. Your total return for this investment would be $1,618, calculated as follows:

$$\text{Total return} = \text{Current return} + \text{Capital gain}$$

$$\$1,618 = \$368 \qquad + \$1,250$$

In this example, the current return of $368 results from the payment of dividends for two years ($1.84 per-share dividend $\times$ 100 shares $\times$ 2 years). The capital gain of $1,250 results from the increase in the stock price from $49 a share to $61.50 a share ($12.50 per-share increase $\times$ 100 shares = $1,250). (Of course, commissions to buy and sell your stock, a topic covered in the next section, would reduce your total return.)

In this example, the investment increased in value and the total return was greater than the current return. For an investment that decreases in value, the total return will be less than the current return. And while it may be obvious, we should point out that the larger the dollar amount of total return, the better.

*annualized holding period yield*   A yield calculation that takes into account the total return, the original investment, and the time the investment is held.

The **annualized holding period yield** calculation takes into account the total return, the original investment, and the time the investment is held. The following formula is used to calculate the annualized holding period yield:

$$\text{Annualized holding period yield} = \frac{\text{Total return}}{\text{Original investment}} \times \frac{1}{N}$$

where

$$N = \text{Number of years investment is held}$$

To illustrate this concept, let's return to your Ford investment, for which the total return was $1,618, the original investment was $4,900, and the holding period was two years. As shown below, the annualized holding period yield for this investment is 16.5 percent for each of the two years you held the investment:

$$\text{Annualized holding period yield} = \frac{\$1,618}{\$4,900} \times \frac{1}{2}$$

$$= 0.165$$

$$= 16.5 \text{ percent}$$

There is no meaningful average for annualized holding period yield because individual investments vary. But an increase in annualized holding period yield is a healthy sign. For instance, an annualized holding period yield of 16.5 percent is better than one of 11 percent. If you are trying to decide whether to sell or hold a stock, the annualized holding period yield can help you decide if it is time to sell.

*earnings per share*   A corporation's after-tax earnings divided by the number of outstanding shares of common stock.

**Earnings per share** are a corporation's after-tax earnings divided by the number of outstanding shares of common stock. For example, assume that in 2000, XYZ Corporation has after-tax earnings of $800,000. As mentioned previously, XYZ has 100,000 shares of common stock. This means XYZ's earnings per share are $8 ($800,000 ÷ 100,000 = $8). Most stockholders consider the amount of earnings per share important because it is a measure of the company's profitability. No meaningful average for this measure exists, mainly because the number of shares of a firm's stock is subject to change via stock splits and stock dividends. *As a general rule, however, an increase in earnings per share is a healthy sign for any corporation and its stockholders.*

The **price-earnings (PE) ratio** is the price of a share of stock divided by the corporation's earnings per share of stock outstanding over the last 12 months. For example, assume XYZ Corporation's common stock is selling for $96 a share. As determined earlier, XYZ's earnings per share are $8. XYZ's price-earnings ratio is therefore 12 ($96 ÷ $8 = 12). The price-earnings ratio is a key factor that serious investors use to evaluate stock investments. *A low price-earnings ratio indicates that a stock may be a good investment, and a high price-earnings ratio indicates that it may be a poor investment.* Generally, you should study the price-earnings ratio for a corporation over a period of time. For example, if XYZ's price-earnings ratio has ranged from 12 to 30 over the past three years, its current price-earnings ratio of 12 indicates that it is a potentially good investment. If XYZ's current price-earnings ratio were 27—toward the high end of the range—it may be a poor investment at this time. Although PE ratios vary by industry, they range between 5 and 35 for most corporations.

The **beta** is an index reported in many financial publications that compares the risk associated with a specific stock issue with the risk of the stock market in general. The beta for the stock market in general is 1.0. The majority of stocks have betas between 0.5 and 2.0. Generally, conservative stocks have low betas and speculative stocks have high betas. For example, assume XYZ Corporation's stock has a beta of 0.50. This means its stock is less responsive than the market. When the market in general increases by 10 percent, XYZ's stock will go up 5 percent. If, on the other hand, ABC Corporation has a beta of 2.0, this means ABC's stock is twice as responsive as the market. When the market in general decreases by 10 percent, ABC's stock will go down 20 percent. Take another look at the Value Line report in Exhibit 14–8. The beta for Reebok International is reported at the top on the left side and is 1.15. This means that if the stock market as a whole goes up 10 percent, the market value of Reebok's stock will increase 11.5 percent. If the value of the stock market as a whole decreases by 10 percent, the market value of Reebok's stock will decrease by 11.5 percent. Thus, the market value of Reebok's stock is slightly more volatile than the stock market as a whole. Because individual stocks generally move in the same direction as the stock market in general, most betas are positive, but it is possible for a stock to have a negative beta. A negative beta occurs when a corporation's stock moves in the opposite direction compared to the stock market in general.

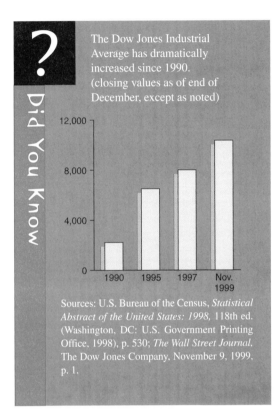

*price-earnings ratio*   The price of a share of stock divided by the corporation's earnings per share of stock outstanding over the last 12 months.

*beta*   An index that compares the risk associated with a specific stock issue with the risk of the stock market in general.

## DAVID JOHNSON ON WHY PEOPLE SHOULD CHOOSE STOCKS

Investments in stocks are growth oriented according to David Johnson, founder of Biznews—a firm that specializes in providing quality, up-to-the-minute financial news and economic analysis to radio and television stations. That is to say, stock investments generally don't pay a big dividend like a certificate of deposit or a bond does, but in return they will grow in value. A GOOD stock portfolio can grow 10 percent, maybe 15 percent a year.

Mr. Johnson is quick to point out another reason for investing in stocks: They can grow on a tax-deferred basis. If you have income from a certificate of deposit or a bond, you stop at the end of each year and pay tax on it. The nice thing about stock investments is that you don't pay any tax until you actually sell the investments. And when you do, assuming you've held those investments for at least 12 months, you pay taxes at a sharply reduced rate. So if you are growth-oriented, if you have a job, and don't have immediate demands for even a small portion of your income, stocks are a great way to build wealth.

To help ensure success, Mr. Johnson believes an investor must have reasonable expectations, be patient, and recognize the need for advice. Few individuals would sit down and craft their own will or fix their own car. Acting independently without professional help when building a diversified investment portfolio can be just as catastrophic. Reasonable expectation, patience, and outside help have proved to be a winning combination.

---

*fundamental theory*
An investment theory based on the assumption that a stock's intrinsic or real value is determined by the company's future earnings.

*technical theory*
An investment theory based on the assumption that a stock's market value is determined by the forces of supply and demand in the stock market as a whole.

*efficient market theory*
An investment theory based on the assumption that stock price movements are purely random; also called the *random walk theory.*

**Sheet 58**

## Investment Theories

Investors sometimes use three different investment theories to determine a stock's value. The **fundamental theory** is based on the assumption that a stock's intrinsic or real value is determined by the company's future earnings. If a corporation's expected earnings are higher than its present earnings, the corporation's stock should increase in value. If its expected earnings are lower than its present earnings, the stock should decrease in value. In addition to expected earnings, fundamentalists consider (1) the financial strength of the company, (2) the type of industry the company is in, (3) new-product development, and (4) the economic growth of the overall economy.

The **technical theory** is based on the assumption that a stock's market value is determined by the forces of supply and demand in the stock market as a whole. It is based *not* on the expected earnings or the intrinsic value of an individual corporation's stock but on factors found in the market as a whole. Typical technical factors are the total number of shares traded, the number of buy orders, and the number of sell orders over a period of time. Technical analysts, sometimes called *chartists,* construct charts that plot past price movements and other market averages. These charts allow them to observe trends and patterns for the market as a whole that enable them to predict whether a specific stock's market value will increase or decrease.

The **efficient market theory,** sometimes called the *random walk theory,* is based on the assumption that stock price movements are purely random. Advocates of the efficient market theory assume the stock market is completely efficient and buyers and sellers have considered all of the available information about an individual stock. Any news on an individual corporation, an oil embargo, or a change in the tax laws that may affect the value of a stock is quickly absorbed by all investors seeking a profit. Thus, a stock's current market price reflects its true value. The efficient market theory rejects

# Financial Planning Calculations

## EVALUATING CORPORATE STOCK

No checklist can serve as a fool-proof guide for choosing a common or preferred stock. However, the following questions will help you evaluate a potential stock investment.

### CATEGORY 1: THE BASICS

1. What is the corporation's name? _____
_____

2. What are the corporation's address and telephone number? _____
_____

3. Have you requested the latest annual report and quarterly report?  ☐ Yes  ☐ No

4. What information about the corporation is available on the Internet? _____
_____

5. Where is the stock traded? _____
_____

6. What types of products or services does this firm provide? _____
_____

7. Briefly describe the prospects for this company. (Include significant factors like product development, plans for expansion, plans for mergers, etc.)
_____
_____
_____

### CATEGORY 2: DIVIDEND INCOME

8. Is the corporation currently paying dividends? If so, how much? _____

9. What is the current yield for this stock? _____

10. Has the dividend payout increased or decreased over the past seven years? _____

11. How does the yield for this investment compare with those for other potential investments? _____
_____

### CATEGORY 3: FINANCIAL PERFORMANCE

12. Is the corporation profitable? What are the firm's earnings per share for the last 3 years? _____
_____

13. Have profits increased over the last seven years? ☐ Yes  ☐ No

14. What is the 52-week high and low for this stock? What is the stock's current price? _____
_____

15. What is the firm's beta? _____

16. What is the firm's current PE ratio? _____

17. How does the firm's PE ratio compare with other firms in general? With other firms in the same industry? _____
_____
_____

18. Are this year's sales higher than last year's sales?  ☐ Yes  ☐ No

19. Have sales increased over the last seven years? ☐ Yes  ☐ No

20. Briefly describe any other information that you obtained from Moody's, Value Line, Standard & Poor's, or other stock advisory services. _____
_____
_____
_____
_____
_____

### A WORD OF CAUTION

When you use a checklist, there is always a danger of overlooking important relevant information. The above checklist is not all-inclusive, but it does provide some very sound questions that you should answer before making a decision to invest in stock. Quite simply, it is a place to start. If you need other information, *you* are responsible for obtaining it and for determining how it affects your potential investment.

both the fundamental theory and the technical theory. According to this theory, it is impossible for an investor to outperform the average for the stock market as a whole over a long period of time.

Before completing this section, you may want to examine the accompanying Financial Planning Calculations box.

Concept Check 14-3

1. What sources of information would you use to evaluate a stock issue?
2. How would you define (1) a blue-chip stock, (2) an income stock, (3) a growth stock, (4) a cyclical stock, (5) a defensive stock, (6) a penny stock, (7) a large-cap stock, and (8) a small-cap stock?
3. What are the formulas for current yield, total return, annualized holding period yield, book value, earnings per share, and price-earnings ratio?
4. Do you think the fundamental theory, the technical theory, or the efficient market theory best describes price movements for the stock market? Why?

# BUYING AND SELLING STOCKS

## Obj. 4
Describe how stocks are bought and sold.

*primary market*
A market in which an investor purchases financial securities, via an investment bank or other representative, from the issuer of those securities.

*investment bank*
A financial firm that assists corporations in raising funds, usually by helping to sell new security issues.

*initial public offering (IPO)*   Occurs when a corporation sells stock to the general public for the first time.

To purchase a pair of Levi Strauss jeans, you simply walk into a store that sells Levi's, choose a pair, and pay for your purchase. To purchase common or preferred stock, you generally have to work through a brokerage firm. In turn, your brokerage firm must buy the stock in either the primary or secondary market. In the **primary market,** you purchase financial securities, via an investment bank or other representative, from the issuer of those securities. An **investment bank** is a financial firm that assists corporations in raising funds, usually by helping to sell new security issues.

New security issues sold through an investment bank can be issued by corporations that have sold stocks and bonds before and need to sell new issues to raise additional financing. The new securities can also be initial public offerings. An **initial public offering (IPO)** occurs when a corporation sells stock to the general public for the first time. During the first 11 months of 1999, 502 companies used IPOs to raise almost $100 billion to fund new business start-ups or finance new corporate growth and expansion.[5] And during November 1999, one corporation—United Parcel Service—raised over $5 billion and currently holds the record as the largest American IPO ever. Other highly visible companies that have sold stock to raise capital include Home Depot, Microsoft, Lucent Technologies, and America Online. Investors bought these stocks through brokerage firms acting as agents for an investment banking firm, and the money they paid for common stock flowed to the corporations that issued the stock. Because these companies used the financing obtained through IPOs wisely, they have grown and prospered, and investors have profited from their IPO investments. However, not all companies that use IPOs to raise capital are good investments.

*Be warned:* The promise of quick profits often lures investors to purchase IPOs. An IPO is generally classified as a high-risk investment—one made in the hope of earning a relatively large profit in a short time. Depending on the corporation selling the new security, IPOs are usually too risky for most people.

*secondary marktet*
A market for existing financial securities that are currently traded among investors.

After a stock has been sold through the primary market, it is traded through the secondary market. The **secondary market** is a market for existing financial securities that are currently traded among investors. Once the stocks are sold in the primary market, they can be sold time and again in the secondary market. The fact that stocks can be sold in the secondary market improves the liquidity of stock investments because the money you pay for stock goes to the seller of the stock.

## Primary Markets for Stocks

How would you sell $100 million worth of common stocks or preferred stocks? For a large corporation, the decision to sell stocks is often complicated, time consuming, and expensive. There are basically two methods.

First, a large corporation may use an investment bank to sell and distribute the new stock issue. Most large corporations that need a lot of financing use this method. If this method is used, analysts for the investment bank examine the corporation's financial position to determine whether the new issue is financially sound and how difficult it will be to sell.

If the investment bank is satisfied that the new stock is a good risk, it will buy the stock and then resell it to its customers—commercial banks, insurance companies, pension funds, mutual funds, and the general public. The investment bank's commission, or spread, ranges from less than 1 percent for a utility firm to as much as 25 percent for a small company selling stock for the first time.[6] The size of the spread depends on the quality and financial health of the issuing corporation. The commission allows the investment bank to make a profit while guaranteeing that the corporation will receive the financing it needs.

If the investment bank's analysts believe the new issue will be difficult to sell, the investment bank may agree to take the stock on a best-efforts basis, without guaranteeing that the stock will be sold. Because the corporation must take back any unsold stocks after a reasonable time, most large corporations are unwilling to accept this arrangement. If the stock issue is too large for one investment bank, a group of investment bankers may form an *underwriting syndicate*. Then each member of the syndicate is responsible for selling only a part of the new issue.

The second method used by a corporation trying to obtain financing through the primary market is to sell directly to current stockholders. Usually promotional materials describing the new stock issue are mailed to current stockholders. These stockholders may then purchase the stock directly from the corporation.

You may ask, "Why would a corporation try to sell its own stock?" The most obvious reason for doing so is to avoid the investment bank's commission. Of course, a corporation's ability to sell a new stock issue without the aid of an investment bank is tied directly to investors' perception of the corporation's financial health.

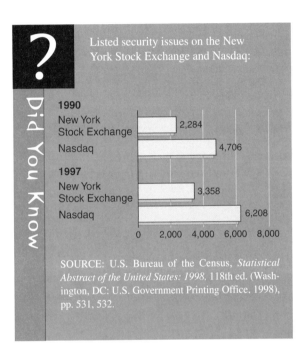

Listed security issues on the New York Stock Exchange and Nasdaq:

**1990**
New York Stock Exchange 2,284
Nasdaq 4,706

**1997**
New York Stock Exchange 3,358
Nasdaq 6,208

SOURCE: U.S. Bureau of the Census, *Statistical Abstract of the United States: 1998*, 118th ed. (Washington, DC: U.S. Government Printing Office, 1998), pp. 531, 532.

## Secondary Markets for Stocks

How do you buy or sell stock in the secondary market? To purchase common or preferred stock, you usually have to work with an employee of a brokerage firm who will buy or sell for you in a securities marketplace, at a securities exchange or through the over-the-counter market.

*securities exchange*
A marketplace where member brokers who represent investors meet to buy and sell securities.

### Securities Exchanges
A **securities exchange** is a marketplace where member brokers who represent investors meet to buy and sell securities. The securities sold at a particular exchange must first be listed, or accepted for trading, at that exchange. Generally, the securities issued by nationwide corporations are traded at either the New York Stock Exchange or the American Stock Exchange. The securities of regional corporations are traded at smaller, regional exchanges. These exchanges are located in Chicago, San Francisco, Philadelphia, Boston, and several other cities. The securities

of very large corporations may be traded at more than one exchange. American firms that do business abroad may also be listed on foreign securities exchanges—in Tokyo, London, or Paris, for example.

The New York Stock Exchange (NYSE) is one of the largest securities exchanges in the world. This exchange lists stocks for over 3,000 corporations with a total market value of about $16 trillion.[7] The NYSE has 1,366 members, or *seats*. Most of these members represent brokerage firms that charge commissions on security trades made by their representatives for their customers. Other members are called *specialists* or *specialist firms*. A **specialist** is an individual on the floor of the exchange who buys *or* sells a particular stock in an effort to maintain an orderly market.

*specialist* An individual on the floor of the exchange who buys or sells a particular stock in an effort to maintain an orderly market.

The cost of a seat is determined largely by sales volume and stock prices on the exchange. The lowest price for a seat on the NYSE in the 1900s was $17,000, paid in 1942. In the late 1990s, a seat sold for approximately $1 million.

Before a corporation's stock is approved for listing on the NYSE, the corporation must meet five criteria:[8]

1. Its annual earnings before income taxes must be at least $2.5 million in the most recent year.
2. It must own net tangible assets valued at $60 million or more.
3. The market value of its publicly held stock must equal or exceed $60 million.
4. At least 1.1 million shares of its common stock must be publicly owned.
5. At least 2,000 stockholders must each own 100 or more shares of its stock.

The American Stock Exchange (AMEX) and various regional exchanges also have listing requirements, but typically these are less stringent than the NYSE requirements. The stock of corporations that cannot meet the NYSE requirements, find it too expensive to be listed on the NYSE, or choose not to be listed on the NYSE is often traded on the American Stock Exchange, on one of the regional exchanges, or through the over-the-counter market.

## The Over-the-Counter Market

*over-the-counter (OTC) market* A network of dealers who buy and sell the stocks of corporations that are not listed on a securities exchange.

*Nasdaq (pronounced "nazzdack")* An electronic marketplace for over 6,000 stocks.

Not all securities are traded on organized exchanges. Stocks issued by several thousand companies are traded in the over-the-counter market. The **over-the-counter (OTC) market** is a network of dealers who buy and sell the stocks of corporations that are not listed on a securities exchange. Today these stocks are not really traded over the counter. The term was coined more than 100 years ago when securities were sold "over the counter" in stores and banks.

Most over-the-counter securities are traded through Nasdaq (pronounced "nazzdack"). **Nasdaq** is an electronic marketplace for over 6,000 different stocks. In addition to providing price information, this computerized system allows investors to buy and sell shares of companies listed on Nasdaq. When you want to buy or sell shares of a company that trades on Nasdaq—say, Microsoft—your account executive sends your order into the Nasdaq computer system, where it shows up on the screen with all the other orders from people who want to buy or sell Microsoft. Then a Nasdaq dealer (sometimes referred to as a *market maker*) sitting at a computer terminal matches buy and sell orders for Microsoft. Once a match is found, your order is completed.

Begun in 1971 and regulated by the National Association of Securities Dealers, Nasdaq is the third largest securities market in the world in terms of volume, trailing only the NYSE and Tokyo Stock Exchange. It is known for its innovative, forward-looking growth companies. Although many securities are issued by smaller companies, some large firms, including Intel, Microsoft, MCI, Apple Computer, and Cisco Systems, also trade on Nasdaq. In 1998, the National Association of Securities Dealers and the American Stock Exchange merged to create the Nasdaq–AMEX Market Group.

## Brokerage Firms and Account Executives

An **account executive,** or *stockbroker,* is a licensed individual who buys or sells securities for his or her clients. (Actually, *account executive* is the more descriptive title because such individuals handle all types of securities, not just stocks.) While all account executives can buy or sell stock for clients, most investors expect more from their account executives. Ideally, an account executive should provide information and advice to be used in evaluating potential investments. Many investors begin their search for an account executive by asking friends or business associates for recommendations. This is a logical starting point, but remember that some account executives are conservative while others are more risk oriented.

Before choosing an account executive, you should have already determined your short-term and long-term financial objectives. Then you must be careful to communicate those objectives to the account executive so that he or she can do a better job of advising you. Needless to say, account executives may err in their investment recommendations. To help avoid a situation in which your account executive's recommendations are automatically implemented, you should be *actively* involved in the decisions of your investment program and you should never allow your account executive to use his or her discretion without your approval. Watch your account for signs of churning. **Churning** is excessive buying and selling of securities to generate commissions. From a total dollar return standpoint, this practice usually leaves the client worse off or at least no better off. Churning is illegal under the rules established by the Securities and Exchange Commission; however, it may be difficult to prove. Finally, keep in mind that account executives generally are not liable for client losses that result from their recommendations. In fact, most brokerage firms require new clients to sign a statement in which they promise to submit any complaints to an arbitration board. This arbitration clause generally prevents a client from suing an account executive or a brokerage firm. Above all, remember you are investing *your* money and you should make the final decisions with the help of your account executive.

## Should You Use a Full-Service or a Discount Brokerage Firm?

Today a healthy competition exists between full-serve brokerage firms and discount brokerage firms. While the most obvious difference between full-service and discount firms is the amount of the commissions they charge when you buy or sell stock and other securities, there are at least three other factors to consider. First, consider how much research information is available and how much it costs. Both types of brokerage firms offer excellent research materials, but you are more likely to pay extra for information if you choose a discount brokerage firm. While most discount brokerage firms don't charge a lot of money for research reports, the fees can mount up over time and can offset the lower commissions they charge to buy or sell stock.

Second, consider how much help you need when making an investment decision. Many full-service brokerage firms argue that you need a professional to help you make important investment decisions. While this may be true for some investors, most account executives employed by full-service brokerage firms are too busy to spend unlimited time with you on a one-on-one basis, especially if you are investing a small amount. Still, the full-service account executive is there to answer questions and make investment recommendations. On the other side, many discount brokerage firms argue that you alone are responsible for making your investment decisions. They are quick to point out that the most successful investors are the ones involved in their investment programs. And they argue that they have both personnel and materials dedicated to helping you learn how to become a better investor.

Finally, consider how easy it is to buy and sell stock and other securities when using either a full-service or discount brokerage firm. Questions to ask include:

1. Can I buy or sell stocks over the phone?
2. Can I trade stocks online?
3. Where is your nearest office located?
4. Do you have a toll-free telephone number for customer use?
5. How often do I get statements?
6. Is there a charge for statements, research reports, and other financial reports?
7. Are there any fees in addition to the commissions I pay when I buy or sell stocks?

## A Sample Stock Transaction

Once you and your account executive have decided on a particular transaction, it is time to execute an order to buy or sell. Today most investors either telephone their account executives or use the Internet and trade online. Let's begin by examining three types of orders used to trade stocks.

*market order*   A request to buy or sell a stock at the current market value.

A **market order** is a request to buy or sell a stock at the current market value. Since the stock exchange is an auction market, the account executive's representative will try to get the best price available and the transaction will be completed as soon as possible.

Exhibit 14–9 illustrates one method for executing a market order to sell stock. You should note two things. First, every stock listed on the NYSE is traded at a specific computer-equipped trading post on the floor of the exchange. A computer monitor above the post indicates current price information for all stocks traded at each trading post. Second, each transaction is recorded, and the pertinent information (stock symbol, number of shares, and price) is transmitted to interested parties through a communications network called a *ticker tape*. A variation of this procedure that is used on the New York Stock Exchange is called the *Super Designated Order Turnaround System* (sometimes referred to as the *Super Dot System*). Orders to buy or sell stock, up to specified sizes in virtually all listed stocks, are transmitted electronically to the proper trading floor post. Then a specialist executes the orders as quickly as market interest and activity permit. Installed to deal with increasing daily stock volume on the New York Stock Exchange, the Super Dot System can handle daily volume exceeding 2 billion shares. Payment for stocks is generally required within three business days of the transaction. Then, in about four to six weeks, a stock certificate is sent to the purchaser of the stock, unless the securities are left with the brokerage firm for safekeeping. Today it is common practice for investors to leave stock certificates with a brokerage firm. Because the stock certificates are in the broker's care, transfers when the stock is sold are much easier. The phrase "left in the street name" is used to describe investor-owned securities held by a brokerage firm.

*limit order*   A request to buy or sell a stock at a specified price.

A **limit order** is a request to buy or sell a stock at a specified price. When you purchase stock, a limit order ensures that you will buy at the best possible price but not above a specified dollar amount. When you sell stock, a limit order ensures that you will sell at the best possible price, but not below a specified dollar amount. For example, if you place a limit order to buy Kellogg common stock for $34 a share, the stock will not be purchased until the price drops to $34 a share or lower. Likewise, if your limit order is to sell Kellogg for $34 a share, the stock will not be sold until the price rises to $34 a share or higher. *Be warned:* Limit orders are executed if and when the specified price or better is reached and *all* other previously received orders have been

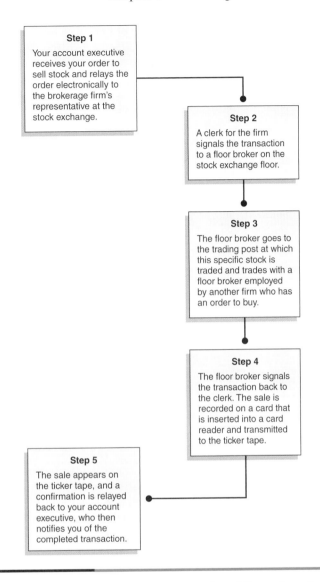

**EXHIBIT 14-9**

Steps in a Typical
Transaction for
Stock Traded on
the New York
Stock Exchange

**Step 1**
Your account executive receives your order to sell stock and relays the order electronically to the brokerage firm's representative at the stock exchange.

**Step 2**
A clerk for the firm signals the transaction to a floor broker on the stock exchange floor.

**Step 3**
The floor broker goes to the trading post at which this specific stock is traded and trades with a floor broker employed by another firm who has an order to buy.

**Step 4**
The floor broker signals the transaction back to the clerk. The sale is recorded on a card that is inserted into a card reader and transmitted to the ticker tape.

**Step 5**
The sale appears on the ticker tape, and a confirmation is relayed back to your account executive, who then notifies you of the completed transaction.

fulfilled. Let's assume you enter a limit order to purchase Microsoft stock at $90. If the stock drops to $90, all purchase orders will be filled in the sequence in which they were received. If the price of Microsoft begins to increase before your order can be filled, you may miss an investment opportunity because you were unable to buy the stock at the specified price.

Many stockholders are certain they want to sell their stock if it reaches a specified price. A limit order does not guarantee this will be done. With a limit order, as mentioned above, orders by other investors may be placed ahead of your order. If you want to guarantee that your order will be executed, you place a special type of limit order known as a stop order. A **stop order** (sometimes called a *stop-loss order*) is an order to sell a particular stock at the next available opportunity after its market price reaches a specified amount. This type of order is used to protect an investor against a sharp drop in price and thus stop the dollar loss on a stock investment. For example, assume you purchased General Motors common stock at $62 a share. Two weeks after making your investment, General Motors is facing multiple product liability lawsuits. Fearing that

*stop order*   An order to sell a particular stock at the next available opportunity after its market price reaches a specified amount.

the market value of your stock will decrease, you enter a stop order to sell your General Motors stock at $56. This means that if the price of the stock decreases to $56 or lower, the account executive will sell it. While a stop order does not guarantee that your stock will be sold at the price you specified, it does guarantee that it will be sold at the next available opportunity. Both limit and stop orders may be good for one day, one week, one month, or good until canceled (GTC).

You can also choose to place a discretionary order. A **discretionary order** is an order to buy or sell a security that lets the account executive decide when to execute the transaction and at what price. Financial planners advise against using a discretionary order for two reasons. First, a discretionary order gives the account executive a great deal of authority. If the account executive makes a mistake, it is the investor who suffers the dollar loss. Second, financial planners argue that only investors (with the help of their account executives) should make investment decisions.

*discretionary order* An order to buy or sell a security that lets the account executive decide when to execute the transaction and at what price.

## Computerized Transactions

While many people still prefer to use telephone orders to buy and sell stocks, a growing number are using computers to complete security transactions. To meet this need, discount brokerage firms and some full-service brokerage firms allow investors to trade online.

A good investment software package can help you evaluate potential investments, monitor the value of your investments, and place buy and sell orders online. As a rule of thumb, the more active the investor is, the more sense it makes to use computers to trade online. Other reasons that justify using a computer include

1. The size of your investment portfolio.
2. The ability to manage your investments closely.
3. The capability of your computer and the software package.

While computers can make the investment process easier and faster, you should realize that *you* are still responsible for analyzing the information and making the final decision to buy or sell a security. All the computer does is provide more information and, in most cases, complete transactions more quickly and economically.

## Commission Charges

*round lot* One hundred shares or multiples of 100 shares of a particular stock.

*odd lot* Fewer than 100 shares of a particular stock.

Most brokerage firms have a minimum commission ranging from $25 to $55 for buying and selling stock. Additional commission charges are based on the number of shares and the value of stock bought and sold. On the trading floor of a stock exchange, stocks are traded in round lots or odd lots. A **round lot** is 100 shares or multiples of 100 shares of a particular stock. An **odd lot** is fewer than 100 shares of a particular stock.

Exhibit 14–10 shows typical charges and services provided by online brokerage firms. Notice that many of the online brokerage firms illustrated in Exhibit 14–10 charge for research information and other investor services. You should also realize that when you choose an online brokerage firm, you will have to make your own decisions.

Generally, full-service and discount brokerage firms charge higher commissions than those charged by online brokerage firms. As a rule of thumb, full-service brokers may charge as much as $1\frac{1}{2}$ to 2 percent of the transaction amount. For example, if you use a full-service brokerage firm like Merrill Lynch or Morgan Stanley Dean Witter to purchase Home Depot stock valued at $10,000, and the brokerage firm charges $1\frac{1}{2}$ percent, you will pay commissions totaling $150 ($10,000 $\times$ 0.015 = $150). In return for charging higher commissions, full-service brokers usually spend more time with

**EXHIBIT 14-10**  Typical Commission Charges and Services Provided by Online Brokerage Firms

| Firm | Cost of Trades | Research | Extras |
|---|---|---|---|
| **Datek Online** | Online trade: $9.99 for up to 5,000 shares. No automated phone trading available. Broker: $25 | Free BigCharts, NewsAlert, and Thomson reports. | Market orders that take more than 60 seconds to execute are free. |
| **DLJdirect** | $20 for up to 1,000 shares and 2 cents per share thereafter | With $100,000 in an account you get free DLJ research. | With $100,000 you get in on DLJ-underwritten IPOs. |
| **Discover Brokerage** | $14.95 for up to 5,000 shares. Broker: $34 minimum | Research reports are free for clients with over $100,000. | Recognized for its excellent options-trading capacities. |
| **E*Trade** | $14.95. Automated phone: Connect fees are 27 cents per minute, but call is free if it takes less than 12 minutes per trade. Broker: $29.95 | $9.95 for reports from securities analysts. | Free unlimited real-time quotes. |
| **Fidelity Investments** | $25 for up to 1,000 shares. Clients with $100,000 in mutual funds or those who have made 12 trades per year can pay $14.95 for up to 1,000 shares. | Subscriptions for quality reports cost $50 a month. | It's hard to beat the mutual-fund screening tools. |
| **National Discount Brokers** | Online: $14.75. Automated phone: $19.95. Broker: $24.95 | Free articles from investment newsletters. | Fast page loads and real-time balance updates. |
| **Charles Schwab** | $29.95 for up to 1,000 shares and then 3 cents per share. Automated phone: 10 percent off broker prices. Broker: maximum $55 for 100 shares or fewer | Reports cost $29.95 a month. | Custom financial plans and personalized advice. |
| **Suretrade** | Online: $7.95 for up to 5,000 shares. Automated phone: $11.95 for up to 5,000 shares. Broker: $32.95 | Free BigCharts, First Call, Reuters, and Zacks. | Low margin rate; 5.75 percent on loans under $100,000. |
| **A. B. Watley** | $9.95 for up to 5,000 shares. Phone $11.95. Broker: $24.95 | Charges a minimum of $1.50 per report. | Simple website and fast execution of transactions. |

Prices for market orders only.
SOURCE: Fred Vogelstein, "Can't Beat 'Em . . .," *U.S. News & World Report,* June 14, 1999, p. 44.

each client, help make investment decisions, and provide free research information. For the same transaction, most discount brokerage firms would charge commissions ranging between $55 to $85. Today discount brokerage firms are popular with many investors who have yet to venture into online trading, want to talk to an employee of the brokerage firm, and prefer to place their transaction orders over the telephone.

While full-service brokerage firms usually charge higher commissions, on some occasions a discount brokerage firm may charge higher commissions. This generally occurs when the transaction is small, involving a total dollar amount of less than $1,000, and the investor is charged the discount brokerage firm's minimum commission charge.

## Securities Regulation

Government regulation of securities trading began as a response to abusive and fraudulent practices in the sale of stocks. Individual states were the first to react early in the 20th century. Later federal legislation was passed to regulate the interstate sale of securities.

### State Regulation

In 1911, Kansas enacted the first state law regulating securities transactions. Within a few years, a number of other states passed similar laws. Most of the state laws provide for (1) registration of securities, (2) licensing of brokers and securities salespeople, and (3) prosecution of any individual who sells fraudulent stocks and bonds. These state laws are often called *blue-sky laws* because they were designed to stop the sale of securities that had nothing to back them up except the "sky."

### Federal Regulation

The Securities Act of 1933, sometimes referred to as the *Truth in Securities Act,* provides for full disclosure of important facts about corporations issuing new securities. Such corporations are required to file a registration statement containing specific information about their earnings, assets, and liabilities; their products or services; and the qualifications of their top management. This act also requires publication of a prospectus, a summary of information contained in the registration statement.

The Securities Exchange Act of 1934 created the Securities and Exchange Commission (SEC). The Securities and Exchange Commission is the agency that enforces federal securities regulations. The 1934 act gave the SEC the power to regulate trading on the New York Stock Exchange and the American Stock Exchange. It also empowered the SEC to make brokers and securities dealers pass an examination before being allowed to sell securities, and it required that registration statements be brought up to date periodically.

Nine other federal acts were passed primarily to protect investors:

*   The Maloney Act of 1938 made the National Association of Securities Dealers (NASD) responsible for the self-regulation of the over-the-counter securities market.
*   The Investment Company Act of 1940 placed investment companies that sell mutual funds under the jurisdiction of the SEC.
*   The Investment Advisers Act of 1940 required financial advisers with more than 15 clients to register with the SEC.
*   The Federal Securities Act of 1964 extended the SEC's jurisdiction to companies whose stock is sold over the counter if they have total assets of at least $1 million or more than 500 stockholders of any one class of stock.
*   The Securities Investor Protection Act of 1970 created the Securities Investor Protection Corporation (SIPC). This organization provides insurance of up to $500,000 per customer, including $100,000 for any cash deposited with a brokerage firm that fails.
*   The Securities Acts Amendments of 1975 eliminated fixed commissions and allowed more competition among brokerage firms.
*   The Insider Trading Sanctions Act of 1984 strengthened the penalty provisions of the 1934 Securities Exchange Act. Under this act, people are guilty of insider trading if they use information that is available only to account executives or other employees of brokerage firms. The act also expanded the SEC's power to investigate such illegal behavior.

- The Insider Trading Act of 1988 made the top management of brokerage firms responsible for reporting transactions based on inside information to the SEC. This act also enabled the SEC to levy fines of up to $1 million for failure to report such violations of the law.
- The Financial Services Modernization Banking Act of 1999 repealed the Glass Steagall Act of 1933 and portions of the Bank Holding Company Act of 1956. This act allows banks to establish one-stop financial supermarkets where customers can bank, buy and sell securities, and purchase insurance coverage.

### Concept Check 14-4

1.  What is the difference between the primary market and the secondary market?
2.  Describe how stock is bought or sold in the secondary market.
3.  Assume you want to purchase stock. Would you use a full-service broker or a discount broker? Would you ever trade stocks online?
4.  What are the two main federal acts that regulate the securities industry? What do they regulate?

## LONG-TERM AND SHORT-TERM INVESTMENT STRATEGIES

### Obj. 5
Explain the trading techniques used by long-term investors and short-term speculators.

Once you purchase stock, the investment may be classified as either long term or short term. Generally, individuals who hold an investment for a long period of time are referred to as *investors*. Typically, long-term investors hold their investments for at least a year or longer. Individuals who routinely buy and then sell stocks within a short period of time are called *speculators* or *traders*.

### Long-Term Techniques

In this section, we discuss the long-term techniques of buy and hold, dollar cost averaging, direct investment programs, and dividend reinvestment programs.

### Buy-and-Hold Technique
Many long-term investors purchase stock and hold onto it for a number of years. When they do this, their investment can increase in value in three ways. First, they are entitled to dividends if the board of directors approves dividend payments to stockholders. Second, the price of the stock may go up. Third, the stock may be split. Although there are no guarantees, stock splits usually increase the future value of a stock investment over a long period of time.

*dollar cost averaging*
A long-term technique used by investors who purchase an equal dollar amount of the same stock at equal intervals.

### Dollar Cost Averaging
**Dollar cost averaging** is a long-term technique used by investors who purchase an equal dollar amount of the same stock at equal intervals. Assume you invest $2,000 in Johnson & Johnson's common stock each year for a period of three years. The results of your investment program are illustrated in Exhibit 14–11. Notice that when the price of the stock increased in 1999, you purchased fewer shares. When the price decreased in 2000, you purchased more shares. The average cost for a share of stock, determined by dividing the total investment ($6,000) by the total number of shares, is $57.64 ($6,000 ÷ 104.1 = $57.64). Other applications of dollar cost averaging occur when employees purchase shares of their company's stock through a payroll deduction plan or as part of an employer-sponsored retirement plan over an extended period of time.

| Year | Investment | Stock Price | Shares Purchased |
|------|-----------|-------------|------------------|
| 1998 | $2,000 | $50 | 40.0 |
| 1999 | 2,000 | 65 | 30.8 |
| 2000 | 2,000 | 60 | 33.3 |
| Total | $6,000 | | 104.1 |

Investors use dollar cost averaging to avoid the common pitfall of buying high and selling low. In the situation shown in Exhibit 14–11, you would lose money only if you sold your stock at less than the average cost of $57.64. Thus, with dollar cost averaging, you can make money if the stock is sold at a price higher than the average purchase price.

### Direct Investment and Dividend Reinvestment Plans

*direct investment plan*
A plan that allows stockholders to purchase stock directly from a corporation without having to use an account executive or a brokerage firm.

*dividend reinvestment plan*   A plan that allows current stockholders the option to reinvest or use their cash dividends to purchase stock of the corporation.

Today a large number of corporations offer direct investment plans. A **direct investment plan** allows you to purchase stock directly from a corporation without having to use an account executive or a brokerage firm. Similarly, a **dividend reinvestment plan** allows you the option to reinvest your cash dividends to purchase stock of the corporation. For stockholders, the chief advantage of both types of plans is that these plans enable them to purchase stock without paying a commission charge to a brokerage firm. (Note: A few companies may charge a small fee for dividend reinvestment, but the charge is less than what most brokerage firms charge.) As an added incentive, some corporations even offer their stock at a small discount to encourage the use of their direct investment and dividend reinvestment plans. Also, with the dividend reinvestment plan, you can take advantage of dollar cost averaging, discussed in the last section. For corporations, the chief advantage of both types of plans is that they provide an additional source of capital. As an added bonus, they are providing a service to their stockholders.

## Short-Term Techniques

In addition to the long-term techniques presented in the preceding section, investors sometimes use more speculative, short-term techniques. In this section, we discuss buying stock on margin, selling short, and trading in options. *Be warned:* The methods presented in this section are quite risky; do not use them unless you fully understand the underlying risks. Also, you should not use them until you have experienced success using the more traditional long-term techniques described above.

### Buying Stock on Margin

*margin*   A speculative technique whereby an investor borrows part of the money needed to buy a particular stock.

When buying stock on **margin,** you borrow part of the money needed to buy a particular stock. The margin requirement is set by the Federal Reserve Board and is subject to periodic change. The current margin requirement is 50 percent and a $2,000 minimum. This requirement means you may borrow up to half of the total stock purchase price as long as you have at least $2,000 in your brokerage firm account. Although margin rules are regulated by the Federal Reserve, margin requirements and the interest charged on the loans used to fund margin transactions may vary among brokers and dealers. Usually the brokerage firm either lends the money or arranges the loan with another financial institution. Investors buy on margin because doing so offers them the potential for greater profits. Exhibit 14–12 gives an example of buying stock on margin.

As Exhibit 14–12 shows, it is more profitable to use margin. In effect, the financial leverage (often defined as the use of borrowed funds to increase the return on an investment) allowed Paul Watson, who is single and 32 years old, to purchase a larger

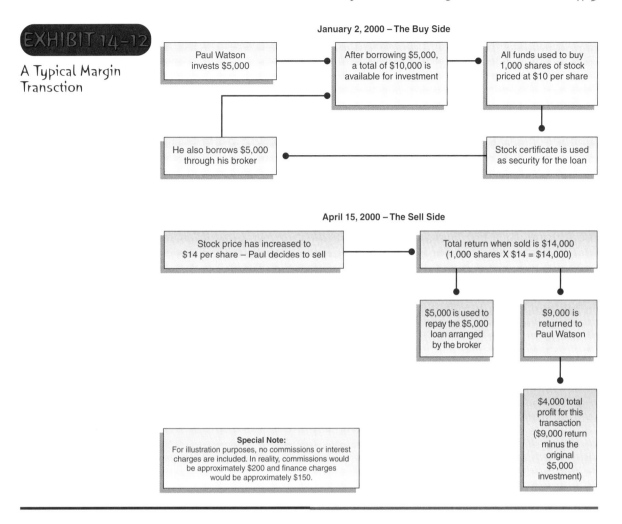

**EXHIBIT 14-12**

A Typical Margin Transction

**January 2, 2000 – The Buy Side**

Paul Watson invests $5,000

After borrowing $5,000, a total of $10,000 is available for investment

All funds used to buy 1,000 shares of stock priced at $10 per share

He also borrows $5,000 through his broker

Stock certificate is used as security for the loan

**April 15, 2000 – The Sell Side**

Stock price has increased to $14 per share – Paul decides to sell

Total return when sold is $14,000 (1,000 shares X $14 = $14,000)

$5,000 is used to repay the $5,000 loan arranged by the broker

$9,000 is returned to Paul Watson

$4,000 total profit for this transaction ($9,000 return minus the original $5,000 investment)

**Special Note:**
For illustration purposes, no commissions or interest charges are included. In reality, commissions would be approximately $200 and finance charges would be approximately $150.

number of shares of stock. Since the dollar value of each share increased, Watson obtained a larger profit by buying the stock on margin.

In this example, Watson's stock did exactly what it was supposed to do: It increased in market value. His stock increased $4 per share, and he made $4,000 because he owned 1,000 shares. His actual profit would be reduced by commissions and the amount of interest his broker would charge for the margin transaction. Had the value of the stock gone down, buying on margin would have increased his loss. For example, Watson would have lost $3,000 if the price of the stock had dropped from $10 a share (the original purchase price) to $7 a share.

If the market value of a margined stock decreases to approximately one-half of the original price, you will receive a *margin call* from the brokerage firm. After the margin call, you must pledge additional cash or securities to serve as collateral for the loan. If you don't have acceptable collateral or cash, the margined stock is sold and the proceeds are used to repay the loan. The exact price at which the brokerage firm issues the margin call is determined by the amount of money you borrowed when you purchased the stock. Generally, the more money you borrow, the sooner you will receive a margin call if the market value of the margined stock drops.

In addition to facing the possibility of larger dollar losses, you must pay interest on the money borrowed to purchase stock on margin. Most brokerage firms charge 1 to 3 percent above the prime rate. Normally, economists define the prime rate as the interest rate that the best business customers must pay. Interest charges can absorb the potential profits if the value of margined stock does not increase rapidly enough and the margined stocks must be held for long periods of time.

## Selling Short

Your ability to make money by buying and selling securities is related to how well you can predict whether a certain stock will increase or decrease in market value. Normally, you buy stocks and assume they will increase in value, a procedure referred to as *buying long.* But not all stocks increase in value. In fact, the value of a stock may decrease for many reasons, including lower sales, lower profits, reduced dividends, product failures, increased competition, and product liability lawsuits. With this fact in mind, you may use a procedure called *selling short* to make money when the value of a stock is expected to decrease in value. **Selling short** is selling stock that has been borrowed from a brokerage firm and must be replaced at a later date. When you sell short, you sell today, knowing you must buy or *cover* your short transaction at a later date. To make money in a short transaction, you must take these steps:

1. Arrange to *borrow a stock certificate* for a certain number of shares of a particular stock from a brokerage firm.
2. *Sell the borrowed* stock, assuming it will drop in value in a reasonably short period of time.
3. *Buy the stock at a lower price* than the price it sold for in step 2.
4. Use the stock purchased in step 3 to *replace the stock borrowed from the brokerage firm* in step 1.

For example, Betty Malone, who is divorced and 28 years old, believes America Online stock is overpriced because of increased competition among Internet service providers and numerous other factors. As a result, she decides to sell short 100 shares of America Online (Exhibit 14–13).

As Exhibit 14–13 shows, Malone's total return for this short transaction was $700 because the stock did what it was supposed to do in a short transaction: decrease in value. A price decrease is especially important when selling short because you must replace the stock borrowed from the brokerage firm with stock purchased (hopefully at a lower market value) at a later date. If the stock increases in value, you will lose money because you must replace the borrowed stock with stock purchased at a higher price. If the price of the America Online stock in Exhibit 14–13 had increased from $90 to $97, Betty Malone would have lost $700.

There is usually no special or extra brokerage charge for selling short, since the brokerage firm receives its regular commission when the stock is bought and sold. Before selling short, consider two factors. First, since the stock you borrow from your broker is actually owned by another investor, you must pay any dividends the stock earns before you replace the stock. After all, you borrowed the stock and then sold the borrowed stock. Eventually, dividends can absorb the profits from your short transaction if the price of the stock does not decrease rapidly enough. Second, to make money selling short, you must be correct in predicting that a stock will decrease in value. If the value of the stock increases, you lose.

## Trading in Options

An **option** gives you the right to buy or sell a stock at a predetermined price during a specified period of time. Options are usually available for three-, six-, or nine-month periods. If you think the market price of a stock will increase

*selling short*   Selling stock that has been borrowed from a brokerage firm and must be replaced at a later date.

*option*   The right to buy or sell a stock at the current market value.

An Example of Selling Short

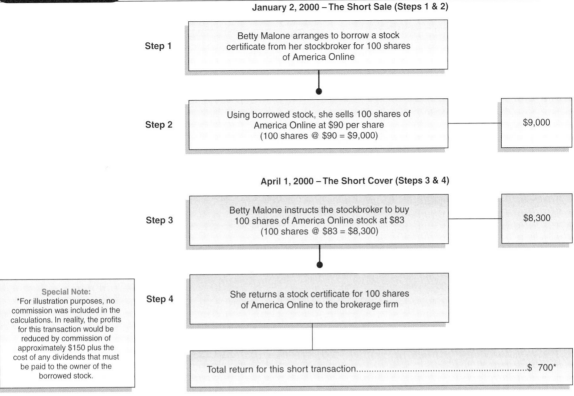

**January 2, 2000 – The Short Sale (Steps 1 & 2)**

**Step 1** — Betty Malone arranges to borrow a stock certificate from her stockbroker for 100 shares of America Online

**Step 2** — Using borrowed stock, she sells 100 shares of America Online at $90 per share (100 shares @ $90 = $9,000) — $9,000

**April 1, 2000 – The Short Cover (Steps 3 & 4)**

**Step 3** — Betty Malone instructs the stockbroker to buy 100 shares of America Online stock at $83 (100 shares @ $83 = $8,300) — $8,300

**Step 4** — She returns a stock certificate for 100 shares of America Online to the brokerage firm

Total return for this short transaction..................................................................$ 700*

**Special Note:**
*For illustration purposes, no commission was included in the calculations. In reality, the profits for this transaction would be reduced by commission of approximately $150 plus the cost of any dividends that must be paid to the owner of the borrowed stock.

during a short period of time, you may decide to purchase a call option. A *call option* is sold by a stockholder and gives the purchaser the right to *buy* 100 shares of a stock at a guaranteed price before a specified expiration date.

It is also possible to purchase a put option. A *put option* is the right to sell 100 shares of a stock at a guaranteed price before a specified expiration date. With both call and put options, you are betting that the price of the stock will increase or decrease in value before the expiration date. If this price movement does not occur before the expiration date, you lose the money you paid for your option.

Because of the increased risk involved in option trading, a more detailed discussion of how you profit or lose money with options is beyond the scope of this book. *Be warned:* Amateurs and beginning investors should stay away from options unless they fully understand all of the risks involved. For the rookie, the lure of large profits over a short period of time may be tempting, but the risks are real.

## Concept Check 14-5

1.  How can an investor make money using the buy-and-hold technique?
2.  What is the advantage of using dollar cost averaging?
3.  Explain the difference between direct investment plans and dividend reinvestment plans.
4.  Why would an investor buy stock on margin?
5.  Why would an investor use the selling-short technique?

## KEY FORMULAS

| Page | Topic | Formula |
|------|-------|---------|
| 457 | Book value | $\text{Book value} = \dfrac{\text{Assets} - \text{Liabilities}}{\text{Number of outstanding shares of common stock}}$ |
| | *Example:* | $\text{Book value} = \dfrac{\$135{,}000{,}000 - \$60{,}000\ 000}{3{,}750{,}000}$ |
| | | $= \$20 \text{ per share}$ |
| 457 | Current yield | $\text{Current yield} = \dfrac{\text{Annual income amount}}{\text{Market value}}$ |
| | *Example:* | $\text{Current yield} = \dfrac{\$3.00}{\$50.00}$ |
| | | $\text{Current yield} = 0.06 = 6 \text{ percent}$ |
| 458 | Total return | $\text{Total return} = \text{Current return} + \text{Capital gain}$ |
| | *Example:* | $\text{Total return} = \$120 + \$710$ |
| | | $\text{Total return} = \$830$ |
| 458 | Annualized holding period yield | $\dfrac{\text{Annualized holding}}{\text{period yield}} = \dfrac{\text{Total return}}{\text{Original investment}} \times \dfrac{1}{N}$ |
| | | $N = \text{Number of years investment is held}$ |
| | *Example:* | $\text{Annualized holding period yield} = \dfrac{\$830}{\$2{,}600} \times \dfrac{1}{4}$ |
| | | $\text{Annualized holding period yield} = 0.08 = 8 \text{ percent}$ |
| 459 | Earnings per share | $\text{Earnings per share} = \dfrac{\text{After-tax earnings}}{\text{Number of outstanding shares of common stock}}$ |
| | *Example:* | $\text{Earnings per share} = \dfrac{\$11{,}250{,}000}{3{,}750{,}000}$ |
| | | $= \$3.00 \text{ per share}$ |
| 459 | Price-earnings (PE) ratio | $\text{PE ratio} = \dfrac{\text{Price per share}}{\text{Earnings per share of stock outstanding over the last 12 months}}$ |
| | *Example:* | $\text{Price-earnings ratio} = \dfrac{\$54}{\$3.00}$ |
| | | $= 18$ |

# Summary of Objectives

**Obj. 1   Identify the most important features of common stock.**

Corporations sell common stock to finance their business start-up costs and help pay for their ongoing business activities. People invest in common stock because of dividend income, appreciation of value, and the possibility of gain through stock splits. Dividend payments to common stockholders must be approved by a corporation's board of directors. In return for providing the money needed to finance the corporation, stockholders have the right to elect the board of directors. They must also approve changes to corporate policies that include (1) an amendment to the corporate charter, (2) the sale of certain assets, (3) possible mergers, (4) the issuance of preferred stock or corporate bonds, and (5) changes in the amount of common stock.

**Obj. 2   Discuss the most important features of preferred stock.**

The most important priority an investor in preferred stock enjoys is receiving cash dividends before any cash dividends are paid to common stockholders. Still, dividend distributions to both preferred and common stockholders must be approved by the board of directors. To make preferred stock issues more attractive, corporations may add a cumulative feature, a participation feature, and/or a conversion feature to these issues.

**Obj. 3   Explain how you can evaluate stock investments.**

A number of factors can make a share of stock increase or decrease in value. When evaluating a particular stock issue, most investors begin with the information contained in daily newspapers or on the Internet. Classification of stocks, stock advisory services, annual reports, quarterly reports, information contained in business periodicals, numerical measures, and the fundamental, technical, and efficient market investment theories can all be used to help evaluate a stock investment.

**Obj. 4   Describe how stocks are bought and sold.**

A corporation may sell a new stock issue through an investment bank or directly to current stockholders. Once the stock has been sold in the primary market, it can be sold time and again in the secondary market. In the secondary market, investors purchase stock listed on a securities exchange or traded in the over-the-counter market. Most securities transactions are made through an account executive who works for a brokerage firm. A growing number of investors are completing security transactions online. In fact, a good investment software package can help you evaluate potential investments, monitor the value of your investments, and place buy and sell orders online. Most brokerage firms charge a minimum commission for buying or selling stock. Additional commission charges are based on the number and value of the stock shares bought or sold and if you use a full-service or discount broker or trade online. Individual states and the federal government have enacted a number of regulations to protect investors.

**Obj. 5   Explain the trading techniques used by long-term investors and short-term speculators.**

Purchased stock may be classified as either a long-term investment or a speculative investment. Long-term investors typically hold their investments for at least a year or longer; speculators (sometimes referred to as *traders*) usually sell their investments within a shorter time period. Traditional trading techniques long-term investors use include the buy-and-hold technique, dollar cost averaging, direct investment plans, and dividend reinvestment plans. More speculative techniques include buying on margin, selling short, and trading in options.

# Financial Planning Problems

1. *Calculating Dividend Amounts.* Betty and John Martinez own 220 shares of Exxon common stock. Exxon's quarterly dividend is $.41 per share. What is the amount of the dividend check the Martinez couple will receive for this quarter?   (Obj. 1)

2. *Determining the Number of Shares after a Stock Split.* In March, stockholders of Cisco Systems Company approved a 2-for-1 stock split. After the split, how many shares of Cisco Systems stock will an investor have if she or he owned 360 shares before the split?   (Obj. 1)

3. *Calculating Total Return.* Tammy Jackson purchased 100 shares of All-American Manufacturing Company stock at $29½ a share. One year later, she sold the stock for $38 a share. She paid her broker a $34 commission when she purchased the stock and a $42 commission when she sold it. During the 12 months she owned the stock, she received $184 in dividends. Calculate Tammy's total return on this investment.   (Obj. 1)

4. *Calculating Total Return.* Marie and Bob Houmas purchased 200 shares of General Electric stock for $95 a

share. One year later, they sold the stock for $110 a share. They paid their broker a $130 commission when they purchased the stock and a $150 commission when they sold it. During the 12 months they owned the stock, they received $280 in dividends. Calculate the total return on this investment.   (Obj. 1)

5. *Determining a Preferred Dividend Amount.* James Hayes owns Ohio Utility preferred stock. If this preferred stock issue pays 6¼ percent based on a par value of $25, what is the dollar amount of the dividend for one share of Ohio Utility?   (Obj. 2)

6. *Calculating the Dividend for a Cumulative Preferred Stock Issue.* Wyoming Sports Equipment issued a $3 cumulative preferred stock issue. In 1999, the firm's board of directors voted to omit dividends for both the company's common stock and its preferred stock issues. Also, the corporation's board of directors voted to pay dividends in 2000.   (Obj. 2)

   a. How much did the preferred stockholders receive in 1999?

   b. How much did the common stockholders receive in 1999?

   c. How much did the preferred stockholders receive in 2000?

7. *Calculating Return on Investment.* Two years ago, you purchased 100 shares of Coca-Cola Company. Your purchase price was $50 a share, plus a total commission of $55 to purchase the stock. During the last two years, you have received the following dividend amounts: $0.56 per share for the first year and $0.68 per share the second year. Also, assume that at the end of two years, you sold your Coca-Cola stock for $61 a share plus a total commission of $60 to sell the stock.   (Obj. 3)

   a. Calculate the current yield for your Coca-Cola stock at the time you purchased it.

   b. Calculate the current yield for your Coca-Cola stock at the time you sold it.

   c. Calculate the total return for your Coca-Cola investment when you sold the stock at the end of two years.

   d. Calculate the annualized holding period yield for your Coca-Cola investment at the end of the two-year period.

8. *Calculating Book Value, Earnings per Share, and Price-Earnings Ratio.* As a stockholder of Bozo Oil Company,

you receive its annual report. In the financial statements, the firm has reported assets of $9 million, liabilities of $5 million, after-tax earnings of $2 million, and 750,000 outstanding shares of common stock.   (Obj. 3)

   a. Calculate the book value of a share of Bozo Oil's common stock.

   b. Calculate the earnings per share of Bozo Oil's common stock.

   c. Assuming a share of Bozo Oil's common stock has a market value of $40, what is the firm's price-earnings ratio?

9. *Using Dollar Cost Averaging.* For four years, Mary Nations invested $3,000 each year in America Bank stock. The stock was selling for $34 in 1997, for $48 in 1998, $37 in 1999, and for $52 in 2000.   (Obj. 5)

   a. What is Mary's total investment in America Bank?

   b. After four years, how many shares does Mary own?

   c. What is the average cost per share of Mary's investment?

10. *Using Margin.* Bill Campbell invested $4,000 and borrowed $4,000 to purchase shares in Wal-Mart. At the time of his investment, Wal-Mart stock was selling for $45 a share.   (Obj. 5)

   a. If Bill paid a $70 commission, how many shares could he buy if he used *only* his own money and did not use margin?

   b. If Bill paid a $100 commission, how many shares could he buy if he used his $4,000 and borrowed $4,000 on margin to buy Wal-Mart stock?

   c. Assuming Bill did use margin, paid a $250 total commission to buy and sell his Wal-Mart stock, and sold his stock for $53 a share, how much profit did he make on his Wal-Mart investment?

11. *Selling Short.* After researching Toro common stock, Sally Jackson is convinced the stock is overpriced. She contacts her account executive and arranges to sell short 200 shares of Toro. At the time of the sale, a share of common stock had a value of $35. Six months later, Toro was selling for $23 a share, and Sally instructs her broker to cover her short transaction. Total commissions to buy and sell the stock were $120. What is her profit for this short transaction?   (Obj. 5)

## Financial Planning Activities

1. *Surveying Investors.* Survey investors who own stock. Then explain, in a short paragraph, their reasons for owning stock.   (Obj. 1)

2. *Determining the Effect of a Stock Split on a Stock's Market Value.* Use the *Reader's Guide to Periodical Literature,* the Internet, and/or issues of *The Wall Street Journal*

to locate a stock that has experienced a 2-for-1 split.   (Obj. 1)

   a. What is the name of the corporation that had the 2-for-1 stock split?

   b. When did the stock split?

   c. What was the price the day before the stock split?

*d.* What was the price the day after the stock split?

*e.* What was the price a month after the stock split?

*f.* At the end of one month, do you think the stock split was good for an individual investor?

**3.** *Interviewing an Account Executive.* Interview an account executive about the cumulative feature, participation feature, and conversion feature of preferred stock. What do these features mean to preferred stockholders?   (Obj. 2)

**4.** *Using Research Information.* Divide a sheet of paper into three columns. In the first column, list sources of information you can use to evaluate stock investments. In the second column, state where you would find each of these sources. In the third column, describe the types of information each source would provide.   (Obj. 3)

**5.** *Using Stock Advisory Services.* Pick a stock of interest to you and research the company at the library by examining the information contained in reports published by Moody's, Standard & Poor's, or Value Line, or business periodicals like *Business Week, Money,* or *Kiplinger's Personal Finance Magazine.* Then write a one- or two-page summary of your findings. Based on your research, would you still want to invest in this stock? Why or why not?   (Obj. 3)

**6.** *Using the Standard & Poor's Personal Wealth Website.* Visit the Standard & Poor's Personal Wealth website and evaluate one of the corporations listed below. To complete this activity, follow these steps.   (Obj. 3)

*a.* Go to www.personalwealth.com.

*b.* Click on *Stocks.*

*c.* Choose one of the following three corporations, enter its stock ticker symbol (in parentheses), and click on the Go button: General Electric Corporation (GE), Johnson & Johnson Corporation (JNJ), Microsoft Corporation (MSFT).

*d.* For your corporation, print out the information for the overview, chart, and vital stats.

*e.* Based on the information included in this research report, would you invest in this corporation? Explain your answer.

**7.** *Using the Internet.* Choose a stock that you think would be a good investment. Then research the stock using the Internet.

*a.* Based on the information contained on the corporation's home page, would you still want to invest in the stock? Explain your answer.

*b.* What other investment information would you need to evaluate the stock? Where would you obtain this information?

**8.** *Conducting Library Research.* Conduct library research on the fundamental theory, the technical theory, and the efficient market theory described in this chapter. How do these theories explain the movements of a stock traded on the NYSE or over-the-counter market?   (Obj. 3)

**9.** *Exploring Career Opportunities.* Prepare a list of questions you could use to interview an account executive about career opportunities in the field of finance. (Obj. 4)

**10.** *Using Long-Term Investment Techniques.* Interview people who have used the long-term investment techniques of buy and hold, dollar cost averaging, direct investment plan, or dividend reinvestment plan. Describe your findings.   (Obj. 5)

**11.** *Analyzing Short-Term Investments.* Prepare a chart that describes the similarities and differences among buying stock on margin, selling short, and trading in options. (Obj. 5)

## LIFE SITUATION CASE

### RESEARCH INFORMATION AVAILABLE FROM MOODY'S AND VALUE LINE

This chapter stressed the importance of evaluating potential investments. Now it's your turn to try your skill at evaluating a potential investment in Reebok International, Ltd. Assume you could invest $10,000 in the common stock of this company. To help you evaluate this potential investment, carefully examine Exhibits 14–7 and 14–8, which reproduce the research reports on Reebok International from Moody's and Value Line, respectively. Both reports were published in the fall of 1999.

### Questions

**1.** Based on the research provided by Moody's and Value Line, would you buy Reebok International stock? Justify your answer.

**2.** What other investment information would you need to evaluate Reebok International common stock? Where would you obtain this information?

**3.** On Thursday, December 16, 1999, Reebok International common stock was selling for $8 a share. Using a newspaper, determine the current price for a share of Reebok common stock. Based on this information, would your Reebok investment have been profitable if you had purchased the common stock for $8 a share? (Hint: Reebok stock is listed on the New York Stock Exchange.)

**4.** Assuming you purchased Reebok International stock on December 16, 1999, and based on your answer to question 3, would you want to hold or sell your Reebok stock? Explain your answer.

# VIDEO CASE: Investing in Stocks
## (Based on Video Program 119)

"If you want to be financially fit, you have to put your money to work for it to grow."

This quote says it all. For many people, investing means parking their money in a savings account and hoping the interest will add up. Although the interest may be enough to keep up with inflation, the fact remains that without a more aggressive strategy, their money will not grow. In search of higher returns, many investors turn to the stock market. Let's start with the basics:

1. When you invest in stock, you become a part owner of the corporation.
2. Your stock investment will grow if the company is prosperous and earns a profit.
3. Your stock investment can decrease in value if the company falls on hard times.
4. There are two types of stocks: common and preferred.
5. As a common stockholder, you receive dividend distributions approved by the corporation's board of directors.
6. As a preferred stockholder, you are guaranteed to be paid dividends before common stockholders receive dividends.
7. The annual return on stocks averaged about 10 percent a year between 1926 and the mid 1990s.

While investing in stocks entails more risk, you can minimize the risk with careful planning and by learning how to research your investments. Before purchasing your first stock, you should learn as much as possible about the stock market and the company that issued the stock you want to buy. Many experts suggest that you begin the search for a stock investment by thinking about the products or services that you purchase regularly.

Then continue your search by reading investment information in magazines and newspapers or using a stock advisory service. You can also use the Internet to research stock investments. Information about the trends, fundamentals, and technical aspects of the stocks that interest you is available through websites like Quicken (www.quicken.com) and the Standard & Poor's site (www.standardpoor.com).

Finally, you can obtain help in making an investment decision by talking with a stockbroker. Generally, stockbrokers are classified as either full-service or discount brokers,

depending on how much help they provide to clients and the amount of commissions they charge for their services.

Once you have made the decision to buy or sell, your stock is transacted on a stock exchange or the over-the-counter market. A stock market (sometimes referred to as a securities exchange) is a marketplace for buying and selling stock. Members of the exchange gather together to purchase or sell stocks for their clients. You can also purchase or sell stocks through Nasdaq (National Association of Securities Dealers Automated Quotation system). As the name implies, Nasdaq is a computerized, electronic system that matches buy and sell orders for specific stocks.

Protection of investors is the primary concern of the Securities and Exchange Commission (SEC). The National Association of Securities Dealers (NASD) also works to protect investors by overseeing the Nasdaq market and the licensing and general regulation of the securities industry. Even with securities regulation, the responsibility for making intelligent investment decisions is still yours. You are the one who must pick the stock and decide when it is time to buy or sell.

## Questions

1. You have accumulated $4,000 that you can use to start an investment program. Would you place your money in a savings account or invest in stock? Explain your answer.
2. Over 3,000 stocks are listed on the New York Stock Exchange, and over 5,000 stocks are traded over the counter. Assuming you decided to invest your $4,000 in two different stocks, what process would you use to identify and screen four or five potential stocks for further research and evaluation?
3. Now that you have narrowed your search down to four or five potential stock investments, what type of research information would you need to make your final decision?

## Creating an E-Plan: Financial Decisions Using the Web

### INVESTING IN STOCKS

For many investors, selection of stocks for their portfolios is an important element that helps achieve various investment goals.

Websites for Investing in Stocks

- Current stock market information and data at **www.personalwealth.com.**
- Information about investing in stocks at **www.fool.com.**
- Stock quotes and other financial data at **www.wsrn.com, quote.yahoo.com, www.quote.com,** and **my.excite.com/ stocks.**
- Information on activities and resources of various stock exchanges: American Stock Exchange at **www.amex. com;** New York Stock Exchange at **www.nyse.com;** and Nasdaq **www.nasdaq.com.**
- Company annual report information at **www.hoovers.com.**
- News about investing in high-tech stocks at **www.newshub.com.**

(Note: Addresses and content of websites change, and new sites are created daily. Use search engines to update and locate websites for your current financial planning needs.)

*PFP sheets: 58, 61*

Short-Term Financial Planning Activities

1. Identify investments goals that might be appropriate for investing in stocks for your life situation.
2. Research potential stocks based on your various financial goals. Consider risk, potential growth, income, and recent market performance. (see PFP Sheet 58)
3. Monitor current economic conditions that may affect the value of individual stocks as well as the stock market as a whole.
4. Compare the cost of various investment broker services. (see PFP Sheet 61)

Long-Term Financial Planning Activities

1. Identify stock investing decisions that might be used for achieving long-term financial goals.
2. Develop a plan for investing in stocks as family and household situations change.

# Investing in Bonds

## For One Investor, Bellsouth Bonds are the Right Call

Before reading this chapter, answer these two questions: (1) Are you tired of the low interest rates offered by banks, savings and loan associations, and credit unions on certificates of deposit? (2) Are you afraid of investing in stocks because of the increased risk?

If you answered yes to both questions, you may want to consider investing in bonds. That's what Barbara Jackson, 27, did in 1999. The low returns offered on certificates of deposit have forced many investors like Jackson to evaluate other investments that offer higher returns.

Jackson considered investing in stocks and mutual funds, but was afraid of losing her $22,000 nest egg. She wanted an investment that was more secure and offered a predictable source of income. That's when she purchased 12 corporate bonds issued by Bellsouth Corporation. Although Bellsouth has used many different bond issues to finance its operations, Jackson chose a bond issue with a 7 percent interest rate and a maturity date in 2005.

Jackson began her search for an investment by thinking about the products she used daily. Since Bellsouth was the company that provided her wireless phone service, and since she was using her wireless phone more and more, she assumed Bellsouth must be rolling in profits. Not content with just a "feeling that the company must be profitable," she researched the company on the Internet. At the Bellsouth website (www. bellsouth.com), she examined the company's financial statements and learned that Bellsouth was indeed profitable: Both sales revenues and profits had increased each year since 1996.

Still not quite sure, Jackson went to the library and found that Moody's Investors Service rated the Bellsouth bonds Aaa and Standard & Poor's rated them AAA. According to both Moody's and Standard & Poor's, bonds with these ratings are judged to be the "best" and are often referred to as *gilt edge*. Continued interest payments and eventual repayment of the principal are assured for bonds with these ratings.

Based on her research, Barbara Jackson decided to purchase 12 Bellsouth bonds at $1,000 each. With commissions, her total investment was $12,110. Each year until 2005, Bellsouth will pay investors who own bonds in this issue $70 per bond in interest payments. And after receiving her first interest check, Jackson believes she made the right decision. In fact, she is looking forward to more interest checks until the bond's maturity in 2005, when the company will repay bondholders $1,000 for each bond they own. (By the way, Jackson also decided to place the remainder of her $22,000 nest egg in a six-month certificate of deposit that paid 5.15 percent.)

## Questions

1. What might make a particular investment, such as Bellsouth bonds, a good investment for one person and a poor one for another person?
2. Barbara Jackson divided her $22,000 nest egg between Bellsouth bonds and a certificate of deposit. Would you have made the same decision?
3. Based on what you've learned thus far, would you buy bonds issued by Bellsouth Corporation? Explain your answer.

SOURCES: Bellsouth website (www.bellsouth.com), December 20, 1999, Bellsouth Corporation, 1155 Peachtree St. NE, Atlanta, GA 30309; *Moody's Bond Survey,* August 1999, Moody's Investors Service, 99 Church St., New York, NY 10007; *Standard & Poor's Stock and Bond Guide,* 1999 edition, Standard & Poor's Corporation, 25 Broadway, New York, NY 10004.

## Learning Objectives

**Obj. 1**  Describe the characteristics of corporate bonds.

**Obj. 2**  Discuss why corporations issue bonds.

**Obj. 3**  Explain why investors purchase corporate bonds.

**Obj. 4**  Discuss why federal, state, and local governments issue bonds and why investors purchase government bonds.

**Obj. 5**  Evaluate bonds when making an investment.

Opportunity costs! Barbara Jackson, the lady in the opening case, took a chance when she purchased 12 corporate bonds issued by Bellsouth Corporation. Her investment, which cost over $12,000, could decrease in value. But because she took the time to evaluate the investment using reliable sources, she could be reasonably certain she would receive interest payments each year and eventual repayment when this bond issue reaches maturity in 2005.

Bellsouth Corporation, the company that issued the bond, also took advantage of the concept of opportunity costs when it sold bonds. It agreed to pay bondholders 7 percent interest until the bonds mature in 2005. It also agreed to repay Jackson's original investment when the bonds mature. In return, Bellsouth obtained the money it needed to provide telecommunications services to its customers, provide more jobs for employees, and ultimately earn larger profits.

We begin this chapter by describing the basic characteristics of corporate bonds that define the relationship between investors, like Barbara Jackson, and corporations, like Bellsouth Corporation, that sell bonds to obtain financing.

## CHARACTERISTICS OF CORPORATE BONDS

**Obj. 1**
Describe the characteristics of corporate bonds.

*corporate bond*
A corporation's written pledge to repay a specified amount of money with interest.

*face value*  The dollar amount the bondholder will receive at the bond's maturity.

A **corporate bond** is a corporation's written pledge to repay a specified amount of money with interest. Exhibit 15–1 on page 484 illustrates a typical corporate bond. Note that it states the dollar amount of the bond, the interest rate, and the maturity date. The **face value** is the dollar amount the bondholder will receive at the bond's maturity. The usual face value of a corporate bond is $1,000, but the face value of some corporate bonds may be as high as $50,000. The total face value of all the bonds in an issue usually runs into millions of dollars (see Exhibit 15–2 on page 485). Between the time of purchase and the maturity date, the corporation pays interest to the bondholder, usually every six months, at the stated interest rate. For example, assume you purchase the $1,000 Mobil Corporation bond illustrated in Exhibit 15–1 and the interest rate for this bond is 8½ percent. Using the following formula, you can calculate the annual interest amount for this Mobil corporate bond:

**EXHIBIT 15-1**

A Typical
Corporate Bond

$$\text{Dollar amount of annual interest} = \text{Face value} \times \text{Interest rate}$$
$$= \$1{,}000 \times 8.5 \text{ percent}$$
$$= \$1{,}000 \times 0.085$$
$$= \$85$$

In this situation, you receive interest of $85 a year from Mobil. The interest is paid semiannually, or every six months, in $42.50 ($85 ÷ 2 = $42.50) installments until the bond matures.

*maturity date*   For a corporate bond, the date on which the corporation is to repay the borrowed money.

The **maturity date** of a corporate bond is the date on which the corporation is to repay the borrowed money. At the maturity date, the bondholder returns the bond to the corporation and receives cash equal to the bond's face value. Maturity dates for bonds generally range from 1 to 30 years after the date of issue. Maturities for corporate bonds may also be classified as short term (under 5 years), intermediate term (5 to 15 years), and long term (over 15 years).

*bond indenture*   A legal document that details all of the conditions relating to a bond issue.

The actual legal conditions for a corporate bond are described in a bond indenture. A **bond indenture** is a legal document that details all of the conditions relating to a bond issue. Often containing over 100 pages of complicated legal wording, the bond indenture remains in effect until the bonds reach maturity or are redeemed by the corporation.

*trustee*   A financially independent firm that acts as the bondholders' representative.

Since corporate bond indentures are very difficult for the average person to read and understand, a corporation issuing bonds appoints a trustee. The **trustee** is a financially independent firm that acts as the bondholders' representative. Usually the trustee is a commercial bank or some other financial institution. The corporation must report to the trustee periodically regarding its ability to make interest payments and eventually redeem the bonds. In turn, the trustee transmits this information to the bondholders along with its own evaluation of the corporation's ability to pay. If the corporation fails to live up to all the provisions in the indenture agreement, the trustee may bring legal action to protect the bondholders' interests.

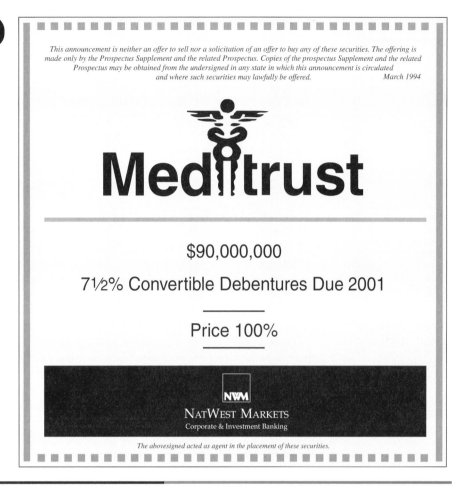

*This announcement is neither an offer to sell nor a solicitation of an offer to buy any of these securities. The offering is made only by the Prospectus Supplement and the related Prospectus. Copies of the prospectus Supplement and the related Prospectus may be obtained from the undersigned in any state in which this announcement is circulated and where such securities may lawfully be offered.*

March 1994

# Meditrust

$90,000,000

7½% Convertible Debentures Due 2001

Price 100%

**NWM**

NATWEST MARKETS
Corporate & Investment Banking

*The abovesigned acted as agent in the placement of these securities.*

## Concept Check 15-1

1. If you needed information about a bond issue, would you go to the library or use the Internet?
2. What is the usual face value for a corporate bond?
3. What is the annual interest amount for a $1,000 bond issued by Zenith Corporation that pays 6¼ percent interest?
4. In your own words, define *maturity date* and *bond indenture*.
5. How does a trustee evaluate the provisions contained in a bond indenture?

## WHY CORPORATIONS SELL CORPORATE BONDS

**Obj. 2**
Discuss why corporations issue bonds.

Let's begin this section with some basics of why corporations sell bonds. Corporations like Meditrust (See Exhibit 15–2) borrow when they don't have enough money to pay for major purchases— much as individuals do. Bonds can also be used to finance a corporation's ongoing business activities. In addition, corporations often sell bonds when it is difficult or impossible to sell stock. The sale of bonds can also improve a corporation's financial leverage—the use of borrowed funds to increase the corporation's return on investment. Finally, the interest paid to bond owners is a tax-deductible expense and thus can be used to reduce the taxes the corporation must pay to the federal and state governments.

While a corporation may use both bonds and stocks to finance its activities, there are important distinctions between the two. Corporate bonds are a form of *debt financing,* whereas stock is a form of *equity financing.* Bond owners must be repaid at a future date; stockholders do not have to be repaid. Interest payments on bonds are required; dividends are paid to stockholders at the discretion of the board of directors. Finally, in the event of bankruptcy, bondholders have a claim to the assets of the corporation prior to that of stockholders.

Before issuing bonds, a corporation must decide what type of bond to issue and how the bond issue will be repaid.

## Types of Bonds

*debenture*   A bond that is backed only by the reputation of the issuing corporation.

Most corporate bonds are debentures. A **debenture** is a bond that is backed only by the reputation of the issuing corporation. If the corporation fails to make either interest payments or repayment at maturity, debenture bondholders become general creditors, much like the firm's suppliers. In the event of corporate bankruptcy, general creditors, including debenture bondholders, can claim any asset not specifically used as collateral for a loan or other financial obligation.

*mortgage bond*
A corporate bond secured by various assets of the issuing firm.

To make a bond issue more appealing to conservative investors, a corporation may issue a mortgage bond. A **mortgage bond** (sometimes referred to as a *secured bond*) is a corporate bond secured by various assets of the issuing firm. A first mortgage bond may be backed by a lien on a specific asset, usually real estate. A corporation can also issue bonds that are backed by stocks and other bonds that it owns and, in some cases, even its operating equipment. A general mortgage bond is secured by all the fixed assets of the firm that are not pledged as collateral for other financial obligations. A secured bond is safer than a debenture because corporate assets or collateral may be sold to repay the bondholders if the corporation defaults on interest or repayment. Because of this added security, interest rates on mortgage bonds are usually lower than interest rates on debentures.

*subordinated debenture*
An unsecured bond that gives bondholders a claim secondary to that of other designated bondholders with respect to both interest payments and assets.

A third type of bond a corporation may issue is called a *subordinated* debenture. A **subordinated debenture** is an unsecured bond that gives bondholders a claim secondary to that of other designated bondholders with respect to interest payments, repayment, and assets. Investors who purchase subordinated debentures usually enjoy higher interest rates than other bondholders because of the increased risk associated with this type of bond.

## Convertible Bonds

*convertible bond*
A bond that can be exchanged, at the owner's option, for a specified number of shares of the corporation's common stock.

A special type of bond a corporation may issue is a convertible bond. A **convertible bond** can be exchanged, at the owner's option, for a specified number of shares of the corporation's common stock. This conversion feature allows investors to enjoy the lower risk of a corporate bond but also take advantage of the speculative nature of common stock. For example, Westinghouse Electric Corporation's $1,000 bond issue with a 2007 maturity date is convertible. Each bond can be converted to 64.5 shares of the company's common stock. This means you could convert the bond to common stock whenever the price of the company's common stock is $15.50 ($1,000 ÷ 64.5 = $15.50) or higher.

In reality, there is no guarantee that Westinghouse bondholders will convert to common stock even if the market value of the common stock does increase to $15.50 or higher. The reason for choosing not to exercise the conversion feature in this example is quite simple. As the market value of the common stock increases, the market value of the convertible bond *also* increases. By not converting to common stock, bondholders enjoy the added safety of the bond and interest income in addition to the increased market value of the bond caused by the price movement of the common stock.

The corporation gains three advantages by issuing convertible bonds. First, the interest rate on a convertible bond is often 1 to 2 percent lower than that on traditional bonds. Second, the conversion feature attracts investors who are interested in the speculative gain that conversion to common stock may provide. Third, if the bondholder converts to common stock, the corporation no longer has to redeem the bond at maturity.

Convertible bonds, like all potential investments, must be carefully evaluated. Remember, not all convertible bonds are quality investments.

## Provisions for Repayment

*call feature*   A feature that allows the corporation to call in or buy outstanding bonds from current bondholders before the maturity date.

Today most corporate bonds are callable. A **call feature** allows the corporation to call in or buy outstanding bonds from current bondholders before the maturity date. In the 1990s, investors saw a large number of bonds called because corporations could replace high-interest bond issues with new bond issues that have lower interest rates. The money needed to call a bond may come from the firm's profits, the sale of additional stock, or the sale of a new bond issue that has a lower interest rate.

In most cases, corporations issuing callable bonds agree not to call them for the first 5 to 10 years after the bonds have been issued. When a call feature is used, the corporation may have to pay the bondholders a *premium*, an additional amount above the face value of the bond. The amount of the premium is specified in the bond indenture; a $10 to $50 premium over the bond's face value is common.

A corporation may use one of two methods to ensure that it has sufficient funds available to redeem a bond issue. First, the corporation may establish a sinking fund. A **sinking fund** is a fund to which annual or semiannual deposits are made for the purpose of redeeming a bond issue. To retire a $100 million bond issue that matures in 2017, Outboard Marine Corporation (OMC) agreed to make annual sinking fund payments of $5 million on April 15 of each year beginning in 1998 and continuing through 2016. Note that Outboard Marine will have made sinking fund payments totaling $90 million ($5 million × 18 years = $90 million) over the 18-year period. From a financial management standpoint, each annual sinking fund payment of $5 million can be invested and is an example of the time value of money (increases in an amount of money as a result of interest earned), a concept stressed throughout this text. At maturity, the $90 million contributed by Outboard Marine *plus* the investment earnings will enable the corporation to pay off this $100 million bond issue.

*sinking fund*   A fund to which annual or semiannual deposits are made for the purpose of redeeming a bond issue.

A sinking fund provision in the bond indenture is generally advantageous to bondholders. Such a provision forces the corporation to make arrangements for bond repayment before the maturity date. If the terms of the provision are not met, the trustee or bondholders may take legal action against the company.

*serial bonds*   Bonds of a single issue that mature on different dates.

Second, a corporation may issue serial bonds. **Serial bonds** are bonds of a single issue that mature on different dates. For example, Seaside Productions used a 20-year, $100 million bond issue to finance its expansion. None of the bonds mature during the first 10 years. Thereafter, 10 percent of the bonds mature each year until all the bonds are retired at the end of the 20-year period.

Detailed information about provisions for repayment, along with other vital information (including maturity date, interest rate, bond rating, call provisions, trustee, and details about collateral), is available from Moody's Investors Service, Standard &

# Financial Planning for Life's Situations

## THE "HOW TO" OF RESEARCHING A BOND

How do you find out whether or not a corporate bond is callable? Where can you find out who the trustee for a specific bond issue is? These are only two of the multitude of questions that concern investors who are trying to evaluate bond investments. Fortunately, the answers are easy to obtain if you know where to look.

Today the most readily available source of detailed information about a corporation, including information about its bond issues, is Moody's *Industrial Manuals.* Individual subscriptions to this series of publications are too expensive for most investors, but the series is available at both college and public libraries. It includes individual manuals on industrial companies, public utilities, banks and financial institutions, and transportation companies. Each manual contains detailed information on major companies in the United States, including the company's history, operations, products, and bond issues.

The following data on a corporate bond issued by Bell Atlantic Company of Maryland will give you an idea of the contents of the "Long-Term Debt" section of a Moody's report.

SOURCE: The information for the Bell Atlantic corporate bond was taken from Moody's *Public Utility Manual,* vol. 1, 1998, p. 2436.

Poor's Corporation, and other financial service companies. Take a look at the information provided by Moody's Investors Service for the Bell Atlantic of Maryland bond illustrated in the Financial Planning for Life's Situations box on this page.

## Concept Check 15–2

1. Why do corporations sell bonds?
2. What are the differences among a debenture, a mortgage bond, and a subordinated debenture?
3. Why would an investor purchase a Westinghouse Electric convertible bond?
4. Describe three reasons a corporation would sell convertible bonds.
5. Explain the methods corporations can use to repay a bond issue.

# WHY INVESTORS PURCHASE CORPORATE BONDS

### Obj. 3

Explain why investors purchase corporate bonds.

In Chapters 13 and 14, we compared the historical returns provided by stocks and bonds. Stocks with a 10.7 percent return before adjusting for inflation have always outdistanced the performance of corporate bonds at a 5.6 percent return and U.S. Treasury bills at a 3.7 percent return. With this fact in mind, you may be wondering why you should consider bonds as an investment alternative. Why not just choose stocks because they provide the highest possible return of the three investment alternatives? The fact is that many corporate and government bonds are safer investments and are often considered a "safe harbor" in troubled economic times. And some investors use corporate and government bonds to diversify their investment portfolios. Basically, investors purchase corporate bonds for three reasons: (1) interest income, (2) possible increase in value, and (3) repayment at maturity.

## Interest Income

As mentioned earlier in this chapter, bondholders normally receive interest payments every six months. As we saw earlier, the dollar amount of interest is determined by multiplying the interest rate by the face value of the bond. In fact, because interest income is so important to bond investors, let's review this calculation. If IBM issues a $7\frac{1}{2}$ percent bond with a face value of $1,000, the investor will receive $75 ($1,000 × 7.5% = $75) a year, paid in installments of $37.50 at the end of each six-month period.

*registered bond*   A bond that is registered in the owner's name by the issuing company.

*registered coupon bond*   A bond that is registered for principal only, and not for interest.

*bearer bond*   A bond that is not registered in the investor's name.

The method used to pay bondholders their interest depends on whether they own registered bonds, registered coupon bonds, bearer bonds, or zero-coupon bonds. A **registered bond** is registered in the owner's name by the issuing company. Interest checks for registered bonds are mailed directly to the bondholder of record. A variation of a registered bond is the registered coupon bond. A **registered coupon bond** is registered for principal only, not for interest. To collect interest payments on a registered coupon bond, the owner must present one of the detachable coupons to the issuing corporation or the paying agent.

A third type of bond is a **bearer bond,** which is not registered in the investor's name. As with a registered coupon bond, the owner of a bearer bond must detach a coupon and present it to the issuing corporation or the paying agent to collect interest payments. *Be warned:* If you own a bearer bond, you can be out of luck if it is lost or stolen. Anyone—the rightful owner or a thief—can collect interest payments and the face value at maturity if he or she has physical possession of the bearer bond or its detachable coupons. While some bearer bonds are still in circulation, corporations no longer issue them.

*zero-coupon bond*   A bond that is sold at a price far below its face value, makes no annual or semiannual interest payments, and is redeemed for its face value at maturity.

A **zero-coupon bond** is sold at a price far below its face value, makes no annual or semiannual interest payments, and is redeemed for its face value at maturity. With a zero-coupon bond, the buyer receives a return based on the bond's increased market value as its maturity date approaches. For example, assume you purchased a Waste Management zero-coupon bond for $350 in 1995 and Waste Management will pay you $1,000 when the bond matures in 2012. For holding the bond 18 years, you will receive interest of $650 ($1,000 face value − $350 purchase price = $650 interest) at maturity.

Before investing in zero-coupon bonds, you should consider at least two factors. First, even though all of the interest on these bonds is paid at maturity, the IRS requires you to report interest each year—that is, as you earn it, not when you actually receive it. Second, zero-coupon bonds are more volatile than other types of bonds. When evaluating such bonds, as in evaluating other types of bonds, the most important criterion is the quality of the issuer. It pays to be careful.

## Dollar Appreciation of Bond Value

Most beginning investors think that a $1,000 bond is always worth $1,000. In reality, the price of a corporate bond may fluctuate until the maturity date. Changes in overall interest rates in the economy are the primary cause of most bond price fluctuations. Changing bond prices that result from changes in overall interest rates in the economy are an example of interest rate risk, discussed in Chapter 13. In fact, there is an inverse relationship between a bond's market value and overall interest rates in the economy. When IBM issued the bond mentioned earlier, the 7½ percent interest rate was competitive with the interest rates offered by other corporations issuing bonds at that time. If overall interest rates fall, the IBM bond will go up in market value due to its higher, 7½ percent, interest rate. On the other hand, if overall interest rates rise, the market value of the IBM bond will fall due to its lower, 7½ percent, interest rate.

When a bond is selling for less than its face value, it is said to be selling at a *discount*. When a bond is selling for more than its face value, it is said to be selling at a *premium*. Generally, investors consult *The Wall Street Journal, Barron's,* the Internet, or a newspaper to determine the price of a bond. Information on how to read bond quotations is provided later in this chapter.

It is also possible to approximate a bond's market value using the following formula:

$$\text{Approximate market value} = \frac{\text{Dollar amount of annual interest}}{\text{Comparable interest rate}}$$

For example, assume you purchase a New York Telephone bond that pays 4⅞ percent interest based on a face value of $1,000. Also assume new corporate bond issues of comparable quality are currently paying 7 percent. The approximate market value is $696, as follows:

$$\text{Dollar amount of annual interest} = \$1,000 \times 4\tfrac{7}{8} \text{ percent}$$

$$= \$1,000 \times 4.875 \text{ percent}$$

$$= \$48.75$$

$$\text{Approximate market value} = \frac{\text{Dollar amount of annual interest}}{\text{Comparable interest rate}} = \frac{\$48.75}{7\%}$$

$$= \$696$$

The market value of a bond may also be affected by the financial condition of the company or government unit issuing the bond, the factors of supply and demand, an upturn or downturn in the economy, and the proximity of the bond's maturity date.

## Bond Repayment at Maturity

Corporate bonds are repaid at maturity. After you purchase a bond, you have two options: You may keep the bond until maturity and then redeem it, or you may sell the bond at any time to another investor. In either case, the value of your bond is closely tied to the corporation's ability to repay its bond indebtedness. For example, the retailer Color Tile and Carpet filed for reorganization under the provisions of the U.S. Bankruptcy Act. As a result, the bonds issued by Color Tile immediately dropped in value due to questions concerning the prospects for bond repayment at maturity. On the other hand, if a corporation establishes a reputation as an aggressive firm with excellent and innovative products, experienced and capable managers, and increasing sales and profits, the value of your bond will increase. Simply put: Other investors will pay more money to get a quality bond that has excellent prospects of repayment at maturity.

**Sample Corporate Bond Transaction for Borden, Inc.**

**Assumptions**

Interest, 8⅜ percent; maturity date, 2016; purchased October 8, 1988; sold October 8, 1999

| Costs when purchased | | Return when sold | |
|---|---|---|---|
| 1 bond @ $680 | $680 | 1 bond @ $1,030 | $1,030 |
| Plus commission | + 10 | Minus commission | – 10 |
| Total investment | $690 | Dollar return | $1,020 |

| Transaction summary | |
|---|---|
| Dollar return | $1,020 |
| Minus total investment | – 690 |
| Profit from bond sale | $ 330 |
| Plus interest ($83.75 for 11 years) | + 921 |
| Total return on the transaction | $1,251 |

## A Typical Bond Transaction

Assume that on October 8, 1988, you purchased an 8⅜ percent corporate bond issued by Borden, Inc. Your cost for the bond was $680 plus a $10 commission charge, for a total investment of $690. Also assume you held the bond until October 8, 1999, when you sold it at its current market value of $1,030. Exhibit 15–3 shows the return on your investment.

After paying commissions for buying and selling your Borden bond, you experienced a capital gain of $330 because the market value of the bond increased from $680 to $1,030. The increase in the value of the bond resulted because overall interest rates in the economy declined during the 11-year period in which you owned the bond. Also, Borden established a reputation for efficiency and productivity during this period. Increased efficiency and productivity help ensure that Borden will be able to repay bondholders when the bond reaches maturity in 2016.

You also made money on your Borden bond because of interest payments. For each of the 11 years you owned the bond, Borden paid you $83.75 ($1,000 × 8.375% = $83.75) interest. Thus, you received interest payments totaling $921. In this example, you made a total return of $1,251, as follows:

$$\text{Total return} = \text{Current return} + \text{Capital gain}$$
$$= \$921 + \$330$$
$$= \$1,251$$

Before investing in bonds, you should remember that the price of a corporate bond can decrease and that interest payments and eventual repayment may be a problem for a corporation that encounters financial difficulties or enters bankruptcy. In addition to purchasing individual bonds, some investors prefer to purchase bond funds. To help you decide whether you should purchase individual bonds or bond funds, read the Financial Planning for Life's Situations box on page 492.

## The Mechanics of a Bond Transaction

Most bonds are sold through full-service brokerage firms, discount brokerage firms, or the Internet. If you use a brokerage firm, your account executive should provide both information and advice about bond investments. Many experts urge you to remember one basic rule: It is always *your* money, and *you* should be the one who makes the final decision to buy or sell a bond. Your account executive's role is to make suggestions and provide information that may enable you to make a more informed decision. As with stock investments, the chief advantage of using a discount brokerage firm or trading

# Financial Planning for Life's Situations

## ARE BOND FUNDS RIGHT FOR YOU?

Simply put, bond funds are an indirect way of owning bonds, debt instruments, and IOUs issued by the U.S. Treasury, corporations, or state, city, and local school districts. Many financial experts recommend bond funds for small investors because these investments offer diversification and professional management. Diversification spells safety because an occasional loss incurred with one bond issue is usually offset by gains from other bond issues in the fund. Also, professional managers should be able to do a better job of picking bonds than individual investors. But before investing, consider two factors. First, even the best managers make mistakes. Second, it may cost more to purchase bond funds than individual bonds. As with most investments, the key to making money with funds is evaluation.

### EVALUATING BOND FUNDS

Martha Hernandez, a working mother with one child, received $44,000 following the death of her grandmother. After some careful planning, she decided to invest $34,000 in two high-quality corporate bond funds. She used the remaining $10,000 to pay off some credit card debts and establish an emergency fund. During the next two years, she earned over 11 percent on her bond investments each year—not bad during a period when CDs were paying between 5 and 6 percent.

Martha's 11 percent return wasn't just luck. She began by establishing an investment goal: Find a safe investment with minimal risk. After establishing her goal, she talked with an account executive at Merrill Lynch and asked for five suggestions that would enable her to attain her goal. Of the five original suggestions, three were conservative bond funds.

Next, Martha took a crucial step that many investors forget: She decided to do her own research and not just rely on the account executive's suggestions. She contacted the firms that managed each of the three bond funds and asked them to mail her both a prospectus and an annual report. After receiving the information, she was able to (1) determine each fund's investment objective, (2) identify the investments each fund contained, and (3) calculate the approximate fees and expenses charged by each fund.

Then she made a trip to the library, where she analyzed the performance of each of the three bond funds in the special mutual fund editions of *Business Week, Kiplinger's Personal Finance Magazine,* and *Money.* Each publication ranked the three bond funds according to the total return for the previous 12 months, 3 years, and 5 years. Although past performance is no guarantee of future performance, it may be one of the best predictors available. Based on the account executive's suggestions and her own research, she chose the "top" two bond funds.

Martha admits that she spent almost 30 hours researching her investments, but believes the time was well spent. When you consider the amount of money she made on her bond fund investments during the first two years—over $7,400—she made almost $250 an hour.

online is lower commissions, but you must do your own research and make the decision to buy or sell a bond issue. As you will see later in this chapter, many sources of information can be used to evaluate bond investments.

Bonds are purchased in much the same manner as stocks. Corporate bonds may be purchased in the primary market or the secondary market. (Remember, in the *primary* market, an investor purchases financial securities, via an investment bank or other representative, from the issuer of those securities. In the *secondary* market, existing financial securities are traded among investors.) In the secondary market, corporate bonds issued by larger, well-recognized companies are traded on either the New York Bond Exchange or the American Bond Exchange. The actual steps involved in purchasing a bond listed on an exchange are similar to the steps required to purchase stocks listed on a stock exchange (see Exhibit 14–9 in Chapter 14). You can also purchase corporate bonds directly from account executives who make a market or maintain an inventory for certain bonds.

Generally, if you purchase a $1,000 bond through an account executive or brokerage firm, you should expect to pay a minimum commission of between $10 and $35. If you purchase more bonds, the commission usually drops to $5 to $20 per bond. You should also expect to pay commissions when you sell bonds.

## Concept Check 15-3

1. Describe the three reasons investors purchase bonds.
2. What are the differences among a registered bond, a registered coupon bond, a bearer bond, and a zero-coupon bond?
3. In what ways can interest rates in the economy affect the price of a corporate bond?
4. Why is the value of a bond closely tied to the issuing corporation's ability to repay its bond indebtedness?
5. How are corporate bonds bought and sold?

# GOVERNMENT BONDS AND DEBT SECURITIES

## Obj. 4
Discuss why federal, state, and local governments issue bonds and why investors purchase government bonds.

In addition to corporations, the U.S. government and state and local governments issue bonds to obtain financing. In this section, we discuss bonds issued by these three levels of government and look at why investors purchase these bonds.

## Treasury Bills, Notes, and Bonds

The federal government sells bonds and securities to finance both the national debt and the government's ongoing activities. The main reason investors choose U.S. government securities is that most investors consider them risk free. In fact, some financial planners refer to them as the ultimate safe investment because their quality is considered to be higher than that of any other investment. Because they are backed by the full faith and credit of the U.S. government and carry a decreased risk of default, they offer lower interest rates than corporate bonds. The U.S. Treasury Department issues four principal types of bonds and securities: Treasury bills, Treasury notes, Treasury bonds, and U.S. government savings bonds. Treasury bills, notes, and bonds can be purchased directly from the 12 Federal Reserve banks or one of their 25 branches. When investors purchase U.S. government securities through the Federal Reserve System, they pay no commission charge. Also, the Federal Reserve System conducts auctions to sell Treasury bills, notes, and bonds. Buyers interested in purchasing these securities at such auctions may bid competitively or noncompetitively. Most individual investors use noncompetitive bids. These bids can be made by phone, by paper form, or using the Internet. If they bid competitively, they must specify the price or interest yield they are willing to accept. If they bid noncompetitively, they are willing to accept the average interest rate and to pay the average price at which the securities are sold.

Finally, Treasury securities may be purchased through banks or brokers, which charge a commission. U.S. government savings bonds can be purchased through the Federal Reserve banks and branches, commercial banks, savings and loan associations, or other financial institutions. U.S. government securities can be held until maturity or redeemed before maturity. Interest paid on U.S. government securities is taxable for federal income tax purposes but is exempt from state and local taxation. Current information on prices and interest rates appears in *The Wall Street Journal* and other financial publications and on the Internet.

### Treasury Bills

A *Treasury bill,* sometimes called a *T-bill,* is sold in a minimum unit of $1,000 with additional increments of $1,000 above the minimum. The maturity for T-bills is 13 weeks, 26 weeks, or 52 weeks.

T-bills are discounted securities, and the actual purchase price you pay is less than the maturity value of the T-bill. Let's assume you purchase a 52-week, $1,000 T-bill with a stated interest rate of 5 percent. To determine the discount amount ($50), multiply the maturity value by the interest rate ($1,000 × 5% = $50). To determine the purchase price ($950), subtract the discount amount from the maturity value ($1,000 − $50 = $950).

In reality, the yield on T-bills is slightly higher than the stated interest rate. In the above example, you received $50 interest on a $950 investment, which represents a 5.3 percent return, as follows:

$$\text{Current yield for a T-bill} = \frac{\text{Discount amount}}{\text{Purchase price}}$$

$$= \frac{\$50}{\$950}$$

$$= 0.053 = 5.3 \text{ percent}$$

### Treasury Notes

A *Treasury note* is issued in $1,000 units with a maturity of more than 1 year but not more than 10 years. Typical maturities are 2, 5, and 10 years. Interest rates for Treasury notes are slightly higher than those for Treasury bills, because investors must wait longer to get their money back and therefore demand more compensation in the form of higher interest. Interest for Treasury notes is paid every six months.

### Treasury Bonds

A *Treasury bond* is issued in minimum units of $1,000 and has maturities ranging from 10 to 30 years. The most common maturity is 30 years. Interest rates for Treasury bonds are generally higher than those for either Treasury bills or Treasury notes. Again, the primary reason for the higher interest rates is the length of time investors must hold Treasury bonds. Like interest on Treasury notes, interest on Treasury bonds is paid every six months.

### U.S. Government Savings Bonds

U.S. government savings bonds were covered in Chapter 5. Here we will provide a quick review.

Generally, Series EE bonds are purchased and held until maturity. The purchase price for Series EE bonds is one-half of their maturity value. Thus, a $100 bond costs $50 when purchased. At the time of publication, Series EE bonds purchased after May 1997 provide a guaranteed return that is based on the yield paid on five-year Treasury notes. The actual interest rate you receive on Series EE bonds is 90 percent of the average yields paid on five-year Treasury notes for the preceding six months.

The interest on Series EE bonds, which some financial planners call *accrued interest,* is exempt from state and local taxes and accumulates free from federal taxation until the bonds are redeemed. Once these bonds are cashed in, the interest on them is subject to federal taxation. As discussed

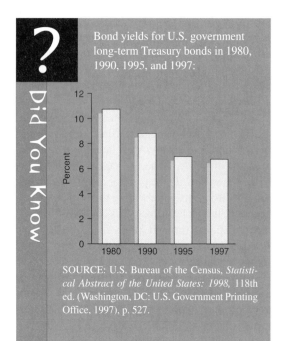

**Did You Know**

Bond yields for U.S. government long-term Treasury bonds in 1980, 1990, 1995, and 1997:

SOURCE: U.S. Bureau of the Census, *Statistical Abstract of the United States: 1998,* 118th ed. (Washington, DC: U.S. Government Printing Office, 1997), p. 527.

### JONATHAN HOENIG: RELEASED FROM BONDAGE

Riddle me this: If a 7-Eleven is open 24 hours a day, 7 days a week, 365 days a year, then *why* do the doors have locks? No answer?

Same question: If stocks have historically outperformed bonds, then why bother making bonds a part of your portfolio? Simple answer: *diversity.*

Buying bonds or other fixed-income investment diversifies a portfolio. By venturing outside the stock market, bond investors are purchasing securities that offer safety and stability. Corporate bonds, bank certificates of deposit, and U.S. Treasury securities pay investors interest income. These interest payments can drastically boost your return, especially when the stock market sags. In addition to interest, the price of bonds itself fluctuates with interest rates. When not held to "maturity," it is quite possible to make money investing in individual bonds.

Generally, you need serious cash to purchase a diversified portfolio of individual bonds, so those looking for fixed-income exposure might want to use bond mutual funds. These funds, which are not federally insured, are offered in a variety of risk profiles.

Thinking safety? In lieu of putting cash under your mattress, try a money market fund. Available through every major fund company, these investments function as really short-term bond funds and are perfect surrogates for the savings account.

in Chapter 5, if the income derived from savings bonds is used to pay college tuition, it is exempt from federal taxation. For more information on U.S. government savings bonds, refer to the material presented in Chapter 5.

## Federal Agency Debt Issues

In addition to the bonds and securities issued by the Treasury Department, debt securities are issued by federal agencies, which include the Federal National Mortgage Association (sometimes referred to as Fannie Mae), the Federal Housing Administration (FHA), the Government National Mortgage Association (sometimes referred to as Ginnie Mae), and the Federal Home Loan Mortgage Corporation (which somehow became known as Freddie Mac).

Although agency debt issues are, for practical purposes, risk free, they offer a slightly higher interest rate than government securities issued by the Treasury Department. Generally, their minimum denomination is $25,000. Securities issued by federal agencies have maturities ranging from 1 year to 40 years, with an average life of about 15 years.

## State and Local Government Securities

*municipal bond*   A debt security issued by a state or local government.

A **municipal bond,** sometimes called a *muni,* is a debt security issued by a state or local government. In the United States, there are 50 state governments. In addition, over 87,000 municipal entities—cities, counties, school districts, and special taxing districts—may sell municipal bonds.[1] Such securities are used to finance the ongoing activities of state and local governments and major projects such as airports, schools, toll roads, and toll bridges, and may be purchased directly from the government entity that issued them or through account executives.

*general obligation bond*
A bond backed by the full faith, credit, and unlimited taxing power of the government that issued it.

State and local securities are classified as either general obligation bonds or revenue bonds. A **general obligation bond** is backed by the full faith, credit, and unlimited

*revenue bond*   A bond
that is repaid from the
income generated by the
project it is designed to
finance.

taxing power of the government that issued it. A **revenue bond** is repaid from the income generated by the project it is designed to finance.

Although both general obligation and revenue bonds are relatively safe, defaults have occurred in recent years. Generally, investment-grade corporate bonds (discussed later in this chapter) have a default rate of about 2 percent. For high-quality municipal bonds, the default rate is generally lower.[2] Even with this fact in mind, investors should still worry about default on interest payments and eventual repayment of municipal bonds. And many people have heard the "horror" stories about investors who owned municipal bonds issued by Orange County (California) or the Washington Public Power Supply. In the mid-1990s, Orange County filed for the largest municipal bankruptcy in American history. Almost as bad was the default by the Washington Public Power Supply on municipal bonds worth $2 billion that caused thousands of investors to lose money.

In the 1990s, default rates were high for tax-exempt bonds used to finance health care facilities. In Florida alone, $20 million in health care bonds went sour just one year after they were issued. Unfortunately, tax-exempt bonds used to fund other government projects have also cost investors millions of dollars.

If the risk of default worries you, you can purchase insured municipal bonds. A number of states offer to guarantee payments on selected securities. Also, there are three large private insurers: MBIA, Inc.; the Financial Security Assurance Corporation; and the Financial Guaranty Insurance Corporation.

Even if a municipal bond issue is insured, however, financial experts worry about the insurer's ability to pay off in the event of default on a large bond issue. Most advise investors to determine the underlying quality of a bond whether or not it is insured. Also, guaranteed municipal securities usually carry a slightly lower interest rate than uninsured bonds because of the reduced risk of default.

Like a corporate bond, a municipal bond may be callable by the government unit that issued it. Typically, some call protection exists. In most cases, the municipality that issues the bond agrees not to call it for the first 10 years. *Be warned:* Your municipal bond may be called if interest rates fall and the government entity that issued the bond can sell new bonds with lower rates. For example, in the late 1990s, thousands of municipal bondholders who purchased high-yielding municipal bonds in the late 1980s have been shocked to have their bonds called. Many were counting on another 10 to 15 years of 12 percent or higher yields to finance their retirement. Although they were repaid the principal invested in the bond that was called, they faced the challenge of reinvesting their money when interest rates were at a 20-year low. If the bond is not called, the investor has two options. First, the bond may be held until maturity, in which case the investor will be repaid its face value. Second, the bond may be sold to another investor. However, it may be difficult to find a buyer for some municipal bond issues.

One of the most important features of municipal bonds is that the interest on them may be exempt from federal taxes. Whether or not the interest on municipal bonds is tax exempt often depends on how the funds obtained from their sale are used. *It is your responsibility, as an investor, to determine whether or not municipal bonds are taxable.* Municipal bonds exempt from federal taxation are generally exempt from state and local taxes only in the state where they are issued. Furthermore, although the interest on municipal bonds may be exempt from taxation, a *capital gain* that results when you sell a municipal bond before maturity and at a profit may be taxable just like capital gains on other investments sold at a profit.

To some extent, the tax advantages associated with municipal bonds have diminished because current tax laws have lowered the maximum federal income tax rate for individuals. (Before those changes were enacted, the maximum rate for individuals was 50 percent!) But even with the lower tax rates, municipal bonds are still very pop-

**EXHIBIT 15-4**

Yields for
Tax-Exempt
Investments

The following information can be used to compare the return on tax-exempt investments with the returns offered by taxable investments.

| Tax-Exempt Yield | Equivalent Yields for Taxable Investments | | | | |
|---|---|---|---|---|---|
| | 15% Tax Rate | 28% Tax Rate | 31% Tax Rate | 36% Tax Rate | 39.6% Tax Rate |
| 4% | 4.71% | 5.56% | 5.80% | 6.3% | 6.6% |
| 5 | 5.88 | 6.94 | 7.25 | 7.8 | 8.3 |
| 6 | 7.06 | 8.33 | 8.70 | 9.4 | 9.9 |
| 7 | 8.24 | 9.72 | 10.14 | 10.9 | 11.6 |
| 8 | 9.41 | 11.11 | 11.59 | 12.5 | 13.2 |
| 9 | 10.59 | 12.50 | 13.04 | 14.1 | 14.9 |
| 10 | 11.76 | 13.89 | 14.49 | 15.6 | 16.6 |

ular among wealthy investors. Because of their tax-exempt status, the interest rates on municipal bonds are lower than those on taxable bonds. By using the following formula, you can calculate the *taxable equivalent yield* for a municipal security:

$$\text{Taxable equivalent yield} = \frac{\text{Tax-exempt yield}}{1.0 - \text{Your tax rate}}$$

For example, the taxable equivalent yield on a 5 percent, tax-exempt municipal bond for a person in the 28 percent tax bracket is 6.9 percent, as follows:

$$\text{Taxable equivalent yield} = \frac{0.05}{1.0 - 0.28} = 0.0694, \text{ or } 6.94 \text{ percent}$$

If this taxpayer had been in the 39.6 percent tax bracket, the taxable equivalent yield for a 5 percent, tax-exempt investment would increase to 8.3 percent. Once you have calculated the taxable equivalent yield, you can compare the return on tax-exempt securities with the return on taxable investments that include certificates of deposit, stocks, mutual funds, and other investment alternatives. Exhibit 15–4 illustrates the yields for tax-exempt investments and their taxable equivalent yields.

**Concept Check 15-4**

1. What are the maturities for a Treasury bill, a Treasury note, and a Treasury bond?
2. How is the interest rate for Series EE savings bonds calculated?
3. What is the difference between a general obligation bond and a revenue bond?
4. What risks are involved when investing in municipal bonds?
5. Assume a taxpayer in the 28 percent tax bracket invests in a 6 percent, tax-exempt municipal bond. Use the above formula to find the taxable equivalent yield.

# THE DECISION TO BUY OR SELL BONDS

**Obj. 5**

Evaluate bonds when making an investment.

One basic principle we have stressed throughout this text is the need to evaluate any potential investment. Certainly corporate *and* government bonds are no exception. Only after you have completed your evaluation should you purchase bonds. Of course, a decision to sell bonds also requires evaluation. In fact, evaluation may be even more crit-ical for bond investments because there are fewer bonds from which to choose. Although

## EXHIBIT 15-5

**Financial Information about Corporate Bonds Available in The Wall Street Journal**

Republished with permission of Dow Jones, Inc. from *The Wall Street Journal*, November 4, 1999; permission conveyed through Copyright Clearance Center, Inc.

# NEW YORK EXCHANGE BONDS

### Quotations as of 4 p.m. Eastern Time
### Friday, January 28, 2000

**Volume $9,685,000**

|  | 2000 | 1999 | 1998 |
|---|---|---|---|
| **SALES SINCE JANUARY 1** (000 omitted) | | | |
|  | $197,143 | $267,622 | $367,124 |

| | Domestic | | All Issues | |
|---|---|---|---|---|
| | Fri. | Thu. | Fri. | Thu. |
| Issues Traded | 176 | 170 | 184 | 178 |
| Advances | 63 | 88 | 64 | 92 |
| Declines | 84 | 56 | 88 | 59 |
| Unchanged | 29 | 26 | 32 | 27 |
| New highs | 1 | 1 | 1 | 1 |
| New lows | 24 | 17 | 24 | 17 |

## Dow Jones Bond Averages

| | −1999− | | −2000− | | | | −−−2000−−− | | | −−1999−− | |
|---|---|---|---|---|---|---|---|---|---|---|---|
| | High | Low | High | Low | | | Close | Chg. | %Yld | Close | Chg. |
| | 106.88 | 96.80 | 97.17 | 94.90 | 20 Bonds | | 95.70 | −0.01 | 7.97 | 106.45 | −0.23 |
| | 104.72 | 94.96 | 95.09 | 93.20 | 10 Utilities | | 93.88 | +0.15 | 7.83 | 104.41 | −0.31 |
| | 109.44 | 98.31 | 99.36 | 96.47 | 10 Industrials | | 97.51 | −0.18 | 8.12 | 108.49 | −0.15 |

### CORPORATION BONDS
### Volume, $9,628,000

| Bonds | Cur Yld. | Vol. | Close | Net Chg. |
|---|---|---|---|---|
| AES Cp 4½05 | cv | 3 | 148 | ... |
| AES Cp 8s8 | 8.6 | 74 | 92½ | ... |
| AMF 10⅞06 | 24.7 | 12 | 44 | − 20½ |
| AMF zr06 | ... | 13 | 33 | − 17 |
| AMR 9s16 | 8.6 | 50 | 104½ | − ⅜ |
| ATT 5⅛01 | 5.2 | 28 | 98⅛ + | ⅛ |
| ATT 7⅛02 | 7.1 | 51 | 100⅛ + | ⅝ |
| ATT 6¾04 | 6.9 | 93 | 97⅞ + | ⅛ |
| ATT 5⅝04 | 6.0 | 305 | 94⅛ | ... |

| Bonds | Cur Yld. | Vol. | Close | Net Chg. |
|---|---|---|---|---|
| Honywll zr03 | ... | 40 | 75¾ + | ⅝ |
| Honywll zr07 | ... | 5 | 56 | + 1⅝ |
| HuntPly 11¾04 | 11.6 | 35 | 101½ + | ⅝ |
| IRT Pr 7.3s03 | cv | 5 | 93 | + ½ |
| IllPwr 6¾05 | 7.2 | 10 | 94¼ + | ⅛ |
| IBM 6⅜00 | 6.4 | 50 | 99¾ | ... |
| IBM 7¼02 | 7.2 | 440 | 100½ − | ⅛ |
| IBM 6.45s07 | 6.8 | 72 | 94½ − | ⅛ |
| IBM 7½13 | 7.4 | 102 | 101⅛ + | 2⅛ |
| IBM 8⅜19 | 7.8 | 45 | 107¾ − | ⅜ |
| IBM 7s25 | 7.6 | 79 | 92⅝ + | ⅛ |

| Bonds | Cur Yld. | Vol. | Close | Net Chg. |
|---|---|---|---|---|
| ReynTob 8s01 | 8.2 | 11 | 98 | + ⅝ |
| ReynTob 7⅝03 | 8.2 | 11 | 93½ + | ¾ |
| ReynTob 8¾04 | 9.4 | 15 | 93 | − 1⅛ |
| ReynTob 9¼13 | 10.2 | 5 | 90⅝ − | ⅝ |
| RobMyr 63 | cv | 15 | 94 | + ¼ |
| Safwy 10s01 | 9.7 | 25 | 103¼ − | ⅜ |
| Safwy 9.65s04 | 9.0 | 187 | 106⅝ | ... |
| Safwy 9.3s07 | 8.7 | 5 | 107⅞ − | ⅜ |
| SouBell 4⅜01 | 4.5 | 20 | 96⅞ | ... |
| StdCmcl 07 | cv | 50 | 48 | − ¾ |
| StdPac 8½07 | 9.1 | 31 | 93¾ − | ¼ |
| StoneC 9⅞01 | 9.9 | 90 | 100⅛ − | ⅛ |
| StoneC 10¾02A | 10.8 | 76 | 99⅞ − | ⅜ |
| StoneC 11½04 | 11.1 | 5 | 103⅜ + | ¼ |
| StoneCn 6¾07 | cv | 10 | 85¼ + | ⅜ |
| TVA 6s00 | 6.0 | 10 | 100⅝ + | ½2 |
| TVA 6⅛03 | 6.3 | 11 | 96¾ − | ¼ |
| TVA 8¼34 | 8.3 | 50 | 99⅜ − | ¼ |
| TVA 7¼43 | 7.7 | 10 | 94⅝ − | ⅝ |
| TVA 6⅞43 | 7.6 | 60 | 90½ | ... |
| Tenet 8s05 | 8.3 | 24 | 96 | − ¾ |
| Tenet 8⅝07 | 9.0 | 55 | 95½ − | ⅜ |
| TerR 4s19 | 5.8 | 20 | 68⅞ − | 4½ |
| TmeWar 8.11s06 | 7.9 | 5 | 102⅞ + | 1⅜ |
| TmeWar 8.18s07 | 8.0 | 23 | 102 | + ¾ |
| TmeWar 9⅛13 | 8.6 | 3 | 106⅝ − | ¾ |
| TolEd 8s03 | 8.0 | 5 | 99½ − | ¼ |
| Tosco 9⅜02 | 9.3 | 10 | 103⅝ − | 1 |
| WsteM 4s02 | cv | 5 | 89½ + | ½ |
| Webb 9¾03 | 10.4 | 142 | 93⅜ + | ½ |
| Webb 9s06 | 10.5 | 58 | 85½ − | ⅝ |
| Webb 9¾08 | 11.3 | 181 | 86½ − | ¾ |
| Webb 10¼10 | 11.5 | 20 | 89¾ + | ¾ |
| WebbDel 9¾09 | 11.1 | 130 | 84⅜ | ... |
| Weirton 10¾05 | 10.8 | 91 | 99⅝ − | ⅛ |
| WhlPit 9⅜03 | 9.0 | 10 | 104 | + ⅛ |
| viKCS En 8⅞e08f | ... | 10 | 36 | − ·1 |

1. The name (often abbreviated) of the issuing firm is AT&T. The bond pays annual interest at the rate of 6¾ percent of the face value, or $1,000 × 6¾% = $67.50 per year. It matures in the year 2004.
2. The current yield, or return, based on today's market price is $67.50 ÷ $978.75, or 6.9 percent.
3. On this day, 93 bonds were traded.
4. The last price for an AT&T bond during the day was $1,000 × 97.875%, or $978.75.
5. The last price paid on this day was 0.125% × $1,000, or $1.25, higher than the last price paid on the previous trading day. In Wall Street terms, the AT&T bond "closed up ⅛" on this day.

**Sheet 59**

*The Wall Street Journal* lists pages and pages of stocks, it provides less than a page for bonds listed on the New York Bond Exchange and the American Bond Exchange. In this section, we examine methods you can use to evaluate bond investments.

## How to Read the Bond Section of the Newspaper

Not all local newspapers contain bond quotations, but *The Wall Street Journal, Barron's,* and many metropolitan newspapers publish complete information on this subject. In bond quotations, prices are given as a percentage of the face value, which is usually $1,000. Thus, to find the actual market price for a bond, you must multiply the face value ($1,000) by the newspaper quote. For example, a price quoted as 84 means a selling price of $1,000 × 84% = $840. Purchases and sales of bonds are reported in tables like that shown at the top of Exhibit 15–5. The highlighted line in Exhibit 15–5 gives the detailed information for an AT&T corporate bond. (The numbers in this list refer to the actual columns in the newspaper quotation.)

For government bonds, most financial publications include two price quotations. The first price quotation, or the *bid price,* is the price a dealer is willing to pay for a government security. The bid price represents the amount that a seller could receive for a government bond. The second price quotation, or the *asked price,* represents the price at which a dealer is willing to sell a government security. The asked price represents the amount for which a buyer could purchase the security. In addition to price quotations, *The Wall Street Journal, Barron's,* and many metropolitan newspapers provide information about the interest rates, maturity dates, and yields of government securities.

## Annual Reports

As pointed out earlier in this chapter, bondholders must be concerned about the financial health of the corporation or government unit that issues bonds. To understand how important financial information is when evaluating a bond issue, consider the following two questions:

* Will the bond be repaid at maturity?
* Will you receive interest payments until maturity?

While it may be difficult to answer these questions with 100 percent accuracy, the information contained in a firm's annual report is the logical starting point. Today there are three ways to obtain a corporation's annual report. First, you can either write or telephone the corporation and request an annual report. (Hint: Many corporations have 800 telephone numbers for your use.) Second, as mentioned in the next section, most corporations maintain a website that contains detailed information about their financial performance. Third, some financial publications provide a reader's service that allows you to use a toll-free telephone number or a postcard to obtain an annual report.

Regardless of how you obtain an annual report, you should look for signs of financial strength or weakness. Is the firm profitable? Are sales revenues increasing? Are the firm's long-term liabilities increasing? In fact, there are many questions you should ask before making a decision to buy a bond. To help you determine the right questions to ask when evaluating a bond issue, examine the Financial Planning Calculations feature on page 500. Also, you may want to examine the bond's rating and perform the calculations described on pages 501–503 before investing your money.

## The Internet

Just as you can use the Internet to evaluate a stock investment, you can use much of the same financial information to evaluate a bond investment. By accessing a corporation's web page and locating the topics "financial information," "annual report," or "investor relations," you can find many of the answers to the questions discussed in the last section. As an added bonus, a corporation may provide more than one year's annual report on its website, so you can make comparisons from one year to another.

When investing in bonds, you can use the Internet in three other ways. First, you can obtain price information on specific bond issues to track your investments. Especially if you live in a small town or rural area without access to newspapers that provide bond coverage, the Internet can be a welcome source of current bond prices. Second, it is possible to trade bonds online and pay lower commissions than you would pay a full-service or discount brokerage firm. Third, you can get research about a corporation and its bond issues (including recommendations to buy or sell) by accessing specific bond websites. *Be warned:* Bond websites are not as numerous as websites that provide information on stocks, mutual funds, or personal financial planning. And many of the better bond websites charge a fee for their research and recommendations. Each of the following websites provides information and educational materials designed to make you a better bond investor:

# Financial Planning Calculations

## EVALUATING CORPORATE BONDS

No checklist can serve as a fool-proof guide for choosing a corporate or government bond. However, the following questions will help you evaluate a potential bond investment. (Usual sources of information include *Moody's Industrial Manuals* and *Standard & Poor's Stock and Bond Guide*.)

### CATEGORY 1: INFORMATION ABOUT THE CORPORATION

1. What is the corporation's name? _____

2. What are the corporation's address and telephone number? _____
_____

3. What type of products or services does this firm provide? _____
_____

4. Briefly describe the prospects for this company. (Include significant factors like product development, plans for expansion, plans for mergers, etc.)
_____
_____
_____
_____

### CATEGORY 2: BOND BASICS

5. What type of bond is this? _____

6. What is the face value for this bond? _____

7. What is the interest rate for this bond? _____

8. What is the annual interest amount for this bond? _____

9. When are interest payments made to bondholders? _____

10. Is the corporation currently paying interest as scheduled?   ☐ Yes   ☐ No

11. What is the maturity date for this bond? _____

12. What is Moody's rating for this bond? _____

13. What is Standard & Poor's rating for this bond? _____

14. What do these ratings mean? _____
_____
_____

15. What was the original issue date? _____

16. Who is the trustee for this bond issue? _____
_____

17. Is the bond callable? If so, when? _____
_____

18. Is the bond secured with collateral? If so, what?
☐ Yes   ☐ No _____

19. How did the corporation use the money from this bond issue? _____
_____

### CATEGORY 3: FINANCIAL PERFORMANCE

20. Has the firm's total debt increased over the last three years?   ☐ Yes   ☐ No

21. Is the corporation profitable? If so, how profitable?
☐ Yes   ☐ No $ _____

22. Have profits increased over the last seven years?
☐ Yes   ☐ No

23. Are this year's sales higher than last year's sales?
☐ Yes   ☐ No

24. Have sales increased over the last seven years?
☐ Yes   ☐ No

25. Briefly describe any other information that you obtained from Moody's, Standard & Poor's, or other advisory services. _____
_____
_____
_____

### A WORD OF CAUTION

When you use a checklist, there is always a danger of overlooking important relevant information. The above checklist is not a cure-all, but it does provide some very sound questions that you should answer before making a decision to invest in bonds. Quite simply, it is a place to start. If you need other information, *you* are responsible for obtaining it and for determining how it affects your potential investment.

**EXHIBIT 15-6** DESCRIPTION OF BOND RATINGS PROVIDED BY MOODY'S INVESTORS SERVICE AND STANDARD & POOR'S CORPORATION

| Quality | Moody's | Standard & Poor's | Description |
|---|---|---|---|
| High-grade | Aaa | AAA | Bonds that are judged to be of the best quality. They carry the smallest degree of investment risk and are generally referred to as *gilt edge*. Interest payments are protected by a large or exceptionally stable margin, and principal is secure. |
| | Aa | AA | Bonds that are judged to be of high quality by all standards. Together with the first group, they comprise what are generally known as *high-grade* bonds. They are rated lower than the best bonds because their margins of protection may be smaller. |
| Medium-grade | A | A | Bonds that possess many favorable investment attributes and are to be considered upper-medium-grade obligations. The factors giving security to principal and interest are considered adequate. |
| | Baa | BBB | Bonds that are considered medium-grade obligations; i.e., they are neither highly protected nor poorly secured. |
| Speculative | Ba | BB | Bonds that are judged to have speculative elements; their future cannot be considered well assured. Often their protection of interest and principal payment is very moderate. |
| | B | B | Bonds that generally lack characteristics of the desirable investment. Assurance of interest and principal payments or of maintenance of other terms of the contract over a long period of time may be low. |
| Default | Caa | CCC | Bonds that are of poor standing. Such issues may be in default or be currently vulnerable to nonpayment. |
| | Ca | CC | Bonds that represent obligations that are highly speculative. |
| | C | | The lowest-rated class in Moody's designation. These bonds are regarded as having extremely poor prospects of attaining any real investment standing. |
| | | C | Standard & Poor's rating given to bonds where a bankruptcy petition has been filed. |
| | | D | Bond issues in default. |

SOURCES: *Moody's Bond Survey,* December 1999, Moody's Investors Service, 99 Church St., New York, NY 10007; *Standard & Poor's Stock and Bond Guide,* 1999 edition, Standard & Poor's Corporation, 25 Broadway, New York, NY 10004.

www.bondsonline.com      www.investingbonds.com
www.tradingedge.com      www.investinginbonds.com
www.moodys.com           www.standardpoor.com
www.ny.frb.org           www.frbsf.org

## Bond Ratings

To determine the quality and risk associated with bond issues, investors rely on the bond ratings provided by Moody's Investors Service, Inc., and Standard & Poor's Corporation. Both companies rank thousands of corporate and municipal bonds.

As Exhibit 15–6 illustrates, bond ratings generally range from AAA (the highest) to D (the lowest). For both Moody's and Standard & Poor's, the first four individual categories represent investment-grade securities. Investment-grade securities are suitable for conservative investors who want a safe investment that provides a predictable source of income. Bonds in the next two categories are considered speculative in nature. Finally, the C and D categories are used to rank bonds that may be in default due to poor prospects of repayment or even continued payment of interest. Although bond ratings may be flawed or inaccurate, most investors regard the work of both Moody's and Standard & Poor's as highly reliable.

Generally, U.S. government securities issued by the Treasury Department and various federal agencies are not graded because they are risk free for practical purposes. The rating of long-term municipal bonds is similar to that of corporate bonds. In addition, Standard & Poor's rates shorter-term municipal bonds maturing in three years or less with the following designations:

SP–1 Strong capacity to pay principal and interest. Those issues determined to possess overwhelming safety characteristics receive a plus (+) designation.
SP–2 Satisfactory capacity to pay principal and interest.
SP–3 Speculative capacity to pay principal and interest.[3]

## Bond Yield Calculations

*yield*   The rate of return earned by an investor who holds a bond for a stated period of time.

For a bond investment, the **yield** is the rate of return earned by an investor who holds a bond for a stated period of time. Two methods are used to measure the yield on a bond investment: the current yield and the yield to maturity.

*current yield*   Determined by dividing the dollar amount of annual interest from an investment by its current market value.

The **current yield** is determined by dividing the dollar amount of annual interest from an investment by its current market value. For bonds, the following formula may help you complete this calculation:

$$\text{Current yield on a corporate bond} = \frac{\text{Dollar amount of annual interest}}{\text{Current market value}}$$

For example, assume you own an AT&T corporate bond that pays 7.5 percent interest on an annual basis. This means that each year you will receive $75 ($1,000 × 7.5% = $75). Also assume the current market price of the AT&T bond is $960. Because the current market value is less than the bond's face value, the current yield increases to 7.8 percent, as follows:

$$\text{Current yield} = \frac{\$75}{\$960}$$

$$= 0.078, \text{ or } 7.8 \text{ percent}$$

This calculation allows you to compare the yield on a bond investment with the yields of other investment alternatives, which include certificates of deposit, common stock, preferred stock, and mutual funds. Naturally, the higher the current yield, the better! A current yield of 10 percent is better than a current yield of 7.8 percent.

*yield to maturity*   A yield calculation that takes into account the relationship among a bond's maturity value, the time to maturity, the current price, and the dollar amount of interest.

The **yield to maturity** that takes into account the relationship among a bond's maturity value, the time to maturity, the current price, and the dollar amount of interest. The formula for calculating the yield to maturity is as follows:

$$\text{Yield to maturity} = \frac{\text{Dollar amount of annual interest} + \dfrac{\text{Face value} - \text{Market value}}{\text{Number of periods}}}{\dfrac{\text{Market value} + \text{Face value}}{2}}$$

For example, assume that on January 1, 1995, you purchased at the current market price of $830 a corporate bond with a $1,000 face value issued by Fruit of the Loom. The bond pays 7 percent annual interest, and its maturity date is 2011. The yield to maturity is 8.7 percent, as follows:

$$\text{Yield to maturity} = \frac{\$70 + \dfrac{\$1,000 - \$830}{17}}{\dfrac{\$830 + \$1,000}{2}}$$

$$= \frac{\$80}{\$915}$$

$$= 0.087, \text{ or } 8.7 \text{ percent}$$

In this situation, the yield to maturity takes into account two types of return on the bond. First, you will receive interest income from the purchase date until the maturity date. Second, at maturity you will receive a payment for the face value of the bond. If you purchased the bond at a price below the face value, the yield to maturity will be greater than the stated interest rate. If you purchased the bond at a price above the face value, the yield to maturity will be less than the stated interest rate. (Remember, the actual price you pay for a bond may be higher or lower than the face value because of many factors, including changes in the economy, increases or decreases in comparable interest rates on other investments, and the financial condition of the company.) Like the current yield, the yield to maturity allows you to compare returns on a bond investment with other investments. Also, like the current yield, the higher the yield to maturity, the better. A yield to maturity of 9 percent is better than a yield to maturity of 7 percent. One additional calculation, times interest earned, is described in the Financial Planning Calculations box on page 504.

## Other Sources of Information

Investors can use two additional sources of information to evaluate potential bond investments. First, business periodicals can provide information about the economy and interest rates and detailed financial information about a corporation or government entity that issues bonds. You can locate many of these periodicals at your college or public library or on the Internet.

Second, a number of federal agencies provide information that may be useful to bond investors in either printed form or on the Internet. Reports and research published by the Federal Reserve System, the U.S. Treasury, and the Department of Commerce may be used to assess the nation's economy. If you want to purchase U.S. Treasury bills, notes, or bonds, or U.S. savings bonds, you can find a great deal of information on the Federal Reserve's websites (www.frbsf.org and www.ny.frb.org). You can also obtain information that corporations have reported to the Securities and Exchange Commission by accessing the SEC website (www.sec.gov). Finally, state and local governments will provide information about specific municipal bond issues.

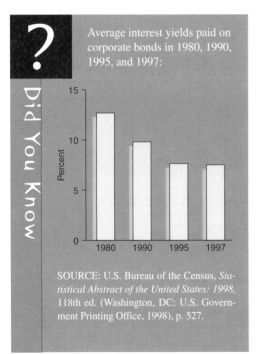

**Did You Know?**

Average interest yields paid on corporate bonds in 1980, 1990, 1995, and 1997:

SOURCE: U.S. Bureau of the Census, *Statistical Abstract of the United States: 1998*, 118th ed. (Washington, DC: U.S. Government Printing Office, 1998), p. 527.

# Financial Planning Calculations

## THE TIMES INTEREST EARNED RATIO: ONE TOOL TO HELP YOU EVALUATE BOND ISSUES

After evaluating Bellsouth Corporation, Barbara Jackson, the investor in the opening case, wanted to purchase the firm's corporate debentures. But she was concerned about the corporation's ability to make future interest payments. To determine Bellsouth's ability to pay interest, she calculated a formula called the *times interest earned ratio,* illustrated below:

$$\text{Times interest earned} = \frac{\text{Operating income before interest and taxes}}{\text{Interest expense}}$$

For example, Bellsouth Corporation had interest expense of $837 million and operating income before interest and taxes of $6,588 million in 1998 (the latest year for which actual figures are available at the time of this publication). The times interest earned ratio for Bellsouth Corporation is 7.87 to 1, as follows:

$$\text{Times interest earned} = \frac{\$6,588 \text{ million}}{\$837 \text{ million}}$$
$$= 7.87 \text{ to } 1$$

Although the average for the times interest earned ratio varies from industry to industry, a higher number is better than a lower number. Bellsouth Corporation is earning slightly over 7.87 times the amount required to pay the annual interest on its long-term notes, bonds, and other financial obligations. With a times interest earned ratio of 7.87 to 1, Bellsouth could experience a "significant" drop in earnings and still meet its financial obligations.

SOURCE: Based on information contained in Bellsouth Corporation's 1998 annual report.

## Concept Check 15-5

1. What is the market value for a bond with a face value of $1,000 and a newspaper quotation of 77¼?
2. What type of information is contained in a corporation's annual report? On a corporation's web page? How could this information be used to evaluate a bond issue?
3. How important are bond ratings when evaluating a bond issue?
4. Why should you calculate the current yield and yield to maturity on a bond investment?
5. How can business periodicals and government publications help you evaluate a bond issue?

## KEY FORMULAS

| Page | Topic | Formula |
|---|---|---|
| 484 | Annual interest | Dollar Amount of Annual interest = Face value × Interest rate |
| | *Example:* | Dollar Amount of Annual interest = $1,000 × 6.75 percent |
| | | = $1,000 × 0.0675 |
| | | = $67.50 |

| 490 | Approximate market value | $$\text{Approximate market value} = \frac{\text{Dollar amount of annual interest}}{\text{Comparable interest rate}}$$ |
|---|---|---|
| | *Example:* | $$\text{Approximate market value} = \frac{\$80}{0.095}$$ $$= \$842.11$$ |

| 494 | Current yield for a T-bill | $$\text{Current yield} = \frac{\text{Discount amount}}{\text{Purchase price}}$$ |
|---|---|---|
| | *Example:* | $$\text{Current yield} = \frac{\$55}{\$945}$$ $$= 0.058 = 5.8 \text{ percent}$$ |

| 497 | Taxable equivalent yield | $$\text{Taxable equivalent yield} = \frac{\text{Tax-exempt yield}}{1.0 - \text{Your tax rate}}$$ |
|---|---|---|
| | *Example:* | $$\text{Taxable equivalent yield} = \frac{0.06}{1.0 - 0.28}$$ $$= 0.0833 = 8.33 \text{ percent}$$ |

| 502 | Current yield for a corporate bond | $$\text{Current yield} = \frac{\text{Dollar amount of annual interest}}{\text{Current market value}}$$ |
|---|---|---|
| | *Example:* | $$\text{Current yield} = \frac{\$75}{\$800}$$ $$= 0.094 = 9.4 \text{ percent}$$ |

| 502 | Yield to maturity | $$\text{Yield to maturity} = \frac{\text{Dollar amount of annual interest} + \dfrac{\text{Face value} - \text{Market value}}{\text{Number of periods}}}{\dfrac{\text{Market value} + \text{Face value}}{2}}$$ |
|---|---|---|
| | *Example:* | $$\text{Yield to maturity} = \frac{\$60 + \dfrac{\$1,000 - \$900}{10}}{\dfrac{\$900 + \$1,000}{2}}$$ $$= 0.074 = 7.4 \text{ percent}$$ |

## Summary of Objectives

**Obj. 1**   **Describe the characteristics of corporate bonds.**

A corporate bond is a corporation's written pledge to repay a specified amount of money with interest. All of the details about a bond (face value, interest rate, maturity date, repayment, etc.) are contained in the bond indenture. The trustee is the bondholder's representative.

**Obj. 2**   **Discuss why corporations issue bonds.**

Corporations issue bonds and other securities to help finance their ongoing activities. Bonds may be debentures, mortgage bonds, subordinated debentures, or convertible bonds. Most bonds are callable. To ensure that the money will be available when needed to repay bonds, most corporations establish a sinking fund. Corporations can also issue serial bonds that mature on different dates.

## Obj. 3  Explain why investors purchase corporate bonds.

Investors purchase corporate bonds for three reasons: (1) interest income, (2) possible increase in value, and (3) repayment at maturity. The method used to pay bondholders their interest depends on whether they own registered bonds, registered coupon bonds, bearer bonds, or zero-coupon bonds. Because bonds can increase or decrease in value, it is possible to purchase a bond at a discount and hold the bond until it appreciates in value. Changes in overall interest rates in the economy are the primary causes of most bond price fluctuations. If you pay too much for a bond or it decreases in value, you can lose money on your investment. You can also choose to hold the bond until maturity and the corporation will repay the bond's face value. Corporate bonds can be bought or sold through account executives who represent brokerage firms.

## Obj. 4  Discuss why federal, state, and local governments issue bonds and why investors purchase government bonds.

Bonds issued by the U.S. Treasury and federal agencies are used to finance the national debt and the ongoing activities of the federal government. The U.S. Treasury issues four principal types of bonds: Treasury bills, Treasury notes, Treasury bonds, and Series EE savings bonds. State and local governments issue bonds to finance their ongoing activities and special projects such as airports, schools, toll roads, and toll bridges. U.S. government bonds can be purchased through Federal Reserve banks and branches, commercial banks, savings and loan associations, and other financial institutions. Municipal bonds are generally sold through the government entity that issued them or through account executives.

## Obj. 5  Evaluate bonds when making an investment.

Some local newspapers, *The Wall Street Journal,* and *Barron's* provide bond investors with information they need to evaluate a bond issue. Detailed financial information can be obtained by requesting a printed copy of the corporation's annual report or accessing its website. It is also possible to trade bonds online and obtain research information via the Internet. To determine the quality of a bond issue, most investors study the ratings provided by Standard & Poor's and Moody's. Investors can also calculate a current yield and a yield to maturity to evaluate bond issues.

The current yield is determined by dividing the dollar amount of annual interest of the bond by its current market value. The yield to maturity takes into account the relationship among a bond's maturity value, the time to maturity, the current price, and the dollar amount of interest.

## Financial Planning Problems

1. *Calculating Interest.* What is the annual interest amount for a $1,000 bond that pays 7¾ percent interest?   (Obj. 1)
2. *Explaining Different Types of Corporate Bonds.* Dorothy Martin wants to invest $10,000 in corporate bonds. Her account executive suggested that she consider debentures, mortgage bonds, and convertible bonds. Since she has never invested in bonds, she is not sure how these types of bonds differ. How would you explain their differences to her?   (Obj. 2)
3. *Evaluating Zero-Coupon Bonds.* List the reasons investors might want to buy zero-coupon bonds. Then list the reasons investors might want to avoid zero-coupon bonds. Based on these lists, do you consider zero-coupon bonds a good alternative for your investment program? Why or why not?   (Obj. 2)
4. *Analyzing Why Investors Purchase Bonds.* In your own words, explain how each of the following factors is a reason to invest in bonds.   (Obj. 3)
   a. Interest income.
   b. Possible increase in value.
   c. Repayment at maturity.
5. *Explaining Different Types of Treasury Securities.* Complete the following table:   (Obj. 4)

| | Minimum Amount | Maturity Range | How Interest Is Paid |
|---|---|---|---|
| Treasury bill | _____ | _____ | _____ |
| Treasury note | _____ | _____ | _____ |
| Treasury bond | _____ | _____ | _____ |

6. *Using the Standard & Poor's Personal Wealth Website.* Use the information provided by the Standard & Poor's Personal Wealth website to answer questions about the following bond issues. To complete this activity, follow these steps.   (Obj. 4)
   a. Go to www.personalwealth.com.
   b. Click on *Bonds.*
   c. Click on *Bond Search.*
   d. Enter the bond ticker symbol (in parentheses) for Chevron Corporation (CHV). Click on the green box to conduct a simple search. After you have obtained information for this bond, click on the green box to conduct a new search. Then enter the symbol for Polaroid Corporation (PRD) and click on the green box to conduct the search for this bond.   (Obj. 4)

*e.* Using the information on the Personal Wealth website, determine the current yield for each bond issue. What does the current yield calculation measure?

*f.* Using the information on the Personal Wealth website, determine the yield to maturity for each bond issue. What does the yield to maturity calculation measure?

*g.* What are Standard & Poor's ratings for each bond. What do these ratings mean?

*h.* Based on your answer to the above questions, which bond would you choose for your investment portfolio? Explain your answer.   (Obj. 4)

7. *Calculating Tax-Equivalent Yield.* Assume you are in the 36 percent tax bracket and purchase a 7 percent, tax-exempt municipal bond. Use the formula presented in this chapter to calculate the taxable equivalent yield for this investment.   (L.O.4)

8. *Evaluating a Corporate Bond Issue.* Choose a corporate bond listed on the New York Bond Exchange, and use *Moody's Industrial Manuals* and *Standard & Poor's Stock and Bond Guide* (available at your college or public library) to answer the following questions about this bond issue.   (Obj. 5)

*a.* What is Moody's and Standard & Poor's rating for the issue?

*b.* What is the purpose of the issue?

*c.* Does the issue have a call provision?

*d.* Who is the trustee for the issue?

*e.* What collateral, if any, has been pledged as security for the issue?

*f.* Based on the information you have obtained, would the bond be a good investment for you? Why or why not?

9. *Calculating Yields.* Assume you purchased a corporate bond at its current market price of $850 on January 1, 1995. It pays 9 percent interest and will mature on December 31, 2004, at which time the corporation will pay you the face value of $1,000.   (Obj. 5)

*a.* Determine the current yield on your bond investment at the time of purchase.

*b.* Determine the yield to maturity on your bond investment.

## Financial Planning Activities

1. *Explaining the Purpose of a Bond Indenture.* Prepare a one-minute oral presentation that describes the type of information contained in a bond indenture.   (Obj. 1)

2. *Investigating a New Bond Issue.* Locate an advertisement for a new bond issue in *The Wall Street Journal, Barron's, The New York Times,* or a local newspaper. Then go to the library or use the Internet to research the corporation or government entity that is issuing the bonds. Based on your research, prepare a two-page report on the issuer. Be sure to describe its financial condition and how it will use the money raised by selling the bonds.   (Obj. 2)

3. *Interviewing an Account Executive.* Talk to an account executive or a banker about the differences among debentures, mortgage bonds, and subordinated debentures. Describe your findings.   (Obj. 2)

4. *Making Investment Decisions.* Assume you just inherited 10 Westinghouse Electric Corporation bonds and each bond is convertible to 64.5 shares of the corporation's common stock.   (Obj. 2)

*a.* What type of information would you need to help you decide whether to convert your bonds to common stock?

*b.* Where would you obtain this information?

*c.* Under what conditions would you convert your bonds to common stock?

*d.* Under what conditions would you keep the bonds?

5. *Analyzing Why Investors Purchase Bonds.* Survey at least two investors who own either corporate or government bonds. Then answer the following questions.   (Obj. 3)

*a.* Why did these investors purchase the bonds?

*b.* How long have they invested in bonds?

*c.* Do they consider their bond issues to be conservative or speculative investments?

*d.* Why did they decide to purchase bonds instead of other investments like certificates of deposit, stocks, mutual funds, or real estate?

6. *Using the Internet to Obtain Investment Information.* Use one of the Internet search engines to locate the website for the Federal Reserve Bank of San Francisco or the Federal Reserve Bank of New York. Then prepare a report that summarizes the information provided on Treasury bills, Treasury notes, and Treasury bonds.   (Obj. 4)

7. *Using the Internet to Obtain Investment Information.* Use one of the Internet search engines to locate the website for the Federal Reserve Bank of San Francisco or the Federal Reserve Bank of New York. Then prepare a report that summarizes the information provided on U.S. government savings bonds.   (Obj. 4)

8. *Reading Financial Information in the Newspaper.* Using information from the local newspaper or *The Wall Street Journal,* answer the following questions on the following bond issues.   (Obj. 5)

Newspaper _____          Date _____

| | Current Yield | Volume | Close Price |
|---|---|---|---|
| IBM 7½ 13 | _____ | _____ | _____ |
| SouBell 7¼ 25 | _____ | _____ | _____ |
| TmeWar 7.48 08 | _____ | _____ | _____ |

9. *Analyzing Yields.* In your own words, describe what affects the current yield and the yield to maturity for a bond.  (Obj. 5)
10. *Evaluating a Bond Transaction.* Choose a corporate bond that you would consider purchasing. Then, using information obtained in the library or on the Internet, answer the questions on the evaluation form presented in the Financial Planning Calculations feature on page 500. Based on your research, would you still purchase this bond? Explain your answer.  (Obj. 5)

## LIFE SITUATION CASE

### A LESSON FROM THE PAST

Back in 1990, Mary Goldberg, a 34-year-old divorcee, got a telephone call from a Wall Street account executive who said that one of his other clients had given him her name. Then he told her his brokerage firm was selling a new corporate bond issue in New World Explorations, a company heavily engaged in oil exploration in the western United States. The bonds in this issue paid investors 13.2 percent a year. He then said that the minimum investment was $10,000 and that if she wanted to take advantage of this "once in a lifetime" opportunity, she had to move fast. To Mary, it was an opportunity that was too good to pass up, and she bit hook, line, and sinker. She sent the account executive a check—and never heard from him again. When she went to the library to research her bond investment, she found there was no such company as New World Explorations. She lost her $10,000 and quickly vowed she would never invest in bonds again. From now on, she would put her money in the bank, where it was guaranteed.

Over the years, she continued to deposit money in the bank and accumulated more than $90,000. Things seemed to be pretty much on track until one of her certificates of deposit (CDs) matured. When she went to renew the CD, the bank officer told her interest rates had fallen and current CD interest rates ranged between 5 and 5¾ percent. To make matters worse, the banker told Mary that only the bank's 36-month CD offered the 5¾ percent interest rate. CDs with shorter maturities paid lower interest rates.

Faced with the prospects of lower interest rates, Mary decided to shop around for higher rates. She called several local banks and got pretty much the same answer. Then a friend suggested that she talk to Peter Manning, an account executive for Smith Barney. Manning told her there were conservative corporate bonds and quality stock issues that offered higher returns. But, he warned her, these investments were *not* guaranteed. If she wanted higher returns, she would have to take some risks.

While Mary wanted higher returns, she also remembered how she had lost $10,000 investing in corporate bonds. When she told Peter Manning about her bond investment in the fictitious New World Exploration, he pointed out that she made some pretty serious mistakes. For starters, she bought the bonds over the phone from someone she didn't know, and she bought them without doing any research. He assured her that the bonds and stocks he would recommend would be issued by real companies, and she would be able to find a lot of information on each of his recommendations at the library. For starters, he suggested the following three investments:

1. ATT 8⅛ 2022 (corporate bond issued by AT&T Corporation with a current market value of $1,030).
2. IBM 7½ 2013 (corporate bond issued by International Business Machines Corporation with a current market value of $1,040).
3. General Electric common stock (listed on the New York Stock Exchange and selling for $51 a share with annual dividends of $0.55 per share).

### Questions

1. According to Mary Goldberg, the chance to invest in New World Explorations was "too good to pass up." Unfortunately, it was too good to be true, and she lost $10,000. Why do you think so many people are taken in by get-rich-quick schemes?
2. During the last part of the 1990s, investors were forced to look for ways to squeeze additional income from their investment portfolios. Do you think investing in corporate bonds or quality stocks is the best way to increase income? Why or why not?
3. Using information obtained in the library or on the Internet, answer the following questions about Peter Manning's investment suggestions. (Hint: For the bond issues, you may want to examine *Moody's Industrial Manuals.* For the stock issue, you can use *Moody's Handbook of Common Stock.*)
   *a.* What is Moody's rating for the AT&T bond?
   *b.* What is Moody's rating for the IBM bond?
   *c.* What do these ratings mean?
   *d.* How would you describe the common stock issued by General Electric?
4. Based on your research, which investment would you recommend to Mary Goldberg? Why?
5. Assuming you recommend one of the above investments, how much of Mary's $90,000 would you invest? What would you do with the remainder of her money?

6. Using a current newspaper, *The Wall Street Journal, Barron's*, or the Internet determine the current market value for each of the three investments suggested in this case. Based on this information, would these investments have been profitable if Mary had purchased the AT&T bond for $1,030, the IBM bond for $1,040, or General Electric stock for $51 a share?

# VIDEO CASE   Investing in Bonds

Which investment is right for you? Stocks? Certificates of deposit? Bonds? Investing your money wisely is one of the most important things you can do. But most people build their portfolios with only one thing in mind: growth. And that usually means investing in stocks. But there may be a place for bond investments in your portfolio. A bond is a loan from the bondholder to the government or corporation that issued the bond. In effect, the investor is loaning money to the bond issuer in exchange for a promise to repay the debt on the maturity date. Between the issue date and the maturity date, the government entity or corporation that issued the bond will pay the bondholder interest.

Investors often turn to bonds because of their safety, stability, and ability to produce income. U.S. Treasury bills, notes, and bonds and U.S. savings bonds are chosen because of their safety. It is also possible to purchase bonds issued by federal agencies and municipal bonds. Interest on municipal bonds, sometimes referred to as "munis," is exempt from federal and many state and local taxes. Because of their tax-free status, the interest rate on munis is often lower than that on taxable bonds. However, their tax-free status actually makes the taxable equivalent yield on these investments comparable to yields provided by taxable bonds.

The methods used to purchase bonds depends on the type of bond. Treasury bills, notes, and bonds are purchased at scheduled auctions sponsored by the federal government at different times of the year. Savings bonds, on the other hand, can be purchased on any day of the year from a financial institution. Like stocks, corporate bonds are purchased through an exchange, such as the New York Bond Exchange or the American Bond Exchange. Once purchased, interest is paid directly to the investor twice a year.

Even though bonds are more conservative investments, you must still consider two risks when evaluating a bond investment: the creditworthiness of the issuer and the ability of the issuer to make interest payments and eventual repayment at maturity. Creditworthiness is often determined by a rating agency. The type of bond that a corporation issues can also affect its creditworthiness. Today corporations issue debenture bonds, mortgage bonds, and subordinated debentures. To minimize risk, some investors prefer to purchase bond mutual funds.

The second risk associated with bond investing is price volatility. A bond can increase or decrease in value because of changes in interest rates. There is an inverse relationship between interest rates in the economy and the value of a specific bond with a fixed interest rate. When interest rates in the economy go down, the value of a specific bond increases. When interest rates in the economy go up, the value of a specific bond decreases. Because long-term bonds experience more interest rate fluctuations than short-term bonds, long-term bonds usually have higher interest rates and provide higher yields.

In addition to evaluating the creditworthiness of bond issuers and the price volatility of bonds, you may want to calculate the bond's taxable equivalent yield, current yield, and yield to maturity. You may also want to use websites like Moody's (www.moodys.com), Standard & Poor's (www.standardpoor.com), and Investing in Bonds (www.investingbonds.com) to evaluate a bond issue.

## Questions

1. According to this case, investors often turn to bonds because of their safety, stability, and ability to produce income. Based on these assumptions, what type of investor would choose bonds for a portion of his or her portfolio?

2. What effect would an increase in overall interest rates have on the value of a bond with a fixed interest rate? What effect would a decrease in overall interest rates have on a bond with a fixed interest rate?

3. Even though bonds are more conservative investments, they still carry risks. What are those risks? How would you go about researching an $8,000 investment in corporate bonds?

# Creating an E-Plan: Financial Decisions Using the Web

## INVESTING IN BONDS

Inclusion of bonds in an investment portfolio can be useful for achieving various financial goals when certain life situations, business conditions, and economic trends arise.

### Websites for Investing in Bonds

- Bonds Online Internet provides information about investing in bonds at **www.bonds-online.com.**
- Current bond investment articles from *Money* magazine at **www.money.com,** *Kiplinger's Personal Finance Magazine* at **www.kiplinger.com,** *Business Week* at **www.businessweek.com,** *Worth* magazine at **www. worth.com,** and *Smart Money* at **www.smartmoney.com.**
- The Federal Reserve Bank of San Francisco offers details for buying U.S. savings bonds and Treasury notes and bonds at **www.frbsf.org.**

(Note: Addresses and content of websites change, and new sites are created daily. Use search engines to update and locate websites for your current financial planning needs.)

*PFP sheet: 59*

### Short-Term Financial Planning Activities

1. Assess various types of bond investments that might be appropriate for your various financial goals and life situation.
2. Compare the recent performance of various corporate bonds that could be appropriate investments for you.
3. Research the recent performance of federal government and municipal bonds. Determine how these might be used in your investment portfolio.

### Long-Term Financial Planning Activities

1. Identify bond investing situations that could help minimize risk.
2. Develop a plan for selecting bond investments in the future.

# INVESTING IN MUTUAL FUNDS

In 1996, Bryan Nations was thinking about investing in the American Fundamental Investors mutual fund. After reading some research material published by Morningstar, a company that specializes in providing information about mutual funds, he decided to invest $5,000 in this fund. Then he made a fatal mistake common to a lot of investors: He forgot about his investment and didn't even look at the statements he received from the investment company. Three years later, he was considering selling his shares in American Fundamental, but he didn't even know the value of his investment.

Then, in his dentist's waiting room, Nations picked up a copy of the September 1999 *Mutual Funds,* and there it was—an article about the American Fundamental Investors mutual fund. The article touted the fund as a real high-flying investment with excellent returns: It had a one-year total return of 22 percent and a three-year total return of 103 percent. So, in the three years since Nations purchased shares in American Fundamental, he had doubled his original $5,000 investment. Based on this information alone, he decided to keep his investment. He also decided that he needed to do a better job of evaluating his investment on a regular basis.

He began his research by going to the website of American Funds (www.americanfunds.com), where he found his fund among all the mutual funds sponsored by the company. He learned that his fund had the following objective: "to provide long-term growth of capital and income primarily through investments in common stocks." There was also information on the fund's past performance, dividends, capital gains, fees and expenses, and Morningstar rating. In addition, Nations was able to print out a complete schedule—six pages—of different investments owned by the fund.

Nations was surprised at how easy it was to find information on his investment. More important, the information he found on the American Funds website supported the material reported in *Mutual Funds* magazine. Those one-year and three-year returns were for real, and his investment really had doubled in value in just three years. After spending more than three hours on the Internet, he not only knew the value of his investment but also had a feeling that this mutual fund would continue to perform well in the future. According to Bryan Nations, this fund was a "keeper."

## Questions

1. Although Bryan Nations doubled his original investment in three years, he now admits that he made mistakes during the first three years he owned shares in the American Fundamental Investors mutual fund. In your own words, what did he do wrong?

2. If you owned shares in the American Fundamental Investors mutual fund, would you use published materials available in the library or sources found on the Internet to monitor your investment? Explain your answer.

SOURCES: "American Fundamental Investors," *Mutual Funds,* September 1999, pp. 86–87; American Funds website (www.americanfunds.com), American Fund Distributors Group, 333 South Hope Street, Los Angeles, CA 90071.

## Learning Objectives

**Obj. 1** Describe the characteristics of mutual fund investments.

**Obj. 2** Classify mutual funds by investment objective.

**Obj. 3** Evaluate mutual funds for investment purposes.

**Obj. 4** Describe how and why mutual funds are bought and sold.

*mutual fund*
An investment chosen by people who pool their money to buy stocks, bonds, and other financial securities selected by professional managers who work for an investment company.

If you ever thought about buying stocks or bonds but decided not to, your reasons were probably like most other people's: You didn't know enough to make a good decision, and you lacked enough money to diversify your investments among several choices. These same two reasons explain why people invest in mutual funds. By pooling your money with money from other investors, a mutual fund can do for you what you can't do on your own. Specifically, a **mutual fund** is an investment chosen by people who pool their money to buy stocks, bonds, and other financial securities selected by professional managers who work for investment companies. Mutual funds are an excellent choice for many individuals. In many cases, they can also be used for retirement accounts, including 401(k), 403(b), traditional individual retirement accounts, and Roth IRAs.

Bryan Nations, the investor in the opening case, did his homework before purchasing shares in the American Fundamental Investors mutual fund. But like many investors, he just assumed his investment would increase in value. Thus, he made two critical mistakes. First, he didn't continue to monitor the value of his investment. Second, he didn't continue to evaluate his investment after his initial purchase. Fortunately for Nations, his mutual fund did earn exceptional returns over the first three years, and his investment doubled in value. While he was lucky, you may not be so fortunate. Make no mistake about this: *Good investors evaluate an investment before purchase. The best investors continue to evaluate their investments after the purchase.*

An investment in mutual funds is based on the concept of opportunity costs, which we have discussed throughout this text. Simply put, you have to be willing to take some chances if you want to get larger returns on your investments. Before deciding whether mutual funds are the right investment for you, read the material presented in the next section.

## WHY INVESTORS PURCHASE MUTUAL FUNDS

**Obj. 1**
Describe the characteristics of mutual fund investments.

Today, investors like—no, love—their mutual fund investments. The following statistics illustrate how important mutual fund investments are to both individuals and the nation's economy:

1. Although the mutual fund concept originated in Europe and then spread to the United States in the late 1800s, mutual funds didn't gain real popularity until the last 25 years.[1]
2. The number of mutual funds grew from 361 in 1970, to over 6,000[2] in 1997, to over 7,500 in late 1999, and continues to increase each year.[3]

3. As of July 1999, the combined value of assets owned by mutual funds in the United States exceeded $6 trillion.[4]

4. In the first seven months of 1999, investors poured $103 billion into mutual fund investments.[5]

5. During the month of July 1999, more than $12.3 billion flowed into mutual fund investments.[6]

No doubt about it, the mutual fund industry is big business. And yet, you may be wondering why so many people invest in mutual funds.

The major reasons investors purchase mutual funds are *professional management* and *diversification*. Most investment companies do everything possible to convince you that they can do a better job of picking securities than you can. Sometimes these claims are true, and sometimes they are just so much hot air. Still, investment companies do have professional fund managers with years of experience who devote large amounts of time to picking just the "right" securities for their funds' portfolios. *Be warned:* Even the best portfolio managers make mistakes. So you, the investor, must be careful!

The diversification mutual funds offer spells safety, because an occasional loss incurred with one investment contained in a mutual fund is usually offset by gains from other investments in the fund. For example, consider the diversification provided in the portfolio of the Alger Capital Appreciation fund, shown in Exhibit 16–1. With over $480 million in assets, this fund contains almost 50 different stock investments spread over 17 different industrial areas. Note that the information contained in Exhibit 16–1 was taken from the fund's semiannual report. If you want more up-to-date information on the composition of investments within the fund or other information about the fund, visit its website at www.algerfund.com.[7]

## Characteristics of Mutual Funds

*investment company*
A firm that, for a management fee, invests the pooled funds of small investors in securities appropriate to its stated investment objectives.

Barron's *Dictionary of Finance and Investment Terms* defines an **investment company** as a firm that, for a management fee, invests the pooled funds of small investors in securities appropriate to its stated investment objectives.[8] Today mutual funds sponsored by investment companies may be classified as either closed-end funds or open-end funds.

*closed-end fund*
A mutual fund whose shares are issued by an investment company only when the fund is organized.

*open-end fund*
A mutual fund whose shares are issued and redeemed by the investment company at the request of investors.

### Closed-End or Open-End Mutual Funds

Approximately 10 percent of all mutual funds are closed-end funds offered by investment companies. A **closed-end fund** is a mutual fund whose shares are issued by an investment company only when the fund is organized. As a result, only a certain number of shares are available to investors. After all the shares originally issued have been sold, an investor can purchase shares only from another investor who is willing to sell. Shares of closed-end funds are traded on the floors of stock exchanges or in the over-the-counter market. Like the prices of stocks, the prices of shares for closed-end funds are determined by the factors of supply and demand, by the value of stocks and other investments contained in the fund's portfolio, and by investor expectations. A special section of *The Wall Street Journal* provides information about closed-end funds.

*net asset value (NAV)*
The current market value of the securities contained in the mutual fund's portfolio minus the mutual fund's liabilities divided by the number of shares outstanding.

Approximately 90 percent of all mutual funds are open-end funds. An **open-end fund** is a mutual fund whose shares are issued and redeemed by the investment company at the request of investors. Investors are free to buy and sell shares at the net asset value. The **net asset value (NAV)** per share is equal to the current market value of securities contained in the mutual fund's portfolio minus the mutual fund's liabilities divided by the number of shares outstanding:

**EXHIBIT 16-1**   Types of Securities Included in the Portfolio of Alger Capital Appreciation Mutual Fund

The Alger Fund
Alger Capital Appreciation Portfolio
Schedule of Investments (Unaudited)
April 30, 1999

| Common Stocks—106.6% | Shares | Value | Common Stocks—(cont.) | Shares | Value |
|---|---|---|---|---|---|
| ADVERTISING—.6% | | | FINANCIAL SERVICES—8.3% | | |
| Outdoor Sytems, Inc.* | 115,000 | $   2,986,620 | Citigroup Inc. | 216,500 | 16,291,625 |
| BIO-TECHNOLOGY—2.0% | | | Kansas City Southern Industries Inc. | 170,100 | 10,131,666 |
| Amgen Inc.* | 158,000 | 9,707,204 | Morgan Stanley Dean Witter & Co. | 137,500 | 13,638,350 |
| | | | | | 40,061,641 |
| BROADCASTING—2.3% | | | | | |
| Cablevision Sytems Corp. Cl. A.* | 142,000 | 10,987,250 | FOOD CHAINS—2.5% | | |
| | | | Fred Meyer, Inc.* | 70,000 | 3,788,750 |
| BUSINESS SERVICES—2.1% | | | Kroger Co.* | 65,000 | 3,530,345 |
| IMS Health Inc. | 341,900 | 10,257,000 | Safeway Inc.* | 85,000 | 4,584,730 |
| COMMUNICATION | | | | | 11,903,825 |
| EQUIPMENT—7.7% | | | | | |
| Ascend Communications, Inc.* | 59,500 | 5,749,188 | INSURANCE—1.3% | | |
| Cisco Sytems, Inc.* | 183,750 | 20,959,076 | American International Group, Inc. | 55,000 | 6,459,090 |
| Motorola, Inc. | 130,000 | 10,416,250 | PHARMACEUTICALS—4.0% | | |
| | | 37,124,514 | Pfizer Inc. | 126,200 | 14,520,951 |
| | | | Schering-Plough Corporation | 102,400 | 4,947,251 |
| COMMUNICATIONS—18.4% | | | | | 19,468,202 |
| America Online Inc. | 159,900 | 22,825,725 | | | |
| Broadcast.com Inc.* | 77,000 | 9,875,250 | RETAILING—17.5% | | |
| Comcast Corp. Cl. A. Special | 206,000 | 13,531,728 | Amazon.com Inc.* | 163,800 | 28,183,918 |
| COX Communications Inc. Cl. A.* | 169,500 | 13,454,063 | Best Buy Company Inc.* | 93,000 | 4,440,750 |
| MCI Worldcom Inc.* | 118,700 | 9,755,716 | Costco Companies Inc.* | 132,000 | 10,683,816 |
| Nextel Communications Inc. Cl. A.* | 183,000 | 7,491,654 | Home Depot, Inc. | 275,000 | 16,482,950 |
| Qwest Communications | | | Office Depot Inc.* | 396,000 | 8,712,000 |
| International, Inc.* | 74,500 | 6,365,131 | Staples Inc.* | 128,475 | 3,854,250 |
| RealNetworks Inc.* | 25,500 | 5,648,250 | Wal-Mart Stores Inc. | 261,000 | 12,006,000 |
| | | 88,947,517 | | | 84,363,684 |
| COMPUTER RELATED & | | | SEMICONDUCTORS—4.7% | | |
| BUSINESS EQUIMENT—6.8% | | | Altera Corporation* | 50,000 | 3,612,500 |
| EMC Corp.* | 117,000 | 12,745,746 | Broadcom Corp. Cl. A.* | 45,000 | 3,470,625 |
| Sun Microsystems Inc.* | 338,000 | 20,216,794 | Linear Technology Corporation | 40,000 | 2,275,000 |
| | | 32,962,540 | Texas Instruments, Incorporated | 50,000 | 5,106,250 |
| | | | Xilinx, Inc.* | 175,000 | 7,984,375 |
| COMPUTER SERVICES—15.7% | | | | | 22,448,750 |
| CNET Inc.* | 98,000 | 12,593,000 | | | |
| eBay Inc.* | 135,800 | 28,263,375 | SEMICONDUCTOR CAPITAL | | |
| Excite Inc.* | 106,600 | 15,563,600 | EQUIPMENT—3.6% | | |
| Yahoo Inc.* | 110,600 | 19,320,493 | Applied Material Inc.* | 193,500 | 10,376,437 |
| | | 75,740,468 | ASM Lithography Holding NV* | 72,000 | 2,808,000 |
| COMPUTER SOFTWARE—5.4% | | | Teradyne, Inc.* | 90,500 | 4,270,514 |
| Intuit Inc.* | 68,500 | 5,899.563 | | | 17,454,951 |
| Microsoft Corporation* | 247,400 | 20,116,836 | Total Common Stocks | | |
| | | 26,016,399 | (Cost $389,094,164)(a) | 10.6% | 514,628,668 |
| CONGLOMERATE—3.7% | | | Liability in Excess of Other Assets | (6.6) | (31,899,475) |
| Tyco International Ltd. | 219,434 | 17,829,013 | Net Assets | 100.0% | $482,729,193 |

SOURCE: Semiannual Report, The Alger Capital Appreciation Fund, April 30, 1999, The Alger Fund, 1 World Trade Center, Suite 9333, New York, NY 10048 (1–800–992–3863).

$$\text{Net asset value} = \frac{\text{Value of the fund's portfolio} - \text{Liabilities}}{\text{Number of share outstanding}}$$

For example, assume the portfolio of all investments contained in the New American Frontiers Mutual Fund has a current market value of $124 million. The fund also has liabilities totaling $4 million. If this mutual fund has 6 million shares outstanding, the net asset value per share is $20:

$$\text{Net asset value} = \frac{\text{Value of the fund's portfolio} - \text{Liabilities}}{\text{Number of shares outstanding}}$$

$$= \frac{\$124 \text{ million} - \$4 \text{ million}}{6 \text{ million shares}}$$

$$= \$20 \text{ per share}$$

For most mutual funds, the net asset value is calculated at the close of trading each day. In addition to buying and selling shares on request, most open-end funds provide their investors with a wide variety of services, including payroll deduction programs, automatic reinvestment programs, automatic withdrawal programs, and the option to change shares in one fund to another fund within the same fund family—all topics discussed later in this chapter.

### Load Funds and No-Load Funds

Before investing in mutual funds, you should compare the cost of this type of investment with the cost of other investment alternatives, such as stocks or bonds. With regard to cost, mutual funds are classified as load funds or no-load funds. A **load fund** (sometimes referred to as an *"A" fund*) is a mutual fund in which investors pay a commission every time they purchase shares. The commission charge, sometimes referred to as the *sales fee,* may be as high as 8½ percent of the purchase price for investments under $10,000. (Typically, this fee declines for investments over $10,000.)

*load fund*  A mutual fund in which investors pay a commission (as high as 8½ percent) every time they purchase shares.

While many exceptions exist, the average load charge for mutual funds is between 3 and 5 percent. Let's assume you decide to invest $10,000 in the First American Large Cap Growth A fund. This fund charges a sales load of 5.25 percent that you must pay when you purchase shares. The dollar amount of the sales charge on your $10,000 investment is $525 ($10,000 × 5.25% = $525). After paying the $525, the amount available for investment is reduced to $9,475 ($10,000 − $525 = $9,475). The "stated" advantage of a load fund is that the fund's sales force (account executives, financial planners, or brokerage divisions of banks and other financial institutions) will explain the mutual fund to investors and offer advice as to when shares of the fund should be bought or sold.

*no-load fund*  A mutual fund in which the individual investor pays no sales charge.

A **no-load fund** is a mutual fund in which the individual investor pays no sales charge. No-load funds don't charge commissions when you buy shares because they have no salespeople. If you want to buy shares of a no-load fund, you must deal directly with the investment company. The usual means of contact is by telephone, the Internet, or mail. You can also purchase shares in a no-load fund from many discount brokers, including Charles Schwab, Jack White & Company, Waterhouse Securities, and E*Trade.

As an investor, you must decide whether to invest in a load fund or a no-load fund. Some investment salespeople have claimed that load funds outperform no-load funds. But many financial analysts suggest there is no significant difference between mutual funds that charge commissions and those that do not.[9] *Since no-load funds offer the same investment opportunities load funds offer, you should investigate them further before deciding which type of mutual fund is best for you.* Although the sales commission should not be the decisive factor, the possibility of saving an 8½ percent load charge is a factor to consider. For example, suppose Barbara Harrington invests $10,000 in a mutual fund that charges an 8½ percent sales fee. Since this fee is deducted in advance, her initial $10,000 investment is reduced by $850. Simply put, she now has $9,150 that she can use to buy shares in this load fund. By comparison, Mary Hernandez decides to invest $10,000 in a no-load mutual fund. Since there is no sales fee, she can use the entire $10,000 to purchase shares in this no-load fund. Depending on the load fund's performance, it may take Barbara a year or more to "catch up" and cover the cost of the sales fee.

## Management Fees and Other Charges

In evaluating a specific mutual fund, you should consider management fees and other charges. The investment companies that sponsor mutual funds charge management fees. This fee, which is disclosed in the fund's prospectus, is a fixed percentage of the fund's asset value. Today annual management fees range between 0.25 and 1 percent of the fund's asset value. While fees vary considerably, the average is one-half of 1 percent of the fund's assets.

*contingent deferred sales load*   A 1 to 6 percent charge that shareholders pay when they withdraw their investment from a mutual fund.

Instead of charging investors a fee when they purchase shares in a mutual fund, some mutual funds charge a **contingent deferred sales load** (sometimes referred to as a *back-end load* or a *"B" fund*). These fees range from 1 to 6 percent, depending on how long you own the mutual fund before making a withdrawal. For example, assume you withdraw $5,000 from B shares that you own in the Aim Balance mutual fund within a year of your original purchase date. You must pay a 5 percent contingent deferred sales fee. Your fee is $250 ($5,000 × 5% = $250). After the fee is deducted from your $5,000 withdrawal, you will receive $4,750 ($5,000 − $250 = $4,750). *Generally,* the deferred charge declines until there is no withdrawal charge if you own the shares in the fund for more than five to seven years. Obviously, this deferred sales fee is designed to discourage early withdrawals. If all other factors are equal, a fund that doesn't charge a contingent deferral sales load is superior to a fund that does.

*12b-1 fee*   A fee that an investment company levies to defray the costs of advertising and marketing a mutual fund.

The investment company may also levy a **12b-1 fee** (sometimes referred to as a distribution fee) to defray the costs of advertising and marketing a mutual fund. Approved by the Securities and Exchange Commission in 1980, annual 12b-1 fees are calculated on the value of a fund's assets and are approximately 1 percent of a fund's assets per year. Note: A true no-load fund has neither a sales fee nor a 12b-1 fee.

Unlike the one-time sales load fees that mutual funds charge to purchase or sell shares, the 12b-1 fee is an ongoing fee that is charged on an annual basis. Note that 12b-1 fees can cost you a lot of money over a period of years. Assuming there is no difference in performance offered by two different mutual funds, one of which charges a 12b-1 fee while the other doesn't, choose the latter fund. The 12b-1 fee is so lucrative for investment companies that a number of them have begun selling Class C shares that charge a higher 12b-1 fee and no sales load or contingent deferred sales fee to attract new investors. When compared to Class A shares (commissions charged when shares are purchased) and Class B shares (commissions charged when withdrawals are made over the first five to seven years), Class C shares, with their ongoing, higher 12b-1 fees, may be more expensive over a long period of time.

By now, you are probably asking yourself, "Should I purchase Class A shares, Class B shares, or Class C shares?" There are no easy answers, but your professional financial adviser or broker can help you determine which class of shares of a particular mutual fund best suits your financial needs. You can also do your own research to determine which

**EXHIBIT 16–2**

Summary of
Expenses Paid
to Invest in the
Vista Growth
and Income
Mutual Fund

SOURCE: Excerpted from
the *Vista Growth and
Income Fund Prospectus,*
January 10, 1998.

**Expense Summary**

|  | Class A Shares |
|---|---|
| **Shareholder Transaction Expenses** | |
| Maximum Sales Charge Imposed on Purchases (as a percentage of offering price) | 4.75% |
| Maximum Deferred Sales Charge (as a percentage of the lower of original purchase price or redemption proceeds)* | None |
| **Annual Fund Operating Expenses (as a percentage of average net assets)** | |
| Investment Advisory Fee | 0.40% |
| 12b-1 Fee** | 0.25% |
| Shareholder Servicing Fee | 0.25% |
| Other Expenses | 0.40% |
| Total Fund Operating Expenses | 1.30% |

**Examples**

| Your investment of $1,000 would incur the following expenses, assuming 5% annual return: | 1 Year | 3 Years | 5 Years | 10 Years |
|---|---|---|---|---|
| Class A Shares[†] | $60 | $87 | $115 | $197 |
| Class B Shares: | | | | |
| Assuming complete redemption at the end of the period[††] [†††] | $70 | $90 | $121 | $198 |
| Assuming no redemptions[†††] | $18 | $57 | $ 97 | $198 |

* The maximum deferred sales charge on Class B shares applies to redemptions during the first year after purchase; the charge generally declines by 1% annually thereafter (except in the fourth year), reaching zero after six years. See "How to Buy, Sell and Exchange Shares."

** Long-term shareholders in mutual funds with 12b-1 fees, such as Class A and Class B shareholders of the Fund, may pay more than the economic equivalent of the maximum front-end sales charge permitted by rules of the National Association of Securities Dealers, Inc.

[†]Assumes deduction at the time of purchase of the maximum sales charge

[††]Assumes deduction at the time of redemption of the maximum applicable deferred sales charge.

[†††]Ten-year figures assume conversion of Class B shares to Class A shares at the beginning of the ninth year after purchase. See "How to Buy, Sell and Exchange Shares."

fund is right for you. Factors to consider include whether you want to invest in a load fund or no-load fund, management fees, and expense ratios. As you will see later in this chapter, a number of sources of information can help you make your investment decisions.

The investment company's prospectus must provide all details relating to management fees, contingent deferred sales fees, 12b-1 fees, and other expenses. Exhibit 16–2 on this page reproduces the summary of expenses (sometimes called a *fee table*) taken from the Vista Growth and Income Fund. Notice that this fee table has three separate parts. The first part describes shareholder transaction expenses. For this fund, the maximum sales charge is 4.75 percent. The second part describes the fund's annual operating expenses. For this fund, the expense ratio is 1.30 percent of the fund's assets. The *expense ratio* is the total management fees, 12b-1 fees, and expenses stated as a percentage of the fund's assets. The third part illustrates the total fees and expenses you would pay on a $1,000 investment assuming a 5 percent annual return and redemption at the end of 1, 3, 5, and 10 years.

Exhibit 16–3 summarizes load charges and no-load charges, Class A, Class B, and Class C shares. In addition, it reports management fees, contingent deferred sales loads, and 12b-1 charges.

| Type of Fee or Charge | Customary Amount |
| --- | --- |
| Load fund | Up to 8½ percent of the purchase |
| No-load fund | No sales charge |
| Management fee | 0.25 to 1 percent per year of the fund's total assets |
| Contingent deferred sales load | 1 to 6 percent of withdrawals depending on how long you own the fund before making a withdrawal |
| 12b-1 fee | Approximately 1 percent of the fund's assets |
| Class A shares | Commission charge when shares are purchased |
| Class B shares | Commission charge when money is withdrawn during the first five to seven years |
| Class C shares | No commission to buy or sell shares of a fund, but higher, ongoing 12b-1 fees |

**EXHIBIT 16-3**

Typical Fees Associated with Mutual Fund Investments

## Concept Check 16-1

1.   What type of information about mutual funds can be found on the Internet?
2.   What are two major reasons investors purchase mutual funds?
3.   How do a closed-end fund and an open-end fund differ?
4.   What are the typical fees charged for a load and no-load mutual fund?
5.   What is the difference among Class A, B, and C shares?
6.   What are the typical management fees, contingent deferred sales loads, and 12b-1 fees?

# CLASSIFICATIONS OF MUTUAL FUNDS

**Obj. 2**
Classify mutual funds by investment objective.

The managers of mutual funds tailor their investment portfolios to the investment objectives of their customers. Usually a fund's objectives are plainly disclosed in its prospectus. For example, the objectives of the Fundamental Investors Mutual Fund are described as follows:

> The fund seeks to make your investment grow and provide you with income over time by investing primarily in common stocks of large, established companies that offer growth potential at reasonable prices.
>
> The fund is designed for investors seeking both capital appreciation and income. An investment in the fund is subject to risks, including the possibility that the fund may decline in value in response to global economic, political and social events. The prices of equity securities will be affected by events involving securities owned in the fund.[10]

While it may be helpful to categorize the 7,500-plus mutual funds into different categories, note that different sources of investment information may use different categories for the same mutual fund. In most cases, the name of the category gives a pretty good clue to the types of investments included within the category. The *major* fund categories are described in alphabetical order as follows:

## Stock Funds

*   *Aggressive growth funds* (sometimes called *capital appreciation funds*) seek rapid growth by purchasing stocks whose prices are expected to increase dramatically in a short period of time. Turnover within an aggressive growth fund is high because managers are buying and selling individual stocks. Investors in these funds experience wide price swings because of the underlying speculative nature of the stocks in the fund's portfolio.

Advice from a Pro

## DEAN BROWN ON WHY INVESTORS CHOOSE MUTUAL FUNDS

Mutual fund investing provides a good way to get started with small amounts of money, at the same time affording the investor professional management, according to Dean Brown, a financial advisor with the Institutional Securities Corporation in Dallas, TX. Mr. Brown also points out that by investing in mutual funds you can diversify your investments to fit your personal goals and objectives. However, the most important advantage is still the ability to get professional management.

When choosing a mutual fund, Mr. Brown recommends that investors rely on research. Research gives investors an understanding of the kind of investment they are making, whether or not they feel comfortable with the choice, and lets them know what the track record for a specific mutual fund is. While research may not be foolproof, it does provide a guide as to what can be expected of a particular fund in the future. Only after an investor has researched a potential investment, is it possible to find a mutual fund that fits the investor's needs, had good management, and has a successful long-term track record.

According to Mr. Brown, many investors are always changing funds and chasing funds that were hot last year. Consequently, they incur more fees, sales charges, and so on. This can make mutual fund investing more expensive and in most cases investors end up with smaller total returns. This is not to say that changes cannot be made in the mutual funds an investor owns. However, it is best to give a well managed fund time to work.

- *Equity income funds* invest in stocks issued by companies with a long history of paying dividends. The major objective of these funds is to provide income to shareholders. These funds are attractive investment choices for conservative or retired investors.

Did You Know

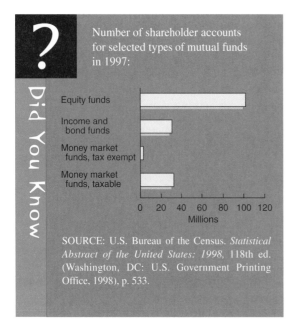

Number of shareholder accounts for selected types of mutual funds in 1997:

SOURCE: U.S. Bureau of the Census. *Statistical Abstract of the United States: 1998*, 118th ed. (Washington, DC: U.S. Government Printing Office, 1998), p. 533.

- *Global stock funds* invest in stocks of companies throughout the world, including the United States. The managers for global funds can invest wherever the opportunities are and are not restricted by national boundaries.
- *Growth funds* invest in companies expecting higher-than-average revenue and earnings growth. While similar to aggressive growth funds, growth funds tend to invest in larger companies that may pay some dividends. As a result, the prices for shares in a growth fund are less volatile compared to aggressive growth funds.
- *Growth and income funds* invest in stocks that provide both a predictable source of dividend income and the potential for dollar appreciation. These funds are generally more conservative than aggressive growth funds and growth funds because they invest in larger and more established companies.
- *Index funds* invest in the same companies included in an index like the Standard & Poor's 500 Stock Index. Since fund managers pick the stocks issued by

the companies included in the index, an index fund should provide approximately the same performance as the index. Also, since index funds are cheaper to manage, they often have lower management fees.

- *International funds* invest in foreign stocks sold in securities markets throughout the world; thus, if the economy in one region or nation is in a slump, profits can still be earned in others. Unlike global funds, which invest in stocks issued by companies in both foreign nations and the United States, a true international fund invests outside the United States.
- *Mid-cap funds* invest in companies with total capitalization of at least $500 million whose stocks offer more security than small-cap funds and more growth potential than funds that invest in large corporations.
- *Regional funds* seek to invest in stock traded within one region of the world, such as the European region, the Latin American region, and the Pacific region.
- *Sector funds* invest in companies within the same industry. Examples of sectors include Health and Biotech, Science & Technology, Computers, and Natural Resources.
- *Small-cap funds* invest in smaller, lesser-known companies with a total capitalization of less than $500 million. Because these companies are small and innovative, these funds offer higher growth potential. They are more speculative than funds that invest in larger, more established companies.
- *Utility funds* invest in companies that provide utility services to their customers. These funds tend to be very conservative because of the stability of sales, profits, and dividends. They are often chosen by retired investors because of their safety.

## Bond Funds

- *High-yield (junk) bond funds* invest in high-yield, high-risk corporate bonds.
- *Insured municipal bond funds* invest in municipal bonds that provide tax-free income and are insured against the risk of default on interest and/or principal by an outside company.
- *Intermediate corporate bond funds* invest in investment-grade corporate debt with maturities between 5 and 10 years.
- *Intermediate U.S. bond funds* invest in U.S. Treasury notes with maturities between 5 and 10 years.
- *Long-term corporate bond funds* invest in investment-grade corporate bond issues with maturities in excess of 10 years.
- *Long-term (U.S.) bond funds* invest in U.S. Treasury and U.S. zero-coupon bonds with maturities in excess of 10 years.
- *Municipal bond funds* invest in municipal bonds that provide investors with tax-free interest income.
- *Short-term corporate bond funds* invest in investment-grade bond issues with maturities between 1 and 5 years.
- *Short-term (U.S.) government bond funds* invest in U.S. Treasury issues with maturities between 1 and 5 years.

## Other Funds

- *Balanced funds* invest in both stocks and bonds with the primary objective of conserving principal. Often the percentage of stocks and bonds is stated in the fund's prospectus.

- *Money market funds* invest in certificates of deposit, government securities, and other safe and highly liquid investments.
- *Stock/bond blend funds* invest in both stocks and bonds to achieve multipurpose objectives that may include flexible income, flexible portfolios, global securities, and convertible securities.

*family of funds*
A group of mutual funds managed by one investment company.

A **family of funds** exists when one investment company manages a group of mutual funds. Each fund within the family has a different financial objective. For instance, one fund may be a government bond fund and another a growth fund. Most investment companies offer exchange privileges that enable shareholders to switch among the mutual funds in a fund family. For example, if you own shares in the Franklin growth fund, you may, at your discretion, switch to the Franklin income fund. Generally, investors may give instructions to switch from one fund to another within the same family either in writing, over the telephone, or via the Internet. The family-of-funds concept makes it convenient for shareholders to switch their investments among funds as different funds offer more potential, financial reward, or security. Charges for exchanges, if any, generally are small for each transaction. For funds that do charge, the fee may be as low as $5 per transaction.

*market timer*   An individual who helps investors decide when to switch their investments from one fund to another fund, usually within the same family of funds.

Many financial analysts suggest that the true mark of a quality mutual fund investment is the fund's ability to increase the investor's return during good times and maintain that return during bad times. To help accomplish this task, a large number of investors have turned to market timers. A **market timer** is an individual who helps investors decide when to switch their investments from one fund to another fund, usually within the same family of funds. Market timers usually charge an annual fee of $1\frac{1}{2}$ to 3 percent of the dollar value of the funds they manage. When evaluating market timers, keep in mind that the services they offer are a relatively recent innovation. Thus, it may be hard to judge their long-term track record accurately. Early research indicates that market timers must be evaluated on their individual investment philosophy and their past performance, and it is impossible to pass judgment on *all* market timers as a group.

## Concept Check 16-2

1. How important is the investment objective as stated in a fund's prospectus?
2. Why do you think fund managers offer so many different kinds of funds?
3. What is a family of funds? How is it related to shareholder exchanges?
4. How does a market timer help people manage their mutual fund investments?

## HOW TO MAKE A DECISION TO BUY OR SELL MUTUAL FUNDS

### Obj. 3
Evaluate mutual funds for investment purposes.

Often the decision to buy or sell shares in mutual funds is "too easy" because investors assume they do not need to evaluate these investments. Why question what the professional portfolio managers decide to do? Yet professionals do make mistakes. The responsibility for choosing the right mutual fund rests with *you*. After all, you are the only one who knows how much risk you are willing to assume and how a particular mutual fund can help you achieve your goals.

If you think there are mutual funds designed to meet just about any conceivable investment objective, you are probably right. Hundreds of mutual funds trade daily under the headings "aggressive growth," "small-cap," and "growth-income." Fortunately, a lot of information is available to help you evaluate a specific mutual fund. Unfortunately, you can get lost in all the facts and figures and forget your ultimate

EXHIBIT 16-4

Common Steps
Used by Investors
to Evaluate Mutual
Funds

☐ **Step 1: Determine your investment objectives.**
For more information, review the material presented in Chapter 13.

☐ **Step 2: Perform a financial checkup to make sure you are ready to invest.**
For more information, review the material presented in Chapter 13.

☐ **Step 3: Obtain the money you need to purchase mutual funds.**
Although the amount will vary, $250 to $2,500 is usually required to open an account
with a brokerage firm or an investment company.

☐ **Step 4: Find a fund with an objective that matches your objective.**
*The Wall Street Journal, Barron's,* and personal finance magazines may help you identify
funds with objectives that match your investment objectives. Also, you can contact, the
investment company and ask for a prospectus and an annual report for a specific mutual
fund. Finally, you can use the Internet to screen mutual funds that are compatible with
your investment objectives.

☐ **Step 5: Evaluate, evaluate, and evaluate any mutual fund before buying or selling.**
Complete the Evaluation of a Mutual Fund form on page 533 before making a decision
to buy or sell a mutual fund. Possible sources of information include newspapers, the
fund's prospectus, the fund's annual report, financial publications, the Internet, and
professional advisory services—all sources described in the remainder of this section.
Be sure to evaluate the fund manager's background and how long the manager has been
managing the fund.

goal: to choose a mutual fund that will help you achieve your financial goals. To help
you sort out all the research, statistics, and information about mutual funds and give
you some direction as to what to do first, we have provided the checklist in Exhibit
16–4. The remainder of this section explains the types of information you can obtain
from each source listed in the exhibit.

## How to Read the Mutual Funds Section of the Newspaper

Most large, metropolitan newspapers, *The Wall Street Journal,* and *Barron's* provide
information about mutual funds. For most investors, the Mutual Funds in Review section of *The Wall Street Journal,* published at the beginning of each month, provides the
most complete financial coverage (see Exhibit 16–5), including information about net
asset value, the fund family and fund name, the fund objective, total return over
selected time periods, rankings, sales load fees (if any), and annual expenses. Coverage
in the regular, daily *Wall Street Journal* and large, metropolitan newspapers and weekly
coverage in *Barron's* are generally less extensive. Much of this same information is
also available on the Internet.

The letters beside the name of a specific fund can be very informative. You can find
out what they mean by looking at the footnotes that accompany the newspaper's
mutual fund quotations. Generally, "NL" means no load, "p" means a 12b-1 distribution fee is charged, "r" means a redemption charge may be made, and "t" means both
the p and r footnotes apply.

In many cases, the search for a no-load fund starts with a newspaper quotation.
Therefore, the NL footnote is especially important. As pointed out earlier, no-load
mutual funds do not charge sales fees. Since no-load funds offer the same investment
opportunities load funds do, financial experts often recommend these funds.

The newspaper coverage described in this section is a good means of monitoring the
value of your mutual fund investments. However, other sources of information provide
a more complete basis for evaluating mutual fund investments.

Financial Information about Mutual Funds Available in the Mutual Funds in Review Section of The Wall Street Journal

**How to Read the Monthly Performance Tables**

Data come from two sources. The daily Net Asset Value (NAV) and Net Change calculations are supplied by the National Association of Securities Dealers (NASD). Performance and cost data come from **Lipper, Inc.**

Though verified, the data cannot be guaranteed by Lipper or its data sources. Double-check with funds before investing.

Performance calculations assume reinvestment of all distributions and are after subtracting annual expenses. But figures don't reflect sales charges ("loads") or redemption fees.

**Total Return**

NAV change plus accumulated income for the period, in percent. Assumes reinvestment of all distributions. Percentages are annualized for periods exceeding one year. Calculations are based on latest data from fund.

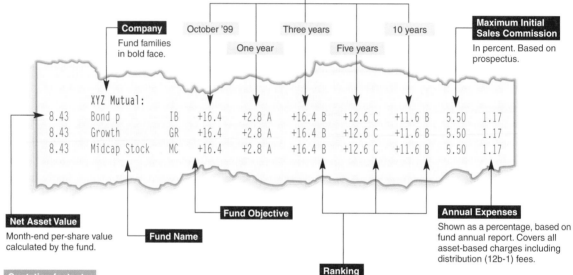

**Company**
Fund families in bold face.

**Maximum Initial Sales Commission**
In percent. Based on prospectus.

**Net Asset Value**
Month-end per-share value calculated by the fund.

**Fund Name**

**Fund Objective**

**Annual Expenses**
Shown as a percentage, based on fund annual report. Covers all asset-based charges including distribution (12b-1) fees.

**Ranking**
Compares performance among funds with same investment objectives and then ranked for time periods listed. Performance is measured from either the closest Thursday or month-end for periods of more than three years. **A** = top 20%; **B** = next 20%; **C** = middle 20%; **D** = next 20%; **E** = bottom 20%.

**Quotation footnotes**

**e**–Ex-distribution, **f**–Previous day's quotation. **g**–Footnotes x and s apply. **i**–No valid comparison with other funds because of expense structure. **j**–Footnotes e and s apply. **k**–Recalculated by Lipper using updated data. **p**–Distribution costs apply, 12b-1. **r**–Redemption charge may apply. **s**–Stock split or dividend. **t**–Footnotes p and r apply. **v**–Footnotes x and e apply. **x**–Ex-dividend. **z**–Footnotes x, e, and s apply. **NA**–Not available due to incomplete price performance or cost data. **NE**–Deleted by Lipper editor; data in question. **NL**–No load (sales commission). **NN**–Fund doesn't wish to be tracked. **NS**–Fund didn't exist at start of period.

## Financial Objectives—Again

In Chapter 13, we talked about establishing investment goals and objectives. In this chapter, we have looked at the investment objectives of mutual funds. Here our aim is to point out the relationship between the two. In establishing your own investment goals and objectives, you must evaluate the personal factors of age, family situation, risk tolerance, income, and future earning power. Only then can you establish short-term, intermediate, and long-term objectives. Now you must find a mutual fund whose investment objectives match your own.

You may want to look at *The Wall Street Journal,* which spotlights a different fund investment category, along with the top performers in each category, on a daily basis. *Barron's,* as pointed out earlier in this section, provides very detailed information, including current market values, historical market values, fund objective, returns, and so on. You can also use the mutual fund screener on the Yahoo Finance website (http://finance.yahoo.com) to identify funds whose objective matches your objective. Finally, as mentioned earlier in this chapter, a mutual fund's prospectus provides a detailed description of the fund's investment objective. *Be warned:* Many mutual funds have developed objectives that sound good but don't really describe the investment philosophy. While the fund's objective is a place to start, you still need to gather as much information as possible about the fund and the investment company that sponsors it.

## Mutual Fund Prospectus

An investment company sponsoring a mutual fund must give potential investors a prospectus. According to financial experts, the prospectus is usually the first piece of information investors receive, and they should read it completely before investing. Although it may look foreboding, a commonsense approach to reading a fund's prospectus can provide valuable insights. In fact, most investors find that a fund's prospectus can provide a wealth of information. As pointed out earlier, the prospectus summarizes the fund's objective. Also, the fee table provides a summary of the fees a fund charges. In addition to information about objectives and fees, the prospectus should provide the following:

- A statement describing the risk factor associated with the fund.
- A description of the fund's past performance.
- A statement describing the type of investments contained in the fund's portfolio.
- Information about dividends, distributions, and taxes.
- Information about the fund's management.
- Information on limitations or requirements the fund must honor when choosing investments.
- The process investors can use to buy or sell shares in the fund.
- A description of services provided to investors and fees for services, if any.
- Information about how often the fund's investment portfolio changes (sometimes referred to as its *turnover ratio*).

Finally, the prospectus provides information about how to open a mutual fund account with the investment company.

## Mutual Fund Annual Report

If you are a prospective investor, you can request an annual report by mail, an 800 telephone number, or the Internet. Once you are a shareholder, the investment company will send you an annual report. A fund's annual report contains a letter from the president of the investment company, from the fund manager, or both. *Caution: Don't forget the role of the fund manager in determining a fund's success.* One important question is how long the present fund manager has been managing the fund. If a fund has performed well under its present manager over a 5-year, 10-year, or longer period, there is a strong likelihood that it will continue to perform well under that manager in the future.

The annual report also contains detailed financial information about the fund's assets and liabilities, statement of operations, and statement of changes in net assets. Next, the annual report includes a schedule of investments. (Take a second look at the schedule of investments for the Alger Capital Appreciation Mutual Fund in Exhibit 16–1.) Finally, the fund's annual report should include a letter from the fund's independent auditors that provides an opinion as to the accuracy of the fund's financial statements.

**PORTION OF THE 1999 MUTUAL FUND SURVEY BY BUSINESS WEEK MAGAZINE**

## Equity Funds

# MUTUAL FUND SCOREBOARD

### How to Use the Tables

| | |
|---|---|
| **A** | SUPERIOR |
| **B+** | VERY GOOD |
| **B** | ABOVE AVERAGE |
| **C** | AVERAGE |
| **C−** | BELOW AVERAGE |
| **D** | POOR |
| **F** | VERY POOR |

**BUSINESS WEEK RATINGS**
Overall ratings are based on five-year, risk-adjusted returns. They are calculated by subtracting a fund's risk-of-loss factor (see RISK) from historical pretax total return. To get a positive rating, the fund must beat the S&P 500 on a risk-adjusted basis. Category ratings are based on risk-adjusted returns of the funds in that category. The ratings are as follows:

**MANAGEMENT CHANGES**
⬤ indicates the fund's manager has held the job at least 10 years; ⬤ indicates a new manager since Dec. 31, 1997.

**S&P 500 COMPARISON**
The pretax total returns for the S&P 500 are as follows: 1998, 28.6%; three-year average (1996-1998), 28.2%; five-year average (1994-98), 24.0%; 10-year average (1989-98), 19.2%.

**CATEGORY**
Each U.S. diversified fund is classified by market capitalization of the stocks in the portfolio and by the nature of those stocks. If the median market cap is greater than $12 billion, the fund is large-cap; from $1.2 billion to $12 billion, mid-cap; and less than $1.2 billion, small-cap. "Value" funds are those whose stocks have price-to-earnings and price-to-book ratios lower than the average of the stocks in their market capitalizations. "Growth" funds have higher than average p-e and p-b ratios. "Blend" funds are those in which the ratios are about average. Hybrids mix stocks and bonds, and possibly other assets. World funds generally include U.S. stocks; foreign funds do not. Sector and regional foreign funds are as indicated.

| FUND | OVERALL RATING (COMPARES RISK-ADJUSTED PERFORMANCE OF EACH FUND AGAINST ALL FUNDS) | CATEGORY (COMPARES RISK-ADJUSTED PERFORMANCE OF FUND WITHIN CATEGORY) | RATING | SIZE ASSETS $MIL. | % CHG. 1997-98 | FEES SALES CHARGE (%) | EXPENSE RATIO (%) | 1998 RETURNS (%) PRE-TAX | AFTER-TAX | YIELD |
|---|---|---|---|---|---|---|---|---|---|---|
| AARP BALANCED STOCK & BOND | | Domestic Hybrid | | 773.5 | 16 | No load | 0.84 | 6.4 | 4.0 | 3.5 |
| AARP CAPITAL GROWTH | C | Large-cap Blend | D | 1550.2 | 27 | No load | 0.87 | 23.7 | 21.1 | 0.4 |
| AARP GROWTH & INCOME ⬤ | B | Large-cap Value | B | 6933.0 | 4 | No load | 0.67 | 6.1 | 3.3 | 2.2 |
| ACCESSOR SMALL TO MID CAP | C | Mid-cap Blend | C | 257.4 | 106 | No load | 1.15 | 15.3 | 13.4 | 0.0 |
| ACORN ⬤ | C− | Mid-cap Growth | B | 3585.0 | −3 | No load | 0.56 | 6.0 | 4.6 | 0.2 |
| ACORN INTERNATIONAL | C− | Foreign | B | 1726.1 | 6 | No load | 1.19 | 15.4 | 14.9 | 0.7 |
| ACORN USA | | Small-cap Blend | | 281.5 | 53 | No load | 1.35 | 5.8 | 4.0 | 0.0 |
| AIM ADVISOR FLEX C ⬤ | B+ | Domestic Hybrid | B | 669.0 | 11 | 1.00** | 2.20† | 12.4 | 10.1 | 1.1 |
| AIM ADVISOR MULTIFLEX C | C | Mid-cap Value | C | 312.6 | −17 | 1.00** | 2.42† | −0.3 | −1.4 | 1.1 |
| AIM AGGRESSIVE GROWTH | D | Small-cap Growth | C | 3069.3 | −17 | 5.50‡ | 1.06† | 5.0 | 4.8 | 0.0 |

Reprinted from the February 3, 1997 issue of *Business Week* by special permission. © 1999 McGraw-Hill Companies, Inc.

## Financial Publications

Investment-oriented magazines like *Business Week, Forbes, Kiplinger's Personal Finance Magazine,* and *Money* are other sources of information about mutual funds. Each of these publications provides an annual survey of mutual funds and ranks them on a number of important investment criteria. Exhibit 16–6 on this page illustrates a portion of *Business Week*'s mutual fund survey for 1999.

A fund's past long-term performance is no guarantee of future success, but it is a valid predictor. To gauge this variable, most annual surveys include information about a fund's total return. In Exhibit 16–6, total returns for 1 year, 3 years, 5 years, and 10 years are reported for each fund included in the survey. Also included in the *Business Week* survey is information about

- The fund's overall rating when compared with *all* other funds.
- The fund's rating when compared with funds in the same category.
- The size of the fund.
- The sales charge and expense ratio for each fund.
- Historical returns over selected time periods for the last 10 years.
- Portfolio data, including turnover, percentage of cash, percentage of foreign investments, PE ratio, and largest holdings.

**EXHIBIT 16-6**   (CONCLUDED)

**SALES CHARGE**
The cost of buying a fund. Many funds take this "load" out of the initial investment, and for ratings purposes, returns are reduced by these charges. Loads may be levied on withdrawals.

**EXPENSE RATIO**
Expenses for 1998 as a percentage of average net assets, a measure of how much shareholders pay for management. Footnotes indicate if the ratio includes a 12(b)-1 plan, which spends shareholder money on marketing. The average is 1.44%.

**PRETAX TOTAL RETURN**
A fund's net gain to investors, including reinvestment of dividends and capital gains at month-end prices.

**AFTERTAX TOTAL RETURN**
Pretax return adjusted for federal taxes. Assumes ordinary income

and capital gains taxed at highest rate applicable in each year; uses 31% tax rate on income since 1993. Capital gains are assumed to be long-term.

**YIELD**
Income distributions as a percent of net asset value, adjusted for capital-gains distributions.

**HISTORY**
A fund's returns relative to all other funds for four periods, which from left to right are: Jan., 1989-June, 1991; July, 1991-Dec., 1993; Jan., 1994-June, 1996; July, 1996-Dec., 1998. The numbers designate which quartile the fund was in during the period: ￭ for the top quartile; ￭ for the second quartile; ￭ for the third quartile; ￭ for the bottom quartile. No number indicates no data for that period.

**TURNOVER**
Trading activity, the lesser of purchases or sales divided by average monthly assets.

**% CASH**
Portion of fund assets not invested in stocks or bonds. A negative number means the fund has borrowed to buy securities.

**% FOREIGN**
Portion of funds assets invested in non-U.S. securities.

**PRICE-EARNINGS RATIO**
The average, weighted price-earnings ratio of stocks in a fund's portfolio, based on last 12 months' earnings.

**UNTAXED GAINS**
Percentage of assets in portfolio that are unrealized and undistributed capital gains. A negative figure indicates losses that may offset future gains.

**LARGEST HOLDING**
Comes from the latest available fund reports.

**RISK**
Potential for losing money in a fund, or risk-of-loss factor. For each fund, the three-month Treasury bill return is subtracted from the monthly total return for each of the 60 months in the ratings period. When a fund has not performed as well as Treasury bills, the monthly result is negative. The sum of these negative numbers is divided by the number of months. The result is a negative number, and the greater its magnitude, the higher the risk of loss. This number is the basis for BW ratings, category ratings, and the RISK column.

**BEST & WORST QUARTERS**
The fund's highest and lowest quarterly returns of the past five years.

| AVERAGE ANNUAL TOTAL RETURNS (%) | | | | | | HISTORY | PORTFOLIO DATA | | | | | | RISK | | | | | TELEPHONE |
|---|---|---|---|---|---|---|---|---|---|---|---|---|---|---|---|---|---|---|
| 3 YEARS | | 5 YEARS | | 10 YEARS | | RESULTS VS. | TURNOVER | CASH | FOREIGN | P-E | UNTAXED | LARGEST HOLDING | LEVEL | BEST | | WORST | | |
| PRETAX | AFTERTAX | PRETAX | AFTERTAX | PRETAX | AFTERTAX | ALL FUNDS | | % | % | RATIO | GAINS (%) | COMPANY (% ASSETS) | | QTR | %RET | QTR | %RET | |
| 13.6 | 11.6 | NA | NA | NA | NA | ￭ | Average | 6 | 14 | 25 | 12 | Ford Motor (2) | | NA | | NA | | 800-322-2282 |
| 26.3 | 23.5 | 18.8 | 16.9 | 16.3 | 14.2 | ￭￭￭￭ | Average | 7 | 8 | 31 | 38 | Schering-Plough (3) | Average | IV 98 | 25.8 | III 98 | -15.4 | 800-322-2282 |
| 19.1 | 16.3 | 18.1 | 15.6 | 16.4 | 14.3 | ￭￭￭￭ | Low | 2 | 15 | 25 | 22 | Ford Motor (3) | Low | II 97 | 15.5 | III 98 | -13.8 | 800-322-2282 |
| 25.1 | 20.8 | 19.9 | 17.0 | NA | NA | ￭￭ | High | 2 | NA | 27 | 16 | Berkshire Hathaway Cl. A (3) | Average | IV 98 | 23.6 | III 98 | -18.6 | 800-759-3504 |
| 17.5 | 15.0 | 12.7 | 10.3 | 16.3 | 14.2 | ￭￭￭￭ | Low | 8 | 10 | 27 | 42 | Liberty Media Cl. A (4) | Average | IV 98 | 17.9 | III 98 | -19.5 | 800-922-6769 |
| 11.7 | 10.8 | 7.9 | 7.3 | NA | NA | ￭￭ | Low | 19 | 94 | 30 | 30 | Tieto Cl B (5) | Average | I 98 | 18.2 | III 98 | -16.1 | 800-922-6769 |
| NA | NA | NA | NA | NA | NA | | Low | 10 | 1 | 23 | 13 | CalEnergy (6) | Very low | | NA | | NA | 800-922-6769 |
| 16.5 | 14.5 | 15.1 | 13.2 | 13.6 | 11.7 | ￭￭￭￭ | Very low | 1 | 10 | 23 | 30 | American Home Products (1) | Very low | II 97 | 11.5 | III 98 | -7.3 | 800-554-1156 |
| 11.4 | 9.8 | 10.7 | 9.5 | NA | NA | ￭￭ | Average | 1 | 27 | 23 | 0 | CarrAmerica Realty (1) | Low | II 97 | 11.3 | III 98 | -14.5 | 800-554-1156 |
| 10.5 | 9.5 | 17.4 | 16.7 | 20.8 | 19.4 | ￭￭￭￭ | Average | 10 | 2 | 33 | 35 | Veritas Software (1) | High | IV 98 | 25.3 | III 98 | -22.8 | 800-347-4246 |

- Risk of loss factor for each fund.
- A toll-free telephone number for each fund.

In addition to annual surveys like the *Business Week* survey, a number of mutual fund guidebooks are available at your local bookstore or public library. You can also order these publications by phone. Some of the more popular publications are

1. Gerald Perritt, *The Mutual Fund Almanac* (1–800–326–6941)
2. Gordon Williamson, *The 100 Best Mutual Funds You Can Buy* (1–800– 748–5552)
3. *Money Letters Mutual Funds Almanac* (1–800–433–1528)
4. *Individual Investor's Guide to Low-Load Mutual Funds*, American Association of Individual Investors (312–280–0170)
5. *Investment Company Institute Directory of Mutual Funds* (202–326–5800)
6. *The Investor's Guide to Low-Cost Mutual Funds*, Mutual Fund Education Alliance (816–454–9422)
7. *Mutual Fund Fact Book*, Investment Company Institute (202–326–5800)
8. Sheldon Jacobs, *The Handbook for No-Load Fund Investors* (1–800–252–2042).

## Professional Advisory Services

A number of subscription services provide detailed information on mutual funds. Standard and Poor's Corporation, Lipper Analytical Services, Morningstar, Inc., Value Line, and Wiesenberger Investment Companies are five widely used sources of such information. Exhibit 16–7 illustrates the type of information provided by Morningstar, Inc., for the Davis NY Venture fund. Although the Morningstar report is just one page long, it provides a wealth of information designed to help you decide if this is the right fund for you. Notice that the information is divided into various sections. At the top, a small box entitled "Historical Profile" contains information about financial return, risk, and rating. Notice that Davis NY Venture is rated 4 stars, Morningstar's above-average rating. The report also provides statistical information over the past 12 years. The middle section of the report provides information about the fund manager(s), performance, risk analysis, and portfolio analysis. The last section at the very bottom describes the investment philosophy of the fund. Generally, the analysis section summarizes Morningstar's research. Here it says,

> On the whole, it's hard not to like this fund. The Davis family and others on the fund's board have a large sum of their own money in the fund.

As you can see, the research information for the Davis NY Venture fund is pretty upbeat. However, other research firms like Lipper Analytical Services, Value Line, and Wiesenberger Investment Companies, as well as Morningstar, Inc., will also tell you if a fund is a poor performer that offers poor investment potential.

In addition, various mutual fund newsletters provide financial information to subscribers for a fee. All of these sources are rather expensive, but their reports may be available from brokerage firms or libraries.

## The Internet

Many investors have found a wealth of information about mutual fund investments on the Internet. Basically, there are three ways to access information. First, you can obtain current market values for mutual funds by using one of the Internet search engines, such as Yahoo. The Yahoo finance page (http://finance.yahoo.com) has a box where you can enter the symbol of the mutual fund you want to research. If you don't know the symbol, you can enter in the name of the mutual fund in the symbol lookup box. The Yahoo finance web site will respond with the correct symbol. In addition to current market values, you can obtain a price history for a mutual fund and a profile including specific holdings that the fund owns.

Second, most investment companies that sponsor mutual funds have a web page. To obtain information, all you have to do is access one of the Internet search engines and type in the name of the fund. Before reading on, take a look at Exhibit 16–8, the opening page for the American Funds Investment Company. Generally, statistical information about individual funds, procedures for opening an account, available literature (including a prospectus and an annual report), and different investor services are provided. *Be warned:* Investment companies want you to become a shareholder. As a result, the websites for *some* investment companies read like a sales pitch. Read between the glowing descriptions and look at the facts before investing your money.

Finally, professional advisory services, covered in the previous section, offer online research reports for mutual funds. A sample of the information available from the Standard & Poor's Personal Wealth website for the Janus Worldwide Fund is illustrated in

## EXHIBIT 16-7   MUTUAL FUND RESEARCH INFORMATION PROVIDED BY MORNINGSTAR, INC.

Published February 24, 2000. Reprinted by permission of Morningstar.

# Davis NY Venture A

| | Ticker | Load | NAV | Yield | Total Assets | Mstar Category |
|---|---|---|---|---|---|---|
| | NYVTX | 4.75% | $28.42 | 0.0% | $16,147.2 mil | Large Value |

**Prospectus Objective:** Growth

Davis New York Venture Fund - Class A seeks growth of capital.

The fund invests primarily in equities issued by companies with market capitalizations of at least $250 million, though it may also hold securities of smaller companies. It may invest in securities of foreign issuers.

Class A shares have front loads; B shares have deferred loads, higher 12b-1 fees, and conversion features; C shares have level loads; Y shares are designed for institutional investors. Prior to Oct. 1, 1995, the fund was named New York Venture Fund.

**Historical Profile**

| | |
|---|---|
| Return | Above Avg |
| Risk | Average |
| Rating | ★★★★ Above Avg |

Investment Style: Equity / Average Stock %

▼ Manager Change
▽ Partial Manager Change

Fund Performance vs. Category Average
■ Quarterly Fund Return
+/- Category Average
— Category Baseline

Performance Quartile (within Category)

| | 1989 | 1990 | 1991 | 1992 | 1993 | 1994 | 1995 | 1996 | 1997 | 1998 | 1999 | 01-00 | History |
|---|---|---|---|---|---|---|---|---|---|---|---|---|---|
| | 9.15 | 8.16 | 10.51 | 11.06 | 11.97 | 11.16 | 14.52 | 17.50 | 22.33 | 25.01 | 28.76 | 28.42 | NAV |
| | 34.75 | −2.90 | 40.55 | 12.04 | 16.09 | −1.93 | 40.56 | 26.54 | 33.68 | 14.73 | 17.59 | −1.18 | Total Return % |
| | 3.06 | 0.22 | 10.07 | 4.42 | 6.03 | −3.24 | 3.03 | 3.59 | 0.33 | −13.85 | −3.45 | 3.84 | +/− S&P 500 |
| | 8.09 | 0.77 | 22.39 | 2.97 | −3.67 | 0.39 | 0.53 | 4.22 | −1.81 | −6.51 | 6.64 | 0.94 | +/− Russ Top 200 Val |
| | 5.28 | 1.87 | 2.34 | 1.62 | 2.36 | 1.00 | 1.34 | 1.24 | 1.31 | 0.47 | 0.01 | 0.00 | Income Return % |
| | 29.46 | −4.77 | 38.21 | 10.41 | 13.73 | −2.93 | 39.22 | 25.30 | 32.36 | 14.26 | 17.58 | −1.18 | Capital Return % |
| | 5 | 26 | 10 | 28 | 33 | 74 | 5 | 10 | 8 | 35 | 10 | 5 | Total Rtn % Rank Cat |
| | 0.40 | 0.17 | 0.19 | 0.17 | 0.26 | 0.12 | 0.15 | 0.18 | 0.23 | 0.11 | 0.00 | 0.00 | Income $ |
| | 0.70 | 0.54 | 0.65 | 0.53 | 0.58 | 0.45 | 1.01 | 0.70 | 0.83 | 0.48 | 0.62 | 0.00 | Capital Gains $ |
| | 0.97 | 0.97 | 0.97 | 0.91 | 0.89 | 0.87 | 0.90 | 0.87 | 0.89 | 0.91 | 0.90 | — | Expense Ratio % |
| | 2.45 | 3.78 | 1.84 | 1.36 | 0.85 | 1.19 | 1.11 | 1.30 | 0.98 | 0.80 | 0.56 | — | Income Ratio % |
| | 58 | 47 | 52 | 26 | 24 | 13 | 15 | 18 | 24 | 11 | 25 | — | Turnover Rate % |
| | 308.2 | 341.9 | 459.0 | 547.9 | 937.7 | 1,090.5 | 1,798.2 | 2,658.8 | 4,655.5 | 6,820.3 | 8,139.4 | 8,106.6 | Net Assets $mil |

| Class | Exp% | Sales Fees | Rec. Hold (Years) |
|---|---|---|---|
| A | 0.90 | 4.75%L | 6.5+ |
| B | 1.74 | 4.00%D,0.75%B | 6.0–6.5 |
| C | 1.72 | 1.00%D,0.75%B | 0.0–6.5 |

### Portfolio Manager(s)

Christopher C. Davis. Since 10-1995. MA 1987 U. of St. Andrews. Davis is a vice chairman with Davis Selected Advisers, his employer since 1990. He has more than 10 years experience in securities analysis. His investment approach has been strongly influenced by working closely with veteran investor Shelby Davis.

Kenneth C. Feinberg. Since 5-1998. BA 1979 Johns Hopkins U.; MBA 1985 Columbia U. Feinberg is a portfolio manager with the Davis Selected Advisors, his employer since 1994. Previously, he was assistant vice president at the Continental Corporation.

### Performance 01-31-00

| | 1st Qtr | 2nd Qtr | 3rd Qtr | 4th Qtr | Total |
|---|---|---|---|---|---|
| 1995 | 10.57 | 12.32 | 11.11 | 1.86 | 40.56 |
| 1996 | 5.23 | 2.62 | 4.91 | 11.69 | 26.54 |
| 1997 | 1.94 | 16.70 | 11.91 | 0.40 | 33.68 |
| 1998 | 8.11 | 2.20 | −14.43 | 21.36 | 14.73 |
| 1999 | 3.20 | 11.97 | −9.00 | 11.83 | 17.59 |

| Trailing | Total Return% | +/− S&P 500 | +/− Russ Top 200 Val | % Rank All Cat | Growth of $10,000 |
|---|---|---|---|---|---|
| 3 Mo | 4.58 | 1.97 | 7.44 | 38 10 | 10,458 |
| 6 Mo | 4.80 | −0.78 | 7.67 | 40 9 | 10,480 |
| 1 Yr | 14.55 | 4.21 | 8.43 | 32 5 | 11,455 |
| 3 Yr Avg | 18.82 | −4.05 | −0.26 | 21 5 | 16,777 |
| 5 Yr Avg | 25.11 | −1.46 | 0.87 | 11 4 | 30,653 |
| 10 Yr Avg | 19.47 | 1.06 | 2.72 | 8 1 | 59,258 |
| 15 Yr Avg | 19.22 | 1.30 | — | 5 1 | 139,648 |

| Tax Analysis | Tax-Adj Ret% | %Rank Cat | %Pretax Ret | %Rank Cat |
|---|---|---|---|---|
| 3 Yr Avg | 17.97 | 3 | 95.5 | 3 |
| 5 Yr Avg | 23.65 | 2 | 94.2 | 5 |
| 10 Yr Avg | 17.49 | 1 | 89.8 | 6 |

Potential Capital Gain Exposure: 31% of assets

### Risk Analysis

| Time Period | Load-Adj Return % | Risk %Rank All Cat | Morningstar Return Risk | Morningstar Risk-Adj Rating |
|---|---|---|---|---|
| 1 Yr | 9.11 | | | |
| 3 Yr | 16.91 | 69 49 | 0.96 0.95 | ★★★ |
| 5 Yr | 23.90 | 68 47 | 1.29 0.89 | ★★★★ |
| 10 Yr | 18.89 | 75 83 | 1.47 1.00 | ★★★★ |

Average Historical Rating (170 months): 4.6★s

¹1=low, 100=high

**Category Rating (3 Yr)**  ① ② ③ ④ ⑤ — Worst ← → Best

| | | Return | High |
|---|---|---|---|
| | | Risk | Average |

| Other Measures | Standard Index S&P 500 | Best Fit Index S&P 500 |
|---|---|---|
| Alpha | −3.3 | −3.3 |
| Beta | 1.01 | 1.01 |
| R−Squared | 89 | 89 |
| Standard Deviation | 21.48 | |
| Mean | 18.82 | |
| Sharpe Ratio | 0.73 | |

### Analysis by Russel Kinnel 02-22-00

Davis New York Venture has been rewarding, but also a little sobering at the same time.

Management's willingness to look beyond traditional value sectors and let its winners ride has enabled the fund to run circles around the large-value group, as well as the S&P 500. In recent years comanagers Chris Davis and Ken Feinberg reacted to sell-offs in Texas Instruments, Oracle, and other tech stocks the same way they did when American Express or Citigroup's shares were depressed. They talked to management, competitors, and customers and crunched the numbers to estimate the value of the business. They liked what they saw and accumulated a position. Over the past couple of years those tech stocks took off and carried the fund to new heights.

Now the sobering bit. As people who spend quality time with company balance sheets and earnings reports, Davis and

Feinberg pride themselves on their ability to tell the opportunities from the value traps. However, they still suffered some nasty blowups in 1999. Bank One and Waste Management imploded even though there were some signs of impending trouble. In addition, Tyco International's accounting methods have come under fire. (Davis and Feinberg have sold most of their holdings in Bank One and Waste Management, but they still believe in Tyco.) Maybe that's just par for the course, but it's a little disconcerting to see a cluster of problems at the same time.

On the whole, though, it's hard not to like this fund. The Davis family and others on the fund's board have a large sum of their own money in the fund. The managers know their companies inside and out. Best of all, this fund has produced great results for quite a long time.

### Portfolio Analysis 01-31-00

| Share change since 12−99 Total Stocks: 107 | Sector | PE | YTD Ret% | % Assets |
|---|---|---|---|---|
| American Express | Financials | 30.4 | −0.75 | 6.74 |
| Texas Instruments | Technology | 64.1 | 11.56 | 5.91 |
| Hewlett−Packard | Technology | 32.4 | −4.84 | 5.77 |
| Citigroup | Financials | 20.1 | 2.36 | 4.58 |
| Wells Fargo | Financials | 17.9 | −1.08 | 4.38 |
| IBM | Technology | 27.3 | 4.06 | 3.83 |
| McDonald's | Services | 26.7 | −7.29 | 3.40 |
| Applied Matls | Technology | 72.6 | 8.34 | 3.16 |
| ⊕ Household Intl | Financials | 11.5 | −5.37 | 3.07 |
| ⊕ Tyco Intl | Industrials | 58.2 | 10.42 | 2.96 |
| Intel | Technology | 46.9 | 20.20 | 2.76 |
| ⊕ Morgan Stanley/Dean Witter | Financials | 16.2 | −6.90 | 2.70 |
| Berkshire Hathaway Cl A | Financials | — | — | 2.70 |
| ⊕ MediaOne Grp | Services | — | 3.50 | 2.45 |
| ⊕ American Home Products | Health | — | 19.91 | 2.44 |
| American Intl Grp | Financials | 32.5 | −3.47 | 2.23 |
| Motorola | Technology | NMF | −7.30 | 2.09 |
| ⊕ Lexmark Intl Cl A | Technology | 40.8 | 4.14 | 1.98 |
| Providian Finl | Financials | 22.3 | −7.34 | 1.69 |
| ⊕ Oracle | Technology | NMF | −10.80 | 1.68 |
| Transatlantic Hldgs | Financials | 11.6 | −3.92 | 1.54 |
| ⊕ Golden West Finl | Financials | 10.3 | −12.10 | 1.42 |
| ⊕ Masco | Industrials | 15.1 | −21.00 | 1.42 |
| Sealed Air (New) | Industrials | — | — | 1.28 |
| SmithKline Beecham ADR | Health | 14.9 | −4.87 | 1.22 |

| Current Investment Style | | Stock Port Avg | Relative S&P 500 Current | Hist | Rel Cat |
|---|---|---|---|---|---|
| Style: Value Blend Growth | Price/Earnings Ratio | 32.1 | 0.89 | 0.86 | 1.26 |
| Size: Large Med Small | Price/Book Ratio | 7.5 | 0.84 | 0.70 | 1.36 |
| | Price/Cash Flow | 24.4 | 1.01 | 0.86 | 1.40 |
| | 3 Yr Earnings Growth | 12.1 | 0.74 | 0.92 | 0.99 |
| | 1 Yr Earnings Est% | 21.4 | 1.17 | — | 1.42 |
| | Med Mkt Cap $mil | 66,945 | 1.0 | 0.9 | 2.18 |

| Special Securities | % assets 01-31-0 |
|---|---|
| Restricted/Illiquid Secs | 0 |
| Emerging−Markets Secs | 0 |
| Options/Futures/Warrants | No |

| Composition % assets 01-31-00 | | Market Cap | |
|---|---|---|---|
| Cash | 4.9 | Giant | 54.8 |
| Stocks* | 93.9 | Large | 27.4 |
| Bonds | 0.0 | Medium | 17.1 |
| Other | 1.2 | Small | 0.7 |
| | | Micro | 0.0 |

*Foreign (% stocks) 2.3

| Sector Weightings | % of Stocks | Rel S&P | 5-Year High | Low |
|---|---|---|---|---|
| Utilities | 0.0 | 0.0 | 8 | 0 |
| Energy | 1.2 | 0.2 | 13 | 1 |
| Financials | 38.1 | 2.9 | 62 | 37 |
| Industrials | 10.2 | 0.9 | 10 | 1 |
| Durables | 0.5 | 0.3 | 4 | 0 |
| Staples | 1.6 | 0.3 | 16 | 2 |
| Services | 9.6 | 0.7 | 14 | 5 |
| Retail | 0.0 | 0.0 | 7 | 0 |
| Health | 5.5 | 0.6 | 15 | 3 |
| Technology | 33.3 | 1.1 | 33 | 6 |

| Address: | 124 E. Marcy Street | Minimum Purchase: | $1000 | Add: $25 | IRA: $250 |
|---|---|---|---|---|---|
| | Santa Fe, NM 87501 | Min Auto Inv Plan: | $1000 | Add: $25 | |
| | 800−279−0279 / 505−983−4335 | Sales Fees: | 4.75%L, 0.25%S | | |
| Web Address: | www.davisfunds.com | Management Fee: | 0.75% max./0.50% min. | | |
| Inception: | 02-17-69 | Actual Fees: | Mgt: 0.54% Dist: 0.23% | | |
| Advisor: | Davis Selected Advisers | Expense Projections: | 3Yr: $751* 5Yr: $955* 10Yr: $1541* | | |
| Subadvisor: | Davis Selected Advisers − NY | Avg Brok Commission: | — Income Distrib: Annually | | |
| NTF Plans: | Fidelity Inst., Datalynx | Total Cost (relative to category): | — | | |

**M**ORNINGSTAR   Mutual Funds

SOURCE: *Morningstar Mutual Funds*, February 24, 2000, p. 18. (Morningstar, Inc., 25 W. Wacker Drive, Chicago, IL 60606).

EXHIBIT 16–8

Opening Page
for the Website
for the American
Family of Mutual
Funds

SOURCE: The above
information was taken
from the Internet on May 7,
2000. (The American
Funds Internet address is
www.americanfunds.com.)

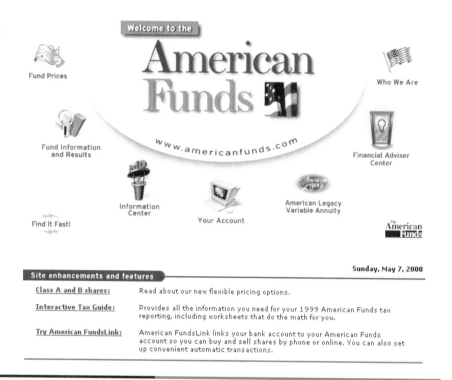

Exhibit 16–9. Note that information about the fund symbol, current NAV, advisor and portfolio manager, and minimum investment amounts is provided. It is also possible to obtain a current quote, chart, and information on returns, risk, holdings, news, and SEC filings by clicking on the appropriate button on the left side of the website. Also, read the Financial Planning for Life's Situations feature on page 532 to see why one couple invested in the Janus Worldwide fund. Many investors have found that the research reports provided by companies like Morningstar, Inc., (www.mornigstar.com), Wiesenberger Thomson Financial Corporation (www.wiesenberger.com), and Lipper Analytical, Inc. (www.lipperweb.com) are well worth the $5 to $10 fee charged for online services. While the information is basically the same as that in the printed reports described in the previous section, the ability to obtain the information quickly without having to wait for research materials to be mailed or to make a trip to the library is a real selling point.

For more information on the evaluation process, study the checklist provided in the Financial Planning Calculations feature on page 533.

## Concept Check 16–3

1. Many financial experts say that purchasing a mutual fund is "too easy." Do you think this statement is true or false? Explain.
2. How can the following help you evaluate a mutual fund?
   a. Newspapers                    e. Financial publications
   b. The fund's objective          f. Professional advisory services
   c. The prospectus                g. The Internet
   d. The annual report
3. Describe the type of information contained in the annual mutual fund survey published by *Business Week*.

**EXHIBIT 16-9**    Information about the Janus Worldwide Fund Available by Accessing Standard & Poor's Personal Wealth Site.

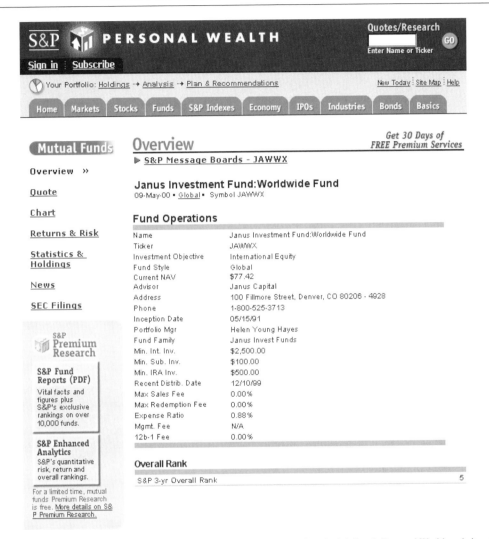

SOURCE: The above information was taken from the Internet on May 9, 2000 (The Standard & Poor's Personal Wealth website address is www.personalwealth.com). Reprinted from the April 4, 2000 edition of *Personal Wealth-Com.* © 2000 by McGraw-Hill Companies, Inc.

## THE MECHANICS OF A MUTUAL FUND TRANSACTION

### Obj. 4
Describe how and why mutual funds are bought and sold.

For many investors, mutual funds have become the investment of choice. In fact, you probably either own shares or know someone who owns shares in a mutual fund—they're that popular! They may be part of a 401(k) or 403(b) retirement account, a SEP-IRA, a Roth IRA, or a traditional IRA retirement account, all topics discussed in Chapter 18. They can also be owned outright by purchasing shares through a brokerage firm or an investment company that sponsors a mutual fund. As you will see later in this section, it's easy to purchase shares in a mutual fund. For $250 to $2,500, you can open an account and begin investing. And there are other advantages that encourage investors to purchase shares in funds. Unfortunately, there are also disadvantages. Exhibit 16–10 summarizes the advantages and disadvantages of mutual fund investments.

## Financial Planning for Life's Situations

### JANUS WORLDWIDE: A DREAM COME TRUE FOR THE GLOVERS

For Mike and Kathy Glover, both in their 30s, the last three years have been like a roller coaster ride. In late 1996, they invested $11,500 in the Janus Worldwide mutual fund. When they made their investment, just about everyone was talking about global investments. The Janus fund seemed to be one of the best and was definitely a high flyer until October 1997. Then the economies in Hong Kong, Indonesia, and other Pacific Rim countries began to experience financial troubles, and investors got scared. The Glovers' Janus fund, like many other global investments in stocks and mutual funds, took a real hit. At that point, they considered selling their Janus Worldwide shares, but they didn't want to lose some of their initial investment.

The Glovers had decided to purchase the Janus Worldwide fund based on research they did in the library and on the Internet. Both admitted they were overwhelmed with the amount of information they found on mutual fund investments. Some of the more interesting articles stressed the need to diversify and place 10 to 30 percent of one's assets in global investments. According to another article, global investors enjoyed two major advantages. First, global investments provide investors with diversification. Second, economies in many nations around the globe are expanding faster than the U.S. economy.

Based on their research, the Glovers decided to go global, but then they had to decide if they wanted to invest in individual stocks issued by foreign companies or global mutual funds. Much of the research they read pointed out that purchasing individual, global stocks was a roadfull of potholes. For starters, evaluating foreign firms may be more difficult than evaluating U.S. firms because reliable accounting information is often scarce. It was easier to get reliable information about global mutual funds. By calling an 800 phone number, they could obtain a prospectus, an annual report, and information about the fund manager. *Business Week, Forbes, Money, Barron's, The Wall Street Journal,* and other financial publications also provided information about global mutual fund investments. For these reasons, most financial planners recommended global mutual funds for people with less than $200,000 to invest.

Now the Glovers are glad they didn't sell their shares in Janus Worldwide. By the end of 1997, just a little over two months after the big downturn in October 1997, their fund had recovered and was worth more than they had paid for it. In late 1999, three years after their purchase of shares in Janus Worldwide, they had averaged between 21 and 22 percent every year, and the value of their investment had increased to almost $20,000.

SOURCES: Yahoo Finance website (http://finance.yahoo.com), September 4, 1999, Yahoo, Inc., 3420 Central Expressway, Santa Clara, CA 95051; Lawrence A. Armour, "A Globetrotter from Denver," *Fortune,* June 23, 1997, pp. 181–82+; Lisa Reilly Cullen, "These First-Class Funds Go Round the World for Profits," *Money,* May 1997, pp. 50–52; and Michael Sivy, "How to Cash In on the Asia Boom," *Money,* May 1997, pp. 108+.

One advantage of any investment is the opportunity to make money on it. In the next section, we examine how you can make money by investing in closed-end funds or open-end funds. We consider how taxes affect your mutual fund investments. Then we look at the options used to purchase shares in a mutual fund. Finally, we examine the options used to withdraw money from a mutual fund.

### Return on Investment

*income dividends*
The earnings a fund pays to shareholders after it has deducted expenses from its dividend and interest income.

As with other investments, the purpose of investing in a closed-end fund or an open-end fund is to earn a financial return. Shareholders in such funds can receive a return in one of three ways. First, both types of funds pay income dividends. **Income dividends** are the earnings a fund pays to shareholders after it has deducted expenses from its dividend and interest income. Mutual fund dividends are usually paid once or twice a year. Second, investors may receive capital gain distributions. **Capital gain distributions** are the payments made to a fund's shareholders that result from the sale of securities in

*capital gain distributions*
The payments made to a fund's shareholders that result from the sale of securities in the fund's portfolio.

## Financial Planning Calculations

### EVALUATION OF A MUTUAL FUND

No checklist can serve as a fool-proof guide for choosing a mutual fund. However, the following questions will help you evaluate a potential investment in such a fund.

#### CATEGORY 1: FUND CHARACTERISTICS

1. What is the value of the assets of this fund? _____

2. What is this fund's Morningstar rating? _____
3. What is the minimum investment? _____
4. Does the fund allow telephone exchanges?
   ☐ Yes   ☐ No
5. Is there a fee for telephone exchanges?
   ☐ Yes   ☐ No

#### CATEGORY 2: COSTS

6. Is there a front-end load charge? If so, how much is it? _____
7. Is there a redemption fee? If so, how much is it? _____
8. How much is the annual management fee? _____
9. Is there a 12b-1 fee? If so, how much is it? _____
10. What is the fund's expense ratio? _____

#### CATEGORY 3: DIVERSIFICATION

11. What is the fund's objective? _____
12. What types of securities does the fund's portfolio include? _____
13. How many securities does the fund's portfolio include? _____
14. How many types of industries does the fund's portfolio include? _____

#### CATEGORY 4: FUND PERFORMANCE

15. How long has the fund manager been with the fund? _____
16. How would you describe the fund's performance over the past 12 months? _____
17. How would you describe the fund's performance over the past 5 years? _____
18. How would you describe the fund's performance over the past 10 years? _____

#### CATEGORY 5: CONCLUSION

19. Based on the above information, do you think an investment in this fund will help you achieve your investment goals?
    ☐ Yes   ☐ No
20. Explain your answer to question 19. _____ _____ _____ _____

#### A WORD OF CAUTION

When you use a checklist, there is always a danger of overlooking important relevant information. The above checklist is not a cure-all, but it does provide some very sound questions that you should answer before making a mutual fund investment decision. Quite simply, it is a place to start. If you need other information, *you* are responsible for obtaining it and for determining how it affects your potential investment.

the fund's portfolio. These amounts generally are paid once a year. Third, as with stock and bond investments, you can buy shares in both types of funds at a low price and then sell them after the price has increased. For example, assume you purchased shares in the Fidelity Large Cap Stock Mutual Fund at $22.50 per share and sold your shares two years later at $25 per share. In this case, you made $2.50 ($25 selling price minus $22.50 purchase price) per share. With this financial information and dollar amounts for income dividends and capital gain distributions, you can calculate a total return for your mutual fund investment. Before completing this section, you may want to examine the actual procedure used to calculate the dollar amount of total return and percentage of total return in the accompanying Financial Planning Calculations box.

**Advantages and Disadvantages of Investing in Mutual Funds**

### Advantages

- Diversification
- Professional management
- Ease of buying and selling shares
- Smaller amount of money often required to open a mutual fund account
- Multiple withdrawal options
- Distribution or reinvestment of income and capital gains
- Switching privileges within the same fund family
- Services that include toll-free telephone numbers, complete records of all transactions, and savings and checking accounts

### Disadvantages

- Purchase/withdrawal costs
- Ongoing management fees and 12b-1 fees
- Poor performance that does not match the Standard & Poor's 500 Stock Index or some other index
- Inability to control when capital gain distributions occur and complicated tax-reporting issues
- Potential market risk associated with all investments
- Some sales personnel are aggressive and/or unethical

---

When shares in a mutual fund are sold, the profit that results from an increase in value is referred to as a *capital gain*. Note the difference between a capital gain distribution and a capital gain. A capital gain distribution occurs when *the fund* distributes profits that result from *the fund* selling securities in the portfolio at a profit. On the other hand, a capital gain is the profit that results when *you* sell your shares in the mutual fund for more than you paid for them. Of course, if the price of a fund's shares goes down between the time of your purchase and the time of sale, you incur a loss.

## Taxes and Mutual Funds

Income dividends, capital gain distributions, and financial gains and losses from the sale of closed-end or open-end funds are subject to taxation. At the end of each year, investment companies are required to send each shareholder a statement specifying how much he or she received in dividends and capital gain distributions. Although investment companies may provide this information as part of their year-end statement, most funds use IRS Form 1099 DIV.

The following information provides general guidelines on how mutual fund transactions are taxed:

- Income dividends are reported, along with all other dividend amounts you have received, on your federal tax return and are taxed as regular income
- If income dividends are less than $400, they are reported on line 9 of Form 1040; if more than $400, income dividends are reported both on line 5 of Schedule B and on the 1040.

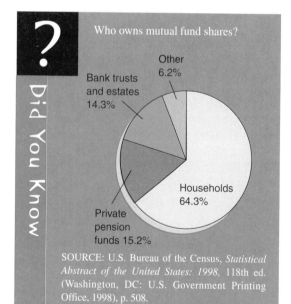

**Did You Know**

**Who owns mutual fund shares?**

Other 6.2%

Bank trusts and estates 14.3%

Households 64.3%

Private pension funds 15.2%

SOURCE: U.S. Bureau of the Census, *Statistical Abstract of the United States: 1998*, 118th ed. (Washington, DC: U.S. Government Printing Office, 1998), p. 508.

## Financial Planning Calculations

### CALCULATING TOTAL RETURN FOR MUTUAL FUNDS

In Chapter 13, we defined total return as a calculation that includes not only the yearly dollar amount of income but also any increase or decrease in market value from the original purchase price of an investment. For mutual funds, you can use the following calculation to determine the dollar amount of total return:

Income dividends
+ Capital gain distributions
+ Change in share market value
Dollar amount of total return

For example, assume you purchased 100 shares of Majestic Growth Fund for $12.20 per share for a total investment of $1,220. During the next 12 months, you received income dividends of $0.45 a share and capital gain distributions of $0.90. Also, assume you sold your investment at the end of 12 months for $14.40 a share. As illustrated below, the dollar amount for total return is $355:

| | |
|---|---|
| Income dividends = 100 × $0.45 = | $   45 |
| Capital gain distributions = 100 × $0.90 = | +   90 |
| Change in share value = $14.40 − $12.20 | |
| = $2.20 × 100 = | + 220 |
| Dollar amount of total return | $ 355 |

To calculate the percentage of total return, divide the dollar amount of total return by the original cost of your mutual fund investment. The percentage of total return for the above example is 29.1 percent, as follows:

$$\frac{\text{Percent of}}{\text{total return}} = \frac{\text{Dollar amount of total return}}{\text{Original cost of your investment}}$$

$$= \frac{\$355}{\$1,220}$$

$$= 0.291, \text{ or } 29.1\%$$

- Capital gain distributions that result from the fund selling securities in its portfolio at a profit are reported on Schedule D as part of your federal tax return and on the 1040.
- Capital gains or losses that result from your selling shares in a mutual fund are reported on Schedule D and the 1040. How long you hold the shares determines if your gains or losses are taxed as a short-term or long-term capital gain. (See Chapter 13 for more information on capital gains and capital losses.)

Two specific problems develop with taxation of mutual funds. First, almost all investment companies allow you to reinvest income distributions and capital gain distributions from the fund in additional shares instead of receiving cash. Even though you didn't receive cash because you chose to reinvest such distributions, they are still taxable and must be reported on your federal tax return as current income. Second, when you purchase shares of stock, corporate bonds, or other investments and use the buy-and-hold technique described in Chapter 14, you decide when you sell. Thus, you can pick the tax year when you pay tax on capital gains or deduct capital losses. Mutual funds, on the other hand, buy and sell securities within the fund's portfolio on a regular basis during any 12-month period. At the end of the year, profits that result from the mutual fund's buying and selling activities are paid to shareholders in the form of capital gain distributions. Unlike with investments that you manage, you have no control over when the mutual fund sells securities and when you will be taxed on capital gain distributions.

To ensure having all of the documentation you need for tax reporting purposes, it is essential that *you* keep accurate records. The same records will help you monitor the value of your mutual fund investments and make more intelligent decisions with regard to buying and selling these investments.

**EXHIBIT 16-11**    Sizing Up the Mutual Fund Supermarkets

| | Total Funds | No-Fee Funds | Charge for Buy/Sell Other No-Loan Funds | Minimum Holding Period for No-Fee Funds | Penalty for Early Sales of No-Fee Funds | Limits on Fund Switches |
|---|---|---|---|---|---|---|
| **Charles Schwab** 1–800–435–4000 www.schwab.com | 1,640 | 1,024 | $39 and up | 180 days | 0.75%, or $39 minimum | No |
| **E*Trade** 1–800–786–2571 www.etrade.com. | 4,300 | 1,187 | $24.95 | 90 days | $24.95 | No |
| **Fidelity** 1–800–544–9697 www.fidelity.com | 3,900+ | 900+ | $35 and up direct; $28.95 online; $28 on Touch-Tone | 180 days | Standard transaction fee | Maximum 15 in 12 mos. or standard fees apply |
| **Jack White** 1–800–233–3411 www.jackwhiteco.com | Roughly 7,500 | 1,300 | $27 direct, $24 online | 90 days | $50, less than $100,000; $100, more than $100,000 | None |
| **Scudder** 1–800–700–0820 www.scudder.com | 8,000+ | 800+ | $35 | 6 months | Standard transaction fee | Yes* |
| **Strong** 1–800–368–1550 www.strong–funds.com | 80 | 80 | $0 | 90 days | $50 | No |
| **Vanguard** 1–800–992–8327 www.vanguard.com | 2,600+ | 948 | $35 | 1 year | 1%, or $50 minimum | Yes* |

*At discretion of brokerage.

SOURCE: Reprinted from the February 1, 1999 issue of *Business Week* by special permission. © 1999 McGraw-Hill Companies, Inc.

## Purchase Options

You can buy shares of a closed-end fund through the New York Stock Exchange, through various other stock exchanges, or in the over-the-counter market. You can purchase shares of an open-end, no-load fund by contacting the investment company that sponsors the fund. You can purchase shares of an open-end, load fund through a salesperson who is authorized to sell them, through an account executive of a brokerage firm, or directly from the investment company that sponsors the fund.

You can also purchase both no-load and load funds from mutual fund supermarkets available through discount brokerage firms. A mutual fund supermarket offers at least two advantages. First, instead of dealing with numerous investment companies that sponsor mutual funds, you can make one toll-free phone call to obtain information, purchase shares, and sell shares in a large number of mutual funds. Second, you receive one statement from the discount brokerage firm instead of receiving a statement from each investment company you deal with. One statement can be a real plus because it provides the information you need to monitor the value of your investments in one place and in the same format. For more information about mutual fund supermarkets and the services they offer, look at Exhibit 16–11.

Because of the unique nature of open-end fund transactions, we will examine how investors buy and sell shares in this type of mutual fund from an investment company.

To purchase shares in an open-end mutual fund from an investment company, you may use four options: regular account transactions, voluntary savings plans, contractual savings plans, and reinvestment plans. The most popular and least complicated method of purchasing shares in an open-end fund is through a regular account transaction. When you use a regular account transaction, you decide how much money you want to invest and when you want to invest, and simply buy as many shares as possible.

The chief advantage of the voluntary savings plan is that it allows you to make smaller purchases than the minimum purchases required by the regular account method described above. At the time of the initial purchase, you declare an intent to make regular minimum purchases of the fund's shares. Although there is no penalty for not making purchases, most investors feel an "obligation" to make purchases on a periodic basis, and, as pointed out throughout this text, small monthly investments are a great way to save for long-term objectives. For most voluntary savings plans, the minimum purchase ranges from $25 to $100 for each purchase after the initial investment. Funds try to make investing as easy as possible. Most offer payroll deduction plans, and many will deduct, upon proper shareholder authorization, a specified amount from a shareholder's bank account. Also, many investors can choose mutual funds as a vehicle to invest money that is contributed to a 401(k), 403(b), or individual retirement account. As mentioned earlier, Chapter 18 provides more information on the tax advantages of different types of retirement accounts.

Contractual savings plans require you to make regular purchases over a specified period of time, usually 10 to 15 years. These plans are sometimes referred to as *front-end load funds* because almost all of the commissions are paid in the first few years of the contract period. You will incur penalties if you do not fulfill the purchase requirements. For example, if you drop out of a contractual savings plan before completing the purchase requirements, you sacrifice the prepaid commissions. Many financial experts and government regulatory agencies are critical of contractual savings plans. As a result, the Securities and Exchange Commission and many states have imposed new rules on investment companies offering contractual savings plans.

*reinvestment plan*
A service provided by an investment company in which shareholder income dividends and capital gain distributions are automatically reinvested to purchase additional shares of the fund.

You may also purchase shares in an open-end fund by using the fund's reinvestment plan. A **reinvestment plan** is a service provided by an investment company in which income dividends and capital gain distributions are automatically reinvested to purchase additional shares of the fund. Most reinvestment plans allow shareholders to use reinvested money to purchase shares without having to pay additional sales charges or commissions. *Reminder:* When your dividends or capital gain distributions are reinvested, you must still report these transactions as taxable income.

All four purchase options allow you to buy shares over a long period of time. As a result, you can use the principle of *dollar cost averaging,* which was explained in Chapter 14. Dollar cost averaging allows you to average many individual purchase prices over a long period of time. This method helps you avoid the problem of buying high and selling low. With dollar cost averaging, you can make money if you sell your mutual fund shares at a price higher than their *average* purchase price.

## Withdrawal Options

Because closed-end funds are listed on securities exchanges or traded in the over-the-counter market, it is possible to sell shares in such a fund to another investor. Shares in an open-end fund can be sold on any business day to the investment company that sponsors the fund. In this case, the shares are redeemed at their net asset value. All you have to do is give proper notification and the fund will send you a check. With some funds, you can even write checks to withdraw money from the fund.

In addition, most funds have provisions that allow investors with shares that have a minimum net asset value of at least $5,000 to use four options to systematically withdraw money. First, you may withdraw a specified, fixed dollar amount each investment period until your fund has been exhausted. Normally, an investment period is three months, and most funds require investors to withdraw a minimum amount, usually $50, each investment period.

A second option allows you to liquidate or "sell off" a certain number of shares each investment period. Since the net asset value of shares in a fund varies from one period to the next, the amount of money you receive will also vary. Once the specified number of shares has been sold, a check is mailed directly to you.

A third option allows you to withdraw a fixed percentage of asset growth. For example, assume you arrange to receive 60 percent of the asset growth of your investment, and the asset growth of your investment amounts to $800 in a particular investment period. For that period, you will receive a check for $480 ($800 × 60% = $480). If no asset growth occurs, no payment is made to you. Under this option, your principal remains untouched.

A final option allows you to withdraw all asset growth that results from income dividends and capital gains earned by the fund during an investment period. Under this option, your principal remains untouched.

Sheet 60

## Concept Check 16–4

1.  How can you make money when investing in mutual funds?
2.  What is the difference among income dividends, capital gain distributions, and capital gains?
3.  How are income dividends, capital gain distributions, and capital gains reported on your federal tax return?
4.  Whom would you contact to purchase a closed-end fund? An open-end fund?
5.  What options can you use to purchase shares in a mutual fund from an investment company?
6.  What options can you use to withdraw money from a mutual fund?

## KEY FORMULAS

| Page | Topic | Formula |
|------|-------|---------|
| 516 | Net asset value | $\text{Net asset value} = \dfrac{\text{Value of a funds portfolio} - \text{Liabilities}}{\text{Number of shares outstanding}}$ |
| | *Example:* | $\text{Net asset value} = \dfrac{\$24,500,000 - \$2,000,000}{1,800,000}$ |
| | | $= \$12.50 \text{ per share}$ |
| 535 | Total return | Income dividends<br>+ Capital gain distributions<br>+ Change in market value<br>Dollar amount of total return |

| | Example: | Dollar amount of | $ 120 |
|---|---|---|---|
| | | | +  80 |
| | | | +320 |
| | | | $ 520 |

| 535 | Percent of total return | $\text{Percent of total return} = \dfrac{\text{Dollar amount of total return}}{\text{Original cost of investment}}$ |
|---|---|---|

$$\text{Example:}\qquad\text{Percent of total return} = \frac{\$\ 520}{\$4{,}500}$$

$$= 0.116, \text{ or } 11.6\%$$

## Summary of Objectives

### Obj. 1   Describe the characteristics of mutual funds investments.

The major reasons investors choose mutual funds are professional management and diversification. Mutual funds are also a convenient way to invest money. There are two types of mutual funds. A closed-end fund is a mutual fund whose shares are issued only when the fund is organized. An open-end fund is a mutual fund whose shares are sold and redeemed by the investment company at the net asset value (NAV) at the request of investors. Mutual funds are also classified as load or no-load funds. A load fund charges a commission every time you purchases shares. No commission is charged to purchase shares in a no-load fund. Mutual funds can also be classified as A shares (commissions charged when shares are purchased), B shares (commissions charged when money is withdrawn during the first five to seven years), and C shares (no commission to buy or sell shares, but higher, ongoing 12b-1 fees). Other possible fees include management fees, contingent deferred sales loads, and 12b-1 fees.

### Obj. 2   Classify mutual funds by investment objective.

The major categories of stock mutual funds, in terms of the types of securities in which they invest, are aggressive growth, equity income, global, growth, growth and income, index, international, mid-cap, regional, sector, small-cap, and utility. There are also bond funds that include high-yield, insured municipal, intermediate corporate, intermediate U.S. government, long-term corporate, long-term U.S. government, municipal, short-term corporate, and short-term U.S. government. Finally, other funds invest in a mix of different stocks, bonds, and other investment securities that include balanced funds, money market funds, and stock/bond blend funds. Today many investment companies use a family-of-funds concept, which allows shareholders to switch their investments among funds as different funds offer more potential, financial reward, or security.

### Obj. 3   Evaluate mutual funds for investment purposes.

The responsibility for choosing the "right" mutual fund rests with you, the investor. The information in newspapers, the financial objectives of the fund, the information in the prospectus and annual reports, financial publications, professional advisory services, and the Internet can all help you evaluate a mutual fund.

### Obj. 4   Describe how and why mutual funds are bought and sold.

The advantages and disadvantages of mutual funds have made mutual funds the investment of choice for many investors. For $250 to $2,500, you can open an account and begin investing. The shares of a closed-end fund are bought and sold on organized stock exchanges. The shares of an open-end fund may be purchased through a salesperson who is authorized to sell them, through an account executive of a brokerage firm, from a mutual fund supermarket, or from the investment company that sponsors the fund. The shares in an open-end fund can be sold to the investment company that sponsors the fund. Shareholders in mutual funds can receive a return in one of three ways: income dividends, capital gain distributions when the fund buys and sells securities in the fund's portfolio at a profit, and capital gains when shares in the mutual fund are sold at a higher price than the price paid. A number of purchase and withdrawal options are available.

## Financial Planning Problems

1. *Calculating Net Asset Value.* Given the following information, calculate the net asset value for the Boston Equity mutual fund.   (Obj. 1)

| | |
|---|---|
| Total assets | $225,000,000 |
| Total liabilities | $5,000,000 |
| Total number of shares | 4,400,000 |

2. *Calculating Net Asset Value.* Given the following information, calculate the net asset value for the New Empire small-cap mutual fund.   (Obj. 1)

| | |
|---|---|
| Total assets | $350,000,000 |
| Total liabilities | $10,000,000 |
| Total number of shares | 17,000,000 |

3. *Calculating Sales Fees.* Jan Throng invested $15,000 in the Aim Charter Mutual Fund. The fund charges a 5.50 percent commission when shares are purchased. Calculate the amount of commission Jan must pay.   (Obj. 1)

4. *Calculating Sales Fees.* Bill Matthews invested $9,800 in the John Hancock growth and income fund. The fund charges a 5.3 percent commission when shares are purchased. Calculate the amount of commission Bill must pay.   (Obj. 1)

5. *Determining Management Fees.* Mike Jackson invested a total of $8,500 in the ABC Mutual Fund. The management fee for this particular fund is 0.70 percent of the total investment amount. Calculate the management fee Mike must pay this year.   (Obj. 1)

6. *Calculating Contingent Deferred Sales Loads.* Mary Canfield purchased the New Dimensions bond fund. While this fund doesn't charge a front-end load, it does charge a contingent deferred sales load of 4 percent for any withdrawals in the first five years. If Mary withdraws $6,000 during the second year, how much is the contingent deferred sales load?   (Obj. 1)

7. *Matching Mutual Funds with Investor Needs.* This chapter classified mutual funds into different categories based on the nature of their investments. Using the following information, pick a mutual fund category that you consider suitable for each investor described and justify your choice.   (Obj. 2)

   *a.* A 25-year-old single investor with a new job that pays $30,000 a year.

   Mutual fund category _____

   Why? _____

   *b.* A single parent with two children who has just received a $100,000 divorce settlement, has no job, and has not worked outside the home for the past five years.

   Mutual fund category _____

   Why? _____

   *c.* A husband and wife who are both in their early 60s and retired.

   Mutual fund category _____

   Why? _____

8. *Finding Total Return.* Assume that one year ago, you bought 100 shares of a mutual fund for $15 per share, you received a $.75-per-share capital gain distribution during the past 12 months, and the market value of the fund is now $18. Calculate the total return for this investment if you were to sell it now.   (Obj. 3)

9. *Finding Percent of Total Return.* Given the information in question 8, calculate the percent of total return for your $1,500 investment.   (Obj. 3)

10. *Using Dollar Cost Averaging.* Over a four-year period, Matt Ewing purchased shares in the Stein Roe Venture Fund. Using the following information, answer the questions that follow. You may want to review the concept of dollar cost averaging in Chapter 14 before completing this problem.   (Obj. 4)

| Year | Investment Amount | Price per Share |
|---|---|---|
| 1999 | $3,000 | $40 per share |
| 2000 | $3,000 | $50 per share |
| 2001 | $3,000 | $60 per share |
| 2002 | $3,000 | $45 per share |

  *a.* At the end of four years, what is the total amount invested?

  *b.* At the end of four years, what is the total number of mutual fund shares purchased?

  *c.* At the end of four years, what is the average cost for each mutual fund share?

# Financial Planning Activities

1. *Deciding If Mutual Funds Are Right for You.* Assume you are 35, are divorced, and have just received a $120,000 legal settlement. Prepare a two-page report on the major reasons you want to invest in mutual funds.   (Obj. 1)

2. *Applying Terms to Mutual Fund Investments.* Using recent newspapers, magazines, mutual fund reports, or the Internet, find examples of the following concepts.   (Obj. 1)
   a. The net asset value for a mutual fund.
   b. An example of a load fund.
   c. An example of a no-load fund.
   d. The management fee for a specific mutual fund.
   e. A fund that charges a contingent deferred sales load.
   f. A fund that charges a 12b-1 fee.

3. *Understanding Fees Associated with Mutual Fund Investments.* Assume you are single, are 28 years old, and have decided to invest $8,000 in mutual funds.   (Obj. 1)
   a. Prepare a chart that shows the typical charges for load funds, no-load funds, management fees, contingent deferred sales loads, and 12b-1 fees.
   b. Calculate the following fees for your $8,000 mutual fund investment: (1) a 5 percent load charge, (2) an annual 0.50 percent management fee, and (3) an annual 1 percent 12b-1 fee.

4. *Matching Mutual Funds with Investor Needs.* This chapter explored a number of different classifications of mutual funds.   (Obj. 2)
   a. Based on your age and current financial situation, which type of mutual fund seems appropriate for your investment needs? Explain your answer.
   b. As people get closer to retirement, their investment goals often change. Assume you are now 45 and have accumulated $110,000 in a retirement account. In this situation, what type of mutual fund would you choose? Why?
   c. Assume you are now 60 years of age and have accumulated $400,000 in a retirement account. Also, assume you would like to retire when you are 65. What type of mutual funds would you choose to help you reach your investment goals? Why?

5. *Using Information to Evaluate Mutual Funds.* Obtain specific information on either the Aim Charter mutual fund or the Aim Value mutual fund. Then describe how each of the following sources of information could help you evaluate one of these mutual funds.   (Obj. 3)
   a. Newspapers.
   b. The fund's investment objective.
   c. The fund's prospectus.
   d. The fund's annual report.
   e. Financial publications.
   f. Professional advisory services.
   g. The Internet.

After researching one of the Aim funds, would you invest in the fund? Why or why not?

6. *Using the Standard & Poor's Personal Wealth Website.* Visit the Standard & Poor's Personal Wealth website and evaluate one of the following mutual funds. To complete this activity, follow these steps.   (Obj. 3)
   a. Go to www.personalwealth.com.
   b. Scroll down to the *Tools* section and click on *Find Funds.*
   c. Choose one of the following three funds, enter its symbol, and click on the "go" button: Aim Charter Mutual Fund/A (CHTRX), Kemper Growth Fund/A (KGRAX), and Washington Mutual Investors Fund/A (AWSHX).
   d. Print out the information for the mutual fund that you chose to evaluate.
   e. Based on the information included in this research report, would you invest in this fund? Explain your answer.

7. *Evaluating Mutual Funds.* Choose one of the following mutual funds and use information from newspapers, magazines, mutual fund reports, or the Internet to complete the mutual fund evaluation form presented in the Financial Planning Calculations feature on page 533. Then answer the following questions.   (Obj. 3)

| Name of Fund | Type of Fund |
| --- | --- |
| Strong Total Return | Growth and income fund |
| Fidelity Select Electronics Fund | Sector fund |
| Highmark Balanced Fund | Balanced fund |
| Janus Mercury Fund | Aggressive growth fund |
| USAA Group S&P Index Fund | Index fund |

   a. Which fund did you choose?
   b. Why did you choose this fund?
   c. Do you think this fund could help you achieve your investment objectives? Explain your answer.

8. *Applying the Concept of Dollar Cost Averaging.* In a one-page report, explain how the concept of dollar cost averaging applies to the options used to purchase mutual funds.   (Obj. 4)

9. *Reading a Prospectus.* Obtain a mutual fund prospectus to determine the options you can use to purchase and redeem shares. Then prepare a chart that illustrates which options can be used to purchase and redeem shares in the fund, and answer the following questions.   (Obj. 4)
   a. Which purchase option would appeal to you?
   b. Assuming you are now of retirement age, which withdrawal option would appeal to you?

# LIFE SITUATION CASE

## THE WRONG MUTUAL FUND?

According to Mike and Della Hanson, a Salt Lake City couple in their middle 30s, mutual funds were one of the biggest disappointments in their lives. In 1996, they invested $11,500 in the Fidelity Select Gold mutual fund. Three years later, their original investment had lost over 20 percent, or about $2,500, during a period when most mutual funds were posting huge profits. What went wrong?

Three years after their investment, the Hansons admitted they had invested money without researching the Fidelity Select Gold fund. They made their investment choice because Mike had heard a "high-powered" financial planner on a radio talk show raving about gold as the "ultimate" safe investment. Over the next two days, Mike convinced Della that gold was an investment that could be trusted, The Hansons would have purchased the gold coins the talk show host was selling, but Mike lost the 800 phone number. For lack of some other way to invest in gold, they decided to purchase shares in the Fidelity Select Gold mutual fund. Besides, they reasoned, shares in a mutual fund would be a better investment than purchasing individual coins because mutual funds provided diversification and professional management. Both thought they were choosing the right investment. What could be better than a mutual fund that "specialized" in gold? Their investment would be a safe choice even if other investments went down in value.

The Hansons also thought that since everybody was investing in mutual funds, they had to be the perfect investment. After all, there were over 7,500 different funds to choose from. Indeed, it seemed almost fashionable to invest in mutual funds. Because of professional management and diversification, there was no need to evaluate a mutual fund. Certainly the fund manager knew more about picking the investments contained in the fund's portfolio than they did. It seemed mutual funds were almost guaranteed to increase in value. But after losing over 20 percent in three years, they realized that "almost guaranteed" was not the same thing as "guaranteed."

At the time of their investment, both had heard good things about Fidelity mutual funds. A number of their friends had opened accounts with Fidelity and had done well. And Fidelity made it so easy! Just fill out an application, send the money, and let the professional managers make all the decisions.

In fact, the Hansons didn't realize that Fidelity, the nation's largest mutual fund family, offered over 100 mutual funds ranging from very conservative to very speculative investments. Simply put, they chose the wrong Fidelity mutual fund. Had the Hansons chosen the Fidelity Select Electronics fund, their original investment would have increased over 50 percent during the same three-year period and been worth over $17,000.

## Questions

1. Often investors indicate that diversification and professional management are the two main reasons they choose mutual fund investments. How important do you consider these two factors? Why?
2. At the time of this publication, Fidelity sells over 100 mutual funds ranging from very conservative to very speculative investments. Why do you think a fund family would offer so many investment alternatives?
3. According to the Hansons, everybody was investing in mutual funds—indeed, it almost seemed fashionable to invest in mutual funds. In your own words, what did the Hansons do wrong?
4. Obtain information about the Fidelity Select Gold fund and the Fidelity Select Electronics fund at the library or via the Internet. Then complete a mutual fund evaluation form (see the Financial Planning Calculations feature on page 533) for each fund and answer the following questions.
   a. What sources of information did you use to evaluate each fund?
   b. What fees must investors pay to invest in each fund?
   c. What is the investment objective for each fund?
   d. How would you describe the fund's financial performance over the past 12 months? The past three years? The past five years?
   e. How would you rate the risk associated with each fund?
   f. Would you invest your money in either of these funds? Justify you answer.

SOURCE: Values for the Fidelity Select Gold fund and the Fidelity Select Electronics fund based on information from The Yahoo Finance website (http://finance.yahoo.com), September 6, 1999, Yahoo, Inc., 3420 Central Expressway, Santa Clara, CA 95051.

# VIDEO CASE   Investing in Mutual Funds

What do long-term investments, tolerance for risk, and investment objectives have in common? Answer: They are all factors that must be considered when establishing a mutual fund investment program.

Today mutual funds are more popular than ever. Basically, a mutual fund allows you to pool your money with other investors to invest in a wide variety of investments. But before you invest, consider the following:

- Diversification and professional management are the main two advantages of mutual funds.
- You can buy shares in a closed-end or open-end mutual fund.
- Mutual funds may be front-end load funds, back-end load funds, or no-load funds.
- Over a long time period, a load fund and a no-load fund perform about the same.
- Mutual funds also charge management fees and 12b-1 fees.

For most mutual fund investors, professional management is an especially important feature. How long has the manager been the manager? Is the fund managed by one person or a group of managers? Is the fund actively or passively managed? Active management means the manager is actively buying and selling the stocks and other securities contained in the fund's portfolio. On the other hand, passive management means the manager matches the stocks and other securities in a fund with some index, like the Standard & Poor's 500 index, and uses a buy-and-hold strategy. The decision to purchase an active managed fund or a passive managed fund is yours. Factors that may help you decide include costs and fees for each type of fund, your risk tolerance, your financial objectives, and your ability to research a fund with a good manager.

To help them decide which fund is right for them, many investors begin with the fund's prospectus. A prospectus defines the fund's objective and provides information about load fees, management fees, and 12b-1 fees. The prospectus also describes the fund's performance over different time periods. Most or all of the same information contained in a printed prospectus can be found on the website of the investment company sponsoring the mutual fund. You can also access websites that contain specific information about individual mutual funds and more general education sites to help you become a better investor.

A decision to sell a mutual fund is complicated by taxation. If your money is invested as part of a 401(k) or 403(b) retirement account, your investment and earnings accumulate tax free until you make withdrawals. For all other accounts, dividends and capital gains distributions are taxable. Dividends are the earnings a fund pays to shareholders after it has deducted expenses from its dividend and interest income. Capital gains distributions are the payments made to a fund's shareholders that result from the sale of securities in the fund's portfolio. Even if you reinvest your dividends and capital gains in the fund, you still have to pay taxes. To determine how much tax you owe, you must keep good records. Then you can use a good software program to determine the amount of tax you owe to the IRS.

## Questions

1. Today mutual funds are more popular than ever. What factors lead investors to choose mutual fund investments?
2. When investing in mutual funds, you can choose a front-end load fund, a back-end load fund, or a no-load fund. What are the differences among the three types of funds? Does one type of fund outperform the other funds?
3. Even with professional management, investors should evaluate a mutual fund investment. Why? How would you go about evaluating a mutual fund investment?
4. What impact does taxation have on a decision to sell shares in a mutual fund?

## Creating an E-Plan: Financial Decisions Using the Web

### INVESTING IN MUTUAL FUNDS

Diversification through the use of mutual funds provides investors with convenience and professional management. The variety of mutual funds contributes to your ability to achieve various financial goals.

Websites for Mutual Funds

- Current mutual fund information and data at **www.personalwealth.com.**
- Current information and financial performance on over 6,000 mutual funds and more than 7,800 stocks at **www. morningstar.net.**
- Information and educational materials and other sources at **www.quicken. com** and **www.bloomberg.com.**
- Current articles on mutual funds from *Money* magazine at **www.money.com,** *Kiplinger's Personal Finance Magazine* at **www.kiplinger.com,** *Business Week* at **www.businessweek.com,** *Worth* magazine at **www. worth.com,** and *Smart Money* at **www.smartmoney. com.**
- Money market fund information at **www.moneyline.com/mlc.**

(Note: Addresses and content of websites change, and new sites are created daily. Use search engines to update and locate websites for your current financial planning needs.)

*PFP sheet: 60*

Short-Term Financial Planning Activities

1. Identify types of mutual funds that might be appropriate for your various financial goals and life situations.
2. Research the recent performance records and costs of various mutual funds that could be appropriate investments for you. (See PFP sheet 60)

Long-Term Financial Planning Activities

1. Identify types of mutual funds that you might use for your long-term financial goals.
2. Develop a plan for selecting and monitoring your mutual fund portfolio.

# 17

# Real Estate and Other Investment Alternatives

## Investing in Indium, Ostrich Farming, and Gemstones

Fraudulent telemarketing firms are selling indium, germanium, selenium, cadmium, and other "strategic metals" at greatly inflated prices. Recently Val Archer received a telephone call from Joe Johnson, an investment adviser. Joe began by assuring Val that "No," he didn't want her to invest a single cent. "Never invest with someone you don't know," he admonished. However, Joe wanted to demonstrate his firm's "research skill" by sharing with Val the forecast that indium was about to experience a significant price increase. Sure enough, the price soon went up.

A second telephone call from Joe didn't solicit an investment either. Joe simply wanted to share with Val a prediction that the price of indium was about to plummet. "Our forecasters will help you decide whether ours is the kind of firm you might someday want to invest with," he added. As predicted, the price of indium subsequently dropped.

By the time Val received a third call, she was a believer. She not only wanted to invest but insisted on it, and with a big enough investment to make up for the opportunities she had missed.

What Val did not know was that Joe had begun with a calling list of 400 names. On the first round of calls, he told 200 prospects that the price of indium would soon go up and the other 200 that it would go down. When the price went up, Joe made a second call to each of the 200 prospects to whom he had given the "correct forecast." Of these, he told 100 that the next price of indium would move up and the other 100 that it would go down.

Once the predicted price decline occurred, Joe had a list of 100 people eager to invest. After all, how could you go wrong with such an infallible source of price forecasts?

Today scam artists like Joe Johnson are turning to the Internet to promote their schemes. They are using online computer services to promote familiar scams such as fraudulent stock offerings and exotic or high-tech investment opportunities such as ostrich farming, gold mining, gemstones, and wireless cable television.

Remember, *never* make an investment decision based solely on information obtained from a single source, whether electronic bulletin board, online chatroom, newspaper or direct-mail ad, telemarketer, or broadcast commercial. The National Fraud Information Center maintains a toll-free Consumer Assistance Service at 1–800–876–7060 to provide consumers with information about telemarketing and online scams. You may also access the Federal Trade Commission on the World Wide Web at http://www.ftc.gov.

### Questions

1. What can you do to protect yourself from investment swindles like this one?
2. What can the federal and state governments do to stop such scams?
3. What other techniques do investment swindlers use?
4. What questions could you ask that might turn off investment swindlers?

## Learning Objectives

**Obj. 1**   Identify types of real estate investments.

**Obj. 2**   Evaluate the advantages of real estate investments.

**Obj. 3**   Assess the disadvantages of real estate investments.

**Obj. 4**   Analyze the risks and rewards of investing in precious metals, gems, and collectibles.

## INVESTING IN REAL ESTATE

### Obj. 1
Identify types of real estate investments.

*direct investment*
Investment in which the investor holds legal title to property.

*indirect investment*
Investment in which a trustee holds legal title to property on behalf of the investors.

Traditionally, Americans have invested in real estate. It is an asset that we can see, touch, and smell, and it is generally a good hedge against inflation. However, as you will see, the choices in real estate investment can be bewildering for the new investor. Furthermore, the Tax Reform Act of 1986 has lessened the appeal of investing in real estate.

Real estate investments are classified as direct or indirect. In a **direct investment,** the investor holds legal title to the property. Direct real estate investments include single-family dwellings, duplexes, apartments, land, and commercial property.

With an **indirect investment,** investors appoint a trustee to hold legal title on behalf of all the investors in the group. Limited partnerships and syndicates, real estate investment trusts, mortgages, and mortgage pools are examples of indirect real estate investments.

Exhibit 17–1 on page 548 summarizes the advantages and disadvantages of the two types of investments.

### Direct Real Estate Investments

**Your Home as an Investment**   Your home is, first, a place to live; second, it is an income shelter if you have a mortgage on it; finally, it is a possible hedge against inflation.

According to David Berson, chief economist at the Federal National Mortgage Association, Americans have about $9.4 trillion invested in single-family homes. Their equity, or the value of what they own outright after mortgage debt, amounts to about $6.5 trillion—some $650 billion more than people hold in stocks, bonds, and mutual funds combined. Generally, people feel driven to buy homes mainly for personal reasons, not as a result of financial analysis. Indeed, according to a study by the National Association of Realtors, the top two reasons most people give for buying are that they "preferred a larger home" or "wanted the tax advantages of homeownership."[1] The Financial Planning for Life's Situations feature on page 549 describes where most Americans put away most of their money.

Home prices generally have climbed steadily over the years. During the past 150 years, owning a home produced a "real," or after-inflation, return of about 2.5 percent a year, roughly the same return yielded by a bond.[2]

**Your Vacation Home**   If you have a vacation home, the after-tax cost of owning it has risen since 1987. How much depends largely on whether the Internal Revenue Service views the property as your second home or as a rental property. It is

**EXHIBIT 17-1**

Types, Advantages, and Disadvantages of Real Estate Investments

deemed a second home as long as you don't rent it for more than 14 days a year. In that case, you can write off your mortgage interest and property tax. If you rent the vacation home regularly, the size of your deductions is determined by whether you actively manage it and by the size of your income. According to one certified public accountant, "The primary reason you buy a vacation home is because you want to use it. Tax reasons . . . are way down on the list."[3]

*commercial property*
Land and buildings that produce lease or rental income.

## Commercial Property

The term **commercial property** refers to land and buildings that produce lease or rental income. Such property includes duplexes, apartments, hotels, office buildings, stores, and many other types of commercial establishments. After a home, the real property investment most widely favored by small investors is the duplex, fourplex, or small apartment building. Many investors have acquired sizable commercial properties by first investing in a duplex and then "trading up" to larger units as equity in the original property increases.

Under current tax laws, deductions such as mortgage interest, depreciation, property taxes, and other expenses of rental property are limited to the amount of rental income you receive. Any excess deductions are considered a passive loss and, with some exceptions, can be used only to offset income from a similar investment such as another rental property. A **passive activity** is a business or trade in which you do not materially participate, such as rental activity. **Passive loss** is the total amount of losses from a passive activity minus the total income from the passive activity.

*passive activity*
A business or trade in which the investor does not materially participate.

*passive loss*   The total amount of losses from a passive activity minus the total income from the passive activity.

## Undeveloped Land

Since the tax law changes of 1986, popular real estate investments, such as suburban garden apartments, no longer appeal to real estate investors. Instead, these investors have been favoring more exotic property, such as undeveloped land.

If land investments have promised tremendous gains, they have also posed enormous risks. With their money riding on a single parcel, investors could end up owning overpriced cropland in the event of a building slowdown or an economic downturn. Furthermore, land usually does not produce any cash flow.

Many investors buy land with the intention of subdividing it. Purchases of this kind are speculative because they involve many risks. You must be certain that water, sewers, and other utilities will be available. The most common and least expensive way to obtain water and sewer service is to hook onto existing facilities of an adjoining city or town.

## Financial Planning for Life's Situations

### HOME IS WHERE THE NEST EGG IS

Where have typical Americans put away most of their money? Hint: not the stock market. The answer is still real estate, according to a study by the Federal Reserve Bank of New York. In 1998, stocks did overtake real estate as the biggest asset among households. But those stockholdings were highly concentrated. According to the Survey of Consumer Finances, only about 50 percent of households in the United States own any stock at all, either directly or indirectly. Most privately held stocks are owned by the richest 10 percent of all households.

On the other hand, two-thirds of all households own their own homes. The house remains the major asset of most households even in later years, when people tend to have more money available for other investments.

The median 25-year-old homeowner has no stocks at all, while the median 55-year-old homeowner has only 3.5 percent of household assets invested in corporate stock. The study, conducted by New York Fed economists Joseph Tracy and Henry Schneider, and Sewin Chan of Rutgers University, concludes that the latest bull market in stocks has had "little effect" on the makeup of the assets of the typical U.S. family. For the average American family, the more important wealth effect may be rising housing prices. According to the National Association of Realtors, housing prices rose 6.1 percent in 1997 and 5.7 percent in 1998.

SOURCE: Reprinted from the August 9, 1999 issue of Business Week by special permission. © 1999 McGraw-Hill Compaines, Inc.

## Indirect Real Estate Investments

Indirect real estate investments include investing in real estate syndicates, real estate investment trusts, and participation certificates.

Bernice R. Hecker, a Seattle anesthesiologist, made her first real estate investment in 1985. She joined a partnership that bought an office building in Midland, Texas. "Why real estate? Probably superstition," she said. "I wanted a tangible asset. I felt I could evaluate a piece of property much more readily" than stocks, bonds, or a cattle ranch.[4]

Dr. Hecker used a real estate syndicate, one of the three basic indirect methods of investing in real estate: (1) Real estate syndicates, partnerships that buy properties; (2) real estate investment trusts (REITs), stockholder-owned real estate companies; and (3) participation certificates sold by federal and state agencies. Indirect real estate investments are sold by most brokerage firms, such as Merrill Lynch.

*syndicate* A temporary association of individuals or firms organized to perform a specific task that requires a large amount of capital.

### Real Estate Syndicates or Limited Partnerships

A **syndicate** is a temporary association of individuals or firms organized to perform a specific task that requires a large amount of capital.[5] The syndicate may be organized as a corporation, as a trust, or, most commonly, as a limited partnership.

The limited partnership works as follows. It is formed by a general partner, who has unlimited liability for its liabilities. The general partner then sells participation units to the limited partners, whose liability is generally limited to the extent of their initial investment, say, $5,000 or $10,000. Limited liability is particularly important in real estate syndicates because their mortgage debt obligations may exceed the net worth of the participants.

In addition to limited liability, a real estate syndicate provides professional management for its members. A syndicate that owns several properties may also provide diversification.

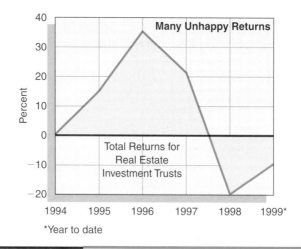

**EXHIBIT 17–2**

Total Returns for
REITs, 1994–99

SOURCES: National
Association of Real Estate
Investment Trusts; *Business
Week*, April 26, 1999, p. 40.
Reprinted from the
August 26, 1999 issue
of *Business Week* by
special permission,
© 1999 McGraw-Hill
Companies, Inc.

Traditionally, real estate syndicates have been tax shelters for the investors. However, the Tax Reform Act of 1986 limited the creativity of real estate syndicators. It hit real estate syndicates particularly hard by preventing losses from "passive" investments in partnerships from offsetting income from other sources. It also limited deductions of interest and depreciation and increased the tax on capital gains.

### Real Estate Investment Trusts (REITs)

*real estate investment trust (REIT)* A firm that pools investor funds and invests them in real estate or uses them to make construction or mortgage loans.

Another way to invest in real estate is the **real estate investment trust (REIT)**, which is similar to a mutual fund or an investment company, and trades on stock exchanges or over the counter. Like mutual funds, REITs pool investor funds. These funds, along with borrowed funds, are invested in real estate or used to make construction or mortgage loans.

There are three types of REITs: *Equity REITs* invest in properties; *mortgage REITs* pool money to finance construction loans and mortgages on developed properties; and *hybrid REITs* are combinations of mortgage and equity REITs.

Federal law requires REITs to

- Distribute at least 95 percent of their net annual earnings to shareholders.
- Refrain from engaging in speculative, short-term holding of real estate to sell for quick profits.
- Hire independent real estate professionals to carry out certain management activities.
- Have at least 100 shareholders; no more than half the shares may be owned by five or fewer people.

You can contact
NAREIT at
1–800–3NAREIT
or at http://www.
nareit.com.

In 1999, REIT stocks fell and have shown few signs of a rebound. (See Exhibit 17–2.) The total return of REITs was −17 percent in 1999.

Recently the National Association of Real Estate Investment Trusts (NAREIT), the Washington, DC–based industry trade group, announced a $2 million ad campaign aimed at luring back investors. "There is tremendous frustration" among many REIT executives who used to see their REITs "do nothing but go up," says Sam Zell, chairman of two of the nation's largest REITs: Equity Office Properties Trust and Equity Residential. His REITs have proven durable in 1999, he says, but adds: "An awful lot of people are depressed." Since 1991, more than 150 REITs have gone public, and the industry's market value has soared from $13 billion to $131 billion.[6]

# Financial Planning for Life's Situations

## REAL ESTATE'S REMARKABLE REVOLUTION

### 1960

Real estate investment trusts created by Congress to let individuals invest in real estate. REITs must distribute at least 95 percent of taxable income to shareholders but can avoid corporate taxes. REITs begin to flourish.

### MID-1970S

REIT market collapses because of high interest rates, excess leverage, and short-term financing. Many REITs go bust. REIT assets slump from $20 billion in 1974 to $7 billion in 1979.

### 1980S

New breed of REIT emerges, with lower leverage, stronger financing, and, after 1986, liberalized powers, thanks to tax changes. Rockefeller Center syndicated as a REIT.

### 1990

Commercial real estate market, hurt by thrift fiasco, collapses. Many empires, like the Reichmann's Olympia & York, go bankrupt. Rockefeller Center files for Chapter 11.

### 1991–92

Banks and other traditional sources cut off lending. Real estate execs seek alternate financing. "Opportunity" or "vulture" funds raise cash to buy distressed properties. Taubman Centers, the holder of shopping centers and malls, pioneers the "umbrella" REIT structure, called the UPREIT, which allows private owners to go public without having to pay capital gains tax.

### 1993–95

Real estate market recovers. In 1993, a record 50 firms, including many old-line families, bring REITs public. REITs proliferate, move rapidly into malls and apartments. Billion of dollars of capital flow into industry.

### 1996

Consolidation phase begins. Simon Property Group and DeBartolo Realty merge, forming biggest REIT, with $3.1 billion market cap. Zell launches first hostile REIT bid. REIT stocks soar.

### 1997

REIT equity market hits $120 billion market cap. Commercial mortgage-backed market reaches $144 billion. Mortimer Zuckerman's Boston Properties launches a $900 million IPO, the biggest REIT ever. First prison REIT, CCA Prison Realty Trust, goes public. REITs start buying up many old-line private real estate companies.

### 1998

REITs growth slows due to fears of overbuilding, recession, and credit crunch. Return on REITs investment falls by 17 percent.

### 1999

REITs still posting negative return on investment. No rebound yet.

Reprinted from 1997 and 1998 issues of *Business Week* by special permission. © 1999 McGraw-Hill Companies, Inc.

You may choose from among more than 300 REITs. Further information on REITs is available from the National Association of Real Estate Investment Trusts, 1129 20th Street, NW, Washington, DC 20036. The Financial Planning for Life's Situations feature summarizes REITs' remarkable history.

**Investing in First and Second Mortgages**   Mortgages and other debt contracts are commonly purchased by more well-to-do investors. The purchaser of a mortgage may take on some sort of risk that is unacceptable to the financial institutions from which mortgage financing is ordinarily obtained. Perhaps the mortgage is on a property for which there is no ready market. The title to the property may not be legally clear, or the title may not be insurable. Nevertheless, many people purchase such mortgages. These investments may provide relatively high rates of return due to their special risk characteristics.

*participation certificate (PC)*   An equity investment in a pool of mortgages that have been purchased by a government agency, such as Ginnie Mae.

**Participation Certificates**   If you want a risk-proof real estate investment, participation certificates (PCs) are for you. A **participation certificate (PC)** is an equity investment in a pool of mortgages that have been purchased by one of several government agencies. Participation certificates are sold by federal agencies such as the Government National Mortgage Association (Ginnie Mae), the Federal Home Loan Mortgage Corporation (Freddie Mac), the Federal National Mortgage Association (Fannie Mae), and the Student Loan Marketing Association (Sallie Mae). A few states issue "little siblings," such as the State of New York Mortgage Agency (Sonny Mae) and the New England Education Loan Marketing Corporation (Nellie Mae).

Maes and Macs are guaranteed by agencies closely tied to the federal government, making them as secure as U.S. Treasury bonds and notes. At one time, you needed a minimum of $25,000 to invest in PCs. Thanks to Maes and Macs mutual funds, you now need as little as $1,000 to buy shares in a unit trust or a mutual fund whose portfolio consists entirely of these securities. Either way, you assume the role of a mortgage lender. Each month, as payments are made on the mortgages, you receive interest and principal by check, or, if you wish, the mutual fund will reinvest the amount for you.

The Financial Planning for Life's Situations feature on page 553 describes various types of participation certificates sold by federal and state agencies.

## Concept Check 17–1

**1.** What web sources are available to protect you from investment scams?
**2.** What are four examples of direct investments in real estate?
**3.** What are four examples of indirect investments in real estate?
**4.** What is a syndicate? A REIT? A participation certificate (PC)?

# ADVANTAGES OF REAL ESTATE INVESTMENTS

**Obj. 2**
Evaluate the advantages of real estate investments.

For many types of real estate investments, blanket statements about their investment advantages and disadvantages are not possible. However, certain types of real estate investments may possess some of the advantages discussed in this section.

## A Hedge against Inflation

Real property equity investments usually (but not always) provide protection against purchasing power risk. In some areas, the prices of homes have increased consistently. For example, prices are rising in the Midwest and in some Western areas, such as Colorado and Texas. "In Colorado Springs, multifamily housing is booming. All the inventory has dried up," says one financial planner.[7]

## Easy Entry

You can gain entry to a shopping center or a large apartment building by investing $5,000 as a limited partner. (A limited partner's liability is restricted by the amount of his or her investment. A limited partner cannot take part in the management of the partnership.) The minimum capital requirements for the total venture may be as high as $1 million or more, which is beyond the limits of a typical real estate investor.

# Financial Planning for Life's Situations

## UNCLE SAM AND HIS FAMILY

The government securities named Maes and Macs can offer safety and relatively high yields.

1. **Ginnie Mae—Government National Mortgage Association (GNMA).** Introduced the first mortgage-backed securities in 1970 and still dominates this market. The residential mortgage-backed securities are packaged in pools and then resold to investors as certificates ($25,000) or as shares by mutual funds. Regular payments to investors are guaranteed by the GNMA, an agency of the Department of Housing and Urban Development. Ginnie Maes are backed by the full faith and credit of the federal government. The average life of mortgages is 12 years.

2. **Freddie Mac—Federal Home Loan Mortgage Corporation (FHLMC).** Issues mortgage-backed securities similar to Ginnie Maes. The pools of fixed-rate home mortgages are made up of conventional home loans rather than mortgages insured by the FHA or the VA. The timely payment of interest and the *ultimate* payment of principal are guaranteed.

3. **Fannie Mae—Federal National Mortgage Association (FNMA).** Issues mortgage-backed securities similar to Ginnie Maes and Freddie Macs. The pools of fixed-rate home mortgages are similar to Freddie Macs but not to Ginnie Maes. Like Ginnie Maes, Fannie Maes guarantee a fair share of interest and principal *every month*. Like Ginnie Maes and Freddie Macs, newly issued Fannie Mae certificates require a minimum investment of $25,000; the older

certificates (whose principal has been partially paid off) require an investment of as little as $10,000.

4. **Sallie Mae—Student Loan Marketing Association.** Created by Congress in 1972 to provide a national secondary market for government-guaranteed student loans. Issues bonds, each backed by Sallie Mae as a whole rather than as specific pools of loans. Sallie Mae bonds are considered as safe as government Treasuries. Brokers sell bonds having minimum denominations of $10,000. You can also buy shares of Sallie Mae *stock;* the corporation is government chartered but publicly owned, and its shares are traded on the New York Stock Exchange.

5. **Sonny Mae—State of New York Mortgage Agency.** Issues bonds backed by fixed-rate, single-family home mortgages and uses proceeds to subsidize below-market-rate mortgages for first-time home buyers. As with ordinary bonds, interest on Sonny Maes is paid only until the bonds mature. Sonny Maes are exempt from federal income tax, and New York State residents do not pay state income tax on them.

6. **Nellie Mae—New England Education Loan Marketing Corporation.** A nonprofit corporation created by the Commonwealth of Massachusetts. Provides a secondary market for federally guaranteed student loans issued in Massachusetts and New Hampshire. The AAA-rated Nellie Mae bonds mature in three years and are sold in minimum denominations of $5,000.

## Limited Financial Liability

If you are a limited partner, you are not liable for losses beyond your initial investment. This can be important if the venture is speculative and rewards are not assured. General partners, however, must bear all financial risks.

## No Management Concerns

If you have invested in limited partnerships, REITs, mortgages, or participation certificates, you need not worry about paperwork and accounting, maintenance chores, and other administrative duties.

## Financial Planning for Life's Situations

### ONLINE REAL ESTATE INVESTMENTS: A PEARL IN EVERY OYSTER?

The explosion of online advertising is one of the most talked-about topics in real estate investing today. But typing the words "real estate investments" when using a popular Internet search engine may yield a list of hundreds of sites, some much more useful than others. This makes it seem easier to find a pearl in an oyster than the investment that's right for you.

"The more information that becomes available on the Internet, the harder it becomes to find the information you're looking for," said Becky Swann, president and founder of Ired.com Inc., a Dallas-based company designed to serve as a "directory of directories" for real estate–related Internet sites.

Here is a brief overview of some of the more useful and creative destinations for sellers and buyers:

**cyberhomes.com**—This site claims to be the only online real estate search service with interactive street-level mapping. Once a property listed for sale has been identified, a click on an icon will provide a Net surfer with a detailed map, complete with street names and area schools.

**www.realtor.com**—The National Association of Realtors in Washington, DC, claims to have the largest real estate site on the Internet, with over 839,000 active listings in the United States and Canada.

**www.chicagotribune.com**—Like most area newspapers, the *Chicago Tribune* maintains and permits free access to its classified real estate investment ads.

**www.pacislands.com**—This site is targeted at the investor looking for hot properties in the South Pacific. It features everything from thumbnail sketches of each area to an animated drawing of a Tahitian belly dancer!

One challenge in searching for an investment on the Internet is that the ease with which you can connect to a site is inversely proportional to its popularity. However, if you have Internet access, it can be easier to find your pearl!

SOURCES: Jay Romano, "http://buyandsellonline.com," *The New York Times,* July 27, 1997, p. 3; Liz Poppens, "Virtual Luau: Site Is a Paradise for Pacific Island Investors," *Chicago Tribune,* July 20, 1997, p. 3C.

## Financial Leverage

*Financial leverage* is the use of borrowed funds for investment purposes. It enables you to acquire a more expensive property than you could on your own. This is an advantage when property values and incomes are rising. Assume you buy a $100,000 property with no loan and then sell it for $120,000. The $20,000 gain represents a 20 percent return on your $100,000 investment. Now assume you invest only $10,000 of your own money and borrow the other $90,000 (90 percent financing). Now you have made $20,000 on your $10,000 investment, or a 200 percent return.

For a brief overview of online real estate investments, see the Financial Planning for Life's Situations feature above.

### Concept Check 17–2

1. What are the advantages of real estate investments?
2. How is financial leverage calculated?

## DISADVANTAGES OF REAL ESTATE INVESTMENTS

Real estate investments have several disadvantages. However, these disadvantages do not affect all kinds of real estate investments to the same extent.

Obj. 3

Assess the
disadvantages of real
estate investments.

## Illiquidity

Perhaps the largest drawback of direct real estate investments is the absence of large, liquid, and relatively efficient markets for them. Whereas stocks or bonds generally can be sold in a few minutes at the market price, this is not the case for real estate. It may take months to sell commercial property or limited partnership shares.

## Declining Property Values

As discussed earlier, real property investments usually provide a hedge against inflation. But during deflationary and recessionary periods, the value of such investments may decline. For example, thousands of developers, lenders, and investors have been victims of a deflation in commercial real estate that began sporadically in the early 1980s. Property values in Southern California, the Northeast, and some other regions are still declining.

## Lack of Diversification

Diversification in direct real estate investments is difficult due to the large size of most real estate projects. REITs, Ginnie Maes, Freddie Macs, and other syndicates, however, do provide various levels of diversification.

## Lack of a Tax Shelter

The Tax Reform Act of 1986 limits taxpayers' ability to use losses generated by real estate investments to offset income gained from other sources. Thus, investors cannot deduct their real estate losses from income generated by wages, salaries, dividends, and interest. In short, the tax shelter aspect of real estate syndicates no longer exists.

## Long Depreciation Period

Before the Tax Reform Act of 1986 went into effect, commercial real estate could be depreciated within 18 years. Under the accelerated cost recovery system (ACRS), adopted in 1980, an investor was allowed to use accelerated depreciation methods to recover the costs. Now investors must use the straight-line depreciation method over $27\frac{1}{2}$ years for residential real estate and over $31\frac{1}{2}$ years for all other types of real estate.

Other provisions of the 1986 act affect real estate investments, and all reduce the value of the tax credits for such investments. Investors are not allowed to take losses in excess of the actual amounts they invest. Furthermore, the investment tax credit has been eliminated entirely for all types of real estate except low-income housing projects.

## Management Problems

Although investments in limited partnerships, REITs, mortgages, and participation certificates do not create management problems, buying and managing individual properties do. Along with the buildings come the responsibilities of management: finding reliable tenants, buying new carpeting, fixing the furnace when it breaks down in the middle of the night, and so on. Many people aren't willing to take on these responsibilities. "This is one reason I dislike small real estate investments," says one financial planner. "There should be a large enough amount of money that it is very important to you and you pay a lot of attention to it. Otherwise it won't work."[8]

If you believe investing in real estate is too risky or too complicated, you might want to consider other tangible investments such as gold and other precious metals, gems, and collectibles. But remember, these investments may entail both risk and reward.

## Concept Check 17-3

1. What are the disadvantages of real estate investments?
2. What depreciation method is used for residential real estate?

# INVESTING IN PRECIOUS METALS, GEMS, AND COLLECTIBLES

**Obj. 4**
Analyze the risks and rewards of investing in precious metals, gems, and collectibles.

When the economy picks up, some investors predict higher inflation. Therefore, many think precious metals such as gold, platinum, and silver will regain some of their glitter. In this section, we discuss several methods for buying precious metals.

## Gold

Gold prices tend to be driven up by factors such as fear of war, political instability, and inflation. On the other hand, easing of international tensions or disinflation causes a decline in gold prices. High interest rates also depress gold prices because they make it very expensive to carry gold as an investment.

Many people have acquired gold directly. Many others have invested in gold through a number of other kinds of investments that serve a variety of purposes. Some of these investments promise quick profits at high risk, others preserve capital, and still others provide income from dividends or interest. But all of them are subject to daily gold price fluctuations. Exhibit 17–3 shows gold price fluctuations between 1976 and April 2000.

**Gold Bullion**    Gold bullion includes gold bars and wafers. The basic unit of gold bullion is one kilogram (32.15 troy ounces of 0.995 fine gold). Coin dealers, precious metals dealers, and some banks sell gold bullion in amounts ranging from 5 grams (16/100 of a troy ounce) to 500 ounces or more. On small bars, dealers and banks add a 5 to 8 percent premium over the pure gold bullion value; on larger bars, the premium is usually 1 to 2 percent. Gold bullion poses storage problems, and unless the gold bar or wafer remains in the custody of the bank or dealer that sells it initially, it must be reassayed (retested for fineness) before being sold.

**Gold Bullion Coins**    You can avoid storage and assaying problems by investing in gold bullion coins. In the early 1980s, before South Africa's political problems intensified, South African krugerrands were the most popular gold bullion coins in the United States. Popular gold bullion coins today include Australia's kangaroo nugget, the Canadian gold maple leaf, the Mexican 50 peso, the Austrian 100 koronas, and the British sovereign. The new American eagle gold coin, the first gold bullion coin ever produced by the U.S. government, was issued in late 1986.

Most brokers require a minimum order of 10 coins and charge a commission of at least 2 percent.

**Gold Stocks**    In addition to investing in gold bullion and gold bullion coins, you may invest in gold by purchasing the common stocks of gold mining companies. Among the gold mining stocks listed on U.S. stock exchanges are those of Homestake

**EXHIBIT 17-3**    FLUCTUATIONS IN THE PRICE OF GOLD SINCE 1976

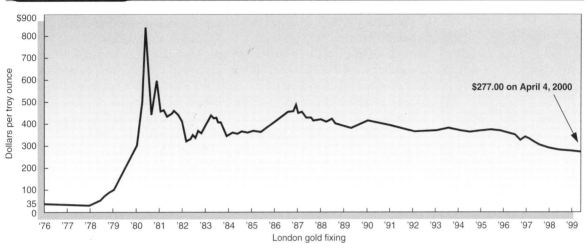

Mining (based in the United States) and Campbell Red Lake and Dome Mines (based in Canada). Because such stocks often move in a direction opposite to that of the stock market as a whole, they may provide excellent portfolio diversification. You may also wish to examine closed-end investment companies with heavy positions in gold mining stocks, such as ARA, Ltd.

## Silver, Platinum, Palladium, and Rhodium

Investments in silver, platinum, palladium, and rhodium, like investments in gold, are used as a hedge against inflation and as a safe haven during political or economic upheavals. During the last 70 years, silver prices ranged from a historic low of 24.25 cents an ounce in 1932, to over $50 an ounce in early 1980, and then back to less than $5.00 an ounce in April 2000.

Three lesser-known precious metals, platinum, palladium, and rhodium, are also popular investments. All have industrial uses as catalysts, particularly in automobile production. Some investors think increased car sales could mean higher prices for these metals. Platinum currently sells for about $500 an ounce and palladium for about $573 an ounce. The rhodium price in April 2000 was about $1,600 per ounce.

As discussed earlier, finding storage for your precious metals can be tricky. While $20,000 in gold, for example, occupies only as much space as a thick paperback book, $20,000 in silver weighs more than 200 pounds and could require a few safe-deposit boxes. Such boxes, moreover, are not insured against fire and theft.

You should remember too that unlike stocks, bonds, and other interest-bearing investments, precious metals sit in vaults earning nothing. And whether you profit on an eventual sale depends entirely on how well you call the market.

## Precious Stones

Precious stones include diamonds, sapphires, rubies, and emeralds. Precious stones appeal to investors because of their small size, ease of concealment, great durability, and potential as a hedge against inflation. Inflation and investor interest in tangible assets helped increase diamond prices 40-fold between 1970 and 1980. A few lucky investors made fortunes, and brokerage and diamond firms took up the investment diamond business.

Whether you are buying precious stones to store in a safe-deposit box or to wear around your neck, there are a few risks to keep in mind. Diamonds and other precious stones are not easily turned into cash. It is difficult to determine whether you are getting a good stone. Diamond prices can be affected by the whims of De Beers Consolidated Mines of South Africa, Ltd., which controls 85 percent of the world's supply of rough diamonds, and by political instability in diamond-producing countries. Moreover, you should expect to buy at retail and sell at wholesale, a difference of at least 10 to 15 percent and perhaps as much as 50 percent.

The best way to know exactly what you are getting, especially if you are planning to spend more than $1,000, is to insist that your stone be certified by an independent geological laboratory, one not connected with a diamond-selling organization. (The acknowledged industry leader in this area is the Gemological Institute of America.) The certificate should list the stone's characteristics, including its weight, color, clarity, and quality of cut. The grading of diamonds, however, is not an exact science, and recent experiments have shown that when the same diamond is submitted twice to the same institute, it can get two different ratings.

Michael Roman, former chairman of the Jewelers of America, a trade group representing 12,000 retailers, stated that his group did not recommend diamonds as an investment and scoffed at the notion that local retail jewelers were realizing huge profits on diamond sales to misguided customers. He also did not believe in certification unless the stone in question is a high-grade diamond weighing at least one carat.

Despite the present rosy scenarios for precious metals and gems, the risks in trading them are sizable. Just ask investors who in 1980 bought gold at as much as $850 an ounce, platinum at $1,040 an ounce, silver at $48 an ounce, and a one-carat diamond at $62,000.

With all diamonds, the absence of color indicates a finer grade.

**Sheet 60**

## Collectibles

*collectibles* Rare coins, works of art, antiques, stamps, rare books, and other items that appeal to collectors and investors.

**Collectibles** include rare coins, works of art, antiques, stamps, rare books, sports memorabilia, rugs, Chinese ceramics, paintings, and other items that appeal to collectors and investors. Each of these items offers the knowledgeable collector/investor both pleasure and the opportunity for profit. Many collectors have discovered only incidentally that items they bought for their own pleasure had gained greatly in value while they owned them.

### Collectibles on the Net

Before the era of the World Wide Web, author and antiques collector David Maloney had to search far and wide to find a 1950s cut-crystal Val St. Lambert pitcher. No one in his hometown of Frederick, Maryland, carries fancy glassware, he says, "and I would spend days driving around to yard sales and little shops." Recently, though, Maloney logged on to the Net and, in only 15 seconds, found a store in Pennsylvania that carries 40 styles of his prized crystal.

Whether you collect glassware, home-run baseballs, or Ming vases, you no longer need to travel to far-flung antiques fairs or pore over trade magazines to add to your collection. The world of collectibles is expanding onto the Web at a geometric rate, bringing unprecedented efficiency and convenience to an art collector's market. The explosion of online collecting and the success of the biggest auction site, eBay, prompted Guernsey's Auction House to open the bidding for Mark McGwire's 70th home-run baseball to online buyers as well as those in the salesroom (it went for $3

# Financial Planning for Life's Situations

## SURFING FOR BOOMERABILIA

Remember those Beatles albums and peace buttons you used to own? That Lamb Chop hand puppet? You can now buy them back and relive your youth via the Internet. Baby boomers moving into their middle years are flocking to the Web in search of memorabilia. "Boomerabilia" include artifacts from the end of World War II through the early 1970s, with an emphasis on TV. Looking to buy or sell a Captain Kangaroo doll or a Batmobile? How about a Beverly Hillbillies car or a Herman Munster puppet? You can find it online.

Most shoppers head for general-auction and collectibles sites, such as eBay and CSM Online (www.csmonline.com). But some sites specialize. Items in their original packaging fetch the most. A WHAM-O hula hoop from the 60s that sold for about $1 can command up to $100 with the original price tag. A Samantha doll from the sitcom "Bewitched," featured in Toy Scouts' (www.toyscots.com) third annual TV and movie auction in the fall of 1999, sold for $4,296. Other hot items include a Lost in Space robot ($1,210), a Dick Clark doll ($634), and a Ben Casey pillowcase ($110). At Time Warp Toys & Collectibles (www.timewarp-toys.com), you'll find cowboys, vehicles, rock-and-roll, and sports items. And at Sentimental Journeys (www.sentimental-journeys.com), nostalgia buffs can find the album Vince Edwards Sings (from the actor who played Ben Casey) for $10 and a Man from U.N.C.L.E. coloring book for $35. Whether it's lunchboxes or Barbie dolls, "American culture from the 50s and 60s is in demand all over the world," says Jane Sorensohn-Kahn, a Barbie collector who writes for *Toy Trader* magazine. With the Net, finding boomer kitsch is a snap.

Reprinted from the February 8, 1999 issue of *Business Week* by special permission. © 1999 McGraw-Hill Companies, Inc.

million to an anonymous phone bidder). And Sotheby's plans to set up shop on the Net for goods under $5,000.

It's easy to see why the Web has such appeal. Buyers can target obscure items with a few keystrokes, and sellers can reach a much larger, more varied market. Of course, online buyers can't kick the tires or size up dealers face to face. But so far, fraud is rare, and preventive measures are increasing.

Although you can find antique armoires and vintage cars, dealers say the Net is best suited to smaller items, such as books, coins, stamps, buttons, and textiles, that can be easily scanned for viewing and shipped by mail. There are three basic ways to go about collecting online, says Maloney, author of *Maloney's Antiques and Collectibles Resource Directory*. You can seek out specialty boutiques, such as Auntie-Dot-Com (www.auntie.com) for leads on dolls; go to auction houses such as Auction Universe (www.auctionuniverse.com); or visit virtual malls such as Buy Collectibles.com (www.buycollectibles.com).

Prices aren't necessarily cheaper on the Web, but it's much easier to compare them, and most sites don't charge a buyer's commission. To purchase an early edition of Mark Twain's *The Adventures of Tom Sawyer*, for example, use a specialty search engine, such as www.bibliofind.com, to view descriptions of dealers' inventories. The site will provide details on the condition, publisher, and price of the book. Most editions of *Tom Sawyer* published in the 20th century sell for about $10, but a first British edition from 1898 lists for $350. Since the Net has opened up a wider market, items that probably wouldn't sell at local antiques show can find an appropriate home.

Still, virtual collecting has drawbacks. Buyers can't examine objects for flaws or trademarks. Many knowledgeable old-time dealers aren't computer literate, while some collectors prefer the thrill of hunting in out-of-the-way junk shops. "The average person still wants to see and feel the antiques," says Terry Kovel, author of *Kovel's*

**EXHIBIT 17-4**

**Where to Bid Online**

Reprinted from the February 8, 1999 issue of *Business Week* by special permission. © 1999 McGraw-Hill Companies, Inc.

| Name | Address | Comments |
|------|---------|----------|
| Auction Universe | www.auctionuniverse.com | Online auction house |
| Buy Collectibles | www.buycollectibles.com | Searchable database |
| Collector Online | www.collectoronline.com | Matches buyers and sellers |
| eBay | www.ebay.com | Web's biggest auctioneer |
| Interactive Collector | www.icollector.com | International dealers |

*Antiques & Collectibles Price List.* "An awful lot of antiques purchases are emotional, because someone walks into a store and sees an object they had as a kid."

A more serious concern, perhaps, is the security risk of buying online when you don't know who's getting your cash or credit card number. But while the security risks of online collecting grab headlines, Kovel says fraud has been negligible. Collectors do take gambles, but for many happy hunters, the increased selection and convenience of shopping on the Web is far outweighing its dangers. Exhibit 17–4 provides some popular websites where you can bid online.[9]

**Caveat emptor**     Collecting can be a good investment and a satisfying hobby, but for many Americans it has recently become a financial disaster. For example, as the market for paintings by Pablo Picasso and Andy Warhol has exploded, forgeries have become a significant problem. Art experts and law enforcement officials say that a new generation of collectors is being victimized by forgeries more sophisticated, more expensive, and more difficult to detect than ever before.

For a rare 1961 Chateau Petrusa, a subtly spicy Merlot, the average price was $2,696 a bottle. (*The Wall Street Journal,* May 2, 1997, p. B8.)

Forgeries or not, art prices are booming. For example, Damien Hirst's *The Lovers,* four jars filled with cow organs in formaldehyde, sold for $229,350, and a plaster cast of the underside of a sink by Rachel Whiteread fetched $220,275. However, a single painting, a van Gogh called *Portrait of Dr. Gachnet,* which sold for an all-time record of $82.5 million in 1990, has been up for sale privately for months. The minimum asking price: $80 million. An 1889 self-portrait believed to be the last painted by van Gogh sold for $71.5 million.

Nostalgia and limited availability will also fuel certain markets. With failed airlines and railroads becoming distant memories, count on Pan Am wing pins and Pullman porter badges to go up in value. Fanaticism, combined with a dwindling supply, will also push up prices of rock-and-roll record albums.[10] (See the Financial Planning for Life's Situations feature on page 559 for more examples.)

Rare-coin scams have increased, and many investors in rare coins have lost most of their investments as a result of fraudulent sales practices. If you are investing in coins, the Federal Trade Commission and the American Numismatic Association urge you to protect yourself by following these rules:

- Use common sense when evaluating any investment claims, and do not rush into buying.
- Make sure you know your dealer's reputation and reliability before you send money or authorize a credit card transaction.
- Do not be taken in by promises that the dealer will buy back your coins or that grading is guaranteed, unless you are confident that the dealer has the financial resources to stand behind these promises.

Advice from a Pro

## PREVENTING FRAUD

Looking for an online investment opportunity that is "unaffected by the volatile stock market," guarantees "virtually unlimited profits," "minimizes or eliminates risk factors," and is "IRA approved"? "Forget it," advises Jodie Bernstein, director of the Federal Trade Commission's Bureau of Consumer Protection. "Claims that an investment is IRA approved are a tip-off to a rip-off. You must be just as careful when investing in opportunities touted on the Net as you are when you make other investments. You should check out these with state securities regulators and other investment professionals." For more information about investing on the Internet, Bernstein suggests that you contact the following organizations:

- Federal Trade Commission (www.ftc.gov).
- North American Securities Administrators Association, Inc. (www.nasaa.org).
- Commodity Futures Trading Commission (www.cftc.gov).
- National Association of Securities Dealers (www.nasd.com).
  - Securities and Exchange Commission (www.sec.gov).
  - National Association of Investors Corporation (www.better-investing.org).
  - InvestorGuide (www.investorguide.com).
  - InvestorWords (www.investorwords.com).
- The Motley Fool (www.fool.com)
- Alliance for Investor Education (www.investoreducation.org).
- The Online Investor (www.investhelp.com)
- National Fraud Information Center (www.fraud.org).

- Get a second opinion from another source about grade and value as soon as you receive your coins. So, before you buy, find out what remedies you will have if the second opinion differs.
- Be cautious about grading certificates, especially those furnished by coin dealers. Grading is not an exact science, and grading standards vary widely.
- Comparison shop. Visit several dealers before buying.[11]

Collecting for investment purposes is very different from collecting as a hobby. Like investing in real estate or the stock market, investing in collectibles should be approached with care. Be especially careful if you buy from online auctions.

Investment counselors caution that collectibles do not provide interest or dividends, that it may be difficult to sell them at the right price on short notice, and that if they become valuable enough, they must be insured against loss or theft.

Exhibit 17–5 on page 562 compares the annual rate of return on various tangible and intangible assets over the past 1, 5, 10, and 20 years.

## Concept Check 17–4

1. What are several methods for buying precious metals?
2. Why do precious stones appeal to investors?
3. What are collectibles?
4. How can you protect yourself from fraudulent practices in the collectibles market?

## EXHIBIT 17-5   IN THE LONG RACE, STOCKS WIN

| Assets | 20 Years | | 10 Years | | 5 Years | | 1 Year | |
|---|---|---|---|---|---|---|---|---|
| | Rank | Return* | Rank | Return* | Rank | Return* | Rank | Return* |
| Stocks | 1 | 13.1% | 1 | 15.5% | 2 | 10.4% | 6 | 2.6% |
| Foreign exchange | 2 | 11.9 | 3 | 13.0 | 1 | 10.6 | 5 | 3.3 |
| Bonds | 3 | 10.2 | 2 | 14.1 | 3 | 9.9 | 10 | 0.7 |
| Stamps | 4 | 9.1 | 10 | −0.9 | 11 | 1.1 | 8 | 1.9 |
| 3-month Treasury bills | 5 | 8.3 | 4 | 6.7 | 4 | 5.6 | 4 | 4.3 |
| Diamonds | 6 | 7.9 | 5 | 5.9 | 9 | 1.4 | 11 | 0.0 |
| Housing | 7 | 6.3 | 6 | 4.1 | 6 | 2.9 | 9 | 1.8 |
| Consumer price index | 8 | 5.7 | 7 | 3.6 | 5 | 3.5 | 7 | 2.1 |
| Farmland | 9 | 4.6 | 9 | −0.7 | 7 | 2.4 | 2 | 6.4 |
| Gold | 10 | 4.5 | 8 | −0.2 | 10 | 1.3 | 3 | 4.7 |
| Oil | 11 | 2.9 | 12 | −5.2 | 12 | −1.9 | 12 | −9.8 |
| Silver | 12 | 1.0 | 11 | −4.9 | 8 | 1.9 | 1 | 31.1 |
| Sotheby's common | 13 | N/A | 13 | N/A | 13 | −3.3 | 13 | −11.4 |

*Average annual return.

SOURCE: Sumner N. Levine, ed., *Business and Investment Almanac, 1995* (Burr Ridge, IL: Richard D. Irwin, 1995), p. 249. © Sumner N. Levine, 1995.

## Summary of Objectives

Obj. 1   **Identify types of real estate investments.**

Real estate investments are classified as direct or indirect. Direct real estate investments, in which the investor holds legal title to the property, include a home, a vacation home, commercial property, and undeveloped land. Indirect real estate investments include real estate syndicates, REITs, mortgages, and participation certificates.

Obj. 2   **Evaluate the advantages of real estate investments.**

Real estate investments offer a hedge against inflation, easy entry, limited financial liability, no management headaches, and financial leverage.

Obj. 3   **Assess the disadvantages of real estate investments.**

Real estate investments may have the disadvantages of illiquidity, declining values, lack of diversification, lack of a tax shelter, a long depreciation period, and management problems.

Obj. 4   **Analyze the risks and rewards of investing in precious metals, gems, and collectibles.**

Some investors prefer to invest in precious metals such as gold, platinum, and silver; precious stones such as diamonds; or collectibles such as stamps, rare coins, works of art, antiques, rare books, and Chinese ceramics. Collectibles do not provide current income, and they may be difficult to sell quickly.

## Financial Planning Problems

1. *Calculating the Return on Investment.* Dave bought a rental property for $200,000 cash. One year later, he sold it for $240,000. What was the return on his $200,000 investment?   (Obj. 2)

2. *Calculating the Return on Investment Using Financial Leverage.* Suppose Dave invested only $20,000 of his own money and borrowed $180,000 (90 percent financing). What was his return on investment?   (Obj. 2)

# Financial Planning Activities

1. *Using the Internet to Obtain Information about Various Types of REITs.* Many REITs now maintain a web page on the Internet. Visit a few websites of REIT companies discussed in this chapter and of the National Association of Real Estate Investment Trusts (NAREIT) at http://www.nareit.com. Then prepare a report that summarizes the various types of REITs available to investors. (Obj. 1)

2. *Assessing the Prices of Single-Family Dwellings.* Interview local real estate brokers and research current business magazines and the business section of the local newspaper to determine if the prices of single-family dwellings in your area have been increasing during the last 10 years. Prepare a written report indicating the reasons for the increase or decrease. (Obj. 1)

3. *Assessing the Investment Potential of Commercial Real Estate.* Research current commercial real estate sections of local newspapers. How many listings do you find for duplexes? For fourplexes and small apartment buildings? Prepare an analysis of the investment potential of these properties. (Obj. 1)

4. *Checking the Availability of Real Estate Limited Partnerships.* Call a few real estate and stockbrokerage firms in your area to find out if any real estate limited partnerships are available for investors. (Obj. 2)

5. *Comparing Mortgage Rates and Terms of a Loan.* Obtain duplex mortgage rates from your local commercial bank, a savings and loan association, and a credit union. Compare these rates and terms such as the down payment, loan costs (points), loan length, and maximum amount available to determine which of the three lenders offers the best financing. (Obj. 3)

6. *Checking Current Prices of Precious Metals.* Listen to business news on radio or television. What are the current quotes for an ounce of gold and an ounce of silver? Are the prices of precious metals going up or down? How do the latest prices compare with the prices quoted in the chapter? What might be some reasons for fluctuations in the prices of precious metals? (Obj. 4)

# LIFE SITUATION CASE

## THE TROUBLE IN PARADISE?

To William D. Sanders, home is a parched, windswept New Mexico ranch that extends over 125 square miles beneath the Sangre de Christo mountains—a world away from the clamor of the real estate industry. The white-haired, denim-clad entrepreneur is patrolling his rugged, high-desert spread from the front seat of a white Ford pickup. "What is great about this place," says the Texas native, his drawl erased by decades spent traveling between cities such as Chicago and London, where he erected companies, "is that you can think."

These days Bill Sanders has plenty to think about. His $20 billion real estate empire, the biggest and most complex in the country, is in serious trouble. There's even a risk it might be dismembered. That would be an enormous comedown for Sanders, who is widely regarded in the industry as the foremost visionary behind the 1990s boom in real estate investment trusts. "He is the senior statesman of our industry," say Mortimer Zuckerman, CEO of REIT Boston Properties. Beyond the real estate world, though, the reclusive Sanders is little known, His extensive talk with *Business Week* over several months was the first in years. Sanders' long-time goal has been to extend his reach across the globe, building giant real estate operating companies. He wants to be the one-stop shop for real estate investors worldwide. But over the years, his empire has suffered big losses because of a bear market that has damaged most real estate equities. The major reason: With real estate at the top of the cycle, investors fear commercial real estate is headed south.

Unfortunately, investors these days hate real estate. Despite the solid cash flow of REITs, the REIT index fell by 23 percent in 1998. One thing that should not be underestimated, however, is Bill Sanders' dedication to REITs. As his pickup travels the dirt tracks of his ranch, Sanders' dream seems as dry as his parched spread.

## Questions

1. Who is regarded as the foremost visionary in real estate investment trusts?
2. What is William Sanders' long-time goal?
3. What has happened to Sanders' empire, and why?
4. Why do today's investors hate real estate investments?

Reprinted from the March 1, 1999 issue of *Business Week* by special permission. © 1999 McGraw-Hill Companies, Inc.

## INTERNET CASE   The Art of Collecting Art

While the expansion of Picasso and Monet onto the Internet may shake things up, serious collectors still rely on the human touch to help them make their moves. "It's hard to collect art," says Jon Weaver, one of *Art & Antiques* magazine's top 100 collectors of 1996. "If you don't know it, you'll get burned." Case in point: Weaver's purchase 12 years ago—before he began collecting—of a Salvador Dali print. It turned out to be a fake.

For some small collectors, the Internet is proving a boon. Ken Raboy, a senior manager at Andersen Consulting in Dallas, haunts online auction sites. He recently made a half-dozen purchases on Artnet.com, many of them at bargain prices. In 1999, he nabbed a Francesco Clemente print for $3,800, right before a major retrospective at New York's Guggenheim Museum started boosting the artist's prices.

The Internet is also convenient for shopping for photographs. Rare prints by classic photographers such as Weegee are skyrocketing in price. One Gustave Le Gray recently went for $840,000 at auction, a record for a photo. In 1998, San Francisco real estate investor Paul Sack bought a night view of Notre Dame in Paris by Maurice Tabard on Artnet.com for $4,025. "For me to go to New York every four weeks to monitor the shows is crazy," he says. "This is more practical."

Price, of course isn't everything when you're buying art. "Don't buy art as an investment," cautions Christoper Burge, head of Christie's.

## Questions

1. How can Jon Weaver and other collectors protect themselves from fraud?
2. Do you believe the Net will make its mark on the art world? Explain your answer.
3. Do you agree with the statement "Don't buy art as an investment"? Explain your answer.
4. What are some Internet sources where collectors can purchase collectibles?

SOURCES: Joan Oleck (edited by Amy Dunkin), "The Art of Collecting Art," *Business Week,* May 17, 1999, pp. 160–62; Stacy Higgenbotham, "Online Bidders, Beware," *Business Week,* August 16, 1999, p. 6; Thane Peterson, "Still Life with Surreal Price Tag," *Business Week,* December 27, 1999, pp. 161–62. Reprinted from the August 16, 1999 issue of *Business Week* by special permission. © 1999 McGraw-Hill Companies, Inc.

## Creating an E-Plan: Financial Decisions Using the Web

### COMPARING OTHER TYPES OF INVESTMENTS

Real estate and collectibles allow investors to achieve greater potential returns. However, these sometimes speculative ventures must be considered carefully in relation to your personal financial situation.

Websites for Real Estate and Other Investments

- Real estate investment information at **www.financenter.com,** and "The Motley Fool" offers **www.fool. com/, www.quicken.com (www.qfn.com),** the Cable News Network financial news service at **cnnfn.com/ index.hmtl,** and the Center for Financial Well Being at **www.healthycash.com/center.**
- Current real estate investments articles from *Money* magazine at **www.money.com,** *Kiplinger's Personal Finance Magazine* at **www.kiplinger.com,** *Business Week* at **www.businessweek.com,** *Worth* magazine at **www. worth.com,** and *Smart Money* at **www.smartmoney.com.**

- Chicago Board of Trade at **www.cbot.com;** Chicago Mercantile Exchange at **www.cem.com.**

(Note: Addresses and content of websites change, and new sites are created daily. Use search engines to update and locate websites for your current financial planning needs.)

*PFP sheet: 60*

Short-Term Financial Planning Activities

1. Identify types of real estate and other investments that might serve your various financial goals and life situation.
2. Compare the cost of buying and operating various types of real estate investments.

Long-Term Financial Planning Activities

1. Identify real estate and other investments that might serve you in the future.
2. Develop a plan for selecting and monitoring real estate and other investments.

## Continuous Case for Part 5

### BUILDING AN INVESTMENT PROGRAM

**Life Situation**
Pam, 43; Josh, 45; children ages 16, 14, and 11

*Financial Goals*
- Evaluate current financial condition
- Build an investment portfolio that considers various risk factors

*Financial Data*

| | |
|---|---|
| Monthly income | $ 4,900 |
| Living expenses | 4,450 |
| Assets | 262,700 |
| Liabilities | 84,600 |
| Emergency Fund | 5,000 |

With approximately 20 years to retirement, Pam and Josh Brock want to establish a more aggressive investment program to accumulate funds for their long-term financial needs. Josh does have a retirement program at work. This money, about $110,000, is invested in various conservative mutual funds. In addition, the Brocks established their own investment program about four years ago, and today they have about $36,000 invested in conservative stocks and mutual funds.

In addition to their investment program, the Brocks have accumulated $11,000 to help pay for the children's college educations. Also, they have $5,000 tucked away in a savings account that serves as the family's emergency fund. Finally, both will qualify for Social Security when they reach retirement age.

### Questions

1. How would you rate the Brocks' financial condition at this stage in their lives?

2. Given the fact that Pam is 43 and Josh is 45 and they have three children who will soon begin their college educations, what investment goals would be most appropriate for this middle-aged couple?

3. According to Pam, "We both know we should have started our investment program sooner, but we always seemed to have 'emergencies' that took what extra money we had." Many investors feel the same way and, to compensate for a late start, often invest in highly speculative investments that promise large returns. Would you recommend such investments to a couple like the Brocks? Explain your answer.

4. Describe the investment portfolio you would recommend for the Brocks. Be sure to include *specific* types of investments (stocks, bonds, mutual funds, etc.), as well as information about the risk factor(s) associated with each investment alternative.

# CONTROLLING YOUR FINANCIAL FUTURE

# 18

# Retirement Planning

## Scope Out Your Social Security Benefits

When Meg Hughes and her husband, Andrew Laurenson, checked their Social Security retirement benefits four years ago, they confirmed a nagging suspicion: They would have to play catch-up to have a comfortable retirement. As a result, they closed their home renovation business in Shepherdstown, West Virginia, and switched to careers that would provide steadier incomes. Hughes became a certified massage therapist, and Laurenson returned to his previous occupation as a social worker.

The document that supplied the couple's wake-up call was the Personal Earnings & Benefit Estimate Statement (PEBES). This six-page mailing from the Social Security Administration (1–800–772–1213; www.ssa.gov) estimates a person's benefits based on the highest 35 years of earnings. "When I got the statement, I realized I would get only about $300 a month in Social Security unless I did something about it," says Hughes, now 54. Laurenson, now 65, would have been entitled to about $600, but his career switch enabled him to draw $886 in monthly benefits when he began collecting Social Security this year.

When making retirement plans for clients, Marilyn Marcosson, a Merrill Lynch vice president in Washington, DC, starts with PEBES. She suggests that clients look at the benefit level and see if they can live on it. Often they say they can't. "That serves as a motivator to make sure savings are moving in the right direction," she says. If you're between 40 and 47 and have worked at least 40 quarters, you've probably gotten your PEBES sometime since October 1, 1999. If you're older than 47 but not yet on Social Security, you should have received a statement within the past four years. Starting in October 1999, a new version, called a Social Security Statement, is being mailed annually to workers.

When reading your PEBES, make sure all income, up to the limit ($72,600 in 1999), is included. Errors such as a missed year could reduce your benefits because Social Security computes the amount using a formula based on your earnings history to date. Spot a slipup? Call the agency, and have your pay stubs, W-2, or—if you are self-employed—1099 form in hand.

Next, you need to determine whether you can live with your benefits. The PEBES shows your monthly estimated benefit under three conditions: if you start collecting at 62, the earliest you can do so; at your "full-retirement age"—65 to 67, depending on your birth date; and at 70. If you choose to draw payments between 62 and your full-retirement age, your benefit will be decreased by as much as 20 percent. If you wait until 70, your benefit can increase as much as 8 percent. You can get a more precise estimate of benefits by using a PEBES order form, which you request either by phone or online. You enter on the form the age at which you plan to retire—say, 64—and your own estimates of your future earnings. You then send it to the agency for calculation. You should get the PEBES back within four weeks after mailing it. Your PEBES could be an eye-opener, even if you don't like everything you see.

## Questions

1. What were Meg Hughes's and Andrew Laurenson's concerns about retirement income?
2. Why did they close their home renovation business?
3. What document served as the couple's wake-up call?
4. How can the Internet assist you in retirement planning?

SOURCE: Adapted from Ellen Hoffman, "Scope Out Your Benefits," *Business Week*, July 19, 1999, p. 120. Reprinted from the July 19, 1999 issue of *Business Week* by special permission. © 1999 McGraw-Hill Companies, Inc.

## Learning Objectives

**Obj. 1** Recognize the importance of retirement planning.

**Obj. 2** Analyze your current assets and liabilities for retirement.

**Obj. 3** Estimate your retirement spending needs.

**Obj. 4** Identify your retirement housing needs.

**Obj. 5** Determine your planned retirement income.

**Obj. 6** Develop a balanced budget based on your retirement income.

## WHY RETIREMENT PLANNING?

**Obj. 1**
Recognize the importance of retirement planning.

Retirement can be a rewarding phase of your life. However, a successful, happy retirement doesn't just happen; it takes planning and continual evaluation. Thinking about retirement in advance can help you anticipate future changes and gain a sense of control over the future.

The ground rules for retirement planning are changing rapidly. Reexamine your retirement plans if you hold any of these misconceptions:

- My expenses will drop when I retire.
- My retirement will last only 15 years.
- I can depend on Social Security and my company pension to pay for my basic living expenses.
- My pension benefits will increase to keep pace with inflation.
- My employer's health insurance plan and Medicare will cover my medical expenses.
- There's plenty of time for me to start saving for retirement.
- Saving just a little bit won't help.

It is vital to engage in basic retirement planning activities throughout your working years and to update your retirement plans periodically. While it is never too late to begin sound financial planning, you can avoid many unnecessary and serious difficulties by starting this planning early. Saving now for the future requires tackling the trade-offs between spending and saving.

### Tackling the Trade-offs

Although exceptions exist, the old adage "You can't have your cake and eat it too" is particularly true in planning for retirement. For example, if you buy state-of-the-art

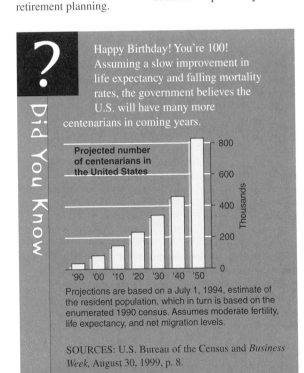

**Did You Know?**

Happy Birthday! You're 100! Assuming a slow improvement in life expectancy and falling mortality rates, the government believes the U.S. will have many more centenarians in coming years.

Projected number of centenarians in the United States

(Thousands: 0, 200, 400, 600, 800)

'90 '00 '10 '20 '30 '40 '50

Projections are based on a July 1, 1994, estimate of the resident population, which in turn is based on the enumerated 1990 census. Assumes moderate fertility, life expectancy, and net migration levels.

SOURCES: U.S. Bureau of the Census and *Business Week*, August 30, 1999, p. 8.

home entertainment systems, drive expensive cars, and take extravagant vacations now, don't expect to retire with plenty of money.

Even though baby boomers are more knowledgeable about saving and investing and can use various methods to manage their assets, the personal savings rate declined from more than 7 percent throughout the 1960s to just under 4 percent in 1998. But the savings crisis may be overstated. In a study conducted for Merrill Lynch & Company, Stanford University economist Douglas B. Bernheim found that, excluding the equity in their houses, baby boomers were saving only about one-third of what they will need in retirement. Yet when housing wealth is included, more than two-thirds of boomers likely will be able to maintain their current standard of living in retirement.[1]

Only by saving now and curtailing current spending can you ensure a comfortable retirement later. Yet saving money doesn't come naturally to many young people. Ironically, although the time to begin saving is when you are young, the people who are in the best position to save are middle-aged.

Seventy-five percent of workers expect to live as well as, if not better than, they do now when they retire, but only 25 percent of those surveyed have begun to save seriously for retirement.[2]

## The Importance of Starting Early

Consider this: If from age 25 to 65 you invest $300 per month and earn an average of 9 percent interest a year, you'll have $1.4 million in your retirement fund. Waiting just 10 years until age 35 to begin your $300-a-month investing will yield about $550,000, while if you wait 20 years to begin this investment, you will have only $201,000 at age 65. Exhibit 18–1 on page 571 shows how even a $2,000 annual investment earning just 4 percent will grow.

For 40 years your life, and probably your family's life, revolves around your job. One day you retire, and practically every aspect of your life changes. There's less money, more time, and no daily structure.

You can expect to spend about 16 to 20 years in retirement—too many years to be bored, lonely, and broke. You want your retirement years to be rewarding, active, and rich in new experiences. It's never too early to begin planning for retirement; some experts even suggest starting while you are in school. Be certain you don't let your 45th birthday roll by without a comprehensive retirement plan. Remember, the longer you wait, the less you will be able to shape your life in retirement.

Retirement planning has both emotional and financial components. Emotional planning for retirement involves identifying your personal goals and setting out to meet them. Financial planning for retirement involves assessing your post retirement needs and income and plugging any gaps you find. Financial planning for retirement is critical for several reasons:

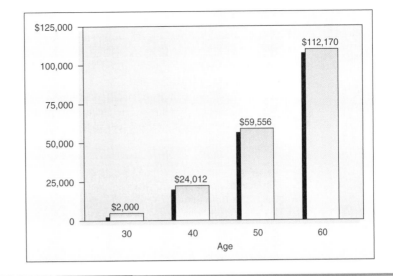

## EXHIBIT 18-1

### It's Never Too Late to Start Planning for Retirement

Start young. A look at the performance of $2,000 per year of retirement plan investments over time even at 4 percent shows the value of starting early. (in 1995 dollars)

1. You can expect to live in retirement for up to 20 years. At age 65, the average life expectancy is 14 years for a man and 19 years for a woman.
2. Social Security and a private pension, if you have one, are most often insufficient to cover the cost of living.
3. Inflation may diminish the purchasing power of your retirement savings. Even a 3 percent rate of inflation will cause prices to double every 24 years.

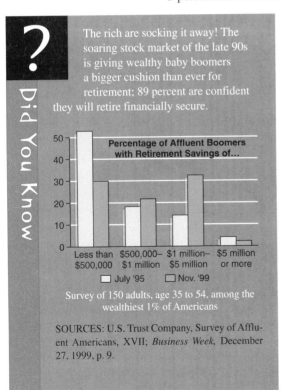

The rich are socking it away! The soaring stock market of the late 90s is giving wealthy baby boomers a bigger cushion than ever for retirement: 89 percent are confident they will retire financially secure.

**Percentage of Affluent Boomers with Retirement Savings of...**

Survey of 150 adults, age 35 to 54, among the wealthiest 1% of Americans

SOURCES: U.S. Trust Company, Survey of Affluent Americans, XVII; *Business Week*, December 27, 1999, p. 9.

You should anticipate your retirement years by analyzing your long-range goals. What does retirement mean to you? Does it mean an opportunity to stop work and relax, or does it mean time to travel, develop a hobby, or start a second career? Where and how do you want to live during your retirement? Once you have considered your retirement goals, you are ready to evaluate their cost and assess whether you can afford them.

## The Basics of Retirement Planning

Before you decide where you want to be financially, you have to find out where you are. Your first step, therefore, is to analyze your current assets and liabilities. Then estimate your spending needs and adjust them for inflation. Next, evaluate your planned retirement income. Finally, increase your income by working part time, if necessary. An attorney, for example, might teach some law courses. Recent articles and other retirement information may be accessed through online computer services. For further information, see Appendix B. Exhibit 18–2 on page 572 shows some good online sources for retirement planning using a personal computer. Also, read the Financial Planning for Life's Situations feature on page 573.

EXHIBIT 18-2

USING A PERSONAL
COMPUTER FOR
RETIREMENT
PLANNING

SOURCE: *Business Week,*
July 19, 1999, p. 110.

**General Websites**

American Savings Education Council (www.asec.org)
Diversified Investment Advisors (www.divinvest.com)
Financenter (www.financenter.com)
401KAFE (www.401kafe.com)
InvestorGuide (www.investorguide.com/retirement.htm)
Longevity Game (www.northwesternmutual.com/games/longevity)
Roth IRA website (www.rothira.com)

**Online Planning Software**

Financial Engines (www.financialengines.com)
Financialplanauditors.com (www.fplanauditors.com)
Quicken.com Retirement (www.quicken.com/retirement)
Vanguard NavitorPlus (majestic4.vanguard.com/GUIDE/DA)

**Software Packages**

Kiplinger's Netwealth (www.Net-Wealth.com) ($29.95)
Microsoft Money99 Financial Suite ($64.95 list)
Quicken Suite 99 ($89.95 list)

## Concept Check 18-1

1.  How can the Internet assist you in retirement planning?
2.  Why is retirement planning important?
3.  What are the four basic steps in retirement planning?

## CONDUCTING A FINANCIAL ANALYSIS

### Obj. 2
Analyze your current
assets and liabilities
for retirement.

As you learned in Chapter 3, your assets include everything you own that has value: cash on hand and in checking and savings accounts; the current value of your stocks, bonds, and other investments; the current value of your house, car, jewelry, and furnishings; and the current value of your life insurance and pensions. Your liabilities are everything you owe: your mortgage, car payments, credit card balances, taxes due, and so forth. The difference between the two totals is your *net worth,* a figure you should increase each year as you move toward retirement. Use Exhibit 18–3 on page 574 to calculate your net worth now and at retirement.

### Review Your Assets

Reviewing your assets to ensure they are sufficient for retirement is a sound idea. Make any necessary adjustments in your investments and holdings to fit your circumstances. In reviewing your assets, consider the following factors.

Housing    If you own your house, it is probably your biggest single asset. The amount tied up in your house, however, may be out of line with your retirement income. You might consider selling your house and buying a less expensive one. The selection of a smaller, more easily maintained house can also decrease your maintenance costs. The difference saved can be put into a savings account or certificates of deposit or into other income-producing investments. If your mortgage is largely or completely paid off, you may be able to get an annuity to provide you with extra income during retirement. In this arrangement, a lender uses your house as collateral to

## Financial Planning for Life's Situations

### THE RETIREMENT TOOLS YOU NEED

If you can manipulate a mouse, you can develop a retirement plan. That's the message from websites and software publishers eager to tap aging baby boomers' financial anxieties and Gen-Xers' fascination with the market. Planning tools are indeed better than ever at crunching numbers, projecting risks, and handling, or at least spotlighting, tricky tax and pension problems. No PC can deliver complete peace of mind about your old age. So even do-it-yourself investors turn to financial advisers for guidance and reassurance. "Eventually, you'll need a higher level of sophistication than you can get from software," says Institute of Certified Financial Planners president Elissa Buie.

Software and the Web, however, can get you rolling. If you're just starting to think about retirement, cruise to the American Savings Education Council to assess your savings personality and "retirement readiness." You'll find dozens of calculators at FinanCenter and InvestorGuide. And everything you wanted to know about Roth IRAs can be found on Brentmark Software's site. Here are your best bets.

Web-based planners are starting to provide services you would expect from personal finance software. Intuit's Quicken.com features a retirement planner that users can link to an online portfolio tracker. Mutual fund giant Vanguard Group's software offers a bonus with simple advice on estate planning.

The newest calculators have their roots in casinos. They use the Monte Carlo method, a mathematical technique for testing thousands of possible investment outcomes to assess your portfolio for worst-case results. While two asset mixes might have the same average return, one may keep you solvent in 90 percent of all possible market forecasts, while with the other you would go broke in 40 percent of the cases. When your retirement's on the line, you need to shoot for the 9-to-1 odds. The best-known Monte Carlo calculator is offered by Financial Engines, founded by economics Nobel laureate William F. Sharpe. Nonmathematicians may be baffled by the Monte Carlo calculators' odds-based output. When you master the charts, however, the results are eye opening—and they are closer to reality than what-if scenarios run on a traditional calculator.

Whatever their algorithms, software planning tools still have one weakness: No program will look you in the eye and say, "Are you following that budget? Have you bought that insurance?" You must find the discipline to plan and follow through within yourself—or hire a human adviser to provide it.

SOURCE: Adapted from Mike McNamee, "Building the Best Retirement Plan," *Business Week,* July 19, 1999, pp. 108–16. Reprinted from the July 19, 1999 issue of *Business Week* by special permission. © 1999 McGraw-Hill Companies, Inc.

---

buy an annuity for you from a life insurance company. Each month, the lender pays you (the homeowner) from the annuity after deducting the mortgage interest payment. The mortgage principal, which was used to obtain the annuity, is repaid to the lender by probate after your death. This special annuity is known as a **reverse annuity mortgage (RAM)** or *equity conversion.*

*reverse annuity mortgage (RAM)*
A mortgage in which the lender uses the borrower's house as collateral to buy an annuity for the borrower from a life insurance company; also called an *equity conversion.*

Chicago-based Senior Income Reverse Mortgage Corporation (1–800–774–6266) offers a free consumers' information kit on reverse mortgages. The kit shows that the amount of money available depends on your age, the value of your home, and interest rates. For example, a 75-year-old couple with a $150,000 home in Chicago or the suburbs could receive a monthly check of about $900 for the next 10 years or $580 for as long as either partner lives in the home.[3]

Life Insurance     You may have set up your life insurance to provide support and education for your children. Now you may want to convert some of this asset into cash or income (an annuity). Another possibility is to reduce premium payments by decreasing the face value of your insurance. This will give you extra money to spend on living expenses or invest for additional income.

**Review Your Assets, Liabilities, and Net Worth**

Net worth: Assets of $108,800 minus liabilities of $16,300 equals $92,500.

| | Sample Figures | Your Figures |
|---|---|---|
| **Assets: What We Own** | | |
| Cash: | | |
|    Checking account | $ 800 | _____ |
|    Savings account | 4,500 | _____ |
| Investments: | | |
|    U.S. savings bonds | | |
|      (current cash-in value) | 5,000 | _____ |
|    Stocks, mutual funds | 4,500 | _____ |
| Life insurance: | | |
|    Cash value, accumulated dividends | 10,000 | _____ |
| Company pension rights: | | |
|    Accrued pension benefit | 20,000 | _____ |
| Property: | | |
|    House (resale value) | 50,000 | _____ |
|    Furniture and appliances | 8,000 | _____ |
|    Collections and jewelry | 2,000 | _____ |
|    Automobile | 3,000 | _____ |
| Other: | | |
|    Loan to brother | 1,000 | _____ |
|      Gross assets | $108,800 | _____ |
| **Liabilities: What We Owe** | | |
| Current unpaid bills | 600 | _____ |
| Home mortgage (remaining balance) | 9,700 | _____ |
| Auto loan | 1,200 | _____ |
| Property taxes | 1,100 | _____ |
| Home improvement loan | 3,700 | _____ |
|    Total liabilities | $ 16,300 | _____ |

**Other Investments**    Evaluate any other investments you have. When you chose them, you may have been more interested in making your money grow than in getting an early return. Has the time come to take the income from your investments? You may now want to take dividends rather than reinvest them.

After thoroughly reviewing your assets, estimate your spending needs during your retirement years.

## Your Assets after Divorce

Any divorce is difficult, particularly when it comes to a division of marital assets. Your pension benefits are considered marital property, which must be divided in a divorce. "Even if a person is not ready to retire, pension benefits are considered a marital asset subject to the division of property," says Howard Sharfstein, a partner in Schulte Roth & Zabel of New York.[4] Any retirement fund money, including a 401(k) plan or a profit-sharing plan, set aside during a marriage and the dollar growth of a pension plan during a marriage are considered marital property.

Division of pension benefits generally depends on the length of the marriage. "In a five-year marriage the percentage of one person's assets given to the spouse is usually

### JONATHAN HOENIG ON RETIREMENT

Retirement? Ah, yes: *retirement.* Better to save now and avoid the deprivation later. You know the spiel: Social Security, a joke; corporate pensions, all but eliminated; job security, gone; the Domino's 30-minute guarantee, abolished. With such an uncertain future, it is best one be prepared.

There are monetary returns, although Hoenig contends that the psychological feeling of safety that regular investing provides trumps all. While the boomers freak about not having saved enough for retirement, young people have time to spare. With a long-term horizon, investing is safe, easy, and relatively hassle free. Mutual funds have made retirement investing more convenient than sleeping through that 9AM class. Automatic investment plans can deduct as little as $25 a month from bank accounts or paychecks. Even pocket cash can get things rockin': Take that double tall latte ($2.39) and raisin cinnamon scone ($1.70) you snag at 'Bucks each morning and put it in an index fund. You'll have over $20,000 before your first midlife crisis. Keep it up until your second, and you'll have accumulated over $110,000—more than enough to pay for intensive therapy and a week in Boca. Systematic

investing is the fiscal equivalent of a tetanus shot: a regular bummer that doesn't hurt as bad as one initially believes.

If you are frightened of investing, worried that a crash or prolonged bear market will turn your retirement into an episode of Good Times, *you must chill!* Don't waste the Xanax worrying about the market, because the fact is that over a long period of time, stocks go up. Over a 20-year time horizon, the market's *worst* performance has been about 2.0 percent. While it might seem you can't afford to invest, the unfortunate reality is that you can't afford not to. With inflation humming along, common stock is the only asset class that will consistently keep you ahead, advises Hoenig.

IRAs, 401(k)s, pension plans—stock 'em full of quality mutual funds and chill. "Home runs" look great on the cover of *Money* magazine, but real wealth is born over time. Compound interest, or the titillating phenomenon of earning interest on interest, provides hefty gains to patient investors. This "get-rich-slowly" scheme won't get your picture in *Barron's* but it will provide for an adequate retirement. $100,000 will buy cases of Geritol once you get to Florida, quips Hoenig.

small," says Sharfstein. "In an eight-year marriage about 25 percent of the monetary assets earned by one partner may be given to the other partner. In a marriage that lasts more than 15 years there's generally a 50-50 split of the marital assets."[5]

*Be warned:* Many retirement-planning strategies accommodate the traditional husband-wife-kids family unit. But millions of nontraditional households have unique retirement needs. Nearly half of all American marriages end in divorce, creating difficulties for millions of adults thinking about their retirement years. Likewise, single parents, gays and lesbians, and individuals who choose to live together outside of marriage all have formidable retirement-planning challenges. See the Financial Planning for Life's Situations feature on page 576 for suggestions.[6]

## Concept Check 18–2

1.   How can you calculate your net worth today and at retirement?
2.   What assets are considered marital assets?

## Financial Planning for Life's Situations

### RETIREMENT PLANNING FOR VARIED LIFE SITUATIONS

- A divorcee should maximize contributions to a retirement plan at work and begin a separate savings account to protect retirement assets.
- A divorcee may consider taking out life insurance on an ex-spouse if he or she is responsible for child support; also, buy disability insurance.
- Revise your estate plan after a divorce. In some states, a divorce doesn't automatically revoke your will or certain trusts if your ex-spouse is a beneficiary.
- An unmarried person should determine if an employer allows a joint-and-survivor benefit for a nonspouse. If so, inform your plan administrator while you're still employed, since the method of distribution can't be switched after you retire.

- An unmarried person should clearly indicate intentions in legally binding documents (be sure to have a will), since blood relatives will usually win in any disputes over assets that arise after death.
- An unmarried person should consider techniques to minimize estate taxes, such as a charitable remainder trust.
- In family situations with strained relationships, a person should consider saving more than the usual 75 to 80 percent of gross preretirement income in anticipation that relatives may not provide future support.

SOURCE: Geoffrey Smith, "Nest-Egg Planning for the Not-So-Average Joe," *Business Week,* July 31, 1997, p. 80. Reprinted from the July 31, 1997 issue of *Business Week* by special permission. © 1999 McGraw-Hill Companies, Inc.

## RETIREMENT LIVING EXPENSES

**Obj. 3**
Estimate your retirement spending needs.

The exact amount of money you will need in retirement is impossible to predict. However, you can estimate the amount you will need by considering the changes you anticipate in your spending patterns and in where and how you live.

Your spending patterns will probably change. A study conducted by the Bureau of Labor Statistics on how families spend money shows that retired families use a greater share for food, housing, and medical care than nonretired families. Although no two families adjust their spending patterns to changes in the life cycle in the same manner, the tabulation in Exhibit 18–4 on page 577 can guide you in anticipating your own future spending patterns.

The following expenses may be lowered or eliminated:

- *Work expenses.* You will no longer make payments into your retirement fund. You will not be buying gas and oil for the drive back and forth to work or for train or bus fares. You may be buying fewer lunches away from home.
- *Clothing expenses.* You will probably need fewer clothes after you retire, and your dress may be more casual.
- *Housing expenses.* If you have paid off your house mortgage by the time you retire, your cost of housing may decrease (although increases in property taxes and insurance may offset this gain).
- *Federal income taxes.* Your federal income taxes will probably be lower. No federal tax has to be paid on some forms of income, such as railroad retirement benefits and certain veterans' benefits. A retirement credit is allowed for some sources of income, such as annuities. You will probably pay taxes at a lower rate because your taxable income will be lower.

Under the U.S. Civil Service Retirement System, your retirement income is not taxed until you have received the amount you have invested in the retirement fund. After that, your retirement income is taxable.

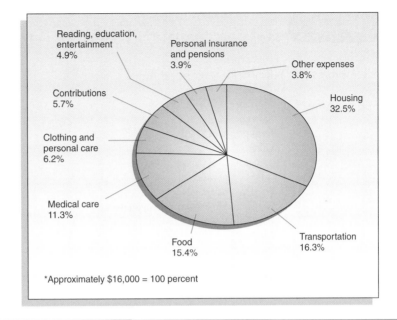

### EXHIBIT 18-4

How an "Average" Older (65+) Household Spends Its Money

SOURCE: U.S. Bureau of Labor Statistics.

Reading, education, entertainment 4.9%
Personal insurance and pensions 3.9%
Other expenses 3.8%
Contributions 5.7%
Housing 32.5%
Clothing and personal care 6.2%
Medical care 11.3%
Food 15.4%
Transportation 16.3%

*Approximately $16,000 = 100 percent

You can also estimate which of the following expenses may increase:

- *Insurance.* The loss of your employer's contribution to health and life insurance will increase your own payments. Medicare, however, may offset part of this increased expense.

  - *Medical expenses.* Although medical expenses vary from person to person, they tend to increase with age.
  - *Expenses for leisure activities.* With more free time, many retirees spend more money on leisure activities. You may want to put aside extra money for a retirement trip or other large recreational expenses.
  - *Gifts and contributions.* Many retirees who continue to spend the same amount of money on gifts and contributions find their spending in this area takes a larger share of their smaller income. Therefore, you may want to reevaluate such spending.

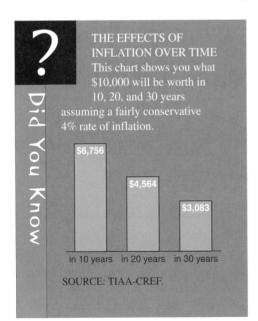

**Did You Know**

**THE EFFECTS OF INFLATION OVER TIME** This chart shows you what $10,000 will be worth in 10, 20, and 30 years assuming a fairly conservative 4% rate of inflation.

$6,756
$4,564
$3,083

in 10 years   in 20 years   in 30 years

SOURCE: TIAA-CREF.

Using the worksheet in Exhibit 18–5 on page 578, list your present expenses and estimate what these expenses would be if you were retired. To make a realistic comparison, list your major spending categories, starting with fixed expenses such as rent or mortgage payments, utilities, insurance premiums, and taxes. Then list variable expenses—food, clothing, transportation, and so on, as well as miscellaneous expenditures such as medical expenses, entertainment, vacations, gifts, contributions, and unforeseen expenses.

Be sure you have an emergency fund for unforeseen expenses. Even when you are living a tranquil life, unexpected events can occur. Build a cushion to cope with inflation. Estimate high in calculating how much the prices of goods and services will rise.

**EXHIBIT 18-5**

Your Monthly
Present Expenses
and Your
Estimated Monthly
Retirement
Expenses

**Monthly Expenses**

| Item | Present | Retirement |
|---|---|---|
| Fixed expenses: | | |
|   Rent or mortgage payment | $_____ | $_____ |
|   Taxes | _____ | _____ |
|   Insurance | _____ | _____ |
|   Savings | _____ | _____ |
|   Debt payment | _____ | _____ |
|   Other | _____ | _____ |
|     Total fixed expenses | _____ | _____ |
| Variable expenses: | | |
|   Food and beverages | _____ | _____ |
|   Household operation and maintenance | _____ | _____ |
|   Furnishings and equipment | _____ | _____ |
|   Clothing | _____ | _____ |
|   Personal | _____ | _____ |
|   Transportation | _____ | _____ |
|   Medical care | _____ | _____ |
|   Recreation and education | _____ | _____ |
|   Gifts and contributions | _____ | _____ |
|   Other | _____ | _____ |
|     Total variable expenses | _____ | _____ |
| Total expenses | _____ | _____ |

## Adjust Your Expenses for Inflation

You now have a list of your likely monthly (and annual) expenses if you were to retire today. With inflation, however, those expenses will not be fixed. The potential loss of buying power due to inflation is what makes planning ahead so important. During the 1970s and the early 1980s, the cost of living increased an average of 6.1 percent a year, though the annual increase slowed to less than 3 percent between 1983 and 1999.

To help you plan for this likely increase in your expenses, use the inflation factor table in the Financial Planning Calculations feature on page 579.

### Concept Check 18-3

1. How can you estimate the amount of money you will need during retirement?
2. What expenses are likely to increase or decrease during retirement?
3. How might you adjust your expenses for inflation?

## PLANNING YOUR RETIREMENT HOUSING

**Obj. 4**
Identify your retirement housing needs.

Think about where you will want to live. If you think you will want to live in another city, it's a good idea to plan vacations now in areas you might enjoy later. When you find one that appeals to you, visit that area during various times of the year to experience the year-round climate. Meet the people. Check into available activities, transportation, and taxes. Be realistic about what you will have to give up and what you will gain.

Where you live in retirement can influence your financial needs. You must make some important decisions about whether or not to stay in your present community and in your current home. Everyone has unique needs and preferences; only *you* can determine the location and housing that are best for you.

# Financial Planning Calculations

## HOW MUCH INFLATION IS IN YOUR FUTURE?

**Estimated Annual Rate of Inflation between Now and Retirement**

| Years to Retirement | 3% | 4% | 5% | 6% | 7% | 8% | 9% | 10% | 11% | 12% |
|---|---|---|---|---|---|---|---|---|---|---|
| 5 | 1.2 | 1.2 | 1.3 | 1.3 | 1.4 | 1.5 | 1.5 | 1.6 | 1.7 | 1.8 |
| 8 | 1.3 | 1.4 | 1.5 | 1.6 | 1.7 | 1.8 | 2.0 | 2.1 | 2.3 | 2.5 |
| 10 | 1.4 | 1.5 | 1.6 | 1.8 | 2.0 | 2.2 | 2.4 | 2.6 | 2.8 | 3.1 |
| 12 | 1.5 | 1.6 | 1.8 | 2.0 | 2.3 | 2.5 | 2.8 | 3.1 | 3.5 | 3.9 |
| 15 | 1.6 | 1.8 | 2.1 | 2.4 | 2.8 | 3.2 | 3.6 | 4.2 | 4.8 | 5.5 |
| 18 | 1.8 | 2.0 | 2.4 | 2.8 | 3.4 | 4.0 | 4.7 | 5.6 | 6.5 | 7.7 |
| 20 | 2.0 | 2.2 | 2.7 | 3.2 | 3.9 | 4.7 | 5.6 | 6.7 | 8.1 | 9.6 |
| 25 | 2.1 | 2.7 | 3.4 | 4.3 | 5.4 | 6.8 | 8.6 | 10.8 | 13.6 | 17.0 |

1. Choose from the first column the approximate number of years until your retirement.

2. Choose an estimated annual rate of inflation. The rate of inflation cannot be predicted accurately and will vary from year to year. The 1997 inflation rate was less than 3 percent.

3. Find the inflation factor corresponding to the number of years until your retirement and the estimated annual inflation rate. (Example: 10 years to retirement combined with a 4 percent estimated annual inflation rate yields a 1.5 inflation factor.)

4. Multiply the inflation factor by your estimated retirement income and your estimated retirement expenses. (Example: $6,000 × 1.5 = $9,000.)

Total annual inflated retirement income: $_____.

Total annual inflated retirement expenses: $_____.

SOURCES: The above figures are from a compound interest table showing the effective yield of lump-sum investments after inflation that appeared in Charles D. Hodgman, ed., *Mathematical Tables from the Handbook of Chemistry and Physics* (Cleveland: Chemical Rubber Publishing, 1959); *Citicorp Consumer Views*, July 1985, pp. 2–3, © Citicorp, 1985; *Financial Planning Tables*, A. G. Edwards, August 1991.

Consider what moving involves. Moving is expensive, and if you are not satisfied with your new location, returning to your former home may be impossible. Consider the social aspects of moving. Will you want to be near your children, other relatives, and good friends? Are you prepared for new circumstances?

## Type of Housing

Housing needs often change as people grow older. The ease and cost of maintenance and nearness to public transportation, shopping, church/synagogue, and entertainment often become more important to people when they retire.

Many housing alternatives exist, several of which were discussed in Chapter 9. Staying in their present homes, whether a single-family dwelling, a condominium, or an apartment, is the alternative preferred by most people approaching retirement. That's what John and Virginia Wolf decided to do after John took early retirement at age 47 from his job as a service manager of a Van Nuys, California, Ford dealership in the late 1970s. Even though the couple had already paid off the mortgage on their small, three-bedroom ranch house and could have moved up into a bigger or fancier place, all John wanted to do was tinker in the garage and dabble in the stock market.[7] A recent survey of over 5,000 men and women revealed that 92 percent wanted to own their homes in retirement.[8]

DeLoma Foster of Greenville, South Carolina, has seen the future, and she wants to be prepared. DeLoma, 69, has osteoporosis, just as her mother did. Although she's not having difficulty now, she knows the debilitating bone condition eventually could make it difficult, if not impossible, to navigate steep stairs, cramped bathrooms, and narrow doorways. So two years ago, she and her husband, Clyde, a 72-year-old retired textile executive, moved into a novel type of home, one that can comfortably accommodate them no matter what disabilities old age may bring. Called a "universal design home," their residence is on the cutting edge of an architectural concept that an aging population may well embrace. The only house of its kind in the neighborhood, it has wide doors, pull-out cabinet shelves, easy-to-reach electrical switches, and dozens of other features useful for elderly persons or those with disabilities. Yet these features are incorporated into the design unobtrusively.

Apart from aesthetics, universal design is appealing because it allows people to stay in their homes as they grow older and more frail. "The overwhelming majority of people would prefer to grow old in their own homes in their own communities," says Jon Pynoos, a gerontologist at the University of Southern California in Los Angeles. Recognizing this trend, building suppliers now offer everything from lever door handles to faucets that turn on automatically when you put your hand beneath the spigot. Remodeling so far is creating the biggest demand for these products. But increasingly, contractors are building universal design homes from scratch, which generally costs less than completely retrofitting an existing house. Philip Stephen Companies in St. Paul, Minnesota, has built six universal design homes in the Southeast, ranging from a 1,240-square-foot ranch in Greer, South Carolina, that sold for $90,000 to the 2,200-square-foot home that DeLoma and Clyde bought for $190,000.

To boost demand, builders are marketing to families of all ages. In Cincinnati, Amherst Homes' sales material stresses that the wide hallways of its $300,000-to-$400,000 homes not only accommodate walkers and wheelchairs but also make it easier to carry bags of groceries and other bulky items. This new setup suits the Fosters just fine. Unlike their peers who are moving into continuing-care communities, they want to stay where they have always lived, near their three children and around people of all ages. They now have a home that can accommodate a wheelchair and even has a room for a nurse if the need arises. "We hope to be able to live here for the rest of our lives," says DeLoma Foster—in comfort and with all the touches they need to ease their daily tasks.[9]

With the many choices available, determining where to live in retirement is itself turning into a time-consuming job. But whether you want to race cars, go on a safari, or stay home to paint, the goal is to end up like Edna Cohen. "Don't feel bad if I die tomorrow," she says. "I've had a wonderful life." Who could ask for more?[10]

Whatever retirement housing alternative you choose, make sure you know what you are signing and understand what you are buying.

**Sheet 62**

## Avoiding Retirement Housing Traps

Too many people make the move without doing enough research, and invariably it's a huge mistake. How can retirees avoid being surprised by hidden tax and financial traps when they move? Pros suggest that you call Right Choice, Inc., in South Hamilton, Massachusetts (1–800–872–2294), or visit the company at www.rsmart.com. The company provides ReloSmart®, an easy-to-use software program that allows you to do unlimited relocation analyses. You can access ReloSmart® for free at www.virtual relocation.com.

## Financial Planning for Life's Situations

### DAD COULDN'T LIVE ALONE

He was the one who had read her bedtime stories, taught her to ride a bike, and left tooth-fairy money under her pillow. So now that her father was 87, widowed, and losing his memory, Judy Balch of Houston wanted to do the right thing. Dad couldn't live alone, and he was too healthy for a nursing home. So Balch and her husband explored four assisted-living facilities (ALFs) that provide housing as well as personal and medical services for the aging. After touring the grounds, quizzing residents, and sampling cuisines, the family settled on a top-tier, $2,800-a-month complex. Two months later, Judy Balch reports that her father is happy in his new home. Not all consumers are as fortunate. The assisted-living industry is booming as aging Americans' quest for new housing options sends them searching for everything from residences offering minimal services to those with nursing homes attached. But the search can be full of pitfalls. A recent General Accounting Office report found that of 60 assisted-living contracts it examined, 20 contained "language that is unclear or misleading." Furthermore, the GAO found that of 622 facilities surveyed in four states, only 65 percent provided a contract prior to the admission decision, and then only if asked. About 10 percent provide no contract at all—and no laws require them to do so. The GAO criticisms didn't end there. The agency cited one Florida contract that made a fuzzy promise to "meet your needs" as an illness progressed. The agreement then specified "changes in physical or mental condition" as reasons for immediate discharge. The GAO further found that 27 percent of the facilities it surveyed had been cited for five or more problems related to quality of care or consumer protection issues, ranging from poor hygiene to failing to notify a doctor when a resident fell.

The government is taking notice. The Senate Special Committee on Aging has asked the nation's 50 governors for details about their states' consumer protection provisions for assisted living. And more states are regulating admissions agreements. If you're on the consumer end of a contract worth hundreds of thousands of dollars, however, you need help now. A good starting point is the federal government's Long-Term Care Ombudsman program, which can be reached via the Elder Care Locator (1–800–677–1116). With volunteers in every state, the program puts consumers in touch with agencies that can help them find ALFs—or resolve complaints against them. Checklists containing questions to ask when reviewing ALFs are available from CCAL (703–841–2333; www.ccal.org), ALFA (703–691– 8100; www.alfa.org), and the American Health Care Association's National Center for Assisted Living (1–800–555–9414; www.ncal.org). The American Association of Retired Persons (202–434–2277; www. aarp.org) offers a publication, *Assisted Living: Weighing the Options*.

Before choosing your option, do a self-assessment, compare fees, check personal services provided, clarify reasons for discharge, and check the owner-corporation's financial strength. Also, ask about manager and staff turnover, and training. If necessary, contact your ombudsman and ask about the facility's grievance procedures.

Finally, visit your aging parent often. It's not only the right thing to do, but it will keep the staff on their toes.

SOURCE: Adapted from Joan Oleck, "Where to Find a Helping Hand," *Business Week,* July 19, 1999, pp. 132–34. Reprinted from the July 19, 1999 issue of *Business Week* by special permission. © 1999 McGraw-Hill Companies, Inc.

Here are some tips from retirement specialists on how to uncover hidden taxes and other costs of a retirement area before moving:

- Write or call the local chamber of commerce to get an economic profile and details on area property taxes.
- Contact the state's tax department to find out state income, sales, and inheritance taxes and special exemptions for retirees. If your pension will be taxed by the state you're leaving, check whether the new state will give you credit for those taxes.
- Subscribe to the Sunday edition of a local newspaper.
- Call a local CPA to find out which taxes are rising.

- Check with local utilities to estimate your energy costs. Visit the area in as many seasons as possible. Talk to retirees and other local residents about costs of health care, auto insurance, food, and clothing.
- Rent for a while instead of buying immediately.

The Financial Planning for Life's Situations feature on page 581 provides some guidelines in choosing an assisted-living facility.

## Concept Check 18-4

1. What are some housing options for retirees?
2. How can retirees avoid retirement housing traps?

## PLANNING YOUR RETIREMENT INCOME

Once you have determined your approximate future expenses, you must evaluate the sources and amounts of your retirement income. Possible sources of income for many retirees are Social Security, other public pension plans, employer pension plans, personal retirement plans, and annuities.

**Obj. 5**
Determine your planned retirement income.

### Social Security

Social Security is the most widely used source of retirement income; it covers 97 percent of U.S. workers. Many Americans think of Social Security as benefiting only retired people. But it is actually a package of protection, providing retirement, survivors', and disability benefits. The package protects you and your family while you work and after you retire. Today more than 44 million people, almost one out of every six Americans, collect some kind of Social Security benefit.[11] The Social Security Administration estimates that 47 percent of individuals age 65 and older would live in poverty without Social Security benefits, four times as many as live in poverty today.

Social Security should not be the only source of your retirement income, however. It should be only a small part of your plan, or you won't live a very exciting retired life. Even the Social Security Administration cautions that Social Security was never intended to provide 100 percent of retirement income.

### When and Where to Apply
Most people qualify for reduced Social Security retirement benefits at age 62; widows or widowers can begin collecting Social Security benefits earlier.

Three months before you retire, apply for Social Security benefits by telephoning the Social Security office at 1–800–772–1213. The payments will not start unless you apply for them. If you apply late, you risk losing benefits.

**Did You Know?**

This chart shows the percentage of final earnings Social Security is estimated to replace. Will you have enough to make up the difference?

#### Your Retirement "Gap"

| Preretirement Salary | Percent of Income Replaced by Social Security | The "Gap" You and Your Employer Must Fill |
|---|---|---|
| $ 20,000 | 45% | 35% |
| 30,000 | 40 | 40 |
| 40,000 | 33 | 47 |
| 60,000 | 25 | 55 |
| 100,000 | 15 | 65 |

SOURCE: TIAA-CREF

**EXHIBIT 18-6**

Age to Receive Full
Social Security
Benefits

SOURCE: *Social
Security: Retirement
Benefits* (Washington,
DC: Social Security
Administration, May
1998), p. 5.

| Year of Birth | Full Retirement Age |
|---|---|
| 1937 or earlier | 65 |
| 1938 | 65 and 2 months |
| 1939 | 65 and 4 months |
| 1940 | 65 and 6 months |
| 1941 | 65 and 8 months |
| 1942 | 65 and 10 months |
| 1943–54 | 66 |
| 1955 | 66 and 2 months |
| 1956 | 66 and 4 months |
| 1957 | 66 and 6 months |
| 1958 | 66 and 8 months |
| 1959 | 66 and 10 months |
| 1960 and later | 67 |

If your full retirement age is above 65 (that is, you were born after 1937), you will still be able to take your retirement benefits at age 62, but the reduction in your benefit amount will be greater than it is for people retiring now.

## What Information Will You Need?

The Social Security office will tell you what proof you need to establish your particular case. Generally, you will be asked to provide the following:

- Proof of your age.
- Your Social Security card or Social Security number.
- Your W-2 withholding forms for the past two years.
- Your marriage license if you are applying for your spouse's benefits.
- The birth certificates of your children if you are applying for their benefits.

## What If You Retire at 62 instead of 65?

Your Social Security benefits will be reduced if you retire before age 65. Currently there is a permanent reduction of five-ninths of 1 percent for each month you receive payments before age 65. Thus, if you retire at 62, your monthly payments will be permanently reduced by 20 percent of what they would be if you waited until 65 to retire. However, if you wait until 65 to collect Social Security, your benefits will not decrease. If you work after 65, your benefits will increase by one-fourth of 1 percent for each month past age 65 that you delay retirement, but only up to age 70.

Because of longer life expectancies, the full retirement age will be increased in gradual steps until it reaches 67. This change starts in 2003 and affects people born in 1938 and later. Look at Exhibit 18–6 to determine your full retirement age.

## Estimating Your Retirement Benefits

Beginning in 1999, the Social Security Administration automatically provides a history of your earnings and an estimate of your future monthly benefits. The statement includes an estimate, in today's dollars, of how much you will get each month from Social Security when you retire—at age 62, 65, or 70—based on your earnings to date and your projected future earnings.

## How to Become Eligible

To qualify for Social Security retirement benefits, you must have the required number of quarters of coverage. The number of quarters you need depends on your year of birth. People born after 1928 need 40 quarters to qualify for benefits.

**EXHIBIT 18–7**

Approximate
Monthly Benefits If
You Retire at Full
Retirement Age
and Had Steady
Lifetime Earnings

SOURCE: *Social
Security: Understanding
the Benefits* (Washington,
DC: Social Security
Administration, January
1999), p. 35.

**Your Earnings in 1998**

| Your Age in 1999 | Your Family | $20,000 | $30,000 | $40,000 | $50,000 | $68,400 or More* |
|---|---|---|---|---|---|---|
| 45 | You | $ 826 | $1,092 | $1,310 | $1,435 | $1,687 |
| | You and your spouse[†] | 1,239 | 1,638 | 1,965 | 2,152 | 2,530 |
| 55 | You | 826 | 1,092 | 1,310 | 1,428 | 1,622 |
| | You and your spouse[†] | 1,239 | 1,638 | 1,965 | 2,142 | 2,433 |
| 65 | You | 767 | 1,016 | 1,197 | 1,269 | 1,373 |
| | You and your spouse[†] | 1,150 | 1,524 | 1,795 | 1,911 | 2,059 |

*Earnings equal to or greater than the OASDI wage base from age 22 through the year before retirement.

[†]Your spouse is assumed to be the same age as you. Your spouse may qualify for a higher retirement benefit based on his or her own work record.

NOTE: The accuracy of these estimates depends on the pattern of your actual earnings, which may vary significantly from those shown here.

**Minimum and Maximum Benefits**   Social Security retirement benefits are based on earnings over the years. Exhibit 18–7 shows approximate monthly Social Security benefits for workers at age 65.

**Taxability of Social Security Benefits**   Up to 85 percent of your Social Security benefits may be subject to federal income tax for any year in which your adjusted gross income plus your nontaxable interest income and one-half of your Social Security benefits exceed a base amount. For current information, telephone the Internal Revenue Service at 1–800–829–3676 for Publication 554, *Tax Benefits for Older Americans,* and Publication 915, *Tax Information on Social Security.*

**If You Work after You Retire**   Your Social Security benefits may be reduced if you earn above a certain amount a year, depending on your age and the amount you earn. You will receive all of your benefits for the year if your employment earnings do not exceed the annual exempted amount.

**Benefits Increase Automatically**   Social Security benefits increase automatically each January if the cost of living increased during the preceding year. Each year, the cost of living is compared with that of the year before. If it has increased, Social Security benefits increase by the same percentage.

**Spouse's Benefits**   The full benefit for a spouse is one-half of the retired worker's full benefit. If your spouse takes benefits before age 65, the amount of the spouse's benefit is reduced to a low of 37.5 percent at age 62. However, a spouse who is taking care of a child who is under 16 or has a disability gets full (50 percent) benefits, regardless of age.

If you are eligible for both your own retirement benefits and for benefits as a spouse, Social Security pays your own benefit first. If your benefit as a spouse is higher than your retirement benefit, you'll get a combination of benefits equal to the higher spouse benefit.

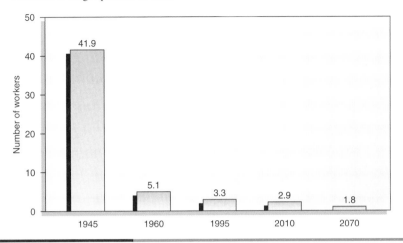

Due to the increase in life expectancy, more people are receiving Social Security benefits for longer periods of time.

**EXHIBIT 18-8**

The Number of Workers per Beneficiary Has Plummeted

SOURCES: Advisory Council on Social Security, 1994–95; *Southwest Economy* (Dallas: Federal Reserve Bank of Dallas, May–June 1997), p. 7.

**Internet Access**   To view and print the Social Security Administration's publications, forms, reports, and program history, with links to information for employers, employees, children, parents, and teachers, visit the agency at www.ssa.gov.

**The Future of Social Security**   According to the Social Security Administration, the Social Security program is financially sound. The Social Security taxes received in recent years exceeded the Social Security benefits that were paid. Such surpluses are expected to continue until the year 2017, at which time a sizable reserve fund is expected to exist.

However, many people are concerned about the future of Social Security. They contend that enormous changes since Social Security started over 65 years ago have led to promises that are impossible to keep. Longer life expectancies mean retirees collect benefits over a greater number of years. More workers are retiring early, thus entering the system sooner and staying longer. The flood of baby boomers who will begin retiring early in the 21st century will mean fewer workers to contribute to the system. In 1945, 45 workers supported every recipient. By 1995, that number had dropped to three. The Social Security Administration estimates the number will drop to two workers by 2050 (see Exhibit 18–8).

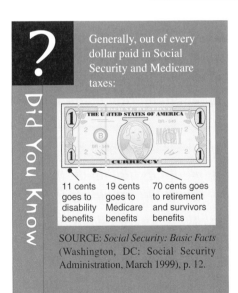

Generally, out of every dollar paid in Social Security and Medicare taxes:

11 cents goes to disability benefits     19 cents goes to Medicare benefits     70 cents goes to retirement and survivors benefits

SOURCE: *Social Security: Basic Facts* (Washington, DC: Social Security Administration, March 1999), p. 12.

## Other Public Pension Plans

Besides Social Security, the federal government administers several other retirement plans (for federal government and railroad employees). Employees covered under these plans are not covered by Social Security. The Veterans Administration provides pensions for many survivors of men and women who died while in the armed forces and disability pensions for eligible veterans. The Railroad Retirement System is the only retirement system administered by the federal government that covers a single private industry. Many state, county, and city governments operate retirement plans for their employees.

## Employer Pension Plans

Another possible source of retirement income is the pension plan your company offers. With employer plans, your employer contributes to your retirement benefits, and sometimes you contribute too. Contributions and earnings on those contributions accumulate tax free until you receive them.

Since private pension plans vary, you should find out (1) when you become eligible for pension benefits and (2) what benefits you will be entitled to. Most employer plans are defined-contribution or defined-benefit plans.

### Defined-Contribution Plan

Over the last two decades, the defined-contribution plan has continued to grow rapidly while the number of defined-benefit plans has generally dropped. A **defined-contribution plan** has an individual account for each employee; therefore, these plans are sometimes called *individual account plans.* The plan document describes the amount the employer will contribute, but it does not promise any particular benefit. When a plan participant retires or otherwise becomes eligible for benefits, the benefit is the total amount in the participant's account, including past investment earnings on amounts put into the account.

*defined-contribution plan* A plan—profit sharing, money purchase, Keogh, or 401(k)—that provides an individual account for each participant; also called an *individual account plan.*

Defined-contribution plans include the following:

1. *Money-purchase pension plans.* Your employer promises to set aside a certain amount for you each year, generally a percentage of your earnings.
2. *Stock bonus plans.* Your employer's contribution is used to buy stock in your company for you. The stock is usually held in trust until you retire, at which time you can receive your shares or sell them at their fair market value.
3. *Profit-sharing plans.* Your employer's contribution depends on the company's profits.
4. *Salary reduction or 401(k) plans.* Under a **401(k) plan,** your employer makes nontaxable contributions to the plan for your benefit and reduces your salary by the same amounts. Sometimes your employer matches a portion of the funds contributed by you. If your employer is a tax-exempt institution such as a hospital, university, or museum, the salary reduction plan is called a *Section 403(b) plan.* These plans are often referred to as **tax-sheltered annuity (TSA) plans.**

*401(k) (TSA) plan* A plan under which employees can defer current taxation on a portion of their salary.

The Tax Reform Act of 1986 retains the $30,000 cap on annual contributions for money-purchase pension plans, stock bonus plans, and profit-sharing plans. Eventually, the annual limit on such plans will increase in response to inflation.

In 1994, the tax act reduced from $30,000 to $9,240 the maximum annual amount an employee can defer for a 401(k) plan. The maximum annual amount you may contribute to a 403(b) plan now ranges from $9,500 up to $12,500 if you have worked for the same employer for 15 years or more. The maximum can be higher in plans to which your employer contributes.

### An Example: How Funds Accumulate

All earnings in a tax-sheltered annuity grow without current federal taxation. Dollars saved on a pretax basis while your earnings grow tax deferred will enhance the growth of your funds (see Exhibit 18–9 on page 587).

### Tax Benefits of a TSA

With a TSA, your investment earnings are tax deferred. Your savings compound at a faster rate and provide you with a greater sum than in an account without this advantage. Ordinary income taxes will be due when

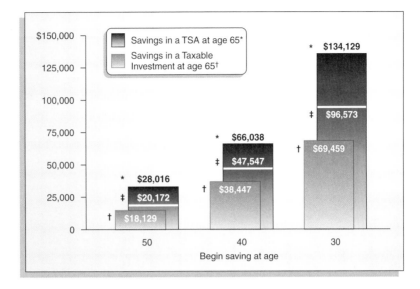

## EXHIBIT 18-9

### An Early Start+ Tax-Deferred Growth = Greater Savings

SOURCE: Massachusetts Mutual Life Insurance Company.

*Tax-deferred growth: Assumes a 28 percent tax bracket, a $100 contribution per month, and a 6 percent tax-deferred annual return.

†Taxable growth: Assumes a 28 percent tax bracket, a $72 contribution ($100 − $28 paid in taxes) per month, and a 6 percent taxable annual return (a 4.32 percent after-tax earnings rate). A 10 percent federal tax penalty may be due on amounts withdrawn before age 59½.

‡Net after 28 percent tax at retirement.

you receive the income. The following table illustrates the difference between saving in a conventional savings plan and a tax-deferred TSA for a single person earning $28,000 a year. Notice how you can increase your take-home pay with a TSA.

|  | Without a TSA | With a TSA |
| --- | --- | --- |
| Your income | $28,000 | $28,000 |
| TSA contribution | 0 | 2,400 |
| Taxable income | 28,000 | 25,600 |
| Estimated federal income taxes | 5,319 | 4,647 |
| Gross take-home pay | 22,681 | 20,953 |
| After-tax savings contributions | 2,400 | 0 |
| Net take-home pay | 20,281 | 20,953 |
| **Increase in take-home pay with a TSA** |  | **$   672** |

What happens to your benefits under an employer pension plan if you change jobs? One of the most important aspects of such plans is vesting. **Vesting** is your right to at least a portion of the benefits you have accrued under an employer pension plan (within certain limits), even if you leave the company before you retire.

### Defined-Benefit Plan

In a **defined-benefit plan,** the plan document specifies the benefits promised to the employee at the normal retirement age. The plan itself does not specify how much the employer must contribute annually. The plan's actuary determines the annual employer contribution required so that the plan fund will be sufficient to pay the promised benefits as each participant retires. If the fund is inadequate, the employer must make additional contributions. Because of their actuarial aspects,

*vesting* An employee's right to at least a portion of the benefits accrued under an employer pension plan, even if the employee leaves the company before retiring.

*defined-benefit plan* A plan that specifies the benefits the employee will receive at the normal retirement age.

defined-benefit plans tend to be more complicated and more expensive to administer than defined-contribution plans.

Companies nationwide are switching their retirement plans to defined contributions from defined benefits. "Paternalistic employers are dying fast—if they're not already dead," says an actuary with an international consulting firm. The result is that "the shift to defined contributions has forced employees to take more responsibility for retirement. They have discretion as to how to invest the money and must make substantive decisions about their own financial futures."[12] It is estimated that by the year 2005, employees will be managing $1.5 trillion of their own retirement money in 401(k) retirement plans.

**Plan Portability**   Some pension plans allow portability. This feature enables you to carry earned benefits from one employer's pension plan to another's when you change jobs.

The Employee Retirement Income Security Act of 1974 (ERISA) sets minimum standards for pension plans in private industry and protects more than 50 million workers. Under this act, the federal government has insured part of the payments promised to retirees from private defined-benefit pensions. ERISA established the Pension Benefit Guaranty Corporation (PBGC), a quasi-governmental agency, to provide pension insurance. The PBGC's board of directors includes the secretaries of the U.S. Departments of Labor, the Treasury, and Commerce.

Use the checklist in Exhibit 18–10 on pages 588–589 to help you determine what your pension plan provides and requires.

## Personal Retirement Plans

In addition to the retirement plans offered by Social Security, other public pension plans, and employer pension plans, many individuals have set up personal retirement plans.

The two most popular personal retirement plans are individual retirement accounts (IRAs) and Keogh accounts.

---

**EXHIBIT 18–10**   Know Your Pension Plan Checklist

**A. Plan Type Checklist**

My plan is a:

*Defined-benefit plan*
☐ Integrated with Social Security.
☐ Nonintegrated.

*Defined-contribution plan*
☐ Integrated with Social Security.
☐ Nonintegrated.

My Social Security benefit:
☐ Will not be deducted from my plan benefit.
☐ Will be deducted from my plan benefit to the extent of _____ percent of the Social Security benefit I am due to receive at retirement.

**B. Contributions Checklist**

My pension plan is financed by:
☐ Employer contributions only.
☐ Employer and employee contributions.
☐ Union dues and assessments.

I contribute to my pension plan at the rate of
$_____ per 1 month 1 week 1 hour or
_____ percent of my compensation.

**C. Vesting Checklist**

My plan provides:
☐ Full and immediate vesting.
☐ Cliff vesting.
☐ Rule of 45 vesting.
☐ Other (specify).

I need _____ more years of service to be fully vested.

---

Continued

## EXHIBIT 18-10    Know Your Pension Plan Checklist (concluded)

### D. Credited Service Checklist

I will have a year of service under my pension plan:
- ☐ If I work _____ hours in a 12-consecutive-month period.
- ☐ If I meet other requirements (specify).

The plan year (12-month period for which plan records are kept) ends on _____ of each year.
I will be credited for work performed:
- ☐ Before I became a participant in the plan.
- ☐ After the plan's normal retirement age.

As of now, _____ [date], I have earned _____ years of service toward my pension.

My plan's break-in-service rules are as follows: _____
_____
_____

### E. Retirement Benefit Checklist

I may begin to receive full normal retirement benefits at age _____.

Working beyond the normal retirement age ☐ will ☐ will not increase the pension paid to me when I retire.

I may retire at age _____ if I have completed _____ years of service. Apart from the age requirement,

I need _____ more years of service to be eligible for early retirement benefits.

The amount of my normal retirement benefit is computed as follows: _____

The amount of my early retirement benefit is computed as follows: _____

My retirement benefit will be:
- ☐ Paid monthly for life.
- ☐ Paid to me in a lump sum.
- ☐ Adjusted to the cost of living.
- ☐ Paid to my survivor in the event of my death (see "Survivors' Benefit Checklist" below).

### F. Disability Benefit Checklist

My plan ☐ does ☐ does not provide disability benefits.

My plan defines the term *disability* as follows: _____
_____

To be eligible for disability retirement benefits, I must be _____ years old and must have _____ years of service.

A determination as to whether my condition meets my plan's definition of disability is made by:

- ☐ A doctor chosen by me.
- ☐ A doctor designated by the plan administrator.
- ☐ The Social Security Administration in deciding that I qualify for Social Security disability benefits.

I must send my application for disability retirement benefits to _____ within ____ months after I stop working.

If I qualify for disability benefits, I will continue to receive benefits:
- ☐ For life, if I remain disabled.
- ☐ Until I return to my former job.
- ☐ As long as I am eligible for Social Security disability benefits.

### G. Survivors' Benefit Checklist

My pension plan ☐ provides ☐ does not provide a joint and survivor option or a similar provision for death benefits.

My spouse and I ☐ have ☐ have not rejected in writing the joint and survivor option.

Electing the joint and survivor option will reduce my pension benefit to _____.

My survivor will receive _____ per month for life if the following conditions are met (specify): _____
_____
_____.

### H. Plan Termination Checklist

My benefits ☐ are ☐ are not insured by the Pension Benefits Guaranty Corporation.

### I. Benefit Application Checklist

My employer ☐ will ☐ will not automatically submit my pension application for me.

I must apply for my pension benefits ☐ on a special form that I get from _____ within _____ months ☐ before ☐ after I retire.

My application for pension benefits should be sent to _____.

I must furnish the following documents when applying for my pension benefits: _____.

If my application for pension benefits is denied, I may appeal in writing to _____ within _____ days.

### J. Suspension of Benefits Checklist

- ☐ I am covered by a single-employer plan or by a plan involving more than one employer that does not meet ERISA's definition of a multiemployer plan.
- ☐ I am covered by a multiemployer plan as that term is defined in ERISA.

SOURCE: *Know Your Pension Plan* (Washington, DC: U.S. Department of Labor, 1992), pp. 5–10.

Income
Ranges and
Deductibility
Limits

|  | AGI—Single Returns | AGI—Joint Returns |
|---|---|---|
| 1999 | $31,000–$41,000 | $51,000–$61,000 |
| 2000 | $32,000–$42,000 | $52,000–$62,000 |
| 2001 | $33,000–$43,000 | $53,000–$63,000 |
| 2002 | $34,000–$44,000 | $54,000–$64,000 |
| 2003 | $40,000–$50,000 | $60,000–$70,000 |
| 2004 | $45,000–$55,000 | $65,000–$75,000 |
| 2005 | $50,000–$60,000 | $70,000–$80,000 |
| 2006 | $50,000–$60,000 | $75,000–$85,000 |
| 2007+ | $50,000–$60,000 | $80,000–$100,000 |

For example, if you filed a single return in 1999 and your AGI is $31,000 or less, your IRA contribution is fully deductible; if your AGI is $35,000, you will still be able to contribute the full $2,000, but only 50 percent will be deductible; and if your AGI is $41,000 or more, your total contribution (maximum $2,000) is nondeductible.

*Individual retirement account (IRA)*
A special account in which the employee sets aside a portion of his or her income; taxes are not paid on the principal or interest until money is withdrawn from the account.

**Sheet 63**

## Individual Retirement Accounts (IRAs)

The **individual retirement account (IRA),** which entails the establishment of a trust or a custodial account, is a retirement savings plan created for an individual. The Taxpayer Relief Act of 1997 includes several provisions designed to help you save for retirement. The act expanded rules on traditional (classic) IRAs and created several new types of IRAs.

The expansion of rules for existing IRAs allows more people to make deductible contributions and gain easier access to their funds. If you are under age 70½ and have earned income, you can contribute up to $2,000 annually to a traditional IRA. If you participate in an employer-sponsored retirement plan, see Exhibit 18–11 for the income ranges that determine what portion of your IRA contribution, if any, would be deductible under the new limits. If your adjusted gross income (AGI) is the lowest number on the range or less, your contribution will be fully deductible; if it is the highest number listed or more, it will be nondeductible. If your income falls somewhere in the middle, it will be partially deductible, depending on the exact amount. These ranges will increase every year until 2007. If your spouse is covered by a retirement plan at work but you aren't, you can still make a fully deductible IRA contribution until your AGI reaches $150,000. New, penalty-free withdrawals are available for distributions made to cover qualified higher education expenses or up to $10,000 for first-time home buyer expenses.

### Regular (Traditional or Classic) IRA

This arrangement lets you contribute up to $2,000 or 100 percent of your income, whichever is less. Whether the contribution is tax deductible depends on your tax filing status, your income, and your participation in an employer-provided retirement plan.

### Roth IRA

With a *Roth IRA,* contributions are not tax deductible, but earnings accumulate tax free. You may contribute up to $2,000 per year (reduced by the amount contributed to a traditional IRA) if you are a single taxpayer with an AGI of less than $95,000 or less than $150,000 if you are filing jointly. You can make contributions even after age 70½. Five years after you establish your Roth IRA, you can take tax-free, penalty-free distributions if you are at least 59½ or will use the fund for first-time home buyer expenses.

Your Roth IRA is exclusively for you. Your interest in the account is nonforfeitable. You can't borrow from your Roth IRA. If you use your Roth IRA as collateral for a loan, the part you pledge as collateral will be taxed as a withdrawal.

You may convert your traditional IRA to a Roth IRA. Depending on your current age and your anticipated tax bracket in retirement, it may be a good idea to convert. Is a tax-deductible IRA or a Roth IRA better for you? If you are saving for a first-time home purchase or retirement at age 59½, and these events are at least five years away, the Roth IRA allows for penalty-free withdrawals as well as tax-free distributions.

**Spousal IRA**    A *spousal IRA* lets you contribute up to $2,000 on behalf of your non-working spouse if you file a joint tax return. As in the traditional IRA, whether or not this contribution is tax deductible depends on your income and on whether you or your spouse participates in an employer-provided retirement plan.

**Rollover IRA**    A *rollover IRA* is a traditional IRA that accepts rollovers of all or a portion of your taxable distribution from a retirement plan or from another IRA. A rollover IRA may also let you roll over to a Roth IRA. To avoid a mandatory 20 percent federal income tax withholding, the rollover must be made directly to a similar employer-provided retirement plan or to an IRA. If you receive the money yourself, you must roll it over within 60 days. However, you will receive only 80 percent of the amount you request as a distribution (distribution minus the mandatory 20 percent withholding tax). Unless you add additional money to the rollover accumulation to equal the 20 percent withheld, the IRS will consider the 20 percent withheld to be taxable income. If you are under 59½, the 20 percent withholding will be considered an early distribution subject to a 10 percent penalty tax. The 80 percent you roll over will not be taxed until you take it out of the IRA.

**Education IRA**    The 1997 act also created a new *education IRA* that allows individuals under certain income levels to contribute up to $500 per year per child under age 18. The contributions are not tax deductible, but they do provide tax-free distributions for education expenses.

You cannot keep money in most retirement plans indefinitely. Except for Roth IRAs, most tax-qualified retirement plans, including 403(b), 401(k), and other IRAs, are required by the IRS to begin what is known as "minimum lifetime distributions" at age 70½. If you have retired, you must either receive the entire balance of your tax-qualified plan or start receiving periodic distributions by April 1 of the year following the year in which you reach 70½ or retire, if later.

The amount of the minimum required distribution is based on your life expectancy at the time of the distribution. The IRS provides single- and joint-life expectancy tables for calculating required distribution amounts. The penalties for noncompliance in this case are severe. Insufficient distributions may be subject to an excise tax of 50 percent on the amount not withdrawn as required.

However, whether or not you are covered by a pension plan, you can still make nondeductible IRA contributions, and all of the income your IRA earns will compound tax deferred until you withdraw money from the IRA. Remember, the biggest benefit of an IRA lies in its tax-deferred earnings growth; the longer the money accumulates tax deferred, the bigger the benefit.

Exhibit 18–12 on page 592 shows the power of tax-deferred compounding of earnings, an important advantage offered by an IRA. Consider how compounded earnings transformed the lives of two savers, Abe and Ben. As the exhibit shows, Abe regularly invested $2,000 a year in an IRA for 10 years, from ages 25 to 35. Then Abe sat back and let compounding work its magic. Ben started making regular $2,000 annual contributions at age 35 and contributed for 30 years until age 65. As you can see, Abe retired with a much larger nest egg—over $192,000 more than Ben's. Moral? Get an early start on your plan for retirement.

## EXHIBIT 18–12    TACKLING THE TRADE-OFFS (SAVING NOW VERSUS SAVING LATER)

| | Saver Abe | | | | Saver Ben | | |
|---|---|---|---|---|---|---|---|
| Age | Years | Contributions | Year-End Value | Age | Years | Contributions | Year-End Value |
| 25 | 1 | $2,000 | $2,188 | 25 | 1 | $   0 | $0 |
| 26 | 2 | 2,000 | 4,580 | 26 | 2 | 0 | 0 |
| 27 | 3 | 2,000 | 7,198 | 27 | 3 | 0 | 0 |
| 28 | 4 | 2,000 | 10,061 | 28 | 4 | 0 | 0 |
| 29 | 5 | 2,000 | 13,192 | 29 | 5 | 0 | 0 |
| 30 | 6 | 2,000 | 16,617 | 30 | 6 | 0 | 0 |
| 31 | 7 | 2,000 | 20,363 | 31 | 7 | 0 | 0 |
| 32 | 8 | 2,000 | 24,461 | 32 | 8 | 0 | 0 |
| 33 | 9 | 2,000 | 28,944 | 33 | 9 | 0 | 0 |
| 34 | 10 | 2,000 | 33,846 | 34 | 10 | 0 | 0 |
| 35 | 11 | 0 | 40,494 | 35 | 11 | 2,000 | 2,188 |
| 36 | 12 | 0 | 37,021 | 36 | 12 | 2,000 | 4,580 |
| 37 | 13 | 0 | 44,293 | 37 | 13 | 2,000 | 7,198 |
| 38 | 14 | 0 | 48,448 | 38 | 14 | 2,000 | 10,061 |
| 39 | 15 | 0 | 52,992 | 39 | 15 | 2,000 | 13,192 |
| 40 | 16 | 0 | 57,963 | 40 | 16 | 2,000 | 16,617 |
| 41 | 17 | 0 | 63,401 | 41 | 17 | 2,000 | 20,363 |
| 42 | 18 | 0 | 69,348 | 42 | 18 | 2,000 | 24,461 |
| 43 | 19 | 0 | 75,854 | 43 | 19 | 2,000 | 28,944 |
| 44 | 20 | 0 | 82,969 | 44 | 20 | 2,000 | 33,846 |
| 45 | 21 | 0 | 90,752 | 45 | 21 | 2,000 | 39,209 |
| 46 | 22 | 0 | 99,265 | 46 | 22 | 2,000 | 45,075 |
| 47 | 23 | 0 | 108,577 | 47 | 23 | 2,000 | 51,490 |
| 48 | 24 | 0 | 118,763 | 48 | 24 | 2,000 | 58,508 |
| 49 | 25 | 0 | 129,903 | 49 | 25 | 2,000 | 66,184 |
| 50 | 26 | 0 | 142,089 | 50 | 26 | 2,000 | 74,580 |
| 51 | 27 | 0 | 155,418 | 51 | 27 | 2,000 | 83,764 |
| 52 | 28 | 0 | 169,997 | 52 | 28 | 2,000 | 93,809 |
| 53 | 29 | 0 | 185,944 | 53 | 29 | 2,000 | 104,797 |
| 54 | 30 | 0 | 203,387 | 54 | 30 | 2,000 | 116,815 |
| 55 | 31 | 0 | 222,466 | 55 | 31 | 2,000 | 129,961 |
| 56 | 32 | 0 | 243,335 | 56 | 32 | 2,000 | 144,340 |
| 57 | 33 | 0 | 266,162 | 57 | 33 | 2,000 | 160,068 |
| 58 | 34 | 0 | 291,129 | 58 | 34 | 2,000 | 177,271 |
| 59 | 35 | 0 | 318,439 | 59 | 35 | 2,000 | 196,088 |
| 60 | 36 | 0 | 348,311 | 60 | 36 | 2,000 | 216,670 |
| 61 | 37 | 0 | 380,985 | 61 | 37 | 2,000 | 239,182 |
| 62 | 38 | 0 | 416,724 | 62 | 38 | 2,000 | 263,807 |
| 63 | 39 | 0 | 455,816 | 63 | 39 | 2,000 | 290,741 |
| 64 | 40 | 0 | 498,574 | 64 | 40 | 2,000 | 320,202 |
| 65 | 41 | 0 | 545,344 | 65 | 41 | 2,000 | 352,427 |
| | | $20,000 | | | | $62,000 | |

| Value at retirement* | $545,344 | Value at retirement* | $352,427 |
|---|---|---|---|
| Less total contributions | $ 20,000 | Less total contributions | $ 62,000 |
| Net earnings | $525,344 | Net earnings | $290,427 |

*The table assumes a 9 percent fixed rate of return, compounded monthly, and no fluctuation of the principal. Distributions from an IRA are subject to ordinary income taxes when withdrawn and may be subject to other limitations under IRA rules.

SOURCE: *The Franklin Investor* (San Mateo, CA: Franklin Distributors, Inc., January 1989).

**EXHIBIT 18-13**

Summary of
Retirement
Plan Options

SOURCE: Adapted from
"12 Easy Retirement
Planning Tips for Women,"
VALIC, An American
General Company, April
1998, p. 20.

| Type of Plan | Plan Features |
| --- | --- |
| Regular or Traditional IRA | • Tax-deferred interest and earnings<br>• $2,000 annual limit on individual contributions<br>• Limited eligibility for tax-deductible contributions<br>• Contributions do not reduce current taxes |
| Roth IRA | • Tax-deferred interest and earnings<br>• $2,000 annual limit on individual contributions<br>• Withdrawals are tax-free in specific cases<br>• Contributions do not reduce current taxes |
| Spousal IRA | • Tax-deferred interest and earnings<br>• Both working spouse and nonworking spouse can contribute up to $2,000 each year<br>• Limited eligibility for tax-deductible contributions<br>• Contributions do not reduce current taxes |
| Rollover IRA | • Traditional IRA that accepts rollovers of all or a portion of your taxable distribution from a retirement plan<br>• You can roll over to a Roth IRA |
| Education IRA | • Tax-deferred interest and earnings<br>• 10% early withdrawal penalty is waived when money is used for higher-education expenses<br>• $500 annual limit on individual contributions<br>• Contributions do not reduce current taxes |
| Employer-sponsored retirement plan (SEP–IRA) | • "Pay yourself first" payroll reduction contributions<br>• Pretax contributions<br>• Tax-deferred interest and earnings |

**Simplified Employee Pension Plans–IRA (SEP–IRA)**   A *SEP–IRA plan* is simply an individual retirement account funded by the employer. Each employee sets up an IRA account at a bank or a brokerage house. Then the employer makes an annual contribution of up to 15 percent of the employee's salary or $30,000, whichever is less.

The SEP–IRA is the simplest type of retirement plan if you are fully or partially self-employed. Your contributions, which can vary from year to year, are tax deductible, and earnings accumulate on a tax-deferred basis. A SEP–IRA has no IRS filing requirements, so paperwork is minimal. Exhibit 18–13 summarizes various retirement plan options.

Your investment opportunities for IRA funds are not limited to savings accounts and certificates of deposit. You can put your IRA funds in many kinds of investments—mutual funds, annuities, stocks, bonds, U.S.-minted gold and silver coins, real estate, and so forth. Only investments in life insurance, precious metals, collectibles, and securities bought on margin are prohibited.

**IRA Withdrawals**   When you retire, you will be able to withdraw your IRA in a lump sum, withdraw it in installments over your life expectancy, or place it in an annuity that guarantees payments over your lifetime. If you take the lump sum, the entire amount will be taxable as ordinary income and the only tax break you will have is standard five-year income averaging. IRA withdrawals made before age 59½ are now subject to a 10 percent tax in addition to ordinary income tax, unless the participant dies or becomes disabled. You can avoid this tax if you roll over your IRA. See the Financial Planning for Life's Situations feature on p. 594.

## Financial Planning for Life's Situations

### AN EARLY DIP INTO YOUR IRA

Once you turn 59½, you have the option to withdraw whatever amount of money you want from your individual retirement account. Do it before then, however, and, with a few exceptions such as the purchase of a first house, death, and disability, you'll face a 10 percent penalty. There is a way around having to pay this substantial fine. A little-used option allows you to take what the government calls substantially equal periodic payments. Anyone can do this anytime, but be careful: You can deplete your retirement fund, and, if you do the math wrong or skip a withdrawal, the Internal Revenue Service can levy a 10 percent penalty against every cent you take. If you are within five years of turning 59½, you are locked into a five-year commitment. If you are younger, you must take money out each year until you reach 59½.

To do it right, Scott Grittenger, a certified financial planner at Strong Capital Management, recommends that you first figure out exactly how much money you will need. Then determine which of three approved IRS methods will get you there. The life expectancy method generally yields the smallest payouts. The annuity method usually nets the highest payouts. Once you've drawn up a plan, don't skip withdrawals or switch methods; otherwise you'll get hit with a penalty.

Here are the downsides to withdrawing too soon:

- The earlier you take money out, the less you will benefit from tax-deferred compounding.
- You cannot change your mind or skip withdrawals.
- If you are within five years of turning 59½, you are locked into a five-year withdrawal commitment.
- If you are younger than 54½, you must take money out until you reach 59½. For a 34-year-old, that means a quarter-century of annual withdrawals.

SOURCE: Adapted from Anne Tergesen, "An Early Dip into Your IRA," *Business Week*, July 19, 1999, p. 126. Reprinted from the July 19, 1999 issue of *Business Week* by special permission. © 1999 McGraw-Hill Companies, Inc.

## Keogh Plans

*Keogh plan* A plan in which tax-deductible contributions fund the retirement of self-employed people and their employees; also called an *H.R. 10 plan* or a *self-employed retirement plan.*

A **Keogh plan,** also known an *H.R.10 plan* or a *self-employed retirement plan,* is a qualified pension plan developed for self-employed people and their employees. Generally, Keogh plans cannot discriminate in favor of a self-employed person or any employee. Both defined-contribution and defined-benefit Keogh plans have tax-deductible contribution limits, and other restrictions also apply to Keogh plans. Therefore, you should obtain professional tax advice before using this type of retirement plan. Whether you have an employer pension plan or a personal retirement plan, you must start withdrawing at age 70½ or the IRS will charge you a penalty.

## Annuities

*annuity* A contract that provides an income for life.

In Chapter 12, you learned what an annuity is and how annuities provide lifelong security. You can outlive the proceeds of your IRA, your Keogh plan, or your investments, but an **annuity** provides guaranteed income for life. Who should consider an annuity? One financial planner uses them for clients who have fully funded all other retirement plan options, including 401(k), 403(b), Keogh, and profit-sharing plans, but still want more money for retirement.[13]

You can buy an annuity with the proceeds of an IRA or a company pension, or as supplemental retirement income. You can buy an annuity with a single payment or with periodic payments. You can buy an annuity that will begin payouts immediately, or, as is more common, you can buy one that will begin payouts at a later date.

To the extent that annuity payments exceed your premiums, these payments are taxed as ordinary income as you receive them, but earned interest on annuities accumulates tax free until the payments begin. Annuities may be fixed, providing a specific income for life, or variable, with payouts above a guaranteed minimum level dependent on investment return. Either way, the rate of return on annuities is often pegged to market rates.

## Types of Annuities

*Immediate annuities* are generally purchased by people of retirement age. Such annuities provide income payments at once. They are usually purchased with a lump-sum payment.

With *deferred annuities,* income payments start at some future date. Interest builds up on the money you deposit. Younger people often use such annuities to save money toward retirement.

A deferred annuity purchased with a lump sum is known as a *single-premium deferred annuity.* In recent years, such annuities have been popular because of the tax-free buildup during the accumulation period.

If you are buying a deferred annuity, you may wish to obtain a contract that permits flexible premiums. With such an annuity, your contributions may vary from year to year.

The cash value of your life insurance policy may be converted to an annuity. If you are over 65 and your children have completed their education and are financially self-sufficient, you may no longer need all of your life insurance coverage. An option in your life insurance policy lets you convert its cash value to a lifetime income.

## Options in Annuities

You can decide on the terms under which your annuity pays you and your family. Exhibit 18–14 on page 596 summarizes the major options and their uses.

### Which Annuity Option Is the Best?

The straight life annuity gives more income per dollar of outlay than any other type. But payments stop when you die, whether a month or many years after the payout begins.

Should you get an annuity with a guaranteed return? Opinions differ. Some experts argue that it is a mistake to diminish your monthly income just to make sure your money is returned to your survivors. Some suggest that if you want to ensure that your spouse or someone else continues to receive annuity income after your death, you might choose the joint-and-survivor annuity. Such an annuity pays its installments until the death of the last designated survivor.

You have still another choice to make: how your annuity premiums are to be invested. With a fixed-dollar annuity, the money you pay is invested in bonds and mortgages that have a guaranteed return. Such an annuity guarantees you a fixed amount each payout period. With a variable annuity, the money you pay is generally invested in common stocks or other equities. The income you receive will depend on the investment results. Exhibit 18–15 on page 596 compares variable and fixed annuities.

An annuity guarantees lifetime income, but you have a choice regarding the form it will take. Discuss all of the possible options with your insurance agent. The costs, fees, and other features of annuities differ from policy to policy. Ask about sales and administrative charges, purchase and withdrawal fees, and interest rate guarantees. Also, as explained in Chapter 12, be sure to check the financial health of the insurance company.

## Will You Have Enough Money during Retirement?

Sheet 64

Now that you have reviewed all the possible sources of your retirement income, estimate what your annual retirement income will be. Don't forget to inflate incomes or investments that increase with the cost of living (such as Social Security) to what they will be when you retire. (Use the inflation factor table in the Financial Planning Calculations box on page 579.) Remember, inflation is a major uncontrollable variable for retirees.

**EXHIBIT 18-14**   INCOME ANNUITY OPTIONS

This exhibit gives you an approximate idea of how different income options compare. The amount of income you actually receive is based on factors such as how you invest, your age, your sex, and the income option you choose. Market conditions at any given time, especially interest rates, influence income amounts.

| Income Option | Description | Common Uses | Typical Monthly Income* |
|---|---|---|---|
| Lifetime income. Also called *life income* or *life only*. | You receive income payments for the rest of your life. The income ceases upon your death. | Provides the most income per dollar invested of any lifetime option. Frequently used by single people with limited sources of additional income. | $923.71 per month for life. |
| Lifetime income with a minimum number of payments guaranteed. Also called *life with period certain*. | You receive income for the rest of your life. If you die before you receive a specific number of payments, your beneficiary will receive the balance of the number of income payments you choose. | Appropriate if you want a life income but dislike the risk of lost income in the event of premature death. People with heirs often consider this option. | $791.49 per month for life, 240-month minimum. |
| Lifetime income for two people. Also called *joint and survivor*. | Income payments are received for as long as either of the two people are alive. Upon the death of either person, income continues as a percentage of the original amount. Common percentages chosen for the survivor are 50, 66⅔, and 100%. | Often chosen by couples, who may choose the 100% option when there is little other income, or 50% or 66⅔% when there is other income. Lifetime income with period certain and installment refund† options are also available for joint-income plans. | $774.06 per month for as long as at least one of the people is alive, assuming the 100% option. |

Note: The numbers above are hypothetical, and your actual income may differ. Only a portion of each payment would be taxable.

*Assumes a 65-year-old male with a 65-year-old spouse invests $100,000 and begins receiving income immediately.

†In an installment refund annuity, you receive an income for the rest of your life. However, if you die before receiving as much money as you paid in, your beneficiary receives regular income until the total payments equal that amount.

SOURCE: *Building Your Future with Annuities: A Consumer's Guide* (Fidelity Investments and U.S. Department of Agriculture, August 1991), p. 12.

**EXHIBIT 18-15**

A Comparison of Variable and Fixed Annuities

| | Variable | Fixed |
|---|---|---|
| Tax-deferred earnings | Yes | Yes |
| Variety of income options | Yes | Yes |
| Annual investment ceiling | No | No |
| Investment flexibility | Yes | No |
| Potential for higher returns | Yes | No |
| Increased investment risk | Yes | No |
| Hedge against inflation | Yes | No |
| Security of principal and earnings | No | Yes |
| Guaranteed interest rate | No | Yes |
| Control over type of investment in the annuity | Yes | No |

**EXHIBIT 18-16**

Sources of Income in Retirement

Social Security provides only 27 percent of the average retiree's annual income. On average, pension income accounts for about 19 percent, slightly less than that provided by Social Security.

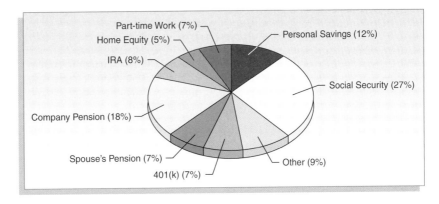

Part-time Work (7%)
Home Equity (5%)
IRA (8%)
Personal Savings (12%)
Social Security (27%)
Company Pension (18%)
Spouse's Pension (7%)
401(k) (7%)
Other (9%)

Now compare your total estimated retirement income with your total inflated retirement expenses. If your estimated income exceeds your estimated expenses and a large portion of your planned income will automatically increase with the cost of living during your retirement, you are in good shape. (You should evaluate your plans every few years between now and retirement to be sure your planned income is still adequate to meet your planned expenses.)

If, however, your planned retirement income is less than your estimated retirement expenses, now is the time to take action to increase your retirement income. Also, if a large portion of your retirement income is fixed and will not increase with inflation, you should make plans for a much larger retirement income to meet your rising expenses during retirement.

Exhibit 18–16 summarizes the various sources of retirement income.

**Concept Check 18-5**

1. What are possible sources of income for retirees?
2. What are examples of defined-contribution plans? How do they differ from defined-benefit plans?
3. What are the two most popular personal retirement plans?
4. What are annuities? What options are available in annuities? Which option is best?

## LIVING ON YOUR RETIREMENT INCOME

As you planned retirement, you estimated a budget or spending plan, but you may find your actual expenses at retirement are higher than anticipated.

The first step in stretching your retirement income is to make sure you are receiving all of the income to which you are entitled. Examine the possible sources of retirement income mentioned earlier to see whether you could qualify for more programs or additional benefits. What assets or valuables could you use as a cash or income source?

To stay within your income, you may also need to make some changes in your spending plans. For example, you can use your skills and time instead of your money. There are probably many things you can do yourself instead of paying someone else to

**Obj. 6**
Develop a balanced budget based on your retirement income.

do them. Take advantage of free and low-cost recreation such as walks, picnics, public parks, lectures, museums, libraries, art galleries, art fairs, gardening, and church and club programs.

## Tax Advantages

Be sure to take advantage of all the tax savings retirees receive. For more information, ask your local IRS office for a free copy of *Tax Benefits for Older Americans*. If you have any questions about your taxes, get free help from someone at the IRS. You may need to file a quarterly estimated income tax return beginning with the first quarter of your first year of retirement or arrange for withholdings on Social Security and pension payments.

## Working during Retirement

You may want to work part time or start a new part-time career after you retire. Work can provide you with a greater sense of usefulness, involvement, and self-worth and may be the ideal way to add to your retirement income. You may want to pursue a personal interest or hobby, or you can contact your state or local agency on aging for information about employment opportunities for retirees.

Over 50 percent of recent retirees want to continue working part time or even full time after retirement, and only 11 percent are worried about outliving their financial resources. There is a rich talent pool of more than 41 million Americans in the 55 to 75 age range, over 50 percent of whom are retired—and many of them are interested in continued employment. These individuals, with their proven skills and abilities, provide a flexible, cost-effective resource that can sustain our productivity gains and economic growth. What drives many of them is the desire to remain productively engaged in life.[14]

If you decide to work part time after you retire, you should be aware of how your earnings will affect your Social Security income. As long as you do not earn more than the annually exempt amount, your Social Security payments will not be affected. But if you earn more than the annual exempt amount, your Social Security payments will be reduced. Check with your local Social Security office for the latest information.

## Investing for Retirement

The guaranteed-income part of your retirement fund consists of money paid into lower-yield, very safe investments. This part of your fund may already be taken care of through Social Security or retirement plans, as discussed earlier. To offset inflation, your retirement assets must earn enough to keep up with, and even exceed, the rate of inflation. Financial Planning for Life's Situations feature on page 599 presents some suggested investment strategies for 30-year-olds, 45-year-olds, and 55-year-olds.[15]

## Dipping into Your Nest Egg

When should you draw on your savings? The answer depends on your financial circumstances, your age, and how much you want to leave to your heirs. Your savings may be large enough to allow you to live comfortably on the interest alone. Or you may need to make regular withdrawals to help finance your retirement. Dipping into savings isn't wrong, but you must do so with caution.

How long would your savings last if you withdrew monthly income? If you have $10,000 in savings that earns 5.5 percent interest, compounded quarterly, you could take out $68 every month for 20 years before reducing this nest egg to zero. If you have

# Financial Planning for Life's Situations

## SPOTS TO STASH YOUR PORTFOLIO

When investing for retirement, asset allocation is very important. You need to put together a diversified portfolio of investments that can protect you against trouble in any one sector.

The Web provides plenty of advice. One of the best online retirement planners is at S&P Personal Wealth at www.personalwealth.com or www.businessweek.com/investor/. Personal Wealth provides at no charge, an individualized plan for retirement-asset allocation. For $9.95 a month, you get access to Standard & Poor's

recommendations for stocks and mutual funds to plug into allocation plans.

As an example of what Personal Wealth can do, *Business Week* asked S&P to come up with model portfolios for three hypothetical people: a 30-year-old man, a 45-year-old woman, and a 55-year-old man. S&P recommends keeping at least half your money in stocks even if you're only 10 years from retirement. If your portfolio is less than $50,000, you're better off using equity mutual funds instead.

### Investment Strategies for Three Stages of Life

**30-Year-old**
- International Stocks 20%
- Small-cap Stocks 25%
- Large-cap Stocks 55%

**45-Year-old**
- International Stocks 15%
- Small-cap Stocks 25%
- Bonds 25%
- Large-cap Stocks 45%

**55-Year-old**
- International Stocks 10%
- Small-cap Stocks 10%
- Large-cap Stocks 30%
- Bonds 50%

### Suggested Funds for the Long Haul. . .

S&P recommends these mutual funds for long-term savers

| Name/Ticker Symbol | S&P Stars** | Total Return* 3-YR | YTD |
|---|---|---|---|
| **Large-Cap** | | | |
| Legg Mason Val.Trust-Pri. LMVTX | 5 | 44.4% | 19.9% |
| Selected American Shs. SLASX | 5 | 30.8 | 18.2 |
| Strong Grth. & Inc. SGRIX | 5 | 31.3 | 15.1 |
| **Mid/Small-Cap** | | | |
| Accessor Small/Midcap ASMCX | 5 | 24.7 | 9.9 |
| Longleaf Pt. Small Cap LLSCX | 5 | 21.6 | 10.1 |
| Weitz Value Portfolio WVALX | 5 | 31.3 | 17.8 |
| **International** | | | |
| Federated Wrld. Int. Sm. Co. A ISCAX | 5 | 30.5 | 40.1 |
| Tweedy Browne Gl. Value TBGVX | 5 | 21.6 | 26.2 |
| UMB Scout Worldwide UMBWX | 5 | 19.6 | 12.3 |
| **Bond** | | | |
| Hotchkis & Wiley Tot. Ret. HWTRX | 5 | 8.1 | −1.7 |
| Sit Tax Free Income SNITX | 5 | 6.7 | −0.8 |
| Strong Corp. Bond STCBX | 4 | 8.6 | −0.9 |

### Suggested Stocks for Growth

S&P thinks these stocks are good long-term bets

| Name/Ticker Symbol | P-E Ratio*** | S&P Stars** | Total Return* 3-YR | YTD |
|---|---|---|---|---|
| **Large-Cap** | | | | |
| Bristol-Myers Squibb BMY | 35.2 | 5 | 50.6% | 8.0% |
| Cisco Systems CSCO | 92.7 | 5 | 72.7 | 44.6 |
| IBM IBM | 34.2 | 5 | 75.9 | 43.8 |
| MCI Worldcom WCOM | 44.7 | 5 | 48.3 | 23.6 |
| **Small/Mid-Cap** | | | | |
| AGCO AG | 18.1 | 5 | −24 | 48.0 |
| Tiffany TIF | 31.9 | 5 | 52.1 | 88.0 |
| Univision Comms. UNV | 104.0 | 4 | NA | 83.3 |
| VISX VISX | 75.8 | 5 | 112.3 | 296.0 |
| **International** | | | | |
| Deutsche Telekom DT | 38.5 | 4 | NA | 28.9 |
| Glaxo Wellcome GLX | 31.7 | 4 | 32.8 | −15.5 |
| Nokia NOK | 46.6 | 5 | 116.4 | 58.1 |
| Repsol REP | 18.1 | 4 | 25.7 | 14.8 |

*Through July 2    **Out of possible 5    ***Estimated 1999 earnings
DATA: Standard & Poor's Corp.

You'll find more on retirement strategies at www.business.week.com/investor/ and www.personalwealth.com

## EXHIBIT 18-17   Dipping into Your Nest Egg

| Starting Amount of Nest Egg | You Can Reduce Your Nest Egg to Zero by Withdrawing This Much Each Month for the Stated Number of Years... | | | | | Or You Can Withdraw This Much Each Month and Leave Your Nest Egg Intact |
| --- | --- | --- | --- | --- | --- | --- |
| | 10 Years | 15 Years | 20 Years | 25 Years | 30 Years | |
| $ 10,000 | $ 107 | $ 81 | $ 68 | $ 61 | $ 56 | $ 46 |
| 15,000 | 161 | 121 | 102 | 91 | 84 | 69 |
| 20,000 | 215 | 162 | 136 | 121 | 112 | 92 |
| 25,000 | 269 | 202 | 170 | 152 | 140 | 115 |
| 30,000 | 322 | 243 | 204 | 182 | 168 | 138 |
| 40,000 | 430 | 323 | 272 | 243 | 224 | 184 |
| 50,000 | 537 | 404 | 340 | 304 | 281 | 230 |
| 60,000 | 645 | 485 | 408 | 364 | 337 | 276 |
| 80,000 | 859 | 647 | 544 | 486 | 449 | 368 |
| 100,000 | 1,074 | 808 | 680 | 607 | 561 | 460 |

Note: Based on an interest rate of 5.5 percent per year, compounded quarterly.

SOURCE: Select Committee on Aging, U.S. House of Representatives.

## EXHIBIT 18-18   Major Sources of Retirement Income: Advantages and Disadvantages

| Source | Advantages | Disadvantages |
| --- | --- | --- |
| **Social Security** | | |
| In planning | Forced savings<br>Portable from job to job<br>Cost shared with employer | Increasing economic pressure on the system as U.S. population ages |
| At retirement | Inflation-adjusted survivorship rights | Minimum retirement age specified<br>Earned income may partially offset benefits |
| **Employee Pension Plans** | | |
| In planning | Forced savings<br>Cost shared or fully covered by employer | May not be portable<br>No control over how funds are managed |
| At retirement | Survivorship rights | Cost-of-living increases may not be provided on a regular basis |
| **Individual Saving and Investing (including housing, IRA, and Keogh plans)** | | |
| In planning | Current tax savings (e.g., IRAs)<br>Easily incorporated into family (i.e., housing)<br>Portable<br>Control over management of funds | Current needs compete with future needs<br>Penalty for early withdrawal (IRAs and Keoghs) |
| At retirement | Inflation resistant<br>Can usually use as much of the funds as you wish, when you wish (within certain requirements) | Some sources taxable<br>Mandatory minimum withdrawal restrictions (IRAs and Keoghs) |
| **Postretirement Employment** | | |
| In planning | Special earning skills can be used as they are developed | Technology and skills needed to keep up may change rapidly |
| At retirement | Inflation resistant | Ill health can mean loss of this income source |

## Financial Planning for Life's Situations

### RETIREMENT CHECKLIST

As you approach retirement, assess your financial condition using the following checklist. Don't wait too long, or you will miss one or more opportunities to maximize your future financial independence.

| | Yes | No |
|---|---|---|
| 1. Do you talk regularly and frankly to family members about finances and agree on your goals and the lifestyle you will prefer as you get older? | ☐ | ☐ |
| 2. Do you know what your sources of income will be after retirement, how much to expect from each source, and when? | ☐ | ☐ |
| 3. Do you save according to your plan, shifting from growth-producing to safe, income-producing investments? | ☐ | ☐ |
| 4. Do you know where your health insurance will come from after retirement and what it will cover? | ☐ | ☐ |
| 5. Do you review your health insurance and consider options such as converting to cash or investments? | ☐ | ☐ |
| 6. Do you have your own credit history? | ☐ | ☐ |
| 7. Do you have a current will or a living trust? | ☐ | ☐ |
| 8. Do you know where you plan to live in retirement? | ☐ | ☐ |
| 9. Do you anticipate the tax consequences of your retirement plans and of passing assets on to your heirs? | ☐ | ☐ |
| 10. Do your children or other responsible family members know where your important documents are and whom to contact if questions arise? | ☐ | ☐ |
| 11. Do you have legal documents, such as a living will or a power of attorney, specifying your instructions in the event of your death or incapacitating illness? | ☐ | ☐ |

SOURCE: Adapted from *Staying Independent,* American Express Consumer Affairs Office and IDS Financial Services Inc.

$40,000, you could collect $224 every month for 30 years before exhausting your nest egg. For different possibilities, see Exhibit 18–17 on page 600.

Exhibit 18–18 on page 600 summarizes major sources of retirement income and their advantages and disadvantages. Finally, use the accompanying Financial Planning for Life's Situations box to assess your financial condition as you approach retirement.

### Concept Check 18–6

**1.** What is the first step in stretching your retirement income?

**2.** How should you invest to obtain retirement income?

# Summary of Objectives

**Obj. 1   Recognize the importance of retirement planning.**

Retirement planning is important because you will probably spend many years in retirement; Social Security and a private pension may be insufficient to cover the cost of living; and inflation may erode the purchasing power of your retirement savings. Many young people professionals are reluctant to think about retirement, but they should start retirement planning now, before they reach age 40.

**Obj. 2   Analyze your current assets and liabilities for retirement.**

Analyze your current assets (everything you own) and your current liabilities (everything you owe). The difference between your assets and your liabilities is your net worth. Review your assets to ensure they are sufficient for retirement.

**Obj. 3   Estimate your retirement spending needs.**

Since the spending patterns of retirees change, it is impossible to predict the exact amount of money you will need in retirement. However, you can estimate your expenses. Some of those expenses will increase; others will decrease. The expenses that are likely to be lower or eliminated are work related expenses, clothing, housing expenses, federal income taxes, and commuting expenses.

**Obj. 4   Identify your retirement housing needs.**

Where you live in retirement can influence your financial needs. You are the only one who can determine the location and housing that are best for you. Would you like to live in your present home or move to a new location? Consider the social aspects of moving.

**Obj. 5   Determine your planned retirement income.**

Estimate your retirement expenses and adjust those expenses for inflation using the appropriate inflation factor. Your possible sources of income during retirement include Social Security, other public pension plans, employer pension plans, personal retirement plans, and annuities.

**Obj. 6   Develop a balanced budget based on your retirement income.**

Compare your total estimated retirement income with your total inflated retirement expenses. If your income approximates your expenses, you are in good shape; if not, determine additional income needs and sources.

# Financial Planning Problems

1. *Preparing a Net Worth Statement.* Prepare your net worth statement using the guidelines presented in Exhibit 18–3. (Obj. 2)
2. *Comparing Spending Patterns during Retirement.* How will your spending patterns change during your retirement years? Compare your spending patterns with those shown in Exhibit 18–4.   (Obj. 3)
3. *Evaluating Housing Options.* Which type of housing will best meet your housing needs in retirement? List the advantages and disadvantages of your choice. Choose two locations and compare the costs.   (Obj. 4)
4. *Calculating IRA Contributions.* Gene and Dixie Sladek both work. They have an adjusted gross income of $40,000, and they are filing a joint income tax return. What is the maximum IRA contribution they can make? How much of that contribution is tax deductible? (Obj. 5)
5. *Calculating Net Pay and Spendable Income.* Assume your gross pay per pay period is $2,000 and you are in the 33 percent tax bracket. Calculate your net pay and spendable income in the following situations.   (Obj. 5)
   a. You save $200 per pay period after paying income tax on $2,000.
   b. You save $200 per pay period in a tax-sheltered annuity.
6. *Calculating Monthly Withdrawals.* You have $50,000 in your retirement fund that is earning 5.5 percent per year, compounded quarterly. How many dollars in withdrawals per month would reduce this nest egg to zero in 20 years? How many dollars per month can you withdraw for as long as you live and still leave this nest egg intact? (Obj. 6)

# Financial Planning Activities

1. *Conducting Interviews.* Survey friends, relatives, and other people to get their views on retirement planning. Prepare a written report of your findings.  (Obj. 1)

2. *Obtaining Information about Reverse Mortgages.* Obtain a consumer information kit from Senior Income Reverse Mortgage Corporation in Chicago (1–800–774–6266). Examine and evaluate the kit. How might a reverse mortgage help you or a family member?  (Obj. 2)

3. *Using the Internet to Obtain Reverse Mortgage Information.*
   a. Visit the website of the American Association of Retired Persons (AARP) at http://www.aarp.org. Locate the AARP Home Equity Information Center, which presents basic facts about reverse mortgages. Then prepare a report on how reverse mortgages work, who is eligible, what you get, what you pay, and what other choices are available to borrowers.
   b. Visit Fannie Mae's website at www.fanniemae. com/Homebuyer to find out about its reverse mortgage program.

4. *Determining Expenses during Retirement.* Read newspaper or magazine articles to determine what expenses are likely to increase and decrease during retirement. How might this information affect your retirement-planning decisions?  (Obj. 3)

5. *Evaluating Retirement Housing Options.* Which type of housing will best meet your retirement needs? Is such housing available in your community? Make a checklist of the advantages and disadvantages of your housing choice.  (Obj. 4)

6. *Writing Letters to Representatives in Congress.* Write a letter urging your representative in Congress to introduce or support legislation repealing the provisions of the present Social Security law that limit the earnings of Americans ages 65 to 69 who must work to provide for their needs.  (Obj. 5)

7. *Requesting Personal Earnings and Benefits Statement.* Obtain Form SSA-7004 from your local Social Security office. Complete and mail the form to receive a personal earnings and benefits statement. Use the information in this statement to plan your retirement.  (Obj. 5)

8. *Balancing a Retirement Budget.* Outline the steps you must take to live on your retirement income and balance your retirement budget.  (Obj. 6)

# LIFE SITUATION CASE

## TO BE YOUNG, THRIFTY, AND IN THE BLACK: THE IMPORTANCE OF STARTING EARLY

Ann Farrell, a 28-year-old hydrogeologist, is one of the lucky ones. As a senior at Smith College in 1991, Farrell attended a seminar on investing early for retirement. "I remembered the figures if you started saving when you were young," she says. Indeed, the payoff is huge. Through compounding, 25-year-olds who invest $2,000 a year and stop at 34 will earn $142,000 more by the time they are 65 than someone who begins investing $2,000 at 35 and contributes $2,000 each year for the next 30 years, according to T. Rowe Price Associates.

Farrell already has $22,000 in her 401(k). That's a nice start compared to most of her peers. Public Agenda, a New York-based market research firm, found that nearly 70 percent of polled adults ages 22 to 32 had saved less than $10,000 for retirement.

When Farrell was a new employee in 1991 at Roux Associates, an environmental consulting firm in Methuen, Massachusetts, she was barred for a year from the company's Fidelity-managed 401(k) plan. Once eligible, she committed 8 percent of her paycheck in the two most aggressive stock funds offered (retirement growth and asset manager). The company matched 50 percent of her pretax contributions, up to 5 percent of her $28,000 salary.

Of course, it helped that her expenses were low. After graduation, Farrell—with only $500 to her name—moved back in with her parents, who charged her $200 a month for rent. She also traveled three out of every four weeks for work. "There is nowhere to spend money on the road," she claims. Still, she had to repay a $10,000 school loan and a $4,000 car loan. She also wanted to build an emergency slush fund. Once she began making headway on these goals, Farrell moved to her own place and gradually increased her pretax contribution to 10 percent. Last year, she upped it to 13 percent (the maximum) of her annual salary, which has hit $40,000). The government allows employees to make a pretax contribution of up to $9,500 a year. Farrell is currently chipping in about $5,000 a year.

Oddly, the lack of growth in environmental consulting has worked to Farrell's benefit. While most Gen-Xers find themselves job hopping every two years or so to get ahead, Farrell stayed put because there wasn't much movement in her industry. So she will become fully vested in her 401(k) this October, after five years in the plan.

But Farrell hasn't exhausted all her retirement savings possibilities. Even though IRA contributions are fully tax deductible only if a single person makes less than $35,000 a year ($50,000 for joint filers), Farrell can still benefit from the tax-deferred growth of the interest on her annual $2,000 contribution. For example, if she contributes $2,000 a year for 30 years, Farrell will earn $47,000 more in a nonde-ductible IRA than in a taxable account, assuming a 28 percent federal tax rate, according to T. Rowe Price Associates.

Farrell has done a lot right, but she has a long road ahead of her. When she makes her next move—she may leave her company and go to business school—she needs to recognize the potholes that exist when protecting her retirement assets. For instance, if she decides to roll over her 401(k), she'll have to examine all of the investment options and rollover requirements. If she doesn't, she could lose her head start on retirement savings.

## Questions

1. What did Ann Farrell learn when she attended a seminar on retirement?
2. How much money did Farrell originally commit to her 401(k) plan? In what funds did she invest her money?
3. What is the maximum contribution Farrell can make to her 401(k) plan?
4. After how long and when did Farrell become fully vested in her 401(k) plan?

SOURCE: Adapted from Toddi Guttner, "To Be Young, Thrifty, and in the Black," *Business Week,* July 21, 1997, p. 76.

## INTERNET CASE   Home Sweet Home

Last year, Inez Gardner noticed that her 87-year-old mother, Mamie, wasn't herself anymore. She would leave the phone off the hook, forget to turn off the oven, and get lost even in familiar places. Gardner, 43, an accountant with the State of Illinois, lived with her mother in Mamie's Evanston, Illinois, home. "My mother had made it clear to us years ago that she wanted to remain in her home," says Gardner. But how could she fulfill that wish and still ensure her mother's safety? It took months, but Gardner and her brothers and sisters found

a solution: a nearby adult day care center where their mother could spend each weekday engaged in a host of supervised activities, such as gardening or sculpting, then return home in the late afternoon. "I don't know how we could have helped her stay at home otherwise," says Gardner. "And she's really happy."

The following table lists several resources that can help people find services for aging family members who choose to live at home:

| Resource | Description |
|---|---|
| **Careguide.com** <br> www.careguide.com | Offers information and assistance in finding and paying for care |
| **Eldercare Locator** <br> 1–800–677–1116 <br> www.aoa.dhhs.gov/elderpage/locator.html | Makes referrals for home care and community services through toll-free number |
| **Extendedcare.com** <br> www.extendcare.com | Search for providers and do research through its online geriatric library |
| **National Association for Home Care** <br> 202–547–7424 <br> www.nahc.org | Features an extensive home care provider locator |
| **National Association of Professional Geriatric Care Managers** <br> 520–881–8008 <br> www.caremanager.org | Find a member list on its website, or order a print directory for $15 |

## Questions

1. For most families, the options for elder care are so numerous that deciding which to use can be bewildering. Do you think Inez made the right choice for her mother?
2. Visit the websites listed in this case. What does each site offer for elderly individuals like Mamie who choose to remain at home?

SOURCE: Adapted from Anne Field, "The Best Old-Age Home May Be at Home," *Business Week,* November 22, 1999, pp. 180–82. Reprinted from the July 21, 1997 issue of *Business Week* by special permission. © 1999 McGraw-Hill Companies, Inc.

## Creating an E-Plan: Financial Decisions Using the Web

### PLANNING FOR RETIREMENT

Long-term financial security is a common goal of most people. Retirement planning should consider both personal decisions (location, housing, activities) and financial factors (investments, pensions, living expenses).

Websites for Retirement Planning

- Retirement planning articles and assistance at **www.lifenet.com** and **www.savingsnet.com.**
- Social Security Administration information and forms at **www.ssa.gov.**
- Roth IRA information at **www.rothira.com** and **www.pensionplanners.com.**
- Information about pension plans at **www.401k.com** and **www.wwebcom.com/retire.**
- Useful investment and retirement planning assistance from American Express at **www.americanexpress.com/401k,** John Hancock at **www.jhancock.com,** Fidelity Investments at **www.personal.fidelity.com/retirement/ toolkit.html,** and T. Rowe Price at **www.troweprice.com/ retirement/retire.html**.
- Retirement and other information from the American Association of Retired Persons at **www.aarp.org.**
- Current retirement articles from *Money* magazine at **www.money.com,** *Kiplinger's Personal Finance Magazine* at **www.kiplinger. com,** *Business Week*

at **www. businessweek.com,** *Worth* magazine at **www.worth.com,** and *Smart Money* at **www.smartmoney.com.**

(Note: Addresses and content of websites change, and new sites are created daily. Use search engines to update and locate websites for your current financial planning needs.)

*PFP sheets: 62–64*

Short-Term Financial Planning Activities

1. Identify personal and financial retirement needs for various stages of your life.
2. Compare the benefits and costs of a traditional IRA, a Roth IRA, and other pension plans (see PFP Sheet 63).

Long-Term Financial Planning Activities

1. Research costs and benefits of various housing alternatives (see PFP Sheet 62).
2. Estimate future retirement income needs and identify appropriate investments to meet those needs (see PFP Sheet 64).
3. Develop a plan for expanding personal interests and increasing contributions to retirement accounts.

# 19

# Estate Planning

## A Plan for the Endgame

Hugh Finn of Louisville, Kentucky, talked to his lawyer about drafting a living will, but never completed one. Then, in 1995, he suffered severe brain damage in an automobile accident and spent three years in a persistent vegetative state. Last year, after his wife moved him to a Virginia nursing home to be close to his parents, she requested that his feeding tube be removed. Other family members objected, and the state of Virginia joined them. The device eventually was withdrawn, and Finn died—but only after an agonizing legal battle that tore his family apart. As a result of that case, some Virginia legislators are trying to restrict family members from making life-and-death decisions for patients who cannot choose for themselves.

Imagine suffering a stroke or being left in a coma as a result of an auto accident. Would you want to be kept on life support, fed through a tube, or given pain-controlling drugs, even if it hastened your death? You have the right to make these choices. But in most states, you must do so in writing. You'll need two documents, called *advanced directives:* a living will that tells doctors and hospitals how you want to be cared for should you become terminally ill, and a health care proxy who designates an advocate who can make sure your wishes are honored. Says Jim Towey, president of the nonprofit group Aging With Dignity: "People have to look at the endgame—and not just in terms of dollars and cents."

Living wills do not give a hospital the right to "pull the plug" without consent of a patient's legal representative. In most states, a decision to end life support requires the approval of two doctors, who must certify that there is no hope of recovery. If you want doctors to exhaust every effort to keep you alive, no matter what, you can also request that in a living will. "You can say: 'I don't want anything done,' or you can

say: 'I want absolutely everything,'" says Bethesda, Maryland, attorney Marilyn Kressel. Whatever its contents, a living will is one legal document that should not be kept in your safe-deposit box. Give copies to your lawyer, your doctor, and your adult children, and take one to the hospital on your next visit.

Putting your wishes in writing does not guarantee that a hospital will honor them, however. To make sure it does, you'll need to appoint a legal representative, usually a relative or friend, who can handle your health care decisions if you cannot. You make this choice by executing a designation of health care proxy, health care surrogate, or medical power of attorney. You might want to make your spouse your representative.

## Questions

1. How can you protect your wishes and your peace of mind with a living will? Visit the U.S. Living Will Registry website at www.uslivingwillregistry.com. The registry electronically stores your wishes and makes them available directly to hospitals.
2. Would you want to be kept on life support? Why or why not?
3. In your opinion, who should have the right to make life-and-death decisions?
4. What two documents do most states need in writing?
5. Should you keep your living will in a safe-deposit box? Why or why not?

SOURCE: Adapted from Howard Gleckman, "A Plan for the Endgame," *Business Week,* March 1, 1999, p. 117. Reprinted from the March 1, 1999 issue of *Business Week* by special permission. © 1999 McGraw-Hill Companies, Inc.

## Learning Objectives

**Obj. 1**   Analyze the personal aspects of estate planning.

**Obj. 2**   Assess the legal aspects of estate planning.

**Obj. 3**   Distinguish among various types and formats of wills.

**Obj. 4**   Appraise various types of trusts and estates.

**Obj. 5**   Evaluate the effects of federal and state taxes on estate planning.

## WHY ESTATE PLANNING?

**Obj. 1**
Analyze the personal aspects of estate planning.

*estate*   Everything one owns.

Your **estate** consists of everything you own. While you work, your objective is to accumulate funds for your future and for your dependents. As you grow older, your point of view will change. The emphasis in your financial planning will shift from accumulating assets to distributing them wisely. Your hard-earned wealth should go to those whom you wish to support and not to the various taxing agencies.

Contrary to widely held notions, estate planning, which includes wills and trusts, is useful not only to rich and elderly people. Trusts can be used for purposes other than tax advantages, such as choosing a guardian for children and avoiding family fights over personal belongings. Furthermore, most people can afford the expense of using them.

This chapter discusses a subject most people would rather avoid: death—your own or that of your spouse. Many people give little or no thought to setting their personal and financial affairs in order.

As you learned in the previous chapter, most people today live longer than those of previous generations and have ample time to think about and plan for the future. Yet a large percentage of people do little or nothing to provide for those who will survive them.

Planning for your family's financial security in the event of your death or the death of your spouse is not easy. Therefore, the objective of this chapter is to help you initiate discussions about questions you should ask before that happens. Does your spouse, for instance, know what all of the family's resources and debts are? Does your family have enough insurance protection?

The question of whether your family can cope financially without your or your spouse's income and support is a difficult one. This chapter can't provide all of the answers, but it supplies a basis for sound estate planning for you and your family.

### What Is Estate Planning?

*estate planning*
A definite plan for the administration and disposition of one's property during one's lifetime and at one's death.

**Estate planning** is a definite plan for the administration and disposition of one's property during one's lifetime and at one's death. Thus, it involves both handling your property while you are alive and dealing with what happens to that property after your death.

Estate planning is an essential part of retirement planning and an integral part of financial planning. It has two components. The first consists of building your estate through savings, investments, and insurance. The second involves transferring your estate, at your death, in the manner you have specified. As this chapter explains, an estate plan is usually implemented by a will and one or more trust agreements.

Nearly every adult engages in financial decision making and must keep important records. Whatever your status—single or married, male or female, taxi driver or corporate executive—you must make financial decisions that are important to you. Those decisions may be even more important to others in your family. Knowledge in certain areas and good recordkeeping can simplify those decisions.

At first, planning for financial security and estate planning may seem complicated. Although many money matters require legal and technical advice, if you and your spouse learn the necessary skills, you will find yourselves managing your money affairs more efficiently and wisely. Begin by answering the questionnaire in the Financial Planning for Life's Situations box on page 609 to see how much you and your family know about your own money affairs. You and your family should be able to answer some of these questions. The questions can be bewildering if the subjects are unfamiliar to you, but after reading this chapter, you'll be able to answer most of them.

## If You Are Married

If you are married, your estate planning involves the interests of at least two people, and more if you have children. Legal requirements and responsibilities can create problems for married people that are entirely different than those of single people. Situations become more complex. Possessions accumulate. The need for orderliness and clarity increases.

Your death will mean a new lifestyle for your spouse. If you have no children or if the children are grown and lead separate lives, your spouse will once again be single. The surviving spouse must confront problems of grief and adjustment. Daily life must continue. At the same time, the estate must be settled. If not, catastrophic financial consequences may result.

If children survive you, making sure that your estate can be readily analyzed and distributed may be even more critical. If relatives or friends are beneficiaries, bequests have to be made known quickly and clearly.

Your desires and information about your estate have to be accessible, understandable, and legally documented. Otherwise, your beneficiaries may encounter problems and your intentions may not be carried out.

## If You Never Married

Never having been married does not eliminate the need to organize your financial affairs. For people who live alone, as for married people, it is essential that important documents and personal information be consolidated and accessible.

Remember that in the event of your death, difficult questions and situations will confront some person at a time of severe emotional strain. That person may not be prepared to face them objectively. Probably the single most important thing you can do is take steps to see that your beneficiaries have the information and the knowledge they need to survive emotionally and financially when you die.

Everyone should take such steps. However, the need to take them is especially great if you are only 5 or 10 years away from retirement. By then, your possessions will probably be of considerable value. Your savings and checking account balances will probably be substantial. Your investment plans will have materialized. If you stop and take a look at where you are, you may be pleasantly surprised at the value of your estate.

# Financial Planning for Life's Situations

### ESTATE PLANNING CHECKLIST

Do you and your family members know the answers to the following questions?

1. Where are your previous years' income tax returns?
2. Where is your safe-deposit box located? Where is the key to it kept?
3. What kinds and amounts of life insurance protection do you have?
4. Can you locate your insurance policies—life, health, property, casualty, and auto?
5. Who are the beneficiaries and contingent beneficiaries of your life insurance policies?
6. What type of health insurance protection do you have, and what are the provisions of your health insurance policy?
7. Do you and your spouse have current wills? Who was the attorney who drafted them? Where are they kept?
8. Do you have a separate record of the important papers you keep in your safe-deposit box? Where is this record located?
9. Do you have a record of your spouse's and children's Social Security numbers?
10. Where is your marriage certificate and the birth certificates of all members of your family?
11. Do you know the name and address of your life insurance agent?
12. Do you know the principal financial resources and liabilities of your estate?
13. Are you knowledgeable about simple, daily, and compound interest rates? About retirement funds and property ownership?
14. Have you given any thought to funerals and burial arrangements?
15. What papers and records will be important to other people when you die?
16. Do you understand the functions of a bank trust department and the meaning of joint ownership?

SOURCE: *Planning with Your Beneficiaries* (Washington, DC: American Council of Life Insurance, Education, and Community Services, n.d.), p. 2.

## New Lifestyles

Millions of nontraditional households have unique estate planning problems. Nearly half of all American marriages end in divorce, creating difficulties for millions of adults contemplating estate planning. Single parents and other single persons all have formidable estate planning challenges. Financial planners and estate attorneys universally offer such households the following smart advice: Plan early, and get expert help. The law provides plenty of protection for married couples, but it is rife with pitfalls for almost everyone else.[1]

Single parents, divorced or not, must plan for their own death as part of retirement and estate planning. David Scott Sloan, chairman of trusts and estates at Sherburne, Powers & Needham, a law firm in Boston, says that simply leaving money to your children can result in a huge estate tax bill, sharply decreasing the funds available if your estate is worth more than $675,000 in 2000 and 2001. Sloan recommends setting up a trust for the children's benefit.

Unmarried couples face formidable retirement and estate planning challenges. A partner lacks any legal right to the companion's assets upon the companion's disability or death or upon the breakup of the partnership. Unmarried couples also cannot use the

**Sheet 65**

so-called marital deduction, which allows spouses to pass on everything they own to their surviving spouse tax free. Only the first $675,000 of an unmarried partner's assets is exempt from estate taxes. Estate planning is even more important for unmarried couples. For example, if no beneficiary is named on your pension plan, the plan sponsor is required to give the proceeds to your closest blood relative. If you want your partner to receive the plan proceeds after you die, make sure he or she is named the beneficiary. Also, check to see if the plan allows unmarried partners to receive joint-and-survivor benefits.

## The Opportunity Cost of Rationalizing

Daily living often gets in the way of thinking about death. You mean to organize things that others need to know in case you die, but you haven't done this yet. One of your rationalizations may be that you are not sure what information you need to provide.

Think about the outcome of your delay. Your beneficiary will meet people who offer specific types of assistance—morticians, clergy, lawyers, insurance agents, clerks of federal government agencies, and so on. These people will probably be strangers—sympathetic, courteous, and helpful, but disinterested. Also, your bereaved beneficiary may find it difficult to reveal confidences to them. Today, however, the information survivors need is as close as the Internet. Visit LIMRA International's home page at www.limra.com, and click on the cover of the booklet, *What Do You Do Now?* LIMRA, a financial services research organization, provides the information free as a public service.

The moral is to plan your estate while you are in good health and think through the provisions carefully. Last-minute "death-bed" estate planning may fail to carry out your wishes.

### Concept Check 19-1

1.  If you needed information about estate planning, would you go to the library or the Internet? Why?
2.  Why is estate planning an important component of financial planning?
3.  Why is estate planning important for single as well as married individuals? For "new" lifestyle individuals?

## LEGAL ASPECTS OF ESTATE PLANNING

### Obj. 2
Assess the legal aspects of estate planning.

When death occurs, proof of claims must be produced or the claims will not be processed. If no thought was given to gathering the necessary documents beforehand (with a sufficient number of copies), a period of financial hardship may follow until proof is obtained. If needed documentation cannot be located, irretrievable loss of funds may occur. Your heirs may experience emotionally painful delays until their rights have been established.

Important papers include the following:

1.  Birth certificates—yours, your spouse's, and your children's.
2.  Marriage certificates—always important, but especially important if you or your spouse were married previously—and divorce papers.
3.  Legal name changes—judgment of court documents pertaining to any legal changes in the names that appear on birth certificates (especially important to protect the adopted children of a previous marriage or children who have been adopted through adoption agencies).

4.  Military service records—the standard DD–214 (Armed Forces of the United States Report of Transfer or Discharge) or any other official statement of your military service details, if appropriate.

Here is a list of additional important documents :

- Social Security documents.
- Veteran documents.
- Insurance policies.
- Transfer records of joint bank accounts.
- Safe-deposit box records.
- Registration of automobiles.
- Title to stock and bond certificates.

You should have several copies of certain documents because when you submit a claim, the accompanying proof often becomes a permanent part of the claim file and is not returned. Remember too that in some circumstances, children may be required to furnish proof of their parents' birth, marriage, or divorce.

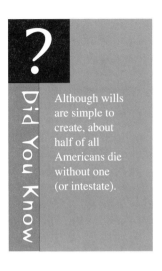

Did You Know ?

Although wills are simple to create, about half of all Americans die without one (or intestate).

## Wills

*will*   The legal declaration of a person's mind as to the disposition of his or her property after death.

One of the most vital documents every adult should have is a written will. A **will** is the legal declaration of a person's mind as to the disposition of his or her property after death. Thus, a will is a way to transfer your property according to your wishes after you die.

Whether you prepare a will before you die or neglect to take that sensible step, you still have a will. If you fail to prepare your own will, the state in which you legally reside steps in and controls the distribution of your estate without regard for wishes you may have had but failed to define in legal form. Thus, if you die **intestate**—without a valid will—the state's law of descent and distribution becomes your copy of the will, as shown in Exhibit 19–1 on page 612.

*intestate*   Without a valid will.

Consider the opportunity cost of a husband and father who died without a will. By default, he has authorized his estate to be disposed of according to the provisions of the fictitious document in Exhibit 19–1. The wording in this exhibit represents a pattern of distribution that could occur unless you prepare a valid will specifying otherwise.

This does not happen only to a husband. It could happen to anyone. To avoid such consequences, make a will! Consulting an attorney for this purpose can spare your heirs many difficulties, especially since the passage of the Economic Recovery Tax Act of 1981. This act created estate planning opportunities and problems for many people. It also created some difficult choices as to types of wills.

### The Effect of Marriage or Divorce on Your Will   If you already have a will and are about to be married or divorced, review your will with an attorney for necessary changes. Upon divorce, only provisions favoring a former spouse are automatically revoked; provisions favoring family members of your ex-spouse, such as stepchildren, nieces, nephews, or in-laws, are not affected.

If you marry after you have made a will, the will is revoked automatically unless certain conditions are met. For example, marriage does not revoke a will if

- The will indicates an intent that it not be revoked by a subsequent marriage.
- The will was drafted under circumstances indicating that it was in contemplation of marriage.

Because your existing will's legal status may be uncertain, you are better off drawing a new will to fit your new circumstances.

EXHIBIT 19-1

The Opportunity
Cost of Not Making
a Will, or What
Will the State Do
to Your Property If
You Die Intestate?

## My Last Will and Testament

Being of sound mind and memory, I, _____, do hereby publish this as my last Will and Testament.

FIRST

I give my wife only one third of my possessions, and I give my children the remaining two thirds.

A. I appoint my wife as guardian of my children, but as a safeguard I require that she report to the Probate Court each year and render an accounting of how, why, and where she spent the money necessary for the proper care of my children.

B. As a further safeguard, I direct my wife to produce to the Probate Court a Performance Bond to guarantee that she exercise proper judgment in the handling, investing, and spending of the children's money.

C. As a final safeguard, my children shall have the right to demand and receive a complete accounting from their mother of all of her financial actions with their money as soon as they reach legal age.

D. When my children reach age 18, they shall have full rights to withdraw and spend their shares of my estate. No one shall have any right to question my children's actions on how they decide to spend their respective shares.

SECOND

Should my wife remarry, her second husband shall be entitled to one third of everything my wife possesses. Should my children need some of this share for their support, the second husband shall not be bound to spend any part of his share on my children's behalf.

A. The second husband shall have the sole right to decide who is to get his share, even to the exclusion of my children.

THIRD

Should my wife predecease me or die while any of my children are minors, I do not wish to exercise my right to nominate the guardian of my children.

A. Rather than nominating a guardian of my preference, I direct my relatives and friends to get together and select a guardian by mutual agreement.

B. In the event that they fail to agree on a guardian, I direct the Probate Court to make the selection. If the court wishes, it may appoint a stranger acceptable to it.

FOURTH

Under existing tax law, certain legitimate avenues are open to me to lower death rates. Since I prefer to have my money used for government purposes rather than for the benefit of my wife and children, I direct that no effort be made to lower taxes.

IN WITNESS WHEREOF, I have set my hand to this, my LAST WILL AND TESTAMENT, this _____ day of _____ 20 _____.

**Cost of a Will**   Legal fees for drafting a will vary with the complexities of your estate and family situation. A standard will costs between $200 and $350. The price varies from place to place, but generally the cost of writing a will is less than that for writing a living trust (to be discussed later in the chapter). Look for an attorney experienced in drafting wills and in estate planning.

## Concept Check 19-2

1. What are the legal aspects of estate planning?
2. What is a will? Why is it an important estate planning tool?
3. How does marriage or divorce affect a will?

# TYPES AND FORMATS OF WILLS     Types of Wills

## Obj. 3

Distinguish among various types and formats of wills.

*simple will*   A will that leaves everything to the spouse; also called an *I love you will.*

A brief review of the types of wills will be helpful, since the tax effects of these wills differ. The four types of wills are the simple will, the traditional marital share will, the exemption trust will, and the stated dollar amount will.

### Simple Will

A **simple will,** sometimes called an *I love you will,* leaves everything to the spouse. Such a will is sufficient for most smaller estates. However, if you have a large or complex estate, especially one involving business interests that you want to pass on to your children, a simple will may not meet your objectives. It may also create higher overall taxation, because everything would be taxed in your spouse's subsequent estate.

For example, in 2001, if your estate was $1.35 million and you left it all to your spouse, there would be no tax at your death. However, there would be a tax of $235,000 at your spouse's death, assuming the value of the estate remains constant. To avoid this, you could use a two-part marital will to split your estate into two halves, resulting in no tax at either death. If your spouse had separate property or if the value of your estate increased, the simple will would create higher taxation.

*traditional marital share will*   A will in which the grantor leaves one-half of the adjusted gross estate to the spouse.

*adjusted gross estate*   The gross estate minus debts and costs.

### Traditional Marital Share Will

The **traditional marital share will** leaves one-half of the **adjusted gross estate** (the gross estate minus debts and costs) to the spouse outright as a marital share. The other half of the adjusted gross estate might go to children or other heirs or be held in trust for the family. A trust can provide the spouse with a lifelong income and would not be taxed at the spouse's death.

Under this type of will, half of your estate is taxed at your death and half at your spouse's death. This results in the lowest overall amount of federal estate taxes on estates above a certain size (twice the exemption amount). However, there are other considerations. State inheritance taxes may be greater, especially at the first death, due to conflicting federal and state exemption and beneficiary classifications. Also, under this type of will, unlike a simple will or an exemption trust, federal estate taxes may have to be paid up front at the first death that will involve the loss of use of money. If your spouse has considerable assets in his or her own right, it might not be prudent to increase your spouse's estate by any amount. In such a situation, a will that equalizes estates might be better. Finally, the nine community-property states severely limit your options as to how to allocate your money.

*exemption trust will*   A will in which everything passes to the spouse except the exemption ($675,000 in 2001).

*probate*   The legal procedure of proving a valid or invalid will.

### Exemption Trust Will

The **exemption trust will** has been gaining in popularity due to its increased exemption ($675,000 since 2000; increases to $1 million by 2006). Under this type of will, everything passes to your spouse with the exception of an amount equal to the exemption, which would pass into trust. The amount passed to your spouse can be by will, trust, or other means. The exemption trust can provide your spouse with a lifelong income.

**Probate** is the legal procedure of proving a valid or invalid will. It is the process by which an executor manages and distributes your property after you die according to your will's provisions. A probate court generally validates wills and makes sure debts are paid. You should avoid probate because it is expensive, lengthy, and public. As you'll read later, a living trust avoids probate and is less expensive, quicker, and private.

There would be little or no tax at your death due to the combination of the exemption and the marital deduction. The exemption amount and any appreciation on it would not be taxed on your spouse's estate.

The main advantage of the exemption trust will is that it eliminates future taxation of the exemption amount and any growth in it. This may be an important factor if property values appreciate considerably.

### Stated Dollar Amount Will

*stated dollar amount will* A will that allows you to pass on to your spouse any amount that satisfies your family objectives.

The **stated dollar amount will** allows you to pass on to your spouse any amount that satisfies your family objectives. These objectives may or may not include tax considerations. For example, you could pass the stated amount of $675,000 (in 2000 and 2001). However, the stated amount might be related to anticipated income needs or to the value of personal items.

State law may dictate how much you must leave your spouse. Most states require that your spouse receive a certain amount, usually one-half or one-third. Some states require that such interests pass outright, and others permit life interests. The stated dollar amount will may satisfy such requirements and pass the balance to others. You may, for example, decide to pass most of your estate to your children, thereby avoiding subsequent taxation of your spouse's estate. It may also make sense to pass interests in a business to children who are involved in the business.

Such plans may increase taxes at your death, since not all of your property passes to your spouse. However, the taxes at your spouse's subsequent death would be lower. You can also leave your spouse an outright amount equal to the exemption with a life estate in the balance, or a life estate in trust.

The stated dollar amount has one major shortcoming: The will may leave specific dollar amounts to listed heirs and the balance to the surviving spouse. Although these amounts may be reasonable when the will is drafted, they can soon become obsolete. What if estate values suddenly decrease due to a business setback or a drop in the stock market? Consider an individual with an extensive equities portfolio who drafted a will in September 1987. After the October 17 market crash, the value of the portfolio may have shrunk by one-third. None of that decrease will be borne by those who were left specific dollar amounts. The entire decrease will be borne by the surviving spouse. Therefore, you should use percentages instead of designated amounts.[2]

### Which Type of Will Is Best for You?

The four types of wills just discussed are your basic choices. Which one is best for you?

Prior to the Economic Recovery Tax Act of 1981, many experts advocated the traditional marital share will. Today many attorneys believe the exemption trust will is best. However, there is no one ideal will. Which will is best for you depends on factors such as the size of your estate, the future appreciation of your estate, inflation, the respective ages of you and your spouse, cash on hand, and—most important—your objectives.

## Formats of Wills

*holographic will* A handwritten will.

*formal will* A will that is usually prepared with an attorney's assistance.

*beneficiary* A person who has been named to receive property under a will.

*statutory will* A formal will on a preprinted form.

Wills may be holographic or formal. A **holographic will** is a handwritten will that you prepare yourself. It should be written, dated, and signed entirely in your handwriting; no printed or typed information should be on its pages. Some states, however, may not recognize a holographic will.

A **formal will** is usually prepared with an attorney's assistance. It may be either typed or on a preprinted form. You must sign the will and acknowledge it as your will in the presence of two witnesses, neither of whom is a **beneficiary** (a person you have named to receive property under the will). The witnesses must then sign the will in your presence.

A **statutory will** is one type of formal will. It is a preprinted form that may be obtained from lawyers and stationery stores. There are serious risks in using this or any

# Financial Planning for Life's Situations

## THE 10 COMMANDMENTS OF MAKING YOUR WILL

1. Work closely with your spouse as you prepare your will. Seek professional help so that your family objectives can be met regardless of who dies first.

2. Write your will to conform with your current wishes. When your circumstances change (for example, when you retire or move to another state), review your will and, if appropriate, write a new one.

3. Do not choose a beneficiary as a witness. If such a person is called on to validate your will, he or she may not be able to collect an inheritance.

4. If you are remarrying, consider signing a prenuptial agreement to protect your children. If you sign such an agreement before the wedding, you and your intended spouse can legally agree that neither of you will make any claim on the other's estate. The agreement can be revoked later, if you both agree.

5. Consider using percentages rather than dollar amounts when you divide your estate. For example, if you leave $15,000 to a friend and the rest to your spouse, your spouse will suffer if your estate shrinks to $17,000.

6. Both you and your spouse should have a will, and those wills should be separate documents.

7. Be flexible. Don't insist that your heirs keep stock or run a cattle ranch. If you do so, they may suffer if economic conditions change.

8. Sign the original copy of your will and keep it in a safe place; keep an unsigned copy at home for reference.

9. Alter your will by preparing a new will or adding a codicil. Don't change beneficiaries by writing on the will itself; this may invalidate the will.

10. Select an executor or executrix who is both willing and able to carry out the complicated tasks associated with the job.

other preprinted form. One risk is that such a form usually requires you to conform to rigid provisions, some of which may not be in the best interests of your beneficiaries. Also, if you change the preprinted wording, you may violate the law regarding wills, which may cause the changed sections or even the entire will to be declared invalid. There is also a risk that the form is out of date with respect to current law. It is always prudent to seek legal assistance in developing these documents.

## Writing Your Will

The way to transfer your property according to your wishes is to write a will specifying those wishes. Joint ownership is no substitute for a will. Although jointly owned property passes directly to the joint owner and may be appropriate for some assets, such as your home, only a will allows you to distribute your property as a whole exactly as you wish. Select a person who will follow your instructions (your *executor* or *executrix*). By naming your own executor, you will eliminate the need for a court-appointed administrator, prevent unnecessary delay in the distribution of your property, and minimize estate taxes and settlement costs. See the accompanying Financial Planning for Life's Situations feature for guidance on important aspects of making a will.

**? Did You Know**

Who can be an executor? Any U.S. citizen over 18 who has not been convicted of a felony can be named the executor of a will.

**Selecting an Executor**    Select an executor or executrix who is both willing and able to carry out the complicated tasks associated with executing a will. These tasks are preparing an inventory of assets, collecting any money due, paying off any debts, preparing and filing all income and estate tax returns, liquidating and reinvesting

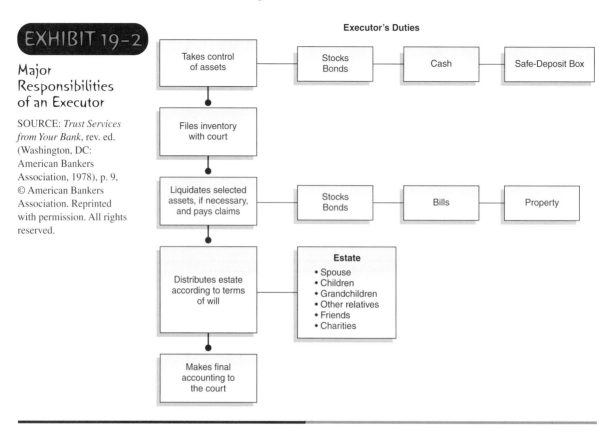

**EXHIBIT 19–2**

Major
Responsibilities
of an Executor

SOURCE: *Trust Services from Your Bank*, rev. ed. (Washington, DC: American Bankers Association, 1978), p. 9, © American Bankers Association. Reprinted with permission. All rights reserved.

**Executor's Duties**

- Takes control of assets → Stocks Bonds → Cash → Safe-Deposit Box
- Files inventory with court
- Liquidates selected assets, if necessary, and pays claims → Stocks Bonds → Bills → Property
- Distributes estate according to terms of will → **Estate** • Spouse • Children • Grandchildren • Other relatives • Friends • Charities
- Makes final accounting to the court

other assets to pay off debts and provide income for your family while the estate is being administered, distributing the estate, and making a final accounting to your beneficiaries and to the probate court.

Your executor can be a family member, a friend, an attorney, an accountant, or the trust department of a bank. Fees for executors, whether professionals or friends, are set by state law. Exhibit 19–2 summarizes typical duties of an executor.

### Selecting a Guardian

*guardian*   A person who assumes responsibility for providing children with personal care and managing the deceased's estate for them.

*trustee*   A person or an institution that holds or manages property for the benefit of someone else under a trust agreement.

In addition to disposing of your estate, your will should name a guardian and/or trustee to care for minor children if both parents die at the same time, such as in an automobile accident or a plane crash. A **guardian** is a person who assumes the responsibilities of providing the children with personal care and of managing the estate for them. A **trustee,** on the other hand, is a person or an institution that holds or generally manages property for the benefit of someone else under a trust agreement.

You should take great care in selecting a guardian for your children. You want a guardian whose philosophy on raising children is similar to yours and who is willing to accept the responsibility.

Most states require a guardian to post a bond with the probate court. The bonding company promises to reimburse the minor's estate up to the amount of the bond if the guardian uses the property of the minor for his or her own gain. The bonding fee (usually several hundred dollars) is paid from the estate. However, you can waive the bonding requirement in your will.

Through your will, you may want to provide funds to raise your children. You could, for instance, leave a lump sum for an addition to the guardian's house and establish monthly payments to cover your children's living expenses.

The guardian of the minor's estate manages the property you leave behind for your children. This guardian can be a person or the trust department of a financial institution, such as a bank. Property that you place in trust for your children can be managed by the trustee rather than by the guardian of the minor's estate.

## Altering or Rewriting Your Will

**Sheet 66**

Sometimes you will need to change provisions of your will. Consider one change involving the marital deduction. The old law limited the amount you could pass to your spouse tax free to one-half of your adjusted gross estate. But the Economic Recovery Tax Act of 1981 created an unlimited marital deduction. You can now pass any amount to your spouse tax free.

If you do have a will, you should review it. This is necessary even if you have already done some planning and your will refers to the old 50 percent marital deduction. Why? The new 100 percent marital deduction is not automatic. Congress would not alter or rewrite your will; this task was left to you. Therefore, unless you change your will or unless your state passes a law making the new definition applicable, you will have to rewrite your will to make the unlimited marital deduction apply. Because many choices are of a personal nature, few, if any, states will get involved. For example, some people may not want to leave the entire estate to their spouse, perhaps for valid tax reasons.

You should review your will if you move to a different state; if you have sold property mentioned in the will; if the size and composition of your estate have changed; if you have married, divorced, or remarried; or if new potential heirs have died or been born.

Don't make any changes on the face of your will. Additions, deletions, or erasures on a will that has been signed and witnessed can invalidate the will.

*codicil*   A document that modifies provisions in an existing will.

If only a few changes are needed in your will, adding a codicil may be the best choice. A **codicil** is a document that explains, adds, or deletes provisions in your existing will. It identifies the will being amended and confirms the unchanged sections of the will. To be valid, it must conform to the legal requirements for a will.

If you wish to make major changes in your will or if you have already added a codicil, preparing a new will is preferable to adding a new codicil. In the new will, include a clause revoking all earlier wills and codicils.

*prenuptial agreement*
A documentary agreement between spouses before marriage.

If you are rewriting a will because of a remarriage, consider drafting a **prenuptial agreement.** This is a documentary agreement between spouses before marriage. In such agreements, one or both parties often waive a right to receive property under the other's will or under state law. Be sure to consult an attorney in drafting a prenuptial agreement.

Wills have existed for thousands of years; the oldest known will was written by the Egyptian pharaoh Uah in 2448 B.C. Recently a new type of will, called a *living will,* has emerged.

## A Living Will

*living will*   A document that enables an individual, while well, to express the intention that life be allowed to end if he or she becomes terminally ill.

A **living will** provides for your wishes to be followed if you become so physically or mentally disabled that you are unable to act on your own behalf. A living will is not a substitute for a traditional will. It enables an individual, while well, to express the

## A Living Will: Example 1

SOURCE: *Don't Wait until Tomorrow* (Hartford, CT: Aetna Life and Casualty Company, n.d.), p. 10.

**To My Family, My Physician, My Lawyer, My Clergyman;**
**To Any Medical Facility in Whose Care I Happen to Be;**
**To Any Individual Who May Become Responsible for**
**My Health, Welfare, or Affairs:**

Death is as much a reality as birth, growth, maturity, and old age—it is the one certainty of life. If the time comes when I, _____, can no longer take part in decisions for my own future, let this statement stand as an expression of my wishes, while I am still of sound mind.

If the situation should arise in which there is no reasonable expectation of my recovery from physical or mental disability, I request that I be allowed to die and not be kept alive by artificial means or "heroic measures." I do not fear death itself as much as the indignities of deterioration, dependence, and hopeless pain. I, therefore, ask that medication be mercifully administered to me to alleviate suffering even though this may hasten the moment of death.

This request is made after careful consideration. I hope you who care for me will feel morally bound to follow its mandate. I recognize that this appears to place a heavy responsibility upon you, but it is with the intention of relieving you of such responsibility and of placing it upon myself in accordance with my strong convictions that this statement is made.

Signed _____

Date _____

Witness _____

Witness _____

Copies of this request have been given to _____

_____

_____

_____

intention that life be allowed to end if he or she becomes terminally ill. Many states recognize living wills, and you may consider writing one when you draw a conventional will. Exhibits 19–3 and 19–4 on page 619 are examples of typical living wills.

To ensure the effectiveness of a living will, discuss your intention of preparing such a will with the people closest to you. You should also discuss this with your family doctor. Sign and date your document before two witnesses. Witnessing shows that you signed of your own free will.

Give copies of your living will to those closest to you, and have your family doctor place a copy in your medical file. Keep the original document readily accessible, and look it over periodically—preferably once a year—to be sure your wishes have remained unchanged. To verify your intent, redate and initial each subsequent endorsement.

Most lawyers will do the paperwork for a living will at no cost if they are already preparing your estate plan. You can also get the necessary forms from nonprofit advocacy groups. Aging With Dignity (www.agingwithdignity.org) lets you download a free, plain-English version called Five Wishes that's valid in 33 states. The group will mail you one for $4 if you send a check to P.O. Box 1661, Tallahassee, Fla., 32302. Another organization, Choice in Dying, provides documents geared to specified states for $5 (1–800–989–9455; www.choices.org). Working through end-of-life issues is difficult, but it can help avoid forcing your family to make a decision in a hospital waiting room—or worse, having your last wishes ignored.[3]

## EXHIBIT 19-4

**A Living Will: Example 2**

SOURCE: *Don't Wait until Tomorrow* (Hartford, CT: Aetna Life and Casualty Company, n.d.), p. 11.

### Living Will Declaration

Declaration made this _____ day of _____ (month, year)

I, _____, being of sound mind, willfully and voluntarily make known my desire that my dying shall not be artificially prolonged under the circumstances set forth below, do hereby declare

If at any time I should have an incurable injury, disease, or illness regarded as a terminal condition by my physician and if my physician has determined that the application of life-sustaining procedures would serve only to artificially prolong the dying process and that my death will occur whether or not life-sustaining procedures are utilized, I direct that such procedures be withheld or withdrawn and that I be permitted to die with only the administration of medication or the performance of any medical procedure deemed necessary to provide me with comfort care.

In the absence of my ability to give directions regarding the use of such life-sustaining procedures, it is my intention that this declaration shall be honored by my family and physician as the final expression of my legal right to refuse medical or surgical treatment and accept the consequences from such refusal.

I understand the full import of this declaration, and I am emotionally and mentally competent to make this declaration.

Signed _____

City, County, and State of Residence _____

The declarant has been personally known to me, and I believe him or her to be of sound mind.

Witness _____

Witness _____

---

A living will can become a problem. A once-healthy person may have a change of heart and prefer to remain alive even as death seems imminent. Living wills call for careful thought, but they do provide you with a choice as to the manner of your death.

## Power of Attorney

*power of attorney*
A legal document authorizing someone to act on one's behalf.

Related to the concept of a living will is a power of attorney. A **power of attorney** is a legal document authorizing someone to act on your behalf. At some point in your life, you may become ill or incapacitated. You may then wish to have someone attend to your needs and your personal affairs. You can assign a power of attorney to anyone you choose.

The person you name can be given limited power or a great deal of power. The power given can be special—to carry out certain acts or transactions—or it can be general—to act completely for you. A conventional power of attorney is automatically revoked in a case of legal incapacity.

## Letter of Last Instruction

In addition to your will, you should prepare a *letter of last instruction*. This document, though not legally enforceable, can provide your heirs with important information. It should contain the details of your funeral arrangements. It should also contain the names of the people who are to be notified of your death and the locations of your bank accounts, safe-deposit box, and other important items listed on pages 610–611.

1. Distinguish among the four types of wills.
2. What are the two formats of wills?
3. What are the steps in writing your will?
4. What is a power of attorney?
5. What is a letter of last instruction?

## TYPES OF TRUSTS AND ESTATES

### Obj. 4
Appraise various types of trusts and estates.

*trustor*   The creator of a trust; also called the *grantor*.

*trust*   A legal arrangement through which one's assets are held by a trustee.

*revocable trust*   A trust whose terms the trustor retains the rights to change.

*irrevocable trust*
A trust that cannot be altered or ended by its creator.

A trust is a property arrangement in which a trustee, such as a person or a bank trust department, holds title to, takes care of, and in most cases manages property for the benefit of someone else. The creator of the trust is called the **trustor** or *grantor*. A bank, as trustee, charges a modest fee for its services, generally based on the value of the trust assets. All trust assets added together are known as an *estate*.

It is a good idea to discuss with your attorney the possibility of establishing a trust as a means of managing your estate. Basically, a **trust** is a legal arrangement through which a trustee holds your assets for your benefit or that of your beneficiaries. "Trusts today are used for everything from protecting assets from creditors to managing property for young children or disabled elders,"[4] according to one tax attorney.

Trusts are either revocable or irrevocable. If you establish a **revocable trust,** you retain the right to end the trust or change its terms during your lifetime. Revocable trusts avoid the often lengthy probate process, but they do not provide shelter from federal or state estate taxes. You might choose a revocable trust if you think you may need its assets for your own use at a later time or if you want to monitor the performance of the trust and the trustee before the arrangement is made irrevocable by your death. If you establish an **irrevocable trust,** you cannot change its terms or end it. The trust becomes, for tax purposes, a separate entity, and the assets can't be removed, nor can changes be made by the grantor. Irrevocable trusts often are used by individuals with large estates to reduce estate taxes and avoid probate. Therefore, an irrevocable trust offers tax advantages not offered by a revocable trust.

### Benefits of Establishing Trusts

Your individual circumstances dictate whether it makes sense to establish a trust. Here are some common reasons for setting up a trust. You can use a trust to

- Reduce or otherwise provide for payment of estate taxes.
- Avoid probate and transfer your assets immediately to your beneficiaries.
- Free yourself from management of your assets while you receive a regular income from the trust.
- Provide income for a surviving spouse or other beneficiaries.
- Ensure that your property serves a desired purpose after your death.

Trustee services are commonly provided by banks and, in some instances, by life insurance companies. An estate attorney can advise you about the right type of trust for you.

### Types of Trusts

There are many types of trusts. Here we discuss 13 types: credit-shelter trusts, grantor retained annuity trusts, (GRATs), disclaimer trusts, marital-deduction trusts, living trusts, self-declaration trusts, testamentary trusts, life insurance trusts, charitable remainder trusts, qualified personal residence trusts, charitable lead trusts, generation-skipping trusts, and spendthrift trusts. Each of these types has particular advantages. Choose the type of trust that is most appropriate for your family situation.

## Credit-Shelter Trust

*credit-shelter trust*
A trust that allows married couples to leave everything to each other tax free.

A **credit-shelter trust** is perhaps the most common estate planning trust. It is also known as a *bypass trust,* a *"residuary" trust,* an *A/B trust,* an *exemption equivalent trust,* or a *family trust.* It is designed to allow married couples, who can leave everything to each other tax free, to take full advantage of the exemption that allows $675,000 (in 2001) in every estate to pass free of federal estate taxes.

The Taxpayer Relief Act of 1997 increased the exemption amounts to $1 million by the year 2006 as follows:

| | |
|---|---|
| 1999 | $ 650,000 |
| 2000 | 675,000 |
| 2001 | 675,000 |
| 2002 | 700,000 |
| 2003 | 700,000 |
| 2004 | 850,000 |
| 2005 | 950,000 |
| 2006 and thereafter | 1,000,000 |

## Grantor Retained Annuity Trust (GRAT)

*grantor retained annuity trust (GRAT)* A trust that shelters valuable assets that can be passed on to heirs with minimal taxes.

If you are worried about estate taxes, consider one of today's most popular alternatives. A **grantor retained annuity trust (GRAT)** not only shelters valuable assets that you can pass on to your heirs with minimal taxes but also lets you receive an annuity for as long as the trust lasts. With proper planning, assets of under $650,000 for a single person, or $1.3 million for a couple, are exempt from taxes. Therefore, you need a net worth of over $1.3 million ($2.0 million for a couple in 2006) and a lawyer specializing in estate planning to make the GRAT strategy worthwhile.[5]

## Disclaimer Trust

*disclaimer trust*  A trust designed for a couple who does not yet have enough assets to need a credit-shelter trust but may need one in the future.

A **disclaimer trust** is appropriate for a couple who does not yet have enough assets to need a credit-shelter trust but may need one in the future. For example, a newly practicing physician who will soon finish paying off college loans might want to take this approach. With a disclaimer trust, the surviving spouse is left everything, but has the right to disclaim some portion of the estate. Anything disclaimed goes into a credit-shelter trust. This approach gives the surviving spouse the flexibility to shelter any wealth from estate taxes. However, if the estate fails to grow as expected, the survivor isn't locked into a trust structure.[6]

## Marital-Deduction Trust

*marital-deduction trust*
A trust that leaves to the spouse any money that does not go into a credit-shelter trust.

With a **marital-deduction trust,** you can leave to your spouse any money that doesn't go into a credit-shelter trust. Whatever the amount, it is free of estate tax when you die, since it qualifies for the marital deduction. Perhaps the most popular form of marital trust is the *qualified terminable interest property trust,* or *Q-TIP.* Here the surviving spouse gets all trust income, which must be distributed at least once a year, and sometimes receives access to the principal as well. When the spouse dies, the assets go to whomever you specified in the trust documents. The trust assets are then taxed as part of the surviving spouse's estate.[7]

## Living or Inter Vivos Trust

*living trust*  A trust that is created and provides benefits during the trustor's lifetime.

A **living trust,** or *inter vivos trust,* is a property management arrangement that you establish while you are alive. Well-structured estate plans often start with a living trust that becomes irrevocable at death, dividing itself into several other types of trusts, such as a credit-shelter trust. You simply transfer some property to a trustee, giving him or her instructions regarding its management and disposition while you are alive and after your death. A living trust has these advantages:

- It ensures privacy. A will is a public record; a trust is not.
- The property held in the trust avoids probate at your death. It eliminates probate costs and delays.
- It enables you to review your trustee's performance and make changes if necessary.
- It can remove management responsibilities from your shoulders.
- It is less subject to dispute by disappointed heirs than a will is.
- It can guide your family and doctors if you become terminally ill or incompetent.

However, a living trust involves higher costs than creating a will, and funding a trust can be time consuming.

## Self-Declaration Trust

*self-declaration trust*
A variation of the living trust in which the creator of the trust is also the trustee.

A **self-declaration trust** is a variation of the living trust. Its unique feature is that the creator of the trust is also the trustee. The trust document usually includes a procedure for removing the creator of the trust as the trustee without going to court. Typically, one or more physicians or family members, or a combination of physicians and family members, have removal power. If the creator of the trust is removed, a named successor trustee takes over.

## Testamentary Trust

*testamentary trust*
A trust established by the creator's will that becomes effective upon his or her death.

A **testamentary trust** is established by your will and becomes effective upon your death. Such a trust can be valuable if your beneficiaries are inexperienced in financial matters or if the potential estate tax is substantial. Like a living trust, a testamentary trust provides the benefits of asset management, financial bookkeeping, protection of the beneficiaries, and minimizing of estate taxes.

Newly acquired property can always be added to your trust. But what if you forget to change the title on some of your assets? A simple pourover will, written when the trust agreement is drafted, is the answer. A *pourover* will is a simple document stating that anything you may have neglected to place in your trust during your lifetime should be placed in it at your death. While assets passing under a pourover will are generally probated, a small amount may be excluded from a probate.

## Life Insurance Trust

*life insurance trust*
A trust whose assets are derived at least in part from the proceeds of life insurance.

In many families, the proceeds of life insurance policies are the largest single asset of the estate. A **life insurance trust** is established while you are living. The trust receives your life insurance benefits upon your death and administers them in an agreed-on manner. Such a trust can be canceled if your family or financial circumstances change or if you wish to make new plans for the future.

Although common estate planning tools, life insurance trusts "aren't for the faint of heart," says one tax attorney. They require careful monitoring so that they don't run afoul of gift tax rules. Basically, current gift tax rules allow you to give away $10,000 a year to an unlimited number of people. The Taxpayer Relief Act of 1997 increased this amount in $1,000 increments, depending on the rate of inflation. For example, a 3 percent average annual inflation rate would mean no increase in the $1,000 amount until the end of the fourth year, when it would become $11,000. If you exceed this amount, you will begin cutting into the lifetime credit that allows you to pass along $675,000 (in 2001) free of federal or gift taxes. Once you exceed this limit, you must pay gift tax.

## THE IMPORTANCE OF ESTATE PLANNING

"Waiting too long can be very costly" say Mitchell H. Miller and Robert E. Blinstrubas of the Miller Blinstrubas Law Offices located in Hinsdale, Illinois. "Everyone makes jokes about the inevitability of death and taxes. Unfortunately, too often people either don't want to think about death and incompetency or they do not have enough information to make informed decisions. Then we'll get the call when a problem occurs, and by then many valuable planning opportunities have been lost." Miller and Blinstrubas are attorneys with a combined 27 years of experience advising their clients about estate planning, asset protection, long-term care, and related issues. They advise that anyone with a home, savings, or minor children should consult an experienced estate planning attorney.

The term *estate planning* generally refers to the legal issues involved in planning for death, incompetency, and reducing or avoiding estate taxes. The process for settling a deceased person's affairs is called *probate*. Probate is a court process with two primary goals: (1) to make sure all debts are paid and (2) to distribute property to the proper recipients. A will is a set of your instructions to a probate court judge for settling your affairs. A will allows you to avoid some of the more expensive aspects of probate. If you have minor children, a will is an absolute necessity for naming guardians, who will raise your children if you and your spouse are deceased. If you don't have a will, your state will give you a will by statute. This is called *intestate probate*. Intestate probate usually takes much longer and is more expensive. Miller and Blinstrubas emphasize that everyone should at least have a will or risk leaving the families with a lot of unnecessary cost and aggravation.

Planning for incompetency may be even more important than planning for death. What will happen if, because of age or illness, you are unable to make decisions for yourself?

Without proper planning, your family will have to deal with a court process called *guardianship* or *conservatorship*. A *guardian* is a court-appointed individual, often a family member, who is legally authorized to handle your affairs. Everything a guardian does must be reported to, and approved by, a judge, at least once a year. Guardianship is expensive, both financially and emotionally, for your family. Everyone should have durable powers of attorney for health care and property management. A *durable power of attorney* is a document that authorizes the person you choose to make decisions for you if you cannot make decisions for yourself. Miller and Blinstrubas also recommend a *living will,* a statement of intent that you do not want your life to be artificially prolonged by a life support system.

Miller and Blinstrubas often recommend a *revocable living trust* as a more modern approach to solving many of the problems of basic estate planning. A properly established living trust avoids probate and guardianship, and may reduce or eliminate estate taxes. When you create a revocable living trust, you establish a new legal "person" that becomes the owner of your property. You do not give up any control of your affairs. Typically, you are the trustee (the manager of your property) and the beneficiary (the person entitled to the property). During your lifetime, there will be no effect on your day-to-day affairs. However, upon your death, because your trust—not you—is the legal owner of your property, there is no need for probate. Your designated successor trustee, typically your spouse or children, takes control of the trust and distributes your property according to your wishes without the cost and time of probate. If you become incompetent, a trust will empower your successor trustees to manage your affairs for you without the need for guardianship. A revocable living trust can also be an invaluable tool to reduce or avoid estate taxes.

*charitable remainder trust*    A trust in which the creator retains the right to the income but transfers the right to a charity upon his or her death.

### Charitable Remainder Trust

With a **charitable remainder trust,** you retain the right to the income but transfer that right to the charity upon death. If you have highly appreciated assets, it is a great way to improve your cash flow during your retirement and pursue a charitable interest at the same time. The biggest drawback is that you have to give away the asset irrevocably.

*qualified personal residence trust (QPRT)*    A trust that allows you to get your home or a vacation home out of your estate.

### Qualified Personal Residence Trust

A **qualified personal residence trust (QPRT)** lets you get your home or vacation home out of your estate. You give your home to a trust but live in it for a term of, say, 10 years. At the end of that time, the home belongs to the continuing trust or to the trust beneficiaries, depending on how the trust is written.

*charitable lead trust*    A trust that pays a specified charity income from a donated asset for a set number of years.

### Charitable Lead Trust

A **charitable lead trust** pays a specified charity income from a donated asset for a set number of years. When the term is up, the principal goes to the donor's beneficiaries with reduced estate or gift taxes. Such a trust has high setup and operating costs, however, which may make it impractical unless the assets involved are substantial. For this reason, it is a vehicle for very wealthy people, allowing them a way to keep an asset in the family but greatly reducing the cost of passing it on.[8]

*generation-skipping trust*    A trust that transfers a beneficial interest between two generations, where one generation is two or more generations subsequent to that of the creator.

### Generation-Skipping Trust

A **generation-skipping trust** allows you to directly leave a substantial amount of money to your grandchildren. That's because the federal government imposes a flat 55 percent tax on everything in excess of $1 million that you leave to your grandchildren's generation. In essence, it allows the government to make up for losing the opportunity to levy estate taxes on the middle generation. Like a credit-shelter trust, a generation-skipping trust can be used at the time of death to preserve the $1 million generation-skipping tax exemption for both spouses.[9]

*spendthrift trust*    A trust that permits the beneficiary to receive small amounts of money at specified intervals.

### Spendthrift Trust

If your beneficiary is too young or unable to handle money wisely, consider a **spendthrift trust.** Here the beneficiary receives small amounts of money at specified intervals. It prevents the beneficiary from squandering money or losing it in a bad investment.

There are still other types of specialized trusts. For example, a *pourover trust* is usually dormant during your lifetime, but can be activated if you become disabled. It can be used to manage your insurance, qualified pension or profit-sharing plan proceeds, and your probate estate. A *Q-DOT (qualified domestic trust)* is for spouses who are not U.S. citizens. It provides the same marital deduction benefit that is available to citizen spouses. A GRUT (grantor retained uniturst) and a *personal residence GRIT (grantor retained income trust)* permit grantors to use favorable rules for determining the amount of gift made to the trust.

As you can see, trusts are complicated; therefore, you should seek a competent estate attorney in preparing this legal document. The purpose of all types of trusts is to preserve your estate for your heirs.

## Estates

As mentioned earlier, your *estate* is everything you own (see Exhibit 19–5 on page 625). It includes all of your property—tangible and intangible, however acquired or owned, whether inside or outside the country. It may include jointly owned property, life insurance and employee benefits, and property you no longer own. Thus, an important step in estate planning is taking inventory of everything you own, such as

**Sheet 67**

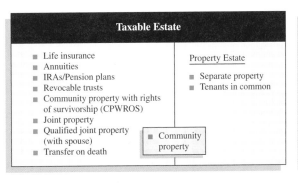

**EXHIBIT 19-5**

What Is Your
Estate?

SOURCE: *Planning Your Estate* (A. G. Edwards & Sons, Inc., 1996), p. 6.

This exhibit shows which assets are included in your probate estate, the much larger number of assets included in your taxable estate, and the very few assets that can avoid both probate and estate taxes.

1.  Cash, checking accounts, savings accounts, CDs, and money market funds.
2.  Stocks, bonds (including municipals and U.S. savings bonds), mutual funds, commodity futures, and tax shelters.
3.  Life insurance, employee benefits, and annuities.
4.  Your home and any other real estate, land and buildings, furniture, and fixtures.
5.  Farms, grain, livestock, machinery, and equipment.
6.  Proprietorship, partnership, and close corporation interests.
7.  Notes, accounts, and claims receivable.
8.  Interests in trusts and powers of appointment.
9.  Antiques, works of art, collectibles, cars, boats, planes, personal effects, and everything else.

*community property*
Any property that has been acquired by either spouse during the marriage.

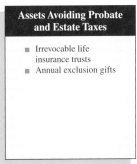

In common-law states (most states), spouses are not considered co-owners of property unless it has been jointly titled. Surviving spouses are entitled to inherit a portion of the deceased spouse's property.

In the community-property states (Arizona, California, Idaho, Louisiana, Nevada, New Mexico, Texas, Wisconsin, and Washington), where each spouse owns 50 percent of the property, half of the community assets are included in each spouse's estate. **Community property** is "any property that has been acquired by either of the spouses during the marriage, but not by gift, devise, bequest or inheritance, or, often, by the income therefrom." In the other, non–community-property states, property is included in the estate of the spouse who owns it. The way you own property can make a tax difference.

Joint Ownership   Joint ownership of property between spouses is very common. Joint ownership may also exist between parents and children, other relatives, or any two or more persons. While joint ownership may avoid *probate* (official proof of a will), creditor attachment, and inheritance taxes in some states, it does not avoid federal estate taxes. In fact, it may increase them.

There are three types of joint ownership, and each has different tax and estate planning consequences. First, if you and your spouse own property as *joint tenants with the right of survivorship (JT/WROS)*, the property is considered owned 50–50 for estate tax purposes and will automatically pass to your spouse at your death, and vice versa. No gift tax is paid on creating such ownership, nor, due to the unlimited marital deduction, is any estate tax paid at the first death. However, this type of joint ownership may result in more taxes overall at the surviving spouse's later death than would be the case with a traditional marital share will, discussed earlier.

Second, if you and your spouse or anyone else own property as *tenants in common,* each individual is considered to own a proportionate share for tax purposes, and only your share is included in your estate. That share does not go to the other tenants in common at your death but is included in your probate estate and subject to your decision as to who gets it. While there are no gift or estate tax consequences between spouse joint owners, gifts of joint interests to children or others can create taxation.

*Tenancy by the entirety,* the third type of joint ownership, is limited to married couples. Under this type of joint ownership, both spouses own the property; when one spouse dies, the other gets it automatically. Neither spouse may sell the property without the consent of the other.

Joint ownership is a poor substitute for a will. It gives you less control over the disposition and taxation of your property. Your state laws govern the types and effects of joint ownership. Some states require that survivorship rights be spelled out in the deed, or at least abbreviated (for example, JT/WROS). Only your attorney can advise you on these matters.

### Life Insurance and Employee Benefits

Life insurance proceeds are free of income tax, excluded from probate, and wholly or partially exempt from most state inheritance taxes. These proceeds are included in your estate for federal estate tax purposes if the policy contains any incidents of ownership such as the right to change beneficiaries, surrender the policy for cash, or make loans on the policy.

Assignment of ownership to your beneficiary or a trust can remove a life insurance policy from your estate. But if your spouse is the intended beneficiary, you do not need to assign ownership, since the proceeds will be free of estate tax due to the marital deduction.

Death benefits from qualified pension, profit-sharing, or Keogh plans are excluded from your estate unless they are payable to it or unless your beneficiary elects the special provision for averaging income tax in lump-sum distributions.

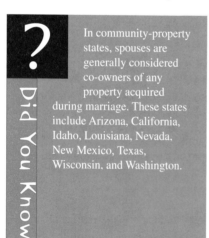

If there is "too much" money in your qualified retirement plan when you and your spouse die, your heirs could lose up to 80 percent in federal and state income taxes, estate tax, and the "excess accumulation" tax. Proper estate planning can minimize such confiscatory taxes.[10]

### Lifetime Gifts and Trusts

Gifts or trusts with strings attached, such as retaining the income, use, or control of the property, are fully included at their date-of-death value, whether your rights are expressed or implied. For example, if you transfer title of your home to a child but continue to live in it, the home is taxed in your estate. Or if you put property in trust and retain a certain amount of control over the income or principal, the property is included in your estate even though you cannot obtain it yourself. Also, if you are the beneficiary of a trust established by someone else and you have general rights to the principal during life or the power to appoint it to anyone at death, that amount is included in your estate.

## Settling Your Estate

If you have had a will drawn, you are *testate* in the eyes of the law, and an executor (named in your will) will carry out your wishes in due time. If you have not named an executor, the probate court (the court that supervises the distribution of estates) will appoint an administrator to carry out the instructions in your will.

| EXHIBIT 19-6 | | Gross Estate | Settlement Costs | Net Estate | Percent Shrinkage |
|---|---|---|---|---|---|
| The Erosion of Probate and Estate Taxes | Elvis Presley | $10,165,434 | $ 7,374,635 | $ 2,790,799 | 73% |
| | John D. Rockefeller | 26,905,182 | 17,124,988 | 9,780,194 | 64 |
| | Clark Gable | 2,806,526 | 1,101,038 | 1,705,488 | 39 |
| SOURCE: Public court records, state probate courts. | Walt Disney | 23,004,851 | 6,811,943 | 16,192,908 | 30 |

If you don't have a will, you become *intestate* at your death. In that case, your estate is put under the control of a court-appointed administrator for distribution according to the laws of the state in which you reside.

## Concept Check 19-4

1. Differentiate among the 13 types of trusts.
2. What is included in an estate?
3. What are the three types of joint ownership?

## FEDERAL AND STATE ESTATE TAXES

**Obj. 5**
Evaluate the effects of federal and state taxes on estate planning.

The tax aspects of estate planning have changed considerably due to recent major changes in the federal tax structure. The maximum tax rate on estates and gifts, for example, is gradually declining. As Exhibit 19–6 shows, estate settlement costs can quickly deplete an estate.

You can reduce your taxable estate by giving away assets to anyone during your lifetime. (But don't give away assets just to reduce your estate tax liability if you may need those assets in your retirement.) No gift tax is due on gifts of up to $10,000 to any one person in any one year. (A married couple, acting together, may give up to $20,000 to one person in one year.)

For example, suppose that on January 2, 2001, Michael gave $10,000 worth of shares of a stock mutual fund to his son. On January 2, 2008, these shares are worth $50,000. As a result of this gift in 2001, Michael has removed from his estate the $10,000 gift plus $40,000 of appreciation, for a total of $50,000. All of this has been accomplished at no gift tax cost.

### Types of Taxes

Federal and state governments levy various types of taxes that you must consider in planning your estate. The four major taxes of this kind are estate taxes, estate and trust income taxes, inheritance taxes, and gift taxes.

### Estate Taxes

*estate tax* A federal tax on the right of a deceased person to transfer property and life insurance at death.

An **estate tax** is a federal tax levied on the right of a deceased person to transmit his or her property and life insurance at death. Estate taxes have undergone extensive revision since the mid-1970s. The Economic Recovery Tax Act of 1981 made important tax concessions, particularly the unlimited marital deduction and the increased exemption equivalent shown in Exhibit 19–7 on page 628.

**EXHIBIT 19-7**

Unified Estate and
Gift Tax Schedule

As of 1999, each individual is entitled to a unified credit of $211,300, which is the amount of tax generated by a transfer of $650,000. In other words, no estate or gift taxes are assessed on the first $650,000 of a person's combined taxable gifts and transfers at death.

**Taxable Estate**

| Over | Not Over | Pay | Percentage on Excess |
|---|---|---|---|
| $      0 | $   10,000 | $        0 | 18 |
| 10,000 | 20,000 | 1,800 | 20 |
| 20,000 | 40,000 | 3,800 | 22 |
| 40,000 | 60,000 | 8,200 | 24 |
| 60,000 | 80,000 | 13,000 | 26 |
| 80,000 | 100,000 | 18,200 | 28 |
| 100,000 | 150,000 | 23,800 | 30 |
| 150,000 | 250,000 | 38,800 | 32 |
| 250,000 | 500,000 | 70,800 | 34 |
| 500,000 | 750,000 | 155,800 | 37 |
| 750,000 | 1,000,000 | 248,300 | 39 |
| 1,000,000 | 1,250,000 | 345,800 | 41 |
| 1,250,000 | 1,500,000 | 448,300 | 43 |
| 1,500,000 | 2,000,000 | 555,800 | 45 |
| 2,000,000 | 2,500,000 | 780,800 | 49 |
| 2,500,000 | 3,000,000 | 1,025,800 | 53 |
| 3,000,000 and over | | 1,290,800 | 55 |

*Example:* Taxable estate    $1,000,000
Gross tax                              345,800
Less credit                          −211,300
Net tax due                      $  134,500

**Unified Estate and Gift Tax Credit**

| Tax Credit | Equivalent Estate |
|---|---|
| $211,300 | $650,000 |

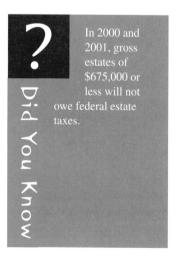

**Did You Know**

In 2000 and 2001, gross estates of $675,000 or less will not owe federal estate taxes.

Under present law, with intelligent estate planning and properly drawn wills, you may leave all of your property to your surviving spouse free of federal estate taxes. The surviving spouse's estate in excess of $675,000 (in 2001) faces estate taxes of from 37 to 55 percent.

All limits have been removed from transfers between spouses during their lifetimes as well as at death. Whatever you give your spouse is exempt from gift and estate taxes. Gift tax returns need not be filed for interspousal gifts. There is still the possibility, however, that such gifts will be included in your estate if they were given within three years of your death.

**Estate and Trust Federal Income Taxes**    In addition to the federal estate tax, estates and certain trusts must file federal income tax returns with the Internal Revenue Service. Generally, taxable income for estates and trusts is computed in much the same manner as taxable income for individuals. Under the Tax Reform Act of 1986, trusts and estates must pay quarterly estimated taxes, and new trusts must use the calendar year as the tax year.

*inheritance tax*  A tax levied on the right of an heir to receive an estate.

## Inheritance Taxes

An **inheritance tax** is levied on the right of an heir to receive all or part of the estate and life insurance proceeds of a deceased person. The tax payable depends on the net value of the property and insurance received. It also depends on the relationship of the heir to the deceased.

Inheritance taxes are imposed only by the state governments. Most states levy an inheritance tax, but the state laws differ widely as to exemptions, rates of taxation, and the treatment of property and life insurance. A reasonable average for state inheritance taxes would be 4 to 10 percent of your estate, with the higher percentages on larger amounts.

Over the past few years, many states have been phasing out their inheritance tax provisions, usually over a period of three or four years. This apparently reflects a desire to retain older and wealthy citizens as residents and to discourage them from leaving the states where they have lived most of their lives to seek tax havens in states such as Florida and Nevada. Increasingly, state legislatures have been questioning the equity of further taxes at death and are opting instead for sales and income taxes to provide state revenues.

*gift tax*  A federal and state tax on the privilege of making gifts to others.

## Gift Taxes

The federal and state governments levy a **gift tax** on the privilege of making gifts to others. A property owner can avoid estate and inheritance taxes by giving property during his or her lifetime. For this reason, the federal tax laws provide for taxes on gifts of property. The tax rates on gifts used to be only 75 percent of the tax rates on estates, but since 1976 the gift tax rates have been the same as the estate tax rates. Indeed, the tax rates are now called *unified transfer tax rates*.

Many states have gift tax laws. The state gift tax laws are similar to the federal gift tax laws, but the exemptions and dates for filing returns vary widely among the states.

As discussed earlier, the federal gift tax law allows you to give up to $10,000 each year to any person without incurring gift tax liability or having to report the gift to the IRS. Note that the Taxpayer Relief Act of 1997 increased this amount in $1,000 increments, depending on rates of inflation in future years. Gifts from a husband or a wife to a third party are considered as having been made in equal amounts by each spouse. Consequently, a husband and wife may give as much as $20,000 per year to anyone without incurring tax liability.

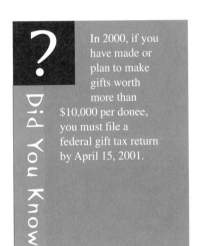

**Did You Know?**

In 2000, if you have made or plan to make gifts worth more than $10,000 per donee, you must file a federal gift tax return by April 15, 2001.

## Tax Avoidance and Tax Evasion

A poorly arranged estate may be subject to unduly large taxation. Therefore, you should study the tax laws and seek advice to avoid estate taxes larger than those the lawmakers intended you to pay. You should have a clear idea of the distinction between tax avoidance and tax evasion. *Tax avoidance* is the use of legal methods to reduce or escape taxes; *tax evasion* is the use of illegal methods to reduce or escape taxes.

The Financial Planning for Life's Situations feature on page 630 explains how wealthy Americans might minimize estate tax through a gifting program.

## Charitable Gifts and Bequests

Gifts made to certain recognized charitable or educational organizations are exempt from gift, estate, and inheritance taxes. Accordingly, such gifts or bequests (gifts through a will) represent one method of reducing or avoiding estate and inheritance taxes.

## Financial Planning for Life's Situations

### DEATH, TAXES, AND THE RICH

Judging from the political furor over "death taxes," wealthy Americans might be expected to go out of their way to minimize the tax bite on their heirs. But a new study shows that the rich largely overlook the simplest way to reduce estate taxes: giving away their property while they're alive.

Fewer than half of the elderly wealthy who could be subject to the estate tax make even $10,000 a year in overall gifts to family members, says economist James M. Poterba of the Massachusetts Institute of Technology. And even many of those givers neglect to take full advantage of tax-free gifts, which can total $10,000 a year to each child or grandchild.

Grants of more than $10,000 per recipient per year are subject to a gift tax. But even at the 55 percent top rate, making a gift is cheaper than leaving funds in an estate. Take a benefactor who has exhausted the $10,000 annual exemption per recipient and has $100,000 more to give. He or she can give $64,500 of it and use the rest to pay the gift tax, while the same $100,000 in an estate would net the heirs only $45,000.

Why don't the wealthy take advantage of these breaks? "The low-wealth wealthy are afraid they'll need their resources for health care," says Poterba. Rules that let heirs escape capital-gains taxes on inherited assets also create an incentive to hang on to appreciated property. But even among the super-rich, he says, "there's just a reluctance to give up control of assets—even if the transfer would lead to substantial tax savings."

SOURCE: Adapted from Mike McNamee, "Death, Taxes, and the Rich," *Business Week*, January 11, 1999, p. 34. Reprinted from the January 11, 1999 issue of *Business Week* by special permission. © 1999 McGraw-Hill Companies, Inc.

## Calculation of Tax

The estate tax is applied not to your total gross estate but to your net taxable estate at death. *Net taxable estate* is your testamentary net worth after subtracting your debts, liabilities, probate costs, and administration costs. These items, all of which are taken off your estate before calculating your tax, are cash requirements to be paid by your estate. The Financial Planning Calculations feature on page 631 provides additional examples of figuring estate taxes.

### Debts and Liabilities
In arriving at your taxable estate, the amount of your debts and other creditor obligations are subtracted. You are liable for the payment of these debts while living; your estate will be liable at your death. Your debts may include mortgages, collateralized loans, margin accounts, bank loans, notes payable, installment and charge accounts, and accrued income and property taxes. They may also include your last-illness and funeral expenses.

### Probate and Administration Costs
Your estate administration costs will include fees for attorneys, accountants, appraisers, executors or administrators and trustees, court costs, bonding and surety costs, and miscellaneous expenses. These administration costs may run 5 to 8 percent of your estate, depending on its size and complexity. While the percentage usually decreases as the size of the estate increases, it may be increased by additional complicating factors, such as handling a business interest.

Next, deductions are made for bequests to qualified charities and for property passing to your spouse (the marital deduction). That leaves your net taxable estate, to which the rates shown in Exhibit 19–7 on page 628 are applied to determine your gross estate tax.

# Financial Planning Calculations

## SAVING ON ESTATE AND GIFT TAXES THROUGH TRUSTS

Example 1 in the table below demonstrates how, upon the death of the surviving spouse, only one unified credit—that of the surviving spouse—will remain to offset the estate tax. The strategy in example 2 produces no estate tax on the first estate and reduces the surviving spouse's potential estate tax by the amount of property in this trust. This trust is known as a *credit-shelter* or *bypass trust*.

### Example 1: $2,600,000 Estate

All to spouse (used full marital deduction in first estate)

First estate (deceased):

| | |
|---|---:|
| Gross estate | $2,600,000 |
| Marital deduction | (2,600,000) |
| Taxable estate | 0 |
| Tentative estate tax | 0 |
| Final tax | 0 |

Second estate (surviving spouse):

| | |
|---|---:|
| Gross estate | $2,600,000 |
| Marital deduction | 0 |
| Taxable estate | 2,600,000 |
| Tentative estate tax | 1,078,800 |
| Estate tax credit | (192,800) |
| Final tax | 886,000 |
| Combined estate taxes | $ 886,000 |

### Example 2: $2,000,000 Outright and in Trust to Spouse, $600,000 to Bypass Trust

Optimal marital deduction

First estate (deceased):

| | |
|---|---:|
| Gross estate | $2,600,000 |
| Marital deduction | (2,000,000) |
| Taxable estate | 600,000 |
| Tentative estate tax | $  192,800 |
| Estate tax credit | (192,800) |
| Final tax | 0 |

Second estate:

| | |
|---|---:|
| Gross estate | $2,000,000 |
| Marital deduction | 0 |
| Taxable estate | $2,000,000 |
| Tentative estate tax | 780,800 |
| Estate tax credit | (192,800) |
| Final tax | 588,000 |
| Combined estate taxes | 588,000 |
| Tax savings | $  298,000 |

SOURCE: David Gerson and Charles Cangro, "Estate & Gift Tax: The Real Tax Problem," *Fundsfocus,* Neuberger Berman Management Inc., Fall 1994, p. 2.

Inheritance and estate taxes in your own state are additional costs, and these costs are not deductible in arriving at your taxable estate. In fact, you may have to pay inheritance taxes in two or more states, depending on the location of your property.

## Paying the Tax

If, after having used various estate tax reduction techniques, you must still pay an estate tax, you should consider the best way to pay it. The federal estate tax is due and payable in cash nine months after your death. State taxes, probate costs, debts, and expenses also usually fall due within that time. These often result in a real cash bind, because people rarely keep a lot of cash on hand. They derived their wealth from putting their money to work in businesses, real estate, or other investments. Estate liquidity—having enough cash to pay taxes and costs without forced sales of assets or heavy borrowing— is often a problem.

One way to handle the estate tax is to set aside or accumulate enough cash to pay it when it falls due. However, you may die before you have accumulated enough cash, and the cash you accumulate may be subject to income tax during your lifetime and to estate tax at your death.

Another way to handle the estate tax is for your family to sell assets to pay taxes. The first assets to be sold might be stocks, bonds, gold or silver coins, and similar liquid assets. However, these assets may be the source of your family's income after your death, and the market for them may be down. Assets such as real estate may also be sold, but prices on forced sales are usually only a fraction of the fair value.

Your family could consider borrowing; however, it is unusual to find a commercial lender that will lend money to pay back-taxes. If you do find one, it may require personal liability. In any event, borrowing does not solve the problem; it only prolongs it, adding interest costs in the process.

Borrowing from the IRS itself in the form of deferred payments or installments may be possible for reasonable cause. Tax extension and installment payment provisions are helpful, but they still leave a tax debt to be paid by your heirs at your death. Paying that debt, even over an extended period of time, could be a real burden and severely restrict their income and flexibility.

Life insurance may be a reasonable, feasible, and economical means of paying your estate tax. Instead of forcing your family to pay off the estate tax and other debts and costs by borrowing or selling, you can, through insurance, provide your family with tax-free cash at a fraction of the cost of borrowing.

**Sheet 68**

## Concept Check 19–5

1. What are the four types of taxes to consider in planning your estate?
2. How is estate tax calculated?
3. What are the various ways to handle the payment of estate tax?

## Summary of Objectives

**Obj. 1**   **Analyze the personal aspects of estate planning.**

Estate planning is an essential part of retirement planning and an integral part of financial planning. The first part of estate planning consists of building your estate; the second part consists of transferring your estate, at your death, in the manner you have specified. The personal aspects of estate planning depend on whether you are single or married. If you are married, your estate planning involves the interests of at least two people, and more if there are children. Never having been married does not eliminate the need to organize your financial affairs.

**Obj. 2**   **Assess the legal aspects of estate planning.**

In the event of death, proof of claims must be produced or the claims will not be processed. Among the papers needed are birth certificates, marriage certificates, legal name changes, and military service records. Every adult should have a written will, which is the legal declaration of a person's mind as to the disposition of his or her property after

death. Thus, a will is a way to transfer your property according to your wishes after you die.

**Obj. 3**   **Distinguish among various types and formats of wills.**

The four types of wills are the simple will, the traditional marital share will, the exemption trust will, and the stated dollar amount will. A will can be simple or complex depending on your personal and financial circumstances.

A *simple will,* sometimes called an *I love you will,* leaves everything to the spouse. Such a will is sufficient for most smaller estates. However, if you have a large or complex estate, a simple will may not meet your objectives. It may also create higher overall taxation, because everything would be taxed in your spouse's subsequent estate.

**Obj. 4**   **Appraise various types of trusts and estates.**

Establishing a trust can be an excellent way to manage your estate. Trusts are revocable or irrevocable. Popular forms of trusts include credit-shelter trusts, grantor retained annuity trusts, disclaimer trusts, marital-deduction trusts, living trusts, self-declaration trusts, testamentary trusts, life insurance trusts, charitable remainder trusts, qualified personal residence trusts, charitable lead trusts, generation-skipping trusts, and spendthrift trusts. An attorney's help is needed to establish a trust.

If you establish a *revocable trust,* you retain the right to end the trust or change its terms during your lifetime. If you establish an *irrevocable trust,* you cannot change its terms or end it. However, an irrevocable trust offers tax advantages not offered by a revocable trust.

Obj. 5  **Evaluate the effects of federal and state taxes on estate planning.**

The tax aspects of estate planning have changed considerably due to recent major changes in the federal tax structure. The four major federal and state taxes you must consider in planning your estate are estate taxes, estate and trust income taxes, inheritance taxes, and gift taxes.

The federal estate tax is due and payable in cash nine months after your death. State taxes, probate costs, debts, and expenses also usually fall due within that time.

## Financial Planning Problems

Refer to Exhibit 19–7 to solve the following problems. (Obj. 5)

1. *Calculating Gross Tax, Amount of Credit, and Net Tax.* Bob and Kathy have a taxable estate of $1,500,000.
   a. What is the gross tax on this estate?
   b. What is the amount of credit?
   c. What is the net tax due?
2. *Calculating Gross Tax, Amount of Credit, and Net Tax.* Mike and Karen have a taxable estate of $3 million.
   a. What is the gross tax on this estate?
   b. What is the amount of credit?
   c. What is the net tax due?

3. *Calculating the Gift Tax.* In 1998, Joshua gave $10,000 worth of AT&T stock to his son. In 2008, the AT&T shares are worth $60,000.
   a. What was the gift tax in 1998?
   b. What is the total amount removed from Joshua's estate in 2008?
   c. What will be the gift tax in 2008?
4. *Calculating the Gift Tax.* In 1999, you gave a $10,000 gift to a friend. What is the gift tax?

## Financial Planning Activities

1. *Preparing a Written Record of Personal Information.* Prepare a written record of personal information that would be helpful to you and your heirs. Make sure to include the location of family records, your military service file, and other important papers; medical records; bank accounts; charge accounts; the location of your safe-deposit box; U.S. savings bonds; stocks, bonds, and other securities; property owned; life insurance; annuities; and Social Security information.  (Obj. 1)
2. *Developing Long-Term Estate Planning Goals.* Develop a list of specific long-term estate planning goals with your family. Discuss how those goals could be achieved even if you or your spouse died unexpectedly.  (Obj. 1)
3. *Drafting a Simple Will.* Draft your simple will, using Exhibit 19–1 as a guideline. Whom will you appoint as a trustee or guardian for your minor children? Why? (Obj. 2)
4. *Comparing Costs of Preparing a Will.* Contact several lawyers in your area to find out how much they would charge to prepare your simple will. Are their fees about the same?  (Obj. 3)

5. *Using the Internet to Obtain Information about Wills.* Visit Metropolitan Life Insurance Company's web page at http://www.lifeadvice.com. Using this information, prepare a report on the following: *(a)* Who needs a will? *(b)* What are the elements of a will (naming a guardian, naming an executor, preparing a will, updating a will, estate taxes, where to keep your will, living will, etc.)? *(c)* How is this report helpful in preparing your own will?
6. *Preparing the Letter of Last Instructions.* Prepare your own letter of last instructions.  (Obj. 3)
7. *Determining Criteria in Choosing a Guardian.* Make a list of the criteria you will use in deciding who will be the guardian of your minor children if you and your spouse die at the same time.  (Obj. 3)
8. *Using the Internet to Obtain Information about Estate Planning.* Visit the Prudential Insurance Company of America website at http://prudential.com/estateplan. Gather information on various estate planning topics such as an estate planning worksheet; whether you need an estate plan; when to update your plan; estate taxes, wills, executors, trusts, etc. Then prepare a report to help you develop your estate plan.  (Obj. 4)

9. *Establishing a Trust.* Discuss with your attorney the possibility of establishing a trust as a means of managing your estate.   (Obj. 4)

10. *Obtaining Information from Your State Department of Revenue.* Ask your state department of revenue for brochures on state inheritance and gift taxes. What are the exemptions and rates of taxes? How are your property and life insurance treated for the purpose of inheritance tax? Of gift tax?   (Obj. 5)

## LIFE SITUATION CASE

### DON'T LET YOUR WINDFALL BLOW AWAY

Warren, a married entrepreneur who owns a successful promotions business in New York City, doesn't yet have kids, but he is already making plans. Last December, Warren received an unexpected inheritance of $1.4 million, after taxes, from his late grandfather. Instead of buying a Porsche or a new home, he did the right thing by his family-to-be and invested it all. "Warren is extremely fastidious," says Lesley Sommers, his financial planner.

Warren did what smart people do with sudden wealth: They decide not to blow it. "Letting your head rule your emotions lets you keep your money, not lose it," says Barbara Levin, director of the Forum for Investor Advice in Bethesda, Maryland, a research group for investment pros. A 1997 Forum survey found that 59 percent of 1,000 respondents who received cash payouts of $20,000 or more had sought professional advice. An equal number had invested every dime. When Warren got his windfall, Sommers invested all but $100,000. Warren says, "she taught me that this [windfall]

should not change where I eat or go on vacation." So if you win the lottery, don't blow it on houses, cars, vacations, and luxury items. Even millions won't go far once the IRS takes its share. Instead, pay off high-interest credit card and other debts that offer no tax deductions. Then find a financial adviser. (A good source is the Certified Financial Planner Board of Standards at 1–888–237–6275; www.cfp-board.org) This professional can help you find a competent estate planner and create an investment plan.

### Questions

1. What did Warren do with his $1.4 million inheritance?
2. What do smart people do with sudden wealth?

SOURCE: Adapted from Joan Oleck, "Don't Let Your Windfall Blow Away," *Business Week On-line,* December 1999, p. 116. Reprinted from the March 1, 1999 issue of *Business Week* by special permission. © 1999 McGraw-Hill Companies, Inc.

## INTERNET CASE   The Threat of the Federal Estate Tax

Ruth W., a 72-year-old widow, has an estate valued at approximately $1,500,000. She was shocked to learn that the federal estate tax at her death could be almost $250,000 if she died in 2001 and more than $100,000 if she lived until 2006.

Ruth is aware that she could reduce the size of her estate by $70,000 a year by making gifts of $10,000 annually to each of her three children and four grandchildren. She needs additional information about estate planning before making her decision.

### Questions

1. What Internet sources are available to help Ruth with her estate planning decisions?
2. What personal and financial factors should Ruth consider before making gifts?
3. Do you think Ruth should consult an estate attorney? Why or why not?

SOURCE: "The Threat of the Federal Estate Tax," *American Institute for Cancer Research,* March 1998, pp. 8–9.

## Creating an E-Plan: Financial Decisions Using the Web

### DEVELOPING AN ESTATE PLAN

Most people do not think they have enough assets to do estate planning. However, the planned transfer of resources with the use of a will, trusts, and other legal vehicles is a necessary phase of your total financial plan.

Websites for Estate Planning

- Estate planning information at **www.webtrust.com.**
- Wills and estate planning information at **www.nolo.com** and **www.mtpalermo.com.**
- Federal estate tax information at **www.irs.ustreas.gov.**
- Estate tax information at **www.lifenet.com/estate.**
- Current estate planning articles from *Money* magazine at **www.money.com,** *Kiplinger's Personal Finance Magazine* at **www.kiplinger.com,** *Business Week* at **www. businessweek.com,** *Worth* magazine at **www.worth.com,** and *Smart Money* at **www.smartmoney.com.**

(Note: Addresses and content of websites change, and new sites are created daily. Use search engines to update and locate websites for your current financial planning needs.)

*PFP sheets: 65–68*

Short-Term Financial Planning Activities

1. Investigate the cost of a will. Decide on the type of will and provisions appropriate for your life situation (see PFP Sheet 66).
2. Using the IRS and other websites, identify recent estate tax law changes that may affect your financial planning decisions.
3. Compare the benefits and costs of different trusts that might be appropriate for your life situation (see PFP Sheet 67).

Long-Term Financial Planning Activities

1. Develop a plan for actions to be taken related to estate planning (see PFP Sheet 65).
2. Identify saving and investing decisions that would minimize future estate taxes (see PFP Sheet 68).

## Continuous Case for Part 6

### PLANNING FOR TOMORROW

**Life Situation**
Pam, 48; Josh, 50; children ages 21, 19, and 16

*Financial Goals*
- Replenish savings and investments used for college costs
- Plan for retirement in about 15 years
- Consider estate planning activities

*Financial Data*

| | |
|---|---|
| Monthly income | $ 5,700 |
| Living expenses | 4,600 |
| Assets | 242,500 |
| Liabilities | 69,100 |

With two children in college, the Brocks once again find their life situation changing. Compared to five years ago, their total assets have decreased from $262,700 to $242,500 due to college expenses. The Brocks' oldest child will graduate next year, but the youngest will enter college in a couple of years. Therefore, the drain on the family's finances will continue.

The family's finances are adequate, but both Pam and Josh are beginning to worry about retirement. Over the years, Josh has taken advantage of different career opportunities. Today his annual salary, $68,400, is higher than it has ever been. But his employment changes have resulted in a smaller pension fund than would be available had he remained with the same organization. The current value of his pension plan is just over $115,000. The investment program he and Pam started

almost 10 years ago is growing and is now worth about $62,000. But they still worry whether they will have enough money to finance their retirement dreams when Josh retires in 15 years. According to Josh, "If I retired today, we couldn't maintain our current lifestyle. In fact, we couldn't even exist."

### Questions

1. How would you rate the Brocks' financial condition at this stage in their lives?
2. Given that Pam is 48 and Josh is 50, what should be their major priorities as they continue planning for retirement?
3. What types of estate planning, if any, should the Brocks consider at this time?

# APPENDIXES

APPENDIXES

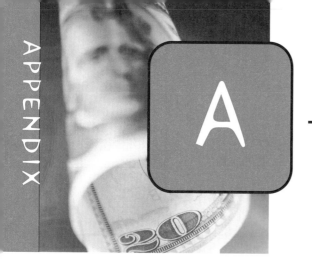

# A

# The Time Value of Money: Future Value and Present Value Computations

"If I deposit $10,000 today, how much will I have for a down payment on a house in five years?"

"Will $2,000 saved a year give me enough money when I retire?"

"How much must I save today to have enough for my children's college education?"

As introduced in Chapter 1 and used to measure financial opportunity costs in other chapters, the *time value of money,* more commonly referred to as *interest,* is the cost of money that is borrowed or lent. Interest can be compared to rent, the cost of using an apartment or other item. The time value of money is based on the fact that a dollar received today is worth more than a dollar that will be received one year from today, because the dollar received today can be saved or invested and will be worth more than a dollar a year from today. Similarly, a dollar that will be received one year from today is currently worth less than a dollar today.

The time value of money has two major components: future value and present value. *Future value* computations, which are also referred to as *compounding,* yield the amount to which a current sum will increase based on a certain interest rate and period of time. *Present value,* which is calculated through a process called *discounting,* is the current value of a future sum based on a certain interest rate and period of time.

In future value problems, you are given an amount to save or invest and you calculate the amount that will be available at some future date. With present value problems, you are given the amount that will be available at some future date and you calculate the current value of that amount. Both future value and present value computations are based on basic interest rate calculations.

## INTEREST RATE BASICS

Simple interest is the dollar cost of borrowing or earnings from lending money. The interest is based on three elements:

- The dollar amount, called the *principal.*
- The *rate of interest.*
- The amount of *time.*

The formula for computing interest is

$$\text{Interest} = \text{Principal} \times \text{Rate of interest} \times \text{Time}$$

The interest rate is stated as a percentage for a year. For example, you must convert 12 percent to either 0.12 or $^{12}/_{100}$ before doing your calculations. The time element must also be converted to a decimal or fraction. For example, three months would be shown as either 0.25 or ¼ of a year. Interest for 2½ years would involve a time period of 2.5.

**Example A**   Suppose you borrow $1,000 at 5 percent and will repay it in one payment at the end of one year. Using the simple interest calculation, the interest is $50, computed as follows:

$$\$50 = \$1,000 \times 0.05 \times 1 \text{ (year)}$$

**Example B**   If you deposited $750 in a savings account paying 8 percent, how much interest would you earn in nine months? You would compute this amount as follows:

$$\text{Interest} = \$750 \times 0.08 \times \text{¾ (or 0.75 of a year)}$$
$$= \$45$$

**Sample Problem 1**   How much interest would you earn if you deposited $300 at 6 percent for 27 months? *(Answers to sample problems are on page 643.)*

**Sample Problem 2**   How much interest would you pay to borrow $670 for eight months at 12 percent?

## FUTURE VALUE OF A SINGLE AMOUNT

The future value of an amount consists of the original amount plus compound interest. This calculation involves the following elements:

$$FV = \text{Future value}$$
$$PV = \text{Present value}$$
$$i = \text{Interest rate}$$
$$n = \text{Number of time periods}$$

The formula for the future value of a single amount is

$$FV = PV(1 + i)^n$$

**Example C**   The future value of $1 at 10 percent after three years is $1.33. This amount is calculated as follows:

$$\$1.33 = \$1.00 (1 + 0.10)^3$$

Future value tables are available to help you determine compounded interest amounts (see Exhibit A–1 on page 644). Looking at Exhibit A–1 for 10 percent and three years, you can see that $1 would be worth $1.33 at that time. For other amounts, multiply the table factor by the original amount.

This may be viewed as follows:

**Example D**   If your savings of $400 earn 12 percent, compounded *monthly,* over a year and a half, use the table factor for 1 percent for 18 time periods. The future value of this amount is $478.40, calculated as follows:

$$\$478.40 = \$400\,(1.196)$$

**Sample Problem 3**   What is the future value of $800 at 8 percent after six years?

**Sample Problem 4**   How much would you have in savings if you kept $200 on deposit for eight years at 8 percent, compounded *semiannually*?

## FUTURE VALUE OF A SERIES OF EQUAL AMOUNTS (AN ANNUITY)

Future value may also be calculated for a situation in which regular additions are made to savings. The following formula is used:

$$FV = \frac{(1 + i)^n - 1}{i}$$

This formula assumes that (1) each deposit is for the same amount, (2) the interest rate is the same for each time period, and (3) the deposits are made at the end of each time period.

**Example E**   The future value of three $1 deposits made at the end of the next three years, earning 10 percent interest, is $3.31. This is calculated as follows:

$$\$3.31 = \$1\,\frac{(1 + 0.10)^3 - 1}{0.10}$$

This may be viewed as follows:

Using Exhibit A–2 on page 645, you can find this same amount for 10 percent for three time periods. To use the table for other amounts, multiply the table factors by the annual deposit.

**Example F**   If you plan to deposit $40 a year for 10 years, earning 8 percent compounded annually, use the table factor for 8 percent for 10 time periods. The future value of this amount is $579.48, calculated as follows:

$$\$579.48 = \$40(14.487)$$

Sample Problem 5    What is the future value of an annual deposit of $230 earning 6 percent for 15 years?

Sample Problem 6    What amount would you have in a retirement account if you made annual deposits of $375 for 25 years earning 12 percent, compounded annually?

## PRESENT VALUE OF A SINGLE AMOUNT

If you want to know how much you need to deposit now to receive a certain amount in the future, use the following formula:

$$PV = \frac{1}{(1 + i)^n}$$

Example G    The present value of $1 to be received three years from now based on a 10 percent interest rate is $0.75. This amount is calculated as follows:

$$\$0.75 = \frac{\$1}{(1 + 0.10)^3}$$

This may be viewed as follows:

Present value tables are available to assist you in this process (see Exhibit A–3 on page 646). Notice that $1 at 10 percent for three years has a present value of $0.75. For amounts other than $1, multiply the table factor by the amount involved.

Example H    If you want to have $300 seven years from now and your savings earn 10 percent, compounded *semiannually*, use the table factor for 5 percent for 14 time periods. In this situation, the present value is $151.50, calculated as follows:

$$\$151.50 = \$300(0.505)$$

Sample Problem 7    What is the present value of $2,200 earning 15 percent for eight years?

Sample Problem 8    To have $6,000 for a child's education in 10 years, what amount should a parent deposit in a savings account that earns 12 percent, compounded *quarterly*?

## PRESENT VALUE OF A SERIES OF EQUAL AMOUNTS (AN ANNUITY)

The final time value of money situation allows you to receive an amount at the end of each time period for a certain number of periods. This amount is calculated as follows:

$$PV = \frac{1 - \dfrac{1}{(1 + i)^n}}{i}$$

Example I　The present value of a $1 withdrawal at the end of the next three years would be $2.49, calculated as follows:

$$\$2.49 = \$1 \left[ \dfrac{1 - \dfrac{1}{(1 + 0.10)^n}}{0.10} \right]$$

This may be viewed as follows:

This same amount appears in Exhibit A–4 on page 647 for 10 percent and three time periods. To use the table for other situations, multiply the table factor by the amount to be withdrawn each year.

Example J　If you wish to withdraw $100 at the end of each year for 10 years from an account that earns 14 percent, compounded annually, what amount must you deposit now? Use the table factor for 14 percent for 10 time periods. In this situation, the present value is $521.60, calculated as follows:

$$\$521.60 = \$100(5.216)$$

Sample Problem 9　What is the present value of a withdrawal of $200 at the end of each year for 14 years with an interest rate of 7 percent?

Sample Problem 10　How much would you have to deposit now to be able to withdraw $650 at the end of each year for 20 years from an account that earns 11 percent?

# USING PRESENT VALUE TO DETERMINE LOAN PAYMENTS

Present value tables can also be used to determine installment payments for a loan as follows:

$$\dfrac{\text{Amount borrowed}}{\text{Present value of a series table factor (Exhibit A–4)}} = \text{Loan payment}$$

Example K　If you borrow $1,000 with a 6 percent interest rate to be repaid in three equal payments at the end of the next three years, the payments will be $374.11. This is calculated as follows:

$$\dfrac{\$1,000}{2.673} = \$374.11$$

Sample Problem 11　What would be the annual payment amount for a $20,000, 10-year loan at 7 percent?

## ANSWERS TO SAMPLE PROBLEMS

1. $300 × 0.06 × 2.25 years (27 months) = $40.50.
2. $670 × 0.12 × ⅔ (of a year) = $53.60.
3. $800(1.587) = $1,269.60. (Use Exhibit A–1, 8%, 6 periods.)
4. $200(1.873) = $374.60. (Use Exhibit A–1, 4%, 16 periods.)
5. $230(23.276) = $5,353.48. (Use Exhibit A–2, 6%, 15 periods.)
6. $375(133.33) = $49,998.75. (Use Exhibit A–2, 12%, 25 periods.)
7. $2,200(0.327) = $719.40. (Use Exhibit A–3, 15%, 8 periods.)
8. $6,000(0.307) = $1,842. (Use Exhibit A–3, 3%, 40 periods.)
9. $200(8.745) = $1,749. (Use Exhibit A–4, 7%, 14 periods.)
10. $650(7.963) = $5,175.95. (Use Exhibit A–4, 11%, 20 periods.)
11. $20,000/7.024 = $2,847.38. (Use Exhibit A–4, 7%, 10 periods.)

## EXHIBIT A-1   Future Value (Compounded Sum) of $1 after a Given Number of Time Periods

| Period | 1% | 2% | 3% | 4% | 5% | 6% | 7% | 8% | 9% | 10% | 11% |
|---|---|---|---|---|---|---|---|---|---|---|---|
| 1 | 1.010 | 1.020 | 1.030 | 1.040 | 1.050 | 1.060 | 1.070 | 1.080 | 1.090 | 1.100 | 1.110 |
| 2 | 1.020 | 1.040 | 1.061 | 1.082 | 1.103 | 1.124 | 1.145 | 1.166 | 1.188 | 1.210 | 1.232 |
| 3 | 1.030 | 1.061 | 1.093 | 1.125 | 1.158 | 1.191 | 1.225 | 1.260 | 1.295 | 1.331 | 1.368 |
| 4 | 1.041 | 1.082 | 1.126 | 1.170 | 1.216 | 1.262 | 1.311 | 1.360 | 1.412 | 1.464 | 1.518 |
| 5 | 1.051 | 1.104 | 1.159 | 1.217 | 1.276 | 1.338 | 1.403 | 1.469 | 1.539 | 1.611 | 1.685 |
| 6 | 1.062 | 1.126 | 1.194 | 1.265 | 1.340 | 1.419 | 1.501 | 1.587 | 1.677 | 1.772 | 1.870 |
| 7 | 1.072 | 1.149 | 1.230 | 1.316 | 1.407 | 1.504 | 1.606 | 1.714 | 1.828 | 1.949 | 2.076 |
| 8 | 1.083 | 1.172 | 1.267 | 1.369 | 1.477 | 1.594 | 1.718 | 1.851 | 1.993 | 2.144 | 2.305 |
| 9 | 1.094 | 1.195 | 1.305 | 1.423 | 1.551 | 1.689 | 1.838 | 1.999 | 2.172 | 2.358 | 2.558 |
| 10 | 1.105 | 1.219 | 1.344 | 1.480 | 1.629 | 1.791 | 1.967 | 2.159 | 2.367 | 2.594 | 2.839 |
| 11 | 1.116 | 1.243 | 1.384 | 1.539 | 1.710 | 1.898 | 2.105 | 2.332 | 2.580 | 2.853 | 3.152 |
| 12 | 1.127 | 1.268 | 1.426 | 1.601 | 1.796 | 2.012 | 2.252 | 2.518 | 2.813 | 3.138 | 3.498 |
| 13 | 1.138 | 1.294 | 1.469 | 1.665 | 1.886 | 2.133 | 2.410 | 2.720 | 3.066 | 3.452 | 3.883 |
| 14 | 1.149 | 1.319 | 1.513 | 1.732 | 1.980 | 2.261 | 2.579 | 2.937 | 3.342 | 3.797 | 4.310 |
| 15 | 1.161 | 1.346 | 1.558 | 1.801 | 2.079 | 2.397 | 2.759 | 3.172 | 3.642 | 4.177 | 4.785 |
| 16 | 1.173 | 1.373 | 1.605 | 1.873 | 2.183 | 2.540 | 2.952 | 3.426 | 3.970 | 4.595 | 5.311 |
| 17 | 1.184 | 1.400 | 1.653 | 1.948 | 2.292 | 2.693 | 3.159 | 3.700 | 4.328 | 5.054 | 5.895 |
| 18 | 1.196 | 1.428 | 1.702 | 2.026 | 2.407 | 2.854 | 3.380 | 3.996 | 4.717 | 5.560 | 6.544 |
| 19 | 1.208 | 1.457 | 1.754 | 2.107 | 2.527 | 3.026 | 3.617 | 4.316 | 5.142 | 6.116 | 7.263 |
| 20 | 1.220 | 1.486 | 1.806 | 2.191 | 2.653 | 3.207 | 3.870 | 4.661 | 5.604 | 6.727 | 8.062 |
| 25 | 1.282 | 1.641 | 2.094 | 2.666 | 3.386 | 4.292 | 5.427 | 6.848 | 8.623 | 10.835 | 13.585 |
| 30 | 1.348 | 1.811 | 2.427 | 3.243 | 4.322 | 5.743 | 7.612 | 10.063 | 13.268 | 17.449 | 22.892 |
| 40 | 1.489 | 2.208 | 3.262 | 4.801 | 7.040 | 10.286 | 14.974 | 21.725 | 31.409 | 45.259 | 65.001 |
| 50 | 1.645 | 2.692 | 4.384 | 7.107 | 11.467 | 18.420 | 29.457 | 46.902 | 74.358 | 117.390 | 184.570 |

## EXHIBIT A-1   (Concluded)

| Period | 12% | 13% | 14% | 15% | 16% | 17% | 18% | 19% | 20% | 25% | 30% |
|---|---|---|---|---|---|---|---|---|---|---|---|
| 1 | 1.120 | 1.130 | 1.140 | 1.150 | 1.160 | 1.170 | 1.180 | 1.190 | 1.200 | 1.250 | 1.300 |
| 2 | 1.254 | 1.277 | 1.300 | 1.323 | 1.346 | 1.369 | 1.392 | 1.416 | 1.440 | 1.563 | 1.690 |
| 3 | 1.405 | 1.443 | 1.482 | 1.521 | 1.561 | 1.602 | 1.643 | 1.685 | 1.728 | 1.953 | 2.197 |
| 4 | 1.574 | 1.630 | 1.689 | 1.749 | 1.811 | 1.874 | 1.939 | 2.005 | 2.074 | 2.441 | 2.856 |
| 5 | 1.762 | 1.842 | 1.925 | 2.011 | 2.100 | 2.192 | 2.288 | 2.386 | 2.488 | 3.052 | 3.713 |
| 6 | 1.974 | 2.082 | 2.195 | 2.313 | 2.436 | 2.565 | 2.700 | 2.840 | 2.986 | 3.815 | 4.827 |
| 7 | 2.211 | 2.353 | 2.502 | 2.660 | 2.826 | 3.001 | 3.185 | 3.379 | 3.583 | 4.768 | 6.276 |
| 8 | 2.476 | 2.658 | 2.853 | 3.059 | 3.278 | 3.511 | 3.759 | 4.021 | 4.300 | 5.960 | 8.157 |
| 9 | 2.773 | 3.004 | 3.252 | 3.518 | 3.803 | 4.108 | 4.435 | 4.785 | 5.160 | 7.451 | 10.604 |
| 10 | 3.106 | 3.395 | 3.707 | 4.046 | 4.411 | 4.807 | 5.234 | 5.696 | 6.192 | 9.313 | 13.786 |
| 11 | 3.479 | 3.836 | 4.226 | 4.652 | 5.117 | 5.624 | 6.176 | 6.777 | 7.430 | 11.642 | 17.922 |
| 12 | 3.896 | 4.335 | 4.818 | 5.350 | 5.936 | 6.580 | 7.288 | 8.064 | 8.916 | 14.552 | 23.298 |
| 13 | 4.363 | 4.898 | 5.492 | 6.153 | 6.886 | 7.699 | 8.599 | 9.596 | 10.699 | 18.190 | 30.288 |
| 14 | 4.887 | 5.535 | 6.261 | 7.076 | 7.988 | 9.007 | 10.147 | 11.420 | 12.839 | 22.737 | 39.374 |
| 15 | 5.474 | 6.254 | 7.138 | 8.137 | 9.266 | 10.539 | 11.974 | 13.590 | 15.407 | 28.422 | 51.186 |
| 16 | 6.130 | 7.067 | 8.137 | 9.358 | 10.748 | 12.330 | 14.129 | 16.172 | 18.488 | 35.527 | 66.542 |
| 17 | 6.866 | 7.986 | 9.276 | 10.761 | 12.468 | 14.426 | 16.672 | 19.244 | 22.186 | 44.409 | 86.504 |
| 18 | 7.690 | 9.024 | 10.575 | 12.375 | 14.463 | 16.879 | 19.673 | 22.091 | 26.623 | 55.511 | 112.460 |
| 19 | 8.613 | 10.197 | 12.056 | 14.232 | 16.777 | 19.748 | 23.214 | 27.252 | 31.948 | 69.389 | 146.190 |
| 20 | 9.646 | 11.523 | 13.743 | 16.367 | 19.461 | 23.106 | 27.393 | 32.429 | 38.338 | 86.736 | 190.050 |
| 25 | 17.000 | 21.231 | 26.462 | 32.919 | 40.874 | 50.658 | 62.669 | 77.388 | 95.396 | 264.700 | 705.640 |
| 30 | 29.960 | 39.116 | 50.950 | 66.212 | 85.850 | 111.070 | 143.370 | 184.680 | 237.380 | 807.790 | 2,620.000 |
| 40 | 93.051 | 132.780 | 188.880 | 267.860 | 378.720 | 533.870 | 750.380 | 1,051.700 | 1,469.800 | 7,523.200 | 36,119.000 |
| 50 | 289.000 | 450.740 | 700.230 | 1,083.700 | 1,670.700 | 2,566.200 | 3,927.400 | 5,988.900 | 9,100.400 | 70,065.000 | 497,929.000 |

## EXHIBIT A-2   Future Value (Compounded Sum) of $1 Paid in at the End of Each Period for a Given Number of Time Periods (an Annuity)

| Period | 1% | 2% | 3% | 4% | 5% | 6% | 7% | 8% | 9% | 10% | 11% |
|---|---|---|---|---|---|---|---|---|---|---|---|
| 1 | 1.000 | 1.000 | 1.000 | 1.000 | 1.000 | 1.000 | 1.000 | 1.000 | 1.000 | 1.000 | 1.000 |
| 2 | 2.010 | 2.020 | 2.030 | 2.040 | 2.050 | 2.060 | 2.070 | 2.080 | 2.090 | 2.100 | 2.110 |
| 3 | 3.030 | 3.060 | 3.091 | 3.122 | 3.153 | 3.184 | 3.215 | 3.246 | 3.278 | 3.310 | 3.342 |
| 4 | 4.060 | 4.122 | 4.184 | 4.246 | 4.310 | 4.375 | 4.440 | 4.506 | 4.573 | 4.641 | 4.710 |
| 5 | 5.101 | 5.204 | 5.309 | 5.416 | 5.526 | 5.637 | 5.751 | 5.867 | 5.985 | 6.105 | 6.228 |
| 6 | 6.152 | 6.308 | 6.468 | 6.633 | 6.802 | 6.975 | 7.153 | 7.336 | 7.523 | 7.716 | 7.913 |
| 7 | 7.214 | 7.434 | 7.662 | 7.898 | 8.142 | 8.394 | 8.654 | 8.923 | 9.200 | 9.487 | 9.783 |
| 8 | 8.286 | 8.583 | 8.892 | 9.214 | 9.549 | 9.897 | 10.260 | 10.637 | 11.028 | 11.436 | 11.859 |
| 9 | 9.369 | 9.755 | 10.159 | 10.583 | 11.027 | 11.491 | 11.978 | 12.488 | 13.021 | 13.579 | 14.164 |
| 10 | 10.462 | 10.950 | 11.464 | 12.006 | 12.578 | 13.181 | 13.816 | 14.487 | 15.193 | 15.937 | 16.722 |
| 11 | 11.567 | 12.169 | 12.808 | 13.486 | 14.207 | 14.972 | 15.784 | 16.645 | 17.560 | 18.531 | 19.561 |
| 12 | 12.683 | 13.412 | 14.192 | 15.026 | 15.917 | 16.870 | 17.888 | 18.977 | 20.141 | 21.384 | 22.713 |
| 13 | 13.809 | 14.680 | 15.618 | 16.627 | 17.713 | 18.882 | 20.141 | 21.495 | 22.953 | 24.523 | 26.212 |
| 14 | 14.947 | 15.974 | 17.086 | 18.292 | 19.599 | 21.015 | 22.550 | 24.215 | 26.019 | 27.975 | 30.095 |
| 15 | 16.097 | 17.293 | 18.599 | 20.024 | 21.579 | 23.276 | 25.129 | 27.152 | 29.361 | 31.772 | 34.405 |
| 16 | 17.258 | 18.639 | 20.157 | 21.825 | 23.657 | 25.673 | 27.888 | 30.324 | 33.003 | 35.950 | 39.190 |
| 17 | 18.430 | 20.012 | 21.762 | 23.698 | 25.840 | 20.213 | 30.840 | 33.750 | 36.974 | 40.545 | 44.501 |
| 18 | 19.615 | 21.412 | 23.414 | 25.645 | 28.132 | 30.906 | 33.999 | 37.450 | 41.301 | 45.599 | 50.396 |
| 19 | 20.811 | 22.841 | 25.117 | 27.671 | 30.539 | 33.760 | 37.379 | 41.446 | 46.018 | 51.159 | 56.939 |
| 20 | 22.019 | 24.297 | 26.870 | 29.778 | 33.066 | 36.786 | 40.995 | 45.762 | 51.160 | 57.275 | 64.203 |
| 25 | 28.243 | 32.030 | 36.459 | 41.646 | 47.727 | 54.865 | 63.249 | 73.106 | 84.701 | 98.347 | 114.410 |
| 30 | 34.785 | 40.588 | 47.575 | 56.085 | 66.439 | 79.058 | 94.461 | 113.280 | 136.310 | 164.490 | 199.020 |
| 40 | 48.886 | 60.402 | 75.401 | 95.026 | 120.800 | 154.760 | 199.640 | 259.060 | 337.890 | 442.590 | 581.830 |
| 50 | 64.463 | 84.579 | 112.800 | 152.670 | 209.350 | 290.340 | 406.530 | 573.770 | 815.080 | 1,163.900 | 1,668.800 |

## EXHIBIT A-2   (Concluded)

| Period | 12% | 13% | 14% | 15% | 16% | 17% | 18% | 19% | 20% | 25% | 30% |
|---|---|---|---|---|---|---|---|---|---|---|---|
| 1 | 1.000 | 1.000 | 1.000 | 1.000 | 1.000 | 1.000 | 1.000 | 1.000 | 1.000 | 1.000 | 1.000 |
| 2 | 2.120 | 2.130 | 2.140 | 2.150 | 2.160 | 2.170 | 2.180 | 2.190 | 2.200 | 2.250 | 2.300 |
| 3 | 3.374 | 3.407 | 3.440 | 3.473 | 3.506 | 3.539 | 3.572 | 3.606 | 3.640 | 3.813 | 3.990 |
| 4 | 4.779 | 4.850 | 4.921 | 4.993 | 5.066 | 5.141 | 5.215 | 5.291 | 5.368 | 5.766 | 6.187 |
| 5 | 6.353 | 6.480 | 6.610 | 6.742 | 6.877 | 7.014 | 7.154 | 7.297 | 7.442 | 8.207 | 9.043 |
| 6 | 8.115 | 8.323 | 8.536 | 8.754 | 8.977 | 9.207 | 9.442 | 9.683 | 9.930 | 11.259 | 12.756 |
| 7 | 10.089 | 10.405 | 10.730 | 11.067 | 11.414 | 11.772 | 12.142 | 12.523 | 12.916 | 15.073 | 17.583 |
| 8 | 12.300 | 12.757 | 13.233 | 13.727 | 14.240 | 14.773 | 15.327 | 15.902 | 16.499 | 19.842 | 23.858 |
| 9 | 14.776 | 15.416 | 16.085 | 16.786 | 17.519 | 18.285 | 19.086 | 19.923 | 20.799 | 25.802 | 32.015 |
| 10 | 17.549 | 18.420 | 19.337 | 20.304 | 21.321 | 22.393 | 23.521 | 24.701 | 25.959 | 33.253 | 42.619 |
| 11 | 20.655 | 21.814 | 23.045 | 24.349 | 25.733 | 27.200 | 28.755 | 30.404 | 32.150 | 42.566 | 56.405 |
| 12 | 24.133 | 25.650 | 27.271 | 29.002 | 30.850 | 32.824 | 34.931 | 37.180 | 39.581 | 54.208 | 74.327 |
| 13 | 28.029 | 29.985 | 32.089 | 34.352 | 36.786 | 39.404 | 42.219 | 45.244 | 48.497 | 68.760 | 97.625 |
| 14 | 32.393 | 34.883 | 37.581 | 40.505 | 43.672 | 47.103 | 50.818 | 54.841 | 59.196 | 86.949 | 127.910 |
| 15 | 37.280 | 40.417 | 43.842 | 47.580 | 51.660 | 56.110 | 60.965 | 66.261 | 72.035 | 109.690 | 167.290 |
| 16 | 42.753 | 46.672 | 50.980 | 55.717 | 60.925 | 66.649 | 72.939 | 79.850 | 87.442 | 138.110 | 218.470 |
| 17 | 48.884 | 53.739 | 59.118 | 65.075 | 71.673 | 78.979 | 87.068 | 96.022 | 105.930 | 173.640 | 285.010 |
| 18 | 55.750 | 61.725 | 68.394 | 75.836 | 84.141 | 93.406 | 103.740 | 115.270 | 128.120 | 218.050 | 371.520 |
| 19 | 63.440 | 70.749 | 78.969 | 88.212 | 98.603 | 110.290 | 123.410 | 138.170 | 154.740 | 273.560 | 483.970 |
| 20 | 72.052 | 80.947 | 91.025 | 102.440 | 115.380 | 130.030 | 146.630 | 165.420 | 186.690 | 342.950 | 630.170 |
| 25 | 133.330 | 155.620 | 181.870 | 212.790 | 249.210 | 292.110 | 342.600 | 402.040 | 471.980 | 1,054.800 | 2,348.800 |
| 30 | 241.330 | 293.200 | 356.790 | 434.750 | 530.310 | 647.440 | 790.950 | 966.700 | 1,181.900 | 3,227.200 | 8,730.000 |
| 40 | 767.090 | 1,013.700 | 1,342.000 | 1,779.100 | 2,360.800 | 3,134.500 | 4,163.210 | 5,529.800 | 7,343.900 | 30,089.000 | 120,393.000 |
| 50 | 2,400.000 | 3,459.500 | 4,994.500 | 7,217.700 | 10,436.000 | 15,090.000 | 21,813.000 | 31,515.000 | 45,497.000 | 80,256.000 | 165,976.000 |

## EXHIBIT A-3   Present Value of $1 to Be Received at the End of a Given Number of Time Periods

| Period | 1% | 2% | 3% | 4% | 5% | 6% | 7% | 8% | 9% | 10% | 11% | 12% |
|--------|------|------|------|------|------|------|------|------|------|------|------|------|
| 1  | 0.990 | 0.980 | 0.971 | 0.962 | 0.952 | 0.943 | 0.935 | 0.926 | 0.917 | 0.909 | 0.901 | 0.893 |
| 2  | 0.980 | 0.961 | 0.943 | 0.925 | 0.907 | 0.890 | 0.873 | 0.857 | 0.842 | 0.826 | 0.812 | 0.797 |
| 3  | 0.971 | 0.942 | 0.915 | 0.889 | 0.864 | 0.840 | 0.816 | 0.794 | 0.772 | 0.751 | 0.731 | 0.712 |
| 4  | 0.961 | 0.924 | 0.885 | 0.855 | 0.823 | 0.792 | 0.763 | 0.735 | 0.708 | 0.683 | 0.659 | 0.636 |
| 5  | 0.951 | 0.906 | 0.863 | 0.822 | 0.784 | 0.747 | 0.713 | 0.681 | 0.650 | 0.621 | 0.593 | 0.567 |
| 6  | 0.942 | 0.888 | 0.837 | 0.790 | 0.746 | 0.705 | 0.666 | 0.630 | 0.596 | 0.564 | 0.535 | 0.507 |
| 7  | 0.933 | 0.871 | 0.813 | 0.760 | 0.711 | 0.665 | 0.623 | 0.583 | 0.547 | 0.513 | 0.482 | 0.452 |
| 8  | 0.923 | 0.853 | 0.789 | 0.731 | 0.677 | 0.627 | 0.582 | 0.540 | 0.502 | 0.467 | 0.434 | 0.404 |
| 9  | 0.914 | 0.837 | 0.766 | 0.703 | 0.645 | 0.592 | 0.544 | 0.500 | 0.460 | 0.424 | 0.391 | 0.361 |
| 10 | 0.905 | 0.820 | 0.744 | 0.676 | 0.614 | 0.558 | 0.508 | 0.463 | 0.422 | 0.386 | 0.352 | 0.322 |
| 11 | 0.896 | 0.804 | 0.722 | 0.650 | 0.585 | 0.527 | 0.475 | 0.429 | 0.388 | 0.350 | 0.317 | 0.287 |
| 12 | 0.887 | 0.788 | 0.701 | 0.625 | 0.557 | 0.497 | 0.444 | 0.397 | 0.356 | 0.319 | 0.286 | 0.257 |
| 13 | 0.879 | 0.773 | 0.681 | 0.601 | 0.530 | 0.469 | 0.415 | 0.368 | 0.326 | 0.290 | 0.258 | 0.229 |
| 14 | 0.870 | 0.758 | 0.661 | 0.577 | 0.505 | 0.442 | 0.388 | 0.340 | 0.299 | 0.263 | 0.232 | 0.205 |
| 15 | 0.861 | 0.743 | 0.642 | 0.555 | 0.481 | 0.417 | 0.362 | 0.315 | 0.275 | 0.239 | 0.209 | 0.183 |
| 16 | 0.853 | 0.728 | 0.623 | 0.534 | 0.458 | 0.394 | 0.339 | 0.292 | 0.252 | 0.218 | 0.188 | 0.163 |
| 17 | 0.844 | 0.714 | 0.605 | 0.513 | 0.436 | 0.371 | 0.317 | 0.270 | 0.231 | 0.198 | 0.170 | 0.146 |
| 18 | 0.836 | 0.700 | 0.587 | 0.494 | 0.416 | 0.350 | 0.296 | 0.250 | 0.212 | 0.180 | 0.153 | 0.130 |
| 19 | 0.828 | 0.686 | 0.570 | 0.475 | 0.396 | 0.331 | 0.277 | 0.232 | 0.194 | 0.164 | 0.138 | 0.116 |
| 20 | 0.820 | 0.673 | 0.554 | 0.456 | 0.377 | 0.312 | 0.258 | 0.215 | 0.178 | 0.149 | 0.124 | 0.104 |
| 25 | 0.780 | 0.610 | 0.478 | 0.375 | 0.295 | 0.233 | 0.184 | 0.146 | 0.116 | 0.092 | 0.074 | 0.059 |
| 30 | 0.742 | 0.552 | 0.412 | 0.308 | 0.231 | 0.174 | 0.131 | 0.099 | 0.075 | 0.057 | 0.044 | 0.033 |
| 40 | 0.672 | 0.453 | 0.307 | 0.208 | 0.142 | 0.097 | 0.067 | 0.046 | 0.032 | 0.022 | 0.015 | 0.011 |
| 50 | 0.608 | 0.372 | 0.228 | 0.141 | 0.087 | 0.054 | 0.034 | 0.021 | 0.013 | 0.009 | 0.005 | 0.003 |

## EXHIBIT A-3   (Concluded)

| Period | 13% | 14% | 15% | 16% | 17% | 18% | 19% | 20% | 25% | 30% | 35% | 40% | 50% |
|--------|------|------|------|------|------|------|------|------|------|------|------|------|------|
| 1  | 0.885 | 0.877 | 0.870 | 0.862 | 0.855 | 0.847 | 0.840 | 0.833 | 0.800 | 0.769 | 0.741 | 0.714 | 0.667 |
| 2  | 0.783 | 0.769 | 0.756 | 0.743 | 0.731 | 0.718 | 0.706 | 0.694 | 0.640 | 0.592 | 0.549 | 0.510 | 0.444 |
| 3  | 0.693 | 0.675 | 0.658 | 0.641 | 0.624 | 0.609 | 0.593 | 0.579 | 0.512 | 0.455 | 0.406 | 0.364 | 0.296 |
| 4  | 0.613 | 0.592 | 0.572 | 0.552 | 0.534 | 0.515 | 0.499 | 0.482 | 0.410 | 0.350 | 0.301 | 0.260 | 0.198 |
| 5  | 0.543 | 0.519 | 0.497 | 0.476 | 0.456 | 0.437 | 0.419 | 0.402 | 0.320 | 0.269 | 0.223 | 0.186 | 0.132 |
| 6  | 0.480 | 0.456 | 0.432 | 0.410 | 0.390 | 0.370 | 0.352 | 0.335 | 0.262 | 0.207 | 0.165 | 0.133 | 0.088 |
| 7  | 0.425 | 0.400 | 0.376 | 0.354 | 0.333 | 0.314 | 0.296 | 0.279 | 0.210 | 0.159 | 0.122 | 0.095 | 0.059 |
| 8  | 0.376 | 0.351 | 0.327 | 0.305 | 0.285 | 0.266 | 0.249 | 0.233 | 0.168 | 0.123 | 0.091 | 0.068 | 0.039 |
| 9  | 0.333 | 0.300 | 0.284 | 0.263 | 0.243 | 0.225 | 0.209 | 0.194 | 0.134 | 0.094 | 0.067 | 0.048 | 0.026 |
| 10 | 0.295 | 0.270 | 0.247 | 0.227 | 0.208 | 0.191 | 0.176 | 0.162 | 0.107 | 0.073 | 0.050 | 0.035 | 0.017 |
| 11 | 0.261 | 0.237 | 0.215 | 0.195 | 0.178 | 0.162 | 0.148 | 0.135 | 0.086 | 0.056 | 0.037 | 0.025 | 0.012 |
| 12 | 0.231 | 0.208 | 0.187 | 0.168 | 0.152 | 0.137 | 0.124 | 0.112 | 0.069 | 0.043 | 0.027 | 0.018 | 0.008 |
| 13 | 0.204 | 0.182 | 0.163 | 0.145 | 0.130 | 0.116 | 0.104 | 0.093 | 0.055 | 0.033 | 0.020 | 0.013 | 0.005 |
| 14 | 0.181 | 0.160 | 0.141 | 0.125 | 0.111 | 0.099 | 0.088 | 0.078 | 0.044 | 0.025 | 0.015 | 0.009 | 0.003 |
| 15 | 0.160 | 0.140 | 0.123 | 0.108 | 0.095 | 0.084 | 0.074 | 0.065 | 0.035 | 0.020 | 0.011 | 0.006 | 0.002 |
| 16 | 0.141 | 0.123 | 0.107 | 0.093 | 0.081 | 0.071 | 0.062 | 0.054 | 0.028 | 0.015 | 0.008 | 0.005 | 0.002 |
| 17 | 0.125 | 0.108 | 0.093 | 0.080 | 0.069 | 0.060 | 0.052 | 0.045 | 0.023 | 0.012 | 0.006 | 0.003 | 0.001 |
| 18 | 0.111 | 0.095 | 0.081 | 0.069 | 0.059 | 0.051 | 0.044 | 0.038 | 0.018 | 0.009 | 0.005 | 0.002 | 0.001 |
| 19 | 0.098 | 0.083 | 0.070 | 0.060 | 0.051 | 0.043 | 0.037 | 0.031 | 0.014 | 0.007 | 0.003 | 0.002 | 0 |
| 20 | 0.087 | 0.073 | 0.061 | 0.051 | 0.043 | 0.037 | 0.031 | 0.026 | 0.012 | 0.005 | 0.002 | 0.001 | 0 |
| 25 | 0.047 | 0.038 | 0.030 | 0.024 | 0.020 | 0.016 | 0.013 | 0.010 | 0.004 | 0.001 | 0.001 | 0 | 0 |
| 30 | 0.026 | 0.020 | 0.015 | 0.012 | 0.009 | 0.007 | 0.005 | 0.004 | 0.001 | 0 | 0 | 0 | 0 |
| 40 | 0.008 | 0.005 | 0.004 | 0.003 | 0.002 | 0.001 | 0.001 | 0.001 | 0 | 0 | 0 | 0 | 0 |
| 50 | 0.002 | 0.001 | 0.001 | 0.001 | 0 | 0 | 0 | 0 | 0 | 0 | 0 | 0 | 0 |

**EXHIBIT A-4**   Present Value of $1 Received at the End of Each Period for a Given Number of Time Periods (an Annuity)

| Period | 1% | 2% | 3% | 4% | 5% | 6% | 7% | 8% | 9% | 10% | 11% | 12% |
|---|---|---|---|---|---|---|---|---|---|---|---|---|
| 1 | 0.990 | 0.980 | 0.971 | 0.962 | 0.952 | 0.943 | 0.935 | 0.926 | 0.917 | 0.909 | 0.901 | 0.893 |
| 2 | 1.970 | 1.942 | 1.913 | 1.886 | 1.859 | 1.833 | 1.808 | 1.783 | 1.759 | 1.736 | 1.713 | 1.690 |
| 3 | 2.941 | 2.884 | 2.829 | 2.775 | 2.723 | 2.673 | 2.624 | 2.577 | 2.531 | 2.487 | 2.444 | 2.402 |
| 4 | 3.902 | 3.808 | 3.717 | 3.630 | 3.546 | 3.465 | 3.387 | 3.312 | 3.240 | 3.170 | 3.102 | 3.037 |
| 5 | 4.853 | 4.713 | 4.580 | 4.452 | 4.329 | 4.212 | 4.100 | 3.993 | 3.890 | 3.791 | 3.696 | 3.605 |
| 6 | 5.795 | 5.601 | 5.417 | 5.242 | 5.076 | 4.917 | 4.767 | 4.623 | 4.486 | 4.355 | 4.231 | 4.111 |
| 7 | 6.728 | 6.472 | 6.230 | 6.002 | 5.786 | 5.582 | 5.389 | 5.206 | 5.033 | 4.868 | 4.712 | 4.564 |
| 8 | 7.652 | 7.325 | 7.020 | 6.733 | 6.463 | 6.210 | 5.971 | 5.747 | 5.535 | 5.335 | 5.146 | 4.968 |
| 9 | 8.566 | 8.162 | 7.786 | 7.435 | 7.108 | 6.802 | 6.515 | 6.247 | 5.995 | 5.759 | 5.537 | 5.328 |
| 10 | 9.471 | 8.983 | 8.530 | 8.111 | 7.722 | 7.360 | 7.024 | 6.710 | 6.418 | 6.145 | 5.889 | 5.650 |
| 11 | 10.368 | 9.787 | 9.253 | 8.760 | 8.306 | 7.887 | 7.499 | 7.139 | 6.805 | 6.495 | 6.207 | 5.938 |
| 12 | 11.255 | 10.575 | 9.954 | 9.385 | 8.863 | 8.384 | 7.943 | 7.536 | 7.161 | 6.814 | 6.492 | 6.194 |
| 13 | 12.134 | 11.348 | 10.635 | 9.986 | 9.394 | 8.853 | 8.358 | 7.904 | 7.487 | 7.103 | 6.750 | 6.424 |
| 14 | 13.004 | 12.106 | 11.296 | 10.563 | 9.899 | 9.295 | 8.745 | 8.244 | 7.786 | 7.367 | 6.982 | 6.628 |
| 15 | 13.865 | 12.849 | 11.939 | 11.118 | 10.380 | 9.712 | 9.108 | 8.559 | 8.061 | 7.606 | 7.191 | 6.811 |
| 16 | 14.718 | 13.578 | 12.561 | 11.652 | 10.838 | 10.106 | 9.447 | 8.851 | 8.313 | 7.824 | 7.379 | 6.974 |
| 17 | 15.562 | 14.292 | 13.166 | 12.166 | 11.274 | 10.477 | 9.763 | 9.122 | 8.544 | 8.022 | 7.549 | 7.102 |
| 18 | 16.398 | 14.992 | 13.754 | 12.659 | 11.690 | 10.828 | 10.059 | 9.372 | 8.756 | 8.201 | 7.702 | 7.250 |
| 19 | 17.226 | 15.678 | 14.324 | 13.134 | 12.085 | 11.158 | 10.336 | 9.604 | 8.950 | 8.365 | 7.839 | 7.366 |
| 20 | 18.046 | 16.351 | 14.877 | 13.590 | 12.462 | 11.470 | 10.594 | 9.818 | 9.129 | 8.514 | 7.963 | 7.469 |
| 25 | 22.023 | 19.523 | 17.413 | 15.622 | 14.094 | 12.783 | 11.654 | 10.675 | 9.823 | 9.077 | 8.422 | 7.843 |
| 30 | 25.808 | 22.396 | 19.600 | 17.292 | 15.372 | 13.765 | 12.409 | 11.258 | 10.274 | 9.427 | 8.694 | 8.055 |
| 40 | 32.835 | 27.355 | 23.115 | 19.793 | 17.159 | 15.046 | 13.332 | 11.925 | 10.757 | 9.779 | 8.951 | 8.244 |
| 50 | 39.196 | 31.424 | 25.730 | 21.482 | 18.256 | 15.762 | 13.801 | 12.233 | 10.962 | 9.915 | 9.042 | 8.304 |

**EXHIBIT C-4**   (Concluded)

| Period | 13% | 14% | 15% | 16% | 17% | 18% | 19% | 20% | 25% | 30% | 35% | 40% | 50% |
|---|---|---|---|---|---|---|---|---|---|---|---|---|---|
| 1 | 0.885 | 0.877 | 0.870 | 0.862 | 0.855 | 0.847 | 0.840 | 0.833 | 0.800 | 0.769 | 0.741 | 0.714 | 0.667 |
| 2 | 1.668 | 1.647 | 1.626 | 1.605 | 1.585 | 1.566 | 1.547 | 1.528 | 1.440 | 1.361 | 1.289 | 1.224 | 1.111 |
| 3 | 2.361 | 2.322 | 2.283 | 2.246 | 2.210 | 2.174 | 2.140 | 2.106 | 1.952 | 1.816 | 1.696 | 1.589 | 1.407 |
| 4 | 2.974 | 2.914 | 2.855 | 2.798 | 2.743 | 2.690 | 2.639 | 2.589 | 2.362 | 2.166 | 1.997 | 1.849 | 1.605 |
| 5 | 3.517 | 3.433 | 3.352 | 3.274 | 3.199 | 3.127 | 3.058 | 2.991 | 2.689 | 2.436 | 2.220 | 2.035 | 1.737 |
| 6 | 3.998 | 3.889 | 3.784 | 3.685 | 3.589 | 3.498 | 3.410 | 3.326 | 2.951 | 2.643 | 2.385 | 2.168 | 1.824 |
| 7 | 4.423 | 4.288 | 4.160 | 4.039 | 3.922 | 3.812 | 3.706 | 3.605 | 3.161 | 2.802 | 2.508 | 2.263 | 1.883 |
| 8 | 4.799 | 4.639 | 4.487 | 4.344 | 4.207 | 4.078 | 3.954 | 3.837 | 3.329 | 2.925 | 2.598 | 2.331 | 1.922 |
| 9 | 5.132 | 4.946 | 4.772 | 4.607 | 4.451 | 4.303 | 4.163 | 4.031 | 3.463 | 3.019 | 2.665 | 2.379 | 1.948 |
| 10 | 5.426 | 5.216 | 5.019 | 4.833 | 4.659 | 4.494 | 4.339 | 4.192 | 3.571 | 3.092 | 2.715 | 2.414 | 1.965 |
| 11 | 5.687 | 5.453 | 5.234 | 5.029 | 4.836 | 4.656 | 4.486 | 4.327 | 3.656 | 3.147 | 2.752 | 2.438 | 1.977 |
| 12 | 5.918 | 5.660 | 5.421 | 5.197 | 4.988 | 4.793 | 4.611 | 4.439 | 3.725 | 3.190 | 2.779 | 2.456 | 1.985 |
| 13 | 6.122 | 5.842 | 5.583 | 5.342 | 5.118 | 4.910 | 4.715 | 4.533 | 3.780 | 3.223 | 2.799 | 2.469 | 1.990 |
| 14 | 6.302 | 6.002 | 5.724 | 5.468 | 5.229 | 5.008 | 4.802 | 4.611 | 3.824 | 3.249 | 2.814 | 2.478 | 1.993 |
| 15 | 6.462 | 6.142 | 5.847 | 5.575 | 5.324 | 5.092 | 4.876 | 4.675 | 3.859 | 3.268 | 2.825 | 2.484 | 1.995 |
| 16 | 6.604 | 6.265 | 5.954 | 5.668 | 5.405 | 5.162 | 4.938 | 4.730 | 3.887 | 3.283 | 2.834 | 2.489 | 1.997 |
| 17 | 6.729 | 6.373 | 6.047 | 5.749 | 5.475 | 5.222 | 4.988 | 4.775 | 3.910 | 3.295 | 2.840 | 2.492 | 1.998 |
| 18 | 6.840 | 6.467 | 6.128 | 5.818 | 5.534 | 5.273 | 5.033 | 4.812 | 3.928 | 3.304 | 2.844 | 2.494 | 1.999 |
| 19 | 6.938 | 6.550 | 6.198 | 5.877 | 5.584 | 5.316 | 5.070 | 4.843 | 3.942 | 3.311 | 2.848 | 2.496 | 1.999 |
| 20 | 7.025 | 6.623 | 6.259 | 5.929 | 5.628 | 5.353 | 5.101 | 4.870 | 3.954 | 3.316 | 2.850 | 2.497 | 1.999 |
| 25 | 7.330 | 6.873 | 6.464 | 6.097 | 5.766 | 5.467 | 5.195 | 4.948 | 3.985 | 3.329 | 2.856 | 2.499 | 2.000 |
| 30 | 7.496 | 7.003 | 6.566 | 6.177 | 5.829 | 5.517 | 5.235 | 4.979 | 3.995 | 3.332 | 2.857 | 2.500 | 2.000 |
| 40 | 7.634 | 7.105 | 6.642 | 6.233 | 5.871 | 5.548 | 5.258 | 4.997 | 3.999 | 3.333 | 2.857 | 2.500 | 2.000 |
| 50 | 7.675 | 7.133 | 6.661 | 6.246 | 5.880 | 5.554 | 5.262 | 4.999 | 4.000 | 3.333 | 2.857 | 2.500 | 2.000 |

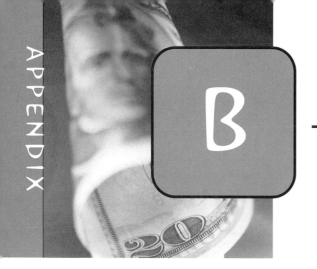

APPENDIX

# B

# Consumer Agencies and Organizations

The following government agencies and private organizations can offer information and assistance on various financial planning and consumer purchasing areas. These groups can serve your needs when you want to

- Research a financial or consumer topic area.
- Obtain information for planning a purchase decision.
- Seek assistance to resolve a consumer problem.

Section 1 provides an overview of federal, state, and local agencies and other organizations you may contact for information related to various financial planning and consumer topic areas. Section 2 lists state consumer protection offices that can assist you in local matters.

## SECTION 1

Most federal agencies may be contacted through the Internet; several websites are noted. In addition, consumer information from several federal government agencies may be accessed at www.consumer.gov

| Topic Area | Federal Agency | State, Local Agency; Other Organizations |
|---|---|---|
| **Advertising**<br>False advertising<br>Product labeling<br>Deceptive sales practices<br>Warranties | Federal Trade Commission<br>Sixth and Pennsylvania Avenue, NW<br>Washington, DC 20580<br>(202) 326–2222<br>(www.ftc.gov) | State Consumer Protection Office<br>c/o State Attorney General or Governor's Office<br>  (see Section 2)<br><br>National Fraud Information Center<br>Box 65868<br>Washington, DC 20035<br>1–800–876–7060<br>(www.fraud.org) |
| **Air Travel**<br>Air safety<br>Airport regulation<br>Airline route | Federal Aviation Administration<br>800 Independence Avenue<br>Washington, DC 20591<br>1–800–FAA–SURE<br>(www.faa.gov) | International Airline Passengers Association<br>Box 660074<br>Dallas, TX 75266<br>1–800–527–5888<br>(www.iapa.com) |

**SECTION 1** (Continued)

| Topic Area | Federal Agency | State, Local Agency; Other Organizations |
| --- | --- | --- |
| **Appliances/Product Safety**<br>Potentially dangerous products<br>Complaints against retailers,<br>  manufacturers | Consumer Product Safety Commission<br>Washington, DC 20207<br>1–800–638–CPSC<br>(www.cpsc.gov) | Council of Better Business Bureau<br>4200 Wilson Boulevard<br>Arlington, VA 22203<br>(703) 276–0100<br>(www.bbb.org) |
| **Automobiles**<br>New cars<br>Used cars<br>Automobile repairs<br>Auto safety | Federal Trade Commission (see above)<br><br>National Highway Traffic Safety Administration<br>400 Seventh Street, SW<br>Washington, DC 20590<br>1–800–424–9393<br>(www.nhtsa.dot.gov) | AUTOCAP/National Automobile Dealers<br>  Association<br>8400 Westpark Drive<br>McLean, VA 22102<br>(703) 821–7144<br><br>Center for Auto Safety<br>2001 S Street, NW<br>Washington, DC 20009<br>(202) 328–7700 |
| **Banking and Financial<br>  Institutions**<br>Checking accounts<br>Savings accounts<br>Deposit insurance<br>Financial services | Federal Deposit Insurance Corporation<br>550 17th Street, NW<br>Washington, DC 20429<br>1–800–934–3342<br>(www.fdic.gov)<br><br>Comptroller of the Currency<br>15th Street and Pennsylvania Avenue, NW<br>Washington, DC 20219<br>(202) 447–1600<br><br>Federal Reserve Board<br>Washington, DC 20551<br>(202) 452–3693<br>(www.federalreserve.gov)<br><br>National Credit Union Administration<br>1775 Duke St.<br>Alexandria, VA 22314<br>(703) 518–6300<br>(www.ncua.gov) | State Banking Authority (see Section 2)<br><br>Credit Union National Association<br>Box 431<br>Madison, WI 53701<br>(608) 231–4000<br>(www.cuna.org)<br><br>American Bankers Association<br>1120 Connecticut Avenue, NW<br>Washington, DC 20036<br>(202) 663–5000<br>(www.aba.com)<br><br>U.S. savings bond rates<br>1–800–US–BONDS |
| **Career Planning**<br>Job training<br>Employment information | Coordinator of Consumer Affairs<br>Department of Labor<br>Washington, DC 20210<br>(202) 219–6060<br>(www.dol.gov) | State Department of Labor or State Employment<br>  Service |
| **Consumer Credit**<br>Credit cards<br>Deceptive credit advertising<br>Truth-in-Lending Act<br>Credit rights of women,<br>  minorities | Federal Trade Commission<br>Sixth Street and Pennsylvania Avenue, NW<br>Washington, DC 20580<br>(202) 326–2222<br>(www.ftc.gov) | Debt Counselors of America<br>(www.dca.org)<br><br>Consumer Credit Counseling Service<br>8701 Georgia Avenue, Suite 507<br>Silver Spring, MD 20910<br>1–800–388–2227<br>(www.nccs.org) |
| **Environment**<br>Air, water pollution<br>Toxic substances | Environmental Protection Agency<br>Washington, DC 20460<br>1–800–438–4318 (indoor air quality)<br>1–800–426–4791 (drinking water safety)<br>(www.epa.gov) | Clean Water Action Project<br>317 Pennsylvania Avenue, SE<br>Washington, DC 20003<br>(202) 547–1196 |

**(Continued)**

| Topic Area | Federal Agency | State, Local Agency; Other Organizations |
|---|---|---|
| **Food**<br>Food grades<br>Food additives<br>Nutritional information | U.S. Department of Agriculture<br>Washington, DC 20250<br>1–800–424–9121<br>(www.usda.gov)<br><br>Food and Drug Administration<br>5600 Fishers Lane<br>Rockville, MD 20857<br>(301) 443–3170<br>(www.fda.gov) | Center for Science in the Public Interest<br>1875 Connecticut Avenue, NW, Suite 300<br>Washington, DC 20009<br>(202) 332–9110<br>(www.cspinet.org) |
| **Funerals**<br>Cost disclosure<br>Deceptive business practices | Federal Trade Commission (see above) | Funeral Service Consumer Arbitration Program<br>11121 West Oklahoma Avenue<br>Milwaukee, WI 53227<br>(414) 541–2500 |
| **Housing and Real Estate**<br>Fair housing practices<br>Mortgages<br>Community development | Department of Housing and Urban Development<br>451 Seventh Street, SW<br>Washington, DC 20410<br>1–800–669–9777<br>(www.hud.gov) | National Association of Realtors<br>430 North Michigan Avenue<br>Chicago, IL 60611<br>(312) 329–8200<br><br>National Association of Home Builders<br>15th and M Streets, NW<br>Washington, DC 20005 |
| **Insurance**<br>Policy conditions<br>Premiums<br>Types of coverage<br>Consumer complaints | Federal Trade Commission (see above)<br><br>National Flood Insurance Program<br>Box 459<br>Landam, MD 20706-0459<br>1–800–638–6620 | State Insurance Regulator (see Section 2)<br><br>American Council of Life Insurance<br>1001 Pennsylvania Avenue, NW<br>Washington, DC 20004-2599<br>1–800–942-4242<br><br>Insurance Information Institute<br>110 William Street<br>New York, NY 10038<br>(212) 669-9250<br>(www.iii.org) |
| **Investments**<br>Stocks, bonds<br>Mutual funds<br>Commodities<br>Investment brokers | Securities and Exchange Commission<br>450 Fifth Street, NW<br>Washington, DC 20549<br>(202) 272–7440<br>(www.sec.gov)<br><br>Commodity Futures Trading Commission<br>2033 K Street, NW<br>Washington, DC 20581<br>(202) 254-8630 | Investment Company Institute<br>1600 M Street, NW<br>Washington, DC 20036<br>(202) 293–7700<br>(www.ici.org)<br><br>National Association of Securities Dealers<br>1735 K Street, NW<br>Washington, DC 20006<br>(202) 728–8000<br><br>National Futures Association<br>200 West Madison Street<br>Chicago, IL 60606<br>1–800–621-3570<br><br>Securities Investor Protection Corp.<br>805 15th Street, NW, Suite 800<br>Washington, DC 20003<br>(202) 371–8300 |

**SECTION 1** (Concluded)

| Topic Area | Federal Agency | State, Local Agency; Other Organizations |
|---|---|---|
| **Legal Matters** <br> Consumer complaints <br> Arbitration | Department of Justice <br> Office of Consumer Litigation <br> Washington, DC 20530 <br> (202) 514–2401 | American Arbitration Association <br> 140 West 51st Street <br> New York, NY 10020 <br> (212) 484–4000 <br><br> American Bar Association <br> 750 North Lake Shore Drive <br> Chicago, IL 60611 <br> (312) 988–5000 <br> (www.abanet.org) |
| **Mail Order** <br> Damaged products <br> Deceptive business practices <br> Illegal use of U.S. mail | U.S. Postal Service <br> Washington, DC 20260-2100 <br> (202) 268–4298 <br> (www.usps.gov) | Direct Marketing Association <br> 6 East 43rd Street <br> New York, NY 10017 <br> (212) 689–4977 |
| **Medical Concerns** <br> Prescription medications <br> Over-the-counter medications <br> Medical devices <br> Health care | Food and Drug Administration (see above) <br> Public Health Service <br> 200 Independence Avenue, SW <br> Washington, DC 20201 <br> 1–800–336–4797 <br> (www.fda.gov) | American Medical Association <br> 535 North Dearborn <br> Chicago, IL 60610 <br> (312) 645–5000 <br><br> Public Citizen Health Research Group <br> 2000 P Street <br> Washington, DC 20036 <br> (202) 872–0320 |
| **Retirement** <br> Old-age benefits <br> Pension information <br> Medicare | Social Security Administration <br> 6401 Security Boulevard <br> Baltimore, MD 21235 <br> 1–800–772–1213 <br> (www.ssa.gov) | American Association of Retired Persons <br> 601 E Street, NW <br> Washington, DC 20049 <br> (202) 434–2277 <br> (www.aarp.org) |
| **Taxes** <br> Tax information <br> Audit procedures | Internal Revenue Service <br> 1111 Constitution Avenue, NW <br> Washington, DC 20204 <br> 1–800–829–1040 <br> 1–800–TAX–FORM <br> (www.irs.gov) | Department of Revenue (in your state capital city) <br><br> The Tax Foundation <br> One Thomas Circle <br> Washington, DC 20005 <br> (202) 822–9050 <br><br> National Association of Enrolled Agents <br> 6000 Executive Blvd. <br> Rockville, MD 20852 <br> 1–800–424–4339 |
| **Telemarketing** <br> 900 numbers | Federal Communications Commission <br> 1919 M Street, NW <br> Washington, DC 20554 <br> (202) 632–6999 <br> (www.fcc.gov) | National Consumers League <br> 815 Fifteenth Street, NW <br> Washington, DC 20005 <br> (202) 639–8140 <br> (www.natlconsumersleague.org) |
| **Utilities** <br> Cable television <br> Utility rates | Federal Communications Commission <br> 1919 M Street, NW <br> Washington, DC 20554 <br> (202) 632–6999 <br> (www.fcc.gov) | State utility commission (in your state capital) |

Information on additional government agencies and private organizations may be obtained from these publications:

*Consumer's Resource Handbook*
   Consumer Information Center
   Pueblo, CO 81009
   www.pueblo.gsa.gov
   (copies available at no charge)

*Consumer Sourcebook*
   Gale Research, Inc.
   Book Tower
   Detroit, MI 48226
   (available in many school and public libraries)

## SECTION 2

This section provides contacts for state consumer protection, banking, and insurance agencies. Many state consumer protection offices may be accessed through the website of the National Association of Attorneys General at www.naag.org.

You may also find the website for your state consumer protection office by using a search engine with the following words: "(state)+consumer+protection+agency."

Some of the most informative state consumer protection websites useful to all consumers include

- The Tennessee Divison of Consumer Affairs at www.state.tn.us/consumer.
- The Florida Department of Agriculture and Consumer Services at www/fl-ag.com.
- The New Jersey Consumer Affair Department at www.state.nj.us/lpa/ca/home.htm.
- The Minnesota attorney general at www.ag.state.mn.us/consumer.

Most state departments of insurance may be accessed on the Internet at www.fdn.net/statedoi.html.

The websites of state tax departments are available at www.taxadmin.org or www.best.com/~ftmexpat/html/taxsites.statelaw.html.

| State Consumer Protection Offices | State Banking Authorities | State Insurance Regulators |
|---|---|---|
| **Alabama** | | |
| Consumer Protection Division Office of Attorney General 11 South Union Street Montgomery, AL 36130 (334) 242–7334 1–800–392–5658 (toll-free in AL) | Superintendent of Banks 401 Adams Avenue, #680 Montgomery, AL 36130 (334) 242–3452 | Insurance Commissioner 201 Monroe Street #1700 Montgomery, AL 36104 (334) 269–3550 |
| **Alaska** | | |
| Consumer Protection Unit Office of the   Attorney General 1031 W. 4th Avenue (#200) Anchorage, AK 99501 (907) 276–8554 | Director of Banking, Securities and   Corporations P.O. Box 110807 Juneau, AK 99811-0807 (907) 465–2521 | Director of Insurance P.O. Box 110805 Juneau, AK 99811-0805 (907) 465–2515 |
| **Arizona** | | |
| Consumer Fraud Division Office of Attorney General 1275 West Washington Street Phoenix, AZ 85007 (602) 542–3702 1–800–352–8431 (toll-free in AZ) | Superintendent of Banks 2910 North 44th St. Phoenix, AZ 85018 (602) 255–4421 1–800–352–8400 (toll-free in AZ) | Department of Insurance 2910 North 44th Street, Suite 210 Phoenix, AZ 85018-7256 (602) 912–8444 1–800–325–2548 (toll-free in AZ) |

**SECTION 2**    (Continued)

| State Consumer Protection Offices | State Banking Authorities | State Insurance Regulators |
|---|---|---|
| **Arkansas**<br>Consumer Protection Division<br>Office of Attorney General<br>200 Catlett Prien<br>323 Center Street<br>Little Rock, AR 72201<br>(501) 682–2341<br>1–800–482–8982 (toll-free in AR) | Bank Commissioner<br>Tower Building<br>323 Center Street, Suite 500<br>Little Rock, AR 72201-2613<br>(501) 324–9019 | Insurance Commissioner<br>1200 West 3rd St.<br>Little Rock, AR 72201-1904<br>(501) 371–2600<br>1–800–852–5494 |
| **California**<br>California Department of Consumer<br>  Affairs<br>400 R Street, Suite 3000<br>Sacramento, CA 95814<br>(916) 445–4465<br>1–800–952–5210 (toll-free in CA) | Superintendent of Banks<br>111 Pine Street, Suite 1100<br>San Francisco, CA 94111-5613<br>(415) 263–8507<br>1–800–622–0620 (toll-free in CA) | Commissioner of Insurance<br>300 Capitol Mall, Suite 1500<br>Sacramento, CA 95814<br>(916) 445–5544<br>1–800–927–HELP (toll-free in CA) |
| **Colorado**<br>Consumer Protection Unit<br>Office of Attorney General<br>1525 Sherman St., 5th Floor<br>Denver, CO 80203-1760<br>(303) 866–5189<br>1–800–332–2071 (toll-free in CO) | State Bank Commissioner<br>Division of Banking<br>1560 Broadway St., Suite 1175<br>Denver, CO 80202<br>(303) 894–7575 | Commissioner of Insurance<br>1560 Broadway St., Suite 850<br>Denver, CO 80202<br>(303) 894–7499 (ext. 4311) |
| **Connecticut**<br>Department of Consumer Protection<br>State Office Building<br>165 Capitol Avenue<br>Hartford, CT 06106<br>(860) 566–2534<br>1–800–842–2649 (toll-free in CT) | Banking Commissioner<br>260 Constitution Plaza<br>Hartford, CT 06103<br>(860) 240–8100<br>1–800–831–7225 (toll-free in CT) | Insurance Commissioner<br>P.O. Box 816<br>Hartford, CT 06142-0816<br>(860) 297–3800 |
| **Delaware**<br>Consumer Protection Unit<br>Department of Justice<br>820 North French Street, 4th Floor<br>Wilmington, DE 19801<br>(302) 577–8600<br>1–800–220–5424 (toll-free in DE) | State Bank Commissioner<br>555 East Lockerman Street, Suite 210<br>Dover, DE 19901<br>(302) 739–4235<br>1–800–638–3376 (toll-free in DE) | Insurance Commissioner<br>841 Silver Lake Boulevard<br>Dover, DE 19901<br>(302) 739–4251<br>1–800–282–8611 (toll-free in DE) |
| **District of Columbia**<br>Department of Consumer and Regulatory<br>  Affairs<br>614 H Street, NW<br>Washington, DC 20001<br>(202) 727–7120 | Superintendent of Banking and Financial<br>  Institutions<br>714 14th St., NW (11th floor)<br>Washington, DC 20005<br>(202) 727–1563 | Superintendent of Insurance<br>441 4th Street, NW<br>One Judiciary Square, 8th Floor<br>Washington, DC 20001<br>(202) 727–8000 (ext. 3007) |
| **Florida**<br>Department of Agriculture and<br>  Consumer Services<br>Division of Consumer Services<br>Mayo Building, 2nd Floor<br>Tallahassee, FL 32399-0800<br>(850) 488–2221<br>1–800–435–7352 (toll-free in FL) | State Comptroller<br>State Capitol Building<br>Tallahassee, FL 32399-0350<br>(850) 488–0370<br>1–800–848–3792 (toll-free in FL) | Insurance Commissioner<br>Plaza Level Eleven—The Capitol<br>Tallahassee, FL 32399-0300<br>(850) 922–3100<br>1–800–342-2762 (toll-free in FL) |
| **Georgia**<br>Governor's Office of Consumer Affairs<br>Two M. L. King, Jr., Drive, SE<br>Suite 356<br>Atlanta, GA 30334<br>(404) 656–3790<br>1–800–869–1123 (toll-free in GA) | Commissioner<br>Banking and Finance<br>2990 Brandywine Road, Suite 200<br>Atlanta, GA 30341-5565<br>(770) 986–1633 | Insurance Commissioner<br>2 Martin L. King, Jr., Drive<br>Atlanta, GA 30334<br>(404) 656–2070<br>1–800–656–2298 (toll-free in GA) |

**SECTION 2**   (Continued)

| State Consumer Protection Offices | State Banking Authorities | State Insurance Regulators |
| --- | --- | --- |
| **Hawaii** | | |
| Office of Consumer Protection<br>Department of Commerce and Consumer<br>  Affairs<br>Box 3767<br>Honolulu, HI 96813-3767<br>(808) 586–2636 | Commissioner<br>Financial Institutions<br>P.O. Box 2054<br>Honolulu, HI 96805<br>(808) 586–2820 | Insurance Commissioner<br>P.O. Box 3614<br>Honolulu, HI 96813<br>(808) 586–2790 |
| **Idaho** | | |
| Consumer Protection Unit<br>Office of Attorney General<br>650 West State Street<br>Boise, ID 83720-0010<br>(208) 334–2424<br>1–800–432–3545 (toll-free in ID) | Director<br>Department of Finance<br>700 West State Street, 2nd Floor<br>Boise, ID 83720-0031<br>(208) 332–8098<br>1–888–346–3376 (toll-free in ID) | Director of Insurance<br>700 West State Street<br>Boise, ID 83720<br>(208) 334–4250<br>1–800–721–3272 (toll-free in ID) |
| **Illinois** | | |
| Consumer Protection Division<br>Office of Attorney General<br>222 South College<br>Springfield, IL 62706<br>(217) 782–0244<br>1–800–642–3112 (toll-free in IL) | Commissioner of Banks and Trust<br>  Companies<br>500 East Monroe Street<br>Springfield, IL 62701<br>(217) 782–3000 | Director of Insurance<br>320 West Washington Street<br>Springfield, IL 62767<br>(217) 782–4515 |
| **Indiana** | | |
| Consumer Protection Division<br>Office of Attorney General<br>402 West Washington Street<br>Indianapolis, IN 46204<br>(317) 232–6330<br>1–800–382–5516 (toll-free in IN) | Director<br>Department of Financial Institutions<br>402 West Washington Street<br>Indianapolis, IN 46204-2759<br>(317) 232–3955<br>1–800–382–4880 (toll-free in IN) | Commissioner of Insurance<br>311 West Washington Street, Suite 300<br>Indianapolis, IN 46204-2787<br>(317) 232–3285<br>1–800–622–4461 (toll-free in IN) |
| **Iowa** | | |
| Consumer Protection Division<br>Office of Attorney General<br>1300 East Walnut Street, 2nd Floor<br>Des Moines, IA 50319<br>(515) 281–5926 | Superintendent of Banking<br>200 East Grand, Suite 300<br>Des Moines, IA 50309<br>(515) 281–4014<br>1–800–972–2018 (toll-free) | Insurance Commissioner<br>Lucas State Office Building, 6th Floor<br>Des Moines, IA 50319<br>(515) 281–5705 |
| **Kansas** | | |
| Consumer Protection Division<br>Office of Attorney General<br>301 West 10th Street<br>Topeka, KS 66612-1597<br>(785) 296–3751<br>1–800–432–2310 (toll-free in KS) | State Bank Commissioner<br>700 Jackson Street, Suite 300<br>Topeka, KS 66603-3714<br>(785) 296–2266 | Commissioner of Insurance<br>420 SW 9th Street<br>Topeka, KS 66612<br>(785) 296–3071<br>1–800–432–2484 (toll-free in KS) |
| **Kentucky** | | |
| Consumer Protection Division<br>Office of Attorney General<br>1024 Capital Center Drive<br>Frankfort, KY 40601-8204<br>(502) 696–5389<br>1–800–432–9257 (toll-free in KY) | Commissioner, Department of Financial<br>  Institutions<br>477 Versailles Road<br>Frankfort, KY 40601<br>(502) 564–3390<br>1–800–223–2579 (toll-free in KY) | Insurance Commissioner<br>215 West Main Street<br>P.O. Box 517<br>Frankfort, KY 40601<br>(502) 564–3630<br>1–800–595–6053 (toll-free in KY) |
| **Louisiana** | | |
| Consumer Protection Section<br>Office of Attorney General<br>State Capitol Building<br>Box 94095<br>Baton Rouge, LA 70804-9095<br>(504) 342–9639<br>1–800–351–4889 (toll-free in LA) | Commissioner<br>Financial Institutions<br>P.O. Box 94095<br>Baton Rouge, LA 70804<br>(504) 925–4660 | Commissioner of Insurance<br>P.O. Box 94214<br>Baton Rouge, LA 70804-9214<br>(504) 342–5900<br>1–800–529–5300 (toll-free in LA) |

**SECTION 2**   (Continued)

| State Consumer Protection Offices | State Banking Authorities | State Insurance Regulators |
| --- | --- | --- |
| **Maine**<br>Consumer and Antitrust Division<br>Office of Attorney General<br>35 State House Station<br>Augusta, ME 04333-0035<br>(207) 624–8527<br>1–800–332–8529 (toll-free in ME) | Superintendent of Banking<br>36 State House Station<br>Augusta, ME 04333-0036<br>(207) 624–8570 | Superintendent of Insurance<br>State House Station Number 34<br>Augusta, ME 04333-0034<br>(207) 624–8475<br>1–800–300–5000 (toll-free in ME) |
| **Maryland**<br>Consumer Protection Division<br>Office of Attorney General<br>200 St. Paul Place, 16th Floor<br>Baltimore, MD 21202-2021<br>(410) 528–8662 | Bank Commissioner<br>500 N. Calvert Street<br>Baltimore, MD 21202<br>(410) 333–6812<br>1–888–784–0136 (toll-free in MD) | Insurance Commissioner<br>525 St. Paul Place<br>Baltimore, MD 21202<br>(410) 468–2000<br>1–800–492–6116 (toll-free in MD) |
| **Massachusetts**<br>Consumer Protection Division<br>Department of Attorney General<br>1 Ashburton Place<br>Boston, MA 02108<br>(617) 727–5765 | Commissioner of Banks<br>100 Cambridge Street<br>Boston, MA 02202<br>(617) 727–3145<br>1–800–495–2265 (toll-free in MA) | Commissioner of Insurance<br>470 Atlanta Avenue<br>Boston, MA 02110-2223<br>(617) 521–7794 |
| **Michigan**<br>Consumer Protection Division<br>Office of Attorney General<br>Box 30213<br>Lansing, MI 48909<br>(517) 373–1140 | Commissioner<br>Financial Institutions Bureau<br>P.O. Box 30224<br>Lansing, MI 48909<br>(517) 373–3460 | Commissioner of Insurance<br>Insurance Bureau<br>611 West Ottawa Street<br>Lansing, MI 48933<br>(517) 373–9273 |
| **Minnesota**<br>Office of Consumer Services<br>Office of Attorney General<br>445 Minnesota St.<br>St. Paul, MN 55101<br>(612) 296–3353 | Deputy Commissioner of Commerce<br>133 East 7th Street<br>St. Paul, MN 55101<br>(612) 296–2135<br>1–800–657–3602 (toll-free in MN) | Commissioner of Commerce<br>133 East 7th Street<br>St. Paul, MN 55101<br>(612) 296–2488<br>1–800–657–3602 (toll-free in MN) |
| **Mississippi**<br>Consumer Protection Division<br>Office of Attorney General<br>Box 22947<br>Jackson, MS 39225-2947<br>(601) 359–4231<br>1–800–281–4418 (toll-free in MS) | Commissioner<br>Department of Banking and Consumer<br>  Finance<br>P.O. Box 23729<br>Jackson, MS 39225-3729<br>(601) 359–1031<br>1–800–844–2499 (toll-free in MS) | Commissioner of Insurance<br>P.O. Box 79<br>Jackson, MS 39205<br>(601) 359–3569<br>1–800–562–2957 (toll-free in MS) |
| **Missouri**<br>Office of Attorney General<br>Box 899<br>Jefferson City, MO 65102<br>(573) 751–3321<br>1–800–392–8222 (toll-free in MO) | Commissioner of Finance<br>P.O. Box 716<br>Jefferson City, MO 65102<br>(573) 751–3242<br>1–800–735–2966 (toll-free in MO) | Director of Insurance<br>301 West High Street, Room 630<br>P.O. Box 690<br>Jefferson City, MO 65102<br>(573) 751–2640<br>1–800–726–7390 (toll-free in MO) |
| **Montana**<br>Consumer Affairs Unit<br>Department of Commerce<br>1424 Ninth Avenue<br>Helena, MT 59620-0501<br>(406) 444–4312 | Commissioner<br>Financial Institutions<br>Box 200546<br>Helena, MT 59620-0546<br>(406) 444–2091 | Commissioner of Insurance<br>126 North Sanders<br>Helena, MT 59620<br>(406) 444–2040<br>1–800–332–6148 (toll-free in MT) |
| **Nebraska**<br>Consumer Protection Division<br>Department of Justice<br>2115 State Capitol, Box 98920<br>Lincoln, NE 68509<br>(402) 471–2682 | Director of Banking and Finance<br>1200 N Street, Suite 311<br>Lincoln, NE 68508<br>(402) 471–2171 | Director of Insurance<br>941 "O" Street, Suite 400<br>Lincoln, NE 68508-3690<br>(402) 471–2201 |

**SECTION 2**    (Continued)

| State Consumer Protection Offices | State Banking Authorities | State Insurance Regulators |
|---|---|---|
| **Nevada** | | |
| Commissioner of Consumer Affairs | Commissioner | Commissioner of Insurance |
| Department of Commerce | Financial Institutions | 1665 Hot Springs Road |
| 1850 East Sahara, Suite 101 | 406 East Second Street | Capitol Complex 152 |
| Las Vegas, NV 89104 | Carson City, NV 89701 | Carson City, NV 89710 |
| (702) 486–7355 | (702) 687–4259 | (702) 687–4270 |
| 1–800–362–5202 (toll-free in NV) | | 1–800–992–0900 (toll-free in NV) |
| **New Hampshire** | | |
| Consumer Protection and Antitrust | Bank Commissioner | Insurance Commissioner |
|   Division | 169 Manchester Street | 169 Manchester Street |
| Office of Attorney General | Concord, NH 03301 | Concord, NH 03301-5151 |
| State House Annex | (603) 271–3561 | (603) 271–2261 |
| Concord, NH 03301-6397 | | 1–800–852–3416 (toll-free in NH) |
| (603) 271–3641 | | |
| **New Jersey** | | |
| Division of Consumer Affairs | Commissioner of Banking | Commissioner |
| P.O. Box 45029 | 20 West State Street, CN-325 | Department of Insurance |
| Newark, NJ 07101 | Trenton, NJ 08625 | 20 West State Street, CN-329 |
| (973) 648–7457 | (609) 292–3420 | Trenton, NJ 08625 |
| | | (609) 633–7667 |
| **New Mexico** | | |
| Consumer and Economic Crime Division | Director | Superintendent of Insurance |
| Office of Attorney General | Financial Institutions Division | P.O. Drawer 1269 |
| P.O. Drawer 1508 | P.O. Box 25101 | Santa Fe, NM 87504-1269 |
| Santa Fe, NM 87504 | Santa Fe, NM 87504 | (505) 827–4601 |
| (505) 827–6060 | (505) 827–7100 | 1–800–947–4722 (toll-free in NM) |
| 1–800–678–1508 (toll-free in NM) | | |
| **New York** | | |
| Bureau of Consumer Frauds and Protection | Superintendent of Banking | Superintendent of Insurance |
| Office of Attorney General | Two Rector Street | 25 Beaver Street |
| State Capitol | New York, NY 10006-1894 | New York, NY 10014 |
| Albany, NY 12224 | (212) 618–6553 | (212) 480–6400 |
| (518) 474–5481 | 1–800–522–3330 (toll-free in NY) | 1–800–342–3736 (toll-free in NY) |
| 1–800–771–7755 (toll-free in NY) | | |
| **North Carolina** | | |
| Consumer Protection Section | Commissioner of Banks | Commissioner of Insurance |
| Office of Attorney General | P.O. Box 10709 | Dobbs Building |
| Department of Justice Building | Raleigh, NC 27605 | P.O. Box 26387 |
| Box 629 | (919) 733–3016 | Raleigh, NC 27611 |
| Raleigh, NC 27602 | | (919) 733–7343 |
| (919) 716–6000 | | 1–800–662–7777 (toll-free in NC) |
| **North Dakota** | | |
| Office of Attorney General | Commissioner of Banking and Financial | Commissioner of Insurance |
| 600 East Boulevard |   Institutions | Capitol Building, 5th Floor |
| Bismarck, ND 58505 | 2000 Schafer Street | 600 East Boulevard Avenue |
| (701) 224–2210 | Bismarck, ND 58501-5305 | Bismarck, ND 58505-0320 |
| 1–800–472–2600 (toll-free in ND) | (701) 328–9933 | (701) 328–2440 |
| | | 1–800–247–0560 (toll-free in ND) |
| **Ohio** | | |
| Consumer Frauds and Crimes Section | Superintendent of Banks | Director of Insurance |
| Office of Attorney General | 77 South High Street, 21st Floor | 2100 Stella Court |
| 30 East Broad Street | Columbus, OH 43266-0121 | Columbus, OH 43215-1067 |
| State Office Tower, 25th Floor | (614) 644–1631 | (614) 644–2658 |
| Columbus, OH 43215-3428 | | 1–800–686–1526 (toll-free in OH) |
| (614) 466–4986 | | |
| 1–800–282–0515 (toll-free in OH) | | |

**SECTION 2**    (Continued)

| State Consumer Protection Offices | State Banking Authorities | State Insurance Regulators |
| --- | --- | --- |
| **Oklahoma**<br>Assistant Attorney General for Consumer Affairs<br>Office of Attorney General<br>4545 N. Lincoln Blvd., Suite 260<br>Oklahoma City, OK 73105<br>(405) 521–3653 | Bank Commissioner<br>4545 North Lincoln Boulevard, Suite 164<br>Oklahoma City, OK 73105<br>(405) 521–2782 | Insurance Commissioner<br>3814 Santa Fe<br>Oklahoma City, OK 73118<br>(405) 521–2686<br>1–800–522–0071 (toll-free in OK) |
| **Oregon**<br>Financial Fraud Section<br>Department of Justice<br>1162 Court Street, NE<br>Salem, OR 97310<br>(503) 378–4732 | Administrator<br>Division of Finance and Corporate Securities<br>350 Winter Street, NE, Room 21<br>Salem, OR 97310<br>(503) 378–4140 | Insurance Commissioner<br>350 Winter Street, NE<br>Salem, OR 97310-0700<br>(503) 947–7984 |
| **Pennsylvania**<br>Bureau of Consumer Protection<br>Office of Attorney General<br>Strawberry Square, 14th Floor<br>Harrisburg, PA 17120<br>(717) 787–9707<br>1–800–441–2555 (toll-free in PA) | Secretary of Banking<br>333 Market Street, 16th Floor<br>Harrisburg, PA 17101-2290<br>(717) 787–6991<br>1–800–PABANKS (toll-free in PA) | Insurance Commissioner<br>1326 Strawberry Square, 13th Floor<br>Harrisburg, PA 17120<br>(717) 787–2317 |
| **Puerto Rico**<br>Department of Consumer Affairs<br>Minillas Station, Box 41059<br>Santurce, PR 00940-1059<br>(787) 721–0940 | Commissioner of Financial Institutions<br>1492 Ponce de Leon Avenue (No. 600)<br>San Juan, PR 00907-4127<br>(787) 723–3131 | Commissioner of Insurance<br>Fernandez Juncos Station<br>1607 Ponce de Leon Avenue<br>Santurce, PR 00910<br>(787) 722–8686 |
| **Rhode Island**<br>Consumer Protection Division<br>Department of Attorney General<br>72 Pine Street<br>Providence, RI 02903<br>(401) 274–4400<br>1–800–852–7776 (toll-free in RI) | Associate Director and Superintendent of Banking and Securities<br>233 Richmond Street, Suite 231<br>Providence, RI 02903-4231<br>(401) 277–2405 | Insurance Commissioner<br>233 Richmond Street<br>Providence, RI 02903-4233<br>(401) 277–2223 |
| **South Carolina**<br>Department of Consumer Affairs<br>Box 5757<br>Columbia, SC 29250–5757<br>(803) 734–9452<br>1–800–922–1594 (toll-free in SC) | Commissioner of Banking<br>1015 Sumter Street, Room 309<br>Columbia, SC 29201<br>(803) 734–2001 | Chief Insurance Commissioner<br>P.O. Box 100105<br>Columbia, SC 24201<br>(803) 737–6150<br>1–800–768–3467 (toll-free in SC) |
| **South Dakota**<br>Division of Consumer Affairs<br>Office of Attorney General<br>500 East Capitol Avenue<br>Pierre, SD 57501-5070<br>(605) 773-4400<br>1–800–300–1986 (toll-free in SD) | Director of Banking<br>State Capitol Building<br>500 East Capitol Avenue<br>Pierre, SD 57501-5070<br>(605) 773–3421 | Director of Insurance<br>Insurance Building<br>118 West Capitol<br>Pierre, SD 57501-2000<br>(605) 773–3563 |
| **Tennessee**<br>Antitrust and Consumer Protection Division<br>Office of Attorney General<br>500 James Robertson Parkway<br>Nashville, TN 37243-0600<br>(615) 741–4737<br>1–800–342–8385 (toll-free in TN) | Commissioner<br>Financial Institutions<br>500 Charlotte Ave., 4th Floor<br>Nashville, TN 37243-0705<br>(615) 741–2236 | Commissioner of Insurance<br>500 James Robertson Parkway<br>Nashville, TN 37243-0565<br>(615) 741–2241<br>1–800–342–4029 (toll-free in TN) |

**SECTION 2**    (Concluded)

| State Consumer Protection Offices | State Banking Authorities | State Insurance Regulators |
|---|---|---|
| **Texas**<br>Consumer Protection Division<br>Office of Attorney General<br>Capitol Station, Box 12548<br>Austin, TX 78711-2548<br>(512) 463–2070 | Banking Commissioner<br>2601 North Lamar<br>Austin, TX 78705<br>(512) 475–1300 | Consumer Services<br>Texas Department of Insurance<br>P.O. Box 149104<br>Austin, TX 78714-9104<br>(512) 463–6464<br>1–800–252–3439 (toll-free in TX) |
| **Utah**<br>Division of Consumer Protection<br>Department of Commerce<br>160 East 300 South, Box 146704<br>Salt Lake City, UT 84114-6704<br>(801) 530–6601<br>1–800–721–7233 (toll-free in UT) | Commissioner<br>Financial Institutions<br>P.O. Box 89<br>Salt Lake City, UT 84110-0089<br>(801) 538–8854 | Commissioner of Insurance<br>3110 State Office Building<br>Salt Lake City, UT 84114<br>(801) 538–3805<br>1–800–439–3805 (toll-free in UT) |
| **Vermont**<br>Assistant Attorney General<br>Public Protection Division<br>Office of Attorney General<br>109 State Street<br>Montpelier, VT 05609-1001<br>(802) 828–5507 | Commissioner of Banking, Insurance and<br>    Securities<br>89 Main Street<br>Montpelier, VT 05620-3101<br>(802) 828–3301 | Commissioner of Banking, Insurance and<br>    Securities<br>89 Main St., Drawer 20<br>Montpelier, VT 05620-3101<br>(802) 828–3302 |
| **Virginia**<br>Antitrust and Consumer Litigation Section<br>Office of Attorney General<br>Supreme Court Building<br>900 East Main Street<br>Richmond, VA 23219<br>(804) 786–2116 | Commissioner<br>Financial Institutions<br>P.O. Box 640<br>Richmond, VA 23218-0640<br>(804) 371–9657<br>1–800–552–7945 (toll-free in VA) | Commissioner of Insurance<br>1300 East Main Street<br>Richmond, VA 23219<br>(804) 371–9967<br>1–800–552–7945 (toll-free in VA) |
| **Washington**<br>Consumer Protection Division<br>Office of Attorney General<br>Box 40118<br>Olympia, WA 98504-0118<br>(360) 753–6210<br>1–800–551–4636 (toll-free in WA) | Supervisor of Banking<br>P.O. Box 41200<br>Olympia, WA 98504-1200<br>(360) 902–8707<br>1–800–372–8303 (toll-free in WA) | Insurance Commissioner<br>Box 40255<br>Olympia, WA 98504-0255<br>(360) 753–3613<br>1–800–562–6900 (toll-free in WA) |
| **West Virginia**<br>Consumer Protection Division<br>Office of Attorney General<br>812 Quarrier Street, 6th Floor<br>Charleston, WV 25301<br>(304) 348–8986<br>1–800–368–8808 (toll-free in WV) | Commissioner of Banking<br>State Capitol Complex<br>Building 3, Room 311<br>Charleston, WV 25305-0240<br>(304) 558–2294<br>1–800–642–9056 (toll-free in WV) | Insurance Commissioner<br>Box 50540<br>Charleston, WV 25305-0540<br>(304) 558–3354<br>1–800–642–9004 (toll-free in WV) |
| **Wisconsin**<br>Division of Trade and Consumer<br>    Protection<br>Box 8911<br>Madison, WI 53708<br>(608) 224–4976<br>1–800–422–7128 (toll-free in WI) | Commissioner of Banking<br>Box 7876<br>Madison, WI 53707-7876<br>(608) 261–9555<br>1–800–452–3328 (toll-free in WI) | Commissioner of Insurance<br>121 East Wilson<br>Madison, WI 53702<br>(608) 266–0103<br>1–800–236–8517 (toll-free in WI) |
| **Wyoming**<br>Office of Attorney General<br>123 State Capitol Building<br>Cheyenne, WY 82002<br>(307) 777–7874 | Manager<br>Division of Banking<br>Herschler Building<br>3rd Floor East<br>Cheyenne, WY 82002<br>(307) 777–7797 | Commissioner of Insurance<br>Herschler Building<br>122 West 25th Street<br>Cheyenne, WY 82002-0440<br>(307) 777–7401<br>1–800–438–5768 (toll-free in WY) |

# ENDNOTES

## CHAPTER 6

1. Peter Pae, "Credit Junkies," *The Wall Street Journal,* December 26, 1991, p. 1.
2. Joseph Weber, "Platinum vs. Platinum: The War over Fat Wallets," *Business Week,* May 3, 1999, p. 152.
3. *Business Review* (Philadelphia: Federal Reserve Bank of Philadelphia, January–February 1992), p. 5.
4. Amy Cortese, "The Ultimate Plastic," *Business Week,* May 19, 1997, pp. 119–22.
5. Marcia Stepanek, "What Smart Cards Couldn't Figure Out," *Business Week,* November 30, 1998, p. 142.
6. *Statistical Abstract of the United States: 1998,* Table 824, p. 524.
7. Experian Consumer Education Department, *Reports on Credit,* 1997.
8. Adapted from *Guide to Online Payments,* Federal Trade Commission, March 1999 (www.ftc.gov).
9. *Cosigning a Loan: Facts for Consumers* (Washington, DC: Federal Trade Commission, Bureau of Consumer Protection, January 1988), p. 1.
10. Experian Consumer Education Department, *Reports on Credit,* March 1999.
11. Adapted from William M. Pride, Robert J. Hughes, and Jack R. Kapoor, *Business,* 6th ed. (Boston: Houghton Mifflin, 1999), pp. 498–500.

## CHAPTER 7

1 . Judy Hammond, "Consumer Credit Counselors Say Debt Recovery Can Take Three to Five Years," *Knight-Ridder/ Tribune Business News,* February 16, 1999.
2. *Debt Counseling,* rev. ed. (AFL-CIO publication no. 140, March 1981).
3. *At Home with Consumers* (Washington, DC: Direct Selling Education Foundation, April 1997), p. 2.
4. *Consumer Corner,* The American Bankruptcy Institute, August 7, 1999, p. 4 (www.abiworld.org).

## CHAPTER 11

1. *U.S. Indstry and Trade Outlook 1999* (Washington, DC: U.S. Government Printing Office, 1999), p. 44.
2. George Anders and Laurie McGinley, "Surgical Strike," *The Wall Street Journal,* May 6, 1997, p. A1.

3. "Federally Funded Health Services: Information on Seven Programs Serving Low Income Women and Children," *Reports and Testimony,* General Accounting Office/HRD-92-73 FS, May 28, 1992, p. 24.
4. *Insurance Handbook for Reporters,* 2d ed. (Northbrook, IL: Allstate Insurance Group, 1985), p. 130.
5. *The Consumer's Guide to Disability Insurance* (Washington, DC: Health Insurance Association of America, September 1991), p. 1.
6. *Source Book of Health Insurance Data* (Washington, DC: Health Insurance Association of America, 1991), pp. 95–96.
7. Eve Tahmincioglu, "The Catch-22 of Long-Term Care Insurance," *Kiplinger's Personal Finance Magazine,* May 1997, pp. 97–102.
8. Peter Weaver, "Long-Term Coverage Eligible for Tax Breaks," *Nation's Business,* February 1997, p. 62.
9. George J. Church, "Backlash Against HMOs," *Time,* April 14, 1997, pp. 32–36.
10. Nancy Ann Jeffrey, "Aetna to Fight Suit by Parent Who Says Deceased Son Was Denied HMO Service," *The Wall Street Journal,* May 14, 1999, p. B4.
11. Peter Weaver, "Managed-Care Patients Gaining Protections," *The AARP Bulletin,* July–August 1999, p. 9.
12. *U.S. Industry and Trade Outlook 1999,* pp. 44–100.
13. Jagadeesh Gokhale, "Medicare: Usual and Customary Remedies Will No Longer Work," *Economic Commentary,* Federal Reserve Bank of Cleveland, April 1997, p. 1.
14. "Mending Medicare: Washington's Real Hot Potato," *Business Week,* March 1, 1999, p. 32.
15. Howard Gleckman and John Carey, "Playing the Medicare Card," *Business Week,* June 14, 1999, p. 52.

## CHAPTER 12

1. *Business Week,* July 5, 1999, p. 93.

## CHAPTER 13

1. The Learning Center: Basics of Smart Investing (Battling Inflation), Standard & Poor's Personal Wealth website (www.personalwealth.com), August 10, 1999, Standard & Poor's Corporation, 25 Broadway, New York, NY 10004.
2. Ibid.

3. Douglas Goldstein and Joyce Flory, *The Online Guide to Personal Finance and Investing* (Burr Ridge, IL: Irwin Professional Publishing, 1997), p. 2.
4. Ibid.

### CHAPTER 14

1. The Learning Center: Basics of Smart Investing, Standard & Poor's Personal Wealth website (www.personalwealth.com), August 16, 1999, Standard & Poor's Corporation, 25 Broadway, New York, NY 10004.
2. Yahoo Finance website (http://finance.yahoo.com), August 16, 1999, Yahoo, Inc., 3420 Central Expressway, Santa Clara, CA 95051.
3. John Downes and Jordan Elliot Goodman, eds., *Dictionary of Finance and Investment Terms* (Houppauge, NY: Barron's Educational Series, 1995), p. 406.
4. The New York Stock Exchange website (www.nyse.com), December 17, 1999, The New York Stock Exchange, 11 Wall Street, New York, NY 10005.
5. John E. Fitzgibbon, Jr. "November to Remember Brings 59 IPOs, Raised $33.9 Billion," Red Herring website (www.redherring.com), December 3, 1999, Red Herring.com News Corporation, 1550 Bryant Street, Suite 450, San Francisco, CA 94103.
6. Downes and Goodman, *Dictionary of Finance,* p. 629.
7. New York Stock Exchange website (www.nyse.com), August 16, 1999, The New York Stock Exchange, Inc., 11 Wall Street, New York, NY 10005.
8. Ibid.

### CHAPTER 15

1. U.S. Department of Commerce, *Statistical Abstract of the United States, 1998,* 118th ed., p. 305.
2. Walter Updergrave, "Bonds: Why You Need Them," *Money,* October 1999, p. 66.
3. Short-Term Credit Ratings, Standard & Poor's website (www.standardpoor.com/ratings/search/index.htm), December 20, 1999, Standard & Poor's Corporation, 25 Broadway, New York, NY 10004.

### CHAPTER 16

1. *1997 Mutual Fund Fact Book* (Washington, DC: Investment Company Institute, 1997), pp. 19, 35.
2. Investment Company Institute website (www.ici.org), September 2, 1999, Investment Company Institute, 1401 H Street, NW, Washington, DC 2005-2184.
3. Ibid.
4. Ibid.
5. Ibid.
6. Ibid.
7. *Semiannual Report,* April 30, 1999, p. 36. The Alger Fund, 1 World Trade Center, Suite 9333, New York, NY 10048.
8. John Downes and Jordan Elliot Goodman, *Dictionary of Finance and Investment Terms* (Hauppauge NY: Barron's Educational Series, 1995), p. 274.
9. Peter Lynch and John Rothchild, *Learn to Earn* (New York: Fireside Publishing, 1995), p. 124.
10. Prospectus for the Fundamental Investors Mutual Fund, December 31, 1999, p. 2, The American Funds, P.O. Box 7650, San Francisco, CA 94120 (1–800–421–0180).

### CHAPTER 17

1. Barbara Donnelly Granito, "How to Manage the Real-Estate Balancing Act," *The Wall Street Journal,* August 12, 1994, p. C13.
2. Ibid.
3. Georgette Jasen, "Second Home Can Be Rewarding, but Not in the Investment Sense," *The Wall Street Journal,* August 23, 1994, p. C1.
4. Joanne Lipman, "Land and Opportunity," *The Wall Street Journal,* December 2, 1995, p. D22.
5. William M. Pride, Robert J. Hughes, and Jack R. Kapoor, *Business,* 6th ed. (Boston: Houghton Mifflin, 1999), p. 105.
6. Stephanie Anderson Forest and Richard A. Melcher, "Can REITs Climb Out of the Rubble?" *Business Week,* April 26, 1999, p. 40.
7. Lynn Asinof, "Real Estate Lures Investors Again after a Deep Slump," *The Wall Street Journal,* October 22, 1992, p. C1.
8. Ibid.
9. Amy Dunkin, "All the World's an Auction," *Business Week,* February 8, 1999, pp. 120–21.
10. Alexandra Peers, "Keep Everything," *The Wall Street Journal,* December 9, 1994. p. R8.
11. *Consumer Alert: Investing in Rare Coins* (Washington, DC: Federal Trade Commission, n.d.).
12. Stacey Higginbothan, "1-Way Patrol: Online Bidders, Beware," *Business Week,* August 16, 1999, p. 6.

### CHAPTER 18

1. Kerry Capell, "How to Retire Successfully," *Business Week,* July 21, 1997, pp. 60–61.
2. "What's in Store for the Future?" *Financial Insights,* September 1992, p. 1.
3. "New Firm Specializes in Reverse Mortgages," *The Wheaton Leader,* March 30, 1994, business section, p. 2.
4. "Retirement Planning after Divorce," *Barron's,* August 31, 1992, p. 74.
5. Ibid.
6. Geoffrey Smith, "Nest-Egg Planning for the Not-So-Average Joe," *Business Week,* July 21, 1997, pp. 78–84.
7. Eric Schine, "There's Never Any Reason for Us to Be Bored," *Business Week,* July 21, 1997, pp. 70–76.
8. Jeanette A. Brandt, "Housing and Community Preferences: Will They Change in Retirement?" *Family Economics Review,* U.S. Department of Agriculture, May 1989, p. 7.
9. Mary C. Hickey, "A Design for Senior Living," *Business Week,* July 19, 1999, p. 136.
10. Schine, "There's Never Any Reason for Us to Be Bored," p. 76.
11. *Social Security: Understanding the Benefits* (Washington, DC: Social Security Administration, January 1997), p. 5.
12. Carol Kleinman, "Firms Shifting Retirement Planning, Risk to Workers," *Chicago Tribune,* January 19, 1992, sec. 8, p. 1.
13. Mary Rowland, "Pick Through the Annuity Tangle," *The New York Times,* February 16, 1992, p. 17.
14. William K. Zinke, "Retirees are a Big Opportunity for Corporate America," *Business Week,* August 16, 1999, p. 8.
15. Mike McNamee, "Good Spots to Stash Your Portfolio," *Business Week,* July 19, 1999, p. 118.

## CHAPTER 19

1. This section is based on Geoffrey Smith, "Nest-Egg Planning for the Not-So-Average Joe," *Business Week,* July 21, 1997, pp. 78–84.
2. Murray Iseman, "Common Estate Planning Fiascoes," *Barron's,* January 2, 1989, p. 27.
3. Howard Gleckman, "A Plan for the Endgame," *Business Week,* March 1, 1999, p. 117.
4. Lynn Asinof, "Trust Funds Are Just for the Rich? Think Again," *The Wall Street Journal,* January 9, 1995, pp. C1, C10.
5. Pam Black, "A GRAT Can Be Great for Saving Your Kids a Bundle," *Business Week On-line,* March 1, 1999, p. 116.
6. Lynn Asinof, *The Wall Street Journal,* January 9, 1995, pp. C1, C10.
7. Ibid.
8. Lynn Asinof, "Estate Planning Techniques for the Rich," *The Wall Street Journal,* January 11, 1985, pp. C1, C18.
9. Ibid.
10. *Looking Beyond Your Current Estate Plan,* American Society of CLU and ChFC, 1997.

# INDEX